Criminal Law

First published 1965
Reprinted 1966, 1967
Second edition 1969
Third edition 1973
Reprinted 1974, 1976, 1977
Fourth edition 1978
Reprinted 1979, 1982
Fifth edition 1983
Reprinted 1984
Reprinted 1986
Sixth edition 1988
Seventh edition 1992
Reprinted 1994, 1995

Criminal Law

by J C Smith CBE, QC, LLD, FBA
of Lincoln's Inn, Honorary Bencher,
Honorary Fellow of Downing College,
Cambridge,
Emeritus Professor of Law,
University of Nottingham

and Brian Hogan LLB
of Gray's Inn, Barrister
Professor of Common Law and Head of Department of Law,
University of Leeds

Seventh Edition

Butterworths
London, Dublin and Edinburgh
1992

United Kingdom	Butterworths a Division of Reed Elsevier (UK) Ltd, Halsbury House, 35 Chancery Lane, LONDON WC2A 1EL and 4 Hill Street, EDINBURGH EH2 3JZ
Australia	Butterworths, SYDNEY, MELBOURNE, BRISBANE, ADELAIDE, PERTH, CANBERRA and HOBART
Canada	Butterworths Canada Ltd, TORONTO and VANCOUVER
Ireland	Butterworth (Ireland) Ltd, DUBLIN
Malaysia	Malayan Law Journal Sdn Bhd, KUALA LUMPUR
New Zealand	Butterworths of New Zealand Ltd, WELLINGTON and AUCKLAND
Puerto Rico	Butterworth of Puerto Rico, Inc, SAN JUAN
Singapore	Reed Elsevier (Singapore) Pte Ltd
South Africa	Butterworths Publishers (Pty) Ltd, DURBAN
USA	Butterworth Legal Publishers, CARLSBAD, California, and SALEM, New Hampshire

Reprinted 1994, 1995

A CIP Catalogue record for this book is available from the British Library.

ISBN 0 406 00313 0
    0 406 00314 9

Typeset by Latimer Trend & Company Ltd, Plymouth.
Reprinted in Great Britain by Clays Ltd, St Ives plc

Preface to the First Edition

It is thought that university teachers and undergraduates will require no explanation or apology for the production of a new text-book on the substantive law of crime. Criminal Law has not received the same detailed and critical examination in university text-books as have other fields of the common law, for example, Contract and Tort. In the university law schools Kenny's *Outlines of Criminal Law* has long held almost unchallenged sway but it is now sixty-three years since the first edition of that classic work appeared. An immense amount of work has been done on the Criminal Law in the meantime, not least by the present learned editor of Kenny, Dr. J. W. C. Turner. There may now be something to be said for a book which makes a completely fresh start. Cross and Jones's *Introduction to Criminal Law*, on the other hand, may be thought too brief for the needs of the undergraduate—though we are full of admiration for the amount of information and learning which those authors have packed into so small a space. Moreover, both of these books deal in a single volume not only with the substantive law but also with Criminal Procedure and Evidence. Dr. Glanville Williams's great work, *Criminal Law: The General Part*, covers only general principles, while other books covering the whole field do not face up to the problems with which the undergraduate is expected to grapple.

We have endeavoured to provide the undergraduate with as complete an exposition of the substantive Criminal Law as he has to guide him in other fields of study. We have excluded Procedure and Evidence from consideration except in so far as these are necessary for an understanding of the law. Only by so doing could we give our subject the kind of treatment we think it demands. Moreover, Evidence is now commonly regarded as a worthy subject of academic study in its own right; and Criminal Procedure is by no means always part of a Criminal Law course.

All the important crimes are examined. Few courses, in or out of universities, perhaps cover so much ground; but the book allows scope for selection. In making the book reasonably comprehensive, we have not been unmindful of the fact that the practitioner commonly, and increasingly, finds assistance in the solution of problems in books designed primarily for students; and the citation of authorities is, therefore, more extensive than the needs of the undergraduate alone would have required. We have drawn freely on the published researches of scholars in the Criminal Law, not only in Britain but also in the Commonwealth and United States. In particular, we would acknowledge our debt, which will be apparent in almost every chapter, to the writings of Dr. Glanville Williams.

We have derived great assistance from many discussions with our colleagues and students at Nottingham and elsewhere; and our thanks are particularly due to Mr. P. R. H. Webb who read the whole of the manuscript. Tribute is also due to the helpfulness and, particularly, the patience of our publishers who waited a long time, without complaint, for the manuscript. Even their tolerance, however, is hardly in the same class as that of our wives, particularly throughout a recent long vacation during which we almost lived in the law library.

The book began as the work of only the first-named author, but the task proved greater than expected and a large proportion of the text has been contributed by the second. It has been revised in common and we each accept responsibility for the whole. We have endeavoured to state the law as at April 30, 1965.

J C SMITH

BRIAN HOGAN

Preface to the Seventh Edition

Our aim in writing this book, as we declared in the preface to the first edition, was to provide the student with as complete an exposition of the criminal law as he had to guide him in other fields of study. We hoped that what we thought to be good for the student would also be good for the practitioners and the courts. Judging by the gratifying frequency with which the work is cited in the law reports, that hope seems to have been fulfilled. But our principal aim is unchanged. Insofar as the book is of value to the practitioner, that is a bonus, but it remains essentially a textbook for the student who wants something more than a superficial understanding of the subject.

Since 1965 there has been an enormous growth in case law. The space now required to expound the law of accessories, for example, with the same degree of completeness as in 1965, is much greater. The time required to expound it in lectures has increased correspondingly and this has led to a reduction in the range of topics covered in degree courses in criminal law. Our book always covered more than any university or polytechnic course and gave some scope for selection by the teacher. It covered some crimes which had not previously received close analysis in criminal law books, like contempt of court. The proportion of the book which is read by the undergraduate student has probably been shrinking over a number of editions and we have decided that substantial pruning is now required.

We believe that we have retained every topic that the degree student is likely to require. We have eliminated other material on the grounds either that there have been no significant developments since the last edition or that the subject cannot be adequately covered in a book of this character. Examples of the first category are bigamy, perjury and treason. We like to think that anyone, student, teacher or practitioner, who needs to study these topics will find the sixth edition of continuing and unimpaired value. Examples of the second category are the law of firearms, which can be fully dealt with only by setting out extensive legislation, and contempt of court where the inquirer is likely to turn to one of the excellent specialised works, like that of Professor Miller, rather than to the necessarily abbreviated acount that we could give.

We have eliminated the separate chapter (7) on "The Effect of Particular Words" but some of the material in that chapter has been incorporated in Chapter 6, "Crimes of Strict Liability." The elimination of Chapter 19, "Offences Relating to the Administration of Justice," meant that a new home had to be found for offences of impeding and compounding the prosecution of arrestable offences. We have dealt with this by breaking up the long chapter (8) on "Modes of Participation in Crime" into Chapter 7, "Parties to Crime," and Chapter 9, "Vicarious Liability and the Liability of Associations," and inserting a new Chapter 8, "Assistance After the Offence." The chapter on "Sexual Offences" (now Chapter 14) has been shortened by the elimination of offences of abduction of women and offences relating to prostitution. The ancillary "Miscellaneous Matters" has been dropped from the Chapter 16 on "Theft and Related Offences" and counterfeiting is omitted from Chapter, 17, "Forgery". "Computer Misuses Offences" is the subject of a new Chapter 19, following 18, "Offences of Damage to Property." Material which we felt should be salvaged from the eliminated chapters on "Offences against Public Morals" and "Offences against the Security of the State" is brought together in a new Chapter 20, "Criminal Libels and Related Offences." Finally, offences under the Public Order Act 1986 are retained in Chapter 21; but anyone seeking our exposition of public nuisance, offences of entering and remaining on property, criminal eviction and harrassment or piracy and hi-jacking will have to turn to the Sixth Edition.

We hope that this surgery will make the book more attractive to students. Of course it is not the book for a student who wants a quick overview of the subject. It never was. We believe that the utility of the book to the practitioner and in the courts will not be significantly impaired because it is our impression that the parts of the book relied on are those concerned with general principles, offences against the person, theft and criminal damage. We trust that in these areas the practitioner will find that he is better served than before.

Developments since the last edition and some re-thinking on our part have required substantial amendments to every chapter of this edition. Although the Criminal Justice Act 1991 has not yet been brought into force, Chapter 1 has received its most thorough revision since the first edition to take account of its provisioins. Other statutes which have required us to make significant modifications are the Criminal Procedure (Insanity and Unfitness to Plead) Act 1991, the Human Fertilisation and Embryology Act 1990, the Criminal Justice Act 1988, especially the provisions relating to assault and battery, the Road Traffic Act 1991 and the Aggravated Vehicle-Taking Act 1992. The Computer Misuse Act 1990, as mentioned earlier, has required a short new chapter. The flood of reported cases touches almost every aspect of the law and we have tried to consider it all and to take due account of it.

Yet again we are indebted to Michael Gunn for careful proof-reading and his perceptive and well-informed advice on matters of substance. We also thank all those who have offered comments on and criticisms of the Sixth Edition. Our publishers, as ever, have been courteous and expeditious and we are grateful to them.

We have tried to state the law as at April 1 1992, except that we have included discussion of provisions of the Criminal Justice Act 1991 and the Road Traffic Act 1991 which have not been brought into force.

J C SMITH

BRIAN HOGAN

Contents

Chapter 11   Incitement, Conspiracy and Attempt 265

PART II. PARTICULAR CRIMES

Chapter 13   Non-Fatal Offences Against the Person   397

Chapter 16 Theft and Related Offences 495

Chapter 19   Computer Misuse Offences   714

Chapter 20   Criminal Libels and Related Offences   723

Abbreviations

The following are the abbreviations used for the principal text-books and legal journals cited in this book. References are to the latest editions, as shown below, unless it is specifically stated otherwise. The particulars of other works referred to in the text are set out in the relevant footnotes.

Andenaes, GPCL — *The General Part of the Criminal Law of Norway* (1965) by Johannes Andenaes.

Archbold — *Criminal Pleading, Evidence and Practice*, by John Frederick Archbold 44th ed (1992) by P J Richardson and others.

Blackstone — *Blackstone's Criminal Practice, 1992* by P Murphy and others

Blackstone, *Commentaries*, i — *Commentaries on the Laws of England*, by Sir William Blackstone, Vol i [4 vols] 17th ed (1830) by E Christian.

Burchell and Hunt, SACLP — *South African Criminal Law and Procedure*, Vol 1, *General Principles* (1983) by E M Burchell, J R L Milton and J M Burchell.

Butler — Report of the Committee on Mentally Abnormal Offenders, 1975, Cmnd 6244.

CLJ — Cambridge Law Journal.

Cal Law Rev — California Law Review.

Can Bar Rev — Canadian Bar Review.

Co 1 Inst — *Institutes of the Laws of England*, by Sir Edward Coke, Vol 1 [4 vols] (1797).

Col LR — Columbia Law Review.

Crime, Proof and Punishment — *Crime, Proof and Punishment*, Essays in honour of Sir Rupert Cross. Edited by C F H Tapper (1981).

Criminal Law Essays — Criminal Law: Essays in honour of J C Smith. Edited by P F Smith (1987).

Crim LR — Criminal Law Review.

CLP	Current Legal Problems.
CLRC/OAP/R	Criminal Law Revision Committee, Fourteenth Report, Offences against the Person, 1980, Cmnd 7844.
CLRC/OAP/WP	Criminal Law Revision Committee, Working Paper on Offences against the Person, 1976.
CLRC/SO/WP	Criminal Law Revision Committee, Working Paper on Sexual Offences, 1980.
Draft Code	*A Criminal Code for England and Wales* (Law Com. No. 177), 1989
East, 1 PC	*A Treatise of the Pleas of the Crown*, by Edward Hyde East, Vol 1 [2 vols] (1803).
Edwards, *Mens Rea*	*Mens Rea in Statutory Offences*, by J Ll J Edwards (1955).
Foster	*A Report on Crown Cases and Discourses on the Crown Law*, by Sir Michael Foster 3rd ed (1792) by M Dodson.
Gordon	*Criminal Law of Scotland* 2nd ed (1978) by G H Gordon.
Griew, *Theft*	*The Theft Acts 1968 and 1978* 6th ed (1990) by Edward Griew.
Hale, 1 PC	*The History of the Pleas of the Crown*, by Sir Matthew Hale, Vol 1 [2 vols] (1736).
Hall, *General Principles*	*General Principles of Criminal Law*, by Jerome Hall (2nd ed, 1960).
Halsbury	*The Laws of England*, by the Earl of Halsbury and other lawyers 4th ed (1973—) by Lord Hailsham of St Marylebone.
Harv LR	Harvard Law Review.
Hawkins, 1 PC	*A Treatise of the Pleas of the Crown*, by W Hawkins, Vol 1 [2 vols] 8th ed (1795) by J Curwood.
Holdsworth, 1 HEL	*A History of English Law*, by Sir William Holdsworth, Vol 1 [14 vols] (1923–64).
Howard, SR	*Strict Responsibility*, by Colin Howard (1963).
J Cr L	Journal of Criminal Law (English).
J Cr L & Cr	Journal of Criminal Law and Criminology (USA).
JSPTL	Journal of the Society of Public Teachers of Law.
Kenny, *Outlines*	*Outlines of Criminal Law*, by C S Kenny 19th ed (1965) by J W C Turner.
LQR	Law Quarterly Review.

LS	Legal Studies, the Journal of the Society of Public Teachers of Law
MACL	*The Modern Approach to Criminal Law*, ed by L Radzinowicz and J W C Turner (1948).
Med Sci & L	Medicine, Science and the Law.
MLR	Modern Law Review.
NZ Essays	*Essays on Criminal Law in New Zealand*, edited by R S Clark (1971).
Phillimore	Report of the Committee on Contempt of Court, 1974, Cmnd 5794.
Pollock and Maitland, 1 HEL	*The History of English Law before the Time of Edward I*, by Sir Frederick Pollock and F W Maitland, Vol 1 [2 vols] 2nd ed.
RCCP	Report of the Royal Commission on Capital Punishment, 1953, Cmd 8932.
Reshaping the Criminal Law	*Reshaping the Criminal Law*. Essays in honour of Glanville Williams. Edited by P R Glazebrook (1978).
Russell	*Crime*, by Sir W O Russell 12th ed (1964) by J W C Turner [2 vols].
Smith, Justification and Excuse	*Justification and Excuse in the Criminal Law* by J C Smith (The Hamlyn Lectures, 1989)
Smith, *Theft*	*The Law of Theft* 6th ed (1989) by J C Smith.
SHC	*Criminal Law: Cases and Materials* 4th ed (1990) by J C Smith and Brian Hogan.
SALJ	South African Law Journal.
Stephen, *Digest*	*A Digest of the Criminal Law*, by Sir James Fitzjames Stephen 9th ed (1950) by L F Sturge.
Stephen, 1 HCL	*A History of the Criminal Law of England*, by Sir James Fitzjames Stephen, Vol 1 [3 vols] (1883).
Street, *Torts*	*The Law of Torts*, by M Brazier (8th ed, 1988).
U Pa Law Rev	University of Pennsylvania Law Review.
Williams, CLGP	*Criminal Law: The General Part*, by Glanville L Williams (2nd ed, 1961).
Williams, TBCL	*Textbook of Criminal Law*, by Glanville L Williams 2nd ed (1983).
YLJ	Yale Law Journal.

Table of Statutes

References in this Table to *Statutes* are to Halsbury's Statutes of England (Fourth Edition) showing the volume and page at which the annotated text of an Act may be found.
Page references printed in **bold** type indicate where the section of an Act is set out in part or in full.

Table of Cases

Cases are listed under the name of the accused whenever the usual method of citation would cause them to be preceded by the abbreviation "R v" signifying that the prosecution was undertaken by the Crown.

E

M

N

Part I

General Principles

1 Crime and Sentence

This book is about the substantive law of crime. That is, it attempts to state and to discuss the law which determines whether any act is a crime or not. The book is not about the procedure by which the law is enforced or the evidence by which criminal offences are proved, except in so far as these matters are inseparable from the discussion of the substantive law. Procedure and evidence are subjects of equal importance which are admirably discussed in other books.

The criminal law is no more an end in itself than the law of procedure and evidence through which it is enforced. Our criminal law has grown up over many centuries and the purposes of those who have framed it, and of those who have enforced it, have undoubtedly been many and various. Consequently, it is not easy to state confidently what are the aims of the criminal law at the present day. The authors of a completely new code of criminal law are, however, in a position to state their objectives at the outset. "The general purposes of the provisions governing the definition of offences" in the American Law Institute's Model Penal Code[1] might be taken as a statement of the proper objectives of the substantive law of crime in a modern legal system. The purposes are:

"(a) to forbid and prevent conduct that unjustifiably and inexcusably inflicts or threatens substantial harm to individual or public interests;
 (b) to subject to public control persons whose conduct indicates that they are disposed to commit crimes;
 (c) to safeguard conduct that is without fault from condemnation as criminal;
 (d) to give fair warning of the nature of the conduct declared to be an offense;
 (e) to differentiate on reasonable grounds between serious and minor offenses."

The reader will judge for himself how far these purposes are fulfilled by English criminal law as he studies the general principles and particular offences discussed in the succeeding chapters. For example, whether our law is confined to forbidding conduct that is "inexcusable", whether it adequately safeguards conduct that is without fault from condemnation as criminal, are matters which are particularly considered in the chapter on "strict liability",[2] but which constantly arise elsewhere.

---

1. Proposed Official Draft, Art. 1 1.02 (1). Cf. Walker, *The Aims of a Penal System*.
2. Below, p. 99.

While the definition of offences can adequately *forbid* unjustifiable and inexcusable conduct, it can rarely prevent it. The Children and Young Persons (Harmful Publications) Act 1955 was said to have been "completely successful" at a time when no prosecution had been brought under it.[3] But this is unusual. The fact that an act is known to be forbidden by the criminal law may, for many persons, be sufficient to ensure that they will not commit such an act but for others this will not be enough. Hence our need for a law of criminal procedure, of evidence – and of sentencing.[4] The mere fact of conviction, being a public condemnation of the conduct in question, has some value in the prevention of crime, but it is far from being sufficient. Some, at least, of the purposes for which the criminal law exists can be fulfilled only through the imposition of sentences. It is therefore desirable at the outset to enquire to what ends sentences are directed – or professedly directed – by those who impose them. When a sentence is to be imposed, the first decision to be made should be as to the object to be achieved by it.[5] Is the aim simply to mete out an appropriate punishment to a wrongdoer? Or is it to deter the wrongdoer and others from committing such offences in the future? Or to protect the public by shutting the offender away? Or is it the reform of the offender? Or a combination of these objects? When this first decision has been made, a second decision – what measure is most appropriate to achieve the desired object? – must follow. It is only with the first decision that we are concerned in this chapter.

1 Crime and Punishment

Crime has always been regarded by the courts as a moral wrong and conduct demanding retribution. The law is based on an assumption that, in the absence of evidence to the contrary, people are able to choose whether to do criminal acts or not and that a person who chooses to commit a crime is responsible for the resulting evil and deserves punishment. The courts have generally seen their task as one of fitting the penalty to the particular degree of iniquity and dangerousness of the offender's conduct on this particular occasion. The sentence should adequately reflect the revulsion felt by citizens for the particular crime. Its purpose is seen not only as punishment but also as a public denunciation of the conduct in question. It may then satisfy the demand for retaliation by the public, or some members of the public, which serious crime sometimes arouses.

The sentence must be proportionate to the offence. The business of the court is to do justice and only by achieving some measure of proportion between one sentence and another can it do justice as between one offender and another. It is difficult to say, in absolute terms, that a particular

---

3. 299 HL Deb. col., 451, 12 Feb. 1969, quoted by Zellick [1970] Crim LR 192.
4. On sentencing generally, see Ashworth, *Sentencing and Penal Policy* (1983); D. A. Thomas, *Principles of Sentencing* (2nd ed.), N. D. Walker, *Sentencing in a Rational Society*.
5. See D. A. Thomas, "Sentencing, The Basic Principles" [1967] Crim LR 455 and 503.

sentence of imprisonment is proportionate to a particular rape or wounding – just as in the civil law it is difficult to put a cash value on the plaintiff's arm when it has been lost through the defendant's negligence. We are not weighing like against like. The courts have to do the best they can. In relative terms, the notion of proportionality is more practicable. It is possible to say that one wounding is worse than another; and that, if the first deserves, say, three years' imprisonment, the other deserves two. And so, once the courts have established a point, or points of departure, it is possible to have an approximate scale within the maximum prescribed. Sometimes a realistic statutory maximum will assist in establishing the scale. If the worst kind of case within the definition of the offence deserves the maximum, what, relatively, does this case deserve?

a) *Moral fault and harm done.* How is the gravity of the offence to be assessed? First, by its wickedness as assessed by the court, guided by the court's assessment of the public view of the case. Courts profess to have regard to public opinion (thoughtful public opinion, not the hysteria which sometimes follows notorious crimes) in assessing sentence. This may be observed in their reaction to public disquiet about the prevalence of rape. The opportunity for the courts to respond has been widened by the new power of the Attorney-General,[6] with leave of the Court of Appeal, to refer to that court a sentence which appears to him to be unduly lenient. The court may then impose the appropriate sentence, whether greater or less.

In assessing gravity the courts have regard not only to the moral fault of the offender but also to the amount of harm he has done. One who attempts to commit a crime is no less blameworthy, and may be no less dangerous, because the attempt happens to fail. In law, a person who attempts to commit a crime is generally liable to the same maximum punishment as one who succeeds. But it is the practice of the courts to punish the attempt less severely than the complete offence. No harm or, at least, less harm, has been done. Similarly, one who attempts to steal a large sum of money but gets away with a trivial amount commits the same offence in law as if he had been entirely successful and is liable to the same maximum penalty; but he is likely to get off much more lightly.

The importance attached to the harm done, though not intended or foreseen, is no less conspicuous in some parts of the substantive law. If D assaults P he is guilty only of a summary offence punishable with three months' imprisonment; but if the same assault, quite unforeseeably, causes actual bodily harm, the offender is guilty of an indictable offence punishable with five years. If a person drives dangerously he is liable to two years' imprisonment. If precisely the same dangerous driving causes death, he is liable to five years. Dangerous driving causing three deaths may be punished more severely than the same dangerous driving causing only one.

"The fact is that in public estimation it is a factor which people in general do take into account. People do regard killing three as more criminal than killing one. That is a fact of life which the court recognises."[7]

6. Criminal Justice Act 1988, s. 36.
7. *Pettipher* (1989) 11 Cr App Rep (S) 321, per Schiemann J, followed in *Chadwick* [1991] RTR 176.

It may be thought that a rational system would assess punishment by reference to the harm intended or foreseen, or, at least, foreseeable, rather than on the chance of what actually happens; but the fact is that the significance in the law of the harm done is increasing. So it is now an offence punishable with five years' imprisonment to cause death by merely careless driving when under the influence of drink or drugs.[8] And this has now been joined by an offence of causing death when "joyriding" as taking a vehicle without the owner's consent is popularly and unhappily called.[9]

The retributive approach to sentencing was for many years out of favour with criminologists who thought it anachronistic and, indeed, barbarous. Recently there has been a change of thought and a "Return to retribution in penal theory."[10] This is at least partly because experience has shown that we simply do not know how to reform offenders and because sentences imposed purely on the basis of prevention of crime may be unfair and oppressive. The attitude of the English judges has changed little, if at all, having always been generally retributivist.

Most important of all, the principle that criminals should "get their just deserts"[11] is central to the statutory framework for sentencing in the Criminal Justice Act 1991. The sentencing court must have constant regard to the "seriousness" of the offence. Custody is not to be imposed unless the seriousness of the offence requires it. If custody is imposed, it must be commensurate with the seriousness of the offence. If the offence is not serious enough to require custody, a non-custodial sentence involving some interference with liberty may be imposed – but only if the offence was serious enough to justify it. The provisions of the Act are examined in more detail below.

b) *The statutory maximum.* It is the almost invariable practice of Parliament to fix a maximum but no minimum sentence and to leave it to the judge or magistrate to decide what sentence in the range from an absolute discharge to the specified maximum it is right to impose. Even where the maximum is imprisonment for life the court may grant an absolute discharge. The only significant exception to this rule is murder where the court has no discretion and is required to impose a sentence of life imprisonment in all cases. Except in the case of murder, the practice of Parliament is based on a recognition of the fact that the imperfections of definition are such that any definition, however carefully drafted, will embrace a wide range of culpability and that there will be some acts falling within it which are morally blameless and deserving of no punishment. Murder is no different from other crimes in this respect but it is still treated differently for historical, emotional and, perhaps, political reasons.

---

8. Road Traffic Act 1991, s. 3, below, p. 484.
9. Below, p. 604.
10. Galligan in *Crime, Proof and Punishment*, 144; Tonry and Morris "Sentencing Reform in America" in *Reshaping the Criminal Law*, 434, 437. But cf. Wootton, *Crime and the Criminal Law* (2nd ed., 1982).
11. *Crime, Justice and Protecting the Public* (Cm. 965), para. 2.1.

c) *The tariff.* The statutory maximum gives very limited guidance to a court. It is useful only when it is not altogether out of proportion to contemporary attitudes to the crime in question. Many maxima have been revised recently but others have remained unchanged since the nineteenth century. Their origins can be traced to the terms of transportation which took the place of capital punishment in the 1820s and 1830s. Even in the case of modern revisions the practice of fixing a maximum high enough to cover the worst type of case results in maxima far above the normal range of sentences. In 1968 Parliament fixed the maximum sentence for theft at ten years – an unrealistically long term which was never imposed. The Criminal Justice Act 1991, s. 26 (1) reduces it to seven years but even this reduced maximum gives no guidance whatever to a magistrates' court and very little to a Crown Court, except in a very unusual case. A proposal in 1978 by the Advisory Council on the Penal System to provide more realistic maxima, based on the actual practice of the courts, found little support.[12]

This is not say that the maxima have no significance beyond the obligation not to exceed them. Where the judge imposed the maximum sentence of two years upon a man convicted of reckless driving in a case where the passengers in the other car narrowly escaped being burnt to death, the Court of Appeal reduced the sentence to 18 months, saying that it was important to bear in mind that Parliament had drawn a distinction between reckless driving and causing death by reckless driving which was punishable with five years' imprisonment.[13]

That decision also demonstrates the principle that the maximum should be reserved for the worst type of case which comes before the court and a sentence which does not allow for this is wrong in principle.[14]

d) *The "merited sentence".* Before 1991 there were many statutory rules regulating the imposition of particular sentences but no general statutory framework. The Criminal Justice Act 1991, coming into force on 1 October 1992, introduces such a framework. Before examining those provisions, it is necessary to look at the position as it had been developed before the Act by decisions of the Court of Appeal. The court stated principles and laid down guidelines, not to impose uniformity of sentence, but to try to achieve uniformity of approach. The decisions established a "tariff" in the sense of a range within which a sentence would be regarded as normal for that offence and outside of which it would be regarded as abnormal and require some special justification if it was to be upheld. Within that range where would be found a sentence appropriate to the circumstances of the particular offence before the court. Many of the principles of sentencing were explicable only on the assumption that such an appropriate sentence existed.

Thus it was held to be wrong to increase the sentence because the offender had insisted on his right to jury trial,[15] or on pleading not guilty, or

---

12. "Sentences of Imprisonment: A Review of Maximum Penalties", 1978.
13. *Staddon* [1992] Crim LR 70.
14. Judges should not, however, use their imaginations to conjure up unlikely worst possible kinds of case: *Ambler* [1976] Crim LR 266.
15. *Jamieson* (1975) 60 Cr App Rep 318.

had conducted his defence in a particular way;[16] but the sentence might be reduced on the ground that he had pleaded guilty.[17] The sentence might be reduced because he had informed against his co-prisoner, but it must not be increased because he did not inform.[18] His good record might be a ground for mitigating the sentence, but his bad record must not be allowed to aggravate it.[19] A fine might be diminished because of his poverty; but it must not be increased because of his wealth.[20]

These rules only made sense if there was an appropriate sentence for the offence from which proper subtractions might be made. That appropriate sentence was to be assessed on the circumstances of the offence, not on what the offender did before (e.g., his good or bad character) or afterwards (e.g., the fact that he pleaded guilty or not guilty). It seems to have been essentially an assessment of what he deserved, of what was necessary to mark the seriousness of what he had done, to provide proper retribution, and to deter the offender from doing it again. It is convenient to call it "the merited sentence". He must not be given a greater sentence than the offence merited but the sentence might be less because of the application of the mitigating factors.

e) *General deterrence and exemplary sentences.* Sometimes the court's aims were not limited to punishing and deterring the offender. They wanted to impose a sentence which would deter others from committing offences of this character.[21] The courts recognised the propriety of the "exemplary" sentence – a sentence intended to make an example of the offender as a warning to others. Even here, however, it was not open to the judge to impose a sentence greater than the merited sentence, but the judge might now disregard some or all of the mitigating factors.

f) *Protection of the public.* The court might also ignore the mitigating factors and impose the whole merited sentence in order to protect the public from the particular offender. Until 1991 there existed, in specified circumstances, a statutory power to impose an "extended term of imprisonment" where the court was satisfied, by reason of the offender's previous conduct and the likelihood of his committing further offences, that it was expedient to protect the public from him for a substantial time. The "extended term" might, but would not necessarily, exceed the statutory maximum. The term was "extended" in the sense that it was longer than the term which would have been imposed if this new power had not existed – it might be

---

16. *Regan* [1959] Crim LR 529; *Harper* [1968] 2 QB 108, [1967] Crim LR 714.
17. *de Haan* [1968] 2 QB 108, [1967] 3 All ER 618 n; *Fraser* [1982] Crim LR 841.
18. *James* (1913) 9 Cr App Rep 142; *Davies* (1978) 68 Cr App Rep 319; *Aramah* (1983) 4 Cr App Rep (S) 407.
19. *Boardman* [1958] Crim LR 626; *Queen* [1982] Crim LR 56.
20. *Thomas* [1967] Crim LR 313, but now see Criminal Justice Act 1991, ss. 18 and 19, below, p. 13.
21. A famous example is the sentence of four years' imprisonment imposed by Salmon J on each of nine youths convicted of assaults and wounding offences on black men. The offenders had no previous convictions. The sentences were upheld by the Court of Criminal Appeal: "the time had certainly come for the courts to put down offences such as these with a heavy hand". See Salmon J in [1960] CLJ 45 at 48 and Asquith LJ's discussion of exemplary sentences in *The Listener*, XLIII at 821, cited in the 6th edition of this book, p. 13.

longer than the offender deserved for the offence he had committed. Even where the court was not exercising this statutory power, it might impose a sentence somewhat greater than the merited sentence in order to protect the public, striking a balance between the needs of public safety and the requirement of fairness to the offender.[1]

g) *Protecting the public by life imprisonment.* Where the maximum sentence for an offence was life imprisonment, the imposition of that maximum was limited in practice to cases where an indeterminate sentence (and, substantially, that is what life imprisonment amounts to) was necessary for the protection of the public. The conditions stated in the leading case of *Hodgson*[2] are (i) the current offence is grave enough to require a very long sentence; (ii) the nature of the offence or the offender's history shows that he is a person of unstable character likely to commit such offences in the future; and (iii) the consequences to others of such offences may be specially serious. The first criterion seems to be rather liberally interpreted where the offender is very dangerous, so that a life sentence was upheld when the appropriate determinate sentence would have been about five years and even where an offence of arson was "relatively minor in its classification".[3]

2 Criminal Justice Act 1991[4]

a) *"Custodial" and "community" sentences.* It is now time to consider the effect of the 1991 Act. Under that Act a sentence, other than a fine, is either a custodial sentence or a community sentence. A custodial sentence means, in relation to a person of or over 21, a sentence of imprisonment and, in relation to a younger person, a sentence of detention in a young offender institution under the Children and Young Persons Act 1933 or of custody for life under the Criminal Justice Act 1982. A community sentence means a sentence of one or more community orders and "community orders" are (i) a probation order; (ii) a community service order; (iii) a combination order (a probation order coupled with an order to perform specified hours of unpaid work); (iv) a curfew order; (v) a supervision order; and (vi) an attendance centre order.

b) *Imposition of custodial sentences.* Section 1 (2) of the 1991 Act provides: "the court shall not pass a custodial sentence on the offender unless it is of the opinion—
  (a) that the offence, or the combination of the offence and one other offence associated with it, was so serious that only such a sentence can be justified for the offence; or
  (b) where the offence is a violent or sexual offence, that only such a sentence would be adequate to protect the public from serious harm from him."

1. *Moore* (1986) 8 Cr App Rep (S) 376; *Zacharcko* [1988] Crim LR 546.
2. (1967) 52 Cr App Rep 113.
3. *Blogg* (1981) 3 Cr App Rep (S) 114.
4. See Criminal Law Review for April 1992 (pp. 229–287) for an analysis of the Act.

The section is headed "Restrictions on imposing custodial sentences" and its effect is that if a non-custodial sentence can be "justified" then custody must not be imposed. It is not sufficient that a custodial sentence would also be justified. Custody must be the only kind of sentence that would be justified. The Act gives no help as to the meaning of "justified". It is tentatively suggested that a non-custodial sentence is justified if the court's opinion is that right-thinking members of the public, properly informed as to the seriousness of the offence, would think it reasonable to impose a non-custodial sentence – or, at least, would not be outraged by it. If, by this test, or whatever test is held to be appropriate, a fine could be "justified" as the sentence for the offence, then a fine it must be.

c) *Imposing a non-custodial sentence when only a custodial sentence is "justified"*. The phrase in paragraph (a), "only such a sentence can be justified", seems to mean that a non-custodial sentence would not be justified, i.e., would be wrong. But there may be mitigating factors, not affecting the seriousness of the offence (e.g., the offender informed on his co-defendant and pleaded guilty), which, by s. 28, the court may, and probably must, take into account, and which might lead it to think that custody is not the only appropriate sentence. Looking only at the seriousness of the offence, custody may be the only justified sentence; but looking at the wider range of considerations, the court may think custody is not the only justified sentence, indeed is not justified at all. In that case it would seem right that a non-custodial sentence should be imposed.

d) *The seriousness of the offence*. In assessing the seriousness of the offence it seems that the court will be undertaking much the same exercise as it did before the Act in deciding on the "merited sentence"; except that now it may consider the offence together with one "associated offence". An offence is "associated" with the one for which the offender is to be sentenced if he is convicted of it in the same proceedings, or sentenced for it at the same time, or he asks for it to be taken into consideration.

The Act gives some guidance as to how to assess the seriousness of the offence. The court must disregard any previous convictions of the offender or any failure of his to respond to previous sentences: s. 29 (1). It is obviously right that a person should not be punished twice for the same offence and that principle was well recognised before the 1991 Act.

On the other hand, the court may take account of aggravating factors of the present offence which are "disclosed by the circumstances of other offences" committed by him. It has been suggested that the disclosure of persistent use of a knife or systematic fraud are aggravating factors which may be taken into account. There is some difficulty in reconciling this with the rule that previous convictions must be ignored. It is also hard to reconcile with the rule that only one associated offence may be considered. If D is convicted on 10 counts of cheque frauds, or if he is convicted on a single count and asks for 9 cheque frauds to be taken into consideration, the court may consider only two of these 10 "associated" offences. If he has 9 *previous* convictions for the same offences may they all be looked at for the purposes of showing that he is a persistent offender?

e) *Mitigating factors*. Section 28 (1) provides that:

"Nothing in [Part 1 of the Act] shall prevent a court from mitigating an offender's sentence by taking into account such matters as, in the opinion of the court, are relevant in the mitigation of sentence."

This presumably allows the court to take account of such matters as that the offender informed on an accomplice or pleaded guilty in deciding whether to impose a custodial sentence. Section 1 (2) does not say that a court must impose a custodial sentence when it is justified by the serious-ness of the offence, only that it must not do so unless it is so justified.

f) *Length of a custodial sentence*. When the court has decided to impose a custodial sentence, s. 2 tells it how to assess the length:

"2) The custodial sentence shall be—

(a) for such term (not exceeding the permitted maximum) as in the opinion of the court is commensurate with the seriousness of the offence, or the combination of the offence and other offences associ-ated with it; or

(b) where the offence is a violent or sexual offence, for such longer term (not exceeding the maximum) as in the opinion of the court is necessary to protect the public from serious harm from the offender."

In deciding whether a custodial sentence is to be imposed at all, it will be remembered that the court is limited to consideration of the present offence and one associated offence; but, once it has decided that a custodial sentence is required, it must, if there are associated offences, take account of all of them.

The problems of interpretation to which the 1991 Act gives rise may be expected to produce much case law. In the meantime, it is instructive to consider the case of *Clugston*,[5] a case decided before the 1991 Act. D pleaded guilty to 23 counts of receiving stolen cheque books and obtaining property by deception and asked for 80 similar offences to be taken into consideration. The Court of Appeal upheld a sentence of three years' imprisonment. He had many previous convictions for dishonesty. In deciding whether only a custodial sentence would be justified under the Act it seems that the court would have to take the one of the 23 offences which it thought to be the most serious, together with one of 102 associated offences and, disregarding the remaining 101 offences and the previous convictions, ask itself if the combination of those two offences required a custodial sentence. If the court decided that only a custodial sentence was justified, it would go on to consider its length. It would no longer be limited to consideration of only one other associated offence. So, once the court had decided that the two selected offences justified custody, it could consider all the 103 offences in deciding how long the custody should be.

If the two most serious offences could justifiably be dealt with by a non-custodial sentence, no custodial sentence could be imposed. The court would then have to go on to consider whether the two chosen offences were serious enough to warrant a community sentence.

5. [1991] Crim LR 857. See commentary by David Thomas.

Although s. 2 (2) is in imperative terms, it seems that it is subject to s. 28 (1) (above), so that the court may impose a sentence which is less than would be commensurate with the seriousness of the offence. The commensurate sentence may be five years but, taking account of the fact, for example, that the offender informed on a co-defendant and pleaded guilty, the court might think two years enough.

g) *"Violent or sexual offences" and other offences*. With respect to the imposition and the length of custodial sentences, the Act makes special provision for a person convicted of a "violent or sexual offence". The general principle is that a custodial sentence may be imposed only if the seriousness of the offence requires it and only for such a term as the seriousness of the offence requires. A person shall go to prison only if he deserves prison and only for such a period as he deserves. But where the offence is a violent or sexual offence he may be sent to prison if that is the only way to protect the public from "serious harm" (which means "death or serious injury, whether physical or psychological, occasioned by further offences"[6]) from him. It seems that the court does not have to be satisfied that the seriousness of the violent or sexual offence which has been committed requires custody. It now may have its eye, not on what the offender has done, but on what he is likely to do. He does not necessarily deserve prison for what he has done – but he has to go there for the protection of the public. And, if he does deserve prison, the term which may be imposed is not limited to what he deserves but may be for such longer term as is necessary to protect the public from serious harm.

It is important therefore to know the meaning of "violent" and "sexual" offences. A "violent offence" is defined (s. 31 (1)) as:

"an offence which leads, or is intended or likely to lead to a person's death or to physical injury to a person and includes an offence which is required to be charged as arson (whether or not it would otherwise fall within this definition)."

So smashing up another's property with a hammer is not a "violent offence" except in circumstances in which it is likely to lead to injury to the person; whereas setting fire to another's property is a "violent offence" even if no danger to the person is intended or likely.

A "sexual offence" is an offence under (i) the Sexual Offences Act 1956 (except buggery and indecency between men which would not be an offence but for the fact that it is committed on a UK merchant ship with a crew member; and offences of living on the earnings of prostitution and brothel keeping); (ii) the Indecency with Children Act 1960; (iii) s. 54 of the Criminal Law Act 1977; and (iv) the Protection of Children Act 1978 (except ss. 4 and 5).

h) *Protecting the public from non-violent, non-sexual offenders*. There may be such offenders from whom the court thinks it expedient to protect the public, so far as it can do so. It cannot, however, impose a sentence greater

6. S. 31 (3).

than is commensurate with the seriousness of the offence and one associated offence. In practice the "commensurate" sentence is likely to be a range rather than a precise period – e.g., if the judge imposed three years in a particular case, the Court of Appeal would not feel able to hold that this was not commensurate; nor would it if the sentence were four years. But neither two years nor five years would be acceptable. So what the judge can do when he thinks a preventive sentence is called for is (i) to go for the top of the range, and (ii) to ignore any mitigating factors there may be. But that is the limit of his powers.

i) *Life sentences.* The Act does not affect the common law principles governing the imposition of discretionary life sentences.[7] When a judge exercises his discretion to impose a life sentence on a violent or sexual offender he may specify in open court the term within that sentence which marks the seriousness of the offence.

j) *Giving reasons for custodial sentences.* The 1991 Act provides that it is the duty of the court to state in open court:
   (i) when it passes a custodial sentence, why the offence is so serious that only a custodial sentence can be justified; or why only such a sentence is adequate to protect the public, and
  (ii) when it passes a custodial sentence which is longer than is commensurate with the seriousness of the offence, why it is necessary to do so to protect the public from serious harm.

k) *Community sentences.* By s. 6 (1) of the Act—
   "A court shall not pass on an offender a community sentence ... unless it is of the opinion that the offence, or the combination of the offence and one other offence associated with it, was serious enough to warrant such a sentence."
Assuming that the offence is punishable with custody, the court must have decided that custody is not required – something less than custody can be "justified". But the offence, though not serious enough to require custody, must be serious enough to warrant a community sentence. If that is the court's opinion, it must then (s. 6 (2)) make the particular order which is, in its opinion—
   "(a) ... the most suitable for the offender; and
   (b) the restrictions on liberty imposed by the order or orders shall be such as in the opinion of the court are commensurate with the seriousness of the offence, or the combination of the offence and other offences associated with it."
So here too the court is bound to have regard to the seriousness of the offence and to impose the restrictions which are deserved, neither more nor less.

l) *Fines.* Before the 1991 Act the principle applied by the courts was that a fine should be fixed by reference to the seriousness of the offence without

---

7. Above, p. 9.

regard to the means of the offender. It might then be reduced because of the offender's poverty but it could not be increased because of his wealth. Thus it might happen that if A and B committed precisely the same offence they would be fined the same amount, say £500, where A had an income of £20,000 and B £100,000. Clearly A would be more severely punished than B. The 1991 Act, ss. 18 and 19, applies a different principle. When a magistrates' court imposes a fine for a summary offence punishable by a fine not exceeding a level on the standard scale[8] or an either way offence punishable by a fine not exceeding the statutory maximum, it shall determine the number of "units" which is commensurate with the seriousness of the offence; and the value of a unit will be the offender's disposable weekly income (calculated in accordance with rules to be made by the Lord Chancellor and subject to a prescribed minimum and maximum). The maximum number of units varies according to the level on the standard scale: level 1 – 2 units; 2 – 5 units; 3 – 10 units; 4 – 25 units and 5 (or a statutory maximum offence) – 50 units.

In other cases – notably fines imposed by the Crown Court – it is simply provided that the court shall take into account the means of the offender as they are known to the court, whether that has the effect of increasing or reducing the amount of the fine.

3 The scale of fines for summary offences

The "statutory maximum"

	Amount of fine
The statutory maximum fine on summary-conviction of an offence triable either way, being the sum prescribed under the Magistrates' Courts Act 1980, s. 32:	£2,000

The standard scale

The standard scale of maximum fines on an adult on conviction of a summary offence, being the sum prescribed under the Criminal Justice Act 1982, s. 37:

Level on the scale	Amount of fine
1	£50
2	£100
3	£400
4	£1,000
5	£2,000

Where there is a change in the value of money, the Secretary of State is empowered by s. 48 of the Criminal Justice Act 1982 to vary the maximum amount of fines, including the amounts specified in the standard scale, as appears to him to be justified by the change.

8. Below, p. 22.

2 The Definition of a Crime[1]

It is now rather unfashionable to begin law books with definitions. One reason for this is the difficulty frequently encountered in defining the subject-matter of a particular branch of the law; and nowhere has this been more greatly felt than in the criminal law. But a book about crimes which does not tell the reader what a crime is allows him to proceed with his own preconceived notions in the matter; and it is well recognised that there is a popular meaning of crime which is different from, and narrower than, the legal meaning. A law book must be concerned with the legal meaning of crime; and the reader is entitled to know what it is, or at least why it is so difficult to tell him.

An attempt to define *a crime* at once encounters a serious difficulty. If the definition is a true one, it should enable us to recognise any *act* (or *omission*) as a crime, or not a crime, by seeing whether it contains all the ingredients of the definition. But a moment's reflection will suffice to show that this is impossible. When Parliament enacts that a particular act shall become a crime or that an act which is now criminal shall cease to be so, the act does not change in nature in any respect other than that of legal classification. All its observable characteristics are precisely the same before as after the statute comes into force. Any attempt at definition of a crime will thus either include the act at a time when it is not a crime, or exclude it when it is. Suicide was a crime until 3 August 1961, when, by the Suicide Act 1961,[2] it became perfectly lawful to kill oneself. Homosexual acts committed in private by male persons who have attained the age of 21 were offences until 27 July 1967, when by the Sexual Offences Act 1967,[3] such acts became permissible. The nature of the acts in question, their morality or immorality and their consequences do not change overnight; but their legal nature does.

1. Kenny, *Outlines of Criminal Law* (15th ed.) Ch. 1; C. K. Allen, "The Nature of a Crime", *Journal of Society of Comparative Legislation*, February, 1931, reprinted in *Legal Duties*, 221; Winfield, *Province of the Law of Tort*, Ch. VIII; Williams, "The Definition of Crime" (1955) 8 CLP 107; Hughes, "The Concept of Crime: An American View" [1959] Crim LR 239 and 331.
2. Below, pp. 379–382.
3. Below, p. 477.

1 Characteristics of a Crime

1 A Public Wrong

It is, of course, possible to point to certain characteristics which are generally found in acts which are crimes. They are generally acts which have a particularly harmful effect on the public and do more than interfere with merely private rights. Sir Carleton Allen writes:

"Crime is crime because it consists in wrongdoing which directly and in serious degree threatens the security or well-being of society, and because it is not safe to leave it redressable only by compensation of the party injured."[4]

This explains why acts have been made crimes either by judicial decision or by legislation, and it does not necessarily accurately represent the present state of affairs. A crime may remain a crime long after it has ceased to be a threat to the security or well-being of society.[5] Thus Allen's proposition tells us what – as he thinks – ought to be criminal rather than what is criminal.

The public nature of crimes is evidenced by the contrast between the rules of civil and criminal procedure. Any citizen can, as a general rule and in the absence of some provision to the contrary, bring a criminal prosecution, whether or not he has suffered any special harm over and above other members of the public. As a member of the public he has an interest in the enforcement of the criminal law. D steals P's watch. P may prosecute him – so may Q, R, S, T or any other citizen.[6] In practice, of course, the vast majority of prosecutions are carried on by the Crown Prosecution Service or other public officers who have no personal interest in the outcome. The individual who starts a prosecution may not discontinue it at will,[7] for it is not only his concern but that of every citizen. The Crown, however, through the entry of a *nolle prosequi* by the Attorney-General, may stay the proceedings at any time[8] without the consent of the prosecutor. If the prosecution succeeds and a sentence is imposed by the court, the instigator of the prosecution has no power to pardon the offender. This belongs to the Crown, representing the public interest in the matter.

All this contrasts sharply with civil wrongs – torts and breaches of contract. There, only the person injured may sue. He (and only he) may freely discontinue the proceedings at any time and, if he succeeds and an award of damages is made in his favour, he may, at his entire discretion, forgive the defendant and terminate his liability.

---

4. *Legal Duties*, at 233–234.
5. Williams, 8 CLP at 126–127.
6. The right of private prosecution is unaffected by the Prosecution of Offences Act 1985; but s. 24 empowers the High Court, on the application of the Attorney-General, to restrain a vexatious prosecutor. The DPP may take over a private prosecution at any stage (s. 6 (2)) and may discontinue a prosecution during its "preliminary stage": s. 23.
7. *Wood* (1832) 3 B & Ad 657.
8. After the indictment has been signed: *Wylie* (1919) 83 JP 295. But the Director of Public Prosecutions may intervene and offer no evidence: *Turner v Director of Public Prosecutions* (1978) 68 Cr App Rep 70 (Mars Jones J), [1978] Crim LR 754; *Raymond v A-G* [1982] QB 839, [1982] 2 All ER 487, CA, [1982] Crim LR 826 and commentary.

Crimes, then, are wrongs which the judges have held, or Parliament has from time to time laid down, are sufficiently injurious to the public to warrant the application of criminal procedure to deal with them. Of course this does not enable us to recognise an act as a crime when we see one. Some acts are so obviously harmful to the public that *anyone* would say they should be criminal – and such acts almost certainly are – but there are many others about which opinions may differ widely. When a citizen is heard urging that, "There ought to be a law against it . . .", he is expressing his personal conviction that some variety of act is so harmful to society that it ought to be discouraged by being made the subject of criminal proceedings. There will almost invariably be a body of opinion which disagrees. But even if *everyone* agreed with him, the act in question would not thereby become a crime. Public condemnation is ineffective without the endorsement of an Act of Parliament or a decision of a court.

2 A Moral Wrong

The second characteristic of crimes which is usually emphasised is that they are acts which are morally wrong. As seen above, the traditional attitude of the common law has been that crimes are essentially immoral acts deserving of punishment. In the early days of the law, when the number of crimes was relatively few and only the most outrageous acts were prohibited – murder, robbery, rape, etc. – this was, no doubt, true. But now many acts are prohibited on the grounds of social expediency and not because of their immoral nature. Especially is this so in the field of summary offences – and summary offences are crimes.[9] Moreover many acts which are generally regarded as immoral – for example, adultery – are not crimes. Thus the test of immorality is not a very helpful one.

Whether an act ought to be a crime simply on the ground of its immoral nature has been the subject of vigorous debate. The view of the Wolfenden Committee on Homosexual Offences and Prostitution was that the enforcement of morality is not a proper object of the criminal law. The function of the criminal law, as they saw it is:

". . . to preserve public order and decency, to protect the citizen from what is offensive or injurious, and to provide sufficient safeguards against exploitation and corruption of others, particularly those who are specially vulnerable . . .

"It is not . . . the function of the law to intervene in the private lives of citizens, or to seek to enforce any particular pattern of behaviour, further than is necessary to carry out the purposes we have outlined."[10]

This view was challenged by Lord Devlin,[11] who argued that there is a public morality which is an essential part of the bondage which keeps society together; and that society may use the criminal law to preserve morality in the same way that it uses it to preserve anything else that is essential to its existence. The standard of morality is that of "the man in the

9. Williams (1955) 8 CLP at 110.
10. (1957) Cmnd. 247, para. 13.
11. The Maccabaean Lecture, "The Enforcement of Morals" (1959) 45 *Proc. of British Academy*, 129 reprinted in *The Enforcement of Morals* (1965) p. 1.

jury box", based on the "mass of continuous experience half-consciously or unconsciously accumulated and embodied in the morality of common sense".

To this it was answered[12] that it is not proper for the state to enforce the general morality without asking whether it is based on ignorance, superstition or misunderstanding; that it is not a sufficient ground for prohibiting an act that "the thought of it makes the man on the Clapham omnibus sick". But if we are not to base criminal law on the general morality, does not this imply that "our law making is or should be controlled by independent Gods of Pure Reason, installed somewhere in our political systems and endowed with power to determine such questions for society, free of the prejudices to which lesser men are subject?"[13] "A free society is as much offended by the dictates of an intellectual oligarchy as by those of an autocrat."[14]

In the midst of this controversy was decided the case of *Shaw v Director of Public Prosecutions*,[15] in which Lord Simonds asserted that
"there remains in the courts of law a residual power to enforce the supreme and fundamental purpose of the law, to conserve not only the safety and order *but also the moral welfare of the state*";
and that the King's Bench was the custos morum of the people and had the superintendency of offences contra bonos mores.

"*Shaw's* case", concludes Lord Devlin, "settles for the purpose of the law that morality in England means what twelve men and women think it means – in other words it is to be ascertained as a question of fact."[16]

Subsequently, however, the particular rule of law that caused the Wolfenden Committee to formulate its general principle[17] – that homosexual conduct between consenting male adults is an offence – was repealed by the Sexual Offences Act 1967. The House of Lords has repudiated the suggestion that it has power to extend the criminal law to enforce good morals.[18] The enforcement of morality, as such, by the criminal law is losing ground.

2 Criminal Proceedings

Because of the impossibility of defining the criminal quality of an act, most writers – and the courts – have been driven to turn to the nature of the proceedings which may follow from its commission.

12. H. L. A. Hart, *The Listener* 30 July 1959, p. 162.
13. Rostow, "The Enforcement of Morals" [1960] CLJ 174 at 189.
14. Devlin, "Law, Democracy and Morality" (1962) 110 U Pa Law Rev 635 at 642 reprinted in *The Enforcement of Morals* (1965) p. 86.
15. [1962] AC 220, [1961] 2 All ER 446; below, p. 291.
16. 110 U Pa Law Rev at 648. See also H. L. A. Hart, *Law, Liberty and Morality*; Hughes, "Morals and the Criminal Law" (1962) 71 YLJ 662. For an excellent discussion of the whole controversy, see Basil Mitchell, *Law, Morality and Religion in a Secular Society* (1967).
17. Above, p. 17.
18. *Knuller (Publishing, Printing and Promotions) Ltd v Director of Public Prosecutions* [1973] AC 435, [1972] 2 All ER 898, below, p. 292.

"The criminal quality of an act cannot be discerned by intuition; nor can it be discovered by reference to any standard but one: is the act prohibited with penal consequences?"[19]

The problem then becomes one of distinguishing criminal proceedings from civil proceedings. Any attempt to distinguish between crimes and torts comes up against the same kind of difficulty encountered in defining crimes generally: that most torts are crimes as well, though some torts are not crimes and some crimes are not torts. It is not in the nature of the act, but in the nature of the proceedings that the distinction consists; and both types of proceeding may follow where an act is both a crime and a tort.[20]

Kenny,[1] in the most celebrated of all attempts to define a crime, directed his attention to ascertaining the essential distinction between civil and criminal procedure. He rejected any distinction based on (i) the degree of activity manifested by the State in the two types of proceeding; for though the "contrast is a genuine and vivid one", it was incapable of being applied with precision;[2] (ii) the tribunals; for both civil and criminal cases may be heard in the magistrates' courts and the House of Lords; (iii) the object of the proceedings; for, while "the object of criminal procedure is always *Punishment*", the award of exemplary damages in civil actions is also punitive; (iv) the nature of the sanctions; for, while criminal sanctions never enrich any individual, it was not true to say that all civil actions do, since some civil actions for penalties could be brought only by the Crown.

Kenny finally seized upon the degree of control exercised over the two types of proceedings by the Crown[3] as the criterion, and defined "crimes" as

"wrongs whose sanction is punitive and is in no way remissible by any private person, but is remissible by the Crown alone, *if remissible at all*."[4]

He thought it necessary to bring in the elements of punishment only to exclude action for the recovery of the Crown's debts or other civil rights; and the italicised words were included so as not to exclude certain crimes which cannot be pardoned.[5]

---

19. *Proprietary Articles Trade Association v A-G for Canada* [1931] AC 310 at 324, per Lord Atkin.

20. A civil action for assault or battery is barred by ss. 44 and 45 of the Offences Against the Person Act 1861 if criminal proceedings brought in the magistrates' court by or on behalf of the victim (i) have been dismissed and a certificate of dismissal has been issued; or (ii) have resulted in conviction and the defendant has paid anything he was ordered to pay or has served any imprisonment imposed. See Stevens and Whitehouse (1991) 155 JP 697.

1. *Outlines of Criminal Law* (15th ed.), Ch. 1.

2. Kenny was greatly troubled at several points in his analysis by the anomalous form of proceeding known as a penal action. This was a civil action which might be brought by any member of the public – a common informer – but its object was the punishment of the defendant; and the successful plaintiff was enriched by the penalty imposed. By the Common Informers Act 1951 such procedure is abolished and any offence formerly punishable by common informer procedure is made punishable on summary conviction by a fine not exceeding the statutory maximum.

The penal action was in no case the *sole* objection Kenny found to any of the rejected definitions; so he would presumably have reached the same result, even if these proceedings had already been abolished.

3. Above, p. 16.

4. Op. cit., at 16.

5. A public nuisance while still unabated and offences under Habeas Corpus Act 1679, s. 11.

Kenny's definition has been much criticised. Winfield[6] thought it led to a vicious circle:

"What is a crime? Something that the Crown alone can pardon. What is it that the Crown alone can pardon? A crime."[7]

Winfield thought it advisable not to accept this part of Kenny's definition; and he concentrated on the question, what is punishment? The answer he arrived at is that: "The essence of punishment is its inevitability . . . no option is left to the offender as to whether he shall endure it or not"; whereas, in a civil case, "he can always compromise or get rid of his liability with the assent of the injured party".[8] Thus we seem to arrive back at the just rejected test of who can remit the sanction.

More substantial is the point made by Williams.[9] If we are going to define crime by reference to procedure, we ought to make use of the whole law of procedure, not just one item of it – the power to remit the sanction. If a court has to decide whether a particular act which has been prohibited by Parliament is a crime, it may be guided by a reference in the statute to any element which exists only in civil, or only in criminal, procedure as the case may be. A crime is:

"an act that is capable of being followed by criminal proceedings, having one of the types of outcome (punishment, etc.) known to follow these proceedings."[10]

This definition is by no means so unhelpful as at first sight may appear; for there are many points of distinction between civil and criminal procedure, and the specification in a statute of any one procedural feature which is peculiar either to the civil or the criminal law will therefore point to the nature of the wrong. The question in issue may well be whether a rule of criminal, or a rule of civil, procedure should be followed.[11] While it may be that no statute or decision gives guidance on this precise point, the procedure test may yet supply the answer if a statute or decision indicates, as the appropriate procedure, some other rule which is peculiar either to civil or to criminal proceedings. Of course, the definition tells us nothing about what acts *ought* to be crimes, but that is not its purpose. Writers who set out to define a crime by reference to the nature of the act, on the other hand, inevitably end by telling us, not what a crime is, but what the writer thinks it ought to be; and that is not a definition of a crime.

3 The Practical Test

From time to time the courts have found it necessary to determine whether a proceeding is criminal or not. Before the Criminal Evidence Act 1898, the

6. *Province of the Law of Tort*, Ch. VIII.
7. Ibid., at 197.
8. Ibid., at 200.
9. 8 CLP 107 at 128.
10. Ibid., at 123.
11. Cf. P. J. Fitzgerald, "A Concept of Crime" [1960] Crim LR 257 at 259–260.

defendant could not give evidence on oath on his own behalf in a criminal case whereas (since the Evidence Act 1851) he had been able to do so in a civil action. If he wished to give evidence the nature of the proceeding had to be ascertained.[12] The same problem could arise today if it were sought to *compel* the defendant to give evidence.[13] But much the most fruitful source of this problem has been the Judicature Act 1873, s. 47, and its successor, the Judicature Act 1925, s. 31 (1) (a), which, until 1968,[14] provided that no appeal should lie to the Court of Appeal "in any criminal cause or matter". The question whether a particular proceeding is a criminal cause or matter has frequently come before the Court of Appeal and the House of Lords. In these cases the test which has regularly been applied is whether the proceedings may result in the punishment of the offender. If it may, then it is a criminal proceeding.[15] As a practical test, this seems to work well enough; but it must always be remembered that it is a rule with exceptions; for some actions for penalties are undoubtedly civil actions, and yet they have the punishment of the offender as their objective; for this reason the test of punishment is jurisprudentially unsatisfactory.[16]

The meaning of punishment itself is not easy to ascertain; for the defendant in a civil case, who is ordered to pay damages by way of compensation, may well feel that he has been punished. It has been suggested[17] that:

"What distinguishes a criminal from a civil sanction and all that distinguishes it . . . is the judgment of community condemnation which accompanies and justifies its imposition."

According to this view it is the condemnation, plus the consequences of the sentence – fine or imprisonment, etc. – which together constitute the punishment; but the condemnation is the essential feature. From this, it is argued that "we can say readily enough what a 'crime' is":

"It is not simply anything which the legislature chooses to call a 'crime'. It is not simply anti-social conduct which public officers are given a responsibility to suppress. It is not simply any conduct to which a legislature chooses to attach a 'criminal' penalty. It is conduct which, if duly shown to have taken place, will incur a formal and solemn pronouncement of the moral condemnation of the community."[18]

But if "the formal and solemn pronouncement" means the judgment of a criminal court (and what else can it mean?) we are driven back to

12. *Cattell v Ireson* (1858) EB & E 91; *Parker v Green* (1862) 2 B & S 299.
13. He is compellable in a civil but not in a criminal case.
14. Appeal now lies to the Court of Appeal (Criminal Division) as provided by the Criminal Appeal Act 1968.
15. E.g., *Mellor v Denham* (1880) 5 QBD 467; *Seaman v Burley* [1896] 2 QB 344; *Robson v Biggar* [1908] 1 KB 672; *Re Clifford and O'Sullivan* [1921] 2 AC 570; *Amand v Home Secretary and Minister of Defence of the Royal Netherlands Government* [1943] AC 147, [1942] 2 All ER 381; *Re Osman (No. 4)* [1991] Crim LR 533.
16. It is thought not to be a substantial objection that exemplary damages may be awarded in some civil cases; for this is merely ancillary to the main object and the occasions for their award are now much restricted: *Rookes v Barnard* [1964] AC 1129 at 1221, [1964] 1 All ER 367 at 407, HL; *Cassell & Co Ltd v Broome* [1972] AC 1027, [1972] 1 All ER 801, HL.
17. By H. M. Hart, "The Aims of the Criminal Law" (1958) 23 Law and Contemporary Problems, 401, 404.
18. H. M. Hart, "The Aims of the Criminal Law" (1958) 23 Law and Contemporary Problems, 405.

ascertaining whether the proceeding is criminal or not. How is the judge to
know whether to make "solemn and formal pronouncement of condemnation" or to give judgment as in a civil action? Surely, only by ascertaining
whether the legislature (or the courts in the case of a common law crime)
have prescribed that the proceedings shall be criminal; and this must
depend, primarily, upon whether it is intended to be punitive.

3 The Classification of Offences

1 Indictable and Summary Offences

For procedural purposes crimes are classified as indictable and summary offences. Summary offences are offences which may be tried by courts having summary jurisdiction and the trial is conducted by magistrates without a jury; all proceedings on indictment, which always take place with a jury, are now brought before the Crown Court.[1] For practical purposes it is the question of trial with or without a jury which is the important distinction between trial on indictment and summary trial. In other respects the course and conduct of the trial is very much the same.

The classification of offences as indictable and summary broadly reflects a distinction between serious and minor crimes. Some offences are so obviously serious that they are triable only on indictment,[2] and some offences are so obviously minor that they can be tried only summarily. But there are very many crimes the gravity of which turns upon the particular circumstances of the case. Recognising this Parliament has from time to time provided for the summary trial of indictable offences and vice versa. Since this was done as occasion demanded without any coherent overall plan it is not surprising that the classification which eventually emerged was found by the James Committee to be "confusing, complicated and anomalous."[3] The Committee had two objectives in mind. One was to simplify the existing classification and the other was to get a better distribution of criminal business between the Crown Court and magistrates' courts with a view to relieving the pressure of work on the former. To these ends the Committee made a number of recommendations which were first given effect by the Criminal Law Act 1977 but are now for the most part to be found in the Magistrates' Courts Act 1980.

In particular the Committee recommended a three fold classification of offences and now the only classes of offence are: (a) offences triable only on indictment; (b) offences triable only summarily; and (c) offences triable either way.

1. Supreme Court Act 1981, s. 46. When the Crown Court sits in the City of London it is known as the Central Criminal Court: s. 8 (3).

2. And some serious offences are more serious than others; consequently provision is made in Supreme Court Act 1981, s. 75 (1) for the allocation of cases as between High Court judges, Circuit judges and Recorders. See Practice Direction (1988) 86 Cr App Rep 142.

3. *The Distribution of Criminal Business between the Crown Court and Magistrates' Courts* (1975) Cmnd. 6323, para. 9.

1 Offences Triable Summarily only

A summary offence is one which, if committed by an adult, is triable only summarily.[4] Such offences are entirely the creation of statute. It is of course open to Parliament to review the appropriate class for a particular offence and the opportunity was taken in the Criminal Law Act 1977, with a view to easing the workload of the Crown Court, of making certain offences (including drink-driving and assaulting constables in the execution of their duty) summary only, though they had formerly been triable either way. Subsequently the Criminal Justice Act 1988 has made summary only the offences of common assault and battery and taking vehicles without consent.

2 Offences Triable only on Indictment

An indictable offence means an offence which, if committed by an adult, is triable on indictment, whether it is exclusively so triable or triable either way.[5] Offences triable only on indictment include any offence punishable by death or imprisonment for life on first conviction, causing death by dangerous driving and the more serious offences under the Theft Act 1968. Generally offences are made indictable only, either because they are of such exceptional gravity or because other reasons, such as anticipated complexity of issues, make them unsuitable for summary trial.

3 Offences Triable Either Way

An offence triable either way means an offence which, if committed by an adult, is triable either on indictment or summarily.[6] The class extends to (i) the offences listed in the Magistrates' Courts Act 1980, Sched. 1; and (ii) offences made triable either way by virtue of any other enactment.[7]

For offences falling under this head the procedure is regulated by the Magistrates' Courts Act 1980. It is for the court to decide, having regard to representations made by the prosecutor and the accused and all the circumstances of the case, which is the more suitable form of trial (s. 19). If the court decides that trial on indictment is more suitable it proceeds to consider the case as examining justices (s. 21). But if the court decides that summary trial is more suitable it cannot so proceed unless (i) having first informed the accused of his right to be tried by jury, the accused consents to be tried summarily; and (ii) the accused is informed that if he is tried summarily and convicted he may be committed to the Crown Court for

---

4. Interpretation Act 1978, Sched. 1. To incite the commission of a summary offence is itself a summary offence (Magistrates' Courts Act 1980, s. 45 (1)); to conspire to commit a summary offence is an indictable offence (Criminal Law Act 1977, s. 3); it is not generally an offence to attempt to commit an offence which is summary only, unless the statute so provides: Criminal Attempts Act 1981, ss. 1 and 3, below, p. 314.
5. Interpretation Act 1978, Sched. 1.
6. Interpretation Act 1978, Sched. 1.
7. Magistrates' Courts Act 1980, s. 17.

sentence if the court is of the opinion that a greater punishment should be inflicted than it has power to impose (s. 20).[8]

The Divisional Court has issued guidelines[9] setting out the sorts of aggravating factors which may make an either way offence more suitable for trial on indictment. Generally, however, an either way offence should be tried summarily unless it has one or more of the specified aggravating factors *and* the sentencing powers of the court (generally the maximum which a magistrates' court may impose is six months' imprisonment and/or a fine of £2,000) are insufficient.

If the court then proceeds to summary trial it may at any time before the conclusion of the prosecution's case discontinue summary trial and proceed to inquire into the charge as examining justices (s. 25 (2)). Conversely if the court has begun to inquire into the charge as examining justices it may at any time decide, having regard to representations made, that the case is after all more suitable for summary trial. If it does so the court may proceed to try the case summarily provided the accused, having first been informed of his right to jury trial, consents to be tried summarily (s. 25 (3) and (4)).

This is, in outline, the normal procedure for dealing with offences triable either way but there are three exceptional cases.

The first is where the prosecution is being conducted by or on behalf of the Attorney General, the Solicitor General or the Director of Public Prosecutions. If any of these officers apply for trial on indictment the court has no say in the matter and must proceed as examining justices (s. 19 (4)).

The second is where the accused is charged with a "scheduled offence". The James Committee had proposed,[10] and again with a view to relieving pressure on the Crown Court, that minor cases of theft and criminal damage should be triable only summarily. This proposal was accepted by Parliament in relation to criminal damage but not in relation to theft on the ground that a conviction for the latter involved a stigma not involved in the former. The outcome is that where on a charge of criminal damage the value of the property does not exceed the relevant sum (currently £2,000) the accused must be tried summarily but, having regard to the loss of the former right to be tried by jury, the maximum punishment which the court can impose is three months' imprisonment and/or a fine of £1,000.

The third exception concerns children and young persons. Where such a person is charged with any offence, other than homicide, he must be tried summarily unless (a) he is a young person (i.e. between fourteen and seventeen) charged with an offence punishable by fourteen years' imprisonment and the court considers that if convicted he should be sentenced to a long period of detention; or (b) he is charged jointly with a person over seventeen in which case the court may, if it considers it necessary in the interests of justice, commit both for trial.[11]

---

8. The circumstances in which D may be committed for sentence are set out in s. 38 of the Act as substituted by s. 25 of the Criminal Justice Act 1991.
9. *Practice Note (National Mode of Trial Guidelines)* (1991) 92 Cr App Rep 142, DC.
10. Cmnd. 6323, paras. 74–105.
11. Magistrates' Courts Act 1980, s. 24.

2 Treasons, Felonies and Misdemeanours: Arrestable Offences

At common law a crime might be classified either as treason, felony or misdemeanour. Originally the distinction between felony and misdemeanour was a distinction between serious and minor offences (the former involving penalties of a different order from the latter)[12] but over the years this distinction, though always broadly discernible, became blurred. The practical importance of the distinction came to lie in certain consequences which turned upon whether the offence was felony or misdemeanour. For example, the general power of arrest without warrant was available only in respect of felonies; only in felonies was the distinction drawn between principals and accessories to the crime; and it was an offence to conceal (misprision), or to agree not to prosecute (compound), a felony, though it was not an offence to conceal a misdemeanour and probably not an offence to compound one.

But now, by s. 1 of the Criminal Law Act 1967, all distinctions between felony and misdemeanour are abolished and, on all matters on which a distinction has previously been drawn, the law is assimilated to that applicable to misdemeanour at the commencement of the Act. Consequently there is no distinction of substance between the former felonies, whether created at common law or by statute, and misdemeanours, and all may be conveniently called "offences". No doubt it would simplify things if it were possible to dispense altogether with any mention of felony and misdemeanour, but this is not possible. The terms appear regularly in pre-1968 cases and the student must know to what they refer. Most of these cases remain unaffected by the abolition of the distinctions between felony and misdemeanour since the law is, in the main, the same for both. And even cases which raise the peculiarities of felony may remain authoritative in other respects. For example, although it is no longer necessary to draw the elaborate distinctions relating to degrees of participation in felony, the cases may remain authoritative as showing the limits of criminal participation in an offence.

It will be appreciated, however, that for some purposes, and especially for the purposes of the law of arrest without warrant, it is necessary to maintain a distinction between those (serious) offences in respect of which it is necessary that there should be a power of arrest without warrant and those (minor) offences in respect of which there is no general need for such a power. The Criminal Law Act 1967, s. 2, accordingly introduced the new concept of the arrestable offence. The definition in that Act has now been replaced and modified[13] by s. 24 of the Police and Criminal Evidence Act (PACE) 1984 where an arrestable offence is defined as any offence "for which the sentence is fixed by law[14] or for which a person (not previously convicted) may be sentenced for a term of five years (or might be so

---

12. See generally, Pollock and Maitland, 2 HEL, Cap. VIII, s. 2.
13. The modification is that common law misdemeanours for which no maximum sentence is prescribed are now included in the definition of arrestable offences. Statutory conspiracy to commit an arrestable offence was made an arrestable offence by s. 3 of the Criminal Law Act 1977.
14. These are murder (Murder (Abolition of Death Penalty) Act 1965, s. 1 (1)); treason (Treason Act 1814, s. 1); piracy with violence (Piracy Act 1837, s. 2).

sentenced but for the restrictions imposed by s. 33 of the Magistrates' Courts Act 1980[15]), and to attempts to commit any such offence." Included in the definition of arrestable offences are certain offences (for example, going equipped for stealing contrary to s. 25 of the Theft Act 1968) which, not carrying five years' imprisonment, would not be arrestable offences in their own right but where a power of arrest without warrant was thought necessary for the proper enforcement of the law. In other respects PACE re-states the law relating to arrest but does not provide a comprehensive code.[16]

Moreover, the Criminal Law Act 1967 created offences in relation to arrestable offences which cannot be committed in respect of other offences. Under s. 4 (1) it is an offence to assist a person guilty of an arrestable offence, and s. 5 (1) creates an offence of agreeing for gain to conceal information relating to an arrestable offence. These offences had their counterparts in the earlier law; the first closely resembles the former offence of being an accessory after the fact to felony, and the latter has features – though very emaciated features – of the former offences of misprision and compounding. The modern classification of arrestable and non-arrestable offences has thus broadly and with much modification superseded the former classification of felonies and misdemeanours.

15. This qualification, introduced by the Criminal Law Act 1977 and continued in PACE, is to make it clear that the power of arrest remains unaffected by the fact that in certain circumstances (as to which see above, p. 25) an indictable offence may be triable only summarily.
16. Apart from retaining the arrestable offence, PACE retains a small number of statutory powers of arrest without warrant (see Sch. 2). There is no power under PACE to arrest without warrant for any other *offence* though an *offender* may be arrested without warrant if the arrest conditions specified in s. 25 are met. PACE leaves unaffected the common law power to arrest for breach of the peace.

4 The Elements of a Crime

It is a general principle of criminal law that a person may not be convicted of a crime unless the prosecution have proved beyond reasonable doubt both (a) that he has caused a certain event or that responsibility is to be attributed to him for the existence of a certain state of affairs, which is forbidden by criminal law, and (b) that he had a defined state of mind in relation to the causing of the event or the existence of the state of affairs. The event, or state of affairs, is called the *actus reus* and the state of mind the *mens rea* of the crime. Though it is absolutely clear that D killed P – that is, he has caused an *actus reus* – he must be acquitted of murder if there is a reasonable possibility that the killing was accidental; for, if that is the case, it has not been proved beyond reasonable doubt that he had the requisite mental element. It was so laid down by the House of Lords in *Woolmington v Director of Public Prosecutions*[1] where it was held, overruling earlier authorities, that it is a misdirection to tell a jury that D must *satisfy* them that the killing was an accident. The true rule is that the jury must acquit even though they are not satisfied that D's story is true, if they think it might reasonably be true. They should convict only if satisfied beyond reasonable doubt that it is *not* true. This rule is of general application[2] and there is only one exception to it at common law – the defence of insanity.[3] To raise other defences at common law – for example, provocation, self-defence, automatism or duress – the accused need do no more than introduce some evidence of all the constituents of the defence; whereupon it is for the Crown to satisfy the jury that those constituents did not exist. If there is evidence of a defence, though it has not been specifically raised by the accused, the judge must direct the jury to acquit unless they are satisfied that the defence has been disproved.[4] A statute may, however, expressly or impliedly[5] impose a burden of proof on the defendant and frequently does so. Where an onus of proof is put upon D, he satisfies it if

---

1. [1935] AC 462; **SHC 42**.
2. *Mancini v Director of Public Prosecutions* [1942] AC 1, [1941] 3 All ER 272; *Chan Kau v R* [1955] AC 206, [1955] 1 All ER 266; *Lobell* [1957] 1 QB 547, [1957] 1 All ER 734 (self-defence); *Bratty v A-G for Northern Ireland* [1963] AC 386, [1961] 3 All ER 523; **SHC 199** (automatism); *Gill* [1963] 2 All ER 688, [1963] 1 WLR 841 (duress). But the onus of proving procedural bars to trial, such as *autrefois convict* or *acquit*, may be on the defendant: *Coughlan* (1976) 63 Cr App Rep 33 at 36.
3. Below, p. 205.
4. *Palmer v R* [1971] AC 814, [1971] 1 All ER 1077 at 1080; **SHC 245**; *Wheeler* (1968) 52 Cr App Rep 28 at 30–31; *Hamand* (1985) 82 Cr App Rep 65.
5. *Hunt* [1987] 1 All ER 1 at 10, 15, HL.

he proves his case on a balance of probabilities – the same standard as that on the plaintiff in a civil action – and he need not prove it beyond reasonable doubt.[6]

The principle that a man is not criminally liable for his conduct unless the prescribed state of mind is also present is frequently stated in the form of a Latin maxim: *actus non facit reum nisi mens sit rea*[7]. It is convenient, for purposes of exposition, to consider the mental element separately from the other elements of the crime. The mental element is traditionally described as the *mens rea* and the other elements as the *actus reus*. The *actus reus* amounts to a crime only when it is accompanied by the appropriate *mens rea*. To cause an *actus reus* without the requisite *mens rea* is not a crime and may be an ordinary, innocent act. For example, the offence of perjury[8] consists in making a statement, whether true or not, on oath in a judicial proceeding, knowing it to be false or not believing it to be true. Thus, every statement on oath in a judicial proceeding is the *actus reus* of perjury. When we say then that a certain event is the *actus reus* of a crime what we mean is that the event would be a crime if it were caused by a person with *mens rea*. The description of it as an *actus reus* implies no judgment whatever as to its moral or legal quality. The analysis into *actus reus* and *mens rea* is for convenience of exposition only. The only concept known to the law is the crime; and the crime exists only when *actus reus* and *mens rea* coincide.

It is not always possible to separate *actus reus* from *mens rea*.[9] Sometimes a word which describes the *actus reus*, or part of it, implies a mental element. Without that mental element the *actus reus* simply cannot exist. There are many offences of possession of proscribed objects and it has always been recognised that possession consists in a mental as well as physical element.[10] The same is true of words like "permits",[11] "appropriates",[12] "cultivates"[13] and many more. Having an offensive weapon in a public place is the *actus reus* of an offence; but whether an article is an offensive weapon depends, in some circumstances, on the intention with which it is carried. In the absence of that intention, the thing is not an offensive weapon and there is no *actus reus*.[14] The significance of this is that any mental element which is part of the *actus reus* is necessarily an element

6. *Carr-Briant* [1943] KB 607, [1943] 2 All ER 156. The Criminal Law Revision Committee and the Law Commission have proposed that the law should be so amended that D would, in these cases, merely have to introduce sufficient evidence to raise the issue (an "evidential burden") whereupon the onus of proof would be on the Crown: Eleventh Report, Cmnd. 4991, paras. 137–142; Draft Code, cl. 13.

7. "Properly translated, this means 'An act does not make a man guilty of a crime, unless his mind be also guilty.' It is thus not the *actus* which is '*reus*' but the man and his mind respectively:" per Lord Hailsham in *Haughton v Smith* [1975] AC 467 at 491–492, [1973] 3 All ER 1109 at 1113–1114. It is, however, convenient to follow the established usage of "*actus reus*". Cf. Lord Simon in *Director of Public Prosecutions for Northern Ireland v Lynch* [1975] AC 653 at 690, [1975] 1 All ER 913 at 934 and Lord Diplock in *Miller* [1983] 2 AC 161, [1983] 1 All ER 978, 979, HL.

8. Perjury Act 1911, s 1 (1), Stephen, *Digest*, 95–96.

9. See A. C. E. Lynch, "The Mental Element in the Actus Reus" (1982) 98 LQR 109.

10. Below, p. 110.

11. Below, p. 104.

12. Below, p. 497.

13. *Champ* (1981) 73 Cr App Rep 367, [1982] Crim LR 108 and commentary.

14. Below, p. 443.

of the offence. It is possible for the courts to dispense with *mens rea* in whole or in part, but, except in the anomalous case of an intoxicated offender,[15] they can never dispense with the *actus reus*. If an offence consists in possessing or permitting, it cannot be proved if D cannot be shown to have possessed or permitted. The court may of course give effect to the word without requiring full *mens rea*, as where it held that D was guilty of permitting the use of an uninsured vehicle where he intended to permit only the use of the vehicle (which was in fact uninsured) or cultivating a cannabis plant where he intended only to cultivate that plant (which was in fact a cannabis plant).

1 The Actus Reus

1 The Nature of an Actus Reus

Since the *actus reus* includes all the elements in the definition of the crime except the accused's mental element,[16] it follows that the *actus reus* is not merely an act. It may indeed consist in a "state of affairs", not including an act at all.[17] Much more often, the *actus reus* requires proof of an act or an omission (conduct). Usually, it must be proved that the conduct had a particular result. In murder, for example, it must be shown that the accused's conduct caused the death. Some crimes do not require evidence of any result. Perjury is committed as soon as D makes a statement on oath which he does not believe to be true. It is irrelevant whether he is believed or not. These different types of offence have been designated[18] "result crimes" and "conduct crimes" respectively. It has been said[19] that in "result crimes" the law is interested only in the result and not in the conduct bringing about the result. Similarly, a well-known definition of *actus reus* is "such result of human conduct as the law seeks to prevent".[20] But a dead man with a knife in his back is not the *actus reus* of a murder. It is putting the knife in the back thereby causing the death which is the *actus reus*. The law is no less interested in the conduct which brings about the result in a "result crime" than in a "conduct crime".[1]

True conduct crimes, such as perjury, are rare. The term has been widely interpreted by Glanville Williams to include rape and abduction – in these crimes, "you do not have to wait to see if anything happens as a result of what the defendant does."[2] If the test is whether you "have to wait

---

15. See *Lipman* [1970] 1 QB 152, [1969] 3 All ER 410, below, p. 368.
16. It should be said that this is not the only possible definition of an *actus reus*, and that a more limited view is taken of it by some writers. It is thought, however, that it is the most useful conception of the *actus reus* and is adopted throughout this book. Cf. Williams, CLGP, 16 and [1958] Crim LR at 830.
17. Below, p. 43.
18. By Gordon, 61.
19. Ibid.
20. Kenny, 17.
1. See Lord Diplock in *Treacy v Director of Public Prosecutions* [1971] AC 537 at 560, [1971] 1 All ER 110 at 120.
2. "The Problem of Reckless Attempts", [1983] Crim LR 365 at 366, 368.

to see" wounding is a conduct crime if committed with a knife but a result crime if committed with a gun, crossbow or catapult. If the distinction is to be made at all (and, while interesting, it is not clear that it has, or should have, any practical consequences) these offences are better regarded as result crimes. A result has to flow from D's physical movements, whether you have to wait for it or not.

Since the Criminal Attempts Act 1981,[3] all indictable offences are now, in a sense, potentially conduct crimes because any act, done with intent thereby[4] to commit an indictable offence may be an indictable attempt to commit it. The *actus reus* of the offence attempted need never happen and may, indeed, be impossible. Its definition serves only to define the *mens rea* of the attempt. A case can be made that the law should always have regard only to the conduct and not to the result. Whether the conduct results in harm is generally a matter of chance and does not alter the blameworthiness and dangerousness of the actor. But the law has not gone so far. If D hurls a stone, being reckless whether he injures anyone, he is guilty of an offence if the stone strikes P but of no offence – not even an attempt – if no one is injured. From a retributive point of view, it might be argued that D should be equally liable in either event. On utilitarian grounds, however, it is probably undesirable to turn the whole criminal law into "conduct crimes". The needs of deterrence are probably adequately served in most cases by "result crimes"; and the criminal law should be extended only where a clear need is established.

The *actus reus* then is made up, generally but not invariably, of conduct and sometimes its consequences and also of the circumstances in which the conduct takes place (or which constitute the state of affairs) in so far as they are relevant. Circumstances, like consequences, are relevant if they are included in the definition of the crime. The definition of theft, for example, requires that it be proved that D dishonestly appropriated property *belonging to another*. If the property belonged to no-one (because it had been abandoned) D's appropriation could not constitute the *actus reus* of theft. However dishonest he might be, he could not be convicted of theft because an essential constituent of the crime is missing.[5]

Sometimes a particular state of mind on the part of the *victim* is required by the definition of the crime. If so, that state of mind is part of the *actus reus* and, if the prosecution are unable to prove its existence, they must fail. If D is prosecuted for rape, it must be proved that P did not consent to the act of intercourse. The absence of consent by P is an essential constituent of the *actus reus*. But in some crimes the consent of the victim is entirely irrelevant. If D is charged with the murder of P, it is no defence for him to show that P asked to be killed.

It is apparent from these examples that it is only by looking at the definition of the particular crime that we can see what circumstances are elements of the *actus reus*. We find this definition, in the case of common

3. As interpreted in *Shivpuri*, below, p. 322.
4. I.e., D intends to cause the result by that act; it is the last act D intends, and needs, to do, not a merely preparatory act. An earlier act is sufficient, if "more than merely preparatory": below, p. 304.
5. He might, however, be convicted of an attempt to steal. Below, p. 317.

law crimes, in the decisions of the courts and, in the case of statutory crimes, in the words of the statute, as construed by the courts. Many factors may be relevant; for example, in bigamy, the fact that D is validly married; in treason committed abroad, that D is a British national (or under the protection of the Crown for some other reason); in handling stolen goods, that the goods have, in fact, been stolen; and so on.

a) *The effect of penalty provisions in determining the elements of the* actus reus. Sometimes it happens that Parliament provides that an offence shall be more severely punishable when a particular fact, say X, is present. The effect is that there are now two offences. The offence with X is a different, graver, offence than the offence without X. X is an element in the *actus reus* or the *mens rea*, or both, of the greater offence. The importance of this is (i) that D can be convicted of the greater offence only if the charge alleges X, and (ii) it is for the jury to decide whether X is proved and to give their verdict accordingly, not a matter for the judge to decide after verdict.[6] It follows that there are now two offences: the original offence (i) with X and (ii) without X. Buggery was a single offence at common law, whether committed with or without consent, with a person of any age or sex, or with an animal. The Sexual Offences Act 1956, s. 12 (1), merely provided that this offence was punishable with life imprisonment. The Sexual Offences Act 1967, however, provided for a new scale of penalties[7] ranging from two years to imprisonment for life, depending on the age and sex of the other person and whether he consented. Until 1984 it was thought that there was a single offence and that it was for the judge to determine, e.g., whether there was consent or not. In *Courtie*[8] the House of Lords laid down the principle stated above and held that buggery with a male aged nineteen with his consent was a different offence from buggery with the same person without his consent, the second offence carrying a higher maximum. Since the indictment had not alleged absence of consent and that issue had not been decided by the jury, D could be convicted of the lesser offence only. Where Parliament provides an elaborate structure of maximum penalties, as in the case of drug offences, the substantive law is correspondingly complex.[9] But the principle is sound. Where proof of fact X entails liability to a higher penalty, the requirements of proof of X should be no less stringent than in the case of the other facts of the offence.

b) Actus reus *and justification or excuse*. In the terminology used by Glanville Williams:[10]

> "*Actus reus* includes ... the absence of any ground of justification or excuse, whether such justification or excuse be stated in any statute creating the crime or implied by the courts in accordance with general principle ...."

6. *Courtie* [1984] AC 463, [1984] 1 All ER 740, HL.
7. Below, p. 481.
8. Above, fn. 6.
9. *Shivpuri* [1987] AC 1 [1986] 2 All ER 334, [1986] Crim LR 536 and commentary; *Ellis, Street and Smith* (1986) 84 Cr App Rep 235, [1987] Crim LR 44, CA, and commentary.
10. CLGP, 19. See also TBCL, Ch. 2.

An alternative view is that of D.J. Lanham:[11]

"As a matter of analysis we can think of a crime as being made up of three ingredients, *actus reus*, *mens rea* and (a negative element) absence of a valid defence."

If the public executioner carries out his duty to hang a convicted traitor or D shoots to kill in reasonable defence, no offence is committed – according to Williams because there is no *actus reus* (or, indeed, *mens rea*) and, according to Lanham, because, though there is both *actus reus* and *mens rea* (the intentional killing of a human being) there is a valid defence. Williams's opinion is attractive both because it seems strange to describe an act which is required or permitted by the law as an *actus reus*[12] and because there are practical difficulties in distinguishing (as Lanham's analysis requires) between the definitional elements of an offence and defence elements. On the other hand, the enumeration of the elements of an offence becomes impossibly cumbersome if it has to include all conceivable defences – as the authors of the draft criminal code put it, "the inapplicability of every exception admitted by the definition of an offence must be treated as an element of it."[13] Moreover, defences may also require mental as well as external elements. Duress is a defence but only, of course, if D is aware of the threatening facts.[14] If the object of the Latin terminology is convenience of exposition, there is much to be said for the Lanham usage and it is generally (but not invariably) followed in this book.[15]

2 An Actus Reus must be Proved

Mens rea may exist without an *actus reus* but, if the *actus reus* of a particular crime does not exist or occur, that crime is not committed. Although D believes that he is appropriating P's property he cannot in any circumstances be guilty of theft if the property belongs to no-one. D has the *mens rea* but the *actus reus*, the other fundamental element of the crime, is lacking. D may assault P with intent to ravish her against her will but, if in fact she consents, his act cannot amount to rape. D may intend to marry during the lifetime of his wife but if, unknown to him, she is dead, he cannot commit bigamy. If D makes a statement, which he believes to be false, for the purpose of obtaining money, he cannot be convicted of obtaining by deception if the statement is, in fact, true. In each case, D may now be convicted of attempting to commit the crime in question.[16]

In *Deller*,[17] D induced P to purchase his car by representing (*inter alia*) that it was free from encumbrances. D had previously executed a document which purported to mortgage the car to a finance company and, no doubt, he thought he was telling a lie. He was charged with obtaining by false

11. [1976] Crim LR 276.
12. But, as noted above, *actus reus* implies no moral judgment, the only point of the analysis being convenience in exposition.
13. Draft Code, vol 2, 7.2, 7.3.
14. Below, p. 232.
15. See below, p. 75. The Latin terms are frequently used by the courts but no detailed analysis has been made by them and it cannot be said that there is a standard judicial usage.
16. Below, p. 317.
17. (1952) 36 Cr App Rep 184; **SHC 3**. Cf. *Brien* (1903) 3 SRNSW 410; *Dyson* [1908] 2 KB 454; below, p. 331.

pretences.[18] It then appeared that the document by which the transaction had been effected was probably void in law as an unregistered bill of sale. If it was void the car *was* free from encumbrances – ". . . quite accidentally and, strange as it may sound, dishonestly, the appellant had told the truth".[19] D's conviction was, therefore, quashed by the Court of Criminal Appeal, for, though he had *mens rea*, no *actus reus* had been established. D could now be convicted of an attempt to obtain by deception.[20]

A case which is sometimes said to be inconsistent with this fundamental principle, but which is worth discussing because it illustrates the difficulties which may arise in connection with its application, is *Dadson*.[1]

D was a constable, employed to watch a copse from which wood had been stolen. He carried a loaded gun. P emerged from the copse carrying wood which he had stolen, and, ignoring D's calls to stop, ran away. D, having no other means of bringing him to justice, fired and wounded him in the leg. He was convicted of shooting at P with intent to cause him grievous bodily harm. It was assumed in this case that it was lawful to wound an escaping felon if this was the only way of arresting him;[2] but stealing growing wood was not, under s. 39 of the Larceny Act 1827, a felony unless P had two previous convictions for the same offence. In fact P had been repeatedly convicted of stealing wood, but D did not know this. Erle J told the jury that the alleged felony, *being unknown to the prisoner*, constituted no justification. On a case reserved the judges thought the conviction right: D was not justified in firing at P because the fact that P was committing a felony was not known to D at the time.

The argument runs that this case is wrong because, if we ignore D's state of mind and look at the actual facts, what he did was lawful; that there was no *actus reus*. It is submitted that this is going too far. It is important to distinguish between two types of "defence" which may be raised. In the first type, D merely denies the existence of an element (other than the *mens rea*) in the definition of the crime. If D makes out the defence he certainly cannot be convicted, whatever his state of mind. This is what happened in *Deller*.[3] In the second type, D admits that all the elements in the definition of the crime have been established and goes on to assert other facts which afford him a defence in law. As appears from the example of duress, above, the establishment of this type of defence may require D to assert the existence of a mental element as well as external facts.

In *Dadson*[4] D did not deny that he shot at P or that he intended to cause him grievous bodily harm. He admitted the necessary constituents of the crime (other than "unlawfulness") but went on to assert other facts which, he alleged, made his act lawful. Whether his act was lawful depended on what were the constituents of the defence which he raised; and the case

---

18. Under s. 32 of the Larceny Act 1916, now replaced by s. 15 of the Theft Act 1968, below, p. 569. The same principles are applicable.
19. (1952) 36 Cr App Rep 184 at 191.
20. Below, p. 317.
    1. (1850) 2 Den 35; *cf. Tooley* (1709) 11 Mod Rep 242 at 251, per Holt CJ; and see Williams, CLGP, 23 et seq., and Burchell and Hunt 115.
    2. On this point, see below, p. 253.
    3. Above.
    4. Above.

decides that the defence, like duress and self-defence, required the assertion not merely of external facts but also of a state of mind. A doctrine of *actus reus* which says that such a course *must* be wrong, as contravening a fundamental principle, is much too constricting. Whether the defence should consist simply in the external facts, or in the facts plus the state of mind, is a matter of policy; and it was a not unreasonable decision of policy to say that a man who deliberately shot another should be guilty of an offence unless he knew of circumstances justifying or excusing his conduct.

Dadson then, is perfectly reconcilable with *Deller*. It does not decide that a man can be convicted where there is no *actus reus*: there was an *actus reus* for D did unlawfully wound P. All that the case decided was that the defence to wounding, "I was arresting an escaping felon", was a defence which required a mental as well as a physical element and, the mental element lacking, the wounding was unlawful.[5]

The Code Team and the Law Commission assumed that *Dadson* was overruled by the Criminal Law Act 1967, s. 2 and PACE 1984, s. 24 which replaced it. Section 24 provides that D may arrest P if (i) P is in the act of committing an arrestable offence, or (ii) D has reasonable grounds to suspect P to be committing such an offence. Having reasonable grounds for suspicion is a separate and distinct ground for arrest: Dadson's act would be lawful (it is said) simply because P was in the act of committing the arrestable offence. But this conclusion overlooks the common law principle, restated in PACE, s. 28 (3), that an arrest is lawful only if "the person arrested is informed of the ground for the arrest at the time of, or as soon as practicable after, the arrest". It follows that a person making an arrest must know of, or at least suspect, the existence of valid grounds for an arrest. Dadson was wholly unaware of such grounds. If the arrest was unlawful, the shooting to effect it was also unlawful.[6]

a) *Justification and excuse.* A distinction is sometimes made between a defence amounting to a justification and a defence amounting only to an excuse: where the circumstances justify the act, it is immaterial that D is not aware of them; where they can merely excuse the act, they do so only if he is aware of them. Force used to make an arrest is said to be justified, not merely excused, so, it is argued, *Dadson* was a cause of justification and is wrongly decided. Duress, which obviously requires awareness, is distinguishable because it merely excuses. But the distinction does not work. A boy who, knowing it is a wicked thing to do, deliberately kills his playmate has a defence if he shows he was aged only nine at the time. He is excused, but no one would say he was "justified" because he was only nine. Is he to be liable for murder if he thought he was ten (when he would have been liable)? Obviously not. He is excused by the fact, whether he knows of it or not. It

---

5. Below, p. 257. For a defence of *Dadson*, see Hall, *General Principles*, 228 and Perkins, *Criminal Law*, 39. And cf. the crime of perjury where D may be convicted if he makes a statement on oath which he believes to be false though it is in fact true.

6. This conclusion derives some support from *Chapman v DPP* [1988] Crim LR 843, DC and commentary; Smith, *Justification and Excuse*, pp. 34–41. On the issue of the principle, see Hogan [1989] Crim LR 679.

is the policy of the law that a child under ten shall not be convicted of crime and the child's mistake cannot be allowed to defeat that policy.

Self-defence is still governed by the common law. Suppose that D shoots at P with intent to murder him and kills him. It turns out that D did so in nick of time because, unknown to D, P was about to shoot D dead. If he had only known he would certainly have had the defence of self-defence. Is D guilty of murder? According to the justification/excuse theory, it depends on whether self-defence provides a justification or an excuse for the use of force. Glanville Williams, who at one time thought self defence merely an excuse, now considers it to be a justification,[7] so he thinks D would have a defence. But can it really be right that a person who has fired a gun at another with intent to murder should be beyond the reach of the law? One answer is that, though not guilty of murder, he is guilty of attempted murder under the Criminal Attempts Act 1981 (since, by that Act, he is to be treated for the purpose of an attempt charge as if the facts were as he believed them to be). But how can it be said that his act was both (i) justified and (ii) attempted murder? What would a jury make of a direction to that effect? The better view is that the *Dadson* principle applies and that it is generally applicable to defences unless policy (as in the case of the nine year old, above) otherwise requires.

3 Analysis of an Actus Reus

Some writers have suggested that "an act" is nothing more than a willed muscular movement – for example, the deliberate crooking of a finger. But if D crooked his finger around the trigger of a loaded pistol which was pointing at P, with the result that P was killed, to say "D crooked his finger" would be a most misleading way of describing D's "act". "Again, suppose a person orally demands money by threats of injury. Can the action of his vocal chords be separated from the resulting sound issuing from his mouth and its intended meaning to the hearer?"[8] We naturally say, "D shot P" or "D demanded money from P". This way of describing the act takes account of the circumstances surrounding the actual movement of the body (in so far as they are relevant) and its consequences (again, in so far as they are relevant), and, for ordinary purposes, it is obviously the sensible way of describing it. But for the purposes of the criminal law it is sometimes necessary to break down an "act", so comprehensively described, into the constituents of (i) the conduct which is the central feature of the crime, (ii) the surrounding material circumstances, and (iii) the consequences. One reason for so doing will soon appear. When we consider *mens rea* we will see that the law's requirements as to the mental state which must be proved are not necessarily the same for each of the different elements in the *actus reus*. To take a crime where the cases show this to be so,[9] s. 20 of the Sexual Offences Act 1956, provides:

---

7. Compare CLGP (1961) 25, (1982) 2 LS 233, 250.
8. *Timbu Kolian v R* (1968) 119 CLR 47 at 69, per Windeyer J. D's act was demanding with menaces.
9. See below, p. 38.

"It is an offence for a person acting without lawful authority or excuse to take an unmarried girl under the age of sixteen out of the possession of her parent or guardian against his will."

Here the conduct which is the central feature of the crime is the physical act of taking away the girl. The material circumstances are:

(i) the absence of lawful authority or excuse;
(ii) that the girl was unmarried and under sixteen;
(iii) that she was in the possession of her parent or guardian.

The material consequence is the removal of the girl from the possession of the parent.[10]

If any one of the circumstances is not present or the consequence does not occur the crime is not committed. Thus if D was acting under the order of a competent court; or if P was married,[11] or seventeen; or if she was not in the possession of any parent or guardian, in none of these cases would there be an *actus reus*.

4 The Conduct must be Willed

If the *actus reus* of the crime includes an act, it must of course be proved that D did that act. Suppose the act is "wounding" and the evidence shows that, while D was holding a knife in his hand, E seized D's hand and, against D's will, plunged the knife still held by D's hand into P. Plainly D is not guilty of wounding because it was not his act. Similarly D would not be guilty of a battery if he was afflicted by St. Vitus' dance and his fist shot out in an uncontrolled spasm and struck P; or if D, startled by an unexpected explosion, dropped a weight, which he was carrying carefully, on to P's foot. If D, while driving, is attacked by a swarm of bees and disabled from controlling the vehicle, he may be held to be no longer "driving".[12] In each of these cases the movement of D's limbs was involuntary in that it did not flow from an exercise by D of his will. The event happened either against or at least without his will. In these examples, D was conscious. If he is unconscious or asleep, he cannot exercise his will, so any movements of his body are involuntary.

There is one exception to the rule that there is no liability for an involuntary act. Where the "act" was done while in a state of intoxication self-induced by taking alcohol or a drug (other than a merely soporific or sedative drug[13]) it will, apparently, be no defence to crimes not requiring a "specific intent", that D was unconscious or otherwise "acting" involuntarily.[14] It has been argued[15] that this is part of a wider rule that automatism

---

10. Williams argues that this is not a consequence and that the offence is not a "result crime" but a "conduct crime" (above, p. 30) ([1983] Crim LR 365 at 368 "The Problem of Reckless Attempts") but is not the removal of the girl from the father's possession as much a "result" as killing or wounding? See above, p. 30. If D and the girl are intercepted by her father at his front door, has not D failed to achieve a result?
11. If under 16, she could be validly married if domiciled abroad at the time of the marriage. See *Mohamed v Knott* [1969] 1 QB 1, [1968] 2 All ER 563.
12. *Hill v Baxter* [1958] 1 QB 277 at 286.
13. *Hardie* [1984] 3 All ER 848, [1985] 1 WLR 64, **SHC 102**, CA.
14. *Lipman* [1970] 1 QB 152, [1969] 3 All ER 410; **SHC 100**; approved in *Director of Public Prosecutions v Majewski* [1977] AC 443, [1976] 2 All ER 142. See below, pp. 231, 368.
15. McKay, "Intoxication as a Factor in Automatism", [1982] Crim LR 146, 147.

induced by D's "fault" is no defence in these cases. "Fault" means doing or omitting to do something which could reasonably be foreseen to be likely to bring about such a state. There is, however, no case which does not involve the use or misuse of drink or drugs and it is thought that this anomalous rule is properly confined to such cases, the basis for it being the grave social danger seen to be presented by intoxicated persons. A diabetic who fails to take sufficient food after a normal dose of insulin may rely on consequent automatism as a defence to a charge of a crime of basic intent, unless he was actually aware of the risk of becoming aggressive, unpredictable and uncontrolled.[16] So too may a person whose condition was due to taking valium (a soporific or sedative drug) even though not on medical prescription.[17] Of course, if the "fault" is in itself sufficient to found liability for the offence charged, then the defendant is properly convicted of it under ordinary principles.[18] An elementary example is where a driver, feeling sleepy, continues to drive until he falls asleep and has an accident. His failure to stop may constitute the fault necessary to convict him of careless, or even dangerous, driving.[19]

Writers dispute whether the voluntariness of D's conduct should be regarded as part of the *actus reus* or as part of the *mens rea*.[20] On the one hand, it is a mental element; on the other, it is said that it is an essential constituent of the act, which is part of the *actus reus*. It has been argued that the classification is important. The argument runs: some offences, known as offences of strict liability, do not require *mens rea*; so that, if voluntariness is part of the *mens rea*, a man charged with an offence of strict liability might be convicted for an involuntary act. But an *actus reus* must be proved, even for an offence of strict liability; so if voluntariness is part of the *actus reus*, no one can be convicted of any crime if his act was involuntary. As the latter result is thought to be not only desirable but to represent the law, voluntariness can only properly be regarded as an element in the *actus reus*. The fallacy in this argument lies in the proposition that offences of strict liability require "no *mens rea*" and the assumption that this means that the whole of the mental element involved in *mens rea* may be lacking.[1] This is not so. If the mental element is part of the *actus reus*, there is certainly no way of dispensing with it;[2] but it does not follow that it must be dispensed with where an offence is held to be one of strict liability.

The leading case on strict liability, *Prince*,[3] decides that D may be convicted of the offence under s. 20 of the Sexual Offences Act 1956 although he believes in good faith and on reasonable grounds that the girl

---

16. *Bailey* [1983] 2 All ER 503; [1983] 1 WLR 760 below, p. 226.
17. *Hardie*, above.
18. The dictum of Martin JA in *Rabey* (1978) 79 DLR (3d) 414, 425 quoted by Mackay as a "typical example of a dictum in support of 'fault liability' ", op. cit. 147, fn. 11 seems to be saying no more than this.
19. *Kay v Butterworth* (1945) 173 LT 191, below, p. 41.
20. Turner (MACL 195 and 199 and Kenny, *Outlines*, 23) thought "voluntariness" an element of *mens rea*. Williams, CLGP, s. 8 and I. Patient, [1968] Crim LR 23 think it part of the *actus reus*.
1. Cf. Howard, SR 1; R. S. Clark, *NZ Essays* at 49; Packer, 126.
2. Above, p. 29.
3. (1875) LR 2 CCR 154; **SHC 108**.

he is taking is over sixteen. We commonly say that no *mens rea* need be proved because the act which D *intends* – to take an eighteen year old girl out of the possession of her parents – is not prohibited by law – it is not an *actus reus*. But although this is an offence "requiring no *mens rea*" it is quite clear that it involves a substantial mental element, apart from the element of voluntariness. D must be proved to have intended to take a girl out of the possession of her parents. If he thought the girl was in no one's possession, he is not guilty. If he thought the girl was a boy, he is probably not guilty. No one suggests, however, that we should say that his knowledge that the girl is in the possession of her parents is part of the *actus reus*. The fact is that even in offences of strict liability, a limited degree of *mens rea* must be proved; and a jurist may, if he chooses, classify the voluntariness of the accused's act as part of the limited degree of *mens rea*. It is a matter of convenience only.

What is clear is that the voluntariness of an act is a more fundamental element of criminal liability than the intention to cause, or foresight of, results of the act which we normally think of as *mens rea*. It is a defence, known as "automatism", that this element has not been proved by the Crown.

"What is missing in these cases appears to most people as a vital link between mind and body; and both the ordinary man and the lawyer might well insist on this by saying that in these cases there is not 'really' a human action at all and certainly nothing for which anyone should be made criminally responsible however 'strict' legal responsibility might be."[4]

a) *Insane and non-insane automatism.* A person who was in a state of automatism at the time he is alleged to have committed the offence cannot be guilty of it and the only question is whether he is to be found simply "not guilty" or "not guilty by reason of insanity". The outcome (which is of great importance) depends on how the automatism was caused. If it was caused by "a disease of the mind" the proper verdict is not guilty by reason of insanity. If it arose from any other cause the verdict is simply not guilty. But whether a cause is a "disease of the mind" is a question of law and that phrase has a wide meaning. Any "internal factor", mental or physical, is, in law, a disease of the mind. So automatism caused by a cerebral tumour or arteriosclerosis, epilepsy or diabetes arises from a disease of the mind. These are all "internal" to the accused. External factors include concussion, the administration of an anaesthetic or other drug, or hypnosis. In a number of cases acts done while sleeping have been treated as non-insane automatism[5] but it has now been held[6] that they are the product of a disease of the mind. In the absence of evidence of any external cause, it is

4. Hart, *Jubilee Lectures*, at 137. Note that Turner, while regarding voluntariness as *mens rea*, thought it a different and more fundamental element than foresight of consequences; MACL 195–205.

5. *Boshears* (1961) Times, 8 February. *Kemp* (1986) Times, 3 May (D strangled his wife while experiencing a condition known as "night terror").

6 *Burgess* [1991] 2 QB 92, [1991] Crim LR 548.

difficult to see how behaviour while asleep could be regarded as not due to an internal factor.

Whether D is found to have been in a state of automatism may depend on the nature of the defence. It will be recalled that the one exception at common law to the rule that the burden of proof is on the prosecution is the defence of insanity. So if D claims that he was in a state of automatism because of an internal factor, he is raising the insanity defence and it will be for him to satisfy the jury on the balance of probabilities that this was so; but if he relies on an external factor and lays a proper foundation for the defence, the onus is on the prosecution to satisfy the jury beyond reasonable doubt that it was not so. If he alleges that his condition was due to the administration of insulin (an external factor) inducing hypoglycaemia (too little blood sugar), he will be acquitted unless the prosecution can disprove the allegation; but if he alleges that it was due to diabetes (an internal factor) causing hyperglycaemia (excessive blood sugar), the onus will be on him to prove the allegation on the balance of probabilities; and, if he succeeds, he will be found not guilty by reason of insanity.[7]

A proper foundation for a defence of non-insane automatism may be laid by introducing evidence from which it may reasonably be inferred that the act was involuntary. Whether such a foundation has been laid is a question of law. Lord Denning has said that the accused's own word will rarely be sufficient,[8] unless it is supported by medical evidence. The difficult questions which arise where there is evidence that the automatism was caused partly by disease of the mind and partly by other factors are considered below.[9]

Automatism has narrow limits as a defence. It is to be confined, according to Lord Denning,[10] to acts done while unconscious and to spasms, reflex actions and convulsions. In *Broome v Perkins*[11] D was held guilty of driving without due care and attention, though in a hypoglycaemic state, because from time to time he apparently exercised conscious control over his car, veering away from other vehicles so as to avoid a collision, braking violently, and so on. The common law never recognised "irresistible impulse" as a defence even where it arose from insanity. A fortiori, it would not be recognised in the case of a sane person. The fact that, as a result of hysterical amnesia or hysterical fugue, D was unaware of "legal restrictions or moral concern", is no defence if he knew the facts which constitute the offence charged.[12] An irresistible craving for drink is not a

---

7. *Hennessy* [1989] 2 All ER 9; [1989] 1 WLR 287, CA *Bingham* [1991] Crim LR 433.

8. In *Dervish* [1968] Crim LR 37, *Cook v Atchison* [1968] Crim LR 266 and *Stripp* (1978) 69 Cr App Rep 318, CA it was held that D's evidence that he had a "blackout" was insufficient to raise the defence; but D's own evidence is enough to raise the defence of provocation: *Whitfield* (1976) 63 Cr App Rep 39, CA.

9. P. 200.

10. In *Bratty* [1963] AC 386, [1961] 3 All ER 523 at 532. It is confined to "involuntary movement of the body or limbs of a person": *Watmore v Jenkins*, above, at 586, per Winn J. In a Canadian case, *Racimore* (1976) 25 CCC (2d) 143 a "failure to remain" after an accident was held to be involuntary because D did not know there had been an accident. This seems to be an unsatisfactory device for introducing a requirement of *mens rea* into an offence of strict liability. Cf. *Davey v Towle* [1973] RTR 328.

11. [1987] Crim LR 271, DC.

12. *Isitt* [1978] Crim LR 159, CA.

defence to a charge of stealing alcohol.[13] If D has punched P it is no defence (though it may mitigate the sentence) to say that this was an immediate and irresistible reaction to provocation by P. But the borderline between this and a "reflex action" must be a fine one. The nature and effect of a reflex action is itself uncertain. In *Ryan v R*,[14] D with one hand pointed a loaded shotgun at P whom he had robbed, while with the other hand he attempted to tie P up. P moved. D was startled and, he said, "involuntarily" pressed the trigger because of a "reflex action". Barwick CJ thought that, if this story had been true, D would not have been responsible in law for the "act" of pressing the trigger; but Windeyer J held that, while that act may have been "involuntary" in a dictionary sense, it was one for which he was responsible in law and not properly analogous to an act done in convulsions or an epileptic seizure. With respect, however, it seems closer to these than to "the sudden movement of a tennis player retrieving a difficult shot; not accompanied by conscious planning but certainly not involuntary".[15]

It is of course very important to identify the precise act for which D is to be held responsible. In *Ryan v R* the pointing of the loaded gun and the placing of the finger on the trigger were clearly voluntary acts and, provided that it could be said that these acts caused death, the accused would be liable for homicide, whether the pressing of the trigger was an act for which he was responsible or not. Similarly in the English civil case of *Gray v Barr*[16] D approached P with a loaded gun and fired a shot to frighten P. D and P grappled together and P fell on the gun and was shot and killed. The trial judge and Salmon LJ thought that the real cause of P's death was the accident of his falling on the gun; whereas Denning MR and Phillimore LJ thought that the cause was D's deliberate act in approaching P with the gun. All the judges agreed, however, that D could properly have been convicted of manslaughter on these facts. The act for which D would be held responsible was not the firing of the fatal shot which was not his act but deliberately approaching P in that threatening way. Again, a man may be immune from liability for an offence involving "driving", though he is sitting at the controls of a moving vehicle, if he is unconscious through an epileptic fit; but, depending on the degree and frequency of epilepsy and the probability that he might have an attack, he might be liable through the conscious act of starting or continuing to drive.[17]

i) *Involuntariness not arising from Automatism*
A person may have full control over his body but no control over events in which it is involved. A driver's brakes fail without his fault and, consequently, he inevitably fails to accord precedence to a pedestrian on a

13. *Dodd* (1974) 7 SASR 151 at 157.
14. (1967) 40 ALJR 488, discussed by I. D. Elliott 41 ALJ 497.
15. Elliott, loc. cit.
16. [1971] 2 QB 554, [1971] 2 All ER 949; below, p. 368. Cf. *Jarmain* [1946] KB 74, [1945] 2 All ER 613; *Blayney v Knight* (1975) 60 Cr App Rep 269, DC.
17. *Hill v Baxter* [1958] 1 QB 277 at 286, [1958] 1 All ER 193 at 197, per Pearson LJ; *McBride* [1962] 2 QB 167, [1961] 3 All ER 6. Similarly where D goes to sleep: *Kay v Butterworth* (1945) 173 LT 191.

pedestrian crossing.[18] Although it is said that this offence is absolute[19] requiring no evidence of negligence, it was held in *Burns v Bidder*[20] that such a driver has a defence. The court equated the driver's situation with that of one stunned by a swarm of bees, disabled by epilepsy,[1] or propelled by a vehicle hitting his car from behind. "Voluntariness" is essential even in so-called crimes of "absolute liability".[2] On the other hand, it seems to have been held that it is no defence that the failure to accord precedence arises inevitably from the unforeseeable behaviour of the pedestrian,[3] but the driver in such a case has no more power to avert the failure than where his brakes fail. It is submitted that D should never be held criminally liable for an "act" or result of an act over which he has no control.

5 Causation

When the definition of an *actus reus* requires the occurrence of certain consequences it is necessary to prove that it was the conduct of the accused which caused those consequences to occur. In murder or manslaughter, for example, it is necessary to prove that the act of the accused caused the death. If the death came about solely through some other cause then the crime is not committed, even though all the other elements of the *actus reus* and the *mens rea* are present.

In *White*[4] it appeared that D put potassium cyanide into a drink called "nectar" with intent to murder his mother. She was found dead shortly afterwards with the glass, three parts filled, beside her. The medical evidence showed that she had died, not of poison, but of heart failure. D was acquitted of murder and convicted of an attempt to murder. Although the consequence which D intended occurred, he did not cause it to occur and there was no *actus reus* of murder. A less obvious example is *Hensler*.[5] There D wrote a begging letter to P, declaring that he was "a poor shipwrecked widow" and telling other lies. P, because he remembered something which had been told him previously, was not deceived but, nevertheless, sent five shillings. D was convicted of an *attempt* to obtain five shillings by false pretences. Once again the consequence which D intended (and which was[6] part of the *actus reus* of obtaining by false pretences) occurred but it was not D's false pretence which caused it to occur. It was as if a rogue, having tried unsuccessfully to break into a safe with an inadequate implement, were to be presented by the owner with the contents. The rogue would have got what he wanted, yet failed to bring about the *actus reus* of the crime.

18. Contrary to Zebra Pedestrian Crossing Regulations 1971.
19. *Hughes v Hall* [1960] 2 All ER 504, [1960] 1 WLR 733.
20. [1967] 2 QB 227, [1966] 3 All ER 29. See the valuable discussion by Patient, loc. cit., above, p. 38, fn 20.
  1. But see now *Sullivan* [1984] AC 156, [1983] 1 All ER 577.
  2. An alternative explanation is the existence of a general defence of "impossibility", below, p. 263.
  3. *Neal v Reynolds* [1966] Crim LR 393. The case is only briefly reported and may be explained on another ground.
  4. [1910] 2 KB 124; **SHC 283**.
  5. (1870) 11 Cox CC 570; below, p. 562.
  6. As it now is of obtaining by deception: below, p. 562.

The problems of D's foresight, on the one hand, and of causation on the other are distinct questions and both may have to be answered in a criminal case. The cases of *White* and *Hensler*, considered above, are both cases where D foresaw a consequence, and that consequence occurred, yet he did not cause it.

Since the problem almost invariably arises in connection with cases of murder and manslaughter, detailed discussion of it is postponed to the chapters on homicide.[7] For the present it is sufficient to note the rule, which is almost invariable, that D should have caused the *actus reus*.[8]

6 A "State of Affairs" as an Actus Reus[9]
A crime may be so defined that it can be committed although there is no "act" in the sense considered above. There may be no necessity for any "willed muscular movement". Instead it may be enough if a specified "state of affairs" is proved to exist. These offences are sometimes called "status"[10] or "situation"[11] offences. Under the Road Traffic Act 1988, s. 4 (2), for example, any person who, when in charge of a motor vehicle on a road or other public place is unfit to drive through drink or drugs, commits an offence. One cannot take charge without consciously doing so, but it is not *taking* charge of the vehicle, or *becoming* unfit which is the offence, but simply *being* in charge and *being* unfit. So long as this state of affairs continues, the *actus reus* of the crime is committed. The *actus reus* may even be in process of being committed while D is sleeping peacefully,[12] for he may still be "in charge". A person commits an offence if, when not at his place of abode, he *has with him* any article for use in the course of or in connection with burglary, etc.[13] So long as he has the article with him, he is committing the offence. Of course, in both of these examples the accused will, almost invariably, have done the acts of taking charge, getting drunk, or taking up the article, but such acts seem, technically, to be no part of the crime.

This has led to extraordinary results in offences of "being found" in a particular situation. In *Larsonneur*[14] D was convicted under the Aliens Order 1920 in that she, "being an alien to whom leave to land in the United Kingdom has been refused" was found in the United Kingdom. She had been brought from Ireland into the United Kingdom against her will in the custody of the police. Notwithstanding the wide condemnation of that decision,[15] a similar result has been reached in respect of the offence under

---

7. See below, pp. 331 et seq.
8. For exceptions, see *Larsonneur* and *Winzar v Chief Constable of Kent*, below.
9. See Glazebrook, "Situational Liability" in *Reshaping the Criminal Law*, 108.
10. Howard, SR Chapter 3.
11. M. D. Cohen, 7 Israel Law Rev 186.
12. *Duck v Peacock* [1949] 1 All ER 318; but see the defence provided by Road Traffic Act 1956, s. 9 (1) proviso, now re-enacted in Road Traffic Act 1988, s. 4 (3).
13. Theft Act 1968, s. 25, below, p. 630.
14. (1933) 24 Cr App Rep 74; **SHC 128**. Cf. *Walters* [1969] 1 QB 255, [1968] 3 All ER 863 (being an incorrigible rogue). See the criticism of *Larsonneur* by Howard, *Strict Responsibility*, 47. For a spirited but unconvincing defence of the case, see Lanham [1976] Crim LR 276.
15. "The acme of strict injustice", Hall, GPCL 329, n. 14; Williams CLGP 11; Howard, *Strict Responsibility*, 47; Gordon, 287; Burchell & Hunt, 114.

s. 12 of the Licensing Act 1872 of being found drunk in a highway. In *Winzar v Chief Constable of Kent*[16] D was taken to hospital on a stretcher but was found to be drunk and told to leave. When he was seen slumped on a seat in the corridor, the police were called and they took him to a police car stationed in the highway outside the hospital. He was convicted of being found drunk in the highway. The words, "found drunk", were held to mean "perceived to be drunk". But "perceive" means "to become aware of" and it seems that the police became aware of D's condition in the hospital and not in the highway. Larsonneur and Winzar were convicted of offences the commission of which was in fact procured by the police; and this seems peculiarly offensive. These offences of "being found" are unusual[17] in that they require an act on the part of the finder but no act or *mens rea* of the defendant. Even "state of affairs" offences ought to require proof that D either caused the state of affairs or failed to terminate it when it was possible to do so.[18] Physical impossibility of compliance with the law should be a defence, at least where it is not proved that the impossibility arose through D's own fault.[19]

It has been held by the Privy Council that the offence of "remaining" in Singapore, having been prohibited from entering that republic, could not be committed by one who was ignorant of the prohibition.[19] It is implicit in the case that to "remain" because detained would not be an offence. It is true that "remaining" may be said to be D's act while "being found" is the act of another; but the substance of the two offences is the same. It was held[20] at common law that "being in possession" was an insufficient act to constitute the *actus reus* of a crime, but there are many cases where, by statute, mere possession is enough. Thus possession of dangerous drugs, explosive substances, firearms and forged bank-notes all constitute the *actus reus* of various crimes. "Being in possession" does not involve an act in the sense of a muscular movement at all, for a man may possess goods

---

16. (1983) Times, 28 March, DC. Cf. *Palmer-Brown v Police* [1985] 1 NZLR 365, CA (D not "found" behaving in a particular way when behaviour occurred some time after encounter with constable).

17. But not unique. Being the parent of a child of compulsory school age is an offence under s. 39 (1) of the Education Act 1944 if the child fails to attend school regularly. It is unnecessary to prove any knowledge or neglect on the part of the parent: *Crump v Gilmore* [1970] Crim LR 28. See also the Prevention of Oil Pollution Act 1971 which provides that the owner or master of a ship is liable if oil is discharged from a British ship in a prohibited sea area. Glazebrook, "Situational Liability" in *Reshaping the Criminal Law*, 108, contends that *Larsonneur* type liability is by no means unusual, pointing, inter alia, to the similarity, from the defendant's point of view, of vicarious liability (on which see below, p. 170).

18. Cf. *Burns v Nowell* (1880) 5 QBD 444 at 454 "... before a continuous act or proceeding, not originally unlawful, can be treated as unlawful by reason of the passing of an Act of Parliament, by which it is in terms made so, a reasonable time must be allowed for its discontinuance ..." Other jurisdictions have avoided the result in *Larsonneur*: *Achterdam* 1911 EDL 336 (Burchell & Hunt 105); *O'Sullivan v Fisher* [1954] SASR 33. In the United States, similar offences have been held unconstitutional; *Robinson v California*, 370 US 660, 8 L Ed 2d 758 (1962) being addicted to the use of narcotics.)

19. *Lim Chin Aik v R* [1963] AC 160, [1963] 1 All ER 223. See also *Finau v Department of Labour* [1984] 2 NZLR 396 (failure to leave New Zealand after revocation of permit not an offence where impossible to leave because of pregnancy). But cf. *Grant v Borg* [1982] 2 All ER 257, [1982] 1 WLR 638, HL, where an immigrant was held guilty of knowingly remaining beyond the time limited although, because of a mistake of law, he may have believed the time had been extended.

20. *Heath* (1810) Russ & Ry 184; *Dugdale v R* (1853) 1 E & B 435.

merely by knowingly[1] keeping them in his house. Possession which is initially lawful may become criminal because of a change of circumstances without any act by D,[2] but only after he has failed to divest himself of possession within a reasonable time.[3] "Being in possession" is simply a state of affairs, which, in certain circumstances, involves criminal liability.

7 Omissions[4]

a) *Offences of mere omission*. Statutes frequently make it an offence to omit to do something. There are many provisions requiring companies and others to submit returns of various kinds and making it an offence to fail to do so. The driver of a vehicle which is involved in an accident causing damage or injury to any person, vehicle or animal must give his name and address to any person having reasonable grounds for requiring him to do so, or report the accident to the police within 24 hours.[5] A motorist who fails to provide a police officer with a specimen of breath when properly required to do so commits an offence.[6] So does a person legally liable to maintain a child if he fails to provide him with adequate food, clothing, medical aid or lodging.[7] Offences of pure omission are also to be found, though rarely, at common law. A police officer was held to be guilty of a common law misdemeanour when, without justification or excuse, he failed to perform his duty to preserve the Queen's peace by protecting a citizen who was being kicked to death.[8]

b) *Offences of omission causing a result*. In the above examples, where the offence is merely the failure to act, there are no special difficulties. Problems arise when the offence requires proof of a result as, for example, in homicide and other offences against the person. Stephen stated the rule for these offences as follows:

"It is not a crime to cause death or bodily injury, even intentionally, by any omission. . . ."[9]

He gave the following famous illustration:

"A sees B drowning and is able to save him by holding out his hand. A abstains from doing so in order that B may be drowned, and B is drowned. A has committed no offence."

Stephen went on to state exceptional cases where the law imposes a duty to act. If A in the example were B's parent, A would have a duty to act and would be guilty of murder. There are two problems here. Can we truly say

---

1. A man may possess a thing in the civil law although he does not know of its existence; but knowledge will usually be required in criminal law: cf. *Warner v Metropolitan Police Commissioner*, below, p. 110; *Cugullere* [1961] 2 All ER 343, [1961] 1 WLR 858; below, p. 449.
2. Cf. *Buswell* [1972] 1 All ER 75, [1972] 1 WLR 64.
3. *Burns v Nowell*, above, fn. 18. *Levine* [1927] 1 DLR 740 is contrary but *Burns v Nowell* is followed in South Africa: Burchell & Hunt 264.
4. Glazebrook (1960) 76 LQR 386; Graham Hughes (1958) 67 YLJ 590.
5. Road Traffic Act 1988, s. 170 (4).
6. Road Traffic Act 1988, s. 6.
7. Children and Young Persons Act 1933, s. 1 (2) (a).
8. *Dytham* [1979] QB 722, [1979] 3 All ER 641.
9. *Digest of the Criminal Law* (4th ed., 1887), Art. 212.

that A has "killed" B or "caused" B's death? and how do we know who is under a duty to act?

c) *Causation*. Stephen apparently saw no difficulty in saying that a death or bodily injury may be caused by omission. Others do. The authors of *Blackstone* are worried about the "But for" test: "it must be established that but for the omission the relevant consequence would not have happened in the way it did".[10] Well, it wouldn't. A would have saved B from drowning. The difficulty is a different one: B's death would have occurred in precisely the same way if A had died or not come on the scene for any other reason so how can he be said to have caused it? He simply allowed it to happen. The cause of B's death was his falling into the water. Nothing else had to happen. He just drowned. If A and strangers, C, D and E had walked by together it is impossible to say that, as a matter of fact, A has caused the death but C, D and E have not. In law, however, as the Draft Code puts it:

"a person causes a result which is an element of an offence when ... (b) he omits to do an act which might prevent its occurrence and which he is under a duty to do according to the law relating to the offence." (Cl. 17 (b).)

d) *Can the offence be committed by omission?* The courts have long accepted without debate that murder and manslaughter are capable of commission by omission. On the other hand they have assumed that assault, another offence at common law, requires an act. The words "kill" and "slay" in an indictment have been held to be satisfied by proof of an omission, so why not "assault"? It is said that if D digs a pit for P to fall into, he commits an assault. Why should it be different if he digs the pit without any such intention and then leaves it unfilled, intending P to fall in? Glanville Williams argues in respect of a similar case that "in such circumstances of act-omission the total conduct should be regarded as an act...".[11] But "should be regarded as" suggests a fiction and criminal liability should not turn on fictions. And it would not meet the case where the hole has been dug by D's gardener and D, hearing that P is coming, decides to leave it unfilled. In *Fagan v Metropolitan Police Commissioner*, where D accidentally drove his car onto a policeman's foot and then intentionally left it there, the majority of the court held that there was an assault on the ground that, because D remained sitting in the car, there was a continuing act, not a mere omission. This again suggests, if not a fiction, a straining of words. Why should it be different if D had got out immediately, leaving the car on the officer's foot? It would be more realistic to recognise that one can "assault", no less than "kill" by omission.

In statutory offences the question is one of construction. Is the verb, in its context, properly construed to include an omission? Glanville Williams has written:

---

10. A1.11.
11. "What should the Code do about Omissions?" (1987) 7 L S 92.

"In my opinion the courts should not create liability for omissions without statutory authority. Verbs used in defining offences and prima facie implying active conduct should not be stretched by interpretation to include omissions. In general the courts follow this principle. They do not say, for instance, that a person 'wounds' another by failing to save him from being wounded, or 'damages' a building by failing to stop a fire. At least, this has never been decided."[12]

But Professor Williams has himself pointed out that the courts often have held offences to be capable of being committed by omission although the enactment did not expressly provide for it.

In *Shama*[13] a conviction for falsifying a document required for an accounting purpose contrary to the Theft Act 1968, s. 17 (1) (a) was upheld where D omitted entirely to fill in a form which it was his duty to complete. In *Firth*[14] a doctor was held to have deceived a hospital contrary to the Theft Act 1978, s. 2 (1) by failing to inform the hospital that certain patients were private patients. "Obstruct", "falsify" and "deceive" are all verbs which the courts have held to be capable of satisfaction by omission. So why not any other verb? The difficulty is to find any principle to limit such construction. In *Ahmad*[15] it was held that the words "does acts" in a modern statute, the Protection from Eviction Act 1977, were to be strictly construed and were not satisfied by proof of an omission. A person commits an offence if he "does acts" likely to interfere with the peace or comfort of a residential occupier with intent to cause him to give up occupation of the premises. D, having done such acts without any such intent, omitted with the required intention to rectify the situation he had created. He was not guilty. Yet even the word "act" may sometimes be satisfied by an omission. It has been held that a man "commits an act of gross indecency" with a child by totally passive submission to an act done by the child.[16]

e) *Offences against the person.* Most cases of homicide by omission have resulted in convictions for manslaughter but there is one case of murder. In *Gibbins and Proctor*[17] a man and the woman with whom he was living were convicted of murder of the man's child by withholding food. By living with the man and receiving money from him for food the woman had assumed a duty towards the child. The judge was held to have rightly directed that they were guilty of murder if they withheld food with intent to cause her grievous bodily harm, as a result of which she died. If the child had sustained grievous bodily harm but not died, it is difficult to suppose that the court would not have held the defendants guilty of an offence under s. 18 of the Offences against the Person Act 1861.[18] The commission of this offence seems to have been an essential constituent of the defendant's

---

12. [1982] Crim LR 773.
13. [1990] 2 All ER 602, [1990] Crim LR 411.
14. (1990) 91 Cr App Rep 217, [1990] Crim LR 326.
15. (1986) 84 Cr App Rep 64, [1986] Crim LR 739. It will be noted that the court did not regard the act plus omission as an act. Cf. "Supervening Fault", below, p. 50.
16. *Speck* [1977] 2 All ER 859.
17. (1918) 13 Cr App Rep 134, CCA.
18. Below, p. 424.

liability, as the case was left to the jury. It would seem strange that causing death should be capable of commission by omission and causing grievous bodily harm not. It would mean that D was not in breach of a duty to act until death occurred when the duty was retrospectively imposed. That is surely unacceptable. As for wounding, though there is no decision, it is hard to see why "wound", a concept of the common law, should be less easily satisfied by omission than is "kill". Assault has been discussed above.

The CLRC recommended that liability for omissions in offences against the person should be confined to murder, manslaughter, and their proposed offences of causing serious injury with intent, unlawful detention, kidnapping, abduction and aggravated abduction.[19] It is not certain how far this is the actual law in relation to the corresponding offences as they now exist. If it is the law, causing injury which is not serious, wounding, and assault are offences incapable of commission by omission.

f) *Offences against property.* The codification team, being obliged to accept the CLRC's recommendations, concluded that, if injury to the person was to be incapable of commission by omission, so, a fortiori, should be damage to property. This leads to the following illustration:

"20(v) D is employed as a night watchman at a factory. His duties are to take all reasonable steps to ensure the safety of the building. D sees that a small fire has broken out. There is an adjacent bucket of sand with which, as he knows, he could easily put out the fire. Having a grievance against his employer, he walks away and lets the fire burn. The factory is destroyed. He is not guilty of arson."

Such a conclusion may be unacceptable to the courts. If so, the remedy is in their hands. "Destroy" and "damage" in the Criminal Damage Act 1971[20] are capable of being construed to include omissions.

g) *Who owes a duty?* Given that the offence is capable of being committed by omission, the next question is, who may be under a duty to act? Since most cases of omission have concerned homicide, the duties so far recognised[1] are duties to preserve life. Parents owe such a duty to their children. Presumably children above the age of responsibility owe a corresponding duty to their parents.[2] Other close relationships, whether of a family, domestic, business, or other nature, possibly impose similar duties. A person who has undertaken to care for a helpless and infirm relative[3] who has become dependent on him may be held to owe a duty, particularly where he is to receive some reward for caring for the other.[4] This category might well be extended to an unrelated person. Persons who jointly engage in a hazardous activity whether lawful – like mountaineering – or unlawful

---

19. Fourteenth Report, paras 252–255.
20. Below, p. 684.
   1. Other than in cases of "supervening fault", below, p. 51.
   2. E.g., a muscular fourteen year old leaves his fainting mother to drown in the notorious shallow pool.
   3. *Marriott* (1838) 8 C & P 425; *Nicholls* (1874) 13 Cox CC 75 (D was P's grandmother).
   4. *Instan* [1893] 1 QB 450 (D was P's niece, living in P's house, consuming food provided at P's expense and not supplying any to P); *Stone and Dobinson* [1977] QB 354, [1977] 2 All ER 341; **SHC 345**, below, p. 372.

– like drug abuse[5] – may also owe duties to one another, though there is no authority to that effect. The holder of a public office requiring him to care for others may incur criminal liability by failing to do so.

A contractual duty may found a duty under criminal law to persons not party to the contract but likely to be injured by failure to perform it.

In *Pittwood*[6] a railway crossing gate-keeper opened the gate to let a cart pass and went off to his lunch, forgetting to shut it again. Ten minutes later a haycart while crossing the line was struck by a train. D was convicted of manslaughter. It was argued on his behalf that he owed a duty of care only to his employers, the railway company, with whom he contracted. Wright J held, however, that

"there was gross and criminal negligence, as the man was paid to keep the gate shut and protect the public ... A man might incur criminal liability from a duty arising out of contract".[7]

h) *Act or omission?* It is not always easy to distinguish between an act and an omission. If a doctor is keeping a patient alive by cranking the handle of a machine and he stops, this looks like a clear case of omission. So too if the machine is electrically operated but switches itself off every 24 hours and the doctor deliberately does not re-start it. Switching off a functioning machine looks like an act; but is it any different in substance from the first two cases?[8] On the other hand, is it any different from cutting the high-wire on which a tight-tope walker is balancing?[9] – which is an act, if ever there was one. Is the ending of a programme of dialysis an omission, while switching off a ventilator is an act? Is the discontinuance of a drip feed, which is keeping a patient alive, by withdrawing the tube from his body an act?[10] and failure to replace an emptied bag an omission? It seems offensive if liability for homicide depends on distinctions of this kind; but it appears to be so.

The doctor is, no doubt, under a duty to make reasonable efforts, in the light of customary medical practice and all other relevant factors, to keep the patient alive.[11] Unfortunately, this does not solve the problem because the content of any duty there may be to keep alive is different from that of the duty not to kill. There is no doubt that parents have a duty to their children; yet, where parents refuse their consent to an operation on a new-born baby, suffering from Down's Syndrome, knowing that without the operation it will die, they are not necessarily guilty of a criminal homicide if

5. The point was not decided in *Dalby* [1982] 1 All ER 916. Cf. *People v Beardsley* (1967) 113 NW 1128.

6. (1902) 19 TLR 37.

7. Wright J said that this was not a mere case of nonfeasance, but of misfeasance. However D's breach of duty was not in opening the gate, but in omitting to close it again. Cf., however, *Smith* (1869) 11 Cox CC 210, where Lush J ruled that there was no duty because D's employer had no duty to provide a watchman. (If D makes a practice of seeing old ladies across the road, he is not responsible if one day he fails to be present and an old lady is killed.) Beynon [1982] Crim LR at 22 suggests that opening and not shutting might be regarded as one "act"; but would it really have been different if the gate had been opened by D's colleague who had just gone off duty? One hopes not.

8. Examples put by Williams [1977] Crim LR 443–452. See also TBCL, 236–237.

9. Kennedy [1977] Crim LR 443 at 452. See the discussion by Helen Beynon [1982] Crim LR 17.

10. Beynon, op. cit.

11. Williams, TBCL, 236.

death ensues. If it were an offence, it would (in the absence of diminished responsibility) be murder because the parents intend the death of the child. In *Re B (A minor)*,[12] when the parents refused their consent, the child was made a ward of court, and the court gave consent as being in the interests of the child. Dunn LJ said that the decision of the parents to allow the child to die was one which everyone accepted as "entirely responsible". It was a decision, it seems, that the parents could lawfully take, so that the death of the child, if it had followed, would not have been an *actus reus*. Indeed, Templeman LJ thought there might possibly be cases "where the future is so certain and where the life of the child is bound to be full of pain and suffering that the court might be driven to a different conclusion" – i.e., to allow the child to die. Yet there is no doubt that if the parents – or anyone – did any positive act to kill the child, they would be guilty of murder. The undoubted duty of parents to preserve the life of their child is different from, and more restricted than, their duty not to kill it.

In *Arthur*,[13] a doctor, having noted that the parents of a Down's Syndrome child did not wish the child to survive, ordered "Nursing care only" and the administration of a drug, allegedly to stop the child seeking sustenance. At the trial of the doctor for attempted murder, Farquharson J directed the jury that it was for them to decide whether "there was an act properly so-called on the part of Dr Arthur, as distinct from simply allowing the child to die". Simply allowing the child to die would apparently have been lawful,[14] and withholding food was, according to the medical evidence put by the judge to the jury, "a negative act" – a mere omission. It is submitted that a better view is that an omission to provide such a child with food and the ordinary necessities of life ought to be equated with an act causing death rather than with an omission to perform an operation or to take some other extraordinary action. The position seems to be the same with a helpless, elderly person, incapable of taking decisions. It may be lawful for his family and the doctor to decide that an operation which would prolong a useless and painful life should not be performed; but it surely cannot be lawful to starve him to death, whether with the assistance of drugs or not.

i) *Termination of a duty*. When the duty arises out of a particular relationship, it will terminate when the relationship ends, as when an employee leaves the service of his employer. It is less clear, when, if ever, the duty of a parent to a child ends. In the case of a normal child it may well be on the attainment of the child's majority, but this could hardly be so in the case of a handicapped and dependent child. In the case of dependent persons generally, one who has undertaken the duty can probably divest himself of it only by passing it on to some responsible authority or other person.

12. [1981] 1 WLR 1421.
13. (1981) unreported, discussed by Gunn and Smith [1985] Crim LR 705 and Kennedy, *Treat Me Right*, Ch. 8.
14. It is submitted that nothing turned on the fact that the charge had been reduced from murder to attempted murder – see [1986] Crim LR 760–762 and Poole and Brahams [1986] Crim LR 383.

j) *Supervening fault*. Where D does an act which puts in peril P's person, his property, his liberty or any other interest protected by the criminal law and D is aware that he has created the peril, he has a duty to take reasonable steps to prevent the harm in question resulting. The act may be done without any kind of fault but, if D fails to intervene, it is undoubtedly his act which is the cause of the harm. For this reason the principle may apply to a wider range of offences than can be committed by simple omission. In *Miller*,[15] D, a squatter in P's house, went to sleep holding a lighted cigarette. He awoke to find the mattress smouldering. He did nothing to put it out but moved into an adjoining room and went to sleep there. The house caught fire. D was convicted of arson contrary to s. 1 (1) and (3) of the Criminal Damage Act 1971. The House of Lords held that the recorder had rightly directed the jury that, when D woke up, he was under a duty to take some action to put the fire out. Lord Diplock said:[16]

"I see no rational ground for excluding from conduct capable of giving rise to criminal liability conduct which consists of failing to take measures that lie within one's power to counteract a danger that one has oneself created, if at the time of such conduct one's state of mind is such as constitutes a necessary ingredient of the offence."

The Court of Appeal had upheld the conviction on a different basis:

"We would only say that an unintentional act followed by an intentional omission to rectify it or its consequences, or a reckless omission to do so when recklessness is a sufficient mens rea for the particular case, should only be regarded in toto as an intentional or reckless act when reality and common sense so require; this may well be a matter to be left to the jury. Further, in the relevant analysis we think that whether or not there is on the facts an element of adoption on the part of the alleged offender of what he has done earlier by what he deliberately or recklessly fails to do later is an important consideration."

The application of this "continuous act" theory would apparently have produced a different result in *Ahmad*.[17] If the appellant could be deemed to have acted intentionally (i.e., with intent to cause the residential occupier to give up occupation) when he rendered the flat uninhabitable, the difficulty of convicting him would have disappeared. This theory, however, involves an undesirable legal fiction. Fictions should have no place in the criminal law. Lord Diplock preferred the "duty" to the "continuous act" theory but only on the ground that the former is easier to explain to a jury. It is submitted, however, that they are different in substance as the example based on *Ahmad* shows.[18]

It is necessary to invoke the *Miller* principle only in the case of a result crime requiring fault where the act causing the result is done without that fault. Where the offence requires no fault, there is no need to rely on it. In

---

15. [1983] 2 AC 161, [1983] 1 All ER 978. See [1982] Crim LR 527 and 773–774.
16. At p. 176, p. 981.
17. Above, p. 47.
18. See commentary [1982] Crim LR 527 and 773–774 and (1984) 4 LS 88 at 91.

Wings Ltd v Ellis[19] D Ltd, a tour operator, published a brochure which, unknown to D, contained misrepresentations. On discovering the truth, D did all they could to correct the errors but, subsequently, P read an uncorrected brochure and booked a holiday in reliance on it. D was convicted under the Trade Descriptions Act 1968, s. 14 (a), making a statement which they knew to be false and, s. 14 (b), recklessly making a false statement. The statement was "made" when it was read by P and, by then, D knew it was false. The Divisional Court, applying *Miller*, quashed both convictions. D had done all that could reasonably be expected to correct the false trade descriptions. The prosecutor appealed in respect of the offence under s. 14 (a) only. The appeal was allowed. Subject to a statutory defence which was not pleaded, the House held that s. 14 (a) created an "absolute" offence.[20] D knew the statement was false and no other fault was required. There was no room for the application of *Miller*. Though any reader of s. 14 would suppose that s. 14 (a) is the more serious offence, 14 (b) requires some element of fault, however "reckless" is interpreted, and Lord Hailsham thought that *Miller* might have been properly held applicable to that.[1]

Where the offence is one requiring fault, whether *mens rea* strictly so-called or negligence, it is submitted that the *Miller* principle is of general application.[2] If D, sitting alone in the passenger seat of a car, were accidentally to knock off the handbrake, so that the car ran away, it is submitted that he could be convicted of murder if he wilfully omitted to put the brake on again, intending the car to run over and kill P. D locks the door of a room, not knowing that P is inside. Having learned that P is within, he omits to unlock the door. Should he not be liable for false imprisonment?[3]

k) *"Easy rescue" statutes.* Many jurisdictions[4] have dealt with the "shallow pool" case by making it an offence for anyone to fail to take steps which he could take without any personal risk to save another from death or injury. But these statutes do not equate omissions with acts. It does not follow that an offender is liable for the harmful result which he ought to have prevented and has allowed to happen. He is not necessarily guilty of homicide if the victim dies.[5]

---

19. [1984] 1 All ER 1046, [1984] 1 WLR 731; revsd [1985] AC 272, [1984] 3 All ER 577, HL.
20. See below, p. 99.
   1. Lord Scarman thought the analogy with *Miller* "ingenious, if far-fetched" and (it is submitted unfairly) an "unhelpful and over-elaborate approach to the interpretation of an act intended to protect the public ..."; [1984] 3 All ER 590–591.
   2. *Green v Cross* (1910) 103 LT 279 – D innocently caught a dog in a trap. Instead of releasing it he left it until it was freed two hours later by the police. Held, Channell J dissenting, that there was evidence on which he could be convicted of "cruelly ill-treating" the dog.
   3. Andenaes, *GPCL of Norway*, 135; and see *Fagan v Metropolitan Police Commissioner* [1969] 1 QB 439, [1968] 3 All ER 442; below, p. 403.
   4. Feinberg, *Harm to Others* (OUP, 1984), C. 4.
   5. Andanaes, GPCL, 132.

2 Mens Rea[6]

Legal historians tell us that until the twelfth century a man might be held liable for many harms, simply because his conduct caused them, without proof of any blameworthy state of mind whatsoever on his part. Under the influence of Canon law and the Roman law, a change gradually took place and the courts began to require proof of an element of moral blameworthiness – "a guilty mind" of some kind. In the developed common law of crime, some such mental element is always necessary, and is known as *mens rea*.

1 Definition of Terms

Mens rea is a technical term. It is often loosely translated as "a guilty mind", but this translation is frequently misleading. A man may have *mens rea*, as it is generally understood today, without any feeling of guilt on his part. He may, indeed, be acting with a perfectly clear conscience, believing his act to be morally, and even legally, right, and yet be held to have *mens rea*. In order properly to appreciate the meaning of the term it is necessary to distinguish between a number of different possible mental attitudes which a man may have with respect to the *actus reus* of the crime in question. These are: (i) intention, (ii) recklessness, (iii) negligence and (iv) blameless inadvertence.

i) *Intention*[7]

Numerous offences are defined so as to require proof of "intention" to cause specified results. It might be expected that the meaning of such a fundamental term would have been settled long ago but this is not so. The cases are inconsistent, judicial opinion has recently changed and there is still some measure of uncertainty. We may begin, however, with one well-settled proposition. Everyone agrees that a person intends to cause a result if he acts with the purpose of doing so. If D has resolved to kill P and he fires a loaded gun at him with the object of doing so, he intends to kill. It is immaterial that he is aware that he is a poor shot, that P is nearly out of range, and that his chances of success are small. It is sufficient that killing is his object or purpose, that he wants to kill, that he acts in order to kill.

One view is that "intention" should be limited to that case – that a result should never be regarded as intended unless it was the actor's purpose, i.e. unless he acted in order to bring about the result. This is often considered to be the ordinary meaning given to the word by people generally. The courts have consistently given the word a wider meaning, sometimes

---

6. Turner, "The Mental Element in Crimes at Common Law", MACL 195; Williams, *The Mental Element in Crime* and CLGP, in Ch. 2; Hart, "Negligence, *Mens rea* and Criminal Responsibility", in *Oxford Essays in Jurisprudence*, 29; Smith, "The Guilty Mind in the Criminal Law" (1960) 76 LQR 78; Ashworth, "Reason, Logic and Criminal Liability" (1975) 91 LQR 102. R. A. Duff, "Certifying Criminal Fault" in *Criminal Law and Justice*, 93; Williams, "Oblique Intention", (1987) CLJ 417.

7. Smith, "Intention in Criminal Law" (1974) 27 CLP 93; J. H. Buzzard, "Intent" [1978] Crim LR 5 and Smith, "A Reply" [1978] Crim LR 14; White, *Misleading Cases*, 47.

described as "oblique" as distinct from "direct" intention.[8] Until recently, the predominant judicial view was that an actor intended a result if he knew that it was a highly probable (or perhaps merely probable) result of his act, although it was not his purpose or object to cause that result. In 1979 Lord Diplock said that the matter had been finally settled in this sense by the decision of the House of Lords in *Hyam v Director of Public Prosecutions*.[9] A majority of the House in *Hyam* was certainly of the opinion that this was the law but the actual decision was that foresight of high probability of serious bodily harm was a sufficient *mens rea* for murder, not that such a state of mind necessarily amounted to an intention to cause serious bodily harm. In *Moloney*,[10] however, the House held that the *mens rea* of murder is intention to cause death or serious bodily harm so it was essential to determine the meaning of "intention". *Moloney* must be read in the light of the explanation of it by the House in *Hancock and Shankland*[11] and by the Court of Appeal in *Nedrick*.[12] When it is so read it appears that:

(1) A result is intended when it is the actor's purpose.
(2) A court or jury may also infer that a result is intended, though it is not desired, when—
   (a) the result is a virtually certain consequence of the act, and
   (b) the actor knows that it is a virtually certain consequence.

a) *Two criticisms.* (i) The fact that the result was a virtually certain consequence of D's act is very good evidence that he knew that it was a virtually certain consequence; but it is difficult to see why it should be regarded as a necessary condition. If D thinks he knows that the result is virtually inevitable because he is making a mistake, why should he be held not to have intended it because it was not, in fact, inevitable? His state of mind is the same in either case. If D fires a gun pointed at P's heart, his intention can hardly be affected by the fact, unknown to D, that P is wearing a bullet-proof vest. The state of mind of a person who thinks he knows is the same as that of a person who actually knows. The difference is in the external circumstances.

(ii) It is emphasised that D's knowledge that the act he is doing is virtually certain to cause the result is not intention to cause that result, but only evidence from which the court or jury may infer intention. "Intention" is, in the end, left undefined. What is this further state of mind which must be inferred? It is not desire that the result be caused because that is expressly ruled out; and that seems to leave nothing. Faced with such a direction, the jury can do no more than decide to call the defendant's awareness of virtual certainty "intention" if they think that, in all the circumstances of the case, he ought to be convicted of the offence charged; and not to call it intention if they think he ought to be acquitted. They are not instructed to *characterise* the state of mind as intention or not, as they

8. Cf. Bentham, *Principles of Morals and Legislation* (Harrison ed., 207).
9. [1975] AC 55, [1974] 2 All ER 41, **SHC 308**, below, p. 57. See [1979] AC at 638.
10. [1985] AC 905, [1985] 1 All ER 1025, **SHC 52**.
11. [1986] AC 455. [1986] 1 All ER 641, **SHC 56**.
12. [1986] 3 All ER 1, [1986] 1 WLR 1025, **SHC 60**.

think fit, but that appears to be all that they can do. If they ask the judge for further directions, what can he do but tell them this? – though he would, no doubt, wrap it up in the usual patter about intention being an ordinary word of the English language and its meaning a question for them.

Lord Lane CJ has recognised the force of this criticism in the debate on the Report of the House of Lords Select Committee on Murder[13] when he stated

"in *Nedrick* the court was obliged to phrase matters as it did because of earlier decisions in our Lordships' House by which it was bound. We had to read very gingerly indeed in order not to tread on your Lordships' toes. As a result, *Nedrick* was not as clear as it should have been. However, I agree with the conclusions of the committee that 'intention' should be defined in the terms set out in paragraph 195 of the report on page 50. That seems to express clearly what in *Nedrick* we failed properly to explain."[14]

The definition referred to is that stated in cl. 18 (b) of the Draft Code: "A person acts 'intentionally' with respect to . . . a result when he acts either in order to bring it about or being aware that it will occur in the ordinary course of events."

This definition would meet both the above criticisms. If this is what the court in *Nedrick* really meant but "failed properly to explain" then there is every reason why it should make amends as soon as possible and reformulate the law on these lines. The Moloney "guidelines" which the court was following have been to some extent discredited and other passages in *Moloney* support the Draft Code definition. Lord Bridge gave a notable example of a man who boards a plane which he knows to be bound for Manchester—the last place he wants to be—in order to escape pursuit: by boarding the Manchester plane, the man "*conclusively* demonstrates his intention to go there, because it is a moral certainty that that is where he will arrive".[15] There is nothing here about this being merely evidence from which the jury might infer intention—intention is *conclusively* demonstrated. Why should not the Court of Appeal prefer this statement to the partly discredited guidelines and apply the Code definition? Unless and until such a step is taken, we must assume that *Nedrick* represents the law.

b) *Results known to be condition of achievement of purpose*. It may be said that no one can ever know that a result is certain to follow from an act. This is why courts and writers are driven to speak of "virtually" or "morally" or "almost" certain results. But a person may know that he cannot achieve his purpose, A, without bringing about some other result, B. If he is to bring about A, he knows he must also, at the same time or earlier, bring about B. It may be that, in any other circumstances, he would much rather B did not happen, indeed its occurrence may be abhorrent to him. But, the choice being between going without A and having A and B, he decides to have A and B. It seems fair to say that he intends to cause B as well as A. Suppose

13. HL Paper 78–I, 1989.
14. HL Official Report, vol. 512, col. 480, 6/11/1989.
15. [1985] AC at 296 (authors' italics).

that P has made a will, leaving the whole of his large estate to D. D loves P but he has an overwhelming desire to enjoy his inheritance immediately. If he gives P what he knows to be a fatal dose of poison, he intends to kill P, though he says truthfully that it causes him anguish. D wishes to injure his enemy, Q, who is standing inside the window of the house of D's friend, P. If, knowing the window to be closed, he throws the stone through it at Q, can it be doubted that he intends to break his friend's window?

Since result A is the actor's purpose, it is immaterial that he is not certain that it will happen. He is not a good shot and he knows the stone may miss – but he intends to strike Q. And, since he knows that, if he strikes Q, it will be because he has broken P's window, he intends to break the window. It seems from these examples that we might safely say that a result known to be a condition of the achievement of the actor's purpose is intended.

Yet even this modest conclusion is not beyond doubt. In *Moloney*[16] Lord Bridge referred with approval to *Steane*[17] where D, who, during the second world war, gave broadcasts which would assist the enemy in order to save himself and his family from the horrors of the concentration camp, was held not to have had an "intent to assist the enemy". Steane may have been a loyal citizen who, in other circumstances, would have wished to do nothing to assist the enemy; but, being faced with the choice, "Assist us – or back to the concentration camp", he chose to assist the enemy. Of course, his purpose was to stay out of the camp; but it seems plain that he knew that his purpose could only be achieved by assisting the enemy. Reading the script was assisting the enemy.[18] In *Ahlers*,[19] a German consul who assisted German nationals to return home after the declaration of war in 1914 was held to have intended only to do his duty as consul. In *Sinnasamy Selvanayagam*[20] the Privy Council said, *obiter*, that if D remained in occupation of his home in defiance of a lawful order to quit, knowing that the owner of the property would be annoyed, his "dominant intention" was simply to retain his home and he was not guilty under the Ceylon Penal Code of remaining in occupation with intent to annoy the owner. In *Gillick*'s case[1] some of the judges seem to have been of the opinion that a doctor, who knew that his provision of contraceptive advice to a girl under sixteen would encourage a man to have sexual intercourse with her, would not be guilty of abetting the offence, because his intention

---

16. [1985] AC 905 at 929.
17. [1947] KB 997, [1947] 1 All ER 813.
18. It might be argued that, even in these circumstances, B is not necessarily a condition of A. Someone might open the window while the stone is in flight towards it. The microphone into which Steane spoke might have been disconnected or the transmitter broken down. Lord Bridge's man who boards the plane for Manchester (the last place he wishes to go to) to escape arrest intends (as Lord Bridge says [1985] AC at 986) to go to Manchester although it is possible that the plane will be diverted to Luton. Even in the case of D who gives P the fatal dose of poison to accelerate his inheritance, it is possible that P will die of natural causes before the poison takes effect: cf. *White* [1910] 2 KB 124, CCA.
19. [1915] 1 KB 616.
20. [1951] AC 83.
   1. *Gillick v West Norfolk and Wisbech Area Health Authority* [1986] AC 112, [1985] 3 All ER 402, [1986] Crim LR 113 HL and commentary. See also *Salford Health Authority, ex p Janaway* [1988] 2 WLR 442, CA.

was to protect the girl, not to encourage unlawful sexual intercourse with her.

In some of these cases, it seems that the concept of intention is strained to do a job for which it is not fitted. Steane's acquittal would more properly have been based on duress and the case envisaged in *Gillick* seems to have been, in substance, one of necessity – a minor encouragement of sexual intercourse was a lesser evil than an unwanted pregnancy in the young girl. In each of these cases, D had an honourable purpose. Where D's purpose is disreputable, the court is most unlikely to interpret intention so narrowly. If Steane, being a chain smoker deprived of cigarettes, had read the script in order to get a packet of Players, it is probable that Lord Goddard CJ would have had no hesitation in holding that, of course, he intended to assist the enemy. Yet, from the point of view of intention, there seems to be no difference between the cases.[2] If this is so, it produces an undesirable distortion of the concept of intention and it would be better if the true reason for the decision were articulated. *Moloney*, however, encourages such decisions – the jury appears to be left a measure of discretion to say whether they think the state of mind should be categorised as intention or not.

It is arguable that intention, in law, should extend to results known or believed by the actor to be conditions of the achievement of his purpose but should go no further. This would give effect to the constantly reiterated opinion of the courts that intention is different from desire. Result B is not desired, at least it is not desired for its own sake; but it is intended. And any overlap with recklessness is avoided. D is not merely taking a risk of causing B; he *knows* or thinks he knows that, if he achieves his aim of causing A, B will happen or have already happened.

c) *Results known to be virtually certain to accompany achievement of purpose.* Result B may also be intended, according to *Moloney*, where B is not a condition of A. It is possible for A (D's purpose) to occur without B also happening, but as D knows, causing A is virtually certain to cause B as well. D, wishing to collect the insurance on a cargo (result A), puts a time bomb in a plane to blow up in mid-Atlantic. He has no wish to kill the crew. It is *possible* for the plane and cargo to be destroyed and the crew to escape – people do occasionally fall from aircraft at great heights and survive – but the possibility is so remote as to be negligible; and D knows that. There is certainly a strong argument for saying that he intends to kill. This is so even if, as D knows, this type of bomb has a 50% failure rate. There is an even chance that nothing will happen. But he wants the explosion (result A) to happen and, if it does, killing (result B) is, as he knows, a virtual certainty. So a jury may (not must) find that there is an intention to kill.

The difficulty is that once we depart from absolute certainty, there is a question of degree and an uncertain boundary between intention and recklessness. In *Hyam*,[3] D, in order to frighten Mrs Booth, her rival for the affections of X, put blazing newspaper through the letter box of Booth's

2. Glanville Williams, *The Mental Element in Crime*, 21.
3. [1975] AC 55, [1974] 2 All ER 41.

house and caused the death of two of her children. Ackner J directed the jury that D was guilty if she knew that it was highly probable that her act would cause at least serious bodily harm; and by their verdict of guilty the jury must be taken to have found that she did know that. In the light of *Moloney*, that direction was wrong but Lord Bridge[4] thought that, on a proper direction, no reasonable jury could have failed to convict Hyam. Is that really so? Might not a jury have been satisfied that D knew this was a highly probable result without being satisfied that she knew it was virtually certain? In *Moloney*,[5] Lord Hailsham and Lord Bridge put the case of a terrorist who plants a time bomb in a public building and gives a warning to enable the public to be evacuated. He knows that it is virtually certain that a bomb disposal squad will attempt to defuse the bomb. The squad does so, the bomb explodes and a member of the squad is killed. It is assumed that this is murder. The bomber intends to endanger the squad's lives (because he knows that it is virtually certain they will attempt to defuse the bomb) but he does not, surely, know that it is virtually certain that one of them will be killed or even seriously injured. It is doubtful if this would be murder even under the "highly probable" formula of *Hyam*. It looks like reckless-ness which is not enough for murder. The example might be justified if it could be proved that the terrorist wants the bomb to go off *at a time* when he knows it is virtually certain that the squad will be attempting to defuse it. That would be indistinguishable from the "bomb-in-the-plane" case, above, where the bomber wants the bomb to go off in mid-Atlantic.

In *Moloney*, D shot his stepfather, whom he loved, when, in the course of a drunken game to establish who was quicker "on the draw" with loaded shotguns, he pulled the trigger in response to a challenge, "if you have [the guts] pull the trigger." He may not have realised that the gun was aimed at point-blank range, at P's head. His conviction was quashed because the judge misdirected the jury that D intended serious bodily harm if he foresaw that it would "probably" happen. Lord Bridge insisted on the need for "a moral certainty", a probability which is "little short of overwhelm-ing" and an act that "will lead to a certain event unless something unexpected supervenes to prevent it".[6] Unfortunately, in summing up his opinion in the form of guidelines for trial judges, he used the term, "natural consequence", to mean a consequence that is virtually certain to ensue.

In *Hancock v Shankland*[7] two striking miners pushed from the parapet of a bridge heavy concrete blocks which struck a taxi taking a working miner to work and killed the taxi-driver. They said they intended to push the blocks on to the middle lane, not the inside lane in which the taxi was travelling, and that they intended to frighten the working miner and prevent him going to work, but not to hurt anyone. At their trial for murder, the judge closely followed the *Moloney* "guidelines". The Court of Appeal held that the conviction must be quashed. The guidelines were defective. The jury might well have understood "natural consequence" to mean "direct consequence" and not to convey the notion of moral certainty

4. [1985] AC at 926, [1985] 1 All ER at 1037.
5. [1985] AC at 913, 927.
6. [1985] AC at 925, 926, 929.
7. [1986] AC 455, [1986] 1 All ER 641.

or overwhelming probability of which Lord Bridge spoke. The House of Lords agreed. Both courts stressed that even awareness that the consequence is virtually certain is not intention, but only evidence from which a jury may infer intention, if they are satisfied beyond reasonable doubt that this is the right inference. The difficulty of applying this rule is considered above.

Although the House in *Moloney* said that they were laying down the law not only for murder but for offences requiring "specific intent" generally (which, here, seems to mean merely offences requiring intent), their approval of *Steane* and the difficulty of reconciling the illustration of the bomber suggests that the word may well be held to bear different shades of meaning in different contexts.

An act may be intentional with respect to circumstances as well as consequences. Intention here means either hope that the circumstance exists – which corresponds to purpose in relation to consequences – or knowledge that the circumstance exists – which corresponds to foresight of certainty in relation to consequences.

"He who steals a letter containing a cheque, intentionally steals the cheque also if he hopes that the letter may contain one, even though he well knows that the odds against the existence of such a circumstance are very great."[8]

If D receives a car which he knows to be stolen, that is an intentional handling of stolen goods even though D would, perhaps, much prefer that the car was not stolen. If, however, D believed merely that it was probable, or highly probable, that the car was stolen, this would not be an intentional handling.

d) *Reform.* There are two possible defects in the definition proposed in the Draft Code.[9] The first is that it does not provide for the case where D knows that the relevant result will occur if but only if he succeeds in achieving some other purpose; and he is not certain that he will achieve that other purpose. This is exemplified by the case of the bomb with the 50% failure rate, above, p. 56. The second, which was revealed by Lord Goff's speech in the debate on the Select Committee Report on Murder, is that in certain, admittedly rather unlikely, circumstances, the definition might mean that a person intended a result which it was his purpose to avoid— which does not seem to be very good sense. The Law Commission[10] now proposes a definition, for the purposes of non-fatal offences against the person, which would avoid both difficulties:

"... a person acts—
(a) 'intentionally' with respect to a result when
    (i) it is his purpose to cause it; or
    (ii) although it is not his purpose to cause that result, he is aware that it would occur in the ordinary course of events if he were to succeed in his purpose of causing some other result."

---

8. Salmond, *Jurisprudence* (11th ed., 1957), 411.
9. Above, p. 55.
10. Law Com. No. 122 (1992) 5.4–5.11 and cl 2 of draft Bill, following Smith, "A Note on Intention" [1990] Crim LR 85.

ii) *Recklessness*[11]

For many crimes, either intention to cause the proscribed result or recklessness whether it be caused is sufficient to impose liability. A person who does not intend to cause a harmful result may take an unjustifiable risk of causing it. If he does so, he may be held to be reckless. Not all risk-taking constitutes recklessness. Sometimes it is justifiable to take a risk of causing harm to another's property or his person or even of causing his death. The operator of an aircraft, the surgeon performing an operation and the promoter of a tightrope act in a circus must all know that their acts might cause death but none of them would properly be described as reckless unless the risk he took was an unreasonable one. The law allows the use of reasonable force in the lawful arrest of an offender or in private defence. If D forces P's car off the road, that cannot be reckless driving if it was reasonable to use that degree of force lawfully to arrest P.[12] If D, doing an act of reasonable self-defence, damages P's window, he is not guilty of reckless criminal damage.[13] Whether it is justifiable to take a risk depends on the social value of the activity involved relative to the probability and the gravity of the harm which might be caused. The question is whether the risk was one which a reasonable and prudent man might have taken. It might be reasonable for D to shoot P's ferocious dog which is attacking his sheep, but it does not follow that it would be reasonable to take a risk of causing injury or death to P – still less a bystander, Q. The test is objective – that is to say, the court or jury lays down the required standard of care. It is impossible to say in general terms that recklessness requires any particular degree of probability of the occurrence of the harm in question. If the act is one with no social utility – for example, a game of "Russian roulette" or an armed robbery – the slightest possibility of any harm should be enough. If the act has a high degree of social utility – for example, the performance of a surgical operation – then only such a very high degree of probability of grave harm as outweighs that utility will suffice to condemn it as a reckless act.

To establish recklessness it is necessary in all cases to show that D took an unjustifiable risk; but the prosecution, in some cases at least, must go further. How much further varies because it is now established that English law recognises two kinds of recklessness, which we have called "Cunningham recklessness" and "Caldwell/Lawrence recklessness" after the leading cases. Broadly, the distinction is that Cunningham recklessness requires proof that D was aware of the existence of the unreasonable risk whereas Caldwell/Lawrence recklessness is satisfied if either (i) he was aware of its existence, or (ii) in the case of an obvious risk he failed to give any thought to the possibility of its existence. Some offences require proof of Cunningham recklessness. Others are satisfied by proof of Caldwell/ Lawrence recklessness. The existence of the dual test is not justified on grounds of policy or principle but it was accepted with equanimity by the

---

11. See D. J. Birch, "The Foresight Saga" [1988] Crim LR 4 and articles referred to therein; White, *Misleading Cases*, 31; and Field and Lynn, "The Capacity for Recklessness", (1992) 12 LS 74.
12. *Renouf* [1986] 2 All ER 449, [1986] 1 WLR 522, 82 Cr App Rep 344.
13. *Sears v Broome* [1986] Crim LR 461, DC.

House of Lords in *Savage and Parmenter*[14] and can only be rectified by legislation, of which there seems little prospect.

This strange state of affairs came about in the following way. In *Cunningham*[15] D tore a gas meter from the wall of the cellar of an unoccupied house to steal the money in it. He left the gas gushing out. It seeped into a neighbouring house and was inhaled by P whose life was endangered. D was convicted under s. 23 of the Offences against the Person Act 1861[16] of maliciously administering a noxious thing so as to endanger life. Because the judge directed the jury that "malicious" meant simply "wicked", D's conviction was quashed. The Court of Criminal Appeal quoted with approval the principle first propounded by Kenny in 1902.[17]

". . . in any statutory definition of a crime 'malice' must be taken not in the old vague sense of 'wickedness' in general, but as requiring either (i) an actual intention to do the particular *kind* of harm that in fact was done, or (ii) recklessness as to whether such harm should occur or not (i.e. the accused has foreseen that the particular kind of harm might be done, and yet has gone on to take the risk of it). It is neither limited to, nor does it indeed require, any ill-will towards the person injured."

The court reiterated: "In our opinion, the word 'maliciously' in a statutory crime postulates foresight of consequence." Cunningham was not guilty unless he knew, when he broke off the gas meter, or left the broken pipe with the gas gushing out,[18] that it might be inhaled by someone. In cases requiring "malice" it is not sufficient that, if D had stopped to think, it would have been obvious to him that there was a risk. He must actually know of the existence of the risk and deliberately take it. In a series of cases, of which the latest is *Parmenter*,[19] convictions of malicious wounding have been quashed because the judge, in directing the jury, took the words of Diplock LJ, "should have foreseen", out of their context in *Mowatt*,[20] thus leading the jury to think that it is enough that D ought to have foreseen. It is not. To be "malicious", D must actually foresee some harm and the fact that he ought to have foreseen is, at best, some evidence that he did foresee.

This was the law applicable to the offence of damage to property under the Malicious Damage Act 1861. The Law Commission in their Report on Criminal Damage[1] made many proposals for the reform of the law but they

14. [1991] 4 All ER 698, HL.
15. [1957] 2 QB 396, [1957] 2 All ER 412.
16. Below, p. 429.
17. *Outlines of Criminal Law* (16th ed., 1952) at 186.
18. See omissions, above, p. 51.
19. [1991] 4 All ER 698 at 706, HL.
20. [1968] 1 QB 421 at 426. This page of the law reports should be stamped with a judicial health warning.

1. Law Com. No. 29 (1970), confirming proposals in Working Paper No. 23 (1969): "Where the Act has been preceded by a report of some official commission or committee that has been laid before Parliament and the legislation is introduced in consequence of that report, the report itself may be looked at by the court for the limited purpose of identifying the 'mischief' that the Act was intended to remedy, and for such assistance as is derivable from this knowledge in giving the right purposive construction to the Act." – *Fothergill v Monarch Airlines Ltd* [1980] 2 All ER 696 at 706, per Lord Diplock. The principle has been applied in numerous cases referred to in this book. The text-book writer is not limited in this way and a wider use of legislative history is made in attempting to discover the true legislative intent.

considered that the mental element, as interpreted in *Cunningham*, was satisfactory. They proposed only that it be "expressed with greater simplicity and clarity" and that this should be achieved by using "intentionally or recklessly" in place of the archaic and misleading "maliciously". Parliament adopted their proposals in the Criminal Damage Act 1971. Unfortunately, the Commission proposed no definition of recklessness and the Act contains none. Before 1981, the Court of Appeal held, though after some hesitation, that "reckless" in the 1971 Act bore the *Cunningham* meaning but in that year, the House of Lords decided in *Caldwell*[2] (Lords Wilberforce and Edmund-Davies dissenting) and in *Lawrence*[3] that, where the statute uses the word "reckless", a different test applies. In *Caldwell* Lord Diplock said that a person is reckless whether any property would be destroyed or damaged—

"... if (1) he does an act which in fact creates an obvious risk that property would be destroyed or damaged and (2) when he does the act he either has not given any thought to the possibility of there being any such risk or has recognised that there was some risk involved and has nonetheless gone on to do it."[4]

The judgment in *Lawrence* was given on the same day but after, and referring to, *Caldwell*. The House was differently constituted but Lords Diplock and Roskill were in both cases. It was held that the test of recklessness was the same for reckless driving (now replaced by dangerous driving) as for criminal damage but what must be risked is different. Unlike criminal damage, reckless driving did not require proof of any result as to which D must be reckless, so it was necessary to invent one; and the House specified injury to the person or substantial damage to property. Lord Diplock formulated the test of recklessness in slightly different terms. The "obvious risk" of *Caldwell* became an "obvious and serious risk" in *Lawrence*.

a) *Analysis of the Caldwell/Lawrence test.* Courts often stress that judgments are not to be construed as if they were statutes but in this instance they seem to have ignored that salutary rule. The Court of Appeal has advised judges that they should direct juries in the exact words of Lord Diplock. In a reckless driving case, it was a fatal misdirection to omit either "obvious" or "serious" in describing the risk. Regrettably, therefore, it is necessary to undertake some textual analysis of Lord Diplock's propositions.

Under both limbs of the direction, as formulated, it must be proved that the risk taken was an "obvious [and serious] risk". The further element of culpability is either:

(a) D's failure to give thought to whether there was "such a risk" (which might be designated "inadvertent recklessness"); or

(b) D's knowledge that there was "some risk" ("advertent recklessness").

2. [1982] AC 341, [1981] 1 All ER 961. For facts, see below, p. 691.
3. [1982] AC 510, [1981] 1 All ER 974. For discussion of these decisions see commentaries at [1981] Crim LR 393 and 410; Syrota [1982] Crim LR 97; Glanville Williams [1982] CLJ 252.
4. [1981] 1 All ER at 967.

b) *Must the risk have been "obvious" in all cases?* While this is the effect of treating the model direction as if it were in a statute, it may not be what Lord Diplock intended. In other parts of his speeches he dealt first with advertent recklessness and applied the test of "obvious [and serious]" only when he came to inadvertent recklessness. This may explain the use of the contrasting phrases, "*any such* [i.e., obvious [and serious]] risk", for inadvertent recklessness and "*some* risk" for advertent recklessness. This makes sense: recklesness is either deliberately taking "*a risk*" of harmful consequences, or failing to recognise *an obvious [and serious] risk*. The relevance of "obvious" is plain, it is that the person who was not aware of the risk ought to have been aware of it. When D was aware of the risk the fact that it was obvious does not have the same relevance. In the one case the culpability consists in ignoring a known (and unacceptable) risk, in the other it consists in failing to advert to the obvious. When, however, Lord Diplock came to formulate the model direction, he inverted the order of his two cases and so stated the rule that "obvious [and serious]" applies to both cases. In principle, the requirement that the risk be "obvious" should not apply to advertent recklessness. Its obvious character would be evidence that D was aware of it, but that is all. If there is a case in which the risk of causing a disaster is not at all obvious but the defendant happens to knows of it he should surely be judged reckless if he takes it and causes the disaster.[5]

c) *Must the risk have been "serious" in all cases?* Unless Lord Diplock intended the recklessness required for reckless driving to be different in some respect from that required for criminal damage, the use of the word "serious" in *Lawrence* simply spelt out what was implicit in *Caldwell*. As subsequent decisions required a judge directing a jury to use the word "serious" in a reckless driving case but not in a case of criminal damage, it ought to follow that there is a difference. But it is submitted that no such difference was intended. Elsewhere in *Lawrence* Lord Diplock speaks of a "real risk" as the requirement. Did he intend that a person should be liable for recklessly causing criminal damage although he took no "real", no "serious", risk? Surely not. Serious must mean "to be taken seriously", "not negligible", a risk which a reasonably prudent person would not take.[6] If so, it is applicable to all forms of recklessness.

d) *Obvious to whom?* Where the risk must be obvious, does that mean obvious to the individual defendant or the reasonably prudent person? There are passages in *Caldwell* which suggest that the individual defendant is meant and powerful arguments have been advanced in favour of this view;[7] but in *Lawrence* the House was plainly looking to the "ordinary prudent motorist" as represented by the jury. It is this test which prevails. The Divisional Court in *Elliott v C*[8] reluctantly felt themselves bound so to

5. This analysis is more fully developed in the commentary on *Reid* (1989) 91 Cr App Rep 263 at [1991] Crim LR 269, 271.
6. *Reid*, above, at p. 270.
7. Glanville Williams [1983] Crim LR 365, Syrota [1982] Crim LR 97. Cf. Field and Lynn (1992) 12 LS 74.
8. [1983] 2 All ER 1005, [1983] 1 WLR 939.

hold. D, a backward fourteen-year-old girl who had been out all night without food or sleep, entered a garden shed, poured white spirit on to the carpet and threw two lighted matches on it. Fire flared up and the shed was destroyed. She was charged with arson of the shed, contrary to s. 1 (2) of the Criminal Damage Act 1971. The magistrates found that she had given no thought to the possibility that the shed might be destroyed by fire and that, in the circumstances, the risk would not have been obvious to her if she had given thought to the matter. The magistrates who had acquitted were directed to convict: the risk would have been obvious to a reasonably prudent man who stopped to think.

The same view was taken by the Court of Appeal with equal reluctance in *Stephen Malcolm R.*[9] A fifteen-year-old boy who had thrown petrol bombs close to a girl's bedroom window was convicted of arson contrary to s. 1 (2) (b) of the Criminal Damage Act 1971. He claimed that he was not reckless whether life would be endangered because he did not realise that, if the bomb had gone through the window, it might have killed the girl. The court held that the judge had correctly applied the test of the ordinary prudent man rejecting the argument that D was reckless only if he did an act which created a risk obvious to someone of his age and with such of his characteristics as would affect his appreciation of the risk.

The test works harshly in these cases of young people. In the case of adults, it will do so in the case of those who lack the capacities of the ordinary prudent person. In *Stephenson*[10] a tramp sheltered in a hollow in a haystack. Feeling cold, he lit a fire in the hollow. The haystack was destroyed. Any reasonable person would have been aware of the risk but Stephenson was suffering from schizophrenia and may not have been aware of it. Because this was not clearly left to the jury, the court – pre-*Caldwell* – quashed his conviction. Even if he had stopped to think it is possible that, because of his condition, he might not have realised that there was a risk of damage. *Stephenson* appears to be overruled by *Caldwell*. How far are we to go in ignoring abnormalities? Is a blind man to be held to have recklessly damaged property because he was unaware of a risk which would have been obvious to a sighted person? And what about temporary handicaps – the person who strikes a match, being unaware because of his heavy cold, that the premises reek with petrol fumes? *Caldwell*, as interpreted in *Elliott v C* and *R*, appears to be a slippery slope to intolerable injustice with no obvious exit.

If it would have appeared to the reasonably prudent person that there was an obvious risk, it is immaterial that a person with expert knowledge not possessed by the defendant would have known that there was no, or no serious, risk. A person may act, reckless whether life is endangered, without there being in fact any danger to life.[11]

e) *Caldwell recklessness as a state of mind.* Lord Diplock considered it axiomatic that *mens rea*, including recklessness, requires proof of the state

9. (1984) 79 Cr App Rep 334.
10. [1979] QB 695, [1979] 2 All ER 1198.
11. *Sangha* [1988] 2 All ER 385 [1988] 1 WLR 519. Cf. the case of the bullet-proof vest discussed in relation to intention, above, p. 54

of the defendant's mind. D must have been aware of the risk or not have given thought to the possibility of its existence – "not giving thought" is a state of mind. Once the obvious (and serious) risk is proved, there seems to be only one way out for the defendant. He can escape only if he considered the matter and decided that there was no risk, or a "negligible" risk. It appears that, if D wishes the court or jury to consider this possibility, he must introduce some evidence of it. In *Lawrence* Lord Diplock said:

"If satisfied that an obvious and serious risk was created by the manner of the defendant's driving, the jury are entitled to infer that he was in one or other of the states of mind required to constitute the offence and will probably do so; but regard must be given to any explanation he gives as to his state of mind which may displace the inference."

The case where D has considered the matter and decided that there is no risk is sometimes referred to as the "lacuna" or "loophole" in the *Caldwell/ Lawrence* principle. But it is an essential element in the theory for, if the lacuna were filled and D held liable where he has given thought, it would no longer be possible to maintain that a state of mind must be proved. Then the prosecution would prove their case by satisfying the jury that D's conduct involved an obvious (and serious) risk. If it matters not whether the defendant was aware of the risk, or never gave thought to the possibility of it, or decided there was no risk, his state of mind is immaterial. Consider *Lamb*.[12] D pointed a loaded revolver at his friend, P, in jest. D and P knew that there were two bullets in the revolver but they believed it was safe to pull the trigger because neither bullet was opposite the barrel. D shot P dead. Neither of them knew that, when the trigger is pulled, the cylinder containing the chambers rotates clockwise before the firing-pin strikes. D's conviction was quashed because of a misdirection by the trial judge but Sachs LJ said, obiter, that "it would, of course, have been fully open to a jury, if properly directed, to find the accused guilty, because they considered his view as to there being no danger was formed in a criminally negligent way". Lamb may well have been guilty of gross negligence but a person who has formed the view that there is no danger is not reckless in the *Caldwell/Lawrence* sense. He is not aware of the risk; and he has not failed to give thought to whether there is a risk or not.

The existence of the lacuna was acknowledged in a reported case for the first time in *Reid*,[13] a case of alleged reckless driving (overtaking) causing death, where Mustill LJ said:

"The defendant was not saying that he recognised the existence of a risk and assessed it as negligible, or that he assessed it as less than serious, whatever precisely that term may mean. So far as he was concerned, there was no risk. *If this was or might have been so, the jury must acquit.*" (Authors' italics.)

In some earlier cases the lacuna was overlooked or avoided. In *Crossman*,[14] D, a lorry driver rejected the advice of the loaders of a piece of heavy machinery on to his lorry that it was unsafe unless chained and sheeted. It

12. [1967] 2 QB 981, [1967] 2 All ER 1282, CA.
13. (1989) 91 Cr App Rep at 269, above, fn. 5.
14. [1986] RTR 49, [1986] Crim LR 406.

was, he said, "as safe as houses." The load fell off and killed a pedestrian. When his argument that reckless driving must have something to do with the handling or control of the vehicle was rejected, he pleaded guilty to reckless driving and his conviction was upheld. Yet if, after his attention had been drawn to the possibility of risk, he really believed that the load was "as safe as houses", he was not reckless in the *Lawrence* sense. In *Chief Constable of Avon and Somerset Constabulary v Shimmen*[15] a self-defence expert on his way from the pub was demonstrating his skill to his friends at narrowly missing a shop window with a kick. He smashed the window. It was unsuccessfully argued that this was a "lacuna" case. D thought he had minimised the risk but he knew there was some risk – so he falls squarely within the second limb of the *Caldwell* test. He said he thought he had "eliminated as much risk as possible by missing by two inches instead of two millimetres". Taking even the slightest risk with the property of another can be justified only if there is some acceptable reason for taking the risk. Probably there was none in this case. D may have considered the known risk "negligible" but that was a question for the court or jury, not for him. If, however, D believes that he has eliminated all risk by some, in fact, inadequate, precaution, he cannot be held reckless. Suppose that *Lamb*[16] had observed that one of the bullets was opposite the barrel and had rotated the chamber anti-clockwise, so the bullet was at "11 o'clock" and then, believing that there was no danger, had pressed the trigger. There is no distinction between that and the actual case. It can make no difference whether D's conclusion that there was no risk arose from his initial contemplation of the circumstances or from steps taken by him to change those circumstances. Nor should D be regarded as reckless if the proportions to which he, mistakenly, believes he has reduced the risk are indeed negligible i.e., the risk which he believes he is taking is one which a reasonable and prudent person might take.

f) *The province of Caldwell/Lawrence recklessness.* Lord Roskill has said that "reckless" should be given the Caldwell meaning in all offences, "unless Parliament has otherwise ordained";[17] but this dictum does not seem to have been accepted by the Court of Appeal and *Savage and Parmenter* now makes it clear that *Caldwell* is by no means of universal application. With the abolition of reckless driving, its sphere of operation may well be limited to criminal damage and manslaughter. Cases where it does not apply are considered below.

g) *Recklessness in rape and indecent assault.* Rape and indecent assault are offences which may be committed recklessly in so far as a man may be guilty of either offence if he is reckless as to whether the woman consents to the sexual intercourse, or indecent act.[18] After *Caldwell* the courts were at

15. (1986) 84 Cr App Rep 7, [1986] Crim LR 800.
16. Above, p. 65.
17. *Seymour* [1983] 2 All ER 1058 at 1064, HL.
18. For rape, the requirement of recklessness is expressed in the Sexual Offences (Amendment) Act 1976, s. 1 (1) and, for indecent assault, it is implied in the Sexual Offences Act 1956, s. 14 (1).

first disposed to hold that *Caldwell* recklessness with an additional requirement of "indifference" was enough.[19] This was found to create immense difficulties for juries and in *Kimber*[20] the Court of Appeal held that, for indecent assault, the law was that recklessness was proved only if D did not believe that P was consenting and "couldn't care less" whether she was consenting or not. This was followed in a rape case, *Satnam S, Kewal S*[1] where it was held that the common law, as stated by the House of Lords in *Morgan*[2] was, following the recommendations of the Heilbron report,[3] intended by Parliament to be incorporated in the Sexual Offences (Amendment) Act 1976. Accordingly, *Caldwell* did not apply. *Caldwell* and *Lawrence* were distinguished as cases where the question was as to the foreseeability of the consequences of the criminal act, whereas in rape the question is "foreseeability ... as to the state of mind of the victim". "Couldn't care less" seems to imply that, at least, the possibility that the woman may not be consenting has crossed the man's mind. If he then proceeds to have intercourse and she is not in fact consenting he is guilty of reckless rape. "Couldn't care less" seems, in one respect, to be too narrow. D may fervently hope that the woman is consenting – he does care, but, it is submitted, not enough.

h) *Recklessness in offences requiring "malice"*. Although the concept of recklessness applied in *Cunningham*[4] was subjected to criticism in *Caldwell*,[5] the former case was distinguished and not overruled. The continuing validity of Cunningham recklessness is confirmed by *Savage* and *Parmenter*.[6] In *W (a minor) v Dolbey*,[7] D, a fifteen-year-old boy, who had been using an air rifle to shoot at bottles, pointed it at P who told him not to. D replied, "There is nothing in the gun, I have got no pellets." D pulled the trigger. There was a pellet in the rifle and it wounded P's forehead. The Divisional Court held that D's conviction for malicious wounding, contrary to s. 20 of the Offences against the Person Act 1861, must be quashed. D did not foresee that any physical harm might come to P and he was not therefore reckless within the principle of *Cunningham*. Since he had considered whether there was a risk and decided there was none, he was probably not *Caldwell*-reckless either. If so, the result would have been the same if he had broken P's spectacles and been charged with criminal damage. It was a "lacuna" case.

i) *Recklessness at common law*. In *Savage and Parmenter*[8] it was recognised that Cunningham recklessness applies generally in offences against the

19. *Pigg* [1982] 2 All ER 591, [1982] 1 WLR 762. CA, a case of an alleged common law attempt to rape. Cf. *Bashir* (1982) 77 Cr App Rep 59 [1982] Crim LR 687, CA.
20. [1983] 3 All ER 316, [1983] 1 WLR 1118.
1. (1983) 78 Cr App Rep 149, [1985] Crim LR 236.
2. [1976] AC 182.
3. Cmnd 6352, 1975.
4. Above, p. 61.
5. Above, p. 62.
6. [1991] 4 All ER 698 at 720, HL.
7. (1983) 88 Cr App Rep 1, [1983] Crim LR 681, DC.
8. [1991] 4 All ER 698 at 707, 711.

person, including assaults. Not all such offences have a definition using the word, "maliciously". "Assault" is not defined at all and, whether an assault is a common law or statutory offence, its constituents are determined by the common law. They include Cunningham, not Caldwell, recklessness.

j) *Recklessness of the intoxicated – "general recklessness"*. The word "reckless" is used in yet another sense, different from those so far considered, in the case of intoxicated offenders. This usage is discussed below.[9]

k) *The future of recklessness*. The existing variation in the meaning of recklessness is indefensible. To take an example based on *W (a minor) v Dolbey*,[10] if D takes an air rifle and, not even considering the possibility that it might be loaded (as is the fact), aims and fires it at P, breaking P's spectacles and destroying his eye, D will be liable for causing criminal damage to the spectacles but will not be criminally liable at all for the destruction of the eye. The law appears to give greater protection to spectacles than to eyes. Yet, although D has committed no crime by destroying P's eye, it appears that he will be guilty of manslaughter if P dies of the injury within a year and a day.

The *Caldwell* test fails to make a distinction which should be made between the person who knowingly takes a risk and the person who gives no thought to whether there is a risk or not. And, on the other hand, it makes a distinction which has no moral basis. The person who, with gross negligence, fails to consider whether there is a risk is liable; but the person who considers whether there is a risk and, with gross negligence, decides there is none, is not liable.[11] The right solution, it is submitted, is to go back to the *Cunningham* test which appears to have been entirely trouble-free in practice.

l) *"Indifference" as an element in recklessness*. The notion of "indifference" has featured prominently in discussions of recklessness. It was much used by the House of Lords in *Morgan*,[12] and is the "couldn't care less" concept of *Kimber* and *Satnam S*.[13] It is submitted, however, that it is not an essential element in recklessness. A person who knowingly takes an unreasonable risk of causing a forbidden result may hope, sincerely and fervently, that it will never happen; but he is, surely, reckless. Where *Caldwell* recklessness applies, there is no room for an additional requirement of indifference, as *Pigg*[14] clearly demonstrated. But it might be otherwise if the *Cunningham* test were restored to general favour.

The problem is that of the person who is unaware that there is a risk, but would not care if he knew there was. He would carry on just the same. He is indifferent. It never crosses his mind that the woman with whom he is about to have sexual intercourse might not be consenting; but it would not

9. P. 226.
10. (1983) 88 Cr App Rep 1, [1983] Crim LR 681.
11. See the discussion of "the lacuna", above, p. 65.
12. [1976] AC 182, below, p. 87.
13. Above, p. 67.
14. Above, p. 67.

make any difference if it did. It never crosses his mind that the statement he is about to make might be false, but he would say it anyway. He may well be thought to be no less reprehensible than one who is aware of the risk and takes it. His case is caught by *Caldwell* but not by *Cunningham* recklessness. There are two difficulties about extending *Cunningham* recklessness to cover this particular case. First, it requires the court or jury to answer a hypothetical question and, second, there is a problem of evidence. How is it to be proved that, if D had given thought, he would not have cared? This seems to call for an inquiry into his general character and habits which our law of evidence does not allow. To do so would savour of convicting him because he is that sort of person, not because of what he has done.

iii) *Negligence*

Before the decisions in *Caldwell* and *Lawrence* it was possible to draw a clear distinction between recklessness and negligence. Recklessness was the conscious taking of an unjustifiable risk, negligence the inadvertent taking of an unjustifiable risk. If D was aware of the risk and decided to take it, he was reckless; if he was unaware of the risk, but ought to have been aware of it, he was negligent. This distinction still holds good in a crime where *Cunningham* recklessness is required; the inadvertent taking of the risk, mere negligence, does not entail liability. Where, however, we are concerned with *Caldwell* recklessness, the inadvertent risk-taker may be held liable – his failure to direct his mind to the possibility of a risk, which would have been obvious to him had he done so, is reckless.

There are, however, still crimes where D may be held liable even if he did consider whether or not there was a risk and concluded, wrongly and unreasonably, that there was no risk, or so small a risk that it would have been justifiable to take it. This is now the hallmark of a crime of negligence. In such a case, D is, of course, a fortiori liable where he unreasonably failed to consider whether there was any risk and the risk was "obvious". There is thus a substantial overlap between recklessness and gross negligence.[15] Indeed the number of instances of gross negligence which do not amount to *Caldwell* recklessness will be very small. Examples may be found in the facts of *Lamb*[16] and *Crossman*.[17]

iv) *Intention, Recklessness and Negligence as to Circumstances*

Intention, recklessness and negligence may all exist with respect to circumstances as well as consequences. Sometimes the law may require intention as to one or more elements of a crime yet be satisfied with recklessness or negligence as to another or others. In obtaining by deception[18] D must intend to obtain, but he may be merely reckless whether the statement he makes is true or false. In rape, D must intend to have sexual intercourse but may be merely reckless whether P consents to his doing

15. Below, p. 372.
16. [1967] 2 QB 981, [1967] 2 All ER 1282, discussed above, p. 65.
17. [1986] RTR 49, above, p. 65.
18. Below, p. 555.

so.[19] It would seem that, in determining whether D's fault amounted to intention, recklessness or negligence, the same criteria should be applied to circumstances as to consequences. So an act is intentional as to a circumstance[20] when D wants the circumstance to exist (where he hopes, perhaps faintly, that the letter he steals contains money, he intends to steal money)[1] or knows that it exists; or, if the broader view of intention[2] is accepted, he is virtually certain that it exists. He is reckless whether a circumstance exists or will exist when it is obvious that it may do so and either he knows that, or (in the case of *Caldwell* recklessness)[3] does not give his mind to it. He is negligent with respect to a circumstance when, as a reasonable man, he ought to know that it exists or will exist and fails to do so, whether he has given thought to the question or not.

v) *Blameless Inadvertence*

Finally, a man may reasonably fail to foresee a consequence that follows from his act – as when a slight slap causes the death of an apparently healthy person; or reasonably fail to consider the possibility of the existence of a circumstance – as when goods, which are in fact stolen, are bought in the normal course of business from a trader of high repute.

2 Basic Mens Rea

Mens rea is a term which has no single meaning. Every crime has its own *mens rea* which can be ascertained only by reference to its statutory definition or the case law. The most we can do is to state a general principle, or presumption, which governs its definition. Before *Caldwell* it could be said that this principle was that, in crimes requiring *mens rea*, as distinct from negligence, the defendant should be liable only for that which he had *chosen* to bring about, or to take the risk of bringing about, i.e., that he intended, or was reckless (in the *Cunningham* sense) whether all the elements of the offence, both results and circumstances, should occur. Because he had so chosen, he could fairly be held responsible for the occurrence of the *actus reus*. His intention or recklessness as to all the elements of the offence was *mens rea* or the basic constituent of it. Since *Caldwell*, the principle can no longer always be said to be based on the idea of choice. The person who gives no thought to the question whether there is a risk cannot be said to have chosen to take that risk.

The general principle is expressed in the draft Code as follows:

"24 (1) Unless a contrary intention appears, a person does not commit a Code offence unless he acts intentionally, knowingly or recklessly in respect of each of its elements. . . ."

---

19. Below, p. 451.
20. This is not the same as saying that the circumstance is intended, because that implies a belief by D that he may be able to influence the existence of the circumstance; below, p. 276.
  1. Salmond, *Jurisprudence* (11th ed.) 411.
  2. Above, p. 53.
  3. In *Pigg* (1982) 74 Cr App Rep 352 at 358 the Court of Appeal rejected an argument that *Caldwell* applied only to consequences and not to circumstances.

Some offences are so defined that only intention with respect to one or more elements is sufficient. Others are defined so as to require only negligence, or no fault at all, with respect to particular elements; limiting, or qualifying the basic *mens rea* which cl. 24 (1) would require.

A concept similar to that embodied in cl. 24 (1) has been designated "basic intent" by Lord Simon in *Director of Public Prosecutions v Morgan*:[4]

"By 'crimes of basic intent' I mean those crimes whose definition expresses (or, more often implies) a *mens rea* which does not go beyond the *actus reus*."

Lord Simon's "basic intent" does not go beyond but (it seems) does not necessarily go as far as the *actus reus* – it may not extend to every element of it. The intent required in *Prince*[5] might thus be a "basic intent" for Lord Simon, but it would not satisfy the principle of cl. 24 (1) above. For this reason, and because it involves recklessness as well as intention, the term "basic *mens rea*" is preferred.

3 The Requirement of an Ulterior Intent

The principle stated in cl. 24 (1), by itself, would amount to a definition of the *mens rea* of many crimes, but it does not meet all cases. A crime is frequently so defined that the *mens rea* includes an intention to produce some further consequence beyond the *actus reus* of the crime in question. Burglary will serve as an example. It is not enough that D intended to enter a building as a trespasser, that is, to achieve the *actus reus* of burglary. It is necessary to go further and to show that D had the intention of committing one of a number of specified offences in the building. The actual commission of one of those offences is no part of the *actus reus* of burglary which is complete as soon as D enters. Causing grievous bodily harm with intent to resist the lawful apprehension of any person,[6] placing gunpowder near a building with intent to do bodily injury to any person,[7] are instances of similar crimes. Where such an ulterior intent must be proved, it is sometimes referred to as a "specific intent".[8] This term, however, is one which should be regarded with caution.[9] It is variously used to mean (i) whatever intention has to be proved to establish guilt of the particular crime before the court;[10] (ii) a "direct" as distinct from an "oblique" intention;[11] or (iii) an intention ulterior to the *actus reus* or (iv) a crime where D may successfully plead lack of the prescribed *mens rea* notwithstanding the fact that he relies on evidence that he was intoxicated at the time.[12] The phrase "ulterior intent" is therefore preferred to describe the third concept. The nature of the ulterior intent required varies widely from crime to crime – an intent to commit one of a number of specified offences

---

4. [1975] 2 All ER 347 at 363; contrasting the term with "ulterior intent" as used in the third edition of this work and below.
5. Above, p. 38.
6. Offences against the Person Act 1861, s. 18.
7. Ibid., s. 30.
8. See Perkins, "A Rationale of *Mens Rea*" (1939) 52 Harv L Rev 905, 924.
9. See Cross, [1961] Crim LR 510.
10. *Director of Public Prosecutions v Beard* [1920] AC 479 at 501–502; below, p. 220.
11. Above, p. 54. *Steane* [1947] KB 997 at 1004, [1947] 1 All ER 813 at 816.
12. Below, p. 220.

in burglary, an intent to cause P to act to his prejudice in forgery, an intent permanently to deprive the owner in theft and so on.

Where an ulterior intent is required, it is obvious that recklessness is not enough. On a charge of wounding with intent to cause grievous bodily harm, proof that D was reckless whether he caused grievous bodily harm will not suffice.[13]

It should again be emphasised that most crimes require only basic *mens rea* and no ulterior intent. In rape, for example, it is enough that the accused intentionally or recklessly perpetrated the *actus reus* – intercourse with a woman without her consent – and no ulterior intention need be proved. The result is that the best we can do by way of a general definition of *mens rea* is as follows: "Intention, knowledge or recklessness with respect to all the elements of the offence *together with any ulterior intent which the definition of the crime requires.*"

4 The variable nature of *mens rea*

Mens rea, as so defined, is not required for all crimes, for (i) even at common law there were many exceptions to it and (ii) statutory crimes are frequently interpreted so as to exclude the necessity for either intention or recklessness with respect to some one or more elements in the *actus reus*.

Sometimes the common law is satisfied by proof of the basic *mens rea* of a lesser offence than that charged. So on a charge of murder it is enough that D intended to cause serious bodily harm. Statutes are sometimes similarly interpreted and on a charge of maliciously inflicting grievous (that is, serious) bodily harm, it is enough that D intended to cause or was reckless whether he caused actual (that is, not serious) bodily harm.[14] Sometimes it is enough to prove only negligence; sometimes even this is not necessary and D may be convicted although he was blamelessly inadvertent as to a circumstance of the *actus reus*. In the latter case we shall say that the crime imposes "strict liability" as to that circumstance.

The offence under s. 20 of the Sexual Offences Act 1956 discussed above[15] will serve as an illustration. It has been held that, as to the circumstance that the girl is under sixteen, the accused may be blamelessly inadvertent and yet may be convicted. In *Prince*,[16] D took a girl out of the possession and against the will of her father and mother. He knew he was doing this; but, as the jury found, he believed her statement that she was eighteen and his belief was reasonable, for she looked very much older than sixteen. In fact, she was under sixteen and D therefore brought about the *actus reus* of the crime. He was not even negligent, let alone reckless or intentional as to the girl's age. In spite of his blameless inadvertence as to this important circumstance in the *actus reus*, D was convicted. Yet in *Hibbert*[17] D took away and seduced a young girl but was acquitted because it was not proved that he knew, or had any reason to believe, that she was in

13. *Belfon* [1976] 3 All ER 46, where this passage was cited at p. 49, [1976] 1 WLR 741, 744.
14. Below, p. 426.
15. See p. 38.
16. (1875) LR 2 CCR 154; **SHC 108**. See Cross, "Centenary Reflections on Prince's Case" (1975) 91 LQR 540.
17. (1869) LR 1 CCR 184.

the possession of her parents. Bramwell B, though upholding the conviction in *Prince*, thought D would have a good defence if he believed he had the father's consent. That the girl is (i) under sixteen, (ii) in the possession of her parents,[18] and (iii) that they do not consent, are circumstances which are equally essential to the existence of an *actus reus*, yet *mens rea*, as the law stands,[19] is required as to (ii) and (iii) but not as to (i).

This seems illogical and unjust. An ideal rule would seem to be that stated at the beginning of this section, requiring intention or recklessness as to *all* the elements in the *actus reus*. Presumably no element is included in the definition of an *actus reus* unless it contributes to the heinousness of the offence. If the accused is blamelessly inadvertent with respect to *any* one element in the offence, and does not, therefore, appreciate the full heinousness of his conduct, is it then proper to hold him responsible for it?

That the law should impose strict liability to one circumstance and yet require *mens rea* as to another in the same crime may be partly a result of historical development for the courts' attitude to the problem of *mens rea*, and especially to how far a requirement of *mens rea* should be imported into statutory offences, has varied from time to time. One element may have fallen to be construed by a court devoted to strict liability, another by a court which adhered to the principles of *mens rea*. This may explain how the law came to be in the state it is, but it certainly does not justify it.

There is a particular difficulty in requiring *mens rea* as to an element in the *actus reus* of a morally indifferent nature. The definition of a crime sometimes draws an arbitrary line as to a person's age, or as to time, weight, size and other matters of degree. Ignorance of the law is no defence and a person who is unaware of the law is unlikely to direct his mind to the question whether the arbitrary line has been crossed in the particular case. There is no reason for the possessor of a shotgun to consider whether the barrel is less than twenty-four inches in length unless he knows that, if it is, possession without a firearms certificate is an offence.[20] Similarly, a person taking a girl out of the possession of her parents may give no thought to the question whether she is under or over sixteen, if he is unaware of the legal significance of that age. The case is different in a material respect from that of the person who has a positive but mistaken belief that the girl is over sixteen. Williams[1] sought to resolve the difficulty by distinguishing between cases of "mistaken belief" (where there is a positive belief) which will negative recklessness and "simple ignorance" (where there is no advertence to the question) which will not. This distinction gains some support from *Caldwell*.[2] D can truly be said to be indifferent as to the circumstance – he does not care whether the barrel of the gun is more or less than twenty-four inches or the girl under or over 16, because he is unaware that it matters. This principle, however, could only be properly

18. So a belief that she was eighteen might now be a defence amounting, since the reduction in the age of majority, to a belief that she was not in anyone's custody: Cross, loc. cit. 553, n. 24.
19. It is arguable that *Hibbert* is inconsistent with *Prince* but it was not overruled in this latter case.
20. Firearms Act 1968, s. 1.
  1. Williams CLGP (1st ed.) 122, (2nd ed.) 151.
  2. Above, p. 62; cf. *Pigg* (1982) 74 Cr App Rep 352 at 358–359.

applicable in respect of age, time, weight, size and other circumstances which everyone knows to exist in some degree. D knows that the barrel has length or that the girl has an age and, ex hypothesi, he does not care what it is. Where the circumstance is not simply a matter of degree but of kind, it is no longer possible to say that D was indifferent. D may buy and deliver to P a book with an attractive cover without looking at the contents and without considering whether it might contain blasphemous and obscene material, but to infer that he was indifferent would be quite unwarranted. When he learnt the facts, he might be quite horrified.[3] Under *Caldwell*, it would seem that the fact that it should have been obvious to him that the book was blasphemous and obscene would be enough to fix him with recklessness, for the references to "indifference" seem to have no substance.[4]

These problems do not arise if the court holds that the crime is one of strict liability with respect to the circumstance in question, as they did in *Prince*.[5]

5 Transferred Malice[6]

If D, with the *mens rea* of a particular crime, does an act which causes the *actus reus* of the same crime,[7] he is guilty, even though the result, in some respects, is an unintended one. D intends to murder O and, in the dusk, shoots at a man whom he believes to be O. He hits and kills the man at whom he aims, who is in fact P. In one sense this is obviously an unintended result; but D did intend to cause the *actus reus* which he has caused and he is guilty of murder. Again, D intends to enter a house, No. 6 King Street, and steal therein. In the dark he mistakenly enters No. 7. He is guilty of burglary.[8]

The law, however, carries this principle still farther. Suppose, now, that D, intending to murder O, shoots at a man who is in fact O, but *misses* and kills P who, unknown to D, was standing close by. This is an unintended result in a different – and more fundamental – respect than the example considered above. Yet, once again, D, with the *mens rea* of a particular crime, has caused the *actus reus* of the same crime; and, once again, he is guilty of murder. So, where D struck O, who fell against P, who also fell and sustained a fatal injury, D was guilty of manslaughter: "The criminality of the doer of the act is precisely the same whether it is [O] or [P] who dies."[9] The application of the principle to cases of this second type is known as the doctrine of "transferred malice".

---

3. The taker of the girl and the possessor of the shotgun might be equally horrified when they learnt *the law*, but that is not the same thing. We are considering recklessness as to facts, not law. Cf. *Mousir* [1987] Crim CR 561 and commentary.
4. Above, p. 68.
5. Above, p. 72.
6. See Ashworth in *Reshaping the Criminal Law*, 77–94 and in *Crime, Proof and Punishment*, 45–70; Williams "Convictions and Fair Labelling" [1983] CLJ 85.
7. See *Hussain* [1969] 2 QB 567, [1969] 2 All ER 1117, [1969] Crim LR 433 and commentary; *Ellis, Street and Smith* [1987] Crim LR 44 and commentary; cf. *Kundeus* (1976) 24 CCC (2d) 276 at 282–283.
8. See *Wrigley* [1957] Crim LR 57.
9. *Mitchell* [1983] QB 741, [1983] 2 All ER 427, CA.

In *Latimer*,[10] D had a quarrel in a public house with O. He took off his belt and aimed a blow at O which struck him lightly, but the belt bounded off and struck P who was standing close by and wounded her severely. The jury found that the blow was unlawfully aimed at O, but that the striking of P "was purely accidental and not such a consequence of the blow as the prisoner ought to have expected" – that is, he was not even negligent with respect to this result. It was held, on a case reserved, that D was properly convicted of unlawfully and maliciously wounding P.

It is important to notice the limitations of this doctrine. It operates only when the *actus reus* and the *mens rea* of the *same* crime coincide. If D, with the *mens rea* of one crime, does an act which causes the *actus reus* of a different crime, he cannot, as a general rule, be convicted of either offence. D shoots at P's dog with intent to kill it but misses and kills P who, unknown to D, was standing close by. Obviously he cannot be criminally liable for killing the dog, for he has not done so; nor can he be convicted of murder,[11] for he has not the *mens rea* for that crime. A similar result follows where D shoots at P with intent to kill him and, quite accidentally, kills P's dog: D is guilty of neither crime. In *Pembliton*[12] D was involved in a fight outside a public house, and, as a result, was charged with maliciously breaking a window. The jury found:

"that the prisoner threw the stone which broke the window, but that he threw it at the people he had been fighting with, intending to strike one or more of them with it, but not intending to break the window."[13]

His conviction was quashed by the Court for Crown Cases Reserved, for there was no finding that he had the *mens rea* of the crime, the *actus reus* of which he had caused. Lord Coleridge pointed out that it would have been different if there had been a finding that he was reckless as to the consequence which had occurred – but there was no such finding. The intent which is transferred must be a *mens rea*, whether intention or recklessness. If D shoots at O with intent to kill, because O is making a murderous attack on him and this is the only way in which he can preserve his own life, he does not intend an *actus reus* (in the broader sense, p. 31, above), for to kill in these circumstances is justified. If, however, D misses O and inadvertently kills P, an innocent bystander, he does cause an *actus reus* but he is not guilty of murder for there is no *mens rea* (in the broader sense) to transfer; the result which he intended was a perfectly lawful one.[14]

It has been suggested by Williams[15] that the doctrine of transferred malice should be applied only where the actual consequence was brought about negligently: that is, where D, when shooting at O, *ought* to have appreciated that there was a risk of killing P. There is, however, no suggestion in the cases that the rule is to be thus limited and it will be noted

10. (1886) 17 QBD 359; **SHC 87**.
11. As to whether it could be manslaughter, see below, pp. 366 ff. and 372.
12. (1874) LR 2 CCR 119; **SHC 86**.
13. Ibid., at p. 120.
14. Below, p. 252; and cf. *Gross* (1913) 23 Cox CC 455, below, p. 354.
15. CLGP 48. He would now abolish the doctrine for criminal damage. It results in "unfair labelling" where the property damaged is more valuable than the property D intended to damage. He would retain it for offences against the person: [1983] CLJ 85. Injury to one person is (presumably) as bad as the same injury to any other person.

that the doctrine was applied in *Latimer* even though there was an express finding that D was not negligent with respect to the consequence which actually occurred. It would, moreover, be illogical to make the commission of a crime requiring *mens rea* depend on the presence or absence of negligence.

Williams regards the doctrine of transferred malice as a "rather arbitrary exception to normal principles". He rejects the argument that "the result is *not* unintended, for the intention was to kill, and the result is a killing." He writes:[16]

> "This argument ... sounds plausible only because part of the real intention is omitted. Although the result in the sense of a killing was intended, the result in the sense of a killing of P was not intended. After all the accused is not indicted for killing in the abstract; he is indicted for killing P; and it should therefore, on a strict view, be necessary to establish *mens rea* in relation to the killing of P."

The answer to this, it is submitted, is that D's act is unintentional only in a respect which is immaterial. The test of materiality in a difference of result is whether it affects the existence of the *actus reus* which D intended. Thus it would be immaterial that D intended to shoot P in the heart but, because of a quite unexpected movement by P, shot him (unintentionally) in the head. The *actus reus* of murder is the killing of a human being – *any* human being – under the Queen's Peace, and his identity is irrelevant.

6 Coincidence of *Actus Reus* and *Mens Rea*[17]

The *mens rea* must coincide in point of time with the act which causes the *actus reus*.[18] "If I happen to kill my neighbour accidentally, I do not become a murderer by thereafter expressing joy over his death. My happiness over the result is not the same as a willingness to commit the illegal act."[19] *Mens rea* implies an intention to do a present act, not a future act.[20] Suppose that D is driving to P's house, bent on killing P. A person steps under the wheels of D's car, giving D no chance to avoid him, and is killed. It is P. Clearly, D is not guilty of murder. One who walks out of gaol while in a state of automatism does not commit the offence of escape[1] by deliberately remaining at large.[2] Suppose that D, having resolved to kill his wife, P, prepares and conceals a poisoned apple with the intention of giving it to her tomorrow. She finds the apple today, eats it and dies. D is not guilty of murder. He might be guilty of manslaughter on the ground that the act of leaving the apple where it might be found was reckless or grossly negligent.[3] If D does an act with intent thereby to cause the *actus reus*, and does so, it is immaterial that he has repented before the *actus reus* occurs. Where

16. CLGP at 135; and see 9 JSPTL at 170–171. S. R. L. Milton (1968) 85 SALS 115.
17. Marston, "Contemporaneity of Act and Intention" (1970) 86 LQR 208; A. R. White, "The Identity and Time of the Actus Reus" [1977] Crim LR 148.
18. *Jakeman* (1983) 76 Cr App Rep 223, [1983] Crim LR 104 and commentary thereon.
19. Andanaes, *CLGP of Norway*, 194.
20. "There is no law against a man's intending to commit a murder the day after tomorrow. The law only deals with conduct": Holmes, *The Criminal Law* (John Harvard ed.) 54.
1. Sixth edition of this work, p. 756.
2. *Scott* [1967] VR 276; discussed by Howard in [1967] Crim LR at 406.
3. Cf. *Burke* [1987] Crim LR 480 and commentary.

D dispatched suitcases which she knew to contain cannabis from Ghana to London, her repentance before the importation took place was no defence.[4]

Where however D has, with *mens rea*, gone beyond mere preparation and is in the course of committing an offence, it should be no answer that the final step was involuntary or accidental – as where D is on the point of pulling the trigger with intent to murder and, being startled by an explosion, does so involuntarily.[5]

Where the *actus reus* is a continuing act, it is sufficient that D has *mens rea* during its continuance.[6] Where the *actus reus* is part of a larger transaction, it may be sufficient that D has *mens rea* during the transaction, though not at the moment the *actus reus* is accomplished. D inflicts a wound upon P with intent to kill him. Then, believing that he has killed P, he disposes, as he thinks, of the "corpse." In fact P was not killed by the wound but dies as a result of the act of disposal. D has undoubtedly caused the *actus reus* of murder by the act of disposal but he did not, at that time have *mens rea*. In an Indian and a Rhodesian[7] case it has been held, accordingly, that D must be acquitted of murder and convicted only of attempted murder. But in *Thabo Meli*[8] the Privy Council held that it was:

"impossible to divide up what was really one series of acts in this way. There is no doubt that the accused set out to do all these acts in order to achieve their plan, and as parts of their plan: and it is much too refined a ground of judgment to say that, because they were at a misapprehension at one stage and thought that their guilty purpose was achieved before it was achieved, therefore they are to escape the penalties of the law."

This suggests that the answer might be different where there was no antecedent plan to dispose of the body and *Thabo Meli* was distinguished on this ground in New Zealand[9] and, at first, in South Africa.[10] But in *Church*[11] the Court of Criminal Appeal applied *Thabo Meli* where D, in a sudden fight, knocked P unconscious and, wrongly believing her to be dead, threw her into the river where she drowned. He was charged with murder and his conviction for manslaughter was upheld. Here there was no antecedent plan. The point was not considered by the court, but it was apparently thought to be enough that the accused's conduct constituted "a series of acts which culminated in [P's] death."

In *Le Brun*[12] the court followed *Church*, holding that it was immaterial that there was no preconceived plan and that the same principles apply to manslaughter as to murder.[13] D, in a quarrel, knocked his wife unconscious

4. *Jakeman*, above Cf. *Wings Ltd v Ellis*, above, p. 52.
5. See commentary on *Burke* [1987] Crim LR 480.
6. *Fagan v Metropolitan Police Comr* [1969] 1 QB 439, [1968] 3 All ER 442; below, p. 403. Cf. *Miller* [1983] 2 AC 161, [1983] 1 All ER 978, HL; *Singh (Gurdev) v R* [1974] 1 All ER 26, [1973] 1 WLR 1444, CA.
7. *Khandu* (1890) ILR 15 Bomb 194; *Shorty* [1950] SR 280.
8. [1954] 1 All ER 373; **SHC** 12. Followed in *Moore and Dorn* [1975] Crim LR 229.
9. *Ramsay* [1967] NZLR 1005.
10. *Chiswibo* 1960 (2) SA 714.
11. [1966] 1 QB 59, [1965] 2 All ER 72.
12. [1991] 4 All ER 673.
13. *In A–G's reference (No. 4 of 1980)* [1981] 2 All ER 617 at 620 the court left open the question whether the principle applies to manslaughter and whether it was part of the ratio decidendi of *Church* that it does so.

and while attempting to drag her body away dropped and killed her. The jury were rightly told that they could convict of murder or manslaughter, depending on the intention with which the blow was struck, if D accidentally dropped P while (i) attempting to move her to her home against her wishes and/or (ii) attempting to dispose of her body or otherwise cover up the assault. The court appears to uphold the conviction on both of two alternative principles.

(a) The "transaction" principle. This appears to be that D is guilty of homicide if he kills during the continuance of the transaction, the sequence of events initiated by the unlawful blow, and that the transaction continues at least during the conduct described under (i) and (ii) above. This suggests that it certainly continues while D is engaged in some kind of wrongdoing arising out of, and immediately following, the unlawful blow. Though the case does not decide this, the result might have been different if D had dropped P in the same manner and at the same time and place while attempting to get her to hospital, or to her home if he had thought that was where she would wish to be taken; or, if he believed her to be dead, while he was attempting to deliver the corpse to the police. Under this principle it is immaterial that the second act is the sole cause of death.

(b) The causation principle. This holds that the initial blow is a cause of death. As that blow was struck with *mens rea*, there is no further problem— D is guilty of murder or manslaughter as the case may be. The second event was also a cause of death but it is clear that there may be more than one cause. This may suggest that Le Brun would have been guilty if P had been similarly dropped by a passer-by who was trying to get her to hospital. But it may be that an intervening act by a third party is regarded as breaking the chain of causation, particularly where it is unforeseeable, whereas the same thing done by the original actor is not.[14] The causation principle was the ratio decidendi of the South African case of *S v Masilela*.[15] D, intending to kill P, knocked him unconscious and, believing him to be dead, set fire to the house. P died from the fumes. If he had not been unconscious he would have been able to walk out, so knocking him unconscious was a cause of death. But it is probable that the chain of causation would be regarded as broken if the house had been set on fire by a tramp who happened to come along after D's departure.

In all these cases the second act was a cause of the death. Where it is impossible to say which act caused death, it has been held that D may be convicted only if it can be proved that he acted with *mens rea* (or other appropriate degree of fault) on both occasions. Where D knocked P downstairs and then, believing that he had killed her, cut her throat in order to dispose of the body, and it was impossible to say which act caused death, it was held that the jury should have been directed that they should convict of manslaughter if they were satisfied *both* (i) that knocking P downstairs was an intentional act which was unlawful and dangerous;[16] *and* (ii) that the act of cutting the throat was one of gross criminal negligence.[17]

14. See the passage, below, pp. 339–340, cited by the court in *Le Brun*.
15. 1968 (2) SA 558 (AD), **SHC 13**.
16. This is manslaughter. Below, p. 366.
17. This may be and, it was assumed in the case, was manslaughter. Below, p. 372.

If manslaughter was committed, it was immaterial that it was impossible to prove on which of these two closely related occasions it occurred.[18] If the jury were not satisfied on both points, there was a 50 per cent chance that this was a case of accidental death, in which case acquittal must follow. But if *Thabo Meli* applies to manslaughter,[19] the direction is too favourable. Assuming it was all one "transaction", it should have been enough to prove that D had the required *mens rea* on the first occasion.

7 Motive not an Element of an Offence

If D causes an *actus reus* with *mens rea*, he is guilty of the crime and it is entirely irrelevant to his guilt that he had a good motive. The mother who kills her imbecile and suffering child out of motives of compassion is just as guilty of murder as is the man who kills for gain. On the other hand, if either the *actus reus* or the *mens rea* of any crime is lacking, no motive, however evil, will make a man guilty of a crime.

A contrary view, it is true, has been put by an American writer:[20]

"Suppose a grave felony is about to be committed under such circumstances that the killing of the offender to prevent the crime would be justified by law, and at that very moment he is shot and killed. If the slayer was prompted by the impulse to promote the social security by preventing the felony he is guilty of no offence; if he had no such impulse but merely acted upon the urge to satisfy an old grudge by killing a personal enemy, he is guilty of murder. The intent is the same in either case – to kill the person; the difference between innocence and guilt lies in the motive which prompted this intent."

It is submitted, however, that (assuming that D knew of the facts which justified the killing) this view is contrary to principle. If it were correct, it would seem to follow that D, the public executioner, would be guilty of murder in hanging X, who had been condemned to death by a competent court, if it were shown that D had postponed his retirement to carry out this particular execution because he had a grudge against X and derived particular pleasure from hanging him. This can hardly be the law. If a surgical operation, though dangerous to life, is clearly justifiable on medical grounds, a surgeon who performs it with all proper skill cannot be said to be guilty of attempted murder, or, if the patient dies, murder, because he hopes the patient will die so that he can marry his wife, or inherit his property, or so that the patient will avoid the thoroughly miserable life he will face if he survives.[1]

Sometimes, when we speak of motive, we mean an emotion such as jealousy or greed, and sometimes we mean a species of intention. For example, D intends (i) to put poison in his uncle's tea, (ii) to cause his uncle's death and (iii) to inherit his money. We would normally say that (iii) is his motive. Applying our test of "desired consequence" (iii) is

18. *A-G's Reference (No. 4 of 1980)* [1981] 2 All ER 617, [1981] 1 WLR 705, CA, [1981] Crim LR 493 and commentary.
19. This question was left open. *Church* suggests that it does; and that seems right in principle.
20. Perkins and Boyce, *Criminal Law* (3rd ed.), 930.
1. See A. T. H. Smith in *Reshaping the Criminal Law*, 95.

certainly also intended. The reason why it is considered merely a motive is that it is a consequence ulterior to the *mens rea* and the *actus reus*; it is no part of the crime. If this criterion as to the nature of motive be adopted then it follows that motive, by definition, is irrelevant to criminal responsibility – that is, a man may be lawfully convicted of a crime whatever his motive may be, or even if he has no motive. The courts are not always consistent in their terminology. If D dismisses E, an employee, who has given evidence against him, in accordance with the terms of E's contract, D will be guilty of contempt of court, it is said, if his "motive" was to punish E for his evidence but not if it was for any other reason – e.g. incompetence or redundancy.[2] Consistency in terminology would suggest that in such a case we should speak of intent or purpose rather than motive. For example, if this variety of contempt were to be defined, the definition might say, "with intent to punish the witness".

In some exceptional cases motive is an element of an offence. In a prosecution for libel, if the civil law defences of fair comment or qualified privilege are available at all,[3] they may, no doubt, be defeated by proof of motive in the sense of spite or ill-will, while in blackmail, contrary to the Theft Act 1968, s. 21,[4] the accused's motive may be relevant in ascertaining whether his demand was unwarranted.[5]

As *evidence*, motive is always relevant.[6] This means simply that, if the prosecution can prove that D had a motive for committing the crime, they may do so since the existence of a motive makes it more likely that D in fact did commit it. Men do not usually act without a motive.

Motive is important again when the question of punishment is in issue. When the law allows the judge a discretion in sentencing, he will obviously be more leniently disposed towards the convicted person who acted with a good motive. When the judge has no discretion (as in murder) a good motive may similarly be a factor in inducing the Home Secretary to grant an early release on licence.

8 Ignorance of the Law is no Defence[7]
In our discussion of the general principles of *mens rea* nothing has been said about whether the accused knows his act is against the law, for, in the great majority of cases, it is irrelevant whether he knows it or not: "... the principle that ignorance of the law is no defence in crime" said Lord Bridge, "is so fundamental that to construe the word 'knowingly' in a criminal statute as requiring not merely knowledge of facts material to the

---

2. *A-G v Butterworth* [1963] 1 QB 696, [1962] 3 All ER 326, CA. Cf. *Rooney v Snaresbrook Crown Court* (1978) 68 Cr App Rep 78, [1979] Crim LR 109.
3. See below, p. 726.
4. See below, pp. 609–610.
5. Cf. *Adams*, below, p. 332; *Chandler v Director of Public Prosecutions*, [1964] AC 763.
6. *Williams* (1986) 84 Cr App Rep 299, CA, not following *Berry* (1986) 83 Cr App Rep 7.
7. See Ashworth, "Excusable Mistake of Law", [1974] Crim LR 652.

offender's guilt, but also knowledge of the relevant law, would be revolutionary and, to my mind, wholly unacceptable."[8] It must usually be proved that D intended to cause, or was reckless whether he caused, the event or state of affairs which, as a matter of fact, is forbidden by law; but it is quite immaterial to his conviction (though it may affect his punishment) whether he *knew* that the event or state of affairs was forbidden by law. This is so even though it also appears that D's ignorance of the law was quite reasonable and even, apparently, if it was quite impossible[9] for him to know of the prohibition in question. It was no defence for a native of Baghdad, charged with an unnatural offence on board a ship lying in an English port, to show that the act was lawful in his own country and that he did not know English law.[10] It was held that a Frenchman might be guilty of murder in the course of duelling in England, even if he did not know that duelling was against English law.[11] In *Bailey*,[12] D was convicted of an offence created by a statute which was passed while he was on the high seas although he committed the act before the end of the voyage when he could not possibly have known of the statute.[13] In each of these cases it might be argued that D at least intended something immoral; but that makes no difference. A motorist's mistaken belief that a constable has no right in the particular circumstances to require a specimen of breath is not a reasonable excuse for not providing the specimen.[14] So, if a statute forbids the sale of a house for a price above a stated figure, D, who helps to negotiate a sale at a price of which he is aware, and which is in excess of the stated figure, has *mens rea* even though he affirmatively believes a sale at the particular price to be lawful.[15] He intends the occurrence of that event which the law forbids. If, on the other hand, D is misled as to the price and believes it to be a figure which is, in fact, below the statutory maximum, then he has no *mens rea*.[16] The event which he now intends is not forbidden by the law. It probably makes no difference that D had received competent legal advice that his conduct would be lawful.[17] The contrary view, it has been said,[18] would

---

8. *Grant v Borg* [1982] 2 All ER 257 at 263, HL but cf. *Curr* [1968] 2 QB 944, [1967] 1 All ER 478, below, p. 269, where the court thought that a woman improperly receiving a family allowance payment was guilty only if she knew that what she was doing "amounted to an offence". But the section required only that she should know that the allowance was not "properly payable".

9. *Bailey*, below.

10. *Esop* (1836) 7 C & P 456.

11. *Barronet and Allain* (1852) Dears CC 51.

12. (1800) Russ & Ry 1.

13. But the judges recommended a pardon. Where a continuing act was made unlawful it was held that a reasonable time must be allowed for its discontinuance and that ignorance of the law was relevant to determine this question: *Burns v Nowell* (1880) 5 QBD 444. Cf. above, p. 44, fn 18.

14. *Reid* [1973] 3 All ER 1020, [1973] 1 WLR 1283, CA. ". . . if you choose at the street side to act out the part of Hampden, you have got to be right:" per Scarman, LJ.

15. *Johnson v Youden* [1950] 1 KB 544, [1950] 1 All ER 300.

16. Ibid.

17. *Cooper v Simmons* (1862) 7 H & N 707; *Crichton v Victorian Dairies Ltd* [1965] VR 49. In *Shaw v Director of Public Prosecutions* [1962] AC 220, [1961] 2 All ER 446, below, p. 291, D had sought advice as to the legality of the publication and evidently believed it to be legal. See also Hall, *GPCL* 387; Burchell & Hunt, 262; Perkins 926; and *Cambridgeshire and Isle of Ely County Council v Rust* [1972] 2 QB 426, [1972] 3 All ER 232, DC.

18. *People v McCalla*, 220 Pac 436 (1923).

result in "the advice of an attorney being paramount to the law." It is no defence that D acted in reliance on an assurance by a competent official that no prosecution would be brought;[19] but that is a most material fact when it comes to sentence. Arguably it might be different where the official advice is that the proposed act is lawful,[20] but the authorities at present are against this view.[1]

Few distinctions have given more difficulty than that between mistake of fact and mistake of law but the point has been little discussed in the present context. The decision in *Brutus v Cozens*[2] that the meaning of an ordinary word in a statute is not a question of law opens up exciting possibilities. If D studies the Public Order Act and concludes that the conduct in which he proposes to indulge is not "insulting", but the court takes a different view, why cannot D rely on his mistake "of fact"? It is thought that such a defence would be unsympathetically received by the courts and, indeed, regarded as subversive of the criminal law;[3] but, accepting (as we must) *Brutus v Cozens*, it is difficult to see that it is bad in principle.

In the case of the most serious crimes the problem does not arise; everyone knows it is against the law to murder, rob or rape. In the case of many less serious crimes, however, a person may very easily, and without negligence, be ignorant that a particular act is a crime. In such cases there will usually be nothing immoral about the act; and the conviction of a morally innocent person requires justification. Various justifications for the rule have been advanced. Blackstone[4] thought that "every person of discretion" may know the law – a proposition which is manifestly untrue today. Austin[5] based the rule upon the difficulty of disproving ignorance of the law, while Holmes,[6] who considered this no more difficult a question than many which are investigated in the courts, thought that to admit the plea would be to encourage ignorance of the law. A modern writer, Jerome Hall,[7] argues that to allow the defence would be to contradict one of the fundamental postulates of a legal order: that rules of law enforce objective meanings, to be ascertained by the courts:

"If that plea [*sc.* ignorance of the law] were valid, the consequence would be: whenever a defendant in a criminal case thought the law was thus and so, he is to be treated as though the law were thus and so, that is, *the law actually is thus and so.*"[8]

---

19. *Arrowsmith* [1975] QB 678, [1975] 1 All ER 463.
20. Williams CLGP, s. 106; Ashworth [1974] Crim LR at 657 ("A Criminal Estoppel?").
  1. *Surrey County Council v Battersby* [1965] 2 QB 194 at 203, [1965] 1 All ER 273; *Cambridgeshire and Isle of Ely County Council v Rust* [1972] 2 QB 426, [1972] 3 All ER 232; *Brook v Ashton* [1974] Crim LR 105; *Bowsher* [1973] RTR 202.
  2. [1973] AC 854, [1972] 2 All ER 1297, HL; below, p. 738.
  3. Cf. *Sancoff v Halford* [1973] Qd R 25. (Belief that books were not obscene is a mistake of law.)
  4. *Commentaries*, iv, 27.
  5. *Lectures on Jurisprudence*, 497.
  6. *The Common Law*, 48.
  7. "Ignorance and Mistake in Criminal Law" (1957) 33 Ind LJ 1. Cf. *General Principles*, 382–383.
  8. 33 Ind LJ at 19. In *Cooper v Simmons* (1862) 7 H & N 707 at 717 Martin B thought that to allow the defence would be "to substitute the opinion of a person charged with a breach of the law for the law itself."

As Hall points out, the criminal law represents an objective code of ethics which must prevail over individual convictions and he therefore argues:[9]

"Thus, while a person who acts in accordance with his honest convictions is certainly not as culpable as one who commits a harm knowing it is wrong, it is also true that conscience sometimes leads one astray. *Mens rea* underlines the essential difference. Penal liability based on it implies the objective wrongness of the harm proscribed – regardless of motive or conviction. This may fall short of perfect justice but the ethics of a legal order must be objective."

Unfortunately, however, much modern legislation is devoid of moral content, apart from the moral obligation to obey the law. One who, being ignorant of the law, sells goods at a price in excess of the maximum fixed by statute could hardly be said to have been led astray by his conscience while the "harm proscribed" lacks "objective wrongness".

The common law rule is not universally followed and the arguments by which it is supported have been found "not very convincing to those used to another system".[10] In Scandinavian criminal law, ignorance of the law is, in varying degrees, a defence. Thus, in Norway, a man will not be excused for ignorance of "the general rules of society which apply to everybody" or "the special rules governing the business or activity in which the individual is engaged". But "a fisherman need not study the legislation on industry"; a servant may be excused for *bona fide* and reasonable obedience to illegal orders of his master; or a stranger for breaking a rule which he could not be expected to know about; or liability may be negatived because the legislation is very new, or its interpretation doubtful. Such rules seem to have much to commend them, compared with the rigid and uncompromising attitude of English law. They seek to relate guilt to moral responsibility in a way in which our rule does not.[11]

9 Mistake of Law may Negative *Mens Rea*

If D, with *mens rea*, causes the *actus reus*, he is guilty and it will not avail him to say that he did not know the *actus reus* was forbidden by the criminal law. But the *actus reus* may be so defined that a mistake of law may result in D's not being intentional or reckless with respect to some element in it and so in his not having *mens rea*. In such a case, his mistake, whether reasonable or not, is a defence. ". . . an honest belief in a certain state of things does afford a defence, including an honest though mistaken belief

---

9. Ibid., at 22.

10. Andenaes. "*Ignorantia Juris* in Scandinavian Law" in *Essays in Criminal Science* (ed. Mueller), 217 at 222. For South African Law see *S v De Blom* 1977 (3) SA 513 (AD) discussed by Turpin, [1978] CLJ 8.

11. An exception to the general rule is created by the Statutory Instruments Act 1946, s. 3. See Lanham, "Delegated Legislation and Publication" (1974) 37 MLR 510. On a charge brought under a statutory instrument it is a defence for D to prove that the instrument had not been issued at the time of the alleged offence; unless the Crown then proves that reasonable steps had been taken to bring it to the notice of the public, or persons likely to be affected by it, or D. See *Defiant Cycle Co Ltd v Newell* [1953] 2 All ER 38. The Privy Council has held that, in a jurisdiction where there is no similar provision, a person who is unaware that a ministerial order applying a prohibition to him has been made may set up his ignorance as a lack of *mens rea*: *Lim Chin Aik v R* [1963] AC 160, [1963] 1 All ER 223; above, p. 44.

about legal rights."[12] Unless the prosecution can prove that the mistake was not made, they have not established the requisite *mens rea*. If D is charged with intentionally or recklessly damaging property belonging to another, his honest belief, arising from a mistake of law, that the property is his own, is a defence. The Court so held, in *Smith*,[13] not because of any special provision in the Criminal Damage Act but by "applying the ordinary principles of *mens rea*". In *Roberts v Inverness Local Authority*[14] D was acquitted of moving a cow from one district to another without a licence because he believed the two districts had been amalgamated into one. Likewise in *National Coal Board v Gamble*[15] it was accepted that a mistake by the weighbridge operator about his right to withhold the ticket (a question of civil law) might be "a genuine belief in the existence of circumstances which, if true, would negative an intention to aid." A person does not "act as auditor of a company at a time when he knows that he is disqualified for appointment to that office" if, through ignorance of the statutory provisions, he does not know he is disqualified.[16]

The crucial question will be, what is the *mens rea* required by the crime? A mistake negativing *mens rea* as to some element in the *actus reus* is no defence if the law does not require *mens rea* as to that element. Bigamy provides a good illustration. The *actus reus* is committed by one who "being married, marries". If D, knowing that he was already married to X, were to marry P, it would certainly be no defence for him to say that he thought the law allowed him more than one wife. He intends, being married, to marry – the *actus reus* – and would simply be saying that he did not know that the *actus reus* was forbidden by the criminal law. If, misunderstanding the law of divorce, he wrongly supposed that his first marriage had been dissolved, he would not intend the *actus reus*. His mistake as to the law of divorce would negative basic *mens rea*; and, if bigamy required basic *mens rea*, it would be a defence. The law, however, is that bigamy does not require *mens rea* as to the element, "being married". The Crown need prove only that D intended to go through the alleged second ceremony; whereupon it is a defence if it appears that D may have believed, on reasonable grounds, that he was not married.[17] So here, exceptionally, the mistake of law is a defence only if it is reasonable. In an Australian case[18] D, a landlord, was charged with wilfully demanding as rent a sum which was irrecoverable under the relevant statute. D wrongly believed that he was entitled to charge any rent he pleased. Three judges thought the belief no defence: it was sufficient that D wilfully demanded that sum of money. But two judges thought that D's belief precluded the *mens rea* required; that a man cannot wilfully demand an *irrecoverable* rent

---

12. *Barrett and Barrett* (1980) 72 Cr App Rep 212 at 216, CA, below, p. 89.
13. [1974] QB 354, [1974] 1 All ER 632, CA; **SHC 542**, below, p. 690.
14. 1889, 27 SLR 198, discussed by Widgery LCJ in *Cambridgeshire and Isle of Ely CC v Rust* [1972] 3 WLR 226 at 231. The LCJ treats the mistake as one of fact; but surely the boundaries of districts are determined by civil law.
15. [1959] 1 QB 11 at 25, per Devlin J. The facts are set out below, p. 134.
16. *Secretary of State for Trade and Industry v Hart* [1982] 1 All ER 817, [1982] 1 WLR 481. Cf. Juries Act 1974, s. 20 (5) (d).
17. Below, p. 217.
18. *Iannella v French* (1968) 119 CLR 84.

unless he knows it is irrecoverable. "The defendant who is not shown in such a case to know that the act is unlawful needs no excuse. The offence has not been proved against him."[19]

This principle will operate only when the definition of the *actus reus* contains some legal concept like "property belonging to another". It has no application where the law fixes a standard which is different from that in which D believes. If he kills a trespasser it is no defence for him to assert that he believed the law allows deadly force to be used to expel trespassers.[20] It does not apply where D refuses, however honestly, to accept the judgment of a court,[1] just as it would be hopeless for him to argue that he did not accept the validity of an Act of Parliament. The principle is probably also confined to the case where the legal concept belongs to the civil law – as the notion of property ownership does – and not to the criminal law.[2] Suppose that X obtains goods from P by deception and gives them to D, who knows all the facts. We have already seen that it will not avail D to say he does not know handling stolen goods is a crime. Equally, it is thought it will not avail him to say that he did not know that it is against the criminal law to obtain goods by deception and that goods so obtained are "stolen" for this purpose. "Stolen" is a concept of the criminal, not the civil law, and ignorance of it is no defence.

On the other hand, the "leave" granted to a visitor to remain in the United Kingdom looks like a civil law concept, but the House of Lords has held that a mistake of law is no answer to a charge of knowingly remaining without leave.[3]

10 Absence of a "Claim of Right" as an Element in *Mens Rea*

Sometimes the *mens rea* of an offence is so defined as to require the absence of a claim of right. In other words, if D believed he had a right to do the act in question, he had no *mens rea* and therefore was not guilty of the crime. This defence will prevail even if D's belief is mistaken and is based upon an entirely wrong view of the law. It is available in a number of important crimes, including theft,[4] criminal damage to property,[5] and a number of other offences requiring wilfulness or fraud. This is in accordance with the ordinary principle that a mistake of law may, indirectly, operate as a defence by preventing the accused from having *mens rea* in acting as he did. It is important to notice the limits within which this defence operates. The mistake must be one which leads the accused to believe he has a right to act as he does; it is not enough that he simply believes his act is not a crime. Here too, the distinction between mistake as to the criminal and as to the civil law seems to be important. Thus if D, having read in an out-of-date

19. At p. 97, per Barwick CJ.
20. Cf. *Barrett and Barrett* (1980) 72 Cr App Rep 212; below, p. 89.
  1. Ibid.
  2. It seems that a distinction between mistakes of civil and mistakes of criminal law was found to be untenable in German law: *Honig* (1963) 54 J Cr L & Cr at 285. But the distinction taken in the text seems to be a necessary consequence of the concept of *mens rea*.
  3. *Grant v Borg* [1982] 2 All ER 257, [1982] 1 WLR 638.
  4. Below, p. 537.
  5. Below, p. 702.

book on criminal law that it is not stealing to take another's title deeds to land,[6] were to take P's deeds, thinking that this was a way in which he could injure P without any risk of being punished, he could, no doubt, be convicted of theft under s. 1 of the Theft Act 1968. He had no claim of right. It would be otherwise if D, owing to a misunderstanding of the law of property, thought that the title deeds were his, and that P was wrongfully withholding them from him. Here, clearly, he had a claim of right. Thus, while a mistake as to the criminal law only will not give rise to a claim of right, an error as to the civil law may do so.

It certainly cannot be asserted with confidence that the absence of a claim of right is a *general* requirement of *mens rea*, as it is in the case of theft and the other crimes referred to above. The question will therefore be considered in relation to specific crimes discussed below.

11 Proof of Intention and Foresight

There was formerly high authority[7] for the view that there is an irrebuttable presumption of law that a person foresees and intends the natural consequences of his acts. Proof that he did an act the natural consequence of which was death, was conclusive proof that he intended to kill, in the absence of evidence of insanity or incapacity to form an intent. To what extent, if at all, this actually represented the law was disputed: but it is now clear beyond all doubt that it is not the law. The question in every case is as to the actual intention of the person charged at the time when he did the act. Section 8 of the Criminal Justice Act 1967 provides:

"A court or jury in determining whether a person has committed an offence,

(a) shall not be bound in law to infer that he intended or foresaw a result of his actions by reason only of its being a natural and probable consequence of those actions; but

(b) shall decide whether he did intend or foresee that result by reference to all the evidence drawing such inferences from the evidence as appear proper in the circumstances."

To what extent intention or foresight need be proved in any particular case depends on the law relating to the crime which is in issue. Section 8 is concerned with *how* intention or foresight must be proved, not *when* it must be proved.[8] On a charge of manslaughter, for example, it remains unnecessary to prove that D intended or foresaw that death was likely to result from his act.[9] The section was once construed so as to affect the substantive law of murder[10] but this was exceptional and it is now clear that it applies only to proof and never affects the substantive law.

---

6. This was the rule at common law.

7. *Director of Public Prosecutions v Smith* [1961] AC 290, [1960] 3 All ER 161; below, p. 347. The decision cannot be technically overruled by the Privy Council but five judges, all members of the House of Lords, declared that it was wrongly decided in *Frankland* [1987] AC 576, PC.

8. *Director of Public Prosecutions v Majewski* [1976] 2 All ER 142 at 151, 170.

9. *Director of Public Prosecutions v Newbury* [1977] AC 500, [1976] 2 All ER 365, HL; **SHC 335.**

10. *Hyam v Director of Public Prosecutions* [1975] AC 55, [1974] 2 All ER 41; **SHC 308**; above, p. 57.

Section 8 is confined to the *result* of D's actions. But no satisfactory distinction can be made between the results of an action and the relevant surrounding circumstances. In this connection at least, no attempt need be made to draw such a distinction because the decision of the House of Lords in *Director of Public Prosecutions v Morgan*[11] establishes that, as a matter of common law, the same principle applies to circumstances. It used to be said that a mistake of fact could be a defence only if it was reasonable but that is refuted by *Morgan*. It may now be taken to be settled that, once it is established that the definition of a crime requires a state of mind – intention, knowledge or *Cunningham* recklessness – with respect to particular elements of an offence, a mistake of fact or of law which is inconsistent with that state of mind is also incompatible with guilt and must lead to an acquittal. In *Morgan* the trial judge stressed to the jury that the *mens rea* of rape was an intention to have intercourse with a woman *without her consent*. Yet he went on to tell them that they could convict if they found that D believed, without reasonable grounds, that P was consenting. This, as Lord Cross pointed out,[12] was to present the jury with "two incompatible alternatives." Lord Hailsham said:[13]

"Once one has accepted, what seems to me abundantly clear, that the prohibited act in rape is non-consensual sexual intercourse, and that the guilty state of mind is an intention to commit it, it seems to me to follow as a matter of inexorable logic that there is no room either for a 'defence' of honest belief or mistake, or of a defence of honest and reasonable mistake. Either the prosecution proves its case or it does not."

The significance of *Morgan*, as the courts have now[14] belatedly recognised, goes far beyond the law of rape. The requirements of "inexorable logic" extend to the criminal law generally. In no case can the judge properly present the jury with "two incompatible alternatives."

The first question in every case is, what *mens rea* does the definition of the crime in question require? Neither section 8 nor *Morgan* (except in the case of rape at common law[15]) affect the answer to this question. What s. 8 and *Morgan* do establish is that a failure to foresee consequences, whether reasonable or not (s. 8), or a failure to know of circumstances, whether reasonable or not (*Morgan*) which negatives the *mens rea* of the offence requires acquittal. Where, on the other hand, the law does not require *mens rea*, s. 8 and *Morgan* have no application. *Prince*[16] and other cases of strict liability are unaffected.[17] So are the bigamy cases which lay down that a mistake as to the existence of the first marriage must be reasonable (the *Tolson* principle).[18] These cases establish as a matter of substantive law that neither intention nor recklessness is required with respect to the element, "being married", in the definition of bigamy.

11. [1976] AC 182, [1975] 2 All ER 347; **SHC 46**; below, p. 451.
12. At 352.
13. At 361.
14. *Beckford v R* [1987] 3 All ER 425, [1987] 3 WLR 611 PC.
15. Rape is now defined by statute. See below, p. 451.
16. Above, pp. 38, 72.
17. Per Lord Hailsham at 362.
18. Lord Hailsham, loc. cit.

It is most important to notice that *Caldwell*[19] is not inconsistent with the law as stated. By broadening the concept of recklessness it establishes that a failure to think about consequences, which would formerly have been inconsistent with recklessness, is sometimes[20] no longer inconsistent with it. *Caldwell*[1] is concerned with the definition of *mens rea* in crimes where the word "reckless" appears. *Morgan* has nothing to say about the definition of the *mens rea* in any crime, except rape at common law. The two cases are about different things. The fundamental principle of *Morgan* is in no way inconsistent with the existence of crimes of negligence, where unreasonable mistakes will be no defence. That is a matter of policy and one which, ideally, should be decided in Parliament when the statutory definitions of crimes are approved.

It was said, with some justification, in 1982 that there had been a "Retreat from *Morgan*".[2] There was a tendency for the courts to say that *Morgan* was concerned only with the law of rape and laid down no general principle. In one case,[3] the Court of Appeal said, obiter, that D might have been convicted of doing an act with intent to evict a residential occupier although he believed that the person he intended to evict was not a residential occupier but a squatter, because there was no reasonable basis for his belief. So to hold would be to defy the "inexorable logic" which Lord Hailsham found compelling in *Morgan*. Happily, the "retreat" has now been stemmed and in *Beckford v R* the Privy Council has said:

"Looking back, *Morgan* can now be seen as a landmark decision in the development of the common law, returning the law to the path upon which it might have developed but for the inability of an accused to give evidence on his own behalf."[4]

It may now perhaps be safely assumed that the courts will give full effect to the principle of the case as described above.

a) *Morgan and Defences*
Beckford v R is of great importance in that it takes the principle of *Morgan* even further than the majority of the House were at that time prepared to go. In *Morgan* the defence was a simple denial of the prosecution's case. By charging rape, the prosecution alleged that D had intercourse with a woman who did not consent and that he either knew that she did not consent or was reckless whether she did so. D denied that he knew or was reckless, as alleged. There is another type of plea, more accurately described as a defence, where D admits the allegations made by the prosecution but asserts further facts which, in law, justify or excuse his action. Self-defence is an example. D admits that he intentionally killed or wounded P but asserts that he did so because P was making a deadly attack on him and this was the only way he could save his own life. It may transpire that D was mistaken. P was not in fact making a deadly attack.

19. Above, p. 62.
20. That is, when *Caldwell* as distinct from *Cunningham* recklessness is in issue.
  1. [1982] AC 341, [1981] 1 All ER 961, above, p. 62.
  2. D. Cowley [1982] Crim LR 198.
  3. *Phekoo* [1981] 3 All ER 84, [1981] 1 WLR 1117.
  4. [1987] 3 All ER 425 at 431, **SHC 241**.

The law has long recognised that D's defence is still good if his mistaken belief of fact was based on reasonable grounds. Directions to juries and dicta in higher courts were consistent in asserting that the defence failed if there were no reasonable grounds for his belief. The majority of the House of Lords in *Morgan* did not intend to interfere with this rule. They were concerned with a mistake as to an element of the offence, this question related to a mistake as to an element of a defence. In *Beckford* the Privy Council rejected this distinction. They approved the ruling of Lane LCJ in *Gladstone Williams*.[5] Discussing the offence of assault, he said:

"The mental element necessary to constitute guilt is the intent to apply unlawful force to the victim. We do not believe that the mental element can be substantiated by simply showing an intent to apply force and no more."

If D believed, reasonably or not, in the existence of facts which would justify the force used in self-defence, he did not intend to use *unlawful* force. *Beckford* clearly applies to all instances of private defence.[6] The principle would seem to apply to defences generally but it is perhaps premature to assert that it will be so applied. In duress, for example, the courts continue to state (though obiter) that D's belief in the alleged compelling facts must be based on reasonable grounds. If, however, D is to be judged on the facts as he believed them to be when he sets up self-defence it is difficult to see why it is different in principle or in policy when he sets up duress. In both cases he is saying that, on the facts as he believed them to be, his act was not an offence. It is submitted that the principle of *Beckford* should be applicable to defences generally.

Of earlier cases, that of the Divisional Court in *Albert v Lavin*[7] must, since *Beckford*, be taken to be wrong in making a distinction in relation to assault between the definitional elements of an offence and the definitional elements of a defence. The same subjective test applies to both. *Barrett and Barrett*[8] is more complex.

D was convicted of assault occasioning actual bodily harm to bailiffs who were executing a warrant to take possession of his house. D intended to assault the bailiffs but claimed that he was justified because he believed the court order had been obtained by fraud, though his application to have it set aside had been unsuccessful. Not surprisingly, this refusal to accept the judgment of the courts was held to be no defence. If D was making a mistake, it was one of law, admittedly the civil law,[9] but of a rather special kind. It does not necessarily follow that the result would have been the same if D had believed the men were not bailiffs at all but imposters, or that the court had made no order. He was entitled to use force to repel a trespasser. An honest and reasonable belief that the men were trespassers should certainly have been an answer; and so, it is submitted (and *Beckford* confirms this), should an honest, even though unreasonable belief, arising from a mistake of fact. *Morgan* was discussed, in relation not to this, but to

5. [1987] 3 All ER 411, (1983) 78 Cr App 276, CA.
6. Below, p. 252.
7. [1982] AC 546, [1981] 1 All ER 628, DC.
8. (1980) 72 Cr App Rep 212.
9. See above, pp. 83–85.

a second point. It was argued that D was justified because he honestly believed that the force the bailiffs were using was excessive. But a mistake as to the amount of force which the law permits is certainly a mistake of law which is incapable of founding a defence. If it were otherwise, every man would, in effect, fix his own standards, whereas standards are fixed by law. *Morgan*, properly understood, had nothing to do with either of these points and the court's remark that it was inapplicable because it related to rape was inapt. Indeed, the court spoke with approval of the *Tolson*[10] principle but, as they phrased it, it was the *Morgan*[11] principle: – "an honest belief in a certain state of things does afford a defence, including an honest though mistaken belief about legal rights" – not, be it noted, an honest *and reasonable* belief. The subjectivist could not ask for more; but the principle was inapplicable here because (i) refusal to accept the validity of a court order, if it is properly called a mistake at all, is not the sort of mistake that a court can, as a matter of policy, admit as a defence; and (ii) standards are conclusively settled by the law.

Although s. 8 requires the court to have regard to *all* the evidence, that is, all the evidence relevant to the question whether D did intend or foresee, the courts have consistently held that evidence that D did not intend or foresee because he had taken drink or drugs is no defence, except in the case of crimes requiring "specific intent". This practice has been reconciled with the words of s. 8 by holding that there is a rule of substantive law that the prosecution need prove no *mens rea* where D relies on evidence that he had taken drink or drugs for the purpose of showing that he lacked any *mens rea*, not being a "specific intent", which the definition of the crime requires in all other circumstances.[12]

It might be thought, at first sight, that proof of intention, foresight and knowledge presents almost insuperable difficulties. Direct evidence of a man's state of mind, except through his own confession, is not available. But the difficulties, in practice, are not so great. If D points a loaded gun at P's head, pulls the trigger and shoots him dead, it is reasonable to infer that D intended and foresaw P's death. A jury might well be convinced by such evidence that D intended to kill. If D offered an explanation of any kind – he thought the gun was unloaded, or he intended to fire above P's head – and the jury thought that it might reasonably be true, then they should acquit him of an intention to kill. If he offered no explanation, as s. 8 makes clear, the jury would not be bound to convict him of having such an intention; they would have to ask themselves whether, in the light of all the evidence, they were satisfied beyond reasonable doubt. Sometimes D's acts may afford apparently overwhelming evidence of his intention to produce a particular result but evidence to the contrary is always admissible and the question must be left to the jury.[13] Similarly, the fact that any reasonable

---

10. See above, p. 87, below, p. 451.
11 Above, p. 87.
12. *Director of Public Prosecutions v Majewski* [1977] AC 433, [1976] 2 All ER 142, HL.
13. *Riley* [1967] Crim LR 656, is a striking instance of the rebuttal of apparently conclusive evidence of an intent. Expert evidence was admitted that D was suffering from psychoneurosis; but in the case of a normal person expert evidence as to the operation of the mind is not admissible. It is a question for the jury: *Chard* (1971) 56 Cr App Rep 268, CA. Cf. *Turner* [1975] QB 834; [1975] 1 All ER 70.

man would, in the circumstances, have known of a fact is cogent evidence that D knew of it.[14]

The difficulty of distinguishing between "he foresaw" and "he ought to have foreseen", "he knew" and "he ought to have known," is not a good reason for not drawing the line at this point. It is an inescapable difficulty when we have a law which requires us to look into men's minds; and such a requirement is essential to a civilised system of criminal law.

"... a lack of confidence in the ability of a tribunal correctly to estimate evidence of states of mind and the like can never be sufficient ground for excluding from enquiry the most fundamental element in a rational and humane criminal code."[15]

14. Sexual Offences (Amendment) Act 1976, below, p. 451.
15. *Thomas v R* (1937) 59 CLR 279 at 309, per Dixon J.

5 Crimes of Negligence[1]

1 Negligence as Failure to Comply with an Objective Standard

Intention, recklessness and negligence all involve a failure to comply with an objective standard of conduct. Where intention or *Cunningham* recklessness[2] is required a state of mind must also be proved. *Caldwell* recklessness too was said by the House of Lords to involve proof of a state of mind; but this is so only in the sense that *not* giving thought is a state of mind.[3] *Caldwell* recklessness may however be negatived by evidence of a state of mind – i.e., that D had given thought to the matter and wrongly concluded that there was no risk.[4] In a crime of negligence such evidence is no answer. Negligence may be conclusively proved by simply showing that D's conduct failed to measure up to an objective standard. It is no answer for him to say, "I considered whether there was a risk and decided there was none." Where the risk is one that he ought to have foreseen, that is an admission of negligence. It is not necessary to prove that D did not foresee the risk. It could never be a defence to a charge of negligence to show that the dangerous act was done recklessly or intentionally. If D were charged with manslaughter and the prosecution's case was that he killed P by gross negligence it is inconceivable that it could be a defence for him to say, convincingly, "I wasn't negligent; I *intended* to kill him" – or "I took a quite deliberate risk of killing him." The more blameworthy state of mind must include the less; so, if D failed to comply with the objective standard, he is liable whatever his state of mind. Negligence is *conduct* which departs from the standard to be expected of a reasonable man. This is not to say that a person's state of mind is always irrelevant when negligence is in issue. He may, for example, have special knowledge which an ordinary person would not possess. The question then is, whether a reasonable man, with that knowledge, would have acted as he did. Behaviour with a revolver which is possibly not negligent in the case of an ordinary person with no special knowledge might be grossly negligent if committed by a firearms

---

1. See Hart, "Negligence, *Mens Rea* and Criminal Responsibility" in *Oxford Essays in Jurisprudence*, 29. The question of liability for negligence in manslaughter and under the Road Traffic Acts is considered in detail below, pp. 372 and 483.
2. Above, p. 61.
3. See Williams [1981] CLJ 252 at 256–258.
4. Above, p. 65.

expert.[5] If D has less knowledge or capacity for foresight than the reasonable man this, it seems, will not generally help him; but if he has more knowledge or capacity for foresight, a higher standard will be expected of him. This principle receives statutory recognition in the Road Traffic Act 1988, s. 2A (3), defining dangerous driving.[6] In deciding whether a driver drove dangerously, the standard is "what would be expected of a competent and careful driver"; and, in determining that standard—

".. . regard shall be had not only the circumstances of which he could be expected to be aware, but also to any circumstances shown to be within the knowledge of the accused."

Writers differ as to whether negligence can properly be described as *mens rea*.[7] If that term is used simply as a compendious expression for the varieties of fault which may give rise to criminal liability, then it does of course include negligence. If it is taken in its more literal sense of "guilty mind", the usage is inappropriate. It is sometimes argued that the absence of foresight or knowledge is just as much a state of mind as its presence;[8] but, since negligence may be proved without establishing anything as to what was going on in D's mind, it seems more appropriate and convenient to restrict the term to intention and recklessness and that is the sense in which it is used in this book. Crimes requiring *mens rea* are contrasted with crimes of negligence.

2 Negligence as the Basis of Liability

There are very few crimes in English law in which negligence is the gist of the offence. Manslaughter has long been the most conspicuous example and, indeed, the only serious crime in this category but it is now uncertain whether even this crime can be committed with less than *Caldwell* recklessness.[9] Generally, in serious crimes, intention or recklessness is required as to the central features of the offence, but negligence with respect to some subsidiary element in the *actus reus* is sometimes enough.

So under s. 19 of the Sexual Offences Act 1956,[10] it is an offence to take an unmarried girl under the age of eighteen out of the possession of her parent or guardian against his will with the intent that she shall have unlawful sexual intercourse with men or with a particular man. It is expressly provided, however, that it is a defence "If he believes her to be of the age of eighteen or over and *has reasonable cause for the belief*". It follows that an honest but unreasonable belief that the girl is over eighteen is no

---

5. Cf. *Lamb* [1967] 2 QB 981, [1967] 2 All ER 1282; **SHC 333** above, p. 65.
6. Below, p. 490
7. Edwards *Mens Rea*, 206.
8. Salmond on *Jurisprudence* (11th ed.) 429. Cf. *Tesco Supermarkets v Nattrass* [1972] AC 153 at 199, per Lord Diplock. *Caldwell*, above.
9. Below, p. 372.
10. *Prince*, above, p. 38, applies, subject to the statutory defence.

defence. Negligence with respect to that element will suffice, though, of course, it must be shown that D intended[11] to take the girl out of the possession of her parent, and had the ulterior intent as to unlawful sexual intercourse.

If there had been a similar provision in the section in issue in *Prince's* case,[12] he would, of course, have been acquitted. But such a provision, as well as catching the negligent person, disposes of another difficult case. It deals satisfactorily with the case of the man who does not advert to the girl's age at all (simple ignorance), for he cannot say that "he believed her to be of the age of eighteen or over". Such a person will have no defence even though he had reasonable ground for believing the girl to be over eighteen[13] and was therefore not negligent.

The rule, once supposed to exist, that a mistake was never a defence unless it was reasonable was capable of turning almost any crime into a crime of negligence; but *Morgan*[14] and *Beckford*[15] have established that there is no such rule. Those decisions do not affect cases where it has been ruled that *mens rea* as to some element of the offence is not required and that only a reasonable mistake will excuse. For example, it has been held that if D goes through a ceremony of marriage, believing wrongly but without reasonable grounds that he is not married because his wife is dead, or his marriage has been dissolved or annulled, he is guilty of bigamy.[16] This, in effect, is to turn bigamy into a crime of negligence so far as this element of the offence is concerned. D is to be held liable because he did not take sufficient care to ascertain that his first marriage was at an end, before going through the second ceremony.

In the examples just considered, the negligence is as to a subsidiary element only. Occasionally, negligence is the central feature of the crime. Under the Road Traffic Act 1988, s. 3, for example, it is an offence to drive a mechanically propelled vehicle on a road without due care and attention or without reasonable consideration for other persons using the road. On a charge of driving without due care, it is clear that negligence is the gist of the offence. This section, it has been held, establishes

"an objective standard, impersonal and universal, fixed in relation to the safety of other users of the highway. It is in no way related to the degree of proficiency or degree of experience to be attained by the individual driver."[17]

So a learner driver, who was "exercising all the skill and attention to be expected from a person with his short experience" but who failed to attain the required standard, was held guilty.[18] The offence may be committed by making an error of judgment of a kind which a reasonably prudent and

11. Cf. *Hibbert*, above, p. 72 and *Hudson*, below, p. 97, fn. 10.
12. Above, p. 38.
13. Cf. *Harrison* [1938] 3 All ER 134.
14. Above, p. 87.
15. [1987] 3 All ER 425, PC.
16. *Tolson* (1889) 23 QBD 168, CCR; *Gould* [1968] 2 QB 65, [1968] 1 All ER 849.
17. *McCrone v Riding* [1938] 1 All ER 157; below, p. 485; *Preston JJ ex p Lyons* [1982] RTR 173, DC, discussed by Wasik, [1982] Crim LR 411.
18. Ibid.

skilful driver would not make.[19] It will be noted that it is not necessary to prove that any harmful consequence ensued; it is enough to show that D drove in a manner in which a reasonable man would not have driven because he would have realised it involved an unjustifiable risk.

3 Degrees of Negligence

It has been said that there can be no

"degrees of inadvertence when that word is used to denote a state of mind, since it means that in the man's mind there has been a complete absence of a particular thought, a nullity; and of nullity there can be no degrees."[20]

It is true that there can be no degrees of inadvertence but there can be degrees of fault in failing to advert. The more obvious the risk, the greater the fault in failing to be aware of it. If negligence is regarded as non-attainment of a required standard of conduct then it is clear that there are degrees of it. One person may fall just short of the required standard, another may fall far short. The existence of degrees of negligence is recognised by s. 2A of the Road Traffic Act 1988 (as substituted by the Road Traffic Act 1991)[1] when it provides that a person drives dangerously if

"(a) the way he drives falls far below what would be expected of a competent and careful driver, and

(b) it would be obvious to a competent and careful driver that driving in that way would be dangerous."

A driver whose driving falls below, but not *far* below what would be expected of a competent and careful driver is negligent and probably guilty of careless driving contrary to s. 3 of the 1988 Act; but he is not sufficiently negligent to be guilty of the more serious offence of dangerous driving.

When gross negligence was recognised as a sufficient fault for manslaughter it was clear that a person might be guilty of the former offence of causing death by dangerous driving but not guilty of manslaughter. The slight degree of negligence which would suffice for the former Road Traffic offence did not amount to "gross" negligence. If manslaughter may still be committed by gross negligence, which is not certain,[2] it remains to be seen whether the new offence of causing death by dangerous driving, where the danger that would be obvious to a competent and careful driver is danger to life, is necessarily manslaughter. Is driving "far below the required standard" gross negligence? Or does it have to be *very* far below? Probably the former.

---

19. *Simpson v Peat* [1952] 2 QB 24, [1952] 1 All ER 447.
20. Kenny, *Outlines*, 39, criticised by Hart in *Oxford Essays in Jurisprudence* who writes at 42: "Negligence is gross if the precautions to be taken against harm are very simple, such as persons who are but poorly endowed with physical and mental capacities can easily take."
1. Below, p. 490.
2. Below, p. 372

4 Should Negligence be a Ground of Liability?

Distinguished academic writers have strongly contended that negligence should have no place in criminal liability. Their arguments for the most part assumed the clear-cut distinction between conscious and inadvertent risk-taking which formerly distinguished recklessness from negligence. Since the advent of *Caldwell* recklessness much inadvertent risk-taking has been brought within the criminal law. Turner acknowledges that negligence connotes that D was

> "in some measure blameworthy, and that we should expect an ordinary reasonable man to foresee the possibility of the consequences and to regulate his conduct so as to avoid them;"[3]

but contends that the moral test, on which criminal liability should be (and, indeed, is) based, is that of foresight of the consequences of one's conduct. Hall goes further and finds it difficult to accept that negligently caused harm reflects a moral fault.[4] He rejects the view that punishment stimulates care, arguing that the deterrent theory postulates a man who weighs the possibility of punishment in the balance before acting; but the inadvertent harm-doer, by definition, does not do this. Hall appears to suggest[4] that the courts themselves do not really believe that punishment deters negligence, pointing out that sentences, even for negligent homicides, are relatively light. He rejects the thesis that negligent persons may be ethically blameworthy in so far as they are insensitive to the rights of others. In the case of negligently caused motor-car accidents, for example, he argues that

> "it seems much more probable that a dull mind, slow reactions, awkwardness and other ethically irrelevant factors were the underlying cause."[5]

Williams[6] acknowledges that "it is possible for punishment to bring about greater foresight, by causing the subject to stop and think before committing himself to a course of conduct;" but thinks that this justification does not go very far and that the law is wise in penalising negligence only exceptionally.

Hart[7] challenges the commonly accepted criterion of foresight. The reason why it is thought proper to punish (in most cases) the man who foresees the forbidden harm is that he can choose to cause it or not; but in some cases of negligence, at least, it may be said,

> " 'he could have thought about what he was doing' with just as much rational confidence as one can say of an intentional wrong-doing, 'he could have done otherwise'."

Hart's approach to negligence, however, differs from that so far generally adopted by the courts. He would not enforce an objective, external and impersonal standard which took no account of the individual's lack of

---

3. MACL 207.
4. *General Principles*, 136.
5. Ibid., at p. 138. And cf. Keedy in 22 Harv L Rev at p. 84: ". . . a man should not be held criminal because of lack of intelligence."
6. CLGP 123.
7. *Oxford Essays in Jurisprudence*, 29.

capacity. He would recognise that punishment might[8] be proper only if two questions are answered in the affirmative:[9]

"(i) Did the accused fail to take those precautions which any reasonable man with normal capacities would in the circumstances have taken?

(ii) Could the accused, given his mental and physical capacities, have taken those precautions?"

The only English case following this approach seems to be *Hudson*.[10] In deciding whether a man who had sexual intercourse with a defective woman, contrary to s. 7 of the Sexual Offence Act, 1956,[11] had "no reason to suspect her to be a defective", the court was bound—

"to take into account the accused himself. There may be cases, of which this is not one, where there is evidence before the jury that the accused himself is a person of limited intelligence, or possibly suffering from some handicap which would prevent him from appreciating the state of affairs which an ordinary man might realise."

The decisions in *Caldwell* and *Lawrence* in 1981 were open to the interpretation that an "obvious" risk meant obvious to the particular defendant but the courts soon put paid to that notion. Obvious means obvious to the reasonable man, even if the defendant is a backward fourteen-year-old schoolgirl.[12]

Hall argues[13] that negligence should be controlled in other ways – by re-examining whether negligent persons should be able to escape completely from the consequences of civil liability by insurance; by more vigorous control of licences to operate dangerous instrumentalities; and by more education and instruction.

The negligent handling of certain instruments – notably motor vehicles – can have such drastic consequences that society is almost bound to adopt any measures which seem to have a reasonable prospect of inducing greater care; and it seems reasonable to suppose that the threat of punishment does have an effect on the care used in the handling of such instruments. There is a trend towards replacing strict liability by liability for negligence.[14] Courts in the Commonwealth have moved ahead of those in England. The lead came from Australia.[15] In Canada, the Supreme Court, in a notable judgment delivered by Dickson J, held that public welfare offences prima facie fall into an intermediate class between offences requiring *mens rea* and offences "of absolute liability". The prosecution need prove only that D caused the *actus reus* but he may escape liability by proving that he took all reasonable care to avoid the commission of the offence.[16] Without going so far as to establish any general principle, in England Parliament has recently

---

8. Hart is not concerned to *advocate* the punishment of negligence, but only to dispel the belief that liability for negligence is a form of strict or absolute liability.

9. Ibid., at p. 46.

10. [1966] 1 QB 448, [1965] 1 All ER 721.

11. Below, p. 464

12. *Elliott v C (a minor)* [1983] 2 All ER 1005, [1983] 1 WLR 939 DC; **SHC 78**. *R, Stephen Malcolm* (1984) 79 Cr App Rep 334 CA; **SHC 81**, above, p. 64.

13. "Negligent Behaviour should be excluded from Penal Liability", 63 Col LR 632.

14. Below, p. 119.

15. *Maher v Musson* (1934) 52 CLR 100; *Proudman v Dayman* (1941) 67 CLR 536.

16. *City of Sault Ste Marie* (1978) 40 CCC (2d) 353, **SHC 130**.

shown an inclination to move in this direction. The Trade Descriptions Act 1968 creates a number of offences, some of which replace earlier offences of strict liability, and provides by s. 24 that it is a defence to prove (i) that the commission of the offence was due (inter alia) to a mistake or accident and (ii) that D "took all reasonable precautions and exercised all due diligence to avoid the commission of such an offence by himself or any person under his control". Thus, though the prosecution do not have to prove negligence, it is a defence for D to show that he was not negligent. Similar steps have been taken in the Misuse of Drugs Act 1971.[17]

Where there is no such express provision in a statute, it is unlikely that the courts will hold it to be implied. It is true that the House of Lords in *Sweet v Parsley*[18] looked favourably on a doctrine developed in Australia:[19]

"When a statutory prohibition is cast in terms which at first sight appear to impose strict responsibility, they should be understood merely as imposing responsibility for negligence but emphasising that the burden of rebutting negligence by affirmative proof of reasonable mistake rests upon the defendant."[20]

– but the courts have shown no inclination to put such a principle into practice. In *Gammon (Hong Kong) Ltd v. A–G of Hong Kong*,[1] the Privy Council, while stressing the need for very high standards of care, regarded the choice as a straight one between *mens rea* and strict liability.

17. Below, p. 110.
18. [1969] 1 All ER 347 at 351, per Lord Reid, at 357, per Lord Pearce and at 362, per Lord Diplock; **SHC 119.**
19. Fn. 15, above.
20. Orchard, "The Defence of Absence of Fault in Australasia and Canada", *Criminal Law Essays*, 114.
  1. [1985] AC 1, [1984] 2 All ER 503 at 509.

6 Crimes of Strict Liability

1 The Position at Common Law and by Statute

Crimes which do not require intention, recklessness or even negligence as to one or more elements in the *actus reus* are known as offences of strict liability or, sometimes, "of absolute prohibition".[1] An example is the Medicines Act 1968, s. 58 (2) which provides that no person shall sell by retail specified medicinal products except in accordance with a prescription given by an appropriate medical practitioner. In *Pharmaceutical Society of Great Britain v. Storkwain Ltd*[2] D supplied specified drugs on prescriptions purporting to be signed by a Dr Irani. The prescriptions were forged. There was no finding that D acted dishonestly, improperly or even negligently. So far as appeared, the forgery was sufficient to deceive the pharmacists without any shortcoming on their part. Yet the House of Lords held that the Divisional Court was right to direct the magistrate to convict.

The term "absolute prohibition" is somewhat misleading in so far as it suggests that an accused whose conduct has caused[3] an *actus reus* will necessarily be held liable. It is common to say that "no *mens rea*" need be proved in the case of these offences: "D can be convicted on proof by P of *actus reus* only."[4] It is only in an extreme case[5] that this is true.[6] The fact is that an offence is regarded – and properly regarded – as one of strict liability if no *mens rea* need be proved as to a single element in the *actus*

1. For discussions of these offences, see L. H. Leigh, *Strict and Vicarious Liability*; Edwards, *Mens Rea*; Sayre, "Public Welfare Offences" (1933) 33 Col LR 55; Howard, SR; Smith and Pearson, "The Value of Strict Liability" [1969] Crim LR 516; Carson, "Some Sociological Aspects of Strict Liability and the Enforcement of Factory Legislation" (1970) 33 MLR 396; Hogan, "Criminal Liability without Fault" (1969, Leeds Univ. Press); Brett, "Strict Responsibility: Possible solutions" (1974), 37 MLR 417.

2. [1986] 2 All ER 635, HL discussed, [1991] Crim LR 892, by B. S. Jackson who shows that the Society's policy was to prosecute only where the pharmacist had not acted with due diligence; but the Society does not have a monopoly of the right to prosecute; and if, in practice, fault is required, should not the decision whether it exists be made in court?

3. In *Kilbride v Lake* [1962] NZLR 590, discussed by Budd and Lynch, [1978] Crim LR 74, D was acquitted of permitting a vehicle not displaying a current warrant of fitness to be on the highway, when the warrant was detached during his absence. The court took the view that there was an *actus reus* (*sed quaere?*) but that D had not caused it and he was not liable even if the offence was one of strict liability. Cf. *Parker v Alder* [1899] 1 QB 20; below, p. 121; *Strowger v John* [1974] RTR 124.

4. Howard, SR 1.

5. *Larsonneur*, above, p. 43.

6. Above, p. 37.

reus,[7] The single element will usually be one of great significance; but it by no means follows that *mens rea* should not be required as to the remaining constituents of the offence. In construing the Hong Kong Building Ordinance, Lord Scarman said, "Each provision clearly requires a degree of *mens rea*, but each is silent whether it is required in respect of all the facts which together constitute the offence created." The Privy Council held that D was liable for deviating in a material way from the approved plan, even though there was no evidence that he knew that his act constituted a material deviation from the plan – liability as to that element was strict.[8] Liability is thus not "absolute" and the term "strict liability" will be preferred throughout this book.

Crimes of strict liability are almost invariably the creation of statute. It is usually said[9] that there were only two exceptions at common law to the rule requiring *mens rea*. These were public nuisance and criminal libel. In the former any employer might be held liable for the act of his employee even though he himself did not know it had taken place; while in the latter a newspaper proprietor was liable for libels published by his employees without his authority or consent. Public nuisance, however, is an anomalous crime and is treated in several respects rather as if it were a civil action than an indictable offence; while in criminal libel the rule has been modified by the Libel Act 1843 which makes it a defence for the defendant to prove that the publication was without his authority, consent or knowledge and did not arise from want of due care or caution on his part. It will be noted, moreover, that both cases are instances of vicarious liability. To these two instances, we must add a third – contempt of court.[10] It is an offence to publish inaccurate reports of the evidence at a trial in such a manner that the jurors might be influenced in their decision, even though the publisher believes in good faith and on reasonable grounds that the reports are accurate.[11] Parliament has expressly recognised the existence of strict liability in this offence by the Contempt of Court Act 1981. "The Strict Liability Rule", as the Act calls it, continues to be a rule of the common law, though it is to some extent qualified by the Act. According to one view, blasphemy is another example of strict liability at common law. A minority of the House of Lords in *Lemon and Gay News Ltd*[12] thought that was the effect of the decision of the majority. The majority denied that this was so. A writing is blasphemous when it has a tendency to shock and outrage Christians. *Lemon* decides that it is unnecessary to prove that D was aware of this tendency. It is sufficient that he intentionally used words which, in fact, are likely to shock and outrage. It is submitted that the minority were right to regard this as the imposition of strict liability. D may be convicted although he is quite unaware that his act has the quality which makes it criminal. No one would deny that strict liability is imposed when a

7. Passage approved by Lord Edmund-Davies in *Whitehouse v Gay News Ltd* [1979] AC 617 at 656, [1979] 1 All ER 898 at 920.
8. *Gammon (Hong Kong) Ltd v A–G of Hong Kong* [1985] AC 1, [1984] 2 All ER 503, PC.
9. But the matter is by no means so clear as is sometimes thought. See below, pp. 729 and 765.
10. *Evening Standard Co Ltd* [1954] 1 QB 578, [1954] 1 All ER 1026.
11. This too is sometimes said to be an instance of vicarious liability.
12. [1979] AC 617, [1979] 1 All ER 898, [1979] Crim LR 311 and commentary.

butcher is convicted of selling meat which is unfit for human consumption although he is unaware of the dangerous character of the meat. The case of the blasphemous libel seems to be the same in principle.[13] A similar decision has been made in respect of the related common law offence of outraging public decency.[14]

Apart from these instances, the common law always required *mens rea*, at least as to the more important elements in the *actus reus*, subject to the qualifications in respect of murder and manslaughter considered below.[15] It is very different with statutory offences. In a great many cases, the courts have held that Parliament intended to impose strict liability and have convicted defendants who lacked *mens rea*, not merely as to some subsidiary matter, but as to the central feature of the *actus reus*.

The validity of the imposition of strict liability was recognised by the House of Lords in *Warner v Metropolitan Police Comr* (1968),[16] the first case on the point to reach the highest tribunal. Only the next year, however, in *Sweet v Parsley*[17] the attitude of the House changed remarkably in favour of a presumption requiring *mens rea* and in 1980 in *Sheppard*[18] Lord Diplock noted that "The climate of both parliamentary and judicial opinion has been growing less favourable to the recognition of absolute offences over the last few decades . . .".[19] Any expansion of strict liability should therefore be strictly scrutinised. Many offences of strict liability are, however, firmly established and recent experience confirms that it would be unrealistic to suppose that the courts will not, from time to time, discover new ones.[20]

The case which has been said[1] to be the first to impose strict liability is *Woodrow*.[2] D was found guilty of having in his possession adulterated tobacco, although he did not know it was adulterated. The prosecution emphasised the purpose of the statute – it was for the protection of the revenue – and the absence of "knowingly" or any similar word. The court relied on a section of the Act which empowered the commissioners of excise to forbear to prosecute where there was no "intention of fraud or of offending against this Act" – the implication being that the crime was still committed even when there was no fraud or intention of offending against the Act. Parke B thought that the prosecution would very rarely be able to prove knowledge; and that the public inconvenience which would follow if they were required to do so would be greater than the injustice to the individual if they were not. Even the exercise of reasonable care would not have saved D; according to Parke B, he was liable even if the adulteration

13. See [1979] Crim LR at 312.
14. *Gibson* [1991] 1 All ER 439, below, p. 748.
15. See pp. 346–348, and 365–375.
16. [1969] 2 AC 256, [1968] 2 All ER 356, **SCH 115**, Lord Reid (whose speech deserves careful study) dissenting on this issue. The case is more fully considered below, p. 110.
17. [1970] AC 132, [1969] 1 All ER 347, HL; **SHC 119**; but the House again imposed liability in *Alphacell Ltd v Woodward* [1972] AC 824, [1972] 2 All ER 475; below, p. 113.
18. [1980] 3 All ER 899 at 906.
19. [1969] 2 AC 256, [1968] 2 All ER 356.
20. A recent example is *Kirkland v Robinson* [1987] Crim LR 643, DC, below, p. 113.
1. By Sayre, op. cit.
2. (1846) 15 M & W 404.

was discoverable only by a "nice chemical analysis".[3] Notwithstanding the subsequent mass of case-law, the considerations taken into account in this early case are very much the same as those which influence the decisions of the courts today.

A number of other well-known cases may be taken as examples. In *Hobbs v Winchester Corporation*,[4] the plaintiff, a butcher, was suing for compensation for certain unsound meat which had been destroyed under the Public Health Act 1875. That Act provided that, where any person sustained damage in relation to any matter as to which he was not himself in default, full compensation should be paid. The question was: was the plaintiff in default? He was unaware, and he could not have discovered by any examination which he could reasonably be expected to make, that the meat was unsound. It was held by the Court of Appeal, reversing Channell J, that the plaintiff was in default because he was guilty of the crime of selling unsound meat. Kennedy LJ said:[5]

"the clear object, the important object [of the statute] . . . is as far as possible to protect the buyer of that which, in the opinion at all events of most people, is a necessity of human life, from buying and consuming meat that is unwholesome and unfit for the food of man; and I should say that the natural inference from the statute and its object is that the peril to the butcher from innocently selling unsound meat is deemed by the legislature to be much less than the peril to the public which would follow from the necessity of proving in each case a *mens rea*.

I think that the policy of the Act is this: that if a man chooses for profit to engage in a business which involves the offering for sale of that which may be deadly or injurious to health he must take that risk, and that it is not a sufficient defence for anyone who chooses to embark on such a business to say 'I could not have discovered the disease unless I had an analyst on the premises.'"

In *Cundy v Le Cocq*[6] D was convicted of selling intoxicating liquor to a drunken person contrary to s. 13 of the Licensing Act 1872. It was proved that D did not know the person was drunk and nothing had occurred to show that he was drunk. While some sections of the Act contained the word "knowingly", s. 13 did not do so. The Divisional Court held that it was not necessary to consider whether D knew, or had means of knowing, or could with ordinary care have detected, that the person served was drunk. If he served a drink to a person who was in fact drunk, he was guilty.

It will be noted that it was established in each of these cases that D was not even negligent. The convictions were upheld notwithstanding D's

---

3. The judges suggested that D might have taken a warranty from the person from whom he bought the tobacco, indemnifying him against the consequences of a prosecution (fine and forefeiture). But there are difficulties about this. In *Askey v Golden Wine Co* [1948] 2 All ER 35 at 38, Denning J said: 'It is . . . a principle of our law that the punishment inflicted by a criminal court is personal to the offender and that the civil courts will not entertain an action by the offender to recover an indemnity against consequences of that punishment."
4. [1910] 2 KB 471, CA.
5. Ibid., at 483.
6. (1884) 13 QBD 207.

blameless inadvertence as to the crucial factor in the *actus reus*. This is a very remarkable and, on the face of it, unjust result, and certainly requires explanation.

2 Recognition of Offences of Strict Liability

Since these offences are almost always the creation of statute, the courts, in enforcing them, profess merely to be implementing the expressed intention of Parliament. This is mere lip-service.

"The fact is that Parliament has no intention whatever of troubling itself about *mens rea*. If it had, the thing would have been settled long ago. All that Parliament would have to do would be to use express words that left no room for implication. One is driven to the conclusion that the reason why Parliament has never done that is that it prefers to leave the point to the judges and does not want to legislate about it."[7]

The courts then have a fairly free hand in this matter. How do they exercise their power? They usually begin with a ritual incantation of the presumption in favour of *mens rea*, commonly the well-known statement by Wright J in *Sherras v De Rutzen*:[8]

"There is a presumption that *mens rea*, or evil intention, or knowledge of the wrongfulness of the act, is an essential ingredient in every offence; but that presumption is liable to be displaced either by the words of the statute creating the offence or by the subject-matter with which it deals, and both must be considered."

This presumption seems to have been generally followed by the courts until the latter part of the nineteenth century. After the case of *Prince*[9] (1875) the courts showed a greater readiness to interpret statutory offences to impose strict liability. It has been said[10] that the doctrine of *mens rea* reached its nadir when even bigamy was held to be a crime of strict liability in *Wheat* (1921),[11] now happily overruled. The trend in the years before *Warner*[12] seems to have been in favour of strict liability; but in *Sweet v Parsley*[13] the House of Lords reaffirmed principles which were beginning to look old-fashioned: ". . . whenever a section is silent as to *mens rea* there is a presumption that, in order to give effect to the will of Parliament, we must read in words appropriate to require *mens rea*;" and ". . . it is a universal

---

7. Devlin, *Samples of Lawmaking*, at 71. Cf. Thornton, *Legislative Drafting* 264. Lord Reid in *Sweet v Parsley* [1969] 1 All ER 347 at 351 and the proposals of the Law Commission, below, p. 122.
8. [1895] 1 QB 918 at 921, below, p. 106.
9. See above, p. 38.
10. Williams, CLGP, 178.
11. [1921] 2 KB 119, overruled by *Gould* [1968] 2 QB 65, [1968] 1 All ER 849.
12. *Warner v Metropolitan Police Comr* above, p. 101.
13. Below, p. 112.

principle that if a penal provision is reasonably capable of two interpretations, that interpretation which is most favourable to the accused must be adopted."[14] According to Lord Diplock,[15] the implication of *mens rea*

". . . stems from the principle that it is contrary to a rational and civilised criminal code, such as Parliament must be presumed to have intended, to penalise one who has performed his duty as a citizen to ascertain what acts are prohibited by law (*ignorantia juris non excusat*) and has taken all proper care to inform himself of any facts which would make his conduct unlawful."

It is difficult to say what effect the recital by the courts of the presumption has on their actual decisions. More important in practice appears to be the weight which they give to the two matters which Wright J said might displace it: (i) the words of the statute, and (ii) the subject-matter.

1 The Offence in its Statutory Context

a) *Verbs importing a mental element.* We have already noticed that a particular verb may imply a mental element.[16] The use of such a verb in the definition of an offence may import a requirement of *mens rea* when the use of a different verb with no such implication would result in an offence of strict liability. It is an offence if a person "uses or causes or permits to be used" a motor vehicle in contravention of certain regulations. "Using", "causing" and "permitting" are three separate offences. In *James & Son Ltd v Smee*[17] the court held that *using* a vehicle in contravention of a regulation (in that it had a defective braking system) was an offence of strict liability; but D was charged with *permitting* the use which, said the court, "in our opinion, at once imports a state of mind". A person might use a vehicle with defective brakes although he had no idea that the brakes were defective; but he could not properly be said to permit use with defective brakes unless he knew that the brakes were defective or, at least, was turning a blind eye to that fact. Unfortunately, the courts act inconsistently in their interpretation of this and similar words. The offence of permitting a vehicle to be used without insurance is committed by a person who lends his car to another on condition that it is only driven by an insured driver, if it is in fact driven by person who is uninsured. The court ignores the ordinary meaning of the word "permit". D who says: "Here is my car, but you must not drive it until you have insurance" is taken to permit what he actually forbids, driving without insurance.[18]

Similar inconsistency is to be found in the interpretation of the verbs, "suffer", "allow" and "cause". It seems that the courts will generally give verbs their natural meaning, including any mental element they imply, unless they consider that social policy requires them to decide otherwise. Probably the danger to the public of uninsured driving is the reason for the

---

14. Per Lord Reid at pp. 349–350.
15. At p. 362.
16. Above, p. 29.
17. [1955] 1 QB 78, [1954] 3 All ER 273, DC. Cf. *Lomas v Peek* [1947] 2 All ER 574.
18. *DPP v Fisher* [1991] Crim LR 787, distinguishing *Newbury v Davis* [1974] RTR 367.

courts' refusal to give effect to what they recognise in another social context to be the natural meaning of the words used by Parliament. But is uninsured driving a greater social evil than driving with defective brakes?

b) *Adverbs: "knowingly"*. The use of an adverb is a more explicit way of making clear that *mens rea* is required. The clearest word is "knowingly". Devlin J has said that "knowingly" only says expressly what is normally implied"[19] – it does expressly what the presumption in favour of *mens rea* would do by implication. The use of the word suggests that Parliament wanted to make sure that the courts would not find some reason for holding the presumption to be excluded – similarly where Parliament provides that it is an offence to "knowingly permit" something to be done. Perhaps the word "permit" would have been sufficient to import *mens rea* – but the draftsman was taking no chances.

When "knowingly" is used, it should be difficult for any court to hold that *mens rea* is not required as to all the elements of the offence, though it might not extend to an exception clause in the definition of the crime.[20]

The requirement of "knowingly" is satisfied by proof of what is sometimes called "wilful blindness": "it is always open to the tribunal of fact, when knowledge on the part of a defendant is required to be proved, to base a finding of knowledge on evidence that the defendant had deliberately shut his eyes to the obvious or refrained from inquiry because he suspected the truth but did not want to have his suspicion confirmed."[1] Sometimes, however, the courts take a stricter view, as in handling stolen goods, below, p. 650.

c) *Wilfully*. The word "wilfully" looks like a "*mens rea* word" and it is sometimes treated as such. D does not "wilfully" obstruct a police officer simply because he does a deliberate act which in fact obstructs the officer; an intention to obstruct must be proved.[2] There are, however, cases in which the courts have imposed strict liability notwithstanding its use. "Wilful" in these cases is held to apply only to the act but not to some circumstance or consequence which is an element of the crime. D was held guilty of wilfully fishing in private water, although he believed there was public right to fish there;[3] of wilfully killing a house pigeon when he shot a bird, believing it was a wild pigeon;[4] and of wilfully destroying an oak tree in contravention of a tree preservation order when he was unaware of the order and believed that permission had been given for the tree to be felled.[5] In these cases, the fishing, the killing of a bird, the cutting down of a tree were all "wilful" acts; but in none of them was the commission of the crime "wilful". In the most important and recent authority, *Sheppard*,[6] Lord Diplock said that if the word is given such a narrow meaning it is otiose

19. *Roper v Taylor's Central Garage (Exeter) Ltd* [1951] 2 TLR 284 at 288.
20. Cf. *Brooks v Mason* [1902] 2 KB 743, DC and *Wings Ltd v Ellis*, above p. 52.
1. *Westminster City Council v Croyalgrange Ltd* [1986] 2 All ER 353 at 359, HL.
2. *Willmott v Atack* [1977] QB 498, [1976] 3 All ER 794, DC.
3. *Hudson v MacRae* (1863) 4 B & S 585, DC.
4. *Cotterill v Penn* [1936] 1 KB 53.
5. *Maidstone Borough Council v Mortimer* [1980] 3 All ER 552, DC.
6. [1981] AC 394, HL.

because, in the absence of the word and even in offences of strict liability, the law requires a voluntary – i.e., a wilful – act. Its use should therefore imply that something more is required. In *Sheppard* it was held that "wilfully" in s. 1 of the Children and Young Persons Act 1933 was not to be limited to requiring an intention to do one of the physical acts described in the section (assault, ill-treat, etc.) but must extend to the consequences ("in a manner likely to cause him unnecessary suffering or injury to health"). D was guilty of "wilful neglect" by refraining from getting medical aid only if he knew there was a risk that the child's health might suffer or, where he was unaware of the risk, if he did not care whether the child might be in need of medical treatment or not. Following *Sheppard*, it is arguable that "wilfully" should be construed to mean wilfully committing the crime; but in practice it is unlikely that the courts will consistently so hold.

d) *Effect of usage of* mens rea *words in some sections but not others.* Where a *mens rea* word is used in one section of a statute but not in another that may suggest that the second creates an offence of strict liability; but Lord Reid has said:

"It is also firmly established that the fact that other sections of the Act expressly require *mens rea*, for example because they contain the word 'knowingly', is not itself sufficient to justify a decision that a section which is silent as to *mens rea* creates an absolute offence."[7]

In *Sherras v De Rutzen*,[8] D was charged with supplying liquor to a constable on duty, contrary to s. 16 (2) of the Licensing Act 1872. The policeman was not wearing his armlet which, it was admitted, was an indication that he was off duty. D, who was in the habit – quite lawfully – of serving constables in uniform but without their armlets, made no enquiry and took it for granted that the policeman was off duty. Section 16 (1) of the Act made it an offence for a licensee *knowingly* to harbour or suffer to remain on his premises any constable on duty. Section 16 (2) did not include the word "knowingly". Yet D's conviction was quashed. Day J said that the only inference to be drawn was that under s. 16 (1) the prosecution had to prove knowledge, while under s. 16 (2) the defendant had to prove he had no knowledge.[9] Wright J made no attempt to reconcile the two sub-sections, contenting himself with pointing out that:[10]

"if guilty knowledge is not necessary, no care on the part of the publican could save him from conviction ... since it would be as easy for the constable to deny that he was on duty when asked, or to produce a forged permission from his superior officer as to remove his armlet before entering the public house."

7. *Sweet v Parsley* [1970] AC 132 at 149, [1969] 1 All ER 347.
8. [1895] 1 QB 918. Cf. *Harding v Price* [1948] 1 KB 695, [1948] 1 All ER 283, DC (a defence to failure to report an accident to show that D did not know accident had occurred, even though word "knowingly" in the Motor Car Act 1903 was omitted when the section was repealed and replaced by the Road Traffic Act 1930).
9. This view was doubted by Devlin J in *Roper v Taylor's Central Garage* (above). If Day J intended to refer to the *evidential* burden only, the *dictum* is unobjectionable. See Edwards, *Mens Rea*, 90–97.
10. [1895] 1 QB 918 at 923.

2 The Offence in its Social Context

a) *"Real" or "quasi" crime?* Here an important matter is whether the court considers the offence to be "a real crime" or a "quasi-crime". Parliament makes no such distinction. An act either is, or it is not, declared by Parliament to be a crime.[11] It is the courts which decide whether it is "real" or "quasi" crime. They do so on the basis that an offence which, in the public eye, carries little or no stigma and does not involve "the disgrace of criminality",[12] is only a quasi-crime. Then, strict liability may be imposed because "it does not offend the ordinary man's sense of justice that moral guilt is not of the essence of the offence".[13] In *Sherras v De Rutzen* Wright J distinguished "a class of acts . . . which are not criminal in any real sense, but are acts which in the public interest are prohibited under a penalty".[14] Since we are assuming a defendant who is morally blameless, no stigma ought to attach to him anyway. In determining whether the offence involves "stigma", it is necessary to consider the case where the offence is committed intentionally. If Parliament prohibits the causing of results because it deems them in some measure harmful, the intentional causing of the harm in question probably deserves some measure of moral condemnation. Some stigma attaches to, or should attach to, the motorist who deliberately leaves his car in a parking space for longer than is permitted by law – it is an anti-social act, likely to cause inconvenience to others. But few people, even "right-thinking" people, would consider such an act so iniquitous, even when done intentionally, that the actor ought to be locked up or even shunned and avoided. Since offences of strict liability do not distinguish between degrees of fault and no fault at all, the conviction fixes the offender with whatever stigma might attach to an intentional offender.[15]

b) *A general or special prohibition?* A second factor which may be of great significance is whether the provision is of general application or relates only to those following a particular trade, profession or special activity. In the latter type of case, the court may be much more ready to hold such a "regulatory offence" to impose strict liability. Lord Diplock put it as follows:[16]

"Where penal provisions are of general application to the conduct of ordinary citizens in the course of their everyday life, the presumption is that the standard of care required of them in informing themselves of facts which would make their conduct unlawful is that of the familiar common law duty of care. But where the subject-matter of a statute is the regulation of a particular activity involving potential danger to public health, safety or morals, in which citizens have a choice whether they participate or not, the court may feel driven to infer an intention of

11. See Ch. 2, above.
12. Per Lord Reid in *Warner v Metropolitan Police Comr* [1969] 2 AC 256 at 272.
13. Ibid. Cf. *Wings Ltd v Ellis*, above, p. 52.
14. [1895] 1 QB 918 at 922.
15. See J. C. Smith, "Responsibility in Criminal Law", in *Barbara Wootton, Essays in Her Honour* (ed. Bean and Whynes, 1986) 141.
16. In *Sweet v Parsley* [1970] AC 132 at 163.

Parliament to impose, by penal sanctions, a higher duty of care on those who choose to participate and to place on them an obligation to take whatever measures may be necessary to prevent the prohibited act, without regard to those considerations of cost or business practicability which play a part in the determination of what would be required of them in order to fulfil the ordinary common law duty of care."

So we find most instances of strict liability in statutes regulating the sale of food, and drugs, the management of industrial activities, the conduct of licensed premises and the like. But the "particular activity" may be one in which citizens generally engage, like driving a car. However, this is something which we choose to do and, as it involves potential danger to others, it is not inconsistent with this statement of principle that some offences regulating the conduct of motorists should be strict.

c) *Possibility of amendment.* According to Devlin J, it is:

"a safe general principle to follow . . . that where the punishment of an individual will not promote the observance of the law either by that individual or by others whose conduct he may reasonably be expected to influence, then, in the absence of clear and express words, such punishment is not intended."[17]

This principle has been re-stated many times, for example by the Privy Council in both *Lim Chin Aik*[18] and *Gammon (Hong Kong) Ltd v A–G of Hong Kong*[19] and by the Divisional Court in *Pharmaceutical Society of Great Britain v Storkwain Ltd.*[20] But, if implemented, it would seem to require negligence, though not perhaps of a high degree, rather than impose strict liability. D, it appears, must be shown to have fallen short in some respect of the standard to be expected of him. But was the principle applied in *Storkwain*? Are pharmacists expected to keep a handwriting expert on the premises to scrutinise the prescriptions? Or to telephone the doctor each time they receive a prescription for confirmation that he wrote it?[1] Obviously the courts do not expect such wholly unreasonable precautions to be taken – but how then can the principle be satisfied in such cases?

d) *Social danger.* Fourthly, and by no means least, the courts are influenced by the degree of social danger which, in their opinion, will follow from breach of the particular prohibition. They take judicial notice of the problems with which the country is confronted. The greater the degree of social danger, the more likely is the offence to be interpreted as one of strict liability. Inflation, drugs, road accidents and pollution are constantly brought to our attention as pressing evils; and in each case the judges have at times invoked strict liability as a protection for society.

17. *Reynolds v Austin & Sons Ltd* [1951] 2 KB 135, [1951] 1 All ER 606, DC.
18. [1963] AC 160 at 174, [1963] All ER 223 at 228.
19. [1985] AC 1 at 14–15 [1984], 2 All ER 503 at 508–509.
20. [1985] 3 All ER 4, approved by the House of Lords, [1986] 2 All ER 635 at 640.
  1. It appears that in *Storkwain* the pharmacist, not knowing Dr Irani, *did* telephone the number on the prescription but it was false and he was deceived by the forger or his accomplice who answered: B. S. Jackson, [1991] Crim LR at 895.

i) *Inflation.* The economic dangers through which the country was passing were the basis of the decision in *St Margaret's Trust Ltd.*[2] In this case D Limited, a finance company, was charged with disposing of a car on hire purchase without a deposit of at least 50 per cent of the purchase price having been paid as required by the Hire Purchase Order[3] then in force. A car dealer and his customers had fraudulently misled D Limited into advancing more than 50 per cent by stating a falsely inflated price for the cars which were the subjects of the transactions. It was admitted that D Limited had acted innocently throughout and supposed that a deposit of at least 50 per cent had been paid. The company was, nevertheless, convicted.

The reasons given by the court had very little to do with the words of the statute. It is true Donovan J said:

"The words of the order themselves are an express and unqualified prohibition of the acts done in this case by St. Margaret's Trust Ltd."

But this means no more than that no such word as "knowingly" was used. He went on:

"The object of the order was to help to defend the currency against the peril of inflation which, if unchecked, would bring disaster on the country. There is no need to elaborate this. The present generation has witnessed the collapse of the currency in other countries and the consequent chaos, misery and widespread ruin. It would not be at all surprising if Parliament, determined to prevent similar calamities here, enacted measures which it intended to be absolute prohibitions of acts which might increase the risk in however small a degree. Indeed that would be the natural expectation. There would be little point in enacting that no one should breach the defences against a flood, and at the same time excusing anyone who did it innocently."[4]

ii) *Dangerous drugs.* Legislation concerning dangerous drugs has had a chequered recent history. Lord Parker declared in 1966[5] that he took judicial notice of the fact that drugs are a great danger today and the Divisional Court imposed strict liability of a most draconian character in a number of cases about that time. D was held to be guilty of being "concerned in the management of premises used for the purpose of smoking cannabis" though he did not know and had no means of knowing that such smoking was taking place.[6] In other cases, it was held that D was guilty of being in unauthorised possession of a drug contrary to s. 1 (1) of the Drugs (Prevention of Misuse) Act 1964 if he knew he had control of a thing which was in fact a dangerous drug, even though he did not know, and had no reason to know, that it was either dangerous or a drug.[7] He might have reasonably believed that he had a bottle of sweets, but that would have been no defence.

---

2. [1958] 2 All ER 289, [1958] 1 WLR 522.
3. SI 1956/180. Revoked – no corresponding order in force.
4. [1958] 2 All ER 289 at 293. Would the floodgates really have opened in this way, if the case had been decided differently?
5. In *Yeandel v Fisher* [1966] 1 QB 440 at 446, [1965] 3 All ER 158 at 161.
6. *Yeandel v Fisher*, above.
7. E.g. *Lockyer v Gibb* [1967] 2 QB 243, [1966] 2 All ER 653.

The first case on strict liability ever considered by the House of Lords, *Warner v. Metropolitan Police Commissioner*[8] concerned possession of prohibited drugs. D, who sold scent as a side-line, collected two boxes which had been left for him at a cafe. One box contained scent, the other controlled drugs. D said he assumed both boxes contained scent. The jury were told that such a belief went only to mitigation. The Court of Appeal agreed. If D was in possession of the box and he knew the box contained something, he was in possession of the contents, whatever they were; and, as it was an "absolute" offence, that was all the prosecution had to prove.

The House of Lords, Lord Reid dissenting, agreed with the courts below that s. 1 (1) of the 1964 Act created an "absolute" offence, not requiring any *mens rea* as such. But it was, of course, necessary to prove the *actus reus*, i.e., possession, and that involved proving a mental element. Lord Guest agreed with the Court of Appeal – D's knowledge that he had a box containing *something* under his control was enough – but the other judges held that more was required. Though D's possession of the box gave rise to a strong inference that he was in possession of the contents, that inference might be rebutted. Their Lordships' opinions are obscure and various but it seems that the inference certainly would be rebutted if (i) D believed the box contained scent, (ii) scent was something of "a wholly different nature" from the drugs, (iii) D had no opportunity to ascertain its true nature, and (iv) he did not suspect there was "anything wrong" with the contents. These issues (or at least some of them, for the majority of the House were far from being in complete accord) ought to have been left to the jury and, as they had not, three judges held that there had been a misdirection but upheld the conviction under the proviso.

Possession is a neutral concept, not implying any kind of blame or fault but experience, especially in the old law of larceny, has shown that, when it becomes the determinant of guilt, it tends to acquire a refined and artificial meaning of great complexity. It seems the most obvious common sense to say that a person firmly grasping a parcel is in possession of it and a distinction between the parcel and its contents is too absurd to contemplate; but, if it is a grave offence merely to possess the contents, courts will strive to find means to say that an innocent person is not in possession, by refining the meaning of that concept. Of course, this problem would not arise if it were held that the offence required some element of fault – possession, as observed, is neutral and in itself incapable of being "fault" – but, sadly, of all the judges involved, only Lord Reid was willing to take this sensible course. The result was another calamitous decision by the House.

The five speeches delivered in *Warner* differ so greatly and it is so difficult to make sense of parts of them that courts in later cases have found it impossible to extract a *ratio decidendi*. The law has been modified by the Misuse of Drugs Act 1971 but the onus remains on the Crown to prove possession and the Act has nothing to say about that concept. It has, however, influenced the approach of the courts. In *McNamara*[9] the Court

8. [1969] 2 AC 256, [1968] 2 All ER 356; **SHC 115**.
9. (1988) 87 Cr App Rep 246, [1988] Crim LR 440 and commentary.

of Appeal, while paying lip-service to the House of Lords, has gone back to the view of the Court of Appeal and the (on this issue) dissenting opinion of Lord Guest. D was in possession of a cardboard box containing cannabis resin. He said he thought it contained pornographic material. Because he knew he was in control of the box and that the box contained something he was in possession of cannabis. The court was able to reach this conclusion without qualm because it no longer followed that D was guilty of the offence. Under the Misuse of Drugs Act 1971, s. 28, it was a defence to prove that he neither believed nor suspected nor had reason to suspect that the thing of which he was in possession was a controlled drug.

McNamara provides a welcome simplification of the law where D knows he has the thing or a container with something in it but claims he thought it was something else. It does not solve the problem when he claims he was unaware of its existence. In *Warner*[10] there was unanimous agreement about a hypothetical case posed earlier by Lord Parker CJ[11] – if something is slipped into a lady's shopping basket and she has no idea that it is there, she is not in possession of it. It is easy to find authority in the vast case law on possession to contradict that proposition but Parker LCJ, the Court of Appeal and the House were entirely confident about it: the lady is in possession of the basket and the known contents but not the thing secretly inserted. The judges shrank from saying that the hypothetical lady was in possession of the thing because they were thinking of a packet of controlled drugs and, if she was in possession, she would have been guilty of a grave offence. If the thing were a box of chocolates dropped in by a friend as a birthday present it is unlikely that they would have hesitated to hold that she was in possession of it. Suppose that, before she discovered it, the box had been removed by a pickpocket, would they have hesitated to hold that it was stolen from her (it was not stolen from anyone else) and that the pickpocket was a thief? Of course not. So far as possession is concerned, there is no rational distinction between the drugs and the chocolates.

In *Lewis*[12] it was held that the judge had not misdirected the jury by telling them that the tenant of a house might be found to be in possession of drugs found on the premises although he did not know they were there, provided he had had an opportunity to find out that they were. But there is no material difference between planting drugs in a person's house and planting them in her basket.[13] The decision seems to contradict the one thing on which their Lordships in *Warner* were unanimous. In introducing the idea of opportunity, the court relied on a statement of Lord Morris. But Lord Morris was dealing with a quite different question: possession, he said, was "being *knowingly in control of a thing* in circumstances which have involved an opportunity (whether availed of or not) to learn or discover, at

10. [1969] 2 AC at 282, 286, 300, 303 and 311.
11. *Lockyer v Gibb* [1967] 2 QB 243 at 248, per Parker LCJ.
12. (1987) 87 Cr App Rep 270, [1988] Crim LR 517 and commentary.
13. "First of all a man does not have possession of something which has been put into his pocket or into his house without his knowledge": *McNamara* (1988) 87 Cr App Rep 246 at 248.

least in a general way, *what the thing is*".[14] In *Lewis*, D was not knowingly in control of the thing.

Warner does not affect the law where the drug was not in a container. D must know he has the thing, but it is not necessary that he should know or comprehend its nature.[15] In *Marriott*[16] D was convicted of being in possession of 0.03 grains of cannabis adhering to a penknife. It was held that the jury had been wrongly directed that he was guilty if he knew he was in possession of the penknife. It was necessary to prove at least that he knew that there was some foreign matter adhering to the knife. The court thought that no further *mens rea* was necessary – so that the accused would be guilty if he thought the matter was tobacco or toffee – but now, under the Misuse of Drugs Act, it would be a defence for him to prove that he neither believed, nor suspected, nor had reason to suspect, that the matter was a controlled drug.

The second case concerning strict liability to reach the House of Lords was *Sweet v Parsley*.[17] On this occasion, the House overruled the cases which decided that being "concerned in the management of premises used for the purpose of smoking cannabis" is an offence of strict liability. D, a schoolmistress, was the subtenant of a farmhouse in the country. She let the rooms, retaining one room for her own use and visiting the farm occasionally to collect rent and see that all was well. Cannabis was smoked in the farmhouse but it was found as a fact that she had no knowledge whatever of this. The Divisional Court nevertheless dismissed her appeal. She was "concerned in the management" and that was enough. The House quashed her conviction. The "purpose" referred to in the section must be that of the person concerned in the management; and D had no such purpose. Only Lord Wilberforce was content to stop with this "prosaic interpretation of the paragraph". The remainder relied, in varying degrees, on a presumption in favour of *mens rea*. The actual decision in *Warner* was not affected,[18] but the attitude of the House, with the exception of Lord Reid, who saw no reason to alter what he had said in the earlier case, is very different. The judges are no less sensitive to the public's view of injustice than to their need for protection; and, for once, a case of strict liability had excited public interest. The public outcry and sense of injustice may not have been without influence.[19]

The corresponding provisions of the Misuse of Drugs Act require *mens rea* and leave the onus of proof, where it belongs, with the Crown. It is an offence if an occupier[20] or person concerned in the management of premises

---

14. [1969] 2 AC at 289 (authors' italics).
15. *Boyesen* [1982] AC 768, [1982] 2 All ER 161. (It is immaterial how minute the quantity is provided only that it amounts to something and D knows he has it.)
16. [1971] 1 All ER 595, [1971] 1 WLR 187.
17. [1970] AC 132, [1969] 1 All ER 347; **SHC 119.**
18. *Fernandez* [1970] Crim LR 277 where it was held to be enough that D knew a package might contain some prohibited article and was prepared to take it, whatever the contents were.
19. ". . . fortunately the press in this country are vigilant to expose injustice . . ." per Lord Reid, at p. 150.
20. The occupier is a person whose degree of control is sufficient to enable him to exclude anyone likely to commit an offence under the Act. It is not limited to persons in legal possession and includes a student with rooms in college: *Tao* [1977] QB 141, [1976] 3 All ER 65.

"knowingly permits or suffers" the smoking of cannabis and other specified activities in connection with drugs. The word "knowingly" is introduced for the first time; but it does not alter the rule under the Dangerous Drugs Act 1965 that knowledge or wilful blindness is enough, but reasonable grounds for suspicion are not.[1]

iii) *Pollution*. In view of the current concern about pollution it is scarcely surprising that a modern example should come from that area. In *Alphacell Ltd v Woodward*[2] the House of Lords held that D Ltd was guilty of causing polluted matter to enter a river, contrary to s. 2 (1) (a) of the Rivers (Prevention of Pollution) Act 1951.[3] They had built and operated settling tanks with an overflow channel into the river and provided pumps designed to prevent any overflow taking place. Because the pumps became obstructed with vegetation, an overflow of polluted water occurred. There was no evidence that D knew that pollution was taking place or that they had been in any way negligent. Lord Salmon stressed the public importance of preventing pollution and the risk of pollution from the vast and increasing number of riparian industries and said:[4]

"If . . . it were held to be the law that no conviction could be obtained under the 1951 Act unless the prosecution could discharge the often impossible onus of proving that the pollution was caused intentionally or negligently, a great deal of pollution would go unpunished and undeterred to the relief of many riparian factory owners. As a result, many rivers which are now filthy would become filthier still and many rivers which are now clean would lose their cleanliness."

In *Atkinson v Sir Alfred McAlpine & Son Ltd*[5] it was held that the company was guilty of failing to give written notice, as required by the Asbestos Regulations 1969, that they were going to undertake work involving crocidolite though they neither knew nor had reason to know that the work involved crocidolite. The court distinguished *Harding v Price*[6] where Lord Goddard CJ, holding that D was not guilty of failing to report an accident, the happening of which he was unaware, said:

"If a statute contains an absolute prohibition against the doing of some act, as a general rule *mens rea* is not a constituent of the offence, but there is all the difference between prohibiting an act and imposing a duty to do something on the happening of a certain event. Unless a man knows that the event has happened, how can he carry out the duty imposed? . . . Any other view would lead to calling on a man to do the impossible."

In *McAlpine*, the court said that, unlike the accident, it was "probably possible" to ascertain whether crocidolite was involved; but since they held

---

1. *Thomas* (1976) 63 Cr App Rep 65, [1976] Crim LR 517.
2. [1972] AC 824, [1972] 2 All ER 475. Cf. *Price v Cromack* [1975] 2 All ER 113, [1975] 1 WLR 988, DC; *Maidstone Borough Council v Mortimer* [1980] 3 All ER 552, above, p. 105; *Kirkland v Robinson* [1987] Crim LR 643, DC (possession of live wild birds an offence of strict liability under the Wildlife and Countryside Act 1981, s. 1 (1) (a), taking into account the outstanding social importance of an Act designed to protect the environment).
3. See now Control of Pollution Act 1974, s. 31.
4. [1972] AC at 848.
5. (1974) 16 KIR 220, [1974] Crim LR 668, DC.
6. [1948] 1 KB 695, [1948] 1 All ER 283, DC, above, p. 106, and below, p. 263.

that the mischief would not be met if "knows or ought to know" were read into the regulation, it is clear that impossibility would not be regarded as a defence.

3 The Severity of the Punishment

It is often argued that the provision for a severe maximum punishment shows that strict liability could not have been intended by Parliament. To some extent, this is in conflict with the principle previously discussed, since the provision for only a slight punishment would suggest that Parliament thought the social danger involved to be slight. Certainly, the courts do not seem to have been deterred in recent years from imposing strict liability in the case of offences carrying heavy maximum sentences – an offence under section 9 (1) (b) of the Dangerous Drugs Act 1964 was punishable with ten years' imprisonment and causing death by dangerous driving was punishable with five. The fact that an offence under s. 58 (2) of the Firearms Act 1968 is punishable with three years' imprisonment did not deter the court from holding that an honest and reasonable belief that the firearm was an antique was no defence.[7] In *Gammon (Hong Kong) Ltd v A–G of Hong Kong*[8] the Privy Council admitted that the fact the offence was punishable with a fine of $250,000 and imprisonment for three years was "a formidable point"; but found "there is nothing inconsistent with the purpose of the ordinance in imposing severe penalties for offences of strict liability".

3 Liability is Strict, not "Absolute"

It was observed at the beginning of this chapter that the need for a mental element is not ruled out completely by the fact that an offence is one of strict liability. It may be necessary to prove that D was aware of all the circumstances of the offence save that in respect of which strict liability was imposed. When the court holds that it is an offence of strict liability to sell meat which is unfit for human consumption, it decides that a reasonable mistake as to that particular fact is not a defence. It does not decide that any other defence is unavailable to D; and indeed, we have seen that a mistake as to other circumstances of the *actus reus* may afford a defence.[9] There is no reason why all other defences should not be available as they are in the case of offences requiring full *mens rea*. Even when the former offence of dangerous driving was thought to impose strict liability[10], it was held to be a defence if D was in a state of automatism when he "drove" the vehicle.[11] It is perfectly clear that a child under the age of ten could in no

7. *Howells* [1977] QB 614, [1977] 2 All ER 417.
8. [1985] AC 1 at 17, [1984] 2 All ER 503 at 511.
9. Above, p. 38.
10. Cf. *Gosney*, below, p. 116.
11. *Hill v Baxter* [1958] 1 QB 277, [1958] 1 All ER 193; *Budd* [1962] Crim LR 49; *Watmore v Jenkins* [1962] 2 QB 572, [1962] 2 All ER 868. See Patient, "Some Remarks about the Element of Voluntariness in Absolute Offences" [1968] Crim LR 23.

circumstances be convicted of an offence of strict liability[12] and it is submitted that a child between ten and fourteen could be convicted only if it were proved that he knew his act was "wrong".[13] It is submitted, therefore, that other general defences – insanity, necessity, duress and coercion – should be available equally on a charge of an offence of strict liability as in the case of any other offence.[14]

Larsonneur[15] and *Winzar v Chief Constable of Kent*[16] establish that lawful compulsion is not a defence to offences of "being found". It does not follow that unlawful duress would not be a defence. If D, being drunk, were forced at gunpoint into the highway he should not be guilty of being found drunk there. Nor does it follow that even lawful compulsion may not found a defence to other, less extreme, cases of strict liability than those of "being found".

4 Arguments for and against Strict Liability

The proliferation of offences of strict liability, while generally deplored by legal writers, has been welcomed by the distinguished social scientist, Lady Wootton, on the ground that "nothing has dealt so devastating a blow at the punitive concept of the criminal process . . ."[17]

"If, however, the primary function of the courts is conceived as the prevention of forbidden acts, there is little cause to be disturbed by the multiplication of offences of strict liability. If the law says that certain things are not to be done, it is illogical to confine this prohibition to occasions on which they are done from malice aforethought; for at least the material consequences of an action, and the reasons for prohibiting it are the same whether it is the result of sinister malicious plotting, of negligence or of sheer accident."[18]

Accepting that the primary function of the courts is the prevention of forbidden acts, there remains the question, what acts should be regarded as forbidden? Surely only such acts as we can assert ought not to have been done. Suppose that a butcher, who has taken all reasonable precautions, has the misfortune to sell some meat which is unfit for human consumption. That it was so unfit is undiscoverable by any precaution which a butcher can be expected to take. Ought the butcher to have acted as he did? Unless we want butchers to stop selling meat, or to take precautions so extreme as

---

12. Below, p. 188.
13. Below, p. 189. Cf. Cave J in *Tolson* (1889) 23 QBD 168 at 182 and Lord Diplock in *Sweet v Parsley* [1969] 1 All ER 347 at 361.
14. For discussion of this question see Sayre, "Public Welfare Offences" (1933) 33 Col Law Rev 55 at 75–78; Howard, *Strict Liability*, Ch. 9.
15. (1933) 24 Cr App Rep 74; **SHC 128**; above, p. 43.
16. (1983) The Times, 28 March, above, p. 44. Cf. *O'Sullivan v Fisher* [1954] SASR 33, discussed by Howard, op. cit. at 193; *Achterdam* 1911 EDL 336 (Burchell & Hunt, 114).
17. *Crime and the Criminal Law* (2nd ed.), 44. See also p. 63, criticised by Hogan, "Criminal Liability without Fault" (Leeds Univ Press, 1967); Hart, *The Morality of the Criminal Law*, 13 et seq.
18. Ibid., at p. 51.

to be unreasonable (like employing an analyst)[19] it would seem that the answer should be in the affirmative; we want butchers, who have taken all reasonable precautions, to sell meat – the act of this butcher was not one which the law should seek to prevent. Some of the judges who upheld the conviction of *Prince* did so on the ground that men should be deterred from taking girls out of the possession of their parents, whatever the girl's age. This reasoning can hardly be applied to many modern offences of strict liability. We do not wish to deter people from driving cars, being concerned in the management of premises, financing hire purchase transactions or canning peas.[20] These acts, if done with all proper care, are not such acts as the law should seek to prevent. The fallacy in the argument lies in looking at the harm done in isolation from the circumstances in which it was brought about. Many acts, which have in fact caused harm, *ought* to have been done. The surgeon performing a justified operation with all proper skill may cause death.

Another argument that is frequently advanced in favour of strict liability is that, without it, many guilty people would escape – "that there is neither time nor personnel available to litigate the culpability of each particular infraction."[1] This argument assumes that it is possible to deal with these cases without deciding whether D had *mens rea* or not, whether he was negligent or not. Certainly D may be convicted without deciding these questions, but how can he be sentenced? Clearly the court will deal differently with (i) the butcher who knew that the meat was tainted; (ii) the butcher who did not know, but ought to have known; and (iii) the butcher who did not know and had no means of finding out. Sentence can hardly be imposed without deciding into which category the convicted person falls. Treating the offence as one of strict liability, in the case of jury trial, merely removes the decision of these vital questions of fact from the jury and puts them in the hands of the judge; in the case of summary trial, it removes the questions from the sphere of strict proof according to law and leaves them to be decided in the much more informal way in which questions of fact relating purely to sentence are decided.[2] *Gosney*[3] illustrates this vividly. On the assumption (held, on appeal, to be wrong) that the former offence of

19. See Kennedy LJ cited above, p. 102 and see below, p. 118.
20. See *Smedleys Ltd v Breed*, below, p. 121. "Obviously any consequence is avoidable by the simple expedient of not engaging in the process at all. But that clearly is not what is meant unless the process itself is open to serious criticism as unnecessary or inefficient:" per Lord Hailsham [1974] 2 All ER 21 at 28.
1. Wechsler, "The Model Penal Code", in *Modern Advances in Criminology* (ed., J. Ll. J. Edwards) (1965), 73. The argument was met by the authors of the Code by "the creation of a grade of offense which may be prosecuted in a criminal court but which is not denominated criminal and which entails upon conviction no severer sentence than a fine or civil penalty or forfeiture".
2. Disputed facts affecting sentence may be decided by the judge in a "Newton hearing" after conviction – see *Newton* (1983) 77 Cr App Rep 13, [1983] Crim LR 178. In some cases judges have preferred the use of additional counts to obtain the jury's decision on important issues of culpability which would not appear from a verdict of guilty on a single count. See *Bashir* (intentional or reckless rape?), below, p. 458, and *Hoof* (intentional or reckless arson?), below, p. 708. This course is not open where the offence is one of strict liability. In *Warner* (above, p. 110) the recorder asked the jury after verdict whether D knew the box contained drugs but they said, reasonably, that they had not decided that question.
3. [1971] 2 QB 674, [1971] 3 All ER 220.

dangerous driving was one of strict liability, the judge, no doubt rightly, excluded evidence alleged to show that D was blameless. If the rules relating to proof at the trial have any value at all, it is extraordinary that they should not be applied to the most important facts in the case. That the sentence should be imposed by the judge on a basis of fact different from that on which the jury convicted is deplorable; but it is always possible in the case of strict liability unless the judge questions the jury as to the grounds of their decision – and there are difficulties about this.[4]

The argument which is probably most frequently advanced by the courts for imposing strict liability is that it is necessary to do so in the interests of the public. Now it may be conceded that in many of the instances where strict liability has been imposed, the public does need protection against negligence and, assuming that the threat of punishment can make the potential harmdoer more careful, there may be a valid ground for imposing liability for negligence as well as where there is *mens rea*. This is a plausible argument in favour of strict liability if there were no middle way between *mens rea* and strict liability – that is liability for negligence – and the judges have generally proceeded on the basis that there is no such middle way. Liability for negligence has rarely been spelled out of a statute except where, as in driving without due care, it is explicitly required. Lord Devlin has explained this:[5]

"It is not easy to find a way of construing a statute apparently expressed in terms of absolute liability so as to produce the requirement of negligence. Take, for example, an offence like driving a car while it has defective brakes. It is easy enough to read into a statute a word like 'wilfully' but you cannot just read in 'carelessly'. You cannot show that no one should carelessly drive a car with defective brakes; you are not trying to get at careless driving. What you want to say is that no one may drive a car without taking care to see that the brakes are not defective. That is not so easy to frame as a matter of construction and it has never been done."

The case against strict liability, then, is, first, that it is unnecessary. It results in the conviction of persons who have behaved impeccably and who should not be required to alter their conduct in any way. Secondly, that it is unjust. Even if an absolute discharge can be given (as in *Ball*)[6] D may feel rightly aggrieved at having been formally convicted of an offence for which he bore no responsibility. It is significant that Ball thought it worthwhile to appeal. Moreover, a conviction may have far-reaching consequences outside the courts,[7] so that it is no answer to say that only a nominal penalty is imposed.[8]

The imposition of liability for negligence would in fact meet the arguments of most of those who favour strict liability. Thus Roscoe Pound,

---

4. Cf. comment on *Lockyer v Gibb* [1966] Crim LR 504 and on *Sheppard* [1981] Crim LR 171 at 172, *Dalas* (1966) Times, 28th September; *Warner* [1967] 3 All ER 93, [1967] Crim LR 528; *Lester* [1976] Crim LR 389; *Foo* [1976] Crim LR 456 and commentaries on these cases.
5. *Samples of Lawmaking*, 76.
6. (1966) 50 Cr App Rep 266.
7. As in the case of *Sweet v Parsley* [1970] AC 132, [1969] 1 All ER 347.
8. This was accepted by the Privy Council in *Lim Chin Aik* [1963] AC 160 at 175 and by Lord Reid in *Warner* [1968] 2 All ER 356 at 366.

in a passage which has been frequently and uncritically accepted as a justification for such offences, wrote:[9]

"The good sense of the courts has introduced a doctrine of acting at one's peril with respect to statutory crimes which expresses the needs of society. Such statutes are not meant to punish the vicious will but to put pressure upon the thoughtless and inefficient to do their whole duty in the interest of public health or safety or morals."

The "thoughtless and inefficient" are, of course, the negligent. The objection to offences of strict liability is not that these persons are penalised, but that others who are completely innocent are also liable to conviction. Though Lord Devlin was sceptical about the possibility of introducing the criterion of negligence in the lecture from which the above quotation is taken, in *Reynolds v Austin*[10] he stated from the bench the principle that strict liability should only apply when there is something that the defendant can do to promote the observance of the law – which comes close to requiring negligence.

If there were something which D could do to prevent the commission of the crime and which he had failed to do, he might generally be said to have failed to comply with a duty – perhaps a high duty – of care; and so have been negligent. One would have thought that what D ought to do would necessarily be limited by what was reasonable. A law requiring one to act unreasonably would seem odd indeed; but Lord Salmon was prepared to take this step in *Alphacell*. The section, he thought,[11]

"encourages riparian factory owners not only to take reasonable steps to prevent pollution but to do everything possible to ensure that they do not cause it."

This suggests that, however vast the expenditure involved, and however unreasonable it may be in relation to the risk, D is under a duty to take all *possible* steps. The factory owner might prefer to take the chance of paying the maximum fine of £200; but a "repetition or continuation of an earlier offence" may lead to liability to imprisonment for six months.[12] By now, the offence might be thought to have lost its character of being "not criminal in any real sense" but it could not cease to be an offence of strict liability; and it would still be no defence that reasonable steps (or, indeed, all possible steps) had been taken. Clearly Lord Salmon was right in saying that there was a great deal more in the case than the fine and costs of the trial, amounting to £44. Yet it may be doubted whether factory owners will in fact do more than is reasonable; and it is questionable whether they ought to be required to do so, at the risk – even though it be unlikely – of imprisonment. The contrary argument is that –

". . . the existence of strict liability does induce organisations to aim at higher and higher standards."[13]

9. *The Spirit of the Common Law*, 52.
10. [1951] 2 KB 135 at 150, [1951] 1 All ER 606 at 612; above, p. 108.
11. [1972] 2 All ER at 491. Cf. *Smedleys Ltd v Breed*, below, p. 121.
12. Criminal Law Act 1967, s. 2 (7).
13. Smith and Pearson, "The Value of Strict Liability" [1969] Crim LR 5 at 16.

Possible developments: a "halfway house?" There are several possible compromises between *mens rea* and strict liability in regulatory offences.

(i) D might be convicted without proof of any *mens rea* by the Crown; but acquitted if *he* proved, on a balance of probabilities, that he lacked *mens rea*; i.e., that he had an honest belief in a state of facts which, had it existed, would have made his act innocent.

(ii) D might be convicted without proof of any *mens rea* by the Crown; but acquitted if he proved on a balance of probabilities that he lacked *mens rea and* was not negligent; i.e., that he had an honest *and reasonable* belief in a state of facts which, had it existed, would have made his act innocent.

(iii) D might be convicted without proof of any *mens rea* by the Crown, unless he tendered credible evidence of an honest and reasonable belief in a state of facts which, had it existed, would have made his act innocent; in which case, the onus would lie with the Crown to prove beyond reasonable doubt that he had no such honest belief or that his belief was not reasonable.

The first view finds support in numerous *dicta* to the effect that, where a section uses the word "knowingly", the onus of proving knowledge is on the Crown, but that where it does not do so, D may clear himself by proving that he had no *mens rea*.[14] This view has, however, been disapproved[15] on a number of occasions, particularly in recent times by the Privy Council[16] and by Lord Pearce.[17] Lord Reid, however, looked favourably upon it in *Sweet v Parsley*.

A "halfway house" has developed in Australia. There are two opinions as to the effect of the Australian cases, corresponding to views (ii) and (iii) above. The view which has been most strongly pressed[18] is (ii) – that the onus of proving reasonable mistake is on D. According to view (iii),[19] D bears only an evidential burden and, when he has introduced some evidence of mistake, the onus of proof is with the Crown.

In *Sweet v Parsley*, Lord Reid[20] seems to have contemplated all three approaches as possible improvements on unmitigated strict liability, but to have thought that *Woolmington*[1] would be an obstacle to the implementation of (i) or (ii). Lords Pearce[2] and Diplock[3] looked with approval on the Australian doctrine; but Lord Diplock, relying on the remarks of Dixon J in the leading case of *Proudman v Dayman*[4] (in fact equivocal on this point),

---

14. *Banks* (1794) 1 Esp 144 (Lord Kenyon); *Prince* (1875) LR 2 CCR 154 at 161–2 (Brett J); *Sherras v De Rutzen* [1895] 1 QB 918 at 921 (Day J); *Harding v Price* [1948] 1 KB 695 at 700, [1948] 1 All ER 283 at 284 (Goddard LCJ); *Reynolds v G. H. Austin & Sons Ltd* [1951] 2 KB 135 at 145, [1951] 1 All ER 606 at 609 (Goddard LCJ).
15. *Roper v Taylor's Central Garages* [1951] 2 TLR 284 (Devlin J).
16. *Lim Chin Aik v R* [1963] AC 160 at 173.
17. *Warner* [1969] 2 AC 256 at 303, [1968] 2 All ER 356 at 386.
18. By Howard, "Strict Responsibility in the High Court of Australia" (1960) 76 LQR 547. Campbell, *NZ Essays* 1, at 16; Orchard in *Criminal Law Essays*, 114.
19. Which is Sir F. Adams' opinion of the Australian doctrine: *NZ Essays* 67, at p. 80 and is supported by *Kidd v Reeves* [1972] VR 563; *Mayer v Marchant* (1973) 5 SASR 567.
20. [1970] AC at 150.
1. Above, p. 28.
2. At p. 158.
3. At p. 164.
4. (1941) 67 CLR 536 at 541.

thought that it represented view (iii). Lord Diplock's opinion involves none of the difficulties with *Woolmington* which Lord Pearce naturally encountered and is preferable in principle. It has been followed by the Court of Appeal in New Zealand.[5] View (iii), it is submitted, has much to commend it; but it was studiously ignored in *Alphacell*[6] and we are still a long way from any replacement by judicial decision of strict liability in English law.

5 Statutory Defences

It is common for the drastic effect of a statute imposing strict liability to be mitigated by the provision of a statutory defence. It is instructive to consider one example. Various offences relating to the treatment and sale of food are enacted by the first twenty sections of the Food Safety Act 1990. Many, if not all, of these are strict liability offences. Section 21 (1), however, provides that it shall be a defence for the person charged with any of the offences to prove that he took all reasonable precautions and exercised all due diligence to avoid the commission of the offence by himself or by a person under his control; but, (s. 21 (5)), where this defence involves an allegation that the offence was due to the act or default of another person, the defendant may not, without the leave of the court, rely on it unless within a prescribed period he has served on the prosecutor a notice in writing giving such information identifying or assisting in the identification of the other person as was then in his possession.

The section goes on to provide for ways in which the defence may be established by a person who neither prepared the food in question nor imported it into Great Britain. In respect of offences under s. 8 (selling food not complying with food safety requirements), s. 14 (selling food not of the nature or substance or quality demanded) and s. 15 (falsely describing or presenting food) such a person is taken to have established the defence under subsection (1) if he satisfies the requirements of subsection (3) or (4):

"(3) A person satisfies the requirements of this subsection if he proves –
(a) that the commission of the offence was due to an act or default of another person who was not under his control, or to reliance on information supplied by such a person;
(b) that he carried out all such checks of the food in question as were reasonable in all the circumstances, or that it was reasonable in all the circumstances for him to rely on checks carried out by the person who supplied the food to him; and
(c) that he did not know and had no reason to suspect at the time of the commission of the alleged offence that his act or omission would amount to an offence under the relevant provision.
(4) A person satisfies the requirements of this subsection if he proves –
(a) that the commission of the offence was due to an act or default of

---

5. *Strawbridge* [1970] NZLR 909 at 916.
6. Above, p. 113.

another person who was not under his control, or to reliance on information supplied by such a person;

(b) that the sale or intended sale of which the alleged offence consisted was not a sale or intended sale under his name or mark; and

(c) that he did not know, and could not reasonably have been expected to know, at the time of the commission of the alleged offence that his act or omission would amount to an offence under the relevant provision."

So if a shopkeeper sells a toffee with a nail in it and is charged with selling food not of the nature or substance or quality demanded,[7] contrary to s. 14, he must satisfy the court that he took whatever precautions a shopkeeper can reasonably be expected to take to avoid such an event and, as this defence apparently alleges that the offence was due to the act or default of the manufacturer, he must have served the required notice on the prosecutor. He may then rely on subsection (3) and, if he can prove the three matters stated in the subsection on the balance of probabilities, the defence is made out. Though the requirements look formidable, this might not be too difficult in this particular example. (a) *Someone* not under the defendant's control was responsible for letting the nail get into the toffee and the defendant is not apparently required to identify the defaulter; (b) a shopkeeper cannot reasonably be expected to unwrap and dissect the toffees he sells; and (c) if the manufacturer is reputable and does not have a record of selling sweets containing foreign bodies, he had no reason to suspect it on this occasion. There may be other circumstances in which it is not so easy to get over the three hurdles but, as subsections (2) to (4) are without prejudice to the generality of the defence under subsection (1), it is open to the defendant to satisfy the court in any other way that, as a matter of fact, he took all reasonable precautions and exercised all due diligence. If he prepared or imported the food, he must do this anyway.

This defence substantially mitigates the requirements of earlier legislation under which the shopkeeper would have had to bring the manufacturer before the court and prove, presumably beyond reasonable doubt, that the offence was due to his act or default. The manufacturer was then strictly liable, however diligent he might have been.[8] He would still be liable to conviction because, by s. 20 of the 1990 Act –

"Where the commission by any person of an offence under any of the preceding provisions of this Part is due to act or default of some other person, that other person shall be guilty of the offence . . ."

– but he might now rely on the defence of due diligence provided by s. 21.

The new section might also provide a defence in another notorious case. In *Parker v Alder*[9] a milk salesman, in pursuance of a contract of sale, delivered some milk in a pure and unadulterated condition to a railway station for carriage to London. Under this contract the ownership in the milk passed when it was delivered in London. When delivered it was found to be adulterated. Some unknown person had added 9% of water. The unlucky defendant, without any fault on his part, had sold adulterated milk and was

---

7. Cf *Lindley v G. W. Horner & Co Ltd* [1950] 1 All ER 234.
8. *Lindley v G. W. Horner & Co Ltd*, supra.
9. [1899] 1 QB 20.

convicted of an offence which is now replaced by s. 14 of the 1990 Act. Statutory defences provided in subsequent food legislation would not have helped him because they required him to identify the person to whose act or default the contravention was due, and that he plainly could not do. Now the only requirements are that he supply such information as is in his possession and prove that he took all reasonable precautions, etc.

Statutory defences do not always take such a complicated form. But they usually impose on the defendant a burden of proving both that he had no *mens rea* and that he took all reasonable precautions and exercised all due diligence to avoid the commission of an offence. Thus one who sells feeding stuffs containing deleterious ingredients is liable even if he proves that the commission of the offence was due to a mistake or an accident or some other cause beyond his control unless he also proves that he took all reasonable precautions, etc.[10] The effect of such provisions is that the prosecution need do no more than prove that the accused did the prohibited act and it is then for him to establish, if he can, that he did it innocently. Such provisions are a distinct advance on unmitigated strict liability; but they are still a deviation from the fundamental principle that the prosecution must prove the whole of their case; and an extensive use of offences of strict liability, even when so qualified, is to be deplored.

6 Proposals for Reform

The Law Commission proposed[11] a Criminal Liability (Mental Element) Bill, now incorporated in the draft Criminal Code,[12] which would provide a definition of intention, knowledge and recklessness[13] and establish a presumption for offences created after the passing of the Bill that intention, knowledge or recklessness should be required as to all the elements of the offence.[14] The onus would then be on Parliament, if it wished to create an offence requiring a lesser degree of *mens rea* or an offence of negligence or strict liability, to make this clear in the enactment. It is Parliament's responsibility to decide the nature of criminal liability. It is better that Parliament should have an actual intention in the matter, rather than a purely mythical one, attributed to it, perhaps many years later, in the haphazard manner inevitably associated with the accidents of litigation.

---

10. Agriculture Act 1970, ss. 73 and 82. See too Weights and Measures Act 1985, s. 34; Trade Descriptions Act 1968, s 24. Post Office Act 1953, s. 63 (1). The provision of a statutory defence may be an indication to the court that an offence of strict liability is intended. Cf. Sexual Offences Act 1956, s. 6, below, p. 462, and Obscene Publications Act 1959, s. 2 (5), below, p. 742.
11. Law Com. No. 89 (1978).
12. Cl. 20, "General requirements of fault", Law Com. No. 177. See pp. 195–196.
13. Above, pp. 53 and 61.
14. Law Com. No. 89 (1978). See also Law Com. Working Paper No. 31.

7 Parties to Crime

1 Accomplices[1]

The person who directly and immediately causes the *actus reus* of a crime is not necessarily the only one who is criminally liable for it. By the Accessories and Abettors Act 1861, s. 8 as amended by the Criminal Law Act 1977:

"Whosoever shall aid, abet, counsel or procure the commission of any indictable offence whether the same be an offence at common law or by virtue of any act passed or to be passed, shall be liable to be tried, indicted and punished as a principal offender."[2]

The effect of s. 1 of the Criminal Law Act 1967[3] is that this provision is now applicable to all offences whether they were formerly felonies or misdemeanours. Those who aid, abet, counsel or procure the commission of an offence are conveniently designated "secondary parties." Secondary liability is derivative; i.e., it derives from the liability of the principal.

"when the law relating to principals and accessories as such is under consideration there is only one crime, although there may be more than one person criminally liable in respect of it ... There is one crime and that it has been committed must be established before there can be any question of criminal guilt of participation in it ..."[4]

The common law of felonies designated the actual perpetrator "the principal in the first degree" and distinguished secondary parties into principals in the second degree – those who participated at the time when the felony was actually perpetrated – and accessories before the fact – those who participated at an earlier time.[5] The abolition of felonies has made no change of substance. No one became liable to conviction, as a result of this reform, who was not liable before it; and no one is exempt from liability

---

1. See generally K.J.M. Smith, *A Modern Treatise on Complicity* (1991).

2. Similar provisions relating to summary trial are to be found in the Magistrates' Courts Act 1980, s. 44.

3. Above p. 26. For proposals for further reform of the law, see Law Commission Working Paper No. 43 and Draft Code, cll. 25–28, Report, Part 9.

4. Russell 128, approved in *Surujpaul v R* [1958] 3 All ER 300 at 301, PC.

5. It was traditional to state that the distinction was that the principal in the second degree was *present* at the commission of the offence; but in fact he might be a considerable distance away – in an American case (*State v Hamilton and Lawrie* 13 Nev 386 (1878) – signals from mountain top), 30–40 miles, so long as he was assisting or available to assist, at the time. Hawkins 2 PC c. 29, ss. 7 and 8; Foster 350.

who was not exempt before. The modes of participation in crime which the law recognises are unchanged.

Notwithstanding the abolition of felonies it continues to be necessary for certain purposes to distinguish the "principal in the first degree" (hereafter, "principal") from secondary participants:

(i) in the case of all offences of strict liability for, even in these cases, secondary parties must be proved to have *mens rea*;[6]

(ii) in all cases where the offence is so defined that it can be committed as a principal in the first degree only by a member of a specified class (e.g. the holder of a justices' licence);[7]

(iii) where vicarious liability is in issue. In some offences vicarious liability may be imposed for the act of another who is a principal or does the act of a principal; but there is no vicarious liability for the act of a secondary party.[8]

The old cases on participation in felonies remain valid authorities on the limits of criminal liability. To be liable, a person who is not the principal must be proved to have aided, abetted, counselled or procured, though it is quite sufficient to show that he did one of these things. All four expressions imply the commission of the offence. "Counselling" must not be taken literally. Mere incitement to commit an offence, not followed by its actual commission, is not "counselling".[9] Secondary parties are liable when and where the offence aided, abetted, counselled or procured is committed. So an employer who sends a lorry, which he knows to be in a dangerous condition, from Scotland to England may be held liable in England for a death caused here because of the lorry's condition.[10]

The law of secondary parties is applicable to all offences, unless expressly or impliedly excluded. It is possible that it is impliedly excluded where statute creates offences of "using or causing or permitting to be used."[11] Occasionally, aiding, etc., is made the principal offence.[12]

1 The Principal

Where there are several participants in a crime the principal is the one whose act is the most immediate cause of the *actus reus*. In murder, for example, he is the man who, with *mens rea*, fires the gun or administers the poison which causes death; in theft, the man, who, with *mens rea*, appropriates the thing which is stolen; in bigamy, the person who, knowing himself to be already married, goes through a second ceremony of marriage; and so on. The *actus reus* may be directly brought about by the act of someone who is not a participant in the crime at all (that is, who has no *mens*

---

6. Below, p. 138. In road traffic offences, where disqualification of the principal is obligatory, disqualification of secondary parties is discretionary: Road Traffic Offenders Act 1988, s. 34 (5).

7. Below, p. 152.

8. Below, p. 177.

9. *Assistant Recorder of Kingston-upon-Hull, ex parte Morgan* [1969] 2 QB 58, [1969] 1 All ER 416, DC.

10. *Robert Millar (Contractors) Ltd* [1970] 2 QB 54, [1970] 1 All ER 577, below, p. 000.

11. *Carmichael & Sons (Worcester) Ltd v Cottle* [1971] RTR 11. Cf. *Farr* [1982] Crim LR 745, CA, and commentary.

12. See Suicide Act 1961, below, p. 379.

rea, or who has some defence, such as infancy or insanity). Such a person is usually described as an "innocent agent" and, in such a case, the principal is the participant in the crime whose act is the most immediate cause of the innocent agent's act. If D sends through the post a letter-bomb to P who is injured by the explosion, the postman who delivers the letter is an innocent agent. So if D, intending to kill P, gives to P's daughter a poison which, he says, will cure P's cold, and she innocently administers the poison, causing P's death, then D is guilty as the principal offender.[13] If the daughter had had *mens rea* then she would, of course, have been the principal. Where D, a collector of money, makes a false statement to his employer's book-keeper, knowing that the statement will be entered in the books, and it is so entered by the innocent book-keeper, D is guilty, as a principal, of falsifying his employer's accounts.[14] Where D dishonestly sets in motion a chain of actions by innocent fellow-employees which he intends to result, and which does result, in his employer's account being debited he may be guilty of theft of the thing in action represented by the bank balance.[15] Where D induces a child, aged eleven, to take money from a till and give it to D, D is a principal only if the child is exempt from criminal liability which, in the case of a child of that age, depends on whether he knows the act is wrong.[16] If the child does know his act is wrong, then he is the principal and D is a secondary party.[17]

There are some crimes to which the doctrine of innocent agency is inapplicable because it is impossible to say that D has personally committed the *actus reus*.[18] Bigamy – except in the case of a marriage by proxy – is the clearest example. Compare it with murder. If D causes an innocent person, E, to kill P, it is right for the law to take the view that *D has killed P* – the *actus reus* of murder; but if D induces E, an innocent person, to go through a marriage with F, which D knows to be bigamous, it is impossible to say that *D has married during the lifetime of his wife* – the *actus reus* of bigamy. He has not done so. In the same category, it is submitted, are rape and other crimes involving sexual intercourse and the *dicta* in *Cogan and Leak*[19] that rape may be committed through an innocent agent are contrary to principle.

It is, of course, perfectly possible to have two or more principals in the first degree in the same crime. If D1 and D2 make an attack on P intending to murder him and the combined effect of their blows is to kill him, plainly both are guilty of murder[20] as joint principals.

---

13. *Anon* (1634), Kel 53; *Michael* (1840) 9 C & P 356; below, p. 344.
14. *Butt* (1884) 15 Cox CC 564.
15. *Stringer and Banks* [1991] Crim LR 639.
16. See below, p. 189. And see *Tyler* (1838) 8 C & P 616 (liability for act of lunatic).
17. *Manley* (1844) 1 Cox CC 104. The child was actually nine. A child under ten is now incapable of crime, so D would be the principal whether the nine-year-old knew the act was wrong or not. See also *Mazeau* (1840) 9 C & P 676.
18. Cf. *Woby v B and O* [1986] Crim LR 183, DC (boys under 18 not guilty of *buying intoxicating liquor in licensed premises* when they sent in an adult to buy it).
19. [1976] QB 217, [1975] 2 All ER 1059, [1975] Crim LR 584 and commentary thereon; below, p. 153. Cf. burglary, below, p. 616.
20. *Macklin and Murphy's* case (1838) 2 Lew CC 225; *Bingley* (1821) Russ & Ry 446 (A and B each forged part of a banknote).

What is the position when the principal himself is not present at the moment of the completion of the crime? If two or more persons conspire to employ an innocent agent both are liable as principals for the agent's acts and it is immaterial that the agent was instructed by the one in the absence of the other. The innocent agent's acts are considered the acts of both conspirators.[1] Where there is no innocent agent, the same considerations cannot apply. D1, in pursuance of an agreement with D2, leaves poison to be taken by P, or sets a trap into which P falls. It is thought that D2 will be liable as a secondary party.

The distinction between a joint principal and an abettor will sometimes be difficult to make. Generally it is immaterial in which capacity D2 is alleged to have participated in the crime. When it is necessary to distinguish, the test would seem to be: did D2 by his own act (as distinct from anything done by D1 with D2's advice or assistance) contribute to the causation of the *actus reus*? Where the *actus* is a "state of affairs",[2] the test is: ignoring D1, does the statutory description of the state of affairs fit D2?

2 Secondary Participation

In *Attorney General's Reference (No. 1 of 1975)* Lord Widgery CJ said:

"We approach s. 8 of the 1861 Act on the basis that the words should be given their ordinary meaning, if possible. We approach the section on the basis also that if four words are employed here 'aid, abet, counsel or procure', the probability is that there is a difference between each of those four words and the other three, because, if there were no such difference, then Parliament would be wasting time in using four words where two or three would do."[3]

The four words had previously been regarded as technical terms and it is clear that they cannot be given their ordinary meaning in all respects. It has sometimes been said[4] that "aid and abet" is a single concept, "aid" denoting the *actus reus* and "abet" the *mens rea*. The natural meaning of s. 8 is however that stated in *A-G's Reference*. Moreover the words do connote a different kind of activity. The natural meaning of "to aid" is to "give help, support or assistance to"; and of "to abet", "to incite, instigate or encourage".[5] It is entirely clear that either type of activity is sufficient to found liability as a secondary party. "Abet", so defined, seems indistinguishable from "counsel". Perhaps there is no difference except that at common law "abet" connoted incitement at the time of the offence and "counsel" incitement at an earlier time. Participation in a conspiracy to commit an offence amounts to counselling if the offence is actually committed.[6]

1. *Bull and Schmidt* (1845) 1 Cox CC 281.
2. Above, p. 43.
3. [1975] 2 All ER 684 at 686.
4. *Lynch v Director of Public Prosecutions for Northern Ireland* [1975] 1 All ER 913 at 941, per Lord Simon quoting the third edition of this work and Devlin J in *National Coal Board v Gamble* [1959] 1 QB 11 at 20; **SHC 160**.
5. Oxford English Dictionary.
6. Stephen, *Digest of the Criminal Law* (9th ed.), Article 28; Williams, CLGP, 363; *Pinkerton v US* (1946) 328 US 640. See, however, Lanham, "Complicity, Concert and Conspiracy" [1980] 4 Crim LJ 276. Secondary participation in a conspiracy (if there is such a thing – see *Crime, Proof and Punishment* at 28–29) might not lead to liability for the ulterior offence.

All four words may be used together to charge a person who is alleged to have participated in an offence otherwise than as a principal in the first degree.[7] So long as the evidence establishes that D's conduct satisfied one of the words, that is enough.

It has also been said that "aiding and abetting" described the activity of the principal in the second degree and "counselling and procuring" that of the accessory.[8] Where it is necessary to distinguish between them, "abet" and "counsel" will be used henceforth to describe the two types of secondary participation. "Aid and abet" has however sometimes been used in relation to acts committed before the actual perpetration of the crime. If we are to have regard to the natural meaning of the words instead of regarding them as technical terms, this is desirable because some such acts are not very happily described either as counselling or as procuring though they merit criminal liability.

3 Secondary Parties: Causation and Consensus

"To procure means to produce by endeavour."[9] "You cannot procure an offence unless there is a causal link between what you do and the commission of the offence."[10] In *A-G's Reference* D2 who had added alcohol to D1's drink without D1's knowledge or consent was held to have procured D1's offence of driving with a blood/alcohol concentration above the prescribed limit[11] if it was proved that D2 knew that D1 was going to drive and that the ordinary and natural result of the added alcohol would be to bring D1's blood/alcohol concentration above the prescribed limit. D2 had caused the commission of the offence. This is in accordance with the natural meaning of "procure".[12] The natural meaning of "abet" and "counsel" on the other hand does not imply any causal element because, unlike "procure", these words do not even imply that the offence has been committed. Instigation, incitement, encouragement, counselling, may all be unsuccessful and they have occurred no less because the offence is not committed. Of course, the law is that the offence must have been committed before anyone can be convicted as an abettor or counsellor of it; but, when the offence has been committed, it is certainly still true to say that D2 "counselled" it, in the ordinary meaning of the word, even if his counsel was ignored by D1; and the same seems to be true of abetting. There is nevertheless the high authority of Stephen for the view that one who counsels or commands (as well as procures) is liable and, by implication liable only, for an offence "which is committed *in consequence* of such counselling, procuring, or commandment".[13] It is clearly the law that an attempt to counsel does not amount to counselling. Proffered advice or

7. *Re Smith* (1858) 3 H & N 227; *Ferguson v Weaving* [1951] 1 KB 814, [1951] 1 All ER 412.
8. *Ferguson v Weaving*, above, at 818–819; **SHC 158**, Stephen, *Digest* (4th ed.), Articles 37–39. *Bowker v Premier Drug Co Ltd* [1928] 1 KB 217 ("aid and abet" implies presence).
9. *A-G's Reference (No. 1 of 1975)* [1975] 2 All ER 684 at 686; **SHC 148**; *Reed* [1982] Crim LR 819. See K.J.M. Smith, "Complicity and Causation" [1986] Crim LR 663; Beynon, "Causation, Omissions and Complicity", [1987] Crim LR 539.
10. Ibid., at 687.
11. Road Traffic Act 1972, s. 6(1); now replaced by Road Traffic Act 1988, s. 5.
12. Cf. Glazebrook "Attempting to Procure" [1959] Crim LR 774.
13. Stephen, *Digest* (4th ed.) Art. 39.

encouragement which has no effect on the mind of the principal offender is not counselling.[14] This is not to say that the counselling must be a cause of the commission of the offence. So to require would be to insist that, but for the counselling, the offence would not have been committed.[15] This would confine counselling (and abetting) much too narrowly. If it were incumbent on the prosecution to prove that the offence would not have been committed but for D2's advice or encouragement it seems safe to say that the point would figure much more prominently in the law reports. On the contrary, the facts of many cases where D2 has been held liable suggest that the offence would have been committed whether he had participated or not and no one seems to have suggested that this should be a defence. There must, however, be some connection between the counselling and the commission of the offence. It is probably not necessary to prove that D1 was influenced in any way by D2 but he must at least be aware that he has the authority, or the encouragement, or the approval, of D2 to do the relevant acts.

"For example, if the principal offender happened to be involved in a football riot in the course of which he laid about him with a weapon of some sort and killed someone who, unknown to him, was the person whom he had been counselled to kill, he would not, in our view, have been acting within the scope of his authority; he would have been acting outside it, albeit what he had done was what he had been counselled to do."[16]

What has been said of counselling applies to abetting.[17] Aiding, likewise, does not imply any causal connection. D2 may come to the assistance of D1 and enable him to commit the offence more easily, earlier, or with greater safety and, if so, he is surely guilty even if the same offence would have been committed if he had not intervened.[18]

In *A-G's Reference (No. 1 of 1975)* D2's act of procuring was done without the knowledge or consent, and perhaps against the will, of D1. The case decides that this is immaterial where "procuring" is relied on. It was suggested that it might be different in the case of aiding, abetting and counselling – that these concepts might require a meeting of minds of secondary party and principal. If counselling and abetting must be operative, as suggested above, this is clearly right. The same does not seem necessarily to follow in the case of aiding, however. If D2 sees D1 committing a crime and comes to his assistance by, for example, restraining the policeman who would have prevented D1 from committing the crime, D2 is surely guilty even though his assistance is unforeseen and unwanted by D1 and unknown to him. The same might apply to aid given beforehand. D2, knowing that D1 is going to meet a blackmailer, P, slips a gun into D1's pocket in the hope that he will kill P – which he does.

To sum up – the law probably is that:

(i) "procuring" implies causation but not consensus;

---

14. *Clarkson* [1971] 3 All ER 344, [1971] 1 WLR 1402 (C–MAC); **SHC 167.**
15. ". . . it does not make any difference that the person [*sc.*, the person counselled] would have tried to commit suicide anyway": *A-G v Able* [1984] 1 All ER 277 at 288, per Woolf J.
16. *Calhaem* [1985] QB 808, [1985] 2 All ER 266, CA, per Parker LJ.
17. See e.g. *Wilcox v Jeffery*; **SHC 167**; below, p. 131; *Du Cros v Lambourne*, below, p. 132.
18. See Le Fave and Scott, *Criminal Law*, 504.

(ii) "abetting" and "counselling" imply consensus but not causation;
(iii) "aiding" requires actual assistance but neither consensus nor causation.

a) *How many modes of participation?* These terminological difficulties complicate the statement of the law. The Draft Code uses the terms "procures, assists or encourages" to describe the whole of the activities which amount to secondary participation. It has been suggested[19] that in substance there are only two kinds of action involved – "intentionally influencing the decision of the primary party to commit the crime and intentionally helping the primary actor to commit the crime". But this does not seem to cover a case like the *A-G's Reference*,[20] where the principal is strictly liable. D2 "procured" D1 to drive with excess alcohol by secretly lacing D1's drink. There was no "decision of the primary party to commit the crime"; and "helping the primary actor to commit the crime" also seems to imply that the purpose of the primary actor is to commit the crime, which was not so. If that kind of case is to be covered, the notion of procuring must also be included.

b) *Causation and commission of the offence as a principal.* If a procurer were taken to have caused the commission of the offence for all purposes he would become a principal. If D2, having procured D1 to murder P, were taken to have caused P's death, i.e., killed P, he would satisfy the definition of murder as a principal. Anyone whose assistance or encouragement in fact caused another to commit a crime would be a principal. The separate body of law of accessory liability is based on the assumption that the accessory does not cause the *actus reus*.[1]

The Draft Code, cl. 17 (3), according provides:

"A person who procures, assists or encourages another to cause a result that is an element of an offence does not himself cause that result so as to be guilty of the offence as a principal except when—
(a) section 26 (1) (c) [innocent agency] applies; or
(b) the offence itself consists in the procuring, assisting or encouraging another to cause the result."

A procurer of an innocent agent to commit a crime is taken to have caused the *actus reus* for all purposes. An alleged procurer of a guilty agent must be proved to have in fact caused the act of the guilty agent; but, in law, he is not regarded as having caused the *actus reus*.

c) *Is causing "procuring"?* Glanville Williams writes of the *A-G's Reference* that "in so far as [it] purports to decide that merely causing an offence can be said to be a procuring of it, it should be regarded as too incautious a generalisation". He quotes *Beatty v Gillbanks*[2] where it was held that the Salvation Army was acting lawfully in holding its meeting in

---

19. Kadish, Essays, 151, supported by Glanville Williams, [1990] Crim LR 7, [1991] Crim LR 930.
20. Above, p. 127.
1. Hart and Honoré, *Causation in the Law* (2nd ed.), 380; Kadish, *Essays*, 143–144.
2. (1882) 9 QBD 308; TBCL 339.

Weston-super-Mare although its officers knew from experience that this would cause a hostile organisation, the Skeleton Army, to attack them. It would be absurd to hold that the Salvationists were liable as secondary parties for the attack on themselves, but they might have known that the attack would result in damage to others, e.g. broken shop windows. There are two possible answers to this criticism: (i) Lord Widgery did not say that "procure" means merely "cause". He said "To procure means to produce by endeavour". The Salvationists may have caused the Skeletons to make the attack (and to break the supposed windows) but these were certainly not results that they were endeavouring to produce. Against this, it might be said that in *A-G's Reference* D's awareness that he was causing the commission of the offence also fell short of proof of an endeavour to cause it; and in *Blakely*[3] the court thought that D2 "procured" a result if he contemplated it as a possible result of his act – which is far removed from endeavouring to produce it. (ii) The Skeletons knew exactly what they were doing and in *A-G's Reference* Lord Widgery made it clear the decision would not necessarily be the same where a driver knew that his drink was laced. The unaware driver "in most instances . . . would have no means of preventing the offence from being committed", the aware driver would. Lord Widgery thus contemplated that the act of the aware driver might break the chain of causation, even for the purposes of secondary liability.

4 The Time Factor

Assistance given before the offence is committed will ground liability so it is only as regards the conclusion of the offence that time becomes important. Assistance given when the principal is no longer in the course of the commission of the offence – to enable him to escape or to reap the benefits of the commission of the offence – does not amount to abetting. Where D1 broke into a warehouse, stole butter and deposited it in the street thirty yards from the warehouse door, D2 who came to assist in carrying it off was held not guilty of abetting in larceny.[4] Assistance given to a murderer, after his victim is dead, to a rapist after the act of intercourse has concluded,[5] or to a bigamist after the second ceremony of marriage, cannot ground liability for the crime in question. One who, without any pre-arranged plan, joins in an attack on P after P has received a fatal injury, is not guilty of homicide (though he may be guilty of an attempt) if his action in no way contributes to P's subsequent death.[6]

5 Presence at the Crime

A person is not guilty merely because he is present at the scene of a crime and does nothing to prevent it.[7] To continue to sit beside the driver of a car

---

3. Below, p. 137.
4. *King* (1817) Russ & Ry 332; see also *Kelly* (1820) Russ & Ry 421.
5. The act does not conclude at the instant of penetration but continues at least as long as the penetration: *Mayberry* [1973] Qd R 211 at 229, (Skerman J, dissenting, p. 286, on this issue); *Kaitamaki* [1985] AC 147, [1984] 2 All ER 435.
6. *S v Thomo* 1969 (1) SA 385 (AD); Burchell & Hunt, 352.
7. *Atkinson* (1869) 11 Cox CC 330; but it is an offence to refuse to assist a constable to suppress a breach of the peace when called upon to do so: *Brown* (1841) Car & M 314.

until the end of a journey after learning that he is uninsured does not amount to abetting his uninsured driving.[8] Continuing to share a room with a person known to be in unlawful possession of drugs is not evidence of abetting, unless encouragement or control is proved.[9] If prohibited drugs, found in a van belonging to a party of tourists, are the property of and under the exclusive control of one of them, the others are not guilty of abetting simply because they are present and know of the existence of the drugs.[10] The abettor must either (i) be present in pursuance of an agreement that the crime be committed or (ii) give assistance or encouragement in its commission. Both assistance or encouragement in fact and an intention to assist or encourage must be proved.[11] When this is proved, it is immaterial that D joined in the offence without any prior agreement.[12] In *Allan*[13] it was held that one who remains present at an affray, nursing a secret intention to help if the need arises but doing nothing to evince that intention, does not thereby become an abettor. Where two drivers, without any previous arrangement between them, enter into competitive driving on the highway so as knowingly to encourage each other to drive at a dangerous speed or in a dangerous manner, the one is liable as a secondary party for a death or other criminal result caused by the other.[14] In the leading case of *Coney*[15] it was held that proof of mere voluntary presence at a prize-fight, without more, is, at the most, only prima facie and not conclusive evidence of abetting the battery of which the contestants are guilty. Presence at such an event is certainly capable of amounting to an actual encouragement. If there were no spectators there would be no fight and, therefore, each spectator, by his presence, contributes to the incentive to the contestants. As Matthew J (dissenting) said:[16]

"The chief incentive to the wretched combatants to fight on until (as happens too often) dreadful injuries have been inflicted and life endangered or sacrificed, is the presence of spectators watching with keen interest every incident of the fight."

Voluntary presence at such an event, then, is some evidence on which a jury might find that the accused was there with the intention of encouraging the fight. Coney's conviction was quashed because the majority of the court thought that the chairman's direction was capable of being understood to mean that voluntary presence was *conclusive* evidence of an intention to encourage. If the direction had made it clear that presence was prima facie evidence only, no doubt the conviction would have been sustained. So in *Wilcox v Jeffrey*[17] it was held that D's presence at a public performance by

8. *Smith v Baker* [1971] RTR 350.
9. *Bland* [1988] Crim LR 41.
10. *Searle* [1971] Crim LR 592 and commentary thereon.
11. *Clarkson* [1971] 3 All ER 344, [1971] 1 WLR 1402; **SHC 167**; *Jones and Mirrless* (1977) 65 Cr App Rep 250, CA.
12. *Rannath Mohan v R* [1967] 2 AC 187, [1967] 2 All ER 58.
13. [1965] 1 QB 130, [1963] 2 All ER 897; **SHC 166**; see also *Tansley v Painter* (1968) 112 Sol Jo 1005.
14. *Turner* [1991] Crim LR 57 and commentary. Williams, TBCL 362, thinks otherwise, citing *Mastin* (1834) 6 C & P 396.
15. (1882) 8 QBD 534.
16. Ibid., at p. 544.
17. [1951] 1 All ER 464; **SHC 167**.

H, a celebrated alien performer on the saxophone, who had been given permission to land only on condition that he would take no employment, was a sufficient aiding and abetting of H in his contravention of the Aliens Order 1920. D's behaviour before and after the performance supplied further evidence of his intention to encourage; for he had met H at the airport and he afterwards reported the performance in laudatory terms in the periodical of which he was the proprietor.

Where the evidence establishes mere presence without any positive act, a prior agreement that the crime be committed must be proved. But if some positive act of assistance or encouragement is voluntarily done, with knowledge of the circumstances constituting the offence, it is irrelevant that it is not done with the motive or purpose of encouraging the crime.[18] So if D2 handed a gun to D1 knowing that D1 intended to shoot P, it would not avail D2 to say that he hoped that D1 would not use the gun.[19]

6 Participation by Inactivity

Where D has a right to control the actions of another and he deliberately refrains from exercising it, his inactivity may be a positive encouragement to the other to perform an illegal act, and, therefore, an aiding and abetting. A husband who stands by and watches his wife drown their children is guilty of abetting the homicide. His deliberate abstention from action gives encouragement and authority to his wife's act.[20] If a licensee of a public house stands by and watches his customers drinking after hours, he is guilty of aiding and abetting them in doing so.[1] Again in *Du Cros v Lambourne*,[2] it was proved that D's car had been driven at a dangerous speed but it was not proved whether D or E was driving. It was held that, nevertheless, D could be convicted. If E was driving she was doing so in D's presence, with his consent and approval; for he was in control and could and ought to have prevented her from driving in a dangerous manner. D was equally liable whether he was a principal or an abettor.[3] The result would presumably have been different if it had been E's own car, for D would then have had no right of control, and could only have been convicted if active instigation to drive at such speed had been proved. In such cases it must be proved that D2 knew of those features of D1's driving which rendered it dangerous and failed to take action within a reasonable time.[4] In *Baldessare*,[5] D1 and D2 unlawfully took X's car and D1 drove it recklessly and caused P's death. It was held that D2 was guilty of manslaughter as an abettor. In this case (as prosecuting counsel put it)

---

18. *National Coal Board v Gamble* [1959] 1 QB 11, [1958] 3 All ER 203; **SHC 167**; below, p. 134.
19. Cf., however, *Fretwell* (1864) Le & Ca 443; below, p. 135.
20. *Russell* [1933] VLR 59.
   1. *Tuck v Robson* [1970] 1 All ER 1171, [1970] 1 WLR 741, DC.
   2. [1907] 1 KB 40; cf. also *Rubie v Faulkner* [1940] 1 KB 571, [1940] 1 All ER 285; *Harris* [1964] Crim LR 54.
   3. Cf. *Swindall and Osborne* (1846) 2 Car & Kir 230: *Salmon* (1880) 6 QBD 79; *Iremonger v Wynne* [1957] Crim LR 624; Williams, CLGP 137, n. 23. There is, however, a difference regarding disqualification; above, p. 124, fn. 6. *Smith v Mellors* [1987] Crim LR 421.
   4. *Dennis v Pight* (1968) 11 FLR 458 at 463.
   5. (1930) 22 Cr App Rep 70.

"The common purpose to drive recklessly was . . . shown by the fact that both men were driving in a car which did not belong to them and the jury were entitled to infer that the driver was the agent of the passenger. It matters not whose hand was actually controlling the car at the time."

If, however, all that can be proved is that the offence was committed either by D1 or by D2, both must be acquitted.[6] Only if it can be proved that the one who did not commit the crime must have aided and abetted it can both be convicted.[7] This is as true where parents are charged with injury to their child as it is in the case of any other defendants. The only difference is that one parent may have a duty to intervene to prevent the ill-treatment of their child by the other when a stranger would have no such duty. It is for the prosecution to prove that the parent who did not inflict the injuries must have aided and abetted the infliction by failure to fulfil that duty or otherwise.

One whose participation in the relevant events does not involve advice or encouragement to commit the crime, and who does not assist the commission in any way, is not liable. Accepting a lift on a motor-cycle known to have been taken without consent does not amount to aiding and abetting the use of the vehicle without insurance.[8] It would have been different if the taking had been a joint enterprise.[9]

7 Mens rea

a) *Intention to aid, etc.* It must be proved that D intended to do the acts which he knew to be capable of assisting or encouraging the commission of the crime. That is not the same thing as an intention that the crime be committed. As Devlin J said:[10]

"If one man deliberately sells to another a gun to be used for murdering a third, he may be indifferent whether the third man lives or dies and interested only in the cash profit to be made out of the sale, but he can still be an aider and abettor."

So it is the intention to do the acts of assistance or encouragement which must be proved. If D has that intention it is no defence that his motives were unimpeachable.[11] In *Lynch v Director of Public Prosecutions for Northern Ireland*, where D2 drove D1 to the place where he knew that D1 intended to murder a policeman, D2's intentional driving of the car was

---

6. *Richardson* (1785) 1 Leach 387, *Abbott* [1955] 2QB 497, 39 Cr App Rep 141.

7. *Russell and Russell* [1987] Crim LR 494; *Lane and Lane* (1986) 82 Cr App Rep 5. For a valuable direction where one of two interrogating police officers has caused injury, see *Forman* [1988] Crim LR 677 (Judge Woods). See generally, Glanville Williams, (1989) 52 MLR 179; Griew, [1989] Crim LR 129. *Gibson and Gibson* (1985) 80 Cr App Rep 24 is misleading and should be used with care. See commentary, [1984] Crim LR 615.

8. *D (an infant) v Parsons* [1960] 2 All ER 493, [1960] 1 WLR 797.

9. *Ross v Rivenall* [1959] 2 All ER 376, [1959] 1 WLR 713. Cf. s. 12(1) of the Theft Act 1968 and *Boldizsar v Knight* [1980] Crim LR 653, below, p. 597.

10. [1959] 1 QB 11 at 23, [1958] 3 All ER 203.

11. Woolf J in *Gillick v West Norfolk and Wisbech Area Health Authority* [1984] QB 581 at 589, [1984] 1 All ER 365 at 373. Woolf J's discussion of the criminal aspects of this case was adopted by Lords Scarman and Bridge in the House of Lords, [1986] AC 112.

aiding and abetting, "even though he regretted the plan or indeed was horrified by it".[12]

There is some difficulty in reconciling the implications of the decision in *Gillick's case*[13] (a civil action for a declaration) with this principle. The House of Lords held that, in certain circumstances, a doctor may lawfully give contraceptive advice or treatment to a girl under the age of sixteen without her parents' consent. The conditions of lawful treatment could include cases where the doctor knew that the provision of the advice or treatment would encourage or facilitate sexual intercourse by the girl with a man. The man, but not the girl, would commit an offence.[14] The doctor's motives would no doubt be unimpeachable, but that is generally no answer. Why is not the doctor (and the parents if they concurred in the advice, for they have no more right than the doctor to aid and abet crime) guilty of aiding and abetting the man's offence? His act may well be facilitated (through the girl's being more ready to have intercourse) and (if he knows of the contraception) encouraged by the doctor's acts.[15] The decision that the doctor's advice is lawful clearly implies that he does not aid and abet a crime but the reason is nowhere clearly stated. It seems most likely that Woolf J and the majority of the House thought he lacked the necessary intention. As noted above,[16] this seems to put an undue strain on the concept of intention. If a mother, knowing that her son is about to embark on an armed robbery and cannot be dissuaded, gives him a bullet-proof vest, with the sole and admirable motive of saving him from death or serious injury, is not her intention to enable him to perpetrate the robbery more safely an intention to aid and abet it? *Gillick's case* is better regarded as being based impliedly, if not expressly,[17] on necessity.

Mere recklessness, still less negligence, whether assistance be given, is probably not enough. D's realisation that he may have left his gun-cupboard unlocked and that his son has a disposition to commit armed robbery, is probably not sufficient to fix D with liability for the armed robbery and homicide which the son commits using one of D's guns. There was no intention to do any act of advice or assistance.

In *National Coal Board v Gamble*,[18] E, a lorry driver, had his employer's lorry filled with coal at a colliery belonging to the defendant Board. When the lorry was driven on to the weighbridge operated by the defendants' servant, F, it appeared, and F so informed E, that its load exceeded by nearly four tons that permitted by the Motor Vehicles (Construction and Use) Regulations. E said he would take the risk, F gave him a weighbridge ticket and E committed the offence by driving the overloaded lorry on the highway. The property in the coal did not pass until the ticket was handed over and, therefore, E could not properly have left the colliery without it. It

12. [1975] Ac 653 at 678, [1975] 1 All ER 913, per Lord Morris, approving the judgment of Lowry LCJ on this point. See **SHC 164**. *Fretwell* (1862) Le & Ca 161, below, p. 135, appears to be a merciful decision and unsound in principle.
13. Above, fn. 11.
14. Sexual Offences Act 1956, s. 6, below, p. 462.
15. For a full discussion of this question, see [1986] Crim LR 114.
16. Pp. 56–57.
17. See J. R. Spencer in *Criminal Law Essays* 148, 164.
18. [1959] 1 QB 11, [1958] 3 All ER 203; **SHC 160**, DC, Slade J dissenting.

was held that the Board, through F,[19] was guilty of the misdemeanour. The decision was based on the assumption that F knew he had the right to prevent the lorry leaving the colliery with the coal. Had he not known this, he should have been acquitted. Presumably F was indifferent whether E drove his overloaded lorry on the road or not – he probably thought that it was none of his business – but F's motive was irrelevant and it was enough that a positive act of assistance had been voluntarily done with knowledge of the circumstances constituting the offence.

This result is in accord with two previous decisions. In *Cook v Stockwell*,[20] D, a brewer, supplied large quantities of beer to some cottages, knowing very well that they were re-selling it, without being licensed to do so, to soldiers quartered near by. In *Cafferata v Wilson*,[1] D, a wholesaler, sold a firearm to E, who kept a general shop, but was not registered as a firearms dealer. Presumably D knew that E was going to re-sell the firearm, which he in fact did. In both cases D was held liable as an accessory to the illegal sale.

In these cases the suppliers were indifferent whether the crime was committed or not. In *Fretwell*[2] D reluctantly supplied an abortifacient to a woman when she threatened to kill herself if he did not do so. He hoped she would not use it but she did so and died. This was self-murder at common law but D was held not liable as an accessory because he was "unwilling that the woman should take the poison". A distinction between indifference and unwillingness of this nature is, however, too uncertain to form the basis of a legal rule.

Fretwell is perhaps best regarded as a case in which the court strained the principles governing the liability of accessories in order to mitigate the severity of the rule which treated suicide as murder.[3] Woolf J regards it "as confined to its own facts".[4]

National Coal Board v Gamble suggests a distinction between the cases (i) where the seller is aware of the illegal purpose of the buyer before ownership has passed to the buyer; and (ii) where the seller learns of that purpose for the first time after ownership has passed but before delivery. In (i) delivery amounts to abetting; in (ii) it does not. The seller is merely complying with his legal duty to give the buyer his own property.

> "In a sense a man who gives up to a criminal a weapon which the latter has a right to demand from him aids in the commission of the crime as much as if he sold or lent the article, but this has never been held to be aiding in law."[5]

This seems a scarcely satisfactory distinction. If D delivers weedkiller to E, knowing that E intends to use it to murder his wife, it would be remarkable if D's guilt turned on whether the ownership passed before or after D learned of E's intention. The important thing is that he knows of it

19. See, however, below, p. 180, fn. 16.
20. (1915) 84 LJKB 2187.
   1. [1936] 3 All ER 149.
   2. Above, p. 134, fn. 12. Cf. Williams, CLGP, §124.
   3. As to which, see below, p. 379.
   4. *A-G v Able* [1984] 1 All ER 277 at 287, citing the 4th edition of the work (1978) pp. 120–121. But cf. *Gillick*, above, p. 134 and *Salford Health Authority*, below, p. 395.
   5. [1959] 1 QB 11 at 20, per Devlin J.

when he makes delivery. It should not be an answer that E has a right to possession of the thing in the civil law because the civil law should not afford a right in such a case.[6] In *Garrett v Arthur Churchill (Glass) Ltd*[7] D, who had bought a goblet as agent of E, was held guilty of being knowingly concerned in the exportation of goods without a licence, when, on E's instructions, he delivered E's own goblet to E's agent who was to take it to America.

"... albeit there was a legal duty in ordinary circumstances to hand over the goblet to the owners once the agency was determined, I do not think that an action would lie for breach of that duty if the handing over would constitute the offence of being knowingly concerned in its exportation."[8]

Probably then the seller is liable whether or not the ownership has passed before delivery. Williams's view, however, is that the seller ought to be liable in neither case. He argues:[9]

"The seller of an ordinary marketable commodity is not his buyer's keeper in criminal law unless he is specifically made so by statute. Any other rule would be too wide an extension of criminal responsibility."

Williams would now accept that:

"... the seller of a motor car would become a party to crime if he knew that the buyer proposed to drive the car himself and was subject to epileptic fits – because danger to life is involved; it is very like selling a revolver to a would-be murderer."[10]

An example given to demonstrate the extravagance of a general rule of liability of sellers is:

"... the vendor of a hotel would become a party to crime if he knew at the time of sale that the purchaser intended to carry on illegal after-hour trading."

A rule based on the nature of the thing as "an ordinary marketable commodity" is not workable. Motor cars and weedkiller are ordinary marketable commodities. A more feasible distinction is one based on the seriousness of the offence contemplated. The example of the sale of the hotel would be less startling if the seller knew that it was to be used as a headquarters for espionage or as a brothel. This is the American approach:

"The gravity of the social harm resulting from the unlawful conduct is used to determine whether mere knowledge of the intended use will be sufficient to carry the taint of illegality."[11]

The disadvantage of this rule is its uncertainty and no such distinction has been taken in English law. The cases suggest a general rule of liability of sellers. This is a fortiori the case with lenders or letters of articles or

---

6. See Williams, CLGP, s. 124 and Smith, [1972]B CLJ 197 at p. 208.
7. [1970] 1 QB 92, [1969] 2 All ER 1141. How far does this go? If X lends a picture to a museum, does the museum really commit an offence if, on demand, it returns the picture to X, knowing that he intends to export it without the licence required by law?
8. [1969] 2 All ER at 1145, per Parker LCJ.
9. CLGP, §124 at p. 373. Cf. TBCL, 293–294.
10. 9 JSPTL (NS) at p. 171.
11. Perkins and Boyce (3rd ed.) 746.

premises intended for unlawful purposes for here the owner has a continuing interest in and right to control the property.[12]

b) *Knowledge of circumstances*. It has frequently been said that the secondary party must know of, or at least turn a blind eye to, any circumstance which is an element of the offence.

"Before a person can be convicted of aiding and abetting the commission of an offence he must at least know the essential matters which constitute that offence. He need not actually know that an offence has been committed, because he may not know that the facts constitute an offence and ignorance of the law is not a defence."[13]

"The essential matters which constitute the offence" are the circumstances existing at the time when the act of secondary participation is done. The *actus reus* may also include certain consequences, but these cannot be "known". To what extent the consequences must be foreseen is considered below.[14] The circumstances of the *actus reus* must be known, but there is some authority for the view that the *mens rea* of the principal offender need not.[15] The word "knows", which is generally used in this context, includes "wilful blindness".

c) *Knowing circumstances to be probable – recklessness*. In *Carter* v *Richardson*[16] where D2, the supervisor of a learner driver, D1, was convicted of abetting D1's driving with excess alcohol, the court said that it was sufficient that D2 knew that it was "probable" that D1 was "over the limit" – that he was, in effect, "reckless" in the Cunningham sense.[17] It may be that this was obiter because the magistrates were satisfied that D2, though obviously unaware of the precise amount of alcohol in D1's blood, knew that it was so great as to be above the limit. It is quite clear that inadvertent Caldwell/Lawrence recklessness is not enough: *Blakely and Sutton v DPP*,[18] where D2, wanting D1 to stay the night with her, laced his drink without his knowledge. D2 knew that D1 would not drive home when she told him, as she intended, of the alcohol he had consumed, but he drove off before she could tell him. D2's conviction for procuring D1's driving with excess alcohol was quashed because the justices may have convicted, applying Caldwell/Lawrence recklessness, on the assumption that it was enough that D2 had not given thought to the possibility of an obvious and

12. For example, the hotelier who lets a room to a man accompanied by a fourteen-year-old girl, knowing that he intends to seduce her. But cf. Gordon, 142–143.
13. *Johnson v Youden* [1950] 1 KB 544 at 546, [1950] 1 All ER 300 at 302, **SHC 157**; per Lord Goddard CJ; see above, p. 80. See also *Ackroyds Air Travel Ltd v Director of Public Prosecutions* [1950] 1 All ER 933 at 936; *Thomas v Lindop* [1950] 1 All ER 966 at 968; *Ferguson v Weaving* [1951] 1 KB 814, [1951] 1 All ER 412; **SHC 158**; *Bateman v Evans* (1964) 108 Sol Jo 522; *Smith v Jenner* [1968] Crim LR 99; *Dial Contracts Ltd v Vickers* [1971] RTR 386; *D. Stanton & Sons Ltd v Webber* (1972) 116 Sol Jo 667, [1972] Crim LR 544 and commentary thereon.
14. See p. 143.
15. Below, p. 152.
16. [1974] RTR 314, discussed by Williams [1975] CLJ 182 and *TBCL*, 309. But in *Giorgianni* (1984) 156 CLR 473 the High Court of Australia held that recklessness is not sufficient on a charge of aiding and abetting.
17. Above, p. 61.
18. [1991] Crim LR 763, DC.

serious risk that he would do so. Though the court deplored the use of the word, "reckless", it seems that the conviction would have been upheld if it had been proved that D2 was aware of a risk that D1 would drive with excess alcohol. If so, this would go further than the decision or dicta (as the case may be) in *Carter v Richardson*, where D2 intentionally encouraged the act of driving and was reckless as to the circumstance. In *Blakely* D2's intention was to create the circumstance (D1's excessive alcohol level), and she was, at worst, reckless whether the act of driving, which it was her object to prevent, occurred. It seems that advertent recklessness as to a circumstance is enough, though because of the treacherous nature of the word "reckless", it is better to speak in terms of awareness of probability.

d) *Abetting an offence of strict liability.* The same *mens rea* is required for secondary participation in an offence of strict liability as for any other offence. The principal offender may, but a secondary party may not, be convicted without *mens rea*. The reason is that secondary participation is a common law notion. It was never necessary for a statute creating an offence to specify that it should also be an offence to aid, etc., its commission. The common law, now codified in the Accessories and Abettors Act 1861,[19] was that so to act created liability to conviction of the offence aided. It is natural that the normal principles of liability at common law should apply. The result, however, is to emphasise the anomalous nature of offences of strict liability, for the alleged aider who has no *mens rea* must be acquitted even if he was negligent[20] whereas the principal who has caused the *actus reus* must be convicted even if he took all proper care.

In *Callow v Tillstone*,[1] D, a veterinary surgeon, was charged with abetting the exposure for sale of unsound meat. At the request of a butcher, G, he examined the carcase of a heifer which had eaten yew leaves and been killed by the farmer just before it would have died of yew poisoning. He gave G a certificate that the meat was sound. The examination had been negligently conducted and the meat was tainted. G, relying on the certificate, exposed the meat for sale and was convicted. The justices, holding that D's negligence had caused the exposure, convicted him of abetting. It was held that his conviction must be quashed.[2] Thus, if Prince[3] had been assisted by a friend, D, who had driven him away with the girl in a hansom cab, it would have been a defence for D (even though it was not for Prince) to show that he believed the girl to be over sixteen or even (at least if he was unaware of the relevance of the age of sixteen) that he did not know what age she was. The same principle must apply, a fortiori, to offences where negligence as to circumstances will found liability. If D2 encourages D1 to marry, both believing honestly but mistakenly and on unreasonable grounds that D1's husband is dead, D1 may be convicted of

---

19. Above, p. 130. Cf. *McCarthy* [1964] Crim LR 225.
20. *Carter v Mace* [1949] 2 All ER 714 DC, is to the contrary, but in *Davies, Turner & Co Ltd v Brodie* [1954] 3 All ER 283, [1954] 1 WLR 1364, DC, that case was said to lay down no principle of law and to be decided on its own particular facts. See J. Montgomerie in (1950) 66 LQR 222.
  1. (1900) 83 LT 411, DC; **SHC 165**.
  2. See also *Bowker v Premier Drug Co Ltd* [1928] 1 KB 217 at 227.
  3. Above, p. 38.

bigamy but D2 cannot be convicted of abetting. This principle applies only to circumstances. Whether a secondary party may be liable for unforeseen consequences is considered below.[4]

e) *Knowledge of type of crime.* Three principles are involved here.

(i) If A aids, abets, counsels or procures B to commit a crime of a certain type, neither party specifying any particular victim, time or place, A may be convicted as a secondary party to any crime of that type which B commits.

(ii) If A aids, abets, counsels or procures B to commit a crime against a particular person, or in respect of a particular thing, A is not liable if B intentionally commits an offence of the same type against some other person, or in respect of some other thing.

(iii) A is, however, equally liable with B for any acts done by B in the course of endeavouring to carry out the common purpose. If the common purpose is to cause grievous bodily harm to C, and B, endeavouring to do so, kills C, both A and B are guilty of murder. If the common purpose is to assault C, and B, endeavouring to do so, kills him, both A and B are guilty of manslaughter. If the common purpose is to wound C (so the case is within principle (ii) above) and B, endeavouring to wound C, wounds D, B is liable under the doctrine of transferred malice;[5] and so, therefore, is A.

The application of these principles is not free from difficulty and principles (i) and (ii) require more detailed consideration.

Principle (i). A leading case is *Bainbridge.*[6] D purchased some oxygen-cutting equipment which was used six weeks later for breaking into a bank at Stoke Newington. D's story was that he had bought the equipment for one Shakeshaft, that he suspected Shakeshaft wanted it for something illegal – perhaps breaking up stolen goods – but that he did not know that it was going to be used for any such purpose as it was in fact used. It was held that it was essential to prove that D knew the type of crime that was going to be committed: it was not enough that he knew that some kind of illegality was contemplated; but that, if he knew breaking and entering and stealing was intended, it was not necessary to prove that he knew that the Midland Bank, Stoke Newington, was going to be broken into. It is the same where information on how to commit a crime of a particular type is given, though neither adviser nor advised has any particular crime in view when the advice is given.[7] Where D opened a bank account for E, giving E a false name, D was convicted of aiding and abetting E in the fraudulent use of the particular forged cheque which E subsequently drew upon the account. D had evinced an intention that the account be used as a vehicle for

4. Below, p. 143.
5. Above, p. 74.
6. [1960] 1 QB 129, [1959] 3 All ER 200, CCA; **SHC 151.**
7. *Baker* (1909) 28 NZLR 536. Williams thinks the case is wrongly decided: CLGP §125. But is it distinguishable in principle from *Bainbridge*? Cf. *McLeod and Georgia Straight Publishing Co Ltd* (1970) 75 WWR 161 (newspaper liable for incitement through article on how to cultivate marijuana). In Scotland, merely giving the name of an abortionist does not amount to participation in the subsequent illegal abortion: *HM Advocate v Johnstone* 1926 JC 89.

presenting forged cheques like the one in fact presented.[8] The House of Lords carried the principle to its logical conclusion in *Director of Public Prosecutions for Northern Ireland v Maxwell*.[9] If D gives assistance to E, knowing that E intends to commit a crime, but being uncertain whether E has crime X, or crime Y, or crime Z, in mind, D will be liable as a secondary party to whichever of those crimes E in fact commits. D drove E to an inn, realising that E intended either to plant a bomb or to shoot persons at the inn. In fact, E intended to plant, and did plant a bomb. D was liable for that offence. He would have been liable for murder if E had shot and killed. It would be otherwise if E had committed another type of crime which was not in D's contemplation when he did the relevant act. Nor is a "general criminal intention" enough. So an intention to abet another in the possession of a bag, whatever its contents may be, is insufficient to found an indictment for abetting the possession of cannabis.[10] If D had guessed that the bag contained either cannabis or some other article, proscribed or not, that should have been enough.

Where D has supplied E with the means of committing or information on how to commit a crime of a particular type, is he to be held liable for all the crimes of that type which E may thereafter commit? What if the Midland at Stoke Newington was the second, third or fourth bank which E had feloniously broken and entered with Bainbridge's apparatus? Williams questions whether D should be subject to such unforeseeable and perhaps far-reaching liability.[11] Yet, once it is conceded that D need not know the details of any specific crime, it is difficult to see why he should be liable for any one crime of the type contemplated and not for others.[12]

Bainbridge and *Maxwell* leave some unsolved problems. Whether a crime is of the same type as another may not always be easy to discover. If D lends a jemmy to E, contemplating that E intends to enter a house in order to steal, is D guilty of any offence if E enters a house intending to rape?[13] Clearly, D cannot be convicted of rape, because that is an offence of a different type; but he is probably guilty of burglary, because burglary was the crime he had in view – though this particular variety of burglary may be abhorrent to him. If D contemplates theft and E commits robbery, D is not guilty of robbery but might be convicted of the theft which is included in it.[14] Is theft an offence of the same type as removing an article from a place open to the public[15] or taking a motor vehicle without authority?[16] Is robbery an offence of the same type as blackmail?

Principle (ii). This principle is most clearly expressed by Hawkins:[17]

"But if a man command another to commit a felony on a particular person or thing and he do it on another; as to kill A and he kill B or to

8. *Thambiah v R* [1966] AC 37, [1965] 3 All ER 661, PC.
9. [1978] 3 All ER 1140, [1978] 1 WLR 1350, HL; **SHC 153**.
10. *Patel* [1970] Crim LR 274 and commentary thereon. Cf. *Fernandez* [1970] Crim LR 277.
11. CLGP, §124.
12. On the question of the withdrawal of an accessory before the fact, see below, p. 153.
13. See below, p. 626.
14. Below, p. 552.
15. Theft Act 1968, s. 11. Below, p. 594.
16. Theft Act 1968, s. 12. Below, p. 597.
17. 2 PC c 29, s. 21. See also Foster 369. Stephen, Digest (4th ed.) Art. 43.

burn the house of A and he burn the house of B or to steal an ox and he steal an horse; or to steal such an horse and he steal another; or to commit a felony of one kind and he commit another of a quite different nature; as to rob J S of his plate as he is going to market, and he break open his house in the night and there steal the plate; it is said that the commander is not an accessory because the act done varies in substance from that which was commanded."

The principle applies where there is a substantial variation from the proposed course of conduct. Hawkins also stated:[18]

"if the felony committed be the same in substance with that which was intended, and variant only in some circumstance, as in respect of the time or place, at which, or the means whereby it was effected, the abettor of the intent is altogether as much an accessory as if there had been no variance at all between it and the execution of it; as where a man advises another to kill such a one in the night, and he kills him in the day, or to kill him in the fields, and he kills him in the town, or to poison him, and he stabs or shoots him."

The distinction depends on whether the variation is one "of substance" and any such distinction must produce difficult borderline cases. In *Dunning and Graham*, an unreported case at Preston Crown Court,[19] D had a grievance against P. E offered to set fire to P's house. D accepted the offer and gave E P's address. E went to P's house, changed his mind, and set fire to P's Mercedes instead. D did not know that P owned such a car. Nevertheless, Macpherson J held that it was open to the jury to convict D on the ground that she must have authorised or envisaged the possibility of property such as a car in the driveway being damaged by fire. If the car had been so damaged as a consequence of E's setting fire to the house, D would have been liable for arson of the car under principle (iii), below. The actual case, however, seems to involve a deliberate variation from the plan. The result might be justified on the basis that D had authorised E to take revenge on P by damaging his property and that it did not really matter to her what the property was. Whether the variation is, or is not, one of substance, depends on the purpose of D as expressed to E.

The South African case of *S. v Robinson*[20] provides a further controversial illustration of the difficulties of applying these principles. D1, D2 and E agreed with P that E should kill P to procure the money for which P's life was insured and to avoid P's prosecution for fraud. At the last moment, P withdrew his consent to die but E nevertheless killed him. It was not proved that D1 and D2 foresaw the possibility that E might kill P even if he withdrew his consent or that they had been reckless whether he did so kill him. It was held that the common purpose was murder with the consent of the victim and that E had acted outside that common purpose. D1 and D2, accordingly, were not guilty of murder – though they were guilty of attempted murder, since E had reached the stage of an attempt before P

18. Ibid., s. 20.
19. December, 1985.
20. 1968 (1) SA 666; **SHC 155**.

withdrew his consent. Holmes JA, dissenting, thought ". . . looking squarely at the whole train of events, the conspiracy was fulfilled in death, and
there is no room for exquisite niceties of logic about the exact limits of the
mandate in the conspiratorial common purpose." It is submitted that the
better view is that of the majority. If E knows that a condition precedent of
the agreement has not been performed, he is no longer engaged on the joint
enterprise. If D agrees with E that E shall murder P if he finds out that P is
committing adultery with D's wife and E, having discovered that P is not
committing adultery, nevertheless kills him, D should not be liable for
murder, though, if this conditional intention is enough, he may be liable for
conspiracy to murder.

Principle (iii). The doctrine of transferred malice applies to secondary
parties as it does to principals.[1] Where E, intending to follow D's advice to
kill X, mistakes Y for X and kills Y, D as well as E is guilty of murder. If D
advises E to burn X's house and E does so but the flames spread and burn
Y's house, D as well as E is guilty of arson of Y's house. The difference
between these cases and those falling under principle (ii) is that here E has
not deliberately departed from the course that D advised or assisted him to
follow; E was attempting to put the agreed plan into execution and D is as
responsible for the unintended results of the acts he has authorised or
encouraged as E.

The old and famous case of *Saunders and Archer*,[2] in its result at least, is
reconcilable with this principle. D1, intending to murder his wife, on the
advice of D2, gave her a poisoned apple to eat. She ate a little of it and gave
the rest to their child. D1 loved the child, yet he stood by and watched it eat
the poison, of which it soon died. It was held that D1 was guilty of murder,
but the judges agreed that D2, who, of course, was not present when the
child ate the apple, was not an accessory to this murder.

If D1 had been absent when the child ate the apple it is thought that this
would have been a case of transferred malice and D2 would have been
liable; but D1's presence and failure to act made the killing of the child, in
effect, a deliberate, and not an accidental, departure from the agreed plan.
It was – as it is well put in Kenny,[3]

"as if Saunders had changed his mind and on a later occasion had used
such poison as Archer had named in order to murder some quite
different person of whom Archer had never heard."

Foster, however, stated the rule rather more widely than this:[4]

"So whenever the principal goeth beyond the terms of the solicitation, *if
in the event the felony committed was a probable consequence of what was
ordered or advised*, the person giving such orders or advice will be an
accessory to that felony."

This would make a counsellor liable for negligence in failing to foresee
what he ought, as a reasonable man, to have foreseen, which, it is

---

1. Hawkins, PC, Ch. 29, s. 22; Foster, *Crown Law*, 370; Stephen, *Digest*, Art. 41, illustration
(1).
2. (1576) 2 Plowd 473.
3. *Outlines*, 112.
4. *Crown Law*, 370. See, to the same effect, Stephen, *Digest*, Art 20.

submitted, would be going too far. It is true that he may be held liable for negligently unforeseen consequences where the principal in the first degree may likewise be held liable[5] but, where the crime is one requiring *mens rea*, it is submitted that actual foresight of the consequences in question must be proved equally for the counsellor as for the abettor. Take the following case: D advises E to steal money from P's house by breaking the gas-meter from the wall. E does so, with the result that the gas escapes and P is injured. It is established that E is guilty of maliciously administering a noxious thing[6] only if he actually foresaw that injury of the particular kind might be caused.[7]

Foster's rule would fix D with liability simply because the result was a probable consequence of his action. It is submitted that the true rule is that the counsellor must have such foresight of the consequence of his action as is necessary for the conviction of the principal in the first degree. In this example, D may be convicted only if he foresaw the likelihood that the coal gas would be administered to someone.

f) *Liability of secondary party for unintended consequences: joint enterprise.* Where two persons embark on a joint unlawful enterprise each is equally liable for the consequences of such acts of the other as are done in pursuance of the agreement. The abettor is, then, liable for unforeseen consequences to the same extent as the principal. So in *Baldessare*,[8] the driver was held liable for the unintended and unforeseen death which he caused and his passenger was equally liable. D was guilty of counselling death by dangerous driving when he instructed his employee to drive a vehicle knowing that it had a dangerously defective tyre and, in consequence, there was an accident and a person was killed.[9] If D1 goes beyond the scope of the joint enterprise, then D2 is not liable for D1's act or its consequences. In *Davies v DPP*[10] two gangs of boys engaged in a fight on Clapham Common. One of them, E, carried a knife with which he inflicted a fatal stab wound. There being no evidence that D, another member of the same gang, knew that E carried a knife, it was held that D, though guilty of a common assault, was not an accomplice in the murder.[11] If E had killed with a blow of his fist, D would have been guilty of manslaughter, because the blow was delivered in pursuance of the agreement. But, because the use of a knife was not within his contemplation at all, he was not responsible for the death which resulted from it.[12]

5. *Baldessare* (1930) 22 Cr App Rep 70.
6. Offences against the Person Act 1861, s. 23; below, p. 429.
7. *Cunningham* [1957] 2 QB 396, [1957] 2 All ER 412; **SHC 67**; below, p. 430, fn. 19.
8. Above, fn. 5.
9. *Robert Millar (Contractors) Ltd* [1970] 2 QB 54, [1970] 1 All ER 577. It would seem that, while the driver might have been convicted even if he had not known of the dangerous state of the tyre if he *ought* to have known of it, the counsellor could only be guilty if he actually knew. The state of the tyre was a *circumstance* which made the driving dangerous and knowledge of the essential circumstances of the offence, as distinct from the consequences, must be proved against secondary parties. See above, p. 137.
10. [1954] AC 378, [1954] 1 All ER 507, HL.
11. Cf. *Murtagh and Kennedy* [1955] Crim LR 315.
12. Cf. *Caton* (1874) 12 Cox CC 624.

The leading case is *Chang Wing-siu*.[13] Three men armed with knives went to a flat to commit a robbery in the course of which P was stabbed to death. The judge directed that D might be convicted of murder if, when he took part in enterprise, he contemplated that one of his accomplices might use a knife with the intention of inflicting serious injury. The Privy Council held this to be a correct direction. Sir Robin Cooke, delivering the judgment of the Board, stated:

"[The principle] turns on contemplation or, putting the same idea in other words, authorisation, which may be express but is more usually implied. It meets the case of a crime foreseen as a possible incident of the common unlawful enterprise. The criminal culpability lies in participating in the venture with that foresight."

Chan was considered in a series of murder cases in the Court of Appeal. It was followed in *Ward*;[14] but *Ward* appears to have been studiously ignored in two subsequent decisions of differently constituted courts[15] which appear to have thought, erroneously, that the law of joint enterprise was affected by the decisions in *Moloney* and *Hancock and Shankland*[16] and that an alleged secondary party must now be proved to have had an intention to kill or cause serious bodily harm. Perhaps it was also felt wrong that a secondary party should be guilty of murder when he was merely, in effect, reckless whether death or serious bodily harm be caused, when the principal was not liable unless he intended one of those results. However, the authority of *Ward* was reasserted in *Slack*,[17] followed with some modification by *Wakely*[18] and *Hyde*.[19] *Hyde* was approved by five Law Lords sitting in the Privy Council in *Hui Chi-ming*.[20] In *Slack* Lord Lane CJ said that B was guilty if he "lent himself to a criminal enterprise, involving the infliction, if necessary, of serious harm or death, or ... had an express or tacit understanding with A that such harm or death should, if necessary, be inflicted ...". In *Wakely* he said that an express or tacit agreement or understanding was necessary and that "mere foresight of the real or definite possibility of violence being used ... is ... not sufficient". But "lending oneself" to an enterprise does not necessarily imply agreement to all that one knows might be done; and Lord Lane reconsidered that statement in *Hyde*:

"If B realises (without agreeing to such conduct being used) that A may kill or intentionally inflict serious injury, but nevertheless continues to participate with A in the venture, that will amount to a sufficient mental element for B to be guilty of murder if A, with the requisite intent, kills in the course of the venture."

At this point it should be noticed that the use of the word, "authorisation" in *Chan Wing-siu* seems misplaced. A contemplated act by an accomplice is

13. [1985] AC 168, [1984] 3 All ER 877, PC.
14. (1986) 85 Cr App Rep 71.
15. *Barr* (1986) 88 Cr App Rep 362, *Smith* [1988] Crim LR 119.
16. Above, p. 58.
17. [1989] QB 775, [1989] 3 All ER 90.
18. [1990] Crim LR 119.
19. (1990) 92 Cr App Rep 131, [1991] Crim LR 133.
20. [1992] 1 AC 34, [1991] 3 All ER 897, PC.

not necessarily an authorised act; and it now seems clear that contemplation is enough.[1]

Chang Wing-siu decides that D need not foresee the event as more probable than not – it is sufficient that he foresees "a substantial risk, a real risk, a risk that something might well happen", something more than "a risk which may have been dismissed by him as altogether negligible".

As to the criticism that the accessory should not be liable for murder when he is merely reckless, there is a difference between (i) recklessness whether death be caused (which is sufficient for manslaughter but not for murder), and (ii) recklessness whether murder be committed. The accessory's recklessness must extend to the principal's *mens rea* of murder. His liability derives from that of the principal and he is a participant in the intentional killing or serious bodily harm which causes death.

It is immaterial that, when embarking on the enterprise, the principal did not himself contemplate the possibility that he might act with intent to kill or cause serious injury. It is sufficient that the accessory contemplated that he might do so, and that he did so in fact.[2]

Though these recent cases all concern murder, the principles are general but the scope for their application may be limited. They obviously apply to a charge under s. 18 of the Offences of the Person Act or of rape if A embarked on an indecent assault, knowing that B might go on to commit rape.

g) *Liability of A where B goes beyond the common design.* If A and B have agreed to commit a common assault on P and B contemplates no more than that and, in the course of that assault, A kills by an act done with intent to kill or cause serious bodily harm, A is guilty of murder but, on the balance of authority, B is not guilty even of manslaughter. If A had killed in the course of carrying out an agreed plan, i.e., the assault, both parties would have been guilty of manslaughter; but B is not responsible for A's unauthorised and uncontemplated departure from the plan. The principle was applied in *Dunbar*[3] where the prosecution's case was that B had hired A to kill P. The jury who convicted A of murder and B of manslaughter must be presumed to have found that B authorised A to cause harm less than serious bodily harm. B's conviction for manslaughter was quashed. It seems that she could not even have been convicted of an assault occasioning actual bodily harm as she was not responsible for the act done, but only of incitement and conspiracy to commit that offence.

---

1. In *Hui Chi-ming* Lord Lowry said, "Their Lordships consider that Sir Robin Cooke used this word . . . to emphasise the fact that mere foresight is not enough: the accessory, in order to be guilty, must have foreseen the relevant offence which the principal may commit *as a possible incident of the common unlawful enterprise* and must, with such foresight, still have participated in the enterprise. The word 'authorisation' explains what is meant by contemplation but does not add a new ingredient."

2. *Hui Chi-ming* [1991] 3 All ER at 910.

3. [1988] Crim LR 693, applying *Anderson and Morris* [1966] 2 All ER 644, 50 Cr App Rep 216 and *Lovesey and Peterson* [1970] 1 QB 352, 53 Cr App Rep 461.

It should be noted, however, that there are two decisions of the Court of Appeal[4] that, in the circumstances described above, B is guilty of manslaughter. These cases appear to be wrongly decided in the light of current opinion in the Court of Appeal; but the matter deserves the attention of the House of Lords.

The principle applied in *Dunbar* is presumably a general principle, not limited to homicide cases. If B has authorised A to inflict slight bodily harm, not contemplating that A might intentionally cause grievous bodily harm but A does so, B is not liable. But what if B incites A to steal P's watch and A, meeting resistance uncontemplated by B, uses force and robs P of the watch? B is not guilty of robbery but should he not be guilty of theft? Perhaps it is sufficient to say that he incited theft and theft has been committed for robbery is an aggravated form of theft. If that is the principle, it would be different where B incites A to take P's car for a "joyride" and A takes the car, intending to steal it. Stealing could not be described as an aggravated form of joyriding. B would not be liable as an accessory to joyriding.

h) *The effect of provocation in the course of a joint enterprise.* In *McKechnie*[5] where the killer acted under a provocation received in the course of carrying out the joint enterprise, it was held that this ruled out any liability of the other parties to it. Presumably the reason is that a person who has lost his self-control can no longer be said to be acting in pursuance of a common purpose. If so, there is some difficulty in reconciling the decision with *Calhaem*.[6] *McKechnie* was distinguished in *Pearson*[7] but there the provocation affected both defendants and occurred before the joint enterprise began.

8 Secondary Participation and Inchoate Offences

It is an offence to incite, or to conspire, or to attempt, to commit an offence.[8] It is not an offence to attempt[9] or, it is submitted, to incite or to conspire[10] to do an act which would involve no more than secondary liability for the offence if it were committed. Knowing that D1 intends to drive his car, D3 urges D2 to "lace" D1's drink with so much alcohol that D1 will inevitably commit an offence under s. 5 (1) of the Road Traffic Act 1988[11] if he drives after consuming the drink. D2 agrees to do so and

---

4. *Betty* (1963) 48 Cr App Rep 6, *Reid* (1975) 62 Cr App Rep 109. Cf. *Murtagh and Kennedy* [1955] Crim LR 315 (Glyn-Jones J).
5. [1992] Crim LR 194.
6. [1985] QB 808, [1985] 2 All ER 266 (B liable as a counsellor of A's act where A killed after "going berserk"), above, p. 128.
7. [1992] Crim LR 193, below, p. 356.
8. Chapter 11, below.
9. Criminal Attempts Act 1981, s. 1(4) (b), below, p. 314; *Dunnington*, [1984] QB 472, [1984] 1 All ER 676, [1984] Crim LR 98, CA. Cf. *Chief Constable of Hampshire v Mace* (1986) 84 Cr App Rep 40, [1986] Crim LR 752.
10. *Hollinshead* [1985] 1 All ER 850 at 857–858, CA. The House of Lords left the question open: [1985] AC 975; [1985] 2 All ER 769. See Smith, "Secondary Participation and Inchoate Offences" in *Crime, Proof and Punishment*, 21. *Po Koon Tai*, Criminal Appeal No. 836 of 1979, Supreme Court of Hong Kong, is to the contrary so far as conspiracy is concerned.
11. Driving or being in charge of a motor vehicle with an alcohol concentration above a prescribed limit.

attempts to, or does, lace the drink. If D1 consumes the drink, drives his car and thus commits the offence under the Road Traffic Act 1988, s. 5 (1), D2 and D3 will be guilty as secondary parties;[12] but if D1 declines the drink, or does not drive the car, D3 is guilty neither of incitement nor of conspiracy and D2 is guilty neither of conspiracy nor of attempt to commit the offence. The act incited, agreed upon, attempted and indeed done, lacing the drink, is not the offence.[13]

In this example, D1 is guilty as the principal offender, notwithstanding his lack of *mens rea*, on the ground that the offence is assumed to be one of strict liability. Where the offence is one requiring *mens rea*, which the actual perpetrator of the *actus reus* lacks, then those who procured him to act will be liable because they, or one of them, will be the principals in the first degree. D3 urges D2 to stage his death and disappear so that D2's wife, D1, may claim the insurance money on D2's life. If D1 was not a party to the fraud and was intended to obtain the money innocently, D3 would be guilty of inciting D2 to obtain for another by deception as the principal offender; D3 and D2 would be guilty of conspiring to commit the offence; and D2 would be guilty of an attempt to do so at the latest when the news of his death reached the insurers.[14] If D1 were a party, D2's acts would not be an offence[15] but the three would be guilty of conspiracy to defraud. Where D1 is guilty of incitement to commit a crime, D2 may be liable for abetting or counselling the incitement. Where D1 is guilty of an attempt to commit a crime, D2 may be liable for abetting or counselling the attempt.[16] In the case of conspiracy, however, one who abets or counsels appears to be a principal in the first degree in the conspiracy.

9 Conviction of Secondary Party and Acquittal of Principal Offender

Even if the alleged principal has been acquitted, a conviction of another as a secondary party may be logical. This is so even if it is assumed[17] that a secondary party may be convicted only when the principal himself is guilty. The acquittal of the alleged principal, so far from being conclusive that no crime was committed, is not even admissible in evidence at a subsequent trial of the secondary parties.[18] A second jury may be satisfied beyond reasonable doubt that the crime was committed upon evidence which the first jury found unconvincing; evidence may be admissible against the secondary party which was not admissible against the principal, or fresh evidence may have come to light or the principal may have been acquitted

---

12. *Attorney-General's Reference (No. 1 of 1975)*, above, p. 126.
13. The adulteration of the drink might possibly amount to the administration of a noxious thing, contrary to the Offences against the Person Act 1861, s. 24, below, p. 429.
14. *Director of Public Prosecutions v Stonehouse*, [1978] AC 55, [1977] 2 All ER 909, HL, below, p. 316.
15. This assumes that *Robinson* [1915] 2 KB 342, CCA, is rightly decided and that these would be preparatory acts and not an attempt to obtain. Below, p. 312.
16. *Hapgood and Wyatt* (1870) LR 1 CCR 221, CCR; *S v Robinson* 1968 (1) SA 666. Cf. Sexual Offences (Amendment Act) 1976, s. 7 (2) (aiding, etc. attempted rape).
17. Contrary to the view expressed below, p. 152.
18. *Hui Chi-ming v R* [1991] 3 All ER 897, PC. Under the Police and Criminal Evidence Act 1984, s. 74, a conviction is now admissible to prove the commission of the offence by the principal: *Turner* [1991] Crim LR 57; but an acquittal proves nothing and is inadmissible.

because the prosecution offered no evidence against him. The position would seem to be the same where the secondary party is tried first and convicted and the principal is subsequently acquitted[19] and when the parties are jointly indicted. In *Hughes*,[20] after the prosecution had offered no evidence against E, he was acquitted and called as a witness for the Crown, with the result that D was convicted by the same jury as an accessory before the fact to E's alleged crime. Where principal and secondary party are tried separately, this result is supported by the analogous rule laid down in *Director of Public Prosecutions v Shannon*[1] that the acquittal of one party to a conspiracy does not invalidate the conviction of the only other party on an earlier or later occasion. *Shannon* left open the question whether the one party may be convicted of conspiracy when the other is acquitted at the same trial;[2] and in *Anthony*[3] it was said, *obiter*, that a jury cannot acquit E and at the same time find D guilty of counselling him to commit the crime. If E and D are tried together and the evidence tending to show that E committed the crime is the same against both, then it would be inconsistent to acquit E and convict D.[4] Where, however, there is evidence admissible against D but not against E that E committed the crime (as, for example, a confession by D that he counselled E to commit the crime and saw him commit it) it would be perfectly logical to acquit E and convict D of counselling him (and of conspiring with him). In *Humphreys and Turner*,[5] which was just such a case, Chapman J held that D might be convicted as a secondary party, distinguishing the dicta in *Anthony* as applicable only to felonies. It is submitted that, since the Criminal Law Act 1967 came into force, the rule stated in *Humphreys and Turner* is applicable to all offences.

10 Conviction of Secondary Party where there is no Principal

It is one thing for a court which is trying D2 alone to reject or ignore the holding of another court that D1 was not a principal in the first degree and to hold that he was; and that, therefore, D2 might be convicted as a secondary party to D1's crime. It is quite another thing for a court to hold at one and the same time, (i) that D1 was, in law, not guilty[6] and (ii) that D2 was guilty, as a secondary party, of D1's crime. These propositions seem to be inconsistent with the derivative nature of secondary liability.[7]

---

19. In *Rowley* [1948] 1 All ER 570, D's conviction was quashed when, after he had pleaded guilty as an accessory after the fact, the alleged principals were acquitted by the jury. But the decision is criticised in *Shannon* [1974] 2 All ER 1009 at 1020 and 1049; below p. 300.
20. (1860) Bell CC 242.
 1. [1975] AC 717, [1974] 2 All ER 1009, HL; below, p. 300.
 2. The point is now settled by the Criminal Law Act 1977, and *Longman and Cribben* (1980) 72 Cr App Rep 121, below, p. 300; but *Shannon* is relevant to the common law governing secondary participation.
 3. [1965] 2QB 189, [1965] 1 All ER 440. Cf. *Surujpaul v R* [1958] 3 All ER 300 at 302–303.
 4. *Surujpaul v R* [1958] 3 All ER 300, [1958] 1 WLR 1050.
 5. [1965] 3 All ER 689 (Liverpool Crown Court). Following in *Sweetman v Industries and Commerce Department*, [1970] NZLR 139. Cf. *Davis* [1977] Crim LR 542, CA and commentary.
 6. Not merely that there was not enough evidence to convict him, but that there was evidence which established his innocence.
 7. Above, p. 123.

a) *Can a secondary party ever be guilty of a greater offence than the principal?*
Since secondary liability is said to derive from that of the principal, it is
hard to see how the secondary party can logically be held to be greater than
that of the principal. Hawkins[8] thought that the offence of the *accessory* can
never "rise higher" than that of the principal, "it seeming incongruous and
absurd that he who is punished only as a partaker of the guilt of another,
should be adjudged guilty of a higher crime than the other". But Hawkins
was speaking of an accessory in the strict sense and he saw no incongruity
or absurdity in a principal in the second degree being guilty of a greater
offence than the principal in the first degree. Such a distinction, depending
on whether the secondary party is present at, or absent from. the commission of the crime does not seem acceptable. If it ever had any validity it
depended on the distinction in the law of felonies between a principal on
the second degree and an accessory which has been abolished.

There are some cases where it seems obvious that a person who, at least,
looks like a secondary party ought to be convicted of a greater offence than
the immediate perpetrator of the *actus reus*. We have already noticed that
offences may be committed through innocent agents and that if D, with
intent to kill, sends a letter-bomb through the post to P who is killed by the
explosion, D is guilty of murder as a principal and E, the postman, is an
innocent agent. Suppose, however, that E notices some wires sticking out
of the parcel and that he is aware that a number of letter-bombs
have been sent by terrorists lately with fatal results. He thinks, "This could
be a letter bomb – but I'm in a hurry, I'll risk it", and pushes the letter
through P's letter box where it explodes and kills P. If these facts are
proved, E behaved recklessly and is guilty of manslaughter. He is no longer
an innocent agent. But it would be absurd if D who sent the letter with
intent to kill should escape liability for murder. Glanville Williams
suggests that a person like our postman should be regarded as a semi-
innocent agent – "he is an innocent agent in respect of part of the
responsibility of the secondary party".[9] Kadish does not like this – "the
ideas of a 'semi-innocent agent' and of responsibility as a composite of parts
seems only to add to the conceptual mystery"[10] – but the expression "semi-
innocent agent" is useful for describing this situation. It does not, however,
explain how the greater can derive from the less.

Kadish discusses the example of D who, intending that E shall kill P,
fabricates provocation which causes E to lose his self-control and kill P. E,
because of the provocation, is guilty only of manslaughter. Kadish's
solution is that here D can properly be said to have caused P's death.
Because E's actions are not "fully voluntary" they do not break the chain of
causation. Once it is established that D caused P's death, "it follows that
the nature of his crime is determined by the culpability with which he
acted". According to Kadish's explanation (though he does not spell this
out), this is not a case of the liability of an accessory rising above that of the
principal. There is no accessory. There is only one homicide but it is well

8. 2 PC s. 29, s. 15.
9. TBCL, 373.
10. *Blame and Punishment* 183.

settled that there may be two causes – and two causers – of a result.[11] D and E have both caused the death and it is both manslaughter, in respect of which E is the principal, and murder, in respect of which D is the principal. This theory would also explain other hypothetical cases that have been discussed.

"[D] hands a gun to [E] informing him that it is loaded with blank ammunition only and telling him to go and scare [P] by discharging it. The ammunition is in fact live (as [D] knows) and [P] is killed. [E] is convicted only of manslaughter. ... It would seem absurd that [D] should thereby escape conviction for murder."[12]

E's act would be regarded as not "fully voluntary" because, through his ignorance of material facts, he was not fully aware of what he was doing or its consequences; so D has caused the death, intending to kill and is a principal murderer.[13]

The absurd result postulated above was thought to follow from *Richards*[14] which the Court of Appeal and Lord Mackay considered to be wrongly decided. D, a woman, hired E and F to beat up her husband "bad enough to put him in hospital for a month". She signalled to E and F when P left the house. They inflicted a wound upon P, not amounting to a serious injury. D was convicted of wounding with intent to cause grievous bodily harm but E and F were acquitted of that offence and convicted of the lesser offence of unlawful wounding. Following the opinion of Hawkins, D's conviction was quashed and a conviction for unlawful wounding substituted. It was assumed that, under the old law of felonies, D would have been an accessory and not a principal in the second degree.[15] The result might have been different if D had been present. *Richards* was heavily criticised and, in view of the disapproval expressed in *Howe*, though only obiter, may not be followed in future. *Richards* found a belated defender in Professor Kadish who argues (i) that D did not cause the actions of E and F because they were not her unwitting instruments but chose to act freely as they did and (ii) she could not be held liable "for an aggravated assault [i.e., an assault with intent to cause grievous bodily harm] that did not take place".[16] Of course D did in one sense cause the actions of E and F – they would never have harmed P if she had not set them on to him; but it is a fair point that she would not be regarded as having caused the result under the ordinary principles of secondary participation (above, p. 129). The postman example is distinguishable because the postman there did exactly what the murderer intended him to do. E and F did not.

---

11. E.g. D shoots at P, intending to kill but only wounds. E treats the wound recklessly and P dies of the maltreated wound. D and E have both caused P's death. D is guilty of murder and E of manslaughter. Both are principals.

12. *Howe* [1986] QB 626 at 641–642, [1986] 1 All ER 833 at 839–840, CA. Lord Mackay agreed with the Court of Appeal who found this example convincing: [1987] AC 417, [1987] 1 All ER 771, HL. See the similar examples in the 5th edition of this work, 140.

13. It is not so clear that the causation theory is a satisfactory explanation of the case where D intends the result and E is reckless whether he causes it – e.g., the postman case, above. It seems to be straining a bit to say that the postman's act is not "fully voluntary".

14. [1974] QB 776, [1973] 3 All ER 1088, CA.

15. Above, p. 123.

16. "Complicity and Causation", (1985) 73 Cal. Law Rev. 323 at 329.

The anomaly of holding D liable for the greater offence is emphasised if it is supposed that P, by some unforeseeable mischance, had died of the slight injury inflicted by E and F. This would have been manslaughter by E and F. If D was guilty of the s. 18 offence, it would follow logically that she was guilty of murder. It may be argued that this would be wrong (though she had the necessary *mens rea*), because no act was ever done with *intent thereby* to kill or cause serious bodily harm – there was no "murderous act". If, however, E and F had acted with intent to do serious bodily harm but succeeded in inflicting only a slight injury it would have been murder by all three if P had died of that. But then the act would have been done in pursuance of a joint enterprise to cause serious bodily harm. In fact it was not so done. For that reason, though not for the reasons given, it may be that the decision in *Richards* was right after all.

The position is more straightforward where D and E both have the *mens rea* for the greater offence but E's liability is reduced for some reason to that of a lesser offence. If E causes the *actus reus* in carrying out the agreed plan but his liability is reduced "for some reason special to himself",[17] such as provocation or diminished responsibility,[18] it seems clearly right that D should not be able to shelter behind E's personal exemption from liability for the greater offence. In the case considered in *Howe*, however, the reduction in E's liability did not depend on a personal consideration of this kind. E's defence was that he had agreed to shoot P out of fear of D, but that, when it came to the event, the gun went off accidentally. The killing was therefore unintentional and amounted to no more than manslaughter. The judge, following *Richards*, directed that, if the jury found E guilty only of manslaughter, then D could at most be guilty of manslaughter. The implication of the decision of the House is that this was wrong. It is submitted that it is right; that the true position is that if E has gone beyond a merely preparatory act and is attempting to commit the crime when he "accidentally" kills, both D and E are guilty of murder; but, if E is doing only a preparatory act when he happens to kill – he is driving to P's house with intent to blow it up when the bomb in his car goes off and kills P who has unexpectedly gone out for a walk – E is liable only for manslaughter and so is D. The killing which occurs is not the killing he intended, though the victim happens to be the same.[19]

b) *Where the "principal" is guilty of no offence.* In *Morris v Tolman*,[20] D was charged with abetting the owner of a vehicle in using that vehicle for a purpose for which the vehicle had not been licensed. The statute (the Roads Act 1920) was so phrased that the offence could be committed only by the licence-holder. It was held that, there being no evidence that the licence-holder had used the vehicle for a purpose other than that for which it was licensed, D must be acquitted. Though he, in fact, had used the

---

17. The phrase used by Lord Mackay in *Howe*, above, p. 150.
18. This case is covered by s. 2(4) of the Homicide Act 1957. D's liability for murder is not affected by E's diminished responsibility.
19. See commentary, [1987] Crim LR 481 at 484.
20. [1923] 1 KB 166.

vehicle, that was not an *actus reus*. Again, in *Thornton v Mitchell*,[1] D, a bus conductor, negligently signalled to the driver of his bus to reverse, so that two pedestrians, whom it was not possible for the driver to see, were knocked down and one of them killed. The driver having been acquitted of careless driving, it was held that the conductor must be acquitted of abetting. Again, there was no *actus reus*. The driver's acquittal shows that he committed no *actus reus*, for careless driving is a crime which requires no *mens rea* beyond an intention to drive and D could not be said to have driven the bus. There would have been no such obstacle in the way of convicting D for manslaughter. That would, at that time, simply have raised the question whether D's negligence was sufficiently great.[2]

An alternative way of looking at these cases would be to say that in each of them D was not liable because he was incapable of being a principal offender, not being a licence-holder or a driver, respectively.[3] This rule, however, would produce unsatisfactory results in a number of situations. It is well settled that a person can be convicted as a secondary party to a crime which he is personally incapable of committing as a principal offender. Thus a woman[4] or a boy under fourteen[5] could be convicted of abetting a rape; a bachelor could be convicted of abetting a bigamous marriage. Should the boy, or the woman or the bachelor be acquitted because the person committing the rape, or the person going through the ceremony of marriage was insane, or lacked *mens rea*, or was exempt from criminal liability for some other reason? D's conduct would certainly be none the less heinous, and though incapable of committing an *actus reus* personally, D would have caused one to occur and have done so with *mens rea*. It does not seem feasible to extend the doctrine of the innocent agent to this situation. If D, through an innocent agent, has killed P, it is not unreasonable for the indictment to state, "D ... murdered P." If D, a bachelor, procures E to go through a ceremony of marriage, it would be quite plainly untrue for the indictment to state, "D ... married ..., during the life of his wife ..." for he did not marry anyone, nor did he have a wife. Is there any reason why the indictment should not state, "E ... married F, during the life of his wife ... D ... was present, aiding, abetting and assisting the said E so to marry"? There are two cases where the result at least supports this view. In *Bourne*,[6] D, by duress, compelled his wife to have connection with a dog. He was charged with abetting her to commit buggery. It was argued that, as the wife could not be convicted, since she acted under the coercion of her husband,[7] he must be acquitted. This argument was rejected. The Court of Criminal Appeal assumed that the wife was entitled to be acquitted, but held that, nevertheless, D's conviction as an abettor could stand. In *Bourne*, according to one view, the wife, though excused by

---

1. [1940] 1 All ER 339. See R. D. Taylor, "Complicity and Excuses", [1983] Crim LR 656, for another way of looking at the problems raised by this case.
2. See above, p. 92, and below, p. 372.
3. See Williams, CLGP, §§120, 129 (4).
4. *Ram and Ram* (1893) 17 Cox CC 609.
5. *Eldershaw* (1828) 3 C & P 396, per Vaughan B. See below, p. 459.
6. (1952) 36 Cr App Rep 125, CCA; **SHC 139**, cf. *Kemp and Else* [1964] 2 QB 341, [1964] 1 All ER 649 and *Matusevich and Thompson* [1976] VR 470.
7. See below, p. 243.

duress, committed the *actus reus* with *mens rea* for she knew exactly what she was doing.[8] Another view, however, is that intentionally to do an act, knowing of circumstances which prevent the act from being a crime, is not *mens rea*.[9] In the second case, *Cogan and Leak*,[10] the decision is based on the assumption that the person committing the *actus reus* lacked *mens rea*. D terrorised his wife, P, into submitting to sexual intercourse with E. The jury were directed, in accordance with the decision of the Court of Appeal in *Morgan*,[11] that E's alleged belief that P was consenting was no defence if it was not based on reasonable grounds. The decision of the House of Lords in *Morgan*[12] was given before E's appeal and, consequently, his conviction had to be quashed; but D's conviction for aiding and abetting was upheld. He had procured E to commit the offence.

"In the language of the law the act of sexual intercourse without the wife's consent was the *actus reus*; it had been procured by (D) who had the appropriate *mens rea*, namely his intention that (E) should have sexual intercourse with her without her consent."

The court preferred to regard D as the principal offender, acting through an innocent agent. There are objections to that,[13] apart from the fact that at that time a man could not be guilty of rape of his own wife.[14] It is simply untrue to say, as an indictment for rape as the principal offender must allege, that "D had sexual intercourse with P without her consent."

Whatever the reasoning and its merits, the result in both *Bourne* and *Cogan and Leak* is that the abetting or counselling of a mere *actus reus* is indictable. The result produced is just and logical. The most formidable objection is that the closely related crime of incitement requires proof that the inciter knew, believed or intended the person incited to have *mens rea*.[15] But the difference is that the inciter is immediately liable for the act of incitement. The secondary party does not become liable as such until the *actus reus* is committed. Aiding, abetting, etc. and incitement are different concepts.

11 Withdrawal by a Secondary Party[16]

Where D has counselled E to commit a crime, or is present, aiding E in the commission of it, it may yet be possible for him to escape liability by withdrawal before E goes on to commit the crime. An effective withdrawal will not, however, affect any liability he may have already incurred for

---

8. Cross (1953) 69 LQR 354. Lord Edmund-Davies in *Lynch v Director of Public Prosecutions for Northern Ireland* [1975] 1 All ER 913 at 952; below, p. 235. See also, Edwards (1953) 69 LQR 226.
9. Above, pp. 32–33.
10. [1976] QB 217, [1975] 2 All ER 1059, [1975] Crim LR 584 and commentary; **SHC 141**. See Buxton "Vicarious Rape" (1975) 125 NLJ 1133, Williams [1975] CLJ 182.
11. [1976] AC 182, [1975] 1 All ER 8; **SHC 46**.
12. Above, p. 87, below, pp. 216, 451.
13. Above, p. 152.
14. See now *R.* [1991] 4 All ER 481, [1991] 3 WLR 767, HL.
15. Below, p. 268.
16. See Lanham, "Accomplices and Withdrawal", (1981) 97 LQR 575 Williams, TBCL, 310–311.

incitement, or conspiracy, or, if the withdrawal took place after E had done more than a merely preparatory act,[17] attempt, to commit the crime.[18]

Mere repentance, without any action, clearly leaves D liable.[19] His "innocent" state of mind at the time of the commission of the crime is no answer. He had *mens rea* when he did the act of counselling or aiding. What is an effective withdrawal may depend on the mode of D's participation in the contemplated offence. If it consisted only in advising or encouraging E to commit the crime, it is enough for him to tell E to desist.[20] If E then commits the crime he does so against E's advice and without his encouragement. It may be that E would never have committed the crime if D had not put it into his head in the first place; but then D may be properly and adequately dealt with by conviction of incitement. If D has counselled more than one person, then it seems that he must communicate his countermand to all of those who perpetrate the offence, for otherwise his counselling remains operative.[1]

To be effective, the communication must be such as "will serve unequivocal notice upon the other party to the common unlawful cause that if he proceeds upon it he does so without the further aid and assistance of those who withdraw."[2] The position might be different where D has supplied E with the means of committing the crime. Arguably, D must neutralise, or at least take all reasonable steps to neutralise, the aid he has given. If E ignores D's countermand and uses the thing or information with which D has supplied him to commit the crime, he has in fact been aided by D in doing so. Aid may be less easily neutralised than advice. Where D2 handed D1 a knife so that he could use it on anyone interfering in a burglary, D2 did not make a sufficient communication of withdrawal when, on the appearance of P, he said "Come on, let's go," and got out through a window. Something "vastly different and vastly more effective" was required and, possibly, nothing less than physical intervention to stop D1 committing the crime would be required.[3]

In that case, the "withdrawal" occurred at a very late stage and it does not follow that it is never possible effectively to withdraw by countermand where aid given by D continues to be effective. In *Grundy*[4] D had supplied E, a burglar, with information which was presumably valuable to E in committing the crime; but, for two weeks before E did so, D had been trying to stop him breaking in. It was held that there was evidence of an effective withdrawal which should have been left to the jury. In *Whitefield*[5] there was evidence that D had served unequivocal notice on E that, if he proceeded with the burglary they had planned together, he would do so

---

17. Below, p. 308.
18. Withdrawal does not affect liability for an attempt; below, p. 317.
19. Hale, 1 PC 618; Stephen, *Digest* (4th ed.), Art. 42 Williams, CLGP, §§ 127; *Croft* [1944] 1 KB 295, [1944] 2 All ER 483; *Becerra*, below, fn. 2.
20. *Saunders and Archer* (1573) 2 Plowd 473.
1. *State v Kinchen* (1910) 52 So 185, quoted by Lanham, op. cit. at 591.
2. *Whitehouse* [1941] 1 WWR 112, per Sloan JA (Court of Appeal of British Columbia) approved in *Becerra* (1976) 62 Cr App Rep 212, CA. Cf. *Fletcher* [1962] Crim LR 551; *Grundy* [1977] Crim LR 543, CA.
3. *Becerra*, above, fn. 2.
4. [1977] Crim LR 543.
5. (1984) 79 Cr App Rep 36.

without D's aid or assistance. The jury should have been told that, if they accepted the evidence, that was a defence. It may be that an effective withdrawal can be made more easily at the preparatory stage than where the crime is in the course of commission, as in *Becerra*. When the knife is about to descend, the only effective withdrawal may be physical intervention to prevent it reaching its target.

If a rejected countermand may be an effective withdrawal, as in *Grundy*, it is arguable that an attempt to countermand should be the same. D has done all in his power to communicate his countermand to E but failed. In all these cases, the countermand has, *ex hypothesi*, failed; and, if the question is whether D has done his best to prevent the commission of the crime, the answer does not depend on the reasons for the failure.[6] It may be argued that, where D has failed to communicate, he can escape only by going to the police; but this was not insisted on in *Grundy* when persuasion failed.

Where D does give timely warning to the police, the effect ought in most cases to be that the crime will be prevented; but this may not always be so and, even where it is, there remains D's potential liability for abetting E's attempt, if E has gone beyond mere preparation. Surely, however, efforts to prevent the commission of the crime by informing the police ought to be an effective withdrawal, whether D has or has not attempted to persuade E to desist. Apart from being the best evidence of repentance, it is conduct which the law should and does encourage.[7]

Withdrawal, it is submitted, must be voluntary. If D is arrested, he can hardly be said to have "withdrawn". His arrest does not undo any aid, advice or encouragement he may have already given and therefore does not absolve him from any potential liability he has already incurred.[8] Of course, it usually precludes any future secondary participation by him;[9] but in this section we are concerned with absolution from the potential liability arising from D's past acts.

It is sometimes suggested that withdrawal is effective only if there is a genuine "repentance". English courts are generally reluctant to go into questions of motive. D may have seen the light, or he may be acting out of malice against his accomplices or because of fear of detection or because he has decided that the risks outweigh the possible rewards. It is submitted that it should make no difference.

12 Victims as Parties to Crime[10]

It has been noted[11] that when a statute creates a crime it does not generally provide that it shall be an offence to aid, abet, counsel or procure it. Such a

---

6. Contra, Lanham 590.
7. Cf. the large "discounts" on sentence which may be earned for information given after D has become liable for and been convicted of the offence. Above, pp. 7–8.
8. *Johnson and Jones* (1841) Car & M 218. *Jackson* (1673) 1 Hale PC 464 at 465 appears contra but is an obscure and unsatisfactory case. See Lanham, op. cit. 577.
9. For a case where it did not, see *Craig and Bentley* (1952) The Times, 10–13th December.
10. Hogan [1962] Crim LR 683; Williams, (1990) 10 LS 245; Criminal Law Revision Committee, Fifteenth Report (Cmnd. 9213), Appendix B.
11. Above, pp. 123 and 138.

provision is unnecessary, for it follows by implication of law. There is, however, one exception to this rule. Where the statute is designed for the protection of a certain class of persons it may be construed as excluding by implication the liability of any member of that class who is the victim of the offence, even though that member does in fact aid, abet, counsel or procure the offence. The principle is stated in the Draft Code (cl. 27(7)) in general terms:

"Where the purpose of an enactment creating an offence is the protection of a class of persons no member of that class who is a victim of such an offence can be guilty of that offence as an accessory"

but it has been applied, so far, only in respect of certain sexual offences.

In *Tyrrell*[12] D, a girl between the ages of thirteen and sixteen, abetted E to have unlawful sexual intercourse with her. This was an offence by E under the Criminal Law Amendment Act 1885, s. 5.[13] It was held, however, that D could not be convicted of abetting because the Act

"was passed for the purpose of protecting women and girls against themselves."[14]

The decisions on sodomy with boys under the age of fourteen seem to be explicable only on the assumption that the courts have applied a similar principle.[15] On the other hand, it has been held that a woman who is not pregnant can be convicted of abetting the use upon herself by another of an instrument with intent to procure her miscarriage, although the clear implication of the statute[16] is that such a woman cannot be convicted of *using* an instrument on herself with that intent.[17] However, a pregnant woman can be convicted under the same section of using an instrument on herself so it cannot be argued that this section was passed for the protection of *women* and it would be curious that Parliament should have intended to protect non-pregnant women from themselves, but not pregnant women.

How far the rule in *Tyrrell* extends has not been settled. The court referred to "women" as well as girls and it may well be that it extends to the offences of procuration of women to be prostitutes and of brothel keeping which were in the 1885 Act and are now in the Sexual Offences Act 1956.[18] It will obviously extend to intercourse with girls under sixteen and defectives;[19] to permitting premises to be used for intercourse with young girls and defectives;[20] and to at least some offences of abduction.[1] It has

---

12. [1894] 1 QB 710.
13. See now Sexual Offences Act 1956, s. 6; below, p. 462. The rule applies to incest with a girl under 16; below, p. 467.
14. Per Lord Coleridge CJ at 712. Both the Chief Justice and Mathew J pointed out that there was nothing in the Act to say that the girl should be guilty of aiding and abetting; but, it is submitted, no importance could be attached to that, for statutes hardly ever do.
15. Below, p. 478.
16. Offences against the Person Act 1861, s. 58; below, p. 388.
17. *Sockett* (1908) 72 JP 428; below, p. 299.
18. Sections 22–24, 28 and 29.
19. Below, pp. 462 and 464.
20. Below, p. 466.
1. Sexual Offences Act 1956, ss. 17–21. The rule was not applied in a Tasmanian case of abduction of a girl under eighteen: *Preston* [1962] Tas SR 141; but this turned on the construction of the Tasmanian Criminal Code.

been held that it applies to the prostitute who abets a man who is living off her earnings.[2]

In all these cases, it seems clear that the protection of the law extends only to a person of the class who is a *victim*. Thus, it is thought, a girl under sixteen could be convicted of abetting E in having intercourse with another girl under sixteen; a boy under fourteen could be convicted of abetting E in sodomy with another boy under fourteen; a prostitute could abet E in keeping a brothel in which she was not a participant, or of living off the earnings of another prostitute.

There are many instances outside sexual offences where laws are passed for the protection of a particular class of persons. For example, there is much legislation protecting tenants from rapacious landlords. In the civil law a tenant who has paid a premium illegally demanded by her landlord is not so tainted with his criminality as to be disabled from asserting her rights under the tenancy;[3] and it is possible that a principle similar to that in *Tyrrell* might be applied if a tenant were charged with abetting the landlord's offence.

13 Instigation for the Purpose of Entrapment[4]

Police or other law enforcement officers or their agents sometimes do acts for the purpose of entrapping, or getting evidence against offenders, which would certainly amount to counselling or abetting an offence if they were not done for that purpose. The difficult question is how far an officer may go without himself incurring liability for the offence. Law enforcement officers have no general licence to aid and abet crime. In *Sang*[5] Lord Salmon said:

"I would now refer to what is, I believe and hope, the unusual case, in which a dishonest policeman, anxious to improve his detection record, tries very hard with the help of an agent provocateur to induce a young man with no criminal record to commit a serious crime; and ultimately the young man reluctantly succumbs to the inducement ... The policeman and the informer who had acted together in inciting him to commit the crime should ... both be prosecuted and suitably punished."

It is not clear that the word "dishonest" adds anything to the postulated facts and it should make no difference that the policeman's motive is hatred of crime. It can hardly be necessary that the man induced to act should be "young"; and it might be even more serious to induce a man with a bad record who was "going straight", for the consequences for him would be worse. The essence of the dictum seems to be that a person who would not

---

2. *Congdon* (1990) 140 NLJ 1221 (Judge Addison); Hogan [1962] Crim LR at pp. 692–693; Williams, 10 LS at 248–249.

3. *Grace Rymer Investments Ltd v Waite* [1958] Ch 831, [1958] 2 All ER 777.

4. Williams, CLGP, § 256; McClean, "Informers and Agents Provocateurs", [1969] Crim LR 527; Heydon, "The Problems of Entrapment" [1973] CLJ 268; Law Commission Working Paper No. 55 and *Report on Defences of General Application* (Law Com No. 83, 1977) where it is recommended that there should be no defence of entrapment but that consideration should be given to the creation of a new *offence* of entrapment. See Ashworth, "Entrapment" [1978] Crim LR 137.

5. (1979) 69 Cr App Rep 282 at 296.

otherwise have committed a crime is induced to do so.[6] It may, however, be lawful to participate in an offence which has already been "laid on" and is going to be committed in any event, in order to trap the offenders.[7] In such a case it makes no difference that the police intervention may have affected the time or other circumstances of the commission of the offence.[8]

By these standards, judges in the past may have shown undue tolerance to incitement of offences by the police. In *Mullins*[9] when D, apparently acting with the authority of the police, attended a treasonable conspiracy, endeavoured to persuade strangers to join in and advocated the use of violence, Maule J rejected an argument that D's evidence required corroboration as that of an accomplice. He said that a person employed by the government as a spy does not deserve to be blamed "if he instigates offences no further than by pretending to concur with the perpetrators". That dictum is of course acceptable; but D's conduct seems to have gone well beyond this, particularly in trying to persuade strangers to join in. Where there is a continuing general conspiracy – e.g., to supply drugs to anyone asking for them – it seems that a law enforcement officer commits no offence by inducing the general conspirators to enter into a particular conspiracy within the ambit of the general conspiracy, e.g., to supply him with specified drugs. In *Edwards*[10] it was said that, because there was an established conspiracy when the officer came on the scene, he was not an agent provocateur[11] and therefore there was no ground for excluding the officer's evidence under s. 78 of PACE 1984 as having an adverse effect on the fairness of the proceedings.[12] Similarly, the court seems to have seen nothing wrong in the conduct of an undercover agent who introduced himself as "a contract killer" to a man who had made it known that he wished his wife to be killed and who thereupon solicited the agent to kill.[13]

It would be wise, however, for police authorities to bear in mind the recommendation of the Royal Commission on Police Powers:[14]

"As a general rule, the police should observe only, without participating in an offence, except in cases where an offence is habitually committed in circumstances in which observation by a third party is *ex hypothesi* impossible. Where participation is essential it should only be resorted to on the express and written authority of the Chief Constable."

Moreover, it cannot be the law that the police may properly participate in a crime to the point at which irreparable damage is done. A policeman who assists E to commit murder in order to entrap him must be guilty of

6. Cf. *Birtles* [1969] 2 All ER 1131n, [1969] 1 WLR 1047.
7. *McCann* (1971) 56 Cr App Rep 359.
8. *McEvilly* (1973) 60 Cr App Rep 150.
9. (1848) 3 Cox CC 526.
10. [1991] Crim LR 45. Cf. *Bickley* (1909) 2 Cr App Rep 53; *Marsh v Johnston* [1959] Crim LR 44, SLT 28 (High Court of Justiciary).
11. Defined by the Royal Commission as "a person who entices another to commit an express breach of the law which he would not otherwise have committed and then proceeds to inform against him in respect of such an offence".
12. This stands on its head the ruling in *Sang* that evidence obtained by trickery after, but not before, the commission of an offence might be excluded by the judge in the exercise of a common law discretion.
13. *Bainbridge* [1991] Crim LR 535.
14. Cmd. 3297 (1928), 116.

murder. It is submitted that the same must be true of any injury to the person, unless it is trivial and P consents to it; and probably to any damage to property, unless the owner consents.

a) *No defence of entrapment.* It is convenient to notice here that the House of Lords decided in *Sang* that there is no defence of entrapment in English law. It was thought to be a necessary corollary that a judge has no discretion to exclude evidence of the commission of an offence which was induced by the trap for such exclusion would indirectly provide the defence which the law did not allow. While the substantive law is unchanged, it may be that the new discretion given to the judge by s. 78 of PACE 1984 will entitle the judge, in some circumstances, to exclude such evidence as having an adverse effect on the fairness of the proceedings.[15]

Entrapment is a matter which may be taken into account in fixing the sentence so, where there was a possibility that a theft might not have been committed but for a police trap, D was sentenced as if he had been convicted of a conspiracy to steal rather than the actual theft.[16] Where the police have facilitated the commission of a crime, this fact must be revealed to the trial court.[17]

With cases of police intervention may be compared that of *Smith*[18] where a private citizen took it upon himself to instigate crime with the object of procuring a conviction and was himself convicted. But even in the case of a private citizen it is a defence that he was acting honestly and solely in order to betray his associates and ensure the recovery of any proceeds of the crime[19] – as where a taxi-driver drives burglars to the scene of the crime, with the intention of fetching police when he has left them there.

15. See commentary on *Edwards*, above, fn. 10.
16. *McCann*, above, p. 158.
17. *Macro* [1969] Crim LR 205.
18. [1960] 2 QB 423, [1960] 1 All ER 256.
19. See *Clarke* (1984) 80 Cr App Rep 344, [1985] Crim LR 209, CA. *Mullins*, above, p. 158.

8 Assistance after the Offence

1 Impeding the Apprehension or Prosecution of Arrestable Offenders[1]

At common law anyone who gave to any party to a felony any assistance whatever, tending to and having the object of, enabling him to evade arrest, trial or punishment, was guilty of the felony as accessory after the fact. The whole of the law relating to accessories after the fact was repealed by the Criminal Law Act 1967 and replaced by s. 4 of that Act:

"(1) Where a person has committed an arrestable offence, any other person who, knowing or believing him to be guilty of the offence or of some other arrestable offence, does without lawful authority or reasonable excuse any act with intent to impede his apprehension or prosecution shall be guilty of an offence [triable either way].

(2) If on the trial of an indictment for an arrestable offence the jury are satisfied that the offence charged (or some other offence of which the accused might on that charge be found guilty) was committed, but find the accused not guilty of it, they may find him guilty of any offence under subsection (1) above of which they are satisfied that he is guilty in relation to the offence charged (or that other offence).

(3) A person committing an offence under subsection (1) above with intent to impede another person's apprehension or prosecution shall on conviction on indictment be liable to imprisonment according to the gravity of the other person's offence, as follows:

(a) if that offence is one for which the sentence is fixed by law, he shall be liable to imprisonment for not more than ten years;

(b) if it is one for which a person (not previously convicted) may be sentenced to imprisonment for a term of fourteen years, he shall be liable to imprisonment for not more than seven years;

(c) if it is not one included above but is one for which a person (not previously convicted) may be sentenced to imprisonment for a term of ten years, he shall be liable to imprisonment for not more than five years;

(d) in any other case, he shall be liable to imprisonment for not more than three years."

---

1. Williams, "Evading Justice" [1975] Crim LR 430.

The effect of *Courtie*[2] is that the section creates four offences, punishable with 10, 7, 5 and 3 years' imprisonment, respectively.

1) *The Actus Reus*

There are two elements in the *actus reus*: (i) an arrestable offence must have been committed by the person (O) whose apprehension or prosecution D is charged with impeding; and (ii) D must have done "any act" with the appropriate intent. No one may be convicted of an attempt to commit this offence.[3]

The arrestable offence alleged to have been committed by O must be specified in the indictment. If, however, it turns out that O was not guilty of the specified offence, D may still be convicted if O was guilty of another arrestable offence of which he might have been convicted on the indictment for the specified offence, under s. 6 (3) of the Criminal Law Act 1967.[4] If, for example, it is alleged that O committed murder and it transpires at D's trial that O was not guilty of murder but was guilty of manslaughter or attempted murder, D may be convicted. It is not necessary to direct the jury to find what offence D thought O had committed, though this may be a material factor in the imposition of sentence.[5] It is immaterial that O has been acquitted at an earlier trial if it can be proved at D's trial that O was guilty. Even where O and D are tried together, O's acquittal should not, in principle, be conclusive if it can be proved, as against D, that O committed the offence.[6] But O's conviction is presumptive evidence that he committed the offence: PACE, 1984, s. 74. Once the arrestable offence has been proved, the remaining element in the *actus reus* – any act – is almost unlimited. There must be an *act* – an omission will not suffice – but it need not be an act having a natural tendency to impede the apprehension or prosecution of an offender. Where the act does not have such a tendency, however, it will be difficult to prove the intent, in the absence of a confession. The common instances of the offence will undoubtedly correspond to the typical ways of becoming an accessory after the fact under the old law – by concealing the offender, providing him with a car, food or money to enable him to escape, or destroying evidence against him. According to the Criminal Law Revision Committee,[7] "The requirement that there should be an attempt to 'impede' a prosecution will exclude mere persuasion not to prosecute". Yet words are no doubt a sufficient act; so that the offence would be committed by intentionally misdirecting police who were pursuing an offender, or making a false statement to a detective.[8]

2. Above, p. 32.
3. Criminal Attempts Act 1981, s. 1 (4) (c).
4. *Morgan* [1972] 1 QB 436, [1972] 1 All ER 348. Quaere whether the same principle is applicable to other provisions allowing conviction of offences other than that charged?
5. Ibid.
6. Cf. *Shannon* [1975] AC 717, [1974] 2 All ER 1009, HL; below, p. 300 and commenting on *Donald* (1986) 83 Cr App Rep 49 [1986] Crim LR 535. Williams [1975] Crim LR at 432.
7. Cmnd. 2659, para. 28.
8. This would amount to other offences as well; see below, pp. 418–422.

An act done through an agent would be sufficient. Indeed, the mere authorisation of the agent would be a sufficient act, when done with intent to impede, to constitute the offence, though the agent never acted on it.

2) *The Mens Rea*

There are two elements in the *mens rea*: (i) D must know or believe the offender to be guilty of the arrestable offence which he had actually committed, or some other arrestable offence; and (ii) D must intend to impede the apprehension or prosecution of the offender.

"Some other arrestable offence" must refer to an offence which O has not committed, for otherwise the words are redundant. If D thinks he has seen O commit a robbery and acts with intent to conceal this, he will be guilty, though O had in fact committed a murder and not a robbery. This is obviously as it should be, where, as in this example, D's belief relates to the transaction which constituted the actual offence. Suppose, however, that unknown to D, O committed murder last week. D believes, wrongly, that O committed bigamy two years ago. If D does an act with intent to impede O's prosecution for bigamy – such as burning O's letters – it would seem very odd indeed that he should be liable only because O committed murder last week – the murder has nothing to do with the case. This suggests that the supposed offence must arise from the same transaction as the actual offence (and, undoubtedly, this will normally be the case) but so to hold would require the imposition of some limitation on the express words of the section.[9]

It is immaterial that D is unaware of O's identity.[10] What if he makes a mistake of identity? If D thinks he sees R committing an arrestable offence and acts, intending to impede his apprehension or prosecution, is he guilty under s. 4 if it was in fact O whom he observed? Perhaps the question should be answered by making a distinction. If D does an act which he intends to assist the person whom he in fact observed, his mistake of identity should be immaterial. For example, he sends a constable, who is pursuing the offender, in the wrong direction. Here D knows that the *person he is assisting* has committed an arrestable offence, and that person has in fact done so. Suppose, on the other hand, that D fabricates evidence the following day so as to provide an alibi for R and this evidence could not, and was of course not intended to assist O, of whom D has never heard. Here he does not intend to assist the person whom he in fact observed. An indictment charging D with doing an act, knowing O to be guilty of an arrestable offence and with intent to impede his prosecution is plainly bad. If R has never committed an arrestable offence, it would seem that D is not guilty under the section;[11] if R once did commit an arrestable offence, then

9. Cf. the discussion of s. 5, below, p. 165.
10. *Brindley* [1971] 2 QB 300, [1971] 2 All ER 698.
11. Nor could D be convicted of an attempt to commit the offence. See Criminal Attempts Act 1981, s. 1 (4) (c), below, p. 314.

D is guilty unless the limitation tentatively suggested in the previous paragraph be imposed.

D must *know or believe*. ". . . some other arrestable offence" must be governed only by "believing" since, *ex hypothesi*, the offence has not been committed and, therefore, D cannot "know" it has. ". . . the offence" – the arrestable offence which has actually been committed – is probably governed both by "knowing" and "believing", but, if "believing" is construed as in handling, it adds little to "knowing".[12] If the word "believing" had not been included "knowing" might well have been construed to include wilful blindness.[13] If D has a mere suspicion that O is an arrestable offender and, shutting his eyes to an obvious means of knowledge, assists him, he can hardly be said to "believe" in O's guilt. Thus recklessness may not be enough and, arguably, the subsection is unduly narrow in this respect.[14]

In order to know or believe that an arrestable offence has been committed, D need know no law. It will be enough that he believes in the existence of facts which, whether he knows it or not, amount in law to an arrestable offence.[15] His ignorance of the law cannot afford a defence.[16] The position is, perhaps, not quite so obvious where D has a positive mistaken belief. D knows that there is a duty not to conceal arrestable offenders, but, knowing what O has done, is wrongly informed that it does not constitute an arrestable offence. Arguably, he now has no *mens rea* on the ground that he has made a mistake of civil law,[17] whether there is a right to arrest being a civil and not a criminal matter.

The act must be done with intent to impede the arrestable offender's apprehension or prosecution. It seems that it must be proved that D's *purpose* was to impede, and that it is not enough that he knew his act would certainly impede if that was not his object or one of his objects; or, as it has been put above, that a "direct" and not merely an "oblique" intention is required.[18] At all events, this seems to be the Criminal Law Revision Committee's view of the clause which became s. 4. Discussing the case of harbouring, they wrote:

"If the harbouring is done with the object of impeding apprehension or prosecution . . . it will be within the offence; if it is done merely by way of providing or continuing to provide the criminal with accommodation in the ordinary way, it will not; and juries will be able to tell the difference."[19]

If this be the correct interpretation of the section, then, as under the old law of accessories after the fact, a handler of stolen goods will not be guilty of an offence under s. 4, even where he knows that his conduct has the effect of impeding the apprehension or prosecution of the thief, if that is not his

12. *Ismail* [1977] Crim LR 557, CA; *Grainge* [1974] 1 All ER 928, CA; *Griffiths* (1974) 60 Cr App Rep 14; CA; below, p. 650.
13. Williams [1975] Crim LR at 435.
14. Above, p. 105.
15. Cf. *Sykes v Director of Public Prosecutions* [1962] AC 528 at 563, [1961] 3 All ER 33 at 42.
16. Above, p. 80.
17. Above, p. 83. But see Draft Code, cl. 25 (3) (b), Law Com. No. 143.
18. Above, p. 53.
19. Cmnd. 2659, para. 30.

object.[20] Nor is D guilty if, by acts done with the object of avoiding his own arrest or prosecution, he knowingly impedes the arrest or prosecution of another.[1] Where there is *prima facie* evidence of the necessary intent, it is for D to lay a foundation for a defence by introducing evidence that his sole purpose was of a different character. In the absence of such evidence, there is no duty to direct a jury to consider whether D might have had a different intent.[2] If D has the dual object of saving himself and the other from arrest or prosecution then, no doubt, he is guilty.

Under the old law, D was guilty as an accessory after the fact if he assisted a felon to evade his punishment by enabling him to escape or to remain at large. It is clearly not an offence under s. 4 to enable a convicted arrestable offender (as opposed to one awaiting trial) to escape from gaol; but this is not important as such acts will amount to other offences.[3] Whether it is an offence to assist such an arrestable offender who has escaped to remain at large depends on the interpretation of "apprehension". Does it extend beyond its obvious meaning of apprehension with a view to prosecution and include the re-arrest of the escaped convicted prisoner? There seems to be no reason why it should not be so interpreted.

Even though the act is done with intent to impede, it is not an offence if there is "lawful authority or reasonable excuse" for it. According to the Criminal Law Revision Committee:[4]

"The exception for 'lawful authority' will cover an executive decision against a prosecution, and that for 'reasonable excuse' will avoid extending the offence to acts such as destroying the evidence of an offence (for example a worthless cheque) in pursuance of a legitimate agreement to refrain from prosecuting in consideration of the making good of loss caused by that offence."

It is possible that the exception may have some application outside this situation.[5] As with the Prevention of Crime Act,[6] it enables the courts to afford a defence in circumstances in which they think it reasonable to do so.

3) *The Sentence*

Section 4 (3)[7] provides for a sliding scale of sentences which is related to the arrestable offence which has actually been committed. Where D believes that some other arrestable offence has been committed, the punishment to which he is liable is fixed according to the *actus reus*, not according to the

---

20. *Andrews and Craig* [1962] 3 All ER 961n.
   1. *Jones* [1949] 1 KB 194, [1948] 2 All ER 964.
   2. *Brindley* [1971] 2 QB 300 at 304.
   3. Prison breaking, escape and rescue are offences at common law. See sixth edition of this work, p. 656.
   4. Cmnd. 2659, para. 28.
   5. Would a wife have a reasonable excuse for assisting her husband? See Pace, "'Impeding Arrest'. A Wife's Right as a Spouse?" [1978] Crim LR 82. According to *Lee Shek Ching v R.* Hong Kong, CA, 1985, No. 53, being O's wife is not, as such, a reasonable excuse.
   6. Below, p. 443.
   7. Above, p. 160.

mens rea. If D acts with intent to impede the apprehension of O whom he believes to have committed malicious wounding[8] (maximum, five years), he is liable to three years' imprisonment if his belief is correct; but if O has in fact committed murder, he is liable to ten years. This is another instance of the penalty being related to the harm, rather than the fault of the offender.[9]

It is clear that the arrestable offence which fixes the maximum under s. 4 must have been committed when the act of impeding takes place. D, rightly believing O to be guilty of malicious wounding, acts to impede his arrest. Subsequently, O's victim, P, dies, and O becomes guilty of murder. D is liable to only three and not ten years' imprisonment.

2 Compounding an Arrestable Offence[10]

The abolition of felonies by the Criminal Law Act 1967 eliminated two common law misdemeanours known respectively as compounding a felony and misprision of felony.[11] The former consisted in an agreement for consideration not to prosecute, or to impede a prosecution for, a felony. The latter consisted simply in an omission to report a felony to the police. In place of these offences s. 5 (1) of the Criminal Law Act enacts an offence, triable either way, as follows:

"Where a person has committed an arrestable offence, any other person who, knowing or believing that the offence or some other arrestable offence has been committed, and that he has information which might be of material assistance in securing the prosecution or conviction of an offender for it, accepts or agrees to accept for not disclosing that information any consideration other than the making good of loss or injury caused by the offence, or the making of reasonable compensation for that loss or injury, shall be liable on conviction on indictment to imprisonment for not more than two years."

This provision is much less far-reaching than the previous law. It is narrower than misprision in that the offence is committed only if D accepts or agrees to accept a consideration for not disclosing the information relating to the arrestable offence. It is narrower than compounding in that it is not now criminal to accept or agree to accept consideration for not disclosing information relating to the arrestable offence, if the consideration is no more than the making good of loss or injury caused by the offence or the making of reasonable compensation for that loss or injury. No one may be convicted of attempting to commit an offence under s. 5 (1).[12]

---

8. Below, p. 424.
9. Above, p. 5.
10. Williams, "Evading Justice" [1975] Crim LR at 609.
11. See the first edition of this book, pp. 539–544.
12. Criminal Attempts Act 1981, s. 1 (4) (c), below, p. 314.

1) *Actus Reus*

There are two elements in the *actus reus*: (i) an arrestable offence must actually have been committed; and (ii) D must accept or agree to accept consideration for not disclosing information which he knows or believes to be material.

The offence is committed only where D "accepts or agrees to accept" the consideration. The situation envisaged is that where an offer is made to D. If the offer comes from D, then he would seem to be guilty also of the much more serious offence of blackmail.[13] Consideration presumably bears much the same meaning as in the law of contract and extends to money, goods, services, or any act or forbearance.

The new offence is wider than misprision and compounding in that it extends to all arrestable offences which, of course, include some crimes which were not felonies; but it is provided by s. 5 (5):

"The compounding of an offence other than treason shall not be an offence otherwise than under this section."

It is thus clear that it is not an offence to agree to accept any consideration for not prosecuting a non-arrestable offence, though whether the resulting contract is enforceable is another matter.

The Act makes no provision for any privileged relationships (such as may have existed under the law of misprision) but proceedings may not be instituted without the consent of the Director of Public Prosecutions.[14]

2) *Mens Rea*

There are two elements in the *mens rea*. It must be proved that (i) D knew or believed that an arrestable offence had been committed and (ii) D intended to accept or to agree to accept consideration other than the making good of loss or the making of reasonable compensation.

Where D's knowledge or belief relates to the arrestable offence which has actually been committed, the application of the section seems quite straightforward. But D's belief may relate to some other arrestable offence which, *ex hypothesi*, has not been committed. Here D's acceptance, or agreement to accept consideration, must relate to the offence which he believes to have been committed and thus not to the offence which has actually been committed since they are different. Under this section D's belief need not – as, under s. 4, it probably must[15] – be that an arrestable offence has been committed by the same person who has in fact committed such an offence. If D wrongly supposes that he has seen an arrestable offence committed by R and accepts consideration for not disclosing what

13. Below, p. 606.
14. Section 5 (3).
15. See above, p. 163.

he saw, he will be guilty if in fact he saw O committing an arrestable offence.

The result is that the argument advanced in connection with s. 4, that D's belief must relate to the transaction which resulted in the actual offence, is much stronger in relation to s. 5. If D wrongly supposes that R has committed an arrestable offence and accepts consideration for not disclosing that fact, his guilt can hardly be established by proving that some time, somewhere, someone committed an arrestable offence – for example, that Dr Crippen committed murder. The offence which D supposes to have been committed must have something to do with the offence which has actually been committed. The most obvious point of connection is that the real and the supposed offence must both arise out of the same transaction. An alternative view might be that it is sufficient if either (i) the two offences arise out of the same transaction or (ii) they both relate to the same person. Unknown to D, O committed murder last week. D believes, wrongly, that O committed bigamy two years ago. O offers money to D "to keep his mouth shut". D, believing that O is talking about the bigamy, accepts. According to the first view put above, D is not guilty; according to the alternative view, he is. It is submitted that the first view is better; according to the second, D's liability depends entirely on chance.

If D's acceptance of consideration relates to the transaction in question, then it seems that it will be immaterial that he is mistaken as to both (i) the nature of the arrestable offence and (ii) the identity of the perpetrator. He supposes he saw R perpetrating a robbery. Actually, he saw O committing murder. If he accepts consideration for not disclosing what he saw he should be guilty.

The Criminal Law Revision Committee stated:[16]

". . . the offence will not apply to a person who refrains from giving information because he does not think it right that the offender should be prosecuted or because of a promise of reparation by the offender. It would be difficult to justify making the offence apply to those cases."

It is difficult to see, however, how it can be a defence for D simply to say that he did not "think it right that the offender should be prosecuted", if he has accepted consideration for not disclosing information. Even if he convinces the court of his views as to the impropriety of the contemplated prosecution he still falls within the express words of the section. He could be acquitted only if the section were interpreted so as to require that D's object or motive be the acquisition of the consideration. As we have seen,[17] on a charge under s. 4, it is probable that a *purpose* of impeding must be proved, but this may be justified by giving a narrow meaning to the ulterior intent specified in that section. No ulterior intent is specified in s. 5 and, consequently, it is difficult to see how the section can be limited in the same way.

16. Cmnd. 2659, para. 41.
17. Above, p. 163.

In the light of the new rules about compounding, it is perhaps a little surprising that the offence of advertising rewards for the return of goods stolen or lost has been retained.[18] Section 23 of the Theft Act provides:

"Where any public advertisement of a reward for the return of any goods which have been stolen or lost uses any words to the effect that no questions will be asked, or that the person producing the goods will be safe from apprehension or inquiry, or that any money paid for the purchase of the goods or advanced by way of loan on them will be repaid, the person advertising the reward and any person who prints or publishes the advertisement shall on summary conviction be liable to a fine not exceeding one hundred pounds."

In so far as an advertisement states that "no questions will be asked", it is only proposing what is perfectly lawful under s. 5 (1) of the Criminal Law Act.[19] It is not clear why this should be an offence because it is done through a public advertisement. Nor is it clear why it should be an offence to offer a reward for the return of stolen goods, even their return by the thief. The promise to pay the reward might be unenforceable for lack of consideration but, if it were actually paid, there would be nothing unlawful about that. Possibly the theory is that, if such advertisements were common, theft might be encouraged in that thieves would have an easy and safe way of disposing of the stolen goods for reward. This cannot apply to an advertisement addressed to the bona fide purchaser offering to recompense him if he will return the stolen goods; this seems quite a reasonable thing to do, especially since the bona fide purchaser commits no offence by retaining the goods for himself.[20]

The section creates a quasi-criminal offence, not requiring *mens rea*, so the advertising manager of a company was liable for the publication of an advertisement which he had not read.[1] "Stolen" bears the wide meaning given to that word by s. 24 (4) of the Theft Act so the bona fide purchaser may indeed have become the absolute owner of the goods where, for example, they have been obtained by deception and the property passed.

3 Refusal to Aid a Constable

It is a common law misdemeanour to refuse to go to the aid of a constable who, on seeing a breach of the peace, calls on D to assist him in restoring the peace. A ticket collector was held to be guilty of the offence when he failed to come to the assistance of a policewoman struggling with a thief. His defence that he had obeyed instructions not to leave his post was not

---

18. The section replaces s. 102 of the Larceny Act 1861 which provided for a penalty of £50 recoverable by a common informer. This was changed to a fine of £100 by the Common Informers Act 1951. The Criminal Law Revision Committee hesitantly recommended the retention of the provision "as advertisements of this kind may encourage dishonesty": Cmnd. 2977, para. 144.
19. Above, p. 165.
20. Above, p. 511 and 648.
  1. *Denham v Scott* (1983) 77 Cr App Rep 210, [1983] Crim LR 558, DC.

accepted.[2] There must be a reasonable necessity for the constable to request assistance. It is no defence that D's aid would have been ineffective. So where a constable requested D to assist him in suppressing a breach of the peace among four or five hundred people at a prize fight, Alderson B directed that D's refusal was an offence.[3] It seems that it was no answer that he had his horses to take care of. Alderson B[4] recognised that physical impossibility or a lawful excuse would be an answer; but it is not clear what would constitute "lawful excuse". Is the citizen required to act where there would be a grave risk of death or serious injury?

2. *Waugh* (1976) Times, 1 October (Knightsbridge Crown Court).
3. *Brown* (1841) Car & M 314. Cf. *Sherlock* (1866) LR 1 CCR 20.
4. In *Brown*, above.

9 Vicarious Liability and Liability of Associations

1 Vicarious Liability[1]

In the law of tort, a master is held liable for all acts of his servant performed in the course of the servant's employment. In the criminal law, a master is generally not so liable. In the leading civil case of *Lloyd v Grace, Smith & Co*,[2] a solicitor's managing clerk, without the knowledge of his employer, induced a widow to give him instructions to sell certain property, to hand over the title deeds and to sign two documents which were neither read over nor explained to her, but which she believed were necessary for the sale. The documents were, in fact, a conveyance to the clerk of the property, of which he dishonestly disposed for his own benefit. It was held that, since the clerk was acting within the scope of his authority, his employer was liable. Now it is very likely that the clerk was guilty of certain criminal offences – perhaps larceny of the title deeds and fraudulent conversion of the money; but it is perfectly clear that his employer could never have been made criminally liable for those acts for which he bore civil liability. An employer is similarly liable in tort where the fraud involves a forgery,[3] and for acts which amount to obtaining by deception, assault and battery, manslaughter and so on; but in none of these cases would he be criminally liable simply on the ground that his servant was acting in the course of his employment. The doctrine of vicarious liability in tort developed in the early part of the eighteenth century, but it was made clear by the leading case of *Huggins*[4] that there was to be no parallel development in the criminal law. Huggins, the warden of the Fleet, was charged with the murder of a prisoner whose death had been caused by the servant of Huggins's deputy. It was held that, though the servant was guilty, Huggins was not, since the acts were done without his knowledge. Raymond CJ said:[5]

---

1. Williams, CLGP, Ch. 7, and "*Mens Rea* and Vicarious Responsibility" (1956) 9 CLP 57; Glazebrook, "Situational Liability" in *Reshaping the Criminal Law* 108; Pace, "Delegation – a Doctrine in Search of a Definition" [1982] Crim LR 627; L. H. Leigh, *Strict and Vicarious Libility*; F. B. Sayer "Criminal Responsibility for the Acts of Another" (1930) 43 Harv LR 689; Baty, *Vicarious Liability* (1916), especially Ch. X. For proposals for the reform of the law, see Law Commission Working Place No. 43.
2. [1912] AC 716, HL.
3. *Uxbridge Permanent Building Society v Pickard* [1939] 2 KB 248, [1939] 2 All ER 344.
4. (1730) 2 Stra 883.
5. Ibid., at 885.

"It is a point not to be disputed, but that in criminal cases the principal is not answerable for the act of the deputy as he is in civil cases: they must each answer for their own acts, and stand or fall by their own behaviour. All the authors that treat of criminal proceedings proceed on the foundation of this distinction; that to affect the superior by the act of his deputy, there must be the command of the superior which is not found in this case."

A master can be held liable for his servants' crimes, as a general rule, only where he is a participant in them within the rules stated in the preceding section. Two exceptions to this have already been noted:[6] in public nuisance and criminal libel a master has been held liable for his servants' acts although he is, personally, perfectly innocent. These were the only exceptions at common law; but now, by statute, there are many such offences.

1 Strict Liability and Vicarious Liability Distinguished

Vicarious liability is by no means the same thing as strict liability. The point requires emphasis for there is an unhappy judicial tendency to confuse the two concepts. A statute may require *mens rea* and yet impose vicarious responsibility. It has already been noted that supplying liquor to a constable on duty is an offence requiring *mens rea*,[7] yet a licensee may be vicariously liable for his servants' act in so doing[8] and the same considerations apply to the offence of suffering gaming to be carried on in licensed premises.[9] Conversely, it is clearly possible for a statute to create strict liability without imposing vicarious responsibility. Once a statute has been held to impose a duty, with strict liability, on a particular person, it is likely to be held that that person is liable for the acts of anyone through whom he performs that duty.[10] Where, however, the duty is not imposed on particular persons but on the public generally, vicarious liability is inappropriate. For example, the former offence of causing death by dangerous driving was, at one time, held to be an offence of strict liability, but it is surely inconceivable that vicarious liability would have been imposed.

As in the case of strict liability, so with vicarious liability it may well be argued that the development is the work of the courts rather than of Parliament. A statute rarely says in terms that one person is to be liable for another's crimes.[11] It is not uncommon, however, for the courts to detect such an intention in statutes which create summary offences. The reason

---

6. Above, p. 100.
7. *Sherras v De Rutzen*, above p. 106.
8. *Mullins v Collins* (1874) LR 9 QB 292.
9. *Bosley v Davies* (1875) 1 QBD 84 (*mens rea* required); *Bond v Evans* (1888) 21 QBD 249 (licensee liable for servants' act); Licensing Act 1872, s. 16.
10. *Dicta* to the effect that an offence of strict liability necessarily imposes vicarious responsibility are not difficult to find: see, e.g., *Barker v Levinson* [1951] 1 KB 342 at 345; [1950] 2 All ER 825 at 827; *James & Son Ltd v Smee* [1955] 1 QB 78 at 95, [1954] 3 All ER 273 at 280, per Slade J. *Bradshaw v Ewart-James* [1983] 1 All ER 12 at 14.
11. A striking example is the Road Traffic Offenders Act 1988 s 64 (5), which provides that the owner of a vehicle (even if a corporation) shall be conclusively presumed to have been the driver at the time of the commission of certain offences and, "accordingly, that acts or omissions of the driver of the vehicle at the time were his acts or omissions."

most commonly advanced by the judges for holding a master liable is that the statute would be "rendered nugatory"[12] – and the will of Parliament thereby defeated – if he were not. Two quite distinct principles, differing somewhat in their effect, underlie the various decisions. In the first place, a person may be held liable for the acts of another where he has delegated to that other the performance of certain duties cast on him by Act of Parliament. In the second place, a master may be held liable because acts which are done physically by the servant may, in law, be the master's acts. These two types of case require separate consideration.

2 The Delegation Principle[13]

A good illustration of the application of this principle may be found in the case of *Allen v Whitehead*.[14] Under the Metropolitan Police Act 1839, s. 44, it is an offence to

"knowingly permit or suffer prostitutes or persons of notoriously bad character to meet together and remain in a place where refreshments are sold and consumed".

D, the occupier of a café, while receiving the profits of the business, did not himself manage it, but employed a manager. Having had a warning from the police, D instructed his manager that no prostitutes were to be allowed to congregate on the premises and had a notice to that effect displayed on the walls. He visited the premises once or twice a week and there was no evidence that any misconduct took place in his presence. Then, on eight consecutive days, a number of women, known to the manager to be prostitutes, met together and remained there between the hours of 8 p.m. and 4 a.m. It was held by the Divisional Court, reversing the Metropolitan Magistrate, that D's ignorance of the facts was no defence. The acts of the servant and his *mens rea* were both to be imputed to his master, not simply because he was a servant, but because the management of the house had been delegated to him.

So in *Linnet v Metropolitan Police Commissioner*[15] it was held, following *Allen v Whitehead*,[16] that one of two co-licensees was liable for the acts of the other in knowingly permitting disorderly conduct in the licensed premises, contrary to s. 44 of the same Act, although the other was neither his servant nor his partner,[17] but simply his delegate in "keeping" the premises.

The argument that vicarious responsibility is necessary to make the statute operative applies with especial force to cases of this type. Where the statute is so phrased that the offence can be committed only by the delegator, there would indeed be a real difficulty in making the statute

---

12. *Mullins v Collins* (1874) LR 9 QB 292 at 295, per Blackburn and Quain JJ; *Coppen v Moore (No. 2)* [1898] 2 QB 306 at 314, per Lord Russell CJ; *Allens v Whitehead*, below.
13. See Pace, "Delegation – A Doctrine in Search of a Definition" [1982] Crim LR 627.
14. [1930] 1 KB 211.
15. [1946] KB 290, [1946] 1 All ER 380.
16. Above, fn. 14.
17. Both were, in fact, the employees of a limited company. The company was not charged, no doubt for the good reason that it was not the licensee.

effective without vicarious liability. Under the Metropolitan Police Act 1839, s. 44, the offence may be committed only by a person "who shall *have or keep* any house . . .". Presumably the manager in *Allen v Whitehead* was not such a person and if, therefore, the absentee "keeper" were not liable for his manager's acts, the statute could be ignored with impunity. The position is the same in many of the offences under the Licensing Acts; only the licensee can commit the offences. The difficulty has been well put by Lord Russell CJ:[18]

"We may take as an illustration the case of a sporting publican who attends race-meetings all over the country, and leaves a manager in charge of his public-house; is it to be said that there is no remedy under this section[19] if drink is sold by the manager in charge to any number of drunken persons? It is clear that there is no machinery by which the person actually selling can be convicted; a penalty can only be inflicted on the licensee."

If the licensee's delegate sub-delegates his responsibilities, the licensee is liable for the sub-delegate's acts,[20] but he is not liable for the acts of an inferior servant to whom control of the premises has not been delegated.[1]

There is some doubt as to the degree of delegation which is necessary to bring the principle into operation. In a leading case, *Vane v Yiannopoulos*,[2] Parker LCJ said that:

"It must be shown that the licensee is not managing the business himself but has delegated the management to someone else . . ."[3]

Lord Evershed[4] agreed with that and Lord Hodson said that the principle:

". . . has never so far been extended so as to cover the case where the whole of the authority of the licensee has not been transferred to another."[5]

Lord Reid appears to have confined the principle to cases where the licensee is absent from the premises leaving another in charge.[6] It was held that the principle was inapplicable in that case where the licensee was on the premises at the time of the offence, but not on the floor where a waitress, whom he had instructed as to her rights to sell intoxicating liquor, made an illegal sale. But in *Howker v Robinson*[7] a licensee who was serving in the public bar was held liable for an illegal sale made by his barman in the lounge. This does not seem to be a case where the whole authority of the licensee had been transferred or where he was not managing the business

18. In *Police Commissioners v Cartman* [1896] 1 QB 655 at 658. Yet when Parliament adds "or his servant" the court holds that the delegation principle still applies to the licensee: *Howker v Robinson*, below.
19. Licensing Act 1872, s. 13. Cf. *Cundy v Le Cocq*, above, p. 102, which establishes that the offence is also one of strict liability.
20. *Crabtree v Hole* (1879) 43 JP 799; *Sopp v Long* [1970] 1 QB 518, [1969] 1 All ER 855.
1. *Allchorn v Hopkins* (1905) 69 JP 355.
2. [1965] AC 486, [1964] 3 All ER 820, HL; **SHC 176**.
3. [1964] 2 QB 739 at 745, [1964] 2 All ER 820 at 823.
4. [1965] AC at 505.
5. At p. 510.
6. At p. 497, Cf. Pace, loc. cit., 629, 636.
7. [1973] QB 178, [1972] 2 All ER 786, DC.

himself. The court regarded the question whether there had been delegation as one of fact, which had been properly decided by the magistrates. *Winson*,[8] which the court followed, was entirely different, for there the licensee visited the premises only occasionally and had a manager who was in control.

In *Howker v Robinson* the degree of delegation was no greater than is essential in any public house with more than one bar and it is submitted that not only does it go too far but it leaves the law in an uncertain state; for it is apparently open to the magistrates to find as "a fact" that there has or has not been delegation where the licensee is on the premises. The principle ought to be confined to the case where the licensee is not doing his job, but has handed it over to another. Where a licensee who is employed by a brewery is suspended, his employer has the right, under an implied term in the contract of employment, to delegate the rights and duties of licensee to another employee. Thus sales of liquor on the licensed premises continue to be lawful and, presumably, the suspended licensee is liable for offences committed by the delegate.[9]

According to Lord Parker, the delegation principle comes into play *only* in the case of offences requiring *mens rea*.[10] Where liability is strict, "the person on whom liability is thrown is responsible whether he has delegated or whether he has acted through a servant." According to this view, if D, the licensee, not having delegated his duties, is serving in the bar and E, the barmaid, without his knowledge, sells liquor (i) to a constable on duty and (ii) to a drunken person, D is liable for the latter but not the former offence, since (i) requires *mens rea* but (ii) does not. If this is right, it is the principle next to be discussed which applies in the case of offences of strict liability. The licensee is the "seller" for this purpose even though he is not the owner of property sold,[11] because, under the Licensing Acts, he is the only person who can lawfully "sell" intoxicating liquor on the premises.[12]

Some doubt was cast on the validity of the delegation principle by the House of Lords in *Vane v Yiannopoullos*.[13] Since there was no delegation in that case their lordships' remarks were *obiter*. Lords Morris and Donovan could find no statutory authority for the doctrine and, though they did not find it necessary to pronounce on its validity, Lord Donovan thought that "If a decision that 'knowingly' means 'knowingly' will make the provision difficult to enforce, the remedy lies with the legislature." Lord Reid found the delegation principle hard to justify; but while it may have been unwarranted in the first instance, it was now too late to upset such a long standing practice. Lord Evershed thought that a licensee may "fairly and

---

8. [1969] 1 QB 371, [1968] 1 All ER 197.

9. *DPP v Rogers* [1992] Crim LR 51, DC.

10. *Winson* [1969] 1 QB 371 at 382, [1968] 1 All ER 197; **SHC 179**.

11. He is not the seller for the purposes of the Sale of Goods Act 1979, s. 1. Pace (loc. cit.) points out that, as Parker J, his lordship, had stated the doctrine applied to the strict liability offence of using an unclean milk bottle: *Quality Dairies (York) Ltd v Pedley* [1952] 1 KB 275, [1952] 1 All ER 380, DC, but the ratio decidendi of that case clearly was that D had "used" the bottle through his agent and so was liable under the second principle, below, p. 175.

12. *Goodfellow v Johnson* [1966] 1 QB 83, [1965] 1 All ER 941, [1965] Crim LR 304 and commentary thereon. (D, a licensee, liable for the sale of watered gin, contrary to the Food and Drugs Act 1955, by barmaid, a servant not of D but of his employer, a brewery.)

13. See fn. 2 on p. 173.

sensibly" be held liable where he has delegated his powers and Lord Hodson expressed no opinion. Subsequent cases[14] show that the doctrine continues unimpaired. Such a long standing principle is perhaps unlikely now to be overruled by the House of Lords. It should not, however, be extended.[15] In *Bradshaw v Ewart-James*[16] the court declined to apply it to the case where the master of a ship delegated the performance of his statutory duty to his chief officer. That, however, was not a case of the full delegation which the doctrine seems to require, for the master remained on board and in command. As the master cannot personally direct the ship for 24 hours a day, some delegation is inevitable.

3 Where the Servant's Act is his Master's Act in Law

The most obvious application of the second principle occurs in the many cases where "selling" is the central feature of the *actus reus*, under statutes like the Trade Descriptions Act, the Food and Drugs Acts and the Fertilisers and Feeding Stuffs Act. Now a "sale" consists in the transfer of property in goods from A to B[17] and the seller, in law, is necessarily the person in whom the property is vested at the commencement of the transaction. It is not a great step, therefore, for the court to say that the employer has committed the *actus reus* of "selling" even though he was nowhere near when the incident took place. In *Coppen v Moore (No. 2)*,[18] D owned six shops, in which he sold American hams. He gave strict instructions that these hams were to be described as "breakfast hams" and were not to be sold under any specific name of place of origin. In the absence of D, and without the knowledge of the manager of the branch, one of the assistants sold a ham as a "Scotch ham". D was convicted, under the Merchandise Marks Act 1887, s. 2(2), of selling goods "to which any . . . false trade description is applied". Lord Russell CJ said:[19]

"It cannot be doubted that the appellant sold the ham in question, although the transaction was carried out by his servants. In other words he was the seller, although not the actual salesman. It is clear also, as already stated, that the ham was sold with a 'false trade description' which was material. If so, there is evidence establishing a prima facie case of an offence against the Act having been *committed by the appellant*".

The court was clearly influenced by the fact that D (like many other employers) carried on his business in a number of branches and could not possibly be in direct control of each one so that, if actual knowledge of the particular transaction had to be proved, he could hardly ever be made liable. The court did not, however, apply the principle of delegation which is to be found in the licensing cases. By construing the Act in accordance

14. *Ross v Moss* [1965] 2 QB 396, [1965] 3 All ER 145; *Winson* [1969] 1 QB 371, [1968] 1 All ER 197.
15. Cf. *Howker v Robinson*, above, p. 173. Yet Bristow J, while considering himself bound by the authorities to apply the delegation principle, hoped that it might be overturned by the House of Lords: [1972] 2 All ER at p. 791.
16. [1983] QB 671, [1983] 1 All ER 12, DC.
17. This is so in the criminal as well as the civil law; *Watson v Coupland* [1945] 1 All ER 217.
18. [1898] 2 QB 306. One partner may similarly be liable for the acts of another: *Davies v Harvey* (1874) LR 9QB 433. Cf. *Parsons v Barnes* [1973] Crim LR 537.
19. Ibid., at 313.

with the principles of the civil law and so holding that D had himself committed an *actus reus*, the court introduced a more far-reaching principle.[20] Comparison with *Allchorn v Hopkins*[1] will show that, under the delegation principle, D would not have been liable for the act of the assistant to whom control of the premises had not been delegated.[2]

There are many cases not involving a sale where a similar principle has been invoked. Just as it is the master who, in law, "sells" goods with which his servant is actually dealing, so too is he "in possession" of goods which are actually in his servant's hands[3] and so can be made liable for offences of "being in possession" (of which there are many[4]) through his servants. A producer of plays "presents" a play even though he may be miles away when it is performed and was liable, under s. 15 of the Theatres Act 1843 (now repealed[5]), if words were introduced, even without his knowledge, which had not been allowed by the Lord Chamberlain.[6]

The owners of a van, supplied to the bailiff of their farm, "keep" a van which is not "used solely for the conveyance of goods or burden in the course of trade" without a licence[7] if the bailiff uses it, without their knowledge or authority, to take his wife for a day out at Clacton.[8] A master "uses" his vehicle in contravention of the Motor Vehicles (Construction and Use) Regulations if his servant so uses it.[9] It is quite understandable that a court should hold that an employer "presents" a play or "keeps" a vehicle, for these verbs are apt to describe his function and inapt to describe that of his servants. It is less clear that this is so in the case of "uses". This could very well refer to the servant's use.

4 Mode of Participation of Master and Servant

In those cases where it is only the licensee, keeper of the refreshment house, or other designated person in whom it is an offence to do the act in question, it is apparent that the licensee, etc., who is held vicariously liable

20. If the same reasoning as that followed in *Coppon v Moore* had been used in the licence case, where the offence involved "selling", a licensee who owned his stock might have been convicted, notwithstanding the absence of delegation. But this reasoning has not been followed: *McKenna v Harding* (1905) 69 JP 354; *Vane v Yiannopoullos* [1965] AC 486, [1964] 3 All ER 820. But see *Goodfellow v Johnson* [1966] 1 QB 83, [1965] 1 All ER 941, [1965] Crim LR 304 and commentary thereon.
1. Above, p. 173, fn. 1.
2. It was within the scope of the servant's authority in *Coppen v Moore*, above, to sell hams. A master is not liable where a servant boy, who has no authority to sell anything, supplies his master's whisky to a customer out of hours: *Adams v Camfoni* [1929] 1 KB 95. In this case there was no sale by the master.
3. Infra.
4. For examples, see above, p. 110.
5. See Theatres Act 1968; below, p. 746.
6. *Grade v Director of Public Prosecutions* [1942] 2 All ER 118. The defendant had in fact been called up for service in the R.A.F. The result would have been different if D had been charged with "causing" the play to be presented: *Lovelace v Director of Public Prosecutions* [1954] 3 All ER 481, [1954] 1 WLR 1468.
7. Contrary to s. 27 of the Revenue Act 1869 (repealed).
8. *Strutt v Clift* [1911] 1 KB 1.
9. *Green v Burnett* [1955] 1 QB 78, [1954] 3 All ER 273; but not where a partner, or person authorised ad hoc, uses the vehicle, if there is also an offence of permitting: *Crawford v Haughton* [1972] 1 All ER 535, [1972] 1 WLR 572, DC; *Garrett v Hooper* [1973] Crim LR 61; *Cobb v Williams* [1973] Crim LR 243.

is a principal for he alone possesses the personal characteristic which is an essential part of the *actus reus* and no one else is qualified to fill that role. The servant who actually performs the act is plainly incapable of being a principal, but it seems that he may be convicted as an abettor,[10] – strange though this appears when he is the only participant in the crime who is present.

Where the *actus reus* does not include a personal characteristic of the master and the servant is capable of being a principal, then it seems that he may be held to be a joint principal with his master. In crimes of "selling" and being "in possession" the court allows the prosecution the best of both worlds by having regard to the legal act when dealing with the master and the physical act when dealing with the servant. So it is held that the servant, as well as the master, "sells"[11] or is "in possession";[12] and the servant whose "use" of a vehicle was held to be use by his master was convicted in *Green v Burnett* (above) as a principal. It is submitted that when the servant is capable of being a principal it is logical to hold him liable as such (for he is the real offender) and not as an abettor.

The precise nature of the delegate's liability is of more than academic interest for two reasons. First, if the crime is one of strict liability, *mens rea* must nevertheless be proved if he is to be convicted as an abettor but not if he is a principal.[13] Secondly, where there is a statutory defence enabling one held vicariously liable to escape if he can bring the "actual offender" before the court, it is difficult to suppose that the production of an abettor (even though he is the real offender) will suffice, but a joint principal certainly will.[14]

5 No Vicarious Liability for Abetting, or Attempting Crimes

Abetting is a common law notion and therefore, as we have seen,[15] requires *mens rea* even where the offence abetted is one of strict liability. For the same reasons there can be no vicarious responsibility for abetting an offence, even though the offence itself may be one imposing vicarious liability. In *Ferguson v Weaving*[16] D, a licensee, was charged with abetting several of her customers in consuming liquor on the licensed premises outside the permitted hours, contrary to the Licensing Act 1921, s. 4. It appeared that she had taken all proper means to ensure that drinking ceased when "Time" was called. But the waiters in the concert room, contrary to their instructions, made no attempt to collect the customers' drinks and, while D was visiting the several other rooms in the premises, the offence

---

10. *Griffiths v Studebakers Ltd* [1924] 1 KB 102; *Ross v Moss* [1965] 2 QB 396, [1965] 3 All ER 145.
11. *Hotchin v Hindmarsh* [1891] 2 QB 181. Cf. *Goodfellow v Johnson* [1966] 1 QB 83, [1965] 1 All ER 941.
12. *Melias Ltd v Preston* [1957] 2 QB 380, [1957] 2 All ER 449.
13. Above, p. 138.
14. *Melias Ltd v Preston*, above.
15. Above, p. 138.
16. [1951] 1 KB 814, [1951] 1 All ER 412; **SHC 158**. See also *Thomas v Lindop* [1950] 1 All ER 966; *John Henshall (Quarries) Ltd v Harvey* [1965] 2 QB 233, [1965] 1 All ER 725. *Provincial Motor Cab Co Ltd v Dunning* [1909] 2 KB 599 overlooks this principle and is a doubtful decision.

was committed. It was assumed that control of the concert room had been delegated. While accepting that the waiters might have been guilty of abetting, the court was emphatic that D could not be. Lord Goddard CJ said:[17]

"She can aid and abet the customers if she knows that the customers are committing an offence, but we are not prepared to hold that their knowledge can be imputed to her so as to make her, not a principal offender, but an aider and abettor. So to hold would be to establish a new principle in criminal law and one for which there is no authority."

Had there been a substantive offence of *permitting* drinking on licensed premises after hours, it is fairly clear that the court could have held D guilty; for in that case the acts, and the *mens rea*, of the servant would have been attributed to her.

An attempt is likewise a common law notion, and it has been said that there can be no vicarious liability for attempting to commit a crime, even though the crime attempted imposes vicarious liability.[18]

6 The Special Position of Corporations[19]

A corporation is a legal person but it has no physical existence and cannot, therefore, either act or form an intention of any kind except through its directors or servants. As each director and servant is also a legal person quite distinct from the corporation, it follows that a corporation's legal liabilities are all, in a sense, vicarious. If a corporation's criminal liability for the acts of its servants and agents were co-extensive with that of a natural person, it could be made liable only for those crimes which fall within the narrow limits which govern the vicarious liability of natural persons. A corporation's liability is in fact much wider than that, and therefore requires separate consideration.

It was formerly thought that a corporation could not be indicted for a crime at all.[20] Personal appearance was necessary at assizes and quarter-sessions and the corporation, having no physical person, could not appear. In the Court of King's Bench, however, appearance by attorney was allowed and a way out of this difficulty was found by removing the indictment into that court by writ of certiorari;[1] but now this is unnecessary and, by statute,[2] a corporation may appear and plead through a representative. A second difficulty which has gone was that at one time all felonies were punished by death and, as the corporation was incapable of suffering the prescribed punishment, there was no point in trying it. Further objections which have been raised are that, since a corporation is a creature of the law, it can only do such acts as it is legally empowered to do, so that any crime is necessarily ultra vires; and that the corporation, having neither

---

17. [1951] 1 KB 814 at 821, [1951] 1 All ER 412 at 415.
18. *Gardner v Akeroyd* [1952] 2 QB 743, [1952] 2 All ER 306.
19. See Williams, CLGP, Ch. 22; R. S. Welch, "The Criminal Liability of Corporations" (1946) 62 LQR 345; L. H. Leigh (1977) 9 Ottawa LR 247. For proposals for reform, see Law Commission Published Working Paper No. 44.
20. *Anon* (1701) 12 Mod Rep 560, per Holt CJ.
1. *Birmingham and Gloucester Rly Co* (1842) 3 QB 223.
2. Criminal Justice Act 1925, s. 33.

body nor mind, cannot perform the acts or form the intents which are a prerequisite of criminal liability. The ultra vires doctrine, however, seems to have been ignored in both the law of tort and crime and to apply only in the law of contract and property,[3] while the minds and bodies of the officers and servants of the corporation have been taken to supply its lack of mental and physical faculties. This has been done in two distinct ways:

(i) By holding that a corporation is vicariously liable for the acts of its servants and agents where a natural person would similarly be liable; for example, in public nuisance at common law,[4] or when a statute imposes vicarious responsibility.[5]

(ii) By holding that (a) in every corporation there are certain persons (designated "controlling officers" in the draft Criminal Code)[6] who control and direct its activities, and (b) those persons, when acting in the company's business, are considered to be the "embodiment of the company"[7] for this purpose. Their acts and states of mind are the company's acts and states of mind and it is held liable, not for the acts of its servants, but for what are deemed to be its own acts.

The type of case where it is most obviously proper that a corporation should be held liable arises where a statute imposes a duty upon a corporation to act and no action is taken. It was in such cases that the earliest developments took place. In 1842, in *Birmingham and Gloucester Rly Co*,[8] a corporation was convicted for failing to fulfil a statutory duty. Four years later, in *Great North of England Rly Co*,[9] counsel sought to confine the effect of that decision to cases of non-feasance where there was no agent who could be indicted, arguing that, in the case of misfeasance, only the agents who had done the wrongful acts were liable. The court held that the distinction was unfounded. Even if it were discoverable, it was incongruous that the corporation should be liable for the one type of wrong and not the other. From holding that a corporation could be liable for breach of a statutory duty it was not a great step forward to impose liability in those cases where a natural person would similarly be liable for his servants' acts – for example in public nuisance at common law, or where statute imposes vicarious responsibility.[10]

a) *Non-vicarious liability of corporations.* The Interpretation Act 1889 defined "person" to include "a body of persons corporate or unincorporate" unless the contrary appears and provided that the definition, so far as it includes bodies corporate, applies to any provision of an Act whenever passed, relating to an offence punishable on indictment or summary conviction. So when any statute makes it an offence for "a person" to do or

3. Cf. Winfield, *Text Book of the Law of Tort* (4th ed.), 128.
4. *Great North of England Rly Co* (1846) 9 QB 315.
5. *Griffiths v Studebakers Ltd* [1924] 1 KB 102; *Mousell Bros Ltd v London and North Western Rly Co* [1917] 2 KB 836.
6. Law Com. No. 143, para. 11–6, and cl. 34.
7. *Essendon Engineering Co Ltd v Maile* [1982] RTR 260, [1982] Crim LR 510.
8. (1842) 3 QB 223.
9. (1846) 9 QB 315.
10. *Mousell Brothers v London and North Western Rly Co* [1917] 2 KB 836; *Griffiths v Studebakers Ltd* [1924] 1 KB 102.

omit to do something, that offence is capable of commission by a corporation, unless the contrary appears. The contrary might appear because the nature of the offence is such that a corporation is physically incapable of committing it as a principal, even through its controlling officers. The fact that the offence requires *mens rea* does not reveal a contrary intention for the state of mind of the corporation's controlling officers, as well as their acts, may be attributed to the corporation. There was a further important development in 1944. In that year it was held in three cases that a corporation may be held liable for acts of its employees which would certainly *not* render liable a natural person in the same situation. The principle has been well stated by Denning LJ:[11]

"A company may in many ways be likened to a human body. It has a brain and a nerve centre which controls what it does. It also has hands which hold the tools and act in accordance with directions from the centre. Some of the people in the company are mere servants and agents who are nothing more than hands to do the work and cannot be said to represent the mind or will. Others are directors and managers who represent the directing mind and will of the company and control what it does. The state of mind of these managers is the state of mind of the company and is treated by the law as such."[12]

A person is not a "controlling officer" simply because his work is brain work and he exercises some managerial discretion, since not all such persons "represent the directing mind and will of the company and control what it does."[13] The manager of a supermarket belonging to a company owning hundreds of supermarkets is not the company's "brains" and does not act as the company.[14] Companies have been held to be not criminally liable for the acts of a depot engineer[15] or a weighbridge operator.[16] In the leading case of *Tesco Supermarkets Ltd v Nattrass*[17] it was said that the company may be criminally liable for the acts only of:

"... the board of directors, the managing director and perhaps other superior officers of a company [who] carry out the functions of management and speak and act as the company,"

per Lord Reid,[18] or of a person:

"... who is in actual control of the operations of a company or of part of them and who is not responsible to another person in the company for the manner in which he discharges his duties in the sense of being under his orders,"

per Viscount Dilhorne:[19]

---

11. *H L Bolton (Engineering) Co Ltd v T J Graham & Sons Ltd* [1957] 1 QB 159 at 172.
12. Thus, it is thought that a company could be guilty of abetting an offence through its managing director – though there is no *vicarious* liability in abetting (above, p. 177). See *Robert Millar (Contractors) Ltd* [1970] 2 QB 54, above p. 124.
13. *Tesco Supermarkets Ltd v Nattrass* [1972] AC 153 at 171, HL, per Lord Reid, 187 per Lord Dilhorne, 200 per Lord Diplock; **SHC 183.**
14. Ibid.
15. *Magna Plant Ltd v Mitchell* [1966] Crim LR 394.
16. *John Henshall (Quarries) Ltd v Harvey* [1965] 2 QB 233, [1965] 1 All ER 725.
17. Above, fn. 13.
18. At p. 171.
19. At p. 187.

Lord Diplock[20] thought that the question is to be answered by

"... identifying those natural persons who by the memorandum and articles of association or as result of action taken by the directors or by the company in general meeting pursuant to the articles are entrusted with the exercise of the powers of the company."

Lord Pearson too thought that the constitution of the company concerned must be taken into account; and Lords Dilhorne, Pearson and Diplock thought that the reference in the "common form" provision, discussed below,[1] to "any director, manager, secretary or other similar officer of the body corporate" affords a useful indication. If those persons who are responsible for the general management of the company delegate their duties to another, then the acts of that other will be the acts of the company.[2]

Once the facts have been ascertained, it is a question of law whether a person in doing particular things is to be regarded as the company or merely as the company's servant or agent.[3] Accordingly the judge should direct the jury that if they find certain facts proved, then they must find that the act and intention of the agent is the act and intention of the company. It is not sufficient to direct that the company is liable for its "responsible agents" or "high executives", for such persons are not necessarily the company.[4] The test is the same whether the offence be serious or trivial.

In the *Tesco* case, the company, being charged with an offence under the Trade Descriptions Act 1968, relied on the statutory defence that they had taken all reasonable precautions and exercised all due diligence and that the commission of the offence was due to the act or default of "another person", namely the branch manager, who had failed to supervise the assistant who actually committed the offence. Since the manager was the "hands" and not the "brains" of the company, it was held that the defence was available. It would have been otherwise if it had been not the manager but a director who had failed in his duty.

In *Director of Public Prosecutions v Kent and Sussex Contractors Ltd:*[5] D Ltd was charged with offences under a Defence of the Realm regulation which required an intent to deceive. The justices found that the transport manager of the company had the requisite intention but dismissed the information on the ground that an act of will or state of mind could not be imputed to the company. The Divisional Court held that there was ample evidence that the *company* had done the act in question, with intent to deceive.

That decision was approved by the Court of Criminal Appeal in *ICR Haulage Ltd,*[6] where the convictions of a company, its managing director

---

20. At p. 200.
1. See p. 175.
2. [1972] AC 153 at 193.
3. [1972] AC 153 at 170, 173, per Lord Reid.
4. *Sporle* [1971] Crim LR 706.
5. [1944] KB 146, [1944] 1 All ER 119.
6. [1944] KB 551, [1944] 1 All ER 691. Cf. *McDonnell* [1966] 1 QB 233, [1966] 1 All ER 193, below, pp. 183 and 297.

and nine other persons of a common law conspiracy to defraud were upheld. Stable J said[7]

"... the acts of the managing director were the acts of the company and the fraud of that person was the fraud of the company."

Now a natural person could never be held vicariously liable for a common law conspiracy, and the case is therefore an excellent illustration of the wider liability of corporations.

In *Moore v I Bresler Ltd*[8] the company was convicted of making certain returns in respect of purchase tax, which were false in material particulars, with intent to deceive, contrary to the Finance (No. 2) Act 1940, s. 35. The returns were actually made by the secretary of the company, and the sales manager of the branch concerned, and were made with the object of concealing the fraudulent sale which these two had made of the company's property. Welch criticises the case[9] on the ground (inter alia) that, in identifying these two agents with the company, the court went too far down the scale, but it may perhaps be justified in this respect on the ground that the company secretary was involved. *Kent and Sussex Contractors* seems more doubtful in that only the transport manager appears to have acted.

b) *A corporation's state of mind.* Where the offence is one of strict liability, the corporation may be held liable for the acts of any of its servants or agents where those acts are, in law, the company's acts, under the principle discussed above;[10] but where the offence requires *mens rea*, it must be proved that a controlling officer had the *mens rea*.[11] Similarly, where a defence requires evidence of a belief or other state of mind, this must usually be the belief or state of mind of a controlling officer;[12] but the belief of one will not suffice if another, especially if he is superior to the first, knows that that belief is ill founded.[13] Probably, as the draft code states, all controlling officers who are concerned in the offence must have the required state of mind. If, however, no controlling officer is involved and all the employees or agents who are involved do have the required state of mind, the defence ought clearly to be available. If a branch manager, not being a controlling officer, finds a controlled drug in supplies delivered to his branch and takes control of it, intending to hand it to the police, the company may surely rely on this intention to establish the defence provided by s. 5(4) of the Misuse of Drugs Act 1971, if it is charged with unlawful possession of the drug.[14]

c) *Limitations on corporate liability.* There are certain existing limitations on the liability of a corporation. (1) It can only be convicted of offences

7. [1944] KB at 559, [1944] 1 All ER at 695.
8. [1944] 2 All ER 515.
9. (1946) 62 LQR at 358.
10. "Where an agent's act is the defendant's act in law," p. 167.
11. *Tesco Supermarkets Ltd v Nattrass* [1972] AC 153 [1971] 2 All ER 127. Draft Criminal Code, cl. 34, (2).
12. *GJ Coles & Co Ltd v Goldsworthy* [1958] WAR 183. See Orchard in *Criminal Law Essays*, 114, 117, 118–119.
13. *Brambles Holdings Ltd v Carey* (1976) 15 SASR 270 at 280.
14. See Law. Com. No. 177, Draft Criminal Code, Appendix B, Example 30 (vi).

which are punishable with a fine. These include most offences;[15] but exclude murder. (2) There are other offences which it is quite inconceivable that an official of a corporation should commit within the scope of his employment; for example, bigamy, rape, incest and, possibly, perjury.[16]

It was at one time thought[17] that a corporation could not be convicted of an offence involving personal violence but in *P & O European Ferries Ltd*[18] Turner J held that an indictment for manslaughter would lie against the company in respect of the Zeebrugge disaster. The persuasive authority of this ruling is not impaired by the judge's subsequent decision that, on the evidence before him, the company had no case to answer. The rejected argument was based on the fact that, from the time of Coke (1601), authoritative books had described manslaughter as "the killing of a human being by a human being".[19]

This definition found its way into the law of some states of the USA and, via Stephen's draft Code Bill of 1880, into the New Zealand Crimes Acts of 1908 and 1961. The effect was that the New Zealand Court of Appeal decided in *Murray-Wright*[20] that a corporation could not be guilty of manslaughter as a principal. Turner J did not follow that decision. Coke's purpose in using the phrase "by a human being" was not to exclude corporations from liability – corporations were not indictable for any crime at that time – but to distinguish killings by an inanimate thing or an animal without the fault of any person. Such killings then had legal consequences but were not murder or manslaughter. Moreover, the requirement of an act or omission by a human being is not peculiar to manslaughter. All crimes are acts or omissions, or the results of acts or omissions, by human beings. It is not manslaughter if a person is killed by an earthquake or a thunderbolt or a wild animal in the jungle. Conspiracy is committed contrary to s. 1 of the Criminal Law 1977 "if a person agrees with any other person" but an agreement between two human beings is required to make a conspiracy.[1] A corporation can be convicted of conspiracy but only if at least one of the human beings is a controlling officer of the corporation acting within the scope of his authority.

---

15. See Magistrates' Courts Act 1980, s. 32 and Powers of Criminal Courts Act 1973, s. 30.
16. Even in some of these cases it is not inconceivable that a corporation might be held liable as a secondary party. E.g., the managing director of an incorporated Marriage Advisory Bureau negotiates a marriage which he knows to be bigamous.
17. *Cory Bros Ltd* [1927] 1 KB 810 (Finlay J, holding that a corporation could not be indicted for manslaughter or an offence under s. 31 of the Offences against the Person Act 1861), a ruling of which Stable J said in *ICR Haulage Ltd* [1944] KB 551, "if the matter came before the court today, the result might well be different".
18. (1990) 93 Cr App Rep 72, [1991] Crim LR 695 and commentary. Streatfeild J ruled that an indictment for manslaughter would lie in *Northern Star Mining Construction Co Ltd* (Glamorgan Assizes, 1 February 1965, unreported) but the corporation was acquitted on the merits. Maurice J's decision in a civil action, *S & Y Investments (No 2) Pty Ltd v Commercial Co of Australia Ltd* (1986) 21 App Rep 204 at 217, required a ruling that a company was guilty of manslaughter.
19. See, e.g., Stephen, *Digest of the Criminal Law* (1st ed., 1877, Art 218 and subsequent editions, *Halsbury's Laws of England* (4th ed., 1990 reissue, 613).
20. [1970] NZLR 476.
1. *McDonnell* [1966] 1 QB 233, [1966] 1 All ER 193.

d) *Aggregation.* A question that was raised but not answered in the *P & O* case is whether it must be proved that an individual controlling officer (whether identifiable or not) was guilty of the crime charged or whether it is permissible to "aggregate" the conduct of a number of officers, none of whom would individually be guilty, so as to constitute in sum, the elements of the offence. It is submitted that it is not possible artificially to create a *mens rea* in this way.[2] Two innocent states of mind cannot be added together to produce a guilty state of mind. Any such doctrine could have no application in offences requiring knowledge, intention or recklessness; but, arguably, there is a place for it in offences of negligence. The company owes a duty of care and if its operation falls far below the standard required it is guilty of gross negligence. A series of minor failures by officers of the company might add up to a gross breach by the company of its duty of care. There is authority for such a doctrine in the law of tort[3] and the concept of negligence is the same in the criminal law, the difference being one of degree – criminal negligence must be "gross". It is immaterial that the doctrine of vicarious liability in tort does not apply in criminal law, because this is a case not of vicarious, but of personal, liability and that is a proper concern of the criminal law. Thus the liability of a corporation for manslaughter may depend on whether manslaughter requires recklessness or may be committed by gross negligence – a matter of some doubt.[4]

e) *Social purpose underlying corporate criminal liability.* This does not appear to have been considered by the English courts. The fine imposed is ultimately borne by the shareholders who, in most cases, are not responsible, in any sense, for the offence. If they really had control over the directors and so over the management of the company, this might afford some justification; but it is generally recognised that they have no such control over large, public companies.[5] Moreover fines may be inflicted on the Boards of nationalised industries, where there are no shareholders and the consumers of the product, who ultimately pay the fine, have no rights whatever to appoint or dismiss the officials concerned.[6]

Since the persons actually responsible for the offence may, in the great majority of cases, be convicted, is there any need to impose this additional penalty? Arguments in favour of corporate liability are that there may be difficulty in fixing individuals with liability where someone among the "brains" of the corporation has undoubtedly authorised the offence. Corporate liability ensures that the offence will not go unpunished and that a fine proportionate to the gravity of the offence may be imposed, when it

---

2. Cf. *Armstrong v Strain* [1952] 1 KB 232, [1952] 1 All ER 139, Devlin J: "You cannot add an innocent state of mind to an innocent state of mind and get as a result a dishonest state of mind."

3. *W B Anderson & Sons Ltd v Rhodes (Liverpool) Ltd* [1967] 2 All ER 850, Cairns J, discussed by M Dean, 31 MLR 322, see especially p. 328; *Salmond on Torts* (19th ed.) 508, *Fleming on Torts* (7th ed.) 603.

4. See below, p. 372. In the *P & O* case Turner J seems to have proceeded on the basis that recklessness must be proved.

5. Pennington, *Company Law* (6th ed.), Part III.

6. In 1951 the Yorkshire Electricity Board was fined £20,000 for contravening a Defence Regulation. It has been suggested that the object of such a prosecution was to demonstrate that nationalised industries are not above the law.

might be out of proportion to the means of the individuals concerned. The imposition of liability on the organisation gives all of those directing it an interest in the prevention of illegalities – and they are in a position to prevent them, though the shareholders are not. Since, moreover, the names of the officers will mean nothing to the public, only the conviction of the corporation itself will serve to warn the public of the wrongful acts – operating buses with faulty brakes, or selling mouldy pies – which are committed in its name. None of these reasons seems to be very compelling and the necessity for corporate criminal liability awaits demonstration.

f) *Statutory liability of officers.* It is now common form to include the following provision in statutes creating offences likely to be committed by corporations:

"Where an offence . . . committed by a body corporate is proved to have been committed with the consent or connivance of, or to be attributable to any neglect on the part of, any director, manager, secretary or other similar officer of the body corporate or any person who was purporting to act in any such capacity, he as well as the body corporate shall be guilty of that offence and shall be liable to be proceeded against and punished accordingly."

Whether a director or other officer is under a duty is a question which can be answered only by looking at the facts of each case; and the onus of proving that there was a duty which has been neglected is on the prosecution.[7]

So far as "consent" and "connivance" are concerned the provision probably effects only a slight extension of the law; for the officer who expressly consents or connives at the commission of the offence will be liable as a secondary party under the principles considered above. There may be a consent which does not amount to counselling or abetting, however; and the words "attributable to any neglect on the part of"[8] clearly impose a wider liability in making the officer liable for his negligence in failing to prevent the offence.

7 Unincorporated bodies

An unincorporated association is not a legal person at common law and therefore could not incur criminal liability though its members could. This is still the position for common law offences. Statutory offences are different. The effect of the Interpretation Act 1889 was that in all enactments relating to offences, whenever passed, the word "person" includes bodies corporate (s. 2) and, in enactments passed after 1889, both bodies corporate *and unincorporate* (s. 19). The Interpretation Act 1978 preserves this position.[9] Since 1889 unincorporate bodies have been able to

7. *Huckerby v Elliott* [1970] 1 All ER 189. "Manager" means someone managing the affairs of the company and not, e.g., the manager of a store: *Tesco Supermarkets Ltd v Nattrass* [1972] AC 153 at 178.

8. These words are omitted from s. 18 of the Theft Act 1968, below, p. 656.

9. Sch. 2, para. 4(5) maintains the existing application of "person" to corporate bodies (and, implicitly, its non-application to unincorporate bodies) in pre-1889 statutes creating offences. The definition of "person" in Sch. 1 applies to all statutes passed after the commencement of the 1889 Act, so that they continue to be capable of commission by unincorporate bodies.

commit any offence under an enactment passed after 1889 which makes it an offence for a "person" to do or omit to do anything which an unincorporate body is capable of doing. The potential liability of unincorporate bodies seems to have been little noticed. In *A-G v Able* Woolf J, dealing with an alleged offence under the Suicide Act 1961 said, "It must be remembered that the [Voluntary Euthanasia Society] is an unincorporated body and there can be no question of the society committing an offence";[10] but since the offence may be committed by "a person" it seems that it may be committed by an unincorporated body. An unincorporated body, being the registered keeper of a vehicle, was held capable of liability as a "person" to fixed penalties for illegal parking under the Transport Act 1982.[11]

Sometimes statutes have made express provision for the liability of unincorporated bodies but it seems that this is unnecessary when the word "person" is used in the definition of the offence. The Banking Act 1987, s. 98 (1) simply assumes, rightly, that offences under the Act may be committed by unincorporated associations.

When an unincorporated association is prosecuted, presumably the court must proceed by analogy to the law relating to corporations. Such associations have officials corresponding to the controlling officers of corporations and it is inconceivable that the association is liable for the act of any one of its members who has no part in the general management of its affairs.

10. [1984] QB 795, [1984] 1 All ER 277, 276, above, p. 135.
11. *Clerk to Croydon Justices, ex p Chief Constable of Kent* [1989] Crim LR 910, DC.

10 General Defences

Where D has caused an *actus reus* with the appropriate *mens rea*, he will generally be held liable. But this is not invariably so for there are certain defences which may still be available even in this situation. As well as special defences which apply in the case of particular crimes, there are certain defences which apply in the case of crimes generally and it is these with which we are concerned in this chapter.

The common law of homicide distinguished between justification and excuse. Some homicides, like that done by the public hangman in carrying out the sentence of the court, were justifiable. Others, like killing by misadventure and without culpable negligence, were merely excusable. In both cases the accused who successfully raised the defence was acquitted of felony but, if the homicide was merely excusable, his goods were forfeited. In 1828 forfeiture was abolished and, ever since, there has been no difference, so far as the defendant is concerned, between the various general defences. If successfully raised, they result in a verdict of not guilty.

Recently, however, there has been a revival of interest in a distinction between justification and excuse.[1] An act is justified when we positively approve of it. It is merely excused when we disapprove of it but think it is not right to treat it as a crime. Clearly such a distinction exists in fact. There are examples which obviously fall into one category or the other. The nine-year-old child who deliberately kills his playmate is excused but no one would say he is justified. Nearly everyone would approve of the conduct of a man who wounds an aggressor when that is the only way he can save the lives of his family. But there is also a large middle ground where there would be no consensus.

No one suggests that there is any difference so far as the acquittal of the person relying on the defence is concerned but it has been argued that the distinction affects third parties in that (i) it is lawful to resist an aggressor whose agression is merely excused but not one whose aggression is justified; and (ii) there may be a conviction for aiding and abetting one who is merely excused[2] but not one who is justified. As Fletcher (whose work

1. Fletcher, *Rethinking Criminal Law*, Ch. 10; Yeo, *Compulsion in the Criminal Law*; Smith, *Justification and Excuse*; Williams, "The Theory of Excuses" [1982] Crim LR 732; Alldridge (1986) 50 J Cr L 274; Robinson (1982) 82 Col Law Rev 199.
2. As in *Bourne* (1952) 36 Cr App Rep 125 and *Cogan and Leak* [1976] QB 217, [1975] 2 All ER 1059, above, p. 152.

inspired the current interest) acknowledges,[3] Anglo-American criminal law has never recognised these (as he thinks) fundamental distinctions. The proposed distinctions bear little resemblance to the justifiable and excusable homicides of the common law and there is disagreement between the protagonists as to which defence should fall into which category.

Applying the theory as expounded by Fletcher, a person arresting "anyone who is in the act of committing an arrestable offence" would be justified but a person arresting "anyone whom he has reasonable grounds for suspecting to be [but who is not in fact] committing such an offence" is merely excused. But both acts are equally "justified" by the law – the Police and Criminal Evidence Act 1984, s. 24(4) (a) and (b), declares that both are acts that a person *may* do. In doing so, he incurs no civil or criminal liability. It is true, however, that the first "arrestee" would not be entitled to use force in self-defence (if the arrestor was using only reasonable force) whereas the second might be.[4]

The law does recognise that a person's act may be excused in the criminal law, while incurring civil liability. A person who makes an unreasonable mistake of fact which, if it were true, would amount to reasonable grounds for suspecting another to be in act of committing an arrestable offence, has a defence to a criminal prosecution for false imprisonment or assault (because he lacks *mens rea*) but remains liable for the corresponding torts: the act done is not the act which the 1984 Act says he *may* do. Here the terminology of justification and excuse seems appropriate. The act is "unlawful", but the actor is excused from criminal liability.

Any attempt to categorise defences as justifications or excuses would, in the present state of the law, be premature and it is not made in the following pages.

1 Infancy

Infants are persons under eighteen years of age. As such, they are (with some exceptions) incapable of making contracts or wills but the law imposes no such limitations on their ability to commit crimes, for, as Kenny put it,

"a child knows right from wrong long before he knows how to make a prudent speculation or a wise will".[5]

For the purpose of the criminal law, infants are divided into three categories.

1 Children under Ten Years

The first category is those who are entirely exempt from criminal responsibility in all circumstances. At common law a child was so exempt until the

---

3. Op. cit., fn 1, above.
4. Below, p. 256.
5. *Outlines*, 80.

day before his seventh birthday.[6] Now responsibility begins on the tenth birthday.[7] The rule is commonly stated as a conclusive presumption that the child is *doli incapax*. Even though there may be the clearest evidence that the child caused an *actus reus* with *mens rea*, he cannot be convicted once it appears that he had not, at the time he did the act, attained the age of ten. Nor is this a mere procedural bar; no crime at all is committed by the infant with the result that one who instigated him to do the act is a principal and not a secondary party.[8] And where a husband and wife were charged with receiving from their son (aged seven years) a child's tricycle, knowing it to have been stolen, it was held that they must be acquitted on the ground that, since the child could not steal, the tricycle was not stolen.[9] Ten is a comparatively low age for the beginning of criminal responsibility; but, as the Ingleby Committee pointed out:[10]

"In many countries the 'age of criminal responsibility' is used to signify the age at which a person becomes liable to the 'ordinary' or 'full' penalties of the law. In this sense, the age of criminal responsibility in England is difficult to state: it is certainly much higher than eight."[11]

2 Children over Nine and under Fourteen Years

A child aged not less than ten but under fourteen years is exempt from criminal responsibility unless the prosecution prove, not only that he caused an *actus reus* with *mens rea*, but also that he did so with what is traditionally called "a mischievous discretion".[12] Hale wrote that this involved proof that the child could "discern between good and evil at the time of the offence committed".[13] The modern test is stated in *Gorrie*.[14] A thirteen-year-old boy was charged with the manslaughter of a schoolmate, who died from an infection resulting from a slight wound with a penknife. Salter J told the jury that they must be satisfied:

"that when the boy did this he knew what he was doing was wrong – not merely what was wrong, but what was gravely wrong, seriously wrong."

This passage was adopted in *J M (a minor) v Runeckles*[15] where the court held that it is not necessary to prove that the child knew that the act was morally wrong; he must know that it is "seriously" wrong in the sense that it is not merely naughty or mischievous. The fact that the offence committed is of such a nature that any normal child of the defendant's age would know it is seriously wrong is not apparently sufficient to rebut the

6. A person now attains a particular age at the commencement of the relevant anniversary of the date of his birth: Family Law Reform Act 1969, s. 9(1).

7. Children and Young Persons Act 1933, s. 50, as amended by the Children and Young Persons Act 1963, s. 16, which raised the age from eight. The Ingleby Committee had recommended that the age be raised to twelve. Cmnd. 1911 (1960).

8. Above, p. 124.

9. *Walters v Lunt* [1951] 2 All ER 645; and cf. *Marsh v Loader* (1863) 14 CBNS 535.

10. Cmnd. 1191, p. 30. For the special rules governing the treatment of children and young persons, see Children and Young Persons Acts 1933, 1963 and 1969; Cross, *The English Sentencing System* (3rd ed.), 75.

11. As the age then was. Above, fn 7.

12. Hale, 1 PC 630.

13. 1 PC 26.

14. (1919) 83 JP 136.

15. (1984) 79 Cr App Rep 255, DC.

presumption unless the prosecution proves that he was of normal mental capacity.[16] The child's appearance alone is not sufficient evidence of normality.[17] But it is not necessary in all cases to call evidence to prove that the defendant is a normal child of his age. His behaviour before and after the offence may be sufficient to show that he knew he was doing something seriously wrong. The fact that the child ran away is not, standing alone, sufficient evidence. A child may run away because it believes it has done something naughty and no more.[18] In 1748 a boy of ten was convicted of murder on evidence which showed that, after killing a five-year-old girl, he had concealed the body and told lies about what happened.[19]

In *J M v Runeckles* the court held that there was ample evidence in the nature of the act (a blow with a milk bottle and a stab with a broken part of it), the fact that D ran away from the police and hid, and the content and handwriting of her statement, these being commensurate with the ability of an average thirteen-year-old. But the younger a child, the stronger is the evidence required to establish mischievous discretion.[20] The requirement applies to offences generally including, presumably, offences of strict liability, e.g., offences relating to the eggs of wild birds under the Wildlife and Countryside Act 1981. But in crimes requiring proof of dishonesty the mischievous discretion rule has no separate part to play. If the prosecution prove dishonesty they have proved the mischievous discretion – that the child knew that honest and reasonable people regarded what he was doing as dishonest.[1] But it may, of course, be more difficult to prove this in the case of a ten year old than a person of thirty.

Since it is now the duty of every court, in dealing with a child or young person, to "have regard to the welfare of the child or young person",[2] and merely retributive punishment is ruled out, it has been argued[3] that this test is now out of date:

"It saves the child not from prison, transportation or the gallows, but from the probation officer, the foster parent, or the approved school. The paradoxical result is that, the more warped the child's moral standards, the safer he is from the correctional treatment of the criminal law."

The Ingleby Committee were impressed by similar arguments and by evidence that, because courts find difficulty in applying the presumption and differ in the degree of proof they require, there is inconsistency in the administration of the law. They recommended that the *doli incapax* presumption be abolished. This recommendation has not been implemented.

The power of the court to make a care order under s. 1(2) of the Children and Young Persons Act 1969 when satisfied that the child "is guilty of an

---

16. *JBH and JH (Minors) v O'Connell* [1981] Crim LR 632, DC; *IPH v Chief Constable of South Wales* [1987] Crim LR 42, DC.
17. *A. v DPP* [1992] Crim LR 34, DC.
18. *A. v DPP*, above.
19. *York* (1748), see Fost 70.
20. *X v X* [1958] Crim LR 805.
 1. *T. v DPP* [1989] Crim LR 498.
 2. Children and Young Persons Act 1933, s. 44(1).
 3. By Williams [1954] Crim LR 493 at 495.

offence excluding homicide" (the "offence condition") was abolished by the Children Act 1989, s. 90. The 1989 Act provides that a supervision order with a residence requirement (six months maximum) may be imposed where a child or young person in respect of whom a supervision order is already in force is found guilty of an offence which, in the case of a person over 21, is punishable with imprisonment and in the opinion of the court is "serious".[4]

When the 1969 Act was passed it was intended that criminal proceedings should be brought only as a last resort and, in the case of infants under fourteen, eliminated altogether. Section 4 provides—

"A person shall not be charged with an offence, except homicide, by reason of anything done or omitted while he was a child"—

but it has not been brought into force. It was intended to raise the minimum age by stages, but it appears that it is unlikely to be raised in the foreseeable future. If section 4 should ever be fully implemented, children between ten and fourteen will continue to be capable of committing crime but not be liable to prosecution, except for homicide.

There is another special rule of exemption for a boy under fourteen in that he cannot be convicted of rape,[5] offences involving sexual intercourse,[6] buggery[7] or, possibly, assault with intent to commit buggery.[8] The rule is theoretically based on a presumption of incapacity but,[9] as no evidence is admissible in rebuttal, it is in effect a rule of law. When a boy has done acts which, but for his age, would amount to one of these offences he may be convicted of an indecent assault. He may also be convicted of abetting another to commit those offences of which he is himself incapable.[10]

3 Persons over Fourteen Years

Above the age of fourteen an infant is presumed to be "responsible for his actions entirely as if he were forty".[11] In the case of these infants the prosecution need prove only the usual *mens rea* required in the case of a person of full age to obtain a conviction. There are however very important differences in the treatment of young persons convicted of crime in the modern law.[12] The Children and Young Persons Act 1969, s. 5, provides for restrictions on the prosecution of young persons. This provision has not been brought into force and there is no intention of bringing it into force at the present time. It would restrict the right to prosecute young persons to

---

4. For further conditions, see s. 122A of the 1969 Act, inserted by the 1989 Act, Sch. 12, para. 23.

5. *Groombridge* (1836) 7 C & P 582.

6. *Waite* [1892] 2 QB 600. Whether a conviction for attempted rape or an offence involving sexual intercourse is possible is considered below, p. 459.

7. *Tatam* (1921) 15 Cr App Rep 132, holding that a boy under fourteen cannot be an accomplice to sodomy. But see below, p. 478.

8. *Philips* (1839) 8 C & P 736 (assault with intent to rape – perhaps no longer an offence), below, p. 459.

9. But see below, p. 459.

10. Above, p. 152.

11. *Smith* (1845) 1 Cox CC 260, per Erle J.

12. Chapter 8; Cross, *The English Sentencing System* (3rd ed.), 75. Criminal Justice Act 1982, Part I and Criminal Justice Act 1991, Part III.

"qualified informants" specified in the Act, who might institute proceedings only subject to regulations made by the Home Secretary and where the informant was of the opinion that the case could not otherwise be adequately dealt with.

2 Insanity[13]

1 Insanity before the Trial

An accused person's sanity may become relevant at two stages before trial on indictment. It is inaccurate to speak of "a defence" in these preliminary proceedings, for the effect of a finding of insanity of the appropriate kind is to prevent the accused being tried at all. It is thought convenient to deal briefly with these matters here, however, because of their very close relationship with the defence of insanity at the trial.

Where D has been committed in custody for trial, and the Home Secretary is satisfied by reports from at least two medical practitioners that he is suffering from mental illness, or severe mental impairment,[14] he may order that D be detained in a hospital, if he is of opinion having regard to the public interest that it is expedient to do so.[15] The Home Secretary exercises this power only

"where the prisoner's condition is such that immediate removal to a mental hospital is necessary, that it would not be practicable to bring him before a court, or that the trial is likely to have an injurious effect on his mental state."[16]

The prisoner is normally brought to trial when he is well enough.[17] The basis for this practice is—

"that the issue of insanity should be determined by the jury whenever possible and the power should be exercised only when there is likely to be a scandal if the prisoner is brought up for trial . . ."[18]

The second stage is when the accused is brought up for trial. He may then be found unfit to plead on arraignment under ss. 4 and 4A of the Criminal Procedure (Insanity) Act 1964.[19] The question at this stage is whether he is able to understand the charge and the difference between pleas of guilty and not guilty, to challenge jurors, to instruct counsel and to follow the evidence. If he is able to do these things, he has a right to be tried if he so

---

13. Walker, *Crime and Insanity in England*; Williams, CLGP, Chapter 10. Proposals for the reform of the law are made in the Report of the Committee on Mentally Abnormal Offenders (The Butler Report – hereinafter Butler) Cmnd. 6244, 1975. Emmins, [1986] Crim LR 605.
14. Mental Health Act 1983, s. 1(1).
15. Mental Health Act 1983, ss. 47, 48.
16. RCCP, Cmd. 8932, p. 76 referring to the corresponding power under the Criminal Lunatics Act 1884. See Butler, para. 3.38.
17. Butler, para. 3.38.
18. RCCP, Cmd. 8932, loc. cit.
19. As substituted by the Criminal Procedure (Insanity and Unfitness to Plead) Act 1991, discussed by S. White, [1992] Crim LR 4. The 1964 Act replaced the Criminal Lunatics Act 1800.

wishes, even though he is not capable of acting in his best interests.[20] The same principle must, theoretically, be applicable where the prosecution contend that D is fit to plead and he denies it; but it might be more leniently applied in such a case.

It was held in *Podola*[1] that a man is fit to plead where an hysterical amnesia prevents him from remembering events during the whole of the period material to the question whether he committed the crime alleged, but whose mind is otherwise completely normal. The court was prepared to concede that a deaf mute is "insane" – the word used in the Criminal Lunatics Act 1800 – but declined

> "to extend the meaning of the word to include persons who are mentally normal at the time of the hearing of the proceedings against them and are perfectly capable of instructing their solicitors as to what submission their counsel is to put forward with regard to the commission of the crime."[2]

But is a person suffering from hysterical amnesia so capable? If the actual facts justify a defence of accident or alibi but D is unable to remember them, the defence, in the absence of volunteer witnesses, cannot be raised. On the other hand it would be unsatisfactory if, for example, there could be no trial of a motorist who had suffered concussion in an accident, alleged to have been caused by his reckless driving, and who could not remember what he did. It would be still less satisfactory in the case of one whose failure to recall the relevant events arose from drunkenness.[3]

The issue may be raised by the judge on his own initiative or at the request of the prosecution or the defence. Where neither party raises the issue, the judge should do so if he has doubts about the accused's fitness.[4] He may resolve his doubts by reading the medical reports, but it is undesirable for him to hear medical evidence.

If the question is raised by either party, or if the judge has doubts, the issue must be tried by a jury.[5] The general rule is that the question of fitness is to be determined as soon as it arises. When it arises on arraignment it will be determined by a jury specially empanelled for that purpose—if the accused is found fit and the trial proceeds it will be tried by a different jury. Where, exceptionally, the question falls to be determined at a later time the judge has a discretion to direct that the issue be determined by a separate jury or by the jury by whom the accused is being

20. *Robertson* [1968] 3 All ER 557, [1968] 1 WLR 1767, CA.
1. [1960] 1 QB 325, [1959] 3 All ER 418; **SHC 188**. The jury had found that Podola was not suffering from hysterical amnesia and the question before the Court of Criminal Appeal concerned the onus of proof of that issue; but the Court held that this question could only arise if the alleged amnesia could in law bring Podola within the scope of s. 2 of the Criminal Lunatics Act 1800. The Court's decision on this point thus appears to be part of the *ratio decidendi* of the case.
2. [1960] 1 QB at 356, [1959] 3 All ER at 433. The word "insane" is not used in s. 4 of the 1964 Act; but the law is unchanged. Cf. Cmd. 2149, p. 7.
3. *Broadhurst v R* [1964] AC 441 at 451, [1964] 1 All ER 111 at 116, PC. Butler (by majority) recommends the retention of the *Podola* rule.
4. *MacCarthy* [1967] 1 QB 68, [1966] 1 All ER 447, discussed by A. R. Poole, "Standing Mute and Fitness to Plead" [1966] Crim LR 6.
5. Criminal Procedure (Insanity) Act 1964, s. 4(5). Butler recommended that the issue should be decided by the judge unless (i) the medical evidence is not unanimous, and (ii) the defence want a jury; paras. 10.20–10.23.

tried.[6] The jury may not find D unfit to plead unless there is written or oral evidence to that effect by two or more registered medical practitioners at least one of whom is approved by the Home Secretary as having special experience in the field of mental disorder.[7]

The general view expressed by witnesses before the Royal Commission on Capital Punishment was that:

"someone who is certifiably insane may often nevertheless be fit to plead to the indictment and follow the proceedings at the trial and that, if he is, he should ordinarily be allowed to do so, because it is in principle desirable that a person charged with a criminal offence should, whenever possible, be tried, so that the question whether he committed the crime may be determined by a jury.[8]

a) *Time of trial of fitness to plead.* It is not sufficient, however, to ensure that all persons who are unfit to plead should not be required to defend themselves against the charge. The case against a person who is undoubtedly unfit to plead may be weak and capable of demolition by cross-examination of the prosecution witnesses by his lawyers. It would be wrong if he were to be found unfit and subjected to the restraints which may follow from that finding without having an opportunity to test the prosecution's case. The matter is now regulated by the Criminal Procedure (Insanity) Act 1964, as amended by the Criminal Procedure (Insanity and Unfitness to Plead) Act 1991. As we have seen, the general rule is that the question of fitness is to be determined by a jury as soon as it arises; but if the judge, having regard to the nature of the supposed disability, thinks that it is expedient and in the interests of the accused to do so, he may postpone consideration of the question of fitness to be tried until any time up to the opening of the case for the defence.[9]

This gives the defence the opportunity to test the prosecution's case. If it is insufficient to justify a conviction, the jury will be directed to acquit and the question of fitness to plead will not be determined. If there is a case to answer, that question will then be determined either by a separate jury or by the jury by whom D is being tried as the judge directs.

Where D is found to be unfit, either on arraignment or at the end of the prosecution case, the trial shall not proceed, or further proceed. If the matter rested there, D might again be subject to restraint though he has done nothing wrong. Even if the prosecution's evidence has been heard and amounts to a case to answer, there may be an answer to it in the shape of evidence – e.g., of alibi – available to the defence. Section 4A (introduced by the 1991 Act) therefore provides that a jury shall decide on the evidence (if any) already given and such evidence as is adduced by the prosecution or

---

6. Criminal Procedure (Insanity) Act 1964, s. 4 (5) as substituted by the Criminal Procedure (Insanity and Unfitness to Plead) Act 1991, s. 2, hereafter "The 1964 Act as amended".
7. The 1964 Act as amended, s. 4 (6).
8. Report, Cmd. 8932, p. 78.
9. The judge must generally exercise his discretion to postpone where there is a reasonable chance that the prosecution case will be successfully challenged: *Webb* [1969] 2 QB 278, [1969] 2 All ER 626. On the other hand, "the case for the prosecution may appear so strong and the suggested condition of the prisoner so disabling that postponement of the trial of the issue would be wholly inexpedient": *Burles* [1970] 2 QB 191, [1970] 1 All ER 642, per Parker LCJ.

the defence whether D did the act or made the omission charged against him. If they are satisfied (presumably beyond reasonable doubt) that he did, they make a finding to that effect. If they are not so satisfied, they return a verdict of acquittal, as if the trial had proceeded to a conclusion.

b) *Onus of proof.* *Podola*'s case decides, overruling earlier authorities, that, where D raises the issue of fitness to plead, the onus of proving that he is unfit is on him. By analogy to the rule prevailing when a defence of insanity is raised at the trial,[10] D is required to prove his case, not beyond reasonable doubt, but on a balance of probabilities. If the issue is raised by the prosecution and disputed by the defence then the burden is on the prosecution and the matter must be proved beyond reasonable doubt.[11] If the issue is raised by the judge and disputed by D, presumably the onus is again on the prosecution.[12]

The effect of *Podola*'s case is that a man may be convicted although a jury was not satisfied that he was capable of making out a proper defence at his trial. Moreover the reasoning of the court has been criticised[13] on the ground, *inter alia*, that the prosecution, in bringing the charge at all, is implicitly alleging that D is fit to stand his trial; and that he, in denying that he is so fit, is merely denying that the prosecution have established all the elements in their case.

c) *Disposal of a person unfit to plead who did the act.* Until the reforms made by the 1991 Act took effect the court had to order that any person found unfit to plead had to be admitted to the hospital specified by the Home Secretary where he might be detained without limitation of time, the power to discharge him being exercisable only with the Home Secretary's consent. Since the 1991 Act a person who is found unfit to plead but not to have done the act or made the omission charged simply goes free. Where he is found to be unfit *and* to have done the act or made the omission a wider range of disposals is now generally available. Where, however, the sentence for the offence to which the finding relates is fixed by law – in effect, murder – the court must make a hospital order restricting discharge without limitation of time. In any other case the court may make (i) a hospital order and an order restricting discharge either for a specified time or without limitation of time; or, in appropriate circumstances, (ii) a guardianship order under the Mental Health Act 1983; (iii) a supervision and treatment order under Sch. 2 of the 1991 Act; or (iv) an order for absolute discharge.[14]

2 Insanity at the Trial[15]

If the accused is found fit to plead or, if that issue is not raised, he may raise the defence of insanity at his trial. A successful defence formerly resulted in

10. See below, p. 205.
11. Per Edmund Davies J at first instance, [1960] 1 QB 325 at 329, [1959] 3 All ER 418 at 442; *Robertson* [1968] 3 All ER 557, [1968] 1 WLR 1767, CA.
12. According to Podola's counsel, Mr Lawton, it had been the normal practice in recent years for the prosecution to call the evidence.
13. By Dean [1960] Crim LR 79 at 82.
14. Section 5 of the 1964 Act as amended.
15. See generally, Williams, CLGP, Chapter 9.

an order that the defendant be admitted to a special hospital where he might be detained indefinitely, but now, by the 1991 Act, the same powers of disposal are available as for a person found unfit to plead, stated above.

It is important to notice that, whereas at the two preliminary stages we were concerned with the accused's sanity *at the time of the inquiry*, at the trial the question concerns the accused's sanity *at the time when he did the act*. The fact that he was insane in the medical sense is not in itself sufficient to afford a defence. There is a legal criterion of responsibility defined by the common law and set out in authoritative form in the "M'Naghten Rules", formulated by the judges in 1843. Daniel M'Naghten, intending to murder Sir Robert Peel, killed the statesman's secretary by mistake. His acquittal of murder[16] on the ground of insanity provoked controversy and was debated in the House of Lords, which sought the advice of the judges and submitted to them a number of questions. The answers to those questions became the famous Rules.[17] Answers to hypothetical questions, even by all the judges, are not, strictly speaking, a source of law; but in *Sullivan*[18] it was accepted by the House of Lords that the Rules have provided a comprehensive definition since 1843.

In one sense the Rules have become obsolete since the abolition of the death penalty and the introduction of the defence of diminished responsibility. Recently they have been invoked by way of defence on only one or two occasions each year. Defendants have been unwilling to rely on the defence, preferring to risk conviction and sentence rather than incur the stigma of an insanity verdict and the indefinite detention which would follow. Some who, on the evidence before the court, were not guilty of the offence, have preferred to plead guilty when it was ruled that the evidence amounted to a plea of insanity and not, as they had claimed, non-insane automatism. The propriety of accepting a plea of guilty by a person who, on the evidence, is not guilty seems doubtful but it has not been questioned in the Court of Appeal and the House of Lords has left the matter open.[19] It is possible that the Rules may be more frequently invoked in future because of the wider powers of disposal. Whereas committal to a special hospital may be regarded as worse than the consequences of conviction, an absolute discharge or a supervision and treatment order may not be. A defendant who is advised that one of these orders is likely to be made in the event of a successful defence may now be willing to raise it, whereas formerly he would not have done so – but the stigma of "insanity" remains. Whatever the effect of the recent changes the Rules remain of great importance both because they provide the legal test of responsibility of the mentally abnormal and because they set a limit to the defences of automatism and, in theory, of diminished responsibility. The basic propositions of the law are to be found in the answers to Questions 2 and 3:[20]

> ". . . the jurors ought to be told in all cases that every man is presumed to be sane, and to possess a sufficient degree of reason to be responsible for

16. 4 St Tr NS 847.
17. 10 Cl & F 200; **SHC 190**.
18. [1984] AC 156, [1983] 2 All ER 673.
19. *Sullivan* [1983] 2 All ER 673 at 676; **SHC 202**.
20. 10 Cl & F at 210.

his crimes, until the contrary be proved to their satisfaction; and that to establish a defence on the ground of insanity, it must be clearly proved that, at the time of the committing of the act, the party accused was labouring under such a defect of reason, from disease of the mind, as not to know the nature and quality of the act he was doing, or, if he did know it, that he did not know he was doing what was wrong."

It will be seen that there are two lines of defence open to an accused person: (i) he must be acquitted if, because of a disease of the mind, he did not know the nature and quality of his act; (ii) even if he did know the nature and quality of his act, he must be acquitted if, because of a disease of the mind, he did not know it was "wrong". The two limbs of the rule require separate consideration but the first question, under either limb, is whether D was suffering from "a defect of reason from disease of the mind". If D was unaware of the nature and quality of his act for some other reason, he will usually be entitled to a simple acquittal on the ground that he lacked the necessary *mens rea*. Moreover the onus of proof will remain on the Crown, whereas it will shift to D once he tenders evidence of a defect of reason arising from disease of the mind. If D was unaware that his act was "wrong" for some other reason, this will generally not amount to a defence at all for neither ignorance of the law nor good motive normally affords a defence.

When a defendant puts his state of mind in issue, the question whether he has raised the defence of insanity is one of law for the judge. Whether D, or indeed his medical witnesses, would call the condition on which he relies "insanity" is immaterial. The expert witnesses may testify as to the factual nature of the condition but it is for the judge to say whether that is evidence of "a defect of reason, from disease of the mind", because, as will appear, these are legal, not medical, concepts.

In the leading case of *Sullivan*,[1] the defence to a charge of assault occasioning actual bodily harm was that D attacked P while recovering from a minor epileptic seizure and did not know what he was doing. The House of Lords held that the judge had rightly ruled that this raised the defence of insanity. D had then pleaded guilty to the charge, of which he was manifestly innocent, and his conviction was upheld.

a) *Disease of the mind*. Whether a particular condition amounts to a disease of the mind within the Rules is not a medical but a legal question to be decided in accordance with the ordinary rules of interpretation.[2] It seems that any disease which produces a malfunctioning of the mind is a disease of the mind. It need not be a disease of the brain. Arteriosclerosis, a tumour on the brain, epilepsy, diabetes, all physical diseases, may amount in law to a disease of the mind if they produce the relevant malfunction. A malfunctioning of the mind is not a disease of the mind when it is caused by some external factor – a blow on the head causing concussion, the consumption of alcohol or drugs, or the administration of an anaesthetic. Contrary to the dictum of Devlin J in *Kemp*,[3] it is clear that the law considers not only the

1. [1984] AC 156, [1983] 2 All ER 673, HL; **SHC 202**.
2. *Kemp* [1957] 1 QB 399 at 406, [1956] 3 All ER 249 at 254, per Devlin J, approved by Lord Denning in *Bratty*, below, p. 199.
3. [1957] 1 QB 399 at 407; **SHC 194**.

state of mind in which D was, but how it came about. Devlin J thought that the object of the inclusion of the words "disease of the mind" was to exclude "defects of reason caused simply by brutish stupidity without rational power"; but it seems the words exclude more than that. In *Quick*[4] D who had inflicted actual bodily harm called medical evidence to show that he was a diabetic and that he was suffering from hypoglycaemia and was unaware of what he was doing. Bridge J ruled that he had raised a defence of insanity, whereupon D pleaded guilty. On appeal it was held that the alleged mental condition was caused not by D's diabetes but by his use of insulin prescribed by the doctor. This was an external factor and the defence of automatism should have been left to the jury. If the condition had been caused by the diabetes then it would seem that the defence would have been insanity.

In *Kemp* D made an entirely motiveless and irrational attack on his wife with a hammer. He was charged with causing grievous bodily harm to her with intent to murder her. It appeared that he suffered from arteriosclerosis which caused a congestion of blood in his brain. As a result he suffered a temporary lapse of consciousness during which he made the attack. It was conceded that D did not know the nature and quality of his act and that he suffered from a defect of reason but it was argued on his behalf that this arose, not from any mental disease, but from a purely physical one. It was argued that, if a physical disease caused the brain cells to degenerate (as in time, it might), then it would be a disease of the mind; but until it did so, it was said, this temporary interference with the working of the brain was like a concussion or something of that sort and not a disease of the mind. Devlin J rejected this argument and held that D was suffering from a disease of the mind. He said:[5]

"The law is not concerned with the brain but with the mind, in the sense that 'mind' is ordinarily used, the mental faculties of reason, memory and understanding. If one reads for 'disease of the mind' 'disease of the brain,' it would follow that in many cases pleas of insanity would not be established because it could not be proved that the brain had been affected in any way, either by degeneration of the cells or in any other way. In my judgment the condition of the brain is irrelevant and so is the question of whether the condition of the mind is curable or incurable, transitory or permanent."

In the earlier case of *Charlson*[6] where the evidence was that D was "acting as an automaton without any real knowledge of what he was doing" as a result of a cerebral tumour, Barry J directed the jury to acquit if the defence might reasonably be true. Devlin J distinguished *Charlson* on the ground that there the doctors were agreed that D was not suffering from a mental disease. As this is a question of law the distinction seems unsound[7]

---

4. [1973] QB 910, [1973] 3 All ER 347, [1973] Crim LR 434 and commentary; **SHC 195**. Cf. *Hennessy* and *Bingham*, above, p. 40.
5. [1957] 1 QB at 407, [1956] 3 All ER at 253.
6. [1955] 1 All ER 859, [1955] 1 WLR 317.
7. A similar argument was rejected in *Sullivan* [1983] 2 All ER 673 at 677. The nomenclature adopted by the medical profession may change but the meaning of "disease of the mind" in the Rules remains unchanged.

and in *Bratty*[8] Lord Denning approved *Kemp* and disagreed with *Charlson*. Lord Denning put forward his own view of a disease of the mind:

"it seems to me that any mental disorder which has manifested itself in violence and is prone to recur is a disease of the mind. At any rate it is the sort of disease for which a person should be detained in hospital rather than be given an unqualified acquittal."

Quick casts some doubt on this dictum. The definition might fit a diabetic, but "no mental hospital would admit a diabetic merely because he had a low blood sugar reaction", and it might be felt to be "an affront to common sense" to regard such a person as insane; yet the Court saw the weakness of the argument, agreeing with Devlin J that the disease might be "curable or incurable . . . transitory or permanent"; and the fact that the Home Secretary might have a difficult problem of disposal did not affect the matter. Lord Denning's dictum has also been criticised on the ground that it is tautologous and that a disease of the mind may manifest itself in wrongful acts other than violence, such as theft.[9]

Cases in other jurisdictions have raised the question whether a "dissociative state" resulting from a "psychological blow" amounts to insane or non-insane automatism. In *Rabey*[10] D, a student who had become infatuated by a girl, P, discovered that P did not regard him particularly highly and reacted by hitting her on the head with a rock that he had taken from a geology laboratory. He was acquitted of causing bodily harm with intent on the ground of automatism. The trial judge accepted that D was in a dissociative state consequent upon the psychological blow of his rejection, which, he held, was an external factor, analogous to a blow to the skull, where the skull is thin, causing concussion. The Ontario Court of Appeal allowed the prosecution's appeal and ordered a new trial. A further appeal to the Supreme Court of Canada was dismissed. That court approved the judgment of Martin J, who took the view that "the ordinary stresses and disappointments of life which are the common lot of mankind do not constitute an external cause . . .".[11] The exceptional effect which this ordinary event had on D "must be considered as having its source primarily in the [D's] psychological or emotional make-up". Notwithstanding the powerful dissent by Dickson J, it is submitted that this is right and that in such a case, if the evidence as to the dissociative state is accepted at all,[12] it should be treated as evidence of insanity. Once the judge has so categorised the defence, the onus of proving on a balance of probabilities that he was in a dissociative state is on D. If he and his medical witnesses are to be believed, he was not guilty, but he is a highly dangerous person. Who is to say that the next ordinary stress of life will not lead him

8. *Bratty v A-G for Northern Ireland* [1963] AC 386 at 410–412, [1961] 3 All ER 523 at 533–534, HL; **SHC 199**.
9. Walker, *Crime and Insanity in England*, 117.
10. (1977) 37 CCC (2d) 461, affirming [1980] SCR 513, 54 CCC (2d) 1. See also *Parnerkar* [1974] SCR 449, (1973) 10 CCC (2d) 253 and cases discussed by Mackay in [1980] Crim LR 350.
11. (1980) 54 CCC (2d) at p. 7.
12. Cf. the scepticism of Williams about the acceptance of the evidence of "overenthusiastic psychiatrists" in relation to the similar case of *Parnerkar* [1974] SCR 449, 10 CCC (2d) 253; TBCL (1st ed.) 612–613.

unconsciously to wield a deadly weapon?[13] Martin J left open the question of the effect of an extraordinary event of such severity that it might reasonably be expected to cause a dissociative state in the average person. This, it is submitted, is a case of non-insane automatism because D has done nothing to show that he is any more dangerous to others than anyone else; and he should be simply acquitted.

b) *"External" and "internal" factors.* The distinction between external causes, which may give rise to a defence of non-insane automatism, and internal factors which can only give rise to a defence of insanity discussed above[14] has been subjected to criticism.[15] There is however some reason in it, in that the internal factor will usually be a continuing condition which may cause a recurrence of the prohibited conduct whereas the external factor – the blow on the head, the injection, the inhalation of toxic fumes,[16] etc. will usually have a transitory effect. Of course, the blow on the head may inflict permanent damage, in which case that damage will be an internal factor, giving rise to a defence of insanity.

The reach of the M'Naghten rules in extending to epileptics and diabetics is wide, but all the cases involve apparently purposive conduct and it may be that the Rules should be limited to cases of that type. A convulsive movement of a person in an epileptic fit may result in injury to person or property but it would seem absurd either to convict the epileptic or hold him to be insane. In *Bratty v A-G for Northern Ireland*,[17] D took off a girl's stocking and strangled her with it. There was medical evidence that he was suffering from psychomotor epilepsy which might have prevented him from knowing the nature and quality of his act. It was held to be evidence of insanity. This is very far removed from a convulsive movement of the body. It is a complex operation which has every appearance of being controlled by the brain. Whether or not D could have prevented himself from acting in this way, he appears to be a very dangerous person and, in the absence of some other form of protection for the public, a simple verdict of acquittal seems inappropriate. Sullivan's conduct, like that of Kemp, Charlson, Quick and Rabey also seems to have been apparently purposive and, though he was less obviously a danger to the public than Bratty, his case may be indistinguishable in principle.

c) *Disease of the mind in combination with other factors.* There are three types of factors which may prevent D from knowing the nature of his act.
   (i) Those tending to an absolute acquittal, such as concussion, the taking of a *medically prescribed* drug or anaesthetic, and other "external" factors, including, in the case of crimes of "specific

---

13. In fact, D's expert witness said D had no predisposition to dissociate; but the court, while bound to take account of medical evidence, may also take account of the facts of the case and apply its common sense to all the evidence.
14. See p. 39.
15. See the dissent by Dickson J in *Rabey* (1981) 114 DLR (3d) 193; Mackay, "Non-Organic Automatism", [1980] Crim LR 350; Williams, TBCL, 671.
16. *Oakley* (1986) 24 CCC (3d) 351 at 362, per Martin JA.
17. [1963] AC 386, [1961] 3 All ER 523.

intent" only, intoxication arising from the voluntary taking of drink or drugs.

(ii) Those tending to an acquittal on the ground of insanity – diseases of the mind.

(iii) Those not amounting to a defence at all – in the case of crimes not requiring specific intent, intoxication arising from the voluntary taking of drink or drugs.

The various factors may operate consecutively or concurrently. There is little authority on the complex questions which may arise and such as there is does not seem well thought out. It is sufficient to demonstrate, however, that this is a practical and not merely an academic problem. Some answers to the questions which may arise are suggested in the sixth edition of this work (pp. 190–191) but the matter is not pursued here.

d) *Defect of reason.* The disease of the mind must have given rise to a defect of reason. It seems that the powers of reasoning must be impaired and that a mere failure to use powers of reasoning which one has is not within the Rules. When D claimed that she had taken articles from a supermarket without paying for them because of absentmindedness resulting from depression, it was held that, even if she was suffering from a disease of the mind, she had not raised the defence of insanity but was simply denying that she had *mens rea*.[18]

e) *The nature and quality of his act.* The phrase "nature and quality of his act" refers to the physical nature and quality of the act and not to its moral or legal quality.[19] Illustrations given by leading writers are:

"A kills B under an insane delusion that he is breaking a jar"[20]

and

"the madman who cut a woman's throat under the idea that he was cutting a loaf of bread."[1]

Of course, a man who was under such a delusion as these, apart altogether from insanity, could never be convicted of murder, simply because he had no *mens rea*. The important practical difference, however, is that, if the delusion arose from a disease of the mind, he will be liable to be (though no longer necessarily) indefinitely detained in a special hospital whereas, if it arose from some other cause, he will go entirely free. A person whose acts are involuntary because he is unconscious does not "know the nature and quality of his act".[2]

f) *Knowledge that the act is wrong.* The question is not whether the accused is able to distinguish between right and wrong in general, but whether he was able to appreciate the wrongness of the particular act he was doing at

18. *Clarke* [1972] 1 All ER 219; **SHC 192**.
19. *Codère* (1916) 12 Cr App Rep 21.
20. Stephen, *Digest* (8th ed.), 6.
 1. Kenny, *Outlines*, 76.
 2. *Sullivan* [1983] 2 All ER 673 at 678, HL.

the particular time. It has always been clear that if D knew his act was contrary to law, he knew it was "wrong" for this purpose. Thus in their first answer the judges in *M'Naghten*'s case said:[3]

". . . notwithstanding the party accused did the act complained of with a view, under the influence of insane delusion, of redressing or revenging some supposed grievance or injury, or of producing some public benefit, he is nevertheless punishable, according to the nature of the crime committed, if he knew at the time of committing such crime that he was acting contrary to law; by which expression we understand your lord-ships to mean the law of the land."

Even if D did not know his act was contrary to law, he was still liable if he knew that it was wrong "according to the ordinary standard adopted by reasonable men".[4] The fact that the accused thought his act was right was irrelevant if he knew that people generally considered it wrong. This again seems to be supported by the Rules:[5]

"If the question were to be put as to the knowledge of the accused solely and exclusively with reference to the law of the land, it might tend to confound the jury, by inducing them to believe that an actual knowledge of the law of the land was essential to lead to a conviction: whereas the law is administered upon the principle that everyone must be taken conclusively to know it, without proof that he does know it. If the accused was conscious that the act was one which he ought not to do, and if that act was at the same time contrary to the law of the land, he is punishable."

A modern case, however suggests that the courts are concerned only with the accused's knowledge of legal wrongness.

In *Windle*,[6] D, unhappily married to a woman, P, who was always speaking of committing suicide and who, according to medical evidence at the trial, was certifiably insane, killed P by the administration of 100 aspirins. He then gave himself up to the police, saying, "I suppose they will hang me for this." A medical witness for the defence said that D was suffering from a form of communicated insanity known as *folie à deux*. Rebutting medical evidence was called, but the doctors on both sides agreed that he knew he was doing an act which the law forbade. Devlin J thereupon withdrew the issue from the jury. So far the decision accords perfectly with the law as stated above but, in the Court of Criminal Appeal, Lord Goddard CJ, in upholding the conviction, said:[7]

"Courts of law can only distinguish between that which is in accordance with the law and that which is contrary to law. . . . The law cannot embark on the question and it would be an unfortunate thing if it were left to juries to consider whether some particular act was morally right or wrong. The test must be whether it is contrary to law. . . .
In the opinion of the court there is no doubt that in the M'Naghten Rules 'wrong' means contrary to law and not 'wrong' according to the opinion

3. 10 Cl & F at 209.
4. *Codère* (1916) 12 Cr App Rep 21 at 27.
5. 10 Cl & F at 210.
6. [1952] 2 QB 826, [1952] 2 All ER 1; **SHC 192**.
7. [1952] 2 QB 826 at 833, 834, [1952] 2 All ER 1 at 1, 2.

of one man or of a number of people on the question whether a particular act might or might not be justified."

It is thought that *Windle*[8] is in accordance with authority in rejecting the arguments of the defence that D should be acquitted if, knowing his act to be against the law, he also believed it to be morally right. But the effect of the *obiter dictum* – it was no more than that – that "wrong" means simply "legally wrong", would seem to be to widen the defence by making it available to a man who knows that his act is morally wrong but, owing to disease of the mind, fails to appreciate that it is also legally wrong. Such a case was not before the court and seems unlikely to arise.

The High Court of Australia has refused to follow *Windle*. In *Stapleton v R*[9] they made a detailed examination of the English law, before and after *M'Naghten* and came to the conclusion that *Windle* was wrongly decided. Their view was that if D believed his act to be right according to the ordinary standard of reasonable men he was entitled to be acquitted even if he knew it to be legally wrong. This would extend the scope of the defence, not only beyond what was laid down in *Windle*, but beyond what the law was believed to be before that case. While such an extension of the law may be desirable, it is difficult to reconcile with the M'Naghten Rules and to justify on the authorities.[10] It is unlikely to be followed by the courts in England.

g) *Insane delusions*. The judges were asked in *M'Naghten*'s case:
"If a person under an insane delusion as to existing facts commits an offence in consequence thereof, is he thereby excused?"
They replied:[11]
". . . the answer must, of course, depend on the nature of the delusion: but making the same assumption as we did before, namely, that he labours under such partial delusion only, and is not in other respects insane, we think he must be considered in the same situation as to responsibility as if the facts with respect to which the delusion exists were real. For example, if under the influence of his delusion he supposes another man to be in the act of attempting to take away his life, and he kills that man, as he supposes, in self-defence, he would be exempt from punishment. If his delusion was that the deceased had inflicted a serious injury to his character and fortune, and he killed him in revenge for such supposed injury, he would be liable to punishment."
This seems to add nothing to the earlier answers. The insane delusions that the judges had in mind seem to have been factual errors of the kind which prevent a man from knowing the nature and quality of his act or knowing it is wrong. The example given seems to fall within those rules.

The proposition that the insane person "must be considered in the same situation as to responsibility as if the facts with respect to which the delusion exists were real" must be treated with caution. It must always be

8. Above, fn. 6.
9. (1952) 86 CLR 358; see also *Weise* [1969] VR 953, especially at 960 et seq., per Barry J.
10. *Stapleton v R* is discussed in a note by N. Morris (1953) 16 MLR 435, which is criticised by Montrose (1954) 17 MLR 383.
11. 10 Cl & F at 211; **SHC 190**.

remembered that there must be an actual *actus reus*, accompanied by the appropriate *mens rea*, for a conviction. Suppose that D strangles his wife's poodle under the insane delusion that it is her illegitimate child. If the supposed facts were real he would be guilty of murder – but that is plainly impossible as there is no *actus reus*.[12] Nor is there any crime in respect of the dog, for there is no *mens rea*. The rule seems merely to emphasise that delusions which do not prevent D from having *mens rea* will afford no defence. As Lord Hewart Cj rather crudely put it, "the mere fact that a man thinks he is John the Baptist does not entitle him to shoot his mother".[13] A case often discussed is that of a man who is under the insane delusion that he is obeying a divine command. Some American courts have held that such a belief affords a defence. Yet if the accused knows that his act is forbidden by law, it seems clear he is liable. Stephen certainly thought that this was so:[14]

"My own opinion is that if a special divine order were given to a man to commit murder, I should certainly hang him for it, unless I got a special divine order not to hang him."

h) *Irresistible impulse.* It is recognised by psychiatrists that a man may know the nature and quality of an act, may even know that it is wrong, and yet perform it under an impulse that is almost or quite uncontrollable. Such a man has no defence under the Rules. The matter was considered in *Kopsch*:[15] D, according to his own admission, killed his uncle's wife. He said that he strangled her with his necktie at her own request. (If this was an insane delusion, it would not, of course, afford a defence under the rules stated above.) There was evidence that he had acted under the direction of his subconscious mind. Counsel argued that the judge should have directed the jury that a person under an impulse which he cannot control is not criminally responsible. This was described by Lord Hewart CJ as a

"fantastic theory . . . which if it were to become part of our criminal law, would be merely subversive."[16]

The judges have steadily opposed the admissibility of such a defence on the ground of the difficulty – or impossibility – of distinguishing between an impulse which proves irresistible because of insanity and one which is irresistible because of ordinary motives of greed, jealousy or revenge. The view has also been expressed that the harder an impulse is to resist, the greater is the need for a deterrent.[17]

The law does not recognise irresistible impulse even as a symptom from which a jury might deduce insanity within the meaning of the Rules.[18] If,

12. Nor, notwithstanding *Shivpuri*, below, p. 321, should an insane delusion entail liability for an attempt.
13. Hewart, *Essays*, 224.
14. 2 HCL 160, n. 1.
15. (1925) 19 Cr App Rep 50, CCA. See also *True* (1922) 16 Cr App Rep 164; *Sodeman* [1936] 2 All ER 1138, PC.
16. (1925) 19 Cr App Rep 50 at 51.
17. As a Canadian judge, Riddell J, put it: "If you cannot resist an impulse in any other way, we will hang a rope in front of your eyes, and perhaps that will help": *Creighton* (1909) 14 CCC 349.
18. *A-G for State of South Australia v Brown* [1960] AC 432, [1960] 1 All ER 734, PC.

however, medical evidence were tendered in a particular case that the uncontrollable impulse, to which the accused in that case had allegedly been subject, was a symptom that he did not know his act was wrong, it would be open to the jury to act on that evidence.[19] But it is not permissible for a judge to make use in one case of medical knowledge which he may have acquired from the evidence in another, in his direction to the jury.[20]

Although the M'Naghten Rules remain unaltered a partial defence of irresistible impulse has, as will appear below,[1] now been admitted into the law through the new defence of diminished responsibility.

i) *Burden of proof.* The M'Naghten Rules laid down that

"every man is presumed to be sane, and to possess a sufficient degree of reason to be responsible for his crimes, until the contrary be proved to [the jury's] satisfaction; and that to establish a defence on the ground of insanity, it must be clearly proved, etc."[2]

It seems from these words that the judges were intending to put the burden of proof squarely on the accused, and so it has always been subsequently assumed.[3] Insanity is stated to be the one exception at common law to the rule that it is the duty of the prosecution to prove the prisoner's guilt in all particulars.[4] He does not have to satisfy that heavy onus of proof beyond reasonable doubt which rests on the prosecution but is entitled to a verdict in his favour if he proves his case on a balance of probabilities, the standard which rests on the plaintiff in a civil action. If the jury think it is more likely than not that he is insane within the meaning of the Rules, then he is entitled to their verdict.

When, however, consideration is given to what has to be proved to establish insanity under the first limb of the Rules, there is an apparent conflict with the general rule requiring the prosecution to prove *mens rea.* This requires proof that the accused was either intentional or reckless with respect to all those consequences and circumstances of his act which constitute the *actus reus* of the crime with which he is charged. But this, in effect, is to prove that the accused *did* know the nature and quality of his act. The general rule, therefore, says that the prosecution must prove these facts; the special rule relating to insanity says that the defence must disprove them. Williams argues[5] that the only burden on the accused is the "evidential" one of introducing sufficient evidence to raise a reasonable doubt in the jury's minds; and that the burden of *proof* is on the prosecution. This solution appears to be the only way of resolving the inconsistency; but, as yet, not even the difficulty, let alone the suggested solution, has been judicially recognised in England.[6]

19. Ibid. See also *Sodeman* (1936) 55 CLR 192 at 203.
20. [1960] AC 432 at 449.
1. See p. 212.
2. 10 Cl & F at 210.
3. *Stokes* (1848) 3 Car & Kir 185; *Layton* (1849) 4 Cox CC 149; *Smith* (1910) 6 Cr App Rep 19; *Coelho* (1914) 30 TLR 535; *Bratty v A-G for Northern Ireland* [1963] AC 386, [1961] 3 All ER 523.
4. *Woolmington v Director of Public Prosecutions* [1935] AC 462; **SHC 42**.
5. CLGP, p. 165.
6. Cf., however, *Cottle* [1958] NZLR 999 at 1019, per North J.

This problem does not arise when the accused's defence takes the form that he did not know that his act was wrong. Here he is setting up the existence of facts which are quite outside the prosecution's case and there is no inconsistency in putting the onus on the accused. It is very strange that the onus of proof should be on the Crown if the defence is based on the first limb of the Rules and on the accused if it should be on the second. Yet the authorities[7] seem clearly to establish that the onus in the case of the second limb is on the accused. It is not possible to argue that the courts really meant the evidential burden, for they have said very clearly that the burden is one of proof "on balance of probabilities", the same standard that the plaintiff in a civil action must satisfy. Whatever may be the position regarding the first limb of the defence then, it seems clear that, under the second, the onus is on the accused.

The anomaly is emphasised by the decision of the House of Lords in *Bratty v A-G for Northern Ireland*[8] that, where the defence is automatism arising otherwise than through a disease of the mind, the burden of proof is on the prosecution. It is difficult to see why a man whose alleged disability arises from a disease of the mind should be convicted whereas one whose alleged disability arises from some other cause, would, in exactly the same circumstances, be acquitted.[9]

j) *The special verdict of insanity and the right of appeal.* Where a defence under the M'Naghten Rules was established, the correct verdict until 1964 was

"guilty of the act or omission charged but insane, so as not to be responsible, according to law, for his actions at the time when the act was done or the omission made."

Despite the form of the verdict it was well settled that it was one of acquittal and no appeal lay from the finding either of guilty of doing the act charged, or of insanity.[10]

The anomalous form of the "guilty but insane" verdict had been repeatedly criticised and, by s. 1 of the Criminal Procedure (Insanity) Act 1964, it is provided that it shall be replaced by a special verdict that "the accused is not guilty by reason of insanity". Although it may seem, at first sight, highly illogical to give the accused a right of appeal from an acquittal, this too was a highly desirable reform which was effected by the 1964 Act. If it were the case that a special verdict of insanity could be found only where D himself had so pleaded, it would be reasonable that there should be no appeal; but this was not the case. Thus it will be recalled that in *Kemp*[11] D's contention was that he should be entirely acquitted, but it was held that the medical evidence established insanity within the M'Naghten Rules. The issue was decided against D, yet he had no right of appeal. A similar position arose where, after the Homicide Act, 1957, D raised the defence of diminished responsibility and the prosecution were thereupon

---

7. *Sodeman v R* [1936] 2 All ER 1138: *Carr-Briant* [1943] KB 607, [1943] 2 All ER 156.
8. [1963] AC 386, [1961] 3 All ER 523; **SHC 199**.
9. The Butler proposals on onus of proof appear below, p. 209.
10. *Felstead v R* [1914] AC 534; *Duke* [1963] 1 QB 120, [1961] 3 All ER 737.
11. Above, p. 198.

allowed to introduce evidence of insanity within the M'Naghten Rules.[12] For these reasons, a right of appeal to the Court of Appeal and the House of Lords is provided by s. 12 of the Criminal Appeal Act 1968, subject to the same conditions as apply in criminal appeals generally. The right of appeal is not limited to the case where the issue is decided against D's contention in the court below. It is now possible for D to appeal against the finding (no longer express but now implicit in the verdict) that he did the act or against the finding that he was insane when he did so.

k) *Function of the jury.* It has been laid down for defences of both insanity and diminished responsibility that:[13]

". . . it is for the jury and not for medical men of whatever eminence to determine the issue. Unless and until Parliament ordains that this question is to be determined by a panel of medical men, it is to a jury, after a proper direction by a judge, that by the law of this country the decision is to be entrusted."

The law regarding insanity, however, is now modified by s. 1 of the 1991 Act which provides that a jury shall not return a special verdict of not guilty by reason of insanity except on the written or oral evidence of two or more registered medical practitioners of whom at least one is approved by the Home Secretary as having special experience in the field of mental disorder. The jury may still have to decide between conflicting medical evidence; but if the medical evidence is wholly in favour of a special verdict (or of diminished responsibility) and there is nothing in the facts or surrounding circumstances which could lead to a contrary conclusion, then a verdict of guilty (or guilty of murder as the case may be) will be upset.[14] If there are facts which, in the opinion of the court, justify the jury in coming to a conclusion different from that of the experts, their verdict will be upheld.

3 Proposals for reform

Almost from the moment of their formulation the Rules have been subjected to vigorous criticism, primarily by doctors, but also by lawyers. The Rules, being based on outdated psychological views, are too narrow, it is said, and exclude many persons who ought not to be held responsible. They are concerned only with defects of reason and take no account of emotional or volitional factors whereas modern medical science is unwilling to divide the mind into separate compartments and to consider the intellect apart from the emotions and the will. In 1923 a committee under the chairmanship of Lord Atkin recommended that a prisoner should not be held responsible.

"when the act is committed under an impulse which the prisoner was by mental disease in substance deprived of any power to resist."[15]

12. Below, p. 210.
13. *Rivett* (1950) 34 Cr App Rep 87 at 94; *Latham* [1965] Crim LR 434; *Walton v R* [1978] 1 All ER 542, [1977] 3 WLR 902; [1977] Crim LR 747, PC.
14. *Matheson* [1958] 2 All ER 87, 42 Cr App Rep 145; *Bailey* (1961) 66 Cr App Rep 31, [1961] Crim LR 828, *Sanders* [1991] Crim LR 781 – all cases concerning diminished responsibility – but the same principle surely applies to insanity.
15. Cmd. 2005.

The recommendation was not implemented. In 1953 the Royal Commission on Capital Punishment[16] made much more far-reaching proposals. They thought that the question of responsibility is not primarily a matter of law or of medicine, but of morals and, therefore, most appropriately decided by a jury of ordinary men and women. They thought that the best course would be to abrogate the rules altogether and—

"leave the jury to determine whether at the time of the act the accused was suffering from disease of the mind (or mental deficiency) to such a degree that he ought not be held responsible."[17]

This meant abandoning the assumption that it is necessary to have a rule of law defining the relation of insanity to criminal responsibility; but the Commission thought this assumption had broken down in practice anyway.[18] As an alternative, which they thought less satisfactory but better than leaving the Rules unchanged, the Commission recommended that a third limb be added to the Rules: that the accused "was incapable of preventing himself from committing it . . ."[19]

The Butler Committee proposed a new approach which has been substantially incorporated in the Draft Code. There would be a new verdict of "not guilty on evidence of mental disorder" – "a mental disorder verdict". As under the M'Naghten Rules, such a verdict would be returned in two types of case: (i) where the mental disorder precludes the required fault (corresponding to the "nature and quality" limb), and (ii) where all the elements of the offence are proved but the mental disorder nevertheless should result in an acquittal (corresponding to the "wrong" limb). The Code reverses the order. Clause 35 provides:

"(1) A mental disorder verdict shall be returned if the defendant is proved to have committed an offence but it is proved on the balance of probabilities (whether by the prosecution or by the defendant) that he was at the time suffering from severe mental illness or severe mental handicap."

"Severe mental illness" is defined in the terms proposed by Butler as follows:

"'severe mental illness' means a mental illness which has one or more of the following characteristics—

(a) lasting impairment of intellectual functions shown by failure of memory, orientation, comprehension and learning capacity;

(b) lasting alteration of mood of such degree as to give rise to delusional appraisal of the defendant's situation, his past or his future, or that of others, or lack of any appraisal;

(c) delusional beliefs, persecutory, jealous or grandiose;

(d) abnormal perceptions associated with delusional misinterpretation of events;

---

16. Cmd. 8932.
17. Ibid., para. 333. Cf. Walker's criticism, op. cit. at 110–111: "By what criterion could one tell whether this or that case 'ought' to have been included? Could the criterion be expressed in words, or was it ineffable?"
18. The Commission was impressed by Lord Cooper's view that "However much you charge a jury as to the M'Naghten Rules or any other test, the question they would put to themselves when they retire is – 'Is this man mad or is he not?'"; Report, para. 322.
19. Cmd. 2005.

(e) thinking so disordered as to prevent reasonable appraisal of the defendant's situation of reasonable communication with others."

"Severe mental handicap" means—

"a state of arrested or incomplete development of mind which includes severe impairment of intelligence and social functioning",

a definition adapted from that in the Mental Health Act 1959.

If the Code had stopped here, as Butler intended, this would have involved a major change of principle in that there need be no causal connection between the mental disorder and the commission of the act. Butler thought that the disorders specified are of such severity that a causal connection could safely be presumed. D's belief that he was John the Baptist, presumably "a grandiose delusional belief", would be a defence to a charge of murdering his mother.[20] More realistically, D would have a defence to a charge of robbing a bank or of dangerous driving because he had a jealous delusional belief that his wife was committing adultery. The Law Commission thought such a result unacceptable and so cl. 35 (2) provides:

"Subsection (1) does not apply if the court or jury is satisfied beyond reasonable doubt that the offence was not attributable to the severe mental illness or severe mental handicap."

The effect is that there is a presumption that the commission of the offence was attributable to the disorder but it is rebuttable by proof beyond reasonable doubt.

Clause 36 provides the other limb of the defence:

"**36.** A mental disorder verdict shall be returned if—

(a) the defendant is acquitted of an offence only because, by reason of evidence of mental disorder or a combination of mental disorder and intoxication, it is found that he acted or may have acted in a state of automatism, or without the fault required for the offence, or believing that an exempting circumstance existed; and

(b) it is proved on the balance of probabilities (whether by the prosecution or by the defendant) that he was suffering from mental disorder at the time of the act."

The clause applies only where the mental disorder (or mental disorder combined with intoxication) is the sole cause of D's condition, lack of fault, or mistake. Like the Rules, it applies to a person who, because of mental disorder, is under a delusion that he is the victim of a deadly attack and kills, as he supposes, in self-defence ("an exempting circumstance").

a) *Onus of proof under the Code*. The onus of proving *mens rea* or, when the issue has been raised, of disproving automatism or belief in an exempting circumstance, is on the prosecution. If they fail in this respect, D must be acquitted and the only question (where there is some evidence of mental disorder) is whether there should be absolute acquittal or an acquittal on evidence of mental disorder. It seems right in principle that D should be entitled to an absolute acquittal, unless the jury are satisfied (either by the prosecution or the defence) that he was suffering from mental disorder; and

20. Above, p. 204, fn. 13.

cl. 36 (b), following Butler, so provides. Under cl. 35 the choice for the jury is between conviction ("the defendant is proved to have committed an offence") and a mental disorder verdict so it might be thought the onus should be on the prosecution to prove one or the other. Butler, however, proposed that, to avoid confusing the jury, the onus of proving mental disorder should again be on the party alleging it, whether prosecution or defence; and cl. 35 follows that proposal.

The M'Naghten Rules still have their defenders and the case for them has been most cogently put by Lord Devlin:

"As it is a matter of theory, I think there is something logical – it may be astringently logical, but it is logical – in selecting as the test of responsibility to the law, reason and reason alone. It is reason which makes a man responsible to the law. It is reason which gives him sovereignty over animate and inanimate things. It is what distinguishes him from the animals, which emotional disorder does not; it is what makes him man; it is what makes him subject to the law. So it is fitting that nothing other than a defect of reason should give complete absolution."[1]

3 Diminished Responsibility[2]

The Homicide Act 1957, s. 2, introduced into law a new defence to murder, known as "diminished responsibility", which entitles the accused not to be acquitted altogether, but to be found guilty only of manslaughter.[3] By s. 2 (2) the Act expressly puts the burden of proof on the defendant and it has been held that, as in the case of insanity, the standard of proof required is not beyond reasonable doubt but on a balance of probabilities.[4] Consideration of this defence is, strictly speaking, out of place here, for it is not a general defence, but applies only to murder. In practice, however, the Rules were rarely relied on outside murder cases because the prospect of indefinite and possibly life-long confinement in a special hospital was worse than the likely sentence for most crimes other than murder. Most defendants would prefer a conviction for manslaughter on the ground of diminished responsibility to an acquittal by reason of insanity, so the importance of the Rules has been greatly reduced since 1957. It remains to be seen whether the new powers of disposal of those found not guilty by reason of insanity will revive their importance.

1. "Mental Abnormality and the Criminal Law" in *Changing Legal Objectives* (ed. R. St J. MacDonald, Toronto, 1963) 71 at 85. Cf. A. F. Goldstein, *The Insanity Defence* (1967).
2. Williams (1960), 1 Med Sci & L., 41; Wootton (1960) 76 LQR 224; Sparks (1964) 27 MLR 9; Walker, *Crime and Insanity in England*, 138–164; Dell, "Diminished Responsibility Reconsidered", [1982] Crim LR 809. Griew, "The Future of Diminished Responsibility" [1988] Crim LR 75.
3. The defence is borrowed from the law of Scotland, where it was a judicial creation, originating in the decision of Lord Deas in *HM Advocate v Dingwall* (1867) 5 Irv 466. See T. B. Smith, [1957] Crim LR 354 and Lord Keith [1959] Jur Rev 109.
4. *Dunbar* [1958] 1 QB 1, [1957] 2 All ER 737. Where the medical evidence of diminished responsibility is based on certain facts, it is for the defence to prove those facts by admissible evidence: *Ahmed Din* (1962) 46 Cr App Rep 239; *Bradshaw* (1985) 82 Cr App Rep 79, [1985] Crim LR 733 and commentary.

Where D, being charged with murder, raises the defence of diminished responsibility and the Crown have evidence that he is insane within the Rules, they may adduce or elicit evidence tending to show that this is so. This is now settled by the 1964 Act, s. 6, resolving a conflict in the cases. The Act also provides for the converse situation. Where D sets up insanity, the prosecution may contend that he was suffering only from diminished responsibility.[5] Where D relies on some other defence, such as provocation, and evidence of diminished responsibility emerges, it seems that the most the judge should do is to draw the attention of D's counsel to it.[6] Diminished responsibility is an "optional defence".

Thus, strangely, the roles of the prosecution and defence may be reversed, according to which of them is contending that the prisoner is insane. It seems clear in principle that the Crown must establish whichever contention it puts forward beyond reasonable doubt.[7] It must follow that D rebuts the Crown's case if he can raise a doubt.

The Act does not deal with the situation where D's abnormality of mind is put in issue otherwise than by pleading insanity or diminished responsibility – for example, by raising the defence of automatism. However, the Criminal Law Revision Committee[8] did not think that the limited provision in the Act should throw any doubt on the right of the prosecution to call evidence in cases such as *Kemp*.[9] The prosecution may not, however, lead evidence of D's insanity where the defence have not put the abnormality of D's mind in issue,[10] even though this course is desired by the defence. The position would seem to be that, where the defence rely on the abnormality of mind of any kind, it is open to the prosecution to allege, and to call evidence to prove, that the abnormality amounts to insanity or diminished responsibility. The prosecution should supply the defence with a copy of any statement or report which a prison medical officer may have made on that crime and should make him available as a defence witness.[11]

As with insanity,[12] the decision is to be made by the jury, not the medical experts. They may reject unanimous medical evidence that D is suffering from diminished responsibility if there is anything in the circumstances of the case to justify them in doing so. There is no statutory requirement of medical evidence, such as is now a condition of an insanity verdict, but it has been held that they may not find that the defendant is suffering from diminished responsibility unless there is medical evidence of an abnormality arising from one of the causes specified in the parentheses in s. 2(1) of the Act.[13] An abnormality arising from some other cause will not suffice. So

5. It had been so held at common law by Elwes J in *Nott* (1958) 43 Cr App Rep 8.
6. *Campbell* (1987) 84 Cr App Rep 255 at 259–260; *Kooken* (1982) 74 Cr App Rep 30.
7. *Grant* [1960] Crim LR 424, per Paull J.
8. Cmnd. 2149, para. 41.
9. Above, p. 198.
10. *Dixon* [1961] 3 All ER 460 n, [1961] 1 WLR 337, per Jones J.
11. *Casey* (1947) 32 Cr App Rep 91, CCA. See Samuels, "Can the Prosecution allege that the Accused is Insane?" [1960] Crim LR 453, [1961] Crim LR 308.
12. Above, p. 198.
13. Below. Cf. *Byrne* [1960] 2 QB 396 at 402; *Dix* (1981) 74 Cr App Rep 306 at 311; *Purdy* [1982] 2 NSWLR 964, Roden J diss.

the word "disease" is important. Alcoholism is enough if it injures the brain, causing gross impairment of judgment and emotional responses, or causes the drinking to be involuntary.[14] Medical evidence is "a practical necessity if the defence is to begin to run at all".[15] Where no medical evidence is called, there will always be the suspicion that medical opinion has been sought and found unfavourable.

1 The Nature of the Defence
The Homicide Act 1957, s. 2, enacts:

> "(1) Where a person kills or is a party to the killing of another, he shall not be convicted of murder if he was suffering from such abnormality of mind (whether arising from a condition of arrested or retarded development of mind or any inherent causes or induced by disease or injury) as substantially impaired his mental responsibility for his acts and omissions in doing or being a party to the killing.
>
> (2) . . .
>
> (3) A person who but for this section would be liable, whether as principal or as accessory, to be convicted of murder shall be liable instead to be convicted of manslaughter."

In early cases where the defence was raised, it was held that it was the duty of the judge, in summing up, simply to read the section to the jury and invite them to apply the tests stated therein without further explanation; it was not for the judge to re-define the definition which had been laid down by Parliament.[16] However, it is now clear that it is the duty of the judge to direct the jury as to the meaning to be attached to s. 2.

In *Byrne*[17] the trial judge directed the jury as to the meaning of s. 2, telling them that difficulty or even inability of an accused person to exercise will-power to control his physical acts could not amount to such abnormality of mind as substantially impaired his mental responsibilities. The Court of Criminal Appeal held that this was a wrong direction and that Byrne's conviction of murder must be quashed. Subsequently in *Terry*[18] the court expressly stated that

> ". . . in the light of [the interpretation that this court put on the section in *Byrne*] it seems to this court that it would no longer be proper merely to put the section before the jury but that a proper explanation of the terms of the section as interpreted in *Byrne* ought to be put before the jury."[19]

The facts of *Byrne*[20] were that D strangled a young woman in a Y.W.C.A. hostel and, after her death, committed horrifying mutilations on her body. Evidence was tendered to the effect that D, from an early age, had been subject to perverted violent desires; that the impulse or urge of those desires was stronger than the normal impulse or urge of sex, so that D

14. *Tandy* (1987) 87 Cr App Rep 45, [1988] Crim LR 308.
15. *Dix*, above, at 311.
16. See *Spriggs*. [1958] 1 QB 270, [1958] 1 All ER 300.
17. [1960] 2 QB 396, [1960] 3 All ER 1; **SHC 314.**
18. [1961] 2 QB 314, [1961] 2 All ER 569.
19. [1961] 2 All ER at 574.
20. [1960] 2 QB 396, [1960] 3 All ER 1; **SHC 314.**

found it very difficult or, perhaps, impossible in some cases to resist putting the desire into practice and that the act of killing the girl was done under such an impulse or urge. The court held that it was wrong to say that these facts did not constitute evidence which would bring a case within the section. Lord Parker CJ said:[1]

"'Abnormality of mind', which has to be contrasted with the time-honoured expression in the M'Naghten Rules, 'defect of reason', means a state of mind so different from that of ordinary human beings that the reasonable man would term it abnormal. It appears to us to be wide enough to cover the mind's activities in all its aspects, not only the perception of physical acts and matters and the ability to form a rational judgment whether an act is right or wrong, but also the ability to exercise will-power to control physical acts in accordance with that rational judgment."

Thus, the defence of irresistible impulse is at last admitted into the law (but only of murder) by way of diminished responsibility. The difficulties of proof, which deterred the judges from allowing the defence under the M'Naghten Rules, remain:

". . . the step between 'he did not resist his impulse' and 'he could not resist his impulse' is, as the evidence in this case shows, one which is incapable of scientific proof. A fortiori, there is no scientific measurement of the degree of difficulty which an abnormal person finds in controlling his impulses."

The only way to deal with the problem is for the jury to approach it "in a broad common-sense way".[2] They are entitled to take into account not only the medical evidence but also the acts or statements of the accused and his demeanour and other relevant material. Even when they are satisfied that D was suffering from abnormality of mind there remains the question whether the abnormality was such as substantially to impair his mental responsibility – a question of degree and essentially one for the jury.

It is not necessary that the impulse on which D acted should be found by the jury to be *irresistible*; it is sufficient that the difficulty which D experienced in controlling it (or, rather, *failing* to control it) was *substantially* greater than would be experienced in like circumstances by an ordinary man, not suffering from mental abnormality.[3] The impairment need not be total, but it must be more than trivial or minimal.[4] Where a doctor testified that an epileptic defendant could be "vulnerable to an impulsive tendency and therefore occasional impulsive acts", it was held that there was no evidence of diminished responsibility because (inter alia) the witness had not said that the impulse would *substantially* impair responsibility.[5] The test appears to be one of moral responsibility. A man whose impulse is irresistible bears *no* moral responsibility for his act, for he has no choice; a man whose impulse is much more difficult to resist than

1. [1960] 2 QB 396 at 403, [1960] 3 All ER 1 at 4.
2. [1960] 2 QB at 404, [1960] 2 All ER 1 at 5, per Lord Parker CJ; *Walton v R* [1978] 1 All ER 542, [1977] 3 WLR 902, PC.
3. *Byrne*, above; *Simcox* [1964] Crim LR 402; *Lloyd* [1967] 1 QB 175, [1966] 1 All ER 107n. But cf. Sparks, op. cit., at 16–19.
4. *Lloyd* [1967] 1 QB 175, [1966] 1 All ER 107n.
5. *Campbell* (1987) 84 Cr App Rep 255 at 259.

that of an ordinary man bears a diminished degree of moral responsibility for his act.

The court has from time to time approved directions following those given in Scottish cases and which, in effect, tell the jury what must be proved is a mental state "bordering on, though not amounting to insanity"[6] or "not quite mad but a border-line case".[7] Care must be taken in giving such a direction to avoid any suggestion that "insanity" in this context bears the very narrow meaning of that form of insanity which is a defence under the M'Naghten Rules. If the word is used at all it must be used in "its broad popular sense".[8] A depressive illness may found diminished responsibility, although it is by no means on the borderline of insanity. To tell the jury in such a case that D must be on that borderline is a material misdirection.[9] In such a case, reference to insanity is best avoided altogether.

It is thought, moreover, that this direction is generally unsatisfactory. It follows Scottish directions but the Scottish law of irresponsibility on the ground of insanity appears to be wider than the M'Naghten Rules[10] and diminished responsibility is now interpreted more favourably to the accused in England than in Scotland.[11] Under English law, persons who are actually insane in the "broad popular sense" may well be outside the scope of the M'Naghten Rules and have to rely on diminished responsibility.

Where the evidence is that D was suffering from an abnormality of mind of which one of the causes is an excess of alcohol, the jury must perform the difficult task of ignoring the effect of the alcohol and determine whether the other factors were sufficient to amount to a substantial impairment. They must be asked: "Has D satisfied you on the balance of probabilities that, if he had not taken drink, (i) he would have killed as he in fact did? and (ii) he would have been under diminished responsibility when he did so?"[12] If it was the drink which caused him to kill, he cannot rely on diminished responsibility. But, if an alcoholic's craving for drink is proved to be irresistible, the resulting abnormality at the time of the killing may be a defence.[13]

2 The Effect of the Introduction of Diminished Responsibility

Diminished responsibility has been pleaded with success in cases where one would have thought there was no chance of a defence of insanity succeeding – mercy killers, deserted spouses or disappointed lovers who killed while in a state of depression, persons with chronic anxiety states, and so on.[14] It is surprising that there was no spectacular increase in the number of persons escaping conviction for murder on the ground of their

6. *HM Advocate v Braithwaite* 1945 JC 55, per Lord Cooper.
7. *Spriggs* [1958] 1 QB 270 at 276, [1958] 1 All ER 300 at 304, per Lord Goddard CJ.
8. *Rose v R* [1961] AC 496, [1961] 1 All ER 859.
9. *Seers* (1984) 79 Cr App Rep 261, CA, following the remarks of the Privy Council in *Rose v R* [1961] AC 496, [1961] 1 All ER 859.
10. Cf. T. B. Smith, *The United Kingdom; The Development of Its Laws and Constitution*, 719.
11. Walker, op. cit., 155–156.
12. *Atkinson* [1985] Crim LR 314, approving the commentary on *Gittens* [1984] QB 698, [1984] 3 All ER 252, in [1984] Crim LR 553 at 554.
13. *Tandy* (1987) 87 Cr App Rep 45.
14. Wootton, *Crime and the Criminal Law*, 86.

mental abnormality. In fact, the proportion of persons committed for trial for murder who escape conviction on the ground of their mental abnormality remained much the same after the Homicide Act as it was before. The proportion found insane on arraignment and the proportion acquitted on the ground of insanity sharply declined. This suggests that persons who were formerly found insane on arraignment or acquitted on the ground of insanity now plead diminished responsibility instead; and that only a very few persons escape conviction who would not have done so before 1957.[15] The difference is that instead of being compelled, as until recently it was, to send the mentally abnormal person to a mental hospital, the court may sentence him to imprisonment, put him on probation or make a hospital order as it thinks appropriate in its discretion. In view of the wide range of types of person who shelter under the umbrella of diminished responsibility, it seems desirable that there should be this flexibility in the means of dealing with them.[16]

3 Hospital Orders

It remains to notice that, of much wider practical importance than either insanity or diminished responsibility, is the courts' power to make hospital orders. Under s. 37 of the Mental Health Act 1983, a person who is proved to have committed an offence may be committed to a mental hospital or to the guardianship of a local social services authority. The offence must be one punishable with imprisonment and offences where the sentence is fixed by law (in effect, murder) are excluded. The order can be made only on the evidence of two medical practitioners (one approved by the Secretary of State as having special experience in the diagnosis or treatment of mental disorder) who agree that detention for treatment or reception into guardianship is warranted.

The Crown Court may, if it thinks it necessary for the protection of the public, make a "restriction order" for an indefinite or a specified period.[17] The offender then may not be discharged, given leave of absence or transferred to another hospital without the consent of the Home Secretary.

The relative importance of hospital orders in practice is seen by the fact that in 1986[18] no person charged with murder was found unfit to plead, only one was acquitted on the ground of insanity, 55 charges of murder were reduced to manslaughter on the ground of diminished responsibility, but hundreds of hospital and guardianship orders are made every year.

4 Mistake[19]

It is settled by the "landmark decision"[20] in *Director of Public Prosecutions v Morgan*[1] that mistake is a defence where it prevents D from having the *mens*

15. Walker, op. cit. 158–160; Butler, Appendix 9.
16. For proposals for reform, see CLRC, Fourteenth Report (Cmnd. 7844), 38–44.
17. Mental Health Act 1983, s. 41.
18. Criminal Statistics, England and Wales, 1986.
19. Keedy, "Ignorance and Mistake in the Criminal Law" (1908), 22 Harv LR 75; Williams, CLGP, Ch. 5; Hall, *General Principles*, Ch. XI; Williams, "Homicide and the Supernatural" (1949), 65 LQR 491; Howard, "The Reasonableness of Mistake in the Criminal Law" (1961), 4 Univ QLJ 45.
20. *Beckford v R* [1987] 3 All ER 425, PC.
  1. [1976] AC 182, [1975] 2 All ER 347; **SHC 46**, above, p. 87.

rea which the law requires for the crime with which he is charged. Where the law requires intention or recklessness with respect to some element in the *actus reus*, a mistake, whether reasonable or not, which precludes both states of mind will excuse.[2] Where the law requires only negligence, then only a *reasonable* mistake can afford a defence; for an unreasonable mistake, by definition, is one which a reasonable man would not make and is, therefore, negligent.[3] Where strict liability is imposed, then even a reasonable mistake will not excuse.[4]

A mistake which does not preclude *mens rea* (or negligence where that is in issue) is irrelevant and no defence. Suppose D believes he is smuggling a crate of Irish whiskey. In fact the crate contains Scotch whisky. Duty is, of course, chargeable on both. D believes he is importing a dutiable item and he is importing a dutiable item. The *actus reus* is the same whether the crate contains Irish or Scotch. He *knows*, because his belief and the facts coincide in this respect, that he is evading the duty chargeable on the goods in the crate. If D had believed the crate to contain only some non-dutiable item, e.g., foreign currency (even if he had mistakenly believed it was dutiable) he would have lacked the *mens rea* for the offence.[5] Mistake of law is generally no defence,[6] for usually knowledge that the act is forbidden by law is no part of *mens rea*; but where the *mens rea* involves some legal concept,[7] or the absence of a claim of right,[8] then it may do so.

The rules are simply an application of the general principle that the prosecution must prove its case, including the *mens rea* or negligence which the definition of the crime requires. The so-called "defence" is simply a denial that the prosection has proved its case. Where the natural inference from D's conduct in the particular circumstances is that he intended or foresaw a particular result, the jury are very likely to convict him if he introduces no testimony that he did not in fact foresee; but the onus of proof remains throughout on the Crown and, technically, D does not bear even an evidential burden,[9] as he does when he raises a defence of automatism.

Mistake has traditionally been treated as a special defence because, before *Morgan*,[10] these principles were rarely recognised. There were many *dicta* that *only* reasonable mistakes would excuse. Lord Lane CJ[11] and the

---

2. See above, p. 87. This remains true after *Caldwell* [1981] 1 All ER 961, above, p. 62. For example, D has sexual intercourse with P, having formed the mistaken belief that P is consenting. Recklessness is negatived and he is not guilty of rape.

3. Above, p. 92. Where *gross* negligence is required, an unreasonable but not grossly unreasonable mistake is a defence.

4. Above, p. 99.

5. See commentary on *Taaffe* [1983] Crim LR 536 at 537, CA, affirmed, [1984] AC 539.

6. Above, p. 80.

7. Above, p. 83.

8. Above, p. 85.

9. Williams, "The Evidential Burden" (1977) 127 NLJ 156 at 158. But there is an evidential burden on D to get a particular mistake before the jury. "Mistake is a defence . . . in the sense that it is raised as an issue by the accused. The Crown is rarely possessed of knowledge of the subjective factors which may have caused an accused to entertain a belief in a fallacious set of facts": *Pappajohn v R* (1980) 52 CCC (2d) 481 at 494, per Dickson J. The judge does not have to direct the jury in every case of murder: "You must be satisfied that D did not believe P was a turkey"; but he must give such a direction if D has testified that, when he fired, he thought P was a turkey.

10. [1976] AC 182 at 192, [1975] 2 All ER 347; **SHC 46**; above, p. 86.

11. *Taaffe* [1983] 2 All ER 625 at 628.

House of Lords[12] have recently, in the light of *Morgan*, doubted the propriety of the requirement of reasonableness in earlier pronouncements by distinguished authorities. Statements that unreasonable mistakes can never excuse may be regarded as discredited but it does not follow that the cases in which they were uttered and applied are wrongly decided. Where the court held that a mistake was not a defence because it was unreasonable, there are two possibilities. The case may be wrongly decided, just as *Morgan* was wrongly decided at first instance and in the Court of Appeal.[13] Alternatively, the case may be taken to have decided that the crime in question was one which did not require *mens rea* as to the element in question. If the court rightly held that only a reasonable mistake would excuse, it held in effect that the law requires only negligence with respect to that element. Thus, in *Morgan*, the House showed no inclination to interfere with the bigamy cases[14] which assert that D's mistaken belief in the death of his first spouse, or the dissolution or nullity of the first marriage, is a defence only if it is reasonable. If that is so, these cases must be taken to fall into the second category and establish that neither intention nor recklessness but only negligence with respect to the existence of the first marriage need be proved. Thus Lord Fraser said, "bigamy does not involve any intention except the intention to go through a marriage ceremony." Lord Cross said; ". . . if the definition of the offence is on the face of it 'absolute' and the defendant is seeking to escape his prima facie liability by a defence of mistaken belief, I can see no hardship to him in requiring the mistake – if it is to afford him a defence – to be based on reasonable grounds." This view of bigamy is that the statute, on its true interpretation, required proof of nothing more than negligence.

In the leading case of *Tolson*[15] D believed on reasonable grounds that her husband had been drowned at sea and, more than five years later, married again reasonably believing herself to be a widow. By a majority of nine to five the court held that she was not guilty, but only because her belief was reasonable. The minority of five, it will be noted, held that the offence was one of strict liability, subject only to the statutory defence of seven years absence. The case can fairly be regarded as one of statutory construction, laying down no general principle. The *dicta* – much cited in subsequent cases – that the common law allowed a defence only if it was honest and reasonable[16] must, since *Morgan*, be regarded as unsound.

One unfortunate aspect of the discussion of the bigamy cases in *Morgan* is that it suggests a very strict approach to the problem of the implication of *mens rea* into statutory offences. The House was concerned with the common law offence of rape; but Lord Cross said that if the Sexual Offences Act had enacted in terms that a man who has sexual intercourse

12. *Westminster City Council v Croyalgrange Ltd* [1986] 2 All ER 353 at 399.
13. [1976] AC 182, [1975] 1 All ER 8; **SHC 46**.
14. *Tolson* (below), *King* [1964] 1 QB 285, *Gould* [1968] 2 QB 65. As the opinions in *Morgan* relating to defences have been reconsidered (above p. 88) so too may the opinions regarding bigamy, if the matter ever arises. The House also accepted the requirement of reasonable grounds for believing the use of force to be necessary in self-defence, but see *Beckford* and *Williams*, above, p. 88.
15. (1889) 23 QBD 168, CCR; **SHC 111**.
16. See, e.g., per Cave J at 181.

with a woman without her consent (the *actus reus* of rape) is guilty of an offence, he might well have held that only a reasonable mistake would be a defence. Presumably the only intention which Lord Cross would have required in this hypothetical case would have been an intention to have intercourse with a woman. These *dicta* therefore suggest that, where a statute uses no words expressly importing *mens rea*, the mental element which the court will require the prosecution to prove will be minimal – to go through a ceremony of marriage, to have sexual intercourse, etc., and that it will then be for the accused to introduce evidence sufficient to raise a doubt whether he did not, on reasonable grounds, have a belief inconsistent with some material element in the *actus reus*. This approach may be admirable where we are concerned with "quasi-criminal", "regulatory" or "welfare" offences; but it is submitted it should have no place in serious crimes.

A better approach, it is submitted, is that of the Court of Appeal in *Smith*.[17] Rejecting an argument that the only mental element required by the Criminal Damage Act 1971 was an intention to damage or destroy property, the Court held: "Applying the ordinary principles of *mens rea*, the intention and recklessness and the absence of lawful excuse required to constitute the offence have reference to property belonging to another." Similarly, in *Westminster City Council v Croyalgrange Ltd*[18] Robert Goff LJ referred to "the ordinary principle that, where it is required that an offence should have been knowingly committed, the requisite knowledge must embrace all the elements of the offence". It is submitted that the ordinary principles of *mens rea* require intention or recklessness as to all the elements of the *actus reus* unless that is excluded expressly or by implication; and the more serious the crime, the more reluctant should the court be to find an implied exclusion.

5 Intoxication

The law in this area has developed principally in cases where D was intoxicated by alcohol. In *Lipman*[19] it was held that the same principles apply to intoxication by other drugs but two recent cases, *Bailey*[20] and *Hardie*,[1] suggest that drugs must be divided into two categories. Where it is common knowledge that a drug is liable to cause the taker to become aggressive or do dangerous or unpredictable things, that drug is to be classed with alcohol. Where there is no such common knowledge, as in the case of a merely soporific or sedative drug, different rules apply. There are

17. [1974] QB 354, [1974] 1 All ER 632; **SHC 542**; below, p. 690.
18. [1985] 1 All ER 740 at 744, DC, affirmed [1986] 2 All ER 353, HL.
19. [1970] 1 QB 152, [1969] 3 All ER 410; **SHC 100**; below, p. 368.
20. [1983] 2 All ER 503, [1983] 1 WLR 760.
 1. [1984] 3 All ER 848, [1985] 1 WLR 64; **SHC 102**.

obvious difficulties about classifying drugs in this way and, if the distinction survives at all, it would not be surprising if it leads to further case-law.

1 Intoxication by Alcohol and "Dangerous" Drugs

Intoxication is not, and never has been, a defence as such. It is no defence for D to say, however convincingly, that, but for the drink, he would not have behaved as he did. One of the effects of alcohol is to weaken the restraints and inhibitions which normally govern our conduct so a man may do things when drunk that he would never dream of doing while sober. But, if he had the *mens rea* required for the crime, he is guilty even though drink impaired or negatived his ability to judge between right and wrong[2] or to resist provocation, and even though, in his drunken state, he found the impulse to act as he did irresistible.

Intoxication also impairs a person's perception and judgment so he may fail to be aware of facts, or to foresee results of his conduct, of which he would certainly have been aware, or have foreseen, if he had been sober. So, intoxication may be the reason why the defendant lacked the *mens rea* of the crime charged. When D relies on evidence of intoxication he does so for the purpose of showing he lacked *mens rea*. This is its only relevance so far as liability to conviction is concerned.

In many of the cases where drunkenness is relevant, the defence, in substance, is one of mistake and the evidence of drunkenness is circumstantial evidence that the mistake was made. Two examples quoted by Lord Denning[3] are: (i) where a nurse got so drunk at a christening that she put the baby on the fire in mistake for a log of wood;[4] and (ii) where a drunken man thought his friend, lying in bed, was a theatrical dummy and stabbed him to death.[5] Lord Denning said there would be a defence to murder in each of these cases. These mistakes were highly unreasonable and, in the case of a sober man, it would be extremely difficult to persuade a jury that they were made. The relevance of the evidence of drunkenness is simply that it makes these mistakes much more credible. Similarly where D denies that he foresaw some obvious consequence of his action. A denial which would be quite incredible in the case of a sober man may be readily accepted when there is evidence that D was drunk.

In the leading case of *Beard* it was said that intoxication was a defence only if it rendered D incapable of forming the *mens rea*.[6] Proof of incapacity is of course conclusive that *mens rea* was not present; but it is now established that it is not necessary to go so far. It is a defence to a sober man that, though he was perfectly capable of forming the intent required, he did not do so on the occasion in question. Equally, a drunken man may be capable, notwithstanding his drunkenness, of forming the intent to kill and yet not do so. The nurse at the christening was capable of forming the intent to tend the fire, so she was probably capable of forming an intent to

2. *DPP v Beard* [1920] AC 479 at 502–504.
3. In *A-G for Northern Ireland v Gallagher* [1963] AC 349 at 381, [1961] 3 All ER 299 at 313; **SHC 98**.
4. (1978) 18 *Gentleman's Magazine*, 570; quoted in Kenny, *Outlines*, 29.
5. (1951) Times, 13 January.
6. [1920] AC 479 at 501–502, HL.

kill. The important thing is that she did not do so – and the drunkenness was highly relevant to rebut the inference which might otherwise have arisen from her conduct. The question is, taking D's intoxicated state into account, did he in fact form the necessary intent?[7] The onus of proof – again contrary to certain *dicta* in *Beard*[8] – is clearly on the Crown to establish that, notwithstanding the alleged intoxication, D formed the intent.[9]

a) *Intoxication and "specific intention"* Evidence of intoxication negativing *mens rea* is a defence—

(i) to crimes requiring a "specific intent"[10] whether the drink or drug was taken voluntarily or involuntarily;

(ii) to all crimes where the drink or drug was taken involuntarily. So if D's lemonade is laced with vodka and he is unaware that he has consumed any alcohol, he can rely on evidence of his drunken condition.[11] Similarly, perhaps, where he has taken drink under duress; and

(iii) to all crimes where the drink or drug is taken voluntarily but in *bona fide* pursuance of medical treatment or prescription. So in *Quick*[12] D could rely on evidence that he had taken insulin, though voluntarily, and it was recognised that an anaesthetic would have a similar effect. This is likely to be rarely applicable to drink but it might apply where, for example, brandy is administered to D after an accident.

The principles do not apply where D is charged with a crime not requiring a specific intent and the drink or drug was taken voluntarily. In *Director of Public Prosecutions v Majewski*[13] the House of Lords has confirmed the rule, obscurely stated in *Beard*,[14] that evidence of self-induced intoxication negativing *mens rea* is a defence to a charge of a crime requiring a specific intent but not to a charge of any other crime. In the case of a crime not requiring "specific intent" D may be convicted if he was voluntarily intoxicated at the time of committing the offence, though he did not have the *mens rea* required in all other circumstances for that offence and even though he was in a state of automatism at the time of doing the act. It is a rule of substantive law that, where D relies on voluntary intoxication as a defence to a charge of a crime not requiring "specific intent", the prosecution need not prove any intention or foresight, whatever the definition of the crime may say, nor indeed any voluntary act.[15] It follows

---

7. *Pordage* [1975] Crim LR 575, CA, following *dicta* in *Sheehan* [1975] 2 All ER 960, [1975] Crim LR 339 and commentary, CA. To the same effect are *Menniss* [1973] 2 NSWLR 113 and *Kamipeli* [1975] 1 NZLR 610.

8. [1920] AC 479 at 502.

9. *Sheehan*, above.

10. Below, p. 223.

11. But what of the much more common case where D has voluntarily taken some drink and his companions surreptitiously add more?

12. Above, p. 198. In *Majewski*, below, the Lord Chancellor pointed out that the drugs taken were not medically prescribed.

13. [1977] AC 443, [1976] 2 All ER 142, [1976] Crim LR 374 and commentary. Williams, 126 NLJ 658; A. D. Gold, "An Untrimmed Beard" (1976) 19 Crim LQ 34; Dashwood, "Logic and the Lords in *Majewski*" [1977] Crim LR 532 and 591.

14. [1920] AC 479.

15. The House approved *Lipman*, below, p. 368.

that s. 8 of the Criminal Justice Act 1967[16] has no application. There is, it appears, an implied qualification to every statute creating an offence and specifying a *mens rea* other than a specific intent. The *mens rea* must be proved – except, we must infer, where the accused was intoxicated through the voluntary taking of drink or drugs.

It seems that this rule applies whatever the degree of intoxication, provided that it prevented D from foreseeing or knowing what he would have foreseen or known had he been sober. It is true that Lord Elwyn-Jones at one point[17] posed the question before the House much more narrowly – as that of a man who "consciously and deliberately takes alcohol and drugs not on medical prescription, but in order to escape from reality, to go 'on a trip', to become hallucinated . . .". Such a person is readily distinguishable from the ordinary "social drinker" who becomes intoxicated in the course of a convivial evening. The former, intending to reduce himself to a state in which he will have no control over his actions, might well be said to be in some sense reckless as to what he will do while in that state. The same cannot be said of the latter. But the general tenor of the speeches, as well as earlier and subsequent cases, is against any such distinction.[18]

The nature of "specific intent" is thus a matter of great importance but a careful scrutiny of the authorities, particularly *Majewski* itself, fails to reveal any consistent principle. In *Majewski*, "specific" was contrasted with "basic intent";[19] but some crimes requiring no ulterior intent – conspicuously murder – are also treated as crimes of "specific intent". Lord Simon suggested that the distinguishing factor is that "the *mens rea* in a crime of specific intent requires proof of a purposive element:" yet there need be no purposive element in the *mens rea* of murder; and rape, which is said not to be a crime of specific intent, obviously requires a purposive element. Lord Elwyn-Jones LC suggested that the test is that crimes not requiring specific intent are crimes that may be committed recklessly. Lord Edmund-Davies, a party to *Majewski*, was dismayed to think that, as a result of *Caldwell*, this opinion has prevailed[20] and it certainly now seems likely that any offence which may be committed either by *Cunningham* or *Caldwell* recklessness will be held an offence of "basic" and not "specific" intent.

The only safe conclusion seems to be that "crime requiring specific intent" means a crime where evidence of voluntary intoxication negativing *mens rea* is a defence; and the designation of crimes as requiring, or not requiring, specific intent is based on no principle but on policy. In order to know how a crime should be classified for this purpose we can look only to the decisions of the courts. These tell us that the following are crimes requiring specific intent.

16. Above, p. 86.
17. [1977] AC 443 at 471.
18. A. C. E. Lynch, "The Scope of Intoxication" [1982] Crim LR 139 (see also p. 418) makes a quite different distinction between "complete intoxication" (to which *Majewski* would apply) and "partial intoxication" (to which it would not); but there are many degrees of intoxication and the suggested distinction seems unworkable.
19. Above, p. 70.
20. Above, p. 62; [1982] AC 341 at 361, [1981] 1 All ER 961 at 972.

Murder,[21] wounding or causing grievous bodily harm with intent,[1] theft,[2] robbery,[3] burglary with intent to steal,[4] handling stolen goods,[5] endeavouring to obtain money on a forged cheque,[6] causing criminal damage contrary to s. 1(1) or (2) of the Criminal Damage Act 1971 where only intention to cause damage or, in the case of s. 1(2), only intention to endanger life, is alleged,[7] indecent assault where proof of indecent purpose is required,[8] an attempt to commit any offence requiring specific intent, and possibly some forms of secondary participation in any offence.[9]

The following are crimes not requiring a specific intent: manslaughter (apparently in all its forms);[10] rape,[11] maliciously wounding or inflicting grievous bodily harm;[12] kidnapping and false imprisonment;[13] assault occasioning actual bodily harm;[14] assault on a constable in the execution of his duty;[15] indecent assault where the act is unambiguously indecent;[16] common assault;[17] taking a conveyance without the consent of the owner,[18] criminal damage where intention or recklessness, or only recklessness, is alleged[19] and possibly an attempt to commit an offence where recklessness is a sufficient element in the *mens rea*,[20] as in attempted rape.[1]

b) *Crimes of specific and basic intent.* A classification of all crimes as offences of either specific or basic intent may be over simplified. Consider the offence under s. 18 of the Offences against the Person Act 1861 of

---

21. *Beard*, above; *Gallagher* [1963] AC 349, [1961] 3 All ER 299; *Sheehan* [1975] 2 All ER 960, [1975] 1 WLR 739, CA.
   1. *Bratty v AG for Northern Ireland* [1963] AC 386, [1961] 3 All ER 523, per Lord Denning; *Pordage* [1975] Crim LR 575, *Davies* [1991] Crim LR 469.
   2. *Ruse v Read* [1949] 1 KB 377, [1949] 1 All ER 398 and *Majewski* per Lord Simon at 152.
   3. As a corollary of theft.
   4. *Durante* [1972] 3 All ER 962, [1972] 1 WLR 1612.
   5. *Durante*, above.
   6. *Majewski*, per Lord Salmon at 158.
   7. *Caldwell* [1981] 1 All ER 961 at 964.
   8. *Culyer* (1992) Times, 17 April, CA, below, p. 470.
   9. *Clarkson* [1971] 3 All ER 344 at 347. But in *Lynch v Director of Public Prosecutions* [1975] 1 All ER 913 at 942, Lord Simon said, approving the decision of the Northern Irish Court of Criminal Appeal, that they held that the *mens rea* of aiding and abetting did not involve a "specific intent". But (i) he may have used the term in a different sense; and (ii) there may be a difference depending on the nature of the alleged secondary liability – an intent to procure is different from an intent to aid; above, p. 128.
   10. *Beard*, *Gallagher* and *Bratty v A-G for Northern Ireland* [1961] 3 All ER at 533, per Lord Denning; *Lipman* [1970] 1 QB 152, [1969] 3 All ER 410.
   11. *Majewski*, above, per Lords Simon and Russell and *Leary v R* (1977) 74 DLR (3d) 103, SCC, discussed, 55 Can Bar Rev 691. But if this is right, *Cogan and Leak* above, p. 153 is wrongly decided; and *Morgan* above, pp. 86, 216 might have been decided shortly on this ground.
   12. *Bratty* at 533, per Lord Denning; *Majewski*, above, per Lords Simon and Salmon.
   13. *Hutchins* [1988] Crim LR 379.
   14. *Bolton v Crawley* [1972] Crim LR 222; *Majewski*, above.
   15. *Majewski*, above.
   16. *Culyer*, fn. 8, above. *Burns* (1973) 58 Cr App Rep 364.
   17. A fortiori.
   18. *MacPherson* [1973] RTR 157, *Gannon* (1987) 87 Cr App Rep 254. *Diggin* (1980) 72 Cr App Rep 204 is not, as at first appeared: [1980] Crim LR 656, an authority on intoxicated taking: [1981] Crim LR 563; but see White, "Taking the Joy out of Joyriding" [1980] Crim LR 609.
   19. Below, p. 692.
   20. Commentary on *Pullen* [1991] Crim LR 457 at 458.
   1. Below, p. 305.

unlawfully and maliciously wounding with intent to resist lawful apprehension. There is abundant authority to the effect that the words "unlawfully and maliciously" when used in s. 20 import only a basic intent, i.e., Cunningham recklessness. Presumably they have the same effect in s. 18. So as far as wounding goes, s. 18 is an offence of basic intent. But the intent to resist lawful apprehension seems a clear case of specific intent. So it seems that a drunken man who intends to resist lawful arrest but, because of his drunkenness, does not foresee the risk of wounding, might be convicted, notwithstanding his lack of Cunningham recklessness. If, on the other hand, because of drunkenness, he does not realise that he is resisting lawful arrest, he must be acquitted.[2] Possibly rape is another example. Recklessness whether the woman is consenting is a basic intent; but presumably there must be an actual intention to have intercourse. But it is difficult to envisage a man, however drunk, having sexual intercourse without intending to do so.

It is fatal for a person charged with a crime not requiring specific intent who claims that he did not have *mens rea* to support his defence with evidence that he had taken drink and drugs. By so doing he dispenses the Crown from the duty, which until that moment lay upon them, of proving beyond reasonable doubt that he had *mens rea*. *Mens rea* ceases to be relevant. Can the Crown escape from this duty by leading evidence, or extracting an admission in cross-examination, that D had taken drink so as to diminish his capacity to foresee the consequences of his acts? According to Lord Salmon[3] in *Majewski* the question the House was deciding was whether the accused could rely *by way of defence* on the fact that he had voluntarily taken drink. But there are other dicta which suggest that D is held liable without the usual *mens rea* because he has taken drink – the taking of the drink is the foundation of his liability[4] – a variety of *mens rea* – though not in the sense in which that term is used in this book. If that be right, there is no reason why the Crown should not set out to prove it instead of seeking to prove *mens rea* in the sense of intention or recklessness.

c) *Finding recklessness, disregarding evidence of intoxication: is it possible?*
Contrary to the view stated above, there is some authority that a jury must be directed to decide whether D was reckless, disregarding the evidence that he was intoxicated. In *Woods*[5] D, charged with rape, claimed that he was so drunk that he did not realise P was not consenting. He relied on s. 1(2) of the Sexual Offences (Amendment) Act 1976[6] which requires the

---

2. *Davies* [1991] Crim LR 469.
3. P. 156.
4. "His course of conduct in reducing himself by drugs and drink to that condition in my view supplies the evidence of *mens rea*, of guilty mind, certainly sufficient for crimes of basic intent:" per Lord Elwyn-Jones LC at 150. "There is no juristic reason why mental incapacity (short of M'Naghten insanity) brought about by self-induced intoxication to realise what one is doing or its probable consequences should not be such a state of mind stigmatised as wrongful by the criminal law; and there is every practical reason why it should be": per Lord Simon at 153.
5. (1981) 74 Cr App Rep 312.
6. Below, p. 451.

jury to have regard to the presence or absence of reasonable grounds for a belief that the woman was consenting, "in conjunction with any other relevant matters". He said his intoxication was a relevant matter. The court said that self-induced intoxication is not "a legally relevant matter" but "the subsection directs the jury to look carefully at all the other relevant evidence before making up their minds on this issue." The evidence of intoxication is undoubtedly logically relevant and may be the most cogent evidence. To ignore it, in coming to a conclusion, is to answer a hypothetical question. It is no longer, "did he believe she was consenting?" and must become, "would he have known she was consenting if he had not been drunk?" This is most obviously so in the case where D's intoxication has rendered him unconscious. Take *Lipman*.[7] How can a judge seriously tell a jury to decide whether D *did* intend to do an unlawful and dangerous act to P – ignoring the undisputed evidence that he was unconscious at the time? Without this "legally irrelevant" evidence, the *only* question the jury can sensibly answer is, "would he have known that such an act was dangerous if he had not been intoxicated?" On facts like those in *Lipman*, there is only one possible answer. It is most regrettable that juries should be faced with questions which are, with all respect, nonsensical, even if their common sense will lead them to consider the only matter really in issue.

d) *Intoxication and Caldwell recklessness.* Where the offence is one of *Caldwell* recklessness, the impact of *Majewski* is reduced. Where, because he was intoxicated, D gave no thought to the existence of the risk, he was reckless and is liable to conviction without the invocation of the rule in *Majewski*. This was the position in *Caldwell* itself. But *Majewski* may still have a significant sphere of operation.[8] D might say that he did consider whether there was a risk and decided there was none. He was then not *Caldwell*-reckless. But, if he would have appreciated the existence of the risk had he been sober, he will still be liable because of *Majewski*. D, about to have intercourse with P, asks himself, "Is she consenting?" and answers the question in the affirmative because, being drunk, he fails to observe what he would have observed when sober. He is not *Caldwell*-reckless but, if rape is a crime not requiring specific intent, he is guilty.

ii) *Majewski and defences.* The *Majewski* rule has been held inapplicable where statute expressly provides that a particular belief shall be a defence to the charge. If D held that belief, he is not guilty, even though it arose from a drunken mistake that he would not have made when sober. In *Jaggard v Dickinson*[9] D had a friend, H, who had invited her to treat his house as if it were her own. When drunk, D went to a house which she thought was H's but which in fact belonged to R, who barred her way. D gained entry by breaking windows and damaging the curtains. Charged

---

7. Below, p. 368.
8. This is overlooked by Lord Diplock at [1981] 1 All ER 968a.
9. [1981] QB 527, [1980] 3 All ER 716. Cf. the unsatisfactory case of *Gannon* (1987) 87 Cr App Rep 254, criticised by Glanville Williams (1990) 140 NLJ 1564, Archbold, 21–123.

with criminal damage, contrary to s. 1(1) of the Criminal Damage Act 1971, she relied on s. 5(2) of that Act[10] which provides that a person has a lawful excuse if he believed that the person entitled to consent to the damage would have done so had he known of the circumstances. D said that she believed that H would, in the circumstances, have consented to her damaging his property. Since s. 1(1) creates an offence not requiring specific intent, D could not have relied on her drunkenness to negative her recklessness whether she damaged the property of another, but, it was held, she could rely on it to explain what would otherwise have been inexplicable and give colour to her evidence about the state of her belief. The court thought this was not the same thing as using drunkenness to rebut an inference of intention or recklessness. It seems, however, to be exactly the same thing.[11] Moreover, thought the court, s. 5(2) provides that it is immaterial whether a belief is justified or not if it is honestly held, and it was not open to the court to add the words "and the honesty of the belief is not attributable only to self-induced intoxication". Yet the courts have not hesitated to add similar words to qualify Parliament's express requirement of "malice", i.e. Cunningham recklessness. The result is anomalous. Where the defendant did not intend any damage to property he may be held liable because he was drunk; but where he did intend damage to property but thought the owner would consent he is not liable, however drunk he may have been. Suppose that D, because he is drunk, believes that certain property belonging to P is his own and damages it. His belief is not a matter of defence under s. 5(2)[12] but negatives recklessness whether property *belonging to another* be damaged.[13] Even though D gave his drunken mind to the matter, and so was not *Caldwell*-reckless, he is liable. If D, being drunk, destroys X's property believing that it is the property of Y who would consent to his doing so, this is a defence; but if he destroys X's property believing that it is his own, it is not.

In relation to common law defences, the law has gone quite the other way. Although it is now settled that when D sets up self-defence, he is to be judged on the facts as he believed them to be, whether reasonably or not,[14] a mistake arising from voluntary intoxication cannot be relied on, according to *O'Grady*,[15] even on charge of murder or other crime requiring specific intent. This was plainly obiter because the appellant had been acquitted of murder and was appealing only against his conviction for manslaughter; but in *O'Connor*[16] the Court, inexplicably, treated it as binding, while quashing the conviction of murder on another ground. The dictum seems, moreover, to have proceeded on the assumption that, on a charge of homicide, self-defence must be either a complete defence or no defence at all, which is not the case;[17] and the court's attention does not appear to have

---

10. Below, p. 694.
11. See above, pp. 219–220.
12. *Smith* (DR) [1974] QB 354, [1974] 1 All ER 632.
13. Ibid.
14. *Gladstone Williams* [1987] 3 All ER 411, 78 Cr App Rep 276, above, p. 89.
15. [1987] 3 All ER 420, [1987] 3 WLR 321 criticised by the Law Commission, Law Com. No. 177, para 8.42, by H. Milgate [1987] CLJ 381 and JCS, [1987] Crim LR 706.
16. [1991] Crim LR 135.
17. Below, p. 252.

been drawn to the recommendations of the Criminal Law Revision Committee, complementing those which the court followed in *Gladstone Williams*.[18] The better view, it is submitted, is that a mistake arising from voluntary intoxication by alcohol or dangerous drugs may found a defence to crime requiring specific intent but not to one of basic intent.

2 Intoxication otherwise than by Alcohol or Dangerous Drugs

In *Bailey*[19] a diabetic failed to take sufficient food after insulin. He caused grievous bodily harm and his defence to charges under ss. 18 and 20 of the Offences against the Person Act was that, because of this failure, he was in a state of automatism. The recorder's direction to the jury that this was no defence was obviously wrong so far as s. 18 was concerned for that is an offence of specific intent. The Court of Appeal held[20] that it was also wrong for s. 20 because "self-induced automatism, other than that due to intoxication from alcohol or drugs, may provide a defence to crimes of basic intent". The court went on:

"The question in each case will be whether the prosecution has proved the necessary element of recklessness. In cases of assault, if the accused knows that his actions or inaction are likely to make him aggressive, unpredictable or uncontrolled with the result that he may cause some injury to others and he persists in the action or takes no remedial action when he knows it is required, it will be open to the jury to find that he was reckless."

The automatism seems to have been treated as arising from the failure to take food, rather than from the taking of the insulin, but the court hinted at a distinction between two types of drug:

"It is common knowledge that those who take alcohol to excess or certain sorts of drugs may become aggressive or do dangerous or unpredictable things. . . . But the same cannot be said, without more, of a man who fails to take food after an insulin injection."

In *Hardie*[1] D's defence to a charge of damaging property with intent to endanger the life of another or being reckless whether another's life be endangered, was that he had taken valium, a sedative drug, to calm his nerves and that this had resulted in intoxication precluding the *mens rea* for the offence. The judge, following *Majewski* and *Caldwell*, directed that this could be no defence. The Court of Appeal quashed the conviction. *Majewski* was not applicable because valium

"is wholly different in kind from drugs which are liable to cause unpredictability or aggressiveness. . . . if the effect of a drug is merely soporific or sedative the taking of it, even in some excessive quantity, cannot in the ordinary way raise a conclusive presumption against the admission of proof of intoxication for the purpose of disproving mens rea in ordinary crimes, such as would be the case with alcoholic intoxication

---

18. See above, fn. 14.
19. [1983] 2 All ER 503, [1983] 1 WLR 760, CA.
20. P. 507.
 1. [1984] 3 All ER 848, [1985] 1 WLR 64.

or incapacity or automatism resulting from the self-administration of dangerous drugs."[2]

These cases then appear to apply where intoxication is self-induced otherwise than by alcohol or dangerous drugs. In these cases the test of liability is stated to be one of recklessness: "If he does appreciate the risk that [failure to take food] may lead to aggressive, unpredictable and uncontrollable conduct and he nevertheless deliberately runs the risk or otherwise disregards it, this will amount to recklessness."[3]

It is clear that the recklessness which must be proved is:

(i) subjective, an actual awareness of the risk of becoming aggressive, etc., not recklessness of the *Caldwell* type; but

(ii) "general" – not requiring foresight of the *actus reus* of any particular crime, such as is required in the case of a sober person charged with an offence of *Cunningham* recklessness. D will be liable for any crime

of recklessness the *actus reus* of which he happens to commit under the influence of the self-induced intoxication. And—

(iii) being aware that one may lose consciousness may be sufficient where a failure to exercise control may result in the *actus reus* of a crime, as in the case of careless or reckless driving.

3 Intoxication causing Insanity or Abnormality of Mind

If excessive drinking causes actual insanity, such as delirium tremens, then the M'Naghten Rules will be applied in exactly the same way as where insanity arises from any other causes:

"... drunkenness is one thing and the diseases to which drunkenness leads are different things; and if a man by drunkenness brings on a state of disease which causes such a degree of madness, even for a time, which would have relieved him from responsibility if it had been caused in any other way, then he would not be criminally responsible."[4]

It has already been seen[5] that there are serious difficulties in defining a "disease of the mind" and the distinction between temporary insanity induced by drink and simple drunkenness is far from clear-cut. The distinction becomes important in the case of a man who does not know that his act is wrong because of excessive drinking. If he is suffering from temporary insanity he is entitled to a verdict of not guilty on the ground of insanity; but if he is merely drunk he should be convicted.[6]

Self-induced intoxication must be ignored in deciding whether D was suffering from such an abnormality of mind as to amount to diminished responsibility unless it is proved that the craving for drink or drugs is in

---

2. P. 853. This overlooks the fact that the *Majewski* principle is stated to be a rule of substantive law and that the Criminal Justice Act 1967, s. 8, precludes conclusive presumptions of intention or foresight. Above, p. 86.

3. *Bailey* [1983] 2 All ER 503 at 507.

4. *Davis* (1881) 14 Cox CC 563 at 564, per Stephen J approved by the House of Lords in *Director of Public Prosecutions v Beard* [1920] AC 479 at 501.

5. Above, pp. 197–200.

6. In a case of simple drunkenness the judge should not introduce the question whether the prisoner knew he was doing wrong – for "it is a dangerous and confusing question" – per Lord Birkenhead in *Director of Public Prosecutions v Beard* [1920] AC 479 at 506.

itself an abnormality of mind.[7] It has been argued[8] that drink can produce a toxic effect on the brain which would be an "injury" within s. 2 of the Homicide Act 1957;[9] but the court thought it very doubtful whether the *transient* effect of drink could amount to an injury. Presumably a permanent injury to the brain produced by drink would be held to be an injury within the section. Difficult questions may arise where a substantial impairment arises as a result of a combination of inherent abnormality and drink.[10]

4 Involuntary Intoxication

Involuntary intoxication is narrowly defined. A person who knew he was drinking alcohol could not claim that the resulting intoxication was involuntary merely because he underestimated the amount of the alcohol he was consuming[11] or the effect it would have on him. Involuntary intoxication is probably confined to the cases where D did not know he was taking alcohol or an intoxicating drug at all, as where his food or drink is laced without his knowledge; and the special case where he becomes intoxicated through taking drugs (including, presumably, alcohol) in accordance with a medical prescription.[12] There is little authority on the subject but it is clear that the rule in *Majewski* does not apply and it follows that involuntary intoxication negativing the *mens rea* of the offence charged, whether specific intent or basic intent, is a defence. Where it does not negative *mens rea*, it will not be a defence even though it may well be that D would not have committed the offence had he not been intoxicated; but it will then, of course, be a substantial mitigating factor.[13]

As intoxication is nearly always voluntary, it is probably for D to raise the issue if he wishes to contend that it is involuntary. The onus of proof will then generally be on the Crown:[14] but the Public Order Act 1986, s. 6(5), for the purposes of offences under that Act, requires D to "show" that his intoxication was not self-induced or caused by medical treatment. This was presumably intended to put the onus of proof on D; but "show", in contrast with "prove" which is used in other sections of the Act, might be taken to impose no more than an evidential burden.

5 Intoxication induced with the Intention of Committing Crime

Has D a defence if, intending to commit a crime, he takes drink or drugs in order to give himself Dutch courage and then commits the crime, having, at the time of the act, induced insanity within the M'Naghten Rules or such a state of drunkenness as to negative a "specific intent"? The problem was raised by *A-G for Northern Ireland v Gallagher*.[15] D, having decided to kill

7. *Fenton* [1975] Crim LR 712; *Carraher v HM Advocate* 1946 JC 108; *HM Advocate v MacLeod* 1956 JC 20.
8. In *Di Duca* (1959) 43 Cr App Rep 167. See also *Dowdall* (1960) *Times*, 22 January.
9. Above, p. 212.
10. See p. 200, above and *Clarke and King* [1962] Crim LR 836.
11. *Allen* [1988] Crim LR 698.
12. Cf. *Quick* [1973] QB 910 and commentary, [1973] Crim LR 436–437.
13. Cf. *Davies* [1983] Crim LR 741 (Swansea Crown Court).
14. *Stripp* (1978) 69 Cr App Rep 318 at 323; *Bailey* [1983] 2 All ER 503 at 507.
15. [1963] AC 349, [1961] 3 All ER 299, **SHC 98**.

his wife, bought a knife and a bottle of whisky. He drank much of the whisky and then killed his wife with the knife. The defence was that he was either insane or so drunk as to be incapable of forming the necessary intent at the time he did the act. The Court of Criminal Appeal in Northern Ireland reversed his conviction for murder on the ground that the judge had misdirected the jury in telling them to apply the M'Naghten Rules to D's state of mind at the time before he took the alcohol and not at the time of committing the act. The majority of the House of Lords apparently did not dissent from the view of the Court of Criminal Appeal that such a direction would be

"at variance with the specific terms of the M'Naghten Rules which definitely fix the crucial time as the time of committing the act."[16]

They differed, however, in their interpretation of the summing up and held that it did direct the jury's attention to the time of committing the act. In that case, of course, it was not necessary to decide the problem because the jury, by their verdict, had found that D had *mens rea* and was not insane.

Lord Denning, however, seems to have taken the view that the Court of Criminal Appeal's interpretation of the summing up was correct and that the direction, so interpreted, was right in law. He said:[17]

"My Lords, I think the law on this point should take a clear stand. If a man, whilst sane and sober, forms an intention to kill and makes preparation for it knowing it is a wrong thing to do, and then gets himself drunk so as to give himself Dutch courage to do the killing, and whilst drunk carries out his intention, he cannot rely on this self-induced drunkenness as a defence to a charge of murder, nor even as reducing it to manslaughter. He cannot say he got himself into such a stupid state that he was incapable of an intent to kill. So also, when he is a psychopath, he cannot by drinking rely on his self-induced defect of reason as a defence of insanity. The wickedness of his mind before he got drunk is enough to condemn him, coupled with the act which he intended to do and did do."

The difficulty about this is that an intention to do an act some time in the future is not *mens rea*.[18] The *mens rea* must generally coincide with the conduct which causes the *actus reus*. If D, having resolved to murder his wife at midnight, drops off to sleep and, while still asleep, strangles her at midnight, it is thought that he is not guilty of murder (though he may be liable for manslaughter on the ground of his negligence). The case of deliberately induced drunkenness, however, is probably different. The true analogy, it is thought, is the case where a man uses an innocent agent as an instrument with which to commit crime. It has been seen[19] that if D induces an irresponsible person to kill, D is guilty of murder. Is not the position substantially the same where D induces in himself a state of irresponsibility with the intention that he shall kill while in that state? Should not the responsible D be liable for the foreseen and intended acts of the irresponsible D? So regarded, a conviction would not be incompatible

16. See [1963] AC 349 at 376, [1961] 3 All ER 299 at 310.
17. [1963] AC 349 at 382, [1961] 3 All ER 299 at 314.
18. Above, p. 76.
19. Above, p. 124.

with the wording of the M'Naghten Rules. The result, certainly, seems to be one required by policy and it is thought the courts will achieve it if the problem should be squarely raised before them.

6 Alternatives to *Majewski*

Majewski had been followed by the Supreme Court of Canada in *Leary*[20] but only by a majority of four to three, a powerful minority holding that D could rely on evidence of intoxication in any case and that there was no distinction between the so-called specific intents and other mental elements prescribed in the definition of crime. In the High Court of Australia in *O'Connor*[1] a majority of four to three agreed with the Canadian minority. So did the South African Appellate Division in *S v Chretien*.[2] The Australian majority were confident that they were not opening the flood-gates to hordes of drunken offenders ravaging the public with impunity; juries would not be taken in by spurious defences that D was drunk. The decision only confirmed the law laid down in the state of Victoria as long ago as 1964 and nothing disastrous had happened there. It is fair to say that Australia is probably alone in common law jurisdictions in departing from *Majewski*, but it is strongly supported by the unanimous decision in *Chretien*.

An alternative course is proposed by the Butler Committee.[3] This would require the creation of a new offence to be called dangerous intoxication. It would never be charged in the first instance but would come into operation only when D was acquitted of a "dangerous" offence – dangerous to the person. It is implicit in the proposal that *Majewski* would be repealed so far as these offences are concerned. Where D relied on evidence of intoxication to show that he did not have *mens rea*, the jury should be directed that, if they were not satisfied he had *mens rea*, but were satisfied that he did the act, they should convict him of this new offence.

This solution was considered by the CLRC in their examination of the law of offences against the person.[4] They found it unsatisfactory in that a conviction would merely record that the defendant had committed a dangerous act while intoxicated. It would be the same crime, whether he killed, or committed an act of rape, or a minor assault. Moreover, the problem of the intoxicated offender is not confined to offences against the person and a reform which is sound in principle should be capable of extension to other offences, such as taking away motor vehicles. But, whatever kind of harm was done, the conviction recorded and the maximum sentence would be the same (one year for a first and three years for a subsequent offence). One view is that this is right because D's fault lies in getting drunk and that is what is recorded against him. What he did afterwards was done by an accident or a mistake, albeit a drunken one, and so without fault in the criminal sense. The law has, however, always

20. [1978] 1 SCR 29, (1977) 33 CCC (2d) 473.
 1. (1980) 54 ALJR 349; see also (1980) 54 ALJR 569.
 2. 1981 (1) SA 1097 (A), discussed by J. M. Burchell, (1981) 98 SALJ 177.
 3. Cmnd. 6244, paras 18.51–18.59.
 4. CLRC/OAP/R, pp. 111–118.

attached and will continue to attach importance to the harm done as well as to the harm intended or foreseen.

The majority of the CLRC thought that the best that could be done was to clarify the rule in *Majewski*, to allow evidence of intoxication to negative the *mens rea* of murder and the *intention* required for any offence, leaving D liable for an offence of recklessness where he had not appreciated a risk which he would have appreciated when sober. To the extent that this would clarify the present obscure distinction between offences of specific and basic intent, it would be an improvement. As under the present law, however, the verdict of a jury would not distinguish between an offender who was reckless and one who was intoxicated but not reckless. This is a material difference, because the two cases may call for different sentences. Moreover, where D is convicted of an offence of recklessness when he was not in fact reckless the verdict does not represent the truth. A minority of the CLRC therefore preferred a modification of the Butler proposal, under which the jury would find a special verdict that the defendant did the act alleged in a state of intoxication. The court would have the same sentencing powers as are available on conviction of the offence charged,[5] in order to ensure that the public could be adequately protected from a dangerous offender.

Ashworth tentatively proposes[6] a radical solution. Given the widely held view that intoxication is the source of much violence and damage, "should the law not go further than the summary offences of public drunkenness and make intoxication itself a serious crime, as a kind of inchoate offence?" Since the fault consists in getting drunk and not (where *mens rea* is negatived) in doing the harm, the suggestion is attractive. But there are difficulties. Since the "criminal" act would be no part of the offence and be admissible in evidence, if at all, only for the purpose of establishing that D was intoxicated, it would follow that there would be a theoretical liability where he did nothing but lie in bed and sleep it off. In practice, it would be unlikely that any prosecution would be brought unless some damage was done and, if evidence of that were admitted, inevitably the court would regard it as a most material factor in fixing sentence. There would also be a difficult question of the degree of intoxication which it is necessary to prove. A quite small amount of alcohol affects judgment and so may in fact have prevented D from foreseeing consequences. Everyone is a little more dangerous when he has had only a small amount to drink but it is impossible to prohibit all taking of alcohol or drugs. Experience with road traffic offences revealed the impossibility of drawing a satisfactory distinction between different degrees of intoxication, even in relation to the special activity of driving. That has been solved by fixing a precise blood/alcohol level for drivers;[7] but it is impossible to suppose that this could be extended to a general law against having a certain percentage of alcohol in the blood. Furthermore we are concerned with all drugs, not merely alcohol.

5. A better proposal might be one which provided for a reduced maximum to mark the general difference in culpability between the reckless and the merely intoxicated offender.
6. [1980] Crim LR 556.
7. Road Traffic Act 1988, s. 5.

There is no obviously right solution; but the minority proposal of the CLRC has the great virtue that it requires the jury to declare the facts as they find them, so giving the judge the best opportunity to impose the right sentence; which, after all, is the object of the whole exercise.

6 Duress and Coercion

1 Duress

a) *Duress: threats and circumstances.* For centuries the law has recognised a defence of duress by threats. The typical case is where D is told, "Do this [an act which would be a crime if there were no defence of duress]—or you will be killed", and, fearing for his life, he does the required act. Quite recently, the law has recognised another form of duress—duress of circumstances. Again, D does the act alleged to constitute the crime out of fear, but this time no one is demanding that he do it. He does it because his life is threatened and his only way of escape is to do the act, which, but for the duress, would be a crime. The compulsion on D to do the act is exactly the same whether the threat comes from someone demanding that he do it, or from an aggressor, or other circumstances. His moral culpability, or lack of it, is exactly the same. It would, it has been rightly said,[8] be "the apotheosis of absurdity" to allow a defence of duress by threats while disallowing it for duress of circumstances where the compulsion on the defendant is exactly the same.

The law relating to duress by threats is now well developed. Duress of circumstances is in its infancy but the law is developing by analogy to duress by threats; and both policy and logic suggest that they should be governed by the same principles. The exposition of duress which follows is based on that assumption and, while it is naturally derived mainly from the threats cases, it also draws on the decisions on duress of circumstances.

Duress by threats is a general defence except that it does not apply to some forms of treason or to murder, or attempted murder, whether as a principal or a secondary party. Though it has not yet been decided, duress of circumstances is probably also a general defence subject to the same exceptions.

b) *Duress and voluntariness.* It has often been said that the duress must be such that D's act is not "voluntary". We are not, however, concerned here with the case where a person is compelled by physical force to go through the motions of an *actus reus* without any choice on his part. In such cases he will almost invariably[9] be guilty of no offence on the fundamental ground that he did no act:

"If there be an actual forcing of a man, as if A by force takes the arm of B and the weapon in his hand and therewith stabs C whereof he dies, this is murder in A but B is not guilty."[10]

Nor are we concerned with the kind of involuntariness which arises from automatism where D is unable to control the movement of his body. When D pleads duress (or necessity) he admits that he was able to control his actions and chose to do the act with which he is charged, but denies responsibility for doing so. He may say, "I had no choice" but that is not strictly true. The alternative to committing the crime may have been so exceedingly unattractive that no reasonable person would have chosen it; but there was a choice. The courts recognise this. Where D is required to kill an innocent person, they insist that he must choose to defy the threat or threatening circumstance—and "threaten" him with conviction for murder and life imprisonment if he does not. In Canada, the Supreme Court (holding that necessity may be an excuse, but not a justification) described the act as "morally involuntary", the "involuntariness" being "measured on the basis of society's expectation of appropriate and normal resistance to pressure".[11] This seems to mean only that even a person of goodwill and reasonable fortitude might have chosen to do the "criminal" act. Since a person, yielding to duress which would have been a defence to any other crime, may be convicted of murder or attempted murder, it is clear that, in law, duress is not inconsistent with a voluntary act or with an intention to do that act and to cause the results which the actor knows will follow. The conviction implies both that the act was voluntary and the result intended.[12] D intends to do the act which, but for the duress, would be a crime.

It is said that D's will must have been "overborne" by the threat.[13] Presumably this means only that he would not have committed the offence but for the threat and that the threat was one which might cause a person of reasonable fortitude to do as he did. If the prosecution can prove that he would have done the same act even if the threat had not been made, it seems that the defence will fail.[14] But the threat need not be the only motive for D's actions. In *Valderrama-Vega*[15] D was under financial pressure and had been threatened with disclosure of his homosexual inclinations – neither matter being capable of amounting to duress – but it was wrong to direct the jury that the threats of death or serious injury also alleged to have been

9. Cf. *Larsonneur*, above, p. 43.
10. Hale, 1 P C 534.
11. *Perka* (1984) 13 DLR (4th) 1; **SHC 232.**
12. *Howe* [1987] 1 All ER 771 at 777, HL, per Lord Hailsham, LC, citing Lords Kilbrandon and Edmund-Davies in *Director of Public Prosecutions for Northern Ireland v Lynch* [1975] AC 653 at 703 and 709–710.
13. Cf. the discussion of *Steane* [1947] KB 997, [1947] 1 All ER 813, above, p. 56.
14. In *DPP v Bell (Derek)* [1992] Crim LR 176, DC, D, in terror of an aggressor, began to drive with excess alcohol. Although he admitted that, before the threat, he intended to drive, it was found as a fact (a finding with which the divisional court could not interfere) that he drove because of terror and so had a defence of duress of circumstances (below, p. 242). But for the threat he might have changed his mind or been persuaded by his passengers not to drive.
15. [1985] Crim LR 220 and commentary.

made must have been the sole reason for his committing the offence. If he would not have committed the offence but for the latter threats, the defence was available even if he acted because of the cumulative effect of all the pressure on him. It is probably going too far to say that it is enough that the threats of death were "the last straw" because the law will look for something more substantial than "a straw" for an excuse; but threats of death or serious bodily harm can never be trivial, so it is probably sufficient to tell the jury that D has the defence if he would not have acted but for the threats. A direction that the defence was available only if D acted *solely* because of the relevant threats was upheld where it was suggested that he might also have been influenced by greed but the court thought it inadvisable to use that word in a summing up.[16]

Duress is a defence because—

". . . threats of immediate death or serious personal violence so great as to overbear the ordinary powers of human resistance should be accepted as a justification for acts which would otherwise be criminal."[17]

Duress by threats has been accepted as a defence to manslaughter,[18] criminal damage,[19] arson,[20] theft,[1] handling,[2] perjury and contempt of court[3] and drug offences;[4] and courts have assumed that it would apply to buggery[5] and conspiracy[6] to defraud. It now seems safe to say that duress may be a defence to any crime, except some forms of treason, murder and, attempted murder. Curiously, duress of circumstances has so far been invoked only in road traffic cases – reckless driving, driving while disqualified, or with excess alcohol – and where the "circumstance" was a threat by another person; but there can be no rational ground for limiting the defence to this type of case. In principle, its scope should be the same as that of duress by threats – i.e., it is a general defence with the same exceptions for treason, murder and attempted murder.

c) *Duress and treason.* Although it is not uncommon for treason to be mentioned as a crime where duress is not a defence, it is quite clear that it may be a defence to at least some forms of treason.[7]

As long ago as 1419 in *Oldcastle*'s case[8] the accused who were charged with treason in supplying victuals to Sir John Oldcastle and his fellow rebels were acquitted on the ground that they acted *pro timore mortis, et quod recesserunt quam cito potuerunt*. The existence of the defence was

16. *Ortiz* (1986) 83 Cr App Rep 173.
17. *A-G v Whelan* [1934] IR 518, per Murnaghan J (Irish CCA); Elliott and Wood (2nd ed.) at 46.
18. *Evans and Gardiner* [1976] VR 517 and (No. 2) 523.
19. *Crutchley* (1831) 5 C & P 133.
20. *Shiartos* (Lawton J, 19 September, 1961, unreported but referred to in *Gill*, below).
   1. *Gill* [1963] 2 All ER 688, [1963] 1 WLR 841, CCA.
   2. *A-G v Whelan* [1934] IR 518.
   3. *K* (1983) 78 Cr App Rep 82, CA.
   4. *Valderrama-Vega* [1985] Crim LR 220, *Ortiz* (1986) 83 Cr App Rep 173.
   5. *Bourne* (1952) 36 Cr App Rep 125.
   6. *Verrier* [1965] Crim LR 732.
7. [1975] 1 All ER at 920, per Lord Morris; 940, per Lord Simon; 944, per Lord Kilbrandon. In *Gotts* [1992] 2 WLR 284 at 300, Lord Lowry excepts "most forms of treason".
   8. (1419) 1 Hale PC 50; 1 East PC 70.

admitted, *obiter*, by Lee CJ in *M'Growther*,[9] a trial for treason committed in the 1745 rebellion and by Lord Mansfield in *Stratton*:[10]

"... if a man is forced to commit acts of high treason, if it appears really force, and such as human nature could not be expected to resist and the jury are of that opinion, the man is not guilty of high treason."

Much more recently, in *Purdy*[11] Oliver J directed a jury that fear of death would be a defence to a British prisoner of war who was charged with treason in having assisted with German propaganda in the second world war. Against this, Lord Goddard CJ said in *Steane*[12] that the defence did not apply to treason, but this remark appears to have been made *per incuriam*.

Treason is an offence which may take many forms varying widely in seriousness and it would be wrong to suppose that threats, even of death, will necessarily be a defence to every act of treason. In *Oldcastle*'s case[13] Hale emphasises that the accuseds' act was *only* furnishing of victuals and he appears to question whether, if they had taken a more active part in the rebellion, they would have been excused. Stephen thought the defence only applied where the offender took a subordinate part.

d) *Duress and murder*. It was stated in the books from Hale onwards that duress could not be a defence to a charge of murder. As Blackstone put it, a man under duress "ought rather to die himself than escape by the murder of an innocent".[14] There was, however, no clear judicial authority in point and in 1969 in *Kray*[15] an inroad was made into the supposed rule when Widgery LJ said that a person charged as an accessory before the fact to murder might rely on duress. In 1975, in *Lynch v Director of Public Prosecution for Northern Ireland*[16] the House of Lords, by a majority of three to two, held that a person charged with aiding and abetting murder – one who would have been a principal in the second degree under the law of felonies – could have a defence of duress. The position of the actual killer was left open and in *Abbott*[17] in 1976, again by three to two, the Privy Council distinguished *Lynch* and held that the defence was not available to the principal offender, the actual killer. This was an illogical and unsatisfactory position because it is by no means always the case that the actual killer is the most dominant or culpable member of a number of accomplices, but he alone was now excluded from the defence. The distinctions involved were technical and absurd.[18] Accordingly, when the matter came before the House in *Howe*[19] there was a strong case for either going forward

9. (1746) Fost 13; 18 State Tr 391.
10. (1779) 1 Doug KB 239.
11. (1946) 10 JCL 182.
12. [1947] KB 997 at 1005, [1947] 1 All ER 813 at 817.
13. (1419), Hale 1 PC 50.
14. Commentaries, iv, 30.
15. [1970] 1 QB 125, [1969] 3 All ER 941.
16. [1975] AC 653.
17. [1977] AC 755, [1976] 3 All ER 140.
18. *Graham* [1982] 1 All ER 801 at 804, per Lane LCJ.
19. [1987] 1 All ER 771, [1987] 2 WLR 568, [1987] Crim LR 480 (sub nom *Burke*) and commentary.

and allowing the defence to all alleged parties to murder, or backward, and allowing it to none. The House chose the latter course, overruling its own decision in *Lynch*. The speeches emphasise different aspects, but the following reasons for the decision appear among them.

(i) The ordinary man of reasonable fortitude, if asked to take an innocent life, might be expected to sacrifice his own.[20] Lord Hailsham would not—

"regard a law as either 'just' or 'humane' which withdraws the protection of the criminal law from the innocent victim and casts the cloak of its protection on the coward and the poltroon in the name[1] of a 'concession to human frailty'."

(ii) One who takes the life of an innocent person cannot claim that he is choosing the lesser of two evils.[2]

(iii) The Law Commission had recommended[3] ten years previously that duress should be a defence to the alleged principal offender, but Parliament had not acted on that recommendation.[4]

(iv) Hard cases could be dealt with by not prosecuting – in some cases the person under duress might be expected to be the principal witness for the prosecution[5] – or by the action of the Parole Board in ordering the early release of a person who would have had a defence if duress had been an available defence.[6]

It is submitted that none of these reasons is convincing.

(i) If the defence were available, it would apply only when a jury thought a person of reasonable fortitude *would* have yielded to the threat. The criminal law should not require heroism. Moreover, there are circumstances in which the good citizen of reasonable fortitude not only would, but probably should, yield to the threat because—

(ii) to do so might clearly be to choose the lesser of two evils, as where the threat is to kill D and all his family if he does not do, or assist in, an act which he knows will cause grievous harm but not death (though, ex hypothesi, it has resulted in death and so constitutes murder).

(iii) Parliament's failure to act on the Law Commission recommendation proves nothing. The government has not given Parliament the opportunity to consider the matter. By parity of reason, Parliament might be taken to have approved of *Lynch*'s case, because there has been no move to overrule it.

(iv) Even if he were not prosecuted, the "duressee" would be, in law, a murderer and, if he were called as a prosecution witness, the judge would be required to tell the jury that he was an accomplice in murder, on whose evidence it would be dangerous to act in the

20. Pp. 779–780.
1. Referring to the fifth edition of this work at p. 215.
2. Lord Hailsham at 780.
3. Report on Defences of General Application (Law Com. No. 83).
4. Lord Bridge at 784 and Lord Griffiths at 788.
5. Lord Griffiths at 790.
6. Lord Griffiths at 791, Lord Hailsham at 780–781.

absence of corroboration. A morally innocent person should not be left at the mercy of administrative discretion on a murder charge.

e) *Attempted murder and other related offences.* In *Howe* only Lord Griffiths[7] expressed a clear view that duress is not a defence to attempted murder but it has since been so held by a majority of three to two in *Gotts*.[8] This is logical. If it were otherwise the effect would be that an act, excusable when done, would become inexcusable if death resulted within a year and a day. But logic would also require the exclusion of the defence on a charge under s. 18 of the Offences against the Person Act 1861 of causing grievous bodily harm with intent because, here also, the offence becomes murder if death results from it. A distinction might be taken between murder committed with intent to kill, where duress would not be a defence, and murder committed with intent to cause serious bodily harm, where it would. This would be reconcilable with the traditional statement of the law – a man "ought rather to die himself than escape by the murder of an innocent" – which seems to postulate a decision to kill; but *Howe* seems too emphatic and uncompromising a decision to allow of any such refinement. *Gotts* indicates that the line is to be drawn below attempted murder, leaving the defence applicable to incitement and conspiracy to murder.

f) *The threat or danger.* Probably the only threat or danger which will found a defence in either type of duress is one of death or serious personal injury.[9] The law is so stated in the draft criminal code (cll. 42 and 43) and in most modern codes. Lord Goddard in *Steane*[10] spoke of violence or imprisonment but in that case duress was held not to be in issue. Widgery LJ in *Hudson*,[11] Lord Lane CJ in *Graham*,[12] and Woolf LJ in *Conway*,[13] all required a threat of death or serious personal injury. Hale required threats of death and so did the judges in *M'Growther*[14] and *Purdy*[15] but those were cases of treason. While the present law appears to be that a threat of serious personal injury is the minimum which is acceptable to found a defence to *any* crime, a higher minimum may be required for crimes of great gravity.

The dictum of Lords Wilberforce and Edmund-Davies no longer applies to killing but is good for other acts:

"... the realistic view is that, the more dreadful the circumstances of the killing, the heavier the evidential burden of an accused advancing such a plea, and the stronger and more irresistible the duress needed before it could be regarded as affording any defence."[16]

---

7. At pp. 780 and 790.
8. [1992] 1 All ER 832, [1992] 2 WLR 284, HL. Lord Lowry, dissenting, thought it is "the stark fact of death" which distinguishes murder from all other offences.
9. Cf. the position under s. 5(2) (b) of the Criminal Damage Act 1971, below, p. 694.
10. [1947] KB 997 at 1005.
11. [1971] 2 QB 202, [1971] 2 All ER 244.
12. [1982] 1 All ER 801, [1982] 1 WLR 294.
13. [1989] QB 290, [1988] 3 All ER 1025.
14. (1746) Fost 13.
15. (1946) 10 JCL 182.
16. *Abbott v R* [1976] 3 All ER at 152.

There is no modern[17] case in which a threat of injury to property has been admitted.[18] In *M'Growther*[19] D, who was a tenant of the Duke of Perth, called witnesses who proved that the Duke had threatened to burn the houses and drive off the cattle of any of his tenants who refused to follow him. Lee CJ directed that this could be no defence. But that was a case of treason and it does not necessarily follow that such a threat would not be enough on some lesser charge. If the evil D caused by submitting to the threat was clearly less than that which would have been inflicted had he defied it, there are cogent reasons for allowing a defence; even if the threat was not of death or even grievous bodily harm. Williams has argued strongly in favour of such a principle, which is, of course, closely analogous to that adopted in the American Model Penal Code in relation to neces-sity.[20] But this would deny a defence to D even though the injury threatened was one which he could not be expected to endure; and there would be grave difficulty in balancing the two evils against one another when they are of a completely different character.[21]

g) *Threats against whom?* Most of the cases naturally involve a threat or danger to the life or safety of the defendant himself, but the defences are not limited to that situation. In *Hurley and Murray*[1] the Supreme Court of Victoria held that threats to kill or seriously injure D's *de facto* wife amounted to duress. In *Conway*[2] the threat was to the passenger in D's car; and in *Martin*[3] D's wife's threat to commit suicide if he did not drive while disqualified was held capable of founding a defence of duress of circum-stances – though in fact it seems to have been one of duress by threats – "Drive or else . . .". So threats against the life or safety of D's family and others to whom he owes a duty almost certainly will, and threats to a stranger probably will, be sufficient evidence of duress. If a bank robber threatens to shoot a customer in the bank unless D, the clerk, hands him the keys, D surely has a defence to a charge of abetting the robbery. The Draft Code allows the defence where the threat is made to the life or safety of D "or another".

h) *An "imminent" threat.* It is generally stated that the threat must be "immediate" or "imminent" and that, if the person under the compulsion is able to resort to the protection of the law, he must do so. When the threat

17. Cf. *Crutchley* (1831) 5 C & P 133.
18. ". . . the threat may be to burn down [D's] house unless the householder merely keeps watch against interruption while a crime is committed. Or a fugitive from justice may say, 'I have it in my power to make your son bankrupt. You can avoid that merely by driving me to the airport.' Would not many ordinary people yield to such threats, and act contrary to their wish not to perform an action prohibited by law? Faced with such anomaly, is not the only answer, 'Well, the law must draw a line somewhere; and, as a result of experience and human valuation, the law draws it between threats to property and threats to the person," per Lord Simon [1975] 1 All ER at 932.
19. Above, p. 235.
20. Below, p. 251.
21. Law Commission Working Paper No. 55, paras. 14–17.
  1. [1967] VR 526.
  2. [1989] QB 290, [1988] 3 All ER 1025, CA, **SHC 224**.
  3. [1989] 1 All ER 652, **SHC 227**.

is withdrawn or becomes ineffective, D must desist from committing the crime as soon as he reasonably can. If, having consumed excess alcohol, he drives off in fear of his life, he commits an offence only if the prosecution can prove that he continued to drive after the terror ceased.[4]

"The only force that doth excuse, is a force upon the person, and present fear of death; and his force and fear must continue all the time the party remains with the rebels. It is incumbent on every man, who makes force his defence to show an actual force, and that he quitted the service as soon as he could."[5]

In *Hurley*, however, D had ample opportunity to place himself under the protection of the police but the court held that the defence of duress might still be available because his *de facto* wife was held as a hostage by his oppressors. Though he himself was physically out of range, the threats against her were presently operative on his mind. *Hudson* goes further. Two young women, called as witnesses for the prosecution, gave false evidence because they had been threatened by a gang with serious physical injury if they told the truth, and they saw one of the gang in the gallery of the court. Duress was accepted as a defence to a charge of perjury. D could have put herself under the protection of the law by informing the court; and there were no threats to third parties. The court thought it immaterial that the threatened injury could not follow at once since (in its opinion) there was no opportunity for delaying tactics and she had to make up her mind whether to commit the offence while the threat was operating. The threat was no less compelling because it could not be carried out there if it could be effected in the streets of Salford the same night. The case thus turns on the point that police protection could not be effective. It extends the possible ambit of the defence widely for there must be few cases where the police can offer effective and permanent protection against such threats.[6]

i) *The facts and the standard – objective or subjective.* In *Howe* the House of Lords answered in the affirmative the question—

"Does the defence of duress fail if the prosecution prove that a person of reasonable firmness sharing the characteristics of the defendant would not have given way to the threats as did the defendant?"

The House held that the correct direction was that stated by Lane LCJ in *Graham*:[7]

"Was [D], or may he have been, impelled to act as he did because, as a result of what he reasonably believed [E] had said or done, he had good cause to fear that if he did not so act [E] would kill him or ... cause him serious physical injury? (2) If so, have the prosecution made the jury sure that a sober person of reasonable firmness, sharing the characteristics of

4. *DPP v Bell (Derek)*, above, p. 234.
5. *M'Growther*, Fost (1746) 13 at 14, per Lee CJ.
6. See comment in [1971] Crim LR 359 and (by Goodhart) in 87 LQR 299 and 121 NLJ 909 and (by Zellick) in 121 NLJ 845. In *K* (1983) 78 Cr App Rep 82, CA, it was held that duress might be available as a defence to contempt of court committed in the witness box by a prisoner who had been threatened with reprisals against himself and his family, by the accused, a fellow prisoner.
7. [1982] 1 All ER 801 at 806, 74 Cr App Rep 235 at 241. Cf. *Lawrence* [1980] 1 NSWLR 122.

[D], would not have responded to whatever he reasonably believed [E] said or did by taking part in the killing?"

The direction contains three objective elements. D must have *reasonably* believed; his belief must have amounted to *good cause* for his fear and his response must be one which might have been expected of a *sober person of reasonable firmness*. It is respectfully submitted that, in the first two respects, this lays down too strict a rule. D should surely be judged on the basis of what he actually believed and what he actually feared. If his actual fear was such that no person of reasonable firmness could have been expected to resist it, he should be excused. He may have been unduly credulous or stupid, but he is no more blameworthy than a person whose fear is based on reasonable grounds. In *Gladstone Williams*[8] the courts have now recognised that, for purposes of private defence, D should be judged on the facts as he believed them to be, whether reasonably or not, and it seems inconsistent in principle to apply a different test for duress. Lack of faith in the jury to detect the "bogus defence" probably lies at the root of the objective requirements. It is much the same as with mistake generally. The more tenuous the grounds for fear, the less likely is D to be believed.[9]

Since duress is (*pace* Lord Hailsham) a concession to human frailty[10] and some are more frail than others, it is arguable that the standard of fortitude required should also vary.[11] *Graham* is however consistent with the general approach of the law in deciding that this is fixed. It is for the law to lay down standards of conduct. When attacked, D may use only a reasonable degree of force in self-defence. In blackmail P is expected to display a measure of fortitude and not to be affected by trivial threats. Under provocation, D must display a reasonable degree of self-restraint. Similarly, *Graham* decides, a person under duress is required to display "the steadfastness reasonably to be expected of the ordinary citizen in his situation".[12] The court relied particularly on the analogy with the law of provocation as laid down in *Camplin*.[13] This suggests that the threat must be one which would overcome the will of a person having the ability to resist threats reasonably to be expected of an ordinary person of the sex and age of the defendant and in other respects sharing such of the defendant's characteristics as the jury think would affect the gravity of the threat to him.

Similar principles probably apply to the doctrine requiring D to escape from duress if possible. His defence will fail if an ordinary person of his sex, age and other relevant characteristics, would have taken an opportunity to escape. Obviously, physical disabilities, for example that he was lame, would be taken into account.[14] Following *Graham*, however, he must presumably be taken to have been aware of opportunities of which he ought

8. [1987] 3 All ER 441, (1984) 78 Cr App Rep 276, above, p. 89, below, p. 253.
9. Cf. Sexual Offences (Amendment) Act 1976, s. 1(2), below, p. 451.
10. *Pace* Lord Hailsham in *Howe* [1987] 1 All ER 771 at 779–780.
11. "It is arguable that the standard should be purely subjective and that it is contrary to principle to require the fear to be a reasonable one": per Lord Simon, [1975] 1 All ER at 931. Cf. Law Commission Working Paper No. 55, paras, 11–13 and Report (Law Com. No. 83) at 2.27–2.28. Cf. *Hudson* [1965] 1 All ER 721 at 724; above, p. 97.
12. 74 Cr App Rep at 241.
13. [1978] AC 705, [1978] 2 All ER 168, below, p. 358.
14. But the fact that he was voluntarily drunk or drugged might be considered irrelevant.

reasonably to have been aware. A better view, it is submitted, is that if he was not in fact aware of the opportunity to escape, he should not be penalised for his stupidity or slow-wittedness.

j) *Duress by an association voluntarily joined.*

"where a person has voluntarily, and with knowledge of its nature, joined a criminal organisation or gang which he knew might bring pressure on him to commit an offence and was an active member when he was put under such pressure, he cannot avail himself of the defence of duress."[15]

In *Sharp* D was a party to a conspiracy to commit robberies who said that he wanted to pull out when he saw his confederates equipped with guns, whereupon E threatened to blow his head off if he did not carry on with the plan. In the course of the robbery, E killed P. D's conviction for manslaughter was upheld after a jury, directed substantially as above, had rejected his defence of duress.

If D joins a group of people whom he knows to be dedicated to violence as a political end, or one which is overtly ready to use violence for other criminal ends, then he will inevitably forfeit any possible defence of duress. The defence is not inevitably barred because the duress comes from a criminal organisation which D has joined. It depends on the nature of the organisation and D's knowledge of it. If he was unaware of any propensity to violence, the defence will not be denied. The court so held in *Shepherd*[16] where D had voluntarily joined a gang of burglars. The question should have been left to the jury to decide whether he could be said to have taken the risk of violence from a member of the gang, simply by joining its activities.

Until these recent decisions there was no English authority on the point, but there was a wealth of persuasive authority in the criminal codes of many common law jurisdictions, the decision of the Court of Criminal Appeal in Northern Ireland in *Fitzpatrick* (duress no defence to a charge of robbery committed as a result of threats by the I.R.A. because D had voluntarily joined that organisation)[17] and the dicta of Lords Morris, Wilberforce and Simon in *Lynch*.[18] If D was compelled to join the violent organisation by threats of death or serious bodily harm then, in principle, he should not be deprived of the defence. Whether any lesser threat should suffice at this stage has not been decided. D's attempt to withdraw from the organisation, when the particular enterprise which resulted in the charge is in contemplation, is too late. But a man who joined the I.R.A. in his youth can hardly be held to have forfeited his right to plead duress by that organisation for life. If he has done all he can to sever his connection with it before the particular incident was in contemplation, should he not be able to rely on the defence?

k) *The onus of proof.* The onus of disproving duress of either kind is on the Crown.[19] If no facts from which duress might reasonably be inferred

15. *Sharp* [1987] QB 853, [1987] 3 All ER 103, per Lane LCJ.
16. (1987) 86 Cr App Rep 47, CA.
17. [1977] NILR 20.
18. [1975] AC 653.
19. *Gill* [1963] 2 All ER 688, [1963] 1 WLR 841, CCA.

appear in the prosecution's case, then D has the "evidential burden" of laying a foundation for the defence by introducing evidence of such facts.

1) *The emergence of duress of circumstances.* The recognition of this defence occurred, more or less by accident, in *Willer*.[20] D was charged with reckless driving after he had driven very slowly on a pavement in order to escape from a gang of youths who were obviously intent on doing violence to him and his passengers. The trial judge declined to leave the defence of necessity to the jury. The Court of Appeal quashed D's conviction. They said that there was no need to decide on any defence of necessity that might have existed because "the offence [sic] of duress arose but was not pursued", as it ought to have been. It should have been left to the jury to say whether D drove "under that form of compulsion, i.e., under duress". But this was not an instance of the previously recognised defence of duress by threats – the youths were not saying, "Drive on the pavement – or else . . .". There is a closer analogy with private defence.[1] But in substance the court was simply allowing the defence of necessity which it purported to dismiss as unnecessary to the decision. It should surely make no difference whether D drove on the pavement to escape from the youths, or a herd of charging bulls, a runaway lorry, or a flood, if he did so in order to escape death or serious bodily harm.

Subsequent cases have not dismissed *Willer* as a case decided *per incuriam*. They have treated it as rightly decided but have recognised the true nature of the defence. In *Conway*,[2] another case of reckless driving. D's passenger, Tonna, had been the target of an attack on another vehicle a few weeks earlier when another man was shot and Tonna had a narrow escape. According to D, when two young men in civilian clothes came running towards D's parked car, Tonna shouted hysterically, "Drive off". D drove off because he feared a deadly attack on Tonna. Being pursued by the two men in an unmarked vehicle, he drove in a manner which the jury adjudged to be reckless. The two men were police officers who wished to interview Tonna. D's conviction was quashed because the defence of duress of circumstances had not been left to the jury.

Willer and *Conway* were followed in *Martin*.[3] D, while disqualified, drove his stepson, who had overslept, to work. He said that he did so because his wife feared that the boy would lose his job if he were late and threatened to commit suicide if D did not drive him. The wife had suicidal tendencies and a doctor stated that it was likely that she would have carried out her threat. The defence ought to have been left to the jury. This, however, seems to be strictly a case of duress by threats, where D is told, "Commit the crime or else . . .". The defence, as with duress by threats, is available only so long as the "circumstances" continue to threaten. It may have been available (though the court did not decide the point) to a driver who drove off with excess alcohol in his blood to escape assailants; but it

20. (1986) 83 Cr App Rep 225.
1. Below, p. 252.
2. [1989] QB 290, [1988] 3 All ER 1025; **SHC 224**.
3. [1989] 1 All ER 652; **SHC 227**.

was not necessary for him to drive the two and a half miles to his home.[4] But where it was found that D, having consumed excess alcohol, drove off in fear of his life, he was guilty of an offence only if the prosecution could prove that he continued to drive after the terror ceased.[5]

If duress of circumstances is a defence to reckless driving (a fortiori to dangerous driving) it ought, logically, be a defence to causing death by reckless (or dangerous) driving. And if it is a defence to causing death by reckless driving it ought also to be a defence to manslaughter for many cases of that offence were, in law, manslaughter, the constituents of the offences being identical.[6]

2 Coercion

Though the terminology used by judges and writers is by no means uniform, the term "coercion" is generally reserved for a special defence that was available at common law only to a wife who committed certain crimes in the presence of her husband. It was then presumed that she acted under such coercion as to entitle her to be excused, unless the prosecution were able to prove that she took the initiative in committing the offence. The exact extent of the defence is uncertain. It did not apply to treason or murder; Hale[7] excluded manslaughter as well and Hawkins ruled out robbery.[8]

Earlier authorities allowed the defence only in the case of felonies but later it seems to have been extended to misdemeanours – but excluding brothel-keeping;

"for this is an offence touching the domestic economy or government of the home in which the wife has a principal share."[9]

Various theoretical justifications were advanced for the rule – the identity of husband and wife, the wife's subjection to her husband and her duty to obey him – but the practical reason for its application to felonies was that it saved a woman from the death penalty when her husband was able, but she was not, to plead benefit of clergy.[10] This reason disappeared in 1692 when benefit of clergy was extended to women, yet the rule continued and its scope increased.

In 1925, however, the presumption was abolished by the Criminal Justice Act 1925, s. 47:

"Any presumption of law that an offence committed by a wife in the presence of her husband is committed under the coercion of the husband is hereby abolished, but on a charge against a wife for any offence other than treason or murder, it shall be a good defence to prove that the offence was committed in the presence of, and under the coercion of, the husband."

At first sight, it would seem that all Parliament has done is to shift the burden of proof. But there are difficulties about this, for the question at

---

4. *DPP v Jones* [1990] RTR 34, DC.
5. *DPP v Bell (Derek)*, above, p. 234.
6. *Seymour* [1983] 2 AC 493, [1983] 2 All ER 1058.
7. 1 PC 45.
8. 1 PC 4; but the editor of the 8th ed. (J. Curwood) doubted this.
9. Blackstone, *Commentaries*, iv, 29.
10. Hale, 1 PC 45; 2 Lew CC 232n.

once arises, proof of what? and it is not very easy to answer. "Coercion" at common law was really a fiction applied when the wife committed a crime in the presence of the husband and there was no evidence of initiative by the wife. The common law gives little guidance as to what is required now coercion is a matter of affirmative proof. One solution is to hold that it simply means the same as duress and puts the wife in the same situation as anyone else. The difficulty about that is that it would appear to put the wife in a *worse* position; for (i) the onus of disproving duress is on the Crown[11] and (ii) duress probably applies to some forms of treason.[12] The first difficulty might be got over by holding that the statute puts on the wife only the evidential burden (which defendants relying on duress have, but wives relying on coercion at common law did not) of introducing so much evidence as might raise a reasonable doubt whether she was under duress. The second difficulty is less easy to get over. Of course, it may be that, owing to the uncertainties of this branch of the criminal law, Parliament thought that duress did not apply to treason or murder and that wives have been put in a worse position by accident.

The better view is that coercion is a wider defence than duress and is available to wives in addition to the general defence.[13] "The Act can be regarded as merely an incomplete statement of the common law, and the common law still exists to supplement its deficiency."[14] This would seem to have been the real intention and the better view. In the debate on the Bill the Solicitor-General told the House that the section gives the married woman

"a rather wider and more extended line of defence than pure compulsion, because coercion imports coercion in the moral, possibly even in the spiritual realm, whereas compulsion imports something only in the physical realm."[15]

The recommendation of the Avory Committee[16] that wives should be put in the same position as persons generally was not adopted. Far from there being the "endless litigation" which one member feared, there are only three reported cases[17] in which the defence has been relied on.[18] It is by no means clear what a wife has to prove to succeed – moral and spiritual, as distinct from physical, coercion are somewhat intangible.

The defence will no doubt be confined, as it was at common law, strictly to the case of husband and wife and will not be extended to an unmarried couple living as man and wife.[19] Yet a woman in such a situation may be as

---

11. Above, p. 242.
12. Above, p. 235.
13. Williams, CLGP, 765. See *Richman* [1982] Crim LR 507 (Bristol Crown Court).
14. Williams CLGP 765, approved by Lord Edmund-Davies [1975] 1 All ER 954. See also Lord Wilberforce at 930.
15. Parl Deb, H of C (1925), 188, col. 875.
16. Cmd. 1677.
17. *Pierce* (1941) 5 JCL 124 and *Richman*, above, fn. 12. Cf. *Bourne* (above, p. 153) where duress rather than coercion seems to have been relied on.
18. Perhaps the view of Mr Greaves-Lord, M.P., has proved correct: ". . . how many women are there who have been coerced like that, who dare go into the witness box in order to convict the very persons under whose coercion the woman had committed the crime?" Parl Deb, H of C, 188, col. 870.
19. *Court* (1912) 7 Cr App Rep 127.

much under coercion as any married woman; while children, to whom no such defence is available, may be even more under the influence of their parents. It does not extend to a wife by a polygamous marriage nor to a woman who wrongly believes she is married to her oppressor.[20]

It is thought that the very absence of cases in which it has been relied on goes a long way towards showing that it is an unnecessary anomaly at the present day. The Law Commission has recommended its abolition.[1]

7 Necessity

As with duress, we are again concerned with situations in which a person is faced with a choice between two unpleasant alternatives, one involving his committing a breach of the letter of the criminal law and the other some evil to himself or others. If the latter evil outweighs any evil involved in the breach of the letter of the law, it is arguable that the actor should have a defence of necessity. The courts have never recognised a defence in these broad terms and to what extent a defence of necessity prevails in English law is uncertain. As early as 1552 Sergeant Pollard in an argument which apparently found favour with the judges of the Exchequer Chamber said that breaking the letter of laws might be justified "where the words of them are broken to avoid greater inconveniences, or through necessity, or by compulsion. . .".[2] More than three hundred years later Stephen thought the law so vague that it was open to the judges to lay down any rule they thought expedient; and that the expediency of breaking the law in some cases might be so great that a defence should be allowed – but these cases could not be defined in advance.[3]

In spite of these doubts, Williams has submitted "with some assurance" that the defence of necessity is recognised by English law[4] and, particularly, by the criminal law,[5] arguing that the

"peculiarity of necessity as a doctrine of law is the difficulty or impossibility of formulating it with any approach to precision."

From an early period some particular instances of necessity have been recognised. It was justifiable (in the conditions of those days) to pull down a house to prevent a fire from spreading,[6] for a prisoner to leave a burning gaol contrary to the express words of a statute and for the crew of a ship or a passenger[7] to jettison the cargo in order to save the lives of the passengers. It has been held that prison officials may – indeed, must – forcibly feed prisoners if that is necessary to preserve their health and, a fortiori, their

20. *Kara* [1988] Crim LR 42, CA.
 1. Law Com. No. 83 (1977), 3.1–3.9.
 2. *Reniger v Fogossa* (1552) 1 Plowd 1 at 18.
 3. 2 HCL 108.
 4. 6 CLP, 216.
 5. CLGP, 724, et seq.
 6. See now the Criminal Damage Act 1971, below, p. 683.
 7. *Mouse's Case* (1608) 12 Co Rep 63.

lives.[8] It was a defence to the statutory felony of procuring an abortion to show that the act was done in good faith for the purpose only of preserving the life of the mother,[9] although at that time there was no provision for such a defence in any statute.[10] A constable may direct other persons to disobey traffic regulations if that is reasonably necessary for the protection of life and property.[11]

a) *The effect of duress of circumstances on a general defence*. The most important of the case-law developments is the emergence of duress of circumstances, which is simply an instance of necessity. It is a welcome development to those who see a general defence of necessity as an essential element in a just system of criminal law. But it has its dangers. The stringent requirements of the defence of duress by threats which it incorporates may inhibit the development of a broader defence of necessity. If the only threat which will found the defence of duress of circumstances to a person charged with driving while disqualified is one of death or serious injury, it seems to follow that no lesser threat can ever found a defence of necessity to that charge. Why insist on a threat of that gravity if the common law recognises some lesser threat as sufficient? So any general defence of necessity would be confined to circumstances threatening death or serious bodily harm. By the same reasoning, the defence of necessity would be subject to the objective tests of *reasonable* belief in facts giving rise to necessity, *good* cause for fear and the response of a person of *reasonable* firmness.[12]

A possible answer to this argument is that the duress defences apply whether or not the evil caused by the "criminal" act is outweighed by the evil involved in the threat – D is excused because his will is overborne; but that necessity applies only, but whenever, the evil caused is outweighed by the evil avoided, overlapping duress. Suppose that in *Martin* D's wife's threat had been, not to kill herself but to leave D; and suppose further that the consequences of her doing so would have been disastrous for D and his family. Duress of circumstances is not open. Should it be a defence for D to demonstrate that the break-up of his marriage would be a social disaster beside which any effect of his driving a short distance while disqualified would pale into insignificance? It seem unlikely that such a defence would get off the ground.

b) *Lesser dangers*. The traditional examples of necessity – escaping from the burning gaol, etc – do involve danger to life. On the other hand, writers from Hale[13] onwards have denied that necessity can be defence to a charge

---

8. *Leigh v Gladstone* (1909) 26 TLR 139 (Alverstone LCJ). The decision is heavily criticised – see Zellick, [1976] *Public Law* at 159 – and no longer applied in practice: **SHC 366**.

9. *Bourne* [1939] 1 KB 687, [1938] 3 All ER 615; below, p. 386. Cf. *Morgentaler* (1975) 20 CCC (2d) 449 (SCC), discussed by Leigh, [1978] Crim LR 151.

10. See now Abortion Act 1967, below, p. 390, and *T v T* [1988] 2 WLR 189, Fam. Div.

11. *Johnson v Phillips* [1975] 3 All ER 682, [1976] 1 WLR 65, DC. Cf. *Wood v Richards* [1977] RTR 201, [1977] Crim LR 295, DC.

12. Above, p. 240.

13. PC 1, 54, and see Blackstone, *Commentaries*, iv. 31.

of theft of food or clothing. In modern times Lord Denning has justified the rule on the ground that—

". . . if hunger were once allowed to be an excuse for stealing, it would open a door through which all kinds of lawlessness and disorder would pass."[14]

In that case, a civil action, it was held that homelessness did not justify even an orderly entry into empty houses owned by the local authority:

"If homelessness were once admitted as a defence to trespass, no one's house could be safe. Necessity would open a door which no man could shut."[15]

Probably it is now the law that if the taking or the entry was necessary to prevent death or serious injury through starvation or cold there would be a defence of duress of circumstances; but if it were merely to prevent hunger, or the discomforts of cold or homelessness, there would be no defence.

There are some cases where what was in substance a defence of necessity was allowed without identifying a threat to life or serious injury. In *Gillick*'s case one of the conditions stated of the lawfulness of the contraceptive advice or treatment given to a girl under sixteen was that, unless she receives it, "her physical or mental health or both are likely to suffer".[16] In *F v West Berkshire Health Authority*[17] it was held that it was lawful to carry out a sterilisation operation on a woman who lacked the mental capacity to consent because otherwise there would be a grave risk of her becoming pregnant which would be disastrous from a psychiatric point of view. Lord Goff founded his judgment on necessity. These cases would, however, involve at most a slight extension of duress of circumstances – comparable to MacNaghten J's interpretation of "preserving the life of the mother" to include preserving her from becoming "a physical or mental wreck" in *Bourne*,[18] a case which must now be regarded as one of duress of circumstances. Lord Goff has also said, "That there exists a defence of necessity at common law, which may in some circumstances be invoked to justify what would otherwise be a trespass to land, is not in doubt. But the scope of the defence is by no means clear." He found it unnecessary to decide the important question raised in that case, whether the defence could justify forcible entry (which would otherwise be a crime) into the private premises of another in the bona fide, but mistaken, belief that there exists an emergency on the premises by reason of the presence there of a person who has suffered injury and who may require urgent attention.[19]

c) *Necessity elsewhere.* In other parts of the common law world a general defence of necessity is now recognised. Many American states have

14. *Southwark London Borough v Williams* [1971] 2 All ER 175 at 179.
15. Ibid.
16. Per Lord Fraser, [1986] AC 112, at 174. See above, p. 134.
17. [1989] 2 All ER 545, HL.
18. [1939] 1 KB 687, [1938] 3 All ER 615, below, p. 386.
19. *Richards and Leeming* (on appeal from 81 Cr App Rep 125), unreported, 10-7-86, HL. The House agreed with Lord Goff's speech. (We are indebted to Mr Anthony Hooper for drawing our attention to this case.) By s. 17(5) of the Police and Criminal Evidence Act "all the rules of common law under which a constable has power to enter premises without a warrant are hereby abolished". But does this abolish a justification which (if it exists at all) is available, not only to constables, but to persons generally?

adopted the provision in the American Model Penal Code.[20] The courts of Victoria have recognised the existence of a general, if limited, defence in *Loughnan*[1] where D's defence to a charge of escaping from prison was that he feared he would otherwise be killed by other prisoners – but the defence was not made out on the facts. In *Perka*[2] the Supreme Court of Canada held that necessity may be an "excuse" but not a "justification" (there seems to be no practical difference except that it perhaps made the court feel better) for an act which is "inevitable, unavoidable and afford(s) no reasonable opportunity for an alternative course of action that does not involve a breach of the law".

d) *Statutory implication of a defence.* In England it has been argued that there is a principle of statutory interpretation—

". . . that it requires clear and unambiguous language before the courts will hold that a statutory provision was intended to apply to cases in which more harm will, in all probability, be caused by complying with it than by contravening it."[3]

This principle, if it exists, seems to be little noticed in modern times. In *Buckoke v Greater London Council*[4] Lord Denning MR said, *obiter*:

"A driver of a fire engine with ladders approaches the traffic lights. He sees 200 yards down the road a blazing house with a man at an upstairs window in extreme peril. The road is clear in all directions. At that moment the lights turn red. Is the driver to wait for 60 seconds or more, for the lights to turn green? If the driver waits for that time, the man's life will be lost."

Lord Denning accepted the opinion of both counsel that the driver would commit an offence against the Road Traffic Regulations if he crossed the red light. But the threat to the fictional man at the upstairs window seems to be no less than the threat to Willer, to the passenger in Conway's car or to Martin. Lord Denning was stating the effect of the law as he then believed it to be; but he added that the hypothetical driver "should not be prosecuted. He should be congratulated"—so he might welcome this development. As Professor Packer says:

". . . it seems foolish to make rules (or to fail to make exceptions to rules) that discourage people from behaving as we would like them to behave. To the extent that the threat of punishment has deterrent efficacy, rules such as these would condition people confronted with dilemmas to make the wrong choice, either through action or inaction. And the actual imposition of punishment would serve no useful purpose since we assume these people are not in need of either restraint or reform."[5]

---

20. Below, p. 251.
 1. [1981] VR 443.
 2. (1984) 13 DLR (4th) 1, **SHC 232**.
 3. Glazebrook, "The Necessity Plea in English Criminal Law" [1972A] CLJ 87 at 93.
 4. [1971] 1 Ch 655, [1971] 2 All ER 254 at 258; **SHC 227**. Statutory regulations now exempt the driver of the fire engine; but a contractor with a ladder on his lorry might find himself in the same position.
 5. Packer, *The Limits of the Criminal Sanction*, 114.

e) *Necessity and murder*. One of the reasons given by the House of Lords in *Howe*[6] for refusing to allow a defence of duress to murder was that it had been decided in the famous case of *Dudley and Stephens*[7] that necessity was not a defence to murder. Whether that was the *ratio decidendi* of the case has been debated. One interpretation of the judgment is that the court found that no necessity existed. But the House of Lords has now held that the case does decide the point and it is fruitless to discuss that question further. Three men and a boy of the crew of a yacht were shipwrecked. After eighteen days in an open boat, having been without food and water for several days, the two accused suggested to the third man that they should kill and eat the boy. He declined but, two days later, Dudley killed the boy who was now very weak. The three men then fed on the boy's body and, four days later, they were rescued. The accused were indicted for murder. The jury, by a special verdict, found that the men would probably have died within the four days had they not fed on the boy's body, that the boy would probably have died before them and that, at the time of the killing, there was no appreciable chance of saving life, except by killing one for the others to eat.

The accused were convicted of murder, but the sentence was commuted to six months' imprisonment.

In *Dudley and Stephens*[8] Lord Coleridge CJ examined the pronouncements of writers of authority and found nothing in them to justify the extension of a defence to such a case as this. Killing by the use of force necessary to preserve one's own life in self-defence was a well-recognised, but entirely different, case from the killing of an innocent person. Moreover,

"If . . . Lord Hale is clear – as he is – that extreme necessity of hunger does not justify larceny, what would he have said to the doctrine that it justified murder?"[9]

Apart from authority, the court clearly thought that the law ought not to afford a defence in such a case. They thought, first, that it would be too great a departure from morality; and, secondly, that the principle would be dangerous because of the difficulty of measuring necessity and of selecting the victim. The second reason is more convincing:

"Who is to be the judge of this sort of necessity? By what measure is the comparative value of lives to be measured? Is it to be strength or intellect, or what? It is plain that the principle leaves to him who is to profit by it to determine the necessity which will justify him in deliberately taking another's life to save his own."[10]

Williams finds as the "one satisfying reason" in the judgment that it was no more necessary to kill the boy than one of the grown men and adds: "To

6. [1987] AC 417 at 429, 453, above, p. 236.
7. (1884) 14 QBD 273; **SHC 228**. On the instructions of Huddleston B the jury found the facts in a special verdict and the judge then adjourned the assizes to the Royal Courts of Justice where the case was argued before a court of five judges (Lord Coleridge CJ, Grove and Denman JJ, Pollock and Huddleston BB).
8. On the case generally, see A. W. B. Simpson, *Cannibilism and the Common Law*.
9. 14 QBD at 283.
10. 14 QBD at 287.

hinge guilt on this would indicate that lots should have been cast . . .".[11] If the boy had agreed to be bound by the casting of lots, he would have been consenting to die; and consent in such a situation may be a defence. Captain Oates took his life when he left Scott and his companions; yet he was regarded, not as a felon, but as a hero. If the boy had not consented, the drawing of lots would be hardly more rational than trial by ordeal – yet more civilised than a free-for-all. In fact, the court disapproved, *obiter*, of a ruling in an American case, *US v Holmes*,[12] that the drawing of lots in similar circumstances would legalise a killing. Holmes, a member of the crew of a wrecked ship, was cast adrift in an overcrowded boat. In order to prevent the boat sinking, the mate gave orders to throw the male passengers overboard and Holmes assisted in throwing over sixteen men. No doubt, if his act was criminal at all, it was murder; but a grand jury refused to indict him for murder and so he was charged with manslaughter. The judge directed that the law was that passengers must be preferred to seamen; only enough seamen to navigate the boat ought to have been saved; and the passengers whom necessity requires to be cast over must be chosen by lot. As this had not been done (none of the officers or crew went down with the ship) the jury found him guilty.

Stephen thought the method of selection "over refined"[13] and Lord Coleridge thought this

"somewhat strange ground . . . can hardly . . . be an authority satisfactory to a court in this country."[14]

The English judges offered no alternative solution and, presumably, their view was that, in the absence of a self-sacrificing volunteer, it was the duty of all to die. This was also the view of the distinguished American judge, Cardozo J:

"Where two or more are overtaken by a common disaster, there is no right on the part of one to save the lives of some, by the killing of another. There is no rule of human jettison."[15]

Arguably, *Dudley and Stephens* is distinguishable if there is no problem of selection. D, a mountaineer who cuts the rope seconds before he would be dragged over a precipice by E, his falling companion, surely commits no offence. There is no question of choosing between D and E. E is going to die in a matter of seconds anyway. The question is whether he alone should die a few seconds earlier, or whether they should both die seconds later.

At the inquest following the Zeebrugge disaster a witness, an army corporal, gave evidence that he and numerous other passengers were trapped in the stricken ferry and in grave danger of drowning. A possible way of escape up a rope ladder was barred by a man, petrified by cold or fear, who could move neither up nor down. After fruitless attempts to persuade him to move, the corporal ordered those nearer to push him off the ladder. They did so, he fell into the water and was not seen again. The trapped passengers were then able to climb up the ladder to safety. The

11. CLGP, 744.
12. 26 Fed Cas 360 (1842).
13. 2 HCL 108.
14. 14 QBD at 285.
15. *Selected Writings*, 390.

coroner expressed the opinion that a reasonable act of self-preservation, or the preservation of others, is "not necessarily murder". So far as is known, no legal proceedings against the corporal were ever contemplated. Unlike the cabin boy, but like the falling mountaineer, the man on the ladder chose himself as the victim by his immobility there. He was preventing the passengers from going where they had a right and a most urgent need to go. He was, unwittingly, imperilling their lives.[16]

In these examples the evil avoided outweighs that caused – one dies instead of two, or instead of many – and there is extreme duress. It would be extraordinary if there were no defence. So, notwithstanding the approval of *Dudley and Stephens* by *Howe*, it would be premature to conclude that necessity can never be a defence to murder.

f) *The American Model Penal Code*. The Code propounds a general defence of necessity:

"Conduct which the actor believes to be necessary to avoid a harm or evil to himself or to another is justifiable, provided that:

(a) the harm or evil sought to be avoided by such conduct is greater than that sought to be prevented by the law defining the offence charged . . ."[17]

No such general principle exists or is likely to be developed by English courts. Edmund Davies LJ has clearly formulated the judicial attitude:

". . . the law regards with the deepest suspicion any remedies of self-help, and permits these remedies to be resorted to only in very special circumstances. The reason for such circumspection is clear – necessity can very easily become simply a mask for anarchy."[18]

Except in cases where necessity has already been recognised as a defence, the courts are likely to be satisfied by their power to grant an absolute discharge in hard cases.[19]

The Law Commission, departing from the views of its Working Party, at one time recommended that there should be no general defence of necessity; and that, for the avoidance of doubt, it should be enacted that any such defence as does exist is abolished.[20] They thought that provision should be made by statute for a defence to particular offences where appropriate.[1]

These recommendations have been subjected to very cogent criticism and the Law Commission's codification team found themselves unable to act on them. The Commission is now persuaded that the defence of duress of circumstances should be provided and it is to be found in cl. 43 of their draft Code. They have expressed no view about the provision of any wider

16. See further, Smith, *Justification and Excuse*, Ch. 3. And cf., self-defence against a nine year old or insane person.
17. Art. 3. Section 3.02. It is subject to qualifications not necessary to be noted here.
18. *Southwark London Borough v Williams* [1971] Ch 734, [1971] 2 All ER 175 at 181; **SHC 211.**
19. Glazebrook, op. cit., 118–119.
20. Report on Defences of General Application (Law Com. No. 83, 1977); criticised by Williams [1978] Crim LR 128; Huxley [1978] Crim LR 141.
1. See for example, Nurses, Midwives and Health Visitors Act 1979, s. 17.

defence of necessity. The Code would leave it open to the courts to develop such a defence at common law.

8 Public and Private Defence

Force causing personal injury, damage to property, or even death may be justified or excused because the force was reasonably used in the defence of certain public or private interests. Public and private defence is therefore a general defence and appropriately considered at this point. The law is to be found in a variety of sources. Defence of the person, whether one's own or that of another, is still regulated by the common law, defence of property by the Criminal Damage Act 1971, and arrest and the prevention of crime by s. 3 of the Criminal Law Act 1967. Because of its haphazard growth, the law contains some inconsistencies and anomalies. The general principle, however, is that the law allows such force to be used as is reasonable in the circumstances of the particular case: and, for the purposes of offences requiring *mens rea*, what is reasonable is to be judged in the light of the circumstances as the accused believed them to be, whether reasonably or not. For example, if D believed that he was being attacked with a deadly weapon and he used only such force as was reasonable to repel such an attack, he has a defence to any charge of an offence requiring *mens rea* arising out of the use of that force. It is immaterial, so far as D's liability for an offence involving *mens rea* is concerned, that he was mistaken and unreasonably mistaken. But if the offence – e.g., manslaughter[2] – is one which may be committed by gross negligence or recklessness, then a grossly negligent or reckless mistake would not excuse.

The question, "Was the force used reasonable in the circumstances as D supposed them to be?" is, with one exception,[3] a question, to be answered by the jury or magistrates. If it was reasonable to cause any harm which could reasonably have been foreseen, D's act is justified or excused, even if it results in some greater harm. For example, D wrestles with P who is trying to steal D's wallet. P dies of a heart attack. D's opinion that it was reasonable is not conclusive but the test of reasonableness, it has been held,[4] is not "purely objective". The force will commonly be used in a moment of crisis. In the case of self-defence the jury should be reminded they must not disregard the state of mind of the defendant altogether.[5] Lord Morris has said:[6]

"If there has been attack so that defence is reasonably necessary it will be recognised that a person defending himself cannot weigh to a nicety the exact measure of his necessary defensive action. If a jury thought that in

---

2. Whether manslaughter may be committed by gross negligence is discussed below, p. 374.
3. See s. 5 of the Criminal Damage Act 1971, below, p. 694.
4. *Whyte*, [1987] 3 All ER 416, CA.
5. Ibid.
6. *Palmer v R* [1971] 1 All ER 1077 at 1078, PC, applied in *Shannon* (1980) 71 Cr App Rep 192, [1980] Crim LR 438 and *Whyte*, above.

a moment of unexpected anguish a person attacked had only done what he honestly and instinctively thought was necessary that would be most potent evidence that only reasonable defensive action had been taken. A jury will be told that the defence of self-defence, where the evidence makes its raising possible, will only fail if the prosecution show beyond doubt that what the accused did was not by way of self-defence.''

These cases relate to self-defence but similar considerations may apply, depending on the circumstances, to force used to prevent crime or to effect an arrest, etc.

The authority for the proposition that D is to be judged on the facts as he believed them to be is *Gladstone Williams*,[7] now approved by the Privy Council in *Beckford v R*.[8] D was charged with an assault occasioning actual bodily harm to P. D's defence was that he was preventing P from committing an assault on Q. But P may have been lawfully arresting Q. The jury was directed that, if P was acting lawfully, D had a defence only if he believed *on reasonable grounds* that P was acting unlawfully. It was held that this was a misdirection. D had a defence if he honestly held that belief, reasonably or not. The court referred to the recommendation of the Criminal Law Revision Committee: "The common law of self-defence should be replaced by a statutory defence providing that a person may use such force as is reasonable in the circumstances as he believes them to be in the defence of himself or any other person.''[9] The court declared that this proposition represented the common law, as stated in *Morgan*[10] and *Kimber*.[11]

It is arguable that this ruling was obiter but, if so, the law has been settled beyond doubt by the decisions which have followed it.[12]

1 Force used in the Course of Preventing Crime or Arresting Offenders

The common law on this subject was both complex and uncertain;[13] but now, by the Criminal Law Act 1967, s. 3:

"(1) A person may use such force as is reasonable in the circumstances in the prevention of crime, or in effecting or assisting in the lawful arrest of offenders or suspected offenders or of persons unlawfully at large.

(2) Subsection (1) above shall replace the rules of the common law on the question when force used for a purpose mentioned in the subsection is justified by that purpose.''

Section 3 states a rule both of civil and criminal law. When the force is "reasonable in the circumstances" it is justified in every sense. No civil action or criminal proceeding will lie against the person using it. The

7. (1984) 78 Cr App Rep 276, CA. But, where D is drunk, see *O'Grady*, above, p. 89.
8. [1987] 3 All ER 425, [1987] 3 WLR 611.
9. Fourteenth Report (Cmnd. 7844), para. 72(a).
10. Above, p. 87.
11. Above, p. 67.
12. *Jackson* [1985] RTR 257; *Asbury* [1986] Crim LR 258, CA; *Fisher* [1987] Crim LR 334, CA; *Beckford v R* [1987] 3 All ER 425, [1987] 3 WLR 611, PC.
13. See the first edition of this book at pp. 230–238.

section says nothing specifically about any criminal liability of the user of the force. When that is in issue the ordinary principles of *mens rea* should apply. The use of force may be unjustified in the civil law because it is not in fact "reasonable in the circumstances"; but D may nevertheless be excused from liability for an offence requiring *mens rea* if it was "reasonable in the circumstances *as he believed them to be*". The Criminal Law Revision Committee,[14] the authors of the section, wrote:

"No doubt if a question arose on clause [now 'section'] 3, the court, in considering what was reasonable force, would take into account all the circumstances, including in particular the nature and degree of force used, the seriousness of the evil to be prevented and the possibility of preventing it by other means; but there is no need to specify in the clause the criteria for deciding the question. Since the clause is framed in general terms, it is not limited to arrestable or any other class of offences, though in the case of very trivial offences it would very likely be held that it would not be reasonable to use even the slightest force to prevent them."

It cannot be reasonable to cause harm unless (i) it was *necessary* to do so in order to prevent the crime or effect the arrest and (ii) the evil which would follow from failure to prevent the crime or effect the arrest is so great that a reasonable man might think himself justified in causing that harm to avert that evil. It is likely, therefore, that even killing will be justifiable to prevent unlawful killing or grievous bodily harm, or to arrest a man where there is an imminent risk of his causing death or grievous bodily harm if left at liberty. The whole question is somewhat speculative. Is it reasonable to kill or cause serious bodily harm in order to prevent rape? Or robbery, when the property involved is very valuable, and when it is of small value?[15] How much force may be used to prevent the destruction of a great work of art? It seems that the question, what amount of force is reasonable in the circumstances? is always for the jury and never a point of law for the judge.[16] If the prosecution case does not provide material to raise the issue, there is an evidential burden on the accused. If that burden is satisfied, the question for the jury is:

". . . Are we satisfied that no reasonable man (a) with knowledge of such facts as were known to the accused or [reasonably][17] believed by him to exist (b) in the circumstances and time available to him for reflection (c) could be of the opinion that the prevention of the risk of harm to which others might be exposed if the suspect were allowed to escape, justified exposing the suspect to the risk of harm to him that might result from the kind of force that the accused contemplated using."[18]

---

14. Cmnd. 2659, para. 23.
15. Where a butcher used a butcher's knife to frustrate the robber of his takings, his action met with the approval of the coroner, though the robber died; (1967), *The Times*, 16 September.
16. *Reference under s. 48A of the Criminal Appeal (Northern Ireland) Act 1968 (No. 1 of 1975)* [1976] 2 All ER 937 at 947, HL, per Lord Diplock.
17. Lord Diplock used the word "reasonably" and, in the light of his often stated opinion, it is likely that he would wish to continue to use it, were he still alive; but his remarks, in the light of *Gladstone Williams* and the cases following it, should be read as if "reasonably" were omitted.
18. Ibid.

The standard of reasonableness should, as noted above, take account of the nature of the crisis in which the necessity to use force arises for, in circumstances of great stress, even the reasonable man cannot be expected to judge the minimum degree of force required to a nicety. In holding quite considerable force to be justified to prevent an obstruction of the highway by a violent and abusive driver, Geoffrey Lane J said:

"In the circumstances one did not use jewellers' scales to measure reasonable force . . ."[19]

The Criminal Law Act 1967 made no reference to the right of private defence – the right to use force in defence of oneself or another against an unjustifiable attack. The right of private defence still exists at common law; but if, and in so far as, it differed in effect from s. 3 of the 1967 Act, it has probably been modified by that section. Private defence and the prevention of crime are sometimes indistinguishable. If D goes to the defence of E whom P is trying to murder, he is exercising the right of private defence but he is also seeking to prevent the commission of a crime. It would be absurd to ask D whether he was acting in defence of E or to prevent murder being committed and preposterous that the law should differ according to his answer. He was doing both. The law cannot have two sets of criteria governing the same situation and it is submitted that s. 3 of the Criminal Law Act is applicable. The Act may be taken to have clarified the common law. Before the Criminal Law Act, the Court of Criminal Appeal equated the defence of others with the prevention of crime. In *Duffy*[20] it was held that a woman would be justified in using reasonable force when it was necessary to do so in defence of her sister, not because they were sisters, but because "there is a general liberty as between strangers to prevent a felony". That general liberty now extends to all offences. The principles applicable are the same whether the defence be put on grounds of self-defence or on grounds of prevention of crime. The degree of force permissible should not differ, for example, in the case of an employer defending his employee from the case of a brother defending his sister – or, indeed, that of a complete stranger coming to the defence of another under unlawful attack. The position is the same where D acts in defence of property, whether his own or that of another, which P seeks to steal, destroy or damage.

Where D is acting in defence of his own person it may be less obvious that he is also acting in the prevention of crime but this will usually be in fact the case. D's purpose is not the enforcement of the law but his own self-preservation; yet the degree of force which is permissible is the same.[1] An inquiry into D's motives is not practicable.[2]

a) *A duty to retreat?* There were formerly technical rules about the duty to retreat before using force, or at least fatal force. This is now simply a factor to be taken into account in deciding whether it was necessary to use force,

---

19. *Reed v Wastie* [1972] Crim LR 221.
20. [1967] 1 QB 63, [1966] 1 All ER 62, CCA.
   1. *Devlin v Armstrong* [1971] NI 13 at 33; *McInnes* [1971] 3 All ER 295 at 302.
   2. Above, p. 79.

and whether the force was reasonable.[3] If the only reasonable course is to retreat, then it would appear that to stand and fight must be to use unreasonable force. There is, however, no rule of law that a person attacked is bound to run away if he can.

A demonstration by D at the time that he did not want to fight is, no doubt, the best evidence that he was acting reasonably and in good faith in self-defence; but it is no more than that. A person may in some circumstances so act without temporising, disengaging or withdrawing; and he should have a good defence.[4]

In *Browne*[5] Lowry LCJ said, with regard to self-defence:

"The need to act must not have been created by conduct of the accused in the immediate context of the incident which was likely or intended to give rise to that need."

b) *Defence against a provoked attack.* Self-defence is clearly not available where D deliberately provoked the attack with the intention of killing, purportedly in self-defence.[6] Where D's act was merely "likely" to give rise to the need, the proposition, with respect, is more questionable. If D did not foresee that his actions would lead to an attack on him, it is submitted that he should not be deprived of his usual right of self-defence. Even if he did foresee the attack, he may still be entitled to act in self-defence if he did not intend it. D intervenes to stop P from ill-treating P's wife. He knows that P may react violently. P makes a deadly attack on D. Surely D's right of self-defence is unimpaired.

c) *Defence against lawful force.* Lowry LCJ also stated in *Browne*:[7]

"Where a police officer is acting lawfully and using only such force as is reasonable in the circumstances in the prevention of crime or in effecting the lawful arrest of offenders or suspected offenders, self-defence against him is not an available defence."

Again it may respectfully be questioned whether this proposition is not too wide. If D, an innocent person, is mistaken, even reasonably, by the police for a notorious gunman and they so attack him that he can preserve his life only by killing or wounding – an attack which would be reasonable if he were the gunman – does the law really deny him the right to resist?[8] Again, if D reasonably supposes that the police are terrorists, he surely

3. *McInnes*, above. But cf. *Whyte* [1987] 3 All ER 416 at 419, CA.
4. This passage was approved by the Court of Appeal in *Bird* [1985] 2 All ER 513 at 516.
5. [1973] NI 96 at 107, CCA, discussed 24 NILQ 527. On "prior fault" generally, see Yeo, *Compulsion*, Ch. 5.
6. Cf. *Mason* (1756) Fost 132; and the corresponding problem in provocation, p. 364.
7. [1973] NI 96 at 107.
8. The judgment of Winn LJ in *Kenlin v Gardner* [1967] 2 QB 510 [1966] 3 All ER 931 is ambivalent. *Albert v Lavin* [1981] 1 All ER 628, [1981] 2 WLR 1070, DC (reversed by the House of Lords on another point) supports the view in the text. And see the draft Criminal Code. cl. 47(3)(b) and (6) (Law Com 143) and *Ansell v Swift* [1987] Crim LR 194 (Lewes Crown Court). The question is elaborately discussed in *Lawson and Forsythe* [1986] VR 515. Young CJ thought it may be reasonable to assume that, in some circumstances, D may defend himself against a lawful attack; McGarvie J said that he may do so, approving the 5th edition of this work, 327–328, but Ormiston J thought self-defence was only lawful against an unlawful attack. Cf. *Fennell* [1970] 1 QB 428, [1970] 3 All ER 215, [1971] Crim LR 581 and commentary; below, p. 417.

commits no crime by resisting, even if the police are in fact acting lawfully and reasonably.

A person is not to be deprived of his right of self-defence because he has gone to a place where he might lawfully go, but where he knew he was likely to be attacked. There is no question of any duty to retreat at least until the parties are in sight of one another and the threat is imminent.[9]

In a very few cases the attacker may not be committing a crime because, for example, he is a child under ten, insane, in a state of automatism or under a material mistake of fact. If D is unaware of the circumstances which exempt the attacker, then s. 3 of the Criminal Law Act will still, indirectly, afford him a defence to any criminal charge which may be brought, provided he is acting reasonably in the light of the circumstances as they appear, reasonably or not, to him; for he intends to use force in the prevention of crime, as that section allows, and therefore has no *mens rea*. Where D does know of the circumstances in question, then s. 3 is entirely inapplicable, but it is submitted that the question should be decided on similar principles. A person should be allowed to use reasonable force in defending himself or another against an unjustifiable attack, even if the attacker is not criminally responsible.

d) *Unknown circumstances of justification.* The test proposed in the Criminal Law Revision Committee's 14th Report and adopted as the law in *Gladstone Williams* is stated exclusively in terms of the defendant's belief. Its terms do not apply where D is unaware of circumstances which, if he knew of them, would justify his use of force. This accords with *Dadson*.[10] This is no accident. The Committee gave careful consideration to the matter and concluded that the *Dadson* principle was correct.[11] Although s. 2 of the Criminal Law Act and s. 24 of PACE which replaced it appear to justify arrest and therefore the use of force necessary to effect it both (i) where the circumstances of justification in fact exist, and (ii) where the arrester suspects on reasonable grounds that they exist, it is clear that no arrest can be lawful unless the arrester suspects, whether on reasonable grounds or not, that the arrestee is committing, or has committed, or is about to commit, an arrestable offence. Under s. 28 (3) of PACE, restating the common law, the arrest is unlawful unless the arrestee is informed of the grounds for it at the time of, or as soon as is practicable after, the arrest. The arrester cannot state such grounds unless he at least suspects their existence. So a person like Dadson who has no suspicion of any valid ground for making an arrest is acting unlawfully, even though such grounds, unsuspected by him, exist in fact. An arrester who suspects without reasonable grounds will not be justified under (ii) above, but he will be justified under (i) if his unreasonable suspicion is well founded. To that extent an arrest on "hunch" is justified.

Although the spheres of private defence and arrest overlap there are clearly occasions when one applies to the exclusion of the other. An officer

---

9. *Field* [1972] Crim LR 435; cf. *Beatty v Gillbanks* (1882) 9 QBD 308.
10. Above, p. 34.
11. The discussion is not included in the Report, Cmnd. 7844, paras 281–287.

pursuing an escaping criminal is unlikely to be able to claim that he was acting in private defence. Where a soldier who had killed the man he was pursuing disclaimed any intention to make an arrest and relied on a claim that he was acting in self-defence which proved to be unfounded, it was no answer to a charge of murder that he would have been justified in shooting in order to make an arrest.[12] A person cannot rely on powers of arrest unless he was acting with the purpose of arresting.

e) *Defence of property*.[13] Where D is charged with criminal damage and his defence is that he was acting in defence of his own property – as where he kills P's dog which, he claims, was attacking his sheep, the matter is regulated by the Criminal Damage Act 1971, which is considered below, p. 698. Where D is charged with an offence against the person, or any other offence, and his defence is that he was defending his property, he will generally be acting in the prevention of crime and, as in defence of the person, s. 3 is likely to be held to provide the criterion. It can rarely, if ever, be reasonable to use deadly force merely for the protection of property. Would it have been reasonable to kill even one of the Great Train Robbers to prevent them from getting away with their millions of pounds of loot, or to kill a man about to destroy a priceless old master? – even assuming that no means short of killing could prevent the commission of the crime.

In the modern case of *Hussey*[14] it was stated that it would be lawful for a man to kill one who would unlawfully dispossess him of his home. Even if this were the law at the time, it would seem difficult now to contend that such conduct would be reasonable; for legal redress would be available if the householder were wrongly evicted. Insofar as the householder was preventing crime, his conduct would be regulated by s. 3 of the Criminal Law Act 1967 which replaces the rules of common law. It is thought that, in any event, the rule in *Hussey* would not extend to a trespasser who did not intend to dispossess the householder, even if the trespasser were guilty of an offence under Part II of the Criminal Law Act 1977.[15]

f) *To what offences is public or private defence an answer?* These defences are most naturally relied on as answers to charges of homicide, assault, false imprisonment and other offences against the person. It is not clear to what extent public or private defence may be invoked as defences to other crimes. Clause 44 of the Draft Code ("Use of force in public or private defence") would not justify or excuse any criminal conduct not involving the use of force (except acts immediately preparatory to the use of such force); but the Code would leave it open to the courts to develop a wider defence at common law. It is not clear to what extent the present law allows these defences to crimes other than those involving the use of force. In *A-G's Reference (No 2 of 1983)*[16] D made and retained in his shop petrol bombs at a time when extensive rioting was taking place in the area. He was

---

12. *Thain* [1985] NI 457 (NI CA), discussed in Smith, *Justification and Excuse*, 34.
13. See Lanham, [1966] Crim LR 426.
14. (1924) 18 Cr App Rep 160, CCA; **SHC 247**.
15. Cf. *Taylor v Mucklow* [1973] Crim LR 750 and commentary.
16. [1984] QB 456, [1984] 1 All ER 988, [1984] Crim LR 289 and commentary, CA.

acquitted of an offence under s. 4(1) of the Explosive Substances Act 1883 of possessing an explosive substance in such circumstances as to give rise to a reasonable suspicion that he did not have it for a lawful object. It was a defence under the terms of the section for D to prove that he had it for a lawful object. The Court of Appeal held that there was evidence on which a jury might have decided that the use of the petrol bombs would have been reasonable force in self-defence against an apprehended attack. If so, D had the bombs for "a lawful object" and was not guilty of the offence charged. Yet it was assumed[17] that he was committing offences of manufacturing and storing explosives contrary to the Explosives Act 1875. The court agreed with the Court of Appeal in Northern Ireland in Fegan[18] that possession of a firearm for the purpose of protecting the possessor may be possession for a lawful object, even though the possession was unlawful, being without a licence. The judgment is strangely ambivalent.

> "[D] is not confined for his remedy to calling in the police or boarding up his premises. He may still arm himself for his own protection, if the exigency arises, although in so doing he may commit other offences. That he may be guilty of other offences will avoid the risk of anarchy contemplated by the reference."

To say "He may do it – but he will commit an offence if he does" seems inconsistent. There is, however, a clear statement that acts immediately preparatory to justifiable acts of self-defence are also justified. This must surely be right. If D becomes caught up in a shoot-out between police and dangerous criminals, picks up a revolver dropped by a wounded policeman and fires in order to defend his own and police lives, it would be astonishing if he had a defence to a charge of homicide but not to possessing a firearm without a licence.[19] Possibly, then, the passage above refers to preparatory, but not immediately preparatory acts. This does not resolve the ambivalence. The law must say whether a person may, or may not, do such acts; and if it says they are crimes, he may not.

The matter must now be considered in the light of the defence of duress of circumstances. A person may save himself from injury by an attacker by using force or by running away and Willer and Conway[20] are cases where this form of self-defence was an answer to a charge of reckless driving. As a matter of policy there is a great deal to be said for encouraging a threatened person to escape, even where that involves committing a minor offence, rather than using force against the aggressor. It now seems that those defendants would have had a defence if they had driven through a red light, or while disqualified, or with excess alcohol, provided that it was necessary to do so in order to escape death or serious bodily harm. The hypothetical user of the revolver was also acting under duress of circumstances. A successful defendant will not care whether his defence is called "duress of circumstances" or "private defence"; but whether the defence succeeds may well depend on how it is categorised, for the former is limited to threats to the person whereas the latter extends to defence of property; and

17. At pp. 992–993.
18. [1972] NI 80.
19. Cf. Georgiades [1989] Crim LR 574.
20. Above, p. 242. See Elliott, "Necessity, Duress and Self-Defence" [1989] Crim LR 611.

the former is governed by an objective test whereas a subjective test is applied to the latter. A disqualified driver who drove his Rolls Royce to avoid its destruction by an aggressor could not plead duress; nor would possession of the revolver without a licence be excused by duress if the possessor's honest belief that life was in danger was not based on reasonable grounds – though his defence to a charge of homicide would not be impaired. For the avoidance of such anomalies, acts immediately preparatory to public or private defence are better regarded as justified or excused by those defences.

The fears of the courts regarding a general defence of necessity[1] probably militate against a recognition that public and private defence may constitute a defence to crime generally; but, where contravention of *any* law is (i) necessary to enable the right of public or private defence to be exercised, and (ii) reasonable in the circumstances, it ought to be excused. It is open to the courts to move in this direction.

g) *Use of force, excessive in the known circumstances.* Where D, being under no mistake of fact, uses force in public or private defence, he either has a complete defence or if he uses excessive force, no defence. If the charge is murder, he is guilty of murder or not guilty of anything. There being no grossly negligent, or *Caldwell*-reckless, mistake of fact, there is no ground for convicting D of manslaughter. He may have believed the force was reasonable but if, even by the relaxed standard applied in this context,[2] it was not, he was making a mistake of law, which is not a defence, and he is guilty of murder. That is the law of England but for thirty years a line of cases in Australia held that killing by excessive force, even where there is no mistake of fact, should be manslaughter and not murder, if some force was justified:

"... if the occasion warrants action in self defence or for the prevention of felony or the apprehension of the felon but the person taking action acts beyond the necessity of the occasion and kills the offender the crime is manslaughter – not murder."[3]

The defence, as stated by the High Court in *Howe*[4] in relation to self-defence, applied where (i) D honestly and reasonably thought he was defending himself; and (ii) homicide would have been justified if excessive force had not been used; but (iii) D used more force than was reasonably necessary. This principle was mainly applied in self-defence cases,[5] but it originated in *McKay*,[6] which concerned the use of excessive force in the arrest of a felon and the defence of property and it is logical that, if it applies at all, it should apply to any of the defences now being considered.[7]

1. Above, p. 247.
2. Above, p. 255.
3. *McKay* (1957) ALR 648 at 649, per Lowe J.
4. (1958) 100 CLR 448; *Bufalo* [1958] VR 363; *Haley* (1959) 76 WN NSW 550; *Tikos (No. 1)* [1963] VR 285 *Tikos (No. 2)* [1963] VR 306.
5. Ibid.
6. [1957] VR 560.
7. It has been argued the principle is of general application and should govern duress, coercion and necessity. Thus, even if duress, coercion and necessity do not afford a complete defence to murder, they might reduce the offence to manslaughter: Morris and Howard, op. cit., 142. The idea is undeniably attractive but it is as yet unsupported by authority.

This doctrine was followed in some Canadian cases[8] but has been rejected by the Supreme Court. The English courts appear to have flirted with it but it has been regarded sceptically by members of the House of Lords[9] and firmly rejected both by the Privy Council[10] and the Court of Appeal.[11] Their Lordships were unconvinced by the Australian cases and saw no need for this refinement of the law:

"If there has been attack so that defence is reasonably necessary it will be recognised that a person defending himself cannot weigh to a nicety the exact measure of his necessary defensive action. If a jury thought that in a moment of unexpected anguish a person attacked had only done what he honestly and instinctively thought was necessary that would be most potent evidence that only reasonable defensive action had been taken. A jury will be told that the defence of self-defence, where the evidence makes its raising possible, will only fail if the prosecution show beyond doubt that what the accused did was not by way of self-defence."[12]

In *Zekevic*[13] the Australian High Court has now overruled its previous decisions on excessive self-defence and followed *Palmer*, bringing Australian law into line with that of England. It did so, not because it thought the principle applied in those cases was a bad one, but because of the complexity which had arisen from the Court's attempt to state the law in a form which took account of the onus of proof. The law was to be changed because it was too difficult for juries to understand and apply. In the meantime, the CLRC was persuaded that *Howe* was right in principle and recommended its adoption in relation to private defence of person and property and the prevention of crime.[14] It is submitted that the soundness of this recommendation is not impaired by *Zekevic*. The Law Commission agrees and cl. 59 of the Draft Code would implement the recommendation. The principle of *Gladstone Williams*[15] – which has not yet been followed in Australia – removes some of the complexity from the law and it ought to be capable of being stated in a form readily comprehensible by juries. The CLRC propose that murder be retained as a separate offence to cater for the most heinous homicides and a man who believes, however foolishly, that his act is justified in law, hardly falls into that category.

9 Superior Orders

Though there is little authority on this question, it is safe to assert that it is not a defence for D merely to show that the act was done by him in obedience

8. *Gee* (1983) 139 DLR 587; *Brisson* (1983) 139 DLR 685.
9. *Reference under s. 48A of the Criminal Appeal (Northern Ireland) Act 1968 (No. 1 of 1975)* [1976] 2 All ER 937 at 956 and 959.
10. *Palmer v R* [1971] AC 814, [1971] 1 All ER 1077, [1971] 1 WLR 1600; **SHC 245**.
11. *McInnes* [1971] 3 All ER 295.
12. *Palmer v R* [1971] 1 All ER 1077 at 1088.
13. *Zecevic v DPP (Vic)* (1987) 61 ALJR 375. See Editorial, [1988] Crim LR 1.
14. CLRC/OAP/R, para. 228. Cf. P. F. Smith [1972] Crim LR 524.
15. Above, p. 253.

to the orders of a superior, whether military or civil. Where a security officer caused an obstruction of the highway by checking all the vehicles entering his employer's premises, it was no defence that he was obeying his employer's instructions.[16] The Australian High Court has held that there is no place for a general defence of superior orders or of the Crown or executive fiat in Australian criminal law.[17] The fact that D was acting under orders may, nevertheless, be very relevant. It may negative *mens rea* by, for example, showing that D was acting under a mistake of fact or that he had a claim of right[18] to do as he did, where that is a defence; or, where the charge is one of negligence,[19] it may show that he was acting reasonably.

The only question (which has been discussed mainly in connection with military orders) is whether orders are a defence where they do not negative *mens rea* or negligence, but give rise to a reasonable mistake of law. *The Manual of Military Law*[20] now asserts as "the better view" that they do not. Dicta in some of the cases suggest that they might. In a South African case[1] which has been much cited, Solomon J said:

"I think it is a safe rule to lay down that if a soldier honestly believes he is doing his duty in obeying the commands of his superior, and if the orders are not so manifestly illegal that he must or ought to have known they are unlawful, the private soldier would be protected by the orders of his superior officer . . ."

The only English authority[2] directly on the point holds that it is not a defence to a charge of murder for D to show that he fired under the mistaken impression that it was his duty to do so. D was, no doubt, making a mistake of law, but there is no finding as to its reasonableness. If mistake of law does not afford a defence where it is reasonable on other grounds, it should not, in principle, afford a defence because it is reasonable as arising from the orders of a superior. If the result is harsh, it is because the rule (if it be the rule[3]) that reasonable mistake of law is not a defence is a harsh general rule.[4]

10 Impossibility[5]

Where the law imposes a duty to act, it has sometimes been held that it is a defence that, through no fault of his own, it was impossible for D to do so.

16. *Lewis v Dickson* [1976] RTR 431, DC.
17. *A v Hayden* (1984) 156 CLR 532.
18. *James* (1837) 8 C & P 131.
19. *Trainer* (1864) 4 F & F 105.
20. (1956) Part I, 117. Nichols "Untying the Soldier by Re-Furbishing the Common Law" [1976] Crim LR 181.
  1. *Smith* (1900) 17 SCR 561; 17 CGH 561. But the case has not always been followed in South Africa. See Burchell and Hunt, 298–9.
  2. *Thomas* (1816) Ms. of Bailey J, Turner and Armitage, *Cases on Criminal Law*, 67. For an instance of a concealed defence of superior orders, see *Janoway v Salford Area Health Authority* [1989] AC 537, [1988] 2 WLR 442, CA; affd on other grounds [1989] AC 537, [1988] 3 All ER 1079, HL, discussed, Smith *Justification and Excuse*, 70–72.
  3. See above, p. 168.
  4. For further discussion, see Stephen, 1 HCL, 204–206; Dicey, *Law of the Constitution* (10th ed.), 302–306; Williams, CLGP, 105.
  5. Williams CLGP, 746–748.

A driver is not liable for failure to report an accident if he does not know the accident has happened.[6] The secretary of a limited company is not liable for failure to annex to an annual return, as required by the Companies Act 1985, a copy of a balance sheet laid before the company in general meeting where there is no such balance sheet in existence: "nobody ought to be prosecuted for that which it is impossible to do."[7] A person is not liable for failure to leave a particular place if he is unaware of the order requiring him to do so.[8] In New Zealand it has been held that a failure to leave the country after the revocation of a permit was not an offence if no airline would carry D because of the advanced state of her pregnancy.[9] Impossibility is a defence to a charge of failure to assist a constable to preserve the peace when called upon to do so.[10]

On the other hand, the failure of a driver to produce a test certificate is not excused by the fact that it is impossible for him to do so, the owner of the vehicle being unable or unwilling to produce it.[11] Failure by the owner of a vehicle to display the excise licence is not excused by the fact that, without any negligence or default on his part, it has become detached in his absence.[12]

We find here the inconsistency which is so common in relation to strict liability. It cannot be asserted, therefore, that any general defence of impossibility is recognised at the present time. It has to be regarded as a question of the interpretation of the particular provision, with all the uncertainty that this entails.

When impossibility might be available as a defence, it will presumably fail if the impossibility has been brought about by D's own default.[13] The defence would also seem to be confined to cases where the law imposes a duty to act and not to cases of commission where the corresponding defence, if any, is necessity.[14]

11 Non-Compliance with Community Law

A defence of which more may be heard in the future is that the provision under which the defendant is charged is invalid because it conflicts with the law of the European Community.[15] In *Dearlove*[16] P charged a substantially higher price for goods which the buyer intended to sell on the home market than for goods intended for export. It was accepted that this policy

6. *Harding v Price* [1948] 1 KB 695, [1948] 1 All ER 283, DC.
7. *Stockdale v Coulson* [1974] 3 All ER 154 at 157, DC, per Melford Stevenson J.
8. *Lim Chin Aik v R* [1963] AC 160, [1963] 1 All ER 223, PC.
9. *Finau v Dept of Labour* [1984] 2 NZLR 396.
10. *Brown* (1841) Car & M 314, per Alderson B.
11. *Davey v Towle* [1973] RTR 328, DC.
12. *Strowger v John* [1974] RTR 124, DC; cf. *Pilgram v Dean* [1974] 2 All ER 751, DC.
13. But cf. *Stockdale v Coulson*, above, and comment at [1974] Crim LR 375.
14. See *Canestra* 1951 (2) SA 317 (AD) and Burchell and Hunt, 293–296.
15. See T. C. Hartley, "The Impact of European Community Law on the Criminal Process", [1981] Crim LR 75.
16. *Dearlove, Druker* (1988) 88 Cr App Rep 279, CA.

contravened Article 85 (1) of the EEC Treaty. D conspired to obtain goods from P at the lower price by dishonestly representing that he intended to export them to Bulgaria. His conviction was upheld because the Theft Act 1968 could not be regarded as a statutory support of the offending pricing policy and the prosecution was brought by the Crown to protect the public. The result would have been the same if P had brought a private prosecution – the nature of the criminal proceedings would have been the same. But the Court accepted that, if the prosecution had undermined the effectiveness of Article 85 (1) or favoured or reinforced the contravention, the appeal would have been allowed. And it might also have been different if the prosecution had been brought under a regulation made to enforce the offending policy.

11 Incitement, Conspiracy and Attempt

1 Incitement

An inciter, it has been said—

"... is one who reaches and seeks to influence the mind of another to the commission of a crime. The machinations of criminal ingenuity being legion, the approach to the other's mind may take various forms, such as suggestion, proposal, request, exhortation, gesture, argument, persuasion, inducement, goading or the arousal of cupidity."[1]

A person may incite another by threats or pressure as well as by persuasion.[2] Incitement may be implied as well as express. To advertise an article for sale, representing its virtue to be that it may be used to do an act which is an offence, is an incitement to commit that offence[3] – even when accompanied by a warning that the act is an offence. But the mere intention to manufacture and sell wholesale a device which has no function other than one involving the commission of an offence is not an intention to incite the commission of that offence.[4]

The mere incitement of another to commit an indictable offence is a common law misdemeanour, whether the incitement is successful in persuading the other to commit, or to attempt to commit the offence or not. It was so held in the leading case of *Higgins*[5] where Lord Kenyon said:[6]

"But it is argued, that a mere intent to commit evil is not indictable, without an act done; but is there not an act done, when it is charged that the defendant solicited another to commit a felony? The solicitation is an act: and the answer given at the Bar is decisive, that it would be sufficient to constitute an overt act of high treason."

The act incited must be one which, when done, would be a crime by the person incited. So in *Whitehouse* it was not an offence at common law for a man to incite a girl of fifteen to permit him to have incestuous sexual

---

1. Holmes, JA in *Nkosiyana*, 1966 (4) SA 655 at 658, AD.
2. *Race Relations Board v Applin* [1973] QB 815 at 827, CA, Civil Div., per Lord Denning MR, followed in *Invicta Plastics Ltd v Clare* [1976] RTR 251, [1976] Crim LR 131, DC.
3. *Invicta Plastics*, above. (Indication that "Radatec" may be used to detect police radar traps is an incitement to an offence under s. 1 (1) of the Wireless Telegraphy Act 1949.)
4. *James and Ashford* (1985) 82 Cr App Rep 226 at 232, distinguishing *Invicta Plastics*, above.
5. (1801) 2 East 5.
6. Ibid., at 170.

intercourse.[7] Though the man commits incest by having intercourse with her, the girl commits no offence by permitting it. The Criminal Law Act 1977, s. 54, makes it an offence for a man to incite a girl under sixteen to have incestuous sexual intercourse with him but the general principle is unaffected. It is not the offence of incitement for anyone to urge a fifteen-year-old girl to have incestuous intercourse with a third party or for a man to urge an unrelated girl of fifteen,[8] or a defective woman,[9] to have intercourse with himself. Arguably, however, the latter cases are attempts by him to commit the offence.[10]

By analogy to *Bourne*[11] and *Cogan and Leak*,[12] it is arguable that incitement to commit the *actus reus* should be an offence.[13] D threatens E with grievous harm if she does not commit the act of buggery with a dog or encourages F to have sexual intercourse with D's wife, telling him, falsely, that she consents to his doing so. The argument that these acts should be aiding and abetting, if the act is committed, may be thought equally cogent that it should be incitement, if it is not. But the present law is that D must know or believe that the person incited has,[14] or intend that he shall have, the *mens rea* of the offence; and an extension of the law which is justifiable when the *actus reus* has occurred may be thought unjustifiable when it is merely in prospect. If such a principle were accepted, it would not affect cases like *Whitehouse* because there is no *actus reus* on the part of the person incited.

In principle, it would seem necessary that the incitement should have been communicated,[15] but the matter is of small practical importance[16] since, in the case of a failure of communication,[17] there would at least be an attempt to incite.[18]

Where under the rule in *Tyrrell*[19] a victim is incapable of being an abettor, he is equally incapable of incitement; but the procedural requirements of the ulterior offence – such as the consent of the Director of Public Prosecutions[20] – do not necessarily apply to a charge of incitement.

---

7. (1977) 65 Cr App Rep 33, CA, below, p. 467.
8. Below, p. 462.
9. Below, p. 464.
10. Incitement of a person to commit an offence is not the offence of attempting to commit that offence; but the incitement of an innocent agent might be. See *Cromack* [1978] Crim LR 217 and commentary, and Smith in *Crime, Proof and Punishment*, 21. The cases posed in the text are different, being, arguably, attempts by D to do the act himself.
11. (1952) 36 Cr App Rep 125, above, p. 152.
12. [1976] QB 217, [1975] 2 All ER 1059, above, p. 153.
13. See R. Leng (1978) 41 MLR 725.
14. *Curr* [1968] 2 QB 944, [1967] 1 All ER 478, CA, **SHC 251**, below, p. 269.
15. *Banks* (1873) 12 Cox CC 393 (letter, suggesting the murder of a child not yet born, intercepted. Held an attempt to incite under Offences against the Person Act 1861, s. 4; (repealed)). Statutory offences of "soliciting" may be different; cf. *Horton v Mead* [1913] 1 KB 154.
16. *Ransford* (1874) 13 Cox CC 9. Section 19 of the Misuse of Drugs Act 1971 expressly makes it an offence to attempt to incite another to commit an offence under that Act.
17. It is of *some* importance, because a magistrates' court has no power to convict of an attempt on a charge of the full offence.
18. An offence at common law: *Chelmsford JJ, ex parte Amos* [1973] Crim LR 437, DC.
19. Above, p. 156. Tyrrell was acquitted of incitement as well as abetting.
20. *Assistant Recorder of Kingston-upon-Hull, ex parte Morgan* [1969] 2 QB 58, [1969] 1 All ER 416.

If the offence incited is actually committed, then, as seen above, D becomes a participant in the offence and may be dealt with accordingly.

1 The Crime Incited

a) *Offences generally*. Incitement to commit any criminal offence, even an offence triable only summarily, amounted to a misdemeanour at common law. It followed that the incitement was triable on indictment and punishable with fine and imprisonment at the discretion of the court.[1] It was highly anomalous that the mere incitement should be regarded as more serious than the actual commission of the offence, even though the use of the greater powers of sentencing might be defensible where the incitement was to commit a large number of summary offences.[2] Now, by the Magistrates' Courts Act 1980, s. 45, any offence consisting in the incitement to commit a summary offence is triable *only* summarily. Incitement to commit an offence triable either way is itself triable either way.[3] Incitement to commit an offence triable only on indictment continues to be triable only on indictment. Where incitement is tried summarily the offender is not liable to any greater penalty than he would be liable to on summary conviction of the completed offence, whether it is a summary offence[4] or an offence triable either way.[5] Where incitement is tried on indictment, it continues to be punishable with fine and imprisonment at the discretion of the court, whatever the penalty for the crime incited.

b) *Other inchoate offences*. An indictment would lie at common law for inciting to conspire but the offences of incitement and attempt to conspire were abolished by s. 5 (7) of the Criminal Law Act 1977. A charge of incitement to attempt to commit an offence would generally be inept because to incite to attempt is to incite to commit. Where, however, in the circumstances known to the inciter, but not to the person incited, the completed act will amount only to an attempt, the contrary is arguable. For example, D gives E a substance which he knows to be harmless, telling E that it is poison and urging him to administer it to P. If E does as requested he will be guilty of an attempt to murder.[6] D could scarcely be said to have incited murder but it is arguable that he should be liable for inciting an attempt to murder. However, the Magistrates' Courts Act 1980, Schedule 1, paras. 34 and 35 appear to be drafted on the assumption that there is no such offence as an incitement to attempt;[7] and it may well be that this is the law. An incitement to incite is an offence except, possibly, when it amounts to an incitement to conspire. To allow an indictment for incitement to

1. By the Magistrates' Courts Act 1952, s. 19 (8) and Schedule 1, para. 20, incitement to commit a summary offence could be dealt with summarily with the consent of the accused.
2. As in *Curr* [1968] 2 QB 944, [1967] 1 All ER 478, CA; **SHC 251**.
3. Magistrates' Courts Act 1980, s. 17 and Sch. 1, para. 35.
4. Criminal Law Act 1977, s. 30 (4).
5. Ibid., s. 28 (1).
6. Below, p. 321.
7. If there is such an offence, its exclusion from the schedules means that it is triable only on indictment even though the offence incited is triable either way or only summarily.

incite in the latter case would, it has been said, amount to an illegitimate evasion of s. 5 (7) of the Criminal Law Act 1977.[8] But the distinction is absurd and a better view would be that incitement to incite is untouched by the 1977 Act.

c) *Counselling and abetting*. There is probably no offence of incitement to counsel or abet an offence.[9] It is true that, in *Whitehouse*, the court did not quash the conviction on that short ground as they might have done; but the Criminal Law Act 1977, s. 30 (4), seems to be drafted on the assumption that there is no such offence and there is one decision to that effect by a circuit judge.[10] D paid E £50 to find someone to assault P. It was held that there was no case to answer on an indictment alleging that D incited E to assault P and that it is not an offence to incite another to become "an accessory before the fact".

There may, however, be an incitement to incite, so D could have been charged with that unless (possibly) E was incited to conspire with X, a person yet unknown; and there may be a conspiracy to incite,[11] an offence of which both D and E would seem to be guilty – so such a situation is far from being without remedy.

2 Mens Rea

As in the case of counselling and abetting, it must be proved that D knew of (or deliberately closed his eyes to) all the circumstances of the act incited which are elements of the crime in question. As with attempts, he must intend the consequences in the *actus reus*. If D incites E to inflict grievous bodily harm upon P, D is not guilty of incitement to murder, though both D and E will be guilty of murder if death should result from the infliction of the intended harm.[12] An intention to bring about the criminal result is of the essence of incitement. There must probably be, in addition, an element of persuasion or pressure,[13] which is not necessary in the case of counselling or abetting. If D sells a gun to E, knowing that E intends to murder P, it is probable that D is guilty of murder if E does kill P;[14] but, if E does not kill P, it would seem impossible, on those facts alone, to convict D of incitement.[15]

Among the circumstances is the *mens rea* of the person incited. If D believes that the person will do the act without the *mens rea* for the crime in question, then he intends to commit that crime through an innocent agent,

---

8. *Evans* [1986] Crim LR 470, CA; *Sirat* (1986) 83 Cr App Rep 41, [1986] Crim LR 245, CA.
9. See Smith, *Crime, Proof and Punishment*, 21 at 29.
10. *Bodin and Bodin* [1979] Crim LR 176 and commentary (Judge Geoffrey Jones).
11. Incitement to conspire was abolished on the recommendation of the Law Commission's Working Party by s. 5 (7) of the Criminal Law Act 1977; but the Commission saw no reason why conspiracy to incite should not continue in the law (Law Com. No. 76, para. 1.44) and it is unaffected by the 1977 Act. The Commission now recommends "that neither incitement nor conspiracy should be excluded from the scope of incitement": Law Com. No. 177, para. 13.15.
12. Cf. *Whybrow* (1951) 35 Cr App Rep 141.
13. Above, p. 265; *Hendrickson and Tichner* [1977] Crim LR 356; *Christian*, below, p. 461. Cf. Buxton (1969) 85 LQR 252 at 256.
14. Above, p. 133.
15. Cf. *James and Ashford* (1985) 82 Cr App Rep 226 at 232, above, p. 265.

if it is capable of being so committed, and may become guilty as the principal or an abettor if the *actus reus* is completed,[16] but he is not guilty of incitement. In *Curr*[17] D was acquitted of inciting women to commit offences under the Family Allowances Act 1945 because it was not proved that the women had the guilty knowledge necessary to constitute that offence. The real question, it is submitted, should have been, not whether the women actually had the knowledge, but whether D believed they had. In that event he should have been guilty. But if he believed that they did not have the guilty knowledge, he was not guilty of incitement, whether they had it or not.[18] If D urges E to accept the gift of a necklace, which is in fact stolen, he is not guilty of inciting E to handle stolen goods if he believes E to be unaware that the necklace is stolen; even though in fact she is so aware.

2 Conspiracy

Conspiracy was a misdemeanour at common law. It was classically, if loosely, defined[19] as an agreement to do an unlawful act or a lawful act by unlawful means. The word "unlawful" was used in a broad sense. It included not only all crimes triable in England, even crimes triable only summarily, but also at least some torts, fraud, the corruption of public morals and the outraging of public decency. In this respect it went far beyond the other inchoate offences of incitement and attempt, where the result incited or attempted must be a crime. For many years the crime of conspiracy was believed to be even more extensive and to include any agreement to effect a public mischief; but in 1974 in *Director of Public Prosecutions v Withers*[20] the House of Lords held that an agreement which did not come within one of the heads referred to above was not indictable as a public mischief.

It is the ultimate aim of the Law Commission that conspiracy shall be confined to agreements to commit crimes.

"The crime of conspiracy should be limited to agreements to commit criminal offences: an agreement should not be criminal where that which it was agreed to be done would not amount to a criminal offence if committed by one person."[21]

This aim has received general approval. Its immediate implementation, however, was not thought to be appropriate because the abolition of conspiracy to defraud would leave an unacceptably wide gap in the law. It

---

16. Above, p. 125.
17. [1968] 2 QB 944, [1967] 1 All ER 478, CA; **SHC 251**.
18. Cf. *Bourne* (1952) 36 Cr App Rep 125; **SHC 139**; above, p. 152.
19. By Lord Denman in *Jones* (1832) 4 B & Ad 345 at 349. But a few years later in *Peck* (1839) 9 Ad & El 686 at 690 he declared, "I do not think the antithesis very correct."
20. [1975] AC 842, [1974] 3 All ER 984. Conspiracy to commit the common law offence of public nuisance continues to be a potential source of expansion of the criminal law. See commentary on *Soul* (1980) 70 Cr App Rep 295, [1980] Crim LR 233, CA.
21. Law Com. No. 76, para. 1. 113; see also Law Commission Working Paper No. 50.

was therefore recommended that conspiracy to defraud should be preserved until the Law Commission could make recommendations for more
comprehensive offences of fraud and these could be implemented. It was
further decided that, pending the outcome of a review of the law relating to
obscenity and indecency, it was undesirable to interfere with the law of
conspiracy to corrupt public morals or to outrage public decency and that
these too should for the present be preserved. The reform effected by the
Criminal Law Act 1977 is therefore a limited and provisional reform.
Notwithstanding some amendment by the Criminal Attempts Act 1981 and
the Criminal Justice Act 1987, it remains an ill-drafted piece of legislation
presenting numerous problems of interpretation and it is to be hoped that a
more thoroughgoing and effective reform will not be long delayed. In the
meantime, it is an offence of conspiracy triable only on indictment to agree:

   (i) to commit any criminal offence triable within the jurisdiction, even
       an offence triable only summarily;
  (ii) to defraud, whether or not the fraud amounts to a crime;
 (iii) to do an act which tends to corrupt public morals or outrage public
       decency, whether or not the act amounts to a crime.

Whether a particular agreement is a conspiracy at common law or a
statutory conspiracy under the Criminal Law Act, or both, is considered
below. In all cases, however, the *actus reus* is the agreement which, of
course, is not a mere mental operation, but must involve spoken or written
words or other overt acts. If D repents and withdraws immediately after
the agreement has been concluded, he is guilty[22] and his repentance is a
matter of mitigation only.

1) *Common Law and Statutory Conspiracies*

Section 1 (1) of the Act creates the offence of statutory conspiracy. It
provides in effect that it is a conspiracy to agree to commit *any* offence; but
s. 1 (1) is subject to the following provisions of Part I of the Act. These
include s. 5 (1) and (2) which (as amended by the Criminal Justice Act
1987) provide:

   "(1) Subject to the following provisions of this section, the offence of
       conspiracy at common law is hereby abolished.
    (2) Subsection (1) above shall not affect the offence of conspiracy at
       common law so far as relates to conspiracy to defraud."

The Act, as originally enacted, caused great difficulty and controversy
over the relationship between statutory conspiracy and conspiracy to
defraud at common law. Eventually the House of Lords decided in *Ayres*[1]
that any agreement the performance of which would involve the commission of an offence must be indicted as a statutory conspiracy to commit that
offence and not as a conspiracy to defraud. Statutory conspiracy and

22. As in the *Bridgewater Case*, unreported, referred to by Lord Coleridge CJ in the *Mogul SS
Case* (1888) 21 QBD 544 at 549.
  1. [1984] AC 447, [1984] 1 All ER 619.

conspiracy to defraud were mutually exclusive. This led to great difficulties for prosecutors. Indictments and convictions for conspiracy to defraud had to be quashed because it was discovered that the carrying out of the agreement necessarily involved the commission of some offence, however trivial. The House substantially modified the effect of *Ayres*, as generally understood, in *Cooke*.[2] That decision brought new difficulties,[3] but, happily, these need not be pursued here because the Criminal Justice Act 1987, s. 12, restores the full scope of conspiracy to defraud at common law:

"(1) If—
   (a) a person agrees with any other person or persons that a course of conduct shall be pursued; and
   (b) that course of conduct will necessarily amount to or involve the commission of any offence or offences by one or more of the parties to the agreement if the agreement is carried out in accordance with their intentions,
   the fact that it will do so shall not preclude a charge of conspiracy to defraud being brought against any of them in respect of the agreement."

Statutory conspiracy and conspiracy to defraud are no longer mutually exclusive. An agreement to commit a crime involving fraud is both a statutory conspiracy and a conspiracy to defraud. The prosecutor will frequently have a choice which should be exercised in accordance with the guidance in the Code for Crown Prosecutors issued by the Director of Public Prosecutions under s. 10 (1) of the Prosecution of Offences Act 1985.

Statutory conspiracies and common law conspiracies to corrupt public morals or to outrage public decency remain mutually exclusive, as the Act makes plain. Where the conduct in which the parties have agreed to engage would amount to the commission of an offence if carried out by a single person, the agreement is a statutory conspiracy. Where it would not amount to an offence if carried out by a single person, it is conspiracy at common law. Recent cases confirming that it is an offence for a single person to do acts tending to corrupt public morals create a doubt whether there is any scope for the operation of common law conspiracy to do these things.[4]

2) *The Mens Rea of Conspiracy*

Conspiracy is a crime where it is more than usually difficult to distinguish between *actus reus* and *mens rea*. The *actus reus* may be said to be an

---

2. [1986] AC 909, [1986] 2 All ER 985.

3. See [1987] Crim LR 114 and *Levitz* (1989) 90 Cr App Rep 33, [1989] Crim LR 714, where Bingham LJ pointed out that the problems apply to conspiracies entered into between the coming into force of the 1977 Act and July 20 1987 when s. 12 of the Criminal Justice Act 1987 took effect.

4. *May* (1989) 91 Cr App Rep 157, CA; *Gibson* [1990] 2 QB 619, CA; *Rowley* [1991] 4 All ER 649, [1991] Crim LR 785, CA, below, p. 748.

agreement: but agreement is essentially a mental operation, though it must be manifested by acts of some kind. "In the case of conspiracy as opposed to the substantive offence, it is what was agreed to be done and not what was in fact done which is all important."[5] Because the mental element looms so large it is convenient to deal with it first.

1 Statutory Conspiracies[6]

The offence of statutory conspiracy is defined by s. 1 (1) and s. 1 (2) of the Act. Section 1 (1) (as amended by s. 5 of the Criminal Attempts Act 1981) provides:

"Subject to the following provisions of this part of the Act, if a person agrees with any other person or persons that a course of conduct shall be pursued which, if the agreement is carried out in accordance with their intentions, either—
(a) will necessarily amount to or involve the commission of any offence or offences by one or more of the parties to the agreement, or
(b) would do so but for the existence of facts which render the commission of the offence or any of the offences impossible,

he is guilty of conspiracy to commit the offence or offences in question."

a) *Intention to carry out the agreement.* The section assumes the existence of an intention of the parties to carry out the agreement. This is not surprising because the essence of conspiracy, like incitement and attempt, is the intent to cause the forbidden result. The Law Commission understood this well enough and their report[7] was quite unequivocal. The Draft Bill, and the Bill which was introduced into Parliament, provided that, where a person was charged with conspiracy to commit an offence, "both he and the other person or persons with whom he agrees must intend to bring about any consequence which is an element of that offence, even where the offence in question may be committed without that consequence actually being intended by the person committing it". Unwisely, this provision was deleted from the Bill because it was thought too complex; but, in agreeing to the amendment, the Lord Chancellor stated: "What has been sought to be done, and what I think has been conceded in the speeches made today, is that the law should require full intention and knowledge before conspiracy can be established."[8]

However, in *Anderson*,[9] Lord Bridge, in a speech with which all of the House agreed, said that it was sufficient that an alleged conspirator had

---

5. *Bolton* (1991) 94 Cr App Rep 74 at 80, per Woolf LJ.
6. For the background to Part I of the Criminal Law Act, see Law Commission Working Papers Nos. 50 (*Inchoate Offences*, 1973), 56 (*Conspiracy to Defraud*, 1974), 57 (*Conspiracies Relating to Morals and Decency*, 1974) and 63 (*Conspiracies to Effect a Public Mischief and to Commit a Civil Wrong*, 1975); and Report, *Conspiracy and Criminal Law Reform* (Law Com. No. 76, 1976). For the interpretation of the Act, see Griew, Annotations to the Act in *Current Law Statutes*; Smith [1977] Crim LR 598 and 638; Elliott [1978] Crim LR 202; and Williams (1977) 127 NLJ 1164 and 1188.
7. Report on Conspiracy and Criminal Law Reform (Law Com. No. 76), paras 1. 25–1. 41. For the common law, see *Mulcahy* (1868) LR 3 HL 306 at 317, per Willes J.
8. HL Deb. vol 379, col. 55.
9. [1986] AC 27, [1985] 2 All ER 961, [1985] Crim LR 651 and commentary.

agreed that the criminal course of conduct be pursued and that it was not necessary to prove that he intended that it should. He was, she said—

"clearly driven by consideration of the diversity of roles which parties may agree to play in criminal conspiracies to reject any construction of the statutory language which would require the prosecution to prove an intention on the part of each conspirator that the criminal offence or offences which will necessarily be committed by one or more of the conspirators if the agreed course of conduct is fully carried out should in fact be committed."

Lord Bridge was concerned with cases like that of the owner of a car, D, who agrees to hire it to a gang for use in a robbery. D may be quite indifferent whether the robbery is committed or not. The answer to that situation is that the gang are certainly guilty of conspiracy for they do intend to carry out the robbery; and D is guilty of abetting the conspiracy by giving encouragement to its continuance.

In *Anderson*, D was convicted of conspiring with a number of other persons to effect the escape of one of them from gaol. D had agreed to supply diamond wire to cut bars but said that he never intended the plan to be put into effect and believed that it could not possibly succeed. It was held that this was no defence. It was clear in that case that two or more of the alleged conspirators did intend to carry out the agreement, so D's conviction could have been upheld on the ground that he aided and abetted that conspiracy – which he undoubtedly did, encouraging the making or continuance of it by his offer of help.[10] But, if no intention need be proved on the part of one alleged principal offender in conspiracy, it need not be proved on the part of another. A conspiracy which no one intends to carry out is an absurdity, if not an impossibility. Moreover, s. 1 (2)[11] requires intention or knowledge as to facts or circumstances constituting an offence, and it would be very remarkable indeed if intention or knowledge were required for circumstances and not for consequences. It is submitted that *Anderson* should not be followed in this respect. It was overlooked or ignored in *Edwards*[12] where D had agreed to supply amphetamine but there was a possibility that he intended to supply ephedrine. It was held that the judge had rightly directed the jury that they could convict of conspiracy to supply amphetamine only if D intended to supply amphetamine – i.e., it was not sufficient that D agreed to supply amphetamine unless he intended to carry out the agreement. In *McPhillips*[13] the Court of Appeal of Northern Ireland, while citing *Anderson*, accepted the proposition in this book[14] that s. 1 (1) of the 1977 Act[15] assumes the existence of an intention of the parties to carry out the agreement. Lord Lowry CJ held that D, who had joined in a conspiracy to plant a bomb, timed to explode on the roof of a hall at 1 am when a disco would be at its height, was not a party to the

10. See commentary on the decision of the Court of Appeal, [1984] Crim LR 551, and, on conspiracy to aid and abet, below, p. 279.
11. Below, p. 277.
12. [1991] Crim LR 45.
13. Unreported, 20 September 1989.
14. 6th ed., 259.
15. Article 9 (1) of the Criminal Attempts and Conspiracy (Northern Ireland) Order 1983 is identical with s. 1 (1).

conspiracy to murder of which his accomplices were guilty because, unknown to his accomplices, he intended to give a warning enabling the hall to be cleared. He did not intend that anyone should be killed. *Anderson* was distinguished relying on Lord Bridge's dictum that a "perfectly respectable citizen" who joins in an agreement "without the least intention of playing any part in the ostensibly agreed criminal objective but rather with the purpose of frustrating and exposing the objective of the other parties" is not guilty of conspiracy. The dictum may be correct[16] but hardly seems to fit McPhillips, whose convictions, arising out of the same facts, for conspiracy to cause explosions and offences under the Explosive Substances Act 1883, were upheld. He was rightly acquitted of conspiracy to murder as a principal simply because he lacked the required intention. More debatable is the decision that he was not guilty as an abettor of the conspiracy to murder. He intentionally gave assistance or encouragement to what he knew to be a conspiracy to murder and that is normally sufficient for liability. This suggests that an intention to frustrate the object of the conspiracy is a special defence. There are clear public policy grounds for allowing such a defence.

b) *Intention to play some part in carrying out the agreement.* According to Lord Bridge in *Anderson*[17] the *mens rea* of conspiracy is established—

"... if, and only if, it is shown that the accused, when he entered into the agreement, intended to play some part in the agreed course of conduct in furtherance of the criminal purpose which the agreed course of conduct was intended to achieve."

No authority was cited for this novel dictum and the Court of Appeal has subsequently held that Lord Bridge is not to be taken as saying what he plainly did say (above); the court said that that participation in conspiracy can be active or passive and D's intention to participate "is established by his failure to stop the unlawful activity".[18] D's liability is, however, complete when he joins the agreement, intending that it be carried out, and his failure to stop it is, at most, evidence of his agreement and intention. There is nothing in the section, nor in the common law, to require participation in the carrying out of the agreement by each conspirator. All that need be contemplated is the commission of the offence "by one or more of the parties to the agreement".

c) *The meaning of "course of conduct".* The words, "the agreement", mean the agreement that a "course of conduct" shall be pursued. We thus have to envisage the contemplated course of conduct as having been pursued and to ask, would it, when completed, necessarily amount to or involve the

---

16. *Edwards* [1991] Crim LR 45, above, p. 158. But cf. *Somchai Liangsiriprasert v United States Government* (1990) 92 Cr App Rep 77 at 82 where the Privy Council left open the question whether law enforcement officers who entered into an agreement to import drugs into the USA with the object of trapping the dealers should be regarded as conspirators.
17. [1985] 2 All ER 961 at 965.
18. *Siracusa* (1989) 90 Cr App Rep 340, [1990] Crim LR 712.

commission of any offence?[19] But the phrase, "course of conduct", is ambiguous. It might mean only the actual physical acts which the parties propose shall be done; or it might include the consequences which they intend to follow from their conduct and the relevant circumstances which they know, or believe, or intend to exist. In *Director of Public Prosecutions v Nock*,[20] a case of common law conspiracy committed before, but decided after, the Act came into force, the House of Lords used the same phrase, "course of conduct", and gave it the former meaning. The defendants resolved to extract cocaine from a particular substance in their possession by subjecting it to a certain process. The substance contained no cocaine. They were held not guilty of conspiracy to produce a controlled drug. The "course of conduct" was the application of that process to that substance; and this would necessarily *not* amount to or involve the commission of the offence of producing a controlled drug.

Section 1 (1) (b), which was added by the Criminal Attempts Act 1981, is designed to ensure that this result does not follow in a case of statutory conspiracy. *Nock* is a case where the "existence of facts" – i.e., that there was no cocaine in the substance – rendered the commission of the offence of producing a controlled drug impossible; and, but for that fact, the course of conduct would necessarily have resulted in the production of a controlled drug. The agreement in *Nock* would therefore now amount to a statutory conspiracy to produce a controlled drug. The phraseology is unhappy – the *absence* of cocaine must be regarded as the existence of a fact – but the effect seems to be that we look at the facts at the time of the agreement as the defendants believed them to be.

Section 1 (1) (b) removes any problem concerning the existence of facts at the time of the agreement and, as a corollary, consequences which depend on the existence of those facts – for example, the production of cocaine. The subsection has nothing to say, however, about (i) other consequences, not dependent on the existence of facts believed by the defendants to exist or (ii) the existence of facts precluding the commission of the crime at the time it is to be carried out. First, consequences. Suppose the defendants agree to kill P by putting poison in his tea. This, surely, must be conspiracy to murder; but the act of putting poison in the tea will not necessarily result in murder. P may decide not to drink it. So, if the course of conduct is putting poison in the tea, it is not conspiracy to murder – which is absurd.[1] Subsection (1) (b) has nothing to say in the matter because there is no question of impossibility. To avoid the absurdity, "course of conduct" must be read to include the intended consequences – in this case, the death of P.[2] So persons deceiving a building society into giving authority for a mortgage are guilty of conspiracy to procure the execution of a valuable security if they believe that this will be the result of

19. Cf. *Barnard* (1980) 70 Cr App Rep 28, [1980] Crim LR 235, CA and commentary.
20. [1978] AC 979, [1978] 2 All ER 654, [1978] Crim LR 483 and commentary.
   1. It would be conspiracy to attempt to commit murder, since putting poison in the tea necessarily amounts to an attempt. The Criminal Attempts Act 1981 does not rule out the possibility of such an offence, but it is an absurd concept. An agreement to attempt to do something is an agreement to do it.
   2. This argument is more fully developed in [1977] Crim LR at 601–602. See also Williams (1977) 127 NLJ 1164 at 1165.

their "course of conduct" even though it will not happen because the society now uses an electronic device not amounting to a "valuable security".[3] "Course of conduct" includes the contemplated result.

Next, circumstances. In determining whether conspiracy is committed, we have to look forward from the time of the agreement – will the pursuance of the agreed course of conduct necessarily amount to or involve the commission of an offence? Circumstances change. The commission of the offence may be perfectly possible at the time of the agreement and become impossible by the time it is to be performed. Where this may happen, how can we say that the pursuance of the course of conduct will *necessarily* amount to or involve the commission of an offence? Defendants agree to receive certain goods, which they know to be stolen, next Monday; but, before next Monday, the goods may cease to be stolen goods by being restored to lawful custody. D1 and D2 may agree to marry next Tuesday, knowing that D1's wife is alive; but, before next Tuesday, she may die. These events may be unlikely, but they are possible, and therefore it cannot be said that the receipt of the goods or the going through the marriage ceremony will necessarily amount to or involve the offences of handling stolen goods and bigamy respectively. If the contemplated receipt, or ceremony, is the "course of conduct", the agreements do not amount to conspiracy to handle or commit bigamy.[4] Clearly they ought to.

The obvious way out of this difficulty is to construe "course of conduct" to include material circumstances which the parties believe will exist, and that is a perfectly reasonable construction.

There are two difficulties about this approach. One is s. 1 (2) of the Act.[5] This provides that a person is not guilty of conspiracy to commit an offence unless he "intends or knows" that circumstances necessary for the commission of the offence shall or will exist at the time when the conduct constituting the offence is to take place. In the examples just given, D cannot "know" that the circumstances will exist because, as we have seen, they may not do so; and it seems strange to say that he "intends" that they shall exist when he has, and knows he has, no control over their existence.[6] He "believes" they will exist; but s. 1 (2) does not use that word. Nevertheless, the result is so obviously the right one that it is almost certain that "intend or know" will be held to include "believe". The circumstance may be held to be intended because it is part of an intended result; or "know" may be construed broadly.

The second difficulty, which applies to both consequences and circumstances, is a new one, arising from the amendment made by the Criminal Attempts Act 1981, which added s. 1 (1) (b). If "course of conduct" includes the circumstances believed by the parties to exist, this provision is entirely unnecessary. It is necessary only if the *Nock*[7] interpretation of "course of conduct" is right. Parliament thus appears to have accepted that

3. *Bolton* (1991) 94 Cr App Rep 74, [1992] Crim LR 57.
4. They might be conspiracies to attempt. See, fn. 1, above.
5. Below.
6. For a further discussion of "intend or know", see the fourth edition of this book, 220–222 and [1977] Crim LR 602–605.
7. Above, p. 275.

interpretation and to have taken the sting out of it, so far as impossibility at the time of the agreement is concerned. The trouble with this approach is that it leaves other stings elsewhere. However, the argument that course of conduct must include intended consequences and foreseen circumstances is so compelling that s. 1 (1) (b) should be regarded as an "avoidance of doubt" provision, strictly unnecessary, but there for the guidance of the unwary. *Nock* is a discredited, though not overruled,[8] decision on the common law and should not be applied to the interpretation of the Act.

d) *Conspiracy to commit strict liability offences.* Section 1 (2) of the Act provides:

"Where liability for any offence may be incurred without knowledge on the part of the person committing it of any particular fact or circumstance necessary for the commission of the offence, a person shall nevertheless not be guilty of conspiracy to commit that offence by virtue of subsection (1) above unless he and at least one other party to the agreement intend or know that the fact or circumstance shall or will exist at the time when the conduct constituting the offence is to take place."

This provision is intended to ensure that strict liability and recklessness as to circumstances have no place in conspiracy. Intention or knowledge as to all the circumstances of the *actus reus* are to be required *even* where the agreement is to commit a crime which may be committed recklessly or a crime of strict liability. It is expressed to apply *only* to such conspiracies. A strict interpretation could thus lead to the conclusion that the intention or knowledge required by the subsection is *not* required where the offence in view *does* require knowledge. There is no express provision in s. 1 (1) requiring intention or knowledge as to circumstances. If D1 and D2 agree to take P out of the possession of her parents without their consent and D1 knows that she is only 15, there is no conspiracy if D2 believes she is 16 (or has no idea what age she is). Liability for this offence may be incurred without knowledge on the part of the person committing it of the fact of the girl's age; so s. 1 (2) is applicable. The following case has been put.

"But suppose in the same situation, D2's belief is that the girl is not in the possession of a parent or guardian (although D1 is under no misapprehension). It seems that D2 is guilty of conspiracy to commit the offence in section 20, Sexual Offences Act 1956, although if they did take the girl, D2 would not be guilty of that offence. Indeed it is precisely because he would not be so guilty, that he is guilty of conspiracy to commit the offence in section 20. Section 1 (2) fails to protect him because it only applies where liability for any offence may be incurred without knowledge ... of any fact or circumstance, and *Hibbert*[9] holds that there is no liability for the offence in section 20 without knowledge of the existence of a parent or guardian."[10]

It is difficult to suppose, however, that Parliament intended that the requirement of *mens rea* should be greater on a charge of conspiring to

8. See below, p. 318.
9. (1869) LR 1 CCR 184, above, p. 72.
10. Elliott [1978] Crim LR 204.

commit an offence of strict liability or recklessness than on a charge of conspiring to commit an offence requiring knowledge.[11] To avoid the "scandalous paradox"[12] revealed by the above example, reliance should be placed on the word "nevertheless" in s. 1 (2). Parliament might be taken to be saying "*Even* where liability for any offence may be incurred without knowledge, knowledge or intent is required on a charge of conspiracy"; and thus implying that, a fortiori, such knowledge or intent is required on a charge of conspiracy to commit an offence requiring knowledge.

e) *Existence of circumstance not known, intended or believed in.* It follows that the parties are not liable for conspiracy to commit any crime the *actus reus* of which includes a circumstance the existence of which they do not intend, or know of, or believe in. Suppose that D1 and D2 have been invited by E to have intercourse with E's wife, P. D1 and D2 confer together and are uncertain whether P is truly consenting or is merely submitting through fear of E. They agree, nevertheless, to have intercourse with her. P in fact is not consenting so, if they carry out the agreement, they will commit rape. Their recklessness whether she consents or not is a sufficient *mens rea* for rape.[13] In the *actual* circumstances, the carrying out of the agreement "will necessarily amount" to rape; but it is not a conspiracy to rape because it would not be rape in the circumstances which the parties intend, or know, or believe, shall or will exist. Recklessness as to circumstances of the *actus reus* is not a sufficient *mens rea* on a charge of conspiracy to commit a crime even where it is a sufficient *mens rea* for the crime itself.

f) *Unforeseen but inevitable consequences.* As noticed above,[14] Parliament deleted the provision in the Bill requiring an intention to cause any consequence which is an ingredient in the crime the parties are alleged to have conspired to commit. It is, however, submitted above that, notwithstanding *Anderson*, the parties must intend that at least one of them will pursue the course of conduct agreed upon. If so, they must be proved to have intended the foreseen consequences. Exceptionally, the agreed course of conduct may be such that it will necessarily cause a consequence not foreseen by the parties. For example, they agree to inflict a particular type of bodily harm, not appreciating that it will necessarily cause death. On a literal interpretation of the Act they are guilty of conspiracy to murder. In principle, that would be a wrong result, because killing is not intended and possibly not even foreseen as a possibility. It is thought that, here too, the answer lies in the construction of "course of conduct".[15] This should be read not only to include the consequences which are intended by the parties, but also to be limited to such consequences, whether they will in fact necessarily result or not. This is justifiable because it is the *agreed*

11. Smith [1977] Crim LR 606; Williams 127 NLJ 1166.
12. Elliott, loc. cit.
13. Sexual Offences (Amendment) Act 1976, below, p. 451.
14. Above, p. 272.
15. Above, p. 274.

course of conduct that we are concerned with; and the agreement does not include causing death.

If D1 and D2 agree to cause grievous bodily harm to P they are guilty of conspiring to commit an offence under s. 18 of the Offences against the Person Act 1861 but they are not guilty of conspiracy to murder although, if they carry out their intention and consequently P dies, they will be guilty of murder.[16] Similarly, an agreement to behave with gross negligence towards P is not a conspiracy to commit manslaughter, even though the parties will be guilty of manslaughter if they carry out the agreement and kill P.[17]

g) *Where only one party has mens rea.* Section 1 (2) makes it clear that, so far as the relevant circumstances are concerned, both parties to the agreement (or, where there are more than two parties, at least two of them) must have *mens rea*. If D1 and D2 agree to take P out of the possession of her parents without their consent and D1 knows that she is only 15, there is no conspiracy if D2 believes that she is 16.

The Law Commission's rejected subsection would have made similar provision for foresight of consequences, but there is no such provision in the Act. If, however, "course of conduct" is construed, as suggested above, to include intended consequences, and only intended consequences, the result is the same. There is no conspiracy to commit a particular crime unless at least two parties to the agreement intend that the consequences which are ingredients of that crime shall be caused. If D1 intends death and D2 intends grievous bodily harm, this is a conspiracy to cause grievous bodily harm but not a conspiracy to murder.

h) *Agreement to do acts of secondary participation.* Persons may agree to do an act which would render them liable to conviction as secondary parties if that offence were committed. Is an agreement to aid and abet an offence a conspiracy? The Criminal Attempts Act 1981[18] makes it clear that there can be no attempt to aid and abet an offence but it leaves open the question whether there can be a conspiracy to do so.[19]

D1 and D2, knowing that E intends to commit a burglary, agree to leave a ladder in a place where it will assist him to do so. E is not a party to that agreement. If E uses the ladder and commits burglary, D1 and D2 will be guilty of aiding and abetting him to do so. Are they guilty of conspiracy to commit burglary? If the course of conduct is placing the ladder, it seems clear that they are not. Placing the ladder is not an offence, not even an attempt to aid and abet burglary, since the Criminal Attempts Act 1981[20]

16. For an argument to the contrary, see 4th ed. of this work, 222–223 and [1977] Crim LR 638–639. Cf. Williams, 127 NLJ at 1169 and TBCL, 357–359.
17. A conspiracy to commit manslaughter seems a theoretical possibility in the case of a suicide pact or where the party to do the killing is suffering from diminished responsibility. Below, p. 300.
18. Section 1 (4) (b).
19. The question is discussed by Smith in *Crime, Proof and Punishment*, 21, 35–36 and 40–41.
20. Below, p. 315.

makes it clear that this is not an offence known to the law. It has been argued above[1] that "course of conduct" should be interpreted to include the consequences intended to follow from the conduct agreed upon, including the action of a third party to the agreement – in that example, P, who takes up the poisoned tea and drinks it. So it might be argued, consistently with that, the course of conduct ought to include E's use of the ladder in committing burglary. If that should be accepted, the next question would be whether the burglary is "the commission of any offence by one or more of the parties to the agreement". E is not a party to the agreement, so the question becomes, do the words "commission of any offence" include participation in the offence as a secondary party? Since all the parties to a conspiracy to commit an offence will be guilty of that offence if it is committed, but s. 1 (1) contemplates that it may be *committed* by only one of them, it is clear that "commission" means commission by a principal in the first degree. It is submitted therefore that an agreement to aid and abet an offence is not a conspiracy under the Act.

The above paragraphs were approved by the Court of Appeal in *Hollinshead*.[2] DD agreed to sell to X "black boxes", devices for altering electricity meters to show that less electricity had been used than was the fact. They expected X to re-sell the devices to consumers of electricity for use in defrauding electricity boards. The House of Lords[3] did not find it necessary to decide the matter and Lord Roskill said that it should be treated as open for consideration *de novo* if the question arises again. But there was clearly an agreement to aid and abet the consumers to commit offences under the Theft Act 1978, s. 2, against the electricity boards and, if that agreement were a statutory conspiracy, it could not under the then prevailing (though now repealed) rule in *Ayres*,[4] be a conspiracy to defraud. By upholding the conviction for conspiracy to defraud, the House implicitly decided that there was no statutory conspiracy and therefore that an agreement to aid and abet the consumers to commit an offence against the boards was not a statutory conspiracy.[5]

This, it is submitted, is the position under the Act. What of the common law? The Supreme Court of Hong Kong has held that there may be a common law conspiracy to aid and abet an offence. In *Po Koon-tai*,[6] the defendants, the owners of a ship in Hong Kong and the captain and crew on the high seas, agreed to land in Hong Kong certain refugees whom they had picked up at sea in desperate circumstances. The refugees were not alleged to be parties to the conspiracy but they committed the principal offence by landing in Hong Kong without permission. It was held that landing the refugees was "an unlawful act". The concept of the unlawful act in common law conspiracy was one of notorious elasticity but an English court might be reluctant to extend it to acts of aiding and abetting if the Criminal Law Act has been correctly interpreted above. The question

1. P. 274.
2. [1985] 1 All ER 850 at 858.
3. [1985] AC 975.
4. Above, p. 270.
5. See commentary on *Hollinshead* [1985] Crim LR 653 at 656.
6. [1980] HKLR 492.

arises only in the fields of fraud, corruption of morals and outraging public decency.

i) *Conditional intention*. The question of conditional intention requires separate consideration, particularly in the light of section 1 (1) of the Act. The parties may agree on alternative courses of action depending on the existence of some fact to be ascertained or some event which may or may not happen. If one of these courses of action involves the commission of a crime and the other does not, is this a conspiracy to commit the crime? Can it be said that, if the agreement is carried out in accordance with their intentions, the course of conduct pursued will *necessarily* amount to or involve the commission of an offence? Is not the agreement carried out in accordance with their intentions if, in the event, they take the non-criminal course? There are two decisions on the point. In *Reed*[7] A and B were held guilty of conspiring to aid and abet suicide[8] where they agreed that A would visit individuals contemplating suicide and either discourage them or actively help them, depending on his assessment of the appropriate course of action. In *Jackson*[9] A and B agreed with C that C should be shot in the leg so that, if he was convicted of the burglary for which he was being tried, the court would deal with him more leniently. They were guilty of conspiring to pervert the course of justice.

In each case, the court held that the following hypothetical case is distinguishable: A and B agree to drive from London to Edinburgh in a time which can be achieved without exceeding the speed limits, but only if the traffic which they encounter is exceptionally light. In this example, as in the two decisions, the parties have apparently agreed that, in a certain event, they will commit a crime. The difference appears to be that exceeding the speed limit is only incidental to the main object of the agreement – getting from London to Edinburgh in a certain time. In the decided cases, procuring the suicide or perverting justice is, in a certain event, to be "the object of the exercise". Are burglars guilty of conspiracy to murder if they set out to commit burglary, having agreed that, if it is necessary to do so in order to complete the burglary or to escape, they will shoot to kill? Presumably not – shooting to kill would be incidental to the achievement of an objective which might be achieved without it. On the other hand, there is clearly a conspiracy where the parties' objective is to commit a crime – but not if it proves too difficult or too dangerous – as where A and B agree that they will abandon their intention to commit burglary in No. 10 King Street if they find the house surrounded by police.

There is little authority at common law on the adequacy of conditional intention. The fact that an agreement is subject to express or implied reservations does not necessarily preclude conspiracy.[10] It is open to the courts to hold that any conditional intention is enough. If the parties

---

7. [1982] Crim LR 819, CA.

8. Aiding and abetting suicide is a substantive offence, so the rule that there is no offence of conspiracy to aid and abet an offence does not apply. Above, p. 279, below, p. 379.

9. [1985] Crim LR 442, CA.

10. *Mills* (1963) 47 Cr App Rep 49, [1963] Crim LR 181, CCA, and commentary. Cf. *Hussein* [1978] Crim LR 219, CA, and commentary, below, p. 548.

contemplate that, in a certain event, they will intentionally commit the unlawful act, they have a conditional intention. They agree to ask P to give them some money and, if he refuses, to make a statement they know to be false in order to persuade him. This would be a conspiracy to defraud. Possibly "conditional recklessness" would also be enough – in the last example, they agree that they will make the statement, realising that they do not know whether it is true or false.

j) *The object of the conspiracy.* An agreement to commit any offence, even an offence triable only summarily, is a conspiracy contrary to section 1 of the Act, triable on indictment.[11] Proceedings for conspiracy to commit any summary offence or offences may not be instituted except by or with the consent of the Director of Public Prosecutions[12] or, where prosecution for the summary offence itself so requires, by or with the consent of the Attorney-General.[13] Probably discretion will be exercised in the light of the reasons given by the Law Commission[14] for retaining the apparently anomalous rule that an agreement to commit a summary offence should be indictable. "We think that the only justification for prosecuting as conspiracy an agreement to commit summary offences is the social danger involved in the deliberate planning of offences on a widespread scale."

Such indictments at common law were particularly objectionable because they enabled the conspiracy to be punished so much more heavily than the actual commission of the summary offence and because they enabled the indictment to be brought after the time limit for the institution of summary proceedings had expired. As appears below, the Act goes some way towards meeting these objections.[15]

There was an exception at common law where the offence punishable summarily was defined so as to consist in an agreement and that agreement would not be a conspiracy at common law or to commit an offence under some other statute. In such a case a conspiracy charge alleges "the very offence which is created by the Act . . . and which the Act makes triable only as a summary offence"; and, therefore, no indictment would lie.[16]

11. There is one exception. An agreement to commit a summary offence, not punishable with imprisonment, is not a conspiracy if the offence is to be committed in contemplation or furtherance of a trade dispute: s. 1 (3). Section 3 of the Conspiracy, and Protection of Property Act 1875 is repealed: s. 5 (11). See [1977] Crim LR at 650.
12. Section 4 (1).
13. Section 4 (2).
14. Law Com. No. 76, para. 1. 85. The Commission refer to *Blamires Transport Services Ltd* [1964] 1 QB 278, [1963] 3 All ER 170 as a typical example of the sort of case they had in mind. The conspiracy to contravene certain provisions of the Road Traffic Acts extended over two years and included a large number of offences, all triable only summarily.
15. In *Blamires* the prosecution was brought several years after the offences had been committed. That would not be possible under the Act; but if the proceedings were instituted within the six-month limitation period, the fine of £1,000 would still be possible. It may be that the agreement, or part of it, amounted to a conspiracy to defraud (it was an agreement to make false records, presumably to deceive inspectors, cause them to act contrary to their duty and thereby, according to *Welham v Director of Public Prosecutions* [1961] AC 103, [1960] 1 All ER 805, to defraud them) in which case it must be indicted as such, and the limitation period is inapplicable.
16. *Barnett* [1951] 2 KB 425, [1951] 1 All ER 917, CCA, holding that there could be no indictment for a conspiracy amounting to a bidding agreement under the Auctions (Bidding Agreements) Act 1927. The agreement was not unlawful apart from the Act. (Offences under the Act are now triable on indictment: Auctions (Bidding Agreements) Act 1969 s. 1 (1)).

Such an agreement appears not to be a conspiracy under section 1 (1)[17] of the Act because it is the agreement itself, and not any course of conduct to be pursued, which amounts to the commission of an offence.[18]

An agreement to break a law which might be made in the future was not indictable at common law.[19] Suppose, however, that the parties agree to pursue a course of conduct which will offend against a statute passed but not in force at the time of the agreement. If, at the time of the agreement, a date has been fixed on which the statute will come into force and, if that date is before the agreed date of the course of conduct, it appears that there is a conspiracy. If the commencement date is fixed after the agreement and is before the agreed date of performance, the continuing agreement will become a conspiracy as soon as the date of commencement is fixed.

i) *Agreement in England to commit an offence abroad.* Section 1 (4) of the Act provides:

"In this Part of this Act 'offence' means an offence triable in England and Wales, except that it includes murder notwithstanding that the murder in question would not be so triable if committed in accordance with the intentions of the parties to the agreement."

This subsection (apart from the exception) codifies the law stated by the House of Lords in *Board of Trade v Owen*, where Lord Tucker justified the rule as follows:[20]

"The gist of the offence being the agreement, whether or not the object is attained, it may be asked why it should not be indictable if the object is situate abroad. I think the answer to this is that it is necessary to recognize the offence to aid in the preservation of the Queen's Peace and the maintenance of law and order within the realm with which, generally speaking, the criminal law is alone concerned."

Thus an agreement in Dover to commit an assault in Calais is not indictable here for the assault would not be triable here. An agreement in Dover there to procure a girl under the age of twenty-one to have unlawful sexual intercourse in Calais with a third person is indictable in England for the procuration, if it occurred, would be triable here.[1] An agreement in England by a British citizen to commit murder abroad is indictable in England apart from the exception in section 1 (4) for murder by a British citizen is indictable in England wherever it is committed.[2] The exception goes further. An agreement in England by aliens to commit murder abroad is indictable here, though the murder, if committed abroad, would *not* be triable here. An agreement in England to obtain property by deception abroad is not indictable as a conspiracy to defraud merely because it will cause loss to a person in England.[3]

17. It would, in any case, probably be a conspiracy to defraud, if it were a conspiracy at all.
18. Cf. s. 5 (6) which declares that *conspiracies* under the enactments shall be governed by the rules laid down by ss. 1 and 2 but shall not also be offences under s. 1.
19. *West* [1948] 1 KB 709, [1948] 1 All ER 718.
20. [1957] AC 602 at 625, [1957] 1 All ER 411 at 415.
 1. Sexual Offences Act 1956, s. 23 (1), below, p. 464.
 2. Below, p. 327. Bigamy by British citizens abroad is also indictable here.
 3. *A–G's Reference No. 1 of 1982* [1983] QB 751, [1983] 2 All ER 721. But see below, p. 290.

ii) *Agreement abroad to commit an offence in England*. The Act makes no express provision for this case. It has been clear since 1973[4] that, at common law, an agreement abroad to commit a crime in England is indictable here if an overt act is done in England in pursuance of the agreement. The Privy Council held in *Samchai Liangsiriprasert v United States Government*[5] that it is unnecessary to prove that any overt act was done in England. The only purpose of requiring an overt act could be to establish the link between the conspiracy and England or to show that the conspiracy was continuing and any other evidence which establishes this is just as good.

iii) *Agreement abroad to commit an offence abroad*. D1 and D2, British citizens in France, agree to kill P in France or to go through a ceremony of marriage there, both knowing that D1 is married. The offences contemplated are triable in England so, literally, these are indictable conspiracies under the Act. It may be, however, that the presumption against the extra-territorial application of the criminal law will exclude agreements not made within the jurisdiction and not intended to have any effect therein but this seems less likely after *Liangsiriprasert*.[6]

2 Common Law Conspiracies

a) *Conspiracy to defraud*. It was stated by the House of Lords in *Scott v Metropolitan Police Commissioner*[7] that:

"... it is clearly the law that an agreement by two or more by dishonesty to deprive a person of something which is his or to which he is or would be or might be entitled[8] and an agreement by two or more by dishonesty to injure some proprietary right of his, suffices to constitute the offence of conspiracy to defraud."[9]

In *Scott* D agreed with the employees of cinema owners that, in return for payment, they would abstract films without the consent of their employers, or of the owners of the copyright, in order that D might make copies infringing the copyright, and distribute them for profit. It was held that D was guilty of a conspiracy to defraud. It was immaterial that no one was deceived; the well-known definition of "defraud" by Buckley J in *Re London and Globe Finance Corporation Ltd*,[10] "to defraud is by deceit to induce a course of action", is not exhaustive. Larceny was an offence which

---

4. *DPP v Doot* [1973] AC 807, [1973] 1 All ER 940
5. (1990) 92 Cr App Rep 77, PC (a case of extradition from Hong Kong to USA, but applying the common law of England), followed in *Sanson* [1991] Crim LR 126 where, however, one of the conspirators had acted in England in pursuance of the conspiracy.
6. Cf. the corresponding problem in attempts, below, p. 316.
7. [1975] AC 819, [1974] 3 All ER 1032.
8. In *Tarling v Government of the Republic of Singapore* (1978) 70 Cr App Rep 77, [1978] Crim LR 490 the House of Lords by a majority held that the intention of company directors to make and retain a secret profit for which they would have been accountable to the shareholders was not evidence of an intention to defraud. See, however, Smith [1979] Crim LR 220 at 225–226.
9. Per Viscount Dilhorne at 1039.
10. [1903] 1 Ch 728 at 732, 733.

had to be committed "fraudulently", but deceit has never been a necessary ingredient of theft. The majority of the authorities relied on were in fact conspiracies to steal or to do acts which included theft, though the defrauding was not necessarily confined to theft. In *Button*[11] DD were convicted of conspiracy to use their employer's vats and dyes to dye articles which they were not permitted to dye in order to make profits for themselves and so to defraud their employer of the profit. The dyes were no doubt stolen; but the employer did not have a proprietary interest in the profit so that the appropriation of it did not constitute a substantive offence.[12] The great majority of agreements to defraud will be agreements to commit offences under the Theft Acts but clearly there are cases amounting to fraud within the definition in *Scott* which are not substantive offences. An example is the appropriation of the profit in *Button*. The Criminal Law Revision Committee considered whether such conduct should be brought within the definition of theft and concluded:

"... although the conduct, when it occurs, is reprehensible enough to deserve punishment, it does not seem to us that it occurs often enough to involve a substantial problem or to require the creation of a new criminal offence."[13]

Parliament presumably accepted this view, as it certainly accepted, after full debate, that temporarily to deprive another of his property should not be theft; yet an agreement so to do is clearly capable of amounting to conspiracy under the decision in *Scott*. Likewise with the case where D1 and D2 agree to shift D1's boundary fence so as to appropriate P's land – an act which is not, by specific decision of Parliament, theft, but evidently a conspiracy to defraud.

It is clear that P is defrauded if he is induced to take an economic risk which he would not have taken but for a deception.[14] It is no answer that D believed that the speculation was a good one and that P had a good chance of making a profit. If P is induced to part with something of economic value, he is probably defrauded even if he does receive the promised return.[15]

The proposition in *Scott* is not an exclusive definition of conspiracy to defraud. It is confined to economic prejudice; but a person is also defrauded if he is deceived into acting contrary to his public duty.[16] So it would be a conspiracy to defraud to agree by deception to induce a public official to grant an export licence,[17] or to supply information[18] or to induce a

---

11. (1848) 11 QB 929.
12. (1956) 19 MLR 39.
13. Cmnd. 2977, p. 29.
14. *Allsop* (1976) 64 Cr App Rep 29, [1976] Crim LR 738, CA and commentary; cf. *Hamilton* (1845) 1 Cox CC 244, *Carpenter* (1911) 22 Cox CC 618.
15. *Potger* (1970) 55 Cr App Rep 42; Smith, *Law of Theft* para. [184].
16. *Welham v Director of Public Prosecutions* [1961] AC 103, [1960] 1 All ER 805; below, p. 291. *Welham* was followed in *Terry* [1984] AC 374, [1984] 1 All ER 65, HL. (D, who uses an excise licence belonging to another vehicle intending to cause police officers to act on the assumption that it belongs to his vehicle, has an intention to defraud, even though he intends to pay the licence fee.)
17. *Board of Trade v Owen* [1957] AC 602, [1957] 1 All ER 411.
18. *Director of Public Prosecutions v Withers* [1975] AC 842, [1974] 3 All ER 984.

professional body to accept an unqualified person as a member,[19] assuming, in each case, that it was the duty of the person so deceived not to do as asked in the actual circumstances of the case. If the public official is persuaded by means other than deception – for example, bribes or threats – to act contrary to his duty, he is obviously not defrauded and the agreement is not a conspiracy unless it can be said that those affected by the breach of duty have been defrauded – e.g. those persons about whom the confidential information is disclosed or, more likely, perhaps, the official's superiors whose duty to keep the information secret has been vicariously violated. Most conspiracies to pervert the course of justice consist in agreements to deceive a public official so that he acts contrary to his duty and are conspiracies to defraud.

Some of their lordships in *Withers*[20] thought that this principle is strictly confined to public officials, and does not extend to the case of a bank manager deceived into breaking his contractual duty. However in *Wai Yu-tsang v R*[1] the Privy Council said that the cases concerned with public duties are not to be regarded as a special category but as examples of the general principle that conspiracy to defraud does not require an intention to cause economic loss. The Board, disapproving Lord Diplock's more restrictive statement in *Scott*,[2] preferred the broad propositions of Lord Denning – "If anyone may be prejudiced in any way by the fraud, that is enough" – and Lord Radcliffe, who agreed with Lord Denning and used similar language, in *Welham*.[3] This seems to open a very broad vista of potential criminal liability and, if followed, may give a new impetus to the Law Commission's prolonged search for a suitable statutory definition of "defraud".

b) *Intention to defraud.* If a person is defrauded when he is "prejudiced" conspirators clearly have a sufficient *mens rea* if it is their purpose to cause that prejudice. There are dicta to the effect that such a purpose is required but in *Wai Yu-tsang* the Privy Council thought this too restrictive and that it is enough that the parties have *agreed to cause* the prejudice. If they have agreed to cause it, i.e., to defraud, they intend to defraud, and it is immaterial that defrauding is not their purpose. The purpose of fraudsters is almost always to make a profit for themselves, not to cause loss to another. They act out of greed, not spite. Since they know that they can make a gain only by causing loss or prejudice, they intend to cause the loss or prejudice, even though they have no wish to cause it and perhaps regret the "necessity" of doing so in order to achieve their object.

In the light of these principles *A-G's Reference (No 1 of 1982)* (the "whisky-label case")[4] is a doubtful decision. The defendants were charged with conspiracy to defraud X Co by causing loss by unlawful labelling, sale and supply of whisky, falsely purporting to be "X label" products. The

19. *Bassey* (1931) 22 Cr App Rep 160, CCA.
20. [1975] AC 842, [1974] 3 All ER 984.
 1. [1991] 4 All ER 664 at 670, PC.
 2. [1975] AC 819 at 840–841.
 3. [1961] AC 103 at 133 and 124 respectively.
 4. [1983] QB 751, [1983] 2 All ER 721, [1983] Crim LR 534 and commentary.

agreement was made in England but the whisky was to be sold in Lebanon. The ratio decidendi was that the trial judge had rightly held that he had no jurisdiction to try the indictment because the contemplated crime in Lebanon (obtaining by deception from the purchasers of the whisky) would not have been indictable in England. One reason for holding that there was no conspiracy to defraud X Co was that this was not the "true object" of the agreement. Damage to X Co would have been "a side effect or incidental consequence of the conspiracy and not its object".[5] This must now be considered in the light of the decision of the House of Lords in *Cooke*.[6] British Rail stewards boarded a train, equipped with their own food which they dishonestly sold to passengers, instead of that provided by their employers, intending to keep the proceeds of sale for themselves. They were probably guilty in law of going equipped to cheat the passengers and, when they sold food to them, of obtaining the price by deception.[7] Whether this was so or not, the House had no difficulty in holding that they were guilty of conspiracy to defraud British Rail. It is true that the House was preoccupied with the problem of distinguishing *Ayres*, the "whisky-label case" was not cited and it does not appear that it was argued that the loss to British Rail was "a side effect or incidental consequence". Nevertheless, it is clear that this was a case where the object of the conspirators was to make a profit out of the customers, not to defraud British Rail. Of course, one must agree with Lord Lane CJ in the "whisky-label case"[8] that, "It would be contrary to principle, as well as being impracticable for the courts, to attribute to defendants constructive intentions to defraud third parties based on what the defendants should have foreseen as probable or possible consequences." Constructive intentions are to be abhorred; but presumably the House in *Cooke* thought that a jury could properly find that the defendants must have known that their conduct would, inevitably, cause loss to British Rail. If so, it was right to hold that they *intended*[9] to defraud BR and it should be immaterial that this was not their purpose. Of course, the intention must be proved. Thus, the use abroad of a stolen cheque book and cheque card is capable of being fraud on a bank in England because the effect is to cause the bank in England to meet its legal or commercial obligation to honour the cheque; but, if D is charged with conspiracy to defraud the bank, the jury must be directed that he appreciated that his conduct would have this effect.[10] Subject to the jurisdictional problem, considered below, it is submitted that, on a proper direction, the whisky-label conspirators might properly have been convicted of conspiracy to defraud the X Co. They were probably much more sophisticated than the BR stewards in *Cooke* and better able to appreciate the effect of their

5. [1983] 2 All ER 724. But in *R v Governor of Pentonville Prison, ex p Osman* (1990) 90 Cr App Rep 281 at 298 it was held, distinguishing the whisky-label case, that a conspiracy to deprive P of dollars in the United States was only the means to effecting the "true object" of the conspiracy which was the defrauding of P in Hong Kong. The distinction is not blindingly obvious.
6. [1986] AC 909, [1986] 2 All ER 985, [1987] Crim LR 114.
7. Below, p. 555.
8. [1983] 2 All ER at 724.
9. Above, p. 54.
10. *McPherson and Watts* [1985] Crim LR 508.

actions on third parties. This applies equally to the facts of the "Chanel case",[11] where the facts were similar.

c) *Prejudice includes putting at risk.* If the conspirators know that the effect of carrying out the agreement will be to put P's property at risk, then they intend prejudice to P and, if they are dishonest, they are guilty of conspiracy to defraud him. This is so notwithstanding that it turns out that P's property is unimpaired, or even that he makes a profit out of the transaction. A clear example would be where the conspirators agree to take P's money without his consent and put it on a horse at 20 to 1. They have agreed to defraud him and the conspiracy is not undone even if the horse wins and, as they intended throughout, they pay half the winnings into his bank account. This, it is submitted is the best explanation of *Allsop*.[12] The judgment is difficult because of its reliance on two dicta of Lord Diplock which were mutually inconsistent and have both since been disapproved; but the decision on the facts is readily explicable. D was a "sub-broker" for a hire-purchase finance company, P. His function was to introduce prospective hire-purchasers who wished to acquire cars. In collusion with others, he filled in application forms with false statements about the value of the cars and the payment of deposits so as to cause P to accept applications for hire-purchase finance which, otherwise, they might have rejected. He expected and believed that the transactions he introduced would be duly completed, so that P would achieve their contemplated profit to the advantage of all concerned, including D who got his commission. His defence was that he did not intend P to suffer any pecuniary loss or be prejudiced in any way. The court found that P was defrauded when he was induced to do the very acts which D intended him to do. P paid an excessive price for cars and advanced money to persons who were not as creditworthy as they were alleged to be. This not merely put him at risk of being defrauded, but actually defrauded him: "Interests which are imperilled are less valuable in terms of money than those same interests when they are secure and protected".[13] The result intended by D was, in law, the defrauding of P; and P was in law defrauded. It is wholly immaterial whether D would have regarded that result as "fraud". If he did not, he was making a mistake of law.

According to this explanation D intended to prejudice P. The facts admitted of no other interpretation. But the judge had directed the jury that they could convict if they were satisfied that D realised that his conduct was *likely to lead* to the detriment or prejudice of P. If this is taken literally, it is sufficient that D is reckless (in the Cunningham sense) whether prejudice – i.e., defrauding – occurs. It is submitted that this would be going too far and take common law conspiracy out of line with statutory conspiracy. In *Wai Yu-tsang* the Privy Council expressed a reluctance "to allow this part of the law to become enmeshed in a

---

11. *Pain, Jory and Hawkins* (1985) 82 Cr App Rep 141.
12. (1976) 64 Cr App Rep 29.
13. (1976) 64 Cr App Rep at 32.

distinction, sometimes artificially drawn between intention and recklessness"; but they then said, of *Allsop* and the instant case, that it is enough that:

"the conspirators have dishonestly agreed to bring about a state of affairs which they realise will *or may* [authors' italics] deceive the victim into so acting, or failing to act, that he will suffer economic loss or his economic interests will be put at risk."

The use of the words, "or may", admit recklessness as a sufficient *mens rea* – it is enough that the parties have taken a conscious risk of causing prejudice. This was probably not necessary to the decision since the trial judge had directed the jury that D was guilty if he knew what he had done "would cause detriment or prejudice to another".

d) *Dishonesty in putting property at risk.* The intention to defraud is readily discernible in *Allsop* where there could be no question of P believing he had any right to do what he did. More difficult is the case where company directors take a risk with the company's property, perhaps hoping to make a large profit and so benefit the shareholders. If the risk taken was such that "no director could have honestly believed . . . it was in the interest of that company that the risk should be taken",[14] then the company is defrauded. Whether a risk is unjustifiable is a question of judgment and a matter of degree. There is no clear dividing line between right and wrong, such as was crossed in *Allsop* when false statements were made or in *Wai Yu-tseng* where the dishonouring of cheques was concealed in a bank account. Whether the risk is so grave that no director could believe it justified is equally a matter of judgment and degree. Conspiracy to defraud thus lacks the precision that we should normally look for in an offence. In *Landy*[15] the Court of Appeal proposed a model of how an indictment should be drawn for the facts of that case. The words italicised by the authors illustrate these points:

"Causing and permitting the Bank to make *excessive* advances to *insubstantial* and *speculative* trading companies incorporated in Liechtenstein and Switzerland, such advances being *inadequately* guaranteed and without *proper* provision for payment of interest."[16]

Dishonesty is an essential constituent of the *mens rea* but there has been controversy about what "dishonesty" means in this context. In *Landy*[17] the court appeared to think that the ultimate test was whether the *defendant* thought his conduct dishonest. In *McIvor*[18] the court reiterated this view, holding that the test in theft is different; but, shortly afterwards in *Ghosh*[19] it was held that the same test should be applied in conspiracy to defraud as in theft. The standard of honesty is that of ordinary decent people and D is dishonest if he realises he is acting contrary to that standard. In theft, D is

14. *Sinclair* [1968] 3 All ER 241, 52 Cr App Rep 618.
15. [1981] 1 All ER 1172, 72 Cr App Rep 237.
16. [1981] 1 All ER at 1179.
17. [1981] 1 All ER 1172 at 1181.
18. [1982] 1 All ER 491, [1982] 1 WLR 409.
19. [1982] QB 1053, [1982] 2 All ER 689. See *Cox and Hodges* [1983] Crim LR 167 and commentary (fraudulent trading).

not dishonest if he believes he has a right to do the act in question and this must also apply in conspiracy. If, however, he knows that no "ordinary decent company director" would take the risk in question, then he knows that the risk is an unjustifiable one and it is dishonest for him to take it.[20] The test proposed in *Sinclair*[1] accords with this. If *no* director could have believed the risk was justified, it follows that the defendant did not; but it would seem right that the jury should be directed that they must find this is so.

e) *Fraud – by whom?* In statutory conspiracy it is expressly provided that the contemplated offence is to be committed "by one or more of the parties to the agreement".[2] In *Hollinshead*[3] the Court of Appeal held that this was a restatement of the common law, so the same principle applied to conspiracy to defraud: the contemplated fraud must be one which is to be perpetrated by one of the parties to the agreement in the course of carrying it out. But complete execution of the agreement to sell the black boxes would not defraud anyone. The parties contemplated that the fraud would be carried out by other persons, not yet ascertained, who would buy the boxes and use them to defraud the electricity boards. The court therefore quashed the convictions for conspiracy to defraud – but they were restored by the House of Lords. The House held that the "purpose" of the defendants was to cause economic loss to the electricity boards. This is difficult to understand. Their purpose was to make a profit by selling the devices to the (as they thought) middleman. Presumably they did not care what happened to the boxes after that. If they had been accidentally destroyed in a fire, they would not consider that their enterprise had failed. On the contrary they might have been pleased at the prospect of selling some more. The House seems to have been much influenced by the fact that the boxes were "dishonest devices" with only one "purpose", which was to cause loss. But "purpose" is here used in the sense of "function". An inanimate thing cannot have a "purpose" (any more than it can be "dishonest") in the sense in which that word is used in the law of conspiracy. However that may be, *Hollinshead* seems to broaden the law of conspiracy to defraud to include the case where the defendants contemplate that the execution of their agreement will enable some third party to perpetrate a fraud.

f) *Jurisdiction over conspiracy to defraud.* An agreement in England to carry out a fraud abroad is not indictable as a conspiracy to defraud in England. But the question remains, where is the fraud committed? Where DD, by acts done abroad, cause P in England to incur obligations to do acts in England, it seems that P is defrauded in England and there is an indictable conspiracy to defraud.[4] But what if the fraud committed abroad merely

20. For a remarkable difference of opinion in the House of Lords as to whether there was evidence of dishonesty, see *Tarling v Government of the Republic of Singapore* (1978) 70 Cr App Rep 77. See, on this case, Smith, [1979] Crim LR 220.
   1. Above, fn. 14.
   2. Criminal Law Act 1977, s. 1(1)(a), above, p. 271.
   3. [1985] 1 All ER 850 at 857, above, p. 280.
   4. *McPherson and Watts* [1985] Crim LR 508, above, p. 287. Cf. *Beck* [1985] 1 All ER 571, [1985] 1 WLR 22.

causes an economic loss to P in England? In the *"whisky-label* case" it seems to be assumed that this is not an indictable conspiracy to defraud. Yet is not P equally defrauded whether the act is done at home or abroad? When, in the near future, British Rail can go through the Channel tunnel will they be any less defrauded by sales made by the dishonest stewards after the train has passed the middle of the Channel?

In cases like *Scott*,[5] the *whisky-label case* and *Cooke* P is caused a loss in two ways. Take *Scott*: (i) Because of the circulation of the pirated copies, P will sell fewer legitimate copies; and (ii) DD intended to keep the profits from the sale of the pirated copies for which, in law, they were bound to account to P.[6] The same applies to the sale of the bogus whisky and food in the other two cases. In the case of the BR stewards, it might be argued that they were continuing to defraud in the second respect in England, because they would fail to account on their return. But that is an evasion of the substance of the matter. The truth is that P is equally defrauded in these cases wherever P does the acts in question. Lord Radcliffe has said:[7]

"Now I think that there are one or two things that can be said with confidence about the meaning of this word 'defraud'. It requires a person as its object; that is, defrauding involves doing something to someone. Although in the nature of things it is almost invariably associated with the obtaining of an advantage for the person who commits the fraud, it is the effect on the person who is the object of the fraud that ultimately determines its meaning."

Just as a person can be killed or wounded only in the place where he is, so, arguably, he can be defrauded only in the place where he is. It may be that this would extend the limits of jurisdiction beyond the traditional understanding of their boundaries; but fraud is now much more international than ever before and, in the absence of clear authority to the contrary, the way may be open for the courts to take this step.[8]

g) *Conspiracy to corrupt public morals.* In *Shaw v Director of Public Prosecutions* the House of Lords (Lord Reid dissenting) held that a conspiracy to corrupt public morals is an offence. D published the Ladies' Directory which advertised the names and addresses of prostitutes with, in some cases, photographs and, in others, particulars of sexual perversions which they were willing to practise. He was convicted of (1) conspiring to corrupt public morals; (2) living on the earnings of prostitution[9] and (3) publishing an obscene article, contrary to the Obscene Publications Act 1959, s. 2 (1).[10] His conviction on all counts was upheld by the Court of Criminal Appeal and the House dismissed his further appeal in respect of

5. Above, p. 284.
6. *Reading v A-G* [1951] AC 507, [1951] 1 All ER 617.
7. *Welham v Director of Public Prosecutions* [1961] AC 103 at 123, [1960] 1 All ER 805 at 808, HL.
8. See also *Tomsett* [1985] Crim LR 369, CA, and commentary and the discussion of *Tarling's case* (1979) 70 Cr App Rep 77 in [1979] Crim LR 221.
9. Contrary to s. 30 of the Sexual Offences Act 1956.
10. Considered below, p. 730. Leave to appeal on that count was refused by the Court of Criminal Appeal. See the puzzling remarks by Lord Reid [1962] AC 220 at 280, [1961] 2 All ER 446 at 460 ; and see [1961] Crim LR 473, n. 2a.

counts (1) and (2). Lord Tucker, with whose speech the majority agreed, was of the opinion that there was an offence of conspiring to commit a public mischief and that the corruption of public morals was a public mischief; but he did not reject the view of the Court of Criminal Appeal that to corrupt public morals is a substantive offence. Lord Simon in *Director of Public Prosecutions v Withers*[11] concluded that there were three possible *rationes decidendi*.

(i) There is a substantive offence of corrupting public morals, so an agreement to do so is a conspiracy.

(ii) The corruption of public morals is a separate head of conspiracy.

(iii) There is an offence of conspiracy to effect a public mischief and the corruption of public morals is a public mischief.

Lord Simon held that it was open to the House to reject *ratio* (iii) and, indeed, the decision does so. Since Lord Tucker did not decide that there is a substantive offence of corrupting public morals, it seems clear that the *ratio* must be taken to be (ii). It is therefore uncertain whether an agreement to corrupt public morals is a statutory conspiracy; but judges of first instance may consider themselves bound by the decision of the Court of Criminal Appeal to hold that it is. *Shaw* was followed in *Knuller*[12] where, Lord Diplock dissenting, the House held that an agreement to publish advertisements to facilitate the commission of homosexual acts between adult males in private was a conspiracy to corrupt public morals, although such conduct is no longer a crime.[13] Lord Reid maintained his view that *Shaw* was wrongly decided but held that it should nevertheless be followed in the interests of certainty in the law. Given the existence of the offence, he thought there was sufficient evidence of its commission here:

"... there is a material difference between merely exempting certain conduct from criminal penalties and making it lawful in the full sense ... I read [the Sexual Offences Act 1967[14]] as saying that, even though it may be corrupting, if people choose to corrupt themselves in this way that is their affair and the law will not interfere. But no licence is given to others to encourage the practice."[15]

In *Shaw*, Lord Simonds used language which suggested that the House was asserting the right to expand the scope of the criminal law:[16]

"In the sphere of criminal law I entertain no doubt that there remains in the courts of law a residual power to enforce the supreme and fundamental purpose of the law, to conserve not only the safety and order but also the moral welfare of the State, and that it is their duty to guard it against attacks which may be the more insidious because they are novel and unprepared for."

11. [1974] 3 All ER 984 at 1003. Above, p. 269.
12. [1973] AC 435, [1972] 2 All ER 898.
13. Below, p. 477.
14. Below, p. 477.
15. [1972] 2 All ER at 904.
16. [1962] AC 220 at 267, [1961] 2 All ER 446 at 452. For a judicial view to the contrary, see Stephen, 3 HCL 359. See Seaborne Davies, *Annual Survey of English Law* (1932), 276–277. For criticism of *Shaw*, see Seaborne Davies (1962), 6 JSPTL (NS) 104; Goodhart (1961) 77 LQR 560; Hall Williams (1961) 24 MLR 626; and [1961] Crim LR 470.

In *Knuller*, however, the House was emphatic that there is no residual power to create new offences. That is a task for Parliament.

"What the courts can and should do (as was truly laid down in *Shaw*'s case) is to recognise the applicability of established offences to new circumstances to which they are relevant."[17]

Moreover, a finding that conduct is liable to corrupt public morals is one not lightly to be reached. It is not enough that it is liable to "lead morally astray." Lord Simon of Glaisdale went so far as to say that—

"The words 'corrupt public morals' suggest conduct which a jury might find to be destructive of the very fabric of society."[18]

h) *Conspiracy to outrage public decency.* A majority of the House in *Knuller* (Lords Reid and Diplock dissenting) held that there is a common law offence of outraging public decency[19] and, consequently, it is an offence to conspire to outrage public decency. The particular offences previously recognised – keeping a disorderly house, mounting an indecent exhibition and indecent exposure – were particular applications of a general rule. It is not an answer to show that outrageously indecent matter is only on the inside pages of a book or magazine which is sold in public. But—

"... 'outrage', like 'corrupt' is a very strong word. 'Outraging public decency' goes considerably beyond offending the susceptibilities of, or even shocking, reasonable people ... [T]he offence is concerned with recognised minimum standards of decency, which are likely to vary from time to time ... [N]otwithstanding that 'public' in the offence is used in a locative sense, public decency must be viewed as a whole; and ... the jury should be invited, where appropriate, to remember that they live in a plural society, with a tradition of tolerance towards minorities, and that this atmosphere of tolerance is itself part of public decency."[20]

Lords Simon and Kilbrandon (Lord Morris dissenting) thought that the jury had not been adequately directed in accordance with these principles and, accordingly, that the conviction must be quashed.

3) *The Actus Reus of Conspiracy*

1 The Agreement
It may be that an agreement in the strict sense required by the law of contract is not necessary[1] but the parties must at least have reached a decision[2] to perpetrate the unlawful object. In *Walker*[3] a conviction was

---

17. [1972] 2 All ER at 932, per Lord Simon of Glaisdale.
18. Cf. Lord Devlin's views, above, p. 17.
19. See below pp. 748–749; following *Mayling* [1963] 2 QB 717, [1963] 1 All ER 687, CCA.
20. [1972] 2 All ER at 936, per Lord Simon.
   1. See Orchard, "Agreement in Criminal Conspiracy" [1974] Crim LR 297 and 335.
   2. Cf. Williams, CLGP, 212.
   3. [1962] Crim LR 458. *Mulcahy v R* (1868) LR 3 HL 306 at 317.

quashed although it was "perfectly clear" that D had discussed with others the proposition of stealing a payroll, because it was not proved that they had got beyond the stage of negotiation when D withdrew.

If A agrees to sell B certain goods, known to both to be stolen, at "a price to be agreed between us", they have not (apart from the question of illegality) reached the stage of a concluded contract.[4] Is there an indictable conspiracy? It is thought that there probably is; though it is arguable that the situation is no different from that where the parties are bargaining as to the price of stolen goods and are clearly, therefore, still at the stage of negotiation.

A single agreement may involve two or more conspiracies. Where the defendants agreed to buy cannabis in Thailand and import it into the UK a conviction in Thailand for conspiracy there to possess cannabis for sale did not bar a prosecution in England for conspiracy to import the cannabis into England. There were two distinct conspiracies and it was immaterial that the evidence proving both might be the same.[5] An agreement by BR stewards to sell their own food on trains instead of BR's and keep the profits is a conspiracy to defraud BR and, it seems, a second conspiracy to cheat the passengers.[6] But where there is a general conspiracy to commit offences of a certain type, agreements to commit particular offences of that type may be treated simply as evidence of the general conspiracy.[7]

It is probably not essential that the agreement should have been made prior to the concerted action. If, when D1 is taking steps towards the commission of a crime D2 comes to his assistance and the two work in concert, they might thereby be held to have conspired;[8] but if D1 is unaware of, or rejects D2's assistance, there is no conspiracy,[9] though D2 might be held to be an abettor of any offence or attempt consummated by D1.[10] The same principles probably apply to statutory conspiracy.

2 Proof of the Agreement

The question of what is a sufficient agreement to found a charge of conspiracy is one of several questions in the criminal law which are aggravated by a confusion between the substantive law and the law of evidence. The actual agreement in most cases will probably take place in private and direct evidence of it will rarely be available. A very frequent way of proving it is by showing that the parties concerted in the pursuit of a common object in such a manner as to show that their actions must have

---

4. *May and Butcher Ltd v R* [1934] 2 KB 17n, HL.
5. *Lavercombe* [1988] Crim LR 435.
6. *Cooke* [1986] AC 909, [1986] 2 All ER 985, HL.
7. *Hammersley* (1958) 42 Cr App Rep 207, "the Brighton Conspiracy Case", discussed in [1958] Crim LR 422–429 where the acts alleged ranged over a period of eight years and involved numerous illegal agreements with other persons, yet the court contrived to hold that only one conspiracy to obstruct the course of justice, evidenced by a large number of overt acts, was disclosed by the indictment. Cf. *Edwards* [1991] Crim LR 45.
8. *Leigh* (1775) 1 Car & Kir 28n. *Tibbits and Windust* [1902] 1 KB 77, CCR.
9. *State v Tally* (1894) 102 Ala 25; Michael & Wechsler's Cases 699; *Hawkesley* [1959] Crim LR 211 (QS).
10. *Rannath Mohan v R* [1967] 2 AC 187, [1967] 2 All ER 58, PC.

been co-ordinated by arrangement beforehand.[11] The danger is that the importance attached to the acts done may obscure the fact that these acts do not in themselves constitute a conspiracy, but are only evidence of it. If the jury are left in reasonable doubt, when all the evidence is in, whether the two accused persons were acting in pursuance of an agreement, they should acquit, even though the evidence shows that they were simultaneously pursuing the same object.[12]

It may not be necessary to show that the persons accused of conspiring together were in direct communication with one another. Thus, it may be that the conspiracy revolves around some third party, X, who is in touch with each of D1, D2, D3, though they are not in touch with one another (a "wheel conspiracy"); or D1 may communicate with X, X with D2, D2 with Y, Y with D3 (a "chain conspiracy"). Provided that the result is that they have a common design – for example, to rob a particular bank – D1, D2 and D3 may properly be indicted for conspiring together though they have never been in touch with one another until they meet in the dock. It must be proved, of course, that each accused has agreed with another guilty person in relation to that single conspiracy.[13]

"What has to be ascertained is always the same matter: is it true to say . . . that the acts of the accused were done in pursuance of a criminal purpose held in common between them?"[14]

These propositions, for which there is ample authority,[15] are stated in the case of *Meyrick*,[16] though that case itself seems a questionable application of them. D1 and D2, night-club proprietors, each offered bribes to a police sergeant, E, to induce him to connive at breaches of the licensing laws. They were convicted of conspiring to, inter alia, contravene the licensing laws.

The jury were directed that there must be a "common design" and, by their verdict of guilty, they so found but it is difficult to see how the evidence justified this finding. The design of each night club proprietor was simply to evade the licensing laws in respect of his own premises.

Meyrick was distinguished in *Griffiths*[17] on the rather unconvincing ground that

11. *Cooper and Compton* [1947] 2 All ER 701; *Hammersley* (1958) 42 Cr App Rep 207. Lord Diplock thinks that it is "a legal fiction" (*Director of Public Prosecutions v Bhagwan* [1970] 3 All ER 97 at 104) and "the height of sophistry" (*Knuller (Publishing, Printing and Promotions) Ltd v Director of Public Prosecutions* [1972] 2 All ER 898 at 921) that the offence lies not in the concerted action but in the inferred anterior agreement; but the law is clear that it is the agreement that is the offence. The concerted action is evidence of the crime, but not the crime itself.
12. Where there are counts for both conspiracy and the ulterior crime and the only evidence of conspiracy is the collaboration of the parties in the completion of the ulterior crime, the only logical verdicts are guilty of both conspiracy and the ulterior crime or not guilty of both. Thus in *Cooper and Compton* [1947] 2 All ER 701, the court quashed a verdict of guilty of conspiracy as inconsistent with a verdict of not guilty of larceny. Conversely, in *Beach and Owens* [1957] Crim LR 687, a verdict of guilty of attempt to pervert the course of justice was quashed as inconsistent with a failure to agree on a conspiracy count.
13. *Ardalan* [1972] 2 All ER 257 at 261.
14. *Meyrick* (1929) 21 Cr App Rep 94 at 102 and *Griffiths* [1966] 1 QB 589, [1965] 2 All ER 448 applied in *Chrastny* [1992] 1 All ER 189, [1991] 1 WLR 1381, CA.
15. See e.g. *Cooper and Compton*, above; *Sweetland* (1957) 42 Cr App Rep 62.
16. See above, fn. 14.
17. (1965) 49 Cr App Rep 279.

". . . the conspiracy alleged [in *Meyrick*] was . . . in relation to a comparatively small geographical area, namely Soho. In view of the size and nature of the locality, there were clearly facts upon which a jury could come to the conclusion that the night club proprietors in that district well knew what was happening generally in relation to the police."[18]

Even if D1 and D2 each knew that the other had made a similar agreement with E, it would seem that there were two conspiracies not one. Paull J has put the following example:

"I employ an accountant to make out my tax return. He and his clerk are both present when I am about to sign the return. I notice an item in my expenses of £100 and say: 'I don't remember incurring this expense.' The clerk says: 'Well, actually I put it in. You didn't incur it, but I didn't think you would object to a few pounds being saved.' The accountant indicates his agreement to this attitude. After some hesitation I agree to let it stand. On those bare facts I cannot be charged with fifty others in a conspiracy to defraud the Exchequer of £100,000 on the basis that this accountant and his clerk have persuaded 500 other clients to make false returns, some being false in one way, some in another, or even all in the same way. I have not knowingly attached myself to a general agreement to defraud."[19]

It is submitted that the position would be no different if the accountant had said: "We do this for all our clients"; there would still have been a series of conspiracies, not one general conspiracy. The convictions in *Griffiths* were indeed quashed on the ground that the evidence, while perhaps sufficient to establish a series of separate conspiracies, did not establish the single "wheel conspiracy" alleged. A count charging a general conspiracy is not bad because the evidence offered to prove it includes subsequent subsidiary conspiracies.[20] If A and B set up an organisation to plant bombs, that is a conspiracy and indictable as such, though the overt acts offered to prove it consist in further agreements to plant particular bombs. Those further agreements are indictable as separate conspiracies, notwithstanding the existence of the general conspiracy;[1] and acquittal or conviction of one such alleged conspiracy is no bar to trial for another.

3 Conspiracy where the Contemplated Offence is Committed

The courts discourage the charging of conspiracy where there is evidence of the complete crime:

". . . when the proof intended to be submitted to a jury is proof of the actual commission of crime, it is not the proper course to charge the parties with conspiracy to commit it, for the course operates, it is manifest, unfairly and unjustly against the parties accused; the prosecutors are thus enabled to combine in one indictment a variety of offences, which, if treated individually, as they ought to be, would exclude the possibility of giving evidence against one defendant to the prejudice of

18. Ibid., at 291.
19. Ibid. Cf. the argument of Maddocks in *Meyrick* (1929) 45 TLR 421 at 422.
20. *Greenfield* [1973] 3 All ER 1050, [1973] 1 WLR 1151.
1. *Coughlan (Martin)* (1976) 63 Cr App Rep 33, [1976] Crim LR 631, CA.

others, and which deprive defendants of the advantage of calling their co-defendants as witnesses."[2]

Though these sentiments have been approved by the Court of Criminal Appeal,[3] it is not at all clear that evidence is admissible on a conspiracy charge which would not be admissible on a joint trial for the complete crime. In both cases D1 may be prejudiced by evidence admissible only against D2. The real objection to conspiracy, as it has been commonly used in recent years, has been pointed out by Williams.[4] It is—

". . . to the use of a conspiracy count to give a semblance of unity to a prosecution which, by combining a number of charges and several defendants, results in a complicated and protracted trial. The jury system is unworkable unless the prosecution is confined to a relatively simple issue which can be disposed of in a relatively short time."

In *Griffiths*[5] a supplier of lime, his accountant and seven farmers were charged with conspiracy to defraud the government of the subsidy payable to farmers for spreading lime on their land. In addition to the conspiracy count, there were 24 other counts alleging substantive offences of false pretences. There were 60 prosecution and 35 defence witnesses and 263 exhibits including accounts and schedules. The jury had to return no less than 78 verdicts and the trial lasted 10 weeks – at the end of which, not surprisingly, all the convictions had to be quashed. But modern conspiracy trials have been much longer and no less complex.

4 Two or More Parties

It must be proved that D conspired with another but the other need not be identified.[6] If the managing director of a company resolves to perpetrate an illegality in the company's name, but communicates this to no one, there is no conspiracy between him and the company. To allow an indictment would be to

"offend against the basic concept of a conspiracy, namely an agreement of two or more to do an unlawful act . . . it would be artificial to take the view that the company, although it is clearly a separate legal entity can be regarded here as a separate entity or a separate mind . . ."[7]

In statutory conspiracies there are three cases in which the requirement of two parties is not satisfied. By section 2 (2) of the Act, a person is not guilty of a statutory conspiracy—

". . . if the only other person or persons with whom he agrees are (both initially and at all times during the currency of the agreement) persons of any one or more of the following descriptions, that is to say—

(a) his spouse;

---

2. Cockburn CJ, in *Boulton* (1871) 12 Cox CC 87 at 93.
3. *West* [1948] 1 KB 709 at 720, [1948] 1 All ER 718 at 723.
4. CLGP, 684; and see *The Proof of Guilt* (3rd ed.), Ch. 9 and "The Added Conspiracy Count" (1978) 128 NLJ 24.
5. Above, p. 296. The headnote is wrong in stating that a "wheel conspiracy" is not known to the law: *Ardalan* [1972] 2 All ER 257 at 262.
6. *Phillips* (1987) 86 Cr App Rep 18, discussed, [1988] Crim LR at 338.
7. *McDonnell* [1966] 1 QB 233, [1966] 1 All ER 193 (Nield J). Cf. *ICR Haulage Co.*, above, p. 181.

(b) a person under the age of criminal responsibility; and

(c) an intended victim of that offence or of each of those offences."

Paragraph (a) almost certainly states the rule of the common law, although no English case has ever so decided.[8] The common law rule was based upon the fiction that husband and wife were one person with one will. The application of the rule to statutory conspiracies is based upon a social policy of preserving the stability of marriage.[9]

The common law rule applies only where the parties are married at the time of the agreement. Marriage after the conspiracy or during its continuance is no defence.[10] Clearly the same rule applies under the Act. A wife is guilty, though she agrees only with her husband, if she knows that there are other parties to the conspiracy.[11]

For the purposes of paragraph (b) a person is under the age of criminal responsibility "so long as it is conclusively presumed by section 50 of the Children and Young Persons Act 1933,[12] that he cannot be guilty of any offence"[13] – that is, he is under the age of ten. The Act makes no provision for the case of a child between ten and fourteen.[14] If such a child has a "mischievous discretion" there is clearly a conspiracy. If such a discretion is not proved the child is not guilty but, if there is an agreement in fact, the adult party probably is. There appears to be no common law authority on agreements with children but principle suggests that the rule should be the same as for statutory conspiracies.

The Act does not define "victim". It is suggested that a person is a victim of an offence when the offence is held to exist for his protection with the effect that he is not a party to that offence when it is committed by another with his full knowledge and co-operation.[15] Thus there would be no conspiracy where D agreed with a girl under sixteen to take her out of the possession of her parents without their consent, or to have sexual intercourse with her, or to have intercourse with a defective. On the other hand, an agreement by an adult to commit buggery with a fourteen year old boy, or to commit an act of gross indecency with a ten year old boy who has a "mischievous discretion" is a conspiracy. In these cases the boy as well as the man will be guilty of the offence if the act takes place so he cannot be regarded as a "victim". Again there seems to be no common law authority in point and the question seems unlikely to arise on a charge of conspiracy at common law since an agreement to defraud with the victim of the fraud is difficult to imagine.

The Act does not deal with other cases where one of two parties to the agreement would not be liable to prosecution for the ulterior offence. It is clear that there may be a conspiracy although only one party is capable of

---

8. See, e.g., Hawkins 1 PC, c. 27, s. 8 and *Mawji v R* [1957] AC 126, [1957] 1 All ER 385, PC. There may be a conspiracy between husband and wife in the civil law: *Midland Bank Trust Co Ltd v Green* (No. 3) [1979] Ch 496, [1979] 2 All ER 193 (Oliver J).

9. Law Com. No. 76, paras, 1.46–1.49.

10. *Robinson's Case* (1746) 1 Leach 37.

11. *Chrastny* [1992] 1 All ER 189, [1991] 1 WLR 1381, CA.

12. Above, p. 188.

13. Section 2 (3) of the Act.

14. Above, p. 189.

15. Above, p. 156.

committing the ulterior offence as a principal. If it can be committed only by the holder of a justices' licence and A, a licensee, agrees with B, a customer who is incapable of committing the offence as a principal, that he, A, will do so, there is a conspiracy to contravene the licensing legislation. The course of conduct will necessarily amount to the commission of the offence by one of the parties. B will be liable as a secondary party if the offence is committed. The controversial case of *Whitchurch*[16] is thus readily explicable. D, believing herself to be pregnant, agreed with two others that they would procure her miscarriage. It was not proved that D was in fact pregnant. A person who unlawfully uses instruments on a woman to procure an abortion commits an offence whether the woman is pregnant or not; but a woman who does the same acts to herself is guilty only if she is in fact pregnant. It was held that all three were guilty of conspiracy and it is submitted that the result would be the same if D had agreed with only one other person. D is guilty as a secondary party if the ulterior offence is committed by using the instruments on her,[17] so she is not a "victim" under the principle of *Tyrrell*.[18] In *Duguid*[19] D agreed with E to remove a child of whom E was the mother from the possession of her lawful guardian. This would have been a crime by D under the Offences against the Person Act 1861, s. 56 but it was provided that a mother should not be liable to prosecution on account of taking her own child. It was held that E's "immunity from prosecution for an act done by herself" was no bar to the conviction of D for conspiracy. The court did not find it necessary to decide whether E could have been convicted of the conspiracy.[20] This suggests that there may be a conspiracy with only one guilty party but the case is far from clear because the court may have accepted the argument of the prosecution that any bar to the prosecution of E was of a procedural nature. The better view is that there must be two conspirators.[21]

The Act does not deal with an agreement with a mentally disordered person so the common law, whatever it may be, applies to all conspiracies. The Law Commission thought express provision unnecessary because "a purported agreement with a person who is so mentally disordered as to be incapable of forming the intent necessary for the substantive offence will not be an agreement within clause 1 (1) of the draft Bill [now, in substance, section 1 (1) of the Act]."[1] This seems to be right in the case of a mentally disordered person who does not know the nature and quality of the proposed act; but a person who, through mental disorder, does not know the proposed act is "wrong" may be perfectly capable of forming the intent

---

16. (1890) 24 QBD 420, criticised by Williams as "gravely wrong for it sets at naught the limitation upon responsibility imposed by Parliament": CLGP, 673. But see Hogan, "Victims as Parties to Crime" [1962] Crim LR 683 and below, p. 389.
17. *Sockett* (1908) 72 JP 428.
18. Above, p. 156.
19. (1906) 21 Cox CC 200.
20. The language used suggests that she might well have been guilty of conspiracy and of secondary participation in the ulterior offence if D had committed it, whether or not she could have been prosecuted.
21. Section 56 has been repealed by the Child Abduction Act 1984, below, p. 441, but the similar problems which could arise under that Act should be resolved n the same way.
  1. Law Com. No. 76, p. 22, note 67.

to commit it with full knowledge of the facts and circumstances.[2] In such a case it is arguable that a mentally normal party to the agreement is guilty of a statutory conspiracy though the mentally abnormal person is not because it is sufficient that the carrying out of the agreement will amount to an offence by *one of the parties*.[3] What is the position where there is an agreement by D1 and D2 to kill where D2 would have a defence of diminished responsibility on a charge of murder? If the killing is to be done by D1 it will be murder and so the agreement is a conspiracy to murder. If it is to be done by D2, D1 will still be guilty of murder by virtue of s. 2 (4) of the Homicide Act 1957.[4] However if, as submitted above,[5] "commission of any offence" means commission as principal in the first degree, this appears to be a conspiracy to commit manslaughter.

Another case with which the Act does not deal specifically is that where E purports to conspire with D but has no intention of going through with the plan. The question was formerly of no practical importance because D could be convicted of an attempt to conspire, but the Act rules that out. The point has not arisen in England but in some jurisdictions it has been decided that there is no conspiracy.[6] It might be argued that, looking at the facts objectively, there is such an agreement as (apart from the illegality) would be enforceable in the law of contract and that therefore there is an *actus reus*. D, who, with *mens rea*, has caused the *actus reus* should be guilty. An answer to this argument is that there is no *actus reus* unless E agrees in fact, i.e. that an actual subjective agreement is required. If *Anderson*[7] is followed and E held to be guilty of conspiracy notwithstanding his lack of intention, the problem disappears.

5 Acquittal of the other Alleged Conspirators

Where D is alleged to have conspired with one other person, E, the acquittal of E, either before or after the trial of D, was no bar to, or ground for quashing, as the case may be, the conviction of D.[8] This was where the parties were tried separately. Where they were tried together there was some doubt whether it was ever right to convict D and acquit E – or vice versa.[9] These doubts are resolved by s. 5 (8) and (9) of the Act which governs both common law and statutory conspiracies:

"5 (8) The fact that the person or persons who, so far as appears from the indictment on which any person has been convicted of conspiracy, were the only other parties to the agreement on which his conviction was based have been acquitted of conspiracy by reference to that agreement (whether after being tried with the person convicted or separately) shall not be a ground for quashing

2. Cf. *Matusevich v R* (1977) 51 ALJR 657 at 670, per Aickin J.
3. Section 1 (1), above, p. 271.
4. Above, p. 151, fn. 18.
5. Above, p. 280.
6. *Harris* [1927] NPD 347 (South Africa); *O'Brien* [1954] SCR 666 (Canada); *Delaney v State* (1932) 164 Tenn 432 (Tennessee); *State v Otu* [1964] NNLR 113 (Nigeria). Cf. *Thomson* (1965) 50 Cr App Rep 1. See Fridman in (1956) 19 MLR 276.
7. Above, p. 272.
8. *Director of Public Prosecutions v Shannon* [1975] AC 717, [1974] 2 All ER 1009, HL.
9. Ibid.

his conviction unless under all the circumstances of the case his conviction is inconsistent with the acquittal of the other person or persons in question.

(9) Any rule of law or practice inconsistent with the provisions of subsection (8) above is hereby abolished."

There may be evidence – usually a confession – which is admissible against D but not against E, which shows that D conspired with E. In these circumstances it is perfectly logical for the jury to be satisfied, as against D, that he conspired with E, but not satisfied, as against E, that he conspired with D. It is only when the evidence against D and E is of equal weight, or nearly so, that the judge should direct the jury that they must either acquit both or convict both – being careful to add that, if they are unsure about the guilt of one, both must be acquitted.[10]

4) *Onus of Proof*

The onus of proof of conspiracy, whether common law or statutory, is on the Crown even where, on a charge of committing the ulterior offence, it would be on the defendant. So on a charge of conspiring to produce a controlled drug (an offence under s. 4 (2) of the Misuse of Drugs Act 1971) the prosecution must prove that D knew that the thing he was producing was the controlled drug alleged although on a charge of committing the offence under the Misuse of Drugs Act the onus of proving lack of knowledge or suspicion would, by s. 28 of that Act, have been on D.[11]

5) *Sentence*

A person convicted of a common law conspiracy was liable to imprisonment and a fine at the discretion of the court; but under the Criminal Justice Act 1987, s. 12, conspiracy to defraud is now punishable with a maximum of ten years' imprisonment. A person convicted of a statutory conspiracy is liable to a sentence of imprisonment for a term not exceeding the maximum provided for the offence which he has conspired to commit.[12] Where the conspiracy is to commit more than one offence, the maximum is the longer or longest of the sentences provided for. Where the offence is triable either way the maximum for conspiracy is the maximum provided for conviction on indictment. Power to impose life imprisonment is provided in the case of conspiracy to commit (i) murder or any other

---

10. *Longman and Cribben* (1980) 72 Cr App Rep 121, [1981] Crim LR 38 and commentary. Cf. the similar problem which arises with secondary parties, above, p. 151. *Roberts* (1983) 78 Cr App Rep 41, [1985] Crim LR 218.
11. *McGowan* [1990] Crim LR 399.
12. Section 3 (3).

offence the sentence for which is fixed by law; (ii) any offence for which a sentence of imprisonment for life is provided and (iii) an indictable offence punishable with imprisonment for which no maximum term is provided.[13]

The power to impose a fine without limit is unaffected by the Act. Section 3 (1) preserves the general power of the Crown Court under the Powers of Criminal Courts Act 1973, s. 30 (1), to impose a fine in lieu of or in addition to dealing with the offender in any other way. A conspiracy to commit an offence punishable with a maximum fine of £10 is thus punishable with a fine without limit except, of course, that it must not be unreasonable in all the circumstances.

6) *Powers of Arrest*

Since the Police and Criminal Evidence Act 1984, s. 24 (1), came into force all offences carrying a maximum of five years imprisonment or more are arrestable offences,[14] whether the maximum derives from an enactment or from the common law. As conspiracy to defraud is now punishable with a maximum of ten years' imprisonment under the Criminal Justice Act 1987, s. 12 (3), it is an arrestable offence. So are common law conspiracies to corrupt public morals or outrage public decency because they are punishable at common law with imprisonment at the discretion of the court.

Statutory conspiracies are arrestable offences if the offence, or one of the offences, which the parties have conspired to commit, is punishable with a maximum of five years or more.

7) *Periods of Limitation*

Section 4 (4) of the Act provides that where—

"(a) an offence has been committed in pursuance of any agreement; and

(b) proceedings may not be instituted for that offence because any time limit applicable to the institution of such proceedings has expired, proceedings under section 1 above for conspiracy to commit that offence shall not be instituted against any person on the basis of that agreement."

One of the objections to conspiracy charges at common law, especially charges of conspiracy to commit a summary offence, is that they enable a limitation period to be evaded. This provision meets that criticism, at least to some extent. Section 4 (4) only applies where the offence has been committed. Thus an agreement to commit an offence which is subject to a period of limitation remains indictable indefinitely if the offence is never

13. Section 3(2).
14. See above, p. 26.

committed and never will be committed because the parties have abandoned the plan. There is no point from which the period of limitation can begin to run.

8) *Rationale of Conspiracy*

Why should the mere agreement to commit an offence be a crime?[15] A commonly accepted reason is that it enables the criminal law to intervene at an early stage to prevent the harm involved in the commission of the ulterior offence.[16] This argument is not completely convincing, however, for it does not explain why agreements differ from other acts manifesting an intention to commit a crime, which are not offences unless sufficiently proximate to amount to attempts. A declaration by one person of his unshakeable resolution to commit a crime and the taking of preparatory steps (not in themselves offences) do not amount to a crime. The law thus attaches importance to the act of agreement, "over and above its value as an indicator of criminal intent."[17] It is a step towards the commission of a crime to which the law has long attached a peculiar significance. The combination of minds, bent on the commission of the unlawful act, is taken to dispense with the need for proximity where only one person is involved.

It is argued that the effect of the combination is to increase the risk that the crime will be committed and the danger to the proposed victim, or to the public. Yet the risk and the danger are not necessarily greater than those arising from the resolve and the preparatory acts of a determined individual. Perhaps the basis, never clearly articulated by our courts, is that there is something inherently wicked in a "plot" to commit crime.[18]

None of this explains why an agreement to do an act, which is not a crime, may be a conspiracy. The traditional explanation is as follows.

"The general principle on which the crime of conspiracy is founded is this, that the confederacy of several persons to effect any injurious object creates such a new and additional power to cause injury as requires criminal restraint; although none would be necessary were the same thing proposed, or even attempted to be done, by any person singly."[19]

This, however, does not explain why the confederacy, however powerful, should be criminal when even the actual achievement of the same injurious object by an individual – or, indeed, by the confederates – is not in itself an offence. The rationale of this aspect of conspiracy is now generally rejected and we are moving to a stage where it will be of historical interest only. ". . . the offence of conspiracy to do an unlawful, though not criminal, act ought to have no place in a modern system of law."[20] The only

15. See Ian H. Dennis, "The Rationale of Criminal Conspiracy" (1977) 93 LQR 39; Williams, CLGP, para. 226; Sayre (1922) Harv LR 393.
16. Law Commission Working Paper, para. 12: "the most important rationale". The Law Commission agreed: Law Com. No. 76, 1.5.
17. Dennis, op. cit., above, fn. 15.
18. See Dennis, op. cit. pp. 51–52.
19. Criminal Law Commission, 7th Report (1843), p. 90.
20. Law Com. No. 76, 1.9.

significant exception to this principle is now the law of conspiracy to defraud; and it is intended that that will go when the law relating to fraud has been amended.

3 Attempt

An attempt to commit any indictable offence was a misdemeanour at common law. The common law[1] was repealed by the Criminal Attempts Act 1981 (in this section of the book referred to as "the Act") which came into force on 27th August 1981. Section 1 (1) of the Act creates a new statutory offence.

"If, with intent to commit an offence to which this section applies, a person does an act which is more than merely preparatory to the commission of the offence, he is guilty of attempting to commit the offence."

1 Mens Rea in Attempts

Exceptionally, *mens rea* is here discussed before *actus reus* because, as has often been remarked,[2] the mental element assumes paramount importance in attempts. The *actus reus* may be a perfectly innocent and harmless act as where D, intending to murder P, puts sugar in his tea, believing that it is not sugar but a deadly poison. The *actus reus* may be *any* act, provided it is done with intent to commit the offence and goes beyond mere preparation.

Where, as is commonly the case, the complete offence may be committed with a *mens rea* falling short of an intention to commit the offence, the requirements of the law on a charge of attempt are stricter. An intention to cause grievous bodily harm is a sufficient *mens rea* for murder, but that is plainly not an intent to commit murder and so is insufficient on a charge of attempted murder. Nothing less than an intention to kill will do.[3] Reckless-ness is a sufficient *mens rea* for most non-fatal offences against the person and for criminal damage and many other offences but it is not a sufficient *mens rea* on a charge of attempting to commit any of them.[4]

As has been seen,[5] however, intention has a variable meaning in the criminal law so the question arises, what does "intent to commit an offence" mean in s. 1 (1) of the Act? It was held in *Pearman*[6] that the word "intent" in section 1 has the same meaning as in the common law of attempts. They applied *Mohan*[7] where the Court of Appeal held that there must be proved—

"... a decision to bring about, in so far as it lies within the accused's power, the commission of the offence which it is alleged the accused

1. See the fourth edition of this book at pp. 246–264.
2. See, e.g., *Whybrow* (1951) 35 Cr App Rep 141; **SHC 275**.
3. Cf. *Whybrow* (1951) 35 Cr App Rep 141; **SHC 275**; *O'Toole* [1987] Crim CR 759, CA.
4. *Millard and Vernon* [1987] Crim LR 393.
5. Above, p. 53.
6. (1984) 80 Cr App Rep 259, CA.
7. [1976] QB 1, [1975] 2 All ER 193; **SHC 276**.

attempted to commit, no matter whether the accused desired that consequence of his act or not."

The concluding words are difficult to reconcile with the main proposition which certainly seems to embody the notion of trying to cause, or striving for, a result.

In *Pearman* the court thought that these words—

"are probably designed to deal with a case where the accused has, as a primary purpose, some other object, for example, a man who plants a bomb in an aeroplane, which he knows is going to take off, it being his primary intention that he should claim the insurance on the aeroplane when the freight goes down into the sea. The jury would not be put off from saying that he intended to murder the crew simply by saying that he did not want or desire to kill the crew, but that was something that he inevitably intended to do. Similarly, for example, a man who is cornered by the police when he is in a car may have the primary purpose of simply escaping from that situation. If he drives straight at the police officers at high speed, a jury is likely to conclude that he intended to injure a police officer and maybe cause him serious grievous bodily harm."[8]

This is the meaning given to intention in the criminal law generally after the series of cases culminating in *Nedrick*[9] and applied by the Court of Appeal in *Walker*,[10] a case of attempted murder. The court condoned the use by the judge of the phrase, "very high degree of probability", but stressed that "virtual certainty" is preferable. These refinements may not have been in point as the jury had convicted on a direction that they must be satisfied that D was *trying* to kill. If he was trying to kill it was immaterial, as a matter of law, whether death was, or was known by D to be, virtually certain, highly probable, or merely possible: a person may intend to kill even though the possibility of doing so is, and he knows it is, remote. Probability is no more than relevant evidence – it is easier to infer that D was trying to kill if he threw P from the window of the 20th floor than if he threw him from the window of 1st floor. It was only if he was *not* trying to kill that the degree of probability assumed the character of a rule of law, and then *Nedrick* requires foresight of virtual certainty and nothing less will do.

This, however does not solve all the problems. The notion of attempt requires an intended result. It does not necessarily require intention with respect to material circumstances. So in *Pigg*,[11] before the Act, it was assumed without argument that a man might be guilty of attempted rape if he tried to have sexual intercourse with a woman, being reckless whether or not she consented to his doing so. Though the point was not spelt out in any case, it is submitted that this was right in principle, at least until *Caldwell* recklessness supplanted *Cunningham* recklessness[12] in the case of some crimes. The *mens rea* of the complete crime should be modified only

8. (1984) 80 Cr App Rep 259 at 263.
9. [1986] 3 All ER 1, 83 Cr App Rep 267, above, p. 54.
10. (1989) 90 Cr App Rep 226, [1990] Crim LR 44.
11. [1982] 2 All ER 591, 74 Cr App Rep 352, [1982] Crim LR 446 and commentary.
12. Above, p. 61.

in so far as it is necessary in order to accommodate the concept of attempt. If recklessness as to circumstances is a sufficient *mens rea* for the complete crime, it should be so for an attempt.

The Law Commission at one time assumed that a distinction between consequences and circumstances would be unworkable and proposed that intention should be required as to all the elements of the offence. The first version of the Draft Criminal Code[13] followed that opinion and stated the rule expressly, using rape as an example. This was criticised as undesirably narrow. The Commission found the criticism persuasive and the Draft Code, cl. 49 (2), now provides:

> "For the purposes of subsection (1) [attempt to commit an offence], an intention to commit an offence is an intention with respect to all the elements of the offence other than fault elements, except that recklessness with respect to circumstances suffices where it suffices for the offence itself."

In *Khan*[14] the court, after considering the conflicting opinions, held that, for the purposes of the Criminal Attempts Act, a man has an intention to commit rape if he intends to have sexual intercourse with a woman, being reckless whether she consents. The decision is limited to attempted rape but consistency will surely require the application of the same principle (as expressed in the Draft Code, above) to other offences where recklessness as to circumstances suffices, conspicuously offences of obtaining by deception. For example, company directors, being uncertain whether they have power to operate nuclear ships (which they do not), issue a prospectus stating categorically that they do have such power. If thereby they obtain money, they will be guilty of doing so by deception. If they fail to do so, they should be guilty of an attempt to obtain.

The recklessness required in rape and obtaining offences is, it is submitted, *Cunningham* recklessness, i.e., advertent, subjective recklessness, and the law should draw the line at this. *Caldwell/Lawrence* recklessness should have no place. It would be wrong to hold that a person intended and attempted to commit a crime when he had not even adverted to an element of it. Still less should strict liability have any place on a charge of attempt. But when strict liability as to a circumstance is imposed there is every reason why recklessness as to that circumstance should suffice. D, being uncertain whether a girl (in fact aged 15) is under or over 16, attempts to take her out of the possession of her parents against their will. He should be held to have a sufficient intention for, and to be guilty of, an offence under the Sexual Offences Act 1956. The section imposes strict liability as to the girl's age so recklessness as to that element of the offence will certainly "suffice", as the Draft Code has it.[15] It would be wrong if liability for attempts should reach farther in the case of an offence which requires recklessness than one which imposes strict liability.

13. Law Com. No. 143.
14. [1990] 2 All ER 783, 91 Cr App Rep 29.
15. What of the person who does not give a thought to whether the girl is under or over sixteen because he does not appreciate the relevance of that age? Perhaps he should be held sufficiently reckless because he knew the girl was of some age and, ex hypothesi, did not care what it was. Cf. commentary on *Mousir* [1987] Crim LR 561 at 562.

Where recklessness will not suffice for the complete offence it is clear that it will not suffice for the attempt. So if D attempts to receive goods, being reckless whether they are stolen, he is not guilty of an attempt to handle stolen goods because the full offence of handling requires knowledge or belief that the goods are stolen goods.

a) *Conditional intent.* Great practical difficulty and much academic debate was caused by the decision of the Court of Appeal in *Husseyn.*[16] The defendants opened the door of a van in which there was a holdall containing valuable sub-aqua equipment. They were charged with attempted theft of that equipment. The judge directed the jury that they could convict if the defendants were about to look into the holdall and, if its contents were valuable, to steal them. The Court of Appeal held that this was a misdirection: "it cannot be said that one who has it in mind to steal only if what he finds is worth stealing has a present intention to steal". This caused particular difficulties in the law of burglary because most persons charged with that crime intend to steal, not some specific thing, but anything they find which they think is worth stealing. The Court of Appeal[17] got over this difficulty by holding that *Husseyn* applied only where, as in that case, the indictment named the specific thing which the defendant was alleged to have attempted to steal. It would have been different, apparently, if the indictment had charged an attempt to steal "some or all of the contents" of the holdall – or car, handbag or house, as the case may be. This purely procedural device was rightly criticised. In *Husseyn*, for example, the only thing in the holdall was the sub-aqua equipment. If the defendant was guilty of attempting to steal "some or all of the contents" he was obviously guilty of attempting to steal the sub-aqua equipment – there were no other contents; but if the indictment charged him with that he had to be acquitted!

a) *Conditional intent under the 1981 Act.* The Act does not expressly do anything about this absurd and unworthy distinction which remains part of the law.[18] The Act does, however, remove the major obstacle to a rational solution to the problem, namely the decision in *Haughton v Smith.*[19] So long as this case remained law, the defendant could only be convicted of attempting to steal something that was in the holdall, car, room or other place, because there could be no attempt to steal something that was not there.[20] In *Husseyn* the jury must have found that D intended to steal anything in the holdall that he found to be of value. If he would have taken the sub-aqua equipment had he found it, he had certainly done an act which was more than merely preparatory to stealing it and he ought to be

16. (1977) 67 Cr App Rep 131n, [1978] Crim LR 219 and commentary; White, *Misleading Cases*, 63.
17. *A–G's References* (Nos. 1 and 2 of 1979) [1980] QB 180, [1979] 3 All ER 143, [1979] Crim LR 585; see also *Walkington* [1979] 2 All ER 716, [1979] Crim LR 526 and commentary.
18. *Smith and Smith* [1986] Crim LR 166, CA.
19. [1975] AC 476, [1973] 3 All ER 1109, below, p. 323.
20. Though there was an understandable inclination on the part of the Court of Appeal to carry on as if that case did not exist. See *Bayley v Easterbrook* [1980] Crim LR 503 and commentary.

found guilty of attempting to do so. It might not, however, be possible for the jury to be satisfied that he would have taken that item. If he would not have taken it, it follows that he was looking for other things – we know not what and perhaps he did not know either – which were not there. He was attempting to steal all right, but his attempt was doomed to failure. This no longer matters since the Act reversed *Haughton v Smith*. He was no different in this respect from the man who attempts to steal from an empty pocket. The only difficulty is about the form of the indictment. The formula approved by the Court of Appeal, "some or all of the contents", is unsatisfactory because the jury may not be satisfied that he intended to steal *any* of the contents and may indeed be satisfied that he did not intend to steal any of them. The indictment would be accurate, however, if it simply stated, "attempted to steal from a holdall". This represents the truth, whether there is anything there that he would have stolen or not. The failure to specify any subject-matter is not an objection because there is in fact no subject-matter to be specified. The defendant must be dealt with on the basis that he intended to take anything he thought worth taking, whatever it might be. The problem is exactly the same in the empty pocket case.

In *Husseyn*, the Court followed *Easom*,[1] where D picked up a woman's handbag in a theatre, rummaged through the contents and put it back having taken nothing. The handbag was attached by a thread to a policewoman's wrist. D's conviction for stealing the handbag and the specified contents – tissues, cosmetics, etc., was quashed because there was no intention permanently to deprive the owner of these. Consequently, the court held, he was not guilty of attempting to steal the handbag or contents. Whether he was rightly acquitted of theft is debated[2] but, assuming he was, he was also innocent of attempting to steal the specific contents, but he was clearly guilty of an attempt to steal what was not there. Plainly, he was looking for money and therefore the handbag was, in effect, empty. *Easom*, too, seems a suitable case for a charge of attempting to steal from a handbag. The court posed a much-discussed example. "If a dishonest postal sorter picks up a pile of letters intending to steal any which are registered, but, on finding that none of them are, replaces them, he has stolen nothing." This is true; but he was then (before *Haughton v Smith*) and is now, guilty of attempting to steal registered letters.

2 Actus Reus in Attempt

Before the Act there was an *actus reus* if the defendant had taken such steps towards the commission of the offence as were properly described as "an attempt" to commit it, in the ordinary meaning of that term. Many steps may be taken towards the commission of a crime which could not properly be so described. D, intending to commit murder, buys a gun and ammunition, does target practice, studies the habits of his intended victim, reconnoitres a suitable place to lie in ambush, puts on a disguise and sets out to take up his position. These are all acts of preparation but could

---

1. [1971] 2 QB 315, [1971] 2 All ER 945.
2. See Williams, TBCL, 651–653 and [1979] Crim LR 530, fn. 3; below, p. 502.

scarcely be described as attempted murder. D takes up his position, loads the gun, sees his victim approaching, raises the gun, takes aim, puts his finger on the trigger and squeezes it. He has now certainly committed attempted murder; but he might have desisted or been interrupted at any one of the stages described. At what point had he gone far enough to be guilty of an attempt? The answer given by the common law was that it was a matter of fact: was the act sufficiently proximate to murder to be properly described as an attempt to commit it? More detailed formulations of the principle proved unsuccessful, being capricious in their operation or simply unhelpful.[3] This is not surprising when it is recalled that the principle has to apply to all crimes and that crimes are very diverse in their nature. The only well-settled rule was that if D had done the last act which, as he knew, was necessary to achieve the consequence alleged to be attempted, he was guilty.[4] The converse, however, did not apply. An act might be sufficiently proximate although it was not necessarily the last act to be done. In *White*[5] D was held guilty of attempted murder by the attempted administration of a dose of poison though he may well have contemplated further doses, and further doses may have been necessary, to kill.

The test stated in s. 1 (1) of the Act is in substance that proposed by the Law Commission.[6] The Commissioners found that there is no "magic formula" to define precisely what constitutes an attempt and that there is bound to be some degree of uncertainty in the law. The proximity test was the only one broadly acceptable. Even its imprecision was not without advantages: "its flexibility does enable difficult cases to be reconsidered and their authority questioned"; and "where cases are so dependent on what are sometimes fine differences of degree, we think it is eminently appropriate for the question whether the conduct in a particular case amounts to an attempt to be left to the jury". The purpose of the proximity test was to prevent too great an extension of criminal liability, by excluding mere acts of preparation. The Commission thought it "undesirable to recommend anything more complex than a rationalisation of the present law". They rejected a definition in terms of proximity because of the danger of a formula which suggested that only the last act could be an attempt. They therefore decided that the formula should direct attention, not to when the commission of the offence begins, but to when mere preparation ends. The preparatory act test is more apt in one respect. "Proximity" suggested that the attempter had to come "pretty near"[7] to success; yet, where the attempt is to do the impossible, success is an infinity away. There is no such

---

3. The most interesting effort was called the "equivocality theory". This is discussed in the fourth edition of this book at 253–255, but it is probably now of only historical interest, so far as English law is concerned.

4. Even this, not very ambitious, rule was doubted by Lord Edmund-Davies in *Stonehouse* [1978] AC 55 at 86, [1977] 2 All ER 909 at 933, but his Lordship's doubts seem to relate to the last act of a secondary party which, admittedly, does not necessarily constitute an attempt. See [1977] Crim LR 547–549.

5. [1910] 2 KB 124; **SHC 283**. See also *Linneker* [1906] 2 KB 99.

6. See Law Com. No. 102, 2.45–2.52. Criticised by Williams, "Wrong Turnings on the Law of Attempt" [1991] Crim LR 416.

7. O. W. Holmes J, *Commonwealth v Kennedy* (1897) 170 Mass. 18.

conceptual difficulty about preparatory acts to do the impossible – by one who does not know it is impossible, of course! It seems that no substantial change in the law was intended. If any change has been made, it is to extend the scope of attempts because, if there is any "middle ground" between mere preparation and a proximate act, an act in the middle ground now constitutes an attempt whereas formerly it did not do so. However, it seems more likely that preparation and commission overlap than that there is any gap between them.

Every step towards the commission of an offence, except the last one, could properly be described as "preparatory" to the commission of the offence. The assassin crooks his finger around the trigger preparatory to pulling it. If the section were so interpreted, only the last act would amount to an attempt – a result which the Law Commission's formula was intended to avoid. The key word is "merely".[8] Not all preparatory acts are excluded. When does an act cease to be *merely* preparatory? The answer, it seems, must be when the actor is engaged in the commission of the offence which he is attempting – as Rowlatt J put it many years ago, when he is "on the job".[9] Whether he is seems to be still, as it was before the Act, the ultimate question.

Whether an act is "more than merely preparatory to the commission of the offence" is a question of fact. In a jury trial, it is of course for the judge to decide whether there is evidence sufficient in law to support such a finding and it is then for the jury to decide (i) what acts the defendant did and (ii) whether they were more than merely preparatory.[10] If the judge decides there is not sufficient evidence, he directs a verdict of not guilty. Where he decides there is sufficient evidence, he must leave both questions of fact to the jury, even where the only possible answer in law is that the defendant is guilty. Where, for example, the evidence is that the defendant has done the "last act", he may not tell the jury that, if they find that D did that act, that *is* an attempt even though, in law, this is so. The judge may express a strong opinion, but he must not appear to take the question of fact out of the hands of the jury.[11]

It has been argued[12] that the judge and jury, in performing their respective functions, are not entitled to have regard to the word "attempt". The question to be determined is, in the words of s. 4 (3), simply whether the defendant "did an act falling within subsection (1) of [section 1]"; and that subsection does not use the word "attempt". While there is great force

8. Griew, *Current Law Statutes*, says that "If 'merely' adds anything at all, it is only emphasis"; but elsewhere in his note he recognises that all acts but the last are in one sense preparatory and that the phrase, "merely preparatory", indicates that "there may, in any criminal transaction, be a point before which it is appropriate to describe the actor as not yet engaged in the commission of the offence but as *only* preparing to commit it". (Our italics.) "Only" equals "merely". Thus, Griew seems to agree that not all preparatory acts are excluded, but only those that are "only" or "merely" preparatory.

9. *Osborn* (1919) 84 JP 63.

10. See s. 4 (3) of the Act, which, in substance, codifies the common law as to the functions of judge and jury: *Stonehouse* [1978] AC 55, [1977] 2 All ER 909.

11. If he does and the jury convict, the conviction is likely to be upheld under the proviso to s. 2 of the Criminal Appeal Act 1968.

12. Griew, *Current Law Statutes*.

in this argument, it is submitted that it should not prevail. As observed above, all acts but the last are preparatory. How then are we to determine whether an act is more than *merely* preparatory? To be more than merely preparatory, it must also be something else. What? Some other concept not mentioned in the section must be invoked to give it a sensible meaning. The answer seems to be that the act must be part of the commission of the intended offence, an act that is done by a defendant "on the job", that it is, in a word, an "attempt".

The Act is, in this respect, a codifying act so, applying *Bank of England v Vagliano*,[13] "the correct approach is to look first at the natural meaning of the statutory words, not to turn back to earlier case law and seek to fit some previous test to the words of the section."[14] The citation of pre-Act cases has been discouraged; but the rule in *Vagliano* recognises that where a provision is "of doubtful import" resort to the previous law is prefectly legitimate – and there is a good deal of doubt about the import of this provision.

Since the Act provides for the first time a statutory definition of attempt, the cases on attempt at common law are no longer binding. They may, however, be regarded as persuasive because the Act is (in this respect) intended to be no more than a rationalisation of the common law.

The test of proximity at common law was expressed in various ways. One way, which gave attempts very narrow scope, was that of Lord Diplock in *Stonehouse* where, having cited the opinion in *Eagleton*[15] that only acts "immediately connected" with the offence can be attempts, he continued:[16] "In other words the offender must have crossed the Rubicon and burnt his boats."

The "Rubicon test" was at first accepted as representing the law under the Act[17] but was rejected in *Gullefer*.[18] In *Jones*,[19] applying *Gullefer*, the court upheld D's conviction of attempted murder where he got into P's car and pointed a loaded sawn-off shot gun at him, despite an argument that D had at least three acts to do: remove the safety catch, put his finger on the trigger and pull it. When he pointed the gun, there was evidence to leave to the jury.

In *Gullefer* Lord Lane also referred to an alternative "test" formulated by Stephen:[20]

"An attempt to commit a crime is an act done with intent to commit that crime and forming part of a series of acts which would constitute its actual commission, if it were not interrupted."

Lord Lane recognised the unhelpful nature of this test. It does not define where the "series of acts" begins. Moreover, many acts which are obviously merely preparatory could be said to be part of such a series. Lord

13. [1891] AC 107 at 144.
14. *Jones* (1990) 91 Cr App Rep 351 at 353, discussed by K. J. M. Smith, [1991] Crim LR 576.
15. (1855) Dears CC 376, 515.
16. [1978] AC 55 at 68.
17. *Widdowson* (1985) 82 Cr App Rep 314 at 318–319.
18. [1990] 3 All ER 882, 91 Cr App Rep 356, note. Cf. *Boyle* (1986) 84 Cr App Rep 270.
19. Above, fn. 14.
20. Digest of Criminal Law (5th ed., 1894), Art. 50.

Lane said the Act requires a "midway course" and that the attempt begins "when the defendant embarks on the crime proper". This seems the same as Rowlatt J's "on the job" test.

It was thought that some pre-Act cases which were considered by judicial and academic critics to take too restrictive a view of attempts might be decided differently under the Act. This now seems unlikely. Notable among the cases is *Robinson*.[1]

D, a jeweller, having insured his stock against theft, concealed some of it on his premises, tied himself up with string and called for help. He told a policeman who broke in that he had been knocked down and his safe robbed. The jewellery was insured for £1,200. The policeman was not satisfied with the story and discovered the property concealed on the premises. D confessed that he had hoped to get money from the insurers. His conviction for attempting to obtain by false pretences was quashed. If this case still represents the law, a judge, on these facts, should direct a jury to acquit of the attempt. Notwithstanding the criticisms, it is by no means clear that this conduct ought to be regarded as more than merely preparatory. The stage had been set; but the business of obtaining money from the insurance company was yet to begin. D was undoubtedly preparing to commit a crime but it is not obvious that he had yet begun to commit it. *Widdowson*, decided under the Act, was a rather similar case and the conviction was quashed. In *Gullefer* D, seeing that the dog he had backed in a greyhound race was losing, jumped onto the track to stop the race. He hoped that the stewards would declare "no race" whereupon punters would be entitled to have their money back and he would recover his £18 stake. His conviction for attempting to steal the £18 was quashed. His act was merely preparatory. It remained for him to go to the bookmaker and demand his money. Like Robinson, he had prepared the ground for his demand but, until he began to make it, he had not, apparently, "embarked on the crime proper", he was not "on the job".

The strict interpretation of the Act appears most vividly in *Campbell*[2] where D was arrested by police when, armed with an imitation gun, he approached within a yard of the door of a post office with intent to commit a robbery therein. His conviction for attempted robbery was quashed: there was no evidence on which a jury could "properly and safely" find that his acts were more than merely preparatory. From the viewpoint of public safety it is an unhappy decision. Though the police may lawfully arrest a person doing such preparatory acts because he is, or they have reasonable grounds for suspecting that he is, about to commit an arrestable offence,[3] they may feel obliged to wait until he has entered the post office and approached the counter before arresting him. The extra danger to post office staff, the public and the officers themselves is obvious.[4]

---

1. [1915] 2 KB 342, 11 Cr App Rep 124, CCA. Cf. *Button* [1900] 2 QB 597, CCR.
2. [1991] Crim LR 268. But cf *Kelly* [1992] Crim LR 181.
3. PACE, s. 24 (7) below, p. 436.
4. Campbell was convicted of the offence of carrying an imitation firearm and in similar cases it may be possible to convict of "going equipped"; but the police may not know whether the suspect is armed or equipped and, whether they know or not, they will naturally wish to obtain a conviction for the more serious offence which they suspect he intends to commit.

In *Comer v Bloomfield*[5] the defendant went a step further than Robinson. Having crashed his van, he pushed it into a nearby wood, reported to the police that it had been stolen and wrote to his insurers stating that the van had been stolen and inquiring whether he could claim for it. He was acquitted by magistrates of attempt to obtain money by deception and the Divisional Court held that the magistrates were entitled to conclude that the making of a preliminary inquiry was insufficiently proximate to the actual obtaining. If the magistrates had convicted the defendant, it may be that the conviction would have been upheld on the ground that there was evidence on which they might find that the act was sufficiently proximate. Some such inconsistency in result must be anticipated when the question is treated as one of fact. Even if *Robinson* does represent the law under the Act, Bloomfield's inquiry might well be held to be evidence of a more than merely preparatory act; D had set about the business of getting money from the insurers.

Perhaps the most striking case of all the common law cases is *Komaroni and Rogerson*[6] where the defendants followed a lorry for 130 miles, waiting in vain for the driver to leave it unattended so that they could steal it. Streatfield J held that this was mere preparation. It seems likely that this would be held to be evidence of an attempt under the Act.

3 Attempt by Omission

A crime of omission where the *actus reus* does not include any consequence of the omission is by its nature incapable of being attempted.[7] This is not true of an offence including a consequence which may be committed by one having a duty to act. If the parents of a child deliberately withhold food from the child with the intent to kill it, they have set out to commit murder.[8] In fact, they are attempting to commit murder but, in the rare case where it cannot be proved that they did any act contributing to the death, it seems probable that, under the Act, they are no longer guilty of that offence.[9] They have done no act, as required by s. 1 (1). Though the government seems to have supposed that an attempt could be charged in such a case,[10] it would require bold judicial interpretation to read "act" to include "omission". Cases will be rare where an intent to commit an offence by omission can be proved. Where it can be so proved, there seems to be an unfortunate gap in the law.

4 Successful Attempts

It has sometimes been argued that failure is essential to the very nature of an attempt so that success precludes a conviction for attempting to commit

---

5. (1970) 55 Cr App Rep 305.
6. (1953) 103 L Jo 97.
7. Below, p. 315.
8. *Gibbins and Proctor* (1918) 13 Cr App Rep 134, above, p. 47. Cf. Gunn and Smith [1985] Crim LR 705 at 706, fn. 9.
9. They are of course guilty of the offence of wilful neglect of a young person under the Children and Young Persons Act 1933.
10. See Dennis [1982] Crim LR 5, 7.

a crime.[11] For a rather technical reason, this was true of attempts to commit felonies at common law. There was a rule that a misdemeanour committed in the course of committing a felony "merged" in the felony. Since an attempt to commit a felony was a misdemeanour, it ceased to exist when the felony was committed. This doctrine was almost certainly abolished, so far as trial on indictment is concerned, as long ago as 1851,[12] though the matter was disputed. With the abolition of felonies by the Criminal Law Act 1967 this doctrine of merger disappeared and s. 6 (4) of the Act provided:

"... where a person is charged on indictment with attempting to commit an offence or with an assault or other act preliminary to an offence, but not with the completed offence, then (subject to the discretion of the court to discharge the jury with a view to the preferment of an indictment for the completed offence) he may be convicted of the offence charged notwithstanding that he is shown to be guilty of the completed offence."

This provision does not extend to summary trial and there was some doubt about the position in magistrates' courts until the Divisional Court held in *Webley v Buxton*[13] that an attempt to commit a misdemeanour does not merge in the completed offence at common law. D, sitting astride a motor-cycle, used his feet to push it eight feet across a pavement. He was charged with attempting to take a conveyance for his own use without the consent of the owner. The slightest movement of the conveyance is enough to constitute the full offence.[14] It was held that, though the justices were satisfied that he was guilty of the full offence, they had properly convicted him of the attempt. The Act makes no provision in the matter, following the recommendation of the Law Commission,[15] so the matter is governed by the common law as stated in *Webley v Buxton*.

As a matter of principle, this seems right. At a certain point in the transaction, D is guilty of an attempt. The attempt may fail for many reasons, or it may succeed. There is no reason why, if it succeeds, it should cease to be the offence of attempt which, until that moment, it was. The greater includes the less. If D is convicted of attempted murder while his victim, P, is still alive and P then dies of injuries inflicted by D, D is now liable to be convicted of murder; but the conviction for attempt is not invalidated. It would, of course, be improper to convict D of both the attempt and the full offence at the same time. To that extent, the attempt merges in the completed offence.

5 Offences which may be Attempted

By s. 1 (4), the section applies to any offence triable in England and Wales as an indictable offence – i.e., any offence triable only on indictment, or

---

11. Hall, GPCL, 577: "... attempt implies failure ...". Fletcher *Rethinking*, 131. In *Commonwealth v Crow* (1931) 303 Pa 91 at 98, the court said "A failure to consummate a crime is as much an essential element of an attempt as the intent and performance of an overt act towards its commission."
12. By the Criminal Procedure Act 1851, s. 12, now repealed by the Criminal Law Act 1977.
13. [1977] QB 481, [1977] 2 All ER 595, [1977] Crim LR 160.
14. Below, p. 598.
15. Law Com. No. 102, 2.113.

triable either way,[16] – except conspiracy, whether common law or statutory,[17] and offences of assisting an arrestable offender or compounding an arrestable offence contrary to ss. 4 (1) and 5 (1) respectively of the Criminal Law Act 1967.[18] It is an offence under the Act, as it was at common law, to attempt to commit the common law offence of incitement.[19] This is to deal with the case where a communication, which would be an incitement if it arrived, is intercepted. The Act makes clear that it is not an offence to attempt to aid, abet, counsel, procure or suborn the commission of an offence:[20] s. 1 (4) (b). Where, however, aiding, etc., is the principal offence as in s. 2 (1) of the Suicide Act 1961[1] or s. 4 of the Sexual Offences Act 1967,[2] an attempt to aid, etc. is an offence. Section 1 (4) (b) does not apply because these are not instances of aiding, etc., *an offence*.

Apart from the statutory exceptions there may be other crimes where an attempt is impossible. Stephen thought there was a large number of such offences[3] but his examples are not wholly convincing. There are five types of offence where no attempt is possible. (1) Where any act done with the appropriate intent amounts to the complete crime.[4] Such crimes are rare but one may be the form of treason known as compassing the Queen's death. The offence requires proof of an overt act but it seems that any act done with intent to kill the Queen would be enough. (2) A crime defined as an omission[5] where the *actus reus* does not include any consequence of the omission, as in the case of misprision of treason or some statutory offences of omission. (3) An offence which may be committed recklessly or negligently but not intentionally. The only example which comes readily to mind is involuntary manslaughter. The essence of this crime is that the killing is unintentional. An intentional killing (in the absence of diminished responsibility, the conditions for infanticide, provocation[6] or a suicide pact) is necessarily murder. Section 1 (1) of the Act requires an intent to commit the offence which D is charged with attempting but an intent to commit involuntary manslaughter is not a concept known to the law. (4) It is difficult to conceive of an attempt where the *actus reus* is a state of affairs, such as "being found" in particular circumstances.[7] (5) At common law it

16. Above, p. 24.
17. Above, p. 267.
18. Above, pp. 160–168. Reasons for excluding the offences under the Criminal Law Act 1967 are given in Law Com. No. 102 at 2.124–2.126.
19. Above, p. 266.
20. *Dunnington* [1984] QB 472, [1984] 1 All ER 676, 78 Cr App Rep 171. For the common law, see Smith, "Secondary Participation and Inchoate Offences", in *Crime, Proof and Punishment*, 21.
1. Below, p. 379. *McShane* (1977) 66 Cr App Rep 97, [1977] Crim LR 737. Smith in *Crime, Proof and Punishment* at 32.
2. Below, p. 479.
3. 2 HCL 227.
4. In *Rogers v Arnott* [1960] 2 QB 244, [1960] 2 All ER 417 it was said that, for this reason, there could be no attempt to commit fraudulent conversion under s. 20 of the Larceny Act 1916; but it seems clear that there may be an attempt to appropriate property belonging to another, i.e., to steal, contrary to s. 1 of the Theft Act 1968, which has replaced fraudulent conversion.
5. Attempt by omission generally is considered, above, p. 313.
6. For attempted infanticide, see *K A Smith* [1983] Crim LR 739, below, p. 384; and for attempt under provocation, *Bruzas* [1972] Crim LR 367, below, p. 351.
7. Above, p. 43.

was doubtful whether an attempt to commit an offence triable only summarily was a crime. Under the Act, it is clear that it is not, unless the provision creating the offence expressly provides that it shall be. Such "an attempt under a special statutory provision" (s. 3 (1) of the Act) is now governed by the same principles as attempts under the Act.

a) *Attempt in England to commit an offence abroad.* Where the offence, if it were completed, would be triable on indictment in England, the attempt is likewise indictable. If D, a British citizen, in England posts a letter bomb to P in France, intending to kill P, he is liable to conviction for attempted murder as soon as the letter is posted;[8] but, if he intends only to injure P, he is not guilty of an attempt to cause him grievous or actual bodily harm. Murder abroad by a British citizen is triable in England but lesser offences against the person are not. If D were an alien, then he could not be tried in England for attempted murder. This seems anomalous, particularly since two aliens acting in concert could since 1977 be convicted of conspiracy in England to commit murder abroad.[9] If D posts a letter in England, attempting to obtain property by deception from P in France, he appears to be guilty of an attempt if he intends that the ownership or possession of the property shall be transferred to him in England;[10] but if both are to be transferred in France (e.g. to D's agent there) it is possible that the completed offence would not be triable in England, in which case there is no indictable attempt.

b) *Attempt abroad to commit an offence in England.* It was settled before the Act by the decision of the House of Lords in *DPP v Stonehouse*[11] that an act done abroad with intent thereby to cause the commission of an offence in England was indictable here, at least if it had an effect in England. D, in Miami, falsely staged his death by drowning with the intent that his innocent wife in England should claim life assurance monies. He was guilty of attempting to enable his wife to obtain by deception. The "effect", to which the majority of the House attached importance, was the communication through the media to her and the insurance companies of the false statement that he had died. Lord Keith insisted that an effect within the jurisdiction was essential but Lord Diplock thought otherwise. Why should the result have been different if D had been rescued from the sea and confessed before any report of his death appeared in England? In *Liangsiriprasert v United States Government*[12] the Privy Council, holding that a conspiracy abroad to commit an offence in England is indictable even though no overt act has been done within the jurisdiction, said, *obiter*, that the same rule applies to the other inchoate offences of incitement and attempt. The Act has nothing to say on the question so it remains a matter of common law. This may be taken to have been settled by *Liangsiriprasert*.

8. Above, p. 308; below, p. 328.
9. Above, p. 283.
10. Smith, *Theft*, para. 196A.
11. [1978] AC 55, [1977] Crim LR 544; **SHC 284**.
12. (1991) 92 Cr App Rep 77 at 87–90.

c) *Attempt abroad to commit an offence abroad.* D, a British citizen, being in France, attempts to kill P in France or, knowing himself to be married, attempts to go through a ceremony of marriage there. If he succeeds he will be liable to conviction in England of murder and bigamy. Exceptionally, English law assumes jurisdiction over these crimes when committed abroad by a British citizen. Literally, then, the attempt is an offence under the Act. It has been argued that the presumption against the extra-territorial operation of the criminal law[13] requires the words "does an act" to be construed as applicable only to acts done within the jurisdiction, or having, or being intended to have, some effect therein; but this argument has less weight after *Liangsiriprasert.* If the court has jurisdiction over the full offence when wholly committed abroad, why not over the attempt?

6 Withdrawal

It is logical that, once the steps taken towards the commission of an offence are sufficiently far advanced to amount to an attempt, it can make no difference whether the failure to complete the crime is due to a voluntary withdrawal by the prisoner, the intervention of the police, or any other reason. In *Taylor*[14] it was held that an attempt was committed where D approached a stack of corn with the intention of setting fire to it and lighted a match for that purpose but abandoned his plan on finding that he was being watched. In some jurisdictions, logic has given way to policy and a defence of free and voluntary desistance is allowed.[15] Following the recommendation of the Law Commission,[16] the Act makes no change in this respect. The principal argument in favour of a withdrawal defence is that it might induce the attempter to desist – but this seems unlikely. The existence of the defence would add to the problems of law enforcement authorities.

4 Impossibility

The problem to be discussed is peculiar to the "inchoate" offences which are the subject of this chapter. If it is impossible to commit a crime, obviously no one can be convicted of committing it. It does not follow that no one can be convicted of inciting another, or conspiring or attempting to commit it. It is a fact that people sometimes do incite, conspire and attempt to do what is impossible. This happens only when the defendant does not realise that what he has in view is impossible, i.e., he is making a mistake of some kind.

The law has long recognised that, in some circumstances, a conviction for incitement, conspiracy or attempt to commit an offence might be proper, although the commission of that offence was impossible. There has

13. See Griew, *Current Law Statutes*, General Note.
14. (1859) 1 F & F 511; See also *Lankford* [1959] Crim LR 209.
15. See Stuart, [1970] Crim LR at 519–521.
16. Law Com. No. 102, 2.131–2.133.

been great controversy about the circumstances in which impossibility will afford a defence and those in which it will not.

One category of case can be shortly disposed of. That is where the crime is "impossible" in the sense that the intended result is not a crime at all but D, because of his ignorance or mistake of criminal law, believes that it is. Here, the law is the same for all three inchoate offences and it is clear that none of them is committed. Suppose that D comes from a land where adultery is a crime and he thinks that it is a crime in England. He may incite the commission of adultery, agree to commit adultery and attempt to commit adultery. The "offence" he has in mind is non-existent, its "commission" is impossible and he has committed no inchoate offence. In *Taaffe*[17] D imported into the United Kingdom certain packages which he believed to contain foreign currency. He thought it was a crime to import foreign currency. It was not. He could not, on those facts, be committed of any offence or of an attempt to commit any offence. The intention to import foreign currency, believing it to be a crime, though morally reprehensible, was not the *mens rea* of any crime – any more than an intention to commit adultery in England is a *mens rea*. The conduct he had in mind was not the *actus reus* of any offence. In fact, Taaffe had committed the *actus reus* of a crime because the contents of the package were cannabis and it is an offence to import cannabis; but there was no *mens rea* to complement that *actus reus*.

In all the other cases to be considered D has the *mens rea* of the ulterior offence – he intends that it shall be committed; but because of some *fact* as to which he is ignorant or mistaken, either—

    (i) the result he intends cannot be achieved, or

    (ii) the result he intends, if achieved, will not be the crime that he believed would be committed.

Into category (i) fall cases where the means used are inadequate to achieve the intended result and where the subject matter or victim of the intended offence does not exist. Category (ii) comprises cases where some circumstance, which is an element of the intended crime, does not exist. D believes that he is committing a crime, because he is making a mistake, not of criminal law, but of fact. For example, he intends that he (or the person incited or with whom he conspires) shall have sexual intercourse with P, whom he believes to be fifteen. P is sixteen and consequently the "result" (intercourse with P) will not be the crime that D intended. At one time,[18] it was thought that the distinction between categories (i) and (ii) was material but, as the law now stands, it has no part to play.

It might be expected that the same general principles of the common law would apply to all cases of of incitement, conspiracy and attempt and this probably was the case.[19] The law now, however, is that

---

17. [1984] AC 539 [1984] 1 All ER 747, HL, [1983] 2 All ER 625, CA. See commentary on the decision of the Court of Appeal, [1983] Crim LR 536.
18. See the first three editions of this work. R. A. Duff, "Attempts and the Problem of the Missing Circumstance" (1991) 42 NILQR 87 and White, *Misleading Cases.*"
19. In *Fitzmaurice* [1983] QB 1083, [1983] 1 All ER 189. CA, followed in *Sirat* (1986) 83 Cr App Rep 41, [1986] Crim LR 245, it was held that the principles stated in *Haughton v Smith* and *Nock* apply to incitement.

(i) incitement and common law conspiracy are governed by the common law;

(ii) statutory conspiracy and attempt are governed by the Criminal Law Act 1977, s. 1 (1), as amended,[20] and the Criminal Attempts Act 1981, s. 1 (2) and (3), respectively.

a) *The common law*. The common law was laid down, for attempts, in *Haughton v Smith*,[1] and for conspiracy, in *Director of Public Prosecutions v Nock*.[2] The result of these decisions is that impossibility is a general defence at common law. It seems that the only exception is that D may be convicted where the impossibility results from the inadequacy of the means used, or to be used, to commit the offence. So, for example, D will not be guilty of incitement where—

(i) The subject matter of the offence does not exist. D incites E to steal from P's safe. P's safe is empty.

(ii) The victim of the offence does not exist. D incites E to murder P. P is already dead.[3]

(iii) The subject-matter of the offence lacks some quality which is an element of the offence. D and E believe a certain diamond to have been stolen. D incites E to receive it. It has not been stolen.[4]

(iv) The victim of the offence lacks some quality which is an element of the offence. D and E believe P to be aged fifteen. In fact she is sixteen. D incites E to have sexual intercourse with her.

On the other hand, D may be guilty of incitement where—

(i) He gives E a jemmy and urges him to use it to break into P's safe and steal a diamond. The diamond is in the safe, but it is impossible to break in with the jemmy.

(ii) He gives E some poison and tells him to administer it to P so as to kill him. The dose is inadequate to kill anyone.

b) *The statutory law*. For statutory conspiracies the law is to be found in the Criminal Law Act 1977, s. 1 (1)[5] as amended by the Criminal Attempts Act 1981 and, for attempts, it is in the Criminal Attempts Act 1981, s. 1 (2) and (3) which provides:

"(2) A person may be guilty of attempting to commit an offence to which this section applies even though the facts are such that the commission of the offence is impossible.

(3) In any case where—

(a) apart from this subsection a person's intention would not be regarded as having amounted to an intent to commit an offence; but

(b) if the facts of the case had been as he believed them to be, his intention would be so regarded, then for the purposes of

20. Above, p. 271.
1. [1975] AC 476, [1973] 2 All ER 896.
2. [1978] AC 979, [1978] 2 All ER 654, above, p. 275.
3. *Sirat* (1986) 83 Cr App Rep 41 at 43.
4. *Haughton v Smith*, above.
5. Above, p. 271.

subsection (1) above he shall be regarded as having an intent to commit that offence."

Subsection (3) is strictly unnecessary but it was wise to include it as a matter of caution. It is unnecessary because under it no one will "be regarded as having an intent to commit that offence" who does not in fact have that intent. It would be wholly wrong to impute a non-existent intent to a defendant and the Act does not do so. In other words the subsection does nothing – except forestall the following fallacious argument.

  (i) D (believing them to be stolen) intends to handle certain goods.
  (ii) Those goods are not stolen.
  (iii) Therefore D does not intend to handle stolen goods.

Subsection (3) says he shall be regarded as having an intent to handle stolen goods. Of course, he has such an intent anyway. The fact that the goods are not stolen, being unknown to him, is wholly irrelevant in determining his intention.

The gist of the two provisions is that for both conspiracy and attempt there must be an intention to commit the offence[6] contemplated, whereupon it is immaterial that it is *in fact* impossible to commit that offence if, in the case of conspiracy, there has been an agreement to commit it and in the case of an attempt, a more than merely preparatory step towards its commission. The provisions have no application to the cases considered above[7] where it is, *in law*, impossible to commit "the offence" D intended to commit.

The proper construction of the Criminal Attempts Act has been a matter of acute controversy but it is now settled by the decision of the House of Lords in *Shivpuri*.[8]

It seems reasonable to assume that the same interpretation will be put on the amended s. 1 (1) of the Criminal Law Act 1977 (statutory conspiracy) for that section was amended by the Criminal Attempts Act 1981, s. 5, to keep the law of attempt and conspiracy in line in this respect.

In the case of attempts, it must be proved that D had an intention to commit the crime in question. Once that is established, the only question is whether, with that intent, he has done an act which is "more than merely preparatory" to the commission of the offence. Since, ex hypothesi, the offence is impossible, it is the offence envisaged by D to which the act in question must be more than merely preparatory. The effect is that the court must ask, "would the act have been more than merely preparatory to the commission of the offence if the facts had been as D believed them to be?"

In the case of conspiracy, it must be proved that D agreed with another or others that a course of conduct be pursued which, in the circumstances believed by the parties to exist, will, in the event of their intention being achieved, amount to or involve the commission of the offence. It has been argued above[9] that this is the only sensible interpretation of the phrase, "course of conduct", and that the amendment by the 1981 Act was strictly unnecessary. The 1981 amendment may, however, be taken to reinforce

6. For conspiracy, pace Lord Bridge in *Anderson*, above, p. 273.
7. P. 317.
8. [1987] AC 1, [1986] 2 All ER 334, [1986] Crim LR 536.
9. P. 274.

this opinion. It is then immaterial that the circumstances are in fact such that the offence is impossible, or that the results can never be achieved.

In the following examples, D will be guilty both of conspiracy and attempt.

(i) D and E agree that they will use D's jemmy to break into P's safe and steal a diamond. D tries to do so. It is quite impossible to break into the safe with that jemmy. D and E are guilty of conspiracy and D of an attempt to steal the diamond. (It is immaterial whether the diamond is in the safe or not.)

(ii) D and E agree that they will administer a poison, which D has acquired, to P in order to kill him. D administers the poison. The poison would not kill anyone. D and E are guilty of conspiracy, and D of an attempt, to murder P.

(iii) D and E agree that they will steal from P's safe. D attempts to break open the safe. It is empty. D and E are guilty of conspiracy, and D of attempt, to steal from the safe.

(iv) D and E agree that they will murder P. D shoots at P's heart but P is already dead. D and E are guilty of conspiracy to murder and D of attempted murder.

(v) D and E agree that they will receive from F certain goods which they believe to be stolen goods. D takes possession of the goods. The goods are not stolen goods. D and E are guilty of conspiracy, and D of an attempt, to handle stolen goods.

(vi) D and E agree that D will have sexual intercourse with P, a girl whom they believe to be aged fifteen. D has sexual intercourse with her. In fact she is sixteen. D and E are guilty of conspiracy, and D of an attempt, to have sexual intercourse with a girl under the age of sixteen.

Examples (iii) and (iv) would not have been offences at common law under the principles established in *Haughton* v *Smith* and *Nock* but those decisions are now generally recognised to have been unduly restrictive. It is the cases exemplified by illustrations (v) and (vi) which have been the subject of much controversy.[10] The reason is that, in these cases, if D succeeds in doing the precise thing that he set out to do, he will not commit a crime. D takes possession of the very goods he intended to take possession of – no other – and that is no offence, for the goods are not stolen goods. D has sexual intercourse with the girl he intends to have intercourse with. She is sixteen and consents so there is nothing unlawful. How then can his taking steps towards the accomplishment of something which is no crime be a conspiracy or an attempt to commit it? Bramwell B ridiculed the idea in *Collins*[11] in 1864. He put the case of D who takes an umbrella from his club, intending to steal it. It turns out to be his own umbrella. Bramwell B thought it absurd that D should be convicted of attempting to steal it. Arguments of this kind prevailed in the House of Lords in *Anderton v*

10. The decisive article which influenced the decision in *Shivpuri* is Glanville Williams, "The Lords and Impossible Attempts", [1986] CLJ 33. For earlier writing, see Hogan [1984] Crim LR 584 and 135 NLJ 454, Williams 135 NLJ 337 and commentaries at [1985] Crim LR 44, 504, [1986] Crim LR 51.
11. 9 Cox CC 497 at 498.

Ryan[12] (1985) but were then rejected in *Shivpuri*[13] (1986) barely a year later.

In *Anderton v Ryan* D bought a video recorder for £110. Later she said to police, "I may as well be honest, it was a stolen one I bought ...". She was charged with handling and attempted handling. The prosecution, presumably believing that they were unable to prove that the recorder had in fact been stolen, offered no evidence on the first charge. The magistrates were not satisfied that the recorder had been stolen, though D believed it had. They dismissed the charge. The Divisional Court allowed the prosecution's appeal[14] but the House of Lords, Lord Edmund-Davies dissenting, restored the decision of the magistrates. The Criminal Attempts Act 1981, s. 1 (3), said Lord Roskill, "does not compel the conclusion that an erroneous belief in the existence of facts which, if true, would have made his completed act a crime makes him guilty of an attempt to commit that crime". Because the House thought the conclusion absurd, they were not going to reach it unless compelled to. In *Shivpuri* D was arrested by customs officials while in possession of a suitcase. He admitted that he knew it contained prohibited drugs. Analysis showed that the material in the suitcase was not a prohibited drug but a vegetable material akin to snuff. He was convicted of attempting to be knowingly concerned in dealing with a prohibited drug, contrary to s. 1 (1) of the Criminal Attempts Act 1981 and s. 170 (1) (b) of the Customs and Excise Management Act 1979. His appeal was dismissed by the Court of Appeal[15] and, overruling *Anderton v Ryan*, by the House of Lords. No distinction is to be drawn between "objectively innocent" acts (taking one's own umbrella, receiving non-stolen goods, handling snuff) and "guilty" acts, for the purposes of the law of attempts. The law is as stated above.[16] Since it must be proved that D intended to commit the crime in question, he is morally at least as bad as the person who actually commits the offence and, where the offence may be committed with some lesser degree of *mens rea*, perhaps worse; and he is as dangerous to whatever interest the particular law is designed to protect as the person who actually commits the offence. It is sometimes objected that he is punished solely for his thoughts but this is not true because it must be proved (in the case of an attempt) that he has taken such steps to put his intention into execution as would (if the facts were as he believed) be more than merely preparatory to the commission of the offence. In the case of conspiracy (not expressly considered in *Shivpuri* but presumably governed by the same principles) he must have agreed with another that the offence be committed – the usual *actus reus* of conspiracy. It is also argued that the conclusion offends against the principle of legality (no one shall be convicted of doing something which has not been declared by the law to be an offence). But the issue in these cases was the proper construction of the statute. If Parliament has said (and the House ultimately decided that it has) that it is to be an offence (attempt) to do any

12. [1985] AC 560, [1985] 2 All ER 355.
13. [1987] AC 1, [1986] 2 All ER 334.
14. [1985] 1 All ER 138, [1984] Crim LR 483.
15. [1985] QB 1029, [1985] 1 All ER 143.
16. P. 319.

more than a merely preparatory act with intent to commit an offence, the law may be criticised for being too wide-ranging; but the conviction of one who does any such act with that intent can no longer be criticised for breaching the principle of legality.

The breadth of the law is such that there may be cases where prosecution would be ill-advised. Bramwell B's man who took his own umbrella would no doubt be surprised to find himself charged with attempting to steal his own umbrella. D who has *succeeded* in having sexual intercourse with P, a sixteen-year-old girl, might be astonished to find himself charged in consequence with *attempting* to have sexual intercourse with a girl under sixteen. As such acts are objectively innocent, the offence is unlikely to come to light unless D advertises the fact that he acted with *mens rea*. There will be other cases, however, where a prosecution is in the public interest. The would-be drug smuggler, exemplified by *Shivpuri*, is an instance. It may well be that their Lordships' change of mind was not uninfluenced by the fact that *Anderton v Ryan* would have required them to turn such dangerous persons loose on the public. Perhaps the most important case in practice is that of the person who receives goods wrongly believing them to be stolen. Mrs Ryan's was an unusual and trivial case. Typical of the case where a prosecution is likely to be brought is *Haughton v Smith* itself. A van, heavily laden with stolen corned beef, was intercepted by the police. Having discovered that the intended recipient was D, the police allowed it to proceed on its way, but under the control of disguised policemen. D received the goods, believing them to be stolen. But the beef ceased to be stolen goods when the police took control of it.[17] The House held that he was not guilty of attempted handling but now he could plainly be convicted. The public interest called for his conviction no less than if the police had never intercepted the goods.

c) *Two doubtful cases.* (i) It has been noted that an intention to commit a non-existent crime arising from a mistake as to the criminal law involves no liability.[18] More arguable is the case where D has an intention to commit an existing offence because he is making a mistake of civil law. Believing that the law requires him to use money for a particular purpose, D dishonestly uses the money for another purpose. If his belief were true, he would be guilty of theft. Actually the law allows him to do what he likes with the money and he commits no substantive offence.[19] He intends to steal and has done his best to do so. In principle, the case is difficult to distinguish from those where the intent to commit an offence is attributable to a mistake of fact; but the use of "facts" in s. 1 (3) (b) is likely to exclude liability.

(ii) The recognition in *Khan*[20] of the reckless-as-to-circumstances attempt raises the spectre of the reckless/impossible attempt.[1] D has intercourse with P who consents, but D is not sure whether she consents or not. Is he guilty of attempted rape? Glanville Williams thinks he must be, but

17. Below, p. 636.
18. Above, p. 317.
19. Commentary on *Huskinson* [1988] Crim LR 620 at 622.
20. Above, p. 306.
  1. Glanville Williams, [1983] Crim LR 365 at 375.

that he should not be prosecuted. A possible answer is that s. 1 (3) of the Act requires us to treat D as if the facts were "as he *believed* them to be" and D does not *believe* that the woman is not consenting but is merely reckless whether she consents or not. The subsection, whatever its purpose or effect, does not apply to this case and, as it is this section which removes the impossibility defence, this affords some ground for holding that the reckless/impossible attempt is still no offence.

d) *Impossibility in future.* It would be rash to predict that *Shivpuri* solves all the problems relating to impossibility except the doubtful cases noted above. The fact that Lord Hailsham, with whom Lord Elwyn-Jones and Lord Mackay concurred, offered reasons why *Anderton v Ryan* was distinguishable (even though they concurred in overruling it) may encourage subsequent attempts to distinguish *Shivpuri* on similar lines. To do so would, however, be to resurrect in a slightly different form arguments which were in substance rejected in *Shivpuri*.[2] It is, of course, anomalous that, for incitement, impossibility should continue to be governed by the common law, particularly as that was left in such an unsatisfactory state by *Haughton v Smith* and *Nock*. It is submitted that the matter would be put on a sound basis by the enactment of the proposal of the Draft Criminal Code, cl. 50 (1).[3]

> "A person may be guilty of incitement, conspiracy or attempt to commit an offence although the commission of the offence is impossible, if it would be possible in the circumstances which he believes or hopes exist or will exist at the relevant time."

2. See the analysis of Lord Hailsham's speech at [1986] Crim LR 539–541.
3. See Law Com. No. 177, 13.50–13.53.

Part II

Particular Crimes

12 Homicide

1 Murder

The classic definition of murder is that of Coke:
> "Murder is when a man of sound memory, and of the age of discretion, unlawfully killeth within any county of the realm any reasonable creature *in rerum natura* under the king's peace, with malice aforethought, either expressed by the party or implied by law, so as the party wounded, or hurt, etc. die of the wound or hurt, etc. within a year and a day after the same."[1]

1) *Who Can Commit Murder*

"A man of sound memory, and of the age of discretion" means simply a man who is responsible according to the general principles which have been discussed above. Such a man is not insane within the M'Naghten Rules; he is over nine and, if under fourteen, he has a "mischievous discretion"; and, since 1957,[2] he does not suffer from diminished responsibility. A corporation cannot be tried for murder because it cannot suffer the only penalty allowed by law, life imprisonment.

2) *Where Murder Can Be Committed*

If the killing is by a British citizen, it need no longer take place within "any county of the realm". Murder and manslaughter are among the exceptional cases where the English courts have jurisdiction over offences committed abroad. By s. 9 of the Offences against the Person Act 1861 and s. 3 of the British Nationality Act 1948 a murder or manslaughter committed by a British citizen on land anywhere out of the United Kingdom may be tried in any county or place in England as if it had been committed there.[3]

---

1. 3 Inst 47.
2. See s. 2 of the Homicide Act 1957, above, p. 212.
3. See CLRC, OAP/WP, p. 67, OAP/R 125.

Homicides on a British ship[4] or aircraft[5] are also triable here, whether committed by a British subject or not; but not those on a foreign ship, outside territorial waters.[6]

3) *Who Can Be The Victim*[7]

Though this matter is traditionally discussed only in relation to murder and does not seem to have arisen in other contexts, it is clear that, in principle, the same rules must apply to assaults and offences against the person generally, Coke's "reasonable creature in *rerum natura*" is simply the "person" who is the victim of an offence in the modern law of offences against the person – i.e., any human being.[8] The problems are at what stage in the process of birth a foetus becomes a person; and at what stage in the process of death a person becomes a corpse. It is not murder to kill a child in the womb or in the process of leaving the womb. At common law it was a "great misprision" (misdemeanour)[9] and it is now an offence under s. 58 of the Offences against the Person Act 1861,[10] or, where the child is capable of being born alive, under the Infant Life (Preservation) Act 1929.[11] The question is whether the child has "an existence independent of its mother". To kill a child before it has such an existence is, under the 1929 Act, child destruction and not murder. To have such an existence the child must have been wholly expelled from its mother's body and be alive. The cord and after-birth need not have been expelled from the mother nor severed from the child. The tests of independent existence which the courts have accepted are that the child should have an independent circulation, and that it should have breathed after birth. But there are difficulties about both these tests.

In *Brain* Park J said:[12]

"... it is not essential that it should have breathed at the time it was killed; as many children are born alive and yet do not breathe for some time after their birth."

And, according to Atkinson, there is no known means of determining at what instant the foetal and parental circulations are so dissociated as to allow the child to live without the help of the parental circulation; and this

---

4. Not only when sailing on the high seas, but also when in the rivers of a foreign territory at a place below bridges, where the tide ebbs and flows and where great ships go: *Anderson* (1868) LR 1 CCR 161.

5. Civil Aviation Act 1982, s. 92.

6. Jurisdiction over offences within territorial waters is given by the Territorial Waters Jurisdiction Act 1878, s. 2. And see Oil and Gas (Enterprise) Act 1982, s. 22.

7. Seaborne Davies, "Child-killing in English Law", MACL 301; Williams, *Sanctity of Life and the Criminal Law*, 19–23; S. B. Atkinson, "Life, Birth and Live Birth" (1904) 20 LQR 134.

8. Draft Code, cl. 53.

9. 3 Co Inst 50. According to Hale, 1 PC 433, "a great crime". Willes J said in 1866 (BPP 21, p. 274) that the crime was obsolete. (See MACL at 310.)

10. Below, p. 388.

11. Below, p. 384.

12. (1834) 6 C & P 349 at 350. But see *C v S* and *Rance v Mid-Downs Health Authority*, below, p. 385.

dissociation may precede birth.[13] There is thus some uncertainty about the precise moment at which the child comes under the protection of the law of murder, though the question does not seem to have troubled the courts in recent years. The last reported case the CLRC could trace was in 1874.[14] The committee recommends that the test should be that the victim should have been born and have an existence independent of its mother.

If the child is poisoned or injured in the womb, is born alive and then dies of the poison or injury, this may be murder or manslaughter.[15] In West[16] Maule J directed the jury:

". . . if a person intending to procure abortion does an act which causes a child to be born so much earlier than the natural time that it is born in a state much less capable of living and afterwards dies as a consequence of its exposure to the external world, the person who by her misconduct so brings a child into the world and puts it merely into a situation in which it cannot live is guilty of murder."

In such a case, D would have had the *mens rea* sufficient, at that time, for murder, since she intended to commit a felony.[17] In modern law, however, a person who intends to kill or cause serious injury to an unborn child does not have the *mens rea* for murder – he does not intend to kill or cause serious injury to a person in being – and should not be liable to conviction of that offence.[18] If the child is born alive and dies of the injury inflicted with that intent he might be guilty of manslaughter if there was an obvious and serious risk (*Caldwell* recklessness, or perhaps, gross negligence) that this might occur. If D's intention was to cause death or serious injury to the mother he would, by "transferred malice", be guilty of murder of the child who was born alive and died of the injury so inflicted.[19] It was held in *Senior*[20] that where the pre-natal injury was caused by gross negligence or with a *mens rea* sufficient only for manslaughter, and death after birth resulted from it a conviction for manslaughter was appropriate. It would be logical to go on to hold that gross pre-natal neglect of the child by the mother, resulting in death after birth, should also be manslaughter; but this step has not been taken, and the rule appears to apply only to acts and not omissions.[1]

Similar problems could arise as to the moment at which life ends, though these do not seem, in practice, to have troubled the courts. Is P dead, and therefore incapable of being murdered, if his heart has stopped beating but a surgeon confidently expects to start it again, by an injection or mechanical

13. 20 LQR at 145.
14. *Handley* (1874) 13 Cox CC 79, followed by Wright J in *Pritchard* (1901) 17 TLR 310. Cmnd. 7844, para. 35.
15. 3 Co Inst 50; Hawkins, 1 PC, c. 31, §16; East, 1 PC 228; contra Hale, 1 PC 433.
16. (1848) 2 Cox CC 500. See also *Kwok Chak Ming* (Hong Kong, 1963) discussed in [1963] Crim LR 748 and Temkin, "Pre-natal Injury, Homicide and the Draft Criminal Code", [1986] CLJ 414.
17. Under 9 Geo. IV, c. 31, s. 13.
18. Cf. Temkin, above, fn. 16, and the Draft Code, cl. 53.
19. Cf. Draft Code, cl. 53.
20. (1832) 1 Mood CC 346.
  1. *Knights* (1860) 2 F & F 46; *Izod* (1904) 20 Cox CC 690; and see the discussion by Davies, MACL at 308–309.

means?[2] Is P dead if he is in a "hopeless" condition and "kept alive" only by an apparatus of some kind?[3] There is, at present, no certain answer to these questions which are being raised in an acute form by heart transplant operations. The current medical view is that the test is one of brain death and that this can be diagnosed with certainty.[4] The law has not yet evolved a definition of its own and the CLRC declined to propose one[5] both because of the fluid state of medical science and the repercussions that such a definition might have on other branches of the law.

All persons appear to be "under the Queen's peace" for this purpose, even an alien enemy, "unless it be in the heat of war, and in the actual exercise thereof."[6] So also it is murder at common law if a man condemned to death be executed by someone other than the officer lawfully appointed, or if the officer lawfully appointed carries out the execution by an unauthorised method, as where he beheads a man condemned to be hanged.[7] In *Page*[8] an argument that an Egyptian national who had been murdered in an Egyptian village by a British soldier was not within the Queen's peace, was rejected.[9]

4) *Death Within a Year and a Day*

This rule seems to have had its origin in the procedure of the ancient appeal of felony, a private prosecution, and to have imposed a limit on the time in which the action must be brought.[10] Time then ran from the day of the death. The rule has changed its nature – time now runs from the day on which the injury which caused death was inflicted – and its function. It has become part of the substantive law of homicide, an arbitrary rule restricting the right of the prosecution to prove that the defendant caused death. If the death occurs after a year and a day there is no *actus reus*. The change had occurred by the time of Coke who wrote:

"... for if he die after that time, it cannot be discerned, as the law presumes, whether he died of the stroke or poison, etc. or a natural death."[11]

2. Williams, *Sanctity of Life and the Criminal Law*, 18.

3. Elliott (1964) 4 Med Sci & L 77; and see ibid., at 550; I. M. Kennedy, "Alive or Dead?" (1969) 22 CLP 102; "Switching Off Life Support Machines", [1977] Crim LR 443; Hogan "A Note on Death" [1972] Crim LR 80; Skegg, "Irreversibly Comatose Individuals: Alive or Dead?" [1964] CLJ 130; and Report of the Broderick Committee (1969) Cmnd. 4810, paras. 808–812.

4. *British Medical Journal* and *The Lancet*, 31 February 1979. Cf. *Malcherek* [1981] 2 All ER 422, [1981] 1 WLR 690, below, p. 336.

5. CLRC/OAP/R, para. 37.

6. Hale, 1 PC 433.

7. Ibid.

8. [1954] 1 QB 170, [1953] 2 All ER 1355 (C–MAC).

9. The real issue in that case was whether the court-martial assembled in the Canal Zone had jurisdiction to try the case. It was admitted that, if D had been brought to this country and tried here, no question could have arisen as to the nationality of the victim. The court-martial was held to have jurisdiction under the Army Act.

10. Yale, "A Year and a Day in Homicide" [1989] CLJ 202.

11. 3 Co Inst 52.

This may have been a sound basis for the rule in Coke's time, but the retention of the rule in the present state of medical science can be justified only on the ground that one who has injured another should not remain indefinitely at risk of prosecution for murder.[12] The rule remains valid, not only for murder, but also for manslaughter and probably for all other forms of criminal homicide – infanticide, suicide in pursuance of a suicide pact[13] (Homicide Act 1957, s. 4 (1)), aiding and abetting suicide[14] (Suicide Act 1961, s. 2 (1)) and causing death by dangerous driving or by careless driving when under the influence of drink or drugs. In *Dyson*[15] D, who had inflicted injuries on a child in November, 1906, and again in December, 1907, was indicted for the manslaughter of the child which died on 5 March 1908. The judge directed the jury that they could find D guilty if they considered death to have been caused by the injuries inflicted in November, 1906. The Court of Criminal Appeal set aside the conviction:

"It is still undoubtedly the law of the land that no person can be convicted of manslaughter where the death does not occur within a year and a day after the injury was inflicted, for in that event it must be attributed to some other cause."[16]

The law takes no note of a part of a day. If the blow is struck at any time on 1 January 1991, death must occur before midnight on 1 January 1992, to be within the rule. Time runs, it is submitted, not from the date of D's act but from that of the infliction of the injury, where these are different. This is in accordance both with the causation rationale of the rule and considerations of policy. For example, D plants a bomb on 1 January 1991. It goes off on 2 January 1992, and gravely injures P. D is guilty of homicide if P dies before 3 January 1993. If the relevant date were that of D's act, he could not be made liable at all.[17]

5) *The Problem of Causation*[18]

The year and a day rule is a convenient starting point for the whole question of causation. What must be caused is some acceleration of death. Since everyone must die sooner or later, it follows that every killing is merely an acceleration of death; and it makes no difference for this purpose that the victim is already suffering from a fatal disease or injury or is under sentence of death. Thus, in *Dyson*, the facts of which are given above, Lord Alverstone CJ said:[19]

12. CLRC, OAP/WP, para. 44, OAP/R, para. 39.
13. *R v Inner West London Coroner, ex p De Luca* [1989] 3 All ER 414 at 416, 417, DC. (Death occurring after more than a year from the day of a self-inflicted injury is not suicide.)
14. Ibid.
15. [1908] 2 KB 454.
16. Ibid., at 456.
17. See CLRC/OAP/R, para. 40. The CLRC recommends, and the Draft Code, cl. 53 (b) provides, that, in the case of pre-natal injury, time should run from the date of birth.
18. Hart and Honoré, *Causation in the Law* (2nd ed.), especially Chs. XII–XIV; Williams, "Causation in Homicide", [1957] Crim LR 429 and 510; Camps and Harvard, "Causation in Homicide – A Medical View", [1957] Crim LR at 576.
19. [1908] 2 KB at 457. And see Hale, 1 PC 428; *Fletcher* (1841) Russell 417; *Martin* (1832) 5 C & P 128 at 130.

"The proper question to have been submitted to the jury was whether the prisoner accelerated the child's death by the injuries which he inflicted in December, 1907. For if he did the fact that the child was already suffering from meningitis from which it would in any event have died before long, would afford no answer to the charge of causing its death."

The administration of pain-saving drugs presents difficult problems. In the case of *Adams*[20] Devlin J directed the jury that there is no special defence justifying a doctor in giving drugs which would shorten life in the case of severe pain: "If life were cut short by weeks or months it was just as much murder as if it were cut short by years." He went on:

"But that does not mean that a doctor aiding the sick or dying has to calculate in minutes or hours, or perhaps in days or weeks, the effect on a patient's life of the medicines which he administers. If the first purpose of medicine – the restoration of health – can no longer be achieved, there is still much for the doctor to do, and he is entitled to do all that is proper and necessary to relieve pain and suffering even if measures he takes may incidentally shorten life."

These passages are not easy to reconcile. If the doctor gives drugs with the object of relieving the pain and suffering of a dying man knowing that the drugs will certainly shorten his life, then he intends to shorten life. If, as Devlin J held, and as must surely be the case, the doctor has a defence, it cannot be because his act has not caused death nor because he did not intend so to do. Perhaps this is a case in which motive affords an excuse.[1] Would not a legatee, who administered the same drugs with the object of hastening his inheritance, be guilty of murder if his action accelerated the death to any appreciable extent?[2]

Alternatively, it may be that there is a defence in these cases only where the drugs are not a "substantial" cause of death; for, if the doctor is entitled to shorten life at all to save pain, presumably he may do this only where death is inevitable within a short time; hence the contrast made by the learned judge between "weeks or months" and "minutes or hours".[3]

1 A Question of Fact and Law

Causation is generally a question of fact for the jury but, in answering the question, they must apply the legal principles which it is the judge's duty to explain to them.[4] According to *Blaue*,[5] where "there is no conflict of evidence and all the jury has to do is to apply the law to the admitted facts, the judge is entitled to tell the jury what the result of that application will be". *Cheshire*,[6] however, shows that, in some cases, the jury may have a

20. [1957] Crim LR 365; (1957) Times, 9 April; Sybille Bedford, *The Best We Can Do*, at 192; Devlin, *Easing the Passing* (1985); Hart and Honoré, op. cit., at 344.
   1. See, for an alternative explanation, Beynon, "Doctors as Murderers", [1982] Crim LR 17.
   2. But the doctor who, following accepted medical practice, administered drugs which shortened life, would not be guilty because he knew that P had left him a legacy and was pleased at the prospect of receiving it sooner. See above, p. 79.
   3. See, for an alternative explanation, Helen Beynon, [1982] Crim LR 17–19.
   4. *Pagett* (1983) 76 Cr App Rep 279, CA.
   5. [1975] 3 All ER 446 at 450, CA, below, p. 338.
   6. [1991] 3 ALL ER 670, [1991] 1 WLR 844, below, p. 341.

substantial role in evaluating the primary facts. The judge may certainly direct the jury that they must acquit where there is no evidence that D caused death, but it is not so clear that he may tell them that they must find that D did cause death (or any other result) even where that is the only reasonable conclusion. If it is not for the judge to decide the issue, still less is it for medical experts. Their function is to inform the court as to the medical facts. It is then for the jury to find the facts and apply the legal principles under the direction of the judge. Thus, the case of *Jordan* has been criticised[7] because medical experts were permitted to say that certain medical treatment, and not a wound inflicted by D, was the cause of P's death.[8] Whether the wound was "a cause", for the purpose of the decision, was a question of law, not of medicine. Certainly it was relevant and proper for the court to know if the medical treatment was effective to cause death, either in conjunction with, or independently of, the wound; and perhaps all that the witnesses intended to say was that the treatment alone was the medical cause of death.

2 The "But For" Principle
The first principle is that D's act cannot be the cause of an event if the event would have occurred in precisely the same way had that act never been done. It must be proved that, *but for*, D's act, the event would not have occurred.[9] In the traditional terminology, the act must be a *sine qua non* of the event. But this is only a starting point. There are many acts which are *sine qua non* of an event but are not, either in law or common sense, the cause of it. If D invites P to dinner and P is run over and killed on the way, P would not have died but for the invitation; but no one would say "D killed P", and D has not caused his death in law. In *Jordan*,[10] the wound was certainly a *sine qua non* of the death for it led directly to the medical treatment, but it did not necessarily follow that it was, in law, a cause of the death. That depended on the application of the further principles considered below.

3 Contributory Causes
It is clear that the act of the accused need not be the sole or the main cause of death. It is wrong to direct a jury that D is not liable if he is less than one-fifth to blame.[11] In *Dyson* it would have been immaterial that the blows would not have caused death but for the meningitis; it was enough that the death would not have been caused by the meningitis at the time when it occurred but for the blows. Contributory causes may be the acts of others including the acts of the deceased himself. The contributory negligence of

7. By Williams at [1957] Crim LR 431 and by Camps and Havard at [1957] Crim LR 582.
8. Cf. *Cato* [1976] 1 All ER 260 at 264, below, p. 367 where the medical experts said it was not for them to state the cause of death; they spoke to facts, and deductions therefrom were for the jury.
9. Even this basic rule may have exceptions, but only in very unlikely circumstances, e.g., D and E, independently and simultaneously, shoot at P. D's bullet goes through P's heart and E's bullet blows his brains out. It seems safe to assume that both will be held to have caused P's death. Cf. Hall, *General Principles* 267.
10. Discussed in detail, below, p. 340.
11. *Hennigan* [1971] 3 All ER 133.

the plaintiff in civil actions of negligence was an absolute defence at common law, but no such principle applied in the criminal law. In *Swindall and Osborn*[12] where one or other of the two accused ran over and killed an old man, Pollock CB directed the jury that it was immaterial that the man was deaf or drunk or negligent and contributed to his own death.

A case in which the negligence of third parties contributed to P's death is *Benge*.[13] D, a foreman platelayer, employed to take up a certain section of railway line, misread the time-table so that the line was up at a time when a train arrived. He placed a flagman at a distance of only 540 yards, instead of 1,000 yards as required by the company's regulations and entirely omitted to place fog signals, although the regulations specified that these should be put at 250-yard intervals for a distance of 1,000 yards. At D's trial for manslaughter it was urged that, in spite of his mistakes, the accident could not have happened if the other servants of the company had done their duty – if the flagman had gone the proper distance or if the engine driver had been keeping a proper look-out, which he was not. Pigott B ruled that this was no defence; if D's negligence mainly or substantially caused the accident, it was irrelevant that it might have been avoided if other persons had not been negligent.

Evidence of P's negligence may, however, be relevant in showing that D was not negligent at all or that his negligence was not gross.

The death is not attributable to the accused if the culpability of his act in no way contributed to it. In *Dalloway*[14] D was driving a cart on a highway with reins not in his hands but loose on the horse's back. A three-year-old child ran into the road a few yards in front of the horse and was struck by one of the wheels and killed. Erle J directed the jury that, if the prisoner had reins and by using the reins could have saved the child, he was guilty of manslaughter; but that, if they thought he could not have saved the child by the use of the reins, then they should acquit him. If D had not been driving the cart at all the incident could not have occurred; and in that sense, he "caused" it; but it was necessary to go further and show that the death was due to the culpable element in his act – the negligence in not using the reins.

4 A Substantial Cause

It is sometimes said[15] that the act must be a "substantial" cause but this seems to mean only that D's contribution must not be so minute that it will be ignored under the "de minimis" principle.[16] It may therefore be misleading to direct a jury that D is not liable unless his conduct was a "substantial" cause.[17] Killing is merely an acceleration of death and factors which produce a very trivial acceleration will be ignored. For example:

12. (1846) 2 Car & Kir 230 above, p. 132. See also *Walker* (1824) 1 C & P 320 (Garrow B).
13. (1865) 4 F & F 504. Cf. *Ledger* (1862) 2 F & F 857.
14. (1847) 2 Cox CC 273.
15. See for example, *Benge*, above, *Smith* [1959] 2 QB 35 at 42–43, [1959] 2 All ER 193 at 198 (below, p. 341); Hall, *General Principles*, 283; Perkins (1946) 36 J Cr L & Cr at 393, and *Criminal Law*, 606–607.
16. *Cato* [1976] 1 All ER 260 at 265–266; ". . . it need hardly be added that [that cause] need not be substantial to render the accused guilty": *Malcherek* [1981] 2 All ER 422 at 428.
17. *Hennigan*, above, p. 334.

D and P are roped mountaineers. P has fallen over a thousand-foot precipice and is dragging D slowly after him. D cuts the rope and P falls to his death five seconds before both P and D would have fallen. Or where two persons independently inflict wounds on P:

"... suppose one wound severed the jugular vein whereas the other barely broke the skin of the hand, and as the life blood gushed from the victim's neck, one drop oozed from the bruise on his finger ... metaphysicians will conclude that the extra drop of lost blood hastened the end by the infinitesimal fraction of a second. But the law will apply the *substantial factor* test and for juridical purposes the death will be imputed only to the severe injury in such an extreme case as this."[18]

These are, perhaps, rather unlikely examples but the principle would apply, for example, to the person visiting the dying man and contributing to his exhaustion by talking with him; and probably to the administration of pain-killing drugs which accelerate death.[19]

The problem of an intervening cause, which is discussed below[20] is sometimes put on the basis of substantial cause. Thus Hall writes:

"For example, a slight wound may have necessitated going to a doctor or drugstore, and *en route* the slightly injured person was struck by an automobile or shot by his mortal enemy. The slight wound, though a necessary condition of the death, did not contribute substantially to it."[1]

5 Intervening Acts or Events

Difficult problems may arise where, after D has inflicted an injury on P, some other act or event intervenes before death.

D is not responsible for the death where P dies as the result of some subsequent act or event which would have caused death in just the same way even if D had not inflicted the injury on P: for example, D administers poison to P but, before it takes any effect on P's body, P dies of a heart attack[2] or is shot dead by E. Here it is clear D is not guilty of homicide, even though the dose of poison was a fatal one. He must be judged by what actually happened, not by what would have happened but for subsequent events.

It is not, however, every intervening act or omission of a causal nature which will relieve D from liability for the subsequent death. There are three different grounds on which he might still be held to have caused the death.

(1) The injury inflicted by D may still be "an operating cause and a substantial cause"[3] of P's death. The intervening act may be a further injury inflicted by E, not in itself mortal, but causing death when combined with the injury inflicted by D. D and E are both guilty of homicide. If P's wound is treated negligently by E, or by P himself, and P dies of the ill-

---

18. Perkins and Boyce, *Criminal Law* (3rd ed.), 779. But cf. *Garforth* [1954] Crim LR 936.
19. Above, p. 332.
20. Below.
1. Hall, *General Principles*, at 283, 393.
2. Cf. *White*, above, p. 309; *Pankotai* [1961] Crim LR 546.
3. *Smith* [1959] 2 QB at 42–43, per Parker LCJ; **SHC 36**; below, p. 341. On "substantial" see above, p. 334.

treated or non-treated wound, D is liable. In *People v Lewis*[4] P, having received a mortal gunshot wound from which he would have died within the hour, cut his throat and died within five minutes. D was held liable for manslaughter on the ground that the original wound was an operating cause. "Here, when the throat was cut, [P] was not merely languishing from a mortal wound; he was actually dying; and after the throat was cut he continued to languish from both wounds. Drop by drop the life current went out from both wounds, and at the very instant of death the gunshot wound was contributing to the event."[5] The application of this principle would have provided a different answer if P had blown his brains out and died instantly for then the bleeding from the original wound would not have been an operating cause. The conviction could then have been upheld only by applying a different principle – that the first act provided a reason for the second[6] – and the court would indeed have decided the case on that ground if they had been satisfied that the first act *was* the cause of the second; but they thought that P's suicide might have been out of remorse or a desire to shield D.

In *Malcherek*[7] D inflicted upon P injuries which resulted in brain damage. She was put on a life support machine. Some days later, after carrying out five of the six tests[8] for brain death prescribed by the Royal Colleges, doctors disconnected the machine and half an hour later she was pronounced dead. The judge withdrew the question of causation from the jury, ruling that there was no evidence on which they could decide that D did not cause P's death. On appeal, it was argued that there was evidence on which the jury could have found that the doctors caused death by switching off the machine. The appeal was dismissed. There was no doubt that the injury inflicted by D was an operating and substantial cause of death. Whether or not the doctors were also a cause of death was immaterial. They were not on trial;[9] D was. It was enough that one cause of P's death was the injury inflicted by D.

(2) P may die as the result of some act or event which would not have occurred but for the act done by D and which is a natural consequence of D's act – that is, it was foreseeable as likely to occur in the normal course of events. Though any injury which D may have inflicted is not an "operating cause" in the sense discussed in the previous paragraph, D is still held to have caused the death. If, however, the act or event was not the natural consequence of D's act, then D is not liable. The propositions are illustrated by the examples given by Perkins:[10]

---

4. 124 Cal 551 (1899) Sup Ct of California.
5. But was the contribution of the gunshot wound substantial or de minimis? Cf. the example given by Perkins, above, p. 335 and Hart and Honoré, 243.
6. Hart and Honoré, op. cit., 244.
7. [1981] 2 All ER 422, [1981] 1 WLR 690. The appeal of *Steel*, heard at the same time was materially the same.
8. There were reasons for not applying the sixth test.
9. The court remarked, obiter, that they thought the suggestion that the doctors had caused the death "bizarre" – they had done their skilful best to save life, but failed and so discontinued treatment.
10. (1946) 36 J Cr L & Cr at 393.

"... if one man knocks down another and goes away leaving his victim not seriously hurt[11] but unconscious, on the floor of a building in which the assault occurred, and before the victim recovers consciousness he is killed in the fall of the building which is shaken down by a sudden earthquake, this is not homicide. The law attributes such a death to the 'Act of God' and not to the assault, even if it may be certain that the deceased would not have been in the building at the time of the earthquake, had he not been rendered unconscious. The blow was the occasion of the man's being there, but the blow was not the cause of the earthquake, nor was the deceased left in a position of obvious danger. On the other hand if the blow had been struck on the seashore, and the assailant had left his victim in imminent peril of an incoming tide which drowned him before consciousness returned, it would be homicide."[12]

P's being drowned in the latter example was a "natural" consequence of D's action – that is, a consequence which might be expected to occur in the normal course of events. P's being killed by the falling building in the former was an abnormal and unforeseeable consequence.

Human intervention, where it consists in a foreseeable act instinctively done for the purposes of self-preservation, or in the execution of a legal duty, does not break the chain of causation. In *Pagett*,[13] D, to resist lawful arrest, held a girl in front of him as a shield and shot at armed policemen. The police instinctively fired back and killed the girl. D was held to have caused her death and to be guilty of manslaughter.[14] Though the court regarded the officers' instinctive act as "involuntary", they also held that neither a reasonable act of self-defence nor an act done in the execution of a duty to prevent crime or arrest an offender, using such force as is reasonable in the circumstances, will break the chain of causation. A truly involuntary act clearly does not break the chain – D so startles E that E involuntarily drops a weight he is carrying which causes damage. There is no true intervening "act" and D has caused the damage. But acts of self-defence or in the prevention of crime are by no means necessarily in this class. It would seem that it cannot be "reasonable" for anyone intentionally to kill P, an innocent person, in order to save his own life[15] or to arrest X; and whether it is reasonable for him to take a risk of killing P must be doubtful. *Pagett* does not deal with the case where the officer's intervening act is unlawful, but it does not necessarily follow that D's act does not continue to be a cause of death. There may be two unlawful causes.

The same principles should apply in determining whether the killing of an innocent bystander, or another policeman, by police bullets should be

---

11. The result would appear to be the same if he were seriously hurt.
12. Cf. *Hallett* [1969] SASR 141 where the court followed this passage in relation to similar facts.
13. (1983) 76 Cr App Rep 279; **SHC 32**.
14. Since the jury acquitted of murder, it must be taken that they were not satisfied D had the necessary *mens rea* as then defined in *Hyam* [1975] AC 55 – that he knew it was probable that the girl would suffer death or grievous bodily harm.
15. *Dudley and Stephens* (1884) 14 QBD 273, above, p. 249; *Howe* [1987] AC 417, [1987] 1 All ER 771, HL. Cf. commentary on *Pagett* [1983] Crim LR 394.

taken to be caused by D. It is obvious that the police marksman also causes death.[16] His liability was not the issue in *Pagett*; but, if the shooting was a reasonable act of self-defence, the result, so far as he was concerned, was accidental death.[17]

Where an intervening act causing death is not foreseeable,[18] it breaks the chain of causation whether it is intentional, negligent or merely accidental. The surgeon to whom the injured P is taken for an operation deliberately kills him; or the ambulance driver, taking P to the hospital, negligently drives into a canal and drowns him; or a careless nurse gives him a deadly poison in mistake for a sleeping pill; or, as in a Kentucky case, *Bush v Commonwealth*,[19] the medical officer attending P inadvertently infects him with scarlet fever and he dies of that. None of these is an act which might be expected to occur in the ordinary course of events and they free D from liability. But if the injured P is receiving proper and skilful medical attention and he dies from the anaesthetic or the operation D will be liable. The receipt of such medical attention may be regarded as the natural consequence of the infliction of the wound. At one time the cases concerning medical treatment seemed to lay down a stricter rule, and this is considered in more detail below.

(3) This third case, if it exists, is in the nature of an exception to the second. According to *Blaue*,[20] in the criminal law, as in the civil, the defendant must "take his victim as he finds him," and this applies to the victim's mind as well as his body. If then, D's act causes P to do an act, or make an omission, which causes P's death, D may be held liable although P's intervening conduct was not the natural consequence of D's act – it was not foreseeable that P was likely so to behave. In *Blaue* D stabbed P, a young girl, and pierced her lung. She was told that she would die if she did not have a blood transfusion. Being a Jehovah's Witness, she refused on religious grounds. She died from the bleeding caused by the wound. D was convicted of manslaughter and argued that P's refusal to have a blood transfusion, being unreasonable, had broken the chain of causation. It was held that the judge had rightly instructed the jury that the wound was a cause of death. Lawton LJ said:[21]

"It has long been the policy of the law that those who use violence on other people must take their victims as they find them. This in our judgment means the whole man, not just the physical man. It does not lie

---

16. *Cf. Malcherek*, above, p. 336.
17. The court said that its comments were confined to homicide: but the same principles must surely apply to a case of wounding.
18. *Dalby* [1982] 1 All ER 916, [1982] 1 WLR 425, below, p. 371 (supply of controlled drug to addict who was likely to take it and suffer harm and who did so and died) seems (*pace Goodfellow* (1986) 83 Cr App Rep 23) to turn on the law of constructive manslaughter (which requires an act causing *direct* harm) rather than any general principle of causation. The case did not decide that D might not have been convicted of manslaughter on the ground of gross negligence.
19. (1880) 78 Ky 268 (Kentucky Court of Appeals).
20. [1975] 3 All ER 446, [1976] Crim LR 648 and commentary. *Smithers* (1976) 34 CCC (2d) 427 (Sup. Ct. of Canada) is to the same effect. Immaterial that death was caused in part by malfunctioning epiglottis, where kick was contributing cause, outside the *de minimis* range.
21. At 450.

in the mouth of the assailant to say that his victim's religious beliefs which inhibited him from accepting certain kinds of treatment were unreasonable. The question for decision is what caused the death. The answer is the stab wound."

In this case, the wound was "an operating cause and a substantial cause," so the dictum was probably unnecessary to the decision. The principle stated, if valid, is capable of wider application. If the victim of a rape were to be so outraged as to commit suicide by shooting herself it might be argued that it was the bullet which caused the death and not the rape. Certainly the rape is not "an operating and substantial cause" in the same sense as the wound in *Blaue*; but the rapist must take his victim as he finds her. His act caused the act which caused her death. In another context the principle that you take your victim as you find him has not been applied. There is a long line of cases in which D has been held to have caused death or injury by so frightening P that P has jumped from a window or a car or behaved in some other manner dangerous to himself.[1] The test of causation to be applied is whether P's reaction was within the range of responses which might be expected from a victim in his situation.[2] If the reaction was "so daft as to make it [P's] own voluntary act" the chain of causation is broken. So it seems D does not have to take a "daft" victim as he finds him – unless, presumably he knows him to be daft – i.e., likely to behave in an extraordinary fashion. The range of responses to be expected will of course vary according to the age and perhaps the sex of the victim.

The *Blaue* principle, if valid, would impose liability upon D for unforeseeable intervening acts causing death and is probably confined to acts or omissions by the victim. If the parents of the victim of the supposed rape were to kill her on the ground that their religion required them to liquidate a defiled daughter, it is thought that D would not be liable for the death. If, however, in *Blaue*, P had been too young to make a decision about a blood transfusion and her parents had succeeded on religious grounds in preventing a transfusion being given, it is thought that the wound would have remained an operating and substantial cause, so D would still have been liable. The parents might also have been guilty of homicide.

An intervening act by the original actor will not break the chain of causation so as to excuse him where the intervening act is part of the same transaction;[3] but it is otherwise if the act which causes the *actus reus* is part of a completely different transaction. For example, D, having wounded P, visits him in hospital and accidentally infects him with smallpox of which he dies.[4]

---

1. *Pitts* (1842) Car & M 284; *Halliday* (1889) 61 LT 701; *Curley* (1909) 2 Cr App Rep 96 at 109; *Lewis* [1970] Crim LR 647; *Mackie* [1973] Crim LR 54 (Cusack J); *Boswell* [1973] Crim LR 307 (Judge Gower); *Daley* (1979) 69 Cr App Rep 39.

2. *Williams and Davis* [1992] Crim LR 198. Cf. *Roberts* (1971) 56 Cr App Rep 95 at 102.

3. See above, p. 77; Russell, 53–60, where the cases are set out; Williams, CLGP, 65; Hart and Honoré, *Causation in the Law*, 333.

4. This paragraph was cited by the court in *Le Brun* (1991) 94 Cr App Rep 101, above, p. 77.

6 Death caused by Medical Treatment of an Injury

The nineteenth century cases[5] held that, where the immediate cause of death is the medical treatment received by P consequent upon his injury by D, D is guilty of homicide, whether the treatment was proper or improper, negligent or not. If the treatment was given bona fide by competent medical officers, evidence was not admissible to show that it was improper or unskilful. In the earlier cases, this rule was applied only where the wound was dangerous to life. Later, and logically, it was extended to less serious injuries.

Those cases must now be regarded in the light of the modern decisions in *Jordan*,[6] *Smith*[7] and *Cheshire*.[8]

In *Jordan* D stabbed P who was admitted to hospital and died eight days later. At the trial,

"it did not occur to the prosecution, the defence, the judge or the jury that there could be any doubt but that the stab caused death."[9]

In the Court of Criminal Appeal, the fresh evidence of two doctors was allowed to the effect that in their opinion death had not been caused by the stab wound, which was mainly healed at the time of the death, but by the introduction (with a view to preventing infection) of terramycin after the deceased man had shown he was intolerant to it and by the intravenous introduction of large quantities of liquid. This treatment, according to the evidence, was "palpably wrong." The court held that if the jury had heard this evidence they would have felt precluded from saying that they were satisfied that the death was caused by the stab wound and they quashed the conviction. The case has been interpreted by Williams[10] as one where the medical treatment was grossly negligent, but he argues[11] that any degree of negligence which would be recognised by the civil courts should be enough. The court did not say in express terms that there was evidence of negligence, gross or otherwise, though it may reasonably be inferred that "palpably wrong" treatment is negligent.

While anxiously disclaiming any intention of setting a precedent[12] they stated the basis of their decision in even broader terms. They were "disposed to accept it as law that death resulting from any normal treatment employed to deal with a felonious injury may be regarded as caused by the felonious injury;" but it was "sufficient to point out here that this was not normal treatment." Surely treatment which is "not normal" is not necessarily negligent, even in the civil law.

The case gave rise to some concern in the medical profession and it was predicted[13] that the result of it would be that if, in future, the victim of a

---

5. Discussed in the sixth edition of this work, 321.
6. (1956) 40 Cr App Rep 152; **SHC 34**.
7. [1959] 2 QB 35, [1959] 2 All ER 193; **SHC 36**.
8. [1991] 3 All ER 670.
9. See (1956) 40 Cr App Rep 152 at 155.
10. [1957] Crim LR at 430.
11. Ibid., at 513.
12. But no court has the right to preclude future courts from considering the effects of its decisions.
13. By Camps and Havard, "Causation in Homicide – A Medical View" [1957] Crim LR 576 at 582–583.

homicidal assault died as a result of the medical treatment instituted to save his life, it would not be considered homicide by the assailant if the treatment could be shown to be "not normal".

Jordan was distinguished by the Court of Criminal Appeal in *Smith*[14] and by the Court of Appeal in *Blaue*[15] as "a very particular case depending upon its exact facts." In *Malcherek* the court thought that if a choice had to be made between *Jordan* and *Smith*, *Smith* was to be preferred; but they did not believe it was necessary to choose. In *Blaue*, *Jordan* was thought to be "probably rightly decided on its facts". It is submitted that this is so. *Smith* is distinguishable. In the course of a fight between soldiers of different regiments, D stabbed P twice with a bayonet. One of P's comrades, trying to carry P to the medical reception station, twice tripped and dropped him. At the reception station the medical officer, who was trying to cope with a number of other cases, did not realise that one of the wounds had pierced a lung and caused haemorrhage. He gave P treatment which, in the light of the information regarding P's condition available at the time of the trial, was "thoroughly bad and might well have affected his chances of recovery." D's conviction of murder was upheld and counsel's argument, that the court must be satisfied that the treatment was normal, and that this was abnormal was brushed aside.

". . . if at the time of death the original wound is still an operating cause and a substantial cause, then the death can properly be said to be the result of the wound, albeit that some other cause of death is also operating. Only if it can be said that the original wounding is merely the setting in which another cause operates can it be said that the death does not result from the wound. Putting it in another way, only if the second cause is so overwhelming as to make the original wound merely part of the history can it be said that death does not flow from the wound."[16]

Jordan was a case where a jury might have found, in the light of the new evidence, that the wound was, or may have been, merely the setting in which medical treatment caused death – as if a nurse had, with gross negligence, administered a deadly poison in mistake for a sleeping pill.

In *Cheshire*[17] the bullet wounds which D inflicted upon P had ceased to be a threat to life and there was evidence that P's death was caused by the tracheotomy performed and negligently treated by the doctors so that it narrowed his windpipe and caused asphyxiation. The court held that the judge had misdirected the jury by telling them only recklessness on the part of the doctors would break the chain of causation but upheld the conviction, asserting that "the rare complication . . . was a direct consequence of the appellant's acts, which remained a significant cause of his death". The test proposed by the court is not easy to apply:

"Even though negligence in the treatment of the victim was the immediate cause of his death, the jury should not regard it as excluding the

---

14. [1959] 2 QB 35 at 43, [1959] 2 All ER 193 at 198.
15. [1975] 3 All ER 446; **SHC 37**. Likewise in *Evans and Gardiner (No. 2)* [1976] VR 523 at 531.
16. Per Lord Parker CJ [1959] 2 QB 35 at 42–43, [1959] 2 All ER 193 at 198.
17. [1991] 3 All ER 670, [1991] Crim LR 709.

responsibility of the accused unless the negligent treatment was so independent of his acts, and in itself so potent in causing death, that they regard the contribution made by his acts as insignificant."

It is difficult to know what "so independent" and "so potent" mean. In all these cases, D's act caused P to undergo the treatment and if that renders it "dependent", D would be taken to have caused death, however outlandish the treatment; but it is clear that this is not intended. There is a similar problem with "potent". Suppose that the tracheotomy would have caused death even if the wound had been completely healed (this is not entirely clear[18]). No greater potency can then be imagined; but it is, at least, unlikely that the court intended that it should follow that D had not caused death. The wound would not have been an operating and substantial cause but the ultimate question is whether D's act was a cause and it is clear that it might be, even if the wound was not.

It is submitted that the following propositions at present represent the law:

(i) Medical evidence is admissible to show that the medical treatment of a wound was the cause of death and that the wound itself was not.[1] This is so whether or not the wound is mortal.

(ii) If a wound was an operating and substantial cause of death, D is guilty of homicide, however badly the wound was treated.[2]

(iii) If a wound was not an operating and substantial cause of death (i.e., it was effectively healed) but P was killed by, e.g., the inadvertent administration of deadly poison by a nurse, the wrongful administration of terremycin, or the ill-treatment of a tracheotomy, D may or may not be guilty of homicide. The test we must now apply is the *Cheshire* independence/potency test. A better test, it is submitted, would be whether the treatment, or the manner of administering it, was so extraordinary as to be unforeseeable – which may be much the same thing as asking whether it was grossly negligent.

Jordan and *Cheshire* were cases where the medical treatment, not the wound, may have been the cause of death. The same principle applies where the wound prevents medical treatment for an independent condition which would have saved life: *McKechnie*[3] where the injuries inflicted by D precluded medical treatment for the duodenal ulcer which killed P. Only an "extraordinary and unusual" medical decision that the life-saving treatment was not possible would have broken the chain of causation.

---

18. Indeed, according to the Court of Appeal (p. 678) the judge directed the jury that the prosecution must prove that "the bullets were one operative and substantial cause of death"; But the bullets (unless they were still in P's body) could not be an *operating* cause, if that is what is meant, in the sense that a wound might be.

1. *Jordan* must be authority for this at least. Moreover at the trial in *Smith* Dr. Camps gave evidence, that, with proper treatment, P's chances of recovery were as high as 75 per cent.

2. But Hart and Honoré, 361, discussing *Blaue*, suppose that P had called for a blood transfusion and the doctor had refused because he wanted to play golf, whereupon P bled to death. They argue that death would have been "caused by the doctor's callousness, not the original wound". Surely it would have been caused by both. The wound would certainly have been an operating and substantial cause.

3. (1991) 94 Cr App Rep 51, [1992] Crim LR 194.

7 The Effect of Neglect by the Injured Person

The common law rule is that neglect or maltreatment by the injured person of himself does not exempt D from liability for his ultimate death. In *Wall's* case,[4] where the former governor of Goree was convicted[5] of the murder of a man by the illegal infliction on him of a flogging of 800 lashes, there was evidence that P had aggravated his condition by drinking spirits. MacDonald LCB, told[6] the jury:

". . . there is no apology for a man if he puts another in so dangerous and hazardous a situation by his treatment of him, that some degree of unskilfulness and mistaken treatment of himself may possibly accelerate the fatal catastrophe. One man is not at liberty to put another into such perilous circumstances as these, and to make it depend upon his own prudence, knowledge, skill or experience what may hurry on or complete that catastrophe, or on the other hand may render him service."

In *Holland*[7] D waylaid and assaulted P, cutting him severely across one of his fingers with an iron instrument. P refused to follow the surgeon's advice to have the finger amputated, although he was told that if he did not his life would be in great danger. The wound caused lockjaw, the finger was then amputated, but it was too late and P died of lockjaw. The surgeon's evidence was that if the finger had been amputated at first, P's life could probably have been saved. Maule J told the jury that it made no difference whether the wound was in its own nature instantly mortal, or whether it became the cause of death by reason of the deceased not having adopted the best mode of treatment. The question was whether, in the end, the wound inflicted by the prisoner was the real cause of death. *Holland* was followed in *Blaue*.[8] The argument[9] that medical science has advanced greatly since 1841 and that a refusal to undergo medical treatment, reasonable then, would be unreasonable now, did not impress the court. Whether P's conduct was reasonable or not was irrelevant.

8 Intended Consequences

It is sometimes said that intended consequences cannot be too remote. This, however, is not always true, for the *sine qua non* rule remains applicable. Thus, in *White*[10] the consequence intended by D – the death of his mother – occurred; but its occurrence had nothing to do with D's act in administering the poison and would have happened just the same if D had done nothing. Even where the *sine qua non* rule is satisfied, the consequence, though intended, may be too remote where it occurs as a result of the intervention of some new cause. So in the cases of *Bush*[11] and *Jordan*[12] it may be that D intended P's death, and P's death occurred; moreover, in

4. (1802) 28 State Tr 51.
5. Twenty years after the event.
6. Ibid., at p. 145.
7. (1841) 2 Mood & R 351.
8. Above, p. 378. Cf. *Mubila* 1956 (1) S A 31.
9. By Hart and Honoré, *Causation in the Law*, at 360.
10. Above, p. 309; **SHC 283**.
11. (1880) 78 Ky 268; above, p. 338.
12. (1956) 40 Cr App Rep 152; **SHC 34**.

neither case would death have occurred without D's act; but in the one case it was caused by scarlet fever and not by D's bullet; and in the other it was caused by medical treatment and not by D's knife. Where the death occurs in the manner intended by D he will be guilty even if the course of events was not what he expected, for example, he shoots at P's head, but the bullet misses, ricochets and kills P by striking him in the back. The case of *Michael*[13] is perhaps a rather extreme example of this:

D's child, P, was in the care of a nurse, X. D, intending to murder the child, delivered to X a large quantity of laudanum, telling her it was a medicine to be administered to P. X did not think the child needed any medicine and left it untouched on the mantelpiece of her room. In X's absence, one of her children, Y, aged five, took the laudanum and administered a large dose to P who died. All the judges held that the jury were rightly directed that this administration by "an unconscious agent" was murder.

Hart and Honoré[14] criticise the case on the ground that the child was

"not in any sense an agent, conscious or unconscious, of the mother, who intended [X] alone to give the poison to the child; but the decision may be justified on the ground that, in our terminology, the act of the child of five did not negative causal connexion between the prisoner's act and the death."

According to this view, the result would have been different if Y had been, not five, but fifteen.

It does not appear that Y knew, from the labelling of the bottle or otherwise, that this was "medicine" for P. If she did know this, and acted on that knowledge, then there seems no difficulty in imputing the death to D, whatever Y's age. No such fact being reported, however, the case must be treated as one where Y's intervention was in no way prompted by D's instructions. Thus, if Y had taken the poison herself, her death would have been just as much caused by D's act as was P's in the actual case; but it would require an extension of the decision to hold D guilty in such a case, for Y's death was not an intended consequence.[15] If such an extension be not made, the result is quite arbitrary, for it was pure chance whether Y administered the poison to P, or to herself or another child.

9 Special Instances of Causation

There are a few instances of causation which require special mention, by reason of the state of the authorities.

a) *Killing by mental suffering or shock.* The view of earlier writers was that the law could take no cognisance of a killing caused merely by mental suffering or shock, because "no external act of violence was offered, whereof the common law can take notice and secret things belong to

---

13. (1840) 9 C & P 356.
14. Op. cit., at 337.
15. But the doctrine of transferred malice (above, p. 74) would support such an extension.

God.''[16] Stephen thought[17] that the fear of encouraging prosecutions for witchcraft was the reason for the rule and that it was "a bad rule founded on ignorance now dispelled."

"Suppose a man were intentionally killed by being kept awake till the nervous irritation of sleeplessness killed him, might not this be murder? Suppose a man kills a sick person intentionally by making a loud noise when sleep gives him a chance of life; or suppose knowing that a man has aneurism of the heart, his heir rushes into his room and roars in his ear, 'Your wife is dead!' intending to kill and killing him, why are not these acts murder? They are no more 'secret things belonging to God' than the operation of arsenic."

This view now represents the law. Hale's proposition was first modified in *Towers*[18] where D violently assaulted a young girl who was holding a four-and-a-half-months'-old child in her arms. The girl screamed loudly, so frightening the baby that it cried till it was black in the face. From that day it had convulsions and died a month later. Denman J held that there was evidence to go to the jury of manslaughter. In the case of an adult person, he said that murder could not be committed by using language so strong or violent as to cause that person to die:

"mere intimidation, causing a person to die from fright by working upon his fancy, was not murder";

but that rule did not apply to a child of such tender years as this;

". . . if the man's act brought on the convulsions or brought them to a more dangerous extent, so that death would not have resulted otherwise, then it would be manslaughter."[19]

This was extended to the case of an adult person by Ridley J in *Hayward*.[20] D, who was in a condition of violent excitement and had expressed his determination to "give his wife something", chased her from the house into the road using violent threats against her. She fell dead. She was suffering from an abnormal heart condition, such that any combination of physical exertion and fright or strong emotion might cause death. Ridley J directed the jury that no proof of actual physical violence was necessary, but that death from fright alone, caused by an illegal act, such as a threat of violence, was enough.

b) *Killing by perjury.* It is sometimes said[1] that it is not homicide if D, by giving false evidence, procures the conviction and execution of P. There is no conclusive authority on the point. In *McDaniel*[2] D and others were in fact convicted of the murder of P by falsely swearing to his guilt of robbery

---

16. Hale, 1 PC 429; and see East, 1 PC 225.
17. *Digest*, 217, n 9.
18. (1874) 12 Cox CC 530.
19. Ibid., at 533.
20. (1908) 21 Cox CC 692.
  1. The earlier authorities said that it was murder; but Coke (3 Inst 48) said that it was "not holden for murder at this day." Foster, *Crown Law* at 131, supported this, citing the case of *Titus Oates* (1685) 10 State Tr 1227, who, he thinks, would certainly have been charged with murder by perjury if that had been a crime. East, 1 PC 333, is non-committal. Hawkins accepted the older view: 1 PC, c. 13, §5, 7.
  2. (1756) 1 Leach 44.

(in order to obtain the reward) for which P was hanged; but judgment was respited "upon a doubt whether an indictment for murder would lie in this case:" and the Attorney-General declined to argue that it would, so the prisoners were discharged. Blackstone wrote[3] that he had

"grounds to believe it was not from any apprehension that the point was not maintainable, but from other prudential reasons."

The "prudential reasons" appear to be

"to avoid the danger of deterring witnesses from giving evidence upon capital prosecutions, if it must be at the peril of their own lives."

East[4] says that Lord Mansfield CJ took the same view of the law and that he and the other judges supported the indictment.

The balance of authority is then, perhaps, against the rule; but if it exists, it is thought that it has nothing to do with causation[5] but it is a rule of policy, closely analogous to that which protects a witness from an action for defamation[6] or for damages for the injury suffered by conviction upon perjured evidence.[7]

6) *The Mens Rea of Murder*

The *mens rea* of murder is traditionally called "malice aforethought". This is a technical term and it has a technical meaning quite different from the ordinary popular meaning of the two words. The phrase, it has been truly said,

"is a mere arbitrary symbol ..., for the 'malice' may have in it nothing really malicious; and need never be really 'aforethought'."[8]

Thus a parent who kills a suffering child out of motives of compassion is "malicious" for this purpose; and there is sufficient aforethought if an intention to kill is formed only a second before the fatal blow is struck. Neither ill-will nor premeditation is necessary.

The meaning of the term is of the utmost importance, for it is the presence or absence of malice aforethought which determines whether an unlawful killing is murder or manslaughter.

"Murder is unlawful homicide with malice aforethought. Manslaughter is an unlawful homicide without malice aforethought."[9]

Malice aforethought is a concept of the common law. It has a long history but, since *Moloney*,[10] it is no longer necessary to explore this in order to expound the modern law. We can now state that it consists in—

(i) an intention to kill any person or,

---

3. *Commentaries*, iv, 196.
4. 1 PC 333, n (a).
5. Cf. Hart and Honoré, *Causation in the Law*, at 405.
6. *Watson v M'Ewen*, [1905] AC 480.
7. *Hargreaves v Bretherton* [1959] 1 QB 45, [1958] 3 All ER 122; *Marrinan v Vibart* [1963] 1 QB 528, [1962] 3 All ER 380.
8. Kenny, *Outlines* (15th ed.) 153.
9. Per Stephen J in *Doherty* (1887) 16 Cox CC 306 at 307.
10. [1985] AC 905, [1985] 1 All ER 1025, above, p. 58.

(ii) an intention to cause grievous bodily harm to any person.

"Intention" has the meaning attributed to it in *Hancock*[11] and *Nedrick*[12] examined above.

"Grievous bodily harm", at one time broadly interpreted to mean any harm sufficiently serious to interfere with health and comfort, must now be applied in its ordinary natural meaning. "Grievous" means "really serious"[13] and the word "really" probably adds nothing but emphasis to the fact that the harm intended must be (actually or really) serious.[14]

In 1960 in the notorious case of *Director of Public Prosecutions v Smith* the House of Lords laid down a largely objective test of liability in murder – the test was "not what the defendant contemplated, but what the ordinary reasonable man or woman would in all the circumstances of the case have contemplated as the natural and probable result". In *Hyam*[15] the House declined to overrule *Smith*, holding that its effect had been modified by s. 8 of the Criminal Justice Act 1967; but in *Frankland and Moore v R*[16] the Privy Council (comprising five judicial members of the House of Lords), acting on the dicta of Lord Diplock in *Hyam*,[17] Lord Bridge in *Moloney*[18] and Lord Scarman in *Hancock*,[19] held that in so far as it laid down an objective test, *Smith* did not represent the common law of England. Though the Privy Council cannot formally overrule a decision of the House of Lords, it can probably be taken, for all practical purposes, that *Smith* is overruled. Section 8 did not, after all, modify the law of murder; and the function of that section in relation to murder, as to all other crimes, is not to define what *mens rea* must be proved, but only *how* the *mens rea* required by the common law or other statutes, is to be proved.

Although the common law of malice aforethought is now fully stated in the rule requiring an intention to cause death or grievous bodily harm, it is necessary to refer to s. 1 of the Homicide Act 1957 which modified the common law.

"(1) Where a person kills in the course or furtherance of some other offence, the killing shall not amount to murder unless done with the same malice aforethought (express or implied) as is required for a killing to amount to murder when not done in the course or furtherance of another offence.

(2) For the purposes of the foregoing subsection, a killing done in the course or for the purpose of resisting an officer of justice, or of resisting or avoiding or preventing a lawful arrest, or of effecting or assisting an escape or rescue from legal custody, shall be treated as a killing in the course or furtherance of another offence."

---

11. [1986] AC 455, [1986] 1 All ER 641, HL; **SHC 56**.
12. [1986] 3 All ER 1, [1986] 1 WLR 1025, CA, above, p. 54; **SHC 60**.
13. *Director of Public Prosecutions v Smith* [1961] AC 290 at 334, [1960] 3 All ER 161 at 171.
14. *Saunders* [1985] Crim LR 230.
15. [1975] AC 55 at 70–71; **SHC 306**.
16. [1987] AC 576 [1987] 2 WLR 1251 on appeal from the Isle of Man, where at the time of the homicides, the English common law, unamended by the equivalent of s. 8 of the Criminal Justice Act 1967, prevailed.
17. [1975] AC 55 at 94.
18. [1985] AC 905 at 921 and 928.
19. [1986] AC 455 at 473.

The purpose of this section was, as the side-note indicates, to limit malice aforethought by the "Abolition of 'constructive malice'". This took two forms. (i) It was murder to kill in the course or furtherance of a violent felony (or possibly any felony) so that an intention to commit the felony (e.g., rape or robbery) was a sufficient *mens rea* where death resulted. (ii) It was murder to kill while attempting to prevent lawful arrest or bring about escape from lawful arrest or custody, so that an intention to do these things was also malice aforethought where the act caused death. Subsection (1) abolishes the first, and subsection (2) the second, form of constructive malice. While eliminating constructive malice, the section leaves in existence "express" and "implied" malice. Although these terms have been used for centuries, their meaning is obscure and is certainly not any ordinary natural meaning that they might bear.[20] In the light of the common law, as we know it to be, "express malice" must be taken to mean the intention to kill and "implied malice" the intention to cause grievous bodily harm. Though the terms remain on the statute book, there is in practice no need to use them and the sooner they are buried the better.

It was at one time argued that s. 1 also abolished intention to cause grievous bodily harm as a head of malice aforethought – an argument which required some other meaning to be given to "implied malice" since that is expressly preserved. The argument was that the only reason why intention to cause grievous bodily harm was malice aforethought before 1957 was that in 1803 Lord Ellenborough's Act created a felony of causing grievous bodily harm with intent to do so. If death resulted, that was murder because, and only because, the killing was in the course or furtherance of that felony. The argument was rejected in *Vickers*[1] but accepted by Lords Diplock and Kilbrandon in *Hyam* where the matter was left open because Lord Cross was not prepared to decide between the conflicting views. In *Cunningham*[2] the House confirmed that intention to cause grievous bodily harm survived the Homicide Act as a head of *mens rea*, having ante-dated Lord Ellenborough's Act as a form of malice aforethought, distinct from constructive malice.

7) *The Sentence for Murder*

Until the Homicide Act 1957 all persons convicted of murder were automatically sentenced to death. By s. 5 of that Act certain types of murder were singled out and designated "capital murder". These continued to be punishable by death, while the remaining types of murder were punishable by imprisonment for life. In effect we had two degrees of murder.

The distinction between the two degrees of murder proved to be most unsatisfactory, and the death penalty for murder was suspended by the

---

20. See Lord Hailsham in *Cunningham* [1981] 2 All ER 863 at 867.
1. [1957] 2 QB 664, [1957] 2 All ER 741, CCA (a court of five judges).
2. [1982] AC 566, [1981] 2 All ER 863, HL.

Murder (Abolition of Death Penalty) Act 1965, which is to continue permanently in force.[3] All persons convicted of murder must now be sentenced to imprisonment for life. The mandatory sentence for murder is unique in English law and the CLRC considered whether the judge should not have a discretion as in all other crimes. They were deeply and almost evenly divided on the issue. Their Report[4] set out the arguments on both sides in some detail but made no recommendation.

Subsequently the matter was considered by a Select Committee of the House of Lords (the Nathan Committee) which recommended, with one dissentient, that the mandatory sentence be abolished. Murder should be punishable with a maximum sentence of life but the judge should have the same discretion to impose lesser sentences as he has for other crimes.[5] The arguments in favour of this course are overwhelming. Murders vary as greatly in their gravity, and murderers in their dangerousness, as for any other crime. The recommendation has not, however, found favour with the government and there seems to be no prospect of its implementation at the present time.

On sentencing a murderer, the judge may recommend to the Home Secretary the minimum period which should elapse before the prisoner is released on licence. The power is rarely exercised and was in practice superseded by a non-statutory procedure under which the trial judge who imposed a life sentence, whether mandatory or discretionary, wrote to the Home Secretary giving his view as to the period necessary to meet the requirements of retribution and deterrence (the "tariff"). The letter was sent through the Lord Chief Justice who added his own views. The date of the formal review of the case by the Parole Board was then fixed, normally three years before the expiration of that period. The Nathan Committee was shocked to learn that in one period of six months in 1988 the Home Secretary (in practice, a junior minister makes the decision) in 63 out of 106 mandatory life sentences set a higher tariff than that indicated by the judge.

Under the Criminal Justice Act 1991, s. 34, a judge imposing a discretionary life sentence may, as part of the sentence, specify the (in effect) tariff period; and, when that period has been served, it will be the duty of the Home Secretary to release the prisoner on licence if the Parole Board has recommended that it is no longer necessary for the protection of the public that he should be confined. This provision does not apply to mandatory life prisoners – i.e. murderers whose cases are still dealt with under the non-statutory procedure. Before the 1991 Act came into force, it was held in the case of a discretionary life prisoner[6] that while the decision on the tariff is for the Home Secretary, a departure from the judicial recommendation is prima facie irrational and liable to be quashed; but if the recommendation appears to be out of line with the established practice of the courts, it is the Home Secretary's duty to consult the Lord Chief Justice afresh. The decision does not deal directly with the position of the

---

3. By virtue of affirmative resolutions of both Houses of Parliament on 16th and 18th December 1969.
4. Fourteenth Report CLRC/OAP/R, pp. 19–27.
5. HL Paper 78–I, (1989).
6. *R v Secretary of State, ex p Walsh* (1991) Times, 18 December.

mandatory life prisoner and whether similar principles apply remains to be seen.

8) *Proposals for Reform*

The Law Commission's proposals for a statutory definition of murder[7] were never implemented. The latest proposal for the reform of the law of murder stems from the CLRC. Their recommendation for a statutory definition of the offence was incorporated in the Law Commission's draft Code as follows:

"A person is guilty of murder if he causes the death of another—
(a) intending to cause death; or
(b) intending to cause serious personal harm and being aware that he may cause death. ...."

This recommendation was endorsed by the Nathan Committee which made its own independent study of, and received much evidence on, the law of murder. The recommendation would make a relatively small change in the law of murder, excluding a person who, notwithstanding his intention to cause serious harm, did not foresee any risk of death. Of greater practical significance was Nathan's endorsement of the Code definition of intention.[8] But, once again, there seems to be little prospect of the implementation of this reform at the present time.

2 Manslaughter

1) *Voluntary and Involuntary*

At common law, all unlawful homicides which are not murder are manslaughter. A wide variety of types of homicide fall within this category, but it is customary and useful to divide manslaughter into two main groups which are designated "voluntary" and "involuntary" manslaughter, respectively. The distinction is that in voluntary manslaughter D may have the malice aforethought of murder, but the presence of some defined mitigating circumstance reduces his crime to the less serious grade of criminal homicide. Where these circumstances are present, then, D may actually intend to kill and do so in pursuance of that intention and yet not be guilty of murder.[9] At common law, voluntary manslaughter occurred in one case only, where the killing was done under provocation. But now, by statute, two further categories must be added. Under the Homicide Act

---

7. *Imputed Criminal Intent: Director of Public Prosecutions v Smith.*
8. Above, p. 55.
9. *A-G of Ceylon v Perera* [1953] AC 200, PC; *Lee Chun Chuen v R* [1963] AC 220, [1963] 1 All ER 73; *Parker v R* [1964] AC 1369, [1964] 2 All ER 641; contra, per Lord Simon in *Holmes v Director of Public Prosecutions* [1946] AC 588 at 598 HL.

1957, killing is now manslaughter and not murder, notwithstanding the presence of malice aforethought, where (i) D is suffering from diminished responsibility;[10] and (ii) where D kills in pursuance of a suicide pact.[11] Diminished responsibility has already been considered, and the problem of the suicide pact is looked at in connection with the new statutory crime of abetting suicide.[12] This section, then, will be devoted to killing under provocation.

2) *Provocation*[13]

In deciding whether D intended death or grievous bodily harm, the jury must consider evidence of provocation with all other relevant evidence.[14] If they are not satisfied that he had the necessary *mens rea*, they must acquit. But even if they decide he did have *mens rea*, provocation may still be a defence to a charge of murder[15] at common law, entitling D to be convicted of manslaughter. The common law rule was stated by Devlin J in what the Court of Criminal Appeal described as a "classic direction", as follows:

"Provocation is some act, or series of acts, done by the dead man to the accused, which would cause in any reasonable person, and actually causes in the accused, a sudden and temporary loss of self-control, rendering the accused so subject to passion as to make him or her for the moment not master of his mind."[16]

The common law rule has been modified by the Homicide Act 1957, s. 3, which provides:

"Where on a charge of murder there is evidence on which the jury can find that the person charged was provoked (whether by things done or by things said or by both together) to lose his self-control, the question whether the provocation was enough to make a reasonable man do as he did shall be left to be determined by the jury; and in determining that question the jury shall take into account everything both done and said according to the effect which, in their opinion, it would have on a reasonable man."

Section 3 does not create or codify, but assumes the existence of, and amends, the common law defence. It does not state the effect of a successful defence – it is by virtue of the common law that the offence is reduced to manslaughter. The section assumes the existence of the dual test: (i) was the defendant provoked to lose his self-control?, a subjective question, and

10. Section 2.
11. Section 4.
12. Below, p. 379.
13. Ashworth, "The Doctrine of Provocation", [1976] CLJ 292.
14. Section 8 of the Criminal Justice Act 1967, above, p. 86; *Williams* [1968] Crim LR 678; *Ives* [1970] 1 QB 208, [1969] 3 All ER 470.
15. Provocation is not a defence to a charge of wounding or any charge other than murder according to *Cunningham* [1959] 1 QB 288, [1958] 3 All ER 711. In *Bruzas* [1972] Crim LR 367 Eveleigh J held that it is not a defence to a charge of attempted murder; but see commentary and CLRC/OAP/R, para. 98.
16. *Duffy* [1949] 1 All ER at 932n.

(ii) was the provocation enough to make a reasonable man do as he did?, an objective question.

The section does not say in respect of what act D must have lost his self-control but it seems obvious that it must be the act of causing death. The question is whether D's responsibility for homicide – i.e., causing death – should be mitigated. If D has lost control in doing the act which caused death, it is quite immaterial, it is submitted, that he regains it immediately afterwards. In *Clarke*[17] D, under some provocation, head-butted and strangled P and then, panicking, placed live wires into her mouth, electrocuting her. She may, however, have been dead before the electrocution. It was held that the judge had rightly declined to tell the jury to ignore the circumstances of the electrocution in considering provocation. The jury must take into account the whole course of D's conduct, "although some factors (e.g., disposal of the body) might be too remote". But if P was already dead when D put the wires in her mouth, the fact that he had now regained his self-control was surely irrelevant. The only possible relevance of acts done after death (or after the infliction of a fatal injury) could be to show that self-control had not been lost when the earlier acts causing death were done – e.g., suggesting that the whole course of conduct was premeditated; but there was no hint of relevance of that kind in *Clarke*. Of course, if the electrocution was a contributory cause of P's death and was done after D had regained his self-control, he was guilty of murder; but the onus was on the Crown to prove this.

One qualification to this might arise where D, under provocation, causes potentially fatal injury to P but, while P is still alive, regains his self-control and deliberately omits to take steps which he knows might save or prolong her life. D would have a duty to act[18] and, if his omission, being unprovoked, resulted in P's earlier death, he might be convicted of murder.

Whether the defendant was provoked to lose his self-control is a question of fact. In accordance with the general rule, it is for the judge to say whether there is any evidence of that fact. Where the defendant yielded to the entreaties of his incurably ill and suffering wife to put an end to her life, it was held that there was no evidence of provocation: D had not lost his self-control.[19] Sufficient evidence may appear in the case presented by the Crown. If not, there is an evidential burden on the defendant. If no evidence that the defendant was provoked to lose his self-control is adduced by the Crown or the defendant, then the judge will withdraw the defence from the jury. Since the burden of proof is on the Crown, evidence which might leave a reasonable jury in reasonable doubt whether or not the defendant was provoked is sufficient. Once the judge has decided there is sufficient evidence that the defendant was provoked, whether or not the defence has been raised expressly by D or his counsel,[20] he must leave it to the jury to answer the questions, (i) *was* the defendant provoked to lose his self-control? and (ii) was the provocation enough to make a reasonable man do as he did? Since the Act, the judge may not withdraw the defence from

17. [1991] Crim LR 383 and commentary.
18. Above, p. 51.
19. *Cocker* [1989] Crim LR 740, discussed by P. R. Taylor [1991] Crim LR 111.
20. *Mancini v Director of Public Prosecutions* [1942] AC 1, [1941] 3 All ER 272.

the jury on the ground that in his opinion there is no evidence on which they could answer the second question in the affirmative.[1]

1 Provocation by things done or said

Since provocation continues to be a defence at common law it might have been held that the words "provoked" and "provocation" in the section bear the limited meaning they had at common law, subject only to the limited changes expressly made by the section. This has not been the approach of the courts. These words have been given their ordinary natural meaning, free of the technical limitations of the common law. In *Doughty*[2] it was held that the judge was bound by the plain words of the section to leave provocation to the jury where there was evidence that the persistent crying of his baby had caused D to lose his self-control and kill it. Whatever the position may have been at common law, the provocation does not have to be an illegal or wrongful act. There must be "things done or things said" and the crying of the baby was presumably regarded as a "thing done". Mere circumstances, however provocative, do not constitute a defence to murder. Loss of control by a farmer on finding his crops destroyed by a flood, a financier ruined by a crash on the stock market or an author on his manuscript being destroyed by lightning, could not, it seems, excuse a resulting killing. "Act of God" could hardly be regarded as "something done" within s. 3. Since, where there is a provocative act, it no longer need be done by the victim, this distinction begins to look a little thin. If D may rely on the defence where the crops or the manuscript were destroyed by an unknown arsonist or the stock exchange crash was engineered by other anonymous financiers, why should it be different where no human agency was involved? The "provocation" is no more and no less.

2 Provocation and Third Parties[3]

a) *By whom the provocation may be given.* Section 3 removes certain limitations on the defence as formulated in *Duffy*. That formulation limited the nature of operative provocation to acts done (i) by the dead man (ii) to the accused. Evidence would thus not be admissible of acts done (i) by third parties or (ii) to third parties. Under s. 3, however, there is no such limitation and the only question seems to be whether the evidence is relevant to the issue – namely whether D was provoked to lose his self-control. The test of relevance should be – would a reasonable man regard the act in question as having a provocative effect on the person charged? So it was held in *Davies* where D killed his wife, P, following upon her

---

1. This seems to be a unique exception to the rule that the judge must not allow a matter of fact (or opinion) to be decided when there is no evidence of it. The CLRC recommends repeal of this rule: CLRC/OAP/R, para. 88.
2. (1986) 83 Cr App Rep 319.
3. See O'Regan, "Indirect Provocation and Misdirected Retaliation" [1968] Crim LR 319.

adultery with Q, that the judge was wrong to direct that P's conduct and, by implication, not Q's, was to be taken into account.[4]

The defence was available, even at common law, if the blow was *aimed* at the provoker. If, by accident, it missed him and killed an innocent person, P, then the doctrine of transferred malice[5] operated and D was guilty of manslaughter only. In *Gross*[6] D, provoked by blows from her husband, fired at him, intending to kill him but missed and killed P. It was held that

"... if the firing at the person intended to be hit would be manslaughter, then, if the bullet strikes a third person not intended to be hit, the killing of that person equally would be manslaughter and not murder."[7]

If D knew it was virtually certain that he would hit P, he would have an independent *mens rea* with respect to P, probably sufficient to fix him with liability for murder[8] at common law; but now the provocation given by the third party would be a defence.

b) *Acts directed against third parties.* Before the Homicide Act 1957 it used to be said that the provocation must consist in something done to the defendant[9] but the Act requires the jury to take into account *everything* both done and said according to the effect which, in their opinion, it would have on a reasonable man; and this is capable of including acts done to third parties if, in the jury's opinion, they would have provoked a reasonable man in the position of the defendant. In *Pearson*,[10] where two brothers, M and W, killed their violent and tyrannical father, the ill-treatment meted out to M over a period of eight years when the older boy, W, was absent from home was relevant to W's defence, particularly as he had returned home to protect M from violence.

3 The Subjective Condition

The jury should be directed to consider the subjective condition first.[11] In deciding this question of fact they are, naturally, entitled to take into account all the relevant circumstances; the nature of the provocative act and all the relevant conditions in which it took place, the sensitivity or otherwise of D and the time, if any, which elapsed between the provocation and the act which caused death. D's failure to testify to his loss of self-control is not necessarily fatal to his case. Provocation is commonly set up as an alternative to the complete defence of self-defence. The admission of loss of self-control would weaken or destroy the alternative defence; and

---

4. [1975] QB 691, [1975] 1 All ER 890. Cf. the earlier decision to the same effect by Lawton J in *Twine* [1967] Crim LR 710, where D's girl friend's conduct caused D to lose his self-control and strike and kill the man she was with.
5. Above, p. 74.
6. (1913) 23 Cox CC 455 (Darling J); and see *Porritt* [1961] 3 All ER 463, [1961] 1 WLR 1372.
7. 23 Cox CC at 456.
8. Above, p. 346.
9. But see *Fisher* (1837) 8 C & P 182 (Park J, obiter) (D coming upon P buggering D's son) and *Harrington* (1886) 10 Cox CC 370 (Cockburn CJ contemplating the possibility of a defence where D found his daughter being violently assaulted by her husband).
10. [1992] Crim LR 193.
11. *Brown* [1972] 2 All ER 1328 at 1333.

the courts recognise that D has a tactical reason for not expressly asserting what may be the truth.[12]

If D is of an unusually phlegmatic temperament and it appears that he did not lose his self-control, the fact that a reasonable man in like circumstances would have done so will not avail D in the least. A traditional example of extreme provocation is the finding of a spouse in the act of adultery;[13] but if D, on so finding his wife, were to read her a lecture on the enormity of her sin and then methodically to load a gun and shoot her, it is probable (for it remains a question of fact) either that the judge would rule that there was no evidence that D lost his self-control or that the jury would find that he did not. In that case, D would be guilty of murder and it would be irrelevant that the jury may think that a reasonable man in like circumstances would lose his self-control.

Although the House of Lords has stated that the Act "abolishes all previous rules as to what can or cannot amount to provocation"[14] it appears that the subjective condition is unchanged. In *Ibrams*[15] and *Thornton*[16] the Court of Appeal has, after *Camplin*,[17] reaffirmed that there must be a "sudden and temporary loss of self-control", as Devlin J put it in *Duffy*,[18] and approved that judge's further words:

"Indeed, circumstances which induce a desire for revenge are inconsistent with provocation, since the conscious formulation of a desire for revenge means that a person has had time to think, to reflect, and that would negative a sudden temporary loss of self-control, which is of the essence of provocation."

In *Thornton*[19] the court rejected an argument that the words "sudden and temporary" are no longer appropriate. It seems that the function of these words is to emphasise to the jury that there must have been no time in which D was able to (and, it is submitted, did) think and reflect between the final provocation and the fatal act. As long as it is made clear that it is the loss of control and not the provocation which must be "sudden", this seems right. The fact that provocative behaviour has continued over a long period does not rule out the defence, provided it has culminated in a sudden explosion. The prolonged nature of the provocation may explain why an incident, trivial when considered in isolation, caused a loss of self-control. The jury are bound by the Act to take into account everything both done and said according to the effect which in their opinion it would have on a reasonable man; and a jury may well think provocative behaviour over a long period would have a cumulative effect on a reasonable man and had

12. *Bullard v R* [1957] AC 635, [1961] 3 All ER 470 n; *Rolle v R* [1965] 3 All ER 582; *Lee Chun Chuen v R* [1963] AC 220, [1963] 1 All ER 73.
13. Killing, in such a case "is of the lowest degree of [manslaughter]; and therefore ... the court directed the burning in the hand to be gently inflicted, because there could not be a greater provocation": Blackstone, *Commentaries*, iv, 192. And see the leading case of *Manning* (1671) T Raym 212.
14. *Camplin* [1978] AC 705, 67 Cr App Rep 14 at 19; **SHC 320**.
15. (1982) 74 Cr App Rep 154; **SHC 326**.
16. [1992] 1 All ER 306, [1992] Crim LR 53.
17. Below, p. 358.
18. [1949] 1 All ER 932nH.
19. Above, fn. 16.

such an effect on the defendant. The remark in *Davies*[20] that a direction that the jury could take account of "the whole course of conduct of [P] right through that turbulent year of 1972" was too generous can be justified only if no reasonable jury could have thought that the course of conduct had an effect on the accused at the flashpoint. "Everything both done and said" must be limited to what is relevant; but everything which may in fact have contributed to the accused's loss of self-control is relevant. If a matter so contributed, it is not open to the judge to rule that it would not have affected a reasonable man. The "temporary" nature of the loss of self-control seems irrelevant, provided only that it extended to the fatal act. D should not be deprived of defence because he continued berserk for days thereafter – but sudden losses of self-control are in practice temporary.

In *Ibrams*, D had received gross provocation but the last act occurred on 7 October. The attack was carefully planned on 10 October and carried out on 12 October. It was held that the judge was right to rule that there was no evidence of loss of self-control. Recent cases seem to give a generous interpretation to this element of the defence. In *Thornton* a wife who had been treated brutally by her husband over a period of months and had earlier declared her intention of killing him, after a fresh provocation went to the kitchen, took and sharpened a carving knife and returned to another room where she stabbed him. The defence was left to, but rejected by, the jury who presumably were satisfied that there was no sudden and temporary loss of self-control. In *Pearson*[1] there was held to be evidence of provocation although the two defendants had armed themselves in advance with the fatal weapon and the killing was a joint enterprise.

Great importance is attached in many of the older cases to the presence of "cooling time" between the act of provocation and the killing.[1]

Cooling time is obviously a fact of very great importance in deciding this particular question; but it should always be remembered that it is not a matter of law, but one item of evidence in answering the question: was D deprived of his self-control when he did the fatal act?

The CLRC (OAP/R, para. 84) proposed no change in what they took to be the present law:

"... the defence applies only where the defendant's act is caused by the provocation and is committed suddenly upon the provoking event, not to cases where the defendant's violent reaction has been delayed; but the jury should continue to take into consideration previous provocations before the one which produced the fatal reaction."

4 The Objective Condition[2]

In the older cases, the courts laid down as a matter of law what was, and what was not, capable of amounting to provocation.[3] It usually consisted of

---

20. (1975) 60 Cr App Rep 253 at 259.
  1. [1992] Crim LR 193, above, p. 354. See a valuable article, "Cumulative Provocation and Domestic Killing" by Martin Wasik [1982] Crim LR 29, discussing, *inter alia*, some cases and practices which are difficult to reconcile with *Duffy* and *Ibrams*.
  2. See Williams, "Provocation and the Reasonable Man" [1954] Crim LR 740; Edwards "Another View" [1954] Crim LR 898.
  3. See, e.g., Hawkins 1 PC c. 13, s. 36; East, 1 PC 233.

a violent act against the defendant, though two other instances were well recognised, that where a husband discovered his wife in the act of adultery and killed either or both of the guilty pair and that where a father found and promptly killed a man committing sodomy with his son.[4] In *Holmes v Director of Public Prosecutions*[5] the House of Lords held that, as a matter of law, a confession of adultery was insufficient provocation where a husband killed his wife; and added that "in no case could words alone, save in circumstances of a most extreme and exceptional character", reduce the crime to manslaughter. The reasonable man did not make his appearance until *Welsh*[6] in 1869. Thereafter even when the act was recognised as capable of amounting to provocation, it probably had to pass the reasonable man test.

This test was applied by the Court of Criminal Appeal in the important case of *Lesbini*.[7] The girl in charge of a firing range in an amusement arcade made some impertinent personal remarks about D. He asked for a revolver, ostensibly to shoot at the range, and shot her dead. At his trial for murder, his defences of accident and insanity were rejected by the jury. On appeal, it was argued that the jury should have been directed on provocation and *Welsh* did not apply where, as in the present case, D suffered from defective control and want of mental balance. Avory J interjected that it would seem to follow from this that a bad-tempered man would be entitled to a verdict of manslaughter where a good-tempered one would be liable to be convicted of murder[8] and the court held that, to afford a defence, the provocation must be such as would affect the mind of a reasonable man, which was manifestly not so in the present case.

Before the Homicide Act the judges took it upon themselves to instruct the jury as to the characteristics of the reasonable man. The defendant might be mentally deficient[9] but the jury still had to consider the effects of the provocation on a normal person. Moreover, he (or she) was normal in body as well as mind. The fact the defendant was seven months pregnant was irrelevant to the application of the objective test.[10] In *Bedder v Director of Public Prosecutions*,[11] D, a youth of eighteen who was sexually impotent, attempted in vain to have sexual intercourse with P, a prostitute. She jeered at him and attempted to get away. He tried to hold her and she slapped him in the face, punched him in the stomach and kicked him in the genitals. D knew of his impotence and had allowed it to prey on his mind. The House of Lords held that the jury had been correctly directed to consider what effect P's acts would have had on an ordinary person, not a man who is sexually impotent. Mental and physical characteristics were, in the view of the House of Lords, inseparable.

The Homicide Act, s. 3 made three changes in the law. (i) It made it clear that "things said" alone may be sufficient provocation, if the jury should be

---

4. *Fisher* (1837) 8 C & P 182.
5. [1946] AC 588, [1946] 2 All ER 124.
6. (1869) 11 Cox CC 336.
7. [1914] 3 KB 1116.
8. For a discussion of this argument, see the fourth edition of this work, 304–306.
9. *Alexander* (1913) 9 Cr App Rep 139.
10. *Smith* (1915) 11 Cr App Rep 81.
11. [1954] 2 All ER 801, [1954] 1 WLR 1119.

of the opinion that they would have provoked a reasonable man, thus reversing *Director of Public Prosecutions v Holmes*.[12] (ii) It took away the power of the judge to withdraw the defence from the jury on the ground that there was no evidence on which the jury could find that a reasonable man would have been provoked to do as D did, reversing *Mancini*.[13] (iii) It took away the power of the judge to dictate to the jury what were the characteristics of the reasonable man, reversing *Bedder*.

It was not until the decision of the House of Lords in *Camplin*,[14] more than 20 years after the Act, that the second and third effects were fully recognised. The Court of Appeal in that case were of the opinion that *Bedder* was binding on them. The House of Lords decided that the effect of s. 3 is to overrule that case and all others which defined any characteristic of the reasonable man except his powers of self-control and the fact that he is sober.

In *Camplin* D, a fifteen-year-old boy, killed P, with a kitchen utensil known as a chapati pan. D's story was that P had buggered him against his will and then laughed at him when he was overcome by shame, whereupon he lost his self-control and made the fatal attack. The trial judge declined the invitation of D's counsel to instruct the jury to consider the effect of the provocation on a boy of fifteen. He directed that the test was the effect of the provocation, not on a reasonable boy, but on a reasonable man. The Court of Appeal held that this was a misdirection and distinguished *Bedder* on the ground that youth, and the immaturity which naturally accompanies youth, are not deviations from the norm, but norms through which everyone must pass. Youth is not a personal idiosyncrasy and certainly not a physical infirmity or disability like Bedder's impotence.[15] The House of Lords dismissed the Director's appeal on the broader ground that *Bedder* is, in effect, overruled by s. 3 of the 1957 Act. Their lordships were much influenced by the fact that, under the Act, words alone may be a sufficient provocation. This accentuates the anomalies, inconveniences and injustices which would flow from a continued application of the *Bedder* principle, for the gravity of verbal provocation will frequently depend on the particular characteristics or circumstances of the person to whom a taunt or insult is addressed. In a case of provocation by words, personal characteristics could not be ignored without absurdity. To allow such characteristics to be taken into account where the provocation was verbal so undermined the *Bedder* principle that it should no longer be followed, whatever the nature of the provocation.

This conclusion, it is submitted, is well justified by the words of the Act. S. 3 is to be given its natural meaning[16] and tells us that the question for the jury is "whether the provocation was enough to make a reasonable man do as [D] did." What is "the provocation"? It seems obviously to be the things done or things said – which may or may not have been a sufficient

12. [1946] AC 588, [1946] 2 All ER 124.
13. [1942] AC 1, [1941] 3 All ER 272.
14. [1978] AC 705, [1978] 2 All ER 168; **SHC 320.**
15. [1978] 1 All ER at 1241.
16. *Davies* [1975] QB 691, [1975] 1 All ER 890.

provocation at common law – which the jury have found to have provoked the accused. The section goes on to direct that the jury—

"shall take into account *everything* both done and said according to the effect which, *in their opinion*, it would have on a reasonable man."

The words we have italicised are inconsistent with the continuance of *Bedder* as a rule of law. "Everything" includes a taunt of impotence where that in fact provoked the accused and the effect of it on a reasonable man is a question for the opinion of the jury

The result of *Camplin*, as Lord Simon pointed out, is to bring the common law, as modified by the Homicide Act, into line with the New Zealand Crimes Act 1961.[17] This provides by s. 169 (2):

"Anything done or said may be provocation if—

(a) In the circumstances of the case it was sufficient to deprive a person having the power of self-control of an ordinary person, but otherwise having the characteristics of the offender, of the power of self-control; and

(b) It did in fact deprive the offender of the power of self-control and thereby induced him to commit the act of homicide."

a) *The relevant "characteristics"*. The reasonable man must now be endowed by the jury with the age, sex and other personal characteristics of the accused, whether normal or abnormal. The characteristics may be taken into account by the jury – it is a matter for their opinion – both in assessing the gravity of the provocation addressed to the accused and in determining what degree of self-control is to be expected of him. The jury should be directed as follows:[18]

"The judge should state what the question is using the very terms of the section. He should then explain to them that the reasonable man referred to in the question is a person having the power of self-control to be expected of an ordinary person of the sex and age of the accused, but in other respects sharing such of the accused's characteristics as they think would affect the gravity of the provocation to him; and that the question is not merely whether such a person would in like circumstances be provoked to lose his self-control but also would react to the provocation as the accused did."

The judge may tell the jury that a man is not entitled to rely on "his exceptional excitability (whether idiosyncratic or by cultural environment or ethnic origin) or pugnacity or ill-temper or on his drunkenness."[19] The judge should remind the jury of any material characteristics of the defendant[20] and may suggest considerations which may influence the jury in forming their opinion but he must make it clear that it is for them and no one else to decide what weight, if any, ought to be given to them. The evidence of witnesses as to how they think a reasonable man with the characteristics of the accused would react to the provocation is not admissible.

---

17. As explained in *McGregor* [1962] NZLR 1069.
18. Per Lord Diplock at p. 175.
19. Per Lord Simon, who did not think this list necessarily exhaustive. *McCarthy* [1954] 2 QB 105, [1954] 2 All ER 262 remains good law.
20. *Burke* [1987] Crim LR 336, CA.

The question of what is meant by "characteristics" was further elucidated by the Court of Appeal in *Newell*,[21] following the judgment delivered
by North J in the New Zealand case of *McGregor*:[1]

"The characteristic must be something definite and of sufficient significance to make the offender a different person from the ordinary run of
mankind, and have also a sufficient degree of permanence to warrant its
being regarded as something constituting part of the individual's character and personality."

By the terms of the decision in *Camplin* and of the New Zealand Crimes
Act, the jury are obviously not entitled to give weight to such permanent
characteristics as unusual excitability or pugnacity of the defendant or his
disposition to lose his temper readily; and transitory states of mind, such as
a mood of depression, excitability or irascibility are equally excluded.

North J went on:

"Moreover, it is to be equally emphasised that there must be some real
connection between the nature of the provocation and the particular
characteristic of the offender by which it is sought to modify the ordinary
man test. The words or conduct must have been exclusively or particularly provocative to the individual because, and only because, of the
characteristic of the offender by which it is sought to modify the ordinary
man test ... In short there must be some direct connection between the
provocative words or conduct and the characteristic sought to be invoked
as warranting some departure from the ordinary man test."

Notwithstanding Lord Diplock's reference to D's age, it is not in every case
that the judge is obliged to mention age. In *Ali*[2] where the provocation was
an attack at a discotheque, the judge did not err by omitting to focus the
jury's attention on the fact that D was aged 20: the gravity of the
provocation to a man was the same whether he was 20, 35 or any other age.
In other circumstances the fact that D was aged 20 might be significant. In
Roberts,[3] where a 23-year-old man suffering from substantial deafness and
consequent impairment to his speech killed as the result of taunts, it was
held that the judge had rightly directed that the hypothetical reasonable
man had those characterisitics; and that he had rightly excluded psychiatric
evidence that immature prelingually deaf persons are subject to irrational
explosions of violence. This evidence seems to go to the exceptional
excitability of D, which *Camplin* does not allow to be taken into account.
The test to be applied by the judge seems to be: in all the circumstances of
this case, could a reasonable jury consider that this characteristic of the
defendant would affect the gravity of the provocation to him?

The jury is now entitled and bound to take into account two classes of
fact: (i) the events which have happened and which might have a tendency
to cause a reasonable man with the relevant characteristics of the defendant
to lose his self-control; and (ii) those relevant characteristics. The two

21. (1980) 71 Cr App Rep 331, [1980] Crim LR 576, CA; **SHC 324**.
  1. [1962] NZLR 1069 at 1081. North J's observations are said to have caused continual
difficulty in New Zealand and to "add needless complexity to the application of [section 169]":
McCarthy (263/91, unreported, 27 February 1992), NZ CA.
  2. [1989] Crim LR 736; **SHC 326**. Similarly, sex may not always be relevant.
  3. [1990] Crim LR 122.

matters are inter-related. The fact that a man is impotent is a relevant characteristic if the alleged provocation consists in taunts of impotence but it would be irrelevant if the provocation were taunts about the defendant's race, religion, stupidity or dishonesty.

In *Newell*, D was a chronic alcoholic who was very depressed by the defection of the young woman with whom he had been living for some time and to whom he was strongly attached. When D and his friend, P, were both very drunk, P made derogatory remarks about the woman which caused D immediately to lose his self-control and make a violent attack on P, killing him. The judge asked the jury: "Would a sober man, in relation to that drunken observation, batter his friend over the head with a nearly two poundweight ashtray?" That was held to be a proper direction. The only matter which could possibly be described as a characteristic was D's chronic alcoholism but, without deciding that it was, the court held that it had nothing to do with the words by which D was said to be provoked.

The application of these principles may make considerable demands on a jury. In *Raven*,[4] D aged 22, had a mental age of approximately nine years, regrettably, no doubt, a permanent characteristic, and had lived in "squats" for two to three years of his life. The jury were directed to consider the reasonable man as having lived the same type of life as D for 22 years, but with his retarded development and mental age.

5 The Relationship between the Provocation and the Mode of Resentment

In *Mancini v Director of Public Prosecutions*[5] D was charged with the murder of P who had been stabbed to death by an instrument with a two-edged blade, a sharp point and sharp sides, at least five inches long. D's story was that P was attacking him with an open pen-knife and MacNaghten J told the jury that, if they believed this story, they should return a verdict of not guilty (on the ground of self-defence.) He did not direct them that, if they rejected the defence of self-defence, they still might find D guilty of manslaughter on the ground of provocation; and D appealed on the ground that he ought to have done so. His conviction was affirmed. By their verdict, the jury had rejected his story of the attack with the pen-knife; and the case had, therefore, to be treated as one in which, at the most, P made an unarmed attack on D. If there had been evidence of provocation, it would have been the judge's duty to direct the jury on it, even though the defence had not been set up;[6] but here there was no evidence. An attack by hand or fist

"would not constitute provocation of a kind which could extenuate the sudden introduction and use of a lethal weapon like this dagger, and there was, therefore, ... no adequate material to raise the issue of provocation."[7]

The House stated the law in general terms as follows:[8]

4. [1982] Crim LR 51 and commentary.
5. [1942] AC 1, [1941] 3 All ER 272, HL.
6. Above, p. 352.
7. [1942] AC at 10, [1941] 3 All ER at 278.
8. [1942] AC at 9, [1941] 3 All ER at 277, per Lord Simon.

"... it is of particular importance ... to take into account the instrument with which the homicide was effected, for to retort, in the heat of passion induced by provocation, by a simple blow, is a very different thing from making use of a deadly instrument like a concealed dagger. In short, the mode of resentment must bear a reasonable relationship to the provocation if the offence is to be reduced to manslaughter."

Clearly such a case could not be decided in this way today. If there was evidence that D was provoked to lose his self-control, the judge could not decline to leave the defence to the jury because the resentment did not bear a reasonable relationship to the provocation. It was in this respect, no doubt, that Lord Diplock in *Camplin* said that *Mancini* is no longer to be treated as an authority on the law of provocation.[9] It would now be wrong to tell the jury, "fists might be answered with fists but not with a deadly weapon",[10] because if fists were answered with a deadly weapon, this would be to take out of the jury's hands a question which is exclusively for them and on which their opinion is decisive. So it has been said that the "reasonable relationship rule" is not a rule of law and that it is wrong for the judge, who has directed them on the subjective and objective conditions, to go on to tell them that there is a third condition, viz that the retaliation must be proportionate to the provocation.[11] Yet in a sense, the reasonable relationship rule still is a rule of law because the defence is made out only if the provocation was enough to make the reasonable man "do as he did". Thus, it would be right for the judge to direct the jury: "If you are satisfied that a reasonable man, though he might have answered with fists, would not have answered with the deadly weapon used by D, then you *must* reject the defence of provocation." This is no more than the application of the words of the section to the facts. The difference, since the Act, is that it is for the jury, not the judge, to decide whether the answer with a deadly weapon was the act of a reasonable man.

Since 1978, the decision in *Camplin* has removed much of the "inequity" said to arise from the test. The main argument, in favour of the test, that the bad-tempered man should be treated in the same way as the good-tempered man, has been subjected to cogent criticism.[12] If the good-tempered man kills when he has not lost his self-control, he deserves to be convicted of murder and no injustice is done to him if the man who has lost his self-control is convicted only of manslaughter. On the other hand, it is the business of the law to lay down standards of conduct and this is a standard of self-restraint, similar to the standards of fortitude and resolution which are required by the law in the defence of duress and blackmail. One difference, however, is that here we are not concerned with criminal liability or no criminal liability, but only with a matter of mitigation – in practice, with untying the judge's hands to enable him to impose an appropriate sentence instead of requiring him to impose the sentence of imprisonment for life. The CLRC has recommended that the question for the jury should be whether, on the facts as they appeared to the defendant,

9. 67 Cr App Rep at 21. See commentary on *Brown* [1972] Crim LR 506.
10. Per Devlin J in *Duffy* [1949] 1 All ER 932n.
11. *Brown* [1972] 2 QB 229, [1972] 2 All ER 1328.
12. Williams, [1954] Crim LR 751; Kenny, *Outlines*, 178.

the provocation can reasonably be regarded as a sufficient ground for the loss of self-control leading the defendant to react against the victim with murderous intent,[13] and that, in answering this question, the defendant should be judged with due regard to all the circumstances, including any disability, physical or mental, from which he suffered.[14] This proposal would remove the objective test and, with it, much unnecessary technicality from the law.

It will be noted that, under section 3 of the Homicide Act, the subjective and objective tests differ. The questions are: (i) did D *lose his self control?* and (ii) was the provocation enough to make the reasonable man *do as D did?* It can hardly have been intended, however, that the jury should consider whether a reasonable man in full control of himself would have done what D did for the logical effect of that would be to eliminate the defence from the law. The objective test must be construed as it was in *Phillips v R:*[15]

"... the question ... is not merely whether in their opinion the provocation would have made a reasonable man lose his self-control but also whether, having lost his self-control, he would have retaliated in the same way as the person charged in fact did."

This assumes that a person who has lost his self-control acts with more or less ferocity according to the degree of provocation which caused the loss of self-control. The Privy Council has rejected the argument—

"... that loss of self-control is not a matter of degree but is absolute; there is no intermediate stage between icy detachment and going berserk. This premise, unless the argument is purely semantic, must be based upon human experience and is, in their Lordships' view, false. The average man reacts to provocation according to its degree with angry words, with a blow of the hand, possibly, if the provocation is gross and there is a dangerous weapon to hand, with that weapon."[16]

Whatever scientific opinion may be,[17] this certainly seems to be the view of human conduct on which the section is based; and the objective condition requires affirmative answers to two questions: (i) would the reasonable man have lost his self-control? and (ii) would he then have retaliated as D did?

6 Provocation arising from a Mistake of Fact

The authorities suggest that, where D is provoked partly as the result of a mistake of fact he is entitled to be treated as if the facts were as he mistakenly supposed them to be. Thus in *Brown*[18] D, a soldier, wrongly, but apparently reasonably, supposed that P was a member of a gang who were attacking him and his comrade. He struck P with a sword and killed him. The judges were clearly of the opinion that this was only manslaughter. In the other cases the mistake arose from drunkenness. In

13. CLRC/OAP/R, para. 81.
14. Ibid., para. 83.
15. [1969] 2 AC 130 at 137, PC; **SHC 328**.
16. Ibid., 137. See White, "A Note on Provocation" [1970] Crim LR 446.
17. Brett, "The Physiology of Provocation" [1970] Crim LR 634.
18. (1776) Leach 148.

Letenock[19] the Court of Criminal Appeal substituted a verdict of manslaughter in the case of a soldier who had stabbed a corporal, where

"The only element of doubt in the case is whether or not there was anything which might have caused the applicant, *in his drunken condition*, to believe that he was going to be struck."[20]

This decision is unaffected by *McCarthy*[1] which was not concerned with a mistake of fact but with the effect of the alcohol on D's self-restraint. So in *Wardrope*,[2] Edmund Davies J told the jury both that the provocation "must be such as to deprive a reasonable man, not a drunken man . . . of self-control" and that

"A person whose mind was so impaired by drink as to imagine himself attacked was entitled[3] to take such steps in defending himself as were necessary to meet the imagined attack as if it were real or not exaggerated. . . ."

It is recognised that a drunken mistake may negative the *mens rea* of murder[4] and it is consistent that such a mistake should be relevant in determining whether the killing should be reduced to manslaughter on the ground of provocation. A drunken mistake is almost inevitably an unreasonable one; and it seems clear that it is immaterial whether the mistake is reasonable or not for this purpose. The jury must look at the reactions of the reasonable man in the circumstances which D supposed to exist.

7 Self-induced Provocation

The jury must be told to take into account everything both done and said according to the effect which, in their opinion, it would have on a reasonable man, even where that which was done and said was a predictable result of D's own conduct. It was so held in *Johnson*,[5] not following dicta of the Privy Council in *Edwards v R*.[6] D's unpleasant behaviour in a nightclub resulted in an attack on him in response to which he killed. He was not precluded from relying on provocation even if the attack was a predictable result of his behaviour.

It has been suggested[7] that such a decision might open a defence for one who *deliberately* induces provocation – D provokes P to do a provocative act so that D may kill him and rely on the defence of provocation. Such a situation seems far-fetched. If it did occur, it should, it is submitted, be decided on the same lines as *A-G for Northern Ireland v Gallagher*[8] – D

---

19. (1917) 12 Cr App Rep 221, CCA.
20. Ibid., at 224.
  1. [1954] 2 QB 105, [1954] 2 All ER 262.
  2. [1960] Crim LR 770.
  3. Wardrope also raised the defence of self-defence and the use of the word "entitled" (cf. *Southgate* [1963] 2 All ER 833) suggests that it was to this defence that the judge was here referring; but he could hardly have intended the jury to consider D's mistake of fact for the purpose of the one defence and not for the other. Such a mistake, properly taken into account for purposes of self-defence, may not lead to a complete acquittal since it is said that drunken mistakes can at best reduce murder to manslaughter.
  4. Above, pp. 220–224.
  5. [1989] Crim LR 738.
  6. [1973] AC 648, [1973] 1 All ER 152, PC.
  7. By Ashworth [1973] Crim LR 483.
  8. Above, p. 229.

should be held liable for the acts which, when unprovoked, he intended to do under provocation. The judge should find there is no evidence that D was provoked.

8 Provocation by a Lawful Act

It has been argued that "The law would be self-contradictory if a lawful act could amount to provocation,"[9] but it is submitted that this proposition will not bear examination.[10] To taunt a man with his impotence or his wife's adultery may be cruel and immoral, but it is not unlawful and it may, surely, amount to provocation. So, we now know, may the crying of a baby.[11] Where P's act is one which he is not merely at liberty to do but which is positively praiseworthy, it is scarcely conceivable that a jury would find that it would provoke a reasonable man to lose his self-control; but under the terms of s. 3 it must be a question for the jury in each case. It is impossible, as a matter of law, to divide acts which P is at liberty to do into classes of "good" and "bad".

3) *Involuntary Manslaughter*

This category includes all varieties of homicide which are unlawful at common law but committed without malice aforethought. It is not surprising, therefore, that the fault required takes more than one form. And, as the limits of malice aforethought are uncertain, it follows inevitably that there is a corresponding uncertainty as to the boundary of manslaughter. The difficulties do not end there, for there is another vague borderline between manslaughter and accidental death. Indeed, Lord Atkin said[12] that

"... of all crimes manslaughter appears to afford most difficulties of definition, for it concerns homicide in so many and so varying conditions ... the law ... recognises murder on the one hand based mainly, though not exclusively,[13] on an intention to kill, and manslaughter on the other hand, based mainly, though not exclusively,[14] on the absence of intent to kill, but with the presence of an element of 'unlawfulness' which is the elusive factor."

The element of "unlawfulness" is no less elusive today than when Lord Atkin spoke. We can say, however, that there are two broad categories of involuntary manslaughter:

(i) manslaughter by an unlawful and dangerous act;
(ii) manslaughter by recklessness, or, possibly, gross negligence.

9. Howard, *Australian Criminal Law* (2nd ed.) 93.
10. See *Browne* [1973] NI 96 at 108, per Lowry LCJ: "I should prefer to say that provocation is something *unwarranted* which is likely to make a reasonable person angry or indignant."
11. *Doughty* (1986) 83 Cr App Rep 319, above, p. 353.
12. In *Andrews v Director of Public Prosecutions* [1937] AC 576 at 581, [1937] 2 All ER 552 at 554–555.
13. See above, p. 347.
14. See above, p. 350.

The constituents òf each of these categories require some degree of analysis.

1 Manslaughter by an Unlawful and Dangerous Act

Coke laid it down that an intention to commit any unlawful act was a sufficient *mens rea* for murder[15] so that if D shot at P's hen with intent to kill it and accidentally killed P, this was murder, "for the act was unlawful". This savage doctrine was criticised by Holt CJ[16] and by the time Foster wrote his *Crown Law*,[17] it appears to have been modified by the proviso that the unlawful act must be a felony. Thus, if D shot at the hen intending to steal it, the killing of P was murder. This was the doctrine of constructive murder which survived until the Homicide Act 1957. From Foster's time there existed a twin doctrine of constructive manslaughter; that any death caused while in the course of committing an unlawful act, other than a felony, was manslaughter. An act was unlawful for this purpose even if it was only a tort, so that the only *mens rea* which needed to be proved was an intention to commit the tort.

The present law is that D is guilty of manslaughter if he kills by an unlawful and dangerous act. The only *mens rea* required is an intention to do that act and any fault required to render it unlawful. It is irrelevant that D is unaware that it is unlawful or that it is dangerous,[18] and that he is unaware of the circumstances which make it dangerous, if a reasonable person would have been aware of them.[19] The meaning of "unlawful" and "dangerous" requires further examination.

a) *The unlawfulness: a crime?* At one time it was thought that the act was sufficiently unlawful if it was a civil wrong, a tort. Thus in *Fenton*[20] where D threw stones down a mine and broke some scaffolding which caused a corf to overturn with fatal results, Tindal CJ told the jury that D's act was a trespass and the only question was whether it caused P's death. Even in the nineteenth century this doctrine was not accepted without reservation by the judges. A notable refusal to follow it is the direction of Field J in *Franklin*.[1] D, walking on Brighton pier, took up "a good sized box" from a refreshment stall and threw it into the sea where it struck a swimmer, P, and killed him. The prosecution argued that, apart from any question of negligence, it was manslaughter if the commission of the tort of trespass against the stallkeeper had caused death. Field J, after consulting Mathew J who agreed, held that the case must go to the jury "on the broad ground of negligence". Expressing his "great abhorrence of constructive crime", Field J asserted that—

---

15. 3 Inst. 56. See Turner, MACL 195 at 212 et seq. for a discussion of the historical development.
16. *Keate* (1697) Comb 406 at 409.
17. (1762) – see p. 258.
18. *Newbury* [1977] AC 500, [1976] 2 All ER 365, *Ball* [1989] Crim LR 730.
19. *Watson* [1989] 2 All ER 865, [1989] Crim LR 733.
20. (1830) 1 Lew CC 179.
1. (1883) 15 Cox CC 163; **SHC 332.**

"The mere fact of a civil wrong committed by one person against another ought not to be used as an incident which is a necessary step in a criminal case."

If it is not enough that the act is tortious, presumably it must be a crime; but even today it is not completely clear that this is the law, though it was so held in *Lamb*.[2] D pointed a loaded gun at his friend, P, in jest. He did not intend to injure or alarm P and P was not alarmed. Because they did not understand how a revolver works, both thought there was no danger in pulling the trigger; but, when D did so, he shot P dead. D was not guilty of a criminal assault or battery because he did not foresee that P would be alarmed or injured. It was therefore a misdirection to tell the jury that this was "an unlawful and dangerous act". It was not, said Sachs LJ, "unlawful in the criminal sense of the word"; and, referring to *Franklin*, "it is not in point to consider whether an act is unlawful merely from the angle of civil liabilities". This opinion is supported by *Jennings*[3] where it was held that carrying an uncovered knife in a public place was not a sufficient unlawful act in the absence of proof that D was carrying it with intent to cause injury: "Walking down the walkway with the knife in his hand [even with intent to frighten] was not a criminal offence which could constitute the 'unlawful' act for this purpose." If the intent had been proved, D would have been committing an offence under the Prevention of Crime Act 1953.[4]

Against these cases must be set the omission of the House of Lords in *DPP v Newbury*[5] to identify any crime rendering the act unlawful. The "unlawful" act was throwing a piece of paving stone from the parapet of a bridge as a train approached. This certainly has every appearance of a criminal act which is perhaps why it was not and, the House thought, could not be, argued that the act was lawful. But the question for the House was whether D could properly be convicted if he did not foresee that his act might cause harm to another. So, despite appearances, the act could not be regarded as an assault or any of the usual offences against the person, all of which require *mens rea*. Unless resort is to be had to the tort of trespass, this leaves as possibilities the offence of endangering passengers contrary to s. 34 of the Offences against the Person Act 1861 or an offence of criminal damage – but an offence against property seems almost as objectionable a basis for convicting of manslaughter as a tort.

"Unlawful" is left as a vague, undefined concept in *Newbury* and this is also true of *Cato*[6] where D caused P's death by injecting him with heroin with his consent. The court accepted that this was not an offence under the Misuse of Drugs Act and assumed for this purpose that it was not an offence under s. 23 of the Offences against the Person Act 1861[7] but said "the unlawful act would be described as injecting the deceased with a mixture of heroin and water which at the time of the injection and for the

2. [1967] 2 QB 981, [1967] 2 All ER 1282; **SHC 233**.
3. [1990] Crim LR 588.
4. Below, p. 443.
5. [1977] AC 500, [1976] 2 All ER 365; **SHC 335**.
6. [1976] 1 All ER 260; **SHC 336**.
7. Below, p. 429. In fact D was convicted of the s. 23 offence so the remarks discussed in the text may be obiter.

purposes of the injection Cato had unlawfully taken into his possession".
The act was thus closely associated with other acts which are offences but it
is submitted that neither this nor the fact that the act excites strong moral
condemnation should be enough to found liability for manslaughter.

The better view, it is submitted, is that in *Lamb* and *Jennings*, i.e., that a
criminal act must be identified and proved, including the appropriate *mens
rea*. So Lord Denning's dictum in the civil case of *Gray v Barr*[8] which was
criticised by Lord Salmon in *Newbury*[9] is correct if it is confined to the case
where the unlawful act relied on is assault or battery. Lord Denning said:
"the accused must do a dangerous act with the *intention* of frightening or
harming someone, or with *realisation* that it is likely to frighten or harm
someone". This is simply to require the *mens rea* of assault or battery.
However, an act which is intended or known to be likely to frighten is not
necessarily a "dangerous" act; and whether it is dangerous, as appears
below, is a question to be answered by an objective test.

b) *Intoxication and the unlawful act.* Where the prosecution rely on an
unlawful act which does not require a specific intent and D was intoxicated
at the time, it is immaterial that he lacked the *mens rea* of the crime in
question and even that he was unconscious: *Lipman*[10] where D killed P by
cramming a sheet into her mouth and striking her while he was on an
L.S.D. "trip" and believed he was in the centre of the earth being attacked
by snakes. Though the jury convicted on the grounds that D was reckless
or grossly negligent when, quite consciously, he took the drugs, the Court
of Appeal upheld the conviction by applying the *Church* doctrine. The
unlawful act was the battery committed on P while D was unconscious.

c) *Unlawfulness arising otherwise than through negligence.* This requirement
is implicit in the rule in *Church*[11]. An act which all sober and reasonable
people would realise entailed the risk (*sc.*, an unjustifiable risk) of harm to
others almost certainly becomes the tort of negligence when harm results
and therefore the reference to "an unlawful act" would be otiose if it did
not mean unlawful in some other respect. This is in accordance with the
well-established rule that negligence sufficient to found civil liability is not
necessarily enough for criminal guilt, that death caused in the course of
committing the tort of negligence is not necessarily manslaughter. But the
limitation goes further than this: there are degrees of negligence which are
criminally punishable which are yet not sufficient to found a charge of
manslaughter. If, then, the unlawfulness, whether civil or criminal, of the
act arises solely from the negligent manner in which it is performed, death
caused by the act will not necessarily be manslaughter. This follows from

8. [1971] 2 QB 554 at 568, above, p. 41. Lord Denning's italics.
9. [1977] AC 500. Cf. Blackstone, p. 109.
10. [1970] 1 QB 152, [1969] 3 All ER 410; **SHC 100**. The case was heavily criticised. See
Hooker [1969] Crim LR 547; Orchard [1970] Crim LR 132; Glazebrook [1970] CLJ 21;
Buxton [1970] *Annual Survey of Commonwealth Law*, 128 and 134. It was not followed in
Australia: *Haywood* [1971] VR 755 (Crockett J) but has now been affirmed by the House of
Lords in *Majewski* (above, p. 220).
11. Below, p. 370.

the decision of the House of Lords in *Andrews v Director of Public Prosecutions*.[12]

In that case Du Parcq J told the jury that if D killed P in the course of dangerous driving contrary to s. 11 of the Road Traffic Act 1930 he was guilty of manslaughter. Lord Atkin (who clearly regarded dangerous driving in the 1930 Act as a crime of negligence)[13] said that, if the summing up had rested there, there would have been misdirection:

"There can be no doubt that this section covers driving with such a high degree of negligence as that, if death were caused, the offender would have committed manslaughter. But the converse is not true, and it is perfectly possible that a man may drive at a speed or in a manner dangerous to the public, and cause death, and yet not be guilty of manslaughter."[14]

Lord Atkin expressly distinguished[15] between acts which are unlawful because of the negligent manner in which they are performed and acts which are unlawful for some other reason:

"There is an obvious difference in the law of manslaughter between doing an unlawful act and doing a lawful act with a degree of carelessness which the legislature makes criminal."

His Lordship's next sentence implies that killing in the course of unlawful acts generally *was* manslaughter:

"If it were otherwise a man who killed another while driving without due care and attention would *ex necessitate* commit manslaughter."

This passage has been severely criticised[16] and it is certainly unhappily phrased. ". . . doing a lawful act with a degree of carelessness which the legislature makes criminal" is a contradiction in terms, for the act so done is plainly not a lawful act. But the distinction evidently intended, viz., between acts which are unlawful because of negligent performance and acts which are unlawful for some other reason, is at least intelligible and, in view of the established distinction between civil and criminal negligence, a necessary limitation.

d) *Omissions as "unlawful acts"*. In *Lowe*,[17] the Court of Appeal held that D is not guilty of manslaughter simply on the ground that he has committed the offence under s. 1(1) of the Children and Young Persons Act 1933 of neglecting his child so as to cause unnecessary suffering or injury to its health, and that neglect has caused death. The Court disapproved *Senior*[18] which, on similar facts, held that this was manslaughter. *Lowe* has now been overruled on its interpretation of the 1933 Act and *Senior* to some extent rehabilitated by *Sheppard*[19] – but not on this point, on which, it is thought, *Lowe* and not *Senior* represents the law. Death had certainly been

---

12. [1937] AC 576, [1937] 2 All ER 552; **SHC 342**.
13. See above, p. 92. The offence of dangerous driving was abolished by the Criminal Law Act 1977 but restored in a new form by the Road Traffic Act 1991, s. 2. Below, p. 489.
14. [1937] AC at 584, [1937] 2 All ER at 556, 557.
15. [1937] AC at 585, [1937] 2 All ER at 557.
16. Turner, MACL at 238.
17. [1973] QB 702, [1973] 1 All ER 805.
18. [1899] 1 QB 283.
19. [1981] AC 394, [1980] 3 All ER 899, 72 Cr App Rep 82, HL.

caused by unlawful and dangerous conduct, but the Court distinguished between omission and commission.

".... if I strike a child in a manner likely to cause harm it is right that if the child dies I may be charged with manslaughter. If, however, I omit to do something with the result that it suffers injury to its health which results in its death, we think that a charge of manslaughter should not be an inevitable consequence even if the omission is deliberate."

If the omission is no more than an act of negligence then it is right that the doctrine of the unlawful and dangerous act does not apply and D is not guilty in the absence of gross negligence; but if the omission is truly *wilful* – a deliberate omission to summon medical aid, knowing it to be necessary, there seems to be no valid ground for the distinction.[20]

e) *The dangerousness*. Until 1966 it was possible to argue that any unlawful act, other than a merely negligent act, causing death was manslaughter; but in that year in *Church* the Court of Criminal Appeal rejected that view. Edmund Davies J. said:

"For such a verdict inexorably to follow, the unlawful act must be such as all sober and reasonable people would inevitably recognise must subject the other person to, at least, the risk of some harm resulting therefrom, albeit not serious harm.[1]

The test of dangerousness is objective. In *Newbury* Lord Salmon stressed:

".... the test is not did the accused recognise that it was dangerous but would all sober and reasonable people recognise its danger."

The test describes the kind of act which gives rise to liability for manslaughter, not the intention or foresight, real or assumed, of the accused. Hence the enactment of s. 8 of the Criminal Justice Act 1967[2] had no effect on the law as stated in *Church*. The question is whether the sober and reasonable man would have appreciated that the act was dangerous in the light, not only of the circumstances actually known to the accused, but also of any additional circumstances of which that hypothetical person would have been aware. So a peculiarity of the victim is relevant if it would have been known to the sober and reasonable observer of the event, even if it was not known to the accused. The burglary of a house in which resides P, a frail 87-year-old man, becomes a "dangerous" act as soon as P's frailty and great age would be apparent to the reasonable observer. The unlawful act continues through the "whole of the burglarious intrusion" so that if P dies of a heart attack caused by D's continuing in the burglary after it has become a dangerous, as well as unlawful, act he will be guilty of manslaughter.[3] Where a petrol station attendant with a weak heart died in consequence of a robbery this was not manslaughter because the observer

---

20. See editorial comment in [1976] Crim LR 529.

1. [1966] 1 QB 59 at 70.

2. Above, p. 86.

3. *Watson* [1989] 2 All ER 865, [1989] Crim LR 733. D's conviction was quashed because causation was not established. P's death may have been caused by the arrival of the emergency services. But did this predictable event break the chain of causation? Cf. commentary, [1989] Crim LR 734. If P has sustained a fatal shock before D has any opportunity to observe his frailty, D's liability seems to depend on whether his acts after he had that opportunity (now "dangerous" acts) contributed to the death.

would not have known of his peculiar susceptibility – the act was not "dangerous".[4]

f) *Fright, shock and harm.* Whether fright is "harm" so that an act which is likely only to frighten amounts to manslaughter if it in fact kills is less clear. In *Reid*[5] Lawton LJ said that "the very least kind of harm is causing fright by threats" – in that case, by the use of firearms – but he was discussing the mental element of an accessory rather than the nature of the act, which is our present concern. The act was, in the opinion of the court, likely to cause death or serious injury and therefore was certainly "dangerous". In *Dawson*[6] the court assumed without deciding that in the context of manslaughter "harm" includes "injury to the person through the operation of shock emanating from fright". So it seems that it is not enough that the act is likely to frighten. It must be likely to cause such shock as to result in physical injury.

g) *Must the unlawful act be "directed at" the victim?* In *Dalby*[7] it was held that

"where the charge of manslaughter is based on an unlawful and dangerous act, it must be an act directed at the victim and likely to cause immediate injury however slight."

D and P were drug addicts. D, who was lawfully in possession of diconal tablets, supplied some to P who took them in a highly dangerous form and quantity and died. D was not guilty because the supply was not an act directed against the person of P and did not cause direct injury to him. But in *Goodfellow*[8] D's argument that he was not guilty of manslaughter because his act was not directed against P was rejected. D, wanting to move from his council house and seeing no prospect of exchanging it, set it on fire, attempting to make it appear that the cause was a petrol bomb. P died in the fire. The court said that *Dalby* decided that no more than that "there must be no fresh intervening cause between the act and the death". The act of burglary which causes the death of the obviously frail householder is not directed at him but it is accepted in *Watson* that it may be manslaughter.[9] In *Ball*[10] the court distinguished some examples posed by D's counsel on the ground that, unlike the case before the court, they were of acts not directed at P. The court therefore expressed no opinion on "the example of a person storing goods known to be stolen; if unknown to him the goods contain unstable explosive which explodes killing another, is that manslaughter?" The answer must surely be no, unless the sober and reasonable

---

4. *Dawson* (1985) 81 Cr App Rep 150. Yet before the Homicide Act 1957 this would have been murder (killing in the course or furtherance of a violent felony) and, according to one theory, Parliament's provision that it was not murder left it manslaughter. See first edition of this work, 19–20. The theory has not taken root.
5. (1975) 62 Cr App Rep 109 at 112.
6. (1985) 81 Cr App Rep at 155.
7. [1982] 1 All ER 916; **SHC 337**.
8. (1986) 83 Cr App Rep 23. The conviction was upheld on the grounds of both unlawful act and reckless manslaughter.
9. Above, fn. 3.
10. [1989] Crim LR 730, CA.

observer would have known of the danger. Only if he would have known would the question whether the act must be directed at P arise. Applying *Goodfellow* and *Watson*, he would be guilty: the act need not be directed at P. But *Dalby* was not in fact based on causation[11] and there is something to be said in favour of the "directed at" requirement. It does not seem appropriate that a person's guilt of homicide should depend on whether he was handling stolen goods or committing criminal damage or burglary. Cases of this sort would be better left to the next category of killing by recklessness or gross negligence.

2 Reckless Manslaughter

For many years the courts have used the terms "recklessness" and "gross negligence" to describe the fault required for involuntary manslaughter, other than constructive manslaughter, without any clear definition of either term. It was not clear whether these terms were merely two ways of describing the same thing, or whether they represented two distinct conditions of fault. The fifth edition of this work adopted the latter view, distinguishing between gross negligence manslaughter, where the gross negligence must be whether death or serious injury be caused, and reckless manslaughter where the recklessness might be as to death, personal injury, whether serious or slight, and[12] possibly any injury to "health or welfare". The matter must now be re-considered in the light of the decisions in *Lawrence* and *Caldwell*[13] and their application to manslaughter by the House of Lords in *Seymour*[14] and by the Privy Council in *Kong Cheuk Kwan v R.*[15] In *Seymour* it was held that the law was the same for manslaughter as for the then statutory offence of causing death by reckless driving[16] and therefore that the *Lawrence* test was applicable, subject in a manslaughter case to the omission of reference to a risk of substantial damage to property. The risk must be of physical injury to some other person. The abolition of the offence of causing death by reckless driving[17] does not affect that ruling. In *Kong Cheuk Kwan* the Privy Council expressly approved[18] of a comment made by Watkins LJ in delivering the judgment of the Court of Appeal in *Seymour*:[19]

"... we are of the view that it is no longer necessary or helpful to make reference to compensation and negligence. The *Lawrence* direction on recklessness is comprehensive and of general application to all offences, including manslaughter involving the driving of motor vehicles recklessly and should be given to juries without in any way being diluted.

---

11. The point of law certified for the House of Lords postulated "an act [not directed against P] which is the substantial cause of the death" and the court left open the question whether D was guilty of manslaughter by gross negligence which it could scarcely have done if it was deciding that D did not cause death.
12. Following *Stone and Dobinson* [1977] QB 354, [1977] 2 All ER 341.
13. [1982] AC 510 and 341 respectively, above, p. 62.
14. [1983] 2 AC 493, [1983] 2 All ER 1058.
15. (1985) 82 Cr App Rep 18, [1985] Crim LR 787.
16. Below, p. 374.
17. Below, p. 489.
18. At p. 26.
19. (1983) 76 Cr App Rep 211 at 216.

Whether a driver at the material time was conscious of the risk he was running or gave no thought to its existence, is a matter which affects punishment for which purposes the judge will have to decide, if he can, giving the benefit of doubt to the convicted person, in which state of mind that person had driven at the material time."

The reference to "compensation and negligence" clearly relates to the classic statement of the gross negligence doctrine by Hewart LCJ in *Bateman*.[20]

"In explaining to juries the test which they should apply to determine whether the negligence, in the particular case, amounted or did not amount to a crime, judges have used many epithets such as 'culpable', 'criminal', 'gross', 'wicked', 'clear', 'complete'. But whatever epithet be used and whether an epithet be used or not, in order to establish criminal liability the facts must be such that, in the opinion of the jury, the negligence of the accused went beyond a mere matter of compensation between subjects and showed such disregard for the life and safety of others, as to amount to a crime against the State and conduct deserving of punishment."

This passage has been criticised[1] on the grounds that (i) it is circular in that it tells the jury to convict if they think that D is guilty of a crime and (ii) it leaves a question of law to the jury. These criticisms are well founded; yet, if we are to have a crime based on a certain degree of negligence, no other test is possible – the jury must say whether the negligence is bad enough to attract criminal liability. The "*Bateman* test" has the virtue that it draws attention to the fact that there exists civil liability for less degrees of negligence and that criminal liability should be reserved for gross aberrations.

Bateman received general approval from Lord Atkin in *Andrews*, though he noted its circular nature[2] and it seems to have been accepted as an authoritative statement until *Seymour*.

If there still exists a gross negligence test, separate from that of *Lawrence* recklessness, *Kong Cheuk Kwan* was surely a case in which the jury ought to have been directed on it. It arose out of a collision in clear sunny weather between two hydrofoils carrying passengers from Hong Kong to Macau and the appellant was in command, and at the helm, of one of them. The clear implication is that there is no such separate test. If so, the law of involuntary manslaughter has been significantly simplified.[3] This conclusion may, however, be premature, for the courts may not have realised the full significance of that step. If the *Lawrence* direction is "comprehensive and of general application" to manslaughter, then so is the "lacuna".[4] *Lamb*[5] who, at the time, the Court of Appeal confidently thought might

---

20. (1925) 19 Cr App Rep 8 at 11. (Negligent medical treatment by a doctor causing death.)
   1. By Turner, MACL 211 Russell, 592–594.
   2. [1937] AC at 583, [1937] 2 All ER at 556 and see the Court of Criminal Appeal [1937] WN 69.
   3. Writers trying to elucidate the law have, however, experienced great difficulty in doing so. See articles at [1983] Crim LR 764 and 776 and [1984] Crim LR 467, 476 and 479.
   4. Above, p. 65.
   5. Above, pp. 65 and 367.

have been convicted of manslaughter on the ground of "criminal negligence", could no longer be so convicted. While the elimination of gross negligence as sufficient fault for manslaughter has been recommended by the Criminal Law Revision Committee[6] and may be no bad thing, it would be a significant change in the law as it was understood to be before *Lawrence* and one to which many judges would certainly be unsympathetic. Moreover, in *Andrews*, Lord Atkin[7] seems to have foreseen the lacuna (or something very like it) and thought it no answer to the charge. In *Goodfellow*, Lane LCJ said that the question in *Kong Cheuk Kwan* was whether the defendant was "guilty of recklessness (or gross negligence)". In fact, the Privy Council said nothing about gross negligence; but the use of the words in parentheses suggests that the Lord Chief Justice was aware of the problem and would not necessarily have regarded *Lawrence* recklessness as the exclusive test if the matter had come before him. In *Ball* the court, *obiter*, assumed the existence of liability for gross negligence.[8] A dual test is justifiable only if there is some difference in the results which have to be proved to have been foreseen or foreseeable. For *Lawrence*, it is "physical injury to some other person" – nothing, be it noted, about injury to "health or welfare". If gross negligence is a separate criterion, then it would seem, as suggested in earlier editions of this work, that it must be negligence as to death or serious injury. If gross negligence as to any injury will suffice, that, as noted earlier, makes nonsense of the *Lawrence* test of recklessness and results in a simple (and savage) test of gross negligence liability for a very serious offence.

In *Jennings v United States Government*[9] the House of Lords rejected the argument that "motor manslaughter" had been abolished by the creation in 1956 of the offences of causing death by dangerous and by reckless driving and the repeal in 1977 of the former offence. "Motor manslaughter" is not a separate legal category. It is just involuntary manslaughter where the implement causing death happens to be a motor vehicle. The law is no different where the death is caused by a gun, a hydrofoil, or a train. Causing death by reckless driving and manslaughter clearly overlapped but were not exactly co-incident for, if D takes an obvious and serious risk of causing substantial damage to property and happens to cause death, he was guilty of the statutory offence, but not of manslaughter. A statement in *Seymour*[10] that "in order to constitute the offence of manslaughter the risk of death being caused by the manner of the defendant's driving must be very high" has been charitably explained in *Kong Cheuk Kwan* as being advice to prosecutors as to the cases in which it was appropriate to charge the common law rather than the statutory offence. That is not what it said.

Reform. The Criminal Law Revision Committee has recommended that involuntary manslaughter be abolished and replaced by a new offence of

6. Fourteenth Report, Cmnd. 7844, para. 121.
7. [1937] AC 576 at 581, [1937] 2 All ER 552 at 555.
8. [1989] Crim LR 730. See commentary.
9. [1982] 3 All ER 104.
10. (1985) 82 Cr App Rep 18 at 25.

causing death recklessly, punishable with a maximum of 14 years imprisonment.[11] "Recklessly" is used in the sense proposed by the Law Commission.[12]

3 Offences Ancillary to Murder

Parliament was not content to leave to the common law the punishment of acts preliminary to murder. The Offences against the Person Act 1861 created offences of conspiracy, solicitation, attempt and threats to murder. The offences of attempt were particularly complicated[13] and were repealed by the Criminal Law Act 1967. Attempts to commit murder are now governed by the Criminal Attempts Act 1981.[14] The conspiracy provision was repealed by the Criminal Law Act 1977 and conspiracy to murder is governed by that Act.

1) *Solicitation*

By s. 4 of the Offences against the Person Act 1861 (as amended by the Criminal Law Act 1977) it is an offence punishable with life imprisonment to

"solicit, encourage, persuade or endeavour to persuade or . . . propose to any person, to murder any other person."

A child in the womb is not a person, so solicitation to kill it while in the womb is not this offence but in *Shephard*[15] D's conviction was upheld when he wrote to a pregnant woman, "When the kiddie is born you must lie on it . . . Don't let it live . . .". The decision seems reasonable on the facts – D *was* soliciting murder – but the court put it on the strange ground that the child was in fact born alive. The implication, that the solicitation was committed only when the child was born alive or would have been undone if the child had been born dead, seems untenable.

This provision adds nothing to the common law of incitement except perhaps on a jurisdictional point. It is expressly provided that the person to be murdered need not be a British subject or within the jurisdiction; but this would generally not be necessary at common law either, since murder by a British citizen is indictable here though committed abroad.[16] The section, however, would catch an alien who, within the jurisdiction, incited

11. CLRC, OAP/R, paras. 88–94. See Draft Code (Law Com. No. 177), cl. 55(c).
12. Law Com. No. 89.
13. See the first edition of this book, pp. 250–253.
14. Above, p. 304.
15. [1919] 2 KB 125, a case found "very hard to follow" in *Tait*, below, p. 377.
16. Above, p. 326. Cf. Greaves's note on the subject in Russell, 612, n. 2.

the commission of murder abroad and who might otherwise be immune under the rule in *Board of Trade v Owen*.[17]

The offence may be committed by the publication of an article in a newspaper and it is immaterial that the readers of the newspapers are not identified.[18] It seems, however, that the offence is not committed unless the mind of the person solicited, etc., is reached. Lord Alverstone CJ so held in *Krause*,[19] applying this limitation even to "endeavour to persuade" which might be thought to cover an unsuccessful attempt to communicate. He held, however, that there was a common law attempt to commit the statutory offence where it was not proved that the offending letters, though sent, had ever reached the addressee.[20] If it is proved that the letter or other publication did reach the addressee, it is not necessary to prove that his mind was in any way affected by it.[1]

In deciding whether the words amount to a solicitation, etc., the jury will take account of (i) the language used; (ii) the occasion on which it was used; (iii) the persons to whom the words were used, and (iv) the circumstances surrounding their use. A soliciting to kill, not merely to do serious harm, must be proved.[2] In *Diamond*,[3] where Coleridge J so directed in leaving to the jury an article extolling the virtues of the assassins of tyrants, the occasion was just after an attempt on the life of the Viceroy of India, and the persons addressed were not "a debating society of philosophers or divines" but "anybody whom the paper would reach in this country or in Ireland."

The proposed victims need not be named, provided that they are a sufficiently well-defined class. Where the indictment used the words "sovereigns and rulers of Europe" Phillimore J thought "rulers" a somewhat vague word, but there were some eighteen or twenty sovereigns in Europe and that was a sufficiently well-defined class.[4]

2) *Threats to Kill*

Section 16 of the Offences against the Person Act 1861 created an offence of making written threats to murder.[5] The Criminal Law Act 1977, Schedule 12, replaces that provision with a new and broader section 16.

"A person who without lawful excuse makes to another a threat, intending that that other would fear that it would be carried out, to kill that other or a third person shall be guilty of an offence and liable on conviction on indictment to imprisonment for a term not exceeding ten years."

17. [1957] AC 602, [1957] 1 All ER 411; above, p. 283.
18. *Most* (1881) 7 QBD 244.
19. (1902) 66 JP 121. Contrast *Horton v Mead*, [1913] 1 KB 154.
20. See also *Banks* (1873) 12 Cox CC 393 at 399, per Quain J.
  1. *Diamond* (1920) 84 JP 211; *Most*, above; *Krause*, above.
  2. *Bainbridge* (1991) No 504/24/90, [1991] Crim LR 535 (not reported on this point).
  3. Above, fn. 17.
  4. *Antonelli and Barberi* (1905) 70 JP 4.
  5. See the third edition of this book, p. 266.

A foetus is not "a third person" and so a threat to a mother to kill the child in her womb is not this offence.[6] If the threat had been to kill the child after it was born the court's inclination would have been to hold that it was still not an offence – if that were an offence why should it not be an offence to threaten a non-pregnant woman to kill any child she might have in the future? – and this, the court thought, "seems to stretch the meaning of 'any third person' altogether too far". Yet, if the point had arisen in relation to the foetus, they would have thought it right to hold that it was an offence, following *Shephard*.[7]

The offence is triable either way.[8] It follows closely the pattern of section 2 of the Criminal Damage Act 1971[9] which relates to threats to destroy or damage property. The threat may take any form[10] and presumably may be implied as well as express.[11] In principle, it is thought that a threat should be "made to another" only when communicated; but, since it has been held that a "demand" is "made" within section 21(1) of the Theft Act when and where a letter containing it is posted,[12] it is at least possible that the same might be decided in the case of a threat. The words "to another" make no difference, since the demand under section 21 must impliedly be made to another.

There would be a lawful excuse for making the threat if, in the circumstances known to D, the killing would be excusable if the threat were carried out, as where D makes the threat in self-defence.[13] A threat to kill may, however, be excusable where actual killing would not. To cause fear of death might be reasonable to prevent crime or arrest an offender whereas actually to kill would be quite unreasonable.[14] In many cases it will be desirable to tell the jury this.[15] Where there is some evidence of a lawful excuse, the onus is on the Crown to prove its absence and the question is always one for the jury.[16]

3) *Concealment of Birth*

This offence when first created by statute in 1623[17] was limited to (i) an illegitimate child who (ii) was born alive and whose body was disposed of so as to conceal its death (iii) by its mother. The current statute, the Offences against the Person Act 1861, s. 60, is subject to none of these limitations; it

6. *Tait* [1990] 1 QB 290, [1989] Crim LR 834.
7. [1919] 2 KB 125, above, p. 375.
8. Criminal Law Act 1977, Sch. 2.
9. Below, p. 708.
10. Below, p. 709.
11. Cf. *Solanke* [1969] 3 All ER 1383, [1970] 1 WLR 1.
12. *Treacy v Director of Public Prosecutions* [1971] AC 537, HL; below, p. 607.
13. See above, p. 252.
14. The two preceding sentences were approved by the Court of Appeal in *Cousins* [1982] 2 All ER 115 at 117.
15. *Cousins*, above.
16. *Cousins*, above.
17. 21 Jac. 1. c. 27.

applies to any child, legitimate or not and whether born alive or not, whose body is disposed of so as to conceal its birth, by anyone. The section provides:

"If any woman shall be delivered of a child, every person who shall, by any secret disposition of the dead body of the said child, whether such child died before, at, or after its birth, endeavour to conceal the birth thereof, shall be guilty of [an offence triable either way] and being convicted thereof shall be liable, at the discretion of the court, to be imprisoned for any term not exceeding two years. . . ."

The expressed object of the original statute was to catch those women who would otherwise escape on a murder charge through the difficulty of proving live-birth and it was provided, indeed, that the woman should suffer death as in the case of murder. Under a later Act,[18] which repealed the 1623 provision, conviction of the new offence thereby created was possible only after an acquittal on an indictment for murder; but the current offence is an independent substantive crime for which an indictment will lie in the first instance. It was formerly the law that a person acquitted of murder, infanticide or child destruction might be convicted, on the same indictment, of concealment of birth; but this rule was abolished by the Criminal Law Act 1967, Sch. 2.

The test of a "secret disposition" seems to be whether there was a likelihood that the body would be found. So, said Bovill CJ, it would be a secret disposition

"if the body were placed in the middle of a moor in the winter, or on the top of a mountain, or in any other secluded place, where the body would not be likely to be found."[19]

If a body were thrown from a cliff top to the sea-shore, it might be a secret disposition if the place were secluded, not if it were much frequented.[20] So where the body was left in a closed but unlocked box in D's bedroom in such a way as to attract the attention of those who daily entered the room, it was held that there was no secret disposition.[1]

The accused must be proved to have done some act of disposition after the child has died. If the living body of the child is concealed and thereafter dies in the place of concealment, this offence is not committed,[2] though it is probable that murder or manslaughter is.

According to Erle J in *Berriman*[3] the child must have

"arrived at that stage of maturity at the time of birth that it might have been a living child";

so that the concealment of a foetus but a few months old would be no offence.[4]

---

18. 43 Geo. 3 c. 58.
19. *Brown* (1870) LR 1 CCR 244.
20. Ibid.
    1. *George* (1868) 11 Cox CC 41. Cf. *Sleep* (1864) 9 Cox CC 559; *Rosenberg* (1906) 70 JP 264.
    2. *Coxhead* (1845) 1 Car & Kir 623 (decided under 9 Geo. 4, c. 31, but the principle is the same); *May* (1867) 10 Cox CC 448.
3. (1854) 6 Cox CC 388 at 390.
4. *Colmer* (1864) 9 Cox CC 506 is to the contrary but is doubted by Russell, 611, n. 69 and Archbold, 19–145.

4) *Other Offences*

It is a common law misdemeanour to dispose of or destroy a dead body with intent to prevent an inquest from being held.[5] It is an offence under the Perjury Act 1911 wilfully to make a false statement relating to births or deaths, or the live birth of a child.[6] And it is a summary offence under the Births and Deaths Registration Act 1953, s. 36, to fail to give information concerning births and deaths when under a duty, as defined in the Act, to do so.

4 Complicity in Suicide and Suicide Pacts[7]

It was felony at common law for a sane person of the age of responsibility to kill himself either intentionally or in the course of trying to kill another.[8] Such a suicide was regarded as self-murder. Though the offender was, in the nature of things, personally beyond the reach of the law, his guilt was not without important consequences at common law, since it resulted in the forfeiture of his property. The results were more important, however, where the attempt failed, for then:

(i) Since D had attempted to commit a felony he was guilty, under ordinary common law principles, of the misdemeanour of attempted suicide.
(ii) If D, in the course of trying to kill himself, killed another, he was guilty of murder under the doctrine of transferred malice.[9]

Though suicide was regarded as "not a very serious crime",[10] an intention to commit it was thus the *mens rea* of murder. Moreover, one who was an accessory or principal in the second degree to the suicide of another was likewise guilty of murder as a secondary party. It followed that the survivor of a suicide pact was also guilty of murder, for, even if he did not actually kill, he was an aider and abettor, or at least an accessory before the fact to the other party's self-murder.

Suicide has now ceased to be a crime by virtue of the Suicide Act 1961 which simply provides that

"The rule of law whereby it is a crime for a person to commit suicide is hereby abrogated."

It inevitably followed that (i) attempted suicide ceased to be criminal; and (ii) that there is no room for the doctrine of transferred malice where D kills P in the course of trying to kill himself, for there is no "malice" to transfer.

---

5. Cf. *Hunter* [1972] Crim LR 369.
6. Perjury Act 1911, s. 4(1).
7. For general discussions, see Williams, *The Sanctity of Life*, Ch. 7; St. John Stevas, *Life, Death and the Law*, Ch. 6; Second Report of the Criminal Law Revision Committee, Cmnd. 1187 (1960).
8. Hawkins, 1 PC 77.
9. *Hopwood* (1913) 8 Cr App Rep 143; *Spence* (1957) 41 Cr App Rep 80. Above, p. 73.
10. *French* (1955) 39 Cr App Rep 192, per Lord Goddard CJ.

In the latter case, D's liability depends on the general principles of murder and manslaughter. Thus, if the death of P were utterly unforeseeable, it would be accidental death; if there was an obvious and serious risk of causing death or serious bodily harm, it may be manslaughter; and, if D himself foresaw this as virtually certain it is murder.[11]

1) *Complicity in Another's Suicide*

Section 2 of the Suicide Act created a new offence:
"A person who aids, abets, counsels or procures the suicide of another or an attempt by another to commit suicide, shall be liable on conviction on indictment to imprisonment for a term not exceeding fourteen years."

The words "aids, abets, counsels or procures", are those used to define secondary participation in crime[12] but here they are used to define the principal offence. The interpretation of the words should be the same.[13] As in the law of secondary participation the words imply that the crime has been committed or attempted.[14] Advising another to commit suicide does not amount to abetting or counselling unless and until that other does commit suicide. Since the aiding, etc., is the principal offence, an indictment will lie for an attempt to aid, etc. so that unsuccessful advice or encouragement is punishable as an attempt.[15] The distribution of a booklet giving advice to any person who wishes to commit suicide on how to do so efficiently and painlessly is not necessarily an offence under the section. In *A-G v Able*,[16] Woolf J refused to grant a declaration that the distribution was unlawful, holding that an offence would be committed only if the distributor intended that the booklet would be used by someone contemplating suicide and that he would be (and in fact was) assisted or encouraged to do so. This is in accordance with the ordinary law of secondary participation.[17]

There were very sound reasons for the abolition of the felony of suicide. The felon was beyond the reach of punishment; the legal sanction was not an effective deterrent – there were some 5,000 suicides a year; and the effect was merely to add to the distress and pain of the bereaved relatives. The most important practical effect of the Act, however, was its repeal by implication of the crime of attempted suicide. This also recognised the realities of the situation for it had been the practice for many years to institute proceedings only where it was necessary for the accused's protection, for example, because no relatives and friends were willing to give help. Thus, in 1959, of a total of 4,980 suicide attempts known to the police (and

---

11. See above, p. 346.
12. Cf. the Accessories and Abettors Act 1861, ss. 2, 8 and the Magistrates' Courts Act 1980, s. 44; above, p. 123.
13. See *Reed* [1982] Crim LR 819, CA; *A-G v Able*, below, fn. 16.
14. Above, p. 124.
15. *McShane* [1977] Crim LR 737, CA, discussed by Smith in *Crime, Proof and Punishment*, 21 at 32–33.
16. [1984] QB 795, [1984] 1 All ER 277, QBD.
17. Above, pp. 126–130. See K. J. M. Smith, [1983] Crim LR 579.

an estimated total of 25,000 actual concealed from the police) only 518 prosecutions were brought. The protection of the attempter may now be secured under Part II of the Mental Health Act 1983.

The new crime of complicity in suicide is one which covers a variety of situations varying almost infinitely in moral culpability; from D who encourages P to commit suicide for the purpose of inheriting his property, to that of D who merely supplies a deadly drug to a suffering and dying P who is anxious to accelerate the end. In order to achieve consistency in the bringing of prosecutions, this is made one of those crimes in which the consent of the Director of Public Prosecutions is required.[18]

2) Suicide Pacts

A party to a suicide pact who aids, abets, counsels or procures the other party to commit suicide is of course guilty of the offence under s. 2 of the Suicide Act.[19]

The survivor of such a pact may, however, have either himself killed the deceased or have procured a third party to do it. Such cases do not fall within the Suicide Act, but within the Homicide Act 1957, s. 4(1), which, as amended by the Suicide Act provides:

"It shall be manslaughter and shall not be murder for a person acting in pursuance of a suicide pact between him and another to kill the other[20] or be party to the other being killed by a third person."

"Suicide pact" is defined by s. 4(3) of the Homicide Act as

"a common agreement between two or more persons having for its object the death of all of them, whether or not each is to take his own life, but nothing done by a person who enters into a suicide pact shall be treated as done by him in pursuance of the pact unless it is done while he has the settled intention of dying in pursuance of the pact."

The onus on a charge of murder of establishing the defence of suicide pact is put by s. 4(2) on the accused and the standard of proof required is the balance of probabilities.

The distinction between complicity in suicide and manslaughter by suicide pact is not entirely satisfactory. The latter, being punishable with life imprisonment, is evidently the more serious crime; yet, since the person guilty of it always intends to die himself, it is difficult to see how it can compare in moral heinousness with the case of D who incites P to die in order that he may live and enjoy P's property.

The distinction between the two crimes may be very fine. If D and P agree to gas themselves and D alone survives, it appears that he will be

---

18. Williams argues in favour of the legalisation of the abetting of a suicide for unselfish reasons: *The Sanctity of Life*, 271–276.
19. Until the enactment of the Suicide Act, this was manslaughter under the Homicide Act 1957, s. 4.
20. If, otherwise than in pursuance of a suicide pact, D kills P at P's request, D is of course guilty of murder. Cf. *Robinson*, above, p. 141.

liable under the Homicide Act if he turned on the tap[1] and under the Suicide Act if P did. It may frequently be difficult to establish who did such an act and this is recognised by the provision in s. 2(2) of the Suicide Act that, on the trial of an indictment for murder or manslaughter, the jury may find the accused guilty of complicity in suicide if that is proved. If D is charged with murder and he establishes on a balance of probabilities that P committed suicide in pursuance of a suicide pact he is entitled to be acquitted of murder and may presumably be convicted of complicity in suicide since he has, in effect, admitted his guilt. If, however, D were charged with complicity and it appeared that he had killed P, he would have to be acquitted.

5 Infanticide[2]

The Infanticide Act 1938, s. 1(1), provides:
"Where a woman by any wilful act or omission causes the death of her child being a child under the age of twelve months, but at the time of the act or omission the balance of her mind was disturbed by reason of her not having fully recovered from the effect of giving birth to the child or by reason of the effect of lactation consequent upon the birth of the child, then, notwithstanding that the circumstances were such that but for this Act the offence would have amounted to murder, she shall be guilty of [an offence], to wit of infanticide, and may for such offence be dealt with and punished as if she had been guilty of the offence of manslaughter of the child."

This enactment replaces a statute of 1922 which confined the defence to a "newly-born" child, a term which the Court of Criminal Appeal had held to be inapplicable to a child of thirty-five days, so that the mother was convicted of murder.[3] The 1922 Act was itself the result of an agitation over very many years during which it was practically impossible to get convictions of murder by mothers of their young children because of the disapproval by public and professional opinion of a law which regarded such killings as ordinary murders. Where a conviction was obtained, the judge had to pronounce a sentence of death which everyone, except perhaps the offender, knew would not be carried out. A number of reasons were advanced why infanticide should be considered less reprehensible than other killings: (i) The injury done to the child was less, for it was incapable of the kind of suffering which might be undergone by the adult victim of a murder; (ii) the loss of its family was less great; (iii) the crime did not create the sense of insecurity in society which other murders caused; (iv) generally, the heinousness of the crime was less, the motive very frequently being the concealment of the shame of the birth of an

---

1. But if D pours out a glass of poison and P takes it, he will be liable under the Suicide Act.
2. Seaborne Davies, "Child-Killing in English Law" (1937) 1 MLR 203; MACL 301; Williams, *The Sanctity of Life*, 25–45.
3. *O'Donoghue* (1927) 20 Cr App Rep 132.

illegitimate child; and (v) where the killing is done by the mother, her responsibility may be reduced by the disturbance of her mind caused by the stress of the birth. It is, of course, the last of these considerations which is the governing one in the present legislation. The killing of an infant by persons other than the mother, or by the mother if the balance of her mind is not disturbed, remains murder.

The Act provides by s. 1(2) that a woman indicted for the murder of her child under the age of twelve months may be acquitted of murder and convicted of infanticide if the conditions of s. 1(1) are satisfied.

Where the charge is murder, an evidential burden on the issue of disturbance will fall on D; but the onus of *proof* remains with the Crown. Where the charge is infanticide, the onus of proving disturbance appears to be on the Crown; but this, of course, is unlikely to be contested.

It appears that the principles on which the Act was based may be no longer accepted and that mental illness is not now considered to be a significant cause of infanticide. In most cases the relationship of incomplete recovery from the effects of childbirth or lactation to the child-killing is remote.[4] When the Infanticide Act was passed, there was no defence of diminished responsibility to murder. The Butler Committee thought that that defence would now probably cover all cases and recommended the abolition of the separate offence of infanticide.[5] The CLRC disagreed, at first on the ground that, so long as the prosecution are unable to charge manslaughter by reason of diminished responsibility, infanticide has the advantage that it avoids the necessity of charging the mother with murder;[6] and later on the ground that diminished responsibility might not cover all the circumstances which in practice may be held to justify an infanticide verdict. According to the Royal College of Psychiatrists, these include "(1) overwhelming stress from the social environment being highlighted by the birth of a baby, with the emphasis on the unsuitability of the accommoda- tion etc; (2) overwhelming stress from an additional member to a household struggling with poverty; (3) psychological injury, and pressures and stress from a husband or other member of a family from the mother's incapacity to arrange the demands of the extra member of the family; (4) failure of bonding between mother and child through illness or disability which impairs the development of the mother's capacity to care for the infant." In order to bring the law into line with its practical operation, and because of the difficulty of establishing a direct connection between giving birth and the imbalance of the woman's mind, the CLRC recommend that the test should be whether the balance of her mind was disturbed by reason of the effect of giving birth to the child *or circumstances consequent upon that birth*.[7] A dissentient view was that the effect would be to make adverse social conditions a defence to child killing.[8] Because of the decision to recommend

4. Butler Report, Cmnd. 6244 at paras. 19.23–19.24.
5. Ibid.
6. CLRC/OAP/WP 26. The committee tentatively suggested that a person apparently suffering from diminished responsibility should be indictable for manslaughter but later withdrew this proposal: CLRC/OAP/R, para. 95.
7. CLRC/OAP/R, paras. 103–106.
8. See Annexes 7 and 8 to the Report.

the broadening of the offence (in law, if not in practice) the Committee abandoned its earlier tentative recommendation that the killing of older children of the family should be infanticide and not murder;[9] and recommended that the maximum penalty should be five years imprisonment and not two, as they had previously been disposed to think.[10]

The Criminal Law Revision Committee thought that, because of the way in which the offence is drafted, it is not possible to charge a person with attempting to commit infanticide[11] but McCowan J has held that such an indictment will lie.[12]

6 Child Destruction and Abortion[13]

1) *Child Destruction*

It has already been observed that it is not murder to kill a child in the womb or while in the process of being born.[14] Though the killing of the child in the womb after quickening was a misdemeanour at common law, the present law on the subject is statutory. Section 58 of the Offences against the Person Act 1861 (subject to the Abortion Act 1967[15]) prohibits attempts to procure miscarriage from any time after the conception of the child until its birth; and s. 1 of the Infant Life (Preservation) Act 1929 prohibits the killing of any child which is capable of being born alive. The two offences thus overlap. Procuring a miscarriage so as to kill a child capable of being born alive may amount to both offences. Killing a child in the process of being born is not procuring a miscarriage and can amount only to child destruction. Section 1 of the Infant Life (Preservation) Act provides:

"(1) Subject as hereinafter in this subsection provided, any person who, with intent to destroy the life of a child capable of being born alive, by any wilful act causes a child to die before it has an existence independent of its mother, shall be guilty of an offence, to wit, of child destruction, and shall be liable on conviction thereof on indictment to imprisonment for life: Provided that no person shall be found guilty of an offence under this section unless it is proved that the act which caused the death of the child was not done in good faith for the purpose only of preserving the life of the mother.

(2) For the purposes of this Act, evidence that a woman had at any material time been pregnant for a period of twenty-eight weeks or more

9. Para. 106.
10. Para. 108.
11. CLRC/OAP/R, para. 113.
12. *K. A. Smith* [1983] Crim LR 739 and commentary.
13. See Williams, *The Sanctity of Life and the Criminal Law*, 139–223 (1958), and "The Legalization of Medical Abortion" *The Eugenics Review*, April, 1964; B. M. Dickens, *Abortion and the Law* (1966).
14. See above, p. 328.
15. See below, p. 390.

shall be prima facie proof that she was at that time pregnant of a child capable of being born alive."

While the actual physical condition in which a foetus would be after birth is a matter for expert medical evidence, whether a foetus at that stage of development can properly be described as "a child capable of being born alive" is a question of law for the court. In *C v S*[16] the medical experts disagreed as to whether a foetus at the stage it will normally have reached by the 18th to the 21st week could be so described. The court held, in the light of the evidence that it would never be capable of breathing, that it could not.[17]

In *Rance v Mid-Downs Health Authority*,[18] a civil action, Brooke J. thought the meaning of the phrase was clear and that a child is "born alive" if—

"after birth, it exists as a live child, that is to say breathing and living by reason of its breathing through its own lungs alone, without deriving any of its living or power of living by or through any connection with its mother."

It is not necessary that the child be capable of survival into old age or even for a period of days. Applying this test, Brooke J was satisfied to "a very high standard of proof" that the particular child was capable of being born alive after 26 weeks of pregnancy and therefore to kill him would have been the offence of child destruction.

The Abortion Act 1967 uses the phrase "protecting the life of the viable foetus" in respect of the provisions of the 1929 Act; but, rejecting the view that "viable" has a different and more restrictive meaning, Brooke J held that it was merely used as convenient shorthand for "capable of being born alive" and its use in 1967 had no effect on the meaning of the 1929 Act.

The jury may convict of this offence on an indictment for murder, manslaughter, infanticide or an offence under s. 58 of the Offences against the Person Act 1861; and on an indictment for child destruction, they may convict of an offence under s. 58 of the Offences against the Person Act 1861.

The Abortion Act 1967 legalises abortion in certain circumstances and subject to certain formalities. It originally provided that it should not affect the offence of child destruction but, as amended by the Human Fertilisation and Embryology Act 1990, s. 5 (1) of the 1967 Act states that

"No offence under [the 1929 Act] shall be committed by a registered medical practitioner who terminates a pregnancy in accordance with the provisions of [the Abortion Act 1967]."

Since this amendment came into effect it is not an offence for a doctor, complying with the terms of the 1967 Act, to cause the death of a child capable of being born alive. If the death of such a child is caused by a doctor who is not complying with the provisions of the 1967 Act, or if it is caused by any other person, then it is prima facie child destruction. If, however, the act is done for the purpose only of preserving the life of the mother, that

16. [1988] QB 135, [1987] 1 All ER 1230, CA.
17. Ibid., at 1238–1239 (Heilbron J). Cf. Wright, [1984] Crim LR 347; Tunkel and Wright, [1985] Crim LR 133.
18. [1991] 1 QB 587, [1991] 1 All ER 801, QBD.

will be a defence to a charge under the 1929 Act but not to a charge under 1861 Act unless the *Bourne* defence of necessity has survived the 1967 Act – a matter of some doubt, considered below.[19]

A wide meaning was given to the words "for the purpose only of preserving the life of the mother" by Macnaghten J in *Bourne*.[20] This was *obiter*, so far as the Infant Life Preservation Act was concerned, since the charge was brought under the Offences against the Person Act 1861; but Macnaghten J took the view that those words represented the common law and were implicit in the 1861 Act by virtue of the word "unlawfully". He said:

"As I have said, I think those words ['for the purpose of preserving the life of the mother'] ought to be construed in a reasonable sense, and if the doctor is of opinion, on reasonable grounds and with adequate knowledge, that the probable consequence of the continuance of the pregnancy will be to make the woman a physical or mental wreck, the jury are quite entitled to take the view that the doctor who under these circumstances and in the honest belief, operates, is operating for the purpose of preserving the life of the mother."[1]

Both before and after this, however, the judge stressed that the test was whether the operation was performed in good faith for the purpose of preserving the *life* of the mother and the passage may be intended to refer only to such inquiries to health as will shorten life for the judge had said:[2]

". . . life depends upon health and health may be so gravely impaired that death results."

Informed medical opinion construed the judgment in the wider sense[3] and this appears to have been vindicated. In *Bergmann and Ferguson*[4] Morris J is reported to have said that the court will not look too narrowly into the question of danger to life where danger to health is anticipated. Then in *Newton and Stungo*[5] Ashworth J stated in his direction to the jury:

"Such use of an instrument is unlawful unless the use is made in good faith for the purposes of preserving the life *or health* of the woman",

adding that this included mental as well as physical health. Newton was acquitted of manslaughter by criminal negligence, but convicted of manslaughter by unlawfully using an instrument and of the offence under s. 58. He did not appeal (obviously the direction was favourable to him) and we thus have no appellate ruling on the question; but it is thought likely that Ashworth J's view would be accepted by the appellate courts.

The criterion of the defence as it has been applied by the courts is a subjective one; that is, the question is not whether the operation is in fact necessary to preserve the life of the mother but whether D believes it to be necessary.[6] In answering this question the court will take account of the size

19. Above, p. 246, below, p. 394.
20. [1939] 1 KB 687, [1938] 3 All ER 615.
1. [1939] 1 KB at 693, 694, [1938] 3 All ER at 619.
2. [1939] 1 KB at 692, [1938] 3 All ER at 617.
3. Havard [1958] Crim LR at 605.
4. (1948) unreported; *The Sanctity of Life*, 154; 1 BMJ 1008.
5. [1958] Crim LR 469, fully considered by Havard in "Therapeutic Abortion" [1958] Crim LR 600.
6. *Bergmann and Ferguson* cited in *The Sanctity of Life*, 165.

of the fee, a large fee being evidence of bad faith;[7] and whether D followed accepted medical practice.[8] What is the position if the operation was in fact necessary, but was performed by D in bad faith, to oblige, as he thought, the mere convenience of the woman and for a high fee? One view might be that there is no *actus reus* here,[9] but it is thought more likely that the defence will be limited to the case of a bona fide belief.[10] Thus, in *Newton*, it does not seem to have been decided that an operation was unnecessary; only that Newton did not bona fide believe it to be necessary.[11]

These cases all relate to s. 58 of the 1861 Act, where they are probably no longer in point.[12] Since they purport to be an interpretation of the proviso in the 1929 Act, however, they cannot be ignored in considering child destruction. On the other hand it is quite possible that the court, when actually confronted with the interpretation of the proviso, might take a stricter and narrower view of what constitutes the preservation of the life of the mother.

2) *Attempting to Procure Miscarriage*

The common law misdemeanour of abortion applied only after the child had quickened in the womb. To procure an abortion before this occurred was no crime. A statute of 1803[13] enacted that it should be a felony punishable by death to administer a poison with intent to procure the miscarriage of a woman quick with child and a felony punishable with imprisonment or transportation for fourteen years to administer poison with a like intent to a woman who was not proved to be quick with child. The distinction between quick and non-quick women gave rise to complications and it disappeared in the re-enactment of the law by the Offences against the Person Act 1837[14] which established the law substantially in its modern form. The current statute is the Offences against the Person Act 1861, which provides by s. 58:

"Every woman being with child who, with intent to procure her own miscarriage, shall unlawfully administer to herself any poison or other noxious thing, or shall unlawfully use any instrument or other means whatsoever with the like intent, and whosoever, with intent to procure the miscarriage of any woman, whether she be or be not with child, shall unlawfully administer to her or cause to be taken by her any poison or

---

7. A significant difference between the case of Newton and that of Stungo (who was acquitted) seems to have been that Stungo took a very small fee, Newton a high one.
8. See Havard [1958] Crim LR at 607, 608.
9. Cf. The discussion of *Dadson*, above, p. 34.
10. Cf. Williams, *The Sanctity of Life*, 166, who would agree with this conclusion on the grounᴅ that the crime is in the nature of an attempt. But it is just as much a substantive crime as burglary.
11. But even if it was necessary to carry out the operation, it was probably not necessary to carry it out in the way it was done – in a consulting room, the patient being sent back to a hotel in a taxi afterwards.
12. Below.
13. 43 Geo. 3. c. 58.
14. 7 Will & 1 Vic. c. 85.

other noxious thing, or shall unlawfully use any instrument or other means whatsoever with the like intent, shall be guilty of an offence, and being convicted thereof shall be liable . . . to imprisonment for life. . . ." The extension of the law was of great practical importance, since most self-induced abortions occur before quickening. Certain modern anti-pregnancy techniques appear to offend against the law because they function after fertilisation of the ovum.[15]

The statute makes it clear beyond all doubt that the offence may be committed by the woman herself as well as by others, the only distinction being that if the woman herself is charged, it must be proved that she is in fact pregnant, whereas this is not necessary if the accused is someone other than the mother herself.

The Act is not confined to the use of a "poison or other noxious thing" or "any instrument"; the "other means" include manual interference, even though no instrument is employed and the medical evidence is that the act could not, in the circumstances, cause a miscarriage.[16] The *actus reus* consists simply in the *administration* of the poison or other noxious thing or the *use* of the instrument or other means.

The Act distinguishes between "poison" and "noxious thing" and it has been held that in the case of something other than a "recognised poison" the thing must be administered in such quantity as to be in fact harmful though not necessarily abortifacient.[17] A sleeping pill has been held not to be noxious;[18] and the administration in harmless quantities of oil of juniper was no *actus reus*;[19] but Denman J said that it would be otherwise if a thing, innocuous when administered in small quantities, were to be administered in such quantities as to be noxious. Field and Stephen JJ thought that if the thing were a "recognised poison" the offence might be committed even though the quantity given was so small as to be incapable of doing harm. The distinction is hardly a logical one for "recognised poisons" may be beneficial when taken in small quantities and in such a case the thing taken is no more poisonous than the oil of juniper was noxious.

It has been observed that the section makes a distinction between the case where the woman administers, etc., the thing to herself and that where it is administered to her by another. In the former case the woman must be proved to be with child, in the latter case, she need not. The importance of this distinction has been diminished by the decision in *Whitchurch*[20] that a woman who is not pregnant may be convicted of conspiring with another to procure her own abortion and by the decision in *Sockett* that such a woman[1] may be convicted of aiding and abetting in the offence of the other, if it is complete. Thus, in effect, the woman will be excused on the ground that she is not with child only in cases where she is not acting in concert with another. While one view is that this interpretation has "set at naught"

15. See Tunkel [1974] Crim LR 461.
16. *Spicer* [1955] Crim LR 772.
17. *Marlow* (1964) 49 Cr App Rep 49 (Brabin J); *Douglas* [1966] NZLR 45. Cf. *Marcus* [1981] 2 All ER 833, below, p. 429.
18. *Weatherall* [1968] Crim LR 115 (Judge Brodrick) below, p. 431.
19. *Cramp* (1880) 5 QBD 307.
20. (1890) 24 QBD 420; above, p. 299.
  1. (1908) 72 JP 428; above, p. 299.

the intention of Parliament,[2] it has been argued elsewhere[3] that it would have been perfectly reasonable for Parliament to discriminate between the non-pregnant woman who calls in the back-street or professional abortion-ist and the non-pregnant woman who administers to herself an abortifa-cient in the solitude of her own bedroom. The point is perhaps not of great practical importance as it appears that it is not the practice to prosecute the mother today.[4]

3) *Knowingly Supplying or Procuring Poison, etc.*

Section 59 of the Offences against the Person Act makes a substantive crime of certain preparatory acts, some of which might amount to counsell-ing or abetting the offence under s. 58. It provides:

"Whosoever shall unlawfully supply or procure any poison or other noxious thing, or any instrument or thing whatsoever, knowing that the same is intended to be unlawfully used or employed with intent to procure the miscarriage of any woman, whether she be or be not with child, shall be guilty of a misdemeanour, and being convicted thereof shall be liable . . . to imprisonment . . . for any term not exceeding five years . . ."

The word "procure", on the first occasion on which it is used in the section, means "get possession of something of which you have not got possession already";[5] so D's conviction was quashed when there was no evidence as to how or when he had come into the possession of the instruments and the judge had directed the jury that the word was

"wide enough to include getting instruments or getting them together or preparing them for use".[6]

This leaves a gap in the legislation. As Crown counsel said:[7]

". . . if a defendant went to a chemist and bought an instrument to abort A, he would have committed an offence, but if he then put the instrument away in a cupboard and later, for the purpose of aborting B went to the cupboard and took the instrument he would not have committed an offence."

The words, "knowing that the same is intended to be unlawfully used" have been construed in an extraordinarily wide sense and one highly unfavourable to the accused. Their natural meaning is surely that some person other than the accused must intend the unlawful user and that the accused must know of that intention. But it has been held that it is enough if the accused *believes* that the poison, etc., is to be so used, so that it is no defence for him to show that the person supplied did not intend to use it[8] or

---

2. Williams, CLGP, 673.
3. Hogan, [1962] Crim LR at 690.
4. Cf. *The Sanctity of Life* at 146; *Peake* (1932) 97 JPN 353.
5. *Mills* [1963] 1 QB 522, [1963] 1 All ER 202, following *Scully* (1903) 23 NZLR 380.
6. [1963] 1 QB at 524.
7. Ibid. at 526.
8. *Hillman* (1863) 9 Cox CC 386, CCR.

that the person supplied was a policeman who had obtained the thing by
false representations about a purely fictitious woman.[9] This construction
was defended by Erle CJ, the rest of the Court concurring, on the
extraordinary ground that

"The defendant knew what his own intention was, and that was that the
substance procured by him should be employed with intent to procure
miscarriage."[10]

This attitude contrasts strikingly with the strict construction of the word
"procure"; and these two cases, which have been dissented from in
Victoria,[11] though followed elsewhere in the Commonwealth,[12] deserve
reconsideration.

4) *The Abortion Act 1967*[13]

The law relating to abortion is modified in important respects by the
Abortion Act 1967. In the Act:

"'the law relating to abortion' means ss. 58 and 59 of the Offences against
the Person Act 1861, and any rule of law relating to the procurement of
abortion."

Section 1 of the Act, as amended by the Human Fertilisation and
Embryology Act 1990, s. 37, provides:[14]

"**1 Medical termination of pregnancy.**—(1) Subject to the provisions of this section, a person shall not be guilty of an offence under
the law relating to abortion when a pregnancy is terminated by a
registered medical practitioner if two registered medical practitioners
are of the opinion, formed in good faith—

(a) that the pregnancy has not exceeded its twenty-fourth week and
that the continuance of the pregnancy would involve risk, greater
than if the pregnancy were terminated, of injury to the physical
or mental health of the pregnant woman or any existing children
of her family; or

(b) that the termination is necessary to prevent grave permanent
injury to the physical or mental health of the pregnant woman; or

(c) that the continuance of the pregnancy would involve risk to the
life of the pregnant woman, greater than if the pregnancy were
terminated; or

9. *Titley* (1880) 14 Cox CC 502 (Stephen J).
10. (1863) 9 Cox CC at 387.
11. *Hyland* (1898) 24 VLR 101.
12. *Scully* (1903) 23 NZLR 380; *Nosworthy* (1907) 26 NZLR 536; *Neil* [1909] St R Qd 225;
Freestone [1913] TPD 758; *Irwin v R* (1968) 68 DLR (2d) 485.
13. See Hoggett, "The Abortion Act 1967", [1968] Crim LR 247: *A Guide to the Abortion Act
1967* (Abortion Law Reform Association). On the working of the Act, see H. L. A. Hart,
"Abortion Law Reform: The English Experience" (1972), 8 MULR 389; M. Simms [1970]
Crim LR 567, 573 and [1971] Crim LR 86; J. M. Finnis, [1971] Crim LR 3.
14. See the valuable discussion of the amended Act by Grubb, [1991] Crim LR 659.

(d) that there is a substantial risk that if the child were born it would suffer from such physical or mental abnormalities as to be seriously handicapped."

(2) In determining whether the continuance of a pregnancy would involve such risk of injury to health as is mentioned in paragraph (a) or (b) of subsection (1) of this section, account may be taken of the pregnant woman's actual or reasonably foreseeable environment.

(3) Except as provided by subsection (4) of this section, any treatment for the termination of pregnancy must be carried out in a hospital vested in the Minister of Health or the Secretary of State under the National Health Service Acts, or in a place for the time being approved for the purposes of this section by the said Minister or the Secretary of State.

(3A) The power under subsection (3) of this section to approve a place includes power, in relation to treatment consisting primarily in the use of such medicines as may be specified in the approval and carried out in such manner as may be so specified, to approve a class of places.

(4) Subsection (3) of this section, and so much of subsection (1) as relates to the opinion of two registered medical practitioners, shall not apply to the termination of a pregnancy by a registered medical practitioner in a case where he is of the opinion, formed in good faith, that the termination is immediately necessary to save the life or to prevent grave permanent injury to the physical or mental health of the pregnant woman."

Where the pregnancy has not exceeded its twenty-fourth week[15] the doctor must balance risks involved in an abortion against the risks to the woman or the children involved in the continuance of the pregnancy and may perform the abortion only if it is his opinion that the latter are greater than the former.

Where the pregnancy has exceeded 24 weeks the risks to the children are no longer a ground for abortion. The abortion can now be justified only on the grounds of risk of grave permanent injury to the woman or her death, or of the birth of a seriously handicapped child. Where the life of the woman is at risk, the doctor must engage in another balancing exercise and may terminate the pregnancy if he is of the opinion that this gives her a better chance of survival: 51/49 is enough. But where the risk is not to her life but of "grave permanent injury" the pregnancy may be terminated only if abortion is "necessary" to prevent this. If the doctor is of the opinion that the woman will certainly suffer grave permanent injury if the pregnancy is not terminated, then termination is, undoubtedly, necessary. It must be assumed, however, that Parliament, in distinguishing between grave permanent injury and death, intended that a higher degree of risk of grave permanent injury than of death is required to justify abortion. If so, termination is not "necessary" simply because the doctor is of the opinion that grave permanent injury is more likely than not, i.e., 51/49 is not enough. Whether necessity can be established somewhere between balance of probabilities and virtual certainty is not clear.

15. It is uncertain when time starts to run. See the discussion by Grubb, [1991] Crim LR 665.

There is a similar problem of determining what is a "substantial" risk of abnormality resulting in "serious" handicap – but these uncertainties have been with us since 1967 without troubling the courts, however much they may have troubled the doctors. Clearly something a good deal less than certainty may amount to a substantial risk and it is thought that most people would regard something well below a 50 per cent chance as substantial in this context.

Section 1(1)(a), on a literal reading, could justify the termination of most pregnancies in their early stages, since some risk is necessarily involved in child-bearing whereas the risks involved in an abortion operation at this stage are very slight.[16] The 1967 Act allowed the interests of the children of the woman's family to be taken into account for the first time. These expressions are not defined in the Act, but it has been argued[17] that "family" means the sociological and not the legal unit, so as to include illegitimate children and perhaps children who have been accepted as members of the family. The view has been expressed[18] that a person over twenty-one could be a child of the family for this purpose if, for example, he were severely subnormal.

a) *Abortion and multiple pregnancies.* Multiple pregnancies may be reduced by killing one or more of the foetuses. The 1990 Act amended s. 5 (2) of the Abortion Act to deal with the matter as follows:

"(2) For the purposes of the law relating to abortion, anything done with intent to procure a woman's miscarriage (or, in the case of a woman carrying more than one foetus, her miscarriage of any foetus) is unlawfully done unless authorised by section 1 of this Act and, in the case of a woman carrying more than one foetus, anything done with intent to procure her miscarriage of any foetus is authorised by that section if—

(a) the ground for termination of the pregnancy specified in subsection (1) (d) of that section applies in relation to any foetus and the thing is done for the purpose of procuring the miscarriage of that foetus, or

(b) any other grounds for termination of the pregnancy specified in that section applies."

So if one or more of several foetuses is identified as being substantially at risk of becoming a child suffering from such a mental or physical abnormality as would lead to its being seriously handicapped, that foetus, or those foetuses, may be aborted. Where no foetus is so identified but the continuance of the multiple pregnancy would satisfy one of the other conditions in s. 1, the doctor may reduce the number of foetuses in order to eliminate or reduce the risk. In this situation, the doctor must select which of a number of healthy foetuses is to die.

---

16. ". . . it follows that a pregnancy may lawfully be terminated in order to secure a relatively small improvement in the woman's medical condition": *A Guide to the Abortion Act 1967*, p. II. The Act is not, however, interpreted in this way by the medical profession and administrators: Hart (1972) 8 MULR at 393–394.

17. Hoggett, op. cit. at 249; *A Guide to the Abortion Act 1967*, p. 6.

18. Ibid.

b) *Good faith of medical opinion*. The Secretary of State for the Social Services has exercised the powers given to him by s. 2 to require the opinion of medical practitioners to be certified in a particular form and notice of the termination of pregnancy and other information to be given. The question of the good faith of the doctors is essentially one for the jury. A verdict of bad faith where there is no evidence as to professional practice and medical probabilities is often likely to be regarded by the Court of Appeal as unsafe; but this depends on the nature of the other evidence.

"An opinion may be absurd professionally and yet formed in good faith; conversely an opinion may be one which a doctor could have entertained and yet in the particular circumstances of a case may be found either to have been formed in bad faith or not to have been formed at all."[19]

If one or both of the doctors has expressed an opinion in bad faith but the operation is performed by a third, D, who is unaware of the bad faith, the conditions of the Act are not satisfied but it is submitted that D has a defence. He lacks *mens rea* for, on the facts as he believes them to be, his act is a lawful one. The doctor in bad faith might, however, be convicted under the doctrine of *Cogan and Leak*.[20]

c) *Termination "by a registered medical practitioner"*. The defences provided by the Act are available "when a pregnancy is terminated by a registered medical practitioner". When the conditions in the Act are satisfied and the pregnancy is terminated by the doctor, there is no *actus reus*. Those who assist him are therefore guilty of no offence. The Act obviously did not contemplate that every action in the steps leading to an abortion would be done personally by the doctor. If, however, the doctor were to delegate more and more of the process to others, there would come a point when it could no longer be said that the pregnancy had been terminated "by a registered medical practitioner" – and at that point it would become unlawful. In *Royal College of Nursing of the United Kingdom v Department of Health and Social Security*,[1] the House of Lords by a majority of three or two, reversing a unanimous Court of Appeal and restoring the judgment of Woolf J, held that a particular process for the extra-amniotic method of termination of pregnancies was lawful, notwithstanding the substantial part played by nurses in that process. According to Lord Diplock, what the Act requires is that—

". . . a registered medical practitioner . . . should accept responsibility for all stages of the treatment for the termination of the pregnancy. The particular method to be used should be decided by the doctor in charge of the treatment for the termination of the pregnancy; he should carry out any physical acts, forming part of the treatment, that in accordance with accepted medical practice are done only by qualified medical practitioners, and should give specific instructions as to the carrying out of such parts of the treatment as in accordance with accepted medical practice are carried out by nurses or other members of the hospital staff

19. *Smith* [1974] 1 All ER 376 at 381.
20. [1976] QB 217, [1975] 2 All ER 1059, above, p. 153.
1. [1981] AC 800, [1981] 1 All ER 545.

without medical qualifications. To each of them, the doctor, or his substitute, should be available to be consulted or called on for assistance from beginning to end of the treatment."

Thus if the doctor were to direct the whole procedure by correspondence or over the telephone, the operation would presumably be unlawful.

Treatment to terminate a pregnancy, which, if the treatment were successful, would be lawfully terminated, is lawful treatment,[2] notwithstanding (as apparently happens in 1 to 2 per cent of cases) an ultimate failure to terminate the pregnancy. If the conditions of the Act are otherwise fulfilled and known to be fulfilled, the steps taken to procure abortion are taken without *mens rea* – there is no intent *unlawfully* to administer anything or *unlawfully* to use any instrument. There is moreover no *actus reus* for the legalisation of an abortion must include the steps which are taken towards it.

d) *Necessity at common law.* The provision in s. 5 (2) of the Abortion Act that, "For the purposes of the law relating to abortion, anything done with intent to procure a woman's miscarriage ... is unlawfully done unless authorised by section 1 of this Act ..." appears to be intended entirely to supercede the law as stated in *Bourne*.[3]

Abortions, and the steps to procure them which are proscribed, are unlawful unless they can be justified by the 1967 Act. It is submitted, however, that this provision cannot have been intended entirely to eliminate the operation of general defences to crime. To take extreme examples, a child under the age of ten or a person within the M'Naghten rules could surely not be convicted of committing or (slightly more likely) abetting an abortion. If this is conceded, then duress by threats ought equally to operate so why not duress of circumstances or necessity? And so we are back to admitting *Bourne's* case into the law. A possible interpretation of the Act would be to allow general defences, other than necessity. Construing s. 5(2) in the light of the previous law, a court might conclude that its obvious purpose was to overrule *Bourne*; and that it would be unreasonable to extend its operation beyond that.

A limited defence of necessity would seem desirable in principle. The defence would necessarily be limited in scope by the fact that, in the great majority of cases where it is necessary to procure an abortion, this is lawful by statute so that there is no room for the operation of any broader defence. But suppose that a qualified doctor who is not a registered medical practitioner and so does not come within the terms of s. 1(4) above, forms the opinion in good faith that immediate termination of a pregnancy is necessary in order to save the life of the mother who is in a remote place and beyond the help of any registered medical practitioner. Is it the law that he must let the woman die when he could save her by terminating the pregnancy?

2. Per Lord Edmund-Davies, citing the 4th edition of this book at 346, [1981] 1 All ER at 573.

3. Above, p. 386. Cf. the Canadian case of *Morgentaler* [1976] 1 SCR 616, (1975) 20 CCC (2d) 449 discussed by L. H. Leigh in [1978] Crim LR 151 and *Davidson* [1969] VR 667 (Menhennit J).

In *Bourne* Macnaghten J took the view that there was not only a right but a duty to perform the operation where a woman's life could be saved only by the doctor procuring an abortion:

"... if a case arose where the life of a woman could be saved by performing the operation and the doctor refused to perform it because of his religious opinions and the woman died, he would be in grave peril of being brought before this court on a charge of manslaughter by negligence. He would have no better defence than a person who, again from some religious reason, refused to call in a doctor to attend his sick child, where a doctor could have been called in and the life of the child could have been saved."[4]

Section 4 of the Abortion Act now provides:

"(1) Subject to subsection (2) of this section, no person shall be under any duty, whether by contract or by any statutory or other legal requirement, to participate in any treatment authorised by this Act to which he has a conscientious objection:

Provided that in any legal proceedings the burden of proof of conscientious objection shall rest on the person claiming to rely on it.

(2) Nothing in subsection (1) of this section shall affect any duty to participate in treatment which is necessary to save the life or to prevent grave permanent injury to the physical or mental health of a pregnant woman."

The same people whose acts are rendered lawful by s. 1 are given by s. 4 the right in conscience to object to performing those same acts. A person cannot claim that right in respect of an act which would not have amounted to an offence before the Abortion Act came into force. So a secretary was not entitled, by s. 4, to refuse to type a letter arranging an abortion rendered lawful by s. 1. It was held that she would not, under the old law, have been guilty of the abortion as a secondary party; her intention would have been merely to carry out her contract of employment, not to counsel or procure.[5]

Section 4(2) does not create any duty, but it does appear to recognise at least the possibility of a duty at common law. The only authority for this appears to be *Bourne*. It will be noted that Macnaghten J dealt only with the case where the woman died, whereas the Act refers to grave permanent injury to physical or mental health. Macnaghten J appeared to regard the doctor's liability as one arising from gross negligence; and this, if a ground of liability at all, is indeed confined to cases where death is caused.[6] There is no general criminal liability for causing grievous bodily harm by gross negligence as distinct from recklessness. If, however, the doctor is under a duty to act, and he knows all the circumstances giving rise to that duty and foresees the consequences of not fulfilling it, it would seem that he has the *mens rea* necessary to found a conviction for causing grievous bodily harm contrary to s. 18 of the Offences against the Person Act 1861.[7] The only doubtful link in this argument appears to be the existence of the duty; but

4. [1939] 1 KB at 693, [1938] 3 All ER at 618.
5. *Janaway v Salford Area Health Authority* [1989] AC 537, [1988] 2 WLR 442, CA, p. 262.
6. Above, p. 372.
7. Below, p. 424.

the Act strengthens the case for its existence. Clearly, a doctor with conscientious objections could fulfil his duty by referring the patient to another doctor who does not have such objections; and it is submitted that the doctor has a duty to do this where an abortion is necessary to save the woman from death or grave permanent injury. The question of a duty to participate in the operation can arise only where there is no effective substitute for the doctor concerned. Where the patient has conscientious objections there can be no duty to perform the operation since, clearly, it can only be lawfully performed with consent.

7 Genocide

The Genocide Act 1969 gives effect to the Genocide Convention, Article II. It is an offence under the Act to commit any of the acts falling within the definition of genocide in Article II. This provides:

"In the present Convention, genocide means any of the following acts committed with intent to destroy, in whole or in part, a national, ethnical, racial or religious group, as such:

(a) Killing members of the group;

(b) Causing serious bodily or mental harm to members of the group;

(c) Deliberately inflicting on the group conditions of life calculated to bring about its physical destruction in whole or in part;

(d) Imposing measures intended to prevent births within the group;

(e) Forcibly transferring children of the group to another group."

The offence is punishable with fourteen years imprisonment unless it consists of the killing of any person, in which case it is punishable with life imprisonment.

13 Non-Fatal Offences against the Person*

1 Offences against the Person: Who is a "Person"?

The "person" who may be the victim of any of the offences discussed in this chapter is a human being. The context excludes associations, whether corporate or unincorporate as victims, though these bodies might be guilty of committing some of the offences as a principal or as an accessory. If a corporation may be guilty of manslaughter[1] there is no reason why it should not be guilty of lesser offences against the person. The meaning of "person" as a victim has been discussed almost exclusively in relation only to murder but it seems clear that the same principles must apply to non-fatal offences. The Draft Code accordingly provides by cl. 53(a) that, for the purposes of the Chapter on Offences against the Person—

"'another' [i.e., the victim] means a person who has been born and has an existence independent of his mother and, unless the context otherwise requires, 'death' and 'personal harm' mean the death of, or personal harm to, such a person."

It seems that this probably represents the common law[2] so that there could be no assault on a foetus or a child in the process of being born; and that statutory offences are to be construed in accordance with it.

2 Assault and Battery

Assault and battery were two distinct crimes at common law and their separate existence (though now, it has been held, as statutory offences) is confirmed by s. 39 of the Criminal Justice Act 1988:

"Common assault and battery shall be summary offences and a person guilty of either of them shall be liable to a fine not exceeding level 5 on the standard scale, to imprisonment for a term not exceeding six months, or to both."

---

* For proposals concerning the reform and codification of this branch of the law, see Law Commission Consultation Paper No. 122, "Legislating the Criminal Code".
1. Above, p. 183.
2. Cf. *Tait*, above, p. 377.

Common assault and battery were indictable offences at common law and under s. 47 of the Offences against the Person Act (hereafter "OAPA") 1861; but this provision of that section was repealed by the 1988 Act, together with ss. 42 and 43 which provided for summary trial – s. 42 where the complaint was made by the party aggrieved, a provision intended for minor offences where the police saw no need to intervene, and s. 43 where the offence was too serious to be sufficiently punished under s. 42. The replacement of all these provision by s. 39, above, is a valuable simplification of the law.

An assault is any act by which D, intentionally or recklessly,[3] causes P to apprehend immediate and unlawful personal violence.[4] A battery is any act by which D, intentionally or recklessly, inflicts unlawful personal violence upon P.[5] But "violence" here includes any unlawful touching of another, however slight, for, as Blackstone wrote:[6]

"the law cannot draw the line between different degrees of violence, and therefore prohibits the first and lowest stage of it; every man's person being sacred, and no other having a right to meddle with it, in any the slightest manner."

As Lane LCJ put it:

"An assault (sc. meaning "battery") is any intentional touching of another person without the consent of that person and without lawful excuse. It need not necessarily be hostile, or rude, or aggressive, as some of the cases seem to indicate."[7]

Presumably the same applies to assault in the strict sense – it is enough that P apprehends some unwanted touching. It is however neither an assault nor a battery for D to pull himself free from P who is detaining him, even though D uses force.[8]

It should be noted that assault and battery are also torts; and many, though not all, of the principles appear to be equally applicable in both branches of the law. Consequently, some of the cases cited below are civil actions.

1 Taking the separateness of assault and battery seriously

The separateness of assault and battery has not been universally recognised.[9] There is a terminological problem in that there is no acceptable verb corresponding to the noun, battery, so that "assaulted" is almost invariably

---

3. *Venna* [1976] QB 421, [1975] 3 All ER 788, CA (a case of battery but the same principle surely applies to assault); *Logdon v Director of Public Prosecutions* [1976] Crim LR 121, DC.
4. A definition in almost identical terms was approved in *Fagan v Metropolitan Police Commissioner* [1969] 1 QB 439, [1968] 3 All ER 442 at 445; **SHC 27**; below, p. 403.
5. *Rolfe* (1952) 36 Cr App Rep 4.
6. *Commentaries*, 3, 120, cited by Goff LJ in *Collins v Wilcock* [1984] 3 All ER 374 at 378, **SHC 353**.
7. *Faulkner v Talbot* [1981] 3 All ER 468 at 471, applied in *Thomas* (1985) 81 Cr App Rep 331 at 334; and see *Collins v Wilcock* [1984] 3 All ER 374 at 379, DC; *Wilson v Pringle* [1987] QB 237, [1986] 2 All ER 440, CA (Civ. Div.), criticised by Wood J. in *T v T* [1988] 2 WLR 189 at 200, 203, Fam Div; *Brown* [1992] 2 WLR 441 at 446, CA.
8. *Sheriff* [1969] Crim LR 260.
9. The CLRC Fourteenth Report, para. 148, treated them as a single offence which may be committed in two ways and the Draft Code, cl. 75, follows the CLRC's recommendation.

used to mean "committed a battery against". Sometimes the term "assault" is used in statutes to mean "assault or battery" but on other occasions both words are used. There is a deplorable inconsistency in the statutory terminology. Even the Criminal Justice Act 1988, having made it crystal clear in s. 39 that there are two offences, goes on in s. 40 (3) (a) to use "common assault" in a context in which it can only sensibly mean "common assault or battery".

There are, however, grave problems of substance as well as terminology which have long been ignored but will have to be faced if we are at last to take seriously the proposition that there are two distinct offences. In *DPP v Little*[10] an information alleging that "L ... did unlawfully assault and batter J" was held to charge two offences and so to be bad for duplicity.[11] Consider the surviving offence under OAPA 1869, s. 47:

"Whosoever shall be convicted of an assault occasioning actual bodily harm shall be liable to [imprisonment for five years]."

In *DPP v Little* the divisional court was in no doubt that this offence included both an assault occasioning actual bodily harm and, much more commonly, a battery occasioning such harm – and this is surely right. It is true that in *Savage*[12] Lord Ackner said in respect of this offence, "It is common ground that the mental element of assault is an intention to cause the victim to apprehend immediate and unlawful violence or recklessness whether such apprehension be caused"; but it is incredible that D, who takes care to ensure that P apprehends nothing and hits him on the back of the head, is not guilty of an "assault occasioning actual bodily". If the word "assault" in the section embraces two offences, it must have the same meaning when used in an indictment or information alleging an offence under the section. It follows that the standard form of indictment—

"AB ... assaulted JN, thereby occasioning him actual bodily harm" alleges two offences and is bad for duplicity. The same considerations apply to indecent and other aggravated assaults. The effect is that thousands of people have been convicted on defective indictments ever since 1861 – but this in no way detracts from the inescapable logic of the argument. Prosecutors would be well advised to draft particulars of an indictment or information so as to make clear that it charges either an assault or a battery, but not both.

2 Common law or statutory offences?

An aggravated assault or battery – i.e., where Parliament has provided for a higher penalty where a specified aggravating circumstance is proved – is a separate offence under the principle of *Courtie*[13] and is necessarily a statutory offence. This applies to an assault or battery occasioning actual bodily harm, contrary to OAPA 1861, s. 47, though until very recently the

10. [1991] Crim LR 900, DC.
11. It was by no means the first case to decide that a charge of assault and/or battery in a single count or information is bad. See *Jones v Sherwood* [1942] 1 KB 127, DC and *Mansfield JJ, ex p Sharkey* [1985] QB 613, [1985] 1 All ER 193, DC.
12. [1991] 4 All ER 698 at 711.
13. [1984] AC 463, [1984] 1 All ER 740, HL, above, p. 32.

standard form of indictment for the offence made no reference to the Act, treating it as an offence at common law, as indeed was universally supposed before *Courtie*. This principle does not apply to common assault or battery – they are "common" precisely because there is no aggravating ingredient – and s. 39 of the 1988 Act does not on its face create any offence but assumes the existence of offences of common assault and battery, merely prescribing the mode of trial and penalty. Nevertheless in *DPP v Little*[14] it was held that common assault and battery have been statutory offences since the enactment of s. 47 of the OAPA 1861. The better view is that s. 47 merely prescribed the penalty for the common law offences of common assault – as statutes do for other common law offences, e.g., murder, manslaughter and conspiracy to defraud.[15] These all continue as offences at common law. Pending review by a higher court, however, the prosecutor is well advised to follow *DPP v Little* and to charge common assault or battery as a statutory offence, contrary to s. 39.

3 Actus Reus of Assault

The typical case of an assault as distinct from a battery is that where D, by some physical movement, causes P to apprehend that he is about to be struck. D rides or drives at P, or acts so as to appear to P to be on the point of striking, stabbing or shooting him. Assault was once regarded as attempted battery. D had embarked on an act which, if not suspended or evaded, would immediately result in an impact of some kind on P. Many attempted batteries are assaults, but this is not necessarily so. D's acts may be unobserved by P, as where D approaches P from behind, or P is asleep, or insensible, or too young to appreciate what D appears likely to do. And there may be an assault where D has no intention to commit a battery but only to cause P to apprehend one.[16]

There is a tendency to enlarge the concept of assault by taking a generous view of "immediacy" and including threats where the impending impact is more remote than in the typical assaults instanced above. In *Lewis*[17] D was held guilty of maliciously inflicting grievous bodily harm and therefore impliedly of an assault,[18] although D was uttering threats from another room. In *Logdon v Director of Public Prosecutions*[19] it was held that D committed an assault by showing P a pistol in a drawer and declaring that he would hold her hostage. In *Smith v Superintendent of Woking Police Station*[20] D committed an assault by looking through the window of a bed-sitting room at P in her night-clothes, intending to frighten her and doing so. The court distinguished the example given in the 4th edition of this book – "There can be no assault if it is obvious to P that D is unable to carry out his threat, as where D shakes his fist at P who is safely locked

14. Above, p. 399.
15. See [1991] Crim LR 900; Archbold, First Supp. to 1992 edition, 19–177.
16. *Logdon v Director of Public Prosecutions* [1976] Crim LR 121.
17. [1970] Crim LR 647, CA.
18. But see now *Wilson* [1984] AC 242, [1983] 3 All ER 448 below, p. 425.
19. Above.
20. (1983) 76 Cr App Rep 234.

inside his car." Kerr LJ said, "That may be so, but those are not the facts of the present case."

There may be an assault although D has no means of carrying out the threat.[1] The question is whether he intends to cause P to believe that he can and will carry it out and whether P does so believe. The question arises where D points an unloaded or imitation gun at P.

If P knows the gun is unloaded or an imitation, there is no assault, for then he could not be put in fear.[2] If P believes it is, or may be a real, loaded gun, there is an *actus reus*, for now he suffers the apprehension which is an essential element of the crime.[3]

It has been generally accepted that mere words cannot constitute an assault. It has been held in Canada[4] that there was no assault where a man with a jacket over his arm went up to the box-office of a theatre and said to the cashier, "I've got a gun, give me all your money or I'll shoot." It would probably have been different if it had been proved that D simulated the pointing of a gun. In England, there seems to be no more authority for the proposition than a dictum of Holroyd J in *Meade and Belt*[5] that "no words or singing are equivalent to an assault". The proposition has been rightly questioned by modern writers.

"If the plaintiff turns a corner to be confronted by a motionless robber who, with gun in hand, commands 'Hands up', why should not this be an assault?"[6]

Moreover,

"The opinion would deny the possibility of an assault (as opposed to a battery) in pitch darkness, when a gesture cannot be seen but menacing words can be heard."[7]

In *Wilson*[8] Lord Goddard said of the accused:

"He called out 'Get out the knives', *which itself would be an assault*, in addition to kicking the gamekeeper."

This was a mere dictum – but it surely counterbalances that in *Meade*? In a civil case, the Court of Appeal held that a threat forcibly to eject P was an assault.[9]

It is clear that a threat to inflict harm at some time in the future cannot amount to an assault[10] – an apprehension of immediate personal violence is essential. As already noted, an oral threat even to murder P, and even if made in his presence, was not an offence until 1977 unless it amounted to an assault.

1. *Pace* Tindal CJ in *Stephens v Myers* (1830) 4 C & P 349.
2. *Lamb*, above, p. 65.
3. *Logdon v Director of Public Prosecutions*, above.
4. *Byrne* [1968] 3 CCC 179 (Br Col C of A). Cf. *Logdon v Director of Public Prosecutions*, supra, where D showed P the gun.
5. (1823) 1 Lew CC 184.
6. Street, *Torts*, 26.
7. Williams [1957] Crim LR at 224.
8. [1955] 1 All ER 744 at 745.
9. *Ansell v Thomas* [1974] Crim LR 31.
10. *Stephens v Myers*, above, fn. 1; and see *Police v Greaves* [1964] NZLR 295; *Fagan v Metropolitan Police Commissioner* [1969] 1 QB 439, [1968] 3 All ER 442; **SHC 27**; below, p. 403, fn. 3.

Whether or not words may amount to an assault, it is clear that they may negative one. In the famous case of *Tuberville v Savage*[11] D laid his hand upon his sword, saying, "If it were not assize time I would not take such language." If D had said nothing, it is clear that the court would have held this to be evidence of an assault; but

"the declaration of [D][12] was, that he would not assault him, the judges being in town."[13]

If the words had not accompanied the act, but followed it, again there would presumably have been an assault, for the words could not undo a crime already constituted by the apprehension aroused in P.

In *Blake v Barnard*,[14] Lord Abinger applied the same principle to the situation where D presented a pistol at P's head and said that if P was not quiet he would blow his brains out. This differs from *Tuberville v Savage* in that D's declared intention not to shoot was conditional on P's doing as he was told. It has been forcefully argued[15] that this is a vital distinction and that D should not have been acquitted of an assault on that ground—

"Otherwise, indeed, the highwayman who says 'Your money or your life,' at the same time presenting a weapon, would not be guilty of assault at common law – a proposition which it is impossible to believe."

Thus in *Read v Coker*,[16] where D and his servants had surrounded P, tucking up their sleeves and aprons, and had threatened to break his neck *if he did not leave the premises*, the Court of Common Pleas had no doubt that this was an assault. Yet P was already a trespasser in that case, having been told to go. The threat amounted to an assault presumably only because it was of excessive force.[17] If P threatens to punch D and D produces a knife, saying that, if P does so, he will "cut him to bits," D is guilty of an assault if the violence he has threatened goes beyond what was reasonably necessary as a means of self-defence.[18]

It has generally been assumed that an act of some kind is an essential ingredient of assault; but a modern case[19] suggests the possibility of an assault by omission. Where D inadvertently causes P to apprehend immediate violence and subsequently wilfully declines to withdraw the threat, his omission might constitute an assault.

Attempt to Assault

It has been questioned whether there can be an attempt to assault, since assault itself was regarded as an attempt to commit a battery. It is

---

11. (1669) 1 Mod Rep 3. But cf. *Light* (1857) Dears & B 332.
12. D was in fact the plaintiff in an action for assault arising out of a fight which followed the incident described.
13. Ibid.
14. (1840) 9 C & P 626.
15. By Williams [1957] Crim LR at 220.
16. (1853) 13 CB 850.
17. Cf. *Osborn v Veitch* (1858) 1 F & F 317 (Pointing a gun at half-cock ("cocking it is an instantaneous act") to resist an unlawful arrest held an assault, because "To shoot a man is not a lawful way of repelling an unlawful assault": per Willes J).
18. *Rozsa v Samuels* [1969] SASR 205. But cf. *Cousins*, above, p. 377.
19. *Fagan v Metropolitan Police Commissioner* [1969] 1 QB 439, [1968] 3 All ER 442, below, p. 403.

submitted that, since assault itself is now wider than attempted battery, there is no reason why there should not be attempt to commit it; as where D points an unloaded gun at P, intending to frighten him, but P, knowing the gun is unloaded, is unperturbed.[20]

4 Actus Reus of Battery

This consists in the infliction of unlawful personal violence by D upon P. It used to be said that every battery involves an assault; but this is plainly not so, for in battery there need be no apprehension of the impending violence. A blow from behind is not any less a battery because P was unaware that it was coming. It is generally said that D must have done some act and that it is not enough that he stood still and obstructed P's passage[1] like an inanimate object. But suppose D is sitting at the corner of a corridor with his legs stretched across it. He hears P running down the corridor and deliberately remains still with the intention that P, on turning the corner, shall fall over his legs. Why should not this be a battery? It would be if D had put out his legs with the intention of tripping up P. There is certainly no battery where D has no control over the incident, as where his horse unexpectedly runs away with him;[2] but this might be put on the ground of lack of *mens rea*. It might be otherwise if D foresaw, when he mounted, that there was an unacceptable risk that this might happen. There may be a battery where D inadvertently applies force to P and then wrongfully refuses to withdraw it. In *Fagan*,[3] where D accidentally drove his mini-car on to a constable's foot and then intentionally left it there, the court held that there was a continuing act, not a mere omission.

Since the merest touching without consent is a criminal offence, the exigencies of everyday life demand that there be an implied consent to that degree of contact which is necessary or customary in the ordinary course.

"Generally speaking, consent is a defence to battery; and most of the physical contacts of ordinary life are not actionable because they are impliedly consented to by all who move in society and so expose themselves to the risk of bodily contact. So nobody can complain of the jostling which is inevitable from his presence in, for example, a supermarket, an underground station or a busy street; nor can a person who attends a party complain if his hand is seized in friendship, or even if his back is (within reason) slapped. Although such cases are regarded as examples of implied consent, it is more common nowadays to treat them as falling within a general exception embracing all physical contact which is generally acceptable in the ordinary conduct of daily life."[4]

20. "Is Criminal Assault a Separate Substantive Crime or is it an Attempted Battery?" (1945) 33 Ky LJ 189; *State v Wilson* (1955) 218 Ore 575; 346 P (2d) 115. See also [1980] Crim LR 780.
1. *Innes v Wylie* (1844) 1 Car & Kir 257.
2. *Gibbon v Pepper* (1695) 2 Salk 637.
3. [1969] 1 QB 439, [1968] 3 All ER 442 above, pp. 46, 77 and 40.
4. *Collins v Wilcock* [1984] 3 All ER 374 at 378, **SHC 353**, per Robert Goff LJ. In *F v West Berkshire Health Authority* [1989] 2 All ER 545 at 563, HL, Lord Goff was more emphatic that the consent rationalisation is "artificial", pointing out that it is difficult to impute consent to those who through youth or mental disorder are unable to give it.

Touching a person for the purpose of engaging his attention has been held to be acceptable[5] but physical restraint is not. A police officer who catches hold of a boy, not for the purpose of arresting him but in order to detain him for questioning, is acting unlawfully.[6] So is a constable who takes hold of the arm of a woman found soliciting in order to caution her. The fact that the practice of cautioning prostitutes is recognised by statute does not imply any power to stop and detain.[7] But to "detain" without any actual touching cannot be a battery. If the detention is effected by the threat of force, then it may be false imprisonment.

For this purpose the person of the victim includes the clothes he is wearing; Parke B ruled that there was a common assault where D slashed P's clothes with a knife:

"surely it is an assault on a man's person to inflict injury to the clothes on his back. In the ordinary case of a blow on the back, there is clearly an assault, though the blow is received by the coat on the person."[8]

It is apparently not necessary that P should be able to feel the impact through the clothes. In *Thomas*[9] where D touched the bottom of P's skirt and rubbed it, the court said, obiter, "There could be no dispute that if you touch a person's clothes while he is wearing them that is equivalent to touching him."

Most batteries are directly inflicted, as by D's striking P with his fist or an instrument, or by a missile thrown by him, or by spitting upon P. But it is not essential that the violence should have been so directly inflicted. Thus Stephen and Wills JJ thought there would be a battery where D digs a pit for P to fall into, or, as in *Martin*,[10] he causes P to rush into an obstruction. It is submitted that it would undoubtedly be a battery to set a dog on another.[11] If D beat O's horse causing it to run down P, this would be battery by D.[12] No doubt the famous civil case of *Scott v Shepherd*[13] is equally good for the criminal law. D throws a squib into a market house. First E and then F flings the squib away in order to save himself from injury. It expodes and injures P. This is a battery by D. If there is no violence at all, there is no battery; as where D puts harmful matter into a drink which is consumed by P.[14]

5 Mens rea of assault and battery

It is convenient to consider the *mens rea* of the two offences together. They are inextricably confused in some of the leading cases but need to be kept

---

5. *Wiffin v Kincard* (1807) 2 Bos & PNR 471; *Coward v Baddeley* (1859) 4 H & N 478. *Donnelly v Jackman* [1970] 1 All ER 987, [1970] 1 WLR 562, where a police officer was held to be acting in the execution of his duty although he persisted in tapping P on the shoulder when P had made it clear that he had no intention of stopping to speak, is "an extreme case": [1984] 3 All ER 374 at 379.
6. *Kenlin v Gardiner* [1967] 2 QB 510, [1966] 3 All ER 931.
7. *Collins v Wilcock*, above, fn. 4.
8. *Day* (1845) 1 Cox CC 207.
9. (1985) 81 Cr App Rep 331 at 334, CA.
10. Below, p. 426.
11. But note the caution of the court in *Dume* (1986) Times, 16 October, CA; Archbold, 19–218.
12. *Gibbon v Pepper* (1695) 2 Salk 637 (obiter).
13. (1773) 2 Wm Bl 892.
14. *Hanson* (1849) 2 Car & Kir 912; but see below, p. 429.

distinct if the separateness of the two offences is to be taken seriously. It was established by *Venna*[15] in 1975 that assault and battery may be committed recklessly as well as intentionally. *Venna* was a case of battery occasioning actual bodily harm but dicta concerning assault were relied on and it is safe to assume that the same principles apply to both offences. The *mens rea* of assault is an intention to cause P to apprehend immediate and unlawful violence, or recklessness whether such apprehension be caused.[16] The *mens rea* of battery is an intention to apply force to the body of another or recklessness whether force be so applied.

a) *What sort of recklessness?* The recklessness proved in *Venna* was subjective, *Cunningham* style, recklessness and the assumption then was that this was what the law required. But there was some doubt about the matter after *Caldwell* was decided in 1981 and subsequent cases insisted that *Caldwell* recklessness was the general rule in the criminal law. There was – and is – no statutory definition of assault, no use of the word "maliciously" to point to *Cunningham* recklessness, or of "recklessly" to point to the *Caldwell* version. Surprisingly, no reported case raised the point until *DPP v K*[17] in 1989 and then the divisional court assumed without argument that *Caldwell* recklessness sufficed. That decision was quickly overruled by the Court of Appeal in *Spratt*[18] which was followed by that court in *Parmenter*.[19] The House of Lords was not asked to decide this point but dicta[20] assume that advertence, i.e., *Cunningham* recklessness, is required; and it seems clear that this is now the law. D must actually foresee the risk of causing apprehension of violence, or the application of it, as the case may be.

b) *Is the* mens rea *interchangeable?* Is it an offence to cause the *actus reus* of battery with *mens rea* only of assault or the *actus reus* of assault with the *mens rea* only of battery? In principle, the answer is no.[21] D waves his fist, intending to alarm P but not to strike him and not foreseeing any risk of doing so; but P does not see D, moves, and is hit. D creeps up behind P intending to hit him over the head without attracting his attention, but P unexpectedly turns round and moves to avoid the blow. Taking the distinction seriously, in the former case D is guilty of attempted assault but not of battery; and in the latter of attempted battery but not of assault. It remains to be seen how seriously the courts will take the separateness of the offences.

15. [1976] QB 421, [1975] 3 All ER 788
16. Cf. *Savage* [1991] 4 All ER 698 at 711, HL.
17. [1990] 1 All ER 331, DC, [1990] Crim LR 321.
18. [1991] 2 All ER 210, [1990] Crim LR 797.
19. [1991 2 All ER 225, [1991] 2 WLR 408.
20. "Where the defendant neither intends nor adverts to the possibility that there will be any physical contact at all, then the offence under s. 47 would not be made out. This is because there would have been no assault, let alone an assault occasioning actual bodily harm" ([1991] 4 All ER at 707): Lord Ackner of course means "no battery". Other dicta show that he recognised that an assault in the strict sense suffices for an offence under s. 47 if it occasions actual bodily harm.
21. Above, p. 70.

c) *Assault and battery by an intoxicated person* Assault and battery are classified as offences of "basic intent" so that it is no defence that D had no *mens rea* because of voluntary intoxication. The reason appears to be that the offences may be committed by recklessness. If, then, an indictment or information specifically alleges an intentional assault or battery, it may be that the offence will be considered to require a "specific intent" and its absence through intoxication will be a defence.[1]

6 Defences to Assault and Battery

1 Consent

a) *Effect of consent.* It is of the essence of both offences that they are done against the will of the victim.[2] Consent therefore negatives either crime and the onus of proving the absence of consent is on the Crown.[3] Fraud does not necessarily negative consent. It does so only if it deceives P as to the identity of the person or the nature of the act.[4] In *Clarence*[5] P consented to intercourse with D and, although she would not have consented had she been aware of the disease from which D knew he was suffering, this was no assault. Where D1, a doctor, by falsely pretending that D2 was a medical student, obtained P's consent to D2's presence at a vaginal examination of P, it was held that there was no assault because the fraud was not as to the nature and quality of what was to be done.[6] Similarly, where a woman consented to the introduction of an instrument into her vagina for diagnostic purposes when the operator was acting only for sexual gratification.[7] In *Burrell v Harmer*[8] consent was held to be no defence to a charge of assault occasioning actual bodily harm, where D tattooed boys aged 12 and 13, causing their arms to become inflamed and painful. The court took the view that the boys were unable to understand the nature of the act. But in what sense did they not understand it? Consent may also be negatived by duress. A threat to imprison P unless he submitted to a beating would probably invalidate P's consent. Possibly a threat to dismiss from employment[9] or to bring a prosecution[10] would have a similar effect. If the test is whether the threat would be sufficient to overcome the will of a reasonably firm person, the outcome must depend to some extent on the relationship between the gravity of the threat and the act to which P is asked to submit. Duress may be implied from the relationship between the parties – for

1. Cf. *Caldwell* [1981] 1 All ER 961 at 964.
2. *Christopherson v Bare* (1848) 11 QB 473. *A-G's Reference (No. 6 of 1980)* [1981] 2 All ER 1057 at 1058.
3. *Donovan* [1934] 2 KB 498, following *May*, [1912] 3 KB 572.
4. But cf. the rule in trespass to land and, therefore, in burglary, below, p. 614.
5. (1888) 22 QBD 23; below, p. 426.
6. *Bolduc and Bird* (1967) 63 DLR (2d) 82 (Sup. Ct of Canada, Spence J diss), reversing British Columbia CA 61 DLR (2d) 494. Cf. *Rosinski* (1824) 1 Mood CC 19.
7. *Mobilio* [1991] 1 VR 339 (Sup Ct of Victoria).
8. [1967] Crim LR 169 and commentary thereon. It is now an offence to tattoo a person under the age of 18, except tattooing by a doctor for medical reasons: Tattooing of Minors Act 1969.
9. *McCoy* 1953 (2) SA 4 (AD) (threat to ground air hostess negativing consent on assault charge).
10. *State v Volschenk* 1968 (2) PH H283 (threat to prosecute held *not* to negative consent on rape charge).

example where D is acting as a schoolmaster, and P is a thirteen year-old pupil.[11] As in rape and indecent assault,[12] submission is not consent. But an unfounded belief in P's consent is a defence, whether the belief is based on reasonable grounds or not, provided only that it is honestly held. "*Cunningham* recklessness" whether P consents is a sufficient *mens rea*.[13]

b) *Limitations on consent*.[14] There are limits to the right of any person to consent to the infliction of physical harm on himself. Consent to being killed is ineffective. It is no defence to a charge of murder for D to say that P asked to be killed. On the other hand, P's consent to D's taking a high degree of risk of killing him is effective where it is justified by the purpose of the act, as it may be in the case of a surgical operation. Where the act has some social purpose, recognised by the law as valid, it is a question of balancing the degree of harm which will or may be caused against the value of that purpose. "Prize fights", though not unlawful as such,[15] have regularly been held to amount to batteries. Any entertainment value they may have is thought by the courts to be outweighed by risks of grave physical injury to the contestants. No prosecutions have been brought in respect of contests conducted with the greatest publicity in accordance with the Queensberry rules and, notwithstanding the clear risk of injury and occasionally death which is involved, it must be assumed that these are lawful. Fights without gloves, or in other circumstances which aggravate the risk of serious injury, are unlawful. In *Coney*[16] Cave J said:

"The true view is, I think, that a blow struck in anger, or which is likely or is intended to do corporal hurt, is an assault, but that a blow struck in sport, and not likely, nor intended to cause bodily harm, is not an assault, and that, an assault being a breach of the peace and unlawful, the consent of the person struck is immaterial. If this view is correct a blow struck in a prize-fight is clearly an assault; but playing with single-sticks or wrestling do not involve an assault; nor does boxing with gloves in the ordinary way, and not with the ferocity and severe punishment to the boxers deposed to in *R v Orton*."[17]

The condition that the blow must be "not intended to cause bodily harm", seems hardly consistent with the rest of the passage. A right hook delivered by Muhammed Ali with the avowed intention of knocking his opponent unconscious could not be said to be not intended to cause bodily harm; yet it appears to be lawful. The assumed value of the sport is taken to justify P's consenting to D's trying to knock him out. Where, however, two youths of 18 and 17 decided to settle an argument by a fight with fists

11. *Nichol* (1807) Russ & Ry 130.
12. Below, pp. 451 and 468.
13. *Morgan* [1976] AC 182, [1975] 2 All ER 347, HL; **SHC 46**; above, pp. 87, 216, and below, p. 451; *Albert v Lavin* [1981] 1 All ER 628, DC. Absence of consent is "a definitional element" of assault. Above, p. 89.
14. Williams, "Consent and Public Policy" [1962] Crim LR 74 and 154.
15. *Pallante v Stadium Pty Ltd (No. 1)* [1976] VR 331.
16. (1882) 8 QBD 534 at 539; above, p. 131.
17. (1878) 39 LT 293. The contestants wore gloves but it was held that the jury were rightly directed that it was a prize-fight if they intended to fight on until one gave in from exhaustion or injury.

(presumably bare) and the one sustained a bleeding nose and bruises to his face it was held that the other was guilty of assault occasioning actual bodily harm.

". . . it is not in the public interest that people should try to cause or should cause each other actual bodily harm for no good reason. Minor struggles are another matter. So, in our judgment, it is immaterial whether the act occurs in private or in public; it is an assault if actual bodily harm is intended and/or caused. This means that most fights will be unlawful regardless of consent."[18]

The court went on to say:

"Nothing which we have said is intended to cast doubt on the accepted legality of properly conducted games and sports, lawful chastisement or correction, reasonable surgical interference, dangerous exhibitions etc. These apparent exceptions can be justified as involving the exercise of a legal right, in the case of chastisement or correction, or as needed in the public interest, in the other cases."

So the shoulder charge, delivered in the course of a game of soccer, which would clearly be unlawful if it were inflicted on an unwilling passer-by, is lawful because P has consented to D's doing what the rules of the game reasonably permit. Prima facie, P has consented to that and nothing more; and therefore *Moore*[19] holding the rules inadmissible in evidence seems a dubious decision. Some players however think they consent to certain acts in breach of the rules which they know are very likely to occur in the ordinary course of play. Proof of breach of the rules ought to establish at least a prima facie case.[20] Consent by boys to rough and undisciplined play may be a defence to a charge of inflicting grievous bodily harm if there is no intention to cause injury. Consent, or a genuine belief in consent, even an unreasonable belief, apparently negatives recklessness: *Jones*[1] where boys were injured by being tossed in the air by schoolmates. The decision recognises that boys have always indulged in rough and undisciplined play among themselves and probably always will; but the non-consenting child is rightly protected by the criminal law.

Consent to a surgical operation for a purpose recognised as valid by the law is effective[2] and this includes a sex-change operation[3] and, presumably, cosmetic surgery and organ transplants. It is otherwise where the purpose is one which the law condemns.

---

18. *A-G's Reference (No. 6 of 1980)* [1981] 2 All ER 1057 at 1059; **SHC 363**. The implication of this passage that causing bodily harm is unlawful though no bodily harm is intended is puzzling. Actual bodily harm may occasionally be caused by a battery not intended to cause harm, as where D's unwanted pat on the head cracks P's eggshell skull; but no question of consent seems to arise in such a case. Perhaps the reference is to reckless assaults. P's consent to take the risk is not an answer unless there is some justification, other than mere consent. Consent to the administration of a noxious thing likely to endanger life is not a defence: *Cato* [1976] 1 All ER 260, [1976] 1 WLR 110. Cf. *McLeod* (1915) 34 NZLR, 430. See commentary at [1981] Crim LR 554.
19. (1898) 14 TLR 229. Cf. *Billinghurst* [1978] Crim LR 553 (Judge Rutter).
20. The rules are admissible in favour of the defence, as tending to negative "malice"; *Bradshaw* (1878) 14 Cox CC 83.
   1. [1987] Crim LR 123, CA.
   2. Stephen, *Digest*, Art. 310. See Skegg, [1974] Crim LR 693 and (1973) 36 MLR 370.
   3. *Corbett v Corbett* [1971] P 83 at 99.

So Coke tells us that in 1604,

"a young strong and lustie rogue, to make himself impotent, thereby to have the more colour to begge or to be relieved without putting himself to any labour, caused his companion to strike off his left hand":

and that both of them were convicted of mayhem.[4] Maiming, even with consent, was unlawful because it deprived the king of a fighting man. In early Victorian times when soldiers, as part of their drill, had to bite cartridges, a soldier got a dentist to pull out his front teeth to avoid the drill. Stephen J thought that both were guilty of a crime.[5] Denning LJ followed these instances in discussing, obiter, the legality of a sterilisation operation:

"When it is done with the man's consent for a just cause, it is quite lawful, as, for instance, when it is done to prevent the transmission of an hereditary disease; but when it is done without just cause or excuse, it is unlawful, even though the man consents to it. Take a case where a sterilisation operation is done so as to enable a man to have the pleasure of sexual intercourse without shouldering the responsibilities attaching to it. The operation is then plainly injurious to the public interest."[6]

Lord Denning's opinion is no longer tenable on the particular point,[7] but it illustrates the continuing and changing influence of public policy. In Cowburn,[8] a man with uncontrollable sexual impulses was willing to undergo a castration operation but the Court of Criminal Appeal declined to give its blessing to the operation as the issue was not before it. The legality of such operations has not been settled by any judicial decision; but it now seems highly improbable that they would be held to be unlawful. Public policy might well be served[9] rather than offended by an operation such as that proposed in Cowburn: but "public policy" is a notoriously elusive and slippery doctrine. It was invoked to justify conviction for a relatively slight degree of harm in Donovan.[10] D, for his sexual gratification, beat a seventeen-year-old girl with a cane in circumstances of indecency. He was convicted of both indecent assault and common assault. The judge failed to direct the jury that the onus of negativing consent was on the Crown, but the Court of Criminal Appeal held that, if the blows were likely or intended to cause bodily harm, this omission was immaterial because D was guilty whether P consented or not. The conviction was quashed because the question whether the blows were likely or intended to cause bodily harm was not put to the jury, and

"There are many gradations between a slight tap and a severe blow . . . ."[11]

4. 1 Co Inst 127a and b.
5. Digest (3rd ed.) 142.
6. Bravery v Bravery [1954] 3 All ER 59 at 67, 68.
7. The National Health Service (Family Planning) Amendment Act 1972 authorised the provision of voluntary vasectomy services.
8. [1959] Crim LR 590. Cf. T v T [1988] Fam 52, [1988] 1 All ER 613, Fam. Div.
9. See Havard [1959] Crim LR 554 at 555: "The Scandinavian experience has shown that voluntary castration is particularly efficacious in these cases and may permit an early rehabilitation in the community."
10. [1934] 2 KB 498.
11. Ibid., at 510. See Leigh, "Sado-Masochism, Consent and the Reform of the Criminal Law" (1976) 39 MLR 130.

In *A-G's Reference (No. 6 of 1980)*[12] the Court of Appeal, while rejecting the tautologous reasoning of *Donovan*,[13] confirmed its effect, namely that the intentional infliction of any degree of bodily harm, however slight,[14] is a battery unless P consents *and* the action can be positively justified by some public interest. In *Brown*[15] sado-masochist homosexual men were convicted of assaults occasioning actual bodily harm on and wounding of one another, contrary to ss. 47 and 20 of the 1861 Act, although the acts were done with consent, there was no permanent injury, no infection and no evidence of medical attention being required. Though many would shrink from such injuries with horror, they apparently brought sexual pleasure to the "victims". This did not amount to a justification or excuse in eyes of the Court of Appeal. As in *Donovan*, the practices did not come into the same category as "manly sports".

2 Necessity
As noticed above, necessity may excuse what would otherwise be an assault, as where D pushes P out of the path of a vehicle which is about to run him down. The fireman, the ambulance man, the surgeon and nurses may all do things to a person rendered unconscious in an accident, or by a stroke, which would ordinarily be battery (or, in the case of the surgeon, wounding or grievous bodily harm) if done without consent; but they commit no offence if they are only doing what is necessary to save life or ensure improvement, or prevent deterioration, in health.[16] Perhaps this is based on the presumption that P would consent if he knew of the circumstances, a principle which excuses conduct in other parts of the criminal law.[17] This is consistent with the view[18] that intervention cannot be justified if it is against P's known wishes. So it seems that a passer-by who prevents P, a sane person, from committing suicide by dragging him from the parapet of a bridge is guilty of battery.[19]

3 Lawful Correction
Parents are entitled to inflict moderate and reasonable physical chastisement on their children; but –

> "If it be administered for the gratification of passion or rage or if it be
> immoderate or excessive in its nature or degree, or if it be protracted
> beyond the child's powers of endurance or with an instrument unfitted
> for the purpose and calculated to produce danger to life and limb . . . ."[20]

12. Above, p. 408.
13. "If an act is unlawful in the sense of being in itself a criminal act, it is plain that it cannot be rendered lawful because the person to whose detriment it is done consents to it. No person can license another to commit a crime."
14. Stephen thought "everyone has a right to consent to the infliction upon himself of bodily harm not amounting to a maim": *Digest of Criminal Law* (4th ed.) 148–149. The influential American Model Penal Code allows consent as a defence where the harm is "not serious".
15. [1992] 2 WLR 441. Leave was given to appeal to the House of Lords.
16. *F. v West Berkshire Health Authority* [1989] 2 All ER 545 at 564, 566, HL, per Lord Goff.
17. E.g., the Theft Act 1968, ss. 2(1) (b), 12(6), Criminal Damage Act 1971, s. 5(2) (b).
18. *F. v West Berks*, above, at 566, per Lord Goff.
19. Cf. Williams, TBCL, 616. Otherwise, perhaps, if P is in police custody: *Kirkham v Chief Constable of the Greater Manchester Police* [1990] 2 QB 283, [1990] 3 All ER 246, CA.
20. *Hopley* (1860) 2 F & F 202 at 206, per Cockburn CJ. Cf. *Smith* [1985] Crim LR 42, CA.

– then it is unlawful. If the chastisement is moderate, it would be impracticable for the courts to inquire very closely into the validity of the parent's motives. Where the force is immoderate, his motives are irrelevant. Immigrant parents must conform to English standards.[1] At common law, school teachers are in the same position as parents with regard to the conduct of the child at, or on its way to or from school.[2] A "member of staff" of a school, as defined in s. 47 (10) of the Education (No. 2) Act 1986 now has no right, by virtue of his position as such, to administer corporal punishment to a "pupil" as defined in s. 47 (5) of that Act. Presumably corporal punishment would still be lawful if administered by a teacher on the authority of a parent. In a school to which the definitions in the 1986 Act do not apply, the common law position continues. Section 1 of the Children and Young Persons Act 1933, which makes it an offence, inter alia, wilfully to assault a person under sixteen, provides that nothing in the section "shall be construed as affecting the right of any parent, teacher, or other person having the lawful control or charge of a child or young person to administer punishment to him."

The ancient right to chastise a servant, an apprentice or (if such a right ever existed), a wife,[3] is now obsolete.

3 Aggravated Assaults

The Offences against the Person Act 1861 singles out certain varieties of assault (and, no doubt, battery) as being especially heinous and provides a more severe punishment for them. Some of these were, no doubt, intended to deal with matters causing public concern at the time, and appear rather curious today.

Thus, obstructing or assaulting a clergyman in the discharge of his duties in a place of worship or burial place, or who is on his way to or from such duties is an offence triable either way, punishable on indictment with two years' imprisonment under s. 36. Assaulting a magistrate or other person in the exercise of his duty concerning the preservation of a vessel in distress or a wreck is an offence punishable on indictment with seven years' imprisonment under s. 37. Such provisions are rarely invoked at the present day and need not be considered further.

1) Assault with Intent to resist Arrest

By s. 38 of the OAPA 1861—

"Whosoever shall assault any person with intent to resist or prevent the lawful apprehension or detainer of himself or of any other person for any offence"

---

1. *Derriviere* (1969) 53 Cr App Rep 637, CA.
2. *Cleary v Booth* [1893] 1 QB 465; *Newport (Salop) JJ* [1929] 2 KB 416; *Mansell v Griffin* [1908] 1 KB 160.
3. *Jackson* [1891] 1 QB 671.

is guilty of an offence triable either way and punishable with two years imprisonment. It may be assumed that the section creates two offences, assault with intent and battery with intent. Threatening the arrester (P) with a club to make him let go of the arrestee would be the assault, poking him with it would be battery. Dragging the arrestee from P's grasp, being reckless whether this causes P to fall to the ground will be a reckless battery with intent if P does fall. D has an intent to prevent "apprehension" when he tries to prevent the arrest taking place, and an intent to prevent "detainer" when he tries to bring the arrest to an end. The section applies only where the arrest is "for any offence"; so it does not apply to an arrest in civil process or for a breach of the peace not amounting to crime. It is immaterial whether the arrest is by a police officer or a citizen; but D's claim that he did not know the arrester was a plain-clothes officer may be crucial where his defence is that he believed he was being attacked by thugs.[4]

The intent must be to resist "lawful" arrest. If D knows of the circumstances which make the arrest lawful, he probably has a sufficient intent even though he believes it to be unlawful: e.g., having read in an out-of-date law book that conspiracy is not an arrestable offence, he resists arrest for conspiracy. The law of arrest is likely to be treated as part of the criminal law for this purpose[5] and his mistake or ignorance of criminal law is no defence.[6] If D wrongly believes in circumstances in which the arrest would be unlawful his mistake of fact negatives the *mens rea*. Whatever the true facts, he does not *intend* to resist *lawful* arrest. It may be that the principle of *Fennell*[7] leaves D liable for common assault or battery but it would be wrong to convict him of the aggravated offence when the aggravating factor is not proved.

2) *Assault on, Resistance to, or Obstruction of Constables*

By s. 51 of the Police Act 1964:

"(1) Any person who assaults a constable in the execution of his duty, or a person assisting a constable in the execution of his duty, shall be guilty of an offence and liable on summary conviction to a fine not exceeding level 5 on the standard scale or to imprisonment for a term not exceeding six months or to both.

(2) Subsection (2) of section 17 of the Firearms Act 1968, shall apply to offences under subsection (1) of this section.

(3) Any person who resists or wilfully obstructs a constable in the execution of his duty, or a person assisting a constable in the execution of his duty, shall be guilty of an offence and liable on summary

4. *Brightling* [1991] Crim LR 364, CA.
5. Cf. cl. 25 (2) (b) of the Code Team's Draft Code (Law Com. No. 143), a provision not included in the Law Commission's draft (Law Com. No. 177).
6. Talfourd J put his decision on this ground in *Bentley* (1850) 4 Cox CC 406.
7. [1971] 1 QB 428, [1970] 3 All ER 215, below, p. 417. Cf. *Ball* (1989) 90 Cr App Rep 378 and commentary at [1978] Crim LR 580.

conviction to imprisonment for a term not exceeding one month or to a fine not exceeding level 3 on the standard scale, or to both."

Though the section is headed "Assaults on Constables", there are three crimes here, only one of which necessarily amounts to an assault. Resistance to a constable may occur without an assault, as where D has been arrested by P and tears himself from P's grasp and escapes.[8] Obstruction, as appears below, embraces many situations which do not amount to an assault. On the other hand, both resistance and obstruction clearly may include assaults. The nature of assault and resistance require no further consideration but obstruction presents problems and is examined in some detail below. The first question – when is a constable[9] acting in the course of his duty? – is common to all three crimes. But the *mens rea* of assault and resistance, on the one hand, and obstruction on the other require separate consideration.

1 A Constable Acting in the Execution of his Duty[10]

When a policeman is acting in the course of his duty is a question which can give rise to difficult problems. A constable directing a motorist to leave the road to take part in a traffic census, before there was a statutory power to do so,[11] was not acting in the execution of his duty since his right at common law to regulate traffic derives only from his duty to protect life and property.[12] There are many things which a constable on duty may do which he is probably not under any "duty" in the strict sense to do; that is, he would commit no crime or tort or even breach of police regulations by not doing it. It might be rescuing a stranded cat or helping to deliver a baby. Older cases[13] suggested that a constable was not in the execution of his duty for the purposes of this section unless he was doing something that he was obliged to do, but in *Coffin v Smith*[14] the divisional court rejected an argument on these lines and doubted those authorities. Officers, who had been summoned to a boys' club to ensure that certain people left, were assaulted. It was held that the officers were there in fulfilment of their duty to keep the peace and were plainly acting in the execution of their duty. In one of the doubted cases, *Prebble*,[15] where a constable at the request of a landlord, turned some persons out of a public house and was held not to be

---

8. *Sheriff* [1969] Crim LR 260.
9. I.e. a person holding the *office*, not the rank of constable. A prison officer acting as such is a constable for this purpose: Prison Act 1952,. s. 8.
10. On the duties of the police, see *Metropolitan Police Commissioner, ex parte Blackburn* [1968] 2 QB 118, [1968] 1 All ER 763, CA, and (*No. 3*) [1973] 2 QB 241, [1973] 1 All ER 324, CA; Lidstone, "A Policeman's Duty not to Take Liberties" [1976] Crim LR 617; U. Ross, "Two Cases on Obstructing a Constable" [1977] Crim LR 187.
11. See now the Road Traffic Act 1988, s. 35.
12. *Hoffman v Thomas* [1974] 2 All ER 233, DC. In the pursuance of that duty, a constable may require a motorist to disobey a traffic regulation: *Johnson v Phillips* [1975] 3 All ER 682, DC; and remove a vehicle to the police station when the driver is arrested: *Liepéns v Spearman* [1985] Crim LR 229. Cf. *Saunders* [1978] Crim LR 98 (Judge Heald) and commentary.
13. *Prebble* (1858) 1 F & F 325 and *Roxburgh* (1871) 12 Cox CC 8. See also *Betts v Stevens* [1910] 1 KB 1 and 4th ed. of this book at 361–372.
14. (1980) 71 Cr App Rep 221.
15. Above, fn. 13.

acting in the execution of his duty, the court found there was no nuisance or danger of breach of the peace, and it may possibly be distinguishable as a case where the officer was doing no more than assist a citizen in the enforcement of private rights. A constable may be acting in the execution of his duty by being present, and by intervening when a breach of the peace occurs or is imminent, but acting outside his duty if he takes it upon himself to expel a trespasser.[16] In a leading case, *Waterfield*,[17] the Court of Criminal Appeal said:

"In the judgment of this court it would be difficult, and in the present case it is unnecessary, to reduce within specific limits the general terms in which the duties of police constables have been expressed. In most cases it is probably more convenient to consider what the police constable was actually doing and in particular whether such conduct was prima facie an unlawful interference with a person's liberty or property. If so, it is then relevant to consider whether (a) such conduct falls within the general scope of any duty imposed by statute or recognised at common law and (b) whether such conduct, albeit within the general scope of such a duty, involved an unjustifiable use of powers associated with the duty."

If the police officer's conduct falls within the general scope of the "duty" to prevent crime and to bring offenders to justice, then it would seem to be within the protection of the statute, if it was lawful. If, in the course of carrying out his duty to prevent crime and to bring offenders to justice, the officer exceeds his powers, then he is no longer acting in the execution of his duty for this purpose.[18] In *McArdle v Wallace*,[19] P was held to be acting in the execution of his duty as a constable when he entered a café to make inquiries regarding some property which he thought might have been stolen. He was told to leave but did not do so and was then assaulted. At the time of the assault he was no longer acting in the execution of his duty since he became a trespasser when he refused to leave: for a constable can hardly have a duty to break the law. A constable who is not acting in the execution of his duty because he is a trespasser begins so to act as soon as circumstances justifying his presence arise – as where he reasonably

---

16. In *Chief Constable of Devon and Cornwall, ex parte Central Electricity Generating Board* [1982] QB 458, [1981] 3 All ER 826, 835 the Chief Constable appeared to take the view that he had no right to intervene to expel trespassers, even where they were committing a criminal obstruction, unless a breach of the peace was imminent. Lawton LJ said the CEGB had no right to call on the police to supply "muscle-power" to remove the obstructors; and if the obstructors allowed themselves to be removed without struggling or causing uproar, "the police will have no reason for taking action, *nor should they*": pp. 836–837. (Authors' italics.)
17. [1964] 1 QB 164 at 170, [1963] 3 All ER 659 at 661.
18. *Ludlow v Burgess* [1971] Crim LR 238, CA; *Pedro v Diss* [1981] 2 All ER 59, 72 Cr App Rep 193. Where D is arrested or detained by an officer unlawfully, for example, where the officer has not used words of arrest or told D the grounds therefor, the officer is not acting in the execution of his duty. Likewise where he searches P without giving reasons: *McBean v Parker* [1983] Crim LR 399; *Brazil v Chief Constable of Surrey* (1983) 77 Cr App Rep 237, DC. Similarly where an officer enters premises, otherwise than in accordance with the power given by PACE, s. 18(1). Cf. *McLorie v Oxford* [1982] 3 All ER 480, [1982] Crim LR 603.
19. [1964] Crim LR 467; cf. *Davis v Lisle* [1936] 2 KB 434, [1936] 2 All ER 213 *Robson v Hallett* [1967] 2 All ER 407; *McGowan v Chief Constable of Kingston-upon-Hull* [1968] Crim LR 34; *Kay v Hibbert* [1977] Crim LR 226, DC. *Jones and Jones v Lloyd* [1981] Crim LR 340, DC.

apprehends a breach of the peace. He does not have to leave the premises and re-enter.[20]

A police officer investigating crime is entitled to speak to any person from whom he thinks useful information can be obtained, even though that person declares that he is unwilling to reply;[1] but the officer has no power to detain for questioning so the use of reasonable force to escape from such detention is not an assault;[2] and the use of excessive force, while a common assault (or wounding, etc.) would not be an offence under s. 51. Where, however, P tapped D on the shoulder, not intending to detain him but in order to speak to him, it was held that P was acting in the course of his duties, though it seems clear that D did not consent to this contact. The court thought that—

"... it is not every trivial interference with a citizen's liberty that amounts to a course of conduct sufficient to take the officer out of the course of his duties."[3]

That the commission of a crime or tort can ever be part of the duty of a constable is an unacceptable proposition; and the case is an "extreme" one,[4] explicable only on the ground that the trespass committed by the constable was a momentary and trivial incident in an otherwise lawful course of conduct. In *Bentley v Brudzinski*,[5] on very similar facts, a different result was reached. Where the question is whether something is trivial or *de minimis*, it is perhaps to be expected that assessments will differ. *Waterfield*[6] is a more difficult case. P, a constable, had been informed that a car had been involved in a serious offence. Evidently acting on the instructions of a superior officer, he attempted to prevent D, the owner of the car, from removing it from the place on the road where it was parked. D drove the car at P, thus assaulting him, in order to remove it. The court held that P was not "entitled" to prevent removal of the car[7] and therefore was not acting in the execution of his duty. The difficulty is that the judgment nowhere specifies in what respect P's act was unlawful. He simply stood in front of the car. It has been pertinently asked, why, if it was not an unlawful act, was it not one that P might properly do in fulfilment of

---

20. *Lamb* [1990] Crim LR 58, DC.

1. Code of Practice C. 38 (1st ed., issued under the Police and Criminal Evidence Act 1984); *Weight v Long* [1986] Crim LR 746.

2. *Kenlin v Gardner* [1967] 2 QB 510, [1966] 3 All ER 931 *Ludlow v Burgess* [1971] Crim LR 238. Cf. *Daniel v Morrison* (1980) 70 Cr App Rep 142, DC.

3. *Donnelly v Jackman* [1970] 1 All ER 987; **SHC 375**, criticised in [1970] Crim LR at 220 and 33 MLR 438; and followed in *Pounder v Police* [1971] NZLR 1808 (constable committing "a trivial trespass"). Cf. *Squires v Botwright* [1972] RTR 462, DC; *Inwood* [1973] 2 All ER 645, CA. See Lanham, "Arrest, Detention and Compulsion" [1974] Crim LR 288.

4. *Collins v Wilcock* [1984] 3 All ER 374 at 378, above, p. 403.

5. [1982] Crim LR 825, DC and commentary.

6. [1964] 1 QB 164, [1963] 3 All ER 659.

7. The case has since been doubted on this point: *Ghani v Jones* [1970] 1 QB 693 at 707, CA. Where a constable in uniform requires a vehicle to stop under s. 163 of the Road Traffic Act 1988, the driver commits an offence if he fails to do so. He has a duty to remain at rest for a reasonable period; but it seems that the constable has no right under the section physically to stop or to detain the driver or vehicle: *Lodwick v Sanders* [1985] 1 All ER 577 at 582–584 [1985] Crim LR 210, per Webster J. But if the constable reasonably suspects the vehicle to be stolen by the driver he is entitled to seize and detain it and arrest the driver: ibid; *Sanders v DPP* [1988] Crim LR 605, DC.

the general duty to bring offenders to justice?[8] It may be, however, that the answer is that P was guilty of obstructing the highway under the Highways Act 1959;[9] but there was no finding that the road was a highway.

Probably the most important application of the provision is in the context of the constable's duty to prevent breaches of the peace which he reasonably apprehends.[10] If it appears (i) that facts existed from which a constable could reasonably have anticipated a breach, as a real and not merely as a remote possibility; and (ii) that he did so anticipate, then he is under a duty to take such steps, whether by arrest or otherwise,[11] as he reasonably thinks are necessary.[12] In *Piddington v Bates*, it was held that P was acting in the course of his duty in forbidding D to join two persons picketing the entrance to certain premises. Notwithstanding the provisions of the Trade Disputes Act 1906, and now the Trade Union and Labour Relations Act 1974,[13] authorising "one or more" persons to picket, the police have a duty to limit the number of pickets if it is necessary to maintain the peace.

Even where no breach of the peace is anticipated, a constable may be under a duty to give instructions to members of the public – for example, to remove an obstruction from the highway – and a deliberate refusal to obey such an instruction may amount to an obstruction of the police. It is in the course of a constable's duty to require pickets to move where they would otherwise obstruct lawful passage on the highway by others.[14]

A constable who makes a lawful arrest is acting in the execution of his duty even though the arrest subsequently becomes unlawful when he fails to communicate the ground to the arrestee.[15]

2 Mens Rea in Cases of Assault and Resistance

The only *mens rea* required is that of assault, or an intention to resist, as the case may be; and it is no defence that D was reasonably unaware that P was a constable, still less that he was on duty. It was so held by a recorder in a direction to a jury in *Forbes*[16] *and Webb* which six judges in *Prince*[17] accepted as correct; and in *Maxwell*[18] *and Clanchy* the Court of Criminal Appeal, holding that there was evidence to support a jury's finding that D knew P was a policeman, said, obiter, that they wished to cast no doubt on *Forbes*; it was followed in *Mark*;[19] and in *Reynhoudt*[20] a majority of the High Court of Australia (Taylor, Menzies and Owen JJ, Dixon CJ and

8. See "The Arrest of a Motor-Car", by P. J. Fitzgerald, [1965] Crim LR 23.
9. Now s. 137 of the Highways Act 1980.
10. *Duncan v Jones* [1936] KB 218.
11. *King v Hodges* [1974] Crim LR 424.
12. *Piddington v Bates* [1960] 3 All ER 660.
13. Section 15.
14. *Kavanagh v Hiscock* [1974] QB 600, [1974] 2 All ER 177, CA, applying *Broome v Director of Public Prosecutions* [1974] AC 587, [1974] 1 All ER 314, HL.
15. *DPP v Hawkins* [1988] 3 All ER 673, [1988] Crim LR 741.
16. (1865) 10 Cox CC 362.
17. (1875) LR 2 CCR 154.
18. (1909) 73 JP 176, 2 Cr App Rep 26.
19. [1961] Crim LR 173 (Judge Maxwell Turner).
20. (1962) 36 ALJR 26.

Kitto J dissenting) arrived at a similar result on the construction of the equivalent provision in Victorian legislation. It is submitted that the better view is that of the dissenting judges in *Reynhoudt* – that at least the chance of P's being a peace officer in the execution of his duty must be foreseen by D when he makes the assault.[1] Such a view avoids any difficulty arising from the fact that s. 36[2] of the 1861 Act uses the words "to the knowledge of the offender", whereas no such words were used in s. 38 or its successor.

Nevertheless, the present English law is that laid down in *Forbes*. This is implicit in *McBride v Turnock*,[3] where D struck at O, who was not a constable, and hit P, who was. Although he had no intention of assaulting P, the Divisional Court held he was guilty of assaulting a constable in the execution of his duty. The *mens rea* for this crime being only that of a common assault, D's "malice" was transferable.[4] No better illustration could be given of the unsatisfactory nature of the rule in *Forbes*.

If D, whether reasonably or not, is unaware that P is a constable and believes in the existence of circumstances of justification or excuse, he should now have a defence.[5] If, however, D knows that P is a constable, it seems that even an honest and reasonable belief that the constable is acting outside the course of his duty will not always be a defence, if the belief is mistaken. In *Fennell*[6] the court assumed that a father might lawfully use reasonable force to free his son from unlawful arrest by the police; but he acted at his peril and, if the arrest proved to be lawful, he was guilty. The court thought it would be otherwise if D mistakenly believed that a relative or friend was in imminent danger of injury and used reasonable force to prevent that.

3 Wilful Obstruction[7]

a) *The meaning of obstruction.* There must be obstruction in fact. An act done with intent to obstruct but which fails to do so is not the offence – but it may be an attempt.[8] A wide interpretation of "obstruction" has been accepted in England. It is not necessary that there should be any interference with the officer himself by physical force or threats. To give a warning to a person who has committed a crime so as to enable him to escape detection by police is enough. Thus in *Betts v Stevens*,[9] D committed the offence by warning drivers who were exceeding the speed limit that there

---

1. This was the view of the majority of the court in *Galvin (No. 2)* [1961] VR 740, overruling *Galvin (No. 1)* [1961] VR 733. Barry J thought actual knowledge necessary. Sholl J adhered to his view in *Galvin (No. 1)* that the offence was one of strict liability. See also *McLeod* (1955) 111 CCC 106.
2. Above, p. 411.
3. [1964] Crim LR 456.
4. Above, p. 74.
5. *Gladstone Williams* [1987] 3 All ER 411, (1984) 78 Cr App Rep 276, above, p. 89. *Mark*, supra, requiring reasonable grounds for the belief, can no longer be regarded as good law.
6. [1971] 1 QB 428, [1970] 3 All ER 215, [1970] Crim LR 581 and commentary, CA; and cf. *Ball* (1989) 90 Cr App Rep 378, [1989] Crim LR 579 and commentary.
7. See Coutts (1956) 19 MLR 411.
8. *Bennett v Bale* [1986] Crim LR 404, DC and commentary.
9. [1910] 1 KB 1.

was a police trap ahead. In the earlier case of *Bastable v Little*[10] it had been held that D was not guilty of the offence when he warned a driver, who was not proved to be committing an offence, of the speed trap. This distinction did not appeal to the divisional court in *Green v Moore*[11] which thought *Bastable v Little* "a very curious decision based on a highly eccentric view of the facts" and one which "should be strictly confined to the facts as the court found them". The court conceded that, if the warning was addressed to motorists who had not exceeded the speed limit and was intended to discourage them from *ever* doing so, the decision was right. But they thought that a more realistic view of the facts was that D intended to warn the drivers to slow down until they had passed through the speed trap, after which they might race away with impunity. So the distinction is between advising a person to *suspend* his criminal activity, so that he will not be found out by the police, which is an offence; and advising him to give it up altogether – in which case he will not be found out by the police – which is not an offence. In *Green v Moore*, D was a probationer constable who "tipped off" the landlord of his local pub that a police "support group" were waiting to catch him in the dastardly act of selling liquor out of hours. Thereafter, naturally, the landlord kept strictly within the letter of the law. D was aware that "the landlord did not give a high priority to the strict observance of licensing hours", and the court construed his warning as one that the sale of liquor out of hours had better be *suspended* until the support group moved on to deal with some other nefarious activity. If he had said, "Fred, the sale of liquor out of hours simply isn't on – give it up, once and for all" – the efforts of the support group would have been equally frustrated, but that would have been no offence. The "suspension theory" can only operate where the person "tipped off" is known or believed to be engaged in a continuing criminal activity or system. If he is dissuaded from persisting in what is or appears to be a "one-off" offence, which he is about to commit, there is no room for the suspension theory. In *Green v Moore*, D knew of the landlord's illegal practice.

Where the police tell an offender to desist from an offence his deliberate refusal may amount to an obstruction, as where D is obstructing the highway and refuses to obey the instructions of a constable to move.[12] It is not necessary that the constable should anticipate a breach of the peace. But a constable has no power to arrest D for obstructing him, unless the obstruction was such that it actually caused, or was likely to cause, a breach of the peace.[13]

Presumably it must be proved that some named officer was obstructed;[14] it would hardly be enough that D warned E in general terms that if he did not stop committing an offence he would be found out; or if he advised E to get a television licence because the detector van was visiting his street next

---

10. [1907] 1 KB 59.
11. [1982] QB 1044, [1982] 1 All ER 428. Cf. *Moore v Green* [1983] 1 All ER 663, DC.
12. *Tynan v Balmer* [1967] 1 QB 91, [1966] 2 All ER 133; *Donaldson v Police* [1968] NZLR 32.
13. *Wershof v Metropolitan Police Comr* [1978] 3 All ER 540 (May J); *Gelberg v Miller* [1961] 1 All ER 291, [1961] 1 WLR 153; *Riley v DPP* [1990] Crim LR 422, DC.
14. *Syce v Harrison* [1981] Crim LR 110.

week – apart from the fact that the operators of the van would not be constables.

Hinchliffe v Sheldon[15] might be thought to go further than *Betts v Stevens*[16] in that it was only suspected, and not proved, that an offence was being committed; but there the warning was tantamount to a physical obstruction.[17] D, a publican's son, shouted a warning to his parents that the police were outside the public house. It was 11.17 p.m. and the lights were on in the bar, so presumably the police suspected that liquor was being consumed after hours. There was a delay of eight minutes before the police were admitted and no offence was detected. *Bastable v Little*[18] was distinguished on the ground that the police had a right to enter the licensed premises under the Licensing Act 1953.[19] Whether an offence was being committed or not, an entry under this statutory right was in execution of their duty; and their *entry* was obstructed.

Lord Goddard CJ defined "obstructing" as

"Making it more difficult for the police to carry out their duties."[20]

This is far wider than was necessary for the decision. But the dictum has been applied in New Zealand in a case where D, a bystander, merely advised E not to answer any questions put to him by P, a police officer, investigating a suspected offence.[1] E was perfectly entitled to remain silent but his doing so undoubtedly made it more difficult for P to carry out his duty of investigating crime. An earlier decision[2] in the Supreme Court of Victoria is to the contrary and is to be preferred. Surely a solicitor who advises his client to say nothing cannot be guilty of an offence, though he undoubtedly makes things more difficult for the police; and why should a solicitor be in a different situation from anyone else?

In England, it has been held that refusal to answer a constable's question, though it undoubtedly makes it more difficult for the police to carry out their duties, does not amount to wilful obstruction: *Rice v Connolly*.[3] The fact that the refusal is expressed in abusive and obscene terms should in principle make no difference.[4] If D's language amounts to some other offence, such as that under the Public Order Act 1986, s. 4,[5] he should be charged with that. *Ricketts v Cox*[6] seems a doubtful decision. The court accepted the finding of the justices that the "totality of [the defendants'] behaviour and attitude at this stage amounted to an obstruction . . .", but

---

15. [1955] 3 All ER 406, [1955] 1 WLR 1207.
16. Above, p. 418.
17. See Coutts, op. cit.
18. Above, p. 418.
19. See now Licensing Act 1964, s. 186(1). The police must have reasonable grounds for suspecting that an offence is being or is about to be committed: *Valentine v Jackson* [1972] 1 All ER 90, [1972] 1 WLR 528.
20. [1955] 3 All ER at 408.
1. *Steele v Kingsbeer* [1957] NZLR 552; distinguished in *Dash v Police* [1970] NZLR 273 (solicited advice, disinterestedly given, to a motorist not to take a breath test, which he was not bound to take; held, not "wilful" obstruction).
2. *Hogben v Chandler* [1940] VLR 285.
3. [1966] 2 QB 414, [1966] 2 All ER 649, DC.
4. See Marshall J in *Rice v Connolly* at 420.
5. Below, p. 757.
6. (1981) 74 Cr App Rep 298, DC.

all that could be added to the total was the abusive, obscene and hostile attitude of the defendants, reprehensible, no doubt, and galling to the officers but still the assertion of an actual right.[7] While the report does refer to some unspecified threat by D, the court attaches no particular significance to it and the decision seems to be based on the generally "obstructive" nature of D's behaviour.

Telling the police a false story is quite different from merely remaining silent and clearly an obstruction.[8] Refusing to reveal the whereabouts of a prohibited drug is not an obstruction; but burying it to hide it from an officer searching for it might be, when the officer's task is made more difficult.[9] These difficulties would not arise if the Act had been held to be limited to physical interference; and it has been held[10] to be so limited in Scotland where "obstruct" has been construed ejusdem generis with "assault" and "resist".[11] D was held not guilty when he told lies to the police to conceal an offence of which he was guilty. There is much to be said in favour of the Scottish view.[12]

One who is guilty of obstruction is, ex hypothesi, in breach of a legal duty; but it is not necessary that the act relied on as an obstruction should be unlawful independently of its operation as an obstruction of the police.[13] It appears that the conferment of powers and imposition of duties on the police, may, impliedly, impose duties on others not to impede the exercise by the police of these powers and duties. The right of a constable to enter licensed premises when he reasonably suspects an offence is being committed implies a duty under the Police Act on the licensee and others to let him in.[14] The right of a constable to require a driver in certain circumstances to provide a specimen of breath[15] implies a duty on the motorist (though he has not been arrested) to remain "there or nearby" until 20 minutes have elapsed since he had his last drink and the constable has had a reasonable opportunity to carry out the test.[16] Since the consumption of further alcohol will render impossible a valid breath test, which it is the constable's right to take, the driver is also under an implied duty not to drink alcohol. So it will amount to obstruction if, knowing that a breath test may be required, the driver runs away or consumes alcohol[17] whether or not the police have arrived on the scene.[18] If, when D is found to have consumed an

7. See commentary at [1982] Crim LR 184. The partial retraction by the commentator at [1982] Crim LR 484 seems unnecessary.
8. *Rice v Connolly* (above); *Mathews v Dwan* [1949] NZLR 1037.
9. See note on *Syce v Harrison* [1981] Crim LR 110n.
10. *Curlett v M'Kechnie* 1938 SCJ 176.
11. The re-arrangement of these offences by the Police Act precludes the application of the *ejusdem generis* rule; but it could have been applied when they were contained in the Offences against the Person Act 1861.
12. See Coutts, op. cit.
13. *Dibble v Ingleton* [1972] 1 QB 480, [1972] 1 All ER 275. See [1972] CLJ 193.
14. *Hinchliffe v Sheldon*, above, p. 419.
15. Road Traffic Act 1988, s. 7.
16. *Director of Public Prosecutions v Carey* [1970] AC 1072 at 1097, [1969] 3 All ER 1662 at 1680.
17. *Dibble v Ingleton* above. *Cunliffe v Bleasdale* [1972] Crim LR 567, per Melford Stevenson J. Cf. *Britton* [1973] RTR 502, CA.
18. *Neal v Evans* [1976] RTR 333, [1976] Crim LR 384.

excess of alcohol, it is the duty of a constable to remove D's car from the highway, there is an implied duty on D to hand over the keys of the car.[19]

Whether a duty thus to co-operate with the police is to be implied depends on whether this is a compelling inference from the nature of the police duty or right. To some extent it is a question of policy – witness the ruling that there is no duty to answer police questions but there is a duty not to give misleading answers.[20] In *Dibble v Ingleton*[1] the court distinguished between "positive acts" which will amount to obstruction and omissions which will not. Of course, here as elsewhere,[2] the law penalises acts more readily than omissions but this is only one factor and omissions may amount to obstruction even when the omission is not an offence independently of s. 51.[3]

b) *Mens rea*. Unlike "assault" and "resist", obstruction must be "wilful". D must intend to behave in such a way as to make it more difficult for the police to carry out their duties. His conduct need be neither hostile to, nor aimed at, the police, as some cases[4] have suggested: *Lewis v Cox*[5] where D persisted in opening the door of a van in which Q, who had been arrested, was about to be driven away. D's purpose was not to obstruct the police but to find out where Q was being taken, but, since he must have known that he was preventing the police officer from driving off, the justices were bound to find that he intended to make it more difficult for them to carry out their duty.[6] Similarly in *Hills v Ellis*[7] where D laid his hand on a constable's arm to draw his attention to the fact that, as D believed, he was arresting the wrong man. *Forbes* is inapplicable to a charge of obstruction. In *Ostler v Elliott*[8] it was held that D's reasonable belief that the police officers were robbers was a defence to wilful obstruction. Since *Gladstone Williams*[9] the only question would be whether the belief was truly held, reasonably or not.

In *Rice v Connolly*[10] it was said that "wilfully" means not only "intentionally" but also "without lawful excuse." This is difficult to follow. "Wilfully" must surely refer to the state of mind of the defendant. But whether he has a lawful excuse for what he does generally depends on D's conduct and the circumstances in which he acts.[11] In that case, D would have been no more "wilful" if he had told a false story. The difference seems to lie in the conduct which the court considers to be permissible.

19. *Stunt v Bolton* [1972] RTR 435, [1972] Crim LR 561.
20. *Rice v Connolly*, above.
  1. Above.
  2. Above, p. 45.
  3. For example, *Stunt v Bolton*, above.
  4. *Willmott v Atack* [1977] QB 498, [1976] 3 All ER 794; *Hills v Ellis* [1983] QB 680, [1983] 1 All ER 667.
  5. [1984] 3 All ER 672, [1985] QB 509.
  6. Cf. the discussion of intention, above, p. 53.
  7. Above, fn. 4.
  8. [1980] Crim LR 584. Note that, if he had assaulted the officers, his reasonable belief that they were not officers would not, in itself, have been a defence to a charge of assaulting them in the execution of their duty. See commentary at [1980] Crim LR 585.
  9. [1987] 3 All ER 411, (1983) 78 Cr App Rep 276, CA, above, p. 89.
10. Above, p. 420.
11. See comment at [1966] Crim LR 390.

"Wilfully" may of course import the absence of any *belief* on D's part of circumstances of lawful excuse. If the story told by D were in fact false, but D believed it to be true, the constable might be obstructed, but he would not be "wilfully" obstructed.

3) *Assault Occasioning Actual Bodily Harm*

By s. 47 of the OAPA 1861:

> "whosoever shall be convicted on indictment of any assault occasioning actual bodily harm shall be liable to imprisonment for not more than five years".

The offence is triable either way. On its face, the section does not appear to create an offence but merely to provide a higher penalty for an assault at common law where actual bodily harm is occasioned. Consequently the offence was treated as a common law offence until the decision in *Courtie*[12], – and indeed for a period thereafter because it took some time for "the penny to drop". We now know that s. 47 created a separate statutory offence[13] or, more accurately, two offences, assault and battery. Lord Ackner in *Savage*[14] at one point describes the *mens rea* of the offence exclusively in terms of the battery and, at another, exclusively in terms of the assault. It is safe to assume that there are two offences and that their constituents, so far as the word "assault" goes, are precisely the same as those of common assault and battery. Once that assault or battery is proved, it remains only to prove that it occasioned actual bodily harm, a question of causation, not requiring proof of any further *mens rea* or fault. This was established in *Roberts*[15] where D in a moving car "assaulted" P by trying to take off her coat (a battery), whereupon she jumped out and sustained injury. It was held that the only question was whether the "assault" caused P's action – only if it was something that no reasonable man could be expected to foresee would the chain of causation be broken.[16] It is now firmly established that this is the law, after a remarkable series of cases had thrown the matter into doubt. In *Spratt*[17] the court, very properly overruling *DPP v K*,[18] held that only *Cunningham*, not *Caldwell*, reckless-ness would suffice to establish the assault but then went on, not referring to *Roberts*, to hold there must be recklessness as to the occasioning of actual bodily harm. *Savage*,[19] decided on the same day, applied the law as stated in *Roberts* but without reference to that case. In *Parmenter*[20] the court, confronted with this conflict, preferred *Spratt*, again without reference to

---

12. [1984] AC 463, [1984] 1 All ER 740, HL, above, p. 32.
13. *Harrow Justices, ex p Osaseri* [1986] QB 589, [1985] 3 All ER 185, DC.
14. [1991] 4 All ER 698 at 707 and 711.
15. (1971) 56 Cr App Rep 95, [1972] Crim LR 27.
16. Cf. *William, Davis*, above, p. 339.
17. [1991] 2 All ER 210, [1990] 1 WLR 1073.
18. [1990] 1 All ER 331, 91 Cr App Rep 23.
19. [1991] 2 All ER 220.
20. [1991] 2 All ER 225, [1991] 2 WLR 408, CA.

Roberts. Hearing appeals in *Savage* and *Parmenter*, the House of Lords held that the law was correctly stated in *Roberts*, reversing *Parmenter* and overruling *Spratt* on this point.[1]

"Bodily harm", according to the House of Lords in *Director of Public Prosecutions v Smith*[2] "needs no explanation. 'Grievous' means no more and no less than 'really serious'." It seems to follow that, under s. 47, the harm need not be really serious. In *Miller*,[3] Lynskey J quoted the statement formerly contained in Archbold:[4]

"Actual bodily harm includes any hurt or injury calculated to interfere with the health or comfort of the prosecutor . . ."

Lynskey J held that this included a hysterical and nervous condition resulting from an assault, taking the view that an injury to the state of a man's mind is actual bodily harm.

The co-existence of this offence with that of maliciously inflicting grievous bodily harm contrary to s. 20 of the same Act, also punishable with a maximum of five years, makes no sense. The prosecutor's task is slightly easier under s. 47 since he does not need to prove even that foresight of slight bodily harm which is necessary under s. 20. He does have to prove an assault or battery which is not necessary under s. 20 but since s. 20 requires proof of a direct application of force this is a distinction with no substantial difference. Section 20 is regarded in practice as the more serious offence. In *Parmenter*[5] the Court of Appeal said that—

"although the sentences imposed in practice for the worst s. 47 offences will overlap those imposed at the lower end of s. 20, nobody could doubt that the two offences are seen in quite different terms, whether by defendants and their advisers contemplating pleas of guilty, or by judges passing sentence under s. 47 on defendants whose pleas of guilty have been accepted by the prosecution, or by subsequent sentencers casting an eye down lists of previous convictions."

4 Wounding and Grievous Bodily Harm

Sections 18 and 20 of the Offences against the Person Act 1861 create offences of wounding and causing or inflicting grievous bodily harm. By s. 18, as amended by the Criminal Law Act 1967:

"Whosoever shall unlawfully and maliciously by any means whatsoever wound or cause any grievous bodily harm to any person with intent to do some grievous bodily harm to any person or with intent to resist or prevent the lawful apprehension or detainer of any person, shall be guilty

1. [1991] 4 All ER 698.
2. [1961] AC 290 at 334, [1960] 3 All ER 161 at 171; Above, p. 347.
3. [1954] 2 QB 282 at 292, [1954] 2 All ER 529 at 534; **SHC 366**. Cf. *Burrell v Harmer* [1967] Crim LR 169 and commentary thereon; above, p. 406.
4. 32nd ed., 959.
5. [1991] 2 All ER at 233.

of [an offence triable only on indictment], and being convicted thereof shall be liable to imprisonment for life."

By s. 20:

"Whosoever shall unlawfully and maliciously wound or inflict any grievous bodily harm upon any other person, either with or without any weapon or instrument shall be guilty of [an offence triable either way] and being convicted thereof shall be liable to imprisonment for five years."

The two sections are closely associated with one another and it is convenient to consider them together. Each creates two offences, one of wounding and the other of causing (s. 18) or inflicting (s. 20) grievous bodily harm.

1) *The Actus Reus*

1 To Wound

In order to constitute a wound, the continuity of the whole skin must be broken.[6] Where a pellet fired by an air pistol hit P in the eye but caused only an internal rupturing of blood vessels and not a break in the skin, there was no wound.[7] It is not enough that the cuticle or outer skin be broken if the inner skin remains intact.[8] Where P was treated with such violence that his collarbone was broken, it was held that there was no wound if his skin was intact.[9] It was held to be a wound, however, where the lining membrane of the urethra was ruptured and bled, evidence being given that the membrane is precisely the same in character as that which lines the cheek and the external and internal skin of the lip.[10]

It was held that there was no wounding under the 1837 Act[11] where P, in warding off D's attempt to cut his throat, struck his hands against a knife held by D and cut them;[12] and where P was knocked down by D and wounded by falling on iron trams.[13] That Act did not contain the words "by any means whatsoever", and it is probable that these cases would now be decided differently. Even under the earlier law, D was guilty where he struck P on the hat with a gun and the hard rim of the hat caused a wound.[14]

It was formerly held that wounding must be the result of a battery but it is probably now sufficient that the wound be directly inflicted whether by a battery or not.[15]

---

6. *Moriarty v Brookes* (1834) 6 C & P 684.
7. *C (a minor) v Eisenhower* [1984] QB 331, (1983) 78 Cr App Rep 48, DC.
8. *M'Loughlin* (1838) 8 C & P 635.
9. *Wood* (1830) 1 Mood CC 278.
10. *Waltham* (1849) 3 Cox CC 442. Contrast *Jones* (1849) 3 Cox CC 441.
11. 7 Will. 4 & 1 Vic. c. 85, s. 4.
12. *Beckett* (1836) 1 Mood & R 526 (Parke B); *Day* (1845) 1 Cox CC 207; above, p. 404. Cf. *Coleman* (1920) 84 JP 112.
13. *Spooner* (1853) 6 Cox CC 392.
14. *Sheard* (1837) 2 Mood CC 13.
15. *Wilson*, below, fn. 1. Cf. *Taylor* (1869) LR 1 CCR 194; *Austin* (1973) 58 Cr App Rep 163, CA.

2 To Cause or Inflict Grievous Bodily Harm

"Grievous bodily harm" was formerly interpreted to include any harm which seriously interferes with health or comfort;[16] but in *Smith*[17] the House of Lords said that there was no warrant for giving the words a meaning other than that which they convey in their ordinary and natural meaning. Grievous bodily harm may cover cases where there is no wounding as, for instance, the broken collarbone in *Wood*.[18] Conversely, there might be a technical "wounding" which could not be said to amount to grievous bodily harm.

Where s. 18 uses the word "cause", s. 20 uses "inflict". The effect is that s. 18 may be wider than s. 20. In a series of cases[19] from 1861 until 1983 it was held or assumed that the words "inflict" and "wound" both imply an "assault". D could be convicted of an offence under s. 20 only if it was proved that he wounded or caused grievous bodily harm by committing an assault. It followed that, when D was charged with an offence under s. 20, he could be convicted on that indictment of common assault, because that was an "included offence". But there was a second line of cases[20] where the alleged requirement of an assault was simply ignored and convictions were upheld although it was very difficult, if not impossible, to discern an assault on the facts.

In 1983, in *Wilson*,[1] the House of Lords resolved the matter by deciding that "inflict" does not, after all, imply assault.[2] The House followed the Australian case of *Salisbury*[3] where it was said that, though "inflict" does not imply assault, it does have a narrower meaning than "cause". Unlike "cause", "inflict" implies the direct application of force. This, however, is almost a distinction without a difference for the direct application of force usually is an assault – or, strictly, a battery, which is probably what "assault" meant in this context. *Wilson* dispenses us from the need to look for an assault in this second line of cases, but the requirement of directness presents equal difficulties. In those cases D was held guilty under s. 20 where, for example, he so frightened P that he jumped through a window[4] or accidentally injured himself by putting his hand through a glass door under[5] "a well-grounded apprehension of violence". Similarly in *Martin*[6] where, shortly before the end of a performance in a theatre. D put out the

16. *Ashman* (1858) 1 F & F 88.
17. [1961] AC 290, [1960] 3 All ER 161; above, p. 347; followed in *Metharam* [1961] 3 All ER 200.
18. Above, fn. 9.
19. *Yeadon and Birch* (1861) 9 Cox CC 91; *Taylor* (1869) LR 1 CCR 194; *Clarence* (1888) 22 QBD 23; *Snewing* [1972] Crim LR 267; *Carpenter* (30 July 1979, unreported, cited [1983] 1 All ER 1004).
20. *Halliday* (1889) 61 LT 701; *Lewis* [1970] Crim LR 647, CA; *Mackie* [1973] Crim LR 54; *Boswell* [1973] Crim LR 307 and *Cartledge v Allen* [1973] Crim LR 530, DC.
1. [1984] AC 242 at 260, [1983] 3 All ER 448 at 455.
2. The House nevertheless contrived to hold that a person charged under s. 20 could be convicted on that indictment of a common assault by virtue of s. 6(3) of the Criminal Law Act 1967 – a much criticised decision but approved by the House in *Savage* [1991] 4 All ER 698 at 711. See Glanville Williams, [1984] CLJ 290 and commentary at [1984] Crim LR 37.
3. [1976] VR 452 at 461.
4. *Halliday* (1889) 61 LT 701.
5. *Cartledge v Allen* [1973] Crim LR 530.
6. (1881) 8 QBD 54 CCR.

lights and placed an iron bar across the doorway. He was convicted of inflicting grievous bodily harm on those injured in the panic. We need no longer search for the invisible assault in these cases, but it is almost equally difficult to discern any *direct* application of force. Certainly force was applied in each case in the sense that there was an impact, causing injury to P. The presence of force in this sense is sufficient to distinguish *Clarence*,[7] the leading authority for the overruled proposition that inflict implies assault. D, knowing that he was suffering from gonorrhea, had intercourse with his wife and infected her. No doubt he had caused her grievous bodily harm but the court held that he had not "inflicted" it because he had not committed an assault. Today, he might be acquitted on the different ground that, because P consented (though in ignorance of his condition), there was no application of force. The actual decision in *Clarence* has not been overruled. In that case, the harm was surely caused "directly" so the distinguishing feature appears to be simply "force". The position appears to be that if force is applied, directly or indirectly by D, harm is "inflicted". If harm is caused without the use of force, it is not inflicted, but, if grievous, and intentionally caused, it may be the subject of an indictment under s. 18.

2) *The Mens Rea*

1 Malice

Both sections contain the word "maliciously". It is settled that this word means "intentionally or recklessly" and "reckless" is used in the *Cunningham*, not the *Caldwell*, sense.[8] The next question is, what is "the particular kind of harm" that must be intended or foreseen? The answer might be expected to be, wounding or grievous bodily harm;[9] but the law has developed differently. It is enough that D foresaw that some physical harm, not necessarily amounting to grievous bodily harm or wounding, might occur.[10] It is not enough, however, that D intended to frighten, whether the charge is one of wounding or inflicting grievous bodily harm.[11] Diplock LJ said in *Mowatt*:[12]

"... the word 'maliciously' does import upon the part of the person who unlawfully inflicts the wound or other grievous bodily harm an awareness that his act may have the consequence of causing some physical harm to some other person. That is what is meant by 'the particular kind of harm' in the citation from Professor Kenny.[13] It is quite unnecessary

7. (1888) 22 QBD 23.
8. Above, p. 62. *Savage* and *Parmenter* [1991] 4 All ER at 721, HL, affirming *Mowatt* [1968] 1 QB 421, [1967] 3 All ER 47; **SHC 69**.
9. Cf. above, p. 70.
10. Above, fn. 8.
11. *Flack v Hunt* (1979) 70 Cr App Rep 51; *Sullivan* [1981] Crim LR 46, CA.
12. [1968] 1 QB 421 at 426, [1967] 3 All ER 47 at 50.
13. *Outlines of Criminal Law* (19th ed.) 211. The citation is the passage approved by the Court of Criminal Appeal in *Cunningham* [1957] 2 QB 396, [1957] 2 All ER 412; **SHC 67**; above, p. 61; below, p. 430.

that the accused should have foreseen that his unlawful act might cause physical harm of the gravity described in [s. 20], i.e., a wound or serious physical injury. It is enough that he should have foreseen that some physical harm to some person, albeit of a minor character, might result."

Where, under s. 18, the charge is of causing grievous bodily harm with intent to do grievous bodily harm, the word "maliciously" obviously has no part to play. Any *mens rea* which it might import is comprehended within the ulterior intent. Even if "wounding" is not foreseen, it is "malicious". Where the charge is of wounding or causing grievous bodily harm with intent to resist lawful apprehension, there is no difficulty in giving meaning to "maliciously" and it is submitted that meaning should be given to that word. A mere intent to resist lawful apprehension should not found liability for a charge of wounding or causing grievous bodily harm. It is submitted that the Court of Appeal went too far in *Mowatt*[14] in saying that "In section 18 the word 'maliciously' adds nothing."

It is clear that there must be proof that the accused actually foresaw the specified result. Any doubt there may have been about this was dispelled by the Criminal Justice Act 1967, s. 8.[15] *Mowatt* was decided before the Act came into force, and certain observations in the case are therefore suspect. It was said[16] that where the act:

". . . was a direct assault which any ordinary person would be bound to realise was likely to cause some physical harm to the other person . . . and the defence put forward on behalf of the accused is not that the assault was accidental or that he did not realise that it might cause some physical harm to the victim, but is some other defence such as that he did not do the alleged act or that he did it in self-defence, it is unnecessary to deal specifically in the summing up with what is meant by the word 'maliciously' in the section."

This suggests that the jury need not be directed on the issue because they are bound to infer that D foresaw the result by reason of its being a natural and probable consequence of his actions. This is directly contrary to the words of s. 8. Under s. 10 of the Criminal Justice Act 1967, formal admissions may be made; but, if D has not admitted his malice, then it is submitted that it must be proved like every other element in the crime. The fact that the evidence appears to the judge to be overwhelming is not a good reason for not leaving it to the jury.

2 The Ulterior Intent

Section 18 alone requires an ulterior intent which may be either an intent to do grievous bodily harm or an intent to resist or prevent the lawful apprehension or detainer of any person. Recklessness is not enough.[17] A count is not bad for duplicity because it specifies the ulterior intent in the alternative; the intents specified "are variations of method rather than

14. [1968] 1 QB 421, [1967] 3 All ER 47; **SHC 69**. See Buxton, "Negligence and Constructive Crime" [1969] Crim LR 112. See also *Ward* (1872) LR 1 CCR 356.
15. Above, p. 86.
16. [1968] 1 QB 421 at 426–427, [1967] 3 All ER 47 at 50.
17. *Re Knight's Appeal* (1968) 12 FLR 81.

creations of separate offences in themselves", according to *Naismith*[18] – though it is difficult to see how an ulterior intent can be equated with a "method".

The intent specified in the indictment must be proved. It is not enough to prove another variety of intent described in the section. So D had to be acquitted where the various counts of the indictment charged intent to murder, to disable, or to do some grievous bodily harm and the jury found that the acts were done to resist and prevent D's apprehension *and for no other purpose*.[19] But if D intends to prevent his apprehension and, in order to do so, intends to cause grievous bodily harm, he may be convicted under an indictment charging only the latter intent. It is immaterial which is the principal and which the subordinate intent.[20]

Intention has the same meaning as in the law of murder[1] so the prosecution must prove either (i) that it was D's purpose to cause grievous bodily harm or, if it was not his purpose, (ii) that he knew that grievous bodily harm was a virtually certain consequence of his act. In case (ii), that is evidence from which the jury may infer that he had the requisite intent.[2]

If D intends to cause grievous bodily harm to O and, striking at O, he by accident wounds another person P, he may be indicted for wounding P with intent to cause grievous bodily harm to O.[3] If D intends to cause grievous bodily harm to O, and strikes the person he aims at who is in fact P, he may be convicted of wounding P with intent to cause grievous bodily harm to P.[4]

The intent to resist lawful apprehension is considered above[5] in relation to s. 38 of the Act.

5 Administering Poison

1) *The Actus Reus*

Sections 23 and 24 of the Offences against the Person Act 1861 create offences, punishable with ten and five years' imprisonment respectively, with a similar *actus reus*. In each case, the definition includes the words –

---

18. [1961] 2 All ER 735, [1961] 1 WLR 952. (C-MAC).
19. *Duffin and Marshall* (1818) Russ & Ry 365; cf. *Boyce* (1824) 1 Mood CC 29.
20. *Gillow* (1825) 1 Mood CC 85.
1. *Bryson* [1985] Crim LR 669; cf. *Belfon* [1976] 3 All ER 46, CA.
2. Above, p. 53.
3. *Monger* [1973] Crim LR 301, per Mocatta J holding that D could not be convicted where the indictment alleged intent to harm P. This is in accord with *Ryan* (1839) 2 Mood & R 213 and *Hewlett* (1858) 1 F & F 91 but contrary to *Hunt* (1825) 1 Mood CC 93 and *Jarvis, Langdon and Stear* (1837) 2 Mood & R 40. Cf. the doctrine of transferred malice, above, p. 74 and comment on *Monger* in [1973] Crim LR 302.
4. *Smith* (1855) Dears CC 559 at 560; *Stopford* (1870) 11 Cox CC 643.
5. P. 412.

". . . unlawfully . . . administer to or cause to be administered to or taken by any other person any poison or other destructive or noxious thing. . . ."[6]

But under s. 23, the *actus reus* includes a further element—

". . . so as thereby to endanger the life of such person, or so as thereby to inflict upon such person any grievous bodily harm . . .".

The words "administer" and "take" are to be construed by the court and not left as a question of fact to the jury.[7] The words are disjunctive and "takes" postulates some "ingestion" by the victim. "Administer" includes "conduct which not being the direct application of force to the victim nevertheless brings the noxious thing into contact with his body", as by spraying CS gas into his face.[8]

A poison is "administered" by D if it is left by him for P who takes it up and consumes it;[9] but it seems that it is not administered until it is taken into the stomach.[10] To leave the poison, intending it to be taken, is an attempt, as Wightman J sensibly instructed a jury,[11] but today the judge would have to leave the question to them.[12]

In *Marcus*,[13] a case under s. 24, "noxious" was broadly interpreted. A substance which may be harmless if taken in small quantities is noxious if administered in sufficient quantity to injure, aggrieve or annoy.[14] The meaning is taken to be coloured by the purpose which D may have in view. It is not necessary that the substance should be injurious to bodily health: "by 'noxious' is meant something different in quality from and of less importance than poison or other destructive things." The court quoted the *Shorter Oxford Dictionary* meaning, "injurious, hurtful, harmful, un-wholesome", and opined that the insertion of the celebrated snail in the ginger beer bottle in *Donoghue v Stevenson*[15] with intent to annoy would have amounted to the offence. It was held that the insertion of sedative and sleeping tablets into a bottle of milk was an attempt to commit an offence under s. 24. While the tablets would cause no more than sedation or possibly sleep, they might be a danger to a person doing such normal but potentially hazardous acts as driving or crossing the street.

The court "explained" *Cato*,[16] a case under s. 23, where it was said that a thing could not be noxious merely because it was harmful if taken in large quantities. That observation was not "explicable" but wrong. The actual

---

6. The meaning of poison, etc., is considered above, p. 388.
7. *Gillard* (1988) 87 Cr App Rep 189 at 194.
8. *Gillard*, above.
9. *Harley* (1830) 4 C & P 369; *Dale* (1852) 6 Cox CC 14. D would more appropriately be charged with "causing . . . to be taken".
10. *Cadman* (1825) *Carrington's Supplement*, 237. The report to the contrary in Ryan and Moody 114 is said to be inaccurate: *Harley* (above) per Parke J: and 6 Cox CC 16 n (c). But see *Walford* (1899) 34 L Jo 116, per Wills J.
11. *Dale* (1852) 6 Cox CC 14.
12. Above, p. 310.
13. [1981] 2 All ER 833, [1981] 1 WLR 774, CA.
14. Following *Hennah* (1877) 13 Cox CC 547 and *Cramp* (1880) 5 QBD 307. Cf. *Marlow* (1964) 49 Cr App Rep 49 (Brabin J).
15. [1932] AC 562.
16. [1976] 1 All ER 260, [1976] 1 WLR 110; **SHC 336**; cf. *Dalby* [1982] 1 All ER 916, [1982] 1 WLR 425, CA.

decision, however, that heroin is a noxious thing even where it is administered to a person with a high tolerance to whom it is unlikely to do any
particular harm, is presumably right. Heroin is noxious because "it is liable
to cause injury in common use".[17] It was no answer that P was experienced
in taking heroin and had a high tolerance; nor was P's consent a defence.[18]

Because the interpretation of "noxious" in s. 24 was coloured by the
words, "injure, aggrieve or annoy", it is arguable that in s. 23 the word
must be read in the light of the fact that the substance must endanger life or
inflict grievous bodily harm, and it is indeed difficult to see how a substance
with a potential only to aggrieve or annoy could result in the *actus reus*.

2) *The Mens Rea*

Under s. 23 the only *mens rea* required is intention or recklessness as to the
administration of a noxious thing. This, at least, is plainly required by the
use in the section of the word "maliciously"; and, of course, it has been so
held in the leading case of *Cunningham*.[19] It may be, however, on present
authority, that the requirement of malice does not extend to the second part
of the *actus* – so as to endanger life or inflict grievous bodily harm.

Section 24 requires an ulterior intent:

"with intent to injure aggrieve or annoy such person".

When a drug is given to P with intent to keep him awake, it seems that
whether this amounts to an intention to injure depends on whether D has a
malevolent or a benevolent purpose. If D, a homosexual man, gives the
drug to P, a small boy, with the motive of ingratiating himself with P or
rendering him susceptible to sexual offences, he has an intent to injure:
Hill.[20] It would probably be otherwise if D's intention was to enable P to
stay awake to enjoy the fireworks or greet his father on return from work.
The administration of a drug to the pilot of an aircraft to keep him awake is
probably not an offence. The administration of the same drug for the
purpose of carrying out a prolonged interrogation may be.[1] This casts
doubt on *Weatherall*.[2] D put a sleeping tablet in P's tea to enable him to
search her handbag for letters proving that she was committing adultery. It
was held that there was insufficient evidence of intent to injure, aggrieve or
annoy: but there was surely evidence of a "malevolent" purpose, as there
would be if D gave P a sleeping tablet with intent to rape her. The test of
malevolence is presumably objective. The paedophile's belief that the

17. [1976] 1 All ER at 268.
18. See also *McShane* [1977] Crim LR 737, CA.
19. [1957] 2 QB 396, [1957] 2 All ER 412; **SHC 67**; D tore the gas meter from the wall of an
unoccupied house to steal money from it. The gas seeped into the neighbouring houses and
was taken by P, whose life was endangered. D's conviction under s. 23 was quashed because
the judge directed the jury only that "malicious" meant "wicked". See now Criminal Damage
Act 1971, s. 1 (2), below, p. 704.
20. (1986) 83 Cr App Rep 386, HL; **SHC 373**.
1. Examples taken from *Hill*, above.
2. [1968] Crim LR 115 (Judge Broderick).

drugged child will enjoy and profit from the sexual experience is unlikely to be regarded as capable of being a "benevolent" purpose.

The contrast between "so as thereby to" in s. 23 and "with intent to" in s. 24; suggests that no *mens rea* is required as to the second part of the *actus* in s. 23; and it was so held in *Cato*. The requirement of "malice" was satisfied by the deliberate injection of heroin into P's body. No foresight of danger to life or the infliction of grievous bodily harm was required.

In *Cunningham*, the court thought the jury should have been told that D must have foreseen that the coal gas might cause injury to someone. They did not say he must have foreseen that life would be endangered. This is an extraordinary result, in that a less culpable state of mind is required for the more serious offence than the less.

By s. 25, a person charged under s. 23 may be convicted of an offence under s. 24. But a person charged under s. 24 may not be convicted of an offence under s. 23.[3]

6 False Imprisonment

False imprisonment, like assault and battery, is both a misdemeanour at common law and a tort. The civil remedy is much more commonly invoked and most of the cases on this subject are civil actions. But, as will appear, it is probable that there are some important distinctions between the crime and the tort.

False imprisonment is committed where D unlawfully and intentionally or recklessly restrains P's freedom of movement from a particular place. "Imprisonment" is probably a wider term than, and includes, "arrest".[4]

1) *The Actus Reus*

1 Imprisonment

The "imprisonment" may consist in confining P in a prison,[5] a house,[6] even P's own house,[7] a mine[8] or a vehicle;[9] or simply in detaining P in a public street[10] or any other place. It is not necessary that he be physically detained. There may be an arrest by words alone, but only if P submits. If P is not

---

3. Cf. *Stokes* (1925) 19 Cr App Rep 71.
4. *Rahman* (1985) 81 Cr App Rep 349 at 353, CA. *Brown* [1977] Crim LR 291, CA, and commentary thereon and articles by Telling [1978] Crim LR 320 and Lidstone [1978] Crim LR 332.
5. *Cobbett v Grey* (1850) 4 Exch 729.
6. *Warner v Riddiford* (1858) 4 CB-NS 180.
7. *Termes de la Ley*, approved by Warrington and Atkin LJJ (1920) 122 LT at 51 and 53.
8. *Herd v Weardale Steel, Coal and Coke Co Ltd* [1915] AC 67.
9. By driving at such a speed that P dare not alight: *McDaniel v State* (1942) 15 Tex Crim 115; *Burton v Davies* [1953] QSR 26.
10. Blackstone, *Commentaries*, iii, 127; *Ludlow v Burgess* [1971] Crim LR 238.

physically detained and does not realise he is under constraint he is not imprisoned.[11] If P agrees to go to a police station voluntarily, he has not been arrested though the constable would have arrested him if he had refused to go.[12] If it is then brought home to P that he will not be allowed to leave until he provides a laboratory specimen, it has been suggested that, though he has never been "arrested", he is "under arrest".[13] If the distinction is valid it would seem to be enough for false imprisonment that P is "under arrest". It is enough that D orders P to accompany him to another place and P goes because he feels constrained to do so. P is not imprisoned if, on hearing D use words of arrest, he runs away or makes his escape by a trick.[14] An invitation by D to P to accompany him cannot be an imprisonment if it is made clear to P that he is entitled to refuse to go. Thus Lord Lyndhurst CB thought there was no imprisonment where D asked a policeman to take P into custody, and the policeman objected, but said that if D and P "would be so good as to go with him", he would take the advice of his superior.[15] The distinction between a command, amounting to an imprisonment, and a request not doing so, is a difficult one.[16] Probably Alderson B went too far in *Peters v Stanway*[17] in holding that P was imprisoned if she went to the police station with a constable voluntarily but nevertheless in consequence of a charge against her.

Though some of the older authorities[18] speak of false imprisonment as a species of assault it is quite clear that no assault need be proved.[19] In *Linsberg*,[20] the Common Sergeant held that P, a doctor, was falsely imprisoned where D locked the door to prevent him leaving a confinement. The restraint need be only momentary, so that the offence would be complete if D tapped P on the shoulder and said, "You are my prisoner."[1] But a battery is not necessarily an imprisonment. In *Bird v Jones*[2] P was involved in

"a struggle during which no momentary detention of his person took place."

It is not an imprisonment wrongfully to prevent P from going in a particular direction, if he is free to go in other directions. This was decided in *Bird v Jones*,[3] where Coleridge J said:

"A prison may have its boundary large or narrow, visible and tangible, or, though real, still in the conception only;[4] it may itself be moveable or fixed: but a boundary it must have. . . ."

---

11. *Alderson v Booth* [1969] 2 QB 216, [1969] 2 All ER 271.
12. *Campbell v Tormey* [1969] 1 All ER 961, [1969] 1 WLR 189.
13. Ibid., per Ashworth J.
14. *Russen v Lucas* (1824) 1 C & P 153.
15. *Cant v Parsons* (1834) 6 C & P 504.
16. Williams in *Police Power and Individual Freedom* at p. 43.
17. (1835) 6 C & P 737, followed in *Conn v David Spencer Ltd* [1930] 1 DLR 805.
18. For example, Hawkins, 1 PC, c. 60, §7; *Pocock v Moore* (1825) Ry & M 321.
19. *Grainger v Hill* (1838) 4 Bing NC 212; *Warner v Riddiford* (1858) 4 CB-NS 180.
20. (1905) 69 JP 107.
  1. *Simpson v Hill* (1795) 1 Esp 431, per Eyre CJ; *Sandon v Jervis* (1859) EB & E 942, ". . . a mere touch constitutes an arrest, though the party be not actually taken;" per Crowder J.
  2. Below.
  3. (1845) 7 QB 742 (Denman CJ dissenting).
  4. For example, P is forbidden to move more than ten yards from the village pump.

It would be otherwise if P could move off in other directions only by taking an unreasonable risk;[5] it could hardly be said that a man locked in a second-floor room was not imprisoned because he could have climbed down the drainpipe.

There is little authority on the question how large the area of confinement may be. It has been suggested that it would be tortious to confine P to a large country estate or the Isle of Man;[6] but it could hardly be false imprisonment to prevent P from leaving Great Britain, still less to prevent him from entering. But a person who has actually landed and is not allowed to leave an airport building is imprisoned.[7] Is P also imprisoned, then, if he is not allowed to leave the ship which has docked in a British port?

It has been held by the Court of Appeal, Duke LJ, dissenting, in *Meering v Graham-White Aviation Co Ltd*[8] that it is irrelevant that P does not know he is imprisoned. Atkin LJ said:

"It appears to me that a person could be imprisoned without his knowing it. I think a person can be imprisoned while he is asleep, while he is in a state of drunkenness, while he is unconscious, and while he is a lunatic ... though the imprisonment began and ceased while he was in that state."

A contrary decision of the Court of Exchequer[9] was not cited and the case has been heavily criticised;[10] but the arguments advanced against awarding damages in this situation are not applicable to the crime. D's conduct may not be damaging to P if P knows nothing about it, but it is not necessarily any less blameworthy for, in most cases, the fact that P remains in ignorance must be a matter of mere chance.

Like other crimes, false imprisonment can be committed through an innocent agent. So D is responsible for the *actus reus* if, at his direction or request, a policeman takes P into custody,[11] or he signs the charge-sheet when the police have said they will not take the responsibility of detaining P unless he does;[12] but merely to give information to a constable, in consequence of which he decides to make an arrest has been held not to be actionable, at all events if D is bona fide.[13] A fortiori, it should not be *criminal*, for lack of *mens rea*; but why should D not be guilty if he deliberately supplies false information to a constable who, acting on his

5. Street, *Torts*, 29.
6. Street, *Torts*, 28. In *Re Mwenya* [1960] 1 QB 241, [1959] 3 All ER 525, a writ of *habeas corpus* was sought for P who was confined to an area of some 1,500 square miles but he was released before it became necessary to decide whether he was imprisoned for the purpose of *habeas corpus*.
7. *Kuchenmeister v Home Office* [1958] 1 QB 496, [1958] 1 All ER 485.
8. (1919) 122 LT 44. Two policemen were stationed outside the door of a room to prevent P leaving. He was effectively imprisoned as if the door had been locked. *Meering* was approved in *Murray v Ministry of Defence* [1988] 2 All ER 521 at 529, 1 HL.
9. *Herring v Boyle* (1834) 1 Cr M & R 377.
10. Williams in *Police Power and Individual Freedom* at 45–46; Street, *Torts*, 31.
11. *Gosden v Elphick and Bennett* (1849) 4 Exch 445.
12. *Austin v Dowling* (1870) LR 5 CP 534. It is otherwise if D signs the charge sheet as a matter of form, when the police are detaining P on their own responsibility: *Grinham v Willey* (1859) 4 H & N 496.
13. *Gosden v Elphick and Bennett*, above; *Grinham v Willey*, above; "We ought to take care that people are not put in peril for making complaint when a crime has been committed," per Pollock CB.

own authority but relying exclusively on D's information, arrests P? D has surely caused the *actus reus* with *mens rea* and may be liable for the ministerial act of the constable as distinct from the judicial act of the magistrate.[14] Where D is initially liable for false imprisonment his liability ceases on the intervention of some judicial act[15] authorising the detention or on any other event, breaking the chain of causation.[16]

Whatever may be the position in the law of tort,[17] it is thought that it would be immaterial in the criminal law that the imprisonment was not "directly" caused by D; and that it would be sufficient that he caused it with *mens rea* – as by digging a pit into which P falls and is trapped.[18]

Another question in the law of tort is whether it is possible falsely to imprison by mere omission in view of the requirement of a trespass. In *Herd v Weardale Steel Coal and Coke Co Ltd*[19] P voluntarily descended into D's mine and, in breach of contract, stopped work and asked to be brought to the surface before the end of the shift. D's refusal to accede to this request was not a false imprisonment: he was under no duty to provide facilities for P to leave in breach of contract. Clearly, the result would be different if D were to take positive steps to prevent P from leaving in breach of contract,[20] as by locking him in a factory. Buckley and Hamilton LJJ[1] thought that mere omission could not have been false imprisonment, even if it occurred when the shift was over. P's only civil remedy would have been in contract; but the House of Lords expressed no opinion on this point.

In *Mee v Cruikshank*,[2] Wills J held that a prison governor was under a duty to take steps to ensure that his officers did not detain a prisoner who had been acquitted. In that case there were acts of imprisonment by the prison officers but they were not the servants of D, the governor, and it seems to have been D's omission which rendered him liable in tort. Surely it ought to be false imprisonment if D, a gaoler, is under a duty to release P at midnight and deliberately omits to unlock his cell until noon the following day?[3] And it ought to make no difference that D's duty to release P arises out of a contract:

---

14. See *Austin v Dowling* (1870) LR 5 C & P 534 at 540.
15. *Lock v Ashton* (1848) 12 QB 871. Cf. *Marrinan v Vibart* [1963] 1 QB 528, [1962] 3 All ER 380.
16. *Harnett v Bond* [1925] AC 669. D's report caused P to be taken to an asylum; D was not liable for the imprisonment after the doctor at the asylum had examined P and decided to detain him. Cf. *Pike v Waldrum* [1952] 1 Lloyds Rep 431.
17. Street, *Torts*, 30.
18. Cf. *Clarence* (1888) 22 QBD 23 at 36, per Wills J.
19. [1915] AC 67, HL.
20. Unless, perhaps, the contract was that P should be entitled to leave only on the fulfilment of some reasonable condition: *Robinson v Balmain New Ferry Co Ltd* [1910] AC 295, PC. *Sed quaere* whether one is entitled to restrain another from leaving even if it is a breach of contract for him to do so? The contract can hardly be specifically enforceable.
  1. [1913] 3 KB at 787 and 793.
  2. (1902) 20 Cox CC 210.
  3. See *Moone v Rose* (1869) LR 4 QB 486; *Lesley* (1860) Bell CC 220; and cf. *Peacock and Hoskyn v Musgrave and Porter* [1956] Crim LR 414 (where damages were awarded for detention by the police, originally justified, but unreasonably prolonged) and *Lambert v Hodgson* (1823) 1 Bing 317.

"If a man gets into an express train and the doors are locked pending its arrival at its destination, he is not entitled, merely because the train has been stopped by signal, to call for the doors to be opened to let him out."[4] But if he is kept locked in for a day at his destination this surely ought to be false imprisonment. And if the technicalities of the forms of action preclude a remedy in tort this is no reason why the omission should not be held to be criminal. The CLRC were of the opinion that the crime of false imprisonment is, and ought to be, capable of commission by omission.[5]

2 Unlawful Restraint

The imprisonment must be "false", that is unlawful. A convicted person sentenced to imprisonment may be lawfully confined in any prison and, as against prison officers so confining him in good faith, he has no "residual liberty". If he is subjected to intolerable conditions he may have other remedies but he cannot sue (or, it may be assumed, prosecute) the officers for false imprisonment.[6] It might, however, be false imprisonment for a fellow prisoner, or an officer acting in bad faith outside the scope of his duty, to lock him in a confined space, such as a hut, within the prison. A parent may lawfully exercise restraint over a child, so long as he remains within the bounds of reasonable parental discipline and does not act in contravention of a court order.[7] Where a girl of 14 or 15 was fostered out by her father with the consent and assistance of the local authority and he abducted her against her will and with intent to take her to her country of origin, it was for the jury to say whether they were satisfied that this was outside the bounds of legitimate parental discipline and correction.[8]

The question most commonly arises in connection with the exercise of powers of arrest. If such powers are exceeded, there is a false imprisonment. The principal powers are as follows.

a) *Arrest by a constable under a valid warrant.* Where the justice lacks jurisdiction to issue the warrant, the constable is statutorily protected[9] from any action if he acts in obedience to it. As the term "action" is inappropriate to a criminal proceeding, a constable could not rely on the Act as a defence to criminal prosecution; but he would probably have a good defence on the ground of lack of *mens rea*.[10] An arrest under warrant for a civil matter is unlawful if the arresting officer does not have the warrant in his possession.[11]

---

4. *Herd v Weardale Steel Coal and Coke Co Ltd* [1915] AC 67 at 71, per Lord Haldane.
5. CLRC/OAP/R, paras. 253, 254.
6. *Hague v Deputy Governor of Parkhurst Prison* [1991] 3 All ER 733, HL. What if the conditions are so intolerable as to found a defence of necessity to a charge of escape (above, p. 248)? Is it false imprisonment to prevent such a prisoner from leaving the prison?
7. *Rahman* (1985) 81 Cr App Rep 349, CA. Cf. *D* [1984] AC 778, [1984] 1 All ER 574, below, p. 438.
8. *Rahman*, above, at 354. In fact, D pleaded guilty, and his appeal was dismissed.
9. The Constables Protection Act 1750.
10. Below, p. 438.
11. *De Costa Small v Kirkpatrick* (1979) 68 Cr App Rep 186, [1979] Crim LR 41.

b) *Arrest by a constable or other person for an arrestable offence.* The Police and Criminal Evidence Act 1984, s. 24 provides:

"(4) Any person may arrest without a warrant—
    (a) anyone who is in the act of committing an arrestable offence;
    (b) anyone whom he has reasonable grounds for suspecting to be committing such an offence.
(5) Where an arrestable offence has been committed, any person may arrest without a warrant—
    (a) anyone who is guilty of the offence;
    (b) anyone whom he has reasonable grounds for suspecting to be guilty of it.
(6) Where a constable has reasonable grounds for suspecting that an arrestable offence has been committed, he may arrest without a warrant anyone whom he has reasonable grounds for suspecting to be guilty of the offence.
(7) A constable may arrest without a warrant—
    (a) anyone who is about to commit an arrestable offence;
    (b) anyone whom he has reasonable grounds for suspecting to be about to commit an arrestable offence."

Section 24 (3) provides that the above subsections apply to conspiring, attempting, inciting, aiding, abetting, counselling or procuring an arrestable offence and that these acts are also arrestable offences.

It will be noted that arrest is always lawful where D reasonably suspects P to be in the act of committing the arrestable offence, even though in fact P is not doing so: but that where D reasonably suspects that P *has committed* an arrestable offence, the arrest is unlawful if that offence has not been committed by anyone, unless D happens to be a constable. This, in effect, re-enacts the rule laid down for arrest for felony in *Walters v W. H. Smith & Sons Ltd.*[12] D suspected on reasonable grounds that P had stolen a number of books from his book stall. He arrested him on a charge of stealing a particular book. Though other books had certainly been stolen, this one had not been stolen by P or anyone else. Because the offence for which the arrest was made had not been committed, D was held liable in damages. The Criminal Law Revision Committee thought it right to preserve the rule, although they pointed out that it may be

"a trap to a private person who is careful instead of precipitate about deciding whether to arrest a person. If, for example, a store detective saw a person apparently shoplifting, he could arrest him under clause 2 (2) [now s. 24 (4)(b) of PACE] on the ground that he had reasonable cause to suspect him of being in the act of committing an arrestable offence, and he would not be liable for unlawful arrest even if it turned out that he was wrong; but if he preferred out of caution to invite the other to the office to give him an opportunity of clearing himself, and then arrested him on being satisfied that he was guilty, the detective would be liable if this turned out to be wrong."[13]

---

12. [1914] 1 KB 595.
13. Cmnd 2659, para. 14.

The justification for the rule is that an increase in the powers of arrest of private persons would not be acceptable to public opinion and that it is desirable, where it is at all doubtful whether an offence has been committed, for a private person to put the matter in the hands of the police.[14] This hardly allows, however, for the case where the citizen has no opportunity to inform the police and must either let the suspected person escape or make an arrest himself.

The powers of arrest of a constable are wider under s. 24 than those of other persons in three respects. An arrest by a constable of a person reasonably suspected of having committed an arrestable offence is not unlawful even though the offence in question has never been committed. Secondly, a constable may arrest a person reasonably suspected to be *about to commit* an arrestable offence, whereas other persons must wait until he is *in the act* of committing the offence. Thirdly, a constable who has made an arrest may do what is reasonable to investigate the matter and discover whether his reasonable suspicions are well founded; but a private person must hand the arrested person over to a constable or magistrate as soon as possible.[15]

c) *Where a constable or other person arrests for breach of the peace committed in his presence, or where he reasonably believes that such a breach will be committed in the immediate future by a person unless he is arrested, or where a breach has been committed and he reasonably believes that a renewal of it is threatened.*[16] There is a breach of the peace whenever harm is actually done or is likely to be done to a person, or in his presence to his property, or a person is in fear of being so harmed through an assault, an affray, a riot, or other disturbance.[17] Public alarm, excitement or disturbance is not of itself a breach of the peace, unless it arises from actual or threatened violence.

d) *Arrest by a constable under the "general arrest conditions".* By s. 25 (1) of the Police and Criminal Evidence Act, a constable who has reasonable grounds for suspecting that any offence which is not an arrestable offence has been committed or attempted, or is being committed or attempted, by X, may arrest X if it appears to him that the service of a summons is impracticable or inappropriate because of the "general arrest conditions" specified in the section. The conditions are, broadly, (i) the constable is unable to ascertain X's true name and address or a satisfactory address for service of a summons; or (ii) the constable has reasonable grounds for believing that the arrest is necessary to prevent X from causing or

---

14. Ibid., para. 15.
15. *Dallison v Caffrey* [1965] 1 QB 348, [1964] 2 All ER 610 at 616–617, CA, per Lord Denning. It is lawful for a private detective to take a suspected shoplifter to his employer for a decision whether to prosecute; *John Lewis & Co Ltd v Tims* [1952] AC 676, [1952] 1 All ER 1203, HL, but it is not, apparently, lawful for the private arrester of a child to take the child to his father to deal with; *Brewin* [1976] Crim LR 742 (Recorder Jowitt) and commentary.
16. *Howell* (1981) 73 Cr App Rep 31 at 36.
17. Ibid. at 37. Lord Denning has said that even the lawful use of force is a breach of the peace: *Chief Constable of Devon* [1981] 3 All ER 826 at 832; but this can hardly subject the person using such force to arrest.

sustaining physical injury to himself, causing physical injury to others, causing loss of or damage to property, committing an offence against public decency, causing an unlawful obstruction of the highway; or to protect a child or other vulnerable person from X.[18]

e) *Arrest under the powers preserved by Schedule 2 of the Police and Criminal Evidence Act 1984.* Numerous statutory powers of arrest without warrant were abolished by s. 26 of the 1984 Act which, however, preserved the powers specified in Schedule 2.

f) *Arrest unlawful, unless information given.* Where a person is arrested, otherwise than by being informed he is under arrest, he must be so informed as soon as practicable afterwards. No arrest is lawful unless the person arrested is informed of the ground of the arrest at the time or as soon as is practicable thereafter; and, where the arrest is by a constable, this is so even where the ground for the arrest is obvious. If the arrested person escapes before it is reasonably practicable for him to be informed that he is under arrest, or the ground for the arrest, the arrest is not rendered unlawful.[19]

2) *Mens Rea*

Since the great majority of the cases are civil actions, there is little authority on the nature of the *mens rea* required for false imprisonment but in *Rahman*[20] the court stated that "False imprisonment consists in the unlawful and intentional or reckless restraint of a victim's freedom of movement from a particular place." This was confirmed by *Hutchins*[1] which held that the offence is one of "basic intent" so that a belief caused by self-induced intoxication that the victim is consenting is no defence. The courts did not specify what kind of recklessness they had in mind; but a common law offence would naturally require *Cunningham* recklessness. This may be taken to be established now that it is settled that assault requires *Cunningham* recklessness.[2] Assault and false imprisonment are both common law offences and are so closely related that it is inconceivable that they should be governed by different principles of *mens rea*. As suggested above, D would not have been criminally liable in *Walters v W H Smith & Son Ltd* because he believed on reasonable grounds that the felony for which he arrested P had been committed; and, today, it should make no difference that there were no reasonable grounds for his belief, so long as it was honestly held. This makes no difference, of course, to the

18. Does this provision imply that any person other than a constable, acting on the same necessity, does so unlawfully? Above, p. 245.
19. These rules, in s. 28 of the 1984 Act, replace the common law as stated in *Christie v Leachinsky* [1947] AC 573, [1947] 1 All ER 567. See *DPP v Hawkins* [1988] 3 All ER 673, [1988] Crim LR 741; *Brosch* [1988] Crim LR 743 and (especially) commentary.
20. (1985) 81 Cr App Rep 349 at 353, CA, above, p. 435.
1. [1988] Crim LR 379.
2. Above, p. 61.

position in the civil law and D remains liable to pay damages to P in the circumstances of that case.

3) Kidnapping

In *R v D*[3] the House of Lords gave an authoritative account of the law of kidnapping.

"First, the nature of the offence is an attack on, and infringement of, the personal liberty of an individual. Second, the offence contains four ingredients as follows: (1) the taking or carrying away of one person by another, (2) by force or by fraud, (3) without the consent of the person so taken or carried away and (4) without lawful excuse. Third, until the comparatively recent abolition by statute of the division of criminal offences into the two categories of felonies and misdemeanours (see s. 1 of the Criminal Law Act 1967), the offence of kidnapping was categorised by the common law as a misdemeanour only. Fourth, despite that, kidnapping was always regarded, by reason of its nature, as a grave and (to use the language of an earlier age) heinous offence. Fifth, in earlier days the offence contained a further ingredient, namely that the taking or carrying away should be from a place within the jurisdiction to another place outside it; this further ingredient has, however, long been obsolete and forms no necessary part of the offence today. Sixth, the offence was in former days described not merely as taking or carrying away a person but further or alternatively as secreting him; this element of secretion has, however, also become obsolete, so that, although it may be present in a particular case, it adds nothing to the basic ingredient of taking or carrying away."

It is the absence of consent of the person taken which is relevant, even where that person is a child. In the case of a young child, lacking the understanding or intelligence to give consent, the absence of consent is a necessary inference. In the case of such a child there may be no force or fraud (unless those words are very broadly construed), as where a baby is taken from a pram outside a shop. But, if it is not kidnapping, it is false imprisonment which is equally punishable so, though it looks a little odd if a baby cannot be kidnapped,[4] no great harm is done. In the case of an older child, it is a question of fact for the jury whether (i) the child has sufficient understanding and, if so, (ii) it in fact consented. Lord Brandon thought that a jury would usually find that a child under 14 lacked sufficient understanding to give consent; but this may underestimate the capacity of the modern child.

It was held in *Reid*[5] that a husband may be convicted of kidnapping his wife and in *D* that a father may be guilty of kidnapping his child. It was recognised that, until modern times, it may be that an indictment of a father for kidnapping his child would have failed because of the paramountcy of his position in the family; but common law principles adapt and

3. [1984] AC 778, [1984] 2 All ER 449, [1984] Crim LR 558.
4. See Glanville Williams, "Can Babies be Kidnapped?" [1989] Crim LR 473.
5. [1973] QB 299, [1972] 2 All ER 1350.

develop in the light of radically changed social conventions and conditions. Lord Bridge held that parental kidnapping includes the case (as in *D*) where the parent acts in contravention of the order of a competent court, leaving open the question whether a parent might be convicted in any other circumstances; but the majority preferred to hold simply that the parent is guilty where he acts "without lawful excuse". What is a lawful excuse is left completely at large; and whether a taking by a parent in other circumstances amounts to kidnapping is likely to be resolved in the same way whether the court proceeds by the route of deciding (as the majority would) whether there is a lawful excuse or by deciding (as Lord Bridge would) whether the offence extends to those further circumstances. If a 12-year-old child refuses to return home from a visit to his grandmother's and his father forcibly carries him off, he surely commits no offence. The majority would say, presumably, because the father has a lawful excuse and Lord Bridge, because kidnapping does not extend to those circumstances. The result is the same. The question must be whether the parent has gone beyond what is reasonable in the exercise of parental authority.

Where P is not D's child and D is not acting in pursuance of any statutory authority or power of arrest, "lawful excuse" is likely to be narrowly confined. In *Henman*[6] D was guilty of attempted kidnapping when he tried to take by force an acquaintance whom he believed to be in moral and spiritual danger from a religious sect to which she belonged. There was no lawful excuse because there was no "necessity recognised by the law as such" for D's conduct.

The crime is complete when P is deprived of his liberty and carried away from the place where he wished to be.[7] The requirements of carrying away and the use of force or fraud seem to be the only factors distinguishing kidnapping from false imprisonment. It seems that every kidnapping is also a false imprisonment but a detention without any taking away or force or fraud (D merely turns the key locking P in the room) is only the latter offence. Where D has carried P away by force or fraud, he may be convicted of both offences.[8] Kidnapping is an aggravated form of false imprisonment[9] so the rules of lawful excuse are, no doubt, the same. Since both offences are common law misdemeanours, punishable with imprisonment or fine at the discretion of the court, the significance of the element of aggravation is that it enables the kidnapper to be labelled as such and given an appropriate penalty.

4) *Taking of Hostages*

The Taking of Hostages Act 1982 creates an offence of exceptional breadth in that it extends to a person of any nationality acting anywhere in the

---

6. [1987] Crim LR 333, CA.
7. *Wellard* [1978] 3 All ER 161, [1978] 1 WLR 921.
8. *Brown* [1985] Crim LR 398, CA (5 years' imprisonment concurrent on both counts upheld).
9. East, 1 PC, 429.

world, or indeed, in outer space. It is committed by anyone who detains another and, in order to compel a State, international governmental organisation or person to do or abstain from doing any act, threatens to kill, injure or continue to detain the hostage. It is punishable with imprisonment for life. Proceedings may not be instituted except by or with the consent of the Attorney-General.

5) *Abduction of Children*

The Child Abduction Act 1984, as amended by the Children Act 1989, creates two offences of abduction of a child under the age of sixteen.

The first offence (s. 1) may be committed only by a person "connected with" the child who takes or sends the child out of the United Kingdom "without the appropriate consent".

A person "connected with" a child is (i) the child's parent; (ii) in the case of a child whose parents were not married at the time of birth, a man in respect of whom there are reasonable grounds for believing him to be the father; (iii) a guardian; (iv) a person in whose favour "a residence order"[10] is in force with respect to the child; or (v) a person having custody. The "appropriate consent" is the consent of *each* of the child's mother, the child's father if he has "parental responsibility"[11] for him, any guardian, any person in whose favour a residence order is in force with respect to the child *and* any person having custody of him; *or* the leave of the court under the Children Act 1989, or, in the case of any person having custody, the leave of the court which awarded custody.

The offence is not committed where a person in whose favour a residence order is in force takes or sends the child out of the United Kingdom for a period of less than one month unless this is a breach of an order under Part II of the Children Act 1989.

The Act provides defences of which D bears an evidential burden and the prosecution the burden of proof where:

    (i) D believes that he has the appropriate consent or that he would have it if the person or persons whose consent is required were aware of all the relevant circumstances; or

    (ii) he has taken all reasonable steps to communicate with those persons but has been unsuccessful; or

    (iii) the other person has unreasonably refused to consent – unless

        (i) that person is one in whose favour there is a residence order in force with respect to the child, or

        (ii) the person taking or sending the child out of the United Kingdom is acting in breach of an order made by a court in the United Kingdom

The second offence (s. 2) is committed where a person who is not the child's mother or, where the parents were married at the time of the birth,

10. As defined in s. 8 (1) of the Children Act 1989.
11. As defined in s. 3 of the Children Act 1989.

his father, or guardian, custodian or a person in whose favour a residence order is in force, without lawful authority or reasonable excuse, takes or detains the child—

(i) so as to remove him from the lawful control[12] of any person having lawful control of him; or

(ii) so as to keep him out of the lawful control of any person entitled to lawful control of him.

"Lawful control" is not defined in the Act and the court in *Mousir*[13] declined to define it, saying that the concept varies according to the person said to have control – e.g., parent, schoolteacher or nanny. If D persuades a fourteen-year-old boy on his way home from school to go to his flat, there is evidence on which a jury can find that he was taken out of his mother's control. The words "so as to" are concerned with the objective consequence, not with D's purpose; so if D has in fact removed the child from lawful control it seems that it will be immaterial that he did not know the child was in anyone's control. But if, as in *Mousir*, the charge is one of attempt, an intent to commit the offence – i.e., remove the child from control – must be proved.[14]

It is provided that it is a defence for D to prove—

(i) where the father and mother were not married at the time of the birth, and he is the child's father or that, at the time of the alleged offence, he believed on reasonable grounds that he was the father; or

(ii) at the time of the alleged offence, he believed that the child had attained the age of sixteen.

The offences under the Act are different in principle from the common law offences of false imprisonment and kidnapping. The essence of the common law offences is that they are acts done without the consent of the person imprisoned or kidnapped whereas the essence of the statutory offences is that they are done without the consent of the person entitled to give the appropriate consent or having lawful control. Though the definition of the second offence does not use the word "consent", it seems clear that a child is not "removed from" or "kept out of" lawful control if the person in control consents to what is done. It is provided that "taking" includes D's inducing the child to accompany him or another and "detaining" includes inducing the child to remain with D or another, and there is no requirement of force or fraud. The child may be ready and willing, but the offence will still be committed.

Notwithstanding this distinction between the offences, it is provided that no prosecution shall be instituted for an offence of kidnapping if it was committed (a) against a child under the age of sixteen and (b) by a person "connected with the child", except by or with the consent of the Director of Public Prosecutions.

Both offences are punishable, on summary conviction, by six months' imprisonment or a fine not exceeding the statutory maximum, or both and, on indictment, by imprisonment for seven years.

---

12. See *Mousir* [1987] Crim LR 561, CA.
13. [1987] Crim LR 561.
14. Commentary on *Mousir* [1987] Crim LR 562.

7 Offensive Weapons

Legislation regulating the possession and use of firearms and offensive weapons is of major importance in the prevention of offences against the person. In earlier editions of this book (see the sixth edition, pp. 416–422) an account was given of the principal offences under the Firearms Act 1968 and other legislation. This is omitted from the present edition and the reader is referred to *Archbold*, Chapter 24, or *Blackstone*, section B12. Consideration is, however, given below to an important offence of general interest, that created by the Prevention of Crime Act 1953.

The Prevention of Crime Act 1953 is, according to its long title:
"An Act to prohibit the carrying of offensive weapons in public places, without lawful authority or reasonable excuse."

It goes much further than the Firearms Act 1968 in that, (i) in general, the mere carrying of the offensive weapon in a public place is an offence without proof of any ulterior intent or the commission of any other offence and (if it is a firearm) without proof that it was loaded or that ammunition was carried; and (ii) it extends to a much wider range of weapons. The Act provides:

"1—(1) Any person who without lawful authority or reasonable excuse, the proof whereof shall lie on him, has with him in any public place any offensive weapon shall be guilty of an offence, and shall be liable—

(a) on summary conviction, to imprisonment for a term not exceeding three months or a fine not exceeding [the statutory maximum], or both;

(b) on conviction on indictment, to imprisonment for a term not exceeding two years or a fine, or both.

(2) Where any person is convicted of an offence under subsection (1) of this section the court may make an order for the forfeiture or disposal of any weapon in respect of which the offence was committed."

1) *Offensive Weapons*

"Offensive weapon" is defined by s. 1 (4), as amended by the Public Order Act 1986, to mean
"any article made or adapted for use for causing injury to the person, or intended by the person having it with him for such use by him or by some other person."

It will be noted that this definition is narrower than that of "weapon of offence" in s. 10 (1) (b) of the Theft Act 1968. It does not include, as the Theft Act does, articles made, adapted or intended for *incapacitating* a person.[15]

There are three categories of offensive weapon: (i) Articles *made for causing injury* would include a service rifle or bayonet, a revolver, a cosh,

15. Below, p. 627; Smith, *Law of Theft*, paras. [365]–[370].

knuckle-duster,[16] dagger, swordstick[17] or flick knife.[18] It has been held that the fact that rice flails are *used* as weapons is sufficient evidence that they are *made* for that purpose:[19] but this seems doubtful. (ii) Articles *adapted for causing injury* would include razor blades inserted in a potato or cap-peak, a bottle broken for the purpose, a chair-leg studded with nails and so on. "Adapted" probably means altered so as to become suitable.[20] It is not certain whether the intention of the adaptor is relevant.[1] Is an *accidentally* broken milk bottle "adapted for use for causing injury to the person"? It is submitted that it is not and that if the article was not adapted with intent, it can only be an offensive weapon in the third category. (iii) It is very important to distinguish the third category of articles which are neither made nor adapted for causing injury, but are carried for that purpose. Whether D carried the article with the necessary purpose is a question of fact.[2] Articles which have been held to be carried with such intent include a sheath-knife,[3] a shot-gun,[4] a razor,[5] a sandbag,[6] a pick-axe handle,[7] a stone,[8] and a drum of pepper.[9] *Any* article is capable of being an offensive weapon; but if it is of such a nature that it is unlikely to cause injury when brought into contact with the person, then the onus of proving the necessary intent will be very heavy.

Articles adapted or intended by the carrier to injure himself. It was held by the Crown Court in *Bryan v Mott*[10] that a bottle broken for the purpose of committing suicide is "adapted" for causing injury to the person. In *Fleming*,[11] on the other hand, the judge ruled that a large domestic carving knife carried by D to injure himself was not "intended" for causing injury to the person: though the Act does not say "another person", that is what it means. The view of the judge in *Fleming* is to be preferred. The question is whether the thing is "an offensive weapon" and since "offensive" implies an attack on another the injury which the adaptor or carrier must

---

16. ". . . bludgeons, properly so-called, clubs and anything that is not in common use for any other purpose but a weapon are clearly offensive weapons within the meaning of the legislature" (the Smuggling Acts): (1784) 1 Leach 342 n (a).
17. [1988] Crim LR 695.
18. An offensive weapon *per se* because judicially noticed as such *Simpson* [1983] 3 All ER 789, [1983] 1 WLR 1494; cf. *Gibson v Wales* [1983] 1 All ER 869, DC, [1983] Crim LR 113 and commentary.
19. *Copus v DPP* [1989] Crim LR 577 and commentary. It was conceded at the trial in *Malnik* [1989] Crim LR 451 that a rice flail was an offensive weapon.
20. Cf. *Davison v Birmingham Industrial Co-operative Society* (1920) 90 LJKB 206; *Flower Freight Co Ltd v Hammond* [1963] 1 QB 275, [1962] 3 All ER 950; and *Herrmann v Metropolitan Leather Co Ltd* [1942] Ch 248, [1942] 1 All ER 294; *Maddox v Storer* [1963] 1 QB 451, [1962] 1 All ER 831; *Formosa* (1990) 92 Cr App Rep 11, [1990] Crim LR 868, CA.
1. *Maddox v Storer* [1963] 1 QB 451, [1962] 1 All ER 831.
2. *Williamson* (1978) 67 Cr App Rep 35, [1978] Crim LR 229.
3. *Woodward v Koessler* [1958] 3 All ER 557.
4. *Gipson* [1963] Crim LR 281; *Hodgson* [1954] Crim LR 379.
5. *Petrie* [1961] 1 All ER 466; *Gibson v Wales* [1983] 1 All ER 869.
6. Ibid.
7. *Cugullere* [1961] 2 All ER 343.
8. *Harrison v Thornton* (1966) 110 Sol Jo 444, [1966] Crim LR 388, DC.
9. 120 JP 250. Also, no doubt, a stiletto heel which can be a very dangerous weapon: (1964) The Times, 25 September.
10. (1975) 62 Cr App Rep 71. The point was not decided by the Divisional Court.
11. [1989] Crim LR 71 (Judge Fricker QC).

contemplate must be injury to another. The cases may, however, be distinguishable if "adapt" does not imply any intention on the part of the adaptor. Breaking the milk bottle in fact makes it more suitable for injuring others, even if the adaptor intends injury only to himself. But such a distinction does not seem justified in principle. In the case of articles "made or adapted", the prosecution have to prove no more than possession in a public place.[12] D will then be convicted unless he can prove, on a balance of probability, that he had lawful authority or reasonable excuse. But if the article falls into the third category the onus is on the prosecution to show that it was carried with intent to injure.[13] The prosecution must satisfy the jury that the article is either offensive *per se* (made or adapted) or, if it is not, that D had it with him with intent. If some of the jury think it is the one, and some of the other, the case, it is submitted, is not made out.[14] The question in *Woodward v Koessler*[15] was whether D intended to "cause injury to the person" if he intended merely to frighten or intimidate by displaying a knife. It is now established that this is too wide. An intention to frighten or to intimidate is not enough. If there is no intention to cause physical injury, there must be an intention to cause injury by shock – and only in very exceptional circumstances could evidence of such an intention be found.[16]

A conditional intention to use the article is sufficient but it must be an intention to use the article in the future. If D sets out from Berkshire intending, if the occasion arises, to use a domestic knife for causing injury in Cornwall, the knife is an offensive weapon so long as it is carried in a public place and the intention continues. Once D believes that there is no possibility of the knife being used for causing injury – because, for example, his purpose has been accomplished – it ceases to be an offensive weapon.[17] It may, therefore, be no offence to carry the knife – whether or not it had been used – from Cornwall back to Berkshire.

After some hesitation, the courts have construed the Act in the light of its long title. It is aimed at the *carrying* of offensive weapons *in public places*. It is not aimed at the actual *use* of the weapon, which can invariably be adequately dealt with under some other offence. In *Jura*[18] D was holding an air rifle at a shooting gallery when, on a sudden provocation, he shot and wounded a woman. It was held that he had a reasonable excuse for *carrying* the rifle though not, of course, for using it in that way. But he had committed one offence, not two. It was as if a gamekeeper at a shooting party were suddenly to lose his temper and shoot at someone. If, then, D is lawfully in possession of the article, whether it be an offensive weapon per se or not, his decision unlawfully to use and immediate use of it does not amount to an offence under the Act. In *Dayle*[19] D took a car jack from the

12. *Davis v Alexander* (1970) 54 Cr App Rep 398.
13. *Petrie* [1961] 1 All ER 466; *Leer* [1982] Crim LR 310.
14. *Flynn* (1985) 82 Cr App Rep 319, [1986] Crim LR 239 and commentary.
15. [1958] 3 All ER 557.
16. *Edmonds* [1963] 2 QB 142, [1963] 1 All ER 828; *Rapier* (1979) 70 Cr App Rep 17.
17. *Allamby* [1974] 3 All ER 126, CA. Cf. *Ellames* [1974] 3 All ER 130.
18. [1954] 1 QB 503, [1954] 1 All ER 696, CA.
19. [1973] 3 All ER 1151.

boot of his car and threw it at P in the course of a fight. In *Ohlson v Hylton*[20] D, a carpenter, took a hammer from his tool bag in the course of a fight and struck P. In neither case was D guilty of an offence under the Act.

It seems that if D is not in possession of the article until an occasion for its use arises and he then takes it up for immediate use, he commits no offence under the Act. The law was so stated in *Ohlson v Hylton*:[1]

"To support a conviction under the Act the prosecution must show that the defendant was carrying or otherwise equipped with the weapon, and had the intent to use it offensively before any occasion for its actual use had arisen."[2]

This interpretation avoids the formidable difficulty which would otherwise arise where D picks up an article in the course of a fight, allegedly for self-defence. The onus of proving that this was an unreasonable step for the purposes of self-defence is on the Crown but, if it was capable of being an offence under the Act, it would be for D to prove he had a reasonable excuse.

An "occasion" has a beginning and it must also have an end.[3] If D picks up a glass to defend himself in the course of a pub brawl he does not commit an offence under the Act; but suppose, when the fight is over, he declines to put the glass down and insists on carrying it home through two miles of streets? Probably the "occasion" has come to an end, and the question is whether D has a reasonable excuse.

2) *Lawful Authority or Reasonable Excuse*

It may be that the existence of lawful authority is a pure question of law, whereas whether there is a reasonable excuse is a question of fact, subject to the usual judicial control.[4] "Lawful authority" presents difficulties. Before the Act, it was presumably generally lawful to be in possession of an offensive weapon in a public place – otherwise there would have been no necessity for the Act. Now it is generally unlawful. "Lawful authority" postulates some legal exception to the general rule of the Act; yet none is provided for and the words themselves are certainly not self-explanatory. In *Bryan v Mott* Lord Widgery CJ said[5] that "lawful authority" refers to those "people who from time to time carry an offensive weapon as a matter of duty – the soldier with his rifle and the police officer with his truncheon." It seems that the "duty" must be a public one – an employer cannot authorise his employees to carry offensive weapons simply by getting them to contract to do so.

---

20. [1975] 2 All ER 490, DC. See also *Police v Smith* [1974] 2 NZLR 32 (guest in restaurant using table knife offensively); *Humphreys* [1977] Crim LR 225, CA (penknife).
    1. [1975] 2 All ER 490 at 496.
    2. *Powell* [1963] Crim LR 511, CCA, and *Harrison v Thornton* [1966] Crim LR 388, DC, appear to be wrongly decided in the light of this principle.
    3. Cf. *Giles* [1976] Crim LR 253 (Judge Jones).
    4. *Peacock* [1973] Crim LR 639; *Leer* [1982] Crim LR 310, CA.
    5. (1976) 62 Cr App Rep 71 at 73, DC.

Whether there is a reasonable excuse is said to depend on whether a reasonable man would think it excusable to carry the weapon[6] and in *Butler*[7] D's argument that he had a reasonable excuse because he never considered whether the swordstick he was carrying was an article made or adapted for causing injury was left to the jury; but that may have been too generous. What did he suppose a swordstick was for, if not injuring people? A possible answer is that he thought it was made as a curio or "collector's item". Generally the courts have construed the provision strictly and exercised close control over magistrates and juries. It is not enough that D's intentions were entirely lawful.[8] It is not necessarily a reasonable excuse that the weapon is carried only for self-defence. To have a defence D must show that there was "an imminent particular threat affecting the particular circumstances in which the weapon was carried."[9] One who is under constant threat, it is said, must resort to the police. He commits an offence if he regularly goes out armed for self-defence. So there was held to be no excuse for carrying an iron bar though D had reasonable cause to fear and did fear that he would be violently attacked and intended to use the bar for defence only.[10] It is not reasonable for an Edinburgh taxi-driver to carry two feet of rubber hose with a piece of metal inserted at one end, though he does so for defence against violent passengers whom taxi-drivers some-times encounter at night.[11] It has been held that possession of a broken milk-bottle (an article adapted for causing injury) is not excused by the fact that D intended to use it to commit suicide.[12] It is an offence for security guards at dance halls to carry a truncheon "as a deterrent" and as "part of the uniform."[13] If, as the court said, "weapons must not be carried as a matter of routine or as part of a uniform," where stand the thousands of men said to be employed by private security forces and to be armed with batons?[14]

Unlawful possession may become lawful if circumstances change so as to give rise to a reasonable excuse. When a person is attacked he may use anything that he can lay his hands on to defend himself, so long as he uses no more force than is reasonable in the circumstances. It may be reasonable to use an offensive weapon that he is unlawfully carrying. When Butler[15] was viciously attacked, his use of the swordstick to defend himself was justified or excused, so possession of it must have become lawful, but that could not undo the offence already committed.[16] The narrow interpretation of reasonable excuse may qualify the important principle that a man cannot be driven off the streets and compelled not to go to a public place where he might lawfully be because he will be confronted by people intending to

6. *Bryan v Mott*, above, p. 445, fn. 10.
7. [1988] Crim LR 695.
8. *Bryan v Mott*, above.
9. *Evans v Hughes* [1972] 3 All ER 412 at 415, DC; *Evans v Wright* [1964] Crim LR 466.
10. Ibid. See also *Bradley v Moss* [1974] Crim LR 430, DC; *Pittard v Mahoney* [1977] Crim LR 169, DC.
11. *Grieve v Macleod* 1967 SLT 70.
12. *Bryan v Mott*, above.
13. *Spanner* [1973] Crim LR 704.
14. 69 Law Soc Gaz 673.
15. Above, p. 447.
16. Smith, *Justification and Excuse*, 117–123.

attack him.[17] If he decides that he cannot go to that place unless armed with an offensive weapon, it seems that he must stay away. He commits an offence if he goes armed.[18]

3) A Public Place

Section 1 (4) of the Prevention of Crime Act 1953 provides:

"'public place' includes any highway and any other premises or place to which at the material time the public have or are permitted to have access whether on payment or otherwise."

This is very similar to the interpretation which has been placed upon s. 192 of the Road Traffic Act 1988 and to the definition of public place, etc., in other Acts.[19] It should always be borne in mind that the same term may bear different meanings according to the context in which it is found and that whether a place is public is a question of fact.[20] A householder impliedly invites persons having legitimate business to walk up his garden path to the door, but this does not render the garden a "public place". The class of persons invited to enter is too restricted to constitute them "the public".[1] On the other hand, the landing of a block of flats has been held to be a public place on the ground that the public had access in fact, whether or not they were permitted to have it.[2] In the absence of a notice restricting entry, there was evidence on which justices could find that the unrestricted access of the public to a council estate extended to the stairways and landings of the flats. The jury are, of course, entitled to draw reasonable inferences; so that where D produced an air pistol in a private dwelling-house which he was visiting, it was open to them to infer that he brought it to or took it away from the house through the public street.[3]

4) Mens Rea

The Court of Criminal Appeal has held that the words "has with him in any public place" mean "*knowingly* has with him in any public place."[4]

"If some innocent person has a cosh slipped into his pocket by an escaping rogue, he would not be guilty of having it with him within the

17. *Field* [1972] Crim LR 435.
18. *Malnik v DPP* [1989] Crim LR 451, DC.
19. E.g. Public Order Act 1936, s. 5.
20. *Theodolou* [1963] Crim LR 573.
  1. *Edwards and Roberts* (1978) 67 Cr App Rep 228, [1978] Crim LR 564 (a case under s. 5 of the Public Order Act 1936).
  2. *Knox v Anderton* (1983) 76 Cr App Rep 156 [1983] Crim LR 114, DC and commentary. Cf. *Heffey* [1981] Crim LR 111 (Judge Nance).
  3. *Mehmed* [1963] Crim LR 780.
  4. *Cugullere* [1961] 2 All ER 343 at 344. Cf. *Warner v Metropolitan Police Commissioner* [1968] 2 All ER 356; **SHC 110**; above, p. 110.

meaning of the section, because he would be quite innocent of any knowledge that it had been put into his pocket."[5]

So D is not guilty, though he has put an offensive weapon in his car if, at the time of the alleged offence, his forgetfulness of its existence or presence in the car is so complete as to amount to ignorance that it is there at all. Whether D must know of the facts which make the thing an offensive weapon within the Act has not been decided. Is D guilty if he has with him in a public place a revolver which he believes to be an imitation but which is real? Analogy with the Firearms Act 1968[6] would suggest that he is, but principle, it is submitted, requires acquittal.

8 Bomb Hoaxes: Criminal Law Act 1977

The bomb hoax, always irritating and sometimes frightening, was dealt with in a variety of ways before 1977. If a demand were made by the hoaxer, it might be treated as blackmail.[7] If, as is usually the case, it involved a threat to damage property, s. 2 of the Criminal Damage Act 1971[8] might be invoked. In other cases, the hoax amounted to the offence of wasting the time of the police.[9] On one occasion at least, the clumsy weapon of public nuisance was used.[10] The Criminal Law Act 1977, s. 51 now provides a special offence.

"**51**—(1) A person who—
   (a) places any article in any place whatever; or
   (b) dispatches any article by post, rail or any other means whatever of sending things from one place to another, with the intention (in either case) of inducing in some other person a belief that it is likely to explode or ignite and thereby cause personal injury or damage to property is guilty of an offence.

   In this subsection "article" includes substance.

(2) A person who communicates any information which he knows or believes to be false to another person with the intention of inducing in him or any other person a false belief that a bomb or other thing liable to explode or ignite is present in any place or location whatever is guilty of an offence.

(3) For a person to be guilty of an offence under subsection (1) or (2) above it is not necessary for him to have any particular person in mind

---

5. Ibid. Cf. *Roper v Taylor's Garages Ltd* [1951] 2 TLR 284 at 288, per Devlin J; above, p. 103; and contrast the cautious approach of the court to a similar problem arising under the Dangerous Drugs Regulations 1953 where the question whether possession must be accompanied by *mens rea* was left open: *Carpenter* [1960] Crim LR 633.
6. *Russell* (1984) 81 Cr App Rep 315, [1985] Crim LR 231, CA. Cf. *Martindale* [1986] 3 All ER 25, [1986] 1 WLR 1042.
7. Below, p. 606. *King* [1976] Crim LR 200.
8. Below, p. 708. *Farrell* [1976] Crim LR 318.
9. Criminal Law Act 1957, s. 5(2). *Bikram* [1974] Crim LR 55.
10. *Madden* [1975] 3 All ER 155, CA; below, p. 764.

as the person in whom he intends to induce the belief mentioned in that subsection.

(4) A person guilty of an offence under this section shall be liable—

    (a) on summary conviction, to imprisonment for a term not exceeding three months or to a fine not exceeding £1,000, or both;

    (b) on conviction on indictment, to imprisonment for a term not exceeding five years."

The gist of the offences is the *mens rea*. The *actus reus* of s. 51 (1) (a) is an act which everyone does every day. Under s. 51(2) the information communicated may in fact be true; it is sufficient that D believes it to be false. If he believes that the information is, or may possibly be, true, then it obviously cannot be an offence to pass it on.

14 Sexual Offences[1]

1 Rape

Section 1 (1) of the Sexual Offences Act 1956 provides:
"It is an offence for a man to rape a woman."
By s. 37, Sch. 2 the maximum punishment is life imprisonment.

That Act told us nothing more about the crime and so its definition was a matter of common law until the law was declared by the Sexual Offences (Amendment) Act 1976.

"**1.** (1) For the purposes of section 1 of the Sexual Offences Act 1956 (which relates to rape) a man commits rape if
   (a) he has unlawful sexual intercourse with a woman who at the time of the intercourse does not consent to it; and
   (b) at the time he knows that she does not consent to the intercourse or he is reckless as to whether she consents to it;
and references to rape in other enactments (including the following provisions of this Act) shall be construed accordingly."

The subsection codifies the law as laid down by the House of Lords in *Director of Public Prosecutions v Morgan*[2] where the argument that an unreasonable belief in consent could not be a defence was rejected. That decision caused widespread but largely unfounded concern which led to the appointment of an advisory group under Heilbron J to consider whether early changes in the law of rape were necessary. The Group made recommendations[3] for important reforms in the law of evidence and procedure on prosecutions for rape; but they concluded that *Morgan* was right in principle and recommended its codification. Much of the criticism of the decision appeared to assume that it meant that D had to do no more than assert that he believed P consented to ensure his acquittal; and, accordingly the Heilbron Group recommended the declaratory provision now to be found in s. 1 (2) of the Act:

"(2) It is hereby declared that if at a trial for a rape offence the jury has to consider whether a man believed that a woman was consenting to sexual intercourse, the presence or absence of reasonable grounds for such a

---

1. CLRC, Fifteenth Report, Sexual Offences, Cmnd. 9213 (1984); Hogan "On Modernising the Law of Sexual Offences" in *Reshaping the Criminal Law* 174. Hughes, "Consent in Sexual Offences" (1962) 25 MLR 319; Koh, "Consent in Sexual Offences", [1968] Crim LR 81.
2. [1975] 2 All ER 347; **SHC 45**; above, pp. 87 and 216.
3. Cmnd. 6352 (1975). See [1976] Crim LR 97.

belief is a matter to which the jury is to have regard, in conjunction with any other relevant matters, in considering whether he so believed."

This, of course, is a matter of common sense, in no way peculiar to rape. Whenever a jury has to decide whether a person knew a fact or foresaw a consequence, the fact that a reasonable man would have known the fact or foreseen the consequence is evidence tending to show that the accused knew or foresaw; but the decision must be made in the light of the whole of the evidence, including the accused's own testimony, if he gives it, that he did not know or foresee as the case may be. It is unfortunate that a matter of common sense should be enacted at all, particularly that it should be enacted in relation to one offence. So long, however, as it is understood that subsection (2) is a public relations provision and does not enact a rule peculiar to rape, it is harmless.

1 The Actus Reus

a) *Unlawful sexual intercourse.* The phrase, "unlawful sexual intercourse", is used in numerous sections of the Sexual Offences Act 1956 to mean "'illicit', i.e., outside the bond of marriage".[4] The word "unlawful" has an important function. If it were not there a man who, by the law of his domicile, is validly married to a girl under sixteen would commit an offence when he had sexual intercourse with her in this country. So would a man whose wife is a "defective". The 1976 Act defines rape "for the purposes of section 1 of the Sexual Offences Act 1956" so it is reasonable to suppose that the phrase was intended to have the same meaning as it has throughout that Act. It was generally accepted in 1976 that, at common law, a man could not be convicted of rape as a principal in the first degree of his wife. Parliament, having considered an amendment to the Bill making it possible for a husband to be convicted of raping his wife, decided to refer the question to the CLRC. It thus appears both from words of the Act and the debate that Parliament's intention, pending the CLRC Report, was to accept the common law for the time being and to restate it. Unfortunately the CLRC was divided on the issue and no legislation was ever enacted. Growing dissatisfaction with this rule led prosecutors and judges to take the initiative. Some judges directed juries that a husband could now be convicted of rape of his wife, others held that this course was not open to them. When the matter came before the Court of Appeal in *R* they ruled[5] that marital rape is an offence; and this decision was upheld by the House of Lords.[6] The "unlawful word" in the 1976 Act, it was held, is "mere surplusage".

The common law rule was based on an absurd fiction that a wife could not retract the consent to intercourse which she gave upon marriage – a proposition which the civil law of marriage had long rejected. We are well rid of it. The issue in *R*, however, was not the common law but the

---

4. *Chapman* [1959] 1 QB 100, [1958] 3 All ER 143, CCA, (s. 19 (1)); *Jones* [1973] Crim LR 710, CA (s. 17 (1)).
5. [1991] 2 All ER 257, [1991] Crim LR 475.
6. [1991] 4 All ER 481, [1992] Crim LR 207.

interpretation of the section. As appears above, this is more debatable. The strongest argument supporting the decision of the House is found in the existence of some exceptions at common law to the husband's immunity. He could be convicted of rape where there had been a judicial separation, a separation by formal agreement, a decree nisi of divorce or nullity, or an undertaking by the husband not to molest his wife. If "unlawful" was interpreted to mean "outside marriage and not otherwise", these exceptions would have been abolished. Parliament would be unlikely to have intended that. But this is not conclusive. "Unlawful" could have been given the qualified meaning, because it is arguable that this is the meaning to be given to it in the rest of the Act.[7] For example, the intercourse of a husband with his fifteen-year-old wife with her consent is not "unlawful" but it might be otherwise if they were judicially separated. Before the decision of the Court of Appeal the matter was the subject of a Law Commission Working Paper[8] and it might have been thought more appropriate to await the Law Commission's recommendations in the light of public comment on the proposals in that paper. The Law Commission has now recommended that the decision in R be confirmed by legislation which would also deal with subsidiary issues requiring attention.[9] In the meantime, it is settled that the law of rape applies within marriage exactly as outside it. The only difference is in the practical problems of proof.

b) *Sexual intercourse*. The phrase "carnal knowledge", formerly favoured in statutes, was replaced in the consolidation by the Sexual Offences Act by "sexual intercourse". Section 44 provides some guidance as to the meaning of that term:

"Where on the trial of any offence under this Act, it is necessary to prove sexual intercourse (whether natural or unnatural), it shall not be necessary to prove the completion of the intercourse by the emission of seed, but the intercourse shall be deemed complete upon proof of penetration only."

By section 7 (2) of the Sexual Offences (Amendment) Act 1976, s. 44, so far as it relates to natural intercourse,[10] applies for purposes of rape. The slightest penetration will suffice and it is not necessary to prove that the hymen was ruptured.[11] The purpose of s. 44 is to remove doubts as to the minimum conduct needed to constitute sexual intercourse. "Complete" is used in the sense of having come into existence, not in the sense of being at an end.[12] Intercourse continues until the man withdraws. In *Kaitamaki*, it was held that it follows that D commits rape if, having penetrated with consent, or believing he has consent, he declines to withdraw on consent

7. As the Draft Code, cl. 87, provides.
8. No. 116, "Rape within Marriage" (1990). See now Report, Law Com. No. 116 (1992).
9. Particularly whether it should be made explicit that the wife is a compellable witness in a marital rape case. It seems that there is little doubt that she is already compellable under PACE 1984, s. 80 (3) (a).
10. *O'Sullivan* [1981] Crim LR 406. There is no such offence as rape *per anum*.
11. *Russen* (1777) 1 East PC 438; *Hughes* (1841) 9 C & P 752; *Lines* (1844) 1 Car & Kir 393.
12. *Kaitamaki* [1985] AC 147, [1984] 2 All ER 435, PC, construing the corresponding provision in the New Zealand Crimes Act 1961, s. 127; *Mayberry* [1973] Qd R 229, above, p. 130.

being revoked or on realising that P does not consent. So rape may be committed by omission. It is debatable whether this is right. Is not penetration without consent an essential part of the *actus reus* which must be accompanied by *mens rea*?[13]

c) *The absence of consent.* The absence of P's consent is an essential part of the *actus reus* and must be proved by the prosecution. Earlier authorities emphasised the use of force; but it is now clear that lack of consent is the crux of the matter and this may exist though no force is used. A subtle change of emphasis occurred in the middle of the nineteenth century in the cases of *Camplin*[14] and *Fletcher*.[15] The test is not "was the act against her will?" but "was it without her consent?" This may seem, as it has to at least one judge,[16] a distinction without a difference; but it emphasises that it is not necessary for the Crown to prove a positive dissent by the woman; it is enough that she did not assent. So convictions were upheld where D had intercourse with a woman whom he had rendered insensible by giving her liquor in order to excite her;[17] and again where D had intercourse with a woman who was asleep.[18]

Inconsistently with this development, courts and writers continued up to 1976 to cite the traditional seventeenth century definition of rape as having intercourse without consent "by force, fear or fraud". The Heilbron Committee,[19] however, adopted the statement of the law in this book and in *Olugboja*[20] the Court of Appeal, while not persuaded that this was wrong, held that, whatever the law may have been before the 1976 Act, Parliament had adopted and incorporated in the Act the statement in the Heilbron report, so that—

"... the question now is simply: 'At the time of sexual intercourse did the woman consent to it?' It is not necessary for the prosecution to prove that what might otherwise appear to have been consent was in reality merely submission induced by force, fear or fraud, although one or more of these factors will no doubt be present in the majority of cases of rape."[1]

There are similar problems with fraud. At present the only fraud recognised as vitiating consent is the impersonation of a husband or deception as to the nature of the act.

Olugboja said that the jury should be directed that consent is to be given its ordinary meaning and, if need be, that there is a difference between consent and submission. This conceals a great difficulty – namely what is

---

13. See the dissent by Woodhouse J in the New Zealand Court of Appeal, [1980] 1 NZLR 59; SHC 21.
14. (1845) 1 Den 89.
15. (1859) Bell CC 63.
16. Lawson J in *Dee* (1884) 15 Cox CC 579 at 595 (Irish CCR).
17. *Camplin* (1845) 1 Den 89.
18. *Mayers* (1872) 12 Cox CC 311; *Young* (1878) 14 Cox CC 114.
19. Cmnd. 6352 (1975), p. 3, citing the 3rd ed., p. 326.
20. (1981) 73 Cr App Rep 344.
  1. 73 Cr App Rep at 350.

the difference between consent and submission? A person submits when he or she yields, or gives in, to pressure of some kind. A woman may reluctantly submit to sexual intercourse only because her fiancé threatens that he will break off their engagement if she does not. Such a case is very far removed from rape but it seems to be be one of submission. At the other extreme, a woman may submit because the man is holding a knife at her throat. This is plainly rape. The distinction cannot, however, be justified by a distinction between consent and submission. In both cases the woman yields because a threat is made. Submission may indeed be induced by a promise. The woman gives in only because the man promises that he will marry her if she does so. No one would say that is rape if the man intends to keep the promise (and it is clearly not rape in law if he does not) but is it not a case of submission? The dictum of Coleridge J in *Day*:[2] "every consent involves a submission; but it by no means follows that a mere submission involves consent", seems, on reflection, to be the wrong way round. A woman who joyously embraces her reluctant lover undoubtedly consents to the intercourse which follows but it would seem inappropriate, to put it mildly, to say that she "submits" to that which she ardently desires and provokes. On the other hand, a woman who gives in to threats does in fact consent, however reluctantly. In *Olugboja*[3] reference is made to an unreported case in which Winn J held that a constable had no case to answer where he induced P to consent to sexual intercourse by threatening to report her for an offence; whereas in *Wellard*[4] D was said to have a previous conviction for rape (for which he was sentenced to six years' imprisonment) by masquerading as a security officer and inducing a girl to consent by threatening to report to her parents and the police that she had been seen having intercourse in a public place.

It is doubtful if the bounds of the crime of rape can be satisfactorily drawn by a distinction between consent and submission. It is so vague that, as the above cases suggest, both judges and juries may have quite different ideas as to its application. The CLRC's recommendation[5] is that sexual intercourse obtained by threats of immediate force against the woman or any other person "should continue to be rape" but that intercourse obtained by other threats, including threats of force which can be carried out only at some time in the future, should not be rape but should be punishable under s. 2 of the Sexual Offences Act 1956[6] with an increased penalty.

Where D had intercourse with a girl of thirteen years of weak intellect, it was held that the jury were rightly told that he was guilty if they were satisfied that the girl was incapable of giving consent or exercising any judgment on the matter.[7] Willes J said[8] that a consent produced by mere

2. (1841) 9 C & P 722 at 724.
3. At 347–348.
4. Above, p. 440, (1978) 67 Cr App Rep 364 at 368. The court made no comment on the propriety or otherwise of the conviction.
5. Fifteenth Report, 2.29.
6. Below, p. 460.
7. *Fletcher* (1859) Bell CC 63.
8. Ibid.

animal instinct would be sufficient to prevent the act from constituting a rape and this was followed by Keating J[9] and approved by Kelly CB.[10] Palles CB, however, described this as a doctrine

"abhorrent to our best feelings, and ... discreditable to any jurisprudence in which it may succeed in obtaining a place."[11]

It is submitted that his view that consent must be an intelligent act is the better view.

No doubt it is also rape to have intercourse with a child too young to understand the nature of the act; but there is no fixed age limit below which consent is impossible as a matter of law.[12] It is a question of fact in each case and therefore it is a misdirection to tell a jury that, as a matter of law, a child of six cannot consent. Yet, since

"... it would be idle for anyone to suggest that a girl of that age had sufficient understanding and knowledge to decide whether to consent or resist"

a conviction may be upheld, notwithstanding such a misdirection.[13] The effect seems to be much the same as if it were a rule of law.

The 1956 Act provides, by s. 1 (2), that

"a man who induces a woman to have sexual intercourse with him by impersonating her husband commits rape."

This provision, re-enacting the Criminal Law Amendment Act 1885, s. 4, reverses a line of decisions[14] culminating in *Barrow*[15] where the Court for Crown Cases Reserved held that the woman's consent to sexual intercourse was a defence even though she was deceived into thinking that D was her husband. However, in *Flattery*[16] four of the five judges in the Court for Crown Cases Reserved thought that *Barrow* ought to be reconsidered; and in *Dee*[17] the Irish Court for Crown Cases Reserved dissented from it and upheld the impersonator's conviction. The *Barrow* line of cases might still be of importance where D obtains intercourse by impersonating some person other than a husband. It is submitted that this should be rape. It is true that, where the husband is impersonated, there is also an error as to the nature of the transaction – it is not marital intercourse but adultery – whereas if D impersonates another, the transaction is both understood to be and is adultery or fornication – but such an error has never been held sufficiently fundamental to found an indictment for rape. Sexual intercourse is, however, a relationship in which personality is supremely important and consent to have intercourse with A is not consent

---

9. In *Fletcher* (1866) LR 1 CCR 39.
10. In *Barratt* (1873) LR 2 CCR 81.
11. In *Dee* (1884) 15 Cox CC 579 at 594.
12. *Harling* [1938] 1 All ER 307 at 308. "It may well be that in many cases the prosecution would not want much evidence beyond the age of the girl to prove non-consent, but in every charge of rape the fact of non-consent must be proved to the satisfaction of the jury": per Humphreys J. By s. 46 of the Sexual Offences Act 1956 "woman" in that Act includes "girl".
13 *Howard* [1965] 3 All ER 684, CCA.
14. *Jackson* (1822) Russ & Ry 487, CCR; *Saunders* (1838) 8 C & P 265; *Williams* (1838) 8 C & P 286; *Clarke* (1854) Dears CC 397.
15. (1868) 11 Cox CC 191.
16. (1877) 2 QBD 410.
17. (1884) 15 Cox CC 579.

to have intercourse with B. The *Barrow* line of cases is presumably authority against this view but it contained a fundamental inconsistency in that it held that D was guilty of an assault; yet consent should have been equally a defence there as in rape and the cases might be treated, as they were in *Dee*, as depending on the narrow view of rape which was rejected in *Fletcher*.[18]

If D had intercourse with P by impersonating, for example, P's fiancé, it is submitted that *Barrow* should be overruled and D convicted of rape.[19]

Where D, by fraud, deceives the woman as to the nature of the transaction, it is well established that this is rape. So in *Flattery*[20] D was convicted where P submitted to intercourse with him under the impression that he was performing a surgical operation. It is an offence under the Sexual Offences Act 1956, s. 3

"for a person to procure a woman, by false pretences or representations, to have sexual intercourse in any part of the world."

It seems probable that this section covers conduct such as that of Flattery but that it also extends to a much wider range of frauds of a much less fundamental character; and it has been held by the Court of Criminal Appeal in *Williams*,[1] a case with substantially the same facts as *Flattery*, that such conduct is still indictable as rape.

Probably any fraud which does not go to the nature of the act or the identity of the man is not sufficient to destroy consent. So misrepresentations by a man as to his wealth, social position or freedom to marry would not render intercourse thereby obtained rape.[2] Even where the woman is induced by fraud to suppose that she is already married to D, her consent to intercourse affords a defence.[3]

The CLRC's recommendation[4] is that it should continue to be rape to obtain sexual intercourse by fraud as to the nature of the act or by impersonation of P's husband and that it should also be rape to obtain intercourse by impersonation of another man. Other cases of obtaining intercourse by fraud should be dealt with under s. 3 of the Sexual Offences Act 1956.[5]

d) *Fundamental mistake not arising from fraud.* Though stress in the cases has been laid on the element of fraud it is thought that this is not the crucial matter; and that if D had intercourse with P, knowing that she was under a

---

18. (1859) Bell CC 63; above, p. 454.
19. But cf. *Collins* [1973] QB 100, [1972] 2 All ER 1105, below, p. 616.
20. (1877) 2 QBD 410.
  1. [1923] 1 KB 340. Williams, TBCL, 561–562, thinks *Williams* "clearly wrong" because it was not proved that P did not know the facts of life and may merely have been persuaded that sex improves breathing; but Hewart LCJ said the girl never consented to an act of sexual intercourse but only to a necessary operation.
  2. See Stephen J in *Clarence* (1888) 22 QBD 23 at 44. Cf. Canadian Criminal Code, s. 298.
  3. *Papadimitropoulos v R* (1958) 98 CLR 249, [1958] ALR 21; **SHC** 378; where it is pointed out that there is no reported instance of an indictment for rape based on the fraudulent character of the ceremony.
  4. Fifteenth Report, 2.24–2.25.
  5. Below, p. 460.

mistake, not induced by him, either as to his identity or as to the nature of the act, that would be rape.[6]

If the man obtains the woman's consent without the use of force, threats or fraud he is not guilty of rape or any offence, though he may have resorted to various other devices – soft lights, sweet music, flattery – and drink. It is a misdirection to tell a jury that D is guilty of rape if he encouraged P to drink in the hope that her resistance would collapse.[7]

2 The Mens Rea

D must know that P does not consent or be reckless whether she consents. There is no doubt that the Heilbron Group had in mind *Cunningham* recklessness.[8]   It appeared for a time as if *Caldwell*[9] had defeated that intention. In *Pigg*,[10] applying *Caldwell*, it was held that "A man is reckless if he was indifferent and gave no thought to the possibility that [P] might not be consenting in circumstances where, if any thought had been given to the matter, it would have been obvious that there was a risk that she was not consenting . . .". It is difficult to understand how a man can be indifferent to something the possibility of which he has not envisaged. In *Satnam S*[11] the court recognised this and other difficulties, pointing out that *Caldwell* was concerned with recklessness as to the consequences of D's act whereas in rape we are concerned with recklessness as to P's state of mind. It was held that the definition of rape should be based on s. 1 of the 1976 Act and *Morgan* without regard to *Caldwell* and *Lawrence*. Though the *mens rea* is formulated in various ways, it seems that there is, in substance, a return to *Cunningham* recklessness. If D is aware that there is any possibility that P is not consenting and proceeds to have intercourse, he does so recklessly. Lord Hailsham in *Morgan* required an "intention of having intercourse, willy-nilly, not caring whether the victim consents or not".[12] Another way of putting it is to ask, "Was D's attitude one of 'I could not care less whether she is consenting or not, I am going to have intercourse with her regardless.'"[13]

It is submitted therefore that the *mens rea* is an intention to have sexual intercourse with P, (i) knowing that P does not consent, or (ii) being aware that there is a possibility that she does not consent.

In *Bashir*[14] it was said that the trial judge had acted "very wisely" in amending the indictment in respect of a single act of alleged rape so that it charged D with knowing that P did not consent in one count and being reckless in a second count. The verdict then assists the judge in the imposition of sentence.

---

6. See *Papadimitropoulos v R* (1958) 98 CLR 249 at 260.
7. *Lang* (1975) 62 Cr App Rep 50, CA. Cf. s. 4 (1) of the Sexual Offences Act 1956, below, p. 440.
8. Above, p. 61.
9. Above, p. 62. Contrast the attention paid to the intentions of the Heilbron Group in *Olugboja*, above, p. 454.
10. [1982] 2 All ER 591, [1982] Crim LR 446 CA, and commentary.
11. (1983) 78 Cr App Rep 149, [1985] Crim LR 236.
12. [1976] AC 182 at 215.
13. *Taylor* (1984) 80 Cr App Rep 327; *Haughian* (1985) 80 Cr App Rep 334.
14. (1982) 77 Cr App Rep 59.

3 Boys under Fourteen; and Women

As noted above,[15] there is an irrebuttable presumption in criminal law[16] that a boy under the age of fourteen is incapable of committing rape, any other crime of which sexual intercourse is an ingredient, or sodomy.[17] This is an absurd rule, capable of producing injustice. If two boys, aged 16 and 13 respectively, were charged with rape of a girl and it was proved that one boy had intercourse with the girl while the other abetted, but it could not be proved which of the boys did the act, both would have to be acquitted because, if it was in fact the 13-year old, the law says it did not happen at all. The CLRC has recommended the abolition of the irrebuttable presumption.[18] There are conflicting *dicta* whether he may be convicted of an attempt. It is submitted that he should be liable to conviction. The law does not say that the completed act is no offence, it says that the completed act can never happen. It does not say that the boy may not try to make it happen. Plainly he may, and, at least since the Criminal Attempts Act 1981, the presumed impossibility should be no answer.[19] This would mitigate the difficulty pointed out above – both boys could be convicted of the attempt. A difficulty in the way of this opinion may be the cases which decided that a boy under 14 could not be convicted of assault with intent to commit rape.[20]

It is clear, however, that a boy under fourteen may be convicted of counselling or abetting a rape,[1] as may a woman.[2]

4 Assault with Intent to Rape

It is uncertain whether this offence exists.[3] There is no doubt that an indictment for assault with intent to rape would lie at common law but it is not certain whether it was a specific offence or an example of a wider common law offence of assault with intent to commit a felony. If the latter, it ceased to exist with the abolition of felonies by the Criminal Law Act 1967 and the repeal of the words in s. 38 of the OAPA 1861 which provided that assault with intent to commit a felony was punishable with two years' imprisonment. It is thought that the better view is that there was no general offence of assault with intent to commit a felony at common law, and that assault with intent to rape was, and is, a specific offence which was not abolished by the 1861 Act or by the repeal of the general statutory offence. Most significantly, it was treated by the draftsman of the 1861 legislation, C. S. Greaves, as continuing to exist after the 1861 Act.[4] Most cases of

15. See p. 191.
16. There is no such presumption in civil cases: *L v K* [1985] Fam 144, [1985] 1 All ER 961. (Ewbank J).
17. *Groombridge* (1836) 7 C & P 582; *Waite* [1892] 2 QB 600, CCR; *Cratchley* (1913) 9 Cr App Rep 232; *Tatam* (1921) 15 Cr App Rep 132.
18. Fifteenth Report, 2.48.
19. Above, p. 317.
20. *Eldershaw* (1828) 3 C & P 396; *Philips* (1839) 8 C & P 736. Cf. Williams, CLGP 634.
  1. *Eldershaw*, above.
  2. *Ram and Ram* (1893) 17 Cox CC 609; above, p. 152.
  3. In *J* (Crown Court at Stafford, 9 June 1986) Turner J held that it does exist and in *P* [1990] Crim LR 323, Pill J held that it does not. In *Lionel* (1982) 4 Cr App Rep (S) 291 an appeal against sentence was dismissed, the assumption that the offence exists not being challenged. See S. Spencer, [1986] Crim LR 110.
  4. *Russell on Crime* (4th ed., 1865, by C. S. Greaves) 927.

assault with intent to rape will amount to attempted rape under the Criminal Attempts Act 1981 but there will be instances where the assault is a "merely preparatory" act.[5] If it exists, it is a common law misdemeanour, punishable by fine or imprisonment at discretion.

2 Other Offences Involving Sexual Intercourse

The meaning given to "consent" in rape left a number of cases where consent was in some way imperfect, but which were not crimes at common law. The law has therefore been supplemented by several statutory crimes involving sexual intercourse where consent has been improperly obtained by threats, false pretences or the administration of drugs; or where the woman, though consenting in fact, is deemed by the law to be incompetent to consent on account of age or mental handicap. Except where otherwise stated the offences are punishable with two years' imprisonment.

1 Procurement of Woman by Threats or by False Pretences
By s. 2 (1) of the Sexual Offences Act 1956:
  "It is an offence for a person to procure a woman, by threats or intimidation, to have unlawful sexual intercourse in any part of the world."
By s. 3 (1) of the Sexual Offences Act 1956:
  "It is an offence for a person to procure a woman, by false pretences or false representations, to have unlawful sexual intercourse in any part of the world."
These offences, which were originally enacted by the Criminal Law Amendment Act 1885, were probably intended to deal with the person who procures the woman to have intercourse with a third party but have been held to apply also to the man who causes the woman to have intercourse with himself.[6] Since the decision in R[7] it is arguable that the word "unlawful" in these sections is "mere surplusage" and that a man may commit either offence against his wife. The offences have such a close affinity with rape that the same principles might be expected to apply. The better view, it is submitted, is that the 1956 Act should be consistently construed so that "unlawful" means outside marriage.

Whereas rape is indictable only if the sexual intercourse takes place within the jurisdiction, here it may take place in any part of the world, but the act of procuring must of course be done[8] within the jurisdiction. The

---

5. Cf. s. 16 (1) (assault with intent to commit buggery), below, p. 479.
6. *Williams* (1898) 62 JP 310 by the Recorder who declined to state a case (s. 3 (1)). Cf. *Cook* [1954] 1 All ER 60, below, p. 465.
7. Above, p. 452.
8. Or, strictly, "begun", because the procuring is complete only when the intercourse takes place.

creation of these offences in no way limited the common law of rape[9] nor does their existence limit the statutory offence which has replaced it.

These offences are not committed unless sexual intercourse actually takes place. Persuading a girl to agree to have intercourse and to accompany a man for that purpose is not "procuring" if the intercourse does not take place; but it is an attempt to procure.[10] "To procure" means to produce by endeavour.[11] Proof that the threats or false pretences induced P to submit to sexual intercourse will inevitably establish this.

These offences can be committed by any person, whether male or female, but a boy under fourteen cannot be convicted of procuring intercourse with himself because of the irrebuttable presumption that he is incapable.[12] It is possible, however, that he might be convicted of an attempt to procure.[13]

a) *Threats.* As has been seen, there is some uncertainty as to what threats are sufficiently grave to negative consent for the purpose of rape. Whatever the limits in rape, it is possible that less grave threats will suffice for this much less serious offence. Threats to injure a third party may be enough.[14] Suppose that, for example, D threatens that, if P does not consent, he will (i) tell the police of a theft she has committed; (ii) tell her father of her previous immorality; (iii) dismiss her from her present employment; (iv) not give her a rise in salary; (v) never take her to the pictures again. Clearly, a line must be drawn somewhere before we reach the last case. Once we go beyond the threats of violence, it is not obvious on what principle the line should be drawn. Perhaps it must be a threat which a person of the age and with the other characteristics of the woman could not reasonably be expected, in the circumstances, to resist.[15]

b) *False pretences.* There is a similar uncertainty about the meaning of false pretences. In *Williams*,[16] Hewart CJ said that "it is obvious" that the words of the section go "far beyond the case of rape". It seems likely that it extends to cases where there is no mistake as to the nature of the act. Certainly cases of impersonation, if they are not rape, will be offences under s. 3. It may be that any false pretence which in fact induces P to give a consent which she would not otherwise have given is enough. But it is just arguable (the property offences involving deception do not support the argument) that the pretence must be one which would influence a reasonable woman. Suppose, for example, that D tells P that intercourse improves the voice, or is a certain cure for rheumatism? Whether the restricted meaning given to "false pretences" under the Larceny Act 1916 applies to s. 3 does not seem to have been decided. If it does, "false pretences" is

---

9. *Williams* [1923] 1 KB 340, CCA (s. 3 (1)).
10. *Johnson* [1964] 2 QB 404, [1963] 3 All ER 577, [1963] Crim LR 860, and commentary thereon. See also Glazebrook, [1959] Crim LR 774.
11. *Christian* (1913) 78 JP 112; *Attorney General's Reference (No. 1 of 1975)* above, p. 126.
12. On the question of an attempt to have intercourse by a boy under fourteen see above, p. 459.
13. See above, p. 459.
14. Cf. *Wilson* (1973) 58 Cr App Rep 304 at 307, CA.
15. Cf. Blackmail, below, p. 606; duress, above, p. 239.
16. [1923] 1 KB 340, above, p. 457.

confined to misrepresentation of present fact and, for example, it would be no offence for D to procure intercourse with P by misrepresenting that it was his intention to marry her.[17] But the words "or false representations" suggest that the wider meaning should be adopted.

The CLRC has recommended that these offences should continue in their present wide terms.[18] Although rarely used, they are useful to deal with the occasional case which does not amount to rape but should not be allowed to fall outside the criminal law. The penalty for the s. 2 offence should be increased to five years and the reference to "false pretences or false representations" should be replaced by "deception".[19]

2 Administering Drugs to Obtain or Facilitate Intercourse

By s. 4 (1) of the Sexual Offences Act 1956:

"It is an offence for a person to apply or administer to, or cause to be taken by, a woman any drug, matter or thing with intent to stupefy or overpower her so as thereby to enable any man to have unlawful sexual intercourse with her."

It will be noted that this offence is complete when the drugs, etc., have been applied, administered, etc., with the ulterior intent;[20] and it is not necessary that intercourse should have taken place or been attempted. No doubt this section also applies to the man who seeks to have intercourse himself, and, clearly, the offence can be committed by any person male or female. Notwithstanding R,[1] the better view seems to be that the section does not apply where the man is the woman's husband.

3 Intercourse with a Girl under Thirteen

By s. 5 of the Sexual Offences Act 1956:[2]

"It is an offence for a man to have unlawful sexual intercourse with a girl under the age of thirteen."

4 Intercourse with a Girl under Sixteen

By s. 6 of the Sexual Offences Act 1956:

"(1) It is an offence [triable either way], subject to the exceptions mentioned in this section, for a man to have unlawful sexual intercourse with a girl under the age of sixteen.

(2) Where a marriage is invalid under section two of the Marriage Act 1949 or section one of the Age of Marriage Act 1929 (the wife being a girl under the age of sixteen), the invalidity does not make the husband guilty of an offence under this section because he has sexual intercourse with her, if he believes her to be his wife and has reasonable cause for the belief.

---

17. Cf. *Dent*, below, p. 561, fn. 10.
18. Fifteenth Report, 2.107–2.112.
19. Below, p. 556.
20. Cf. *Shillingford* [1968] Crim LR 282.
1. Above, p. 452.
2. This replaces the Criminal Law Amendment Act 1885, s. 4.

(3) A man is not guilty of an offence under this section because he has unlawful sexual intercourse with a girl under the age of sixteen, if he is under the age of twenty-four and has not previously been charged with a like offence, and he believes her to be of the age of sixteen or over and has reasonable cause for the belief.

In this subsection, 'a like offence' means an offence under this section or an attempt to commit one, or an offence under paragraph (1) of section five of the Criminal Law Amendment Act 1885 (the provision replaced for England and Wales by this section)."

The offence under s. 5 is punishable with life imprisonment. Since they were amended by the Criminal Law Act 1967, the offences under ss. 5 and 6, which were formerly mutually exclusive, overlap, so that a man who has intercourse with a girl under thirteen commits both offences. In these sections there can surely be no doubt that the word "unlawful" is not surplusage. It is inconceivable that a man should be guilty of an offence simply by having intercourse with a woman who is his lawful wife.

It is clear that these sections must be read in the light of *Prince*.[3] It follows that a belief that the girl is over thirteen, no matter how reasonable it may be, will not afford a defence to a charge under s. 5 and that a belief that the girl is over sixteen is a defence to a charge under s. 6 only if it is reasonable and held by a man under twenty-four who has not previously been charged with a like offence. The defence is available only to one who has an actual belief that the girl was over sixteen; reasonable cause for such a belief does not afford a defence to one who never directed his mind to the question of the girl's age.[4] A man is "charged" for the purposes of this section when he first appears before a court having jurisdiction to determine the matter.[5] Thus, if the other conditions of the defence are satisfied, D will not be guilty of an offence under the section if he has unlawful sexual intercourse with a girl under sixteen after being committed for trial for a like offence, even though he be convicted of the first offence before the second one comes before the court of trial; otherwise if he appears before the court of trial for the first offence before he commits the second. Presumably the rationale of the sub-section is that the defence should be available to a young man who has not had brought to his attention in a formal way the serious consequences of a mistake as to the girl's age. If so, does not the restrictive interpretation of "charge" extend the defence too far? When D has been committed for trial he is well aware of the risks involved in his conduct.

When the present offence was originally enacted in 1885 the age of marriage for a girl was fixed by the common law at twelve and it so remained until the Age of Marriage Act 1929 which raised it to sixteen.[6] Intercourse with a girl under sixteen is now necessarily unlawful, except in

3. (1875) LR 2 CCR 154; **SHC 108**; above, pp. 38, 72; see especially per Blackburn J at 171.
4. *Banks* [1916] 2 KB 621; *Harrison* [1938] 3 All ER 134. Yet the Criminal Law Amendment Act in terms required only "reasonable cause to believe" and made no mention of actual belief. A fortiori, then, this interpretation must apply to the present statute.
5. *Rider* [1954] 1 All ER 5, per Streatfeild J.
6. See now the Marriage Act 1949, s. 2.

the case of a marriage valid under a foreign law. In the latter case there is no *actus reus* under s. 5 or s. 6.[7]

The onus of proving (on a balance of probabilities) all the elements of a defence under sub-ss. (2) or (3) of s. 6 is on the accused.[8] Thus a jury ought to convict a man if they thought that there was an even chance that he believed on reasonable grounds that the girl was his wife or that the conditions of sub-s. (3) were fulfilled.[9]

5 Procuration[10] of Girl under Twenty-One

It is no crime to have unlawful sexual intercourse with a girl over the age of sixteen. But, by s. 23 (1) of the Sexual Offences Act 1956:

"It is an offence for a person to procure a girl under the age of twenty-one to have unlawful sexual intercourse in any part of the world with a third person."

Again, there can be no doubt that "unlawful" must mean outside marriage. Otherwise a marriage guidance counsellor who persuaded a twenty-year old woman to have intercourse with her husband would commit an offence.

As already noted in connection with other sections, procuration implies causation by the endeavours of the accused and the offence is not complete until intercourse takes place.[11] It is likely that the principle of *Prince*[12] is again applicable, so that a reasonable belief that the girl is over twenty-one will afford no defence.

A man who procures a girl under twenty-one to have intercourse with himself commits no offence; but if he agrees with a third person that the third person shall procure the girl for him, then he may be convicted under this section as an abettor and also of conspiracy to commit an offence under this section.[13]

6 Intercourse with a Defective

Section 7 of the Sexual Offences Act 1956, as amended by the Mental Health Act 1959, provides:

"(1) It is an offence, subject to the exception mentioned in this section, for a man to have unlawful sexual intercourse with a woman who is a defective.

---

7. *Alhaji Mohamed v Knott* [1969] 1 QB 1, [1968] 2 All ER 563, [1968] Crim LR 341 and commentary thereon.
8. Section 47 of the Act provides: 'Where in any of the foregoing sections the description of an offence is expressed to be subject to exceptions mentioned in the section, proof of the exception is to lie on the person relying on it."
9. For proposals for reform of the law, see CLRC/SO/WP, 24–28.
10. The Act uses "procurement" in ss. 2, 3 and 9 and "procuration" in ss. 22 and 23 but it does not appear that there is any difference in the meaning of these terms. Cf. *Broadfoot* [1976] 3 All ER 753, CA.
11. *Johnson* [1964] 2 QB 404, [1963] 3 All ER 577; *Mackenzie and Higginson* (1910) 6 Cr App Rep 64.
12. (1875) LR 2 CCR 154; above pp. 38, 72.
13. *Mackenzie*, above, following *Whitchurch*, above, p. 299.

(2) A man is not guilty of an offence under this section because he has unlawful sexual intercourse with a woman if he does not know and has no reason to suspect her to be defective."

By s. 45, as amended, "'defective' means a person suffering from a state of arrested or incomplete development of mind which includes *severe impairment of intelligence and social functioning.*"[14] The italicised words do not give examples of deficiency but specify two conditions which must be present in every case for a person to be "defective". They are not terms of art. Severe impairment is to be measured against the standard of normal persons.[15] "Unlawful" in this section and in s. 9 (below) must mean outside marriage. It cannot be that a man commits an offence by having intercourse with his wife whom he knows to have become a defective.

7 Procurement of a Defective
By s. 9 of the Sexual Offences Act 1956:
   "(1) It is an offence, subject to the exception mentioned in this section, for a person to procure a woman who is a defective to have unlawful sexual intercourse in any part of the world.
   (2) A person is not guilty of an offence under this section because he procures a defective to have unlawful sexual intercourse, if he does not know and has no reason to suspect her to be a defective."

Procurement (or "procuration")[16] implies causation by the endeavours of the accused so that it would seem that a girl is not procured to have intercourse if the initiative comes from her.[17] The problem can hardly arise under s. 2 or s. 3 when false pretences or duress have been proved. But it may arise under s. 9.

It is not clear that this section applies, as do ss. 2, 3 and 23, to the case of a man who procures a defective to have intercourse with himself. In *Cook*[18] Stable J held that D had no case to answer although one morning he asked P to go back to bed and then went and had intercourse with her. The judge pointed out that while the Mental Deficiency Act 1913 made it an offence to have intercourse with a mental defective in an institution or out on licence, there was in that Act no such provision for mental defectives generally. Stable J did not, however, clearly rule that it was no offence for D to procure P to have sexual intercourse with D, but seems rather to have held that the element of persuasion involved in procuration was lacking.[19] Any gap in the law revealed by this case is now closed by s. 7[20] and any procuration by D of P to have sexual intercourse with himself is an offence under that section. Only in one situation is the question whether s. 9

14. Cf. the definition of "severe mental impairment" in Mental Health Act 1983, s. 1(1).
15. *Hall* (1987) 86 Cr App Rep 159, [1987] Crim LR 831, CA. For onus of proof, see above, p. 464, fn. 8.
16. See above, p. 461, fn. 10.
17. See above, p. 461, fn. 11.
18. [1954] 1 All ER 60.
19. "He did not get the girl to come into his house. He did not get her away from her mother." But surely there was evidence that D procured P *to have intercourse*?
20. See above, p. 464.

applies to this case now of importance; some attempts to procure may not amount to attempts to have intercourse.[1]

It is clear that, under ss. 7 and 9, it would be a defence for D to establish that he reasonably[2] did not advert to the question whether P was a defective or not. It would not be necessary for him to prove that he considered the question and decided she was not.[3]

8 Sexual Intercourse with Mentally Disordered Patients

Without prejudice to s. 7 of the Sexual Offences Act 1956 and subject to a similar exception, it is an offence under s. 128 of the Mental Health Act 1959, punishable with two years' imprisonment, for an officer, employee or manager of a hospital or mental nursing home to have sexual intercourse with a woman receiving treatment in the hospital or home or, if the intercourse is on the premises, who is receiving treatment there as an out-patient. Similarly in the case of a man having intercourse with a woman who is a mentally disordered patient subject to his guardianship or in his custody or care.

9 Permitting Use of Premises for Intercourse

Sections 25, 26 and 27 of the Sexual Offences Act 1956 create offences ancillary to those in ss. 5, 6 and 7 respectively. Where the owner or occupier of premises, or any person who has or acts or assists in the management or control of any premises, induces or knowingly suffers to resort to or be on those premises, for the purpose of having unlawful sexual intercourse with men or with a particular man—

(i) a girl under thirteen, he is, by s. 25, guilty of an offence punishable with life imprisonment;

(ii) a girl under sixteen or

(iii) a woman who is defective, he is, by ss. 26 and 27 respectively, guilty of an offence punishable with two years' imprisonment. The offence under s. 26 is triable either way.

If "unlawful" means outside marriage in ss. 5, 6 and 7, it must bear the same meaning here. Although each of these sections uses the expression "induce or knowingly suffer", it is not clear that *mens rea* is required for s. 27 alone provides for an exception:

"A person is not guilty of an offence under this section because he induces or knowingly suffers a defective to resort to or be on any premises for the purpose mentioned, if he does not know and has no reason to suspect her to be a defective."

It is implicit in this that D may "knowingly suffer" a defective to be on the premises, although he does not know she is a defective, if he has reason[4] so to suspect. If, as might reasonably be expected, "knowingly suffer" bears the same meaning in each of these closely related provisions, it would follow that D might likewise "knowingly suffer" girls under thirteen and

1. See [1963] Crim LR at 861.
2. But see *Hudson* [1965] 1 All ER 721; and comment at [1965] Crim LR 172.
3. Contrast the position under s. 6 and *Harrison*, above, p. 463.
4. Cf. above, p. 104.

sixteen respectively to be on the premises for the purpose of intercourse, although he believes them to be over those ages; and in the absence of the exception which applies to s. 27, it may be immaterial that that belief is a perfectly reasonable one – that is, *Prince*[5] is applicable and a person who knowingly suffers *girls* (of whatever age) to be on his premises for this purpose does so at his peril.[6] In *McPherson*[7] it was held that in such circumstances, D may be guilty of *inducing*, if not knowingly suffering, the girls to be there.

10 Incest

There remains one offence involving sexual intercourse which does not depend in any way upon a deficiency in the consent of the woman. This is incest, which consists in sexual intercourse between persons within a specified degree of consanguinity. Incest was not a crime at common law or at all until 1908, but was dealt with by the ecclesiastical courts. The Marriage Act 1949, Schedule 1, sets out the degrees of relationship within which marriage is prohibited and, if celebrated, void, but it is only in the case of a much narrower range of relationships that sexual intercourse is a criminal offence. The law is now to be found in ss. 10 and 11 of the Sexual Offences Act 1956:

"**10.**–(1) It is an offence for a man to have sexual intercourse with a woman whom he knows to be his grand-daughter, daughter, sister or mother.

(2) In the foregoing subsection 'sister' includes half-sister, and for the purposes of that subsection any expression importing a relationship between two people shall be taken to apply notwithstanding that the relationship is not traced through lawful wedlock.

11.–(1) It is an offence for a woman of the age of sixteen or over to permit a man whom she knows to be her grandfather, father, brother or son to have sexual intercourse with her by her consent.

(2) In the foregoing subsection 'brother' includes half-brother, and for the purposes of that subsection any expression importing a relationship between two people shall be taken to apply notwithstanding that the relationship is not traced through lawful wedlock."

Where the female is, and is alleged by the indictment to be, a girl under thirteen, the offence is punishable with life imprisonment and an attempt to commit it with seven years. In other cases, the maximum is seven years for the full offence and two years for an attempt. A prosecution for incest or attempted incest may not be commenced except by or with the consent of the Director of Public Prosecutions.

The statute makes it clear[8] that the prohibition applies equally to illegitimate as to legitimate blood relationships, so that D may be convicted

---

5. Above, pp. 38, 72.
6. This construction is supported by the legislative history of the section. See [1980] Crim LR 655–656. But for another view, see Williams, [1981] Crim LR 796.
7. [1980] Crim LR 654.
8. Cf. *Winch* [1974] Crim LR 487.

of incest with his illegitimate grand-daughter, etc. Presumably the basis of the law is eugenic.

It would seem that a consent by a woman sufficient to negative a charge of rape will not necessarily amount to a permission to the man for the purpose of this offence. In *Dimes*[9] it was held that D's acquittal of rape on the ground of P's consent did not necessarily mean that P was an accomplice in incest:

"There is a distinction between submission and permission."[10]

Mens rea must be proved; so D has a defence if he believes that his wife's daughter, P, is the child of an adulterer.[11]

Probably a significant reason for the existence of this offence is the horror and disgust that the idea of it arouses. That, according to the principles of the Wolfenden report,[12] which have gained wide acceptance, is not a good reason for its retention in the law. Another practical reason may be that the genetic risks of incest appear to be very high. The law does not, however, prohibit sexual intercourse by a person with a serious hereditary disease where the genetic risks may be even higher. That is not a conclusive argument, because the offence of incest imposes a relatively slight restriction on liberty – it excludes the right to have intercourse, not altogether, but only with close relatives; and it applies to everyone. If the offence of incest in its present form were to be abolished, it would probably be thought necessary to provide protection for persons under 21 from the lustful attentions of other members of the family.[13]

It is an offence under section 54 of the Criminal Law Act 1977, punishable summarily with six months' and on indictment with two years' imprisonment, for a man or boy to incite to have sexual intercourse with him a girl under the age of sixteen whom he knows to be his grand-daughter, daughter, sister or half-sister. Again, it is immaterial that the relationship is illegitimate. A girl under sixteen who permits incestuous intercourse commits no offence and, consequently, the incitement was not an offence at common law.[14] It is still no offence to incite a girl under sixteen to have incestuous sexual intercourse with a third party.

3 Indecent Assault and Indecency with Children

By s. 14 of the Sexual Offences Act 1956—

"It is an offence . . . for a person to make an indecent assault on a woman";

and by s. 15—

---

9. (1911) 7 Cr App Rep 43.
10. But cf. above, p. 454.
11. *Carmichael* [1940] 1 KB 630, [1940] 2 All ER 165. Cf. *Baillie-Smith* (1977) 64 Cr App Rep 76, CA.
12. See above, p. 17.
13. CLRC, Fifteenth Report, 63–73.
14. *Whitehouse* (1977) 65 Cr App Rep 33; above, p. 265.

"It is an offence for a person to make an indecent assault on a man."

As amended by the Sexual Offences Act 1985, offences under both sections are punishable with ten years' imprisonment. The offences are triable either way. "Assault" here means assault[15] or battery. The law was correctly stated in this respect by the Crown in the Court of Appeal in *Court*:[16]

"The offence of indecent assault included both a battery, or touching, and psychic assault without touching. If there was touching, it was not necessary to prove that the victim was aware of the assault or of the circumstances of indecency. If there was no touching, then to constitute an indecent assault the victim must be shown to have been aware of the assault and of the circumstances of indecency."

The law is stated in terms of a single offence; but given that assault and battery are distinct offences[17] it appears that each section creates two offences. The elements of the offences are the same as those of common assault and battery with the addition of circumstances of indecency. The *actus reus* of assault is the apprehension caused in the mind of the victim and, if the assault is to be an indecent assault, that apprehension must include apprehension of indecency. In the case of an indecent battery P need not be aware of the indecency of the act or circumstances or, indeed, of the battery itself. The indecent touching of a sleeping or unconscious person is an indecent battery.

Neither offence is committed unless D does something to P or causes P to apprehend that D is going to do something to him. In *Fairclough v Whipp*[18] it was held that D was not guilty where he invited a nine-year-old girl (who could not give an effective consent) to touch his exposed penis. The *ratio decidendi* seems to be that an invitation to somebody to touch the invitor cannot amount to an assault. But this is unlikely to be significant in the case where P is sixteen or over. His compliance will then constitute consent to the contact – unless, for example, it is demanded at knife-point and then the production of the knife will supply the assault and the demand the circumstances of indecency. Some of the cases involving children have held that a hostile intention is required; but it is clear that hostility is not an element in common assault or battery and it is submitted that this is equally so in indecent offences. D's attitude may be affectionate – unduly so – but if P does not consent and he knows this, or is reckless, he is guilty.

The assault or battery need not be indecent in itself provided that it is "accompanied by circumstances of indecency of the part of [D]": *Beal v Kelley*[19] where, after P, a boy of fourteen, had declined D's invitation to

15. *Rolfe* (1952) 36 Cr App Rep 4, where D moved towards a woman with his penis exposed, inviting her to have connection with him but did not touch her.
16. [1987] 1 All ER 120 at 122.
17. Above, p. 397.
18. [1951] 2 All ER 834. It has been argued that this was wrong because "A battery may be committed if the impact is occasioned by the movement of the victim himself against some stationary matter, provided that the accused has intentionally caused that impact . . ."; A. N. Macksey, "The Criminal Law and the Woman Seducer" [1956] Crim LR at pp. 453 and 542. Cf. the argument by D. W. Elliott in relation to s. 20 of the Offences against the Person Act 1861, [1974] Crim LR 15. Earlier cases supported this view: *Police v Marchant* (1938) 2 J C L 324; *Boxer* (1944) discussed at 8 J C L 168–170.
19. [1951] 2 All ER 763, approving Archbold (32nd ed.) s. 2981.

touch his penis, D took P's arm and dragged him towards himself. D's argument that this was merely a common assault with an indecent motive was rejected. The act of pulling another towards oneself is not indecent, but the act could not be divorced from its circumstances. Similarly with the example of the knife-point invitation, above.

a) *Consent.* Consent negatives assault but, in the case of indecent assault, only if P is sixteen or over, As in the case of rape, a consent exacted by force of fraud as to the nature of the transaction[20] or, presumably, as to identity, is not a defence. Nor, according to *Donovan,*[21] is consent a defence if the probable consequence of the alleged assault is the infliction of bodily harm; and that decision seems to have received confirmation of its result, if not its reasoning.[1]

b) *The mens rea of indecent assault.* The matter was considered by the House of Lords in *Court*[2] where Lord Ackner, with whom the majority agreed, answered the certified question as follows:

"On a charge of indecent assault the prosecution must prove (1) that the accused intentionally assaulted the victim, (2) that the assault, or the circumstances accompanying it, are capable of being considered by right-minded persons as indecent, (3) that the accused intended to commit such an assault as is referred to in (2) above."

This suggests that, unlike assaults generally, recklessness is not enough. Intention is said to be required both as to the assault and the indecency. If it is an offence of "specific intent", a drunken D who tore off P's clothes, not knowing what he was doing, would be guilty of battery but not indecent battery. This conclusion, however, may be unwarranted.[3] As appears below, in some cases the intention required is no more than an intention to do the act which is objectively judged to be indecent; and presumably it is sufficient, as in rape, that D is reckless whether P consents.

The speeches in *Court* reveal a rather more complex position as follows:

(i) Where the manner or the external circumstances of the assault include no element of indecency, the assault is not an indecent assault, however indecent the purpose of the offender.

(ii) Where the manner or the circumstances of the assault are unambiguously indecent, the assault is an indecent assault, whether the offender has an indecent purpose or not, provided only that he is aware of the external circumstances.

(iii) Where the manner or the external circumstances of an assault are ambiguous, the assault is an indecent assault only if the offender has an indecent purpose.

In case (i), no reasonable observer of the event would think he was witnessing an indecent assault. In case (ii), any reasonable observer of the event would be quite sure he was witnessing an indecent assault. In case

20. *Case* (1850) 1 Den 850.
21. [1934] 2 KB 498.
  1. *A-G's Reference (No. 6 of 1980)*, above, p. 408.
  2. [1988] 2 All ER 221, HL, [1988] Crim LR 537 and commentary.
  3. See *Culyer* (1992) Times, 17 April, CA, above, p. 222.

(iii), a reasonable observer would think, "This may be an indecent assault or it may not. Why is he doing it?"

An example of case (i) is *George*.[4] D attempted to remove a girl's shoe from her foot because this gave him sexual gratification. Streatfeild, rejecting an argument that D's indecent motive made this an indecent assault, held that there were no circumstances of indecency. In *Thomas*[5] it was held that touching the bottom of a girl's skirt was not indecent, though D may have had an indecent purpose. Even when D behaved indecently while assaulting a boy he was held not guilty of an indecent assault because he did not handle the boy indecently and his indecent behaviour was unseen by and unknown to the boy.[6] The example of case (ii) given by the House is that of a man who strips a woman against her will in public. It is then irrelevant whether he does so for his personal sexual gratification, or because he is a misogynist, or because he wishes to embarrass or humiliate her. His intention to do those unambiguously indecent acts is a sufficient *mens rea*. *Court* itself provides an example of case (iii). D, an assistant in a shop, pulled a girl aged twelve who was in the shop across his knee and spanked her on the bottom outside her shorts. When asked why he did it, he said "Buttock fetish". The question was whether this answer was admissible in evidence. The House, Lord Goff dissenting, held that it was because, the act being ambiguous, it was necessary to prove an indecent intention. If D had pulled the girl's shorts down, it may be that the facts would have come within case (ii) and the evidence would have been inadmissible because the question whether his intention was indecent would not have been in issue. If D's purpose had been purely disciplinary, this would have been a defence on the actual facts, but not on the supposed variation. Lord Goff, dissenting, held that indecent assault does not require proof of an indecent purpose and, accordingly, the evidence was inadmissible.

c) *Indecent assault on children and defectives; and indecency with, children.*
Sections 14 and 15 provide that a person under sixteen or who is a defective cannot give any consent which would prevent an act being an assault for the purposes of these sections. If D does not know and has no reason to suspect that P is a defective, P's consent is a defence, although P is in fact a defective.[7] There is no similar provision with respect to persons under sixteen so once again it is clear that *Prince*[8] is applicable and that a reasonable belief that P is over that age is not a defence if he or she is in fact under it.

Where D has gone through a form of marriage with a girl under sixteen and the marriage is invalid, his "wife's" consent to indecent acts is a defence, although she is under sixteen, if D believes on reasonable grounds that she is his wife.[9] There is no similar provision in s. 15 with respect to a woman who has gone through a form of marriage with a boy under sixteen

4. [1956] Crim LR 52.
5. (1985) 81 Cr App Rep 331.
6. *Johnson* [1968] SASR 132 (Bray J).
7. Sections 14 (4) and 15 (4); and see *Hudson*, above, p. 97.
8. (1875) LR 2 CCR 154; **SHC 108**; above, pp. 38, 72.
9. Section 14 (3) which is in similar terms to s. 6 (2), above, p. 462.

and the implication would seem to be that she would have no defence. Perhaps such a case is unlikely to arise, but it is possible, and the omission of the defence from s. 15 seems to be an oversight.

Where a man under the age of twenty-four is charged under s. 6 with intercourse with a girl under sixteen and establishes a defence on the ground that he reasonably believed her to be over sixteen, he may be convicted on a second count for an indecent assault under s. 14.[10] In *Laws*[11] the Court of Criminal Appeal rightly said that

"it is indeed a grotesque state of affairs that the law offers a defence upon the major charge but excludes that defence if the minor charge is preferred."

Yet the anomaly was re-enacted, after these observations, in the consolidation of the law in 1956.

A not dissimilar curiosity is that boys under fourteen, who must be acquitted of any charge involving sexual intercourse because of their presumed incapacity, may be convicted of indecent assault on evidence that they did in fact have intercourse.[12] This discrepancy seems less objectionable, however, since the acquittal on the major charge is on a "technicality", whereas an acquittal under s. 6 (3) is based on the absence of *mens rea* or even negligence.

d) *Hostility*. It was held in a series of cases[13] involving consenting children that there was no assault because no hostile act was done to the child. This appears to ignore the statutory rule that the child's consent is irrelevant. The Court of Appeal has since held in *M'Cormack*[14] that an indecent act done to a girl of fifteen, with her consent and without hostility, is an indecent assault (i.e., battery) and in *Faulkner v Talbot*[15] Lane LCJ said that an assault "need not be hostile or rude or aggressive, as some of the cases seem to indicate". It seems that the earlier cases can be justified, if at all, only on the ground that the courts thought that nothing indecent was done by D to P. This was the approach of the Court in *Sutton*[16] where it was held that the touching of naked boys under sixteen by D, who was taking pornographic photographs, was not indecent since the touching was merely to indicate a pose.

Where, as in *Burrows*,[17] both the persons concerned are male, a charge of gross indecency under s. 13[18] will lie; but where one of the parties is a

---

10. *Forde* [1923] 2 KB 400; *Keech* (1929) 21 Cr App Rep 125; *Maughan* (1934) 24 Cr App Rep 130.
11. (1928) 21 Cr App Rep 45 at 46.
12. *Waite* [1892] 2 QB 600; *Williams* [1893] 1 QB 320.
13. *Burrows* [1952] 1 All ER 58n; *DPP v Rogers* [1953] 2 All ER 644, 37 Cr App Rep 137, DC; *Williams v Gibbs* [1958] Crim LR 127.
14. [1969] 2 QB 442, [1969] 3 All ER 371. Similarly in the case of a boy under sixteen: *Kallides* (CA unreported, referred to in [1977] 3 All ER at 479).
15. [1981] 3 All ER 468, [1981] 1 WLR 1528, 74 Cr App Rep 1, DC; **SHC 388**.
16. [1977] 3 All ER 476, CA, [1977] Crim LR 569 and commentary thereon. See the Protection of Children Act 1978 which creates offences of taking, permitting to be taken, possessing or publishing, indecent photographs of persons under 16 and *Owen* [1988] 1 WLR 134, [1988] Crim LR 120, CA.
17. Above, fn. 13.
18. Below, p. 480.

female and D does nothing to P there is no possible charge under the Sexual Offences Act.[19] The Divisional Court pointed out the necessity for an amendment of the law on several occasions and now, by the Indecency with Children Act 1960—

> "Any person who commits an act of gross indecency with or towards a child under the age of fourteen, or who incites a child under that age to such an act with him or another, shall be liable on conviction on indictment to imprisonment for a term not exceeding two years or on summary conviction to imprisonment for a term not exceeding six months, to a fine not exceeding [£2,000] or both."

Since this makes mere incitement the offence, it is immaterial that the child does not act on the invitation to touch the accused. Inactivity on D's part is enough if, in the opinion of the jury, it amounts to an invitation to the child to start, or to continue, conduct amounting to gross indecency.[20] The offence would also be committed if D suggested to two children, at least one of whom was under fourteen, that they should commit a gross indecency together.

e) *Assaults by Women.* Under ss. 14 and 15 of the Sexual Offences Act 1956 it is an offence for "a person" to commit an indecent assault and it is clear that this includes a woman as well as a man. It was held in *Hare*[1] that a woman who instigated a twelve-year-old boy to have intercourse with her and infected him with venereal disease was guilty of an offence under s. 62 of the Offences against the Person Act 1861, the predecessor of the present s. 15. This was in spite of the fact that ss. 61–63 of the 1861 Act were headed "Unnatural Offences". The court held that the words of the heading could not control the plain meaning of the statute.[2] In the present Act, ss. 14 and 15 fall under the heading "Assaults" and not under "Unnatural Offences".

It is not an offence for a woman to induce or permit a boy under the age of sixteen to have sexual intercourse with her. If she does so and there is no evidence that she did anything more than lie passively, no offence is committed. If, however, before, during or after the sexual intercourse, she does to the boy any act which would be an indecent assault if it were done without his consent – such as touching his penis – then she is guilty of an indecent assault although he does consent to or encourage the act in question. It is strange that an act which is merely a prelude or a postlude to sexual intercourse should be an offence when the sexual intercourse is not but, given that s. 15 applies to an act by a woman, the conclusion is inevitable. The section, as interpreted, states in effect that a woman commits an indecent assault if she indecently handles a boy under sixteen

---

19. It might be indecent exposure at common law or under the Vagrancy Act 1824, below, p. 474.
20. *Speck* [1977] 2 All ER 859, CA.
  1. [1934] 1 KB 354.
  2. That headings and sidenotes are not part of the Act and cannot be used as an aid to construction has now been held by the House of Lords in *Chandler v Director of Public Prosecutions* [1964] AC 763, [1962] 3 All ER 142. C. K. Allen criticises the principle of interpretation applied in *Hare* as "the extreme of literalism": *Law in the Making* (7th ed.) 524.

with his consent and it is impossible to say that what was an assault when it was done ceases to be an assault when the episode culminates in sexual intercourse.[3]

In *Hare* the court said obiter that a woman might be guilty of an indecent assault on another woman. This seems to have been held by Lopes J in *Armstrong*;[4] and, indeed, there is no reason for interpreting "person" more narrowly in s. 14 than in s. 15.[5]

It has been suggested that

"*Hare* is an authority for the proposition that an indecent assault may be committed passively."[6]

It is submitted, however, that this is not so, for a woman's part in voluntary sexual intercourse, particularly where she is the instigating party, may reasonably be presumed to involve the doing by her of acts, which, if done without consent, would be battery.

4 Indecent Exposure[7]

1 Indecent Exposure at Common Law

a) *The actus reus*. It is a common law misdemeanour[8] to commit an act outraging public decency in public and in such a way that more than one person sees, or is at least able to see, the act. The most common way of committing this offence is by indecently exposing the body.

A wide view is taken of "in public". In *Wellard*[9] Grove J said that a public place is one where the public go, no matter whether they have a right to or not. But earlier cases seem to go farther than this. D may himself be on private premises, to which the general public do not have access, and so may those who see him. In *Bunyan and Morgan*,[10] D was in the parlour of a public house and was witnessed through the window of another room of the house; and in *Thallman*[11] D was on the roof of a private house and could be seen only from the windows of other houses. These could hardly be described as places "where the public go" yet both were convicted. It is

---

3. *Faulkner v Talbot* (1981) 74 Cr App Rep 1, DC.

4. (1885) 49 JP 745.

5. The Wolfenden Committee found no instance of an assault by one female on another "which exhibits the libidinous features that characterise sexual acts between males". In most cases where a woman is convicted under s. 14 it is as aider and abettor of a man in an assault upon another woman: Cmnd. 247, p. 38.

6. Macksey [1956] Crim LR at 355. In *Mason* Veale J held that *Hare* was not authority for this proposition, the court being solely concerned with the question whether a woman can commit an indecent assault.

7. See report of Home Office Working Party on Vagrancy and Street Offences; Leigh, [1975] Crim LR 413.

8. *Sidney* (1663) 1 Sid 168; *Knuller*, above, p. 292.

9. (1884) 14 QBD 63.

10. (1844) 1 Cox CC 74.

11. (1863) 9 Cox CC 388.

doubtful if "in public" adds anything to the requirement that two or more persons must have been able to see the act.[12]

It has been held to be no offence where only one person was able to see that act;[13] but it has never been held that two persons must have actually seen it. In *Elliot*[14] it was submitted that it was enough that D exposed himself in a place where he might have been seen, although *no one* saw him. The court was evidently divided, three to two (but which way does not appear) and asked for the case to be re-argued. They later changed their minds and no judgment was delivered. *Mayling*[15] the Court of Criminal Appeal did not go farther than to say that it is clear that more than one person must *at least have been able* to see the act; but two persons actually saw it in that case. The point is therefore not settled. It seems artificial to insist on two persons having seen the act; but, if this is not required, what is the test? Must two persons have been present? Or is it enough that D exposed himself in a street or at a window where two or more persons might have been expected to pass by and see him though no one did? As a practical matter, of course, there will almost invariably be one witness of the act, for otherwise it would not be provable except by confession.

It is not necessary to prove that anyone was actually disgusted or annoyed. This was decided in *Mayling*,[16] where the court pointed out that a requirement of actual disgust would be incompatible with a rule that the offence could be established by proof that persons could have seen, but did not see, the act. Probably the exposure must grossly transgress generally accepted bounds of decency and tend gravely to offend the average person.[17] Whether it does so will depend on time, place and circumstance.

b) *The mens rea.* It is unnecessary to prove any sexual motive or any intention to insult or annoy. Lady Godiva would have been guilty, notwithstanding her admirable motives, at least if there had been two peeping Toms. In *Crunden*[18] D was convicted when he undressed and swam (presumably naked) opposite the East Cliff at Brighton in view of a row of houses. It was held irrelevant that his object was to procure health and enjoy a favourite recreation, not to outrage decency or corrupt the public morals.

It is submitted that it must at least be proved that D intended that, or was reckless whether, the exposure might be seen by two or more persons who do not consent to see it. In *Bunyan and Morgan*[19] the recorder seems to have held that negligence would suffice and that, although D had been seeking

---

12. Cf. Lord Denham CJ in *Watson* (1847) 2 Cox CC 376 at 377: "... a nuisance must be public; *that is*, to the injury or offence of several," and Willes J in *Harris and Cocks* (1871) 11 Cox CC 659 at 661. See also Lord Coleridge CJ and Huddleston B in *Wellard* as reported in 15 Cox CC 559 at 562, 563.
13. *Reubegard* (1830) cited in 1 Den 344; *Webb* (1848) 1 Den 338; *Watson*, above; *Farrell* (1862) 9 Cox CC 446.
14. (1861) Le & Ca 103.
15. [1963] 2 QB 717, [1963] 1 All ER 687.
16. Ibid.
17. *Moloney v Mercer* [1971] 2 NSWLR 207 (Taylor J) and *Knuller*, above, p. 292.
18. (1809) 2 Camp 89; *Reed* (1871) 12 Cox CC 1.
19. (1844) 1 Cox CC 74.

privacy, it was enough that there was a reasonable probability of his being discovered. This seems to be contrary to principle.

The offence may be committed by a female as well as a male person,[20] and the exposure need not necessarily be to persons of the opposite sex. If, however, three men were to bathe together naked, in a place in which they would reasonably expect not to be observed by anyone else, it is thought that no offence would be committed because this could not be said to outrage public decency. But it is quite otherwise if a man masturbates himself in the view of other men.[1] Is the offence committed if a mixed party of men and women bathe naked together? It is thought not (unless they are liable to be observed by others) because their consent negatives the outraging of decency. If it were not so, nudist camps would be illegal.

2 Indecent Exposure under the Vagrancy Act 1824

By s. 4 of the Vagrancy Act 1824:

"... every person wilfully, openly, lewdly and obscenely exposing his person with intent to insult any female ... shall be deemed a rogue and vagabond. ...."

The offence is punishable summarily by three months' imprisonment or a fine not exceeding level three on the standard scale; or, on a second conviction and committal to the Crown Court for sentence, by one year's imprisonment.

Unlike the common law offence this crime is limited to exposure by a male to female and requires an ulterior intent to insult. The word "person" means "penis"[2] so that—

"however deliberate be the intent to insult the female, and however great the insult she feels, the exposure of the backside is not within the section."[3]

The section was formerly limited to public places, but this limitation was removed by the Criminal Justice Act 1925 s. 42. The exposure is committed "openly" even though it occurs in D's own bedroom.[4] The vast majority of charges of indecent exposure are brought under this Act.[5]

5 "Unnatural" Offences[6]

1 Buggery

Buggery at common law consists in intercourse per anum[7] by a man with a man or woman;[8] or intercourse per anum or per vaginam[9] by a man or a

---

20. *Elliot* (1861) Le & Ca 103.
1. For example, *Mayling*, above.
2. *Evans v Ewels* [1972] 2 All ER 22, DC; contra, *Norton v Rowlands* [1971] CLY 2384 (QS).
3. *Sexual Offences* (ed. Radzinowicz), 427.
4. *Ford v Falcone* [1971] 2 All ER 1138.
5. *Sexual Offences* 427.
6. Some may regard this term as offensive, but it is the heading in the Act.
7. Other unnatural forms of intercourse are not within the meaning of the term: *Jacobs* (1817) Russ & Ry 331; but may amount to indecent assault or an act of gross indecency; see below, p. 480.
8. *Wiseman* (1718) Fortes Rep 91.
9. East says "in any manner": 1 PC 480.

woman[10] with an animal. It can be committed by a husband with his wife.[11] As in rape, penetration must be proved, but emission need not.[12]

Consent is no defence. Indeed, the consenting party is also guilty of the offence, not merely as an abettor but as a principal offender.[13] The person effecting the intercourse is known as the "agent" and the other party as the "patient".

Buggery has never been defined by statute and its elements are still governed by the common law. At common law it was a single offence, whatever the age or sex of the parties, whether or not they both consented and whether or not an animal was involved. This was unaffected by the Sexual Offences Act 1956 s. 12 (1) which provided:

"It is an offence for a person to commit buggery with another person or with an animal."

That subsection, incorporating the common law of buggery, is still the basis of the law, but it is now qualified by the Sexual Offences Act 1967, which provides that it is not an offence for consenting men, who have attained the age of twenty-one, to commit buggery in private. The Act introduced a new scale of penalties[14] according to the circumstances of the particular buggery. The effect of *Courtie*[15] is that, since 1967 (though no one seems to have realised this until 1984) there are four distinct statutory offences of buggery, punishable with life, ten years, five years and two years respectively.

Section 1 of the Sexual Offences Act 1967 provides[16] that it shall not be an offence for a man to commit buggery or gross indecency with another man provided that:

(i) the act is done in private,
(ii) the parties consent and
(iii) the parties have attained the age of twenty-one.

An act is not done in private for this purpose if (i) more than two persons take part or are present; or (ii) the act is done in a lavatory to which the public have or are permitted to have access, whether on payment or otherwise. Where these conditions are not satisfied, whether a place is private seems to be a question of fact and the jury must take into account all the circumstances – the nature of the place, the time, the lighting, the likelihood of a third person coming on the scene and so on.[17]

A person suffering from severe mental handicap[18] cannot consent for the purposes of the Act. It is a defence for D to prove "that he did not know

10. *Bourne* (1952) 36 Cr App Rep 125; **SHC 139**; above, p. 152. Cf. Coke, 3 Inst 59 ". . . a great lady had committed buggery with a baboon and conceived by it . . ."!
11. *Jellyman* (1838) 8 C & P 604.
12. *Reekspear* (1832) 1 Mood CC 342; *Cozins* (1834) 6 C & P 351. Where penetration is impossible, D may be convicted of an attempt. See *Brown* (1889) 24 QBD 357 and p. 317, above.
13. Stephen, *Digest*, Art. 221.
14. Below, p. 481.
15. [1984] AC 463, [1984] 1 All ER 740, above, p. 32.
16. Section 1.
17. *Reakes* [1974] Crim LR 615. (The commentary should refer to proof beyond reasonable doubt, *not* proof on a balance of probabilities.)
18. This means the same as "defective" in Sexual Offences Act 1956, s. 45. Above, p. 465, fn. 14.

and had no reason to suspect" P to be suffering from severe mental handicap. It seems probable that it would be no defence to show that D1 believed D2 to be over twenty-one if he was in fact under that age.[19]

The Act expressly puts on the Crown the onus of proving that the act was

   (i) not done in private, or

  (ii) without consent or

 (iii) that any party was under twenty one.

There is, however, an evidential burden on D to raise these issues.[20]

An act of buggery or gross indecency continues to be an offence where it is done on a United Kingdom merchant ship by a member of the crew of that ship with another man who is a member of the crew of that or any other United Kingdom merchant ship.[1] The Act does not affect the provisions of the Army Act 1955, or the Air Force Act 1955, under which disgraceful conduct of an unnatural kind is punishable with two years' imprisonment,[2] or the Naval Discipline Act 1957[3] under which disgraceful conduct of an indecent kind is similarly punishable.

A consenting party under twenty-one continues to be guilty of an offence but proceedings against him for participating in any buggery or gross indecency may not be instituted except with the consent of the Director of Public Prosecutions.[4]

It continues to be an offence under s. 12 (1) of the 1956 Act for a man to commit buggery with a woman,[5] though both parties consent, or for a man or a woman to commit buggery with an animal, whether in private or not. And although a homosexual act between adult males in private is no longer an offence, there may be a conspiracy to corrupt public morals by publicly encouraging such acts.[6]

It seems to be the law that a person under fourteen, whether male or female, cannot be convicted as a principal offender either as agent or as patient.[7] Clearly, as regards the female and the male patient this does not depend upon any presumption of sexual incapacity. Coke,[8] Hale[9] and East[10] put this rule upon the child's want of discretion; but, if this is so, then the child over ten ought to be liable to conviction on proof of mischievous discretion. However, in *Tatam*[11] the Court of Criminal Appeal ruled that three boys under fourteen with whom D had committed buggery were not accomplices, "being unable at law to commit that offence." This

19. Cf. *Prince* (1875) LR 2 CCR 154; **SHC 108**; above, pp. 38, 72.
20. *Spight* [1986] Crim LR 817, CA and commentary.
  1. Section 2.
  2. Section 66 of both Acts.
  3. Section 37.
  4. If consent is not obtained, any proceeding is a nullity: *Angel* [1968] 2 All ER 607n, [1968] Crim LR 342; but consent is not required on a charge of incitement to commit the offence: *Assistant Recorder of Kingston-upon-Hull, ex p Morgan* [1969] 1 All ER 416.
  5. *Harris* (1971) 55 Cr App Rep 290, CA.
  6. *Knuller v Director of Public Prosecutions* [1973] AC 435, [1972] All ER 898; **SHC 265**; above, p. 292.
  7. Cf. Hogan, [1962] Crim LR 683; Williams, [1964] Crim LR 686.
  8. 3 Inst. 59.
  9. 1 PC 670.
10. 1 PC 480.
11. (1921) 15 Cr App Rep 132.

presumably means that they could be convicted neither as principals nor as abettors. Yet, somewhat remarkably, it seems that a child under fourteen could be convicted of abetting D to commit buggery upon P. This was held in *Cratchley*,[12] where a boy of under ten, who kept watch, was held not to be an accomplice in the buggery of P by D but only on the ground of lack of evidence of guilty knowledge.[13] If the child's immunity really depends on presumed lack of discretion, the presumption ought equally to be rebuttable, or irrebuttable, whether D is the patient or the abettor of a buggery upon another. The only basis on which the present rule can be justified is that the law is designed to protect the patient[14] – which seems to be contrary to fact. It may well be that the present rule is due to a misunderstanding by the courts and subsequent writers of Hale, Coke and East who probably meant no more than that a person under fourteen is not liable unless a mischievous discretion is proved.

Where the agent is a boy under fourteen, the patient, if over fourteen, may nevertheless be convicted,[15] a result difficult to reconcile with the conclusive presumption of incapacity.

2 Procuring Others to Commit Lawful Homosexual Acts

Section 4 of the Sexual Offences Act 1967 creates a new offence, triable either way and punishable on indictment with two years' imprisonment, of procuring another man to commit with a third man an act of buggery which, by reason of s. 1 of the Act, is not an offence.

3 Assault with Intent to Commit Buggery: and Attempts

By s. 16 (1) of the Sexual Offences Act 1956:

"It is an offence for a person to assault another person with intent to commit buggery."

The offence is punishable with ten years' imprisonment. An attempt to commit buggery is likewise punishable, though it is no longer[16] a statutory offence. Most cases under s. 16 (1) will also amount to an attempt but there may be occasional instances where the statutory provision is useful, as where D assaults P, intending to carry him off and commit buggery some hours later.[17] Here the act would probably not be sufficiently proximate to be an attempt but would amount to the statutory offence. On the other hand an attempt covers cases obviously not within the statute, as where D attempts buggery with an animal or, perhaps, approaches a sleeping P and does a sufficiently proximate act which does not amount to an assault or battery.

12. (1913) 9 Cr App Rep 232.
13. The case is distinguishable from *Tatam*, above, only on the assumption that, in the latter case, none of the boys aided and abetted the buggery of another.
14. Cf. *Tyrrell*, above, p. 156.
15. *Allen* (1849) 1 Den 364. It is perhaps not surprising that the court was anxious to uphold the conviction in that case: D induced a boy of twelve to bugger him.
16. It was formerly included in s. 62 of the Offences against the Person Act 1861. Now the only statutory reference to attempt is in the Second Schedule to the 1956 Act, providing for the punishment.
17. And cf. *Lankford* [1959] Crim LR 209.

The necessity for an assault also means that consent must be a defence to a charge under the section, and this even though the other party be under sixteen (for there is here no statutory provision to the contrary) but old enough to understand the nature of the act;[18] but where a charge under s 16 (1) would fail only because of consent, the act is almost certainly an indecent assault under s. 15 by the one party where the other is under sixteen. And, whatever the age of the parties, it may amount to a gross indecency under s. 13.[19] Consent would be no defence, however, to a charge of attempt to commit buggery and here both parties might be convicted if their acts were sufficiently proximate.

Whether a boy under fourteen may be convicted of attempted buggery depends on the same arguments as are considered above[20] in relation to attempted rape.

4 Indecency between Men

By s. 13 of the Sexual Offences Act 1956:

"It is an offence [triable either way] for a man[1] to commit an act of gross indecency with another man, whether in public or private, or to be a party to the commission by a man of an act of gross indecency with another man, or to procure the commission by a man of an act of gross indecency with another man."

As noted above,[2] this is now qualified by the Sexual Offences Act 1967, s. 1. This Act also provides, by s. 4 (3), that it shall not be an offence under s. 13 of the 1956 Act for a man to procure the commission *with himself* of an act of gross indecency by another man where that act, by reason of s. 1 of the 1967 Act, is not an offence. It continues to be an offence under s. 13 for a man to procure another man to commit with a third man an act of gross indecency, though the act, by reason of s. 1 of the 1967 Act, is not an offence. The effect of *Courtie*[3] is that there are two offences of gross indecency – (i) by a man of or over twenty-one with a man under that age (five years) and (ii) other offences (two years).

It is an offence under the Criminal Attempts Act 1981 to attempt to procure the commission of an act of gross indecency by one man with another;[4] or to incite another to procure such an act,[5] at least if it is not an incitement to conspire[6] and, possibly, even if it is.

The nature of "gross indecency" does not seem to have been further defined by the courts, save that it has been held that[7] there is no need for actual physical contact, if two men concert to behave in an indecent manner. It is enough that

---

18. *Wollaston* (1872) 12 Cox CC 180: consent negatives an assault. The point seems to have been overlooked in *Cratchley*.
19. Below.
20. Above, p. 459.
1. "Man" includes "boy": s. 46.
2. See p. 477.
3. [1984] AC 463, [1984] 1 All ER 740, above, p. 32.
4. *Chief Constable of Hampshire v Mace* (1986) 84 Cr App Rep 40, [1986] Crim LR 752, CA.
5. *Bentley* [1923] 1 KB 403.
6. *Sirat* (1985) 83 Cr App Rep 41, [1986] Crim LR 245, above, p. 268.
7. *Hunt* [1950] 2 All ER 291.

"two men put themselves in such a position that it can be said that a grossly indecent exhibition is going on."

According to the evidence before the Wolfenden Committee:[8]

"... the offence usually takes one of three forms; either there is mutual masturbation; or there is some form of intercrural contact; or oral-genital contact (with or without emission) takes place. Occasionally the offence may take a more recondite form; techniques in heterosexual relations vary considerably, and the same is true of homosexual relations."

The distinction between "indecency" and "gross indecency" is not clear. It has been suggested, as an example, that if

"two male persons kissed each other under circumstances which showed that the act was immoral and unnatural",

this would be indecent but not grossly indecent.[9]

The offence requires the co-operation of two men acting in concert.[10] If D's indecent act is directed against another person who does not consent, the act cannot amount to an offence under the section.[11] If D's act is directed towards procuring the co-operation of the other in the act of indecency, then it may amount to an attempt to commit an offence under the section, if the other is unwilling to collaborate. The act may also of course be an indecent assault.[12]

Where the charge is one of *procuring*, the same considerations apply as where that term is used elsewhere in the Act.[13]

5 Penalties for Buggery and Gross Indecency

The Sexual Offences Act 1967, s. 3, provides a new scale of penalties for, and, following *Courtie*, series of offences of, buggery and gross indecency as follows:

Buggery
  (i) If with a boy under the age of sixteen or with a woman or an animal – life.
  (ii) If with a man who is sixteen or over who did not consent – ten years.
  (iii) If with a man between sixteen and twenty-one who consented where D is twenty-one or over – five years.
  (iv) (a) If with a man of twenty-one or over who consented (whatever D's age) – two years.
      (b) If with a man of sixteen or over who consented and D is under twenty-one – two years.

Attempted buggery
  (i) If with a boy under the age of sixteen or with a woman or an animal – ten years.[14]

---

8. Cmnd. 247, p. 38. See also *Sexual Offences* (ed. Radzinowicz), 349.
9. *The Criminal Law Amendment Act* (4th ed.) (1963), by Mead and Bodkin, cited in *Sexual Offences*, p. 349.
10. *Hornby and Peaple* [1946] 2 All ER 487.
11. *Preece and Howells* [1976] Crim LR 392, CA.
12. *Pearce* (1952) 35 Cr App Rep 17, CA.
13. Above, p. 461. See also *Jones* [1896] 1 QB 4; *Bentley* [1923] 1 KB 403.
14. Sexual Offences Act 1967, s. 3 (1) and Powers of Criminal Courts Act 1973, s. 18 (2).

   (ii) If with a man of sixteen or over – the maximum for the completed offence (above).[15]

Committing or procuring gross indecency

   (i) If by a man of or over twenty-one with a man under that age – five years.

   (ii) In other cases two years.

The draughtsman of the 1967 Act was probably unaware that he was creating a series of offences and might have drafted them differently had he been able to foresee *Courtie*. The effect is that the offences are mutually exclusive – a man buggering a fifteen-year-old boy believing him to be sixteen (and vice versa) intends to commit one offence and commits another – raising the 'kind of problems faced by the court in *Prince*[16] and suggesting that the offences are likely to be construed to impose strict liability with respect to age and, perhaps, to sex – but not, it is to be hoped, consent.

15. Ibid.
16. Above, pp. 38, 72.

15 Road Traffic Offences[1]

The advent of the motor vehicle created problems with which the existing law was ill-equipped to deal. The threat of proceedings for manslaughter might deter the motorist from driving with wilful disregard for human life, but where some harm less than death was caused other offences against the person were hardly pertinent at all. These offences, in the main, require that the harm should be caused intentionally or recklessly. It is rare for a motorist to intend harm though perhaps not so rare for him to be reckless as to whether or not he causes harm, particularly if recklessness does not require the driver to be aware of the obvious risk which he is taking. Though the motorist who causes harm may often be at fault, the harm he causes is ordinarily both undesired and unforeseen by him. But it must not be thought that there is little or no room for offences of intention and recklessness in road traffic. There are many offences (such as speeding, driving whilst unlicensed, driving whilst uninsured) where the offence is ordinarily committed intentionally or recklessly though it does not follow that such offences will require proof of intention or recklessness. Generally it is only in relation to the causing of harm to the person or property that the motorist is neither intentional nor reckless.

There were some provisions of statutes which applied to motorists, but only, as it were, by chance. Under the Highway Act 1835, s. 72, for example, it was an offence to drive any carriage on the pavement and this could be applied to the motor carriage, and under the Town Police Clauses Act 1847, s. 28, the furious driving of any horse or carriage was an offence and this was applied to motorists. And it is still an offence under s. 35 of the Offences against the Person Act 1861 for a person, having charge of a carriage or vehicle, to cause bodily harm by wanton or furious driving.[2] But for the main part the law barely concerned the motorist at all. There were no tests of driving proficiency, no registration requirements, no compulsory insurance, and virtually no driving offences. The common law could not fill gaps like these and the result is that for practical purposes the regulation of road traffic is almost entirely statutory.

---

1. Department of Transport, Home Office, *Road Traffic Law Review Report*, HMSO, 1988, hereinafter referred to as the *North Report*. Spencer "Road Traffic Law: A Review of the North Report" [1988] Crim LR 707.

2. This provision is not a dead letter; see *Cooke* [1971] Crim LR 44, QS where D could not be charged under the Road Traffic legislation because the offence was not committed on a road, and *Mohan* [1976] QB 1, [1975] 2 All ER 193, CA; **SHC 276**. The *North Report* recommended the repeal of s. 35.

The legislation is considerable and it is neither possible nor appropriate in a work of this kind to deal in a comprehensive way with the plethora of offences created. Attention is accordingly concentrated on careless driving, dangerous driving and causing death by dangerous driving since a discussion of these contributes to an understanding of the general principles of the criminal law.

1 Careless Driving

At common law negligence is only rarely the basis for criminal liability. *Gross* negligence was once the basis for manslaughter but the present status of manslaughter by gross negligence is very much in doubt.[3] It may be that at least in some cases[4] a mistake of fact affords a defence only if it is reasonable as well as honest and where that is the case criminal liability is incurred though D has been no more than negligent. It is otherwise not an offence to harm the person or property of another by negligent conduct. It is, however, an offence to drive a mechanically propelled vehicle carelessly and the offence does not require (though a prosecution is unlikely without[5]) harm to person or property. Why, if it is not an offence negligently to cause injury with "a garden fork, hedge trimmer or even a chainsaw"[6] should it be an offence to cause harm (or even not to cause harm) by the negligent use of a motor vehicle? The *North Report* concedes that there is not a great logical difference between the careless use of a chainsaw or a vehicle but defends the offence of careless driving on the grounds that:

"... the careless use of chainsaws does not contribute to over 5,000 deaths every year. It is because the danger associated with the widespread use of motor vehicles is so great that society has decided to attempt to restrain the use of vehicles so as to reduce this danger. And there are parallels between road traffic law and other bodies of regulatory law covering areas of activity such as health and safety at work, and building standards. Some of these areas of law contain offences which could be the result of mere carelessness such as, for example, polluting a river or leaving a machine unguarded. The common element between such offences is the degree of danger that may be caused to innocent parties."[7]

Some may find this reassurance convincing, others less so. The assumption appears to be that without an offence of careless driving road deaths attributable to this source would be significantly more than 5,000, but the assumption remains unproven.

---

3. See above, p. 372.
4. E.g., bigamy, see above, p. 94. See generally above, p. 88.
5. "One widespread complaint was of the mechanical nature of the prosecution decision – a bad case of careless driving may not go to court because no personal injury was caused, and conversely a very trivial case of carelessness may lead to prosecution simply because injury was caused": the *North Report*, 5.27.
6. *North Report*, 5.29.
7. *North Report*, 5.30.

To the suggestion that careless driving ought not to be a criminal offence because drivers are already constrained to drive as best they can by a well grounded fear for their own safety and their wish to avoid an accident and its consequences (not least the loss of a no claims bonus the cost of which may exceed any fine the court imposes) the *North Report* replied that if the offence of careless driving were to be abolished then:

"... at least part of it would have to be replaced or there would be some serious instances of bad driving which would go unpunished. In our view it is likely that the issues here are confused by the amount of attention which is focussed on the common shorthand term for this offence – careless driving. But what is required to establish the section 3 offence is more than this. The course of driving must be found to be lacking in *due* care or *reasonable* consideration. Cases where no accident is caused, involving momentary inattention for example, by a driver with an unblemished driving career should not, in our opinion, lead to an appearance in court. But a series of bad overtaking decisions might, if such driving came to police attention, warrant prosecution, even if no accident resulted."[8]

This passage is puzzling. It suggests that the offence of careless driving should be retained because it will deal with cases of "bad" driving which are not bad enough to qualify as "very bad" driving within the offence of dangerous driving. It also suggests that carelessness per se does not suffice for the s. 3 offence; the emphasis on *"due* care" and *"reasonable* consideration" suggesting that more than mere carelessness is required to constitute the offence. This is a novel suggestion and does not appear to be one articulated in the existing case law.

Section 3 of the Road Traffic Act 1988, as substituted by s. 2 of the Road Traffic Act 1991, provides:

"If a person drives a mechanically propelled vehicle on a road or other public place without due care and attention, or without reasonable consideration for other persons using the road or place, he is guilty of an offence."

The offence is summary only and is punishable by a fine at level 4.[9]

The substituted section extends the offence in two respects, first by substituting "mechanically propelled vehicle" for "motor vehicle", and secondly, by the addition of "or other public place" to "road".[10] Otherwise the law is unchanged.

In order to determine whether the offence of careless driving is committed, the test, as Lord Goddard CJ said in *Simpson v Peat*[11] is: was D exercising that degree of care and attention that a reasonable and prudent driver would exercise in the circumstances? The relevant standard, according to Lord Hewart CJ,

"is an objective standard, impersonal and universal, fixed in relation to the safety of other users of the highway. It is in no way related to the

---

8. *North Report*, 5.31.
9. Disqualification is discretionary and the offence carries 2–5 penalty points.
10. The *North Report* recommended these extensions for the offence of dangerous driving (8.10, 8.12) but not for careless driving.
11. [1952] 2 QB 24, [1952] 1 All ER 447 at 449, DC.

degree of proficiency or degree of experience attained by the individual driver."[12]

It is accordingly no defence that a learner driver is doing his best if the care exercised falls short of that to be expected from the reasonably competent driver;[13] nor is any special standard applicable to experienced drivers, such as police drivers who may be trained to meet exacting standards of proficiency,[14] and even though they may have to cope with emergencies which are not the lot of ordinary drivers.[15] Faced by an emergency the issue is not whether by taking some other course of action harm may have been avoided but whether D's reaction to the emergency was a reasonable one.[16]

Another view of the nature of liability for careless driving was given by Lord Diplock in *Lawrence*.[17] "Section 3", he said,

"creates an absolute offence in the sense in which that term is commonly used to denote an offence for which the only mens rea needed is simply that the prohibited physical act (actus reus) done by the accused was directed by a mind that was conscious of what his body was doing, it being unnecessary to show that his mind was also conscious of the possible consequences of his doing it. So s. 3 takes care of this kind of inattention or misjudgment to which the ordinarily careful motorist is occasionally subject without its necessarily involving any moral turpitude, although it causes inconvenience and annoyance to other users of the road."

This is a puzzling passage. Offences of "absolute", perhaps more properly called "strict", liability are ordinarily contrasted with offences requiring a fault element, including offences which require proof of negligence.[18] In the case of an absolute offence it can be no defence to show that all reasonable care was taken but where an offence, such as careless driving, requires proof of negligence the prosecution must necessarily fail unless a want of due care is established.

There is a sense in which liability for careless driving might be said to be absolute. If D's driving falls short of the standard expected from the reasonably prudent driver, not only is it no defence for D to show that he

---

12. *McCrone v Riding* [1938] 1 All ER 157 at 158, DC. The standard is the same as that applied in a civil action for negligence – "the obligation in the criminal law on the . . . driver cannot be the subject of a more stringent test than his liability in civil law": *Scott v Warren* [1974] RTR 104, DC, per Lord Widgery CJ at 107. References in a criminal case to rules of civil law affecting the onus of proof (such as res ipsa loquitur) are probably best avoided though it is open to justices to infer negligence from facts affording no other reasonable explanation.

13. *McCrone v Riding* [1938] 1 All ER 157; *Preston JJ, ex p Lyons* [1982] RTR 173, [1982] Crim LR 451, DC. See Wasik [1982] Crim LR 411. Inexperience may be relevant to sentence: *Mabley* [1965] Crim LR 377.

14. *Woods v Richards* (1977) 65 Cr App Rep 300, DC.

15. In coping with such emergencies the police driver owes the ordinary duty of care to other persons lawfully (*Gaynor v Allen* [1959] 2 QB 403, [1959] 2 All ER 644, DC) or unlawfully (*Marshall v Osmond* [1983] QB 1034, [1983] 2 All ER 225, DC) on the highway. The test is whether D is driving with due care *in all the circumstances*, including the emergency with which he is faced (*Woods v Richards* (1977) 65 Cr App Rep 300, DC) and the nature of the unlawful conduct with which he has to deal (*Marshall v Osmond*).

16. *R v Bristol Crown Court, ex p. Jones* (1986) 83 Cr App Rep 109, DC.

17. [1981] 1 All ER 974 at 981, HL.

18. Cf. his Lordship's view as expressed in *Tesco Supermarkets Ltd v Nattrass* [1971] 2 All ER 127 at 155, HL: "negligence connotes a reprehensible state of mind – a lack of care for the consequences of his physical acts on the part of the person doing them."

was doing his level best but also it is no defence for him to show that it was in fact impossible for him to do any better. Drivers, being human, will inevitably make some errors of judgment in their driving lives but the assumption is, and for practical reasons must be, that the reasonably prudent driver makes none. In truth, the "reasonably prudent driver" is not the average driver but a mean standard. In this limited sense careless driving might be said to be an absolute offence but it is not clear that it is in any sense helpful to so classify it. The general basis on which persons are punished for offences of negligence is that they could have done better, whereas people may be punished for offences of absolute liability even though they have taken all reasonable care.

Lord Diplock does, however, recognise that no liability can be incurred unless what was done by D was directed by a mind conscious of what he was doing. This is merely a particular instance of a general principle governing criminal liability. If D is unforeseeably afflicted by an epileptic seizure when driving he cannot be convicted of careless driving. D may thereby create considerable dangers for other road users, which perhaps explains why some cases seem to show a marked lack of sympathy to drivers raising automatism,[19] but without a real ability to control his actions D cannot be convicted of careless driving.

Nor must it be thought that, as Lord Diplock's dictum might be taken to imply, the offence of careless driving requires proof of inconvenience or annoyance to other road users. Careless driving is a conduct crime and not a result crime;[20] consequently it may be committed though no one is affected by the careless driving in question.

All the circumstances (which cannot be exhaustively stated but include such factors as the state of the road, the volume of traffic, weather conditions and so on) need to be considered by the justices in determining whether D's driving falls short of the relevant standard and the question is essentially one of fact for them. Only where the justices reach a decision which no reasonable bench could reach on those facts will the High Court interfere.[1] Consequently the High Court may uphold a decision to convict (or acquit) if it is one which may reasonably be reached on the facts and even though, had the decision been to acquit (or convict), that decision would equally have been upheld.[2] In criminal cases, as in civil actions for negligence, the courts resist any attempt to elevate "to the status of propositions of law what really are particular applications to special facts of propositions of ordinary good sense".[3]

The point may be illustrated by reference to cases involving the Highway Code. While the Code contains many precepts of good driving, and while the Act itself provides[4] that a failure to observe its provisions may be relied

19. *Watmore v Jenkins* [1962] 2 QB 572, [1962] 2 All ER 868, DC; *Broome v Perkins* [1987] Crim LR 271, DC.
20. Above, p. 30.
  1. *Bracegirdle v Oxley* [1947] KB 349, [1947] 1 All ER 126, DC.
  2. *Jarvis v Fuller* [1974] RTR 160, DC. The same principles apply to a charge of inconsiderate driving: *Dilks v Bowman-Shaw* [1981] RTR 4.
  3. *Easson v London and North Eastern Rly Co* [1944] 2 All ER 425 at 426, CA, per du Parcq LJ.
  4. S. 38 (7).

on in both criminal and civil proceedings as tending to establish or negative liability, it does not lay down for drivers a regime of inflexible imperatives. Since each case turns on its own particular facts it does not *always* (though it may usually) follow that a driver is necessarily careless in driving at such a speed that he cannot stop in the distance he sees to be clear,[5] nor in leaving insufficient braking distance between his vehicle and another's,[6] nor in failing to look behind before reversing,[7] though these are all precepts of driving practice set out in the Code.

Nor is D's driving necessarily careless merely because it constitutes some other driving offence. While the speed at which a vehicle is driven is often a relevant factor, it does not necessarily follow that D is guilty of careless driving merely because he is exceeding a speed limit.[8] Nor does it follow that a driver who is guilty of the offence of failing to accord precedence to a pedestrian on a crossing is guilty of careless driving.[9]

Since the test is objective, and what is relevant is the driver's conduct, it cannot matter that the failure to exercise due care arose from a deliberate act of bad driving on D's part.[10] This is not to say that subjective factors must always be ruled out of account. Though no account is to be taken of such subjective factors as experience and skill,[11] knowledge of circumstances may be a relevant factor. It is clear, for example, that D could be convicted of careless driving where, because of his familiarity with the vehicle, he realises that it has a tendency to pull to the right when the brakes are applied at high speed,[12] while someone who was unfamiliar with the vehicle, and who was reasonably unaware of this tendency, could not.

Section 3 creates two distinct offences, careless driving and inconsiderate driving. In many cases the facts would constitute either offence but they are not identical since the latter, unlike the former, may be committed only where other persons are using the road. Inconsiderate driving is the more appropriate offence where, for instance, D drives his car through a puddle which he might have avoided and drenches pedestrians. It must be the driving which is inconsiderate; other inconsiderate conduct, such as kicking a cyclist,[13] will not do.

For the purposes of s. 3, and no doubt for the purposes of ss. 1 and 2, "other persons using the road" includes the passengers in a vehicle driven by D.[14]

---

5. *Jarvis v Fuller* [1974] RTR 160.
6. *Scott v Warren* [1974] RTR 104, DC. Cf. *Preston JJ, ex p Lyons* [1982] RTR 173, DC.
7. *Hume v Ingleby* [1975] RTR 502, DC.
8. *Quinn v Scott* [1965] 2 All ER 588, [1965] 1 WLR 1004, DC.
9. *Gibbons v Kahl* [1956] 1 QB 59, [1955] 3 All ER 345, DC.
10. *Taylor v Rogers* (1960) 124 JP 217, [1960] Crim LR 271, DC.
11. Presumably no account is to be taken of age although D may lawfully drive a motor car at seventeen years and a motor cycle at sixteen. No doubt the same "impersonal and universal" standard would be applied. But what of careless cycling under s. 29 where D may be only ten years? In civil cases generally a child must exercise the care to be expected of a child of his age but where a child is engaged in an activity such as cycling on a road there is much to be said for holding him to the standard of the reasonably experienced cyclist. But a child of ten to fourteen years is criminally liable only if he knows his act to be wrong: above, p. 191. How is this doctrine to be applied in the case of negligent crimes?
12. *Haynes v Swain* [1975] RTR 40, [1974] Crim LR 483, DC.
13. *Downes v Fell* [1969] Crim LR 376, DC.
14. *Pawley v Wharldall* [1966] 1 QB 373, [1965] 2 All ER 757.

2 Dangerous Driving

Until the law amended by the Criminal Law Act 1977 it was an offence to drive a motor vehicle "recklessly, or at a speed or in a manner dangerous to the public". Although the three offences carried the same penalty, reckless driving was considered the more serious. But it would not be unfair to say that the courts failed to find a satisfactory definition for either offence, nor did they articulate a clear distinction between the two. Perhaps the best that could be said was that dangerous driving was driving that was worse than careless driving and that reckless driving was driving that was even worse than that.

The James Committee[15] noted the confused state of the law. The Committee said:

"The most unsatisfactory motoring offence at present is dangerous driving. At one end of the scale it may verge on reckless driving, at the other it may be barely distinguishable from driving without due care and attention."

The Committee's proposed solution[16] was to have only two offences, reckless driving and "a single composite offence covering the existing offences of dangerous driving, driving without due care and attention and driving inconsiderately". The legislative solution adopted was simply to abolish dangerous driving.

What was still wanting was a definition of recklessness in the context of reckless driving and this was provided by the House of Lords in *Lawrence*.[17] It is no longer necessary to rehearse this decision in the context of driving offences since it is superseded by the offence of dangerous driving which, unlike its predecessor in title, is given a detailed definition.

It is, however, worth noting some of the reasons[18] which led to the rejection of the *Lawrence* test because it sheds some light on the purport of the new offence of dangerous driving.

Essentially the *North Report* found the *Lawrence* test to be too narrow in that it left too many cases of bad driving to be dealt with simply as careless driving. The Report says:[19]

"In terms of behaviour on the road the sort of driving which we believe ought to be treated more seriously would include . . . such activities as driving in an aggresssive or intimidatory fashion which might involve, for example, sudden lane changes, cutting into a line of vehicles or persistently driving much too close to a vehicle in front. The present reckless driving offence is too narrowly framed reliably to catch those guilty of this kind of bad driving, *particularly in that it requires investigation of the driver's state of mind at the relevant time, evidence of which may be hard to obtain.*"

The italics have been supplied because, to some at least, it is not immediately apparent why in an offence carrying two years' imprisonment

---

15. *The Distribution of Criminal Business between the Crown Court and Magistrates' Courts*, Cmnd. 6323, paras. 123, 124 and Appendix K.
16. Appendix K, para. 6.
17. [1982] AC 510, [1981] 1 All ER 974, HL, above, p. 62.
18. *North Report*, 5.7–5.11.
19. At 5.15.

on conviction on indictment (and five years' imprisonment should death be fortuitously caused) the driver's state of mind should be irrelevant. It would surely be relevant to the sentencer who would be inclined to award a sentence towards the lower end of the scale if he concluded that the driver was merely thoughtless and towards the higher end of the scale if he concluded that the driver had deliberately put at risk the persons or properties of others. And why should it be more difficult to obtain evidence as to the driver's state of mind when he is wielding a motor car than when he is wielding a garden fork, hedge-trimmer or chainsaw?

The *North Report* also criticises the *Lawrence* test in that it exculpates the driver who gave thought to the risk but foolishly concluded there was none, the so-called lacunae or loophole.[20] This is an acceptable criticism of *Lawrence* to the extent that there is no rational ground for distinguishing between the driver who foolishly gives no thought to there being any risk and the driver who gives thought to the risk and foolishly concludes that there is none.

The *North Report* concluded that there should be a new 'very bad' driving offence which would be objective and would articulate the relevant standard. Section 2 of the Road Traffic Act 1988, as substituted by s. 1 of the Road Traffic Act 1991, accordingly provides—

"**2A**—(1) For the purposes of sections 1 and 2 above a person is to be regarded as driving dangerously if (and, subject to subsection (2) below, only if)—

(a) the way he drives falls far below what would be expected of a competent and careful driver, and

(b) it would be obvious to a competent and careful driver that driving in that way would be dangerous.

(2) A person is also to be regarded as driving dangerously for the purposes of sections 1 and 2 above if it would be obvious to a competent and careful driver that driving the vehicle in its current state would be dangerous.

(3) In subsections (1) and (2) above 'dangerous' refers to danger either of injury to any person or of serious damage to property; and in determining for the purposes of those subsections what would be expected of, or obvious to, a competent and careful driver in a particular case, regard shall be had not only to the circumstances of which he could be expected to be aware but also to any circumstances shown to have been within the knowledge of the accused.

(4) In determining for the purposes of subsection (2) above the state of a vehicle, regard may be had to anything attached to or carried on or in it and to the manner in which it is attached or carried."

The offence requires a consideration of the following matters.

1) *The Relevant Standard for Dangerous Driving*

In relation to the *driving* of the vehicle the relevant standard is entirely objective. It must be proved (i) that the way D drives falls "far below" what

---

20. As to which, see above, p. 65.

would be expected of a competent and careful driver; *and* (ii) that it would be obvious to a competent and careful driver that driving in that way would be dangerous. The requirements at (i) and (ii) are obviously intended to be additional and are not meant to be two ways of expressing the same thing. Careless driving may well create a risk of injury to the person or of serious damage to property but careless driving which does not fall far below what would be expected of a competent driver does not suffice. Conversely, driving might fall far below the standard of the competent driver and yet not create a risk of injury to the person nor of serious damage to property. Moreover the danger of the relevant harm must be "obvious" to the competent and careful driver and this requires more than that to the competent and careful driver the danger would have been foreseeable; the situation must be one where the competent and careful driver would say that the danger was plain for all to see.

Clearly the magistrates or the jury have to make a value judgment as to whether D's driving falls "far below" the standard of the competent and careful driver. Opinions of magistrates and juries may, and no doubt will, differ on how far below is "far below" but, as with careless driving, appellate courts are unlikely to interfere with what are said to be decisions "of fact and degree" unless the decision is patently unreasonable. There will thus be an element of chance in whether D is convicted of dangerous or careless driving. Viewed as a matter of principle the driving should be considered independently of the harm in fact caused; it is the nature of the driving and its potential to cause the stated harms that is the criterion in a conduct crime such as dangerous driving is.[1]

2) *Driving a Vehicle in a Dangerous State*

The *North Report* recommended that dangerous driving—

"should cover the fact that the vehicle is driven at all, as well as how it is driven. This is necessary so as to include within the offence those who decide to drive when either they themselves or their vehicles are wholly unfit to be on the road as well as those who, despite being fit to drive and having properly maintained vehicles, drive very badly."[2]

Section 2A(2) implements this recommendation in respect of the state of the vehicle but not in respect of the state of the driver. It would thus constitute dangerous driving to drive a car which a competent and careful driver would realise had defective brakes, but would not constitute dangerous driving *as such* to drive while unfit through drink, or when tired, or when subject to epileptic fits.

1. Cf. *Krawec* (1984) 6 Cr App Rep (S) 367, CA, holding that in cases of careless driving leading to death, the unforeseen and unexpected consequences are not normally relevant to penalty, the primary consideration being the extent to which the driving falls below the standard of the reasonable driver. The *North Report* (5.22) recommended that the dangerous driving offence "should look directly and objectively at the quality of the driving . . . – was the driving really bad? – without needing to consider how or what the driver had thought about the possible consequences . . .".

2. At 5.22 (iv).

In determining the state of the vehicle s. 2A(4) provides that regard may be had to anything attached to or carried on or in the vehicle and to the manner in which it is attached or carried. This provision may have been unnecessary but it prevents any possible argument that the "state" of the vehicle refers only to its mechanical state and does not extend, for example, to an improperly secured trailer or an insecure load.[3]

3) *The Relevant Danger*

The danger created must be of "injury to any person or of serious damage to property". As to the latter it is odd, given that the essence of the offence is very bad driving; that the offence is committed (assuming in a particular case that no danger of personal injury is created) only where the very bad driving creates a danger of "serious" harm to property since very bad driving remains very bad driving if it creates a danger of any damage to property. And when does damage become *serious*? £50's worth? £100's worth? £500's worth? Perhaps the courts will take refuge in the formula that "it is all a matter of fact and degree".

4) *The Relevance of Knowledge*

The test of dangerous driving is largely objective: did D's driving fall far below the standard of the competent and careful driver and would it have been obvious to a careful and competent driver that driving in that way would be dangerous? Even in the case where the driving takes the form of driving a vehicle in a dangerous state D cannot defend himself by showing that he was unaware of the defect in the vehicle, or that he thought the load was secure, if it would have been obvious to a careful and competent driver that the vehicle was defective or that the load was insecure.

D's knowledge of circumstances is, however, relevant where he is in fact aware of dangers that would have escaped the notice of the careful and competent driver. If D is reasonably unaware, for example, of the tendency of a car to swerve to the right when braked hard, D cannot be held to have driven dangerously or even carelessly, but once D becomes aware of this tendency he may properly be held to have driven dangerously if it would then be obvious to a competent and careful driver that to drive the car with this tendency would be dangerous.[4] Similarly, D's actual knowledge of an uneven road surface may count against him though other drivers would be unaware of the hazard.

3 Causing Death by Dangerous Driving

By s. 1 of the Road Traffic Act 1988, as substituted by s. 1 of the Road Traffic Act 1991—

3. Cf. *Crossman* [1986] RTR 49, CA (insecure load), above, p. 65.
4. Cf. *Haynes v Swain* [1975] RTR 40, DC, above, p. 488.

"A person who causes the death of another person on a road or other public place is guilty of an offence."

The offence is triable only on indictment and is punishable by imprisonment for five years and/or a fine.

At common law, and it is still the law, a motorist who by his driving causes death may be convicted of manslaughter.[5] In practice juries have been reluctant to convict motorists of manslaughter save in the most exceptional circumstances[6] so in 1956 it was made a statutory offence to cause death by driving a motor vehicle on a road "recklessly, or at a speed or in a manner dangerous to the public". Following the recommendations of the James Committee this offence, like the offence of reckless and dangerous driving,[7] was truncated to causing death by reckless driving. The House of Lords subsequently recognised that the offences of manslaughter and causing death by reckless driving were coextensive in law[8] while accepting that in fact juries were more likely to convict of the causing death offence. Under the law as substituted, however, causing death by reckless driving is superseded by causing death by dangerous driving, a more broadly based offence.

The *North Report* canvasses the arguments for and against a causing death offence.[9] Essentially the argument against a causing death offence is that whether the dangerous driving causes death may be entirely fortuitous. An identical instance of dangerous driving, say a sudden unsignalled lane change at high speed on a motorway, may in the first case cause death, in a second cause injury short of death, and in a third, perhaps owing to the skill of other drivers, may cause no harm whatsoever. Why should the first driver be singled out for an offence carrying five years' imprisonment while the others are at risk only of imprisonment for two years?

The countervailing argument is essentially that the seriousness of the consequences (most especially death) does affect the seriousness of offences. An obvious example is unlawful act manslaughter where, for instance, a common assault, attracting a maximum of six months' imprisonment, may become, if death results, manslaughter punishable by imprisonment for life.

The *North Report* refers also to public opinion which strongly supports the view that account should be taken of consequences and which was accordingly strongly in favour of retaining a causing death offence.[10] The *North Report* found the countervailing arguments persuasive. The *Report* says:

"Taking all these arguments into consideration, we have concluded that, on balance, an offence of causing death by very bad driving, however defined, should be retained. Two main factors have influenced our

5. *Jennings v United States Government* [1983] 1 AC 624, [1982] 3 All ER 104, HL.
6. See *Seymour* [1983] 2 AC 493, [1983] 2 All ER 1058, HL.
7. See above, p. 489.
8. *Jennings*, above.
9. At 6.1–6.9.
10. The *North Report* also recommended, and s. 3 of the Act introduces, an offence of causing death by *careless* driving where the driver is unfit through drink or drugs or whose blood/alcohol level exceeds the prescribed limit. The offence is indictable only and carries 5 years' imprisonment.

thinking. To abolish the offence in the absence of compelling reasons for doing so would mean that some cases of very bad driving were not dealt with with appropriate seriousnss. Repeal of section 1 would be seen as a down-grading of bad driving as a criminal activity. This is not a message which we wish to convey. Secondly, though logic might pull us towards arguments in favour of abolition, neither English nor Scots law in fact relies entirely on intent as the basis for offences. There seems to be a strong public acceptance that, if the consequence of a culpable act is death, then this consequence should lead to a more serious charge being brought than if death had not been the result. We concur with this view. *We recommend that a separate causing death offence be retained, but that it be reformulated in terms consistent with our recommended very bad driving offence.*"[11]

It is respectfully submitted that the *Report* made the wrong recommendation. It is true that there are offences, such as unlawful act manslaughter and murder where D's intent is to cause serious bodily harm, where the fact that death is caused elevates what would otherwise be a lesser offence to a greater offence but the preferred solution[12] is surely to remove such anomalies and not to add to them.

However that may be, the offence under s. 1 requires the prosecution to establish (i) that D has committed the offence of dangerous driving (discussed above); and (ii) has thereby caused the death of another person. As to (ii) the relevant principles appear to be the same as for causation in homicide generally and these are discussed elsewhere.[13] In this connection it may be noted that D may be convicted of the causing death offence even though it would not have been obvious to a careful and competent driver that there was any danger of personal injury so long as there was an obvious risk of serious damage to property; this seems a particularly unwarrantable extension of liability for an unforeseen death.

11. At 6.9.
12. Cf. the Draft Criminal Code Bill under which unlawful act manslaughter would disappear (vol 1, Appendix A, cl. 55) and which would enact that an intent to cause serious bodily harm would suffice for murder only if D is aware that he may cause death. See also *Report of the Select Committee on Murder and Life Imprisonment*, 1989, vol 1, para. 76.
13. Above, p. 331. In this context, however, it needs to be noted that it is not enough that D brings about a death *while* driving dangerously; the dangerous driving must be the *cause of* the death. Cf. *O'Neale* [1988] Crim LR 122, CA; *Hand v DPP* [1991] Crim LR 473, DC.

16 Theft and Related Offences

The law of theft was codified by the Theft Acts 1968 and 1978.[1] These Acts provide a code relating to virtually all offences against property involving fraud, with the notable exception of forgery. On two previous occasions, in the Larceny Acts of 1861 and 1916, the law relating to theft has been the subject of major legislation but the Theft Acts of 1968 and 1978 are quite unlike these earlier enactments. In general terms it may be said that the aim of the Acts of 1861 and 1916 was to consolidate the various statutory provisions and to state these in a convenient and accessible form. The Theft Acts of 1968 and 1978 proceed on another basis altogether. Although the Criminal Law Revision Committee, which was charged with the task of reforming the law,[2] saw that there were advantages in retaining the old system with some necessary amendment to repair its defects, they decided that the time had come

"for a new law of theft and related offences, based on a fundamental reconsideration of the principles underlying this branch of the law and embodied in a modern statute."[3]

In practice the Larceny Act 1916 was often construed on the tacit assumption that there was no intention to alter the previous law and the earlier case law lost little or no authority. Such an approach to the Theft Acts is wholly wrong, and any assumption that there was no intention to alter the previous law would be completely misconceived. If codification of the kind exemplified by the Theft Acts is to operate effectively it must be "within its field the authoritative, comprehensive and exclusive source of that law".[4] If a code is not so regarded it is in danger of failing to develop or reform the law.[5]

Only in very limited circumstances would reference to authorities on the former law of larceny be appropriate. An instance would be where the Theft Acts use expressions taken from the earlier legislation which have

---

1. See Smith, *The Law of Theft*, 6th ed. (hereinafter Smith, *Theft*); Griew, *The Theft Acts 1968 and 1978*, 6th ed. (hereinafter Griew, *Theft*).
2. See Eighth Report, *Theft and Related Offences* Cmnd. 2977, HMSO; hereinafter referred to as Cmnd. 2977, and Thirteenth Report (1977), Cmnd. 6733; hereinafter referred to as Cmnd. 6733.
3. Cmnd. 2977, para. 7.
4. Scarman, *Codification and Judge-Made Law* (1966) at p. 7.
5. Ibid., p. 8.

acquired a settled meaning. In connection with the offence of blackmail, for example, the CLRC decided to retain "menaces" rather than to substitute "threats" because "menaces" had acquired a settled meaning which the CLRC thought should be retained. Strictly, the earlier authorities are no longer binding but they would most likely be followed.

Moreover, it needs to be appreciated that, while the law of theft is generally concerned with invasions of the proprietary interests of others, the law of mine-and-thine is not to be found in the Theft Acts but in the civil law. In the early years of the interpretation of the legislation some courts showed impatience with arguments based on "the finer distinctions in civil law"[6] but whether property "belongs to another" for the purposes of theft "is a question to which the criminal law offers no answer and which can only be answered by reference to civil law principles".[7] Equally the Acts provide no definition of what constitutes "a proprietary right or interest" for the purposes of s. 5. nor who is a "trustee or personal representative" for the purposes of s. 4 of the 1968 Act. Cases concerning Theft Acts offences frequently involve consideration of "the finer distinctions in civil law".[8]

In the interpretation of the Acts the courts have aimed to give words and expressions their ordinary meaning so as to avoid undue technicality and subtlety. This is a sensible approach clearly enough but it has led, and not only in the context of the Theft Act,[9] to the practice of leaving the interpretation, at least of "ordinary" words and expressions, to be decided by the jury.[10] This may be a less desirable development. The interpretation even of ordinary words would seem to be pre-eminently a matter for the court if consistency of interpretation is to be achieved. To leave interpretation in the hands of the jury is to risk juries taking different views on comparable facts. Even such ordinary words in the Theft Act as "dishonesty", "force", "building" etc. may involve definitional problems on which a jury requires guidance if like is to be treated as like. But there is House of Lords authority[11] for this innovation in the interpretation of statutes and it looks as though we shall have to live with it for some time yet.

6. *Baxter* [1971] 2 All ER 359 at 363, CA: *Morris* [1983] 3 All ER 288 at 294, HL.
7. *Dobson v General Accident Fire and Life Assurance Corpn plc* [1989] 3 All ER 927 at 937, CA, per Bingham LJ.
8. See *Shadrokh Cigari* [1988] Crim LR 465, CA, below, p. 530; *Wheeler* (1990) 92 Cr App Rep 279, CA, below, p. 527. See also Smith, "Civil Law Concepts in the Criminal Law" [1972B] CLJ 197; Williams, "Theft, Consent and Illegality" [1977] Crim LR 127 and 205.
9. See Glanville Williams, "Law and Fact" [1976] Crim LR 472; Elliott, "Law and Fact in Theft Act Cases" [1976] Crim LR 707.
10. See the discussion of dishonesty, below, p. 536.
11. *Brutus v Cozens* [1973] AC 854, [1972] 2 All ER 1297. But in *Chandler v Director of Public Prosecutions* [1964] AC 763, [1962] 3 All ER 142, HL; Lord Radcliffe said, at 149, "The Act of Parliament [the Official Secrets Act 1911] in this case has introduced the idea of purpose as a determining element in the identification of the offence charged *and lawyers therefore, whose function it is to attribute meaning to words and to observe relevant distinctions between different words, cannot escape from this duty* merely by saying that 'purpose' is a word which has no sharply defined context. They must do the best they can to find what its content is in the context of this Act." – italics supplied.

A last point by way of introduction. The Theft Act 1968 has not proved quite the success that was hoped for.[12] One offence proved so troublesome that it had to be replaced in the 1978 Act,[13] and in some other respects cracks are beginning to show through. The legislation, and the administration of criminal justice accordingly, would benefit from a review.

1 Theft

By s. 1 (1) of the Theft Act 1968:

"A person is guilty of theft if he dishonestly appropriates property belonging to another with the intention of permanently depriving the other of it; and 'thief' and 'steal' shall be construed accordingly."

And by s. 7 of the Act, as substituted by s. 26 of the Criminal Justice Act 1991, the offence is punishable by seven years' imprisonment.

There is much about this definition which is self-explanatory and the vast majority of instances which actually occur will be covered without further elaboration. It is worth noting that before turning to the elaboration.

1) *The Actus Reus*

The *actus reus* of theft consists (1) in the appropriation of (2) property (3) belonging to another.

1 Appropriation[14]

By s. 3 (1) of the Theft Act 1968:

"Any assumption by a person of the rights of an owner amounts to an appropriation, and this includes, where he has come by the property (innocently or not) without stealing it, any later assumption of a right to it by keeping or dealing with it as owner."

Broadly, appropriation, in the context of the Theft Act, conveys the idea of annexing something or treating something as if it were one's own. But while this notion is conveyed by appropriation it is important to keep in mind that s. 3 (1) itself provides the only relevant definition and according to this subsection "*any* assumption by a person *of the rights* of an owner" amounts to an appropriation.

---

12. While the statistic is a crude one and may to some extent be explained by other factors, a LEXIS search shows that reported appeals more than doubled in the first ten years of the operation of the Theft Act 1968 as against the last ten years of the Larceny Act 1916. A comparable search relating to the Malicious Damage Act 1861 and the Criminal Damage Act 1971, however, shows a six-fold increase in reported appeals.
13. See below, p. 571.
14. See Koffman, "The Nature of Appropriation" [1982] Crim LR 331; Stuart, "Reform of the Law of Theft" (1967) 30 MLR 609.

a) *Appropriation as an unauthorised act*. The meaning of appropriation was considered by the House of Lords in *Morris*[15] and, even if it is not the last word on the matter, it provides a convenient starting point. The case concerned the appeals of D and E against their convictions of theft. Both had perpetrated what is now the common fraud of label-switching in a self-service store, substituting a lower price label for a higher price label on goods which they were about to purchase, the only difference being that D was arrested after he had paid the lower price at the check-out while E was arrested before he had passed through the check-out. D could therefore have been convicted of obtaining the goods by deception contrary to s. 15 of the Act and his counsel argued that it was "somewhat anomalous" that he was liable to be convicted of obtaining by deception goods which he had already stolen. E might have been convicted of attempting to obtain by deception if his conduct was sufficiently proximate but his counsel denied that it was and further submitted that E had not appropriated the goods merely by switching the price labels.

Both the Court of Appeal[16] and the House of Lords dismissed their appeals but the House of Lords did so on a view of appropriation significantly narrower than that of the Court of Appeal and a comparison may be helpful. The Court of Appeal considered that the appropriation took place when D and E removed the articles from the shelves with intent to take them through the check-out without paying the proper price for them. This was a usurpation of one of the owner's rights. Notwithstanding that the owner might consent to their removing the goods from the shelves it was nevertheless a taking for their own use and accordingly an appropriation. The goods had therefore been appropriated *before* the label-switching took place; the label-switching was treated as a second appropriation, as a "later assumption of a right . . . by keeping or dealing with it as owner".

This was to give the widest possible meaning to appropriation. It meant that any assumption of control with intent to treat the property as one's own would be an appropriation even though there was no *overt* conduct on D's part to which P would take exception,[17] and that appropriation would be theft if done with the required intent. The House of Lords preferred a narrower view. Delivering a speech in which all their lordships concurred, Lord Roskill said:[18]

"In the context of s. 3 (1), the concept of appropriation involves not an act expressly or impliedly authorised by the owner but an act by way of adverse interference with or usurpation of those rights."

It seems clear that this was to define appropriation in narrower terms and that the appropriation took place when D and E switched the labels[19] and not when D and E removed the goods from the shelves with intent to switch the labels. Hence, and considering earlier shoplifting cases, the

15. [1984] AC 320, [1983] 3 All ER 288; **SHC** 404.
16. [1983] 2 All ER 448.
17. P would of course take exception to D's conduct if he knew of D's intentions.
18. [1983] 3 All ER 288 at 293.
19. *Anderton v Wish* (1980) 72 Cr App Rep 23, [1980] Crim LR 319, DC, which is to this effect, was approved.

House approved *McPherson*[20] and *Eddy v Niman*.[1] In the former there was held to be an appropriation where D removed goods from the shelves and placed them not in the wire basket as the owner would have approved but in her own shopping bag, an action clearly not authorised by the owner and adverse to the owner's right. In the latter D, bent on stealing goods, placed them in the basket provided but then lost his nerve and abandoned the basket in the shop. It was held that there was no appropriation because nothing was done that was inconsistent with the owner's rights.

However Lord Roskill thought[2] that in *Eddy v Niman* Webster J went too far in saying[3] that there must be "some overt act . . . inconsistent with the true owner's rights" since Lord Roskill thought that the act need not necessarily be overt. This is a puzzling observation[4] and it puzzled the Court of Appeal in *Fritschy*.[5] P, who had authorised D to remove Krugerrands from London to Switzerland, became suspicious when he heard no more from D so he called in the police. D was charged with stealing the Krugerrands in England and the judge directed the jury that they might convict if satisfied that when D collected them in London he intended to dispose of them regardless of P's rights. The Court of Appeal quashed D's conviction and referring to Lord Roskill's view that the act need not necessarily be overt said:

"We have found this comment difficult to understand and we were tempted to say that some subsequent act on the part of an accused person, for example in the present instance disposing of the goods in Switzerland, could be evidence to justify a finding of an earlier appropriation: in this instance at the time when [D] received the Krugerrands [in London]. But having regard to Lord Roskill's earlier requirement of an act by way of adverse interference with or usurpation of an owner's rights, we found this conclusion impossible. There was here no evidence of any act by [D] within the jurisdiction that was not authorised by [P]. That, in the light of . . . *Morris* is fatal to the charge of theft."

The essence of appropriation would therefore seem to lie in conduct of D's which is observable as conduct that is inconsistent with or is a usurpation of the owner's rights; a simple way of looking at it might be to ask: was what D did something that he was not authorised by the owner to do?[6]

It may of course be argued that while a shopkeeper authorises an honest customer to take goods from shelves and place them in the receptacle provided, he does not authorise dishonest customers to do so. Commonly shoplifters place goods in the receptacle merely so that they can move them to a less well observed part of the store to effect a transfer of goods to their

20. [1973] Crim LR 191, CA.
   1. (1981) 73 Cr App Rep 237, [1981] Crim LR 502, DC. See ATH Smith, "Shoplifting and the Theft Acts" [1981] Crim LR 586.
   2. [1983] 3 All ER 228 at 294.
   3. (1981) 73 Cr App Rep 237 at 241.
   4. But consider appropriation by keeping or dealing as owner, below, p. 501. And cf. *A-G's Reference (No. 1 of 1983)* [1985] QB 182, [1984] 3 All ER 369, CA, below, p. 529.
   5. [1985] Crim LR 745.
   6. "The question is – and is only – whether the defendant acted in relation to the [property] in a manner which the owner would have the right to act": *Stein v Henshall* [1976] VR 612 at 615.

own persons. The answer would seem to be that the *conduct* of the shoplifter *is* authorised so long as it falls within the conduct permitted of shoppers. It is not merely that as a practical matter it will be difficult or impossible to prove an intent to steal until D acts in an unauthorised fashion for in some cases such proof will not be difficult to come by. In *Skipp*[7] D, posing as a genuine haulage contractor, collected loads from three separate places and then made off with them. On these facts a jury would inevitably have concluded that he intended to steal each of the loads as he collected it. Paradoxically D's counsel contended for this conclusion since D had been convicted on a single count for stealing all three loads and it was argued that the count was bad for duplicity. It was held there was only one appropriation which took place after the collection of the three loads at the point where D diverted them from their true destination. Until then D had done nothing which was inconsistent with the rights of the various owners since he was doing only what he was authorised to do.

To the same effect is *Meech*[8] though factually more complex. D was asked by P to bank and cash a cheque but because the cheque was for £1,450 the bank asked D to wait until it was cleared. Before clearance D discovered that P had dishonestly acquired the cheque so he resolved to cheat P by staging a fake robbery, to be effected by his confederates E and F, while D was taking the proceeds to P. This was done but the fraud was discovered and D, E and F were convicted of theft. On appeal E and F argued that D had stolen the money when he withdrew it from the bank with dishonest intent and that while they might have been liable as handlers they were not liable as thieves. It was held, however, that the appropriation took place at the time of the staged robbery for it was then that "the performance of the obligation [by D to P] finally became impossible".[9] *Skipp* and *Meech* were approved in *Morris*.[10]

On the other hand Lord Roskill in *Morris*[11] doubted the "difficult case" of *Dip Kaur v Chief Constable of Hampshire*.[12] There D was looking at shoes, some pairs priced £6.99 and some pairs priced £4.99, when she noticed that a £6.99 pair carried a £6.99 price-tag on one shoe and a £4.99 tag on the other. Making no attempt to conceal the price-tags she presented the shoes hoping the cashier would see only the £4.99 tag and charge that price. The cashier did but D's conviction for theft was quashed on the grounds that the contract of sale was merely voidable and not void. The reason which Lord Roskill gave for his disapproval of the case, that it is "on any view wrong" to introduce the niceties of the civil law into this branch of the criminal law, cannot, with respect, be accepted and it is difficult to

---

7. [1975] Crim LR 114, CA.

8. [1974] QB 549, [1973] 3 All ER 939, CA. Cf. *Peter Jackson Pty Ltd v Consolidated Insurance of Australia Ltd* [1975] VR 480 where it was held that a servant authorised to take money to a bank did not steal it until he departed from the authorised route to the bank though he intended to steal from the outset.

9. It would also seem that *Hircock* (1978) 67 Cr App Rep 278, CA, holding that a hire-purchaser was guilty of stealing a car only when he departed from the terms of the agreement, is inferentially approved by *Morris*.

10. [1984] AC 320, [1983] 3 All ER 288.

11. [1983] 3 All ER 288 at 294.

12. [1981] 2 All ER 430, [1981] 1 WLR 578, DC.

see how the decision in *Dip Kaur* is inconsistent with the view of appropriation advanced in *Morris*. D had done nothing with the shoes, either in presenting them to the cashier or in accepting delivery of them, that she was not authorised to do. D had of course tricked the cashier into delivering them but so did D in *Skipp* trick the deliverers into handing over goods by posing as a genuine haulage contractor.

Probably inconsistent with *Morris* is *Monaghan*[13] where D's conviction for theft was upheld when she took away money from a customer and placed it in her employer's till without ringing it up, intending to remove the money later in the day. It is difficult to see that she *did* anything she was not authorised to do unless it can be said that she was authorised to put money in the till only after ringing up the purchase. On the other hand a shop assistant is clearly not authorised to sell goods other than at the price she knows that her employer requires for them and if she marks the goods at less than their true value[14] or charges the customer less than their true value[15] she appropriates the goods.

b) *Appropriation by keeping and dealing*. To assume the rights of another would seem clearly to require conduct on D's part demonstrating such an assumption and so would a dealing. It is difficult to conceive of an assumption or dealing where D has done nothing at all in relation to the goods and even though he has made up his mind to steal the goods.[16] Does "keeping", however, go somewhat further?

Suppose that D, having borrowed P's cycle for a period, resolves on the expiry of the period to keep it. It would clearly be an appropriation to refuse to return it on demand,[17] or to deny P access to it, or for D claim it as his own. Such conduct shows that he is keeping it as owner. It would also constitute appropriation if D were to use the cycle after the expiry of the loan because this is an assumption of one of the owner's rights.[18] But what if D on the expiry of the loan merely leaves the cycle where it is in his garage hoping that P will forget about it and intending to keep it. At first sight it would seem inconsistent with *Morris* to say that D has appropriated the cycle since there is no conduct in relation to the cycle, and a mere mental resolution to steal cannot be an appropriation. But once the period of loan has elapsed D's possession is no longer authorised; his possession is now adverse to the owner's rights. Literally the case falls within the section since D is "keeping ... it as owner" and there would appear to be no warrant for giving the words other than their plain meaning. Of course

13. [1979] Crim LR 673, CA. *Monaghan* was not considered in *Morris*.
14. *Pilgram v Rice-Smith* [1977] 2 All ER 658, [1977] 1 WLR 671, DC; *A-G of Hong Kong v Chan Nai-Keung* [1987] i WLR 1339; [1988] Crim LR 125, PC.
15. In *Bhachu* (1976) 65 Cr App Rep 261, CA, the court thought the appropriation took place when the customer removed the goods but, following *Morris*, it would seem that the appropriation took place when the assistant rang up the lower price. Cf. *A-G of Hong Kong v Chan Nai-Keung* [1987] I WLR 1339, [1988] Crim LR 125, PC.
16. But see *A-G's Reference (No. 1 of 1983)* [1985] QB 182, [1984] 3 All ER 369, CA, below, p. 529.
17. Cf. *Wakeman* (1912) 8 Cr App Rep 18.
18. On which see below. Very little may be required to show that D has assumed the owner's rights. Cf. *Walters v Lunt* [1951] 2 All ER 645; DC; *Poynton* (1862) 9 Cox CC 249.

proof of D's intention may be hard to come by but, assuming an admission by him, he satisfies the requirement of keeping as owner. It may be that in *Morris* Lord Roskill had appropriation by keeping as owner in mind when he said that the act of appropriation need not necessarily be overt.[19]

c) *Appropriation and the rights of an owner.* Section 3 (1) provides that "Any assumption of the rights of an owner" amounts to an appropriation. The Act does not provide, nor does English law otherwise provide, any definitive statement as to what are the rights of an owner[20] but, leaving that aside for now,[1] the phrase is, perhaps, capable of two interpretations. It might mean any assumption of *all* the rights of an owner, or it might mean an assumption of *any* of the rights of an owner. Clearly the latter view would give a more expansive view of appropriation than the former.

Counsel for D in *Morris* argued for the former interpretation. Certainly it looks odd to say that D has stolen an article when he subsequently acknowledges P's ownership of the article by offering to buy it from P, albeit at a price which, as D knows, P did not put it on offer. Lord Roskill dealt shortly with the point:[2]

"[I]f one reads the words 'the rights' at the opening of s. 3 (1) literally and in isolation from the rest of the section, the submission of counsel for [D] undoubtedly has force. But the later words 'any assumption of a right' in sub-s. (1) and the words in sub-s. (2) 'no later assumption by him of rights' seem to me to militate strongly against the correctness of the submission. Moreover the provisions of s. 2 (1) (a)[3] also seem to point in the same direction. It follows therefore that it is enough for the prosecution if they have proved in these cases the assumption by the defendants of *any* of the rights of the owner of the goods in question . . .''

This view has been criticised[4] but, as appears from *Morris*, it represents the current thinking of both the House of Lords and the Court of Appeal. Merely to damage goods (to scratch the paintwork of a car for example) would be an appropriation (an assumption of a right of the owner) though it would not, standing alone, amount to theft for other reasons. Oddly enough Lord Roskill in *Morris*[5] thought that a mischief-maker who swapped labels in a store merely to cause confusion would not, without more, be appropriating the goods. Clearly the mischief-maker would not be guilty of theft but the act, which is one which only the owner may lawfully do or authorise, seems clearly to amount to an appropriation within the general definition advanced in *Morris*. So, too, there would seem to have been an appropriation in *Easom*[6] where D sifted through the contents of P's

---

19. See above, p. 499.
20. For a general discussion of an owner's rights see Honoré, *Oxford Essays in Jurisprudence*, 112–120.
   1. See appropriation as conversion, below, p. 503.
   2. [1983] 3 All ER 288 at 293. In this matter the House followed the Court of Appeal which had set aside the doubts it expressed in *Oxford v Peers* (1980) 72 Cr App Rep 19. *Morris* was followed in *Chan Man-sin v A-G of Hong Kong* [1988] 1 All ER 1, PC.
   3. Below, p. 537.
   4. Smith, *Theft*, para. 36.
   5. [1983] 3 All ER 288 at 293.
   6. [1971] 2 QB 315, [1971] 2 All ER 945, CA.

handbag (tissues, cosmetics etc.) and, finding nothing worth his while to take, returned it to its former place. D's conviction for stealing the handbag and its contents was inevitably quashed since he did not intend to steal these.[7] But it would seem clear that what he did amounted to an appropriation of the handbag and its contents because what he did was not authorised by the owner.

d) *Appropriation and conversion.* The Criminal Law Revision Committee took the view that "appropriates" meant the same as "converts" in the former offences of fraudulent conversion under s. 20 (1) (iv) of the Larceny Act 1916.[8] Consequently it might be permissible in this context to have regard to decisions on the meaning of conversion in the former law of larceny though, as it turns out, there are few helpful decisions in point. Some help might be gleaned from decisions on what constitutes conversion for the purposes of the law of tort but the analogy, if it is to be pursued at all, must be pursued with some caution. "Appropriates" has a statutory definition in s. 3 (1) and while this may not be an exhaustive definition[9] the interpretation given to it which extends it to any assumption of any of the owner's rights would seem to give to appropriation an ambit significantly wider in the criminal law than conversion bears in the law of tort. Moreover the policies of the criminal law and the civil law differ in that the criminal law emphasises the conduct and intentions of D whereas the civil law places the emphasis on some serious interference in fact with the property and this may lead to conduct being treated as an appropriation which would not amount to conversion in the civil law.[10]

e) *Appropriation and possession.* The most common form of appropriation, and by far, is by an unauthorised taking by one who is not in possession from the owner who is in possession. Originally larceny was confined to such takings, an unfortunate straightjacket on the offence loosened only gradually by judicial ingenuity and legislative intervention. All that is behind us and appropriation is in no way geared to possession. A person in or out of possession can appropriate property and the test of appropriation is the same for both cases: has D assumed any of the rights of the owner?

A person lawfully in possession of another's property may accordingly appropriate that property by doing with it something he is not authorised

---

7. No doubt D intended to steal money, should he have found any, and he could have been convicted of attempting to steal money. See above, p. 307.

8. Cmnd. 2977, para. 35. The Committee apparently preferred "appropriates" only on the ground that "converts" was a lawyer's word which was not as meaningful to the layman as "appropriates".

9. The CLRC regarded it (Cmnd. 2977, para. 34) as a partial definition as did Lord Roskill in *Morris* [1983] 3 All ER 288 at 292.

10. In *Jackson* (1864) 9 Cox CC 505, Martin B thought that many acts (none were specified) might amount to the tort of conversion but not the crime. In *Bonner* [1970] 2 All ER 97n at 98, it appears that Edmund Davies LJ did *not* accept a submission that there must be a conversion for the purposes of the civil law before there could be an appropriation. In *Rogers v Arnott* [1960] 2 All ER 417 at 419, Donovan J thought the analogy between civil and criminal conversion was "misleading" because the tort is not actionable without special damage.

to do. Where P deposits jewels with D for safe custody it would be an appropriation for D to wear the jewellery. A fortiori it would be an appropriation for D to pledge or sell the jewellery. Where P hires a car to D for a period, D appropriates the car if he uses it after the period has expired.[11]

So a person not in possession of property may appropriate that property by assuming any of the owner's rights. In *R v Governor of Pentonville Prison, ex p Osman*[12] D's extradition from England was sought by Hong Kong (where the law of theft is the same as it is in England) on various charges, including theft, and it was necessary to determine whether D had appropriated property in Hong Kong. What D had done in Hong Kong, and had done without authorisation, was to transmit telex messages to a bank in the United States instructing the bank to debit one account and credit another. It was held that the appropriation, the assumption of the right of the owner to dispose of his property, took place in Hong Kong for it was in Hong Kong that D did the act which was intended to usurp the rights of the owner, and it inevitably follows from the case that, had the telex been sent from England, the appropriation would have taken place here. That being so it could make no difference, in the view of the court, whether or not the bank in the United States complied with the instruction.[13] The conclusion is, with respect, correct. It is the "assumption" of, in the sense of unwarranted claim to or pretension to have, the rights of an owner that is the essence of appropriation.

Accordingly it would seem that D may appropriate property where he is not in possession of it and does not seek to take possession of it. For D to destroy goods in situ would amount to an appropriation[14] since this is obviously an assumption of the owner's rights even though D never had nor acquires possession of the property. Suppose, then, that D sells the crown jewels, securely guarded in the Tower of London, to a gullible tourist. A clear case of deception but has D appropriated the crown jewels? The issue, in less extravagant but nevertheless engaging circumstances, arose in *Pitham and Hehl*.[15] D, knowing that his friend P was in prison and in no position to interfere, took E1 and E2 to P's house where he purported to sell P's furniture to them. The issue was whether E1 and E2 were properly convicted as handlers[16] and this required of course that there was *stolen* furniture for them to handle which in turn required an appropriation

---

11. In *Jackson* (1864) 9 Cox CC 505 where D, who had been lent P's coat for a day, was found some days later wearing the coat on a ship bound for Australia. Martin B held that there was no evidence of a conversion of the coat. This decision *may* be consistent with the civil cases on conversion for there is apparently no case holding that a mere excess of permitted use constitutes a conversion (Street, *Torts*, at p. 45) but it would seem clear that D has now appropriated the coat by assuming the right to use it when he is not authorised to do so.
12. [1989] 3 All ER 701, 90 Cr App Rep 281, DC.
13. In this the court in *Re Osman* declined to follow *Tomsett* [1985] Crim LR 369, CA, in which it was assumed, without argument, that an appropriation occurs only when D's act takes effect on the property.
14. Were D charged with theft it might be difficult to prove that he was acting dishonestly and he would be more appropriately charged under the Criminal Damage Act 1971.
15. (1977) 65 Cr App Rep 45, [1977] Crim LR 285, CA.
16. See below, p. 646.

of the furniture. Lawton LJ, on behalf of the court, dealt with the matter quite shortly:[17]

"What was the appropriation in this case? ... What had [D] done? He had assumed the rights of the owner. He had done that when he took [E1 and E2 to P's house] showed them the property and invited them to buy what they wanted. He was then acting as the owner. He was then, in the words of the statute, 'assuming the rights of the owner'. The moment he did that he appropriated [P's] goods to himself. The appropriation was complete."

Assuming that D in *Pitham* purported to be the owner, or to have the owner's authority, and was at least at the outset so treated by E1 and E2,[18] the decision, that there was an *appropriation*,[19] may be defended.[20] Had D taken a tenancy of P's house during P's sojourn in prison a purported sale of the furniture, of which he was now in possession, would constitute an appropriation. It can hardly be less an appropriation because D merely appears to be in possession of the furniture. P is at risk of losing his furniture if E1 and E2 remove the property or of having a claim brought against him if they do not remove it before P's return. In neither case are P's rights usurped in the sense that P's title to the furniture is lost but his rights are clearly interfered with and that interference arises because D has purported to assume P's rights as owner.

In *Pitham*, it is assumed, D was in apparent possession of the furniture and was in a position to deliver the furniture to E1 and E2. In the example concerning the crown jewels D is not in apparent possession of the jewels and is in no position to deliver them to the gullible tourist. Because the illustration is a preposterous one (and D is anyway guilty of obtaining by deception) it is tempting to say that the conclusion that D has appropriated the crown jewels is equally preposterous. But the definition of appropriation in s. 3 (1) makes no reference to possession; any assumption of any right of an owner suffices and, with or without possession, a purported sale by D of P's property seems to be an assumption of P's rights as owner.

Williams, however, regards it as "jurisprudentially preposterous"[1] to say that where D is not in possession of property he can steal[2] that property when he is in no position to transfer ownership or make delivery of the property[3] because the purported sale is a wholly nugatory effort to usurp

---

17. (1977) 65 Cr App Rep 45 at 49.

18. Perhaps an unlikely conclusion in view of the fact that D, E1 and E2 gained entry to the house by breaking a window and the preferable interpretation of the facts is that E1 and E2, abetted by D who was paid for his help, went to the house to steal the furniture. See Williams, TBCL, at p. 763; Smith, *Theft*, para. 28.

19. But whether there was a *theft* additionally involves a consideration of the intent permanently to deprive which is considered below, p. 547.

20. For the purposes of the civil law of conversion a mere sale which does not involve a transfer of ownership or a delivery of possession is not a conversion: *Lancashire Wagon Co v Fitzhugh* (1861) 6 H & N 502; *Consolidated Co v Curtis & Son* [1892] 1 QB 495 at 498, per Collins J. But, as pointed out above, p. 503, appropriation bears a significantly wider meaning than conversion.

1. TBCL at p. 765. Cf. Elliott [1991] Crim LR 736, n. 21.

2. But, see above, fn. 19, the issue here is only whether D *appropriates* the property.

3. If as a result of the "sale" the buyer takes the property away, D would be guilty of theft through an innocent agent. Cf. *Stringer and Banks* [1991] Crim LR 639, CA.

one of the powers of the owner.[4] The argument is not without force but s. 3 (1) says that any assumption of the rights of an owner (and to purport to sell another's property would appear to be such an assumption) "amounts to" an appropriation. "Amounts to" here seems to mean "is". There would seem to be no warrant for qualifying the wording by some such requirement that the assumption must in fact threaten P's title to, or enjoyment of, the property.

If it is the case, as it is argued here that it is, that D may appropriate property without ever having or acquiring possession then some strange results ensue. D intends to hijack a lorry containing video-recorders if he can find a buyer for the goods. E, who assumes that D is the owner or is authorized by the owner, in good faith agrees to buy them. D has now appropriated the goods though the lorry is in Nottingham and he is in Leeds and much needs to be done before he can get his hands on the goods.

f) *Appropriation and consent.* An act is not authorised by P merely because it is something which P expects, or even hopes, that D will do. Where P has reason to suspect that his property is being stolen, he may lay a trap (as by placing marked property in an accessible place) in order to catch D on whom the suspicion has fallen. D appropriates the marked property as soon as he takes possession of it; P has fully anticipated that D will take the property but D's appropriation is not authorised. But suppose that P goes further than this. Suppose that D suggests to E that E should take P's property and hand it to D at an arranged place. E tells P of the plan and P, with a view to catching D red-handed, authorises E to deliver the property as arranged.[5] Here P has consented to D having possession but he has not authorised the appropriation and D becomes a thief when he takes delivery of the goods from E.

It would be quite different if P authorised the appropriation. If P, learning of the plan from E, whimsically decided to make D a gift of the property that D was minded to steal and instructed E to deliver it, D would not be guilty of theft[6] since D cannot appropriate property in which he now has the entire proprietary interest. In this illustration P knows all the facts and has decided to make D the owner of the property; nothing thereafter done by D can amount to an appropriation of it. Similarly, if property is delivered under a contract of sale, D is not a thief if he then decides to make off with the goods without paying for them.[7]

Sometimes, of course, P is tricked into parting with the property. P gives money to D because D falsely tells him that he is collecting for charity, or P delivers goods to D in return for a cheque D knows to be worthless. Whenever a deception is used to obtain property the wisest course is to resort to s. 15 of the 1968 Act which is specifically designed to meet the case but it is nevertheless necessary to consider whether D is a thief.

4. But in *Chan Man-sin v A-G of Hong Kong* [1988] 1 All ER 1, PC, it was held that there could be an appropriation though in law the owner did not lose his property.
5. These are essentially the facts of *Turvey* [1946] 2 All ER 60, CCA, where D's conviction for larceny under the former law was quashed.
6. Though he may be convicted of attempting to steal.
7. D may be guilty of making off without payment, below, p. 582.

Consider the difficult case of *Lawrence*.[8] On arrival in London P, an Italian student who spoke little English, showed a piece of paper to D, a taxi-driver, on which was written an address. The address was not far away and the normal fare would have been about 50p, but D said it was a long way off and would be expensive. When P tendered a £1 note D said this would not be enough and from P's wallet, which P was holding open, he took a further £1 note and a £5 note. On appeal against D's conviction for theft it was argued that D had not stolen the money because P had consented to its being taken by D. This argument was based on a requirement in the former law of larceny that a taking must be without the consent of the owner, and it seemed to get the case off on the wrong footing. P's consent to the *taking* as such would no more be a bar to a conviction of theft than the consent of the employer who set the trap so that D could be caught red-handed. The Court of Appeal held that P's consent was, as such, no defence, and when the House of Lords was asked whether s. 1 (1) of the Theft Act was to be construed as though it contained the words "without the consent of the owner" it answered with an emphatic No, and expressed surprise that the question should have been asked at all.

But this does not end the matter. There are two further problems to consider.

The first is whether P has consented, not merely to the *taking* of his property, but to parting with his entire interest in it. If P has transferred his entire proprietary interest then D cannot be convicted of theft;[9] this is so even though D is acting dishonestly. The point is illustrated by *Edwards v Ddin*[10] where D, who had just had three gallons of petrol put in his tank by an attendant at a garage, drove off without paying. It was held that D could not be convicted of theft. The ownership of the petrol passed when it was poured into D's tank so that when D drove off the petrol was entirely his; there was no property belonging to another of which he could divest P.[11]

It is not clear whether D in *Edwards v Ddin* intended from the outset to cheat P or whether he made up his mind to do so only after the petrol had been placed in his tank but, so far as the offence of theft is concerned, it could, on the view of the law submitted here, make no difference.[12] On the former hypothesis D has tricked P into delivering the petrol and no doubt P never would have consented to make D the owner of the petrol had he known that D was not going to pay for it. P was cheated into transferring ownership but he nevertheless intended to transfer it. This may be a simple case but anyone familiar with the civil cases on fraud and mistake will know

8. [1971] 1 QB 373, [1970] 3 All ER 933, CA; affirmed sub nom. *Lawrence v Metropolitan Police Comr*. [1972] AC 626, [1971] 2 All ER 1253, HL; **SHC 402**.
9. Unless the case is caught by s. 5(4) which is considered below, p. 527.
10. [1976] 3 All ER 705, 63 Cr App Rep 218, DC; *Greenberg* [1972] Crim LR 331, QS; and *Corcoran v Whent* [1977] Crim LR 52, DC, are to the same effect. See further below, p. 529.
11. The position is the same at a self-service filling station. If D, intending not to pay, fills his tank with petrol and makes off, the property in the petrol passes and he may not be convicted of theft. In *McHugh* (1977) 64 Cr App Rep 92, CA, it was assumed, wrongly it is submitted, that D would be guilty of theft.
12. But on the view of the law taken by the Court of Appeal in *Lawrence* [1971] 1 QB 373 at 375, [1970] 3 All ER 933, below, p. 532 – that facts which would establish a charge of deception may also support a charge of theft – it would make a difference and D could be convicted of theft. See further below, p. 532.

that it is not always easy to determine whether the fraud does or does not have the effect of preventing the transfer of ownership from P to D. This may become a crucial question *if D is charged with theft*. In practice the difficulty can be circumvented if D has made a deception and thereby induced P to transfer the property to him.[13] If in *Edwards v Ddin* it could have been shown that all along D did not intend to pay that would have been a deception as to his intention to pay and by that deception he obtained the petrol. Similarly, it is submitted, *Lawrence*[14] would have presented no problems had D been charged with deception. By his conduct he represented that £1 would not suffice for the fare and by that deception he obtained the money. It is then quite unnecessary to determine whether D obtained ownership of the money because the offence under s. 15 may be committed whether D obtains ownership *or* possession *or* control.

The moral is plain. If D has by fraud caused P to part with his property the simple and sensible course is usually to charge him with deception contrary to s. 15. But this course was not adopted in *Lawrence* and it was therefore necessary to determine whether ownership of the money passed from P to D. If it did then it could not be shown that D appropriated property belonging to another, and whether it did depended on P's intention. Clearly the ownership of the first £1 (D was not charged with stealing this) passed to D by delivery. The ownership of the £6 would have equally passed by delivery by the same token. As it happened, however, P did not deliver the money; it was taken from P's wallet by D and when he took the money it was at that very moment still the property of P. It is only necessary that the property should belong to another at the instant of appropriation and, as Viscount Dilhorne put it, "[T]he money in the wallet which [D] appropriated belonged to [P]."[15]

The second problem is whether P's consent to what is done by D prevents D's conduct from amounting to an appropriation. In *Lawrence* Viscount Dilhorne, while accepting that D's belief in P's consent is relevant on the issue of dishonesty, apparently denied that consent could ever be relevant to the issue of appropriation:

> "Belief or the absence of belief that the owner had ... consented to the appropriation is relevant to the issue of dishonesty, not to the question whether or not there has been an appropriation."[16]

But a consideration of what P has consented to is surely relevant in considering whether D has done something in relation to the property that he is not authorised to do for until D has done something he is not authorised to do there can be no appropriation: *Morris*.[17] In what respect was D in *Lawrence* dealing with the money in an unauthorised way? In *Morris* Lord Roskill said, "That there was in [*Lawrence*] an appropriation was beyond question."[18] But perhaps it is not quite beyond question.

---

13. And whether or not there is a deception D may in such cases commit the offence of making off without payment contrary to s. 3 of the 1978 Act.
14. [1972] 1 QB 373, [1971] 2 All ER 1253, HL; **SHC 402**.
15. [1971] 2 All ER 1253 at 1255.
16. [1971] 2 All ER 1253 at 1255.
17. [1984] AC 320, [1983] 3 All ER 288, above, p. 498.
18. [1983] 3 All ER 288 at 292.

Suppose that in *Lawrence* D had somehow conveyed to P that the correct fare was £5 and P had handed over £5. P has been defrauded of course but nothing done thereafter by D with the money can amount to an appropriation since it becomes D's money. However, it is to be noted that in *Lawrence* Viscount Dilhorne did not think that P had consented: "In my opinion, the facts of this case to which I have referred fall far short of establishing that [P] consented."[19] If it was the case, then, that P had really no idea of what D was taking from his wallet or was too bewildered or timid to protest the taking,[20] then the way is open to holding that there was an appropriation and on that ground[1] the decision may be defended.

g) *Lawrence or Morris?* It is not an easy matter to effect a reconciliation of the *Morris* view of appropriation with the decision in *Lawrence*[2] and the grounds suggested in the preceding section may appear tenuous. The Civil Division of the Court of Appeal was faced with the problem in *Dobson v General Accident Fire and Life Assurance Corporation plc*.[3] D arranged over the telephone to purchase from P a watch and a ring for £5,950, and called the following day to collect them, giving P a building society cheque which later proved worthless. P's insurance policy covered him for theft (which was accepted to mean theft as defined in the Theft Act 1968) but the insurers argued that in these circumstances D had not committed theft.

On the *Morris* view it would appear that there was no appropriation since D had done nothing that was not authorised by P. But the court was inclined to the *Lawrence* view and held that this was a case of theft, a conclusion justified on the grounds that either (i) the ownership in the items never passed to D;[4] or (ii) that property passed on delivery but at the moment of delivery the items still belonged to P;[5] or (iii) that though P *consented* to the items being taken by D, he did not *authorise* D to take them. This last ground might be considered attractive because *Morris* describes appropriation as an unauthorised act whereas *Lawrence* says the owner's consent is not a bar to conviction but on examination the distinction appears unworkable. How can it sensibly be said in *Dobson* that P, who had entered into a contract of sale (albeit voidable for fraud) under which he parted with the property in the items, had consented to the goods being taken by D but had not authorised him to take them? If *Dobson* is correctly

19. [1971] 2 All ER 1253 at 1254.
20. "It may well be that when [in cross-examination through an interpreter] P used the word 'permitted', he meant no more than that he had allowed the money to be taken. It certainly was not established at the trial that he had agreed to pay a sum far in excess of the legal fare for the journey and so had consented to the acquisition by [D] of the £6": [1971] 2 All ER 1253 at 1254.
   1. Alternatively it may be said that when P proffered the wallet he authorised D only to take the correct fare and in taking more than that D was doing what he was not authorised to do. Contra, Williams [1977] Crim LR 208n.
   2. But see Halpern, "The Appropriate Appropriation" [1991] Crim LR 426.
   3. [1990] 1 QB 274, [1990] Crim LR 271, CA.
   4. On this premise a conviction for theft may be justifiable but the case seems clearly to be one where D obtained a voidable title to the items.
   5. Just as in *Lawrence* the money in P's wallet belonged to P at the moment when D laid his hands on it.

decided then, to all intents and purposes, obtaining by deception is submerged in theft.

The distinction found no favour with the Criminal Division of the Court of Appeal in *Gomez*.[6] Here D, an assistant manager, given a cheque by E which D knew to be worthless, nevertheless obtained authority from P, the manager, to supply goods to E in return for the cheque. D's conviction for stealing the goods was quashed. On the court's analysis of the transaction, with respect the correct one, there was a contract, albeit voidable, under which there was a transfer of property to E with the express authority and consent of P and accordingly there could be no appropriation. Referring to *Dobson* the court said that the distinction between authorisation and consent, if it existed, created refinements that should play no part in determining guilt or innocence.

So *Gomez* recognises that deception is not submerged in theft and that at least the ordinary case of obtaining by deception (and buying goods with a worthless cheque is about as ordinary as they come) cannot amount to theft because nothing is done by D that is not authorised by P which is fatal to proof of an appropriation. The court made a passing reference to *Lawrence* but showed no obvious enthusiasm for it and, it may be said, nailed its colours firmly to the *Morris* mast. Subsequently, however, a differently composed count, while following *Gomez*, expressed a preference for *Lawrence*.[7]

h) *Appropriation, consent and intimidation.* Where P is obliged to hand over property because he has been intimidated by D into so doing, P might be said to assent to the handing over but he is unlikely in any real sense to assent to the appropriation of his property by D, and accordingly D may be convicted of theft. Difficulty arises where D demands that P transfer ownership to him, as by forcing P to make a gift or sale of the property. It might be thought on principle that P does not in fact transfer ownership. There is no real intention on P's part to do so; the property still belongs to him and D may be convicted of stealing it.

It is thought that this is the position of law. Though there are cases supporting the view that duress renders a contract voidable rather than void,[8] it has been cogently argued[9] that duress ought to render a contract void. Textbook writers who formerly favoured the voidable theory now express themselves more cautiously.[10] If duress renders a contract voidable only, then D would not commit theft because ownership would be transferred notwithstanding the intimidation, and the property would belong to D, not to P.

Again the problem may be obviated: this time by charging D with blackmail contrary to s. 21 of the Act. In this sort of situation D is making

---

6. [1991] 3 All ER 394, 93 Cr App Rep 156, CA.
7. *Shuck* [1992] Crim LR 209, CA.
8. *Whelpdale's Case* (1604) 5 Co Rep 119a; *Barton v Armstrong* [1976] AC 104, [1975] 2 All ER 465, PC.
9. By Lanham, "Duress and Void Contracts" (1966) 29 Mod LR 615. And see Hooper, "Larceny by Intimidation" [1965] Crim LR 532 and 592.
10. See, e.g., Cheshire, Fifoot and Furmston's, *The Law of Contract* (12th ed.), 309; Treitel, *The Law of Contract* (8th ed.), 363.

an unwarranted demand with menaces and, so far as blackmail is concerned, it does not matter whether D obtains ownership or not. The problem would not be obviated, however, by charging D with robbery under s. 8 since robbery is merely an aggravated form of stealing. Suppose that D wishes to purchase a particular painting from P but P is unwilling to sell. D thereupon threatens P with violence unless he does sell so P hands over the painting and receives payment. D might now be convicted of blackmail, but can he be convicted of theft or robbery? It is submitted that he can. The civil cases, such as they are, are hardly decisive since the result in them would have been the same whether the contract was considered void or voidable. It is difficult to resist the conclusion that:

". . . in all contracts it is essential that there should be consent. Not even the officious by-stander would care to testify that a person with a gun to his head appeared to consent to the transaction in hand, whatever kind of contract was involved."[11]

So far it has been assumed that the duress takes the form of physical harm to P, actual or threatened. But what if the threat is not one to use physical violence? Suppose, for example, that D, a newspaper proprietor, tells P that unless P pays him money he will attack the creditworthiness of P's business in his newspaper, and P pays the money demanded.[12] This is best treated as a case of blackmail, but could D also be convicted of stealing the money? Does D become the owner of the money or does the money still belong to P? Again an earlier case implies that ownership does not pass to D in this situation, but the particular point was not argued.[13] Much might depend on the nature of the threat;[14] not every threat will necessarily nullify P's assent to the appropriation. The common sense approach would be

". . . to pose the question 'was there consent' or perhaps 'would the officious by-stander say that [P] consented to the transaction?' This would be a question of fact in each case, though the nature of the threat would always be a very important factor."[15]

In cases of doubt, however, it would be better, if the facts will support it, to charge blackmail or deception.

i) *The exception in favour of bona fide purchasers.* Notwithstanding that there is no general limitation on liability for theft in favour of persons acquiring property innocently in the first place, s. 3 (2) of the Act imposes a particular limitation in favour of bona fide purchasers. Section 3 (2) provides:

11. Lanham, "Duress and Void Contracts" (1966) 29 MLR 615, 619. Cf. *McGrath* (1869) LR 1 CCR 205; *Lovell* (1881) 8 QBD 185; and see further Smith, *Theft*, paras. 45, 46.
12. Cf. *Boyle and Merchant* [1914] 3 KB 339, CCA.
13. *Boyle and Merchant*, see last footnote.
14. Cf. *Chapman* [1974] Crim LR 488, CA. D was convicted of theft when by his "overbearing conduct" he caused P, an elderly man, to sell property to him.
15. Lanham, op. cit., 621. And see above, p. 406. Cf. *Clear* [1968] 1 QB 670, [1968] 1 All ER 74, CA – "[T]here is no intent to steal unless there is an intent to take without the true consent of the [owner] . . . But there can be such an intent without that person being deprived of 'that element of free, voluntary action which alone constitutes consent' in the words used by Wilde B".

"Where property or a right or interest in property is or purports to be transferred for value to a person acting in good faith, no later assumption by him of rights which he believed himself to be acquiring shall, by reason of any defect in the transferor's title, amount to theft."

The Criminal Law Revision Committee explained this exception as follows:[16]

"A person may buy something in good faith, but may find out afterwards that the seller had no title to it, perhaps because the seller or somebody else stole it. If the buyer nevertheless keeps the thing or otherwise deals with it as owner, he could . . . be guilty of theft. It is arguable that this would be right; but on the whole it seems to us that, whatever view is taken of the buyer's moral duty, the law would be too strict if it made him guilty of theft."

The exception is in favour only of a person acquiring his interest in good faith and for value. It would extend to a pledgee or a person acquiring a lien as well as a buyer of property; but if a pledgee, having discovered the pledgor's lack of title, were to, say, destroy the property he might be guilty of theft because he is assuming rights greater than those which he believed he had acquired. Nor is the bona fide purchaser of property he discovers to be stolen guilty of handling if he disposes of it to an innocent person P[17] but the property remains stolen and if D, by representing himself as having title to the property, induces P to buy it, D may be guilty of obtaining by deception.[18]

j) *Appropriation as a continuing act.* For certain purposes it may be important to determine whether appropriation is an instantaneous act, or whether it is a continuing one and, if so, for how long it continues.

At one extreme it might be suggested that the appropriation continues so long as the stolen property continues to be in D's possession. This would create obvious difficulties with the offence of handling. Handling is a more serious offence than theft and is constituted by receiving (and other dealings in) stolen goods "otherwise than in the course of the stealing".[19] If the appropriation continued while the thief had possession there would be little or no scope for handling so the notion that appropriation continues so long as the thief has possession must be rejected.

At the other extreme it may be suggested that appropriation is an instantaneous act. This view was apparently taken in *Pitham and Hehl*[20] where D invited E and F to make offers for P's furniture. It was held that by offering P's furniture for sale D stole it; the property instantly became stolen property and it was held that E and F could be convicted of handling because their receiving was not in the course of the stealing.

---

16. Cmnd. 2977, para. 37.
17. Below, p. 648
18. See *Wheeler* (1990) 92 Cr App Rep 279, CA. D did not obtain by deception in selling stolen goods to P but only because the sale, though not the delivery, took place before D became aware that they were stolen.
19. Below, p. 646.
20. (1976) 65 Cr App Rep 45, CA, above, p. 504.

The third possibility is that appropriation continues for so long as the thief can sensibly be regarded as in the act of stealing. This was the view taken in *Hale*[1] where the court rejected an argument that D and E were not guilty of robbery in using force against P seconds after property had been seized ... The appropriation was of course complete when the property was seized but it could fairly be regarded as continuing during the time taken to remove it from the house. This view, with respect, is sensible and ought to be the one which is preferred.

2 Property

The property which may be stolen is defined in s. 4 of the Theft Act 1968, and the broad effect of this section is that all property may be stolen subject to certain exceptions in relation to land, wild growth and wild creatures. Section 4 (1) provides the general definition:

"'Property' includes money and all other property, real or personal, including things in action and other intangible property."

The one limitation on the generality of this definition, apart from the specified exceptions, is that the property must be capable of appropriation. It is easy enough to visualise how tangible property, such as land or goods, may be appropriated, but the definition also extends to intangible property and it may be as well to illustrate how intangible property may be appropriated. The short answer, of course, is that intangible property may be appropriated by any assumption of the rights of an owner in respect of it.[2] Thus a debt might be appropriated by D where he causes the bank[3] to debit P's account and to credit his own.[4] D may not yet have withdrawn from his account the money so credited, but he has already appropriated the debt which the bank owes to P. So if D causes the Q company to transfer P's shares into D's name in the company's books, D has appropriated the shares. In *Kohn*[5] D, an accountant, given cheques by his employers to meet their liabilities, drew cheques on their accounts for his own purposes. His conviction for theft was upheld; the employers' bank accounts were choses in action (i.e. each employer was owed the money that stood to his credit) and to cause the accounts to be diminished[6] was an appropriation of the chose belonging to the employers. On the other hand where D, knowing that his own account is overdrawn, uses his banker's card so that the bank is obliged to meet cheques drawn by him, D does not

---

1. (1978) 68 Cr App Rep 415, [1979] Crim LR 596, CA, below, p. 554. Cf. *Gregory* (1982) 74 Cr App Rep 154, CA.
2. See *Storrow and Poole* [1983] Crim LR 332.
3. It is not enough that D himself by making false entries in the bank's books or by interfering with the bank's computerized accounts causes other accounts to be diminished and his own account to be enhanced for this does not involve an application by D of the choses in action belonging to the other customers: *Thompson* [1984] 3 All ER 565, [1984] 1 WLR 962, CA.
4. *Chan Man-sin v A-G for Hong Kong* [1988] 1 All ER 1, PC; below, p. 547; *ex p Osman* [1989] 3 All ER 701, DC, above, p. 504.
5. (1979) 69 Cr App Rep 395, CA. See further Griew, "Stealing and Obtaining Bank Credits" [1986] Crim LR 356.
6. But there may be an appropriation though the account has not been diminished: *ex p Osman* [1989] 3 All ER 701, DC, above, p. 504.

steal from the bank.[7] The bank is obliged to meet the cheque and its funds are thereby diminished but no thing in action has been appropriated; nothing which the bank owes to X has been transferred to Y.

To things in action s. 4(1) adds "and other intangible property" to stretch even further the reach of the law of theft. An illustration is provided by *A–G of Hong Kong v Chan Nai-Keung*,[8] the law of theft in Hong Kong being identical in this particular to the law of England. The export of textiles from Hong Kong was prohibited except under licence, and exports were regulated by a quota system. An exporter who, in a given year, could not meet his quotas could sell his surplus export quotas to an exporter who could, and there was a flourishing market in these quotas. D, a director of the A exporting company, without the authorisation of the A company, sold surplus quotas at a gross undervalue to the B exporting company in which D had an interest as a director. It was held that the quotas, though they were not things in action, were nevertheless "other intangible property"—the quotas were things of value which could be bought and sold and by knowingly selling them at an undervalue D had appropriated them.[9]

On the face of it all property is capable of appropriation but there was formerly doubt whether electricity was capable of appropriation since the dishonest use, wasting or diverting of electricity is a separate offence under s. 13 of the Theft Act, and the Criminal Law Revision Committee observed that:

"This has to be a separate offence because owing to its nature electricity is excluded from the definition of stealing in . . . [s.] 1 (1) of the [Act]."[10]
The Committee's view was endorsed in *Low v Blease*[11] where it was held that, electricity not being property capable of appropriation, D could not be convicted of burglary in entering premises and making a telephone call from them. It has also been held[12] that confidential information, though it has a value and can be sold, is not property within s. 4 (1); accordingly an undergraduate was not guilty of theft where he unlawfully acquired an examination paper and returned it after he had read its contents.[13] While it does seem to be the case that the "theft" of information is a serious problem for which the civil law may not provide adequate remedies, it would also seem, as Griew observes,[14] that the Theft Act is not the appropriate instrument to deal with this specialised kind of mischief.

a) *Limitations on the theft of land.* It should be appreciated at the outset that it would have been technically possible to make land stealable in general, since land is just as capable of appropriation as goods; such limitations as there are arise from policy considerations. Take, for example, the case (which has apparently occurred from time to time) where D moves the

7. *Navvabi* [1986] 3 All ER 102, [1986] 1 WLR 1311, CA.
8. [1987] 1 WLR 1339, [1988] Crim LR 125, PC.
9. See above, p. 501.
10. Cmnd. 2977, para. 85, below, p. 551.
11. [1975] Crim LR 513, DC.
12. *Oxford v Moss* (1978) 68 Cr App Rep 183, [1979] Crim LR 119.
13. But see commentary at [1979] Crim LR 119.
14. *Theft*, 2. 19. See further Hammond, "Theft of Information" (1984) 100 LQR 252.

boundary fence between his and P's property and thus annexes some of P's land. Supposing this is done dishonestly there are no obstacles in the way of treating this as theft. D has appropriated land belonging to P with intent to deprive him permanently of it. But the Criminal Law Revision Committee, for a number of reasons[15] (such as that appropriating land by encroachment was not so widespread or socially evil that civil remedies were insufficient,[16] the civil law might give D a good title by occupation for twelve years and it would be odd if he remained even theoretically guilty of theft for ever afterwards), felt that such a case ought not to be treated as theft and s. 4 (2) gives effect to this view. Section 4 (2) of the Theft Act 1968 provides:

"A person cannot steal land, or things forming part of land and severed from it by him or by his directions, except in the following cases, that is to say—

(a) when he is a trustee or personal representative, or is authorised by power of attorney, or as liquidator of a company, or otherwise, to sell or dispose of land belonging to another, and he appropriates the land or anything forming part of it by dealing with it in breach of the confidence reposed in him; or

(b) when he is not in possession of the land and appropriates anything forming part of the land by severing it or causing it to be severed, or after it has been severed; or

(c) when, being in possession of the land under a tenancy, he appropriates the whole or part of any fixture or structure let to be used with the land.

For purposes of this subsection 'land' does not include incorporeal hereditaments; 'tenancy' means a tenancy for years or any less period and includes an agreement for such a tenancy, but a person who after the end of a tenancy remains in possession as statutory tenant or otherwise is to be treated as having possession under the tenancy, and 'let' shall be construed accordingly."

(i) *Appropriation by trustees etc.*[17] The rule here is that land, or things forming part of the land, are capable of being stolen. Thus a trustee may appropriate land held in trust by an unauthorised disposition. Of course an unauthorised dealing is not of itself theft since the other requirements of the offence must be present. If, for example, a trustee is authorised to sell the land only to A and he sells it to B because B is offering a much better price, the unauthorised sale by the trustee may not be dishonest.

(ii) *Appropriation by persons not in possession.* Here, as has been shown, the rule is that land as such cannot be stolen by a person not in possession. However a person not in possession can steal anything forming part of the land by severing it or by appropriating it after it has been severed. Thus it may be theft where D helps himself to the topsoil in P's garden, or to a gate, or to rose bushes, or even to

---

15. Cmnd. 2977, paras. 40–44.
16. But the Committee observed (ibid., para. 42) that moving boundaries was a "real problem, especially in crowded housing estates." Cf. the offence under s. 11 (below, p. 593) which seems to owe its origin to *three* known instances of its occurrence.
17. See Brazier, "Criminal Trustees?" (1975) 39 Conv (NS) 29.

growing grass.[18] In each case the appropriation is complete upon severance,[19] but where the thing is already severed, as where the gate is lying in P's yard for repair, the appropriation would be complete, at the latest, when D takes control of it.

(iii) *Appropriation by tenants of fixtures.* A tenant cannot steal the land of which he stands possessed nor things forming part of the land. If D, a tenant, removes topsoil from the demised premises to sell to a neighbour he is appropriating property of another (the landlord) but he is not guilty of theft. But if D's son, who is living with D, removes the topsoil for the same purpose the son would be guilty of theft because he is not "in possession" of the land although he happens to live there.

A tenant may be guilty of theft, however, where he appropriates (and here severance is not required) any fixture or structure let to be used with the land. A fixture here means something annexed to land for use or ornament, such as a washbasin, cupboards or fireplace, and a structure seems to mean some structure of a moveable or temporary character, such as a garden shed or a greenhouse. A house would not be a structure in this sense.

b) *Limitations on the theft of things growing wild.* Section 4 (3) of the Act provides:

"A person who picks mushrooms growing wild on any land, or who picks flowers, fruit or foliage from a plant growing wild on any land, does not (although not in possession of the land) steal what he picks, unless he does it for reward or for sale or other commercial purpose.

For purposes of this subsection 'mushroom' includes any fungus, and 'plant' includes any shrub or tree."

In some ways it might be thought that s. 4 (3) is rather an unnecessary provision. It exempts from liability for theft one who picks wild mushrooms, or one who picks flowers, fruit or foliage "*from* a plant" (thus a person who takes the whole plant may be convicted of theft) growing wild on land unless done for sale or other commercial purpose. Picking holly branches round about Christmas time for the purpose of sale may amount to theft as may picking elderberries for making wine if the purpose is to sell the wine. The whole matter might have been left to the common sense of the prosecutor who would hardly institute proceedings where the appropriation was trivial. Of course this would leave the aggrieved landowner free to take proceedings in such trivial cases, but generally under the criminal law the person aggrieved is free to take proceedings in the most

---

18. In 1972 a man was prosecuted at Leeds Crown Court for stealing Cleckheaton railway station by dismantling and removing it. He was acquitted on the merits, the jury accepting that on this bold enterprise he was acting under a claim of right. But railway stations are stealable by severance.

19. Note that if D is caught in the act of severing he is guilty only of an attempt. By attempting to sever D is of course assuming the rights of an owner and in other circumstances, (above, p. 497), this alone constitutes a complete appropriation. But in this case the effect of the subsection is to insist upon severance to complete the theft.

trivial case and this does not apparently lead to any serious abuse. However, the Criminal Law Revision Committee thought that

"a provision could reasonably be criticized which made it even technically theft in all cases to pick wild flowers against the will of the landowner."[20]

c) *Limitations on the theft of wild creatures.* Section 4 (4) of the Act provides:

"Wild creatures, tamed or untamed, shall be regarded as property; but a person cannot steal a wild creature not tamed nor ordinarily kept in captivity, or the carcase of any such creature, unless either it has been reduced into possession by or on behalf of another person and possession of it has not since been lost or abandoned, or another person is in course of reducing it into possession."

Wild animals while at large are not owned by anyone, nor does a landowner have a proprietary interest in such animals even where they constitute game. The landowner has the right to take wild animals and once a wild animal is caught or killed it immediately becomes the property of the landowner where this takes place, but he has no proprietary interest in such animals while at large. Technically the person catching or killing the animal would not, at that precise moment, be guilty of theft since he is not then appropriating the property of another. But since, as has been shown,[1] a person may commit theft, even where he has come by the property innocently, by any subsequent assumption of ownership, there would be no difficulty in finding such an assumption at a later stage. Indeed, unless the catcher immediately releases it, or the killer does nothing about appropriating the carcase, each would, but for s. 4(4), be guilty of theft.

Though this would be the position under the general law of theft, s. 4 (4) creates an exception which is, substantially, in favour of poaching because it was thought unacceptable to turn poaching into theft. Thus if D takes rabbits running wild on P's land he is not guilty of theft, though he may commit an offence in relation to poaching, and in this case it does not become theft though the poacher takes the rabbit for purposes of sale.

It is, however, possible to steal wild creatures where these have been tamed or are ordinarily kept in captivity. A tiger may be stolen from a zoo, and if it has escaped it may be stolen while at large because it is "ordinarily" kept in captivity. Wild animals may also be stolen when they are in process of being reduced into possession by or on behalf of another. A lazy poacher who picks up the pheasants shot from the skies by P is a thief, as is a gamekeeper who keeps for himself a pheasant which he shot for his employer. And if P, having shot a pheasant, cannot find it in the brush and gives up the search, a subsequent appropriation by D makes him a thief from the landowner.[2]

---

20. Cmnd. 2977, para. 47. The Wildlife and Countryside Act 1981 makes it an offence to kill, possess or sell certain creatures; and to pick, uproot or destroy certain wild plants.
  1. Above, p. 501.
  2. As to abandonment, see below, p. 535.

3 Belonging to Another

At first sight it is a perfectly obvious proposition that a man may steal only the property of another. But appearances can be deceptive. In the vast majority of cases there is of course no difficulty. D snatches P's handbag; the handbag is owned and possessed by P and clearly D has appropriated property belonging to P. In some cases, however, it may not be quite so clear to whom the handbag belongs or whether it belongs to anyone at all.

Moreover property in a given case may belong to both D and P; they may, for example, be joint owners of the property. Obviously there is no reason in principle why D should not be treated as a thief if he dishonestly appropriates P's share. This was the view taken by the Court of Appeal in *Bonner*[3] where it was held that a partner can steal partnership property.

It is easy enough to accept the good sense of the idea that D may steal property belonging to himself if it also belongs to another, but there are also situations in which, though the property in law belongs only to D, it is desirable that his dishonest appropriation of it should be treated as theft. Take a simple illustration suggested by the facts of *Hassall*.[4] There members of a club paid sums of money each week to D, the treasurer, on the understanding that the following Christmas D would return to each member the total sum paid in; but in fact D misappropriated the money. In this situation D becomes the owner of the money (it was never expected that D should return to each member the identical coins given him) and the relationship between D and the members is essentially that of trustee and beneficiaries. Here is a situation where the property in law belongs to D, but it is a case in which D ought to be treated as a thief and ought not to be allowed to shelter behind his legal ownership. Accordingly, s. 5 provides that in some cases, notwithstanding that D is the owner of the property, the property shall be treated as belonging to another so long as that other has some proprietary right or interest in the property. Once more the basic idea is simple enough to grasp but it can lead to difficulties in application.

This, in broad outline, explains the purport of s. 5. The section may now be looked at in more detail.

a) *Property belonging to another: the general rule.* Section 5 (1) of the Theft Act 1968 provides:

"Property shall be regarded as belonging to any person[5] having possession or control of it, or having in it any proprietary right or interest (not being an equitable interest arising only from an agreement to transfer or grant an interest)."

In the ordinary case property is stolen from one who both owns and possesses it by one who has no interest in the property whatever. Section 5 (1) covers this case of course but it goes much further. Suppose that P

---

3. [1970] 2 All ER 97, [1970] 1 WLR 838.
4. (1861) Le & Ca 56.
5. The person to whom the property belongs will usually be known and identified in the indictment, but if the owner is unknown D may be charged with stealing the property of a person unknown provided that this does not result in D being unable to ascertain the nature of the case he has to meet. Cf. *Gregory* [1972] 2 All ER 861 at 866, CA (handling property of person unknown); and see *Anglim and Cooke v Thomas* [1974] VR 363 at 374 (SC of Victoria).

lends a book to Q and that Q is showing the book to R when D snatches the book from R's hands and makes off with it. Here D has stolen the book from R (who has control of it), and Q (who has possession of it), and P (who also has a proprietary interest – ownership – in it).

As we have just seen it does not matter that the property happens to belong to D in one of these senses if at the same time it also belongs to P and it is D's intention dishonestly to deprive P permanently of his interest. Thus in the above illustration if R were dishonestly to appropriate the book he would steal it from both P and Q,[6] and if Q were to dishonestly appropriate the book he would steal it from P.

Conversely D, an owner, may steal the book from P, his bailee. While the book is in P's possession it belongs to P for the purposes of s. 5 (1) which does not place any limitations on the class of persons who may steal from him. Of course the circumstances in which D's appropriation of his own property will amount to theft will not be of common occurrence since D may easily be able to show a claim of right.[7] But consider *Turner (No. 2)*.[8] D had left his car with P for repair, promising to pay for the repairs when he returned to collect the car the following day. D, however, returned a few hours later and surreptitiously took back his car. Although D claimed that he was entitled to do as he did, it was clear from the circumstances that he was acting dishonestly, and his conviction for stealing the car from P was affirmed.

At first sight this seems obviously right because D was out to cheat P of his repairer's lien; even as against the owner D the car could be properly regarded as belonging to P so long as he had his lien. Unfortunately the trial judge told the jury to disregard the question of the lien and the case is accordingly authority for saying that D may steal from his own bailee at will, that is although D is entitled to determine the bailment *at any time*. Such a bailee so long as he remains in possession undoubtedly has a proprietary right or interest against third parties, but it seems odd to regard him as having such an interest against the bailor when the latter has decided, whether by notice or otherwise, to determine the bailment. That P has lawful possession of the property is not in itself enough. So in *Meredith*,[9] where D surreptitiously removed his car from a police pound where it had been lawfully placed by the police for causing an obstruction, it was held that D could not be convicted of stealing the car. The police were lawfully in possession of it so that a third party could have stolen it from them but as against D they had no right to retain it though they did have a right to enforce the statutory charge for its removal. The police, unlike the repairer in *Turner (No. 2)*,[10] were not bailees of the car but (disregarding the repairer's lien) the repairer in *Turner (No. 2)* seems to have been in a position analogous to that of the police in *Meredith*.

6. Cf. *Thompson* (1862) Le & Ca 225. D made off with a sovereign which P handed him to buy a ticket for her because she was unable to make her way through the crowd before a ticket office. This would be theft by D. Cf. *Rose v Matt* [1951] 1 KB 810, [1951] 1 All ER 361, DC.
7. Below, p. 537.
8. [1971] 2 All ER 441, CA; **SHC 424**.
9. [1973] Crim LR 253 CC; **SHC 426**.
10. [1971] 2 All ER 441, above.

(i) *Possession or control*. To a degree possession and control may overlap, and it is not important to pursue any possible distinction between them because property is treated as belonging to P if he has either possession or control. It is the limits of these concepts which are important, not the difference between them.

Possession requires both an intention to possess and some degree of dominion in fact. If P and D both see a wallet on the pavement, both may have the same intent to possess it, but until one of them seizes it neither has possession. Once P seizes it he has both possession and control. If he hands it to D just to show D what he has got, it would normally be said that P retains possession while D has control.

Possession and control are not, however, always as clear cut as in this illustration. There P's intent existed in respect of a specific article and he reduced it into his actual control – he had it in his hands. But it is not necessary to have, or ever to have had, control of a thing in this sense in order to have possession. An Electricity Board may have possession of the coins inserted in a domestic meter although the Board does not know at any given moment how many coins, if any, are in the meter.[11] Similarly, a householder normally has possession of the whole contents of his house even though he cannot itemise his goods. He may consign unwanted articles to his attic or cellar and forget about them, but he still retains possession. It is not, then, essential that P's intent should exist in respect of a specific thing: it may be enough for P's intent to exist in respect of all the goods situate about his premises. In *Woodman*[12] P sold all the scrap metal on certain disused business premises to Q; Q removed most of it but left some as being too inaccessible to be worth the expense of removal. D then entered the premises to take some of this scrap and was held to have been rightly convicted of its theft. P continued to control the site and his conduct in erecting fences and posting notices showed that he intended to exclude others from it; that was enough to give him control of the scrap which Q did not wish to remove.[13]

(ii) *Any proprietary right or interest*. Property is also to be regarded as belonging to any person having in it "any proprietary right or interest". Obviously, then, property may be stolen from the owner although at the time of the appropriation the owner is not in possession or control; and even though the owner may never have been in possession or control. If O sells goods to P (ownership passing to P) and O remains in possession of them, a dishonest appropriation of the goods by D will be theft from both

---

11. Cf. *Martin v Marsh* [1955] Crim LR 781. But see [1956] Crim LR 74.
12. [1974] QB 754, [1974] 2 All ER 955, CA; **SHC 422** See also *Hibbert v McKiernan* [1948] 2 KB 142, [1948] 1 All ER 860, DC (theft of golf balls lost on club premises); *Williams v Phillips* (1957) 41 Cr App Rep 5, DC (theft of refuse from dustbins).
13. Cf. *Rowe* (1859) 8 Cox CC 139, where D, employed to clean out P's canal, was convicted of stealing in appropriating iron found by him on the bed of the canal. For a case holding that P became the owner of coins thrown into his fountain for luck, see (1964) Times, 8th August. But cf. *Bridges v Hawkesworth* (1851) 21 LJQB 75, which is authority for the proposition that a person finding property in the public part of a shop is entitled to the property as against the shopkeeper; consequently the property so found does not belong to the shopkeeper and cannot be stolen from him. Cf. *Parker v British Airways Board* [1982] 1 All ER 834, CA. Presumably the finder of goods on the highway is entitled to the goods as against the highway authority. For a general discussion of the finder's rights as against the landowner see Street, *Torts*, 40.

O and P.[14] Moreover a dishonest appropriation of the property by O may constitute theft of the property by O from P though O has never been out of possession of the property; O has usurped P's proprietary right in the property. Similarly P, by a surreptitious and dishonest removal of *his* property from O's premises (it may be assumed that P intends to avoid paying for the property) steals from O because he usurp's O's interest in the property.[15]

The matter may be further illustrated by reference to the unusual facts of *Hancock*.[16] The case concerned treasure trove which may be shortly defined as articles of gold or silver hidden by an owner with a view to their subsequent recovery. Such treasure belongs to the successors in title of the depositor but, in the likely event that the successors cannot be traced, the trove belongs to the Crown and may therefore be stolen from the Crown. In *Hancock*, D, using a metal detector, had found some Celtic silver coins on the site of an ancient temple. It was not clear whether the coins constituted treasure trove (they might have been deposited with an intent to recover them or they might have been votive offerings left with no intention to recover them) and, at D's trial for theft, the trial judge directed the jury that the Crown had a proprietary right in the coins on the basis that the Crown had an interest in ascertaining whether the coins were treasure trove and that the key issue was whether there was a real possibility that the coins were treasure trove.

D's conviction was inevitably quashed. While on a proper direction the jury could have convicted D of theft if they were satisfied that the coins constituted treasure trove and D knew that,[17] the trial judge was wrong to rule that the Crown had a proprietary right because it had an interest in determining whether the coins constituted treasure trove or not. The court said:[18]

"[T]he Crown's entitlement to the property, itself depends on and cannot take effect until there has been a determination [whether the property is treasure trove or not] by a coroner's jury or by some other tribunal."

Another point discussed in *Hancock* was whether, in a case where the property found by D may or may not be treasure trove, it is preferable to charge D with stealing from the owner of the land. The court advised against this, partly because it might be difficult to prove dishonesty[19] and partly because of the unsatisfactory state of the authorities concerning the ownership of property found in or on the land of another.[20] With respect,

14. Frequently the thief will have no idea of the identity of the owner, or owners, of the property; it suffices that he knows the property belongs to *another*.
15. Cf. *Rose v Matt* [1951] 1 KB 810, [1951] 1 All ER 361, DC (pledgor of clock dishonestly retook it from pledgee).
16. [1990] 2 QB 242 [1990] Crim LR 125, CA.
17. Is it enough that D realises the coins might or might not be treasure trove but resolves to appropriate them anyway?
18. [1990] 3 All ER 183 at 187.
19. D might claim, on the basis of 'finders keepers', that as against the landowner he has a better right to the property, but the surreptitious use of a metal detector on another's land would likely undermine such a claim.
20. See fn. 13, above.

this is not a formidable objection because the authorities at least establish
that where an owner intends to exclude trespassers from his land he intends
to exclude them from taking anything in or on it, and the landowner's
intention to exclude gives him, as against the trespasser, a proprietary
interest in whatever happens to be in or on his land.

D may appropriate property which belongs to P in any of the senses
described in s. 5 (1). It does not matter that P's interest is precarious or that
it may be short-lived; wild birds reared by P may belong to P although they
may "betake themselves to the woods and fields" as soon as they are old
enough to fly,[1] and flowers left on a grave remain the property of the
leaver.[2] It does not matter that someone exists who has a better right to the
property than P: a thief may steal from a thief.[3] Any power to exclude
others, however small, will suffice.

(iii) *Equitable interests* "Any proprietary right or interest" extends to
both legal and equitable proprietary interests. Where property is subject to
a trust it belongs to both the trustee (legal interest) and beneficiary
(equitable interest) and it may be stolen from either.[4] But in the case of
equitable interests s. 5 (1) introduces a limitation, and property is not to be
regarded as belonging to a person who has an equitable interest arising only
from an agreement to transfer or grant an interest. The limitation is of no
great practical importance. In some circumstances an agreement to sell may
give the intending buyer an equitable interest in the property[5] and this
provision makes it clear that the seller cannot commit theft by reselling the
property to another.

b) *Trust property.*[6] Section 5 (2) of the Theft Act 1968 provides:
"Where property is subject to a trust, the persons to whom it belongs
shall be regarded as including any person having a right to enforce the
trust, and an intention to defeat the trust shall be regarded accordingly as
an intention to deprive of the property any person having that right."

In the ordinary case appropriation of trust property by a trustee is covered
not only by this subsection but also by s. 5 (1) because the beneficiary
ordinarily has a proprietary interest and accordingly the trust property
belongs to the beneficiary within s. 5 (1). But in some exceptional circumstances there may be no ascertained beneficiary. This occurs in the case of
"purpose" trusts whether charitable[7] or private,[8] where the object is to
effect some purpose rather than benefit ascertainable individuals. To meet

---

1. Cf. *Shickle* (1868) LR 1 CCR 158.
2. *Bustler v State* 184 SE 2d 24 (1944) (SC of Tennessee). Cf. *Edwards and Stacey* (1877) 13
Cox CC 384.
3. Cf. *Clarke*, referred to at [1956] Crim LR 369–70; *Meech* [1974] QB 549, [1973] 3 All ER
939, CA; above, p. 500.
4. See further s. 5 (2), below.
5. See Smith, *Theft*, paras. 66–67.
6. Brazier, "Criminal Trustees?"(1975) 39 Conv (NS) 29.
7. E.g., where money is given to D in trust for the improvement of schools in a particular
locality.
8. E.g., where money is given to D in trust for the maintenance of a tomb, or for the upkeep
of animals.

such cases s. 5 (2) goes further than s. 5 (1) by providing that the property is to be treated as belonging to anyone who has a right to enforce the trust.[9]

c) *Property received for a particular purpose*. It has already been mentioned[10] that it is in some circumstances right that D should be convicted of theft notwithstanding that he is the legal owner of the property, and the case of *Hassall*[11] was given as an illustration of the kind of situation envisaged. In *Hassall*, though D became the legal owner of the money paid in, it would be clear, even to someone who knew no law, that D was not free to do what he liked with the money. He was under an obligation to deal with the money in a particular way. He might have kept the money in a box or he might have kept it in an account at the bank, but, one way or another, he had to keep the fund in existence. Consequently D's dishonest appropriation of the fund would now amount to theft by virtue of s. 5 (3)[12] which provides:

"When a person receives property from or on account of another, and is under an obligation to the other to retain and deal with that property or its proceeds in a particular way, the property or proceeds shall be regarded (as against him) as belonging to the other."

It is easy enough to appreciate that in *Hassall* D was under an obligation to deal with the money deposited in a particular way but it is more difficult to say, in general terms, when a person "is under an obligation to the other to retain and deal with that property or its proceeds in a particular way." The obligation referred to is a *legal* obligation, a moral or social obligation will not do.[13] The essential notion is that D must be under a fiduciary obligation with regard to the property which he receives. The idea of fiduciary obligation conveys accurately the essential requirement: the property, though it may be owned only by D, must be earmarked in D's hands for certain purposes of P's.

---

9. In the foregoing examples this would be, respectively, the Attorney-General and the person entitled to the residue of the estate.
10. Above, p. 518.
11. (1861) Le & Ca 56; above, p. 518.
12. It would seem to be the case that D's appropriation of the money would amount to theft even without s. 5 (3). The depositors surely retain a proprietary right or interest in the money deposited in such circumstances. Indeed in all cases falling within s. 5 (3) it seems clear that the person from, or on whose account, the property is received would have a proprietary right or interest and thus the case would be covered by s. 5 (1). However, s. 5 (3) does make the point explicitly clear.
13. *Gilks* [1972] 3 All ER 280, CA; *Mainwaring* (1981) 74 Cr App Rep 99. But in *Cullen* (1974) unreported (No. 968/C/74) D's conviction was upheld where, living with P as his wife, she appropriated money given her for housekeeping – notwithstanding *Balfour v Balfour* [1919] 2 KB 571, the court found a "plain" legal obligation. But where people, not members of a family, share premises and the outgoings, it becomes easy to infer that legal relationships are intended so that if one of their number, given money or cheques to meet the outgoings, appropriates the money or cheques the case falls within s. 5 (3): *Davidge v Bunnett* [1984] Crim LR 297, DC. In *Meech* [1974] QB 549, [1973] 3 All ER 939, CA, the facts of which are given above, p. 500, it was concluded that D was under a legal obligation to pay the proceeds of the cheque to P. No doubt D was properly convicted because P had a proprietary right or interest in the money but it is questionable whether D was under a legal obligation in respect of the proceeds of the cheque because P would have been unable to recover them in a civil action.

Take a simple case of loan. P lends D £10 – and, having received the money, D dishonestly decides never to repay P and subsequently denies that P made the loan. D is not guilty of theft. Clearly D is acting dishonestly and the view might be taken that his case is indistinguishable from that of a Hassall who misappropriates £10 from his workmates' holiday fund; but he is not a thief under the Theft Act. He does not appropriate property belonging to another, and the property (the £10) cannot under the Act be regarded as belonging to another since he was under no obligation whatever to deal with it in a particular way. It was D's to deal with as he liked.

But suppose that D had agreed to do certain work for P and that P made D an advance of £10 on the agreed price for the job. If D does not do the work, and never intended to do it, it may be that D can be convicted of obtaining the £10 by deception; but he cannot be convicted of stealing the £10. Again the money belongs only to him, and, although it was advanced to him in connection with a particular transaction, it was not received by him to deal with in a particular way. D may again spend the £10 as he likes. However it is just in this sort of situation that D, in order to ensure an advance payment, will tell P that he needs cash in advance in order to procure materials for the job. When this happens D will often be guilty of obtaining the money by deception, but he is also guilty of theft because he is now under an obligation to deal with the money in a particular way.

Consequently, whether property has been received under an obligation to deal with it in a particular way depends upon the particular circumstances of the case. If, for example, P were to pay a deposit to D, a trader, for goods to be supplied under a contract of sale, the normal inference from such a transaction would be that D is under no obligation to deal with the deposit in a particular way. D might well pay the deposit into his trading account but he could draw on that account as he wished and would not be obliged to keep in existence a fund representing P's deposit. If, on the other hand, P were to give D, his secretary, £100 with instructions to go to a travel agency and purchase a ticket for a flight, the normal inference would be that D is under an obligation to deal with the £100 in a particular way. In such a case it would normally be clearly envisaged by both parties that D will apply that particular £100 to the purchase of the ticket; but in the first illustration it would not normally be envisaged by the parties that the trader will apply the deposit to the particular purpose of purchasing the goods that P has ordered.

The difficulties are well illustrated by *Hall*.[14] D, a partner in a firm of travel agents, had received money from P and others as deposits for air trips to America. The flights never materialised and the deposits, which had been paid into the firm's general trading account, were never returned. The Court of Appeal had no difficulty in accepting the jury's verdict that D had acted dishonestly in spending this money, but quashed D's conviction for theft on the ground that D had not received the money under an obligation to deal with it in a particular way. The court reached this conclusion with obvious reluctance—

14. [1972] 2 All ER 1009, CA; **SHC 427**; and see *Hayes* (1976) 64 Cr App Rep 82.

"Nevertheless, when a client goes to a firm carrying on the business of travel agents and pays them money, he expects that in return he will, in due course, receive the tickets and other documents necessary for him to accomplish the trip for which he is paying, and the firm are 'under an obligation' to perform their part to fulfil his expectation and are liable to pay him damages if they do not. But, in our judgment, what was not here established was that these clients expected them 'to retain and deal with that property or its proceeds in a particular way', and that an 'obligation' to do so was undertaken by [D]. We must make clear, however, that each case turns on its own facts. Cases could, we suppose, conceivably arise where by some special arrangement (preferably evidenced by documents), the client could impose on the travel agent an 'obligation' falling within s. 5 (3)."[15]

The case shows that it is not enough that a debtor dishonestly dissipates his assets so that when the time comes for payment he has no funds from which to meet his obligations, and it makes no difference that the debtor has dissipated *his* funds in order to defeat his creditors.

A liability to pay P is accordingly not enough unless D is obliged to keep a fund representing that property in existence. If an employee receives a bribe in contravention of his duty to his employer, the employer may recover the amount of the bribe in a civil action; but the employee cannot steal the bribe by keeping it for himself since the employer acquires no proprietary interest in the bribe or its proceeds.[16] Similarly, if an employee makes a secret profit by selling at his employer's shop goods of his own or of a third party, the employee does not steal the profit by keeping it to himself.[17] The employer may recover the profit by action but he does not acquire any proprietary interest in the monies received or their proceeds.

The contract of sale or return is worth noting in this connection. In the ordinary case of sale or return P delivers goods to D on the terms that D will return them within a certain time unless D decides to buy them. Should D sell the goods to a third party he makes himself, vis-à-vis P, the buyer of the goods and must pay the agreed purchase price to P. Suppose then that P delivers jewellery to D which D sells to Q and then absconds with the purchase price. D cannot be convicted of stealing the jewellery for he has not appropriated it.[18] Does D steal the proceeds? It is submitted that he does not because his only obligation is to pay P the agreed purchase price;[19] he is not, when he receives the money from Q, under any obligation to deal with it in any particular way. In other words, the buyer under a sale or return transaction is in the same position as any other purchaser of goods who has not paid the price: he is no more than P's debtor for the price.

It might be thought that another reason why the buyer under a contract of sale or return is not under an obligation to deal with the proceeds in a particular way is that he receives the proceeds from Q and not from P. But this will not do. Section 5 (3) applies when D receives property "from or on

15. [1972] 2 All ER 1009 at 1011.
16. *Powell v MacRae* [1977] Crim LR 571, DC; *Police v Leaming* [1975] 1 NZLR 471.
17. *A-G's Reference (No. 1 of 1985)* [1986] QB 491, [1986] 2 All ER 219, CA.
18. See above, p. 497.
19. Cf. Hughes, "Sale or Return, Agents and Larceny" [1963] Crim LR 312, 411.

account of another" and clearly D may receive property from Q on the account of P.[20]

Thus it is not necessary that the fiduciary duty should arise out of the transaction between D and the person delivering the property to him; it is enough that D's fiduciary duty arises out of a relationship with a person other than the deliveror. To go back to the sale or return illustration: D's immunity there was not based on the fact that he received the money from Q; it was based on the fact that he did not receive the money from Q on P's account. It would be another matter if D had been simply an agent for the sale of the jewellery. Then D would not become the buyer of the jewellery at all, and the money paid by Q would belong to P and not to D. In this situation D might in fact become the owner of the money (as where it is expected that D will account for the money but is not expected to hand over the very coins and notes which he receives); nonetheless D has a duty to keep the fund of money in existence and his appropriation of it may amount to theft.

The essence of the matter is that D is under a legal obligation to P, whether the property comes into D's hands from P or from a third party, to retain and deal with *that* property, or the property into which *that* property may be converted by D, in a particular way. The fact that the deliverer of the property to D is unaware of the relationship between D and P which places D under a duty to account to P for the property delivered or its proceeds is no bar to D's conviction for theft if D is so obliged. Conversely, the fact that the deliverer expects D to account for the property to P does not necessarily involve the conclusion that D is under an obligation to account for *that* property or its proceeds to P. Those who sponsor D in an event where the proceeds are to go to a charity no doubt expect that the money they give to D will be accounted for to the charity but it was held in *Lewis v Lethbridge*[1] that D did not steal the money he received from his sponsors by failing to account for it to the charity.[2] No doubt when the state pays out housing benefit to D to enable D to pay his rent the expectation is that D will use the money to pay his landlord but it was held in *Huskinson*[3] that D was not guilty of theft where he spent some of the money received as housing benefit on himself. There was nothing in the relevant legislation suggesting that D should pay *that* money or its proceeds to the landlord. Vis-à-vis the landlord D could have met his legal obligation to pay the rent from any source, such as an unexpected win on the pools.

Although property may be received from any source, what is critical is the nature of the arrangement, express or implied, between D and P. Where D, a broker, is engaged to collect premiums on behalf of P, D may steal the premiums if the agreement provides that they vest in P[4] but not if

20. Cf. *Grubb* [1915] 2 KB 683.
   1. [1987] Crim LR 59, DC.
   2. Perhaps a surprising conclusion. The normal expectation of donors would be that D would keep the money donated, or their proceeds, separate from his own money. Clearly if the money is collected by D on behalf of a charity in a collecting box, D's dishonest appropriation of the contents of the box would be theft. The money delivered in *Lewis v Lethbridge* was just as surely earmarked for the chairty.
   3. [1988] Crim LR 620, DC.
   4. *Brewster* (1979) 69 Cr App Rep 375, CA.

the agreement merely makes D P's debtor for the amount of the premiums paid.[5] In both cases the broker has been dishonest and in both the insurer is the loser but in the first case the broker is a thief and in the second he is not; a distinction which may be effected by a few strokes of the pen in the agreement between P and D.

From the foregoing discussion it may be seen that whether property has been entrusted for a particular purpose may involve complex questions of law and fact. On principle (a) where the transaction is wholly in writing it ought to be for the judge to rule as a matter of law whether there has been an entrusting for a particular purpose; and (b) where the transaction is oral, or partly oral and partly in writing, it ought to be for the judge to rule what may in law amount to an entrusting for a particular purpose and for the jury to determine whether the property was so entrusted in fact.[6] *Mainwaring*[7] contains an unequivocal statement to this effect—

"Whether or not an obligation arises is a matter of law, because an obligation must be a legal obligation. But a legal obligation arises only in certain circumstances, and in many cases the circumstances cannot be known until the facts are established. It is for the jury, not the judge, to establish the facts.

What, in our judgment, a judge ought to do is this: if the facts relied upon by the prosecution are in dispute he should direct the jury to make their findings on the facts, and then say to them: 'If you find the facts to be such-and-such, then I direct you as a matter of law that a legal obligation arose to which s. 5 (3) applies.'"

It was accordingly held in *Mainwaring* that the trial judge was wrong to direct the jury that the defendants were as a matter of law under an obligation. His direction was based on the interpretation of certain receipts and had the issue been exclusively governed by the interpretation of these documents, it is submitted that he would have been right to rule on their effect. But in that case the issue turned on further factors, such as whether certain monies had or had not been paid; the resolution of these facts was the province of the jury and the judge should have instructed them on which findings they might find that the money had been received under an obligation to deal with it in a particular way.[8] In determining whether there is a legal obligation the intentions of the parties must of course be considered, and it may also be relevant to consider such factors as the relationship between them, the nature of the property, previous similar dealings between them, and business practice in similar transactions.[9]

d) *Property got by mistake.* Section 5 (4) of the Theft Act provides:

"Where a person gets property by another's mistake, and is under an obligation to make restoration (in whole or in part) of the property or its

5. *Robertson* [1977] Crim LR 629 (Judge Rubin QC).
6. Cf. *Hall* [1972] 2 All ER 1009 at 1012, 1013.
7. (1981) 74 Cr App Rep 99 at 107, CA. Suggestions to the contrary appearing in *Hayes* (1977) 64 Cr App Rep 82, CA, may now be disregarded.
8. It is necessary to prove that D knew of the facts from which the legal obligation arises; the knowledge of an employee or agent cannot be imputed to him: *Wills* (1990) 92 Cr App Rep 297, CA.
9. *Wakeman v Farrar* [1974] Crim LR 136, DC.

proceeds or of the value thereof, then to the extent of that obligation the property or proceeds shall be regarded (as against him) as belonging to the person entitled to restoration, and an intention not to make restoration shall be regarded accordingly as an intention to deprive that person of the property or proceeds."

This provision may be explained by reference to the facts of *Moynes v Coopper*.[10] In this case D, a labourer employed by P, was given an advance of pay by the site agent amounting to £6 19s. 6½d. Unaware that this advance had been made, P's wages clerk paid D the full weekly wage of £7 3s. 4d. and D dishonestly kept all of the money.

The difficulty with this case is that in law the whole of the £7 3s. 4d. belongs to D. The wages clerk made a mistake of course, but his mistake was not such as would prevent ownership of all the money passing to D. Had the clerk known of the advance he would have paid D only 3s. 9½d; nevertheless the clerk did intend to pay the full amount, and he was authorised as P's wages clerk to pay wages. The case is now covered by s. 5 (4) and D steals the excess payment if he dishonestly appropriates it; although D becomes the owner of the money he is under a legal obligation, at the very least, to repay the value of the excess payment.

But why, it may be asked, is all this trouble taken to deal with this particular kind of debtor? In terms of moral turpitude only the finest shading separates a Moynes from the ordinary debtor who dishonestly decides not to repay his loan. Under the former law Moynes was in fact acquitted, but in view of the criticism which his acquittal attracted it was no doubt felt necessary to bring such conduct within the net of the criminal law.

It may be helpful to consider a mistake of common occurrence in giving too much change. Suppose that a barman makes an error and gives to a customer more change than he is entitled to. The customer realises that a mistake has been made but nevertheless dishonestly[11] decides to keep the excess. Section 5 (4) makes the customer a thief if, but only if, the customer is under a legal obligation to make restoration (in whole or in part) of the money *or* its proceeds *or* the value thereof. The Theft Act provides no guidance on when the customer incurs such an obligation; that can only be determined by reference to the relevant civil law.

The barman may have made one of a variety of mistakes. He may (i) deliver the correct change but to the wrong person; or (ii) having correctly calculated the change as 20p, hand the customer a £1 coin thinking it a 20p piece; or (iii) incorrectly calculate the change due as £1 when it should have been 20p and pay £1 to the customer. Section 5 (4) covers all three cases but it is not strictly necessary to cover cases (i) and (ii) because in these cases the barman's mistake is such that ownership does not pass. The barman retains a proprietary right in the money and s. 5 (1) provides for them.

---

10. [1956] 1 QB 439, [1956] 1 All ER 450.
11. It is assumed here that such an appropriation is dishonest but it is a matter on which, perhaps, views may differ, see below, p. 536.

Case (iii) is different. The barman has made a mistake but he has not made a mistake as to whom he is paying the money, nor as to the amount paid. The customer becomes the owner of the money and unless some special provision is made for the case he cannot be convicted of theft. The case is not covered by s. 5 (3) because the customer is under no legal obligation to retain and deal with *that* money or *its* proceeds in a particular way. The customer is, however, obliged to make restoration (to the *value* of 80p in the illustration given) but the obligation does not extend to the coin delivered or its proceeds. Section 5 (4) does of course cover the situation where D is under an obligation to make restoration of the property or its proceeds (and thus there will be some overlap between s. 5 (4) and s. 5 (3)) but s. 5 (4) extends to the case where D's obligation is to restore an amount (the value) equivalent to the sum by which he has been mistakenly enriched.

Section 5 (4) was applied in *A-Gs Reference (No. 1 of 1983)*.[12] D's salary was paid into her bank account by direct debit and on one occasion her employers mistakenly overpaid her by £74.74. The question for the court was: assuming that she dishonestly decided not to restore that money, would she have been guilty of theft. In law she became the owner of the money and, as Lord Lane CJ pointed out, had no special provision been made for the case that would have been an end to the matter. But s. 5 (4) provided for the case. While she, as owner of the chose in action against the bank, was not under an obligation to restore the chose or its proceeds, she was under an obligation to restore the value thereof to her employers.

But it is important to consider why D was under an obligation to make restoration. It is settled law that if owing to a mistake of fact P believes that he is legally obliged to make a payment when he is not, he is entitled to recover the equivalent of the sum so paid.[13] The issue whether D was under a legal obligation was resolved without difficulty in this case but it will be appreciated that it will not always be so straightforward. The law of unjust enrichment[14] is not free from considerable subtlety. This may mean that D's liability for theft may turn upon a consideration of fine points of civil law remote from the central question of D's dishonesty. But this is not the only context in which complex issues of civil law may have to be determined. But while theft must take account of the civil law of mine and thine, s. 5 (4) goes to the very limit in treating property which in law belongs to D as belonging to P provided P has a right of restitution of the value of that property.

There was no evidence in *A-Gs Reference* that D had spent the money that was overpaid or that she had done any act in relation to it. But to meet a possible argument that in doing nothing D cannot intend permanently to deprive the owner, s. 5 (4) further provides that an intention not to make restoration shall be regarded as an intention permanently to deprive.[15]

The foregoing discussion of s. 5 (4) assumes, as seemingly did the CLRC, that the entire proprietary interest passes to D who is no more than

12. [1985] QB 182, [1984] 3 All ER 369, CA.
13. *Norwich Union Fire Insurance Society Ltd v William H Price Ltd* [1934] AC 455.
14. See Goff & Jones, *The Law of Restitution* (3rd edn., 1986), Ch. 3.
15. But this does not cover a further point. Was there an appropriation? See above, p. 497.

a debtor. No doubt this is so at *law* but the position appears to be different in *equity*. In *Chase Manhattan Bank NA v Israel–British Bank (London) Ltd*[16] the X bank by mistake paid $2 million to the Y bank for the account of the Z bank which subsequently went into liquidation. The X bank was of course entitled to a dividend in the liquidation but it sought to recover the whole of its loss. It was held by Goulding J that a person who pays money (or, presumably, delivers any property) to another under a mistake of fact retains an equitable interest[17] in the money and the conscience of the recipient is subject to a fiduciary duty to respect his proprietary right. Accordingly the X bank was entitled to the restoration of the whole of the money mistakenly paid and was not relegated to claiming a dividend in the liquidation.

If this decision is correct, and it appears to have met with approval, it would seem that s. 5 (4) was strictly unnecessary. In *Moynes v Coopper* P retained an equitable interest in the money overpaid and D, on these facts, could now be convicted of theft even if s. 5 (4) had not been enacted.

The *Chase Manhattan* principle was relied on by the Court of Appeal in *Shadrokh–Cigari*.[18] The O bank had in error credited a child's account at the P bank with £286,000 instead of £286. D, the child's guardian, got the child to sign authority for the issue by the P bank of drafts and when D was arrested only £21,000 remained in the account. Upholding D's conviction for theft from the P bank, the court said that the drafts belonged to the bank and although legal ownership passed to D by delivery, the bank retained an equitable interest by virtue of the *Chase Manhattan* princple and D had appropriated property belonging to another within s. 5 (1). It was accordingly not necessary to rely on s. 5 (4) though that subsection provided an alternative route to conviction.

Section 5 (4), or the *Chase Manhattan* principle, applies though only part of the property is got by mistake. In *Moynes v Coopper*[19] D appropriated only the amount by which he was overpaid. In such a case it would be impossible to identify the coins which represented the overpayment but the prosecution is not required to do so because the property is sufficiently identified if it is proved to be part of an identifiable whole. This principle was applied in *Davis*.[20] By a computer error D was sent two cheques a month in respect of housing benefit when he was entitled to only one. It was held that where D had cashed these cheques he could be convicted of stealing the proceeds (the cash) of one of the cheques and it was not necessary for the prosecution to establish which proceeds he had stolen and which he had not.

It will be evident from the foregoing discussion that "obligation" in s. 5 (4) can only refer to a legal obligation imposed by the civil law. This is confirmed by *Gilks*[1] though the case has its complications. P, a bookmaker, mistakenly believing that D had backed a winning horse, overpaid D on the

---

16. [1981] Ch 105, [1979] 3 All ER 1025.
17. Section 5(1) extends to equitable interests, see above, p. 518.
18. [1988] Crim LR 465, CA.
19. Above, p. 528.
20. (1988) 88 Cr App Rep 347, CA.
 1. [1972] 3 All ER 280, [1972] 1 WLR 1341, CA.

bets he had placed and D, aware of the error, dishonestly decided not to return the overpayment. Since P had made no mistake either as to the amount or the recipient, ownership of the money passed to D. The court was clear that s. 5 (4) was inapplicable. This being a wagering transaction P had no right of restitution in respect of the overpayment so D could be under no legal obligation to make restoration. But the court went on, relying upon an antique and questionable authority under the law of larceny,[2] to uphold D's conviction on the grounds that since P would not have made the overpayment but for his mistake, ownership in the money did not pass to D. This is at odds with the civil law and the holding needs to be reconsidered.

Thus far it has been assumed that P's mistake is self-induced and not induced by any deception on D's part. There is clearly no warrant for drawing any such distinction under s. 5 (4): if property is got by mistake, however induced, D may be convicted of theft *provided* the other elements in the subsection are met. It follows that in some cases D may be convicted of either deception or theft. *Cundy v Lindsay*[3] provides a convenient example of such a case. There the rogue Blenkarn, having induced P to believe that he was dealing with the respected firm of Blenkiron & Co., dishonestly made off with goods consigned by P to Blenkiron & Co. The effect of Blenkarn's fraud was to induce a fundamental mistake; P never intended to deal with Blenkarn so ownership never passed to him. When Blenkarn got his hands on the goods they were still the property of P[4] and Blenkarn could be convicted of theft as well as deception.

In *Cundy v Lindsay* the effect of the fraud was to render the contract void or, more properly stated, the fraud prevented a contract from being formed. More usually fraud renders a contract voidable, that is to say that there is a contract which may (notice *may* not *must*) be set aside by the defrauded party. A classic example is provided by *King's Norton Metal Co Ltd v Edridge, Merrett & Co Ltd*[5] where the rogue Wallis induced P to sell and consign goods on credit to him by pretending that he ran a prosperous business. A clear case of obtaining by deception but the question is whether it is also theft by virtue of s. 5 (4). No doubt if Blenkarn and Wallis were in a prison cell together they would be hard put to find any distinction between their frauds but students of the law of contract will know that there was an important difference so far as the civil law is concerned. It is submitted here that there is an equally important distinction so far as the criminal law is concerned. Wallis, unlike Blenkarn, becomes the owner of the goods; they are *his* goods until such time as P elects to set aside (and he may if he wishes choose to confirm) the contract. But until such time as P sets aside the contract D is under no obligation to make restoration of the goods or their proceeds or the value thereof. He has an obligation to pay the price for the goods but that is a personal obligation he has to P; until such time as the contract is set aside the goods are his. Section 5 (4) requires that

2. *Middleton* (1873) LR 2 CCR 38.
3. (1878) 3 App Cas 459, HL.
4. Blenkarn may be convicted of theft without resort to s. 5 (4); at the time of the appropriation of the property P is still the owner.
5. (1897) 14 TLR 98, CA.

at the time of the appropriation D "is" under an obligation; it is not enough that he may become under an obligation. When the contract is set aside by P, D will become under an obligation to restore the goods to P for they are now P's goods and not D's and an appropriation after the contract has been set aside may amount to theft.[6]

The effect of s. 5 (4), it is submitted, is that while it may enable some cases of deception to be treated as theft, it falls way short of enabling all cases of deception to be treated as theft. Some cases of deception may also be treated as theft without resort to s. 5 (4). The House of Lords in *Lawrence*[7] might have provided definitive guidance on the matter but did not. The Court of Appeal in that case[8] thought that as a result of its decisions all cases of deception might be charged as theft but it has clearly resiled from this view in *Gomez*.[9] It is accordingly submitted that where D, by deception, induces P to part with his entire proprietary interest (albeit under a voidable contract) D may be guilty of obtaining by deception but not of theft.[10]

e) *Property of corporations.* Property may of course belong to a corporation just as much as to an individual, and may be stolen from a corporation. Normally the legal personality of a corporation continues, notwithstanding changes in membership, until the corporation is dissolved, but in the case of a corporation sole (a bishop of the Established Church for example) a vacancy may occur owing to the death of the incumbent. Section 5 (5) accordingly provides:

"Property of a corporation sole shall be regarded as belonging to the corporation notwithstanding a vacancy in the corporation."

This subsection accordingly provides for a very special case but it may be convenient here to consider other problems which arise in connection with corporations and theft.

Theft is a crime which a corporation may commit provided the conditions for corporate criminal liability are met.[11] Thus if the directors of a company were dishonestly to appropriate property belonging to a rival firm to use in the company's business, the company as well as the directors may be convicted of theft. Nor is there any bar to convicting a director, even if he is the majority shareholder, of stealing from the company.[12] A director is no more entitled to appropriate the company's typewriter than is his secretary. But what if D and E are the sole directors of and shareholders in the company – may D and E steal the typewriter if they take it for their own purposes? May D and E use the company's assets for any purpose of their

---

6. Once again, though, there would be no need to rely on s. 5 (4); D is simply appropriating property belonging to another.
7. [1972] AC 626, [1971] 2 All ER 1253, HL, above, p. 506.
8. [1971] 1 QB 373, [1970] 3 All ER 933, CA.
9. [1991] 3 All ER 394, 93 Cr App Rep 156, CA.
10. See further, Griew, "Theft and Obtaining by Deception" [1979] Crim LR 292; Williams, "Theft and Voidable Title" [1981] Crim LR 666; Smith "Theft and Voidable Title: A Reply" [1981] Crim LR 677.
11. Above, p. 178.
12. Cf. *Bonner* [1970] 2 All ER 97n, [1970] 1 WLR 838, above, p. 518.

own though they know that the company's creditors will be defeated thereby without danger of conviction for theft?[13]

If X is in business on his own account he is free to dispose of the assets of the business (for they are his assets) as he wishes and no question of theft can arise even if he dissipates the assets to defeat creditors. If Y and Z form a partnership it is established that either may steal from the other by appropriating the other's share.[14] But it is clear that Y and Z together cannot steal the partnership property (for it is their property) and again even if done to defraud creditors.

Where a company is involved it is not so straightforward.[15] D and E may be the sole directors of and shareholders in DE Ltd but the assets of the company are not theirs; the company is a separate legal entity and is the owner of its own assets. On the face of it D and E may steal the assets of DE Ltd (may appropriate property of *another*) by using the assets for their own purposes. But if D and E do not own the assets of DE Ltd, they control its affairs; DE Ltd can only speak and act through D and E.

The problem was first considered in *A–G's Reference (No 2 of 1982)*[16] which raised the question whether D and E, the sole directors of and shareholders in a number of companies could steal the assets of these companies where both consented to disbursements made by the companies to either of them. In substance what D and E were doing was using the assets to support an extravagant private life style knowing this would inexorably lead to the bankruptcy of the companies. In this case it was conceded that all the elements of theft were present save for dishonesty[17] and whether there was an appropriation of the assets was not directly addressed.

The issue was directly addressed by the High Court of Victoria in *Roffel*[18] where *A–G's Reference (no 2 od 1982)* was found to be of no assistance. It was held that where D, the sole director and shareholder, used the company's assets for private purposes he was not guilty of theft because, following *Morris*,[19] there was no appropriation of the assets. The same conclusion was favoured by the Court of Appeal in *McHugh and Tringham*[20] where the court said[1]—

"(4) An act done with the authority of the company cannot in general amount to an appropriation. Such authority may be—(a) express, or (b) implied. (5) Where the actor is beneficially entitled to the entire issued share capital (or at least the entire voting share capital) of the company it

13. Such conduct may amount to the offence of defrauding creditors contrary to the Insolvency Act 1986, s. 207 but this carries only two years' imprisonment which may be thought inadequate for some cases.
14. *Bonner* [1970] 2 All ER 97n, [1970] 1 WLR 838 CA, above, p. 518.
15. See Sullivan, "Company Controllers, Company Cheques and Theft" [1983] Crim LR 512; Nessen, "Company Controllers, Company Cheques and Theft – An Australian Perspective" [1986] Crim LR 154; Elliott, "Directors' Thefts and Dishonesty" [1992] Crim LR 732.
16. [1984] QB 624, [1984] 2 Ali ER 216, CA. The reference was from [1982] Crim LR 829. See Dine [1984] Crim LR 397; Sullivan [1984] Crim LR 405.
17. As to which see below, p. 536.
18. [1985] VR 511. See Smith (1985) Crim LJ 320.
19. [1984] AC 320, [1983] 3 All ER 288, HL, above, p. 498.
20. (1989) 88 Cr App Rep 385, CA; **SHC 409**.
   1. At P. 393.

may be that his act is not an appropriation because—(a) his act is equivalent to an act of the company, and his intent is the intent of the company, so there can be no circumstances in which any of his acts is unauthorised; and/or (b) since he has the irresistible power to determine what policies the company shall pursue, there is nothing which he himself may do in the company's name which could in practice be unauthorised."

But a differently constituted Court of Appeal in *Philippou*,[2] which made no reference to *McHugh and Tringham*, held that D and E, again sole directors and shareholders who had used the company's assets for private purposes, were properly convicted of theft. The court thought that though appropriation was conceded in *A–G's Reference (No. 2 of 1982)* there can have been "no doubt" that appropriation was established in that case. This was a case where *Lawrence*[3] was determinative. So when Lord Roskill said in *Morris*[4] that appropriation involved an act not expressly or impliedly authorised by the owner, the court in *Philippou* said[5]—

"he cannot be understood as saying that the prosecution must prove that the appropriation alleged was without the authority of the owner, for that would be directly contrary to what was said in *Lawrence*."

And *Roffel* was expressly disapproved.

So once more an acute conflict of judicial views. Which is preferable? It may be said that the conduct of the defendants in all four cases (defeating the claims of creditors by lining their own pockets) was deplorable. But it is not enough that conduct is deplorable; the elements constituting theft must be made out. It is clear beyond a peradventure that if the defendants had been trading on their own account they could not be convicted of stealing the assets of the business though they were using the assets for private purposes in the knowledge that creditors of the business would be defeated. nor, had they set up partnerships, would they have been guilty of theft provided that all the partners agreed to the dissipation of the assets of the partnership. Can it make a sensible distinction that the defendants choose to trade as a company of which they are the sole directors and in which they are the sole shareholders?[6] It is thought not and that the view expressed in *Roffel* and in *McHugh and Tringham* is to be preferred.

D is not a thief where he spends his own money on himself even if it is done to defeat creditors. It can make no difference that D gives his money to E for E to spend on himself, whether E is aware of D's impending insolvency or not.[7] By parity of reasoning, if DE Ltd makes a gift of its

---

2. (1989) 89 Cr App Rep 290, CA; **SHC 411**.
3. [1972] AC 626, [1971] 2 All ER 1253, HL, above, p. 506.
4. [1984] AC 320 at 332, [1983] 3 All ER 288 at 293, HL. And see above, p. 509; the appeal to the HL in *Gomez* may resolve the matter.
5. (1989) 89 Cr App Rep 290 at 299.
6. If there are additional directors and/or shareholders who are kept in the dark, the position would be different and D may properly be convicted of stealing the assets of the company.
7. There are provisions in the Insolvency Act 1986 (ss. 339 and 341) under which the court may, on the application of the trustee in bankruptcy, make such order as it thinks fit for restoring the position to what it would have been if the debtor had not entered the transaction in question. But at no stage does the trustee have a proprietary right or interest in the assets given to E nor any right of restitution in respect of them.

assets to F, F cannot steal them.[8] In principle it can make no difference that DE Ltd makes the gift to D and E, the sole directors and shareholders.

f) *Ownerless property*. A person cannot steal property that is not owned by another at the time of the appropriation. If there is no person to whom the property belongs in any of the senses set out in s. 5, that property cannot be stolen.

Though "property" and "belonging to another" are widely defined in the Act it would still appear to be the law that a corpse cannot be stolen. In *Doodeward v Spence*,[9] a decision of the High Court of New South Wales where the English authorities are examined, it was held that, while there could be no right of property in a corpse buried in the ordinary way, a proprietary interest could be acquired by one who expended work and skill on the corpse with a view to its preservation on scientific or other grounds. Since the rule of common law is hardly one dictated by logic or by practical considerations (there is no reason why the executors should not at least have possession of the corpse[10]), the limitation suggested in *Doodeward v Spence* seems a sensible one. While it may not be a practical problem in this context, it would be surprising if tissue removed from a dead body for the purpose of a transplant was not at least in the lawful possession of the surgeon.[11]

Property that is capable of belonging to another may be ownerless because it has never been made the subject of ownership. D can commit no offence in taking a swarm of bees not previously owned by another. Conversely, property which has at one time been owned may become ownerless by abandonment. But abandonment is not something to be lightly inferred: property is abandoned only when the owner is indifferent to any future appropriation of the property by others. It is not enough that P has no further use for the goods. A farmer who buries diseased animals has no further use for them but he would clearly intend that others should not make use of them and retains ownership of the carcases.[12] A householder who puts rubbish in his dustbin has no further use for the rubbish but he puts it there to be collected by the corporation and not as an invitation to all comers to help themselves.[13] Nor is property abandoned because the owner has lost it and has given up the search. A wife may have

8. The Insolvency Act contains provisions parallel to those in the last note applicable to companies.

9. (1908) 95 R (NSW) 107. See A. T. H., Smith, "Stealing the Body and its Parts" [1976] Crim LR 622.

10. Cf. the Human Tissue Act 1961 which, for the purposes of authorising the removal of tissue from a dead body, speaks of "the person lawfully in possession of his body after his death".

11. Cf. *Welsh* [1974] RTR 478, CA where a driver who had provided a specimen of urine for analysis and subsequently poured the specimen down the sink was convicted of stealing the urine. In *Rothery* [1976] RTR 550, CA where a driver provided a specimen of blood which he subsequently removed, his conviction for stealing the capsule and its container was affirmed; apparently he was not charged with stealing the contents (that is his own blood) but it would seem that he would have no answer to such a charge.

12. Cf. *Edwards and Stacey* (1877) 36 LT 30.

13. Cf. *Williams v Phillips* (1957) 121 JP 163.

lost her wedding ring and long since given up the search but she will not have abandoned it.

2) *Mens Rea*

An appropriation of property belonging to another amounts to theft if it is done (1) dishonestly, and (2) with the intention of permanently depriving the other of it.

1 Dishonesty[14]

Everyone has some idea of what is honest and what is dishonest conduct. Perhaps no two people would have absolutely identical views, but most people would find that their views substantially coincide. And it may be safely guessed, the views of most other people would substantially coincide with those of the law. After all, the law seeks here only to represent the standards of right thinking members of society generally. Consequently the bulk of cases give rise to no problems whatever. But there is in some cases – as always – room for some difference of view, as where D appropriates money to which he believes himself morally entitled, or where he appropriates money which he intends to repay, or goods which he intends to replace.

"Dishonestly" in the Theft Act 1968 replaces the requirement in the former law that D should act "fraudulently and without a claim of right made in good faith". The Criminal Law Revision Committee felt that "dishonestly" was a better word than "fraudulently", being easier for the layman to understand.[15] In this instance some reference to the cases on fraudulent conduct is inevitable in order to elucidate what is dishonest conduct. Such cases are no longer authoritative of course, but in so far as they are indicative of attitudes to the conduct in question it would be hard to gainsay their relevance. It is unlikely that attitudes will change very much on this issue whether the relevant adverb is "fraudulently" or "dishonestly".

The Committee thought that "dishonestly" would probably stand without definition,[16] but decided on a partial definition. Section 2 accordingly provides:

"(1) A person's appropriation of property belonging to another is not to be regarded as dishonest—

    (a) if he appropriates the property in the belief that he has in law the right to deprive the other of it, on behalf of himself or of a third person; or

---

14. See Harvey, "What Does Dishonesty Mean" [1972] Crim LR 312; Elliott, "Dishonesty Under the Theft Act" [1972] Crim LR 625; Elliott "Dishonesty in Theft: A Dispensable Concept" [1982] Crim LR 395; Campbell, "The Test of Dishonesty in *Ghosh*" (1984) 43 LJ 349; Griew, "Dishonesty – the Objections to *Feely* and *Ghosh*" [1985] Crim LR 341; Elliott, "Directors, Theft and Dishonesty" [1991] Crim LR 232.
15. Cmnd. 2977, para. 39.
16. Loc. cit.

(b) if he appropriates the property in the belief that he would have the other's consent if the other knew of the appropriation and the circumstances of it, or

(c) (except where the property came to him as trustee or personal representative) if he appropriates the property in the belief that the person to whom the property belongs cannot be discovered by taking reasonable steps.

(2) A person's appropriation of property belonging to another may be dishonest notwithstanding that he is willing to pay for the property."

a) *Belief in legal right.* D does not commit theft where he appropriates property in the belief that he is in law entitled to deprive P of the property. Thus if D mistakenly believes that he owns P's umbrella, his appropriation of it would not be dishonest whether his mistake, or ignorance, is of fact or law. Moreover, s. 2 (1) (a) makes it clear that D will not commit theft where he appropriates P's umbrella in the belief that it belongs to E on whose behalf D is acting.[17] It may be that E dishonestly told D that the umbrella was his; nevertheless if D acts in good faith he will not be guilty of theft though E will be.

Of course it is all very easy and all very reasonable to make mistakes about umbrellas. One umbrella often looks uncommonly like another. But what if D's mistake is unreasonable? D may make an unreasonable mistake of fact or law, or he may unreasonably believe that he has a legal right which the law does not recognise at all. Suppose, for example, that D, honestly believing that upon marriage a wife's property belongs in law to her husband, sells his wife's clothes. His belief is (probably) unreasonable and the law recognises no such claim. It seems clear, however, that he would not be guilty of theft. The Act says that D's appropriation is not to be regarded as dishonest "if he appropriates the property in the belief that *he* has in law the right to deprive the other of it". It would be difficult to read into this any objective requirement of reasonableness. Support for this view is afforded by *Small*[18] where it was held a misdirection to tell the jury that D would not be acting dishonestly if he reasonably believed the goods had been abandoned. Strictly a person who believes property to be abandoned cannot intend to appropriate the property *of another* and the issue of dishonesty does not arise, but the case contains a clear ruling that while the reasonableness of a belief is a factor to be considered in determining whether it is honestly held, the issue is whether the belief was so held and not whether it is reasonable.

b) *Belief in the other's consent.* Obviously D is not acting dishonestly where, as he knows, P is willing that D should appropriate his property and deprive him permanently of it. It may happen, however, that P is not in fact given the opportunity to express assent or dissent, but D believes that he would have done so had he been asked. Section 2 (1) (b) makes it clear that D is not a thief if he believes that P would have assented. Again, the single

17. Cf. *Knight and Roffey* (1781) 2 East PC 510.
18. [1987] Crim LR 778, CA, Cf. *Kell* [1985] Crim LR 239, CA.

criterion appears to be the honesty of D's belief and it does not matter that it is in the circumstances unreasonable.[19]

But D must believe not only that P would have consented to the appropriation but that P would have consented to the appropriation in the particular circumstances. D may believe that his next-door neighbour would consent to his appropriating a pint of milk from his doorstep when D himself had forgotten to leave an order for the milkman; but may believe that his neighbour would not consent to D's appropriating the milk in order to sell it at a profit to a thirsty hitch-hiker who is passing by.

c) *Belief that property has been lost.* Property which has been lost, as opposed to abandoned, continues to belong to the loser and accordingly anyone appropriating lost property would normally be appropriating property belonging to another. But where the owner of lost property cannot be found by taking reasonable steps no one regards the appropriation of that lost property as dishonest; better that D should have the use of it rather than it be put to no use at all. Section 2 (1) (c) provides accordingly.

Here again it seems clear enough that if D honestly believes that the person to whom the property belongs cannot be traced by taking reasonable steps, he is not a thief, although any reasonable person would have appreciated that the owner could be traced by taking the most simple measures.[20] D may be stupid in not appreciating that the owner of the wig he finds on the floor of the law court cannot be traced by taking reasonable steps, but stupidity is no substitute for dishonesty. What are reasonable steps would depend on the circumstances, including of course the value of the thing found and the place where it is found. It may be that when D finds, say, a number of banknotes he believes that the owner cannot be traced, but some days later learns of facts which lead him to believe that the owner can be traced. If D now appropriates the money he is acting dishonestly and may be convicted of theft. If, however, D is fortunate enough to have spent the money before he learns that the owner might be traced he cannot be convicted of theft. His appropriation when it took place was not dishonest and now, when he might have acted dishonestly, there is nothing left to appropriate.

d) *Other cases.* Section 2 (1) contains only a partial definition and conduct is not to be regarded as dishonest simply because it cannot be brought within the subsection. Nor does it follow from this subsection that D's conduct is necessarily dishonest because D knows that he had no legal right to the property or that P does not consent or that the owner can be traced.

Two further subsections touch on the question of dishonesty. One is s. 1 (2) which provides:

"It is immaterial whether the appropriation is made with a view to gain or is made for the thief's own benefit."

19. *Small*, last note.
20. Ibid.

Normally, of course, people steal to gain something for themselves,[1] but this subsection makes it clear that an appropriation may amount to theft although this motive is lacking.

"The subsection will prevent argument that it is not theft to take something which is useless to the taker or to take something with the intention of immediately destroying it."[2]

Thus it may be theft for D to destroy or hide away ledgers belonging to P because the ledgers provide evidence that D's friend has been misappropriating P's money.[3]

The other provision is s. 2 (2) which states:

"A person's appropriation of property belonging to another may be dishonest notwithstanding that he is willing to pay for the property."

This subsection meets a possible argument that an appropriation cannot amount to theft by virtue only of the fact that D is willing to pay for the property. Obviously all the circumstances must be considered along with D's willingness to pay. In an old case[4] a traveller met a fisherman and, upon the latter's refusal to sell him any fish, took some from him by force and threw down money much above its value. It was doubted whether the traveller was acting dishonestly but it is thought that in circumstances such as these the traveller could now be convicted of theft or of robbery. Certainly it would be an undesirable principle that D should be able to take what he wants from another without fear of any criminal sanction provided only that he is willing to pay. Nevertheless, as will appear, it is possible to imagine circumstances in which it is arguable that D's intention to pay, or to repay, shows that he is not acting dishonestly.

e) *Cases for which no provision is made in the partial definition of dishonesty.* The Theft Act does not, then, provide an exhaustive definition of dishonesty.[5] As a practical matter the definition covers most situations of any common occurrence, but there are other situations where the question of dishonesty may be said to be at large. It is prudent to heed Hale's warning that in cases of stealing,

"the variety of circumstances is so great, and the complications thereof so mingled, that it is impossible to prescribe all the circumstances evidencing a felonious intent, but the same must be left to the due and attentive consideration of the judge and jury."[6]

Hale, however, offered no precise guidance on the respective functions of judge and jury, nor does the Theft Act offer any guidance on the matter. Essentially there would appear to be three possible approaches. The first would require the judge as a matter of law to define dishonesty. He must of course leave the determination of the facts to the jury but he would instruct

---

1. As to gain see s. 34 (2) of the Act, below, p. 611. Note that where s. 4 (3) applies (above, p. 516) D commits theft only where, in effect, he has a view of gain.
2. Cmnd. 2977, Annex. 2.
3. Cf. *Cabbage* (1815) Russ & Ry 292.
4. *The Fisherman's Case* (1584) 2 East PC 661.
5. For an argument that "dishonestly" might have been exhaustively defined, see MacKenna, "The Undefined Adverb in Criminal Statutes" [1966] Crim LR 548, 553.
6. 1 PC 509.

the jury that if they find the facts to be this then D is dishonest but if they find the facts to be that then D is not dishonest. This would enable divisional courts, the Court of Appeal and even the House of Lords to state what is and what is not dishonest so that a single standard could be articulated.

A second approach is to put the matter entirely in the hands of the jury. In its extreme form this approach would simply ask the jury to consider whether D believed, and however outrageous his conduct appeared to the rest of us, he was acting dishonestly and accordingly D's views of what is honest or dishonest become paramount. The courts did toy for a while with this approach[7] but it has obvious dangers. Are we really to say, for example, that someone who genuinely believes that it is all right to rob the rich in order to feed the poor is not a thief? Are we to say that someone who knows that his standards are at odds with the rest of society cannot be convicted of theft because he believes that he is right and the rest of us are wrong?

The third approach, the via media, which Hale would have apparently approved, is to share the task between judge and jury. The judge lays down the guidelines, the jury applies them to the facts of the particular case. This is now the received wisdom endorsed by the Court of Appeal in *Ghosh*.[8] The court, accepting that the law was in "a complicated state", sought to put the law on a clear footing. It was held that the jury should be directed that D acts dishonestly if (i) his conduct would be regarded as dishonest by the ordinary standards of reasonable and honest people; and (ii) D realises that his conduct is so regarded. If (i) and (ii) are met, it matters not that (iii) D himself does not regard his conduct as dishonest.[9]

To the extent that *Ghosh* is a rejection of the second approach[10] it is, perhaps, to be welcomed but it still leaves problems in its wake.

As to (i) the issue is pre-eminently one for the jury—

"Jurors, when deciding whether an appropriation was dishonest can be reasonably expected to, and should, apply the current standards of ordinary decent people. In their own lives they have to decide what is and what is not dishonest. We can see no reason why, when in a jury box, they should require the help of a judge to tell them what amounts to dishonesty . . . It is clear in our judgment that the jury should have been

---

7. *Boggeln v Williams* [1978] 2 All ER 1061, [1978] 1 WLR 873, DC. See also *Feely* [1973] QB 530, [1973] 1 All ER 341, CA; *Landy* [1981] 1 All ER 1172, [1981] 1 WLR 355, CA; *McIvor* [1982] 1 All ER 491, [1982] 1 WLR 409, CA.

8. [1982] QB 1053, [1982] 2 All ER 689; **SHC 435**.

9. Arguably *Ghosh* swallows up the partial definition of dishonesty in s. 2(1) in that if D acts under a claim of right or believes that P would have consented to the appropriation, no reasonable and honest person would regard his conduct as dishonest but, where the facts warrant it, the attention of the trier of fact (the jury or the magistrates) should be called to the terms of s. 2(1): *Wootton* [1990] Crim LR 201, CA. A *Ghosh* direction is not always necessary: *Price* (1989) 90 Cr App Rep 409, [1990] Crim LR 200, CA; *Green* [1992] Crim LR 292, CA; but where it is it should be given to the letter: *Ravenshad* [1990] Crim LR 398, CA.

10. The second approach was taken by the New Zealand Court of Appeal in *Williams* [1985] 1 NZLR 294 where *Ghosh* was not followed. The court held that a jury should be directed that D does not act dishonestly, even where it is proved that he knows that he is acting contrary to his legal obligations, if it is reasonably possible that D was (subjectively) acting honestly, however mistakenly. But in *Salvo* [1980] VR 401 the Supreme Court of Victoria adopted the first approach. It was held that it is for the trial judge to tell the jury, having regard to the alleged facts, what are the constituents of dishonesty.

left to decide whether the defendant's alleged taking of money had been dishonest. They were not, with the result that a verdict of guilty was returned without having given thought to what was probably the most important issue in the case."[11]

No doubt any jury would take the view that it is dishonest to claim payment for work that has not been done,[12] or that it is dishonest to travel on buses intending to avoid payment. In *Ghosh* the court was of the view that a jury would equally have no difficulty in deciding that it is dishonest to rob the rich to feed the poor, or that it is dishonest for anti-vivisectionists to remove animals from laboratories.

But a jury can only surmise as to what conduct is regarded by ordinary people as dishonest. No evidence can be led on this issue so the jurors have only their own knowledge and experience to guide them. This is not to suggest that juries would be capricious but juries might legitimately differ on how they believe that ordinary people would regard the conduct in question.[13]

Consider the "borrowing" cases.[14] It sometimes happens that people take money from others without their consent but with a view to repaying it.[15] D may take some small change from the firm's petty cash to pay a taxi-driver who cannot change D's £10 note;[16] E may take a few pounds from the firm's till to lay a wager on a horse;[17] F may take several hundred pounds from the firm's safe to pay for a family holiday.[18] Whether these takings would be considered dishonest by ordinary people would no doubt involve a consideration of such factors as the amount involved, whether the firm had expressly prohibited "borrowing", whether the taking was open or clandestine and so on. On the propriety and honesty of such "borrowing" views may differ widely.[19] Consider the following case supposed by Lawton LJ delivering the judgment of the Court of Appeal in *Feely*:[20]

---

11. *Feely* [1973] 1 All ER 341 at 345.
12. *Ghosh* [1982] QB 1053, [1982] 2 All ER 689.
13. Consistency of result could be achieved if (i) was regarded as a question of law for the judge, but, following the fashion set by the House of Lords in *Brutus v Cozens* [1973] AC 854, [1972] 2 All ER 1297, (see above, p. 496), the issue is treated as one of fact for the jury. See Griew, *Dishonesty and the Jury* (Leicester UP, 1974). Consider the so-called cash-in-hand transaction under which D provides services (plumbing, decorating etc) for E on the basis that there will be no record of the transaction. The advantage to E is that he does not pay VAT, and to D that he does not account for the transaction to the Revenue. The practice is widespread. While it is not suggested that D and E are guilty of theft, are they acting "dishonestly"? Would the transaction be regarded as dishonest by the standards of ordinary reasonable and honest people? It is confidently submitted that views would differ on this.
14. For a general discussion of the "borrowing" cases see Lowe, "The Fraudulent Intent in Larceny" [1956] Crim LR 78; Smith, "Fraudulent Intent in Larceny" [1956] Crim LR 238; Elliott, "Dishonesty Under the Theft Act" [1972] Crim LR 625.
15. In such cases D does not borrow the money; he deprives P permanently of the money he takes intending to repay an equivalent amount; *Velumyl* [1989] Crim LR 299, CA.
16. An example instanced in *Feely* [1973] QB 530, [1973] 1 All ER 341.
17. *Sinclair v Neighbour* [1967] 2 QB 279, [1966] 3 All ER 988, CA.
18. *McIvor* [1982] 1 All ER 491, [1982] 1 WLR 409, CA.
19. In *Sinclair v Neighbour* [1966] 2 QB 279, [1966] 3 All ER 988, where D took the money to lay a wager on a horse, the trial judge thought that the action was reprehensible but not dishonest. In the CA Sachs LJ was firmly of the view that D's conduct was dishonest but Sellers LJ thought that views might differ.
20. [1973] 1 All ER 341 at 346.

"It is possible to imagine a case of taking by an employee in breach of instructions to which no one would, or could reasonably, attach moral obloquy; for example that of a manager of a shop, who having been told that under no circumstances was he to take money from the till for his own purposes, took 40p from it, having no small change himself, to pay for a taxi hired by his wife who had arrived at the shop saying that she only had a £5 note which the cabby could not change. To hold that such a man was a thief and to say that his intention to put the money back in the till when he acquired some change was at the most a matter of mitigation would tend to bring the law into contempt. In our judgment a taking to which no moral obloquy can reasonably attach is not within the concept of stealing either at common law or under the Theft Act 1968."

At first sight this seems to be an example of robust common sense. No one would regard this conduct by the employee, though apparently in breach of the employer's instruction to take not a penny from the till, as dishonest. But just suppose that the employer is present in the shop that day and, told by the employee that he is strapped for change to pay the taxi driver, he yet resolutely refuses to allow the employee to take the 40p. The employee thereupon knocks the employer senseless and takes the 40p. Are we to say, assuming the employee intends to repay the 40p, that the employer has not been robbed (i.e. that his 40p has not been stolen by force)? This would be an astonishing conclusion. Strapped for change to pay a taxi driver, is D entitled to forcibly deprive any passer-by he meets of the 40p he requires without fear of conviction for theft or robbery because he intends to repay? The answer must be a resounding No. This is not to say that Lawton LJ's employee is to be convicted of theft. However vehement an employer's instructions not to take money from the till, an employee may yet face circumstances where he can honestly say that if his employer had in mind the circumstances that have occurred (e.g. the temporary inability to find change for the taxi driver) the employer would have consented and the employee's salvation is thus provided by s. 2 (1) (b). If, however, the employee knows that the employer would under no circumstances whatever allow an employee to use the employer's money for the employee's own convenience,[1] it is difficult to see how the appropriation can be other than dishonest.

On the *Ghosh* view, however, a jury may, using no more than its own intuition in the matter, take the view, or may not take the view, that such an appropriation is dishonest. It is by no means impossible that differently composed juries may take different views. Having regard to the serious consequences of a conviction for theft it cannot be right that on the same facts a jury in Leeds may acquit while a jury in Nottingham may convict.

As to (ii) the jury must be satisfied that D realises his conduct is so regarded. In *Ghosh*[2] the court supposed the case of a man who comes from a country where all public transport is free and he assumes it is the same here so he boards a bus with no intention of paying. He is not to be regarded as

---

1. Bank managers, as the simplest inquiry shows, view with horror the notion that employees of the bank may in *any* circumstances use the bank's money for their own purposes.
2. [1982] 2 All ER 689 at 696.

acting dishonestly because he is unaware of the circumstances which render this conduct dishonest and is therefore unaware that his conduct would be regarded as dishonest.

This is entirely understandable; no one would wish to condemn the unwitting foreigner's conduct as dishonest. But does this open the door to the modern Robin Hood who thinks that ordinary people do not consider robbing the rich to feed the poor to be dishonest; or the anti-vivisectionist who is convinced that ordinary people up and down the country do not regard freeing animals from laboratories to be dishonest? The answer must be that it does. Commenting on *Boggeln v Williams*,[3] where D had reconnected his electricity supply after the Electricity Board had disconnected it for failure to pay bills, the court in *Ghosh* said[4] that such a case—

"will depend on the view taken by the jury whether the defendant may have believed what he was doing was in accordance with the ordinary man's idea of honesty. A jury might have come to the conclusion that the defendant in that case was disobedient or impudent, but not dishonest in what he did."

No doubt the circumstances in which D can claim to act honestly where his conduct is considered generally to be dishonest will be rare. But not, perhaps, unheard of. Not everyone has the sort of upbringing that acquaints him with community standards of what is honest and what is dishonest. Some may be totally unaware of what the community standards are and others may have the most outlandish ideas of what they are. *Ghosh* does not tell us how to deal with the former and assumes that we must accept the latter. No doubt jurymen try to take a commonsense view, but one man's common sense may not be the same as another's.

The correct approach, it is respectfully submitted, is the first approach though it has to be said that, following *Feely* and *Ghosh*, this view has been rejected by English courts.[5] It should be for the judges to define dishonesty against the background of the partial definition in s. 2. They may get it wrong but they are subject to correction by appellate courts. Arguably the appellate courts may get it wrong but they are subject to scrutiny and they can change their minds. At all events the meaning of dishonesty is then open for public scrutiny. Before *Brutus v Cozens*[6] no one would have doubted, and without in any way interfering with the jury's prerogative to find the facts, that it was the judge's function to explain the law including, most obviously it might be thought, the meaning of words in statutes. There is now a judicial movement to pass the buck to the jury where the word (and "dishonesty" is an archetypal word in this context) is an "ordinary" English word. It is this development which has confused the meaning of dishonesty and, it may be added, much else besides. The direction in *Ghosh* goes some of the way to recognising the problem but falls short of resolving it.

---

3. [1978] 2 All ER 1061, [1978] 1 WLR 873.
4. [1982] 2 All ER 689 at 969.
5. See also *Melwani* [1989] Crim LR 565, CA.
6. [1973] AC 854, [1972] 2 All ER 1297, CA. See Elliott, "*Brutus v Cozens*, Decline and Fall" [1989] Crim LR 323.

f) *Dishonesty: vis-à-vis whom?* Elliott[7] writes—

"There must be a focus for dishonesty, and in theft the focus must be the owner of the property."

With respect this seems entirely right. Take the simplest of examples. If D, knowing that his insolvency is imminent, decides to spend what money he has left on a holiday in Spain rather than meet his obligations to his landlord or his milkman, his disposition of *his own* money cannot be regarded as dishonest because D is aware that his creditors will not be paid. Where, as in cases such as *A–G's Reference (No. 2 of 1982)*, *McHugh and Tringham* and *Philippou*,[8] the owners of a company dissipate its funds on themselves, it may fairly be said that this is dishonest vis-à-vis the creditors; the creditors have been cheated or ripped off. But the wording of the offence, "dishonestly appropriates property belonging to another", seems clearly to require dishonesty in relation to that other, the owner, and dishonesty vis-à-vis a third party cannot suffice.

2 Intention Permanently to Deprive

Theft requires an intention permanently to deprive the other of his property, and while the Theft Act contains provisions making it an offence in certain cases to use the property of another,[9] it should be noted that even in these instances the offence created is not theft. Stealing at common law always required an intention permanently to deprive and that requirement is now expressed in the basic definition of theft in s. 1 (1) of the Act.[10]

There need not, of course, be any permanent deprivation in fact; D may be guilty of theft even though P is never in any danger of losing his property so long as D appropriates with the intent.[11] Conversely, the fact of permanent deprivation is insufficient if there was no intent. But it must be clear that the facts – the history of what D did with the goods – will often have an important bearing on the proof of D's intent. If, for instance, D was found respraying the car which he took from P without his permission, the jury is likely to favour the inference that D's intent was to deprive P permanently of it. If, on the other hand, D had taken P's lawn-mower without permission, and left it in full view of P's house after he had used it to mow his own lawn, the jury is likely to favour the inference that it was not D's intent to deprive P permanently of it. In every case it is for the jury to determine, on the evidence, whether D did so intend, so that where the evidence as to D's intent is circumstantial the judge will instruct the jury that they *may* infer the intent from evidence pointing to that conclusion, but it would be an error of law for the judge to direct that because the evidence points to that conclusion they *must* infer the intent, and the conviction may be quashed on appeal. The meaning of the intent to deprive permanently and its relation to the accompanying problem of proof may be

---

7. "Directors Theft and Dishonesty" [1991] Crim LR 732.
8. Discussed above, p. 533.
9. See below, p. 593.
10. For an argument that temporary deprivation should be theft see Williams, [1981] Crim LR 129.
11. Cf. *Egginton* (1801) 2 Leach 913.

illustrated by reference to the situation in which D takes P's goods and then abandons them. Suppose, for instance, that D takes P's car and subsequently abandons it. If D's intention was to use the car for some temporary purpose then he does not steal it. Nor need D take any steps to return the car, so it follows that as a matter of fact it is often difficult to make out a case of car stealing because it will be difficult for P to show (even if D has been apprehended in possession) that it was D's intent to steal the car rather than use it temporarily.[12] It is less difficult where what D has taken is P's umbrella. If D takes P's car in Nottingham and abandons it in London it would be virtually impossible to get a conviction of theft; if D does the same with P's umbrella a conviction of theft is a virtual certainty. It is not a case of treating cars and umbrellas differently for the jury will be asked to apply the same test to both. Everyone knows that if an umbrella is borrowed in Nottingham and abandoned in London it will be lost forever to its owner, and ordinarily D will know and intend this.

In the general run of cases there are no problems, other than evidential ones, in establishing that D intended permanent deprivation, that he intended to make the property his own. But substantial difficulties can arise. It is obvious, for example, that if D dishonestly appropriates a bottle of whisky which he drinks he has deprived P of it; less obvious, perhaps, where D takes a rail ticket which he intends to return to British Rail at the end of his journey, or where he pawns goods belonging to P intending to redeem and restore them to P at some future stage. It is to meet problems of this kind that s. 6 was introduced.[13] Section 6 does not contain an exhaustive definition of the intent permanently to deprive, it merely clarifies its meaning in certain respects. In most cases it will be unnecessary to go beyond s. 1 (1) and unwise to do so.[14] Section 6 is there to deal with a number of difficult cases of uncommon occurrence. The section provides:

"(1) A person appropriating property belonging to another without meaning the other permanently to lose the thing itself is nevertheless to be regarded as having the intention of permanently depriving the other of it if his intention is to treat the thing as his own to dispose of regardless of the other's rights, and a borrowing or lending of it may amount to so treating it if, but only if, the borrowing or lending is for a period and in circumstances making it equivalent to an outright taking or disposal.

(2) Without prejudice to the generality of subsection (1) above, where a person, having possession or control (lawfully or not) of property belonging to another, parts with the property under a condition as to its return which he may not be able to perform, this (if done for purposes of his own and without the other's authority) amounts to treating the property as his own to dispose of regardless of the other's rights."

a) *Disposal regardless of the other's rights*. In the foregoing illustration concerning the umbrella it is assumed that D knows the umbrella will be lost forever to P and that he intends this. D thus means P permanently to

---

12. Hence it was made a statutory offence merely to take P's car without P's consent.
13. See Spencer, "The Metamorphosis of Section 6 of the Theft Act" [1977] Crim LR 653.
14. *Warner* (1970) 55 Cr App Rep 93, CA; *Cocks* (1976) 63 Cr App Rep 79, CA.

lose the thing and there is no problem whatever concerning intent. But it might be that when D disposes of P's property he is merely indifferent as to whether it will be recovered by P; D might even hope that the property will somehow be restored to P, but realises that in the circumstances this is unlikely. Where D is thus indifferent it may be difficult to say that he is "meaning the other permanently to lose the thing itself". However s. 6 (1) provides that D is nevertheless to be regarded as having the intention of permanently depriving P of it if "his intention is to treat the thing as his own to dispose of regardless of the other's rights".

Note that it is not enough that D is treating the property as his own. In borrowing P's property without P's consent and using it there is an appropriation of the property and D is treating it as his own; but he does not steal the property unless he intends, in addition, to treat it as his own to dispose of regardless of P's rights. Any such disposal will suffice.

Suppose, for example, that D appropriates property belonging to P intending all along to sell it back to P.[15] He will certainly be guilty of obtaining by deception if he carries through his fraud, but it is necessary to decide whether he is a thief when he appropriates the property. It seems clear enough that he is, for he intends to treat the property as his own to dispose of regardless of P's rights. It can hardly be argued that he is not treating the property as his own to dispose of since D proposes to represent to the true owner himself that he is the owner or is authorised by the owner to sell. Nor can it be seriously argued that he is not acting regardless of the owner's rights. D is of course aware of the owner's rights and it is his very awareness which shows that he is acting regardless of them. In such a case this is a clear usurpation of dominion by D since he affects to be the owner.

Contrast *Holloway*.[16] D, who was employed by P to dress skins and was paid by the piece, took some already dressed skins from P's warehouse and then claimed payment for dressing them. Here D, though guilty of obtaining or attempting to obtain by deception, does not steal the skins. He does not mean P to be permanently deprived of them nor does he treat them *as his own* to dispose of regardless of P's rights; all along D acknowledges that the skins belong to P.[17] The fact that D obtains a payment from P for the restoration of his property (for example, the deposit paid in respect of empty bottles belonging to P) does not make D guilty of theft if the payment is one which P is in any event obliged to pay for the restoration of his property;[18] that D has come by the bottles dishonestly does not make him a thief from P.

Section 6 (1) states that a person treating property as his own to dispose of "*is* to be regarded" as having an intent permanently to deprive even though he does not in fact intend that the owner should be deprived in fact. The case instanced above where D appropriates P's property with a view to selling it back to him provides a convenient illustration. Here D "is to be

---

15. Cf. *Hall* (1849) 1 Den 381.
16. (1849) 1 Den 370.
17. It may be there is a more fundamental reason why Holloway would not now be guilty of stealing the skins; there may be no appropriation of the skins. Cf. Smith, *Theft*, para. 53.
18. *Johnstone, Comerford and Jalil* [1982] Crim LR 454 (Mr Recorder Chadwick). Cp. *Pick* [1982] Crim LR 238 (Judge Jolly).

regarded" as intending permanently to deprive though it is part of his fraud that P's property should be restored to him, albeit only after P has paid for it. In such a case, however, P is in at least some danger of being permanently deprived of his property for if, for whatever reason, he refuses to buy back his goods, it can hardly be supposed that D would thereupon make a present of them to P and he would no doubt seek to dispose of the property elsewhere. There is really no difficulty in saying that D intends permanent deprivation where he appropriates P's property with a view to its sale at a profit to D, and permanent deprivation is no less intended because D has P in mind as one of the possible buyers. Even before the Theft Act 1968 came into force it was held that in such a case D intended permanently to deprive.[19]

But what if P is at no risk of being deprived of his property? The example has been given above[20] of the rogue who sells the crown jewels to a gullible tourist. It was argued that the rogue appropriates the jewels because to purport to sell another's property (whether or not the seller is in possession) is an assumption of a right of an owner; the issue here is whether the rogue can be said to intend to deprive the owner permanently of the jewels. On a literal interpretation of s. 6 (1) the rogue may be said to be deemed to have such an intention because he "is" to be so regarded in disposing of them regardless of the owner's rights.

In such a case as this D would not have been guilty of larceny under the former law[1] and in *Lloyd* Lord Lane CJ said[2] that the court "would try to interpret s. 6 in such a way as to ensure that nothing is construed as an intention permanently to deprive which would not prior to the 1968 Act have been so construed". This advice was not apparently conveyed to the Privy Council which in *Chan Man-sin v A–G of Hong Kong*[3] gave the equivalent provision to s. 6 in the Hong Kong Theft Ordinance its literal interpretation. D by the use of forged cheques caused accounts to be debited and other accounts which he controlled to be credited to the tune of some $HK4.8m. Convicted of theft of the things in action, he argued on appeal that since the bank to which he had presented the forged cheques had no authority to honour them and were in law obliged to restore the debited accounts, there could be no debt owed to the debited account holders which D could steal. It was held that by presenting and negotiating the cheques D had appropriated the things by assuming to deal with them as owner. And even if D contemplated that the fraud would be discovered and the balances restored to their owners, he was, as the relevant provision specifies, "nevertheless to be regarded as having the intention of permanently depriving" the owners "if it is his intention to treat the thing as his own to dispose of regardless" of the rights of the owner.[4]

19. *Hall* (1849) 1 Den 381.
20. P. 504.
1. Bloxham (1943) 29 Cr App Rep 37, CCA. But for a different reason – there would be no taking and carrying away of the crown jewels.
2. [1985] 2 All ER 661 at 666.
3. [1988] 1 All ER 1, [1988] Crim LR 497, PC.
4. *Downes* (1983) 77 Cr App Rep 260, [1983] Crim LR 819, CA and *Bagshaw* [1988] Crim LR 321, CA also indicate that Lord Lane's "restrictive" view of s. 6 may be at variance with a literal interpretation of the section.

Chan Man-sin may nevertheless be distinguished from the case of the rogue who "sells" the crown jewels to the gullible tourist. Although D in *Chan Man-sin* may have realised that his fraud would come to light and the balances restored, there was a risk, which D no doubt hoped would materialise, that his fraud would remain undiscovered and in that event the owners would have been permanently deprived.[5] The fraudster selling the crown jewels, on the other hand, knows that the guillible tourist will never get his hands on the crown jewels; there is no risk of deprivation whatsoever. The difficulty is that when the relevant circumstances specified in s. 6 exist D "*is* to be regarded", not "*may* be regarded" as having that intent. It may be, however, that it is unrealistic to say that D has acted "regardless" of P's rights when what he has done poses no threat whatsoever to P's rights.

It would be different if in pursuance of the sale of P's property D delivers possession of the property to the buyer or puts the buyer in a position where he can take possession of it[6] and here D steals the goods (appropriates with intent permanently to deprive) when the sale takes place.

b) *Conditional intention.* A problem which has much exercised the courts in recent years has been that of so-called conditional intent.[7] The problem concerned whether D could be convicted of theft, or of an attempt, where he had no specific property in mind but had resolved to steal if there was anything to be taken or if the property on examination proved to be worth his while to take. The problem was further complicated by the House of Lords decision in *Haughton v Smith*[8] which held that the crime of attempt could not be committed where the *actus reus* was, other than as to means, physically impossible to achieve.

The difficulty created by *Haughton v Smith* has been removed by the Criminal Attempts Act 1981 and physical impossibility is no longer a bar to a conviction for an attempt.[9] The other difficulty has been shown to be not one of substance. D must of course be proved to have an intention to steal but D may have such an intention though his implementation of it is subject to certain conditions (for example, that he is not being observed, or that the goods he seeks are in the place he thinks them to be). So if D looks through P's handbag intending to steal money, he no less intends to steal money though he has no means of knowing that there is any money there and, in the result, the handbag contains no money. If D opens P's car, or a box belonging to P, intending to steal anything that may prove of value, he may be convicted of attempting to steal property belonging to P though, in the result, he finds nothing in the car or box that he considers worth stealing.[10]

---

5. Cf. Griew, *Thet*, 2–150.
6. Cf. *Pitham and Hehl* (1976) 65 Cr App Rep 45, [1977] Crim LR 285, CA, above, p. 504.
7. See *Easom* [1971] 2 QB 315, [1971] 2 All ER 945, CA; *Husseyn* (1977) 67 Cr App Rep 131, CA; *Walkington* [1979] 2 All ER 716, [1979] 1 WLR 1169, CA; *A-G's References (Nos. 1 and 2 of 1979)* [1980] QB 180, [1979] 3 All ER 143, CA. See above, p. 307.
8. [1975] AC 476; [1973] 3 All ER 1109.
9. See above, p. 317.
10. Above, p. 307. Cf. *Bayley and Easterbrook* [1980] Crim LR 503, CA.

D cannot of course be charged with attempting to steal, and still less of stealing, property which he is not minded to appropriate. If D's only interest in looking through P's handbag is money, he cannot be convicted of attempting to steal the remaining contents of the handbag. Thus care may be required in drafting the charge in such cases but if D is bent upon stealing the fact that he has not yet found what he is looking for, or that it is not there, cannot mean that he lacks an intention to steal.

c) *Borrowing or lending.* Where D merely borrows P's umbrella and uses it without P's consent there is an appropriation, but if D intends to return the umbrella to P at some future date – definite or indefinite – he would not be "meaning" P permanently to lose it. Nor, by merely intending to use the umbrella indefinitely, does he intend to treat it as his own *to dispose of* regardless of P's rights. However s. 6 (1) provides that a borrowing or lending may amount to so treating it "if, but only if, the borrowing or lending is for a period and in circumstances making it equivalent to an outright taking or disposal".

Suppose, then, that D intends to return the property in a year's time, five years' time or fifty years' time. Would the borrowing in any or all of these cases amount to an outright taking? On the whole it would seem that this provision was not inserted to leave it to the court to determine how long a period of borrowing is equivalent to an outright taking. If D intends to return the property at some future stage then, without more, it is difficult to see how this could be equivalent to an outright taking – it necessarily falls short of an outright taking.[11] Moreover this sort of problem is not merely academic, it is almost fanciful. People do not ordinarily borrow property for one, five or fifty years as the case may be; property is either borrowed (i.e. D intends to return it) or it is appropriated permanently.

So it is reasonable to suppose that the draftsman had some other sort of case in mind. This is borne out by the fact that the borrowing or lending must be "for a period *and* in circumstances" making it equivalent to an outright taking or disposal. Something *more* than a borrowing is contemplated. "Borrowing," said Lord Lane CJ in *Lloyd*:[12]

"is *ex hypothesi* not something which is done with an intention permanently to deprive. [The second half of s. 6 (1)], we believe, is intended to make it clear that a mere borrowing is never enough to constitute the necessary guilty mind unless the intention is to return the 'thing' in such a changed state that it can truly be said that all its goodness or virtue is gone."

The provision, then, is aimed at the sort of case where D borrows P's theatre season ticket and uses it to gain admission to the whole series of performances. It would thus apply to the case where D takes a railway ticket in order to get a free ride; he intends that the ticket should be restored to P at the end of his journey, but the ticket is now worthless and

11. So in *Warner* (1970) 55 Cr App Rep 93, [1971] Crim LR 114, CA, it was held that the trial judge was wrong in directing the jury that D could be convicted of theft if he intended to retain the property indefinitely.
12. [1985] 2 All ER 661 at 667, CA; **SHC 442**. Cf. *Coffey* [1987] Crim LR 498, CA.

his borrowing of it has been for a period and in circumstances making it equivalent to an outright taking. The same argument may be applied to a cheque which D obtains from P. In the ordinary course of events the cheque will be cashed and returned to the drawer, P, so there is no permanent deprivation of the cheque as a piece of paper. But, as *Duru*[13] makes clear, this ignores that the cheque has left P's hands as something of value and is returned to him as a mere scrap of paper. In such a case D has patently treated the cheque as his own to dispose of regardless of P's rights.

But there are difficulties. Suppose, for example, that D borrows a season ticket and uses it for nineteen out of the twenty performances for which it is valid and then returns it to P for the last performance. Is this use by D equivalent to an outright taking? If it is so treated then the courts would again be faced with considerable difficulties in drawing the line. More important, if it is admitted that something short of an intention to use the ticket to view all twenty performances will suffice (say ten or fifteen) then dishonest use will in some circumstances amount to theft. A principle that was firmly kept out at the front door will have been allowed in at the back.

d) *The thing*. Rather curiously s. 6 (1) speaks of "the thing" where it might have been expected to use "the property". The explanation may be that the draftsman sought to make it clear that the kind of case provided for was one where P is to get the thing itself, in a literal sense, restored to him but it is D's intention that the thing shall be worthless in the real sense. The thing (the cancelled cheque, or used rail or season ticket) is restored to P but the article as property of value is not restored to him.

e) *Parting with property under a condition as to its return*. Section 6 (2) is meant to provide for the case where D (who will most often be a bailee of the property though the position is the same here even if D has taken the property in the first place without P's consent) pledges P's property without P's authority. If D intends to redeem the property and return it to P in due course he would not ordinarily be said to mean to deprive P permanently of the property. The difficulty with such cases arises because it may be uncertain whether D will be able to redeem the goods – the very fact that he has pawned them tends to show that he is lacking in funds. Accordingly s. 6 (2) provides that D is to be treated as having an intention permanently to deprive P if he parts with the property under a condition "which he *may* not be able to perform".

The subsection clearly implies that if D parts with the property, by pledging or otherwise, under a condition as to its return which he knows he can perform then D would not be guilty of theft. Yet in such a case D, by pledging P's property without authority, is treating the property as his own to dispose of regardless of P's rights within s. 6 (1) and s. 6 (2) is expressed to be without prejudice to the generality of s. 6 (1). Presumably, though, s. 6 (1) is to be read subject to s. 6 (2) to this extent otherwise s. 6 (2) would be devoid of any worthwhile meaning.

13. [1973] 3 All ER 715, CA; cf. *Downes* (1983) 77 Cr App Rep 260, CA. *Duru* was a prosecution under s. 15 but the same principles are applicable.

f) *Deprivation of the owner's interest.* Normally a thief intends to deprive permanently in the fullest sense, that is, he intends to make the property his own. In such a case it does not matter that the person from whom the property is stolen is the owner or a person, such as a bailee, who has a limited interest. But it might happen that D, while not intending to deprive the owner permanently of the property, nevertheless intends to deprive, say, a bailee of his interest. For example, knowing that P has hired a car for the duration of his holiday, D appropriates the car for the period of that holiday intending to return it to the owner. Since theft is the dishonest appropriation of property belonging to another with the intention of depriving that other permanently of it, and since the property belongs to the bailee, it seems that D will be guilty of theft if, knowing of P's limited interest as bailee, he dishonestly deprives him permanently of it.[14]

2 Abstracting Electricity

It has been shown[15] why the Criminal Law Revision Committee thought it necessary to make special provision for electricity and the view that electricity is not property capable of being appropriated has been confirmed by the courts.[16] Section 13 accordingly provides:

"A person who dishonestly uses without due authority, or dishonestly causes to be wasted or diverted, any electricity shall on conviction on indictment be liable to imprisonment for a term not exceeding five years."

No doubt this provision will ordinarily be applied to the case where D dishonestly[17] uses some device to by-pass his electricity meter, but it is in fact capable of some curious applications.[18] Strictly there might be an offence under this section where D borrows an electrically driven, hand-operated, milk float, though there would be no theft of the float nor an offence of taking a conveyance under s. 12.[19] But proceedings under s. 13 in such a case are perhaps very unlikely; there might be some reluctance to prosecute when the substance of what D does is not criminal even though there is technically some incidental offence.[20] Moreover, in this sort of situation, it may be that D does not at all advert to the fact that he is causing the electricity to be used.

14. Late in the afternoon of a Christmas Eve a well-known shop ran out of turkeys. While the backs of the earlycomers who had secured a turkey were turned, latecomers removed turkeys from their baskets into their own which the latecomers subsequently paid for at the check-out. Did the latecomers steal the turkeys? Were they acting dishonestly?
15. Above, p. 514.
16. *Low v Blease* [1975] Crim LR 513, DC.
17. See *Boggeln v Williams* [1978] Crim LR 242, 122 Sol Jo 94, DC, above, p. 540.
18. Cf. Smith, *Law of Theft*, paras. 306.
19. See below, p. 597.
20. Prosecutions have been brought for stealing the petrol consumed where D has borrowed a motor vehicle, but this was never regarded as satisfactory and the offence of taking motor vehicles was introduced. Cf. *Low v Blease*, above, p. 514, where it was apparently assumed that a dishonest user of a telephone may commit the offence under s. 13.

It was perhaps for these reasons that the law was amended by the Theft Act[1] to create a specific offence of dishonestly using a public telephone or telex system with intent to avoid payment.[2] This gets at the substance of the mischief and avoids any difficulty.

It is enough under s. 13 that D dishonestly causes electricity to be wasted or diverted; he need not be shown to have made any use of the electricity for himself. An employee who out of spite for his employer puts on all the lighting and heating appliances in the office would commit the offence, but a fellow employee, or even a stranger, who, knowing what D has done, chooses to stay in the office to enjoy the warmth, would not.

3 Robbery[3]

By s. 8 of the Theft Act 1968:

"(1) A person is guilty of robbery if he steals, and immediately before or at the time of doing so, and in order to do so, he uses force on any person or puts or seeks to put any person in fear of being then and there subjected to force.

(2) A person guilty of robbery, or of an assault with intent to rob, shall on conviction on indictment be liable to imprisonment for life."

As defined robbery is essentially an aggravated form of theft; and if there is no theft, or attempted theft, there can be no robbery or attempted robbery. So it would not be robbery where D by force takes a car from P in the belief that he has the legal right to it;[4] or where D by force takes a car from P not intending to deprive P permanently of it. In the first case D may be guilty of an assault, and in the latter of both an assault and an offence under s. 12 of the Theft Act, but in neither case is he guilty of robbery.

The offence of robbery is complete when the theft is complete, that is when the appropriation is complete. So in *Corcoran v Anderton*[5] where D and E sought to take P's handbag by force, it was held that the theft was complete when D snatched the handbag from P's grasp though it then fell from D's hands and the defendants made off without it. It is arguable that the theft in such a case is complete when D struggles with P for possession of the handbag for by that conduct he is assuming the rights of an owner. In the case of robbery the appropriation must normally be by taking since it is difficult to imagine realistic situations in which robbery might be effected by other modes of appropriation.[6]

1. Now Telecommunications Act 1984, s. 42. But this does not cover 999 calls since no payment is involved; it is, however, an offence under s. 5 (2) of the Criminal Law Act 1967 to cause any wasteful employment of the police.

2. Punishable, on summary conviction, by six months' imprisonment and/or a fine not exceeding the statutory maximum; and, on indictment, by two years' imprisonment. As to the intent, cf. *Corbyn v Saunders* [1978] Crim LR 169, DC.

3. See Andrews, "Robbery" [1966] Crim LR 524.

4. Cf. *Skivington* [1968] 1 QB 166, [1967] 1 All ER 483; *Robinson* [1977] Crim LR 173, CA.

5. (1980) 71 Cr App Rep 104, [1980] Crim LR 385.

6. See Andrews, op. cit., 527, for possible instances.

1 Use or Threat of Force in Order to Steal

Any use or threat of "force" against the person suffices. "Force" is undefined and in the prevailing climate of judicial opinion it can come as no surprise that it has been identified as an ordinary English word the meaning of which is to be determined by the jury.[7] But no jury could reasonably find that the slight physical contact which might be involved where D picks P's pocket would amount to a use of force. But very little may be required to turn a case of theft into one of robbery and to push or nudge the victim so as to cause him to lose his balance is capable of being a use of force.[8]

Under the former law robbery was thought of as stealing accomplished by force against the person, the force being used to overpower P's resistance and not merely to seize the property.[9] The CLRC appeared to have the same distinction in mind for they said that they would "not regard mere snatching of property, such as a handbag, from an unresisting owner as using force for the purpose of the definition".[10] The distinction was meant to be conveyed by the words in s. 8, ". . . if he steals . . . and in order to do so, he uses force on any person or seeks to put any person of being then and there subjected to force". But in *Clouden*[11] the distinction was rejected and D's conviction for robbery was upheld where he wrenched a shopping basket from P's hand and ran off with it. In the view of the court the former distinction could not stand with the words of the section and it was open to a jury to find on these facts that force had been used on P with intent to steal. *A fortiori* it will be robbery where, for example, a struggle, even a fleeting one, takes place for possession of a handbag,[12] or where an earring is snatched tearing the lobe of the ear.[13]

A threat of force may be implied as well as express. So long as D intends P to understand, and P does so understand, that force will be used against him if he seeks to prevent the theft, the theft is accomplished by the threat of force. Where D threatens P with force unless P complies with D's demands and at a later stage takes property from an unprotesting P, D may be convicted of robbery if he intends, and P understands, the threat to continue, even though D's original threats were not made for the purpose of taking P's property.[14]

It is not necessary that the force used or threatened should amount to an assault. D may threaten a use of force and satisfy the requirements of the offence of robbery although P is not made to apprehend the immediate infliction of force on him which is necessary to constitute an assault.[15] Since "force" is an ordinary word it is for the jury to determine its meaning as a matter of fact.[16]

---

7. *Dawson and James* (1976) 64 Cr App Rep 170, CA.
8. *Dawson*, last note.
9. *Gnosil* (1824) 1 C & P 304; *Harman's Case* (1620) 2 Roll Rep 154.
10. Cmnd. 2977, para. 65.
11. [1987] Crim LR 56, CA.
12. *Corcoran v Anderton* (1980) 71 Cr App Rep 104, [1980] Crim LR 385, DC.
13. Cf. *Lapier* (1784) 1 Leach 320.
14. *Donaghy and Marshall* [1981] Crim LR 644 (Judge Chavasse).
15. *Tennant* [1976] Crim LR 133, CC.
16. *Dawson and James* (1976) 64 Cr App Rep 170, CA.

2 On Any Person

In most cases of robbery D will use or threaten force against the person to whom the property belongs. But the offence is not so limited. Provided the force is used or threatened *in order* to steal it will be robbery.

"If, for example, the only force used at the time of the [Great Train Robbery] in 1963 had been on a signalman, this would under the [Act] have been sufficient."[17]

It does not matter that the person against whom the force is used or threatened has no interest whatever in the property; it would be robbery to overpower the same signalman because his signal-box overlooks a factory from which the thieves wish to steal and they fear that he will notice them and raise the alarm. It might amount to robbery where D threatens to use force on Q in order to overcome P's reluctance to part with his money, as where D holds P's child over a river and threatens to throw her in unless P hands over his wallet[18] but such a case is more naturally treated as one of blackmail under s. 21 of the Act.

3 Immediately Before or At the Time of Stealing

Strictly interpreted this expression might suggest that force used only a second after the theft is technically complete would not suffice for robbery, a view which may be said to receive further support from the requirement that the force be used "in order to steal". The argument was advanced in *Hale*.[19] D and E entered P's house and while D was upstairs stealing a jewellery box, E was downstairs tying up P. The Court of Appeal declined to quash their convictions for robbery though the appropriation of the jewellery box might have been completed before the force was used. The appropriation, said the court, should be regarded as a continuing act and it was open to the jury on these facts to conclude that it continued while P was tied up. The matter needs to be looked at in a common sense way; while the force must be used at the time of the theft and in order to steal, the theft needs to be looked at in its entirety.

But a line has to be drawn somewhere. If, having taken property from P without using or threatening force, D is stopped by a police officer in the street outside and knocks him down in order to avoid arrest, this would not amount to robbery. Force used to retain possession of property not obtained by force would not ordinarily be thought of as robbery.[20] Even on a broad view the use of force is neither at the time of, nor in order to commit, the theft.[1]

"Immediately before" must add something to "at the time of" the theft. Clearly if a gang overpower P, the nightwatchman, at the main gate of a factory, this would be a use of force immediately before the theft, although some minutes must elapse before the gang reaches the part of the factory

---

17. Cmnd. 2977, para. 65. Cf. *Smith v Desmond and Hall* [1965] AC 960, [1965] 1 All ER 976.
18. Cf. *Reane* (1794) 2 Leach 616.
19. (1978) 68 Cr App Rep 415, [1979] Crim LR 596, CA. Cf. *Gregory* (1982) 74 Cr App Rep 154, [1982] Crim LR 229, CA.
20. *Harman's Case* (1620) 2 Roll Rep 154.
  1. Cf. Cmnd. 2977, para. 65.

where the safe is housed.[2] And it can make no difference that P is not present in the factory at all; it would be robbery where some members of the gang by force detain P at his home while their confederates open the safe in the factory.

It is not enough that D gets P to part with property by threatening to use force on another, and future, occasion. This may well amount to blackmail but the fact that P is intimidated or frightened is not in itself enough for robbery unless he is put in fear of being "then and there" subject to force. But suppose a gang by threats of force persuade P, the factory nightwatch-man, to stay away from work the following evening, and on that evening they steal from the factory uninterrupted. At the time of the theft the threat of force still operates on P's mind; he stays at home because he is afraid of what will happen if he goes to work. But this does not seem to amount to robbery. At the time of the theft P is not put in fear of being "then and there" subjected to force.

It does not seem to be possible to put any particular temporal limit on "immediately". All the circumstances have to be considered including the time when, and the place where, the force was used or threatened in relation to the theft. Force converts theft into robbery only when its use or threat is in a real sense directly part of the theft, and is used in order to accomplish the theft.

4 Mens Rea

Obviously robbery requires at least an intent to steal. But it seems to require more than this. It could be argued that if D intends to steal it will be robbery if in fact there is some use of force, or if in fact he puts someone in fear, whether he intends to do so or not. But it seems clear that D must use or threaten force *in order* to steal, and a merely accidental use of force would not be done in order to steal.[3] It is enough that D seeks to put another in fear of being subjected to force. Fear here means to apprehend, and it would be no less a robbery because P was not afraid. Even if P does not apprehend that he will be subjected to force (because, perhaps, plain-clothes policemen are present and D has walked into a trap), it will be robbery if D sought to make him fear. But it would not be enough that P is in fact put in fear unless D intended to put P in fear. A timorous witness to a smash and grab raid might well fear that the thieves will turn on him, but if the thieves do not intend to put him in fear of being there and then subjected to force the offence cannot amount to robbery.

4 Offences Involving Deception

At common law it was never an offence, as such, to obtain property by deception. In more robust – or less sophisticated – times, it was not apparently regarded as particularly grave to obtain property by swindling.

2. It would surely be open to the jury so to find. Cf. *Hale* (1978) 68 Cr App Rep 415, [1979] Crim LR 596, above.
3. Cf. *Edwards* (1843) 1 Cox CC 32.

In a case in 1704,[4] Holt CJ, holding that it was not stealing where D obtained £20 from P by pretending that he was authorised by Q to collect it, observed, "Shall we indict one man for making a fool of another?" But by 1757 a statutory offence of obtaining property by false pretences had been created. The offence is now defined in s. 15 (1) of the Theft Act:

"A person who by any deception dishonestly obtains property belonging to another, with the intention of permanently depriving the other of it, shall on conviction on indictment be liable to imprisonment for a term not exceeding ten years."

Although property is widely defined for the purposes of s. 15, and includes things in action, there are many common frauds where, though D does not obtain any specific property belonging to P, he nevertheless obtains something of value. D might, for example, obtain a night's lodgings at an hotel by deception or by deception persuade his creditor to defer the payment of a debt. Frauds of this kind were first made criminal by the Debtors Act 1869 which made it an offence to obtain credit by fraud. The Debtors Act was superseded by s. 16 of the Theft Act 1968 which created an offence of obtaining a pecuniary advantage by deception. This offence gave rise to many difficulties in its interpretation (being memorably described by Edmund Davies LJ[5] as "a judicial nightmare") and, following recommendations of the Criminal Law Revision Committee,[6] s. 16 (2) (a) was repealed and superseded by offences of obtaining services by deception and of evasion of liability by deception in ss. 1 and 2 of the Theft Act 1978. The offence of obtaining a pecuniary advantage by deception is, however, retained and may be committed in the ways specified in s. 16 (2) (b) and (c). These offences have common features relating to (i) the deception; (ii) the obtaining; and (iii) dishonesty. In this section these matters are taken first and are followed by a treatment of those matters, which relate in the main to the nature of what is obtained, where the offences diverge.

1) *The Deception*[7]

By s. 15 (4):

"For the purposes of this section 'deception' means any deception (whether deliberate or reckless) by words or conduct as to fact or as to law, including a deception as to the present intentions of the person using the deception or any other person."

Section 16 (3) expressly incorporates this definition for the purposes of the offence under s. 16 (1), and it is incorporated by s. 5 (1) of the Theft Act 1978 for offences under ss. 1 and 2 of that Act.

1 Deliberate or Reckless Deception

In line with general theory concerning criminal liability D may be convicted not only where he knows that what he represents as true is

---

4. *Jones* (1704) 2 Ld Raym 1013.
5. In *Royle* (1971) 56 Cr App Rep 131 at 136.
6. 13th Report (1977) Cmnd. 6733 (hereinafter Cmnd. 6733). See also CLRC Working Paper, *Section 16 of the Theft Act 1968* (1974).
7. See A. T. H. Smith, "The Idea of Criminal Deception" [1982] Crim LR 721.

untrue[8] but also where he represents as true that which, as he is aware, may or may not be true. Of course D cannot be convicted of deception should what he represents to be true turn out to be true[9] because P would not have been deceived. Clearly there would be no offence where D represents as true that which he believes to be true but which, as he ought as a reasonable man to have known, is false. Recklessness ordinarily involves a subjective awareness which is absent from negligence.[10] Moreover the offence of deception requires dishonesty and negligence is no substitute for dishonesty.[11]

2 Words or Conduct

The deception may take the form of either words or conduct.[12] Usually the words or conduct will involve an express assertion of a fact which is untrue, but sometimes the words or conduct of D may be intended to imply certain facts though there is no express assertion of those facts. An obvious case is where D obtains goods or services by giving a cheque in payment. The giving of a cheque does not imply that D then has funds in the bank to meet it for he may have authority to overdraw his account; but he does represent as fact that the cheque is a valid order for the payment of its amount at the bank on which it is drawn.[13] D may therefore be convicted of an offence only if he knows that it will not be met or is reckless whether it is or not.

In *Hamilton*[14] it was held that where D presents a withdrawal slip (and a cheque is indistinguishable in principle) he additionally represents that the bank is indebted to him for the amount stated. Since D knew that his "credit" with the bank was the proceeds of forged cheques, that representation was untrue and it had caused the bank to honour the withdrawal slip where, had it known the true state of affairs, it would not have done so.

A case which is difficult to reconcile with these principles is *Greenstein*.[15] D and others applied to P for large numbers of shares and with each application they sent a cheque to cover the purchase price. They knew that

8. Cf. The Rehabilitation of Offenders Act 1974. D would not be guilty of an offence in, for example, obtaining employment by concealing a "spent" conviction.
9. Cf. *Deller* (1952) 36 Cr App Rep 184, CCA; above, p. 33; but he may commit an attempt.
10. Given the requirement for dishonesty, it is thought that *Caldwell* recklessness cannot apply to deception offences. Contra Archbold, 18–102.
11. *Staines* [1975] Crim LR 651, CA. Cf. *Derry v Peek* (1889) 14 App Cas 337. And see below, p. 568. The Financial Services Act 1986, s. 47, imposes criminal liability for "the reckless making (dishonestly or otherwise)" of statements in certain circumstances. But under s. 15 of the Theft Act dishonesty is of course required in all cases.
12. *Harris* (1975) 62 Cr App Rep 28, CA, booking in at hotel implies an intention to pay. Cf. *Barnard* (1837) 7 C & P 784 – D, knowing it was the practice for Oxford shops to extend credit to students, obtained goods on credit by stating that he was a student. Bolland B said that even if nothing had passed in words the jury might find a pretence in the fact that D wore a cap and gown.
13. *Halstead v Patel* [1972] 2 All ER 147 at 151, DC. Cf. *Hazelton* (1874) LR 2 CCR 134. In *Charles* [1976] 3 All ER 112, HL, Lord Diplock, at p. 113, and Viscount Dilhorne, at p. 116, with whom Lords Salmon and Fraser of Tullybelton agreed, thought that there was in effect only one representation, that the cheque would be honoured on presentation. A postdated cheque similarly involves a representation that it will be honoured on the due date: *Gilmartin* [1983] QB 953, [1983] 1 All ER 829, CA.
14. (1991) 92 Cr App Rep 54, [1990] Crim LR 806, CA.
15. [1976] 1 All ER 1, [1975] 1 WLR 1353, CA.

they did not have funds in the bank to meet the cheque at the time of the application, but they also knew from experience that they would be allocated only a proportion of the shares applied for and that when the shares were allocated P would return a cheque for the difference between their cheque for the full purchase price and the actual purchase price. This return cheque they would immediately bank so that their own cheque, which was presented after the allocation of shares, would be met either on first or, at worst, second presentation. They had been told by their bankers that this practice was irregular and they knew that P would not have issued the shares had P realised that by their scheme they were getting for themselves a larger proportion of shares than bona fide applicants. Indeed to combat this practice which is known as "stagging" P had in some cases asked applicants to give an assurance that their cheques would be met on first presentation and the defendants had given this.

The defendants claimed that they did not dishonestly obtain the shares by deception because their experience in these stagging operations showed that the cheques would be met. But it was held that in so far as the defendants represented that each cheque was a valid order it was not, because, as they knew, they had no authority whatever to draw cheques for these large amounts – cheques which could only be met if the defendants succeeded in deceiving P into thinking that their applications were genuine. Yet a cheque does not cease to be a valid order merely because D does not have the funds to meet it provided it is in his expectation (however arrived at) that there will be funds in the bank to meet it on presentation. But in those cases where the defendants had given an assurance that the cheque would be met on first presentation it might be thought that the road to conviction was plainer. After all they knew there was at least a risk that the cheques would not be met until second presentation and were accordingly reckless in giving that undertaking. This argument found favour with the court. But the definition of deception, though it includes statements of intention, does so only where the statement is untrue as to the *present* intentions of D. How can a statement that a cheque will be met on first presentation some time hence amount to a statement of the present intentions of the defendants?[16]

At all events it may be seen that the giving of a cheque, without more, involves certain implicit representations of fact. These days it is common to use a cheque card when paying by cheque and the nature of the representation involved in using a cheque card was examined by the House of Lords in *Charles*.[17] Essentially cheque cards are issued by banks to overcome the reluctance of payees to accept cheques which they fear may be dishonoured on presentation. Provided certain simple conditions are fulfilled the bank guarantees that cheques up to a certain amount will be honoured. Consequently when a cheque card is used D cannot be guilty of deception in representing that the cheque will be met; even if D knows that there will be no funds to meet the cheque and that he has no authority to overdraw he also knows that the cheque will be honoured by his bank. But in *Charles* it

16. See Smith, *Theft*, para. 177.
17. [1977] AC 177, [1976] 3 All ER 112.

was held that where D draws a cheque using a cheque card he represents to the payee that as between himself (D) and his bank he is authorised to use the card. If, therefore, D's authority to use the card has been withdrawn or if D uses the card to cash cheques beyond the amount authorised by his bank, there is a deception.

It is not enough, however, to show that certain facts may be reasonably inferred from D's words or conduct. But given that D intends (or is reckless whether) his words and conduct should impliedly represent other facts to P, and they do so, there is no difficulty in finding that D has deceived P. Under a contract of sale the seller may charge whatever he can get for his goods and does not imply that his price is fair. But where parties are in a position of trust and, as D knows, P has left it to him to make a fair charge, D, in making an exorbitant charge, may commit the offence for he implicitly represents the exorbitant charge as a fair one; D's silence when making the exorbitant charge is as eloquent as if he said he was going to make only a modest profit.[18]

Where a statement of fact is properly inferred from D's words or conduct there is no difficulty in finding a deception. But what if D, realising that P has deceived himself, takes no steps to undeceive him? Suppose that D offers a boat for sale knowing that the hull is rotten. He is under no obligation to reveal defects in goods which he sells and he cannot be guilty of an offence though he knows that P buys the boat believing the hull to be sound.[19] But what if D had at some stage during the negotiations honestly represented the hull to be sound only to discover before the actual sale that it was rotten?[20] In such a case there seems no reason why D's representation should not be regarded as a continuing one so that if he goes through with the sale without correcting the error he obtains P's money on the basis of a representation which he now knows to be false. So in *Director of Public Prosecutions v Ray*[1] it was held that where a meal is ordered in a restaurant the customer represents that he will pay on presentation of the bill and that representation continues until the bill is paid. Hence if the customer changes his mind and decamps just before the presentation of the bill, it can be said that a representation, true when it was made, has become false and it may be relied upon as a deception if it deceives the waiter.

This may be an extreme instance of the application of the principle concerning continuing representations but the principle is sound in itself. Suppose, for example, that D is in receipt of social security benefits calculated on the basis that she is separated from her husband[2] and, notwithstanding that she has returned to her husband, she continues to draw benefit at the higher rate. It would be only common sense to regard her original representation that she was separated from her husband as a continuing one, and in continuing to draw benefit she is representing as

18. *Silverman* (1988) 86 Cr App Rep 213, [1987] Crim LR 574, CA.
19. It would be otherwise if D had moved the boat from the slipway into the water in order to conceal the rotten state of the hull, cf. *Schneider v Heath* (1813) 3 Camp 506.
20. Cf. *Incledon v Watson* (1862) 2 F & F 841.
1. [1974] AC 370, [1973] 3 All ER 131, HL.
2. Cf. *Moore v Branton* [1974] Crim LR 439, DC.

true that which is now palpably false. Similarly where D, a doctor, has an arrangement with the NHS under which he is to pay for services provided by the NHS to his private patients, his failure to disclose that certain patients are private patients, thereby causing the NHS to make no charge, is an operative deception.[3]

3 Fact or Law

The deception will nearly always be one of fact but s. 15 (4) makes it clear that a deception as to law suffices. So a lawyer might commit the offence where, dishonestly intending to prefer one beneficiary to another, he represents to the executors that "heirlooms" in the testator's will means all the personal chattels of the testator.

A statement of fact is not the same thing as a statement of opinion but as a practical matter it is often difficult to distinguish the two. Regard has to be had, so far as the offence of deception is concerned, to D's knowledge and intentions, and the effect produced in the mind of P. If D says in a testimonial concerning X that X is honest this would normally be taken as a statement of opinion, but it is a statement of fact to the extent that it will be taken to imply that D knows of no circumstances which show X to be dishonest. Thus if D knows that X is dishonest his statement is untrue in point of fact,[4] and it can make no difference that he expresses himself in the form, "It is my opinion that X is honest."

But in ordinary commerce people are given to making extravagant claims about the quality of property in order to induce its sale. It may often happen that D knows that (or does not care whether) his claim is untrue. Take, for example, the case of *Bryan* (1857),[5] where D obtained money from P by pledging with him certain spoons which D represented as being of the best quality, equal to Elkington's A (this being a high quality silver spoon manufactured by Elkington), and to have as much silver on them as Elkington's A. D's spoons were in fact of very inferior quality, and were not worth the sum advanced. D was convicted of obtaining by false pretences, the jury finding that he knew his representations to be untrue. It was held, quashing D's conviction, that dishonestly to exaggerate the quality of goods was not within the offence; in so far as there was a representation of fact – that the spoons pledged were silver spoons – this was true, even though they did not have the quality represented.

But there is much force in the dissenting judgment of Willes J in this case.[6] He regarded as crucial the fact that D's representation was dishonestly made with intent to defraud P, and to the extent that D claimed his spoons had on them as much silver as Elkington's A it could be demonstrated, as D well knew, that they had not. To the more general argument that to uphold D's conviction might interfere with the course of trade,

3. *Firth* [1991] 91 Cr App Rep 217, [1990] Crim LR 326, CA.
4. Cf. *Smith v Land and House Property Corpn* (1884) 28 Ch D 7.
5. Dears & B 265.
6. Ibid., at 280.

Willes J replied that the court ought to prevent trade being carried out in this fashion.

It would seem to be quite open to a court to uphold a conviction for deception under s. 15 of the Theft Act on facts like these. D knew perfectly well, as the jury found, that his spoons were not as good as Elkington's A and to that extent there was an assertion of fact. Willes J might have been ahead of the commercial morality of his time but there is no reason to suppose that standards of fair dealing might have improved since then.[7]

This is not to say that any person who knowingly exaggerates the quality of his goods will commit the offence of deception. Regard must be had to the effect produced in the mind of P. There is a deal of give and take in commercial transactions and P is unlikely to be deceived by mere puffs. On the sale of a car it is thought that D would not be guilty of deception when he asserts that the car is "a good runner" for no one is really deceived by puffs of this kind.

4 Statements of Intention

In the tort of deceit it has long been the rule that a false statement of intention is actionable. In *Edgington v Fitzmaurice*,[8] where the directors of a company were held liable for falsely stating in a prospectus that the company was raising money to improve buildings when the real object was to use the money to discharge existing liabilities, Bowen LJ said:

"There must be a misstatement of an existing fact; but the state of a man's mind is as much a fact as the state of his digestion. It is true that it is very difficult to prove what the state of a man's mind at a particular time is, but if it can be ascertained it is as much a fact as anything else. A misrepresentation as to the state of a man's mind is therefore a misstatement of fact."[9]

In view of this it might be thought unnecessary to provide expressly in s. 15 that deception included "a deception as to the present intentions of the person using the deception or any other person", but it was probably necessary to do so because, under the former law it had been held[10] that a false statement of intention was not a false pretence. The directors in *Edgington v Fitzmaurice*[11] would thus now be liable under the criminal as well as the civil law; and, it might be noted, the case provides an example of a deception as to the intentions of another person, namely, the company.

It is accordingly enough that D merely orders goods on credit having no intention to pay. It is of course right that such a person should be convicted but care must be taken that these offences are not employed against the recalcitrant debtor. Mere failure to pay a debt is no proof of dishonest

---

7. Cf. *Jeff and Bassett* (1966) 51 Cr App Rep 28. Note that the Trade Descriptions Act 1968 deals in a comprehensive way with false descriptions applied to goods and services "in the course of a trade or business".
8. (1885) 29 Ch D 459, CA.
9. Ibid., at 483.
10. *Dent* [1955] 2 QB 590, [1955] 2 All ER 806, CCA.
11. (1885) 29 Ch D 459, CA.

intent and the jury must be carefully directed on drawing the line between the dishonest customer and one who bites off more than he can chew.[12]

2) *The Obtaining*

To establish an offence under ss. 15 or 16 of the 1968 Act or ss. 1 and 2 of the 1978 Act it must be shown that the false representation deceived P and operated to enable D to obtain the property, pecuniary advantage, the service or the evasion of liability.

The authorities clearly favour the view that offences of deception require some person to be deceived.[13] It is not possible to deceive a machine. If D operates a cigarette machine with a washer he may be convicted of stealing the cigarettes[14] but is no more guilty of an offence under s. 15 than one who uses a screwdriver. So if D uses a false token on a parking meter in order to get free parking,[15] or on an automatic turnstile to get a free ride on a train,[16] he commits no offence under s. 2 of the 1978 Act. But if the machine is controlled or supervised by P and as a result of D's dishonest use of the machine P is caused to do or refrain from doing something then it can be said that D has obtained by his deception.

The deception must then operate on the mind of P and *cause* him to part with the property or confer the pecuniary advantage. The deception need not be addressed personally to P and it is enough that it is contained in a newspaper or prospectus and causes members of the public to act on it.

Obviously these offences cannot be committed, though there may be an attempt, where P is not taken in by the deception even though he does in fact part with the property or confer the advantage.[17] Even where P is deceived there can be no offence unless he is caused by it to do or refrain

---

12. Cf. *Ingram* [1956] 2 All ER 639 at 641, per Donovan J. In *Carpenter* (1911) 76 JP 158, the jury found D guilty of obtaining credit by fraud but added a recommendation to mercy on the grounds of his age and optimistic temperament.

13. "For a deception to take place there must be some person or persons who will have been deceived.": *Director of Public Prosecutions v Ray* [1973] 3 All ER 131 at 137, per Lord Morris. See also *Aston and Hadley* [1970] 3 All ER 1045 at 1048, per Megaw LJ; *Welham v Director of Public Prosecutions* [1960] 1 All ER 805 at 808, per Lord Radcliffe.

14. Cf. *Hands* (1887) 16 Cox CC 188.

15. Cf. *Davies v Flackett* (1972) 116 Sol Jo 526, DC; where D on leaving a car park which required paying 5p in a machine to raise the exit barrier, drove off without paying when he saw the barrier being held open by a stranger. The court left open whether an offence could be committed without a human mind, but it is thought that this would now provide the best ground for the decision. See Bystander, "Deceiving a Machine" (1972) 69 Law Soc Gaz 416; Smith, "Some Comments on Deceiving a Machine" (1972) 69 Law Soc Gaz 576.

16. Frauds of this kind may be covered by other legislation. The Road Traffic Regulation Act 1967, s. 42 (4), makes it a summary offence (£50 fine) to operate a parking meter other than by using the proper coin; the Regulation of Railways Act 1889, s. 5 (3), makes it a summary offence (£50 fine) to travel with intent to avoid payment of fare.

17. *Hensler* (1870) 11 Cox CC 570, above, p. 42. This is not to suggest that P must be totally convinced of the truth of D's representation. As Griew (*Theft*, 7–41) rightly points out, a person is deceived by a representation if, though he has certain doubts about its truth, he nevertheless accepts it and acts on it.

from doing something. In *Laverty*[18] a stolen car, the number plates of which had been changed by D, was sold to P and the deception alleged was that the car did not bear its original number plates. It was held that D's conviction could not stand on that deception. P bought the car because he thought that D was authorised to sell it, and provided he was so authorised, there was no evidence to show that P would have minded at all that the car did not bear its original plates.[19] But in *Sullivan*[20] D's conviction was upheld where he sold dartboards advertising himself as the "actual maker" of them. This was a lie because he was not the maker but it is difficult to see how this lie would have induced the purchasers to buy the dartboards and in *Laverty* the court said that it was "very anxious not to extend the principle in *Sullivan* more than is necessary."[1]

Another case where it is not at first sight easy to see the causal connection between the deception and the obtaining is *Director of Public Prosecutions v Ray*.[2] Here it was held that D, a customer in a restaurant, was rightly convicted of obtaining a pecuniary advantage by deception when, after a meal had been consumed but before the bill had been paid, he decamped from the premises while the waiter was out of the dining room. While it can be accepted that the waiter would not have left the room had he known that a customer had changed his mind about paying, it does not follow that he left the room because he assumed that D's original representation that he would pay remained unchanged. But a majority of the House of Lords held otherwise. The waiter was variously described as being put off his guard[3] or lulled into a false sense of security[4] so that there was evidence on which the justices could properly conclude that the deception induced the waiter to leave the room thereby enabling D to evade the debt.[5] In such cases as these it is of course proper to examine or cross-examine P with a view to proving or disproving that his mind was affected by the deception. *Director of Public Prosecutions v Ray* does not establish that the customer must necessarily obtain by deception in these circumstances, only that on the evidence before the justices it was proper to infer that this customer did.[6] To this extent the question whether the deception is an effective cause of the obtaining is a question of fact[7] though there is, as always, a preliminary

---

18. [1970] 3 All ER 432, CA.
19. It is otherwise where D alters the number plates (e.g. alters the last letter from H to M) and causes P to believe that the car is less old than it is.
20. (1945) 30 Cr App Rep 132, CCA.
  1. [1970] 3 All ER 432 at 434. But cf. *Etim v Hatfield* [1975] Crim LR 234, DC, where *Sullivan* was followed and *Laverty* was distinguished. There was an obvious deception in *Etim v Hatfield* because D presented demands through the Post Office for social security benefits to which he was not entitled, and the difficulty in the case arose from the fact that no Post Office employee was called to give evidence. But whoever the clerk was he *must* have paid the money only because of the deception.
  2. [1974] AC 370, [1973] 3 All ER 131, HL; **SHC 448**.
  3. [1973] 3 All ER 131 at 136, per Lord MacDermott.
  4. [1973] 3 All ER 131 at 142, per Lord Hodson.
  5. Evasion of a debt is no longer a "pecuniary advantage" (see now s. 3 of the Theft Act 1978, below, p. 582) but the discussion in the text remains unaffected.
  6. D would not have committed this offence if he had decamped while the waiter was in the room. It is not enough that there is a deception *followed by* the obtaining unless the deception, by operating on P, is a *cause* of the obtaining. This point seems to have been overlooked in *McHugh* (1977) 64 Cr App Rep 92, CA.
  7. Cf. *Hayat* [1976] Crim LR 508, CA.

question of law as to whether the facts are reasonably capable of supporting the inference drawn.

It would seem to follow that if P says he did not care whether D's representation was true or false the case against D must fail because his deception cannot be an effective cause of the obtaining. The issue arose for consideration in *Charles*.[8] D had purchased gambling chips at a casino by using his cheque card to cash cheques to a total value of £750 and it was argued that D's deception in falsely representing that he was authorised to use the card was not an effective cause in inducing P, an employee of the casino, to accept the cheques. P admitted that he accepted cheques from customers only where a cheque card was produced because, as he put it, "It is the bank who takes the risk . . . we make no inquiries as to a customer's credit-worthiness or as to the state of his account with the bank." It would seem to follow therefore that D's deception did not cause P to accept the cheques. In view of this evidence it is surprising that the House of Lords considered that P accepted the cheques only because he was deceived by D into believing that D had authority to use the card. It is true that P admitted that he would not have cashed the cheques had he known that D was *not* authorised, but on his own admission P did not know this, *nor was there any evidence that he cared to find out about it*. On the facts *as interpreted by the House* the conviction could be upheld; *if* P had accepted the cheques because he was deceived into thinking that D had authority then the case could be regarded as one of obtaining by deception.

The courts returned to the problem in *Lambie*.[9] D was the holder of a credit card (Barclaycard) with a stipulated credit limit of £200. Knowing that she was over this limit, D tendered her card to P, a shop assistant employed by Q, to purchase goods to the value of £10.50. Having ascertained that D's name was not on the stop-list and made the other routine checks of the card and the voucher to ascertain that all was in order, P delivered the goods. In her evidence P said that when a credit card was produced she had no means of knowing what was the stipulated limit nor of knowing anything of the holder's dealings with the bank issuing the card. "I am only concerned," she said, "that my store gets paid," and she knew that if the transaction was carried out in the proper way then her store would be paid.

Quashing D's conviction for obtaining a pecuniary advantage by deception, the Court of Appeal sought to distinguish *Charles* on the grounds (i) that P did not in fact rely on the false representation (that D was authorised to use the card) made by D; and (ii) that a credit card differed from a cheque card in that the former, though not the latter, involved a prior contract between the bank issuing the credit card and the retailer.

These distinctions were rejected by the House of Lords which restored D's conviction. As to (ii) it was held, rightly with respect, that there was no relevant distinction for this purpose between a cheque card and a credit card; both amount to guarantees by the bank which can be enforced by someone accepting them according to their terms. As to (i) it was held (in

8. [1977] AC 177, [1976] 3 All ER 112, HL.
9. [1981] 1 All ER 332, [1981] 1 WLR 78; CA; [1982] AC 449, [1981] 2 All ER 776, HL.

the teeth of P's evidence) that the *only* inference to be drawn from P's evidence was that she was induced to part with the goods by D's implicit representation that D was authorised to use the card for had P known that D was not authorised to use the card then P would not have gone through with the transaction.

The decisions in *Charles* and *Lambie* have been subject to criticism.[10] Both cases ignore the fact that in neither was P induced to part with property on any assumption that D's use of the card was authorised. P's evidence in *Lambie* made clear (and P's evidence in *Charles* was hardly less clear) that she was concerned only that the shop was paid and she knew that if she followed certain procedures, which had nothing to do with D's creditworthiness other than making sure that D was not on the stop-list, the shop would be paid whatever D's position was vis-à-vis Barclaycard.

In neither *Charles* nor *Lambie* did the House of Lords question the requirement that the deception must cause the obtaining. The House was saying that the requirement is satisfied where, had P known the true facts, he would not have dealt with D. No doubt, in both *Charles* and *Lambie*, P would not have dealt with D had he known that D lacked authority but this is not the same thing as saying that P dealt with D because he believed that D had authority; P dealt with D in both cases *only* because he knew that if a certain procedure was followed he (or his employer) would be paid. That is the attraction of cheque cards and credit cards, and that is why the banks thought to invent them.

If, then, these cases throw no doubt on the requirement that the deception must be the cause of the obtaining, they must be regarded as special exceptions to the requirement. The decisions in *Charles* and *Lambie* were no doubt influenced by the opportunities for fraud which were perceived as following from the use of cheque cards and credit cards and, unless the requirement that the deception must cause the obtaining is to be brushed aside, must be confined to these situations.[11]

Of course D may be deceived by an implied pretence just as much as an express one so long as he is induced to part with property or confer a pecuniary advantage. The question is whether the deception, whether express or implied, is an operative cause of the obtaining. In this connection, consider the decision of the Court of Appeal in *Rashid*.[12] D, a British Rail steward, was found in possession of sliced loaves and a bag of tomatoes when about to board a train. On a charge of going equipped to cheat contrary to s. 25, the prosecution's case was that D intended to obtain money from passengers by passing off his own sandwiches as those of British Rail and pocket the proceeds. The conviction was quashed owing to various misdirections but the court was of the opinion that the offence could be proved only if an effective and operative deception was practised without which the passengers would not have purchased D's sandwiches.

10. See Smith, [1980] Crim LR 725, [1981] Crim LR 712; Williams, TBCL at p. 846.
11. In *Kassim* [1991] 3 All ER 713 at 721, Lord Ackner, in a passing reference to the cheque and credit card frauds, appears to hint that he is not convinced that there is an offence under s. 15—"Such cases," his lordship said, "obviously give rise to the difficulty of establishing an operative deception."
12. [1977] 2 All ER 237, 64 Cr App Rep 201.

The court thought that on a proper direction no jury would have convicted because it would be a matter of "complete indifference" to the passengers what was the origin of the sandwiches so long as they were value for money.

Yet if the passengers had known that D was perpetrating a fraud on his employers, would they have purchased the sandwiches? No doubt the passenger may not consciously advert to the origin of the sandwiches, but the case is not on all fours with the cheque card case where P is moved to accept the cheque by the bank's guarantee of payment irrespective of D's authority. Had he thought about it, the passenger would have assumed that he was buying British Rail sandwiches and it is because of this implied representation that he is induced to buy. Not surprisingly in *Doukas*[13] the Court of Appeal, on facts essentially similar to *Rashid*, declined to follow the opinion expressed in that case. D, a waiter, was found in possession of bottles of wine which he planned to sell to his employer's customers for his own profit, and his conviction for going equipped to cheat was upheld. The jury was entitled to find that the hypothetical customer, who must be reasonably honest, would not lend his support to a swindle being conducted by D against his employers.[14]

It is possible to argue that a buyer who purchases goods without consciously adverting to their origin has not been deceived though he has been defrauded. It may be said that to be deceived a man must be induced into an affirmative belief that something is true which is false. Against this it can be argued that people enter into many routine transactions on certain implicit assumptions whether they are consciously adverted to or not. One who buys goods assumes that the buyer is either the owner or is authorised to sell whether he consciously thinks about it or not. It must follow that if he deals with British Rail or with an hotelier he must assume that the goods emanate from British Rail or the hotelier. And it cannot be a matter of indifference to him whether the goods supplied belong to British Rail or the hotelier. Quite apart from the fact that he would not lend himself to a fraud in purchasing goods supplied by an employee, he would not willingly forgo his legal remedies against British Rail or the hotelier should the goods prove to be defective. So too a tenant or lodger will assume that a person letting premises is authorised to let since his own position is precarious if that person is a trespasser who is not authorised to let.[15]

It is a self-evident proposition from the foregoing discussion that the deception must precede the obtaining of the property or pecuniary advantage. Thus where D bought petrol and, on then being asked by the attendant whether it was to be charged to D's firm, replied that it was and it was so charged, it was held that D could not be convicted on that representation[16] of obtaining the petrol by deception. D had already obtained ownership and possession[17] of the petrol before the representation

---

13. [1978] 1 WLR 372, [1978] 1 All ER 1061, CA.
14. But cf. the observations of Lord Bridge in *Cooke* [1986] 2 All ER 985 at 990.
15. *Edwards* [1978] Crim LR 49, CA, and commentary.
16. Had the prosecution been able to prove that from the outset D intended to avoid paying for the petrol D could have been convicted.
17. D might obtain ownership of property without deception and then get possession of that property from P by deception (cf. *Phillips v Brooks Ltd* [1919] 2 KB 243) and in such a case he may be convicted under s. 15.

was made.[18] On these facts D might today be convicted of evading a liability by deception because the debt was evaded by, and consequent upon, the deception.

In many cases D obtains property by making both true and false representations, and here D may be convicted of the offence if the representations which are false are an effective, though not necessarily the exclusive, cause of the obtaining. If, for example, D obtains money from P by representing, falsely, that he holds high military rank, and by representing, truly, that the money is required for investment in a company,[19] his deception may be held to be an effective cause of P's parting with his money since he parts with it on the basis that D is a man of standing. But it does not follow that the deception is an effective cause of the obtaining simply because P would not have parted with his property had he been aware that a representation made by D was false. In *Clucas*,[20] D and E falsely represented to P, a bookmaker, that they were acting as commission agents on behalf of several other persons and in that way P was induced to take from them a bet on credit; the horse backed won and P paid on the bet. It was held under the former law that D and E did not obtain the winnings by their false pretence and it is arguable that they would not now obtain the winnings by deception.[1] It was quite clear in this case that P would not have accepted the bet had he known that D and E were not acting for others – indeed at one stage P suspected that all was not as it appeared and was unwilling to pay without further assurances – but the reason why he paid up was that they had backed a winning horse.

With the facts of *Clucas* it is instructive to contrast the facts of *Button*.[2] D had entered races, for which prizes were offered, in the name of E and gave particulars of former running performances which were true of E and which were only modest; on the basis of this D was given a favourable handicap and he romped home in both his races. So much so that suspicion was aroused and the upshot was that D did not stay to take the prize. It was held that D could be convicted under the former law of an attempt to obtain by false pretences, and it seems that he would now be convicted of an attempt to obtain by deception. Here the deception was the effective cause of D winning the race and thereby qualifying for the prize, whereas the deception in *Clucas* in no way improved D's chances of picking the winner. There is a ruling in *Lewis*[3] that where D gets employment by deception (in that case D falsely represented that she was a qualified teacher) he cannot be convicted of obtaining his salary by deception because he is paid in respect of the work done and not in respect of his appointment. *Lewis* was doubted in *King*.[4] The matter, said the court, fell to be determined as one of fact and that where D and E persuaded P to engage them to fell some trees

18. *Collis-Smith* [1971] Crim LR 716, CA.
19. Cf. *Hamilton* (1845) 1 Cox CC 244.
20. [1949] 2 KB 226, [1949] 2 All ER 40, CCA.
  1. But *King*, below, fn. 4, inferentially casts doubt on *Clucas*. D and E in *Clucas* would now commit the offence under s. 16 of the 1988 Act, below, p. 571
  2. [1900] 2 QB 597.
  3. (1922) Somerset Assizes, Rowlatt J: Russell, at 1186n. The case is specifically provided for in s. 16, below, p. 571.
  4. [1987] QB 547, [1987] 1 All ER 547, CA.

by falsely claiming that they were from a firm of tree surgeons and that the felling was necessary to prevent damage, they were properly convicted of an attempt to obtain by deception. This seems entirely right since without the false representations they would not have been given the contract. On the other hand it cannot be supposed that where D gets employment by deception he continues down the years to obtain his salary by deception when his performance is found by his employer to be satisfactory. When the deception ceases to be an operative cause of obtaining the salary is presumably a matter of fact for the jury to determine.

The deception is no less the cause of the obtaining though it would not have deceived a reasonably prudent person so long as it in fact deceives P. D cannot escape the consequences of his dishonesty by showing his victim to have been unusually gullible.[5]

3) *Dishonesty*

Offences involving deception, under both the 1968 and 1978 Acts, require dishonesty. Although no definition of dishonesty is provided, nor is there any adaptation of the partial definition of dishonesty in s. 2, it would seem right that dishonesty should bear, so far as possible, the same meaning for offences of deception as it has for theft. Accordingly:

"Owing to the words 'dishonestly obtains' a person who uses deception in order to obtain property to which he believes himself entitled will not be guilty; for though the deception may be dishonest, the obtaining is not. In this respect ... the offence will be in line with theft, because a belief in a legal right to deprive an owner of property is for the purpose of theft inconsistent with dishonesty and is specifically made a defence by the partial definition of 'dishonestly' in [s.] 2 (1) (a). (The partial definition in [s.] 2 (1) is not repeated in [s. 15 (1)]. It would be only partly applicable to the offence of criminal deception, and it seems unnecessary and undesirable to complicate the [Act] by including a separate definition in [s.] 15.)"[6]

And no doubt the same general considerations apply to s. 16 and to ss. 1 and 2 of the 1978 Act. Consequently reference may be made to the discussion of dishonesty in connection with theft.[7] *Ghosh*[8] (where the charge was laid under s. 15) is of particular relevance and the considered restatement of the law in that case must apply throughout the Acts.

Obviously the partial definition of dishonesty in s. 2 (1), other than in s. 2 (1) (a), can have little application to obtaining offences but it would surely be permissible for the judge to tell the jury that D *may* act dishonestly for the purposes of deception offences though he does not obtain the property

5. Cf. *Giles* (1865) Le & Ca 502.
6. Cmnd. 2977, para. 88. *Woolven* (1983) 77 Cr App Rep 231, CA, confirms the CLRC's thinking. Cf. *Williams* (1836) 7 C & P 354. See *Parker* (1910) 74 JP 208; below, p. 672.
7. Above, p. 536.
8. [1982] QB 1053, [1982] 2 All ER 689, CA, above, p. 540.

with a view to gain or for D's own benefit,[9] or notwithstanding that he intends to pay for the property.[10] The Criminal Law Revision Committee obviously thought the partial definition provided an analogy for deception cases because, in the passage cited above, the analogy is used to support their view that D would not be acting dishonestly in using a deception to obtain property to which he believes himself to be entitled.[11]

In other cases the *Ghosh* doctrine presumably governs. No doubt, as with theft, the jury will experience no difficulty in most cases in determining whether D's conduct is dishonest according to the standards of ordinary decent people, but there are bound to be some cases where the question of dishonesty does not admit of an obvious answer. If, for example, the directors in *Edgington v Fitzmaurice*[12] were to be charged with obtaining money by deception no jury could reasonably decide that it was other than dishonest for them to state that the money was required to expand the business of the firm when it was really required to pay off pressing creditors. But suppose the company was experiencing what the directors believed to be a short term cash-flow problem and in order to maintain public confidence and preserve the jobs of their employees they raised money by untruthfully stating that it was required for expansion. Is it at all fanciful to suggest that a jury in Birmingham might view that quite differently from one in London?

4) *Obtaining Property by Deception: Section 15*

1 Property Belonging to Another

The offence [under s. 15] may be committed in respect of any "property belonging to another". By s. 34 (1) of the Theft Act, s. 4 (1)[13] and s. 5 (1)[14] – which contain the primary definitions of "property" and "belonging to another" – are applied generally for the purposes of the Act.

Consequently "money and all other property, real or personal, including things in action and other intangible property" may be obtained by deception, and the limitations imposed by s. 4 on property which may be stolen do not apply to deception. So far as land is concerned the most obvious case is that of an imposter claiming trust property or a deceased person's estate,[15] but it would extend to any case where D by deception obtains the whole of another's interest in land. So far as things in action are concerned D might commit the offence where, for example, by deception

9. Cf. s. 1 (2).
10. Cf. s. 2 (2). See *Potger* (1970) 55 Cr App Rep 42, CA; where it was held that an intention to give full value did not necessarily negative dishonesty. Cf. *Balcombe v Desimoni* [1972] ALR 513.
11. So that D in *Parker* (1910) 74 JP 208, below, p. 672, would not be guilty of an offence under s. 15 in obtaining payment of a debt owed by P by sending P a letter purporting to come from P's superiors. Cf. *Williams* (1836) 7 C & P 354.
12. (1885) 29 Ch D 459, above, p. 561.
13. Above, p. 513.
14. Above, p. 518.
15. Cmnd. 2977, para. 91.

he induces P to transfer or assign a debt, a copyright or patent, or other intangible property.

Since "property belonging to another" is to be given the same meaning it has for theft under s. 5 (1),[16] it follows that D may commit an offence under s. 15 where by deception he obtains property of which he is the owner. If, for example, in circumstances such as occurred in *Rose v Matt*,[17] D had by deception induced P to part with possession of the clock, he could be convicted of the offence under s. 15.

2 Ownership, Possession or Control
Section 15 (2) provides:

"For the purposes of this section a person is to be treated as obtaining property if he obtains ownership, possession or control of it, and 'obtain' includes obtaining for another or enabling another to obtain or retain."

Frequently D obtains ownership, possession and control of the property but the obtaining of any one of these suffices. If D by deception induces P to sell goods to him the offence is complete when ownership is transferred which may occur before the goods are delivered. If D by deception obtains a loan of the property the offence is complete, if all the other requirements are met, when D gets possession or control of them.

Most often D will obtain the goods for himself but the offence is also committed where D obtains for another or enables another to obtain or retain. Thus the offence might be committed where, for example, D by deception induces P to transfer the ownership in property to E; or where by deception D induces P, who has lent goods to E, not to enforce his right to recover goods from E. In such cases E may be a confederate but D may commit the offence whether E is a confederate or not.

But D would commit no offence under s. 15 where, for example, owing P £10, he dishonestly tells P that he has paid him and that P must have forgotten about it. Here D does not obtain any property belonging to P.[18] Nor would D commit this offence where he enables himself to retain property belonging to P, as where he tells P that he has lost a book which P lent him.[19] He might commit deception by telling P that E has lost the book which P lent to E, for this might enable E to retain the book; but not by telling P that E has repaid a loan which P made to E because this does not enable E to retain property belonging to P.

3 Mens Rea
Those elements of *mens rea* which are common to the offences under ss. 15 and 16, and ss. 1 and 2 of the 1978 Act, *viz.* the making of a deliberate or reckless deception and dishonesty, have been discussed elsewhere. In addition the offence under s. 15 requires an intention permanently to deprive and an intention to obtain the property. As to the former s. 15 (3)

16. Above, p. 518.
17. Above, p. 519.
18. But D commits an offence under s. 2 of the 1978 Act; below, p. 576.
19. But D would be guilty of stealing the book.

provides that s. 6 applies with the necessary adaptation of the reference to appropriating and reference may be made to the discussion elsewhere.

There must, lastly, be an intention to obtain the property for oneself or another by the deception. If, for example, during the course of negotiations for the purchase of goods on credit D tells P what he thinks to be an inconsequential lie (say that he was on active service during the war) he would not commit this offence though P is in fact induced to let him have the goods on credit because he is an ex-serviceman. D did not intend by the deception to obtain the goods. Nor would it be enough that D intends to cause loss to P unless he intends to obtain the property for himself or another.[20]

5 Obtaining a Pecuniary Advantage by Deception: Section 16

It was pointed out at the beginning of this section that the offence of obtaining a pecuniary advantage under s. 16 (2) (a) was found to create such formidable difficulties of interpretation that it has been repealed and replaced by new offences under ss. 1 and 2 of the 1978 Act. Otherwise the offence of obtaining a pecuniary advantage is retained but it may be committed only in the ways specified in paragraphs (b) and (c).[1]

Section 16 provides:

"(1) A person who by any deception dishonestly obtains for himself or another any pecuniary advantage shall on conviction on indictment be liable to imprisonment for a term not exceeding five years.

(2) The cases in which a pecuniary advantage within the meaning of this section is to be regarded as obtained for a person are cases where—

(b) he is allowed to borrow by way of overdraft, or to take out any policy of insurance or annuity contract, or obtains an improvement of the terms on which he is allowed to do so; or

(c) he is given the opportunity to earn remuneration or greater remuneration in an office or employment, or to win money by betting.

(3) For the purposes of this section 'deception' has the same meaning as in section 15 of this Act."

The definition of pecuniary advantage in s. 16 (2) is an exhaustive one. Proof that some pecuniary advantage was obtained by D will not suffice unless it falls within the definition; and if the case falls within the definition it is irrelevant that D in fact obtained no pecuniary advantage since the section states that D is *deemed* to have obtained the advantage if its terms are met.[2]

---

20. See Smith, *Theft*, para. 214. Cf. *Balcombe v Desimoni* [1972] ALR 513.

1. But only one offence is created: *Bale v Rosier* [1977] 2 All ER 160, [1977] 1 WLR 263. The charge must specify the pecuniary advantage which D is alleged to have obtained: *Aston and Hadley* [1970] 3 All ER 1045, [1970] 1 WLR 1584, CA.

2. *Director of Public Prosecutions v Turner* [1973] 3 All ER 124 at 126, per Lord Reid.

1 Overdrafts and Insurance Policies

D may commit an offence, by virtue of s. 16 (2) (b), where by deception he is allowed to borrow by way of overdraft; as where he tells his banker that he requires the credit to enable him to sell goods abroad when he intends to purchase a car. An overdraft is ordinarily regarded as a facility whereby a person may, if he so wishes, overdraw his account to a stated limit.[3] Where a loan is arranged with a bank (say for the purchase of a car) this would not be regarded as an overdraft. It has been held that D is "allowed" to borrow by way of overdraft where by use of the cheque guarantee card issued to him by the bank, the bank is bound to honour cheques issued by D to an amount in excess of that standing to D's credit.[4]

The paragraph also applies to insurance policies and annuity contracts obtained by deception,[5] as where D secures a policy, or a policy on better terms, by falsely stating that he is a non-smoker where this is material to the issue of the policy or its terms.

2 Opportunity to Earn by Employment or Win by Betting

As has been shown the offence of obtaining by deception contrary to s. 15 is not committed unless the deception is an effective cause of the obtaining of the property. Consequently that offence may not committed where D by deception induces a bookmaker to take bets on credit since it is the backing of the winning horse that is the effective cause of the obtaining.[6] The case is now expressly covered by s. 16 (2) (c) and the offence may be committed whether D is allowed to bet on credit or cash terms.

Section 16 (2) (c) may well have been introduced because of a ruling in *Lewis*[7] that D cannot be convicted of obtaining his salary by deception because his salary is paid in respect of work done and not in respect of the appointment. This ruling has been doubted[8] and it may well be that the case is covered by s. 15. Nevertheless, paragraph (c) continues to provide for the case where D obtains employment, or greater remuneration in that employment, by deception.

Paragraph (c) refers to "office or employment". An office can be held by one who is employed and if that office carries additional remuneration this offence may be committed if it is obtained by deception. But an office may exist without any contract of service, as where D is appointed chairman of a voluntary society and if that office is remunerated, as by an honorarium, it would be an offence to obtain the opportunity to earn that remuneration by

---

3. So the offence is complete when D obtains the facility to overdraw; it is not necessary that D should have used the facility: *Watkins* [1976] 1 All ER 578 (Crown Court).
4. *Waites* [1982] Crim LR 369, CA. This seems a surprising decision as it would surely astonish bankers to learn that by issuing such cards they are *allowing* their customers to borrow by way of overdraft to an unspecified amount. But *Waites* was followed in *Bevan* (1986) 84 Cr App Rep 143, [1987] Crim LR 129, CA.
5. The offence may be committed although, as a result of the deception, D could not enforce the contract against P: *Alexander* [1981] Crim LR 183, CA.
6. Cf. *Clucas* [1949] 2 KB 226, [1949] 2 All ER 40; above, p. 567. But *King*, below, fn. 8 and above, p. 567 casts doubt on this.
7. Above, p. 567.
8. In *King* [1987] QB 547, [1987] 1 All ER 547, CA, above, p. 567.

deception. In *McNiff*[9] it was held that the tenancy of a public house was not an office. Nor had the tenant obtained the opportunity to earn remuneration in employment because the tenant earns the opportunity to earn money by his own efforts and is not remunerated by the brewery. Since an office may exist without a contract of service there would seem to be no reason for confining "employment" to cases where there is a contract of service. Giving "employment" its ordinary meaning it would seem to extend to contracts for services and it was so held in *Callender*.[10]

3 Mens Rea

Those elements of *mens rea* which are common to the offences under both s. 15 and s. 16, viz. the making of a deliberate or reckless deception and dishonesty, have been discussed elsewhere. In addition the offence under s. 16 requires an intention to obtain the pecuniary advantage for oneself or another. It is not enough that D obtains a pecuniary advantage unless his deception was made in order to gain it; nor is it enough that D's deception inflicts some pecuniary loss on P unless it was made in order to obtain for D or another the pecuniary advantage.

6 Obtaining Services by Deception

Section 1 of the Theft Act 1978 provides—

"(1) A person who by any deception dishonestly obtains services from another shall be guilty of an offence.

(2) It is an obtaining of services where the other is induced to confer a benefit by doing some act, or causing or permitting some act to be done, on the understanding that the benefit has been or will be paid for."

By s. 4 the offence is triable either way; on summary conviction it is punishable by imprisonment for a term not exceeding six months and/or a fine not exceeding the prescribed maximum (presently £1,000), and on indictment by imprisonment for a term not exceeding five years and/or a fine.

The notion behind this offence is that a person's labour is something of economic value. Labour is not property but a man may contract for value to provide it. It is therefore made an offence by deception to obtain the services of another.

1) *Deception*

Section 5 (1) provides that "deception" has the same meaning as in s. 15. Two further points may be noted. One is that the deception must cause P to

9. [1986] Crim LR 57, CA.
10. (1992) *Times*, 9 April.

provide the services on the understanding that they will be paid for. It is not an offence for D by deception to cause P to provide services without charge. A reason for this might be that in such a case P has suffered no economic loss because no price has been put on his services but the offence may otherwise be committed notwithstanding that P suffers no economic loss. If D gets P to mow his lawn by pretending that he has sprained his ankle but at the same time offers P £10 for the job, the offence will be committed when D does the job if he is in part induced to do so because he believes the story of the sprained ankle. But as with the offence under s. 15 of the 1968 Act,[11] a person's conduct may be dishonest notwithstanding that he intends to pay for the service. No doubt a jury would be reluctant to find D's conduct dishonest where no economic loss is in fact caused and the deception plays only a minor part in influencing P to act but a conviction in such circumstances can be supported.

The other point is that the service be obtained by deceiving P. It is not enough that the service is obtained by stealth and that a charge for the service is avoided. D does not commit this offence where he secretly enters a cinema or cricket ground or where he induces a taxi-driver to carry him by threats.

2) *Services*

"Services" is widely defined.[12] It is constituted by:
  (a) any act done by P provided that (a) it confers a benefit on someone other than P, and (b) it is done on the understanding that it has been or will be paid for; or
  (b) any act which P causes or permits to be done whether by D or another provided that (a) it amounts to a benefit or confers a benefit on someone other than P, and (b) it is caused or permitted on the understanding that it has been or will be paid for.

This is a wide definition. Typically it will extend to cases where D by deception induces P to provide him with board and lodging, or to provide an amenity such as the use of social or sporting facilities, or to provide goods on hire. In such cases as these P would be seen as providing what would ordinarily be thought of as a service but it is to be noted that s. 1 (2) provides the definition of service and it appears to go further than what is ordinarily understood as a service. *Any* act which meets the stated criteria *is* a service. While a sale of goods is not usually thought of as a provision of services, P does an act (delivers goods) which confers a benefit and, though more naturally thought of as falling within s. 15 of the 1968 Act, it seems clearly to fall within this section. An obtaining of goods on hire-purchase

---

11. See *Potger* (1970) 55 Cr App Rep 42, CA, above, p. 569.
12. The CLRC initially had in mind a narrower offence involving deception as to the prospect of payment (see Working Paper, paras. 26–29 and 31–34) but this was rejected by Parliament and the Committee's redraft took account of Parliament's expressed preference for an offence of obtaining services, widely defined.

terms is an obtaining of services,[13] and it cannot be a relevant difference that the purchase price is paid at once rather than in instalments.[14] Accordingly there would seem to be a considerable overlap between this offence and the offence under s. 15 of the 1968 Act, and the offence will also overlap with the offences under s. 16 of the 1968 Act.

P must, however, be induced to do some *act*; a mere omission will not suffice. But this limitation is not likely to be of any great practical significance since the offence extends to inducing P to cause or permit some act to be done. Permission may be given by passive acquiescence as where P allows D to park a car in P's lot or allows D to take a boat which is offered for hire.

Where D induces an act which confers a benefit the offence is complete when P does the act; where D induces P to permit an act it is arguable that the offence is complete when the permission is given but it is submitted that a preferable view is that the offence is complete only when an act is done pursuant to that permission. The latter view seems more consistent with the wording of s. 1 (2): "causing or permitting some act to be done".

3) *The Benefit*

In typical cases proving that a benefit has been conferred will present no difficulty; the very fact that the act induced is on the understanding that it has been or will be paid for is pregnant evidence that it confers a benefit. People do not undertake to pay for lodgings, sporting facilities or the hire of chattels unless a benefit is conferred. That benefit need not be conferred on D; it is enough that P is induced to confer a benefit on another.

"Benefit" cannot mean something which turns out to be to D's profit or to be beneficial to him; it must refer to something which in law is regarded as a benefit. An apt test would seem to be whether the benefit would constitute consideration sufficient to support a contract. It would appear to follow from this that if the alleged benefit would constitute an illegal consideration for the purposes of the law of contract, it cannot be a benefit for the purposes of this offence.[15] This is not to suggest that an enforceable contract is required between P and D before an offence may be committed. The section does not suggest any such limitation. If, for example, a minor by deception induces P to provide non-necessary services P cannot enforce payment by D. There is, however, no reason why the services cannot constitute a benefit for clearly they do constitute a benefit; there is also an "understanding" that they will be paid for and accordingly there is no reason why D should not be convicted of the offence.

13. *Widdowson* (1986) 82 Cr App Rep 314, CA.
14. In *Halai* [1983] Crim LR 624, CA, it was held that a mortgage advance was not a service because it was a lending of money for property. *Halai* was distinguished in *Widdowson* but not convincingly (see comment at [1986] Crim LR 233); lending money is an act which confers a benefit on D and it is "paid for" in interest charges. Cf. *Bolton* [1992] Crim LR 57, CA.
15. See Smith, *Theft*, para. 233.

4) *The Understanding*

The offence, as has been pointed out, is not committed where by deception P is induced to provide services without charge for there is no understanding that such services will be paid for. Where there is an understanding that the services have been or will be paid for,[16] it will ordinarily be an understanding that D has paid or will pay for an act done by P. But the offence is not so limited and extends to the situations where the understanding is that E has paid or will pay for the service (as where D represents that his employer will pay his hotel bill) and where the understanding is that Q has been or will be paid (as where P, an employee, is induced to do an act on the understanding that Q, his employer, has been or will be paid for it).

5) *Payment*

In the ordinary run of case the understanding will be that the services will be paid for in monetary form (cash, cheque or credit card). Suppose, however, that D by deception induces P to provide services in return for services or goods, for example, that if P digs D's garden then D will paint P's house or will provide P with a power drill. "Paid for" presumably has the same meaning as "payment" and it does not strain the ordinary meaning of the word to extend it to recompense in forms other than money. Payment may be said to describe any of the ways in which an obligation may be discharged.[17] On this view D in the examples given would commit the offence.

6) *Dishonesty*

The offence requires dishonesty and reference may be made to the discussion of this matter above.[18]

7 Evasion of Liability by Deception

Section 2 of the Theft Act 1978 provides—
    "(1) Subject to subsection (2) below, where a person by any deception—

---

16. No price needs to be fixed; it is enough that the parties understand that by ordinary commercial practice the service is to be paid for.
17. Cf. *White v Elmdene Estates Ltd* [1959] 2 All ER 605 at 610, per Lord Evershed MR.
18. At pp. 536 and 568.

(a) dishonestly secures the remission of the whole or part of any
existing liability to make a payment, whether his own liability or
another's; or

(b) with intent to make permanent default in whole or in part on any
existing liability to make a payment, or with intent to let another
do so, dishonestly induces the creditor or any person claiming
payment on behalf of the creditor to wait for payment (whether
or not the due date for payment is deferred) or to forgo payment;
or

(c) dishonestly obtains any exemption from or abatement of liability
to make a payment;

he shall be guilty of an offence.

(2) For purposes of this section 'liability' means legally enforceable
liability; and subsection (1) shall not apply in relation to a liability that
has not been accepted or established to pay compensation for a wrongful
act or omission.

(3) For purposes of subsection (1) (b) a person induced to take in
payment a cheque or other security for money by way of conditional
satisfaction of a pre-existing liability is to be treated not as being paid but
as being induced to wait for payment.

(4) For purposes of subsection (1) (c) 'obtains' includes obtaining for
another or enabling another to obtain."

The offence is triable and punishable in the same way as the offence under
s. 1.

The offence[19] under s. 2 was intended by the CLRC to penalise much of
the conduct which was within s. 16 (2) (a) of the Theft Act 1968 which it
replaces. In broad terms s. 2 deals with the dishonest debtor. It does not
make it an offence dishonestly to resolve not to pay a debt, nor does it make
it an offence to take measures (avoiding contact with the creditor, moving
house, for example) though these measures are taken with a view to evading
liability to meet the debt.[20] The section deals with the person who *by
deception* dishonestly seeks to evade a liability to make payment, or to get
the creditor to wait for or forgo payment, or to obtain an exemption from or
abatement of a liability to make payment.

1) *Securing Remission of a Liability*

Section 2 (1) (a) envisages that there is an existing liability and that D by
deception secures the remission of the whole or part of that liability. "An
example", said the CLRC,[21]

19. It is not clear whether the section creates one offence or three. S. 16, which it replaces, was
held to create one offence (*Bale v Rosier* [1977] 2 All ER 160, [1977] 1 WLR 263, DC). In *Holt*
[1981] 2 All ER 854, [1981] 1 WLR 1000, CA, Lawson J was not sure whether the paragraphs
simply described different ways of committing the same offence or whether there were
conceptual differences. While the paragraphs overlap, it would seem they have different
functions and it seems preferable to regard the section as creating three offences: see Smith,
Theft, para. 237.
20. Such conduct may be an offence under s. 3, below, p. 582.
21. Cmnd. 6733, para. 13.

"would be where a man borrows £100 from a neighbour and, when repayment is due, tells a false story of some family tragedy which makes it impossible for him to find the money; this deception persuades the neighbour to tell him that he need never repay the loan."

On the face of it this seems an obvious case falling within s. 2 (1) (a); P certainly intends to remit the debt and believes that he has done so. But in law the debt is not remitted for if D's fraud is discovered P may still claim his £100; moreover P's claim continues undiminished during the period when he remains deceived. So far as the debt of £100 is concerned no change has been brought about by D's fraud which in law causes the debt to be remitted. Only if the paragraph is read so as to be satisfied where P *believes* the debt to be remitted would this case fall within it and such an interpretation (though it would achieve the result intended by the CLRC) would be a bold one.

It was held in *Jackson*[22] that there was an offence under paragraph (a) where D obtained petrol from P by tendering a stolen credit card. That P would thereafter look to the authority issuing the card for payment meant, in the view of the court, that D had secured the remission of a liability. It may fairly be said that D had done so notwithstanding that, in the unlikely eventuality of the authority declining to pay, D's liability to pay would have revived. But a mere agreement by a creditor that he will not enforce a legal liability does not destroy the debt in law.[23]

While this view of paragraph (a) robs it of much of its intended effect the fraudster can take little comfort from that since such cases fall within paragraph (b) in that P has been induced to forgo payment; "forgo" is entirely apt to describe what it is that P is induced to do in such a situation.[1] Of course paragraph (b) additionally requires an intent to make permanent default but proof of that would be easy to come by where D has persuaded P to remit the debt.

Paragraph (a) assumes an existing liability which P is persuaded to remit. It cannot therefore apply where D persuades P that there was no existing liability as, for example, where P, unsure to which of his friends he lent £10 at a party – in fact it was D – is persuaded by D that he must have lent the money to someone else. Such a case, however, falls within paragraph (b).

2) *Inducing Creditor to Wait for or Forgo Payment*

The operation of s. 2 (1) (b) may be illustrated by reference to the facts of *Director of Public Prosecutions v Turner*.[2] D, who owed P some £38 for work done and was being pressed for payment, told P that he had no ready cash

---

22. [1983] Crim LR 617, CA.
23. *Re Charge Card Services Ltd* [1989] Ch 497, [1988] 3 All ER 702, CA.
  1. In *Holt* [1981] 2 All ER 854, [1981] 1 WLR 1000, counsel submitted that paragraph (a) required the legal consequence that the debt be extinguished while under paragraph (b) the forgoing of a liability did not require that the liability be extinguished. Lawson J found "great difficulty in introducing these concepts into the construction of the subsection".
  2. [1974] AC 357, [1973] 3 All ER 124, HL.

and persuaded P to accept a cheque knowing that it would be dishonoured. Such conduct falls within s. 2 (1) (b) if, and only if, D intends to make permanent default on the debt. If, as seemed likely in *Turner* itself, D simply wanted to rid himself temporarily of the importunings of his creditor in order to give himself a breathing space, and was bent on settling the debt at a later stage, he would not commit an offence.

The effect of D's deception must be to make the creditor "wait for . . . or forgo" payment. "Forgo" appears to require that P in some way desists from looking for payment. It would be apt to cover the case where P, a waiter in a restaurant, is falsely told by D, a diner, that Q, another waiter, has taken payment for the meal.[3] "Wait" is more apt to cover the case whereby a strategem (for example sending his son to the door to say "Daddy's out", or returning bills marked "Not known at this address") D delays his creditor. The creditor in such cases does not forgo payment but is made to wait for it.

Section 2 (3) provides that where P is induced to accept a worthless cheque in payment, as happened in *Turner*, he is to be treated as not being paid and being induced to wait for payment. Strictly the acceptance of a cheque as payment suspends the creditor's remedies until the cheque is either honoured or dishonoured; this provision, however, provides that for the purpose of s. 2 (1) (b) the creditor is induced to wait for payment.

The "existing liability" referred to in paragraph (b) (and in paragraph (a)) can be only the liability of the person who makes default.[4]

3) *Obtaining an Exemption from or an Abatement of Liability*

Section 2 (1) (c) differs from s. 2 (1) (a) and (b) in that the latter assume an existing liability and a subsequent deception, whereas (c) is concerned with a deception which induces P to confer an exemption from or abatement of a *prospective* liability.[5] The provision was explained by the CLRC[6]—

"The ratepayer who makes a false statement in order to obtain a rebate to which he is not entitled is acting dishonestly and is practising a deception in order to obtain an abatement of his liability to pay rates and, accordingly, would be guilty of an offence under clause 2 (1) (c). The wording of this provision, 'where a person by any deception . . . dishonestly obtains any exemption from or abatement of liability to make a payment' is intended to cover cases where the deception has induced the victim to believe that there is nothing due to him or that the amount due to him is less than would be the case if he knew the true facts. Another example of the application of this part of clause 2 is the case where a person by deception obtains services at a reduced rate (for example, air travel at a special rate for students when the traveller is not a student)."

3. *Holt* [1981] 2 All ER 854, [1981] 1 WLR 1000.
4. *Attewell-Hughes* [1991] 4 All ER 810, [1991] Crim LR 437, CA.
5. *Firth* (1990) 91 Cr App Rep 217, [1990] Crim LR 326, CA.
6. Cmnd. 6733, para. 15.

There is, however, a difficulty with the operation of paragraph (c) of the same nature as that which, as it has been suggested,[7] applies to paragraph (a). Suppose D, a ratepayer, makes false statements in order to secure a reduction in his rates and the rating authority accordingly assess his rates at £200 rather than the proper rateable value which is £300. D does not thereby obtain an "abatement of liability" because his liability to pay £300 continues undiminished. Of course at some stage the rating authority will make a demand for £200 and at that stage they will, as a result of the continuing deception by D, be induced to forgo part of the existing liability to pay £300 and the case falls within paragraph (b). But strictly, and though this was not the result intended by the CLRC, the case does not fall within paragraph (c) which is, on this view, likely to be of only limited application. Again the gap is not a serious one because at a later stage D will normally commit an offence under paragraph (b) and, indeed, by submitting the false claim to the rating authority he would appear to be guilty of an attempt.

In *Sibartie*,[8] however, it was held that D was guilty of an attempt to commit the offence under paragraph (c) where, on passing a ticket inspector, he flashed (i.e. held it up so briefly that the inspector could not read it) an invalid season ticket. The court said the proper approach to paragraph (c) was to consider its "ordinary meaning" and ask whether D's conduct came within that. D could be taken as representing that he was the holder of a valid ticket, that he was not under a liability to pay, and was thus trying to obtain an exemption from his liability to pay the fare. So he was but, assuming he successfully deceives the inspector, he has not persuaded the inspector to remit the liability but rather to believe there is no liability. And whatever liability D has is not in law remitted. What D has done is to persuade the inspector to forgo a payment which is due and the case falls within paragraph (b).

4) *Legally Enforceable Liability*

By s. 2 (2) an offence under s. 2 (1) may be committed only where the liability is legally enforceable.[9] The section thus has no application to a "liability" which is unenforceable because it is illegal or against public policy or is for any other reason unenforceable; a minor cannot commit an offence under this section if the transaction to which it relates is one that is unenforceable against him.

Nor does s. 2 (1) apply in relation to a liability which has not been accepted or established to pay compensation for a wrongful act or omission. "Without this provision", said the CLRC,[10]

"there would be room for argument that subsection (1) (a) of the clause applies where, for example, a person lies about the circumstances of an

---

7. See above, p. 578.
8. [1983] Crim LR 470, CA.
9. There is an existing liability notwithstanding that a court order is required before it can be enforced: *Modupe* [1991] Crim LR 530, CA.
10. Cmnd. 6733, para. 16.

accident in order to avoid the bringing of civil proceedings for negligence against him. We think that the dividing line is reached where liability is not disputed even though the amount of that liability is. On this basis it would be an offence under clause 2 (1) (a) for an antique dealer to lie about the age and value of jewellery sent to him for valuation which had been lost as a result of his admitted negligence, but not for him to lie about the circumstances of the loss in disputing an allegation of negligence. We see no justification for extending the criminal law to cases where the existence of any liability is disputed: the claimant can launch civil proceedings if he thinks he had been deceived when he absolved the other party from liability."

The "dividing line" is a fine one. The jeweller commits an offence under the section if by deception he induces P to settle on the basis that the jewellery is worth £100 when it is worth £500, but not if by deception he induces P to believe that he has not been negligent so that P drops his claim altogether.

8 Cheating

Cheating was a misdemeanour at common law and was developed most vigorously during the eighteenth century and it appears to require a large and liberal definition to encompass the authorities. Hawkins[11] defined cheating as

". . . deceitful practices, in defrauding or endeavouring to defraud another of his own right by means of some artful device, contrary to the plain rules of common honesty."

The common law offence of cheating still retains some importance because though s. 32 (1) of the Act abolishes cheating (along with common law offences against property) it does so only "except as regards offences relating to the public revenue". The punishment is imprisonment and/or a fine without limit.

As a practical matter the offence of cheating has been used, on any scale at all, only in connection with frauds against the public revenue. In *Hudson*[12] the Court of Criminal Appeal upheld D's conviction on a charge of making false statements to the prejudice of the Crown and the public revenue with intent to defraud where it appeared that D had falsely stated to the Inland Revenue the profits of his business. It was argued that the indictment disclosed no offence known to the law, but the court, relying on dicta of Lord Mansfield CJ in *Bembridge*,[13] and statements by Hawkins[14] and East,[15] held that it was an offence for a private individual, as well as a public officer, to defraud the Crown and public. The argument that there

11. 1 PC 318.
12. [1956] 2 QB 252, [1956] 1 All ER 814, discussed by "Watchful" [1956] BTR 119.
13. (1783) 22 State, Tr 1 at 156.
14. 1 PC 322.
15. 2 PC 821.

was no such offence was raised again in *Mulligan*[16] and was just as forthrightly rejected by the Court of Appeal.

The Criminal Law Revision Committee was minded to abolish the offence and its retention was the result of special pleading by the revenue authorities who wished to retain it for serious revenue frauds where penalties under other provisions were seen by them as inadequate. Perhaps, too, the revenue was attracted by the expansive terminology of Hawkins' definition. At all events the revenue's fondest hopes for cheating must have been realised by *Mavji*.[17] D had dishonestly evaded value added tax to the tune of over £1,000,000. Charged, as he might have been, under s. 38 (1) of the Finance Act 1972 with the fraudulent evasion of tax he would have been liable to a maximum of two years' imprisonment and/or a fine of £1,000 or three times the tax whichever was the greater. Convicted, as he was, of cheating he was sentenced to six years' imprisonment and made criminally bankrupt in the sum of £690,000. The Court of Appeal, affirming D's conviction and sentence, rejected counsel's submission that cheating required a positive act such as a deception and not merely an omission to make a VAT return. The court held that D was under a duty to make such a return and his failure to do so with intent to cheat the revenue of money to which it was entitled constituted the offence.

So to hold was, with respect, a novel extension of the offence. *Hudson*,[18] which was treated in *Mavji* as the leading case, appears to assume that cheating requires the use of a false representation or false device. Even the expansive language of Hawkins is conditioned by the requirement "by means of some artful device". What artful device was employed by D in *Mavji*?

9 Making off without Payment[19]

By s. 3 of the Theft Act 1978—

"(1) Subject to subsection (3) below, a person who, knowing that payment on the spot for any goods supplied or service done is required or expected from him, dishonestly makes off without having paid as required or expected and with intent to avoid payment of the amount due shall be guilty of an offence.

(2) For purposes of this section 'payment on the spot' includes payment at the time of collecting goods on which work has been done or in respect of which service has been provided.

16. [1990] Crim LR 427, CA.
17. [1987] 2 All ER 758, [1987] 1 WLR 1388, CA. *Mavji* was followed in *Redford* (1989) 89 Cr App Rep 1, CA.
18. Above.
19. See Spencer, "The Theft Act 1978" [1979] Crim LR 24, 35; Syrota, "Annotations to Theft Act 1978" in Current Law Statutes.

(3) Subsection (1) above shall not apply where the supply of the goods or the doing of the service is contrary to law, or where the service done is such that payment is not legally enforceable.

(4) Any person may arrest without warrant anyone who is, or whom he, with reasonable cause, suspects to be, committing or attempting to commit an offence under this section."

By s. 4 the offence, which is triable either way, is punishable on summary conviction by imprisonment and/or a fine not exceeding the prescribed maximum (presently £2,000), and on indictment by imprisonment for a term not exceeding two years and/or a fine.

This offence aims to deal in a simple and straightforward way with conduct commonly called "bilking' . It deals with the man who, having consumed a meal in a restaurant, or filled the tank of his car with petrol, or having reached his destination in a taxi, decamps without paying. These cases, as we have seen,[20] for all their factual simplicity create considerable difficulties in relation to offences of theft and deception. There are no such difficulties under s. 3. There is no requirement whatever that D's conduct should otherwise amount to theft or deception or even that he has practised any deception.

It might be noted that the offence creates an exception to the general principle that it is not an offence dishonestly to avoid the payment of a debt. The exception is, however, limited and understandable. In the ordinary case a dishonest debtor can be coerced into payment without employment of criminal sanctions; where bilking is involved it is usually a matter of enforcement on the spot or never. Hence by s. 3 (4) a power of arrest is conferred for, without this, the enforcement of the law would be jeopardised.

1) *Makes off*

"Makes off' might be thought of as having a pejorative connotation implying some stealth in the person making off. Certainly it extends to such cases (the diner who waits till the manager leaves the room or decamps via the cloakroom) but it cannot be confined to such cases. A motorist who drives off after filling his tank with petrol is properly said to make off though it is done openly and without stealth; so too a heavyweight boxer whose departure cannot be prevented by a timorous P. "Makes off" appears to mean simply that D leaves one place (the place where the payment is required) for another place. Nor does the offence require that D should have made off from P's premises such as an hotel or a restaurant; the spot from which D makes off is simply the place where payment is required[21] and may be a newsvendor's stand or an ice-cream van on the

---

20. See, for example, *Director of Public Prosecutions v Ray* [1974] AC 370, [1973] 3 All ER 131, HL, above, p. 559; *Edwards v Ddin* [1976] 3 All ER 705, [1976] 1 WLR 942.
21. Payment may be legitimately required at more than one spot: *Moberly v Alsop* (1991) *Times*, 13 December, DC.

highway. If D has not left the first place he has not made off but if he is in the process of leaving there may be an attempt.[1]

If D leaves with P's consent it may be more difficult to say that D has made off. Suppose that D, having determined never to pay, gives his correct name and address to P and is allowed to go. It would seem difficult to say that D had made off; D has left without paying but the offence requires something more than that. Suppose, though, that E, who also intends never to pay, gives a false name and address to P and is allowed to go. The cases differ in that D can be traced and coerced into payment while E cannot be traced at all. Spencer[2] argues that the difference is material. The mischief aimed at, he says, is the bilking customer who cannot be traced and he supports this by reference to the power of arrest afforded P; it would be highly undesirable if P could arrest a customer of whose identity he is aware, that power being required for the unidentifiable bilker.

Spencer's argument has force but is not easy to square with the language of s. 3. Assume that D is P's best customer of many years' standing. One day D determines not to pay and decamps from the premises via the lavatory window. All the elements of the offence appear to be present unless it is to be said that D did not make off. It may puzzle us all to wonder why D should have thought that he could get away with it but he seems clearly to have made off. A customer in a wheelchair would surely make off if he decamps without paying though he does not at all fancy his chances of outpacing the restaurateur.

Nor does s. 3 obviously give rise to the interpretation that D does not make off if he gives a correct identification but E does make off if he gives a false one. Suppose in the latter case that P orders a taxi for E and bids him a cheery farewell. Can it really be said that E has made off?[3]

If, however, P permits D to leave the spot where payment is required for a purely temporary purpose (for example to answer a telephone call or to collect his wallet from his overcoat which he has deposited in the cloak-room) expecting him to return to settle up, it is submitted that D commits the offence if he then decamps. In such cases P has not consented to D leaving without paying. So where P, a taxi driver, permits D to leave so that D, as he claims, may go into his house to get the fare it would appear that D, if he then decamps, has made off within the section.

2) *Goods Supplied or Service Done*

The offence requires that the goods be *supplied* or that a service be *done*. Most obviously goods are supplied where P delivers them to D but the offence cannot be limited to the case of delivery by P. Petrol is clearly

---

1. *Brooks and Brooks* (1983) 76 Cr App Rep 66, [1983] Crim LR 188, CA; making off, said the Court, "may be an exercise accompanied by the sound of trumpets or a silent stealing away after the folding of tents".
2. [1983] Crim LR 573.
3. Cf. *Hammond* [1982] Crim LR 611, below, p. 586.

supplied to D at a self-service filling station though D supplies himself and, by the same token, goods taken from the shelves in a self-service store are supplied.[4] Supplied in this context connotes goods proffered by P and accordingly taken by D. Hence it would not be an offence under this section (though it may be theft) for D to take goods in a shop which is not self-service; such goods are not proffered until tendered by P or his assistant. It is thought that goods may be supplied though D has a dishonest intent from the outset and accordingly steals the goods; it can hardly have been intended that theft and making off should be mutually exclusive since the effect would be mischievous.

Where service is concerned the service must be "done". Obvious examples of a service done is the provision of hotel accommodation or a meal in a restaurant but it will also apply to the collection of goods, such as clothes, shoes or cars, on which work has been done. A service may be done (as goods may be supplied) though nothing is done by P other than proffering the service of which D takes advantage, as where D is permitted to park his car on P's lot.

There is no definition of "service" in s. 3 as there is of "services" in s. 2 but it is not easy to see that any difference of significance was intended and reference may be made to the discussion above.

3) *Unenforceable Debts*

The offence under s. 3, unlike the offence under s. 1, cannot be committed where the supply of the goods or the doing of the service is contrary to law; or where the service done is such that payment is not legally enforceable. The reason for the distinction is that while the aim of s. 1 is to punish fraud, the aim of s. 3, as seen by the CLRC,[5] is to protect legitimate business. Thus it is no offence for D to make off from a brothel, or from a betting shop without paying for services rendered.

Whether a supply of goods or services is contrary to law or whether payment for a service is not legally enforceable involves a consideration of the general law and cannot be detailed here. But the distinction which the section makes may be illustrated by reference to an impecunious minor. If a landlord supplies intoxicating liquor to a minor the transaction is contrary to law and the minor commits no offence in making off without payment. If the minor has a service provided which is not a "necessary" (say flying lessons) he commits no offence in making off since payment for the service is not legally enforceable. If the minor is supplied with non-necessary goods (say eleven fancy waistcoats) and makes off he commits the offence; while payment for the waistcoats is not legally enforceable, the supply of these *goods* is not contrary to law.

---

4. *Contra* Griew, *Theft*, 12.09, and A. T. H. Smith [1981] Crim LR 590.
5. Cmnd. 6733, para. 19.

4) *Without Having Paid*

Normally this case presents no problems; D has either paid or he has not. But two points may be made. The first is where D pays by cheque supported by a cheque card or uses a credit card. It may be that as between D and his bank he is exceeding his authority but it is submitted that P is none the less paid. In the result it may be the bank that has to pay for the goods or service supplied by P to D but, so far as P is concerned, he is paid for he knows that, whatever the state of D's finances, he will get his money.

The second concerns payment by a worthless cheque, that is a cheque that D knows will not be met. In this case (unlike the first) P looks to D for payment and, believing that he has been paid, allows D to leave. It has been argued that a bad cheque is no more a payment than counterfeit money[6] but in *Hammond*[7] the trial judge thought there was a difference in that one who takes a cheque without a cheque card knows he is taking a risk. He further suggested that if P takes such a cheque and allows D to depart, it cannot be said that D makes off. It would follow that if P unwittingly accepts counterfeit money and allows D to depart, no more can D be said to make off.

The difficulty of the case, then, lies not so much in saying that D has left "without having paid", for a payment in counterfeit money or by a worthless cheque is not a payment, but in the effect which the apparent payment has on P. If as a result he agrees to D's departure it is difficult to say that D makes off.

5) *Mens Rea*

The offence requires that D should make off (i) dishonestly; (ii) knowing that payment on the spot is required or expected from him; and (iii) with intent to avoid payment.

1 Dishonestly

Reference may be made to the general discussion of dishonesty. It does not matter at what stage D decides to act dishonestly so long as he is dishonest when he makes off. While dishonesty is a question for the jury D would not be dishonest in refusing to pay for goods or a service genuinely believed by him to be deficient.

2 Knowing that Payment on the Spot is Required or Expected of Him

The offence is concerned only with cases where payment on the spot is required. Such transactions are difficult to define in abstract terms but

---

6. Griew, *Theft*, 12.14.
7. [1982] Crim LR 611 (Judge Morrison).

usually easy enough to identify.[8] They can be identified by regard to normal trading practices though these may in particular instances be modified by the course of dealing between the parties.[9] If D honestly believes that the transaction is on credit terms, he cannot be convicted of this offence for he is not acting dishonestly and he does not *know* the transaction to be a spot transaction. And where D believes that payment is to be made by another (for example, where he believes that E will pay for the meal) he does not commit the offence because he neither acts dishonestly nor does he know that payment is to be required of him.[10]

3 Intention to Avoid Payment

Unlike s. 2 (1)(b) of the 1978 Act with which s. 3 invites comparison, the latter does not in terms require an intention to make permanent default and commentators tended to favour the view that, and always providing that D was acting dishonestly, an intention temporarily to avoid payment would suffice. *Allen*[11] holds, and rightly it is respectfully submitted, that the offence requires an intention to make permanent default. D had left an hotel without settling his bill and the trial judge directed the jury that all that was required was an intention to make default at the time payment was required. The Court of Appeal held, however, that an intention to make permanent default was required because s. 3 required both (i) a making off without paying on the spot; and (ii) an intent to avoid payment. In view of the requirement in (i), (ii) made sense only if permanent default was intended. The House of Lords endorsed this view and drew further support for it by reference to the fact that the Criminal Law Revision Committee had intended permanent default to be necessary.[12]

10 False Accounting and Other Frauds

1) *False Accounting*

By s. 17 of the Theft Act:

"(1) Where a person dishonestly, with a view to gain for himself or another or with intent to cause loss to another,—

(a) destroys, defaces, conceals or falsifies any account or any record or document made or required for any accounting purpose; or

---

8. S. 3 (1) provides that it includes "payment at the time of collecting goods on which work has been done or in respect of which service has been provided". But this seems to have been added *ex abundanti cautela* and adds nothing. See Smith, *Theft*, para. 245.

9. It cannot be enough that P requires a payment to be made on the spot, e.g. seeing D who owes him £10 lent a month ago, P demands payment on the spot. The reference is to those transactions where payment customarily follows immediately upon the provision of the goods or service.

10. *Brooks and Brooks* (1983) 76 Cr App Rep 66, [1983] Crim LR 188, CA.

11. [1985] AC 1029, [1985] 1 All ER 148, HL.

12. Cmnd. 6733, para. 18.

(b) in furnishing information for any purpose produces or makes use of any account, or any such record or document as aforesaid, which to his knowledge is or may be misleading, false or deceptive in a material particular;

he shall, on conviction on indictment, be liable to imprisonment for a term not exceeding seven years.

(2) For purposes of this section a person who makes or concurs in making in an account or other document an entry which is or may be misleading, false or deceptive in a material particular, or who omits or concurs in omitting a material particular from an account or other document, is to be treated as falsifying the account or document."

Where D falsifies any document or record made for an accounting purpose he might often commit offences independently of this section. He might, for example, commit forgery or he might commit, or attempt to commit, an offence under s. 2 of the 1978 Act. But the offence under s. 17 is wider than forgery or evading liability in some respects.

1 Actus Reus

The offence may be committed by any person who falsifies etc. any document "made or required" for an accounting purpose. A document is "made" for an accounting purpose where that is the purpose of the document; but a document may be "required" for an accounting purpose though made for some other purpose so long as it is required, if only in part, for an accounting purpose.[13] This is understandable but in *Shama*[14] it was held that "required" extended to a document which it was D's duty to complete on completion of the transaction but which he had not filled in at all. D was an international telephone operator who, following each call, had to fill in a *separate* charge ticket, dishonestly failed to complete charge tickets in respect of certain calls. Obviously had there been a single sheet or ledger on or in which D recorded the details of all calls and D had omitted to record some calls, the document he submits to his employer would be false by reason of the omissions. The court thought it would be odd if D could escape conviction simply because each transaction was recorded in a separate document rather than in one document recording the calls seriatim. The result may be odd but it is difficult to see how a total failure to enter a transaction on a separate document falls within s. 17. Clearly D has not *made* an entry in that document for no document was ever made; nor has he omitted an entry in that document because *that* document never existed.[15]

The offence may be committed whether or not the person to whom the document is addressed accepts or acts on it.

---

13. *A–G's Reference (No. 1 of 1980)* [1981] 1 All ER 366, [1981] 1 WLR 34, CA.
14. [1990] 2 All ER 602, [1990] Crim LR 411, CA.
15. Presumably D at the end of his shift returned a bundle of charge tickets to his employers. Effectively it was his work record for the shift and was required for an accounting purpose. The "record" might be regarded as a single document though it records each transaction on a separate page; on this view the document would be false by omitting to record some of the transactions.

"Any account or any record" is wide enough to include a mechanical accounting device such as a computer, a taximeter,[16] or a turnstile which records paying customers.[17] The admission of two persons through one movement of the turnstile amounts to falsification by the omission of a material particular. The section further extends to any document, so long as it is made or required for *any* accounting purpose, though the document itself is not in the nature of an account and though the falsification does not relate to figures. So if D enters in a hire-purchase proposal false particulars relating to a company director, the case would fall within the plain words of s. 17 (1)(a). If D, or E, were to use that document in furnishing information to P, the case would fall within s. 17 (1)(b) if the information was material. The information is so material if it is something that matters to P in making up his mind about action to be taken on the document.[18] D or E may commit the offence in furnishing information not only where they know of the falsification, but also where they know that the document *may* be false or misleading in a material particular; evidently wilful blindness suffices.

But some account of P's must be falsified by D or as a result of information provided by D. It is not enough that D is, as by selling his own property as P's, cheating P if that transaction is not recorded in any account of P's.[19]

2 Mens Rea

The *mens rea* of the offence requires that D (i) intentionally or recklessly falsifies etc. the document, or so uses a document knowing [20] it is false; and (ii) does so dishonestly and with a view to gain for himself or another, or with intent to cause loss to another.

So far as dishonesty is concerned reference may be made to the discussion elsewhere. No doubt dishonesty should be interpreted here so as to accord with the meaning given it in other sections of the Act.

So far as view to gain and intent to cause loss are concerned "gain" and "loss" are defined in s. 34 (2) (a) which is discussed elsewhere.[1] In this context it may be worth emphasising that there might be a view to gain or an intent to cause loss in falsifying the account although the gain or loss has already taken place. "Gain", for instance, includes a gain by keeping what one has, so it is clear that D would commit an offence under s. 17 where, having already appropriated property of P's, he destroys, defaces, conceals or falsifies an account so that he will not be found out, or to put off the evil day when he will be called to account: *Eden*.[2] But in *Choraria and Golechha*[3] it was held that D and E did not have a view to gain where, having secured a discounting facility with the P bank for their trade bills, they presented trade bills to the bank relating to transactions that had never taken place.

---

16. Cf. *Solomons* [1909] 2 KB 980.
17. *Edwards v Toombs* [1983] Crim LR 43, DC.
18. *Mallett* [1978] 3 All ER 10, [1978] 1 WLR 820, CA.
19. *Cooke* [1986] AC 909, [1986] 2 All ER 985, HL.
20. Which may include wilful blindness as to falsity.
   1. See below, p. 611. Cf. *Lee Cheung Wing v R* [1992] Crim LR 440, PC.
   2. [1971] Crim LR 416, CA.
   3. [1989] 3 All ER 908, [1990] Crim LR 865, CA.

This was done to make the bank believe that the account was in credit and to induce the bank to forbear to sue on earlier bills which had not been falsified. "The obtainment of the desired forbearance", said the court, "neither gave the defendant, nor allowed him to retain, anything upon which he could draw, or convert into cash or goods." But the bank had asserted that it would not have advanced money had the truth been known. It is not easy to reconcile this decision with *Eden.* By putting off the evil day when D will be called to account, that is to pay tomorrow that which he would otherwise have to pay today, would seem clearly to constitute a "gain" to D.

In this connection it is worth considering the facts of *Wines,*[4] where D falsified accounts to exaggerate the profit which the radio department, of which he was in charge, was making in order to induce his employer to continue his employment. In such a case there may be no appropriation, or intended appropriation, of any money or goods belonging to the employer, but clearly D is acting dishonestly, and it seems he has both a view to gain (he does this to keep his job and its salary) and an intent to cause loss (in so far as it causes him to continue to operate an uneconomic department).

2) *False Statements by Company Directors*

Section 19 of the Act provides:

"(1) Where an officer of a body corporate or unincorporated association (or person purporting to act as such), with intent to deceive members or creditors of the body corporate or association about its affairs, publishes or concurs in publishing a written statement or account which to his knowledge is or may be misleading, false or deceptive in a material particular, he shall on conviction on indictment be liable to imprisonment for a term not exceeding seven years.

(2) For purposes of this section a person who has entered into a security for the benefit of a body corporate or association is to be treated as a creditor of it.

(3) Where the affairs of a body corporate or association are managed by its members, this section shall apply to any statement which a member publishes or concurs in publishing in connection with his functions of management as if he were an officer of the body corporate or association."

In two senses the offence created by this section is a narrow one. Firstly, it may be committed only by an officer[5] of a body corporate or unincorporated association. Secondly, it may be committed only where the intent is to deceive[6] members or creditors of the corporation or association about its affairs. But in another sense the offence is a wide one for it extends to the

---

4. [1953] 2 All ER 1497, CCA.
5. The officers of a body corporate are frequently defined in the articles or by-laws of a corporation.
6. As to intent to deceive, see *Welham v Director of Public Prosecutions* [1961] AC 103, [1960] 1 All ER 805, HL.

publication of any written statement or account which may be misleading in a material particular. It is not necessary to show that there is any view to gain or intent to cause loss in publishing the statement or account, though no doubt either or both will often be present. The offence might be committed where an officer, in order to inspire confidence in the company, falsely publishes that a well-known person has been appointed to the board. Possibly the offence might be committed where an officer publishes in the accounts a payment as having been made to the Conservative Party where it has in fact been paid to the Labour Party.

3) *Suppression of Documents*

By s. 20:

"(1) A person who dishonestly, with a view to gain for himself or another or with intent to cause loss to another, destroys, defaces or conceals any valuable security, any will or other testamentary document or any original document of or belonging to, or filed or deposited in, any court of justice or any government department shall on conviction on indictment be liable to imprisonment for a term not exceeding seven years.

This provision is not likely to be of great practical importance; it was included because—

"It seemed to us that it might provide the only way of dealing with a person who, for example, suppressed a public document as a first step towards committing a fraud but did not get so far as attempting to commit the fraud. In accordance with the scheme of the [Act] the offence is limited to something done dishonestly and with a view to gain or with intent to cause loss to another."[7]

4) *Procuring the Execution of a Valuable Security*

By s. 20:

"(2) A person who dishonestly, with a view to gain for himself or another or with intent to cause loss to another, by any deception procures the execution of a valuable security shall on conviction on indictment be liable to imprisonment for a term not exceeding seven years; and this subsection shall apply in relation to the making, acceptance, indorsement, alteration, cancellation or destruction in whole or in part of a valuable security, and in relation to the signing or sealing of any paper or other material in order that it may be made or converted into, or used or dealt with as, a valuable security, as if that were the execution of a valuable security.

7. Cmnd. 2977, para. 106.

(3) For purposes of this section 'deception' has the same meaning as in section 15 of this Act, and 'valuable security' means any document creating, transferring, surrendering or releasing any right to, in or over property, or authorising the payment of money or delivery of any property, or evidencing the creation, transfer, surrender or release of any such right, or the payment of money or delivery of any property, or the satisfaction of any obligation."

In *Danger* (1857)[8] D made out a bill of exchange payable to himself and then by deception induced P to accept it. D was convicted under a provision[9] which made it an offence "by any false pretence [to] obtain . . . from any other person any chattel, money or valuable security". D's conviction was quashed. All D obtained was P's signature, the property in the document remained in D throughout. Parliament quickly moved to fill this gap in the law and, with subsequent amendments enlarging its ambit, s. 20 is the successor to the original provision.[10] D in *Danger* would now obviously fall foul of this provision and the offence would be complete when P accepted the bill of exchange by signing it. But s. 20 extends to the "execution" of a valuable security and this applies to its "making, acceptance, indorsement, alteration, cancellation or destruction". The reach of this provision was considered by the House of Lords in *Kassim*.[11]

D opened an account at the P bank in a false name and address. In this name D was given cheque books, a cheque guarantee card and an Access card. Not surprisingly D went on a spending spree and when he was apprehended he had overdrawn on the account by £8,338 and had a debit on the Access card of £943. The P bank was of course obliged to foot the bill.

D was charged with, and convicted of, offences under s. 20. On appeal his argument, a restrictive view of s. 20, was that "execution" required that P should do something to the face of the document. This restrictive view was supported by academic opinion.[12] While this restrictive view is obviously correct to the extent that inducing P by deception to make, accept, indorse etc a valuable security clearly falls within the offence, the Crown argued for the wider view that "execution" extended to giving effect to or carrying out the terms of the document, in this case by meeting the obligations by honouring the cheques and the Access payments. This view was supported by decisions of the Court of Appeal in *Beck*[13] and in *Kassim*[14] though that court had appeared to favour the restrictive view in *Nanayakkara*.[15]

The House of Lords came down in favour of the narrower view. Lord Ackner said:[16]

8. 7 Cox CC 303, CCR.
9. 7 & 8 Geo 4, cap 29, s. 53.
10. An account of the legislative history of s. 20 is given in *Kassim* [1991] 3 All ER 713 at 717.
11. Last note.
12. By Griew, *Theft*, 11-15–11.18, endorsed by Smith, *Theft*, para. 270.
13. [1985] 1 All ER 571, [1985] 1 WLR 22, CA.
14. [1988] Crim LR 372, CAL
15. [1987] 1 All ER 650, [1987] 1 WLR 265.
16. [1991] 3 All ER 713 at 720.

"I respectfully agree with the Court of Appeal's decision in the *Nanayakkara* case that the 1968 Act was not intended to make any changes in the law and that 'acceptance' does not have the wide meaning attributed to it in *R v Beck* but has a narrower technical meaning. It refers to the drawee's act of writing on the bill and signing his assent to the order of the drawer.

It is however also clear from the legislative history of s. 20 (2) that 'execution' . . . has as its object a wide variety of documents including bills of exchange and other negotiable instruments. The subsection contemplates acts being done to or in connection with such documents. It does not contemplate and accordingly is not concerned with giving effect to the documents by the carrying out of the instructions which they may contain, such as the delivery of goods or the payment out of money."

Kassim clarifies the interpretation of s. 20 (2) in an important respect but there are further difficulties with the interpretation of s. 20 (3). In *Benstead and Taylor*[17] it was held that an irrevocable letter of credit[18] was a valuable security within s. 20 (3) because it created a right in property. The decision has been criticised.[19] because "any right to, in or over property" assumes some existing property to which the document gives to D, the beneficiary, a right. A letter of credit creates a right (D may draw on the credit) but it is not a right to, in or over property.

In *King*[20] D and others colluded in a fraud on the P bank whereby P was induced to make mortgage advances on false valuations of the property. P authorised payment in each case by issuing a clearing house automated payment order (a CHAPS order). The court, affirming the convictions of the defendants held that the CHAPS order was a valuable security but this conclusion is open to the same objections as in *Benstead*. Like the letter of credit the CHAPS order created a right but it did not create a right to, in or over property.[1]

11 Temporary Deprivation

In general it is not an offence dishonestly to use the property of another unless there is an intention to deprive the other permanently of the property. There is a case to be made out for creating a general offence (which need not necessarily be termed theft) of dishonest use, but the Criminal Law Revision Committee decided against any such course and

17. (1982) 75 Cr App Rep 276, [1982] Crim LR 456, CA.
18. A letter of credit is an order usually written by one banker to another requiring the other to give credit up to the amount specified in the order to the beneficiary named in the order.
19. By Smith, *Theft*, para. 272.
20. [1992] 1 QB 20, [1991] Crim LR 906, CA.
1. In *Kassim* [1991] 3 All ER 713 at 721, Lord Ackner expressed his approval of *King* but his approval was concerned with whether the CHAPS order was "executed" as clearly it had when it was signed by officials of the P bank.

their view, though subject to vigorous assault in Parliament, was accepted. The Committee were of the opinion – and, it is submitted, were quite rightly of the opinion – that such a considerable extension of the criminal law was not called for by any existing serious evil.[2] But there are particular cases in which temporary deprivation of property is a serious evil. The taking of motor vehicles (which was first made an offence by s. 28 of the Road Traffic Act 1930) is one obvious instance; and the taking of vessels (which was first made an offence by s. 1 of the Vessels Protection Act 1967) is another. These offences are now dealt with in s. 12 of the Theft Act which extends the offence to a much wider range of conveyances.

To the offence of taking conveyances the Theft Act adds a further and new offence of temporary deprivation; that of removing articles from places open to the public. Before the Act there had been a number of notorious "removals" such as the removal from the National Gallery of Goya's portrait of the Duke of Wellington, and the Committee thought the problem "serious enough to justify the creation of a special offence".[3]

1) *Removal of Articles from Places Open to the Public*

Section II of the Theft Act 1968 provides:

"(1) Subject to subsections (2) and (3) below, where the public have access to a building in order to view the building or part of it, or a collection or part of a collection housed in it, any person who without lawful authority removes from the building or its grounds the whole or part of any article displayed or kept for display to the public in the building or that part of it or in its grounds shall be guilty of an offence. For this purpose 'collection' includes a collection got together for a temporary purpose, but references in this section to a collection do not apply to a collection made or exhibited for the purpose of effecting sales or other commercial dealings.

(2) It is immaterial for purposes of subsection (1) above, that the public's access to a building is limited to a particular period or particular occasion; but where anything removed from a building or its grounds is there otherwise than as forming part of, or being on loan for exhibition with, a collection intended for permanent exhibition to the public, the person removing it does not thereby commit an offence under this section unless he removes it on a day when the public have access to the building as mentioned in subsection (1) above.

(3) A person does not commit an offence under this section if he believes that he has lawful authority for the removal of the thing in question or that he would have it if the person entitled to give it knew of the removal and the circumstances of it.

---

2. Cmnd. 2977, para. 56.
3. Ibid, para. 57 (ii).

(4) A person guilty of an offence under this section shall, on conviction on indictment, be liable to imprisonment for a term not exceeding five years."

1 Actus Reus

On the face of it the offence under s. 11 is one of some complexity; the intention was to deal with a specific mischief and care has been taken to confine the operation of the section to that mischief. The following points arise for consideration.

a) *Public access to a building in order to view.* The public must have access to the building and the access must be *in order* to view the building (or part of the building) or a collection (or part of a collection) housed in it. The public might have access to a building (a shopping precinct or arcade for example) where collections are from time to time exhibited in the lanes connecting the shops; but here access exists in order to shop and it is only incidental to access that the public may view the collection. If, however, the collection is housed in a part of the precinct and access is given to that part so that a collection may be viewed, it would be within the section.

Access must be public access; access limited to a particular section of the public will not suffice.[4] It does not matter that the public are required to pay for the privilege of access, whether the purpose of imposing the charge is merely to cover expenses or to make a profit.[5] But the access must be to a building or part thereof. So if D removes a statuette displayed in the open in a municipal park this would not be within the section. If, however, the park consists of a building and its grounds, and the public have access to the building in order to view, D's removal of the statuette would be within this section.

Normally, no doubt, D will have entered in consequence of the owner's invitation[6] to the public to view. But, so long as the public have access to view, D may commit the offence although he entered as a trespasser, or although he is the owner's guest and is temporarily residing in the building.

b) *Articles displayed or kept for display.* The offence proscribes the removal of any articles displayed or kept for display, and is not confined to works of art. The coronation stone in Westminster Abbey (something which the Committee expressly considered[7]) is clearly for this purpose an article displayed to the public though it is not a work of art. The criterion is only whether the article, which may be priceless in either sense of the term, is displayed or kept for display to the public.

"Display" here is presumably used in the sense of exhibit and not merely in the sense of able to be seen; the article must be displayed or exhibited *to the public*.[8] Consequently the removal of a fire extinguisher would not be

4. But the exclusion of a particular class, for example, the exclusion of children from an exhibition considered unsuitable for them, would not prevent access being public access.
5. But see below, p. 596.
6. *Barr* [1978] Crim LR 244 (Deputy Judge Lowry) and commentary.
7. Cmnd. 2977. Cp. *Barr* [1978] Crim LR 244, CA.
8. So linked in *Barr*.

within the section even though it can be seen by members of the public,[9] but it would be within the section if the fire extinguisher was exhibited as an example of an early type of extinguisher, or was in fact an up-to-date extinguisher which was exhibited as an example of good design.

It is enough that the article, though not displayed, is "kept" for display, as where a painting is kept in the gallery's store-room.[10]

c) *Removal.* To complete the offence the article must be removed from the building or from its grounds. But the removal, as s. 11 (2) makes clear, need not be during the times at which the public have access. If the collection is permanently[11] exhibited (which would be the case, for example, with municipal galleries and museums) removal at any time, even on a bank holiday when the building is closed to the public, may amount to an offence. But if the exhibition is temporary only, the removal must take place on a day when the public have access to the building in order to view.

d) *Commercial exhibitions.* As has been seen,[12] s. 11 applies notwithstanding that the owner charges the public for admission, and even though he admits the public only to make profit. But, whether the owner charges for admission or not, the section does not apply where the owner admits the public only to view a collection,[13] where the collection is "made or exhibited for the purpose of effecting sales or other commercial dealings".

It may seem odd that the law draws this distinction between exhibitions for commercial and non-commercial purposes. The reason given for it is that, but for this restriction upon the offence, it would be very wide indeed, and would have created a very substantial exception to the general principle that temporary deprivation should not be a criminal offence.[14] It would have meant, for example, that a removal from the premises of the ordinary commercial bookseller would have been an offence.

As it stands the limitation applies only where the collection is made or exhibited *for the purpose* of sale or other commercial dealings. If then a commercial bookseller, for the purpose of encouraging local art, arranges exhibitions in a room of his bookshop to which the public are admitted, the removal by D of the paintings, or of any other article displayed or kept for display in his premises, would fall within the section. Nor can it make any difference that the artists themselves hope that the exhibition of their work will lead to its sale.

---

9. Cf. Smith, *Theft*, 279.
10. Cf. *Durkin* [1973] QB 786, [1973] 2 All ER 872, CA.
11. In this context "permanently" means for an indefinite period: *Durkin* [1973] 1 QB 786, [1973] 2 All ER 872, CA.
12. Above, p. 595.
13. Note that if the owner admits the public to view the building as well as the collection D may commit the offence by removing anything displayed (including articles forming part of the collection) although the collection is exhibited for commercial purposes. Cf. Smith, *Theft*, para. 284.
14. The clause as originally drafted would have excluded not only the case where the public was invited to view the contents for a commercial object, but also where the public was invited to view the building for a commercial object. The latter limitation was removed; cf. last footnote.

2 Mens Rea

D must intend to remove the article from the building or its grounds. Dishonesty is not required but D would not be guilty of an offence if he removed an article in the belief (and clearly the test of D's belief is here subjective) that he had lawful authority or that the person entitled to give consent would have done so.[15] Strictly it would be an offence for D to remove a statuette from the house to the garden because he thinks the setting better, provided he believes the person entitled to give consent would not have done so.

2) *Taking Conveyances*[16]

Section 12 of the Theft Act 1968 provides:

"(1) Subject to subsections (5) and (6) below, a person shall be guilty of an offence if, without having the consent of the owner or other lawful authority, he takes any conveyance for his own or another's use or, knowing that any conveyance has been taken without such authority, drives it or allows himself to be carried in or on it.

(2) A person guilty of an offence under subsection (1) above shall be liable on summary conviction to a fine not exceeding level 5 on the standard scale, to imprisonment for a term not exceeding six months, or to both.

(3) [Repealed.]

(4) If on the trial of an indictment for theft the jury are not satisfied that the accused committed theft, but it is proved that the accused committed an offence under subsection (1) above, the jury may find him guilty of the offence under subsection (1) and if he is found guilty of it, he shall be liable as he would have been liable under subsection (2) above on summary conviction.

(5) Subsection (1) above shall not apply in relation to pedal cycles; but, subject to subsection (6) below, a person who, without having the consent of the owner or other lawful authority, takes a pedal cycle for his own or another's use, or rides a pedal cycle knowing it to have been taken without such authority, shall on summary conviction be liable to a fine not exceeding level 3 on the standard scale.

(6) A person does not commit an offence under this section by anything done in the belief that he has lawful authority to do it or that he would have the owner's consent if the owner knew of his doing it and the circumstances of it.

(7) For purposes of this section—

(a) 'conveyance' means any conveyance constructed or adapted for the carriage of a person or persons whether by land, water or air, except that it does not include a conveyance constructed or

15. See further in connection with the offences under s. 12; below, p. 600.
16. See White, "Taking the Joy out of Joy-Riding" [1980] Crim LR 609.

adapted for use only under the control of a person not carried in or on it, and 'drive' shall be construed accordingly; and

(b) 'owner', in relation to a conveyance which is the subject of a hiring agreement or hire-purchase agreement, means the person in possession of the conveyance under that agreement."

1 Taking for Own or Another's Use

The offence is committed where D "takes any conveyance for his own or another's use." It is not enough that D uses the conveyance for some purpose (say to sleep or shelter in it) since he must also take it. It has accordingly been held that the offence can be completed only by a taking, that is some movement, however slight, of the conveyance.[17] In the case of a motor vehicle the taking will be most frequently accomplished by driving but the taking may be accomplished in some other way, as by pushing or towing or even by removing the conveyance on a transporter. In *Pearce*[18] D's conviction was upheld when he took an inflatable dinghy and drove off with it on his trailer; the court rejecting an argument that the offence could be committed only where D took the conveyance by moving it in its own medium. The essence of the offence was thought by the Criminal Law Revision Committee to be stealing a ride.[19] Strictly, however, D may steal a ride without committing this offence. A hitch-hiker who jumps on to the back of a passing lorry literally steals a ride but does not commit the offence since in no sense has he *taken* the vehicle for his own or another's use. So too if D, without boarding the conveyance, releases the handbrake of a car so that it runs down an incline, or releases a boat from its moorings so that it is carried away by the tide, this would not fall within the section.[20] In neither case is the conveyance taken by D for his own or another's use.

Considering these last two examples the Court of Appeal in *Bow*[1] expressed the firm view that the reason why D was not guilty of an offence was that although the conveyance had been moved, it would not have been used as a conveyance. In other words "use" means, and means only, use as a conveyance. No doubt in the vast majority of cases D's purpose in taking the conveyance is to betake himself from one place to another but it is not entirely clear that the offence is, or ought to be, confined to such takings. In *Pearce* it does not clearly appear why D took the dinghy but in *Marchant and McCallister*[2] the Court of Appeal assumed that the conviction was based on D's intended use of the dinghy as a conveyance and confirmed that taking a conveyance with intent to use it on some future occasion as a conveyance sufficed.[3] *Bow* suggests, and *Marchant* appears clearly to

---

17. *Bogacki* [1973] QB 832, [1973] 2 All ER 864, CA. Cf. *Miller* [1976] Crim LR 147, CA and *Diggin* (1980) 72 Cr App Rep 204, [1980] Crim LR 656, CA. Without actual movement there may be an attempt to take.
18. [1973] Crim LR 321, CA.
19. Cmnd. 2977, para. 84.
20. Even though the owner temporarily loses the use of his car or boat and is equally inconvenienced.
  1. (1977) 64 Cr App Rep 54, [1977] Crim LR 176 and commentary; **SHC 474**.
  2. (1985) 80 Cr App Rep 361.
  3. Equally a conditional intent (e.g. an intent to use should it prove suitable) will suffice.

confirm, that if D in *Pearce* had some use other than use as a conveyance in mind (e.g. to use it as a paddling pool for his children) he could not be convicted under s. 12. *Stokes*[4] is to the same effect. There it was held that D did not commit the offence where he pushed P's car around the corner to make P think it had been stolen.[5] The courts have interpreted s. 12 (1) as though the words "as a conveyance" had been inserted after "use". But on the face of it "use" is capable of extending to uses other than use as a conveyance.[6] The mischief aimed at is surely that the use of the conveyance is denied to P and it can be of no account to him to what use D puts it.

Even if use is restricted to use as a conveyance any such use suffices. It is enough that D releases a boat from its moorings so that he can be carried downstream in it.

So in *Bow*, where D released the handbrake of P's car and coasted some 200 yards down a narrow road in order to make egress for his own car, it was conceded that no distinction could be drawn between driving the motor and allowing it to coast. But it was argued that D had not used the car as a conveyance, merely to move it as an obstruction. The court accepted that to push an obstructing vehicle a yard or two to get it out of the way would not involve the use of the vehicle as a conveyance,[7] but where the vehicle was necessarily used as a conveyance, the taker cannot be heard to say that it was not for that use. Yet D did not use P's car in order to convey himself from one end of the lane to the other. It so happened that to remove it as an obstruction required its removal not for 2 yards but for 200. It is not easy to see why, if all D is doing is to remove a conveyance as an obstruction, the distance involved should make all that difference.[8]

Thus far it has been assumed that D is not in possession or control of the conveyance but it may happen that D already has lawful possession or control and the question arises whether D can be said to "take" the conveyance by using it in an unauthorised way. Suppose, for example, that D, authorised to use P's van in the course of P's business, uses the van to take his family to the seaside. It seems clear that under this section he may commit the offence for he now "takes [the van] for his own . . . use". D does not have the consent of P for the taking for his own use. This was the view taken by the Court of Appeal in *McGill*,[9] a case decided under s. 217 of the Road Traffic Act 1960. D, given permission to use P's car to drive E to the station and on condition that he returned it immediately, subsequently drove it elsewhere and did not return it for some days. D's conviction for taking the car without the consent of the owner, in relation to his use after the trip to the station, was upheld. The same result must follow under this provision of the Theft Act where there is no requirement for driving away

4. [1983] RTR 59, LA.
5. The outcome of the case may have been different had D got into the car and steered it round the corner.
6. See White, op. cit. at p. 611.
7. In such circumstances D might in any case have lawful authority for the removal, see below, p. 600.
8. In *Bow* D was probably engaged in a poaching expedition and P's car had been deliberately placed to block D's egress. But if D finds a vehicle blocking the highway he is presumably entitled to remove it whether he is on his way to or from a crime.
9. [1970] RTR 209, CA.

and where the emphasis is squarely placed on taking "for his own or another's use". So in *McKnight v Davies*[10] the conviction of a lorry driver was upheld when instead of returning the lorry to the depot at the end of the working day he used it for his own purposes and did not return it till the early hours of the following morning.

McGill and *McKnight v Davies* were cases where the use by D was wholly at variance with the terms of the bailment or the terms of the employment so there was no difficulty in finding a taking for D's own use. It is thought, however, that not every deviation by a bailee from the terms of the bailment, or of an employee from the terms of his employment, would constitute a taking for his own use. There must be a use which is so at variance with the terms of the contract as to show that D has replaced use on behalf of another by use on his own behalf.[11] But there is an exception in the case of a hirer under a hire-purchase agreement. His unauthorised use cannot amount to an offence because by s. 12 (7) he is treated as owner for the purposes of the section.

2 Without Owner's Consent or Lawful Authority

The ordinary run of case where D takes P's vehicle without reference to P presents no problem. It follows from the discussion in the previous paragraph that where D has made reference to P, and has obtained P's permission to use the vehicle for a particular purpose and for a given time, D may be convicted of the offence if he uses it beyond that time for a different purpose: *McGill*.[12] There is no difficulty in such a case in saying that D has taken the vehicle for his own use, and that particular use is clearly one to which P has not consented.

McGill is a clear case. Suppose, however, that D had falsely represented that he was licensed to drive in order to borrow P's car for the trip to the station. There is perhaps no compelling reason why D should not be guilty of the offence since he knows perfectly well that P has "consented" only because he has been misled. But on a strict interpretation of the section all that is required is that P should have consented to D taking the car for the trip to the station (the taking for D's own use) and to this P may be said to have consented even though he would never have consented had he known that D was unlicensed. The point arose in *Whittaker v Campbell*.[13] D and E required a vehicle to transport goods but D was not licensed to drive and E had only a provisional licence. Somehow they came into possession of T's licence and D, representing himself as T, hired a vehicle from P. Their convictions for taking a vehicle without consent were quashed. The court

---

10. [1974] RTR 4, DC; **SHC 476**.
11. "Not every brief, unauthorised diversion from his proper route by an employee in the course of his working day will necessarily involve a 'taking' of the vehicle for his own use.": *McKnight v Davies* [1974] RTR 4 at 8, per Lord Widgery CJ. See also *Wibberley* [1966] 2 QB 214, [1965] 3 All ER 718, CCA; *Phipps* [1970] RTR 209, CA. In determining whether an employee has taken his employers' vehicle it would seem proper to consider whether for civil purposes D is acting in the course of his employment.
12. [1970] RTR 209, CA; above.
13. [1984] QB 318, [1983] 3 All ER 582, DC; **SHC 478**.

thought that while there might be a taking without consent where the owner is by force compelled to part with possession, where he is induced to do so by fraud it could not be said "in commonsense terms" that he had not consented to the taking. The court then considered whether the offence would be committed where the fraud is such as to induce a fundamental mistake and thought that it would not make sense, having regard to the mischief at which the offence was aimed, to have D's liability turn upon whether the transaction was voidable for fraud or void for mistake. The distinction, as students of the law of contract will know, is a troublesome one and on the "commonsense" view there may be something to be said for not burdening students of the criminal law with it. But suppose that D personates P's brother on the telephone and induces P to agree the loan of his car to his brother and to leave the keys in an accessible spot while P is out of town. If D then avails himself of his trick to take possession of the car while P is away, it would be an astonishing conclusion to say that P had consented to D taking his car.

In *Whittaker v Campbell* there was no suggestion of any misrepresentation as to the use to which D and E proposed to put the vehicle and their actual use was within the terms of the hire.[14] Suppose, however, that D obtains possession by specifying a use to which he knows P will consent while having in mind a use to which he knows P would not consent. D might, for example, secure P's consent to the use of his vehicle for the transportation of goods from Leeds to London knowing that P would not consent had he known that the goods were stolen. The case is essentially indistinguishable from *Whittaker v Campbell*. P has consented to the use of his vehicle for that journey though he would not have agreed to incur criminal liability as a handler of stolen goods. Suppose, though, that D's purpose is not to drive to London and back but to take the vehicle on a fortnight's holiday to the south of France. The point arose in *Peart*.[15] D persuaded P to lend him a van by pretending that he needed it for an urgent appointment in Alnwick and that he would return it by 7.30 p.m. In fact D wanted the van for a journey to Burnley where he was found with the van by the police at 9.00 p.m., and he knew all along that P would not have consented to this use. It was held, quashing D's conviction, that P's consent was not vitiated by the deception since P had merely been deceived as to the purpose for which the car was to be used and reliance was placed on this decision by the court in *Whittaker v Campbell*.

But there are difficulties with *Peart*. By reason of the direction given to the jury by the trial judge, the Court of Appeal had to consider the position at the time when the van was borrowed in the afternoon –

"There was no issue left to [the jury] whether, in this particular case, there could have been a fresh taking ... at some time after it was

14. In *Singh v Rathour (Northern Star Insurance Co Ltd, third party)* [1988] 2 All ER 16, CA, a civil case where the issue was whether D was insured under his policy which covered him when driving any vehicle "provided he had the consent of the owner", it was held that D did not have the consent of the owner where he was aware that the consent given did not extend to the use to which he put the vehicle.
15. [1970] 2 QB 672, [1970] 2 All ER 823, CA.

originally taken away at 2.30 p.m. The consent which has to be considered is thus a consent at the time of taking possession of the van with licence to drive and use it."[16]

It seems then that even if he did not commit an offence at the time of the taking he would, like the defendants in *McGill* and *McKnight v Davies*,[17] have done so as soon as he departed from the Alnwick road and set course for Burnley. There is, however, a difference. In *McGill* and *McKnight v Davies* there was no evidence that the defendants had the unauthorised use in mind when they obtained possession but that proof was not lacking in *Peart* – D frankly admitted it – and it is submitted the case ought to be reconsidered. *Given* the use for a journey to which P had consented, D *took* it for a journey for which no consent was given. As a practical matter it will often be necessary to prove a departure from the stated use in order to prove that D intended to use the vehicle in other than the authorised way but this cannot affect the substantive law.

D commits no offence where he takes a vehicle, even without the consent of the owner, when acting under "other lawful authority". This is appropriate to cover cases where local authorities or the police are authorised under various statutory powers to remove vehicles. No doubt D would be acting lawfully in moving P's vehicle a few yards so that he can obtain access to the highway for his own vehicle, even though he may know that P does not consent to the removal.[18]

It may fairly be assumed that general defences such as self-defence and duress are available on a charge of this offence.

3 Conveyance

"Conveyance" as defined by s. 12 (7) (a) has been held to contemplate a mechanical contrivance of some kind. While it includes such conveyances as cars and motor-cycles, it does not include horses;[19] horses are clearly not constructed, though they may be suitable, for the carriage of persons, and the argument that they might be adapted by the use of halter and bridle was rejected.

Because the essence of the offence was thought to be stealing a ride,[20] conveyance is defined, in effect, to exclude conveyances which are not meant for riding.[1] Thus, though it would be an offence to take an aircraft, hovercraft or railway engine, it is not an offence within this section to take a handcart or certain kinds of milk-float which, though power driven, are operated by a person who is not carried in or on it. A bath chair may fall within the definition but not a perambulator.

---

16. [1970] 2 All ER 823 at 824. It seems surprising that the proviso was not applied.
17. Above, p. 600.
18. But see *Bow* (1977) 64 Cr App Rep 54, CA, above, p. 599.
19. *Neal v Gribble* (1978) 68 Cr App Rep 9, [1978] RTR 409.
20. Cf. Cmnd. 2977, para. 84. Earlier (para. 82) the Committee seemed to have viewed the mischief of the offence as the danger, loss and inconvenience which often result from it. See Hansard, H.L. Vol. 290, col. 141.
  1. But on this see above, p. 598.

4 Driving or Being Carried

Where D takes a conveyance without consent or other lawful authority, it is an offence for E, knowing the conveyance has been so taken, to drive it or allow himself to be carried in or on it. A hitch-hiker would not be guilty of an offence where, unknown to him, the driver is using his employer's van, contrary to his instructions, to go to Blackpool for the day. If the driver tells the hitch-hiker that he is so using the van then the hitch-hiker will be liable if he allows himself to be carried further.[2] E's mere presence in the conveyance, knowing that it has been taken without consent or authority, does not suffice unless he allows himself to be "carried" in or on it and this requires some movement of the conveyance.[3]

It could happen that D believes he has authority to take the conveyance but E knows he has not. In such a case E would be guilty of an offence since he knows it was taken without authority. And no doubt E knows the conveyance has been taken without authority, and may be convicted under this provision, though he knows that D has in fact stolen the conveyance.[4]

5 Pedal Cycles

Section 12 (5) creates an offence of taking pedal cycles which is broadly similar in its incidents to the offence under s. 12 (1). A small difference is that the offence under 12 (5) is not committed by one who allows himself to be carried on the cycle knowing that it has been taken without authority. And, of course, the offence is summary only.

6 Mens Rea

Section 12 (6) provides that a person does not commit an offence by anything done in the belief that he has lawful authority to do it or that the owner would have consented. The test of belief appears clearly to be subjective. If D honestly believes that P has consented to his use of P's car, it is not relevant to inquire whether P did in fact consent or whether P would have consented had he known that D was uninsured,[5] or even that D was unlicensed to drive. If D takes a vehicle "without having the consent of the owner" and does not believe that the owner would have consented had he known of the taking, he may be convicted though the owner subsequently says that he would have consented;[6] the offence is constituted not by taking a conveyance without the owner's consent, but in taking it without *having* the consent of the owner. If D takes a conveyance not caring whether the owner would or would not have consented, it would seem that he may be convicted for, in such a case, he does not *believe* that the owner would have consented. But where E is charged with driving or allowing himself to be carried in a conveyance taken by D, it must be shown that E *knew* that D had taken the conveyance without authority; presumably

---

2. *Boldizsar v Knight* [1980] Crim LR 653, DC.
3. *Miller* [1976] Crim LR 147, CA; *Diggin* (1980) 72 Cr App Rep 204, [1981] RTR 83, CA.
4. Cf. *Tolley v Giddings* [1964] 2 QB 354, [1964] 1 All ER 201, DC.
5. *Clotworthy* [1981] RTR 477, CA.
6. *Ambler* [1979] RTR 217, CA.

wilful blindness on E's part will suffice but it may be[7] that nothing short of actual knowledge will suffice. Hence E would be acquitted where he thinks it quite possible that D might have taken the vehicle without authority but makes no inquiries to ascertain whether this is so or not.

Taking a conveyance has been held to be a crime of basic intent so that evidence of intoxication is not relevant as tending to show that D lacked mens rea.[8]

3) *Aggravated Vehicle Taking*

The so-called "joyrider" (or "twocker") is liable to a fine not exceeding level 5 on the standard scale and/or six months' imprisonment under s. 12. The same penalties apply to any person who, knowing that the conveyance has been taken without consent, drives the vehicle or allows himself to be carried in or on it.

The taker is additionally liable for any offence involved in taking the vehicle (most obviously criminal damage caused in making access to the conveyance and in interfering with the locks and the electrics in order to get it started) and the driver, whether or not he is the original taker, is liable for any offence committed whilst driving the vehicle (e.g. driving whilst uninsured, careless driving, dangerous driving). And, of course, a person who allows himself to be carried in or on a conveyance may be liable as a secondary party to these further offences under the principles which govern aiding and abetting.[9]

It might be thought that the existing law was entirely adequate to deal with the taker, those who subsequently drive the taken conveyance and those who allow themselves to be carried in or on it. In the normal case the fine of £2,000 and/or six months' imprisonment is adequate. In the abnormal case where the driver drives dangerously, or kills whilst driving dangerously, a count can be added for that and again the punishment (imprisonment for two or five years respectively) would seem to be adequate.

But the abnormal case is not now so abnormal. The taking of motor vehicles has apparently increased to an extent that has been described as epidemic. And, so it is said, have the risks. Young lads (the takers are usually young lads) create additional hazards by using the vehicle to demonstrate their driving "skills" or become involved in high speed chases when pursued by the police. The hazards of either are obvious.

Even so, it might be countered, the existing law is adequate in the sense that the penalties provided for, say, dangerous driving or causing death by

---

7. Cf. *Tolley v Giddings* [1964] 2 QB 354, [1964] 1 All ER 201. Cf. the offence of handling; below, p. 650.

8. *MacPherson* [1973] RTR 157, CA; *Gannon* (1988) 87 Cr App Rep 254, CA. For a contrary view see White, op. cit. at p. 618.

9. Above, p. 126.

dangerous driving provide a sufficient penalty for these offences.[10] But there is another problem which concerns proof. Was it D or E or F who damaged the vehicle? One or more of them may claim that the damage was done before he joined the enterprise. And where, as not infrequently happens, the vehicle is found burned out, all three say that this must have been done by someone else after they had abandoned the vehicle.

It is to deal with these problems and what is seen as a rapidly growing social menace that s. 12A of the Theft Act 1968, as inserted by the Aggravated Vehicle-Taking Act 1992 provides:

"**12A.**—(1) Subject to subsection (3) below, a person is guilty of aggravated taking of a vehicle if—

(a) he commits an offence under section 12 (1) above (in this section referred to as a "basic offence") in relation to a mechanically propelled vehicle; and

(b) it is proved that, at any time after the vehicle was unlawfully taken (whether by him or another) and before it was recovered, the vehicle was driven, or injury or damage was caused, in one or more of the circumstances set out in paragraphs (a) to (d) of subsection (2) below.

(2) The circumstances referred to in subsection (1)(b) above are—

(a) that the vehicle was driven dangerously on a road or other public place;

(b) that, owing to the driving of the vehicle, an accident occurred by which injury was caused to any person;

(c) that, owing to the driving of the vehicle, an accident occurred by which damage was caused to any property, other than the vehicle;

(d) that damage was caused to the vehicle.

(3) A person is not guilty of an offence under this section if he proves that, as regards any such proven driving, injury or damage as is referred to in subsection (1)(b) above, either—

(a) the driving, accident or damage referred to in subsection (2) above occurred before he committed the basic offence; or

(b) he was neither in nor on nor in the immediate vicinity of the vehicle when that driving, accident or damage occurred.

(4) A person guilty of an offence under this section shall be liable on conviction on indictment to imprisonment for a term not exceeding two years or, if it is proved that, in circumstances falling within subsection (2)(b) above, the accident caused the death of the person concerned, five years.[11]

(5) If a person who is charged with an offence under this section is found not guilty of that offence but it is proved that he committed a basic offence, he may be convicted of the basic offence."

The offence has features which depart markedly from the principles which ordinarily govern liability at least for serious crimes.

10. It is not suggested that the answer or solution lies in the penalty, merely that the penalty is adequate in relation to the crime. The answer lies in a foolproof (or is it expert-proof?) immobilising device.
11. But if the offender is under 17, as most seem to be, the maximum is one year's youth custody.

The prosecution must first prove that D has committed the basic offence (i.e. the offence under s. 12 (1) of the 1968 Act which is described above) in relation to a mechanically propelled vehicle—the offence does not apply to conveyances generally.

Secondly, the prosecution must prove that at any time after the vehicle was unlawfully taken (proof of the identity of the taker is not required) and before it was recovered (i.e. restored to the owner or other lawful custody: s. 12A (8)) the vehicle was driven or injury or damage was caused in one or more of the circumstances specified in s. 12A (2). These circumstances, apart from dangerous driving which requires a measure of fault,[12] require no proof of fault on the part of D, or D and others involved in the enterprise, merely that either injury to the person or damage to property was owing to the driving, or that damage was caused to the vehicle taken. There is strict liability in respect of all these consequences. Moreover, each of the participants in the enterprise commits the offence though he was not driving the vehicle. A case of guilt by association.

So if D and E commit the basic offence each is liable if either causes injury or damage when driving the vehicle. More remarkably, if during the enterprise D chooses to damage the vehicle by slashing the seats, E commits the offence under s. 12A though he does not abet D in slashing the seats or even if E tries to dissuade D from so doing. Even if E is no longer in the vehicle, he may be walking away from it when D decides to set fire to it, E is liable provided he is still "in the immediate vicinity" of the vehicle. Not only guilt by association but guilt by approximation.

Section 12A(3) deals with a problem of proof. The prosecution may prove, or D may admit, that D committed the basic offence but D may claim that he had left the enterprise before the injury or damage was done or that he joined the enterprise after the injury or damage had been done. In such circumstances it is for D to prove on the balance of probability that the dangerous driving or the accident or the damage took place before he committed the basic offence; or that, having committed the basic offence, he was no longer in nor on nor in the immediate vicinity of the vehicle when one of those events took place.

12 Blackmail[13]

Originally the word blackmail was used to describe the tribute paid to Scottish chieftains by landowners in the border counties in order to secure immunity from raids on their lands. In the early stages of its development the crime of blackmail seems to have been pretty well coextensive with robbery and attempted robbery,[14] but over the years the definition has been

---

12. See above, p. 489.
13. MacKenna, "Blackmail" [1966] Crim LR 467; Hogan, "Blackmail" [1966] Crim LR 474; C. R. Williams, "Demanding with Menaces: A Survey of the Australian Law of Blackmail" (1975), 10 Melb LR 118, especially at pp. 136–144.
14. Winder, "The Development of Blackmail" (1941) 5 MLR 21.

extended to embrace more subtle methods of extortion. The law is now set out in s. 21 of the Theft Act:

"(1) A person is guilty of blackmail if, with a view to gain for himself or another or with intent to cause loss to another, he makes any unwarranted demand with menaces; and for this purpose a demand with menaces is unwarranted unless the person making it does so in the belief—

(a) that he has reasonable grounds for making the demand; and

(b) that the use of the menaces is a proper means of reinforcing the demand.

(2) The nature of the act or omission demanded is immaterial, and it is also immaterial whether the menaces do or do not relate to action to be taken by the person making the demand.

(3) A person guilty of blackmail shall on conviction on indictment be liable to imprisonment for a term not exceeding fourteen years."

1 The Demand

A demand may take any form, and, no doubt, may be implicit as well as explicit. D may be guilty of blackmail where, for example, he apprehends P in the act of stealing and conveys to P, without any formal demand, that if P pays him money he will hear no more of the matter.[15] The humblest form of request may be a demand if it contains a menace which is to materialise on failure to comply with the request.[16] But, whether express or implied, there must be a demand. If, having caught P in the act of stealing, D receives and accepts an offer to buy his silence, D might commit the offence of withholding for gain information relating to an arrestable offence but he would not be guilty of blackmail.

Normally the demand will be for money or other property but s. 21 (2) provides that "the nature of the act or omission demanded is immaterial". This is not as far reaching as may appear at first sight because in any event the offence can be committed only if D has a view to gain or an intent to cause loss, and this refers to gain or loss in money or other property.[17] The provision seems to have been included[18] to forestall a possible argument that D's demand must be for some specific property. D might, for example, demand with menaces that he be given employment or demand that P append his signature to a valuable security provided by D;[19] in such cases he may be guilty of blackmail if he acts with a view to gain although he does not demand any property of P.

A demand may be complete though it has not been communicated to P because, say, P is deaf; and a demand by letter is made when it is posted.[20]

---

15. Cf. *Collister and Warhurst* (1955) 39 Cr App Rep 100, CCA.
16. Cf. *Robinson* (1796), 2 East P.C. 1110, where the words "Remember, Sir, I am now only making an appeal to your benevolence" were held in the circumstances capable of importing a demand.
17. Theft Act, s. 34; below, p. 611.
18. Cf. Cmnd. 2977, Annex 2.
19. Cf. *Phipoe* (1795) 2 Leach 673, where Mrs. Phipoe armed with a carving knife "in the French language threatened, amidst the most opprobious expressions, to take away [P's] life" unless he signed a promissory note on paper and with materials provided by her.
20. *Treacy v Director of Public Prosecutions* [1971] AC 537, [1971] 1 All ER 110, HL.

2 Menaces

The word "menace" is an ordinary English word which in many cases will convey its own meaning to a jury without need for elaboration.[1] On one view it might connote only threats of violence to persons or property, but under the former law relating to blackmail "menace" was given a much wider meaning. In this case it seems clear that it was intended to retain the former law; the Criminal Law Revision Committee was of course well aware of the meaning "menace" had acquired and deliberately chose to use this word when they might have chosen some other.[2]

In *Thorne v Motor Trade Association*,[3] Lord Wright said[4] that a menace was a threat of "any action detrimental to or unpleasant to the person addressed". This is of course to define menace very widely. The Committee chose menaces in preference to threats because, "notwithstanding the wide meaning given to "menaces" in *Thorne's Case* . . . we regard that word as stronger than "threats", and the consequent slight restriction on the scope of the offence seems to us right". In view of Lord Wright's definition of menaces it might be thought that any distinction between menaces and threats is wholly illusory, but it does perhaps serve to emphasise that the law will not treat as a menace words or conduct which would not intimidate or influence anyone to respond to the demand. So in *Harry*[5] where the organisers of a student Rag had written to shopkeepers offering them immunity from any "inconvenience" resulting from Rag activities, the trial judge ruled that there was not sufficient evidence of a menace. Some shopkeepers had complained of the veiled threat in the letter but this menace was not, to use the words of Sellers LJ in *Clear*,[6] "of such a nature and extent that the mind of an ordinary person of normal stability and courage might be influenced or made apprehensive so as to accede unwillingly to the demand."

This is not to say that there can be no menace unless P is intimidated. D may be guilty of blackmail where he threatens to assault P unless P pays him money, though P is in no way frightened and squares up to D with the result that D runs away.[7] D has in fact made a demand with menaces which would cause a person of ordinary firmness to accede to it and P's *subsequent* refusal to accede to it cannot relieve D of liability.

Conversely there may be a menace where a person of ordinary firmness would not accede to the demand where, to D's knowledge, the particular victim, owing to such factors as infirmity, youth, timidity or even plain cowardice, will accede to the demand.[8] Indeed, the blackmailer will often select his victim precisely because he is aware of the victim's vulnerability.[9] If D intends that his menace should operate on the mind of P and knows of

---

1. *Lawrence and Pomroy* (1971) 57 Cr App Rep 64, CA.
2. Cmnd. 2977, para. 123.
3. [1937] AC 797, [1937] 3 All ER 157, HL.
4. [1937] AC at 817, [1937] 3 All ER at 167.
5. [1974] Crim LR 32 (Judge Petre); **SHC 483**.
6. [1968] 1 All ER 74 at 80, CA.
7. Cf. *Moran* [1952] 1 All ER 803n, CCA.
8. *Clear* [1968] 1 All ER 74 at 80, CA; *Garwood* [1987] 1 All ER 1032, [1987] 1 WLR 319, CA.
9. Cf. *Tomlinson* [1985] 1 QB 706, CCR.

circumstances that will make P unwillingly accede to the demand, D may properly be convicted of blackmail.

3 Unwarranted Demand

Not every demand accompanied by a menace will amount to blackmail. It will be appreciated at once that it ought not to be blackmail to demand payment of a debt and to threaten civil proceedings in the event of failure to comply. There is a menace (a threat of action detrimental to or unpleasant to the person addressed) but it is in the circumstances a perfectly lawful demand accompanied by a justifiable threat. At the other extreme a demand by D for property to which he is not legally entitled accompanied by a threat to kill P would be thought of as an obvious instance of blackmail.

But between these two extremes less clear cut cases emerge. D may threaten to post P as a defaulter unless he pays a gaming debt;[10] D may threaten to publish memoirs which expose discreditable conduct of P's unless P buys them from her;[11] or D may threaten to expose P's immoral relationship with her unless P pays money which he had promised her.[12] Whether the conduct in any or all of these cases *ought* to be blackmail might give rise to a good deal of argument, but the solution provided in s. 21 (1) of the Theft Act is that D's demand will be unwarranted unless made in the belief (a) that there are reasonable grounds for making it, *and* (b) that the use of the menaces is a proper means of enforcing the demand.

The test is then essentially a subjective one. Suppose that D has had an immoral relationship with P and P promises that he will pay D £100 for the favours which he has received; P fails to keep his promise whereupon D threatens to expose the relationship to P's wife unless he pays.[13] D's liability would now turn upon whether she believed that she had reasonable grounds for demanding the £100, *and* believed that her threat to expose P's immorality was a proper way of enforcing the demand. All the circumstances have to be taken into account in so far as they are relevant as tending to show or negative that her belief was genuine. D might have believed (wrongly) that she was legally entitled to the £100 and that it was lawful for her to threaten to expose P to get it; if that were her belief she would surely believe the demand reasonable and the menace proper. She might have believed she was morally entitled to enforce payment in this way, and this would be enough provided she believed in fact that this was reasonable and proper. One person (a lawyer for example) might feel that he was morally entitled to something and yet recognise that his moral claim would not afford him reasonable grounds for making the demand. Another person might genuinely think that his moral right affords him reasonable grounds. In practice, it may be thought, D does not think precisely in terms of the legality or morality of his conduct, but more in terms whether it is, in a broad way, reasonable.

10. Cf. *Norreys v Zeffert* [1939] 2 All ER 187, KBD.
11. Cf. the case discussed in Lord Denning's *Report*, Cmnd. 2152, 31–36.
12. Cf. *Bernhard* [1938] 2 KB 264, [1938] 2 All ER 140, CCA..
13. Cf. *Bernhard* [1938] 2 KB 264.

In *Harvey, Ulyett and Plummer*[14] D and his confederates paid P £20,000 for what P claimed was a consignment of cannabis but which turned out to be "a load of rubbish". Incensed by this swindle, the defendants kidnapped P's wife and child and made threats of serious bodily harm to them and to P unless the money was returned. No doubt a lawyer (or even a tolerably well informed layman) would have appreciated that in these circumstances the money was not recoverable since it was paid in pursuance of an illegal contract. Such a person might have difficulty in forming a belief that he has reasonable grounds for the demand. But in *Harvey* the particular defendants no doubt felt that they had been swindled ("ripped off to the tune of £20,000" as the trial judge put it) and it was for the jury to determine whether as a matter of fact they believed that their demand was reasonable.

It has been argued[15] that it is not right that D's own moral standards should determine the rightness or wrongness of his conduct; that the law should give "efficacy to the defendant's moral judgments whatever they may be".[16] The answer to this may be that as a practical matter most people do act according to generally accepted legal and moral standards, and the cases must be rare where D can *genuinely* rely on his own moral standards where these are seriously at odds with accepted standards. If D knows that the threat he proposes is to commit a crime, he cannot accordingly maintain that he believes such a threat to be proper.[17] It is not enough that D feels that his conduct is justified or that it is in some way right for him; "proper" in this context involves a consideration of what D believes would be generally thought of as proper. It is not enough that D believes his conduct to be justified, that it is in some way right for him, if he does not also believe that his conduct would be generally regarded as proper. The test of D's belief is of course a subjective one but that belief refers to an external standard; D cannot, therefore, take refuge in his own standards when he knows that these are not thought proper by members of society generally.

Conversely, and because of the subjective nature of the test, D may be guilty of blackmail where he thinks he has no reasonable grounds for his demand or that the use of the menaces is improper, even though, viewed objectively, his demand is perfectly reasonable and his threat perfectly proper. Concentrating to this extent on D's state of mind as the criterion of criminality may be something of an innovation in English criminal law, but cases where the matter arises must inevitably be rare.

Section 21 (2) provides that it is immaterial whether the menaces relate to action to be taken by the person making the demand. Consequently if D makes a demand of P and threatens that E will assault P if he does not comply, this may amount to blackmail. Perhaps this was clear enough without express provision for it, but the provision was included to prevent any possible argument.[18]

---

14. (1981) 72 Cr App Rep 139, CA.
15. By MacKenna J "Blackmail" [1966] Crim LR 467, 469.
16. See *Lambert* [1972] Crim LR 422 (Newcastle Crown Court); **SHC 489**, where Judge John Arnold appears to have accepted that this is the effect of the section.
17. *Harvey, Ulyett and Plummer* (1980) 72 Cr App Rep 139, CA.
18. Cmnd. 2977, Annex 2.

4 View to Gain or Intent to Cause Loss

It has been noted above[19] that the requirement of a view to gain or intent to cause loss operates as a limiting factor on the offence of blackmail. Many might describe as blackmail a threat by D to prosecute P for theft unless she has sexual intercourse with him, but this, though it may constitute some other offence,[20] would not amount to blackmail under s. 21 (1) of the Act. The Theft Act is concerned with invasions of economic interests, and gain and loss are defined accordingly in s. 34 (2) (a):

". . . 'gain' and 'loss' are to be construed as extending only to gain or loss in money or other property, but as extending to any such gain or loss whether temporary or permanent; and—

(i) 'gain' includes a gain by keeping what one has, as well as a gain by getting what one has not; and

(ii) 'loss' includes a loss by not getting what one might get, as well as a loss by parting with what one has."

In the ordinary case of blackmail D will have both a view to gain and an intent to cause loss; by demanding money from P by threats D will ordinarily wish to gain the money for himself and cause the loss of it to P. But either suffices. D may commit the offence where he intends to cause loss to P without making a gain for himself; as where, by threats, he demands that Q destroy property belonging to P. And clearly in this case D intends to cause loss to "another" though the person threatened is not the person to whom the loss is caused.

Conversely there may be a view to gain although there is no intent to cause loss. D might demand that P appoint him a director in P's company; here D has a view to gain for himself but it may well be that, far from intending to cause P loss, he intends to bring him increased profits.

Most often D's view to gain will be transparently obvious since a blackmailer's prime objective is normally to get money or other property from P. And normally D will intend to deprive P permanently of the property. Section 34 (2) (a) makes it clear, however, that gain and loss extend to a temporary, as well as a permanent, gain or loss. D might be guilty of blackmail, for example, where by threats he demands that P make a loan of property. But will any view to gain – no matter how remote – suffice?[1] Clearly there may be a view to gain although the gain is not to materialise for a period of time, or even though the gain may never materialise.

D might by threats cause P to destroy Q's will on the assumption that this will be to D's financial advantage; it can make no difference that Q is on his death bed or is in the best of health, or that Q has made another will revoking the one destroyed. The essence of blackmail is the demand with menaces and the offence is then complete whether D succeeds thereafter in making a gain or not.[2] What seems to be important is that D should have

---

19. At p. 607.
20. See above, p. 460. There is a view to gain where D at gun point demands that a doctor gives him an injection of morphine (morphine is property) to relieve pain: *Bevans* (1987) 87 Cr App Rep 64, [1988] Crim LR 236, CA.
1. See Smith, *Theft*, para. 330.
2. Cf. *Moran* [1952] 1 All ER 803n, CCA.

the view of gain in his mind when he makes the demand; the fact that it has crossed his mind at some stage that there may be a gain involved might not be enough. One of his objectives in making the demand (though he may well have others) must be to make a gain for himself. Equally where it has to be shown that D *intended* to cause loss to another, it would not be enough that D foresaw some likelihood of loss unless he also intended to cause the loss.

Sub-paragraphs (i) and (ii) of s. 34 (2) (a) were introduced to meet a possible argument that D would not be acting with a view to gain, or with intent to cause loss, where the gain or loss had already taken place. For example, D, who owes P £10, might by threats demand that P forgo his claim; it is now quite clear[3] that D is acting with a view to gain.

A further problem is whether D can be said to have a view to gain or intent to cause loss where he acts under a legal claim of right to the property demanded. Suppose that D, who is in fact owed £10 by P, threatens to expose to P's employers the fact that P is a homosexual unless P pays the debt. Obviously D can satisfy the requirement that he believes he has reasonable grounds for making the demand, but it may be supposed (as must almost invariably be the case) that D does not believe that the use of the menace is a proper means of reinforcing the demand.

It was clearly intended by the Criminal Law Revision Committee that D might be guilty of blackmail if he failed to meet either of the criteria in paragraphs (a) and (b) of s. 21 (1), and irrespective of whether D acted under a legal claim of right to the property demanded:

"The essential feature of the offence will be that the accused demands something with menaces when he knows either that he has no right to make the demand or that the use of the menaces is improper. This, we believe, will limit the offence to what would ordinarily be thought should be included in blackmail. The true blackmailer will know that he has no reasonable grounds for demanding money as the price of keeping his victim's secret: *the person with a genuine claim will be guilty unless he believes that it is proper to use the menaces to enforce his claim.*"[4]

The offence of blackmail is, however, governed in all cases by the requirement of view to gain or intent to cause loss, and it can be argued[5] that where D demands property to which he is *legally* entitled, he has no view to make a gain for himself or to cause loss to another; D makes no gain in getting what he is legally entitled to, and P sustains no loss in paying his lawful debts. In other statutory contexts gain is sometimes treated as economic gain or profit, but it has also been said to mean acquisition and is not necessarily to be equated with profit.[6] To give it the latter meaning in the context of the Theft Act would certainly be consistent with the

---

3. Or is it? See *Choraria and Golecha* [1989] 3 All ER 908, [1990] Crim LR 865, CA, above, p. 589.

4. Cmnd. 2977, para. 121, italics supplied.

5. Hogan, "Blackmail" [1966] Crim LR 474, 476. Cf. Smith *Theft*, paras 323–325, cf. Griew, *Theft*, 13.37.

6. Cf. Smith, *Theft*, para. 325 and authorities there cited. Cf. *Blazina* [1925] NZLR 407 on the meaning of "extort or gain" in the New Zealand Crimes Act 1908.

Committee's intentions,[7] and in *Lawrence and Pomroy*,[8] where D and E were convicted of blackmail in making threats to recover a debt, it appears to have been assumed by the Court of Appeal, though the point was not directly argued,[9] that D and E had a view to gain.

5 Unlawful Harassment of Debtors

Section 40 of the Administration of Justice Act 1970 creates an offence of unlawful harassment of debtors, which, because it may overlap blackmail, may be noted at this point. The offence, which is summary only and is punishable by fine,[10] is committed by one who, with the object of coercing another person to pay money claimed as a debt under a contract, (a) harasses the debtor by demands which by reason of their frequency or manner of making are calculated to subject the debtor or members of his household to alarm, distress or humiliation; or (b) falsely represents that criminal proceedings lie for non-payment; or (c) falsely represents that he is authorised in some official capacity to enforce payment; or (d) utters a document falsely represented to have an official character.

Clearly, and whatever may be the position in relation to the offence of blackmail, it can be no defence to a charge under this provision that the debt was owed. The offence was created to curb the growing practice of enforcing the payment of debts in a fashion that is unreasonable, unfair or improper; such as where a creditor calls at the debtor's house to make a demand and is accompanied by a brace of large, fierce and hungry-looking alsatians. The offence is wider than blackmail in that it may cover conduct that the creditor believes to be proper as a means of enforcing the debt. Under paragraph (a) it is enough that the demands are "calculated to" cause distress, and this will probably be interpreted to import an objective standard (calculated in the eyes of reasonable people) so that it will be no defence that D himself did not calculate to cause distress.

13 Burglary and Aggravated Burglary

1) *Burglary*

Section 9 of the Theft Act provides:
"(1) A person is guilty of burglary if—

---

7. As expressed in the passage cited at n. 5, above. But the Committee also characterised blackmail as an offence of dishonesty (cf. paras. 118 and 122) and one who demands that to which he believes he is legally entitled is not acting dishonestly: cf *Skivington* [1968] 1 QB 166, [1967] 1 All ER 483, CA, and *Robinson* [1977] Crim LR 173, above, p. 552.
8. (1973) 57 Cr App Rep 64, CA.
9. But the point was argued in *Parkes* [1973] Crim LR 358 (Judge Dean); **SHC 490**, where it was ruled that a person demanding money undoubtedly owed to him did have a view to gain.
10. Level 5 on the standard scale.

(a) he enters any building or part of a building as a trespasser and with intent to commit any such offence as is mentioned in subsection (2) below; or

(b) having entered any building or part of a building as a trespasser he steals or attempts to steal anything in the building or that part of it or inflicts or attempts to inflict on any person therein any grievous bodily harm.

(2) The offences referred to in subsection (1) (a) above are offences of stealing anything in the building or part of a building in question, of inflicting on any person therein any grievous bodily harm or raping any woman therein, and of doing unlawful damage to the building or anything therein.

(3) A person guilty of burglary shall on conviction on indictment be liable to imprisonment for a term not exceeding—

(a) where the offence was committed in respect of a building or part of a building which is a dwelling, fourteen years;

(b) in any other case ten years.

(4) References in subsections (1) and (2) above to a building, and the reference to in subsection (3) above to a building which is a dwelling, shall also apply to an inhabited vehicle or vessel, and shall apply to any such vehicle or vessel at times when the person having a habitation in it is not there as well as at times when he is."[11]

1 The Actus Reus

a) *Enters.* The common law rules relating to entry were developed with not a little ingenuity and a fondness for technicality. Broadly[12] an entry at common law was constituted by (i) the entry of any part of D's body within the building; or (ii) the insertion of an instrument for the purpose of abstracting property but not if inserted merely to further entry by D. It was assumed in Parliament that the common law rules would continue to apply.[13] But it is questionable how far the incorporation of all the common law's technicality would be consistent with the ordinary interpretation of s. 9 that D is guilty of burglary only if "he enters any building" with intent to commit, or "having entered any building . . . he" commits, the specified offences.

Whether a person can properly be described as being outside a building, or in the process of entry, or as being inside the building, may be said to be determinable in a commonsense way. On a commonsense view a person standing outside a building with one hand inside the door frame would not be regarded as being in the building (though he may be regarded as in the process of entry and thus guilty of attempt) while a person standing inside a building with his hand outside the door frame would be regarded as being in the building.

11. Subsections (3) and (4) are as substituted by the Criminal Justice Act 1991.
12. For more detailed discussion see earlier editions of this work and Smith, *Theft*, paras. 343–345.
13. 290 HL (5th series) cols. 85–86.

This view gains some support from *Collins*.[14] Here it was crucial to know whether D had entered a building (in his case via a bedroom window) before or after an invitation to enter had been made. The Court of Appeal appeared to approach the problem in a commonsense way—

"Unless the jury were entirely satisfied that [D] made an *effective and substantial entry* into the bedroom without [P] doing or saying anything to cause him to believe she was consenting to his entering it, he ought not to be convicted of burglary."[15]

No reference was made to the common law rules of entry but there was at least an implicit rejection of the common law rule that entry by any part of D's body sufficed[16] since the entry must be "effective and substantial".

In *Brown*,[17] however, the Court of Appeal said that "substantial" was an unhelpful addition to "effective" and that the jury ought to be asked only to consider whether the entry was effective. It was held here that the jury was entitled to find that there had been an effective entry where D, though standing on the pavement outside a shop, had the top half of his body through a broken window and was rummaging among the goods inside. But effective for what purpose? The court cannot have meant effective for the purpose of committing the ulterior offence since, on this view, D would not have been guilty of burglary if the goods he sought to steal inside were beyond his reach. This cannot be right. Nor does it make any more sense to say that the entry must be effective for the purposes of constituting an entry since such a direction could only bemuse a jury. It makes more sense, however, to say that an entry must have been effected and leave it to the jury to decide in a commonsense way whether D is sensibly to be regarded as being outside the building, in the process of entry, or as having entered.[18] The offence, it might be noted, is not to commit theft at a time when D is trespassing. In *Brown* D unquestionably trespassed and did so with intent to steal but the offence requires *entry by D* as a trespasser.

This leads on to a consideration whether, in conformity with s. 9, it can be said that D enters a building when he inserts within a building an implement for the purposes of forcing a lock or catch. If this is done by D as part of a plan to enter the building which is then interrupted, D is clearly guilty of attempt but even at common law this was not regarded as a complete entry. But may it be said (as it was at common law and might be said to be at least inferentially supported by *Brown*) that if the implement is inserted for the purpose of abstracting goods that this constitutes an entry by D? If the implement is regarded as an extension of D's arm, it makes little sense to say that it is not an entry if done to effect an entry but is an entry if done to abstract goods. There is not even the slightest hint of any

14. [1973] QB 100, [1972] 2 All ER 1105, CA; **SHC 492**.
15. [1972] 2 All ER 1105 at 1111, per Edmund Davies LJ; italics supplied.
16. Otherwise, remarked Odgers in [1972A] 30 Camb LJ, "burglary may well . . . vary with the length of a part much more private than the prisoner's foot".
17. [1985] Crim LR 212, CA.
18. This could result in different juries taking different views on the same facts and a preferred view would be for the judge to direct the jury on which factual bases D would have or have not entered; the facts are for the jury, the law for the judge. But this view is out of favour with the judges.

such distinction in s. 9. It is accordingly submitted that either both should constitute entry by a trespasser or neither and it is thought that the courts will prefer the view that both should do so.

But what if D uses an innocent agent? It may be supposed that D employs a boy under the age of criminal responsibility to enter buildings and abstract property. The boy, of course, is guilty neither of burglary nor theft but it is clear law that D may perpetrate at least some crimes by using another as his tool or agent.[19] The answer in this context, it is submitted, turns upon the interpretation to be given to s. 9. This says that a person is guilty of burglary if "*he enters* any building as a trespasser . . . or *having entered* as a trespasser he . . ."* (italics supplied) and the question is whether these words are apt to extend to entry by another on his behalf. If they do, they must equally extend to the case where D trains a dog, or even a programmed robot, to enter premises to abstract goods. Essentially the boy under age, the dog and the robot are instruments and the arguments adduced in the preceding paragraph are applicable. All such cases must be regarded as constituting an entry by D or none so regarded, and again it is thought that the courts will favour the view that all such cases constitute an entry.

b) *As a trespasser*. Trespass is a legal concept and resort must be made to the law of tort in order to ascertain its meaning.[20] It would appear that as a matter of civil law any intentional, reckless or (possibly) negligent entry into a building is a trespass if the building is in fact in the possession of another who does not consent to the entry. In all cases of burglary it must be shown that D entered the building as a trespasser in the civil law. If there is no civil trespass then there can be no burglary. If, for example, D is dragged by his drunken friends into P's house and D steals a vase there, D would be guilty of theft but not of burglary.

But while it is essential that D is a trespasser in the civil law, this alone is not enough. Liability in tort is strict to the extent that a mistake, even a reasonable one, is no defence. D is no less a trespasser although he mistakenly believes that the house he enters is his own, or mistakenly believes that he has a right of entry. But to commit burglary *mens rea* is required and, in this particular, this requires that D know (or be reckless as to) the facts which constitute him a trespasser. In *Collins*[1] D, having discovered that P was lying asleep and naked on her bed, stripped off his clothes and climbed on to the window sill of the bedroom. At this moment P awoke and, mistakenly believing that the naked form at the window was her boyfriend, beckoned D in. D then got into P's bed and it was only after D had intercourse with her that P realised her error. D's conviction for burglary (entering as a trespasser with intent to commit rape) was quashed because the trial judge had, in terms, indicated to the jury that it would

---

19. See above, p. 125.
20. Salmond and Heuston on *Torts* (19th ed.) 46; Winfield on *Tort* (13th ed.), 359; Street, *Law of Torts* (8th ed.), 15, 65.
  1. [1973] QB 100, [1972] 2 All ER 1105, CA; **SHC 492**.

suffice if D's conduct amounted to a trespass in the civil law. "In the judgment of this court," said Edmund Davies LJ—

"there cannot be a conviction for entering premises 'as a trespasser' within the meaning of s. 9 . . . unless the person entering does so knowing that he is a trespasser and nevertheless deliberately enters, or, at the very least, is reckless whether or not he is entering the premises of another without the other party's consent."[2]

In relation to the particular facts of this case the issue whether D was a trespasser or a lawful visitor would seem to involve a consideration of two matters: (i) D's belief as to P's (the girl's) authority to authorise his entry to the premises; and (ii) whether that authority was given before or after he had entered the premises.

The second matter is the easier to deal with and may be disposed of simply. It may be assumed that P had the necessary authority and further assumed that as D stood on the ladder outside the window he had determined to have intercourse with P by force. If he had reached P's bedside before any invitation had been extended to him he would already be guilty of burglary for he had already entered with intent to rape and P's subsequent consent could not alter that. But he would not be guilty of burglary had the invitation been extended while he still stood on the ladder.[3] One difficulty of the case, which has been discussed above, lay in determining whether he had entered before or after the invitation was made.

Once D has entered as a lawful visitor he cannot commit burglary though he thereafter commits any or all of the offences specified in s. 9. In the civil law there is a doctrine, trespass *ab initio*, by virtue of which one who enters premises under the authority of the law becomes a trespasser, and is deemed to have trespassed from the moment of entry, if he abuses his authority. *Collins*,[4] however, settled that whatever the status of this quaint doctrine in the civil law, it had no application to the offence of burglary.

Having lawfully entered premises D may become a trespasser if, required to leave by the occupier, he fails to leave within a reasonable time. Assuming that D does not do so and thereafter steals he would steal while trespassing but would not commit burglary unless he thereafter entered another part of the building and stole there. Burglary requires entry of a building or part as trespasser.

The first point is not so easily disposed of. An entry is not trespassory if the person entitled to consent to it gives his consent. Who is that person is determined by reference to the civil law. Trespass is an interference with possession. Burglary is therefore committed against the person in possession of the building, or part of the building, entered. Where the premises are let, the burglary is committed against the tenant and not against the

2. [1972] 2 All ER 1105 at 1110.
3. Provided he understood the invitation as one extended to him (i.e. he was unaware of P's mistake as to his identity) to have consensual intercourse causing him to abandon his intention to have intercourse by force. Supposing, for example, that D's purpose was to set fire to the house he would enter as a trespasser despite the invitation for the purposes of intercourse. See further below, p. 619.
4. [1972] 2 All ER 1105 at 1111.

landlord. Even if the tenant is only a tenant at will, he may maintain trespass. So may a deserted wife, even if she has no proprietary interest in the matrimonial home.[5] The guest at a hotel does not usually have possession of his room, nor does a lodger.[6] Where D breaks into the hotel bedroom, or the lodger's room, he commits burglary against the hotelier or the landlord, not against the guest or lodger. If the hotelier enters the guest's room, or the landlord the lodger's with intent to steal, this is not burglary because there is no trespass. Depending on the terms of the contract, the position may be similar where an employee occupies premises belonging to his employer for the more convenient performance of his duties as servant.[7]

Obviously the person who is in lawful possession of the premises may give the relevant consent but that person, unless he is the sole occupant of the premises, will expressly or impliedly authorise others to permit entry to the premises. An occupier of a house may authorise his wife and children to invite others to the house and these others become lawful visitors even though the occupier is unaware of their entry. A company may authorise employees to permit others to enter the premises and may give to one employee a more extensive authority than another. Rarely will the occupier set out the authority of others in writing and the extent of their authority will have to be determined from the practice of the parties. If D is in fact authorised to enter he cannot enter as a trespasser though he believes he is not authorised. In such a case, D may be guilty of attempt.

Just as the occupier can confer authority, he may withhold or limit it. He may, for example, forbid his spouse ever to invite to the house his mother-in-law, or he may tell his daughter that her boyfriend is not to step over his threshold.

But what becomes of significance here is not merely whether the occupier has authorised entry by D, or authorised another to permit D's entry, but what D's perceptions are about the authorisation. Burglary requires *mens rea* which for this purpose requires that he knows (or at least be reckless as to) the facts which constitute him a trespasser. If D mistakenly believes that the occupier has consented to his entry, or mistakenly believes that the occupier has authorised another to consent to his entry, he lacks the necessary *mens rea* for entry as a trespasser and cannot be convicted of burglary, however unreasonable his belief.[8]

In *Collins* it was argued that P, the daughter, could not give an effective consent to D's entry since it was P's mother and not she who was the occupier and that D knew that (or was reckless whether) the mother would not have assented to his entry in the dead of night to have sexual

---

5. *National Provincial Bank v Ainsworth* [1965] AC 1175, [1965] 2 All ER 472, HL, but see now Matrimonial Homes Act 1983.

6. It is necessary to look at the particular contract; it *may* give the lodger possession: Street, *Torts* (8th ed.) 70.

7. *Mayhew v Suttle* (1854) 4 E & B 347; *White v Bayley* (1861) 10 CBNS 227.

8. It is assumed here that an honest belief in consent to entry suffices. An argument might be advanced, following the *Caldwell* doctrine, that D is reckless if there is a serious risk that the occupier has not authorised the entry and D gave no thought to such risk, but if D has considered the issue and formed the view that he is authorised this case falls outside *Caldwell*.

intercourse with her daughter. The court said that whatever the position was in the law of tort, it was "unthinkable" to accept such a proposition in the criminal law. With respect, the court went astray here. No doubt had D in *Collins* called to deliver a newspaper in the afternoon and P had invited him in for a cup of tea he would have assumed that she was authorised to do so and he would not then enter as a trespasser even if, unknown to D, the occupier (P's mother in this case) had expressly forbidden her to invite any male into the house. But this was not quite what happened in *Collins*. If D had known that P was not the occupier he may properly be regarded as entering as a trespasser had he known (or was reckless whether) the occupier would not have consented to a naked stranger climbing through her bedroom window to have intercourse with her daughter in the dead of night. If D had believed that the occupier would have consented or had believed that the occupier had delegated to P the authority to consent to an entry in these circumstances then he would not enter as a trespasser for the purposes of the law of burglary. But if he did not believe (or was reckless whether) the occupier was consenting, or had authorised P to consent to, his entry there seems no difficulty in holding that he entered as a trespasser.

The courts returned to the problem in *Jones and Smith*.[9] D, P's son, was no longer living with P but he was a welcome visitor to P's house and, according to P, was free to enter at any time. One night D, together with his friend E, entered P's house and stole two televisions. Although P loyally maintained at the trial that his son was always free to enter the family home, the Court of Appeal held that the jury was entitled to conclude that in entering his father's house with intent to steal D had knowingly exceeded the permission given to him and D's conviction for burglary was affirmed.

The problem in *Jones and Smith* was not on all fours with that in *Collins*. The equivalence really concerns the position of D in *Collins* and E in *Jones and Smith*. E in *Jones and Smith* could hardly have thought, any more than D in *Collins*, that the occupier would have consented to his entry to steal the television receiver. To show that he had not entered as a trespasser E would have had to have argued that he believed that the son, D, was authorised to permit friends to enter his father's house to steal television receivers. This would be a preposterous argument and was not advanced.[10] The real issue in *Jones and Smith* on trespassory entry thus concerned D and the question was whether he believed that the "general" permission given by his father extended to an entry in the dead of night to steal property from his father's house. On the facts the jury were entitled to conclude, despite his father's assertions to the contrary, that the father would not have consented to this entry and that D was aware of that.[11]

The view taken of trespassory entry in *Jones and Smith* is certainly consistent with the civil cases which define trespass for the purposes of the

---

9. [1976] 3 All ER 54, [1976] 1 WLR 672, CA.
10. An argument which seems to have been advanced was that E entered the house at the invitation of D with no intention to steal. Had this been accepted E, if he had believed that D was authorised to permit E's entry, would not have entered as a trespasser.
11. Since E had entered as a trespasser and D was aware that he had so entered a simpler course would have been to find E guilty as principal and D as abettor thus short-circuiting the discussion whether D was a trespasser.

law of tort.[12] If a person authorised to enter one part of the premises enters another, or authorised to enter for one purpose enters for another, he becomes a trespasser. So the High Court of Australia construing a similar provision in *Barker v R*[13] held that D entered P's house as a trespasser where, given permission to enter the house to keep an eye on things while P was away, he entered the house to steal P's property. There is of course the difference between the civil and criminal law in that for liability under the latter *mens rea* is required; it must be proved not only that D exceeded his authority but that he was aware (or was reckless whether) he had done so.

The view that, subject to the requirement for *mens rea*, the civil concept of trespass applies has its critics. Dissenting in *Barker v R*, Murphy J said[14] that it led to the conclusion that a guest invited to another's house for dinner would become a burglar if he had entered with intent to steal a teaspoon. It would mean, to take another example, that a shoplifter would be guilty of burglary so soon as he enters a shop since he enters for a purpose alien to the shopkeeper's invitation.

It does not do to dismiss such cases as fanciful on the grounds that proof that the guest or the shoplifter had formed the intent to steal on entry would be hard to come by; it might be much less than difficult if the shoplifter is wearing a specially adapted coat. Are such persons really to be treated as burglars? Williams argues[15] that they should not and if a person is authorised to enter premises his entry should not become trespassory for the purposes of burglary merely because D has determined to avail himself of the invitation to commit one of the specified crimes. Moreover, as Murphy J added, if the wide view is adopted determining the nature of the authorisation, and whether D's intent is alien to it, may raise issues more suitable for metaphysics than for a criminal trial.

It is submitted that the arguments, in concentrating on whether D had exceeded the terms of his authorisation, have perhaps neglected a consideration of what P's reaction would have been had he known of D's intentions. It does not follow that P would inevitably exclude D from his premises though he knows of D's intent to steal. Restaurateurs would not necessarily turn away a customer even though they know that he is prone to stealing spoons. Shopkeepers do not necessarily refuse admission even to known shoplifters and commonly simply warn their staff that a known shoplifter is in the store in order that precautions may be taken. It is at least implicit in *Smith and Jones* that if the jury had believed the father's assertion that his son was free to enter the house even to steal the television receiver then the son's entry would not have been trespassory.

It is thought that it is not helpful in this context to distinguish between a general invitation to enter premises (where the entry is not to be regarded

---

12. *Taylor v Jackson* (1898) 78 LT 555; *Hillen and Pettigrew v ICI (Alkali) Ltd* [1936] AC 65, HL; *The Carlgarth* [1927] P 93, CA, at 110, per Scrutton LJ; *Gross v Wright* [1923] 2 DLR 171; *Farrington v Thompson and Bridgland* [1959] VR 286. Cf. *Byrne v Kinematograph Renters Society Ltd* [1958] 2 All ER 579, [1958] 1 WLR 762. Helpful surveys of the relevant authorities can be found in the judgments in *Barker v R* (1983) 57 ALJR 426.
13. (1983) 57 ALJR 426.
14. (1983) 57 ALJR 426 at 432.
15. TBCL 847.

as trespassory though D has purposes in mind which he realises would lead to his exclusion had P known of them) and an invitation limited to a particular purpose or purposes (where the entry is to be regarded as trespassory if D enters for other than the stated purposes).[16] It is respectfully submitted that the court in *Jones and Smith* was right to reject the submission that a person who enters premises under a general permission can never be a trespasser.[17] However general the terms in which an invitation is expressed (e.g. my house is open to you at any time for any purpose) it can hardly be sensibly supposed that this includes the occasion when you enter to do me serious bodily harm or to burn my house to the ground.

Similar considerations apply where D obtains entry by fraud. D may, for example, obtain entry by pretending that he is the person authorised to read the gas or electricity meter. Were D a genuine official of the gas or electricity board he would, under the principles discussed above, enter as a trespasser despite being given permission to enter if he does so with a secret intention to commit one of the specified offences. D can hardly be in any better a position if he is not a genuine official but gains entry by pretending that he is.

In *Collins* it was said:

"We hold that, *for the purposes of s. 9* of the Theft Act 1968, a person entering a building is not guilty of trespass if he enters it without knowledge that he is trespassing . . ."[18]

but it may be that there is a significant distinction between the offence under s. 9 (1) (a) and under s. 9 (1) (b). Suppose that D enters P's house mistakenly believing it to be his own. Realising his mistake D is about to leave when he sees P's umbrella, and, on impulse, he steals it. Clearly D is not a burglar by virtue of s. 9 (1) (a), but is the case covered by s. 9 (1) (b)? He did not enter the building with knowledge that he was a trespasser, but when he steals he then knows that he entered as a trespasser. At the time when the crime is committed, which under s. 9 (1) (b) is the time of the commission of the ulterior offence and not the time of entry, it would seem that he has *mens rea* in respect of all the constituents of the offence.

c) *Any building or part of a building*. The meaning of "building" in various statutes has frequently been considered by the courts.[19] Clearly the meaning of the term varies according to the context and many things which have been held to be buildings for other purposes will not be buildings for the purpose of the Theft Act – for example, a garden wall, a railway embankment or a tunnel under the road. According to Lord Esher MR, its "ordinary and usual meaning is, a block of brick or stone work, covered in by a roof".[20] It seems clear, however, that it is not necessary that the

---

16. Cf. Pace [1985] Crim LR 716 at 718.
17. [1976] 3 All ER 54 at 58.
18. [1972] 2 All ER 1105 at 1109. Italics supplied.
19. See *Manning and Rogers* (1871) LR 1 CCR 338.
20. *Moir v Williams* [1892] 1 QB 264. Cf. Byles J in *Stevens v Gourley* (1859) 7 CBNS 99 at 112 – "a structure of considerable size and intended to be permanent or at least to endure for a considerable time"; **SHC 499**.

structure be of brick or stone to be a building within this Act. Clearly all dwelling houses are intended to be protected and these may be built of wood; while "the inhabited vehicle or vessel" which is expressly included is likely to be built of steel or of wood.

To be a building the structure must have some degree of permanence, permanence relating to the nature of the structure rather than the residence of the occupier. But moveable structures, leaving aside the special provision the Act makes for inhabited vehicles and vessels, which are intended for permanent use as offices, workshops and stores (portakabins) may fairly be regarded as buildings though their intended use on a given site is only temporary. It is generally assumed that a tent cannot be a building, notwithstanding that it is occupied on a particular site indefinitely, but a structure may be a building even though its construction is flimsy.

To constitute a building the structure does not need to be one occupied by people. Farm outbuildings, such as stables, barns or silos, though they are used to house animals or products are buildings for the purposes of burglary, as are factory buildings and stores. Similarly the detached garage, toolshed or greenhouse standing in the grounds of a dwelling.

But what of the building in process of construction? At what point in the process of erection does a structure become a building? In *Manning and Rogers*,[1] Lush J said:

". . . it is sufficient that it should be a connected and entire structure. I do not think four walls erected a foot high would be a building."

In that case all the walls were built and the roof was on, so it was obvious that the structure was a building. But is a roof essential to a building? It would be strange if a multi-storied block of flats was not a building because only the roof remained to be put in place.[2] It would be stranger still if it was not burglary to enter and steal from a house the roof of which had been blown off in a hurricane.

Lines must be drawn and it will not always be easy to draw these lines.[3] The temptation for the courts may be to say, following *Brutus v Cozens*,[4] that "building" is an ordinary word the meaning of which is "a matter of fact and degree" to be determined by the trier of fact. As a matter of law, which the definition of words in a statute undoubtedly is, it must be for the judge to rule which brick or slate is necessary to constitute the structure a building while it is for the jury to say whether that brick or slate is in place.

    (i) *The extent of a "building".* – Under the old law, the entry had to be into a particular dwelling house, office, shop, garage, etc. A single structure might contain many dwelling houses – for example a block

---

1. (1871) LR 1 CCR 338.
2. Cf. Byles J. in *Stevens v Gourley* (1859) 7 CBNS 99 at 112 who defined a building as "a structure of considerable size and intended to be permanent or at least to endure for a considerable time".
3. Contrast *B and S v Leathley* [1979] Crim LR 314 (Carlisle CC) and *Norfolk Constabulary v Seekings and Gould* [1986] Crim LR 167 (Norfolk CC). In the former it was held that a freezer container detached from its chassis, resting on railway sleepers and used to store frozen food, was a building; while in the latter it was held that two similar containers, still on their wheeled chassis, remained vehicles though they were, as in the first case, being used by a supermarket to provide temporary storage space.
4. [1973] AC 854, [1972] 2 All ER 1297, HL.

of flats – many offices, shops or garages. If D got through the window of Flat 1 with intent to pass through it, go upstairs and steal in Flat 45, the breaking and entering of Flat 1 was neither burglary nor housebreaking for D did not intend to commit a felony therein.[5] It was probably not even an attempt, not being sufficiently proximate to the intended crime. If D broke into a flat above a jeweller's shop with intent to break through the ceiling and steal in the shop, he could be convicted of burglary in the flat only if it could be said that he broke and entered the flat with intent to commit a felony therein, namely to break and enter the shop.[6] The difficulty about this argument is that while the breaking may reasonably be said to have occurred in the flat, the entering, strictly speaking, took place in the shop. On that view, there was no intent to commit a felony in the flat and it was not, therefore, burglary or house-breaking to break and enter it.

It is not entirely clear how this situation is affected by the Theft Act. It really depends on what is the extent of a "building".[7] In its ordinary natural meaning, this term could certainly include a block of flats. If that meaning be adopted, D's getting into the window of Flat 1 as a trespasser with intent to pass through it, go upstairs and steal in Flat 45 is an entry of a building as a trespasser with intent to steal therein – that is, it is burglary. Similarly the intending jewel thief would be guilty of burglary when he entered the flat above the jeweller's shop as a trespasser. The effect would be to make the full offence of what was previously, at the most, an attempt, and probably was only an act of preparation. There seems no good reason, however, why the law should not be extended in this way. On the contrary, there is everything to be said for enabling the police to intervene at the earliest possible moment to prevent such offences; and for forestalling defences such as "I had no intention to steal in the flat – I was only using it as a passage to another flat which I never reached". It is submitted therefore that the word "building" should be given its natural meaning.

(ii) *Part of a building*. – It is sufficient if the trespass takes place in part of a building so that one lodger may commit burglary by entering the room of another lodger within the same house, or by entering the part of the house occupied by the landlord. A guest in a hotel may commit burglary by entering the room of another guest. A customer

---

5. Cf *Wrigley* [1957] Crim LR 57.

6. Cf. comment on *Wrigley*, last note, at [1957] Crim LR 58. An intention to break through the floor would not be sufficient ulterior intent if damage to the building was contemplated.

7. In *Hedley v Webb* [1901] 2 Ch 126, Cozens-Hardy J held that two semi-detached houses were a single building for the purpose of determining whether there was a sewer within the meaning of the Public Health Act 1875, s. 4. In *Birch v Wigan Corporation* [1953] 1 QB 136, [1952] 2 All ER 893, the Court of Appeal (Denning LJ dissenting) held that one house in a terrace of six was a "house" within the meaning of s. 11 (1) and (4) of the Housing Act 1936 and not "part of a building" within s. 12 of that Act. But, since the sections were mutually exclusive, the house could not be both a "house" and "part of a building" for the purpose of the Act. Otherwise, Denning LJ would have been disposed to say that the house was both and Romer LJ also thought that "for some purposes and in other contexts two 'houses' may constitute one building". Cf. Smith, *Theft*, paras. 353–361.

in a shop who goes behind the counter and takes money from the till during a short absence of the shopkeeper would be guilty of burglary even though he entered the shop with the shopkeeper's permission. The permission did not extend to his going behind the counter.[8]

What is "a part" of the building may be a difficult and important question. Take a case put by the Criminal Law Revision Committee.[9] D enters a shop lawfully[10] but conceals himself on the premises until closing time and then emerges with intent to steal. When concealing himself he may or may not have entered a part of the building to which customers are not permitted to go; but even if he did commit a trespass at this stage, he may not have done so with intent to commit an offence in that part of the building into which he has trespassed. For example, he hides in the broom cupboard of a supermarket, intending to emerge and steal tins of food. Entering the broom cupboard, though a trespass committed with intent to steal, is not burglary, for he has no intent to steal in the part of the building which he has entered as a trespasser. When he emerges from the broom cupboard after the shop has closed, he is a trespasser and it is submitted that he has entered a part of the building with intent to steal. He is just as much a trespasser as if he had been told in express terms to go, for he knows perfectly well that his licence to remain on the premises terminated when the shop closed.[11] Suppose, however, having entered lawfully, he merely remained concealed behind a pile of tins of soup in the main hall of the supermarket. This was not a trespass because he had a right to be there. When he emerged and proceeded to steal, still in the main hall of the supermarket, was he entering another part of the building? It is submitted that every step he took was "as a trespasser", but it is difficult to see that he entered any part of the building as a trespasser; the whole transaction took place in a single part of the building which he had lawfully entered.

The word "part" has no precise meaning in relation to buildings. Its significance for the purpose of the section is that a man may lawfully enter one part of a building, yet be a trespasser if he sets foot upon another. This was the view taken in *Walkington*.[12] D, having entered a department store, entered an area bounded by a moveable three-sided counter where he opened a till. It was held that there was evidence on which the jury could find that the counter area was a part of the building from which the public were excluded and that if D knew that, he entered it as a trespasser. Buildings, it

8. *Walkington* [1979] 2 All ER 716, [1979] 1 WLR 1169, CA.
9. Cmnd. 2977, para. 75.
10. I.e., without intent to steal; above, p. 620.
11. The Criminal Law Revision Committee thought "The case is not important, because the offender is likely to go into a part of the building where he has no right to be, and this will be a trespassory entry into that part". But he has no right to be in any part of the building after closing time and the only question, it is submitted, is whether he went into *another* part.
12. [1979] 2 All ER 716, [1979] 1 WLR 1169, CA.

now seems clear, fall into two parts: those parts where D is entitled to be and those where he is not.

If D is lawfully in Flat 1 and, without leaving the building, he enters Flat 2 as a trespasser with intent to pass through it into Flat 3 and steal therein, his entry into Flat 2 does not constitute burglary if each flat is regarded as a separate part. He has not entered *Flat 2*, with intent to steal *therein*. Yet, as we have seen, if he had entered Flat 2 from outside the building as a trespasser, there would have been no problem; he would have entered the *building* as a trespasser with intent to steal *therein*. Perhaps it may fairly be said, however, that the building is in two parts: one part comprising the flat, where D is lawfully present, and the other part comprising *all* the remaining flats, where D may not lawfully go. On this view D would commit burglary by entering as a trespasser that part (i.e. the remainder of the building) with the appropriate intent.

(iii) *Inhabited vehicle or vessel.* – The obvious cases which are brought within the protection of burglary by this provision are a caravan or a houseboat which is someone's home. There seems to be no reason whatever why a home should lack the ordinary protection of the law because it is mobile and this extension is welcome. Its limits should be noted. "Inhabited" implies, not merely that there is someone inside the vehicle, but that someone is *living* there. My saloon car is not an inhabited vehicle because I happen to be sitting in it when D enters against my will. The caravan or houseboat which is a man's home is, however, expressly protected, whether or not he is there at the time of the burglary. He may, for example, be away on his holidays.

The provision is not free from difficulty. Many people now own "dormobiles" or motorised caravans which they use for the ordinary purposes of a motor car during most of the year but on occasions they live in them, generally while on holiday. While the vehicle is being lived in, it is undoubtedly an inhabited vehicle. When it is being used for the ordinary purposes of a motor car it is submitted that it is not an inhabited vehicle. The exact moment at which the dormobile becomes an inhabited vehicle may be difficult to ascertain.[13]

Very similar problems will arise in connection with boats with living accommodation. Ships where the passengers or crew sleep aboard are clearly covered. The person who trespasses into a passenger's cabin on the *Queen Elizabeth II* in order to steal is clearly guilty of burglary.[14]

According to ordinary principles, D should not be convicted unless he knew of the facts which make the thing entered "a

---

13. Cf *Bundy* [1977] 2 All ER 382, [1977] 1 WLR 914, CA, below, p. 632.
14. Presumably, in such a case, the trespass is committed against the owners since, under modern conditions, they, and not the master, are in possession of the ship: *The Jupiter (No. 3)* [1927] P 122 at 131; affd. [1927] P 250. The passengers would seem to be in the same situation as the guests in a hotel. See above, p. 618.

building" in law, just as *Collins*[15] shows that D must know (or be reckless as to) the facts which constitute him a trespasser. Suppose D enters a dormobile parked by the side of the road. If he knew that P was living in the vehicle, there is no problem. But what if he did not know? It would now seem that he must be acquitted of burglary, unless it can be shown that he was at least reckless whether anyone was living there or not; and this involves showing that the possibility was present to his mind.

2 Mens Rea

a) *Intention to enter as a trespasser. Collins*[16] shows that it must be proved on a charge of burglary that D knew (or was reckless as to) the facts which, in law, make his entry trespassory. It would follow that if D sets up an honest belief in a right to enter, it would be for the Crown to prove that the belief was not held.

b) *The ulterior offence.* It must be proved that D, *either*
   (i) entered with intent to commit one of the following offences:
       (a) stealing,
       (b) inflicting grievous bodily harm,
       (c) rape,
       (d) unlawful damage to the building or anything therein;
       or
   (ii) entered and committed or attempted to commit one of the following offences:
       (a) stealing,
       (b) inflicting grievous bodily harm.
For these purposes D has one of the relevant intents though his intent is conditional – that he will steal if there is anything worth stealing in the building, or that he will cause grievous bodily harm to P if P is there. That there is nothing in the building worth stealing or that P is out of town is no bar to D's conviction.[17]
   (i) *Stealing.* – This clearly means theft, contrary to s. 1. This includes obtaining by deception to the extent that this offence may be charged as theft.[18] The rogue in *Dobson v General Accident Fire & Life Assurance Corpn plc*,[19] assuming the case correctly decides that he was guilty of theft, was also guilty of burglary.
   (ii) *Grievous bodily harm.* – Section 9 (1) (b), unlike s. 9 (1) (a), does not require the infliction of the grievous bodily harm to be an offence.[20] Such harm may be inflicted (for example, by accident or in self-

---

15. [1973] QB 100, [1972] 2 All ER 1105; **SHC 492**; above, p. 616.
16. [1973] QB 100, [1972] 2 All ER 1105.
17. *A-G's References (Nos. 1 and 2 of 1979)* [1979] 3 All ER 143, CA. See the discussion above, p. 307.
18. Above, p. 531.
19. [1990] 1 QB 274, [1989] 3 All ER 927, CA, above, p. 509.
20. The bill as drafted by the Criminal Law Revision Committee, and as introduced into Parliament, did so expressly provide. That the Act does not, is an accidental result of an amendment.

defence) without its being an offence. It was argued in *Jenkins*[1] that an indictment alleging that D entered as a trespasser and "inflicted grievous bodily harm upon [P] therein" was bad, because no offence was alleged. This argument, rightly as the court thought, was abandoned but it is not clear why the court so thought. It may have been (i) because para. (b) does not require the infliction to be an offence; or (ii) that it does so require but it is sufficient to follow the words of the section without specifying the offence. The latter, it is submitted, is the only tenable construction for it would be a surprising view that made even a trespasser guilty of burglary by lawfully (or inadvertently) inflicting the harm.

If para. (b) requires the commission of an offence, it is necessary to determine to which offence it refers. It must extend to the offences under ss. 20 and 23 of the Offences against the Person Act since both use the expression "inflict any grievous bodily harm". But *Jenkins* decides that, however "inflicts" is to be interpreted in the context of s. 20,[2] it is not to be confined in this context to conduct involving an assault. It is accordingly suggested that the offence under s. 18 of the 1861 Act must also be included, as must murder since the greater must include the less. If D is charged under para. (a) proof that he entered with *intent* to commit one of these offences will be required; under para. (b) recklessness would suffice if recklessness suffices for the particular offence.

(iii) *Rape*. – This offence has been sufficiently considered above. Entry with intent to rape is a species of burglary which might produce some rather odd-looking examples of that crime. For example, D drags P into a barn or persuades her to go into the barn with him, with intent to rape her. If D is trespassing in the barn, this is burglary.[3]

(iv) *Unlawful damage to the building or anything therein*. – Again the causing of the damage must amount to an offence. It might be any of the offences of causing damage created by the Criminal Damage Act 1971. In the case of every one of the offences which is likely to be invoked under this provision, the *actus reus* must be committed intentionally or recklessly.

Where the charge is one of entering with intent, it follows that an actual intent at the time of entry to cause the harm in question must be proved. In many such cases D's intent may be conditional at the time of entry, in the sense that he intends to steal if there is anything worth stealing, or intends to cause grievous bodily harm if P, his enemy, happens to be in the building. Such a conditional intent is now no bar to a conviction for burglary.[4]

1. [1983] 1 All ER 1000, CA. Cf. Smith, *Theft*, para. 369.
2. See *Wilson (Clarence)* [1983] 1 All ER 993, above, p. 425: *Jenkins* and *Wilson* were reversed by the House of Lords [1984] AC 242, [1983] 3 All ER 448 but on grounds which do not affect the discussion in the text.
3. More generally, however, burglary does not require that the ulterior offence should concern the occupier. If D and E, squatters, occupy P's house, it would strictly amount to burglary were D to steal E's wallet or to inflict on E grievous bodily harm.
4. See above, p. 307.

2) *Aggravated Burglary*

By s. 10 of the Theft Act:

"(1) A person is guilty of aggravated burglary if he commits any burglary and at the time has with him any firearm or imitation firearm, any weapon of offence, or any explosive; and for this purpose—

    (a) 'firearm' includes an airgun or air pistol and 'imitation firearm' means anything which has the appearance of being a firearm, whether capable of being discharged or not; and

    (b) 'weapon of offence' means any article made or adapted for use for causing injury to or incapacitating a person, or intended by the person having it with him for such use; and

    (c) 'explosive' means any article manufactured for the purpose of producing a practical effect by explosion, or intended by the person having it with him for that purpose.

(2) A person guilty of aggravated burglary shall on conviction on indictment be liable to imprisonment for life."

The reason given by the Criminal Law Revision Committee for the creation of this offence is that "burglary when in possession of the articles mentioned . . . is so serious that it should in our opinion be punishable with imprisonment for life. The offence is comparable with robbery (which will be so punishable). It must be extremely frightening to those in the building, and it might well lead to loss of life."[5]

1 The Articles of Aggravation

"Firearm" is not defined in the Act, except to the extent that it includes an airgun or air pistol. The term is given a very wide meaning by the Firearms Act 1968, but since that statutory definition has not been incorporated in the Theft Act it is submitted that the word should not be given a meaning any wider than that which it naturally bears; and that, therefore, the term "imitation firearm" be similarly limited.

The definition of "weapon of offence" is wider than that of "offensive weapon" in s. 1 (4) of the Prevention of Crime Act 1953,[6] in that it includes (as well as everything within the 1953 Act) any article made for *incapacitating* a person, any article adapted for *incapacitating* a person, and any article which D has with him for that purpose. Articles *made* for incapacitating a person might include a pair of socks made into a gag, and articles *intended* for incapacitating a person might include sleeping pills to put in the nightwatchman's tea, a rope to tie him up, a sack to put over his head, pepper to throw in his face, and so on.

The definition of "explosive" closely follows that in s. 3 (1) of the Explosives Act 1875 which, after enumerating various explosives, adds:

". . . and every other substance, whether similar to those above mentioned or not, used or manufactured with a view to produce a practical effect by explosion or by a pyrotechnic effect . . ."

---

5. Cmnd. 2977, para. 80.
6. Above, p. 444.

It will be observed that the definition in the Theft Act is narrower. The Explosive Substances Act, if read literally, is wide enough to include a box of matches – these produce a "pyrotechnic effect"; but it seems clear that a box of matches would not be an "explosive" under the Theft Act. The main difficulty about the definition – and this is unlikely to be important in practice – lies in determining the meaning of "practical effect". Perhaps it serves to exclude fireworks which, so it has been said in connection with another Act, are "things that are made for amusement".[7]

2 "At the Time" of Commission of Burglary

It must be proved that D had the article of aggravation with him *at the time* of committing the burglary. Where the charge is one of entry with intent this is clearly at the time of entry. Where the charge is one of committing a specified offence, having entered, it is at the time of commission of the specified offence. It is not enough to prove an armed entry by D as a trespasser unless that entry is accompanied by one of the specified intents. If, then, D, having no such intent at the time of entry, discards his weapon and thereafter commits one of the specified offences he is not guilty of aggravated burglary though he would be so guilty if he re-armed himself for this purpose.[8]

3 "Has with Him"

The expression "has with him" appears in the Prevention of Crime Act 1953[9] and the contexts of that Act and s. 10 of the Theft Act are so similar that decisions under the one will govern the interpretation of the other. It was accordingly held in *Stones*,[10] following *Cugullere*,[11] that "has with him" means "*knowingly* has with him". The prosecution is thus required to prove that D knew that the article had the relevant characteristics specified in paragraphs (a), (b) or (c). In the case of paragraph (b), for instance, this requires proof that either D knew that the article was made or adapted for use for causing injury, or that, if not so made or adapted, it was intended by him for such use. In the former case it would appear that the prosecution is not additionally required to prove that D intended to use the weapon in the course of the burglary; it is sufficient that D knows that he has with him a weapon so made or adapted. In the latter case it must be proved that the article was intended by D for use for causing injury but, it was held in *Stones*, once the prosecution has established that, it is not necessary to show that D intended so to use it in the course of the burglary. D's conviction was accordingly upheld in *Stones* where at the time of the burglary he had with him an ordinary kitchen knife which, he claimed, he was carrying to use in self-defence in case he was attacked by a gang. The mischief at which the section is aimed, said the court, is that if a burglar has a weapon which

---

7. *Bliss v Lilley* (1862) 32 LJMC 3, per Cockburn CJ, and Blackburn J; but Wightman J thought that a fog-signal was a "firework". Cf *Bouch* [1982] 3 All ER 918, CA.
8. *Francis* [1982] Crim LR 363, CA.
9. Above, p. 443.
10. [1989] 1 WLR 156, 89 Cr App Rep 26, CA.
11. [1961] 2 All ER 343, [1961] 1 WLR 858, CCA, above, p. 444.

he intends to use to injure some person unconnected with the premises burgled, he might nevertheless be tempted so to use it if challenged during the course of the burglary. And clearly a conditional intent to use a weapon suffices for the offence.

Decisions under the Prevention of Crime Act[12] have established that the law is directed against those who take weapons about with them for an offensive purpose. From them it appears that D would not commit an offence under s. 10 in using his jemmy to attack a householder if it was taken solely to effect entry and with no thought to use it as a weapon; and still less would D commit this offence in seizing something nearby, such as a candlestick, and using this to attack another who surprised him in the act of burglary. But if D arms himself and then proceeds to the commission of the offence, he may properly be said to have with him an article for use in the course of or in connection with the burglary though he has so armed himself only moments beforehand. In *O'Leary*[13] D, having entered P's house as a trespasser, took up a kitchen knife and proceeded upstairs where by use of the knife he forced P to hand over property. It was held that he was rightly convicted of aggravated burglary. Burglary is committed under s. 9 (1) (b) at the time when the ulterior offence is committed, and before its commission in this case D had armed himself for use in connection with it.

14 Possession of Articles for Housebreaking, etc.

By s. 25 (1) and (2) of the Theft Act:
"(1) A person shall be guilty of an offence if, when not at his place of abode, he has with him any article for use in the course of or in connection with any burglary, theft or cheat.
(2) A person guilty of an offence under this section shall on conviction on indictment be liable to imprisonment for a term not exceeding three years."
This provision is expressed to be directed against acts preparatory to:
   (i) burglary contrary to s. 9;
   (ii) theft contrary to s. 1;
   (iii) criminal deception contrary to s. 15[14];
   (iv) taking and driving away a conveyance, contrary to s. 12[15].

1) *The Actus Reus*

The *actus reus* consists in the accused's having with him any article. Clearly the article need not be made or adapted for use in committing one of the

12. *Dayle* [1973] 3 All ER 1151, CA; *Ohlson v Hylton* [1975] 2 All ER 490, DC. See above, p. 446.
13. (1986) 82 Cr App Rep 341, CA.
14. By s. 25 (5), "cheat" means an offence under s. 15.
15. By s. 25 (5), "theft" in this section includes an offence under s. 12 (1).

specified offences. It is sufficient that the *mens rea* is proved in respect of the article, that is, that the accused intended to use it in the course of, or in connection with, one of the specified offences. The heading to the section is misleading in referring to "implements" of housebreaking. "Article", which is used in the section and is therefore the governing word, is much wider than implement. Thus the article may be a tin of treacle intended for use in removing a pane of glass, or a pair of gloves to be worn to avoid leaving fingerprints, and it is implicit in recent decisions that it may be a sliced loaf and a bag of tomatoes[16] or bottles of wine[17] which D intends to pass off as the property of his employer.

The offence is thus very wide in its scope. But there must be some limits. Thus D can hardly be committing an offence by wearing his shoes or any other item of everyday apparel. Yet it was argued above that gloves for the avoidance of fingerprints would entail liability.[18] This suggests that the article must be one which D would not be carrying with him but for the contemplated offence. If it is something which he would carry with him on a normal, innocent expedition, it should not fall within this section. So there might be a difference between a pair of rubber gloves and a pair of fur-lined gloves which D was wearing to keep his hands warm on a freezing night, even though he did intend to keep them on so as to avoid leaving fingerprints. The latter pair of gloves is hardly distinguishable, for this purpose, from D's overcoat which seems to fall into the same category as his shoes. If D is carrying a pair of plimsolls in his car to facilitate his cat-burgling, this seems a plain enough case; but what if he has simply selected his ordinary crepe-sole shoes for wear because they are less noisy than his hobnails?

The expression "has with him"[19] is the same as in s. 10 (1) (b) of the Act. Questions as to D's knowledge of the nature of the thing can hardly arise here, since it must be proved that he intended to use it in the course of or in connection with one of the specified offences. No doubt D has an article with him if it is in his immediate possession or control; so that he will be guilty if the article is only a short distance away and he can take it up as he needs it; as where a ladder has been left in a garden by an accomplice and D enters the garden intending to use the ladder to make an entry. If the article is found in D's car some distance from the scene of the crime this will be evidence that D was in possession of the article when driving the car. The tenor of recent decisions on the interpretation of "has with him" indicates that mere momentary possession will not suffice,[20] as where D is apprehended on picking up a stone which he intends to use to break a window in order to commit burglary. But in *Minor*[1] it seems to have been decided that D may be convicted of going equipped (in this case to steal petrol from cars) though he did not take the equipment (petrol cans and a hose) with

---

16. *Rashid* [1977] 2 All ER 237, 64 Cr App Rep 201, CA.
17. *Doukas* [1978] 1 All ER 1061, [1978] 1 WLR 372, CA.
18. Cf. *Ellames* [1974] 3 All ER 130, CA; below, p. 632, where gloves were included in the charge.
19. See above, p. 629.
20. Above, pp. 446 and 629.
1. [1987] 152 JP 30, DC.

him and somehow came across it while he was removing the cap from the petrol tank of a car. It appears to have been regarded as enough that the theft "was to be posterior to the acquisition of the articles". On this view the burglar who picks up a nearby stone to break a window would commit the offence of going equipped but it is respectfully submitted that "has with him" requires more than that the acquisition of the article should precede the theft.

"Place of abode" connotes a place, that is a site, where D lives.[2] Clearly no offence is committed when D has articles for housebreaking etc. in his own home, but place of abode is apt to cover the whole of the premises where D lives so that D does not commit the offence by having the articles in his garage or even in his car while that is on his premises. Once D steps into the street with the articles or drives off with them in his car the offence may be committed. Though a car or a caravan may constitute a place of abode while stationary at some site, they can never constitute a *place* of abode while D is in transit and if he then has the articles with him he may commit the offence.[3]

2) *Mens Rea*

The *mens rea* for the offence would appear to consist in:
  (i) knowledge that one possesses the article; and
  (ii) an intention to use the article in the course of or in connection with any of the specified crimes.

It was held in *Ellames*[4] that the intent to use must necessarily relate to use in the future so that D was not guilty of this offence where the evidence showed only that he was in possession of certain articles (masks, guns, gloves, etc.) after a robbery and was trying to get rid of them. But given an intent to use the article in the future the expression "in the course of or in connection with" any burglary, theft or cheat is wide enough to cover not only articles intended for use in the perpetration of the crime but also articles intended for use before or after its commission. The string used by D in *Robinson*[5] to tie himself up as part of his preparation to defraud the insurers could properly be said to be intended for use "in connection with" the commission of the crime of deception. Equally a car intended for use to make an escape after the commission of a robbery falls within the offence. But the article must be intended for some direct use in connection with the crime and it has been held that D's possession of a stolen driving licence so that he could obtain a job which would give him an opportunity to steal is not within the offence.[6]

---

2. *Bundy* [1977] 2 All ER 382, CA.
3. *Bundy* [1977] 2 All ER 382, CA.
4. [1974] 3 All ER 130, CA.
5. [1915] 2 KB 342; above, p. 312.
6. *Mansfield* [1975] Crim LR 101, CA.

In *Ellames*[7] the view was expressed that D could commit the offence where he possessed the articles for future use by another, so that D would have been guilty in that case had he been hiding away the guns etc. for their future use by others. And it was also the view of the court that it was not necessary to show that D intended the article to be used in connection with a particular theft or cheat; the section requires only intended use in connection with *any* burglary, theft or cheat. No doubt a conditional intent (for example, possessing a jemmy to use if necessary) suffices but D must have made up his mind, even if only contingently, to use the article. If D had not so determined he does not commit the offence.[8]

Section 25 (3) provides:

"Where a person is charged with an offence under this section, proof that he had with him any article made or adapted for use in committing a burglary, theft or cheat shall be evidence that he had it with him for such use."

This is probably no more than enactment of the general rules regarding proof of intent.[9] It puts upon D an evidential burden. If he offers no explanation then the jury may be told that there is evidence upon which they may find that he had the necessary intent; but it is submitted that they should be told so to find only if satisfied beyond reasonable doubt that he in fact had that intent.[10] If D does offer an explanation then the jury should be told to acquit if they think it may reasonably be true and to convict only if satisfied beyond reasonable doubt that the explanation is untrue.[11]

Where the article in question is not made or adapted for use in any specified offence, mere proof of possession without more will not amount to prima facie evidence – i.e., the case will have to be withdrawn from the jury. It is a question of law for the judge, at what point proof of other incriminating circumstances amounts to a case fit for submission to the jury.

15 Handling Stolen Goods

By s. 22 of the Theft Act:

"(1) A person handles stolen goods if (otherwise than in the course of the stealing) knowing or believing them to be stolen goods he dishonestly receives the goods, or dishonestly undertakes or assists in their retention, removal, disposal or realisation by or for the benefit of another person, or if he arranges to do so.

7. [1974] 3 All ER 130, [1974] 1 WLR 1391, CA.
8. So in *Hargreaves* [1985] Crim LR 243, CA, the jury were misdirected when told they could convict if satisfied that D might have used the article.
9. Cf. Criminal Justice Act 1967, s. 8; above, p. 86.
10. Cf. the case where the alleged receiver is proved to have been in possession of recently stolen property and offers no explanation: *Abramovitch* (1914) 11 Cr App Rep 45, CCA.
11. The decision in *Patterson* [1962] 2 QB 429 that the onus of proof under the Larceny Act 1916, s. 28 was on the accused, was based on the express wording of that section and is entirely inapplicable to the new provision.

(2) A person guilty of handling stolen goods shall on conviction on indictment be liable to imprisonment for a term not exceeding fourteen years."

1) *The Actus Reus*

The questions which require consideration are: what are "goods"? when are they "stolen"? and what is "handling"?

1 Stolen Goods
By s. 34 (2) (b):
> ". . . 'goods', except in so far as the context otherwise requires, includes money and every other description of property except land, and includes things severed from the land by stealing."

It will be noted that this definition differs from and is narrower than the definition of "property" for the purposes of theft in s. 1 (1). Since, however, land generally is excluded from theft by s. 4 (1), the effect seems to be that, with small exceptions to be discussed below, the property which can be the subject of handling is co-extensive with that which can be the subject of theft.

a) *Things in action.* Things in action are expressly mentioned in s. 4 (1) and not in s. 34 (2) (b). They must however be included in the words "every other description of property except land". The remaining question is whether the context of s. 22 *requires* the exclusion of things in action. If s. 22 were confined, like the old law, to *receiving*, no doubt the context would so require. The context might be said to so require if a thing in action could not be handled in *all* the ways specified in s. 22 (1) since it may be assumed that it was intended that anything which could be handled under the sub-section could be handled in all the ways specified or in none. If "receiving" in s. 22 is given the same meaning as it bore under the former law (where it referred to taking control of a physical thing) it would not be apt to apply to things in action. Expressions such as "realisation" or "disposal" are, however, entirely apt to include dealings with things in action. But if "receiving" is given its ordinary meaning unfettered by connotations drawn from the earlier law (and there would seem to be no good reason for so fettering it) there is no reason why D cannot receive a thing in action. If D opens a bank account into which he pays stolen money and subsequently assigns the balance to E, it does not seem to be an abuse of language to say that E receives that balance.

The Court of Appeal appears to be prepared to take this view. In *A-G's Reference (No. 4 of 1979)*[12] it was said—
> "[I]t is clear that a balance in a bank account, being a debt, is itself a thing in action which falls within the definition of goods and may therefore be

12. [1981] 1 All ER 1193 at 1198, [1981] Crim LR 51 and commentary.

goods which directly or indirectly represent stolen goods for the purposes of s. 24 (2) (a)."

It is submitted that this view is in accord with the interpretation of the Act and makes good sense.

b) *Land.* "Land" which is stolen contrary to s. 4 (2) (b)[13] can always be the subject of handling since the stealing necessarily involves severance of the thing in question. A fixture or structure which is stolen contrary to s. 4 (2) (c), on the other hand, may or may not be severed from the land. Only if it is severed can it be the subject of handling. If E, an outgoing tenant, dishonestly sells to D, the incoming tenant, a fixture belonging to P, D cannot be guilty of handling (whether or not his act is in the course of stealing) if the fixture is not severed; nor, of course, is F guilty of handling if he, knowing all the facts, takes over the premises, including the fixture, from D; yet he has knowingly taken possession of a stolen fixture.

Land which is stolen contrary to s. 4 (2) (a) will rarely be capable of being handled since the kind of conduct contemplated by s. 4 (2) (a) will not normally involve severance.

Land may be the subject of both obtaining by deception and blackmail, both of which are stealing for this purpose.[14] Again, severance may or may not take place and handling is possible only if it does so.

c) *Meaning of "stolen".* By s. 24 (4):

"For purposes of the provisions of this Act relating to goods which have been stolen (including subsections (1) to (3) above) goods obtained in England or Wales or elsewhere either by blackmail or in circumstances described in section 15 (1) of this Act shall be regarded as stolen; and 'steal', 'theft' and 'thief' shall be construed accordingly."

By s. 24 (1):

"The provisions of this Act relating to goods which have been stolen shall apply whether the stealing occurred in England or Wales or elsewhere, and whether it occurred before or after the commencement of this Act, provided that the stealing (if not an offence under this Act) amounted to an offence where and at the time when the goods were stolen; and references to stolen goods shall be construed accordingly."

Thus goods are "stolen" for the purposes of the Act if:

(i) they have been stolen contrary to s. 1;

(ii) they have been obtained by blackmail contrary to s. 21.

(iii) they have been obtained by deception contrary to s. 15 (1);

(iv) they have been the subject of an act done in a foreign country which was (a) a crime by the law of that country and which (b), had it been done in England, would have been theft, blackmail or obtaining by deception contrary to s. 1 or s. 21 or s. 15 (1) respectively.

13. Above, p. 515.
14. Below.

d) *The "thief" must be guilty*. If the alleged thief is not guilty, then the handler cannot be convicted for there are no *stolen* goods for him to handle.[15] So if the alleged thief turns out to have acted under a claim of right to the property, then the goods appropriated cannot be stolen goods and there can be no conviction for handling them,[16] even though D believed the goods had been stolen.[17] In such circumstances, however, the receiver is now guilty of attempting to handle stolen goods;[18] or of stealing the property.

If the appropriator of the goods is guilty of theft, it is submitted that the goods appropriated may be the subject of handling although the appropriator is immune from prosecution by reason, for example, of diplomatic immunity.[19] The thief could be prosecuted for the theft if diplomatic immunity were waived. The handler may be convicted whether that immunity is waived or not – unless, of course, he too is entitled to diplomatic immunity.

It is submitted that the question whether the thief was guilty must be decided on the evidence of that fact produced at the trial of the handler.[20] Thus the fact that the "thief" has been acquitted is no bar to the prosecution of an alleged handler of the goods which he has been acquitted of stealing and should not even be admitted as evidence that the goods were not stolen. On the other hand, the fact that the alleged thief has been convicted establishes that the goods are stolen unless D can prove otherwise on the balance of probabilities.[1] The fact that D believed the goods to be stolen cannot, in itself, constitute proof that the goods were stolen;[2] but admissions on matters of fact within D's knowledge (for example, that the goods were purchased at a gross undervalue, that identifying marks had been removed from articles) may be such as to entitle the jury to conclude that the goods were stolen.[3]

2 When Goods Cease to be Stolen

By s. 24 (3) of the Act:

"But no goods shall be regarded as having continued to be stolen goods after they have been restored to the person from whom they were stolen or to other lawful possession or custody, or after that person and any other person claiming through him have otherwise ceased as regards those goods to have any right to restitution in respect of the theft."

---

15. But cf. *Close* [1977] Crim LR 107, CA.

16. *Walters v Lunt* [1951] 2 All ER 645, thus remains good law.

17. *Haughton v Smith* [1975] AC 476, [1973] 3 All ER 1109, HL, remains good law on this point.

18. *Shivpuri* [1987] AC 1, [1986] 2 All ER 334, HL, overruling *Anderton v Ryan* [1985] AC 560, [1985] 2 All ER 355, HL.

19. Cf *Dickinson v Del Solar* [1930] 1 KB 376; *AB* [1941] 1 KB 454; *Madan* [1961] 2 QB 1, CCA.

20. Cf *Dabek* [1973] Crim LR 527, CA.

1. PACE, 1984, s. 74, reversing the rule in *Hollington v Hewthorn* [1943] KB 587, [1943] 2 All ER 35. The rule was abolished for civil proceedings by the Civil Evidence Act 1968.

2. *A-G's Reference (No. 4 of 1979)* [1981] 1 All ER 1193, [1981] 1 WLR 667, CA.

3. *McDonald* (1980) 70 Cr App Rep 288, [1980] Crim LR 242, CA; *Hulbert* (1979) 69 Cr App Rep 243, CA; *Korniak* (1983) 76 Cr App Rep 145, [1983] Crim LR 109, CA.

It is obvious that goods which have once been stolen cannot continue to be regarded as "stolen" so long as they continue to exist thereafter. A line must be drawn somewhere; and the Act draws it in the same place as did the common law. So if the stolen goods are taken from the thief by the owner or someone acting on his behalf, or by the police,[4] and subsequently returned to the thief so that he may hand them over to a receiver, the receiver will not be guilty of handling because the goods are no longer stolen goods.[5]

Difficult questions may continue to arise whether goods have in fact been "restored to the person from whom they were stolen or to other lawful possession or custody". It cannot be enough that P (the owner or his agent) knows that D has stolen the goods and follows D to his destination so that the handler can be caught red-handed;[6] nor that in such circumstances P marks the goods after the theft for the purpose of their identification in the hands of the handler.[7] A more difficult case is *King*.[8] A parcel containing the stolen goods (a fur coat) was handed by E, the thief, to a policeman who was in the act of examining the contents when the telephone rang. The caller was D, the proposed receiver. The policeman discontinued his examination, D was told to come along as arranged, he did so and received the coat. It was held that D was guilty of receiving stolen goods on the ground that the coat had not been reduced into the possession of the police – though it was admitted that there was no doubt that, in a very few minutes, it would have been so reduced, if the telephone had not rung. The case has, however, been criticized. It is easy to see that if the police are examining a parcel to see whether it contains stolen goods they do not take possession of the contents until they decide that this is what they are looking for.[9] In *King*, however, E had admitted the theft of the coat and produced the parcel. One might have expected, therefore, that the policeman had in fact made up his mind to take charge of it before the telephone rang. The decision presumably proceeds on the assumption that he had not done so. On that assumption the decision would presumably be the same under the Theft Act[10] for it was held in *Re A-G's Reference (No. 1 of 1974)*[11] that whether the police officer has taken possession depends primarily on the intentions of the police officer. In that case a police officer, correctly suspecting that goods in the back of a car were stolen, immobilised the car by removing the rotor arm and kept watch until D returned to the car. He questioned D and in view of the unsatisfactory nature of D's replies arrested him. It was held that the jury ought to have been asked to consider whether the officer had decided before D's appearance to take possession of the goods or whether he was of an entirely open mind,

4. *Re A-G's Reference (No. 1 of 1974)* [1974] QB 744, [1974] 2 All ER 899, CA; **SHC 504**.
5. Cf. *Dolan* (1855) Dears CC 436; *Schmidt* (1866) LR 1 CCR 15; *Villensky* [1892] 2 QB 597.
6. In *Haughton v Smith* [1975] AC 476, [1973] 3 All ER 1109, where the police accompanied the driver of a van containing stolen goods to its destination in order to trap the handler, Lords Hailsham and Dilhorne questioned whether the prosecution was right to concede that the goods had been restored to lawful custody.
7. *Greater London Metropolitan Police Comr v Streeter* (1980) 71 Cr App Rep 113, DC.
8. [1938] 2 All ER 662, CCA.
9. Cf. *Warner v Metropolitan Police Comr* [1969] 2 AC 256, [1968] 2 All ER 356, HL.
10. In *Re A-G's Reference (No. 1 of 1974)* [1974] 2 All ER 899 at 904, Lord Widgery CJ said that *King* "might be thought to be a rather bold decision".
11. [1974] QB 744, [1974] 2 All ER 899, CA; **SHC 504**.

intending to decide when he had questioned D. Possession[12] requires both
an intent to possess and some act of possession. To immobilise a car does
not necessarily involve an intent to possess it or its contents but, along with
other circumstances, it may afford evidence of such an intent.

It is now quite clear that the goods cease to be stolen in the case where the
police are acting without the authority of the owner for they are clearly in
"other lawful possession or custody of the goods".[13] Indeed, it would seem
to be enough that the goods fall into the possession of any person provided
that person intends to restore them to the person from whom they were
stolen.

Section 24 (3) also provides that the goods lose their character of stolen
goods if the person from whom they were stolen has ceased to have any
right to restitution in respect of the theft. Whether a "right to restitution"
exists is a question of civil law, and now turns on the provisions of the
Torts (Interference with Goods) Act 1977. By s. 3 of this Act, in an action
for wrongful interference with goods, courts are empowered, inter alia, to
order delivery of the goods to the claimant. The remedy is discretionary
(s. 3 (3) (b)) and it would appear that the claimant would be ordinarily
confined to damages. Nevertheless it is thought that the phrase "right to
restitution" in s. 24 (3) of the Theft Act extends to any case in which the
claimant *may* obtain an order for the specific restitution of the goods. Thus
goods continue to be stolen so long as the claimant is entitled to seek the
return of his goods in an action for wrongful interference.[14]

The provision seems to have been intended to bear a still wider meaning.
The Criminal Law Revision Committee explained it as follows:[15]

"This is because, if the person who owned the goods when they were
stolen no longer has any title to them, there will be no reason why the
goods should continue to have the taint of being stolen goods. For
example, the offence of handling stolen goods will . . . apply also to goods
obtained by criminal deception under [s. 15]. If the owner of the goods
who has been deceived chooses on discovering the deception to ratify his
disposal of the goods he will cease to have any title to them."

It is clear that "title" is here used in a broad sense to include a right to
rescind. The Committee clearly has in mind a case where property passes
from P to D at the moment when the goods are obtained by deception. In
such a case, P, strictly, has no "title" and his right to recover the goods (or
much more likely, their value) will only arise on his rescinding the
contract.[16] Such a potential right it is submitted, is clearly a "right to
restitution" within the Act.

---

12. For the purposes of s. 24 (3) possession *or control* suffices. Arguably in both the above cases
the police officer had at least control of the goods but control, like possession, must involve an
intent to take charge.
13. Cf. the dictum of Cresswell J in *Dolan* (1855) Dears CC 436 that goods retained their
stolen character in this situation. Presumably the police in *King* were acting with the owner's
authority. The point is not discussed, but it would seem likely that the theft had been reported
to the police by the owner.
14. *A-G's Reference (No. 4 of 1979)* [1981] Crim LR 51 and commentary.
15. Cmnd. 2977, para. 139.
16. Cf. Smith, *Theft*, para. 89, where it is argued, in relation to s. 5 (4), that a person holding
property under a voidable title is not "under an obligation to make restoration"; above, p. 531.

3 Goods Representing those Originally Stolen may be Stolen Goods

By s. 24 (2) of the Act:

"For the purposes of those provisions references to stolen goods shall include, in addition to the goods originally stolen and parts of them (whether in their original state or not),—

(a) any other goods which directly or indirectly represent or have at any time represented the stolen goods in the hands of the thief as being the proceeds of any disposal or realisation of the whole or part of the goods stolen or of goods so representing the stolen goods; and

(b) any other goods which directly or indirectly represent or have at any time represented the stolen goods in the hands of a handler of the stolen goods or any part of them as being the proceeds of any disposal or realisation of the whole or part of the stolen goods handled by him or of goods so representing them."

The Criminal Law Revision Committee stated[17] of this provision:

"It may seem technical; but the effect will be that the goods which the accused is charged with handling must, at the time of the handling or at some previous time, (i) have been in the hands of the thief or of a handler, and (ii) have represented the original stolen goods in the sense of being the proceeds, direct or indirect, of a sale or other realisation of the original goods."

This section does two things. It provides for goods representing the stolen goods to be notionally treated as stolen goods but it also places limitations on the circumstances in which the *proceeds* of stolen goods continue to be stolen.

The effect is best explained by example. Suppose D steals an Austin car and subsequently that car passes, by way of sale or exchange or otherwise, through the hands of E, F and G. The Austin remains stolen until such time as it ceases to be stolen by virtue of s. 24 (3), i.e. until the Austin is restored to the owner or other lawful custody or until the owner ceases to have a right to restitution in respect of the Austin. It follows that until such time any person acquiring the Austin may be convicted of handling it if he acquires it knowing or believing it to be stolen. This is so even though the person subsequently acquiring the Austin, say G, acquires the Austin from a person, say F, whose acquisition of the car did not constitute handling because he acquired it innocently.

The position with regard to the *proceeds* of stolen goods (the Austin) is different. Assume that D exchanges the Austin with E for a Bentley. The Bentley is now notionally stolen because it directly represents the proceeds of the stolen Austin *in the hands of the thief*, D. Assume that E was aware that the Austin was stolen and he exchanges it with F for a Citroën. The Citroën is now notionally stolen because it represents the proceeds of the stolen Austin *in the hands of the handler*, E.

Assume, then, that D sells the Bentley to H who buys in good faith for £5,000. The Bentley now ceases to be stolen goods and once *notionally* stolen goods cease to be stolen goods they cannot revert to being notionally stolen because they are subsequently acquired by someone aware of their provenance.

The £5,000 in D's hands, however, is notionally stolen because it indirectly represents the proceeds of the stolen Austin and a recipient of all or part of the £5,000 would, if aware of its provenance, be guilty of handling. The position may be a little more complex where D banks the £5,000. If the £5,000 represents all that D has in the account, money which D draws from the account is stolen goods and a receiver of it, having the requisite knowledge, would be guilty of handling. Where, however, D has other innocently acquired money in his account, say a further £5,000, it may be difficult to prove that a cheque drawn for £2,000 that is cashed by E represents the proceeds of the stolen £5,000. It is not enough to establish that the recipient believed that the cheque for £2,000 represented proceeds of the stolen £5,000—that it represented his share of the ill-gotten £5,000.[18] This will establish the recipient's *mens rea* but it must additionally be proved that D intended the £2,000 to represent the proceeds of the stolen money.[19]

4 Forms of Handling

The term "handling" has been adopted because "receiving" – the only way of committing the offence under s. 33 (1) of the Larceny Act 1916 – is now one of several ways in which the new offence can be committed. These are:

(i) *Receiving* the goods.

(ii) *Undertaking* the retention, removal, disposal or realisation of the goods by or for the benefit of another person.

(iii) *Assisting* in the retention, removal, disposal or realisation of the goods by or for the benefit of another person.

(iv) *Arranging* to do (i), (ii), (iii).

It has been decided that s. 22 creates only one offence.[20] Since that offence may be committed in four or six or even eighteen ways, a contrary decision would have had a disastrously complicating effect on the section, giving wide scope to possible objections on the ground of duplicity.

a) *Receiving*. All forms of handling other than receiving or arranging to receive are subject to the qualification that it must be proved that D was acting "for the benefit of another person". If there is no evidence of this – as will frequently be the case – then it must be proved that D *received* or *arranged to receive* the goods and evidence of no other form of handling will suffice. The Act does not define receiving in any way and it must be assumed that all the old authorities remain valid.

To establish receiving, it must be proved, then, that D took possession or control of the stolen property or joined with others to share possession or

---

18. *A–G's Reference (No. 4 of 1979)* [1981] 1 All ER 1193, [1981] 1 WLR 667, CA.
19. But it would seem that the recipient is guilty of an attempt to handle.
20. *Griffiths v Freeman* [1970] 1 All ER 1117, DC. But see also *Ikpong* [1972] Crim LR 432, CA and *Willis and Syme*, ibid., and *Deakin* [1972] 3 All ER 803, CA; *Nicklin* [1977] Crim LR 221, CA. But in *Bloxham* [1982] 1 All ER 582, at 584, Lord Bridge thought it "well settled" that this section creates two offences.

control of it. "Receiving" the thief who has the goods in his possession does not necessarily amount to receiving the goods. If the thief retains exclusive control, there is no receiving.[1] There may, however, be a joint possession in thief and receiver, so it is unnecessary to prove that the thief ever parted with possession – it is sufficient that he shared it with the alleged receiver. In *Smith*[2] it was held that a recorder had correctly directed a jury when he told them that if they believed "that the watch was then in the custody of a person with the cognizance of the prisoner, that person being one over whom the prisoner had absolute control, so that the watch would be forthcoming if the prisoner ordered it, there was ample evidence to justify them in convicting . . ." Lord Campbell CJ said that if the thief had been employed by D to commit larceny, so that the watch was in D's control, D was guilty of receiving. In such a case D was an accessory before the fact to larceny and today he would be guilty of theft. If the facts were as put by Lord Campbell, when did D become a receiver? As soon as the theft was committed? If so, we have the extraordinary result that D became guilty of both theft and receiving at the same moment. But, if this moment is not selected, it is difficult to see what other is appropriate. This may, however, appear less anomalous under the new law than under the old. Virtually all handling is now theft, so it is the general rule that the two offences are committed simultaneously. In the ordinary case, however, the offence is handling because there has been a previous theft. The peculiarity of the present problem is that there has been no *previous* theft so it may be that D becomes a handler only by some act done *after* the theft.

As is clear from *Smith*, actual manual possession or control by D need not be proved. It is enough if the goods are received by his servant or agent with his authority.[3] The receipt may be for a merely temporary purpose such as concealment from the police.[4] It is unnecessary that the receiver should receive any profit or advantage from the possession of the goods. If D took possession of the goods from the thief without his consent, this was formerly only larceny (from the thief) and not receiving.[5] There seems to be no reason why it should not be both theft and handling under the Act, since it is clear that the two offences can be committed by one and the same act.

It continues to be essential for the judge to give a careful direction as to possession or control.[6] If the only evidence against D is that he ran away on being found by the police in a house where stolen property had been left, there would appear to be no case to leave to a jury. Likewise where the evidence is consistent with the view that D went to premises where stolen goods were stored with the intention of assuming possession, but had not actually done so[7] or where the only evidence of receiving a stolen car is that

1. *Wiley* (1850) 2 Den 37.
2. (1855) Dears CC 494.
3. *Miller* (1854) 6 Cox CC 353.
4. *Richardson* (1834) 6 C & P 335.
5. *Wade* (1844) 1 Car & Kir 739.
6. *Frost and Hale* (1964) 48 Cr App Rep 284, CCA.
7. *Freedman* (1930) 22 Cr App Rep 133, CCA. But this might be sufficient evidence of an arrangement to receive.

D's finger-print was found on the driving mirror.[8] The mere fact that the stolen goods were found on D's premises is not sufficient evidence. It must be shown that the goods had come either by invitation or arrangement with him or that he had exercised some control over them.[9] D is not necessarily in possession of a stolen safe simply because he assists others in trying to open it.[10]

b) *Arranging to receive*. Where it is impossible to prove an actual receipt, the evidence may show that D has arranged to receive the goods. Where D has merely made preparations to receive and has not yet reached the stage of an attempt to do so, the preparations may constitute a sufficient arrangement. The difficulties in a case like *King*[11] will be overcome if it appears that the arrangement to receive was concluded before there was a possibility of the goods ceasing to be stolen. Presumably it is enough if the proposed receipt is by a servant or agent. It must be made after the theft, since D must know or believe the goods to be stolen when he makes the arrangement.[12]

Though there is no such express requirement, it is difficult to envisage an arrangement which does not involve an agreement with another. Such an agreement will almost always amount to a conspiracy to receive so the extension of the law effected by this provision is less far-reaching than might appear. Clearly, however, an arrangement made with an innocent person is enough, as is an arrangement which does not involve another party at all, if that can be envisaged.

The offence of handling is complete as soon as the proposed receipt is arranged. It is immaterial (except as to sentence) that D repents or does nothing in pursuance of the arrangement.

c) *Undertaking and assisting*. The provisions of the Act relating to handling by *undertaking* and *assisting* extend the law to cover cases which were formerly not criminal at all. They are far-reaching and overlapping. "Undertaking" presumably covers the case where D sets out to retain, etc., the stolen goods, on his own initiative and appears more apt to describe the activity of the seller of stolen goods rather than that of the buyer. "Assisting" seems more apt to cover the case where D joins the thief or another handler in doing so.[13]

How this provision extends the ambit of the former law may be illustrated by reference to former cases where the conduct in question did not amount to receiving as it was then defined. D negotiates the sale to F of goods which he knows to have been stolen by E. D is never in possession or control of the goods.[14] He would appear to have undertaken or assisted in

---

8. *Court* (1960) 44 Cr App Rep 242, CCA.
9. *Cavendish* [1961] 2 All ER 856, CCA.
10. *Tomblin* [1964] Crim LR 780, CCA.
11. Above, p. 637. And similarly the difficulties of *Haughton v Smith* [1975] AC 476, [1973] 3 All ER 1109, HL, above, p. 319.
12. *Park* (1988) 87 Cr App Rep 164, CA.
13. But cf. *Deakin* [1972] 3 All ER 803, CA.
14. Cf. *Watson* [1916] 2 KB 385.

the disposal of stolen goods. D assists E to lift from a van a barrel of gin which he knows to have been stolen by E or another. Even if he never has possession or control[15] he has assisted or undertaken the removal of the stolen goods. D's fifteen-year-old son, E, brings home a bicycle which he has stolen. D assists in its retention if (i) he agrees that E may keep the bicycle in the house, or (ii) he tells the police there is no bicycle in the house, or (iii) he gives E a tin of paint so that he may disguise it.

D lights the way for E to carry stolen goods from a house to a barn, so that he may negotiate for the purchase of them.[16] D has assisted in the removal of the goods and would be no less liable to conviction (though his sentence might be lighter) if that was the full extent of his intended dealing with the goods.

The undertaking or assisting must under the Act relate to the retention etc. of the goods. Merely to use goods known to have been stolen does not suffice because use alone does not assist in their retention etc. So where D brings stolen equipment to his garage and E uses that equipment knowing it to have been stolen, E does not thereby assist D to retain the equipment.[17] But consider *Kanwar*.[18] D brought home some furnishings which E, his wife, knowing them to be stolen, used to furnish parts of their house. The police entered the house under a search warrant without any thought of arresting E; but when E lied to them about the provenance of the furnishings she was arrested, charged, and subsequently convicted of assisting D to retain the furnishings. On appeal it was recognised that proof of use was not proof of assisting, but E's conviction was upheld on the grounds that (i) assistance did not have to take the form of physical assistance and that merely verbal assistance would do; and (ii) telling lies to the police (even though the police were not taken in by them) amounted to such assistance when made for the purpose of protecting D. Point (i) must be right because D may be assisted to retain stolen goods by lies told by E which put the police off the scent. As to point (ii) the court said[19]—

"It would be absurd if a person dishonestly concealing stolen goods for the benefit of a receiver could establish a defence by showing that he was caught in the act. In the present case, if, while the police were in one part of the house, [E], in order to conceal the painting had put it under a mattress in the bedroom, it would not alter the nature of her conduct that the police subsequently looked under the mattress and found the picture because they expected to find it there or that they had caught her in the act of putting it there."

At first sight this is a common-sense view but it involves reading s. 22 (1) as though it read that something done *with intent to* assist etc. constitutes handling; literally interpreted, however, the subsection appears to require something that in fact assists etc.[20]

15. *Gleed* (1916) 12 Cr App Rep 32, CCA; *Hobson v Impett* (1957) 41 Cr App Rep 138, CCA.
16. *Wiley* (1850) 2 Den 37.
17. *Sanders* (1982) 75 Cr App Rep 84, CA. The fact that E had used the equipment would be some evidence that he had *received* it.
18. [1982] 2 All ER 528, [1982] Crim LR 532, CA, and commentary.
19. [1982] 2 All ER at 529.
20. Since E would be in any case guilty of an attempt to assist etc., the point is not of practical importance.

What becomes clear, then, is that E does not undertake or assist in the retention etc. by D simply because E is thereby advantaged. A wife does not assist in the *retention* of a TV receiver which she knows to be stolen by her husband *merely* because she watches programmes on it; nor does she assist in the *retention* of paintings which she knows to be stolen by him *merely* because she decides how they might be displayed to best effect. If the husband purchases Buckingham Palace with stolen money, his wife does not assist in retention or disposal of the stolen money though she can hardly wait to take up residence. Nor would the wife assist in the disposal of the stolen money merely because her husband insists that the palace be conveyed to them in their joint names. In *Coleman*,[1] though the premises purchased with the money were much less grandiose, it was held that a husband (in this case it was the wife who had stolen the money) could not be convicted of handling on proof only that a flat was purchased with the stolen money which was conveyed to both himself and his wife. It would have been different if the husband had given advice as to the disposal of the stolen money. It would have sufficed to convict him had he negotiated for the purchase of the flat, or if he had advised her to invest in real estate rather than leave the money on deposit at the bank, or even if he had encouraged her to buy the flat. But passive acquiescence by E in D's retention etc. of stolen property does not, as such,[2] render E a handler however much E may benefit from the enjoyment and use of the property.

d) *Arranging to undertake or assist.* The extension of the law to undertaking and assisting is far-reaching, but the Act goes still further. The mere arrangement to do any of the acts amounting to undertaking or assisting amounts to the complete offence of handling. So it would presumably be enough that D agreed to negotiate the sale of the stolen goods, to lift down the barrel of stolen gin or to do any act for the purpose of enabling E to retain, remove or dispose of the stolen goods. "Receiving", "undertaking" and "arranging" all suggest that some conduct is required though as little as a nod or a wink might suffice in particular circumstances. "Assisting", however, may be constituted by inactivity provided it is in circumstances where that inactivity does in fact provide assistance.[3]

Take a simple case. D, a wife, could hardly be constituted a handler because E, her husband, each dawn returns to *his* house with the fruits of the night's burglaries. As has been shown above, D would not become a handler even if she used the goods, provided such use did not involve assistance in their retention etc. Knowledge of the whereabouts of stolen goods cannot constitute D a handler; nor does D become a handler simply by refusing to answer police questions as to the whereabouts of the goods[4] since there is no obligation to help the police with their inquiries.[5] So in

1. [1986] Crim LR 56, CA.
2. But cf. handling by omission, below.
3. See above, p. 132.
4. Though D may become a handler (assist in the retention of the goods) if lies are told to put the police off the scent: *Kanwar* [1982] 2 All ER 528, [1982] 1 WLR 845 above, p. 643.
5. See above, p. 420.

Brown,[6] where E secreted stolen goods in D's flat and told D he had done so, it was held a misdirection to tell the jury that assisting in the retention of the goods could be inferred from D's refusal to reveal the presence of the stolen goods when questioned by the police about them.

The conviction in *Brown* was, however, upheld by applying the proviso. D had tacitly, if not expressly, permitted E to hide the goods on his premises and had thereby assisted in their retention. This is not to say that knowledge of the presence of stolen goods on his premises constitutes the occupier a handler. Obviously D does not assist in the retention of stolen goods because he invites to his premises E who, to D's knowledge, is wearing a stolen overcoat even if D puts it in the cloakroom for the duration of E's stay. But if D's premises are used, as they were used in *Brown*, to house the goods and D allows them to remain there he can properly be said to be assisting in their retention just as plainly as if he had initially given permission. What is important here is that D has control of premises and has chosen to allow their use for the storage of stolen goods.

Pitchley[7] is to the same effect. E, D's son, gave D stolen money telling him that he had won it on the horses and D paid it into his bank account. Two days later D became aware that the money was stolen but he did nothing about it until questioned by the police four days later. D's conviction for handling by assisting in the retention of the stolen money[8] was upheld because he had continued to retain possession after he became aware that the money was stolen. D had assumed control of the money and had, with guilty knowledge, retained control for the benefit of E.[9]

5 Otherwise than in the Course of the Stealing

Whatever the form of handling alleged, it must be done "otherwise than in the course of the stealing". This provision was obviously necessary if a great many instances of theft were not automatically to become handling as well. Without the provision, virtually every instance of theft by two or more persons would have been handling by one or other or, more likely, both of them, since they would inevitably render mutual assistance to one another in the removal of the goods. Given the decision to keep handling as a separate crime, the provision was, then, necessary – but it adds further unfortunate complications to an already complicated offence.

The expression "in *the course of* the stealing" suggests that regard must be had to the enterprise of which the theft forms part. This might vary from a few seconds, as where a pocket is picked, to several hours, as where a lorry is loaded up with goods stolen at a warehouse. During the course of the enterprise all the participants would more properly be regarded as thieves rather than handlers. Thus if D is within a warehouse passing goods which he has stolen to his accomplice E who stands in the street outside, E

---

6. [1970] 1QB 105, [1969] 3 All ER 198, CA.

7. (1973) 57 Cr App Rep 30, CA; **SHC 510**. Cf. *Tamm* [1973] Crim LR 115.

8. The decision overlooks the fact that when D acquired his knowledge there was no longer any "stolen" money to handle (see Smith, *Theft*, para. 418) but this does not affect the point at issue.

9. Cf. theft by "keeping [goods] as owner", above, p. 501.

would be a thief but not a handler.[10] On the other hand, if D steals the goods from the warehouse and delivers them to E some hours later at E's house some miles away, E would be a handler rather than a thief.[11]

The meaning of "in the course" of the stealing for the purposes of handling was considered by the Court of Appeal in *Pitham and Hehl*.[12] D, knowing that P was in prison and in no position to interfere, planned to steal furniture from P's house. He told E1 and E2 that he had furniture to sell, took them with him to P's house, and there sold them such furniture as they wished to buy at a considerable under-value. It was held by the Court of Appeal that D stole the furniture when he appropriated it by inviting E1 and E2 to buy it;[13] the way was thus open to upholding the conviction of E1 and E2 for handling because the handling took place *after* the appropriation was complete and was therefore not in the course of stealing. On the face of it this decision seems to render the words "in the course of the stealing" entirely nugatory. While stealing may be an instantaneous rather than a continuing act,[14] "in the course of the stealing" must mean something more. If in *Pitham and Hehl* E1 and E2 had known that D planned to steal the furniture and had gone to P's house to help him to steal it, it surely could not be realistically argued that their acts were not in the course of the stealing. As it happened there was no proof that they knew that D planned to steal – it was only when the furniture was offered to them at an under-value that they realised that D had stolen the furniture. This made their conduct look more like handling than stealing; nevertheless it is difficult to see how they could be said to have handled the furniture "otherwise than in the course of the stealing."[15]

If D had stolen the furniture at some earlier stage so that the purchase and removal by E1 and E2 could be said to be a separate transaction it would have been proper to convict them of handling. Inevitably a line has to be drawn somewhere and there are bound to be difficult borderline cases. Perhaps the best test that suggests itself if whether D was "on the job" – the job being the enterprise of which the theft is part and parcel – at the time when the acts alleged to constitute E a handler took place. Had this test been applied in *Pitham and Hehl*, the commonsense answer would appear to be that the thief, D, was still on the job when the furniture was "handled" by E1 and E2.

The suggested test has uncertain edges. Is D on the job (in the course of stealing) when he walks down the garden path with the stolen goods? When he drives home with them? When he shows them to his wife? It will usually be easy to conclude that D is on the job when he is still on the premises

10. Cf. *Perkins* (1852) 5 Cox CC 554; *Coggins* (1873) 12 Cox CC 517.
11. Cf. *Kelly* (1820) Russ & Ry 421. The cases in this note and the last were decided under the former law of larceny but the CLRC said (Cmnd. 2977, para. 131) that its provision was "in accordance with the present [now the former] law of receiving".
12. (1977) 65 Cr App Rep 45, CA.
13. The offer to sell was an assumption of P's rights and therefore an appropriation, see above p. 504.
14. See above, p. 512. But cases under this former law of larceny accepted that E was not a receiver merely because he received the goods after the larceny by D was technically complete.
15. Cf. *Hale* (1978) 68 Cr App Rep 415, [1979] Crim LR 596 distinguished in *Gregory* (1982) 74 Cr App Rep 154, CA.

from which the goods are stolen, but it will depend on the circumstances. If D and E agree to steal from their employer P and in pursuance of the plan D steals goods which he places in E's locker so that E may remove them from the premises, E would appear to be a thief rather than a handler even though some time elapses between D's appropriation of the goods and E's removal of them. It is one enterprise for the theft of P's goods. If, however, D steals P's goods and secretes them on the premises, a subsequent arrangement with E for E to remove them from the premises more naturally constitutes E a handler.[16] E is not a party to the theft.

6 For the Benefit of Another Person

Where a person steals goods it will ordinarily be with a view to some benefit to himself.[17] If D steals money he will spend it to his own benefit; if he steals goods he will use the goods to his own benefit or sell them and use the proceeds to his own benefit. When D disposes of stolen goods, a benefit usually accrues to another; the purchaser of the stolen car may be said to be benefitted by his use of the stolen car, the dealer who purchases the stolen TV receiver may make a profit on its resale, and so on. In such cases D has assisted in the disposal or realisation of the stolen goods and thus (irrespective of whether the purchaser or dealer is aware that the goods are stolen) would be guilty of handling unless some further qualification were introduced into the offence.

This qualification is provided, or was intended to be provided, by the requirement that the disposal etc. be "by or for the benefit of another person". In the illustration just given a benefit had accrued to the purchaser and the dealer but the disposal etc. is done by D for his own benefit and is not, or ought not to be considered, for their benefit simply because some profit may incidentally accrue to them.

The Criminal Law Revision Committee was concerned that the thief should not become a handler simply because he did one of the acts of disposing etc.; such an act makes the thief a handler only if it is "by or for the benefit of another"—

"[S]ince the offence will apply only to undertaking or assisting in the disposal or other dealing 'by or for the benefit of another person', *a thief will not be guilty of handling by keeping or disposing of the goods for his own benefit.*"[18]

---

16. *Cf. Atwell and O'Donnell* (1801) 2 East PC 768. D1 and D2 bent on stealing some of their employer's property moved it nearer the warehouse door during the course of the morning. Later that day E1 and E2 arranged to buy the goods from them and all returned later that evening to take away the goods from the warehouse. It was held that E1 and E2 were thieves and not receivers; the theft was a continuing transaction as to those (E1 and E2) who joined the plot before the goods were finally removed from the warehouse. Assuming this case was correctly decided under the former law of larceny, it is submitted that if these facts were to recur that E1 and E2 are handlers and not thieves. The theft (the appropriation) is complete hours before E1 and E2 become aware of it and their handling of the goods must be otherwise than in the course of the stealing.

17. This is not to suggest that theft requires any such view of benefit.

18. Cmnd. 2977, para. 131. Italics supplied.

Section 22 (1) is, however, somewhat unfortunately drafted.[19] It contemplates that handling (otherwise than by way of receiving) may be committed by undertaking or assisting in one of the specified acts (disposing, realising etc.) by *or* for the benefit of another.

Fortunately the House of Lords in *Bloxham*[20] has held that s. 22 (1) is to be interpreted in accordance with the intentions of the Criminal Law Revision Committee. It could not be said, therefore, that a disposal by D for his own benefit was for the benefit of another simply because some profit accrued to the other. Accordingly where D, an innocent purchaser of a stolen car, subsequently realised it was stolen and sold it to P, he did not sell the car "for the benefit of another". Nor, of course, would it make any difference that D had initially stolen the car rather than acquired it innocently. The 1968 Act strives to maintain a distinction between thieves and handlers and a thief is not to attract the heavier penalties accorded to the handler by disposing of stolen goods for his own benefit. This is not to say that a thief cannot in any circumstances handle the goods which he steals and the circumstances in which he may do so are examined in the following two sections.

7 Innocent Receipt and Subsequent Retention with Mens Rea

If D receives the stolen goods innocently, either, that is, believing them not to be stolen or knowing them to be stolen but intending to return them to the true owner, of course, he commits no offence.[1] Suppose he subsequently discovers the goods to be stolen or decides not to return them to the true owner or disposes of them. He has dishonestly undertaken the retention of or has disposed of stolen goods knowing them to be stolen. Whether he is guilty of an offence depends on a number of factors.

(1) Where D does not get ownership of the goods. (The normal situation where goods are stolen.)
  (i) D gives value for the goods
    (a) D retains or disposes of the goods for his own benefit. This is not theft because of s. 3 (2);[2] nor is it handling by undertaking, assisting or arranging since it is not for the benefit of another.[3] D might be guilty of handling by aiding and abetting the receiving by the person to whom he disposes of the goods, if that person has *mens rea*.
    (b) D retains or disposes of the goods for the benefit of another. This is not theft (s. 3 (2)) but is handling.
  (ii) D does not give value.
    (a) D retains or disposes of the goods for his own benefit. This is theft but not handling unless it amounts to aiding and abetting receipt by another.

---

19. See Blake, "The Innocent Purchaser and s. 22 of the Theft Act" [1972] Crim LR 494; Spencer, "The Mishandling of Handling" [1981] Crim LR 682; Smith, *Theft*, para. 421.
20. [1983] AC 109, [1982] 1 All ER 582, HL; **SHC 516**.
 1. *Alt* [1972] Crim LR 552, CA.
 2. Above, p. 511.
 3. *Bloxham* [1983] 1 AC 109, [1982] 1 All ER 582, HL.

    (b) D retains or disposes of the goods for the benefit of another. This is theft and handling.
  (2) Where D gets ownership of the goods. (Because the rogue obtained them by deception and acquired a voidable title or because of some exception of the nemo dat rule.)
    (a) D gives value for the goods.

Retention or disposal of the goods cannot be theft since P had no property in the goods, nor handling since P has lost his right to restitution,[4] his right to rescind being destroyed on the goods coming into the hands of D who was a bona fide purchaser for value.

    (b) D does not give value.

Again this cannot be theft, since P has no property in the goods, but it may be handling since P's right to rescind and secure restitution of his property is not extinguished by the goods coming into the hands of one who does not give value. It will be handling if this is so *and* D either aids and abets a guilty receipt by another or disposes of the goods for the benefit of another.

8 Handling by the Thief[5]

The common law rules regulating the liability of a thief to a charge of receiving goods feloniously stolen by him were complicated. The present position appears to be that any thief may be convicted of handling goods stolen by him by receiving them – if the evidence warrants this conclusion.[6] In the majority of cases the thief can only be guilty of handling by receiving where he is abetting the receipt by another because he is already in possession or control and therefore cannot receive as the principal offender. In some circumstances, however, a thief might be convicted of handling the stolen goods by receiving them as the principal offender. For example, D steals goods and, in the course of the theft, delivers them to E. Two days later E returns the goods to D.

9 Advertising for the Return of Stolen Goods

By s. 23 of the Theft Act 1968 it is an offence publicly to advertise for the return of stolen goods indicating that no questions will be asked about how the person returning the goods came by them. The antecedents of this offence go back to 1828 and it was retained, after some hesitation on the part of the CLRC, because it was thought that advertisements of this kind might encourage dishonesty.[7] Though such advertisements may encourage dishonesty in others, dishonesty is not required of the perpetrator. Indeed the offence has been held to be one of strict liability so that the advertising manager of a newspaper in which such an advertisement appeared committed the offence though he was unaware that it had appeared in the paper.[8]

---

4. Above, p. 636.
5. A. T. H. Smith, "Theft and/or Handling" [1977] Crim LR 517.
6. *Dolan* (1976) 62 Cr App Rep 36, CA; *Stapylton v O'Callaghan* [1973] 2 All ER 782, DC.
7. Cmnd. 2977, para. 144.
8. *Denham v Scott* (1983) 77 Cr App Rep 210, DC.

2) *The Mens Rea*

1 Knowledge or Belief[9]

It must be proved that the goods were stolen and that D handled them "knowing or believing them to be stolen goods." The Criminal Law Revision Committee thought that this provision would extend the law:

"It is a serious defect of the present law that actual knowledge that the property was stolen must be proved. Often the prosecution cannot prove this. In many cases indeed guilty knowledge does not exist, although the circumstances of the transaction are such that the receiver ought to be guilty of an offence. The man who buys goods at a ridiculously low price from an unknown seller whom he meets in a public house may not *know* that the goods were stolen, and he may take the precaution of asking no questions. Yet it may be clear on the evidence that he believes that the goods were stolen. In such cases the prosecution may fail (rightly, as the law now stands) for want of proof of guilty knowledge."[10]

It may be accepted that it would be a serious defect to confine D's liability to the case where he *knows* the goods are stolen. In one sense it may be questioned whether D can ever know that the goods are stolen. Even if D witnesses the "theft" he cannot know that the "thief" may not be acting under, say, a claim of right or under duress. But to give "knowing" such a restricted meaning in this context would be unrealistic. For practical purposes D may be said to know that goods are stolen when from the available facts he concludes they are stolen and either does not consider whether they may not be stolen, or, having considered the possibility, he discounts it. "Believing" was added to enlarge D's liability beyond the case where he knows the goods to be stolen. The question concerns the extent of that enlargement.

Take the Committee's example of the man who buys goods at a ridiculously low price from an unknown seller in a pub. At one extreme he may conclude that the goods are not stolen, in which case he incurs no liability; or at the other he may conclude that the goods are stolen with no ifs or buts, in which case he knows the goods are stolen. Between the two extremes he may consider that there is merely a risk that the goods are stolen, or he may conclude that while he does not know the goods are stolen (he may here refrain from asking questions to put the matter beyond doubt) he is as sure as may be that they are. In both cases D takes a risk that the goods are stolen; low in the first case, high in the second.

Looked at as a matter of principle, ought a person who acquires goods aware of a risk that they may be stolen to be considered a handler if the goods turn out to be stolen? Williams argues that such a rule would be an undue restraint on commerce. "People", he says,[11] "must be free to buy unless they positively know that the goods are stolen. The public interest in

---

9. See Griew, "Consistency, Communication and Codification – Reflections on Two Mens Rea Words" in *Reshaping the Criminal Law*, ed. by Glazebrook, 1978, at p. 57.
10. Cmnd. 2977, 64. Cf *Woods* [1969] 1 QB 447, [1968] 3 All ER 709, CA.
11. TBCL at p. 875. See further Williams, "Handling, Theft and the Purchaser who takes a Chance" [1985] Crim LR 432.

free trade is greater than the public interest in attempting to close every possibility of stolen goods being sold." Spencer, on the other hand and while he accepts that one who merely takes a risk that goods are stolen should not be a handler, argues[12] that D ought to be accounted a handler if he concludes that it is more probable than not that the goods are stolen and that "believing" should be so interpreted.

The courts have been sorely troubled by the interpretation of "knowing or believing". One way of tackling (or avoiding) the problem is to adopt the judicially popular stance of saying these are ordinary English words and their interpretation can be left to the jury without enlargement or explanation by the trial judge. This view has judicial support. In *Harris*[13] Lawton LJ said on behalf of the Court of Appeal:

"In our judgment the words 'knowledge or belief' are words of ordinary usage in English. In most cases, but not all, all that need be said to a jury is to ask them whether that which is alleged by the prosecution, namely receipt, knowing or believing that the goods were stolen, has been established."

But, and assuming the correctness of this approach, the court recognises that while it will do for most cases[14] it will not do for all. *Harris* was a case where the jury were told that if the only inference to be drawn from the facts was that the goods were stolen they were entitled to infer that D knew or believed them to be so. This was regarded by the Court of Appeal as a straightforward case where the jury needed to be directed only in the words of the statute. In at least some cases, however, the issue may not be so straightforward. The inference that the goods were stolen may be less compelling or D may claim that he was less than sure that the goods were stolen and in such cases the meaning of "knowing or believing" needs to be explained to the jury.

The cases are clear that it is a misdirection to tell the jury that it is enough that D suspected that the goods were stolen;[15] mere recklessness as to the provenance of goods does not constitute knowledge or belief. It is also a misdirection to say that D knows or believes where D thinks it more probable than not that the goods are stolen.[16] And care must be taken in expressions along the lines of closing the mind to the obvious. While knowledge or belief *may* be inferred from the fact that D deliberately closed his eyes to the circumstances,[17] it is a misdirection to say that D knows or believes goods to be stolen if, suspecting that goods are stolen, he deliberately shuts his eyes to the consequences.[18] The vice of such a

12. "Handling, Theft and the Mala Fide Purchaser" [1985] Crim LR 92 and 440.
13. (1987) 84 Cr App Rep 75 at 78. See also *Grainge* [1974] 1 All ER 928, [1974] 1 WLR 619, CA; *Smith* (1977) 64 Cr App Rep 217, CA; *Reader* (1978) 66 Cr App Rep 33, CA.
14. *Toor* (1986) 85 Cr App Rep 116, CA.
15. *Grainge* [1974] 1 All ER 928, [1974] 1 WLR 619, CA; still less does it suffice to prove the circumstances were such that D ought to have realised the goods were stolen: *Atwal v Massey* [1971] 3 All ER 881.
16. *Reader* (1978) 66 Cr App Rep 33. Cp. *Spencer* [1983] QB 771, [1985] 1 All ER 673, [1985] Crim LR 101 and 440.
17. *Griffiths* (1974) 60 Cr App Rep 14 at 18, CA.
18. *Griffiths* (1974) 60 Cr App Rep 14, CA; *Ismail* [1977] Crim LR 557, CA; *Smith* (1977) 64 Cr App Rep 217, CA; *Pethick* [1980] Crim LR 242, CA; *Bellenie* [1980] Crim LR 437, CA; *Moys* (1984) 79 Cr App Rep 72, CA.

direction is that they may lead a jury to equate suspicion with knowledge or belief.

These cases merely indicate what does not constitute knowledge or belief. In *Hall*[19] Boreham J, delivering the judgment of the Court of Appeal, concluded that the time had come to give guidelines on the appropriate directions to be given to the jury:

"We think that a jury should be directed along these lines. A man may be said to know that goods are stolen when he is told by someone with first hand knowledge (someone such as the thief or the burglar) that such is the case. Belief, of course, is something short of knowledge. It may be said to be the state of mind of a person who says to himself: 'I cannot say I know for certain that these goods are stolen, but there can be no other reasonable conclusion in the light of all the circumstances, in the light of all that I have heard and seen.' Either of those two states of mind is enough to satisfy the words of the statute. The second is enough (that is, belief) even if the defendant says to himself: 'Despite all that I have seen and all that I have heard, I refuse to believe what my brain tells me is obvious.' What is not enough, of course, is mere suspicion. 'I suspect that these goods may be stolen, but it may be on the other hand that they are not.' That state of mind, of course, does not fall within the words 'knowing or believing'."

While it may be accepted that D knows goods are stolen when so informed by one who has first hand knowledge (provided D believes him of course!) this is merely an example of a case where D has knowledge and it is not a definition of knowledge. It is submitted that D knows goods are stolen when he concludes that they are and either does not consider the possibility that they may not be or considers that possibility and dismisses it. Prima facie "believing" adds something to "knowing",[20] but, according to *Hall*, not very much. The first example given by Boreham J, that of the man who says he cannot be sure but there is no other reasonable conclusion, might be said to know the goods are stolen because he has considered the possibility they are not and discounted it. The second example of the man who refuses to believe what his brain tells him is obviously problematical. D might receive goods from his mother in circumstances which all point to their being stolen and yet refuse to believe that his mother could be a thief.[1] It was once thought to be obvious that the sun went round the earth but some people were not entirely convinced. People can, and do, believe in the preposterous. The essence of belief is conviction and doubts are not inconsistent with conviction. A person may believe, and be properly said to believe, that he knows the way from X to Y notwithstanding that just to be on the safe side he takes a road map with him. So D may believe goods to be stolen provided that that is his conviction and notwithstanding that he has

---

19. (1985) 81 Cr App Rep 260 at 264.
20. Williams, TBCL at p. 875, says that "believing" was an unnecessary and therefore misleading addition to the section. It might equally be said that "knowing" is surplusage in that it conveys nothing that would not be conveyed by "believing".
  1. Conversely a man may believe goods to be stolen though all the available evidence points the other way and if the goods are in fact stolen he may be convicted of handling.

not dismissed from his mind the possibility that they may not be stolen after all.

But if D knows or believes that the goods which he handles are stolen goods, it need not be proved that D realised the nature of those goods. If D handles a container knowing that it contains stolen goods he commits the offence though he is surprised to discover that the container has contents other than those he imagined;[2] and it would seem to make no difference, provided the goods are in fact stolen, that D is misled as to their nature.

2 Dishonesty

Dishonesty was an essential ingredient of the old crime of receiving though it was not expressed in the statute. The inclusion of the word "dishonestly"[3] thus makes no change in the law. D may receive goods knowing or believing them to be stolen and yet not be guilty if, for example, he intends to return them to the true owner or the police.[4] A claim of right will amount to a defence, but it will be difficult to establish such a claim where D knows or believes the goods to be stolen except in the case put above, where he intends to return the goods to the owner.

3 Proof of Mens Rea

The common law rules concerning proof of *mens rea* on a receiving charge hold good under the Act. Accordingly, where D is found in possession of recently stolen property the judge may direct the jury that they *may* infer guilty knowledge or belief if D offers no explanation of his possession or if they are satisfied beyond reasonable doubt that any explanation he has offered is untrue. The onus of proof remains on the Crown throughout, and, whether D offers an explanation or not, he should be convicted only if the jury are satisfied beyond reasonable doubt that he had the guilty knowledge or belief.[5]

Because of the difficulty of proving guilty knowledge, the Larceny Act provided for the admission of certain evidence on a receiving charge which would not be admissible in criminal cases generally. The Theft Act has corresponding provisions. By s. 27 (3):

"Where a person is being proceeded against for handling stolen goods (but not for any offence other than handling stolen goods),[6] then at any stage of the proceedings, if evidence has been given of his having or arranging to have in his possession the goods the subject of the charge, or of his undertaking or assisting in, or arranging to undertake or assist in, their retention, removal, disposal or realisation, the following evidence shall be admissible for the purpose of proving that he knew or believed the goods to be stolen goods:

2. *McCullum* [1973] Crim LR 582, CA.
3. Cf. *Ghosh* [1982] QB 1053, [1982] 2 All ER 689, CA; above, p. 540.
4. Cf. *Matthews* [1950] 1 All ER 137, CCA.
5. *Abramovitch* (1914) 11 Cr App Rep 45, CCA; *Aves* [1950] 2 All ER 330, CCA; *Hepworth*, [1955] 2 QB 600, [1955] 2 All ER 918, CCA.
6. Cf. *Anderson* [1978] Crim LR 223 (Judge Stroyan).

(a) evidence that he has had in his possession, or has undertaken or assisted in the retention, removal, disposal or realisation of, stolen goods from any theft taking place not more than twelve months before the offence charged;[7] and

(b) (provided that seven days' notice in writing has been given to him of the intention to prove the conviction) evidence that he has within the five years preceding the date of the offence charged been convicted of theft or of handling stolen goods."[8]

16 Miscellaneous Matters

1) *Husband and Wife*

For many purposes husband and wife occupy a special position under the law and have special rules relating to themselves. This was so under the former law of larceny but now s. 30 of the Theft Act 1968 provides:

"(1) This Act shall apply in relation to the parties to a marriage, and to property belonging to the wife or husband whether or not by reason of an interest derived from the marriage, as it would apply if they were not married and any such interest subsisted independently of the marriage.

(2) Subject to subsection (4) below a person shall have the same right to bring proceedings against that person's wife or husband for any offence (whether under this Act or otherwise) as if they were not married, and a person bringing any such proceedings shall be competent to give evidence for the prosecution at every stage of the proceedings.

(3) (Repealed.)

(4) Proceedings shall not be instituted against a person for any offence of stealing or doing unlawful damage to property which at the time of the offence belongs to that person's wife or husband, or for any attempt, incitement or conspiracy to commit such an offence, unless the proceedings are instituted by or with the consent of the Director of Public Prosecutions:

Provided that—

(a) this subsection shall not apply to proceedings against a person for an offence—

(i) if that person is charged with committing the offence jointly with the wife or husband; or

(ii) if by virtue of any judicial decree or order (wherever made) that person and the wife or husband are at the time of the offence under no obligation to cohabit; and

(b) (Repealed.)"

---

7. As to which see *Bradley* (1979) 70 Cr App Rep 200, CA, [1980] Crim LR 173, and commentary.

8. These provisions have attracted both judicial and academic criticism: see *Fowler* (1987) 86 Cr App Rep 219, [1987] Crim LR 769, CA.

The substantial effect of s. 30 (1) is to make spouses liable in respect of offences against each other's property as though they were not married. Consequently either spouse may, for example, steal property belonging to the other. It may just be worth pointing out here that while it is clear that a spouse may steal property belonging exclusively to the other, it is equally clear that a spouse may steal property jointly owned with the other spouse since one co-owner may steal from another.[9]

By s. 30 (2) one spouse may prosecute the other, subject to s. 30 (4), for *any* criminal offence whether that offence is committed by a spouse on the person or property of the other, or whether by a spouse against a third party. A wife might, for example, prosecute her husband for stealing property belonging to a child of the marriage or for assaulting his mother-in-law.

While it is desirable that a spouse should have the general protection of the criminal law from depredations by the other, it will be appreciated that an over-readiness to institute proceedings by the one against the other, or by a third party against one spouse for an offence on the other spouse, can only be divisive, and hardly conducive to the continuation of a satisfactory domestic relationship. It is for this reason that s. 30 (4) provides that proceedings may not be instituted except by or with the consent of the Director of Public Prosecutions.[10] But note that the Director's consent need only be sought where the offence consists of "stealing or doing unlawful damage to property which at the time of the offence belongs to that person's wife or husband". Neither a wife nor a police officer, then, would need the Director's leave to institute proceedings for an assault on the wife by the husband, nor to prosecute the husband in respect of *any* offence committed by him on a third party.

Moreover, the Director's leave is not required in the two cases excepted by s. 30 (4) (a). The idea behind these exceptions is that in neither case does the risk of vexatious or divisive proceedings – which is the basis for the Director's control – exist. Thus a husband may, without the Director's leave, bring proceedings in respect of an appropriation of his property at a time when he was no longer bound to cohabit. And a third party may similarly bring proceedings where the spouses are jointly charged in respect of an offence relating to property belonging to one of them; an example of this might be where H sets fire to his house in order to endanger the life of another[11] and W aids him in the enterprise.

2) *Corporations and Their Officers*

So far as offences under the Theft Act generally are concerned, the liability of corporations for them falls to be determined in accordance with the

9. Above, p. 518.
10. *Withers* [1975] Crim LR 647.
11. See below, p. 704.

general principles applicable to the liability of corporations for crime.[12] Where a corporation commits a crime it must be the case that the crime has been committed by a person, or persons, in control of the corporation's affairs.[13] Such persons are of course liable in accordance with the ordinary principles governing liability for crime. In this particular s. 18 contains a special provision relating to the offences of obtaining property by deception, obtaining a pecuniary advantage by deception, and false accounting. The section provides:

"(1) Where an offence committed by a body corporate under section 15, 16 or 17 of this Act is proved to have been committed with the consent or connivance of any director, manager, secretary or other similar officer of the body corporate, or any person who was purporting to act in any such capacity, he as well as the body corporate shall be guilty of that offence, and shall be liable to be proceeded against and punished accordingly.

(2) Where the affairs of a body corporate are managed by its members, this section shall apply in relation to the acts and defaults of a member in connection with his functions of management as if he were a director of the body corporate."

This provision was explained by the Criminal Law Revision Committee as follows:[14]

"The [section] follows a form of provision commonly included in statutes,[15] where an offence is of a kind to be committed by bodies corporate and where it is desired to put the management[16] under a positive obligation to prevent irregularities, if aware of them. Passive acquiescence does not, under the general law, make a person liable as a party to the offence, but there are clearly cases (of which we think this is one) where the director's responsibilities for his company require him to intervene to prevent fraud and where consent or connivance amount to guilt."

The inference from this seems to be that, but for some such provision, the director might not in some circumstances be liable under the general principles governing liability for crime. Suppose, for example, that D, a director, learns that E, a fellow director, proposes to raise an overdraft from a bank by stating that it is required to enable the company to purchase plant when it is required to pay off creditors, but that D does nothing about it and the overdraft is authorised by the bank. The effect of s. 18 appears to be that D incurs criminal liability in respect of the obtaining of the pecuniary advantage by deception because the offence has been committed with his consent. There would be no need to show that D communicated to E his approval of the deception. Possibly, however, D would be liable under general principles for he has a clear duty to control the actions of E in this

12. See above, p. 178.
13. A corporation may of course be vicariously liable for crimes even though the crime is not committed by a person in control of its affairs: see above, p. 171. But vicarious liability would not apply in connection with offences under the Theft Act.
14. Cmnd. 2977, para. 104.
15. See further, above, p. 185.
16. Note that s. 18 imposes criminal liability only on the management; this may include (s. 18 (2)) any member who is in fact in control even though he may not formally hold a managerial post.

situation and his deliberate failure to perform his duty may make him an abettor.[17]

Restitution. Section 28 of the Theft Act 1968 and other statutory provisions relating to the restitution of stolen property are not discussed in this edition. See sixth edition, 639–644; Griew, *Theft*, Ch. 16; Smith, *Theft*, 225–234.

17. See above, p. 132. *Tamm* [1973] Crim LR 115, CA.

17 Forgery

Forgery and counterfeiting are now regulated by the Forgery and Counterfeiting Act 1981. This Act is largely based upon the recommendations of the Law Commission,[1] and forms part of the programme for the codification of the criminal law. Earlier legislation, in particular the Forgery Act 1913 and the Coinage Offences Act 1936, is repealed and the offence of forgery at common law is abolished. It follows that decisions under the former law are no longer binding though they may retain some persuasive authority and, in this text, may be referred to as vehicles for discussion.

Counterfeiting is discussed in the sixth edition of this work, pp. 669–676, but is omitted from this edition.

1 Forgery

The forging of documents in itself rarely brings any advantage to the forger. The forgery is usually done as a preparatory step to the commission of some other crime, most often a crime involving deception, which will result in some material advantage (most obviously money or other property) to the forger. Since preparatory acts, falling short of attempts, are not as such made criminal by the law, it has been cogently argued[2] that, with the exception of special cases such as banknotes and coins, there is no need for a separate offence of forgery. The Law Commission did not accept this view. In its view—

> "There is a number of reasons for not accepting the soundness of this premise. In the many and varied activities of modern society it is necessary to rely to a large extent on the authenticity of documents as authority for the truth of the statements which they contain."[3]

1. Law Com. No. 55, *Report on Forgery and Counterfeit Currency* (1973). See also the Commission's Working Paper No. 26, *Forgery* (1970). As to official reports, see above, p. 61, n. 1.
2. By Griew [1970] Crim LR 548 and Glazebrook [1970] Crim LR 554. Yet many statutes create offences of possessing even apparently innocuous articles with intent to commit crimes.
3. Law Com. No. 55, para. 14. When introducing the Bill to the House of Lords (HL, Vol. 416, col. 605) Viscount Colville declined to enter "the philosophical ... or jurisprudential discussions" about the need to have an offence of forgery. To him it was right that forgers "who, after all, are a special form of criminal that we tend to recognise as such" should have legislation directed against them. The circularity of this reasoning was apparently lost on their lordships. Lord Elwyn-Jones favoured the retention of forgery because it was a fact that "forgeries do run into thousands each year as crimes".

While the Commission recognised that it was unnecessary to rely on forgery where property was obtained by the use of forged documents, the necessity for an offence of forgery was strikingly illustrated by the kind of person who has in his possession numbers of forged documents (such as passports, credit cards, railway season tickets, even Cup Final tickets) where it would not be possible to bring home a charge of attempting to commit any offence. Perhaps it might be added, as a reason for retaining forgery, that it has long been regarded as a serious offence; history is on the side of the Law Commission.

1) *The Subject Matter of Forgery*

A person is guilty of forgery if he makes a false instrument and for this purpose "instrument" is defined by s. 8—

"(1) Subject to subsection (2) below, in this Part of this Act 'instrument' means—

(a) any document, whether of a formal or informal character;

(b) any stamp issued or sold by the Post Office;

(c) any Inland Revenue stamp; and

(d) any disc, tape, sound track or other device on or in which information is recorded or stored by mechanical, electronic or other means.

(2) A currency note within the meaning of Part II of this Act is not an instrument for the purposes of this Part of this Act.

(3) A mark denoting payment of postage which the Post Office authorise to be used instead of an adhesive stamp is to be treated for the purposes of this Part of this Act as if it were a stamp issued by the Post Office.

(4) In this Part of this Act 'Inland Revenue stamp' means a stamp as defined in section 27 of the Stamp Duties Management Act 1891."

The terms "writing", "document" and "instrument" have been traditionally used in the criminal law to denote the subject matter of forgery. At common law the preference was for "writing", under the Forgery Act 1913 it was for "document", under the new legislation "instrument" is given pride of place but this is immediately defined to include "any document, whether of a formal or informal character".

An instrument will normally be written on paper but may be written on any material and the writing may consist in letters, figures or any other symbols used for conveying information. "Instrument" might convey the notion that the document must be of a formal nature (wills, deeds etc.) but since s. 8 (1) (a) extends to documents of an "informal" character this notion would clearly be too restrictive. It has been held under earlier legislation that a forged letter purporting to come from an employee and requesting money from the employer,[4] a telegram which had been ante-dated in order to defraud a bookmaker,[5] a certificate of competency to

4. *Cade* [1914] 2 KB 209, CCA.
5. *Riley* [1896] 1 QB 309, CCR.

drive,[6] and a football pools[7] coupon were all documents and there is no reason to suppose that they would not be considered instruments within s. 8 (1) (a). It may often be relevant to ask, though it is not suggested as an exclusive test, whether the document is of such a kind that the recipient is expected to act on it in some way.

However widely defined, "instrument" cannot extend to manufactured articles as such. In common parlance a replica of a Stradivarius may be said to be a forgery but a violin cannot be regarded as a document. Nor is a painting as such a document. On the other hand an authentication certificate, purporting to come from an acknowledged expert and which ascribes that painting to a particular artist, is a document which may be forged,[8] and it is no less a document because it is pasted to the back of, or even directly written on the back of, the canvas. What, then, if D produces a facsimile Constable or Turner and further signs the painting in the style of the artist? In *Closs*[9] it was argued that the signature was, in effect, a certificate authenticating the work and as such it would constitute a forgery. The argument was rejected. Cockburn CJ asked—

"If you go beyond writing where are you to stop? Can sculpture be the subject of forgery?"[10]

The court went on to regard the signature as no more than a mark put upon the painting by the artist with a view to identifying it. *Closs* was decided at common law and, on essentially similar facts, a ruling was given in *Douce*[11] that the signature constituted a document within the 1913 Act because it purported to convey information about the picture. The Law Commission proposed to settle this argument in favour of *Closs* by defining "instrument" as "an instrument *in writing*"[12] but the Commission's wording has been modified in the Act.[13] If it were the practice of an artist to write on the back of his paintings the date and place of origin of his paintings and then add his signature, it would seem clear enough that this writing constitutes a document; if so there can only be the finest of lines between this and a signature on the face of the painting.

Perhaps an analogy is provided by the case where D alters the final letter on (i) the number plates, and (ii) the vehicle excise licence of his car.[14] The former may be done to induce an intending purchaser to believe that the car is less old than in fact it is.[15] The number plates tell a lie but essentially this lie is as to the age of the car and it is thought that the number plates do not constitute a document for they are not intended to be acted on otherwise

6. *Potter* [1958] 2 All ER 51, [1958] 1 WLR 638 (Paull J).
7. *Butler* (1954) 38 Cr App Rep 57, CCA.
8. *Pryse-Hughes* (1958) Times, 14 May.
9. (1857) Dears & B 460, CCR.
10. (1857) Dears & B 460 at 466.
11. [1972] Crim LR 105, QS.
12. Law Com. No. 55, para. 23, italics supplied.
13. Crystal-Kirk "Forgery Reforged" (1981) 49 MLR argues the painting in *Closs* falls within the 1981 Act.
14. See *Clifford v Bloom* [1977] RTR 351, DC; *Clayton* (1980) 72 Cr App Rep 135, [1981] Crim LR 186, CA.
15. The proffered explanation in *Clayton*, last note, was that D did not wish his friends to think he had come down in the world.

than as an identifying mark.[16] The vehicle excise licence is, however, a document; there is no difficulty in saying that it tells a lie about itself because it purports to have been issued in respect of a vehicle identified by a particular number when it was not so issued.

To be the subject of forgery the document, in the view of the Law Commission, must usually contain messages of two distinct kinds—

"The essence of forgery, in our view, is the making of a false document intending that it be used to induce a person to accept and act upon the message contained in it, as if it were contained in a genuine document. In the straightforward case a document usually contains messages of two distinct kinds – first a message about the document itself (such as the message that the document is a cheque or a will) and secondly a message to be found in the words of the document that is to be accepted and acted upon (such as the message that a banker is to pay a specified sum or that property is to be distributed in a particular way). In our view it is only documents which convey not only the first type of message but also the second type that need to be protected by the law of forgery."[17]

On this view it would not be forgery to make a false copy of a celebrity's autograph since the autograph conveys only one message (viz. about the genuineness of the signature) and there is no second message about the genuineness of the piece of paper on which the autograph is written. But where a cheque is forged by the insertion of a false signature two messages are conveyed; one that the signature is genuine and the other that the signature validates the order for the payment of money.

In this connection *Smith*[18] is worth comment. D had sold baking powder in wrappers substantially resembling the wrappers of one George Borwick, a well-known manufacturer of baking powder. It was held that the wrappers were not forgeries since they were not documents. The same result would appear to follow on the Law Commission view. The wrappers conveyed only one message, that they were George Borwick wrappers, and conveyed no further message concerning the genuineness of the document. They may have conveyed a second message about the lineage of the baking powder but there was no second message conveying the notion that the *wrapper* was to be accepted and acted upon.

The Law Commission was minded, and so provided in its Draft Bill, to exclude from the definition of "instrument" documents of historical interest only or as collector's items, but this does not form part of the Act. Suppose then that D makes a false copy of Shakespeare's will with a view to selling it as genuine. It is of course clear that if D makes a false copy of his father's will with a view to securing the inheritance for himself, this is a forgery. Both wills are made false with a view to dishonest gain but the Shakespeare will differs in one important respect. It is not produced with a view to affecting the devolution of Shakespeare's property and if P buys it he will do so not because the will, *qua* will, is going to affect his or anyone else's interests but merely for the intrinsic value of that piece of paper.

16. But it is an offence under the Road Vehicle (Registration and Licensing) Regulations 1971 fraudulently to alter number plates.
17. Law Com. No. 55, para. 22.
18. (1858) Dears & B 566, CCR.

The essence of "instrument" or "document" is peculiarly difficult to define. To constitute an instrument for the purposes of forgery, the document must do more than merely convey information; it must be of such a nature that the information contained in it[19] as a document is intended to be acted on in some way, usually, though not necessarily exclusively, by purporting to affect the rights or interests of some person or persons.

By s. 8 (1) (d) the definition of "instrument" embraces "any disc, tape, sound track or other device on or in which information is recorded or stored[20] by mechanical, electronic or other means". This extension, if extension it be,[1] must be regarded as entirely right in an age when so much documentation is so processed. The extension will of course be in the same terms. If D produces a recording of what purports to be Mr Gladstone's voice, he is not guilty of forgery though he intends to defraud purchasers; the recording is no more a document for the purposes of the Act than the false Shakespeare will. Nor is D, a bank teller, guilty of forgery merely by causing false entries to be made in the bank's computer any more than he would be guilty of forgery in making false entries in the bank's ledgers.[2] Nor is E guilty of forgery if he obtains access to information stored in a computer by sending electronic signals which cause the computer to accept him as an authorised user.[3] If, however, D and E cause entries to be made which purport to be made or authorised by one who did not make them, they may be guilty of forgery.

2) *The Forgery*

By s. 9 of the Act—

"(1) An instrument is false for the purposes of this Part of this Act—
   (a) if it purports to have been made in the form in which it is made by a person who did not in fact make it in that form; or
   (b) if it purports to have been made in the form in which it is made on the authority of a person who did not in fact authorise its making in that form; or
   (c) if it purports to have been made in the terms in which it is made by a person who did not in fact make it in those terms; or
   (d) if it purports to have been made in the terms in which it is made on the authority of a person who did not in fact authorise its making in those terms; or
   (e) if it purports to have been altered in any respect by a person who did not in fact alter it in that respect; or

19. A document may be comprised of more than one part, e.g. a letter may be taken together with its envelope.
20. Cf. *Gold and Schifreen* [1988] AC 1063, [1988] 2 All ER 186, HL, below, p. 675.
   1. It has never been of any account in the law of forgery on what material, or in what symbols or code, the information is recorded.
   2. Cf. *Re Windsor* (1865) 6 B & S 522.
   3. *Gold and Schifreen* (1987) 3 All ER 618, [1987] 3 WLR 803. See below, p. 675. But in these last two cases D will probably commit an offence under the Computer Misuse Act 1990.

(f) if it purports to have been altered in any respect on the authority of a person who did not in fact authorise the alteration in that respect; or

(g) if it purports to have been made or altered on a date on which, or at a place at which, or otherwise in circumstances in which, it was not in fact made or altered; or

(h) if it purports to have been made or altered by an existing person but he did not in fact exist.

(2) A person is to be treated for the purposes of this Part of this Act as making a false instrument if he alters an instrument so as to make it false in any respect (whether or not it is false in some other respect apart from that alteration)."

1 Falsity in General

The definition given by s. 9 of "falsity" is exhaustive and the governing notion is that the document must not only tell a lie, it must also tell a lie about itself.[4] Telling a lie does not become a forgery because it is reduced to writing; it is the document which must be false and not merely the information in it.

In its ordinary application the distinction is easy enough to grasp. If an applicant for a job falsely states his qualifications in his letter of application, the letter is not a forgery; but if he writes a reference which purports to come from his employer, the reference is a forgery. The reference is false within s. 9 (1) (a) because it purports to have been made in the form in which it is made by a person (the employer) who did not make it in that form. A cheque is similarly false if D signs it in the name of P.

The application of s. 9 (1) (a) is straightforward and no serious difficulties are likely to be encountered in the application of the next three cases instanced in the sub-section. Paragraph (b) deals with the case where D makes a document which purports to be made on P's authority (even though it does not purport to be made by P himself) when P's authority has not been given. It can make no difference, incidentally, if D has the same name as P provided that D intends his signature, or his authorisation, to be taken for the signature or authorisation, of P.

Paragraphs (c) and (d) in effect parallel (a) and (b) in relation to cases where P has in fact made or authorised the instrument in certain terms but D alters those terms. Thus (c) extends to the case where P draws a cheque for £10 and D makes the amount appear as £100; while (d) deals with the case where P, having authorised D to make out the cheque for £10, D in fact enters, £100.

Paragraphs (e) and (f) contain further parallel provisions in relation to alterations. Usually the maker of an instrument is at liberty to alter it (he may, for instance, alter the name of the payee or the amount to be paid on a cheque); but where another alters it, the alteration purporting to be made or authorised by the maker, the other makes a false instrument. In this

---

4. The aphorism appears to have been coined by Kenny, *Outlines*, 375.

connection the facts of *Hopkins and Collins*[5] provide a convenient illustration. D and E, the secretary and treasurer of a football supporters' club, received monies raised by members and made disbursements on behalf of the club. Over a period of time they (i) entered in the books amounts less than were paid in; (ii) entered amounts in excess of what was paid out; and (iii) altered certain of the entries. It is clear that their accounts were inaccurate but to keep inaccurate accounts is not a forgery. The accounts tell a lie but to be false within s. 9 (1) (e) or (f) they must tell a lie about themselves. So far as (i) and (ii) are concerned the accounts merely told a lie; they purported to be the accurate accounts of D and E when they were the inaccurate acounts of D and E. But what of (iii), the alterations? Paragraphs (e) and (f) do not render a document false merely because it has been altered; the alteration is a forgery only if it purports to be made or authorised by one who did not make or authorise it. Thus so long as the alterations were made or authorised by D and E they were not forgeries.

Suppose, however, that only D, the secretary, had been acting dishonestly, and suppose further that only E, the treasurer, was authorised to keep the accounts. If D, without E's authority, altered entries so that the alterations appeared to have been made or authorised by E, the accounts would be forged. To constitute a forgery the hand of Jacob must purport to be the hand of Esau.

A document is accordingly not forged merely because it contains false information and has been prepared by D to perpetrate a fraud. If D, with a view to defrauding P, procures E to execute documents which are to be used to convince P that D is a man of substance or of good character, the documents, so long as they purport to be executed by E, are not forged even though the transactions or facts to which they purport to relate are a complete sham.[6]

But a case which appears to be at odds with the foregoing is *Donnelly*.[7] D, a jeweller, at E's behest, gave E a written valuation of certain items of jewellery, the valuation stating that D had examined the jewellery. In fact there was no jewellery to be valued: the valuation was a sham and part of a plan to defraud insurers. Upholding D's conviction for forgery the Court of Appeal said that it was only concerned to determine whether the valuation certificate was a false instrument by virtue of s. 9. The court held that it was because it fell foul of s. 9 (1) (g) in that it had been made "otherwise in circumstances" in which it was not in fact made. "In our judgment," said the court[8] –

"the words coming at the end of paragraph (g) 'otherwise in circumstances ...' expand its ambit beyond dates and places to *any* case in which an instrument purports to be made when it was not in fact made. This valuation purported to be made *after* [D] had examined the items of jewellery. ... He did not make it after examining these items because they did not exist. That which purported to be a valuation after

5. (1957) 41 Cr App Rep 231, CCA.
6. Cf. *Dodge and Harris* [1972] 1 QB 416, [1971] 2 All ER 1523, CA.
7. (1984) 79 Cr App Rep 76.
8. At p. 78.

examination of items was nothing of the kind: it was a worthless piece of paper."

Obviously the valuation certificate told a lie, but did it tell a lie about the *circumstances* in which it was made? If it did then a begging letter in which the beggar, or someone on his behalf, falsely states that he is bedridden or unemployed, is equally a forgery because the circumstances to which the writer alludes are untrue. This would be a remarkable extension of the law of forgery as previously understood but *if* this is the conclusion to which s. 9 (1) (g) inexorably leads then it would have to be accepted.[9]

This construction is, however, open to serious question, and, it is submitted, cannot stand with the decision of the House of Lords in *More*[10] where Lord Ackner, in a speech with which all their lordships agreed, firmly stated that s. 9 (1) requires the document to tell a lie about itself. "It is common ground," he said[11]—

"that the consistent use of the word 'purports' in each of the paragraphs (a) to (h) inclusive of s. 9 (1) of the Act imports a requirement that for an instrument to be false it must tell a lie about itself, in the sense that it purports to be made by a person who did not make it (or altered by a person who did not alter it) or otherwise purports to be made or altered in circumstances in which it was not made or altered."

While *Donnelly* receives no mention in *More*, it must be clear that the former cannot stand with the latter; the valuation certificate in *Donnelly* told a lie but did not tell a lie about itself.[12]

Paragraph (g) of s. 9 (1) deals with the case where the document purports to be made or altered on a date or at a place or otherwise in circumstances where it was not in fact made or altered. This would deal, for example, with the case where D alters the date on a will or deed to make it appear to antedate another will or deed.[13] Nor is the will or deed any less false because it is D's own will or deed; a will or deed which purports to be executed on the 1st of the month tells a lie about itself if it was in fact executed on the 10th and D, provided he acts with *mens rea*, is guilty of forgery.[14]

2 Falsity and Non-existing Persons

Much the most difficult provision in s. 9 (1) is paragraph (h). Most frequently false documents purport to be made or authorised by some

---

9. Counsel for the Crown in *Donnelly* conceded that the valuation certificate would not have been a forgery either at common law or under the Forgery Act 1913 but argued that it was now a forgery by virtue of s. 9 (1) (g).

10. [1987] 3 All ER 825, [1987] 1 WLR 1578 discussed below, p. 667.

11. At p. 830.

12. For another view see Leng, "Falsity in Forgery" [1989] Crim LR 687.

13. Cf. *Wells* [1939] 2 All ER 169, 27 Cr App Rep 72, CCA; D was convicted of forgery where he altered the date on a settlement so as to ante-date the provisions of an Act of Parliament in order to avoid the payment of tax on the settlement.

14. Under the 1913 Act there was a requirement that a document must be forged in a *material* particular. Arguably on facts such as those in *Wells*, last note, D would not have been guilty of forgery in ante-dating the settlement if he had failed to ante-date it sufficiently to avoid the tax. There is now no requirement for materiality and D on facts such as *Wells* may be guilty of forgery even though the alteration does not achieve its intended effect. D may also be guilty of forgery if he alters it to make it false in any respect whether or not it is false in some other respect: s. 9 (2).

existing person known to the person intended to be affected by the contents of the document. Sometimes, however, D may find it equally, or better, suits his purpose to invent the name of a person by whom the document purports to be made. Suppose, for instance, that D and E apply for a job and in order to bolster their prospects D falsely makes a reference purporting to come from Sir George X while E falsely makes a reference purporting to come from Sir Peter Y. In fact there is no Sir George X who is merely D's invention, but there is a Sir Peter Y who was formerly E's employer. E's reference is clearly a forgery and, on the face of it, there is no reason why D's case should be treated any differently; certainly D's case falls within s. 9 (1) (h).

But consider the facts of *Hassard and Devereux*.[15] D, a company bookkeeper made out cheques to a company creditor, B.S.A., and after the cheques had been signed by directors, he altered the cheques to B. S. Andrews and handed them to his confederate, E. Obviously these cheques were forgeries (s. 9 (1) (b)) and we are not concerned with them. D and E now needed to cash these cheques so they gave them to F who opened an account in the name of B. S. Andrews, F representing herself as Andrews and giving her correct address. F then drew a cheque on this account. While F's conviction for forgery under the 1913 Act was upheld and was a questionable decision under that Act, the question which now arises is whether this cheque is a forgery by virtue of s. 9 (1) (h). It might be said that the case falls literally within the paragraph; the cheque purports to be made by an existing person (B. S. Andrews) who did not in fact exist.

Yet any person may assume an alias. Authors frequently do. If, for example, an author called X chooses to write under the name of Y and has his royalties paid to Y in which style he opens a bank account, is he guilty of forgery if he draws cheques on that account in the name of Y? The answer must be an obvious No. Y is not someone who does not exist; he is someone who does exist, Y being a mere alias for X. Clearly if the bank knows that X and Y are one and the same person there can be no question of forgery. It can hardly become forgery because the bank is unaware of the true name of Y, knowing him only in the style of Y. Nor can the cheques be regarded as forgeries because X has opened a bank account in the name of Y to avoid paying tax on his royalties.

It is suggested, therefore, that the assumption of an alias by D, by which alias he is known to P, falls outside s. 9 (1) (h), and documents presented by D to P in the style of his alias are not documents which are made by a person who did not in fact exist.

A somewhat similar problem is presented by the facts of *Martin*.[16] D, whose name was Robert Martin and who was well known to P, purchased from P a pony and trap, giving in payment a cheque. The cheque was signed in P's presence but was, unnoticed by P at the time, signed in the style of William Martin and was drawn on a bank at which D had no account. Literally the case might be said to fall within s. 9 (1) (h) but viewed realistically P knew precisely who had made and signed the cheque;

15. [1970] 2 All ER 647, [1970] 1 WLR 1109, CA.
16. (1879) 6 QBD 34, CCR.

whatever signature appeared on the cheque P knew that the maker was D. The document in the circumstances did not tell a lie about itself and it is thought that it would not constitute a forgery.

To go back to *Hassard and Devereux*. No doubt the bank, had it been aware that B. S. Andrews was not F's real name, would not have honoured the cheque or, at least, would have required a convincing reason why it should. But the bank was not misled by anything which appeared on the face of the cheque into thinking that it was honouring a cheque other than the cheque of the person presenting it for payment whether that person chose to call herself F or B. S. Andrews. The cheque does not purport to be made by an existing person who does not exist; it purports to be made by an existing person who chooses to assume one name rather than another.

This seems clearly to follow from *More*.[17] D came by a cheque made out to M.R. Jessell with which he opened an account at a building society in the name of Mark Richard Jessell and later drew on that account by completing a withdrawal form in the name of Mark Richard Jessell. Affirming D's conviction for forgery, the Court of Appeal held that the withdrawal form came within s. 9 (1) (h) since it purported to have been made by an existing person who did not in fact exist. The House of Lords disagreed and quashed the conviction. As Lord Ackner pointed out[18]—

"[D] was a real person. . . . The withdrawal form clearly purported to be signed by the person who originally opened the account and in this respect it was wholly accurate. Thus, in my judgment, it cannot be validly contended that the document told a lie about itself. . . ."

This, with respect, is entirely right. It follows that while there is no mention in *More* of *Hassard and Devereux* (presumably because the latter is a decision under the repealed 1913 Act) if the facts of *Hassard* were to recur a conviction for forgery under the 1981 Act could not be sustained.

This does not mean that s. 9 (1) (h) is devoid of effect though the scope for its application is probably not extensive. It would apply where D makes a document purporting to emanate from E (E being purely a fiction in the sense that neither D nor any accomplice of D's is going to assume the alias of E and represent himself as such to P) the case must fall within s. 9 (1) (h) and D is guilty of forgery.[19] Thus the case instanced at the beginning of this section, where D presents to P a reference purporting to emanate from Sir George X, there being no Sir George X, would be one of forgery. Another case falling within the paragraph might be where D writes begging letters to P apparently emanating from distressed ex-servicemen called X, Y and Z, where X, Y and Z are merely figments of D's imagination.

All in all it would seem that paragraph (h) can apply only in restricted circumstances and it may be that Williams was right in suggesting[20] that we ought to be spared the complexity which arises from the application of the law of forgery to documents in the name of fictitious persons.

17. [1987] 3 All ER 825, [1987] 1 WLR 1578, HL.
18. [1987] 3 All ER 830.
19. Cf. *Gambling* [1975] QB 207, [1974] 3 All ER 479, CA.
20. [1974] Crim LR 71 at 80.

3 Falsity by Omission

At first sight it may seem odd to suggest that forgery may be committed by omission since if anything requires positive and painstaking effort it might be said that this is so of the craft[1] of the forger. But appearances can be deceptive. Though such cases may be of rare occurrence, it is possible to predicate cases of forgery by omission. If, for example, P, a blind man, dictates his will to D and D, with a view to gain for himself or another or with intent to cause loss to another, omits certain provisions, the will appears to be a forgery. The will purports to be made or authorised in the terms in which it is made by a person (P) who did not in fact make or authorise its making in those terms and thus falls within s. 9 (1) (c) or (d). In order for an omission to constitute forgery its effect must be to render the document false within s. 9 (1), that is, it must result in the document telling a lie about itself. If in *Hopkins and Collins*[2] D and E had simply failed to enter in the club's books monies which were paid in by members, the accounts would not be forged. Their accounts would be inaccurate but they would not be false within any of the definitions in s. 10 (1); they would remain what they purported to be: a statement of accounts prepared by D and E.

3) *Mens Rea: Intent to Prejudice*

Sections 1–5 of the Act create various offences involving forgery. For purposes of convenience the *mens rea* of the various offences may be regarded as having two aspects. There is first of all the mental element required in relation to the making, using or possession of the false instrument and this aspect is considered in relation to the specific offences in the next section. The second aspect, which governs the offences under ss. 1–4 and certain of the offences under s. 5, is the requirement that D should intend that P should be induced, by reason of accepting the false instrument as genuine, to do some act to his own or another's prejudice. It is this aspect which is discussed in this section. Before turning to this, however, it follows that as the *mens rea* of forgery has these two aspects, it is necessary that it be proved both that D intended to make etc. the false instrument and that he intended thereby to induce another to act to his prejudice. In *Tobierre*[3] it was accordingly held that D's conviction was to be quashed where the trial judge appeared to have directed the jury that it was enough that D intended a false instrument to be accepted as genuine and did not, or did not adequately, explain that it must be proved also that D intended another to thereby act to his prejudice.

By s. 10 of the Act which *exhaustively* defines "induce" and "prejudice"—

---

1. Regrettably the photocopier and even kitchen cleansers (which can be used to remove signatures from credit and cheque cards) have brought forgery within the reach of the artisan as well as the artist.
2. (1957) 41 Cr App Rep 231, CCA, above, p. 664.
3. [1986] 1 All ER 346, [1986] 1 WLR 125, CA; *Garciá* (1987) 87 Cr App Rep 175, CA.

"(1) Subject to subsections (2) and (4) below, for the purposes of this Part of this Act, an act or omission intended to be induced is to a person's prejudice if, and only if, it is one which, if it occurs—

(a) will result—
  (i) in his temporary or permanent loss of property; or
  (ii) in his being deprived of an opportunity to earn remuneration or greater remuneration; or
  (iii) in his being deprived of an opportunity to gain a financial advantage otherwise than by way of remuneration; or
(b) will result in somebody being given an opportunity—
  (i) to earn remuneration or greater remuneration from him; or
  (ii) to gain a financial advantage from him otherwise than by way of remuneration; or
(c) will be the result of his having accepted a false instrument as genuine, or a copy of a false instrument as a copy of a genuine one, in connection with his performance of any duty.

(2) An act which a person has an enforceable duty to do and an omission to do an act which a person is not entitled to do shall be disregarded for the purposes of this Part of this Act.

(3) In this Part of this Act references to inducing somebody to accept a false instrument as genuine, or a copy of a false instrument as a copy of a genuine one, include references to inducing a machine to respond to the instrument or copy as if it were a genuine instrument or, as the case may be, a copy of a genuine one.

(4) Where subsection (3) above applies, the act or omission intended to be induced by the machine responding to the instrument or copy shall be treated as an act or omission to a person's prejudice.

(5) In this section 'loss' includes not getting what one might get as well as parting with what one has."

Essentially "prejudice" may be of two kinds, viz. the causing of economic loss or the causing of conduct in contravention of a duty.

1 Economic Loss

Usually an instrument is forged with a view to the economic benefit (in terms of money or other property) of the forger and consequential economic loss to the victim. Gain and loss are usually two sides of the same coin but the section treats separately of loss caused and advantage gained.

Most obviously D intends to induce P to act, or omit to act, to his prejudice if as a result P will be deprived, permanently or temporarily, of property (s. 10 (1) (a) (i)). This is most commonly the forger's intention and is typically instanced by the forgery of cheques, credit cards and other instruments in order to induce another to act to his prejudice. So if D falsifies a cheque guarantee card to induce P to part with money, or falsifies a credit card to induce Q to part with goods, he may be convicted of forgery. The fact that Q may, as is often the case with credit cards, claim reimbursement from R (a bank) cannot mean that Q has not been induced to act to his prejudice; Q has lost, and D intended to induce the loss of, the goods.

In practice most cases will be covered by s. 10 (1) (a) (i) but the section goes on to deal with other cases of much less frequent occurrence. Section 10 (1) (a) (ii) deals with the sort of case where P is seeking, say, employment or promotion in employment, and D writes a letter to the employer purporting to come from someone whose opinion is respected by the employer and which is intended to ensure that P does not get the post or the promotion. Such cases may be of limited occurrence but when they occur an instrument has been made false with a view to P's prejudice and there is no reason why they should not fall within the ambit of forgery.

Section 10 (1) (a) (iii) may have been included *ex abundanti cautela*. A case may be supposed where D and E are bidding for a contract to supply vehicle components to P. D might forge a letter purporting to come from someone who has done business with E which asserts that E cannot be relied on to keep delivery dates. If E does not get the contract he has not been deprived of property within s. 10 (1) (a) (i). Nor might the case fall within s. 10 (1) (a) (ii) since "remuneration" ordinarily connotes a payment for services rendered and may not be apt to cover the case where someone loses his profit margins under a contract for the supply of goods. Accordingly sub-paragraph (iii) was included to make it clear that such a case falls within the Act.

Section 10 (1) (b) is concerned with financial advantage and there is no need to prove loss to any particular victim. Usually that advantage will accrue to the forger or an accomplice but an offence may be committed though the beneficiary is unaware of the fraud. If D forges a testimonial with a view to securing the employment, or promotion, of someone in P's firm, it does not matter whether that someone is D himself, or someone who has procured the forged testimonial or someone who is wholly ignorant of D's action. The case falls within s. 10 (1) (b) (i) since "somebody" is given an opportunity to earn remuneration or greater remuneration. Nor does it matter that the someone who gets the job, or the promotion, fully justifies the remuneration, or greater remuneration, or, indeed, brings financial gain to P.

Section 10 (1) (b) (ii) deals with the case where a financial advantage, otherwise than by way of remuneration, is sought. So if in the bidding for a contract D forges a letter extolling the virtues of his own (or another bidder's) products an offence may be committed. Again, it cannot matter that D's (or the other's) products are in fact the best and the cheapest. The section makes it clear that an act or omission intended to be induced "is" to another's prejudice if the case falls within the section.

Normally D may falsify an instrument with a view to giving himself (or another) an advantage over other competitors, or seek to disadvantage another competitor, but a case may fall within s. 10 though D is the sole applicant for a job or a sole bidder for a contract.

2 Performance of Duty

Under the former law it was unclear how far the *mens rea* of forgery extended beyond an intent to cause economic loss. The argument is now, in a sense, settled by s. 10 (1) (c) – a victim is prejudiced if it is intended that he should accept a false instrument as genuine "in connection with his performance of any duty".

In formulating this provision the Law Commission sought,[4] on the one hand, to include such cases as forging a security pass to gain access to premises, forging a certificate of competency to drive, and forging documents in such circumstances as *Welham v Director of Public Prosecutions*[5] where documents were forged not with the intention of causing financial loss but with the intention of avoiding statutory restrictions on borrowing. On the other hand, the Commission wished to exclude cases where the prejudice was trivial or inconsequential, such as a forged invitation to a social function done with the intention of raising a laugh at the victim's expense.

The Act seeks to achieve this balance by the employment of the concept of "duty". "Duty" here must refer to a legal duty and cannot extend to what might be regarded as a social or moral duty. It will extend, however, to a duty arising under contract as well as a duty imposed by law independently of contract. Thus such cases as *Harris*[6] (where papers were forged to secure the release of a prisoner from jail); *Toshack*[7] (where a seaman forged a certificate of good conduct so that the Trinity House examiners would let him take an examination); *Moah*[8] (where a testimonial was forged to gain admission to the police force); and *Bassey*[9] (where a student forged papers to gain admission to the Inner Temple) would all fall within s. 10 (1) (c).

But where it is not intended to induce anyone to act in contravention of a duty no offence is committed under the Act. The Law Commission instances the case of the bogus invitation to a party with a view to raising a laugh. It is understandable that the heavy hammer of forgery should not be used on so small a nut,[10] even though real inconvenience may be caused.[11]

It is not enough that an instrument is falsified with a view to deceiving P unless there is an intention to induce an act or omission which constitutes "prejudice" as defined. It would not constitute forgery, for example, to falsify a birth certificate if D's *only* object is to convince people of his legitimacy, or to falsify a degree certificate if D's *only* object is to make his friends believe that he has had a university education. And to constitute forgery D must intend by the false document to prejudice the victim or some other party; it is not enough that acceptance of the false document will result in someone doing, or not doing, something to D's prejudice. Literally "a person's prejudice" in s. 10 might be read as including D

---

4. Law Com. No. 55, paras. 28-37.
5. [1961] AC 103, [1960] 1 All ER 805, HL.
6. (1833) 1 Mood CC 393, CCR.
7. (1849) 1 Den 492.
8. (1858) Dears & B 550, CCR.
9. (1931) 22 Cr App Rep 160, CCA.
10. Yet the heavy hammer would be applicable if the invitation was intended to induce a doorman or butler to admit the bearer to the party.
11. What if the bogus invitation was sent as a means of getting P out of the way while D burgles his premises? Has D, by reason of getting P to accept the invitation as genuine, induced an act which, if it occurs, will result in P's loss of property within s. 10 (1) (a) (i)?

himself but in *Utting*[12] the Court of Appeal rightly regarded such a submission as absurd.

3 Claim of Right

This issue may be conveniently introduced by reference to the facts of *Parker*,[13] a decision under the former law. D, who had made a loan of £3 to P and was unable to get payment from P, wrote P a letter, purporting to come from the War Office, which asked P to give D's demand his best attention without delay. On these facts D has obviously made a false instrument within s. 9 but he is not guilty of forgery by reason of s. 10 (2) which provides that an act which a person has an enforceable duty to do (or an omission which he has an enforceable duty not to do) is to be disregarded for the purposes of the section. Arguably P suffers no "prejudice" within s. 10 (1) if he is merely made to pay that which he already owes[14] but s. 10 (2) puts the matter beyond doubt. The "enforceable duty" must of course be one which is imposed by law or arises under contract.

In *Parker* the debt was in fact owing but it is submitted that an honest belief[15] in entitlement suffices even if the belief is unreasonable. But it is not enough that D genuinely believes that his action is justified.[16] D may feel that he has been unfairly overlooked for promotion on previous occasions but if on the next occasion he falsifies a testimonial intending to induce P to promote him all the requirements of forgery are satisfied. The Law Commission said:

> "If a person makes a false instrument intending that it be used as genuine to prejudice another by inducing him to act contrary to his duty it is irrelevant that that person may genuinely believe that he is entitled to what he is trying to obtain. However firmly he may believe, for example, that he is entitled to a driving licence, he intends another to act contrary to his duty if he intends to induce him to issue such a licence against a false certificate of competency to drive, as it is the issuing officer's duty to issue a licence only against the presentation of a valid certificate of competence."

Suppose, then, that D forges the acceptance to a bill of exchange in the name of E and claims that when he did so he intended all along to meet the bill and has in fact now paid the bankers who honoured the bill so that no actual loss has been sustained by anyone.[17] The case appears to fall within the Act. By the forged signature D has induced the bankers to honour the bill and by this D gains a financial advantage.[18] D cannot be relieved of liability by s. 10 (2) because it cannot be asserted that the bankers have any

---

12. [1987] Crim LR 636.
13. (1910) 74 JP 208, CCC.
14. Cf. the discussion in connection with blackmail, above, p. 612.
15. The Law Commission, Law Com. No. 55, para. 35 considered adding "dishonestly" to the mental element but did not think that it was "either necessary or helpful".
16. Cf. *Hagan* [1985] Crim LR 598, CA, holding it irrelevant that D may have made no personal gain from the property obtained and may have applied it to entirely worthy causes. The case was decided under the 1913 Act but the same result would follow under the 1981 Act.
17. These are the facts of *Geach* (1840) 9 C & P 499.
18. In effect D obtains credit or time to pay.

enforceable duty to honour a forged bill; had the bankers known that they were in the position of accepting a bill without the usual security of an acceptor they would have been in duty bound to reject it.

It follows that while a claim of legal right may negative an intent to cause another to act to his prejudice, it is not ordinarily relevant to consider whether D was acting dishonestly. Some might say that the forger of the acceptance to a bill who all along intends to meet the bill is not acting dishonestly, but this would not affect his liability for forgery since he has intentionally made a false instrument with intent thereby to induce another to do that which it is his duty not to do. This is confirmed by *Campbell*.[19] E, a plausible rogue, told D that having returned a car to a seller, the only way the seller could repay the purchase price was for him to make out a cheque in a fictitious name. D then obliged E by endorsing the cheque in the fictitious name to herself and paying it into her account, later drawing out the money which she paid to E. It was never doubted but that D had been duped and that she thought she was acting honestly in that no one would be the loser. Affirming her conviction for forgery the Court of Appeal said that the trial judge was right to rule that dishonesty was not a necessary element of forgery. Both elements of the *mens rea* were present here; she intended the bank to accept the false signature on the cheque as genuine and by reason thereof to cause the bank to do that which it was its duty not to do. It was thus irrelevant that she intended no permanent or temporary loss to the bank.

But suppose that in *Campbell* E's plausibility had been such that she convinced D that the drawer of the cheque had authorised D to endorse it in his name. Obviously if D signs an instrument "D on behalf of X" wrongly but honestly believing that he has X's authority to do so, the instrument is not a forgery; it has not been made false so as to appear genuine. At common law the same result obtained where D, wrongly but honestly believing that he had X's authority, simply signed the instrument in the name of X.[20] But by s. 9 (1) (a) such an instrument is literally false since it purports to be made in the form in which it is made by a person who did not make it in that form. Yet an instrument may be valid though not signed by the maker so long as it is signed on his authority. A will is valid notwithstanding that another signs it in the testator's name so long as it is signed by the direction and in the presence of the testator; and a bill of exchange is valid if the drawer's signature is written on it by another with the drawer's authority. If the instrument is valid because the signature is authorised, it would be absurd to say that it is a false instrument and such an instrument may properly be regarded as being *made* by the person, P, authorising the use of his signature. If, however, D does not have P's authority to sign, though D believes that he has, the instrument would be invalid. Nevertheless it is submitted that D would not be guilty of forgery either because D does not intend to make the instrument purport to be other than an instrument *made* by P, or because, believing the instrument to be valid, D cannot intend another to act on it to his prejudice. But if on

19. (1985) 80 Cr App Rep 47, CA; **SHC 527**.
20. *Forbes* (1835) 7 C & P 224; *Clifford* (1845) 2 Car & Kir 202.

these facts D honestly believed he was authorised by E to accept in E's name he would not intend the bankers to do anything to their own, or any other person's, prejudice.[1] Similarly D would not be guilty of forgery where he enters a larger amount in a bill or cheque where he is authorised to enter a smaller amount if he honestly believes he is authorised to enter the larger amount.[2]

4 Forgery and Machines

Normally an instrument is forged with a view to causing loss to a person, or bringing a gain to a person, or causing a person to act in contravention of a duty. But nowadays D may use a forged instrument to cause a machine to operate to his advantage. Forgery postulates that "somebody" is induced to accept a false instrument as genuine and by reason of that to do or refrain from doing some act, and thus may not be apt to cover such cases. "The increasing use of more sophisticated machines", said the Law Commission,[3]

> "has led us to include within 'instruments' capable of being forged the discs, tapes and other devices mentioned in paragraph 25, which may cause machines into which they are fed to respond to the information or instructions upon them, and, of course, there are machines which are designed to respond to an instrument in writing. It is necessary, therefore, to make provision to cover in such cases the intention to cause a machine to respond to a false instrument as if it were a genuine instrument. There also has to be provision for treating the act or omission intended to flow from the machine responding to the instrument as an act or omission to a person's prejudice."

Sections 10 (3) and (4) implement the Commission's view. Take a simple illustration. If D uses a false instrument (say a cash card) to obtain cash from a machine (a bank's cash dispenser) he steals the money.[4] While this would seem to be enough to meet the case the position under the Act is that D is guilty of forgery if he made the instrument for this purpose, or of using a false instrument if he is not the maker. He is apparently so guilty though no *person* is ever induced to treat the false card as genuine;[5] the false card was made with a view to "inducing *the machine* to respond" to the false card as genuine (s. 10 (3)), and by s. 10 (4) the prejudice resulting "*shall* be treated" as an act to a person's prejudice.

---

1. Cf. *Forbes* (1835) 7 C & P 224.
2. Cf. *Clifford* (1845) 2 Car & Kir 202.
3. Law Com. No. 55, para. 36.
4. Cf. *Hands* (1887) 56 LT 370, DC, above, p. 562.
5. In the Explanatory Notes to the Draft Bill (Law Com. No. 55) the Commission said of its provision (which is not reproduced in *identical* terms in the Act) that it "is required to deal with those cases where the false instrument, whether it be an instrument in writing or a disc, tape, sound track or other device, is made or used to cause a machine to respond to it as if it were a genuine instrument. The use of a false card to cause a bank's cash dispensing machine to pay out money would not be within [section] 3 standing alone as there would be no intention of inducing somebody to accept it as genuine and to act upon it." And see now the Computer Misuse Act 1990 which in the instances discussed above will usually offer an alternative route to conviction.

In many cases where D, by the use of false instruments or otherwise, causes a machine to record information as made or authorised by one who did not make it, some person will be induced to act on it as genuine and the case is one of forgery in the ordinary way. However, with the increasing mechanisation of accounting, it may be the case, and may increasingly become the case, that D achieves his purpose in having his or another's account credited with monies though no *person* is ever deceived. D may still be convicted of a forgery offence because he has induced the machine to accept the false as genuine and the resulting prejudice is treated as being to a person.

These cases are ones where economic loss is caused. But prejudice is not confined to economic loss and extends to causing a person to act in contravention of a duty since "prejudice" referred to in s. 10 (4) is a reference to any of the forms of prejudice in s. 10 (1). If D causes the bank's computer to accept information which purports to be made or authorised by one who did not make or authorise it with a view to inducing P (an employee of the bank) to act in contravention of his duty this is forgery in the ordinary way. But we are also to contemplate, presumably, that the computer can be induced to act in contravention of its duty! If, then, D makes a false pass to gain access to premises (for example, to a car park or a building) via a machine which is programmed to respond to authorised passes, the case appears to fall literally within these provisions; the machine has accepted the false pass as genuine and its response is to be treated as a response to a person's prejudice.

The difficulties are illustrated by *Gold and Schifreen*.[6] Here D and E, two skilled 'hackers', obtained unauthorised access to P's computer on which information was stored by causing the computer to accept them as authorised users. The House of Lords agreed with the Court of Appeal that their convictions for forgery should be quashed on two grounds. One was that the signals which caused the computer to treat them as authorised users were never 'recorded or stored' within the Act; they appeared only momentarily on a screen and were then immediately expunged. The other reason was that the extension of forgery to discs, tapes etc. did not alter the need for the requirement that for forgery the document must tell a lie about itself. Here, it seems, D and E simply caused the computer to accept *them* as authorised users. In effect they simply told a lie (viz, we are authorised users) and the case might be likened to D writing a password on a piece of paper which tricks the sentry into admitting him.

The court in *Gold* was evidently unhappy about what it regarded as a procrustean attempt to use the Act for situations for which it was not designed.[7] There are certainly difficulties here and it may be that the effect of s. 10 (3) and (4) is not quite so far reaching. Take again the case where D uses a false cash card to get money from the dispenser. At some subsequent stage P, a bank employee, will react to the information stored in the dispenser and D intends P then to act to his own or another's prejudice. At this stage P cannot be induced so to act by accepting the false cash card as

6. [1988] 2 All ER 186, HL.
7. See the Computer Misuse Act 1990, below, p. 714, which deals with the problem.

genuine for he cannot have seen it; that would normally require that D could not be convicted of a forgery offence but s. 10 (3) meets this difficulty by providing that references to a false instrument include a reference to inducing a machine to respond to a false instrument as genuine. The false information, in effect, becomes the false instrument which P is induced to accept as genuine. On this view the "act or omission intended to be induced" in s. 10 (4) is P's (a person's) act or omission following upon the machine responding to the false instrument.

5 Causation

Forgery extends not merely to the case where by reason of accepting the false instrument as genuine P is intended to be induced to act, or fail to act, to his prejudice but also to the case where P is intended to be caused so to act, or not to act, to the prejudice of any other person. As has been shown,[8] a false testimonial may be sent by D to P in order to induce P to appoint D, or to appoint E or not to appoint F, and all three situations fall within the ambit of forgery. But it is not enough that the false instrument results in prejudice to someone; the prejudice must result from a person (or persons) having accepted the false instrument as genuine and being induced thereby to do or refrain from doing something to his or another's prejudice. Prejudice clearly results to F if as a result of the false reference F is not considered for the job and is denied the opportunity to earn remuneration, but the offence lies, not in F being prejudiced, but in P being induced to act to F's prejudice.

Suppose that D wishes to acquire a vehicle from P, a dealer, and because D does not have the wherewithal he is referred by P to Q, a finance company, to arrange a hire-purchase of the vehicle. D signs the hire-purchase proposal in the name of R, R being a creditworthy individual which D is not. Having satisfied himself that R is creditworthy, Q confirms the proposal with P and P delivers the vehicle.[9] Supposing that P is prejudiced by delivering the vehicle to D,[10] it would not be apt to allege in an indictment that D has made a false instrument intending to induce P to act to his prejudice. The victim must be a person who, by reason of being induced to treat the false instrument as genuine, does something (or fails to do something) to his own or another's prejudice. The case presents no problems if D is charged with inducing Q to act to his own or another's prejudice in that D gains from Q a financial advantage otherwise than by way of remuneration.[11]

---

8. Above, p. 666.
9. These are the facts of *Hurford* [1963] 2 QB 398, [1963] 2 All ER 254, CCA.
10. It may be that P is not prejudiced since he may be able to claim the whole of the price of the vehicle from Q.
11. Hence the Law Commission (Law Com. No. 55, para. 47) saw no need to reproduce the offence under s. 7 of the 1913 Act of demanding property under or by virtue of forged instruments.

4) *The Offences*

1 Forgery

By s. 1 of the Act—

"A person is guilty of forgery if he makes a false instrument, with the intention that he or another shall use it to induce somebody to accept it as genuine, and by reason of so accepting it to do or not to do some act to his own or any other person's prejudice."

By s. 6 the offence is triable either way; on summary conviction it is punishable by six months imprisonment and/or a fine of Level 4 and on trial on indictment by ten years imprisonment and/or a fine.[12]

Forgery is committed where D makes an instrument with the intention that somebody shall be induced to accept it as genuine. It is not enough, therefore, that D makes a copy of an instrument if his intention is to represent it as a copy; were it otherwise the photo-copier would have made us a nation of forgers. Nor would it suffice, it is submitted, that, subsequently realising that the copy is good enough to pass as the original, D decides to pass it as the original. The definition requires that D *makes* the false instrument with the requisite intent.

2 Copying a False Instrument

By s. 2 of the Act—

"It is an offence for a person to make a copy of an instrument which is, and which he knows or believes to be, a false instrument, with the intention that he or another shall use it to induce somebody to accept it as a copy of a genuine instrument, and by reason of so accepting it to do or not to do some act to his own or any other person's prejudice."

The offence is triable and punishable in the same way as forgery under s. 1.

The commission of this offence requires (a) that the instrument that is copied is in fact a false instrument;[13] and (b) that D "knows or believes"[14] it to be false. In addition (c) the copy must be made with the intention of inducing someone to accept it as a copy of a genuine instrument.

It is not an offence simply to copy an instrument known or believed to be false if the copy is made to pass as a copy of a false instrument. At a trial for forgery copies of the allegedly false instrument may be photocopied for the convenience of judge and counsel and it can hardly be supposed that this falls within s. 2. The operation of the section may be illustrated by reference to the facts of *Harris*.[15] D, who owed money to P, had acquired a receipt to which P's signature had been forged. He told P that he had paid the debt and when P questioned this, D photocopied the forged receipt and sent the copy to P. Such conduct clearly falls within s. 2. Strictly it is arguable that a photocopy of a false instrument made with the intention of being passed *as a copy* of a false instrument does not tell a lie about itself

---

12. The offence is finable on indictment by virtue of s. 30 of the Powers of Criminal Courts Act 1973.
13. Just as for handling, above, p. 635, it must be proved that the goods are in fact stolen. If the instrument is not false but is believed by D to be false there may be an attempt, above, p. 304.
14. As to which see above, p. 650.
15. [1966] 1 QB 184, [1965] 3 All ER 206n, CA.

and courts elsewhere[16] have been disposed to take this view. Only where the copy is made to pass as the original false instrument would the copy tell a lie about itself. The point is, however, no longer of importance in view of s. 2; the offence is committed if D intends to pass the photocopy as a copy of a genuine instrument. But if D intends to pass off his copy of the false instrument as the false instrument itself this is forgery under s. 1 and does not fall within s. 2.

3 Using False Instruments and Copies

By s. 3—

> "It is an offence for a person to use an instrument which is, and which he knows or believes to be, false, with the intention of inducing somebody to accept it as genuine, and by reason of so accepting it to do or not to do some act to his own or any other person's prejudice."

And by s. 4—

> "It is an offence for a person to use a copy of an instrument which is, and which he knows or believes to be, a false instrument, with the intention of inducing somebody to accept it as a copy of a genuine instrument, and by reason of so accepting it to do or not to do some act to his own or any other person's prejudice."

Both offences are triable and punishable in the same way as forgery under s. 1.

The offence under s. 3 in substance replaces the former offence, under s. 6 of the Forgery Act 1913, of uttering. Under s. 6 a person who "uses, offers, publishes, delivers, disposes of, tenders in payment or exchange, exchanges, tenders in evidence or puts off" was guilty of uttering. This extravagance of language is now replaced by the single verb "uses" but this does not import any restriction on the ambit of the offence. The Law Commission was aware[17] that "uses" is the paramount verb, was so regarded by the courts,[18] and would do duty for the remaining expressions in the earlier legislation.

Any use of the false instrument will suffice. While the actual making of the false instrument can hardly be regarded as a use of it, its communication to another is clearly a use of it. No doubt it would be enough that it is left in a position where P will see it and it may be enough that it is sent to another.[19]

The use is not restricted to the maker of the false instrument. It is equally an offence for someone who did not make the false instrument to use it with the appropriate intent, whether or not there is any collaboration with the maker.

---

16. *Chow Sik Wah and Quon Hong* [1964] 1 CCC 313 (Ontario Court of Appeal); *Tait* [1968] 2 NZLR 126 (New Zealand Court of Appeal).
17. Law Com. No. 55, para. 49.
18. Cf. *Harris* [1966] 1 QB 184, [1965] 3 All ER 206n, CA.
19. Cf. *Harris*, last note. There is clearly a use of a false witness statement when it is sent forward along with other documentation relating to the case. Cf. *A-G's Reference (No. 2 of 1980)* [1981] 1 All ER 493, [1981] 1 WLR 148, CA.

Whether making a copy of a false instrument, without any further steps taken to communicate it to another, constitutes a use of a false instrument[20] is no longer of importance in view of the fact that it would in any case be an offence under s. 2. Strictly, though, the case seems to fall within s. 3. While it can hardly be said that D in forging a document purporting to be made by P is "using" the very document he forges, there is no reason why E, who comes across D's forgery and photocopies it with the appropriate intent, should not be regarded as using D's forged instrument. In the ordinary use of language he has used the instrument which was forged by D. There may thus be a use of a false instrument though it is not communicated to another.

Little needs to be said about s. 4 which parallels s. 3 in relation to the use of a copy of the false instrument. It is submitted that copying a false instrument does not constitute a use *of the copy* within s. 4. As has just been indicated this may constitute a use of the false instrument within s. 3; at the stage of copying D may properly be said to have used the original forged instrument but he can hardly be said to be *using* the copy which he makes.

4 Possession Offences

By s. 5 of the Act—

"(1) It is an offence for a person to have in his custody or under his control an instrument to which this section applies which is, and which he knows or believes to be, false, with the intention that he or another shall use it to induce somebody to accept it as genuine, and by reason of so accepting it to do or not to do some act to his own or any other person's prejudice.

(2) It is an offence for a person to have in his custody or under his control, without lawful authority or excuse, an instrument to which this section applies which is, and which he knows or believes to be, false.

(3) It is an offence for a person to make or to have in his custody or under his control a machine or implement, or paper or any other material, which to his knowledge is or has been specially designed or adapted for the making of an instrument to which this section applies, with the intention that he or another shall make an instrument to which this section applies which is false and that he or another shall use the instrument to induce somebody to accept it as genuine, and by reason of so accepting it to do or not to do some act to his own or any other person's prejudice.

(4) It is an offence for a person to make or to have in his custody or under his control any such machine, implement, paper or material, without lawful authority or excuse.

(5) The instruments to which this section applies are—

(a) money orders;

(b) postal orders;

(c) United Kingdom postage stamps;

(d) Inland Revenue stamps;

---

20. A point canvassed but left open in *Harris*, last note.

    (e) share certificates;

    (f) passports and documents which can be used instead of pass-
        ports;

    (g) cheques;

    (h) travellers' cheques;

    (j) cheque cards;

    (k) credit cards;

    (l) certified copies relating to an entry in a register of births,
        adoptions, marriages or deaths and issued by the Registrar
        General, the Registrar General for Northern Ireland, a regis-
        tration officer or a person lawfully authorised to register mar-
        riages; and

    (m) certificates relating to entries in such registers.

(6) In subsection (5) (e) above 'share certificate' means an instrument
entitling or evidencing the title of a person to a share or interest—

    (a) in any public stock, annuity, fund or debt of any government or
        state, including a state which forms part of another state; or

    (b) in any stock, fund or debt of a body (whether corporate or
        unincorporated) established in the United Kingdom or else-
        where."

The offences under s. 5 (1) and (3) are triable and punishable in the same
way as forgery under s. 1. The offences under s. 5 (2) and (4) are also triable
either way and are punishable on summary conviction with the same
maxima of six months imprisonment and/or a fine of £1,000; on trial on
indictment, however, these offences carry a maximum of two years imprisonment and/or a fine.

    Section 5 penalises the possession of the instruments specified in s. 5 (5).
The list is exhaustive so that it is not an offence under this section to
possess a false instrument as such (say a false testimonial or will) unless it is
one of the instruments specified.

    Section 5(3) also penalises the possession of any "machine or implement,
or paper or any other material, which to [D's] knowledge has been specially
designed or adapted[1] for the making of an instrument" to which the section
applies. It is accordingly not enough that D possesses implements with
which he intends to make an instrument unless the implements are *specially*
designed or adapted to make one of the *specified* implements. It is no
offence to possess a pen though D's intention is to use it to make one of the
specified instruments; nor is it an offence to possess a household cleanser in
order to falsify one of the specified instruments[2] since neither the pen nor
the cleanser are specially designed, nor need they be adapted, for the
making of a false instrument. It is of course not possible to provide an
exhaustive list of the machines, implements, paper or other materials which
are specially designed or adapted for making instruments to which the
section applies; it is for the prosecution to establish that the implement etc.
is so designed or adapted and that D knew that. "Knowledge" in this sub-

---

    1. As to which see the discussion, above, p. 444.
    2. Certain household cleansers can be used to remove the holder's signature from credit cards
thus enabling D to sign the holder's signature in his own hand which can be easily reproduced
by D.

section is not coupled with "belief" as it is elsewhere in the section and generally in offences under the Act. Clearly "knowledge" is more restricted than "knowledge or belief" but the boundary between the two is somewhat speculative.[3]

It is only necessary to show that the implement etc. has been specially designed or adapted to make an instrument to which the section applies, not that the machine etc. has been designed or adapted to make *false* instruments. No doubt it will often be D's intention that he or another should so use it, but it suffices that the implement etc. is specially designed or adapted to produce any of the specified instruments. Very commonly cheque books are stolen and may be found in the custody or control of D; if D has one of the relevant states of mind he is guilty of an offence since the paper or other materials used are specially designed for the making of cheques and cheques are included in the specified instruments.

D must be proved to have "custody or control" of the false instrument or of the implement etc. which is specially designed or adapted for its making. The Law Commission, not entirely unreasonably, is reluctant to plump for "possession" because of the technicalities which have come to be associated with that concept.[4] The Commission prefers "custody or control" as it did with criminal damage and reference may be made to the discussion in that context.[5]

While s. 5 creates four offences, there are in essence two pairs of offences. All four offences have the common element of custody or control of instruments or implements. The offences under s. 5 (1) and (3) are more serious than those under s. 5 (2) and (4) in requiring proof that D has the instrument intending to induce another to accept it as genuine and thereby to do, or not to do, something to his own or another's prejudice, or has the implement with a view to its use to produce an instrument with like intent. This intent has already been discussed.[6] The offences under s. 5 (2) and (4) differ only, but differ markedly, in relation to the mental element that needs to be established. Under these provisions it is enough that D has custody or control of a specified instrument which he knows to be false, or a proscribed implement, "without lawful authority or excuse".

Lawful authority or excuse is not defined in the Act and its use in other contexts[7] affords no grounds for thinking that, so far as D is concerned, it will be generously interpreted. No doubt a police officer who in the course of his duty seizes false documents or implements has lawful authority for his custody, as does a private citizen who gains such custody with a view to delivering them to the police or other proper authority.[8] Lawful authority must extend not only to those authorised by law but also to those who plan to act in accordance with law. "Excuse" is more difficult to define. It must extend to cases other than those where D has available to him some general defence to crime (for example, insanity, infancy or duress) for otherwise its

3. See above, p. 650.
4. See above, p. 110.
5. Below, p. 710.
6. Above, p. 668.
7. See above, p. 446.
8. Cf. *Wuyts* [1969] 2 QB 474, [1969] 2 All ER 799, CA.

inclusion would be meaningless. What is capable of being an excuse must be a matter of law for the judge, but there is little in the decided cases by way of guidance[9] and the issue must turn on what the court believes is reasonable. It is thought unlikely that a court would consider it an excuse that a false instrument or an implement of forgery is kept as a curio. Where D is charged under s. 5 with having control of an implement it would appear to be necessary to prove that D knows it to be specially designed or adapted. Knowledge of falsity is required for the offence under s. 5 (2) and knowledge that the implement is so designed or adapted is required for the offence under s. 5 (3); and by s. 5 (4) the custody of any *such* machine etc. is an offence.

The onus of proving lack of lawful authority or excuse lies on the prosecution. Once the prosecution has proved that D had custody of (a) an instrument he knew to be false, or (b) an implement specially designed or adapted, there would be an evidential burden on D to proffer an explanation. If D does adduce some evidence of lawful authority or excuse it will be for the prosecution in the ordinary way to satisfy the jury that D has no authority or excuse.

9. Cf. *Dickins v Gill* [1896] 2 QB 310, DC, where it was held in a case under the Post Office (Protection) Act 1884, s. 7 that the proprietor of a philatelist newspaper had no lawful authority or excuse for possessing a die which he made in order to produce black and white illustrations of a postage stamp in his newspaper.

18 Offences of Damage to Property

The principal offences of damage to property are governed by the Criminal Damage Act 1971 which replaced the prolix and complicated provisions of the Malicious Damage Act 1861. Like the Theft Acts of 1968 and 1978 the Criminal Damage Act is an entirely new code, and it must be approached and interpreted in the same fashion.[1] The Criminal Damage Act is in the main the work of the Law Commission and reference to the papers of the Commission is helpful in understanding the underlying policies and in elucidating the provisions of the Act.[2]

One thing that is worth noting at the outset is that the Law Commission wished to keep the policies and concepts of the law of damage to property in line with the law of theft. Complete parity for theft and criminal damage is neither practicable nor desirable, but it is important that there should be no conflict of principle if the criminal code as a whole is to be consistent and harmonious. Thus, to take a simple example, while land cannot in general be stolen, there is no need for any similar limitation in relation to offences of criminal damage; on the other hand, it is clearly desirable that if it is not an offence to pick another's wild mushrooms, it should be no more an offence to destroy or damage them.

1 Destroying or Damaging Property of Another

By s. 1 (1) of the Criminal Damage Act 1971:

"A person who without lawful excuse destroys or damages any property belonging to another intending to destroy or damage any such property or being reckless as to whether any such property would be destroyed or damaged shall be guilty of an offence."

And by s. 4 the offence is punishable by imprisonment for ten years.

---

1. See above, pp. 495–497.
2. See Law Com. No. 29, *Offences of Damage to Property* (1970). See also Law Commission Working Paper No. 23, *Malicious Damage*. As to official reports, see above, p. 61, fn. 1.

1) *Destroy or Damage*

The expression "destroy or damage" was commonly used in the Malicious Damage Act 1861 and it would seem that previous decisions on the meaning of these words, though no longer binding, must retain a persuasive value.

What is contemplated by "destroy or damage" is actual destruction or damage; that is, some physical harm, impairment or deterioration which can be usually perceived by the senses.[3] It was for this reason that intangible property was excluded from the definition of property.[4] It is not enough to show that what has been done amounts to a civil wrong, as for example a trespass to land or goods for neither requires proof of actual damage. It was held in *Eley v Lytle* (1885)[5] that D was guilty of no offence when, during a game of football, he ran over P's land and the only evidence of actual damage was that he had committed a trespass. It seems clear that the same result would follow under the Criminal Damage Act. Actual damage, however, need only be slight. Grass can be damaged by trampling it down,[6] and is easily and rapidly damaged by football, cricket, or even bowls.[7] And even sterner stuff is susceptible of damage, as where a stalagmite is broken away.[8]

A thing may be damaged though nothing is actually broken or deformed. A car is damaged just as much by uncoupling the brake cable as by cutting it with a pair of pliers. So a machine may be damaged by removing some integral part,[9] or by tampering with some part so that it will not work although no part is removed or broken,[10] or by running it in an improper fashion so that impairment will result.[11] These principles apply just as much to land as to chattels. To dump rubbish on another's land, even though there is no tangible hurt to the land beneath the rubbish, may be to damage the land if the owner is put to expense in removing the rubbish before the land can be put to his uses.[12] If property, whether real or personal, is rendered unfit for a use to which it might be put, it may sensibly be said to have been damaged. This is not to say that property is damaged merely by a denial of its use. It could not be said that a house or

---

3. But no doubt an unrechargeable battery is damaged by exhausting the charge. The damage cannot be perceived by the eye but it has been rendered useless. It has been held that a card containing a computer programme is damaged by erasure of the programme: *Cox v Riley* (1986) 83 Cr App Rep 54, DC. But as to the modification of computers and computer material see below, p. 714.
4. See below, p. 687.
5. 50 JP 308, DC.
6. *Gayford v Choulder* [1898] 1 QB 316, DC.
7. Cf. *Laws v Eltringham* (1881) 8 QBD 283, DC, below, p. 687, fn. 8.
8. See (1964) The Times, 12 September.
9. Cf. *Tacey* (1821) Russ & Ry 452.
10. Cf. *Fisher* (1865) LR 1 CCR 7, DC, and see *Getty v Antrim County Council* [1950] NI 114 (dismantling). Though a machine or a structure may be damaged by the removal of a part or by dismantling, it does not necessarily follow that the *parts* are damaged by the removal or dismantling; if the parts are undamaged D can be charged only with damaging the whole: *Woolcock* [1977] Crim LR 104 and 161; *Morphitis v Salmon* [1990] Crim LR 48, DC.
11. Cf. *Norris* (1840) 9 C & P 241.
12. In *Lloyd* [1991] Crim LR 904, DC, the court took the view that a car was not damaged by placing a wheel clamp on it.

car is damaged by the theft of the keys to the front door or ignition keys even though the owner may be put to expense before he can put the house or car to their intended uses.[13] On the other hand property may be damaged though there is no interference with its performance if it is rendered less valuable.[14] A car is damaged if the paintwork is scratched and food is damaged by spoiling as where milk is watered.[15]

But different things may be damaged in different ways. In *Samuels v Stubbs*,[16] Walters J said:

"It seems to me that it is difficult to lay down any very general and, at the same time, precise and absolute rule as to what constitutes 'damage'. One must be guided in a great degree by the circumstances of each case, the nature of the article and the mode in which it is affected or treated. ... It is my view, however, that the word ... is sufficiently wide in its meaning to embrace injury, mischief or harm done to property, and that in order to constitute 'damage' it is unnecessary to establish such definite or actual damage as renders the property useless, or prevents it from serving its normal function. ..."

The learned judge then held that a "temporary functional derangement" of a policeman's cap resulting from its being jumped upon constituted damage though there was no evidence that the cap might not have been restored to its original state without any real cost or trouble to the owner.

The approach of Walters J was favoured in *Hardman v Chief Constable of Avon and Somerset Constabulary*[17] where it was held that pavement drawings in water soluble paint constituted damage to the pavement where the local authority was involved in expense in removing them with high-pressure water jets. This seems entirely right. No one would maintain that property which has been daubed by slogans or drawings was not damaged simply because the elements would eventually remove all trace of them or because the householder could remove them more quickly with soap and water. *Samuels v Stubbs* is, perhaps, a less clear case. If an article is accidentally trodden upon (and for the purpose of determining whether there has been damage it can make no difference that it is intentionally trodden upon) and the owner finds that it takes a matter of moments to press it back into shape, surely he would say that no harm had been done. In *"A" (a juvenile) v R*[18] it was held that spitting on a policeman's raincoat did not damage the raincoat where the spittle could be removed by a wipe with a damp cloth. No doubt it would have been otherwise had the material been capable of being stained by the spittle.[19]

---

13. *Henderson and Battley* (1984), CA unreported but extensively cited in *Cox v Riley* (1986) 83 Cr App Rep 54, DC, [1986] Crim LR 460, CA.
14. Cf. *Foster* (1852) 6 Cox CC 25. Cf. *King v Lees* (1949) 65 TLR 21, DC, (passenger urinating in taxi held to have caused injury for purposes of the London Hackney Carriage Act, s. 41).
15. Cf. *Roper v Knott* [1898] 1 QB 868, DC.
16. [1972] 4 SASR 200 at 203.
17. [1986] Crim LR 330 (Judge Llewellyn Jones & Justices).
18. [1978] Crim LR 689 (Judge Streeter & Justices).
19. But would the policeman have been unduly fastidious to insist that even a rainproofed material should be dry-cleaned after it had been spat upon?

While it may be difficult to lay down "any very general and, at the same time, precise and absolute rule as to what constitutes 'damage'", it is submitted that it goes too far, as some of the cases suggest,[20] to say that it is a matter of fact and degree to be determined by the trier of fact in a commonsense way. Once the facts have been determined and the degree of harm ascertained, it is submitted that it is then a question of law whether damage has been established. It is here pertinent to keep in mind, as did Walters J in *Samuels v Stubbs*,[1] the difference between fact and law. Counsel for the defendant argued that the finding "of fact" of the trial court ought not to be disturbed, only to be met with the withering reply that not only was it the practice of Australian courts to distinguish between the determination of the evidence (a matter of fact) and the determination of the inferences to be drawn from those facts (a matter of law) but that this view was based on respected English authorities. In particular it had not escaped Lord Dunedin's notice that "there must be a discrimination as to what is the class of evidence being dealt with; whether the result arrived at depends on the view taken of conflicting testimony, or depends upon the inferences to be drawn from the fact as to which there [can be] no controversy."[2] This point is likely to be lost on English courts given their present predilection for regarding the interpretation of "ordinary" words (and "damage" is about as ordinary a word as is to be found) as a matter of fact. It is nevertheless firmly asserted here that it cannot be right for "damage" to be given one meaning in Berkeley Square and another meaning in Bermondsey.

How D regards his conduct is irrelevant if damage is caused in fact. P's painting may be damaged by D's additions though D regards them as improvements.[3]

"Destroy" clearly goes beyond damage and does not contemplate half measures. To destroy, of structures means to pull down or demolish, of crops or growing things to lay waste, of machines to break up, and of animals to deprive of life.[4]

2) *Property*

S. 10 (1) of the Criminal Damage Act provides:

"In this Act 'property' means property of a tangible nature, whether real or personal, including money and—

(a) including wild creatures which have been tamed or are ordinarily kept in captivity, and any other wild creatures or their carcases if, but only

---

20. *Roe v Kingerlee* [1986] Crim LR 735, DC; *Henderson and Battley*, CA, unreported but approved in *Cox v Riley* (1986) 83 Cr App Rep 54, DC; *Morphitis v Salmon* [1990] Crim LR 48, DC.

1. [1972] 4 SASR 200 at 201.

2. *Dominion Trust Co v New York Life Insurance Co* [1919] AC 254 at 257, PC.

3. Nor is D's motive (e.g. painting fig leaves over parts he considers indelicate) relevant. Cp. *Fancy* [1980] Crim LR 171, CC.

4. Cf. *Barnet London Borough Council v Eastern Electricity Board* [1973] 2 All ER 319, DC.

if, they have been reduced into possession which has not been lost or abandoned or are in the course of being reduced into possession; but
(b) not including mushrooms growing wild on any land or flowers, fruit or foliage of a plant growing wild on any land.

For the purposes of this subsection 'mushroom' includes any fungus and 'plant' includes any shrub or tree."

The exceptions in paragraphs (a) and (b) are of course to keep the law of damage to property in line with the law of theft.[5] But while there is a substantial measure of correspondence in the definitions of property for theft and damage, there are two significant differences.

In the first place land, which in general cannot be stolen, may be the subject of criminal damage. The policies which favour exempting land from the offence of stealing[6] do not apply to the offences of damaging property. The distinction also has the support of history, for while land has always been excepted from definitions of stealing there has never been any such limitation in offences of damage to property. It is, then, still the law that while D cannot steal his neighbour's croquet lawn by annexing it, he may commit criminal damage by turning it over to vegetable marrows.

Secondly, while intangible property has now been brought within the subject matter of theft, it is still excluded from the definition of property for the purposes of criminal damage. "Offences of criminal damage to property," said the Law Commission,

"in the context of the present law connote physical damage in their commission, and for that reason we have not included intangible things in the class of property, damage to which should constitute an offence."[7]

Consequently such intangible property as easements and profits, patents and copyright, are excluded for the purposes of criminal damage.[8]

3) *Belonging to Another*

The offence under s. 1 (1) may be committed only where D destroys or damages property "belonging to another". Here again the policy of the law of criminal damage, which must be to protect interests in addition to ownership, is very much the same as that for the law of theft. Consequently s. 5 of the Theft Act[9] has a substantially similar counterpart in s. 10 of the Criminal Damage Act which provides:

"(2) Property shall be treated for the purposes of this Act as belonging to any person—

5. But note that the destruction of, or damage to, wild animals and plants may be an offence under other legislation; see for example the Wildlife and Countryside Act 1981 and the Badgers Act 1973, as amended by the Wildlife and Countryside (Amendment) Act 1985.
6. See above, p. 514.
7. Law Com. No. 29, para. 34.
8. Cf. *Laws v Eltringham* (1881) 8 QBD 283, DC. D and others had been charged with damaging Newcastle Town Moor by playing bowls upon it. It was held that the property could not be laid in the freemen who had merely the (incorporeal) right of herbage; the property ought to have been laid in Newcastle Corporation as the freeholder.
9. See above, pp. 517–536.

(a) having the custody or control of it;

(b) having in it any proprietary right or interest (not being an equitable interest arising only from an agreement to transfer or grant an interest); or

(c) having a charge on it.

(3) Where property is subject to a trust, the person to whom it belongs shall be so treated as including any person having a right to enforce the trust.

(4) Property of a corporation sole shall be so treated as belonging to the corporation notwithstanding a vacancy in the corporation."

It is, then, enough that P has some proprietary interest in the property which D damages, and it does not have to be shown that P is the owner of the property; D may, for example, damage property of which P is the lessee or bailee. Further, D may commit an offence where the property belongs to him provided that P also has a proprietary interest in the property. In such cases it may be difficult to prove that D acted with *mens rea* or without lawful excuse,[10] but, given that, D may commit criminal damage though he both owns and possesses the property. Just as a co-owner of property may steal it by appropriating the other's share,[11] a co-owner may commit criminal damage by destroying or damaging the property.

But P must have some *proprietary* right or interest in the property.[12] Where property is insured the insurer acquires an interest in the property, but the interest is not a proprietary one.[13] If D destroys his own property which he has insured with P, he does not destroy property belonging to another even though he may have destroyed it with a view to making a dishonest claim against P.[14]

Property is also treated as belonging to a person who has a charge on it. This expression does not, in terms, appear in s. 5 of the Theft Act and was included in the Criminal Damage Act because the Law Commission thought

"it should be made clear that a person who has a charge on property should be regarded as having a sufficient interest in the property to entitle him to the protection of the criminal law for damage done to it by the owner who subjected it to the charge."[15]

But it is not clear in what circumstances the creation of a charge, whether legal or equitable and whether on real or personal property, would not create a proprietary right or interest.

It will be noted that the definition of property belonging to another in the Criminal Damage Act, s. 10, contains no provision equivalent to s. 5 (4) of the Theft Act – property got by another's mistake. This distinction can be of no practical importance; the getting of property by another's mistake

10. See below, p. 694.

11. *Bonner* [1970] 2 All ER 97n, [1970] 1 WLR 838, CA, above, p. 518.

12. See above pp. 520–522.

13. An insurer has an interest in the *safety* of the insured property but, without more, this does not constitute a proprietary interest. Cf. *Lucena v Crauford* (1806) 2 Bos & P NR 269, HL, per Lawrence J at 302.

14. Cf. *Denton* [1982] 1 All ER 65, [1981] 1 WLR 1446, CA, below, p. 695.

15. Law Com. No. 29, para. 39.

may well excite acquisitive instincts but it is unlikely to excite an outburst of vandalism.

Where D is the owner of property in which no other person has any proprietary right or interest, his destroying or damaging it cannot amount to an offence under s. 1 (1). Nor generally is it an offence to damage one's own property apart from the special case dealt with in s. 1 (2).[16] It is no offence for D to destroy a work of art which he owns, or to lay waste his plentiful stocks of food at a time of acute shortage. Such acts may be properly described as wanton but they are not criminal because there is at present no case for making them criminal. But where such a case does exist, and cruelty to animals provides an illustration, particular offences can be created which extend to harm by an owner to his own property.[17]

4) *Mens Rea*

Section 1 (1) requires that the destruction or damaging of the property should be intentional or reckless, and without lawful excuse.

1 Intention and Recklessness[18]

"In the area of serious crime," said the Law Commission,

"the elements of intention, knowledge or recklessness have always been required as a basis of liability ... We consider, therefore, that the same elements as are required at present should be retained, but that they should be expressed with greater simplicity and clarity. In particular, we prefer to avoid the use of such a word as 'maliciously',[19] if only because it gives the impression that the mental element differs from that which is imposed in other offences requiring traditional *mens rea*. It is evident that from such cases as *R v Cunningham*[20] and *R v Mowatt*[1] that the word can give rise to difficulties of interpretation. Furthermore, the word 'maliciously' conveys the impression that some ill-will is required against the person whose property is damaged."[2]

By "traditional *mens rea*" it is clear that the Law Commission meant to convey that liability for damage was predicated upon conduct of D which was intended by D to cause the damage in question or was foreseen by D as creating a risk of causing that damage.

This view certainly governs *intentional* damage. It is not enough that D intended to do the act which caused the damage unless he intended to cause the damage; proof that D intended to throw a stone is not proof that he

---

16. Below, p. 704.
17. Protection of Animals Act 1911, s. 1.
18. Cf. the general discussion of intention and recklessness, above, Ch. 4.
19. "Maliciously" was the expression most commonly used in the Malicious Damage Act 1861 to describe *mens rea*.
20. [1957] 2 QB 396, [1957] 2 All ER 412, CA, **SHC 67**, above, p. 61.
 1. [1968] 1 QB 421, [1967] 3 All ER 47, HL, **SHC 69**, above, p. 427.
 2. Law Com. No. 29, para. 44.

intended to break a window.[3] Nor is it enough that D intends to damage property if he does not intend to damage property *of another*. Since D commits no offence under s. 1 (1) of the Act in damaging or destroying his own property, it follows in principle that he ought to be guilty of no offence where he destroys P's property under the mistaken impression that it is his own. Whether D's mistake is one of fact or law he commits no crime for he lacks *mens rea*, and this view was firmly endorsed by the Court of Appeal in *Smith*.[4] Upon the termination of his tenancy of a flat D had caused £130 worth of damage in removing wiring which he had himself installed and boarded over. In law the landlord became the owner of the wiring and boarding as fixtures, and the trial judge directed the jury that D could have no lawful excuse since he had in law no right to do as he did. D's appeal against conviction was allowed. James LJ said on behalf of the court:[5]

"Applying the ordinary principles of *mens rea*, the intention and reck- lessness and the absence of lawful excuse required to constitute the offence have reference to property belonging to another. It follows that in our judgment no offence is committed under this section if a person destroys or causes damage to property belonging to another if he does so in the honest though mistaken belief that the property is his own, and provided that the belief is honestly held it is irrelevant to consider whether or not it is a justifiable belief."

The mistake in *Smith* appears to have been a mistake as to the civil law; D knew all the facts and drew the wrong conclusion of law from them. The result is the same so far as criminal liability is concerned whether the mistake is one of fact or law so long as the mistake negatives *mens rea*.[6] Consequently D commits no offence in pulling down a house if he honestly believes the house is his whether his mistake is one of fact or law and however egregious his error may have been.[7]

Nor can it make any difference in destroying or damaging what is, or what he believes to be, his own property, that D's conduct might be described as wanton (as where he destroys a work of art) or that the property is destroyed for the purposes of a crime of fraud (as where property is destroyed to defraud insurers). If D does not intend to destroy or damage property of *another*, nothing can render him liable to a charge under s. 1 (1). In *Appleyard*[8] where D, the managing director of a company, set fire to the company's premises, it was argued that he could not be convicted of arson since he was "in effect" the owner of the premises. D's conviction for arson was upheld apparently on the basis that he was not the owner of the premises and knew that he was not. Had D believed that he owned the company's premises then he could not have been convicted whatever his motive (to defraud insurers or creditors, to inflict loss on the shareholders) may have been.

3. Cf. *Pembliton* (1874) LR 2 CCR 119, **SHC 86**.
4. [1974] QB 354, [1974] 1 All ER 632, CA; **SHC 542**.
5. [1974] 1 All ER 632 at 636.
6. See generally above, p. 83.
7. Cf. *Langford* (1842) Car & M 602.
8. (1985) 81 Cr App Rep 319, [1985] Crim LR 723 CA.

The Act extends liability not merely to damage which is caused intentionally but also damage which is caused recklessly. That recklessness in this context was meant to connote foresight of consequences is apparent from the Law Commission's Report. This is reinforced by the Law Commission's proposed definition of recklessness[9] which, as Lord Edmund Davies pointed out,[10] was surely in the draftsman's mind when he drafted the Criminal Damage Act.

But this was not the view taken in *Caldwell*.[11] There D had formed a grievance against P, the proprietor of a residential hotel, and, having got very drunk, decided to revenge himself by setting fire to the hotel though, fortunately, the fire was discovered and extinguished before serious harm was done.[12]

Caldwell establishes that D is reckless for the purposes of s. 1 (1) of the Act (damage to property) and for the purposes of s. 1 (2) of the Act (endangering life by damaging property)[13] if his conduct (1) creates an obvious risk of damage to property (or of endangering life by damaging property); and (2) he either (a) gives no thought to the possibility of there being any such risk, or (b) recognising that there is some risk goes on to take it.

For the purposes of establishing liability under 2 (a), the cases of *Elliott v C*[14] and *Stephen Malcolm*,[15] loyally following *Caldwell*, show that whether there is an obvious and serious risk of damaging property (or endangering life thereby) is to be determined by what a reasonable man would have appreciated; it matters not that D was incapable of appreciating the risk, and in applying the test of what is reasonably foreseeable the reasonable man is not to be notionally invested with characteristics of D, such as immaturity or exhaustion or mental incapacity, as might affect his ability to appreciate the risk. The test is thus entirely[16] objective.

Where D adverts to the issue of risk his liability is to be determined under 2 (b). Having adverted to the risk of damage to property it would seem that D might either (i) decide upon reflection that there is no risk; or (ii) decide to take the risk.

Case (ii) appears to present no problems. D has chosen to accept the risk and must take the consequences. Two points may, however, be made. The first is that in formulating the proposition contained in 2 (b) above, Lord Diplock omitted the bracketed word "unjustifiably". This seems to have been an oversight. It can hardly be supposed, for example, that a police officer pursuing escaping gunmen would be guilty of criminal damage to

---

9. "A person is reckless if, (a) knowing that there is a risk that an event may result from his conduct or that circumstances may exist, he takes that risk, and (b) it is unreasonable for him to take it, having regard to the degree and nature of the risk he knows to be present": Working Paper No. 31, *The Mental Element in Crime*. See now Law Com. No. 89, *Report on the Mental Element in Crime*.

10. *Caldwell* [1981] 1 All ER 961 at 969, HL.

11. [1981] 1 All ER 961; SHC 72.

12. The case is discussed extensively above, p. 62 et seq.

13. For the sake of completeness the same definition of recklessness applies to damage by fire (arson) under s. 1 (3). Cf. *Hardie* [1984] 3 All ER 848 at 851, CA.

14. [1983] 2 All ER 1005, [1983] 1 WLR 939 DC; SHC 78.

15. (1984) 79 Cr App Rep 334, CA; SHC 81.

16. Some possible exceptions are canvassed above, p. 63.

their car because he realised that in using his car to force them to a halt there was a risk of the collision which did in fact result.[17] The second is that D may be convicted if he realises that his conduct involves *a* risk of damage to property. Thus in *Chief Constable of Avon and Somerset Constabulary v Shimmen*[18] where D, while demonstrating his skills in Korean arts, put his foot through a shop window, it was held that his belief that he had eliminated as much risk as possible showed that he realised that there was still some risk and he could accordingly be convicted of criminal damage. No doubt the smallness of a risk may be a factor, along with others, in determining whether it is justifiable to take that risk; but, and in the absence of other factors, it is not acceptable to take *any* risk of breaking another's window.

Case (i) literally falls outside the propositions stated by Lord Diplock in *Caldwell* and *Lawrence*. In *Shimmen* the court thought it might be arguable that a lacuna exists and that one who adverts to the risk and concludes there is none would not be reckless in the *Caldwell* sense. Delivering the judgment of the court in *Reid*,[19] Mustill LJ was, though speaking *obiter*, more forthright and said that one who recognised the existence of a risk but who concluded there was none (or that the risk was negligible or less than serious) must be acquitted.[20] Thus it appears that had Shimmen, having considered whether there was a risk of breaking the window, had concluded, however crassly, that there was none,[1] he would be entitled to an acquittal.

A further issue that needs to be mentioned is the effect of intoxication in relation to offences of criminal damage. It appears that an allegation under subsection (1) or (2) of an intention to cause damage or, under subsection (2) of an intention to endanger life, is an allegation of a specific intent;[2] whereas, if intention *or* recklessness, or only recklessness,[3] is alleged under either subsection, the offence is one of basic intent.

The wide interpretation of recklessness reduces the significance of the distinction by diminishing the number of occasions on which intoxication may negative it; but it may still be important. D claims that, because he was drunk, he was firmly convinced that the property he damaged was his own,

17. Nor could it make any difference that the officer gave no thought to there being any such risk though a reasonable person would have perceived the risk as serious and obvious. The justification for risk-taking is assessed independently of what D thought or did not think.
18. (1986) 84 Cr App Rep 7, [1986] Crim LR 800, DC.
19. (1990) 91 Cr App Rep 263, CA.
20. See further above, p. 65.
   1. Shimmen had not formed the view that there was no risk but he might genuinely have believed that the risk was negligible or less than serious. On the view expressed in *Reid* Shimmen might thus be entitled to an acquittal unless it can be said that a risk is always 'serious' if there is not a shred of justification for taking it.
   2. Cf. *Caldwell* [1981] 1 All ER 961 at 967, per Lord Diplock. Lord Edmund-Davies's opinion (p. 972) was that all arson under subsection (2) is an offence of specific intent but he thought that the prediction of Professor Glanville Williams (TBCL, 431) "that *all* crimes of recklessness except murder will now be held to be crimes of basic intent ..." had been promptly fulfilled by the decision of the majority. And murder is no longer an exception.
   3. Where the prosecution relies on intention and recklessness in the alternative, these should be embodied in different counts of the indictment: *Hardie* [1984] 3 All ER 848, [1985] 1 WLR 64, CA.

not P's. He is not *Caldwell*-reckless: but, if recklessness is alleged and is a basic intent, he is guilty.[4]

It needs to be stressed at this point perhaps that negligence which will ground civil liability will not suffice to support a charge of criminal damage. Where the charge is brought under s. 1 (1) the risk of damage must be "obvious". While it is clear that the defendant may be liable though it was not "obvious" to him, it is equally clear that a risk is not obvious merely because it is foreseeable and would result in civil liability.

It would appear that the doctrine of transferred malice[5] applies, so that if D intends, or is reckless as to, damage to property of A he may be liable where he in fact causes damage, neither intentionally nor recklessly, to property of B.

"The intention or the recklessness need not be related to the particular property damaged, provided that it is related to another's property. If, for example, a person throws a stone at a passing motor car intending to damage it, but misses and breaks a shop window, he will have the necessary intention in respect of the damage to the window as he intended to damage the property of another. But if in a fit of anger he throws a stone at his own car he will not have the requisite intention. In the latter case the question of whether he has committed an offence will depend upon whether he was reckless as to whether any property belonging to another would be destroyed or damaged."[6]

Williams suggests[7] that transferred malice would not apply where D, bent on damaging property other than by fire, accidentally starts a fire in circumstances where there is no obvious and serious risk of fire. This, with respect, seems an acceptable conclusion. Arson is a separate offence carrying a higher punishment than damage caused by other means and its *mens rea* requires not merely the intentional or reckless damaging of property but the intentional or reckless damaging of property *by fire*. A fortiori, D would not commit an offence of criminal damage where he throws a stone at P but misses him and breaks a window, unless of course D was reckless as to the risk of breaking the window.[8]

Obviously *mens rea* cannot be supplied by an afterthought. If D inadvertently breaks P's window he cannot become liable when, having learned that P is a tax inspector, he rejoices in the harm caused. On the other hand, if D inadvertently sets fire to P's property and subsequently becomes aware[9] that he has done so, he may be criminally liable if, intending or being reckless that *further* damage ensue to P's property, he lets the fire take its course when it lies within his power to prevent or minimise that further damage.[10]

---

4. The same principles govern if the offences are charged as arson. The view expressed in *O'Driscoll* (1977) 65 Cr App Rep 50, CA, that the offence under s. 1 (2) was not a crime of basic intent must now be read subject to *Caldwell*.
5. See above, p. 74.
6. Law Com. No. 29, para. 45.
7. (1983) 42 CLJ 85, 86.
8. Cf. *Pembliton* (1874) LR 2 CCR 119.
9. It is not enough that D ought to have been aware, or was not aware because he gave no thought to it: *Miller*, next note.
10. *Miller* [1983] 2 AC 161, [1983] 1 All ER 978, HL. See above, p. 51.

2 Lawful Excuse

The Law Commission took the view that in most cases

> "there is a clear distinction between the mental element and the element
> of unlawfulness, and in the absence of one or other element no offence
> will be committed, notwithstanding that damage may have been done to
> another's property. For example, a police officer who, in order to execute
> a warrant of arrest, has to force open a door of a house is acting with
> lawful excuse although he intends to damage the door or the lock. On the
> other hand a person playing tennis on a properly fenced court who
> inadvertently hits a ball on to a greenhouse roof, breaking a pane of glass,
> acts without lawful excuse, but will escape liability because he has not the
> requisite intention."[11]

This distinction drawn by the Law Commission between the "mental
element" and the element of "unlawfulness" may be a distinction of
convenience but it is a distinction generally adopted in this work because it
is convenient to consider separately, so far as the situation admits, the issue
of intention or recklessness as to the damaging of the property, and the
various grounds of exculpation or justification that may exist for damage
deliberately done.

Under the former law it was not always clear in what circumstances it
was justifiable to damage or destroy the property of another. Strictly the
Criminal Damage Act 1971 is to be interpreted without reference to the
earlier law, but it is of course impossible to legislate, as it were, in a
vacuum; and there is always a risk that policies implicit in the earlier law
will continue to flourish unless new policies are clearly articulated. Consequently s. 5 of the Act provides a partial definition of "lawful excuse"
which contains the new policies and makes a clean break with the earlier
law. The section in part provides—

> "(2) A person charged with an offence to which this section applies[12]
> shall, whether or not he would be treated for those purposes of this Act
> as having a lawful excuse apart from this subsection, be treated for
> those purposes as having a lawful excuse—
>
> (a) if at the time of the act or acts alleged to constitute the offence he
> believed that the person or persons whom he believed to be
> entitled to consent to the destruction of or damage to the property
> in question had so consented, or would have consented to it if he
> or they had known of the destruction or damage and its circum-
> stances; or
>
> (b) if he destroyed or damaged or threatened to destroy or damage
> the property in question . . . in order to protect property belong-
> ing to himself or another or a right or interest in property which
> was or which he believed to be vested in himself or another, and
> at the time of the act or acts alleged to constitute the offence he
> believed—
>
> (i) that the property, right or interest was in immediate need of
> protection; and

---

11. Law Com. No. 29, para. 49.
12. The section applies to an offence under s. 1 (1); as to other offences see below.

(ii) that the means of protection adopted or proposed to be adopted were or would be reasonable having regard to all the circumstances.

(3) For the purpose of this section it is immaterial whether a belief is justified or not if it is honestly held.

(4) For the purposes of subsection (2) above a right or interest in property includes any right or privilege in or over land, whether created by grant, licence or otherwise."

a) *Belief in consent*. Section 5 (2) (a) here very much follows the pattern of s. 2 (1) (b) of the Theft Act 1968,[13] and it is obviously right that it should since the parallel between theft and criminal damage is at this point exact. As appears to be the case with theft, D's belief is judged by the single criterion that it be honestly held; a point which, if it is not clear enough from the wording of s. 5 (2) (a), is put beyond doubt by s. 5 (3).

Most obviously this provision covers the case where D believes that the owner has consented to the destruction or damage, or would have consented if asked. So in *Denton*[14] it was held that D was not guilty of arson in setting fire to his employer's mill where D believed that his employer had encouraged him to do so in order to make a fraudulent claim against the insurers. The provision also covers the case where D believes that P is a person entitled to consent to the destruction or damage who has consented or would have consented if asked. Thus, for example, an employee destroying or damaging property belonging to the firm would commit no offence where he believed that some person in authority (say a foreman) was entitled to consent, and had consented or would have consented if asked.[15] The provision would also cover the case where D comes across an injured animal and, believing that the owner would have consented had he been able to contact him, D kills the animal to put it out of its misery.

b) *Defence of property*. A man is of course entitled to take measures to protect his own property, real or personal, from harm caused by, or by the use of, property belonging to another whether animate (such as trespassing cattle) or inanimate (such as a caravan). If, for example, a dog is attacking sheep it may be shot if this is a necessary measure to protect the sheep. No one would deny the right of D, where property is in fact at risk, to take reasonable defensive measures even though these measures involve damaging the property of others.

But the Act goes much further than this. D has a lawful excuse within s. 5 (2) (b) not only where D's conduct, objectively viewed, is reasonable. Under the obviously subjective terms of the section D has a lawful excuse if (i) he destroyed or damaged the property in question in order to protect property which he *believed* to be vested in himself or another; (ii) he *believed* the property to be in immediate need of protection; and (iii) he *believed* that the means of protection adopted were reasonable having regard to all the

---

13. See above, p. 537.
14. [1982] 1 All ER 65, [1981] 1 WLR 1446, CA.
15. Cf. *James* (1837) 8 C & P 131.

circumstances. It is of course for the prosecution to disprove these matters so long as D meets the evidential burden by laying a foundation for his claim to lawful excuse.

Take an extreme case. Roskill LJ said in *Hunt*:[16]

"Let it be supposed that the roof of some famous cathedral or building, like Westminster Abbey, was in danger due to a defective beam suffering from dry rot; let it be supposed that the authorities are doing nothing to repair it; let it be supposed that some person, acting in good faith, is horrified at this lack of attention. In order to draw attention to what he regards as a dangerous position, he goes and sets fire to a hassock. Is that seriously to be said not to be an offence of criminal damage because it is done to draw attention to the defective beam on the roof of the Abbey?"

It may be further supposed that the beam is sound and that D's belief that it is suffering from dry rot is entirely unreasonable. D's liability involves a consideration of the three issues set out above.

i) *Acting in order to protect property*. It must be shown that D did not destroy or damage the property in question (the hassock) "in order to protect property" (the Abbey roof). If D destroys or damages property for any reason other than the protection of property he cannot have a lawful excuse within s. 5 (2) (b).[17] In *Hunt*[18] D, who assisted his wife in her post as deputy warden of a block of flats for old people, set fire to some bedding in order, as he claimed, to call attention to the defective state of the fire alarm. It was held that the trial judge had properly withdrawn his defence of lawful excuse from the jury. As the court viewed it, whether an act was done "in order to protect property" involved an objective assessment: was the act done one which protected, or was capable of protecting, property? The answer to this question, in the opinion of the court, was a very clear No.

Hunt was followed in *Ashford and Smith*[19] and in *Hill and Hall*.[20] These cases were factually similar. The defendants had been convicted of possessing articles without lawful excuse intending to damage property, their intention being to cut the perimeter fence surrounding military facilities. On appeal an argument advanced on their behalf was that they had acted in order to protect property because, in the event of hostilities, these facilities would be subject to attack thus putting at risk the property of those living nearby. If, it was argued on their behalf, the defendants could compromise the security of these facilities, the authorities might be persuaded to remove them. In both cases the trial judge declined to put their claim to lawful excuse to the jury and the Court of Appeal held that he was right to do so. In *Hill and Hall* the court said that the jury had to determine, first, what was in D's mind (a subjective test) and, second, to decide whether as a matter of law it could be said that what was proposed to be done (to cut the

16. (1978) 66 Cr App Rep 105 at 108, CA.
17. Cf. *Phillips v Pringle* [1973] 1 NSWLR 275 (CCA of New South Wales, action pursuant to a UN resolution against racialism not a lawful excuse for damaging goalposts).
18. (1978) 66 Cr App Rep 105, CA.
19. [1988] Crim LR 682, CA.
20. (1989) 89 Cr App Rep 74, CA.

fence) could amount to something done to protect homes in the vicinity of the facilities. The court thought that it would not because the cutting of the fence was too remote from the eventual aim of protecting property.

But these cases, on this aspect of the defence of lawful excuse, are not beyond criticism.[1] To determine whether D acted "in order to protect property" it is necessary to determine what D's purpose is, and it is no less D's purpose to protect property though the action taken is misguided, incapable of giving effect to that purpose, or even if it has the opposite effect and in fact imperils the property sought to be protected. The hassock burner's concern is with the Abbey roof and, however futile his action, his undoubted purpose is to protect it. Nor is it any less D's purpose to protect property because the protection of the property is to serve some other purpose, as in *Hunt* where it was to secure the safety of the residents or as in *Hill and Hall* where it was to bring about nuclear disarmament.

ii) *The immediate need for protection.* The defence is denied to D if he does not believe that the property is in "immediate" need of protection. An additional ground given for affirming the convictions in *Hill and Hall* was that there was no evidence that D believed that a nuclear strike was imminent ("I don't expect a nuclear bomb to fall today, or tomorrow", she said in evidence) and on this ground the decision may be supported. In *Hunt* the court refrained from expressing an opinion on the scope of the words "in immediate need of protection". No doubt, if asked, D would have said that he did not expect a fire to break out today or tomorrow (other of course than the one he started) but *Hunt* is perhaps distinguishable from *Hill and Hall* in this respect. People do not instal or repair a fire alarm because they consider a fire to be imminent but because there is an ever-present risk of fire. If a fire officer is asked when a defective fire alarm should be repaired he must inevitably say as soon as possible; he is not likely to say that next week or next month will do. There is no such urgency to take measures against a nuclear strike.

The issue to be determined is: did this defendant believe that the property was in immediate need of protection? If the hassock burner believes, and in the teeth of all the evidence, that the collapse of the Abbey roof is imminent then he satisfies this requirement. On the other hand, if the hassock burner believes that the roof will collapse in, say, six months' time, it is thought that his belief that this is sufficiently "immediate" will not avail him.

iii) *Belief in the reasonableness of the action.* Once again the subjective terms of s. 5 (2) (b) need to be emphasised. There is no requirement that D's belief be reasonable, still less that D's conduct must meet some objective standard of reasonableness. But it does mean that D must believe that it was reasonable for him to do as he did. In theory D might justify laying waste an oil refinery because he believes its effluent is damaging his geraniums. But asked the question (and it would seem a legitimate question

1. See [1988] Crim LR 682, [1989] Crim LR 136.

to ask)[2] – do you honestly believe that ordinary commonsense people, similarly circumstanced, would consider your action reasonable? – a No from him would be fatal to his defence, and a Yes is unlikely to be found credible by a jury. Similarly with the hassock burner. He would need to be completely out of touch with reality to believe this was an acceptable way to protect property.

Hunt might be different. There was some evidence that efforts had been made to get the Council to repair the alarm but these had proved unavailing. D may thus have reached the end of his tether and his claim that he believed the action reasonable might carry some credibility.

iv) *Prophylactic measures in defence of property.* A common case calling for the protection of property is where a dog is worrying livestock. In such a case there will ordinarily be lawful excuse for the killing of the dog within s. 5 (2) (b). But the *civil* law goes further. The Animals Act 1971, s. 9 (3) (a), provides that D incurs no civil liability in just this situation provided that D is a person entitled to act for the protection of the livestock and that he gives notice within 48 hours to the officer in charge of a police station of the killing or injury. But s. 9 (3) (b) then goes on to provide that D also incurs no civil liability for the killing of the dog where

"the dog *has been*[3] worrying livestock, has not left the vicinity and is not under the control of any person and there are no practicable means of ascertaining to whom it belongs."

In such a case D's sheep might not be strictly in "immediate" need of protection and the killing might be essentially a prophylactic measure. But it would be odd if D was criminally liable where he may be exempted from civil liability; it would involve D having to incriminate himself in order to take advantage of the civil defence. It is submitted that in these circumstances D would commit no criminal offence.[4]

D may not destroy or damage property of another because he honestly believes that harm may occur to his property at some time in the future. On the other hand it is not in general and as such unlawful for D to take defensive measures in relation to his own property.[5] It is an offence under s. 31 of the Offences against the Person Act 1861 to set traps so as to endanger life, and it is an offence under s. 1 (2) of the Criminal Damage Act 1971 to destroy or damage property in order to endanger life,[6] but it is not otherwise an offence merely to take defensive measures (to set broken glass on walls, erect spiked fences etc.) for the purpose of discouraging or preventing incursions by persons or their property. In such cases the question of criminal liability can arise only where some harm is caused to the person or property of another. So far as harm to another's property is concerned,[7] D will ordinarily have taken his defensive or protective measures at some stage before his property was in "immediate need of

2. Cf. the offence of blackmail, above, p. 610.
3. Italics supplied.
4. See the discussion of *Workman v Cowper*, below, p. 703.
5. Above, p. 258.
6. Below, p. 708.
7. Harm to the person is dealt with above, pp. 253 and 406.

protection", and when the harm occurs D may be absent and unaware of it. It is submitted that where what D has done is a normal method of protecting property, say a barbed wire fence erected by a farmer, he would not be liable though a trespasser tears his best suit in climbing through the fence, and notwithstanding that D himself could not have justified ripping open the trespasser's suit as a use of reasonable force to eject him. But where D adopts unusual defensive measures, say traps calculated to maim animals, it would normally not be difficult to show that he did not honestly believe this was a reasonable way to protect his property.

A measure frequently adopted for the protection of property is the keeping of a guard dog. The Animals Act 1971 provides that a person is not civilly liable for damage caused if the animal is kept for the protection of persons or property and "keeping it there for that purpose was not unreasonable."[8] The Act also provides that no liability is incurred to any person who has "voluntarily accepted the risk thereof."[9] The Guard Dogs Act 1975 now makes it a summary offence, punishable by a fine at level 3, to use or permit the use of a guard dog (i.e. a dog kept for the purpose of protecting persons or property or a person guarding the same)[10] unless a person capable of controlling the dog, the handler, is present and controlling it, except where the dog is secured and not at liberty to go about the premises.[11] But it is further provided that the Act shall not be construed as conferring any civil right of action, or as derogating from any remedy (whether civil or criminal) in proceedings instituted otherwise than by virtue of the Act.[12]

In *Cummings v Grainger*,[13] a civil action, it was held by the Court of Appeal that it was not unreasonable for an owner to keep an unsecured alsatian guard dog on enclosed business premises, and that he was not liable to a trespasser who entered the premises at night having seen the notice "Beware of the dog" on the gate. The attention of the court was drawn to the provisions of the Guard Dogs Act but Lord Denning MR concluded that they did not affect civil liability and so far as reasonableness was concerned they had no application. If these facts were to recur the owner would now commit an offence under the Guard Dogs Act in permitting the use of an uncontrolled guard dog, but the question remains whether he would be liable for an offence against the person or, if property is damaged, under the Criminal Damage Act. So far as the latter is concerned the issue is whether the owner believed that the keeping of an uncontrolled guard dog was reasonable having regard to all the circumstances. In *Cummings v Grainger* the Court of Appeal was firmly of the view that the keeping of an uncontrolled guard dog was not, in the circumstances of that case, unreasonable; and conduct is not necessarily unreasonable even though it involves a breach of the criminal law.[14] No doubt in determining whether D

8. Section 5 (3) (b).
9. Section 5 (2).
10. Section 7.
11. Section 1. *Hobson v Gledhill* [1978] 1 All ER 945, [1978] 1 WLR 215, DC.
12. Section 5 (2).
13. [1977] QB 397, [1977] 1 All ER 104, CA.
14. Cf. *Buckoke v Greater London Council* [1971] 1 Ch 655, [1971] 2 All ER 254, CA, above, p. 248.

thought the measure was reasonable regard would be had to D's knowledge of the risk of accidental as opposed to deliberate trespass, of the risk to children not capable of looking properly to their own protection, of the propensities of the particular dog and similar factors. What is important is that at this point the civil and criminal laws should not set different standards.

v) *Protecting the interests of others.* In most cases no doubt D will be the owner of the property which he seeks to protect, but even if D is not the owner he will not incur criminal liability if he honestly believes himself to be the owner and the other circumstances exist. By s. 5 (4) property is expressly defined to include any right or privilege in or over land. Consequently D may commit no crime where, honestly but mistakenly believing he has a right of way across P's land, he tears down a hut erected by P which, as D thinks, obstructs his imagined right of way.

Moreover, D is in the same position though the right or interest which he believes himself to have in the property which he protects is not a right or interest which is recognised by law since, by s. 5 (3), it is immaterial whether a belief is justified or not so long as it is honestly held. Suppose, for example, that D has a right to kill and take game on O's land, and D kills P's dog which he sees chasing and destroying game. In such a case there is in law no right or interest in property to protect; until D himself reduces the game into his possession he has no proprietary interest in it whatever. But if D believes he has a right or interest in the game, he would incur no criminal liability in killing P's dog provided the other circumstances exist.[15] In such a case as this D's belief that he has a right in property to protect is understandable, but even if D's belief is absurd it is good for this purpose if honestly held.

The position is essentially the same where D claims no right or interest in the property which he protects, but acts to protect the property of another. An employee who caused damage to P's property in defending property belonging to his employer would commit no offence given his belief that the measures were reasonable and were immediately needed. But there need be no nexus whatever between the person intervening to protect the property and the owner of it. An officious bystander who chooses to intervene to protect the property of another will be free from criminal liability if he acts honestly in the same terms.

c) *Cases not falling within the Act.* By its terms s. 5 (2) recognises that there may be other circumstances which would constitute lawful excuse on a charge of criminal damage, and s. 5 (5) further provides:

"This section shall not be construed as casting any doubt on any defence recognised by law as a defence to criminal charges."

It is clear that certain general defences (such as infancy, insanity, duress) are available on a charge of criminal damage and these are discussed

---

15. On the facts of *Gott v Measures* [1948] 1 KB 234, [1947] 2 All ER 609, DC, D would now be acquitted.

elsewhere in this work.[16] But some particular matters call for further discussion here.

d) *Self-defence and necessity (duress of circumstances)*. So far as necessity is concerned the law relating to defence of property is a particular, and well defined, instance where necessity is recognised as a defence, as is the case with defence of the person. The question remains as to how far it is permissible to destroy or damage property on the grounds of necessity in circumstances not involving defence of property. As a starting point it must be obvious that just as harm to the person may be justified on the grounds of self defence of the person, so too the destruction of or damage to property may be justified in defence of the person.[17]

In so far as the attack involves the commission of a crime, as will be commonly the case, the situation would be covered by s. 3 of the Criminal Law Act 1967,[18] which provides that a person may use such force as is reasonable in the circumstances in the prevention of crime. If, then, P sets his dog to attack D, D would not commit an offence of criminal damage if in using reasonable force to defend himself he killed the dog. But s. 3 does appear to import an objective requirement of reasonableness,[19] and D could not rely upon this section where the force used is unreasonable even though D himself honestly believed it was reasonable. Thus there appears to be the odd situation that if D is defending his property it is enough that he honestly believed that the force used was reasonable, but if he is defending his person his honest belief will not save him unless the force used was in fact reasonable in the circumstances.[20]

Now suppose that P's dog, quite unknown to P, chances to attack D. Here s. 3 of the Criminal Law Act can have no application since D is not seeking to prevent the commission of any crime. If D kills the dog, is the test that he must have honestly believed this was reasonable or must it have been reasonable in the circumstances? Perhaps at this level of refinement the answer can be of relevance only to the academic, but the discussion shows, not only that there are loose ends as between the law relating to defence of the person and the law relating to defence of property, but there is a significant difference in that the former is mainly objective while the latter is largely subjective. The difference was seen by the Law Commission which observed:

"We appreciate that our extended definition of lawful excuse introduces a less stringently framed defence than that of self-defence, where the force used must be reasonable when looked at objectively. There may therefore be the anomaly that different tests will apply to self-defence against bodily injury, but we do not think that this is sufficient reason to dissuade us from the present recommendation in this context."[1]

16. Ch. 10. As to intoxication see above, p. 218 et seq.
17. So if D lawfully repelling an attack by E causes E to fall through F's window, D cannot be convicted of criminal damage to F's window: *Sears v Broome* [1986] Crim LR 461, DC.
18. See above, p. 253.
19. See above, p. 254.
20. Perhaps, then, D should say that he feared for the safety of his trousers rather than his ankles.
1. Law Com. No. 29, para. 52.

It may also be noted that s. 5 (2) (b) of the Criminal Damage Act provides a wider defence in connection with offences of damage to property than is afforded by the common law defence of duress of circumstances. It appears to be the case at present that duress of circumstances is available only where D faces a threat of death or serious bodily harm or, possibly, imprisonment.[2] But s. 5 (2) (b), where it applies, permits a purely utilitarian calculation.

Suppose there is a flood affecting the property of X and Y and the fire brigade is called. Their assessment is that while X's house is not in danger there will be serious damage to Y's house by flooding unless X's fence is knocked down to allow the floodwaters to recede. A few pounds worth of damage needs to be done to the fence in order to prevent damage of several hundred pounds to the house. The firemen ask X for permission to knock down the fence, which he refuses, but the firemen nonetheless knock down the fence.[3] It seems transparently clear that the firemen have a lawful excuse for causing the damage; they are protecting Y's property which is in immediate need of protection and no one would deny that damaging the fence is reasonable in the circumstances. But if, additionally, the firemen have to restrain X because he resists their efforts to knock down the fence they would not be able to avail themselves of the defence of duress of circumstances since there is no threat of any harm to the person, let alone death or serious injury. Nor would it seem that the firemen have any other defence since X would commit no crime, if he uses no more force than is reasonable, by using force to defend his property or to eject trespassers. Harm to the person cannot be justified merely on utilitarian principles (that the harm sought to be avoided is greater than the harm inflicted) but damage to property may be so justified.

e) *Claim of right*. It is clear that D cannot commit an offence under s. 1 (1) of the Act in destroying or damaging property which is, or which is believed to be, his own. The position would appear to be the same where D, though he does not believe he is the owner of the property which he destroys or damages, nevertheless acts under a claim of legal right. In *Twose*,[4] a case decided under the old law, where it appeared that persons living near a common had occasionally burnt the furze in order to improve the growth of the grass, it was accepted that D's belief in a right to burn the furze would be a good defence though there was no such right. Here D's belief was at least understandable, but in *Day*,[5] again under the old law, it was held that D was not guilty of an offence in maiming sheep belonging to P which he had distrained where he did so in the honest belief that he was entitled to do so upon P's refusal to pay compensation for damage done by the sheep. It would seem clear that cases such as these would be decided in the same way under the Criminal Damage Act where the clear emphasis is upon honest belief in right without any objective qualification.

2. See above, p. 237.
3. The illustration is based on fact except that X readily gave his permission.
4. (1879) 14 Cox CC 327.
5. (1844) 8 JP 186.

In similar vein it is thought that a person who destroys or damages property found by him in circumstances where he believes the owner cannot be traced by taking reasonable steps can no more be convicted of criminal damage than he can be of theft by appropriating the property.

f) *Other cases.* While the foregoing discussion deals with the more obvious categories of lawful excuse for damage to property there are certainly other cases. Moreover "lawful excuse", like "lawful authority or reasonable excuse,"[6] may have an inbuilt elasticity which enables courts to stretch it to cover new situations so that it is never possible to close the categories that might constitute lawful excuse.

Clear cases arise where there is statutory authority for the destruction or damage.[7] The more general problem is set by the sort of facts that occurred in *Workman v Cowper.*[8] D had shot a foxhound, the owner of which was unknown at the time of the shooting, and which was running wild on common land. There was no evidence that the dog was attacking, or likely to attack, sheep, but it was the lambing season and D thought it best, attempts to catch the dog having failed, to shoot it. On such facts as these D might now bring himself within the terms of s. 5 if he honestly believed that the owner would have consented, or if he had honestly believed that his sheep were in need of immediate protection. But since owners of healthy and expensive foxhounds do not readily consent to their destruction and there was no evidence that the dog was going to attack sheep, it may be assumed that D could not bring his conduct within s. 5. Nor was there anything to suggest that the dog had been abandoned so that D could claim that he did not intend to destroy property belonging to another. On the other hand, D could no doubt claim that he was acting honestly and that what he did was reasonable as a prophylactic measure – the dog, after all, might start attacking sheep. It is interesting to note that in the case itself the magistrates thought that D had acted reasonably and the Divisional Court had some sympathy for their conclusion. D was in fact convicted and it is thought that on similar facts he could still be convicted. Although there may be many who think that what D did was reasonable, even prudent, D was not acting in defence of property and it seems a necessary inference from s. 5 (2) (b) that unless his property is in immediate need of protection (or D honestly believes that it is) there can be no lawful excuse. But if D manages to catch the dog there is a procedure available authorising its destruction within seven days of capture if efforts to trace the owner fail.[9] There is, in effect, a loophole in lawful excuse through which an agile, friendly and healthy dog may avoid a premature death.

6. See above, p. 446.
7. For example, statutory provisions for the destruction of dangerous, diseased or injured animals (Halsbury's Statutes, Vol. 2, *tit.* Animals); damage to property incidental to arrest, search and seizure (Police and Criminal Evidence Act 1984); where property is lawfully seized under statutory powers it would seem that in certain cases (firearms, offensive weapons, drugs) the police would have lawful excuse for destroying the property although the statute may not give an express power to destroy.
8. [1961] 2 QB 143, [1961] 1 All ER 683, DC.
9. Dogs Act 1906, s. 3.

Another situation, which experience shows to be provocative of trouble, concerns the unlawful parking of vehicles on private premises. The landowner may take reasonable measures to remove the vehicle since it constitutes a trespass but this is rarely practicable. Obviously the landowner cannot take a sledgehammer to the offending vehicle, however tempting this may be, and among the means adopted have been pasting adhesive paper across the windscreen or clamping the vehicle. Strictly these measures do not protect property (the car park or the forecourt or driveway) which is in immediate need of protection since the parked vehicles cause no damage and are merely an inconvenience to the landowner and persons who are authorised to park.

It would seem to be the case that putting adhesive paper on the windscreen constitutes damage. The vehicle is rendered unfit for use until time and labour are expended on the removal of the paper. In *Lloyd v DPP*[10] the court was of the opinion that there was no evidence in that case that the clamping of D's car had damaged it. But whether the clamping of the car itself constitutes damage is debateable.[11] To deny another the use of his property is, as such, not to damage it. A landowner who, finding another's car parked unlawfully on his premises, does not damage the other's car by boxing it in so that it cannot be driven away and clamping seems analogous to this.

The actual issue in *Lloyd* was different. D, a trespasser, had parked his car on P's land aware of notices which said that the cars of trespassers would be clamped and that there would be a charge of £25 for removal. D returned to find his car clamped and, having refused to pay the £25 for its removal, he later removed the clamp himself by using a disc cutter. It was held that D was rightly convicted of criminal damage in respect of the clamp. D argued that the clamping constituted a trespass (and on that issue authorities were cited to the court going back to the Year Books) but the court held that even if it was D had consented to it.[12] If D, who is lawfully parked in a park which he knows closes at 10 pm, returns after 10 pm and breaks down the doors to retrieve his car, he can hardly justify the damage to the doors by saying that he needed his car to get home; a trespasser cannot be in a better position. Exceptionally such a person might have a lawful excuse if he was unexpectedly delayed and needed his car for an errand of mercy because he might then believe that the owner of the park would have consented to the damage had he known of the circumstances.

2 Destroying or Damaging Property with Intent to Endanger Life

S. 1 (2) of the Criminal Damage Act 1971 provides—
   "A person who without lawful excuse destroys or damages any property, whether belonging to himself or another—

10. [1992] 1 All ER 982, [1991] Crim LR 904, DC.
11. Cf. [1991] Crim LR 906.
12. The court said D had consented to the *risk* of being clamped but that is the same as consenting to the clamping.

(a) intending to destroy or damage any property or being reckless as to whether any property would be destroyed or damaged; and

(b) intending by the destruction or damage to endanger the life of another or being reckless as to whether the life of another would be thereby endangered.

shall be guilty of an offence."

By s. 4 the offence is punishable by imprisonment for life.

This offence has no obviously traceable parents in the former law,[13] and it may be that it exhibits the hybrid features that are supposed to mark out those of doubtful stock. The Law Commission said of this offence:

"This proposed offence gives effect to our view that the policy of the criminal law is, and should continue to be, to select certain offences as attracting exceptionally high maximum penalties, because those offences are accompanied by aggravating factors. There are examples of this approach in section 8–10 of the Theft Act 1968 dealing with robbery, burglary and aggravated burglary, which may be regarded as theft accompanied by aggravating circumstances . . . We think that the proper criterion should be related to the endangering of life, a concept which appears in section 2 of the Explosive Substances Act 1883 and in section 16 of the Firearms Act 1968. It is not, therefore, a novel one likely to give rise to difficulties of interpretation, and we think that it correctly expresses the necessary seriousness. It is true that in adopting the criterion of endangering life there may still be some overlapping with offences against the person. It may be that when the Criminal Law Revision Committee completes its review of the law of offences against the person it will be necessary to look again at this matter."[14]

So the offence has features both of an offence against property and an offence against the person. In some circumstances (as where D severs the brake cable of P's car intending P to drive to his death) the offence will overlap with the offence of attempted murder, but it is wider than attempted murder in two respects. One is that it does not require the intent to kill which is necessary on a charge of attempted murder:[15] intention or recklessness as to the endangering of life will suffice. On facts such as those occurring in *Cunningham*,[16] for example, it could well be that when D severed the gas pipe he did not intend to asphyxiate P but was reckless whether her life would be endangered; he would not be guilty of attempted murder but he would be guilty of the offence under the Criminal Damage Act.[17] The other is that the offence under the Criminal Damage Act may be

13. A possible ancestor is the offence of setting traps so as to endanger life under s. 31 of the Offences against the Person Act 1861, above, p. 698, but this need not and usually would not, involve damage to property. The Law Commission itself referred to s. 2 of the Explosive Substances Act 1883 (causing an explosion likely to endanger life or cause serious injury to property), and s. 16 of the Firearms Act 1968 (possession of firearm with intent to endanger life or cause serious injury to property); but damaging property is not the gist of either offence.
14. Law Com. No. 29, paras. 21 and 27.
15. See above, p. 304.
16. [1957] 2 QB 396, [1957] 2 All ER 412, above, p. 61.
17. And also, of course, of the offence under s. 23 of the Offences against the Person Act 1861. It might be noted in passing that the toxic elements are now removed from gas used for domestic purposes and natural gas does not contain them; hence domestic gas can cause death only by asphyxiation, and even this risk is almost nil. But there remains a very high risk of explosion which is a serious danger to life.

committed where the acts done by D are too remote to constitute an attempt[18] to murder. If, for example, D were to sever the brake cable of O's car intending thereafter to induce P to drive the car to his death, D's act of damaging the car might be too remote to support a charge of attempting to murder P but it would support a charge under the Act.

But even though the offence under s. 1 (2) of the Criminal Damage Act is in some respects wider than attempted murder it is difficult to see how, as a practical matter, these differences would amount to much. Moreover, attempted murder is in one respect wider than the offence under the Act in that it extends to all acts of attempt and it is not confined to acts involving damage to property.

Certain general features of the offence under s. 1 (2), (such as destruction or damage, property, intention and recklessness) are the same as for the offence under s. 1 (1) which has already been discussed. The following additional matters need to be discussed in relation to the offence under s. 1 (2).

1 Intention and Recklessness

Intention and recklessness in relation to destroying or damaging property has been discussed above.[19] What is said there applies, *mutatis mutandis*, to intention and recklessness in relation to endangering the life of another,[20] and reference may also be made to the general discussion of intention and recklessness elsewhere in this book.[1] It need not be shown that life was in fact endangered by the damage (D may, for example, believe that the building to which he sets fire is occupied when it is not) nor that the damage in fact done created any risk to life so long as D, by damaging the property, intended or was reckless as to the endangering of life.[2] But in this particular it should be noted that there must be a causal connection between the destroying or damaging of the property and the endangering of life. If, to extend an example used above, D were to damage the lock in the process of entering P's garage in order to sever the brake cable of P's car, there would be no offence under s. 1 (2). D intends to damage the lock and he further intends to endanger P's life, but he does not intend "by the destruction or damage to endanger the life of" P. It is only when D damages the brake cable that he would commit the offence under s. 1 (2). So in *Steer*[3] it was held that the offence was not committed where D loosed off some shots at P and his wife as they stood at their bedroom window. While the shooting clearly endangered the lives of P and his wife and also caused damage by smashing the bedroom window, it was not *by* the damage to the window that their lives were endangered. On the other hand, it may be that if, having destroyed or damaged property belonging to P (e.g. having set fire to P's premises), D subsequently realises that P's life is in danger, D would commit the offence under s. 1 (2) if, provided it lies within D's power to

---

18. See above, p. 308.
19. At p. 689.
20. *Hardie* [1984] 3 All ER 848, [1985] 1 WLR 64, CA.
    1. Above, pp. 53–69.
    2. *Sangha* [1988] 2 All ER 385, CA; *Dudley* [1989] Crim LR 57, CA.
    3. [1987] 2 All ER 833, [1987] 3 WLR 205, HL.

prevent or minimise the further harm, he then omits to do so, intending that or being reckless whether, P's life should be endangered.[4]

2 Lawful Excuse

Since the gist of the offence under s. 1 (2) lies in endangering life by destroying or damaging property, it is understandable that D may commit the offence whether he creates a risk to life by destroying or damaging the property of another or by destroying or damaging his own. The risk is just the same whether D severs the brake cable on P's car, or severs the brake cable on his own car before lending it to P to drive.

It is equally understandable that the partial definition of lawful excuse in s. 5 (2) should not be applicable to an offence of this nature, and s. 5 does not apply to offences under s. 1 (2). It can be appreciated that it ought not to be a defence to an offence of this nature that, say, D, with the assent of E, severed the brake cable on E's car before lending it to P to drive. Equally, D ought to have no lawful excuse in damaging property, although done for the purpose of protecting other property, where in so doing he knowingly creates a risk to life.

Clearly, then, the intention in framing the offence under s. 1 (2) was that certain matters (such as destruction by D of his own property, destruction with owner's consent, destruction in defence of property) which constitute lawful excuse where D is charged with an offence under s. 1 (1) do not constitute lawful excuse where D is charged under s. 1 (2). This does not mean that in no circumstances can there be a lawful excuse where D is charged under s. 1 (2), because s. 1 (2) expressly states that the offence may be committed only by one "who *without lawful excuse* destroys or damages any property". It follows that there may be circumstances, presumably of an exceptional character, where D would have lawful excuse for destroying or damaging property even though he does it realising that he may endanger life. An exceptional case of this character would be where D damages property in self defence; if it is legitimate for D to kill in order to prevent himself being killed, D would not commit an offence under s. 1 (2) because he happened to use, and damage, property belonging to another in killing his attacker.[5] Similarly, the police might have lawful excuse for damaging property where this was done to prevent the commission of a serious crime against the person, even though what was done might endanger the life of the criminal. And if necessity is a defence where D chooses to put one life at risk in order to save many others,[6] it would extend to damaging property to do so.

4. *Miller* [1983] 1 All ER 978, HL, above, p. 51. Cf. *Fuller* [1974] Crim LR 134, CA. D pleaded guilty to damaging property being reckless whether life would be endangered though warned by his brother of danger arising from fractured gas pipe only after he had returned home. Appeal was against sentence only.

5. Cf. *Sears v Broome* [1986] Crim LR 461, DC, above, p. 701.

6. See above, p. 251.

3 Arson

The Law Commission took the view that there should be no separate offence of arson, that is, of destroying or damaging property by fire,[7] and simply provided in the Draft Bill that an offence committed under s. 1 (1) by fire should be punishable on indictment by imprisonment for life. In so far as arsonists may be frequently mentally unbalanced and in so far as fire-raising creates extra hazardous risks, this seemed a sensible way to meet the case and avoided complication of the substantive law. But this way of meeting the case proved unacceptable to Parliament,[8] and s. 1 (3) of the Act provides—

"An offence committed under this section by destroying or damaging property by fire shall be charged as arson."

And by s. 4 it is punishable by imprisonment for life.

The provision is a mandatory one – "*shall* be charged as arson" – and where D destroys or damages property by fire the proper course would appear to be to charge him with an offence under s. 1 (1) and (3), or an offence under s. 1 (2) and (3) as appropriate.[9]

The general features of arson are the same as for the offences under s. 1 (1) and s. 1 (2) except that the destruction or damage be by fire. For the offence to be complete some property must be destroyed or damaged by fire. The damage may of course be quite insignificant (it would be enough, for example, that wood is charred[10]) but there must be some damage by fire; it would not be enough that property is merely blackened by smoke though there might well be an attempt in such a case. D must intend, or be reckless as to, destruction or damage *by fire*. So if D, abetted by E, throws a bottle which, unknown to E, D has filled with petrol in order to set fire to P's house, D may be convicted of arson but E may not.[11] E, however, may be convicted of simple criminal damage in respect of any damage caused by the throwing of the bottle.

4 Threats to Destroy or Damage Property

Section 2 of the Criminal Damage Act 1971 provides—

"A person who without lawful excuse makes to another a threat, intending that that other would fear it would be carried out—

(a) to destroy or damage any property belonging to that other or a third person; or

---

7. Law Com. No. 29, paras. 28–33.

8. See HC, Vol. 817, col. 1433 et seq. The reasons given for singling out damage by fire would be equally applicable to singling out damage by explosives; that "arson" is such a splendidly evocative term cannot have been unimportant in securing its retention.

9. Where D is charged under s. 1 (2) and (3) there should be separate counts of arson with intent to endanger life and of arson being reckless that life is endangered so that in relation to sentencing the court has the verdict of the jury: *Hoof* (1980) 72 Cr App Rep 126, CA.

10. Cf. *Parker* (1839) 9 C & P 45.

11. Cooper (G) and Cooper (Y) [1991] Crim LR 524, CA.

(b) to destroy or damage his own property in a way which he knows is likely to endanger the life of that other or a third person; shall be guilty of an offence."

The offence is punishable by ten years' imprisonment: s. 4 (2).

1 The Conduct Threatened

In order to constitute an offence under this section the conduct threatened must be conduct which would be an offence under s. 1 of the Act. D would commit the offence, therefore, where, without lawful excuse, he threatened to destroy or damage the property of another (whether property of the person threatened or of a third party), or where he threatened to destroy or damage his own property in a way which he knows is likely to endanger the life of another (whether the life of the person threatened or the life of a third party).

If D is charged under s. 2 (a) "lawful excuse" has the meaning ascribed to it by s. 5 so that D would not commit an offence where, for example, he threatens to shoot P's dog should he find it marauding his sheep.[12] But by s. 5 (1) the partial definition of lawful excuse in the section does not apply to an offence

"involving a threat by the person charged to destroy or damage property in a way which he knows is likely to endanger the life of another. . . ."

This does not mean that there cannot be a lawful excuse for an offence under s. 2 (b), merely that the partial definition of lawful excuse in s. 5 cannot apply.[13] Where D threatens to destroy property of another with intent to endanger life he would have to be charged under s. 2 (a), and cannot be charged under s. 2 (b). Curiously, it would seem that if D is in such a case charged under s. 2 (a) there would be a lawful excuse if it appeared that he believed the owner would have consented to the threatened destruction or damage (s. 5 (2) (a)), but if he is charged under s. 2 (b) it would not be a lawful excuse that he was threatening to destroy his own property. But the distinction can be of small practical importance; if D threatens to destroy P's property in order to endanger the life of Q then it would be difficult to show that D honestly believed that P would have consented to the threatened destruction "had [P] known of the destruction or damage *and its circumstances*".[14]

2 The Threat

The threat may take any form. The Law Commission said:

"There seems to be no good ground, for limiting threats to written threats, for a telephonic threat, particularly if repeated, can cause more alarm in the recipient than any written threat. If the law is to be extended to cover telephonic threats, then logically there is no reason why it should not be extended to all threats, however made. The only limitation

---

12. See generally above, p. 695.
13. As to what may therefore constitute a lawful excuse, see above, p. 707.
14. Section 5 (2) (a), italics supplied.

that needs to be imposed is that the threats should be intended to create a fear that what is threatened will be carried out."[15]

This last limitation needs to be imposed because the gist of the offence is the threat and, given that D intends that P should believe that the threat will be carried out, there ought to be no requirement that D himself should have intended to carry his threat into effect. And if D intends that P would fear the threat would be carried out, D commits the offence notwithstanding that P knows the threat to be an idle one or is not intimidated by it. It would seem that the threat need not be a threat to do the damage immediately, but immediacy may be a relevant factor, along with other circumstances, in determining whether there is something that can be called a threat.

5 Possession Offences

By s. 3 of the Act—
"A person who has anything in his custody or under his control intending without lawful excuse to use it or cause or permit another to use it—
(a) to destroy or damage any property belonging to some other person; or
(b) to destroy or damage his own or the user's property in a way which he knows is likely to endanger the life of some other person;
    shall be guilty of an offence."

The offence is punishable by imprisonment for ten years: s. 4 (2).

In line with the offence of threatening under s. 2, the possession of the thing must be for the purpose of committing an offence under s. 1 of the Act. There is of course no need for the commission of an offence of destruction or damage, but there must be an intent to use the thing, or allow another to use it, for the purpose of committing what would be an offence under s. 1.[16] Accordingly the same provisions apply, mutatis mutandis, in relation to lawful excuse as apply to charges under s. 2.[17]

1 Custody or Control

Although it is convenient to talk of this offence as one of possession, the section speaks only of custody or control.

"Having regard to the difficulties inherent in the concept of possession, we prefer the idea of custody or control. These words are both to be found in the Statute Book, and together provide a better concept than 'possession', which is a technical term of some difficulty."[18]

---

15. Law Com. No. 29, para. 55.
16. *Fancy* [1980] Crim LR 171, CC.
17. Above, p. 694.
18. Law Com. No. 29, para. 59.

It may well have been a wise decision to eschew the term "possession", but what really helps to simplify the situation is the clear requirement for *mens rea*.

As the Law Commission observe:

"Problems which may arise where a substance, such as a stick of gelignite, is slipped into a person's pocket without his knowledge will be wholly academic, because if that person has no knowledge of its presence he cannot have an intention to use it or permit or cause another to use it. If he has no intention to use it or permit or cause it to be used, he does not commit an offence. . . ."[19]

But there must be custody or control; a mere intention to use something to commit an offence of criminal damage will not suffice. D may be about to pick up stones from the highway to throw through a shop window, but since at this stage he does not have custody or control of the stones he commits no offence under this provision. D need not of course be the owner of the thing in order to have custody or control of it, but he must have the charge of it. Where D is charged with permitting E to use the thing D must be in a position where, as against E, he might properly have prevented E from using it.

2 The Things Used

The section imports no limitation on the things which may be possessed with intent to commit criminal damage – "anything" may do for the purpose.

"The essential feature of the proposed offence is to be found not so much in the nature of the thing – for almost any every-day article, from a box of matches to a hammer or nail, can be used to destroy or damage property – as in the intention with which it is held."

Clearly the nature of the thing may have significance in proving that D possessed the thing with intent to commit criminal damage (the possession of a box of matches may be one thing and the possession of a ton of dynamite quite another) but given that the intent can be proved the nature of the thing is immaterial.

At this point it may be noted that under s. 6 of the Act a search warrant may be issued to a constable where it appears there is reasonable cause to believe that a person has anything in his control or custody or on his premises for the purpose of committing an offence under s. 1. This power of search was explained by the Law Commission[20] as being parallel to the power to search for stolen goods under s. 26 of the Theft Act 1968. On one view the power of search is a wide one since it extends to anything, but it is always limited by the requirement that there must be reasonable cause to believe that the thing has been used or is intended for use in committing an offence of criminal damage.

19. Ibid.
20. Law Com No. 29. Appendix A, notes to clause 6

3 Mens Rea

The offence may be committed only where D intends to use, or cause or permit another to use, the thing to destroy or damage property. It is not enough that D realises that the thing may be so used: he must intend or permit such use. But it is not necessary that D should intend an immediate use of the thing; the offence is aimed at proscribing what is essentially a preparatory act and it is therefore enough that D possesses with the necessary intent even though he contemplates actual use of the thing at some time in the future. And it would also seem to be clear that a conditional intent (an intention to use the thing to cause damage should it prove necessary) will suffice.[1]

6 Kindred Offences

In keeping with the aim of codification[2] the Criminal Damage Act 1971 contains, as near as may be, the whole of the law relating to damage to property. The Act accordingly abolishes the common law offence of arson, repeals most of the provisions of the Malicious Damage Act 1861, repeals the Dockyards Protection Act 1772, and a large number of statutory provisions containing miscellaneous offences of damage to property.

But the Criminal Damage Act leaves untouched the Explosive Substances Act 1883. The Law Commission had at first planned to repeal s. 2 (causing an explosion likely to endanger life or to cause serious injury to property) and s. 3 (possessing explosives with intent to endanger life or cause serious injury to property, and doing any act to cause an explosion likely to endanger life or cause serious injury to property) since these might easily have been brought within the scheme of the Criminal Damage Act. But in the end the Law Commission did not do this because it was felt that the Explosive Substances Act belonged to the area of public order offences, and its replacement should be considered in the context of a review of offences relating to public order. This means that on given facts there may be an offence both under the Criminal Damage Act and the Explosive Substances Act, and it should be noted that there are differences in relation to the *mens rea* that has to be established.

The Criminal Damage Act does not repeal the following provisions of the Malicious Damage Act 1861: s. 35 (placing wood etc. on rail lines or obstructing signals with intent to obstruct or overturn any engine); s. 36 (obstructing railway engines); s. 47 (exhibiting false signals with intent to endanger any ship); s. 48 (concealing or removing buoys provided for the guidance of shipping): and the retention of these offences has made necessary the further retention of general provisions of the Malicious Damage Act relating to malice (s. 58) and jurisdiction (s. 72). It will be seen

---

1. *Buckingham* (1976) 63 Cr App Rep 159, CA; cf. *Bentham* [1973] QB 357, [1972] 3 All ER 271, CA.
2. See above, p. 683.

that none of these offences would necessarily (or even ordinarily) involve damage to property, though the ultimate aim may be to cause damage to property. Frequently such acts might amount to an attempt to commit criminal damage, but in so far as the acts might be merely preparatory these provisions render the preparatory acts criminal.

Nor does the Act repeal offences of damage arising under other legislation where the liability for the damage may be grounded in negligence or where there is strict liability for the damage. In particular cases there may be thought valid policy reasons for imposing criminal liability for damage to property caused negligently,[3] or even for imposing strict liability for offences of damage to property.[4] These offences are perhaps best considered in relation to a review of criminal liability for negligence and a review of strict liability.

7 Miscellaneous Matters

While the maximum punishments provided by the Act for offences of damage tried on indictment (broadly, ten years for the simple offence, and life imprisonment for aggravated offences) may seem high, this was done merely to provide for the worst sort of case within each class and it was not intended in any way to alter present sentencing practice. The Act provides for summary trial of offences under s. 1 (1), s. 2 and s. 3, and in practice most offences will be so tried.[5] There used to be a complex rule relating to the ouster of the jurisdiction of magistrates in cases of damage involving title to real property, but this rule has now been abolished. In addition, all courts are empowered by s. 35 of the Powers of Criminal Courts Act 1973 (as amended by the Criminal Law 1977, s. 60) to make a compensation order (a magistrates' court may not award more than £2,000 on any one order) for loss of, or damage to, property.

3. E.g., s. 59 (c) of the Post Office Act 1953 punishes "carelessness, negligence or other misconduct" which may lead to injury to a postal packet.
4. An e.g. may be s. 60 of the Post Office Act 1953 – Placing dangerous substances against a letter box etc. "likely to injure the box".
5. As to summary trial of offences of damage when the value does not exceed £2,000, see above, p. 25. As to offences of damage triable either way see the Magistrates' Courts Act 1980, Sch 2.

19 Computer Misuse Offences[1]

The impact of computer technology on society has of course been profound. From simple beginnings in arithmetical calculations it has spawned immense data retrieval systems; systems controlling traffic by land, sea and air; systems indispensable to the functioning of industry, banking and commerce. All to the common good, or nearly all to the common good because, inevitably, some will use the technology for anti-social purposes. These may range from simple nosey-parkering, as where the hacker gains access to computer systems just for the fun of it, or for industrial espionage, or for perpetrating frauds, or for disrupting systems with serious commercial consequences, or for disrupting traffic control systems which may put limb and life at risk.

The law before the Computer Misuse Act could deal with some of these problems. Appropriating property belonging to another is no less theft because it is done not by picking a pocket but by causing a computer to debit one account and to credit another. Should someone cause death or injury not with a blunt instrument but by interfering with a traffic control system, he would be equally liable to conviction of an offence against the person.

But there were gaps to which the Law Commission addressed itself in a Working Paper published in 1988.[2] At this stage the Law Commission was primarily concerned with unauthorised access to computing systems (hacking) though it noted other problems such as the inapplicability of deception offences to computers.[3] The problem with hacking was that nosey-parkering (gaining unauthorised access to the correspondence, personal details, business records of another) is not an offence; invasion of privacy and industrial espionage are not, as such, offences. Is there a special case for making nosey-parkering by way of hacking into a computer system a criminal offence? The Law Commission thought that there was and in this it was overwhelmingly supported by commentators on the Working Paper.

The proposal in the Law Commission's Working Paper to criminalise unauthorised access was thus generally applauded. But before the publication of its final *Report*[4] the Commission conducted further discussions with

---

1. Wasik, *Crime and the Computer*, Clarendon Press, 1991.
2. Working Paper No. 110, *Computer Misuse*.
3. Cf. the similar problems in relation to forgery, above, p. 674.
4. Report No. 186, *Computer Misuse*, Cmnd. 819, 1989.

computer and software manufacturers and with computer users in banking and commerce which convinced the Commission of the need not only for a summary offence of unauthorised access (hacking) but also for two further offences, which may be tried on indictment, of unauthorised access with intent to commit or facilitate the commission of further offences and of unauthorised modification of computer material.

1 Unauthorised Access to Computer Material

By s. 1 of the Computer Misuse Act 1990:

"(1) A person is guilty of an offence if—
 (a) he causes a computer to perform any function with intent to secure access to any program or data held in any computer;
 (b) the access he intends to secure is unauthorised; and
 (c) he knows at the time when he causes the computer to perform the function that that is the case.
(2) The intent a person has to have to commit an offence under this section need not be directed at—
 (a) any particular program or data;
 (b) a program or data of any particular kind; or
 (c) a program or data held in any particular computer."

The offence is punishable on summary conviction by six months' imprisonment and/or a fine not exceeding level 5 on the standard scale.

This is the most far reaching of the offences under the Act. The idea, in effect, is to close the door in the hacker's face. The offence is committed though the hacker has no sinister purpose and is no more than a nosey-parker. But why should it be an offence to access files held in the office computer but not an offence to access files held in the filing cabinet? The Law Commission thought it best to close the door altogether on the hacker in order to deter the hacker who *might* be contemplating fraud, or who *might* go on to commit some further offence or who *might*, because of his skills, be recruited by others with more sinister motives. With respect, these are not convincing reasons; conduct is not properly penalised because it *might* lead to the commission of an offence. One reason for criminalising such conduct is that the proprietor of the system which is accessed by an unauthorised user may be put to considerable expense to repair his defences.[5] Of course the proprietor of files incurs expense repairing his defences if an intruder breaks into his office to look through the files. But there is a difference in that the intruder in the latter case must break into the office; he cannot access the files, as he can in the case of computer held material, from a distant part of the country or even, as events have shown,

---

5. The Law Commission instanced a case where the restoration of a system following unauthorised access required 10,000 hours of the time of skilled staff.

from the other side of the world. Computer systems are always vulnerable to the determined hacker. In a world that is increasingly dependent on computers, and the integrity of computer systems, it appears entirely right that the criminal law should be employed to discourage the hacker.

1) *Actus Reus*

The *actus reus* consists in causing a computer to perform any function. The Act does not define 'computer', the Law Commission taking the view that to have done so would be "foolish". Perhaps so but a court, though it might be foolish to attempt a comprehensive definition, may be required to decide whether a particular contrivance is a computer. Most obviously a computer is something that computes but computers have long since done more than merely mathematical calculations and may be used to store other information which can be processed for a wide variety of purposes ranging from legal research (LEXIS), traffic control or manufacturing purposes. It is tentatively suggested that the defining characteristics of a computer are the abilities of the appliance (i) to store information; (ii) to retrieve the information so stored; and (iii) to process that information. Hence the abacus and the slide-rule are not computers;[6] they can be used to make calculations but they have no "memory" and cannot themselves process information. It is submitted that it is insufficient that a machine is programmed to perform a function or number of functions. A washing machine may be programmed to perform several varieties of wash but is not, on this view, a computer; it can only obey instructions and not process them. A computer can select a course of action on the basis of instructions given or information received. A machine which ensures that traffic lights will show red or green at stated intervals is not a computer; a machine which varies the intervals in response to information about traffic density is.

But it may be that some would argue for a wider definition. A computer may be thought of as any machine which responds to signals (now usually electronic) to perform programmed functions. On this view the unauthorised user of the washing machine or microwave oven would commit the offence under s. 1. But such machines are not sold as, nor are they considered to be, computers. The appropriate charge for the unauthorised user of a dishwasher or microwave oven would appear to be the dishonest abstraction of electricity contrary to s. 13 of the Theft Act 1968 rather than unauthorised access to computer material under s. 1 of the Computer Misuse Act.

Given that the machine is a computer, the *actus reus* is complete if it is caused to perform "any" function. It is accordingly enough to switch on

---

6. But not because they are mechanical; computers are now electronic but Babbage's computer was no less a computer because it was mechanical.

the computer though it may be difficult to prove *mens rea* if this is all that D has done.

2) *Mens Rea*

D must cause a computer to perform a function with intent to secure access to any program or data held in any computer, knowing that the access he intends to secure is unauthorised.

By s. 17 "access" is widely defined and includes any "use" of a computer. In practice it will usually be necessary to establish that D has secured access as so defined in order to establish *mens rea* but the offence is complete on causing a computer to perform any function with intent to secure access.

D must "know"[7] that the access he intends to secure is unauthorised. By s. 17 (5) D's access is unauthorised if—

(i) he is not himself entitled to control access of the kind in question to the program or data; *and*

(ii) he does not have consent to access by him of the kind in question to the program or data from any person who is so entitled.

If D believes, however unreasonably, that he is entitled to control access or that his access is authorised by someone entitled to control access, he cannot know that his access is unauthorised. More difficult is the case where D is unsure whether he is entitled to control access or, much more likely, he is unsure of the extent of his authorisation to access a computer, but decides nonetheless to access the computer without checking on his authorisation. If, as will usually be the case, D could readily ascertain the nature and extent of his authority but chooses not to do so and decides to take the risk that his access is unauthorised, and his access is in fact unauthorised, it may be that he does not *know* his access is unauthorised but this is only because he does not want to know. It is submitted that wilful blindness of this kind is enough to constitute knowledge. At the other extreme, the fact that it crosses D's mind that he might possibly be exceeding his authority would not suffice for knowledge.

The offence may be committed though D is authorised to access one computer, computer X, if he does so to access another, computer Y, to which he does not have authorised access. Here again proof of the offence would be very difficult without proof that D has accessed computer Y, but the offence is complete when D has accessed computer X with intent to access computer Y.

Equally, the offence may be committed when D, authorised to access the computer for certain purposes, exceeds his authorisation.

The offence requires both (i) that the access intended by D is in fact unauthorised; and (ii) that D knows that his access is unauthorised. If D believes his access is unauthorised when it is in fact authorised he does not

---

7. See generally above, p. 105.

commit the offence. Nor is he guilty of an attempt since the offence is summary only.

The essence of the offence under s. 1 is causing a computer to perform a function with intent to secure unauthorised access. No particular computer needs to be targeted by D and it is enough that he is out fishing without a licence. Indeed, it is enough that he sets out to fish without a licence.

2 Unauthorised Access with Intent to Commit or Facilitate Further Offences

By s. 2 of the Act—
  "(1) A person is guilty of an offence under this section if he commits an offence under section 1 above ('the unauthorised access offence') with intent—
    (a) to commit an offence to which this section applies; or
    (b) to facilitate the commission of such an offence (whether by himself or by any other person);
    and the offence he intends to commit or facilitate is referred to below in this section as the further offence."
The section applies to arrestable offences generally and is punishable on indictment with five years' imprisonment. The offence requires proof of the s. 1 offence together with an intent to commit an arrestable offence or to facilitate the commission of such an offence by another. By s. 2 (3) it is immaterial whether the ulterior offence is to be committed at the time of access or on some future occasion.

In practical terms the offences most likely to be intended or facilitated by D will be offences against property involving dishonesty but all arrestable offences are included.[8] As to the former it might have been thought that the Theft Acts were adequate to deal with the case with a possible amendment to deal with deception offences in relation to machines. This was how the Law Commission initially viewed the matter but it had second thoughts and concluded that it would be preferable to extend the criminal law to the hacker before he had committed a substantive offence under the Theft Acts or had reached the stage of an attempt. Like s. 1, s. 2 is accordingly aimed at preparatory conduct. Thus, to take examples given by the Law Commission, the hacker who, with intent to steal, is searching for the password to enter an account might not be guilty of an attempt to steal, and the hacker who seeks confidential information in order to blackmail would clearly not be guilty of an attempt to blackmail. Both, however, would commit the substantive offence under s. 2.

The Law Commission thought that the s. 2 offence bore "some relation to an attempt"[9] in that the ulterior offence needs only to be intended and

---

8. A traffic control system might be entered with intent to injure or even kill. Hacking with intent to commit treason is, perhaps, somewhat fanciful.
9. Law Com. No. 186, para. 3.58.

not effected and accordingly s. 2 (4) provides that the offence may be committed though commission of the ulterior offence is impossible. Strictly, it is submitted, this provision is unnecessary but it may save argument.

Since the offence under s. 2 is a substantive offence there may, in turn, be a conspiracy to commit, or an incitement to commit, or an attempt to commit the offence. Given the preparatory nature of the offence, however, there is little scope for the operation of attempt.[10]

3 Unauthorised Modification of Computer Material

By s. 3 of the Act—

"(1) A person is guilty of an offence if—

(a) he does any act which causes an unauthorised modification of the contents of any computer; and

(b) at the time when he does the act he has the requisite intent and the requisite knowledge."

(2) For the purposes of subsection (1) (b) above the requisite intent is an intent to cause a modification of the contents of any computer and by so doing—

(a) to impair the operation of any computer;

(b) to prevent or hinder access to any program or data held in any computer; or

(c) to impair the operation of any such program or the reliability of any such data.

(3) The intent need not be directed at—

(a) any particular computer;

(b) any particular program or data or a program or data of any particular kind; or

(c) any particular modification or a modification of any particular kind.

(4) For the purposes of subsection (1) (b) above the requisite knowledge is knowledge that any modification he intends to cause is unauthorised."

It is, and remains, an offence under the Criminal Damage Act to destroy or damage a computer or its software as by taking a hammer to them and causing damage that can be perceived by the senses. Difficulties arise, however, where there is no perceptible physical damage but where D, say, interferes with programmes to render the computer incapable, or less capable, to carry out the functions the programmes are designed to perform. This may be done without causing any physical damage.

Take a simple case where D erases data held on a disc. The disc is rendered less valuable to P but the information lost to P, being *intangible* property, cannot be the subject of a charge under the Criminal Damage Act. Provided the disc remains unharmed and can be re-used to store

10. Reaching for the switch?

information, there is no *tangible* damage to the disc. So it appears that D might escape liability under the Criminal Damage Act though he has inflicted a loss on P that will take time and expense to repair or may even be irreparable. The computer thus opened up, it seemed, opportunities for mischief-makers to inflict considerable inconvenience on computer users and considerable economic loss on their owners,[11] without fear of any criminal sanction.

In *Cox v Riley*,[12] however, it was held that D was guilty of criminal damage where he erased the program from a plastic circuit card which operated a saw to cut wood to programmed designs. D's counsel argued that the program was not "property of a tangible nature" within the Criminal Damage Act. In this he was no doubt right but, in the view of the court, it failed to take account of the fact that D was charged not with damaging the program but with damaging the plastic card. And in Whiteley[13] it was held that D was properly convicted of criminal damage to computer discs where he gained unauthorised access to an academic computer system and by altering their magnetic particles caused them to delete and add files. His counsel's argument that only intangible information on the discs had been damaged was rejected; the discs had been damaged because their usefulness had been impaired.

These decisions might be viewed as bringing computer misuse, because of its obvious potential for harm, within the Criminal Damage Act by procrustean means,[14] but it is submitted that both decisions were defensible under the Act. The plastic circuit card in *Cox v Riley*, though it may not have been rendered useless and could have been reprogrammed to perform its original function, was temporarily unable to perform the function it was designed to perform. Though the disc was not damaged, it was rendered incapable of performing one of its programs and the case seems indistinguishable from *Fisher*.[15] Similarly, in *Whiteley*[16] the computer, though not itself damaged, had been rendered inoperable by tampering with its control mechanisms, the programs on the discs. That the discs could be restored is irrelevant since temporary impairment suffices.

The Law Commission, however, took the view that the problem of computer misuse should be tackled directly. It might have been possible to deal with the problem by amending the Criminal Damage Act to include interference with data and programs. But the Commission decided on the creation of a new offence for two reasons. One was that "the theoretical difficulties posed by applying the concept of damage to intangible property such as data or programs"[17] would render the law unacceptably uncertain. The other was that criminal damage may be committed recklessly and the Commission did not think that the new offence should extend to a person who recklessly modified computer material.[18] In addition, as will appear,

11. See Wasik, op. cit., Ch. 5.
12. (1986) 83 Cr App Rep 54, DC.
13. [1991] Crim LR 436, CA.
14. See Wasik, op. cit., pp. 137–145.
15. (1865) LR 1 CCR 7, above, p. 684.
16. [1991] Crim LR 436, CA.
17. Law Com. No. 186, para. 3.62.
18. See below.

the Commission sought to clarify the relationship between the modification offence under s. 3 of the Computer Misuse Act and the offence of criminal damage under the Criminal Damage Act.

1) *Actus Reus*

Essentially s. 3 is concerned with the sabotaging of computer systems by any of the acts specified in s. 3 (2). Unauthorised use is insufficient unless it results in a modification of the contents of a computer but any such modification will suffice. Causing a computer to debit P's bank account and credit D's[19] is such a modification because the data concerning P's account is now unreliable.

2) *Mens Rea*

As noted, the offence requires an *intent* to cause an unauthorised modification; recklessness does not suffice. The reason given by the Law Commission[20] was that it did not wish to extend the offence to the person who inadvertently modified the contents of a computer. It is less clear that the offence should not extend to the person who adverts to the risk of modifying the contents of a computer but the Commission apprehended, no doubt rightly, that recklessness in the context of the Computer Misuse Act would have been given the same (*Caldwell*) meaning it has for criminal damage. The Commission thought that such a person would already be guilty of the basic unauthorised access offence but this will not necessarily be the case; the mere fact that D recklessly modifies the contents of a computer does not involve the conclusion that his access is unauthorised.

D's intent need not be directed at any particular computer or program. Nor does this offence require that D himself should access, or intend to access, a computer. The Commission gave the example[1] of X who puts into circulation a disc which he knows to be infected[2] which passes through the hands of Y and Z to V whose files and data are corrupted by its use. X would be guilty of the offence if he intends to cause an unauthorised modification of "any" computer. The same result would of course obtain by the application of the principle of transferred malice.[3] The offence is complete only when the contents of V's computer are modified but by putting the infected disc into circulation X would be guilty of an attempt.

---

19. Cf. *Thompson* [1984] 3 All ER 565, [1984] 1 WLR 962, CA.
20. Law Com. No. 186, para. 3.62.
  1. Law Com. No. 186, para. 3.70.
  2. Said to be a "substantial and serious" problem.
  3. Above, p. 74.

3) *The Relationship between Section 3 and Criminal Damage*

Assuming that *Cox v Riley* and *Whiteley*[4] correctly hold that the modification of the circuit card and the discs by the removal or alteration of electronic particles stored therein constitutes criminal damage there would be an overlap between the offence of criminal damage and the offence under s. 3 of the Computer Misuse Act. The Law Commission thought that such an overlap would be unfortunate partly because it would cause confusion and partly because a person might be exposed to different penalties for the same conduct. Section 3 (6) accordingly provides:

"For the purposes of the Criminal Damage Act 1971 a modification of the contents of a computer shall not be regarded as damaging any computer or computer storage medium unless its effect on that computer or computer storage medium impairs its physical condition."

This provision is intended to reverse the effect of *Cox v Riley* and no doubt prosecutors will heed s. 3 (6) and use the Criminal Damage Act only where the "physical condition" of the computer or computer storage medium is impaired. One reason given by the Law Commission for this is that it would not be right to expose offenders to potentially higher penalties by continuing to use the 1971 Act.[5] Perhaps so, but it seems odd that, to take the case of the hacker instanced by the Law Commission[6] whose electronic vandalism required 10,000 hours of skilled work to repair, that he should be liable to five years' imprisonment under the 1990 Act whereas if he had used a hammer to cause the same loss (or even a penny's worth) he would be liable to ten years under the 1971 Act. Moreover, the offence under the 1971 Act extends to recklessly caused damage. If the aforesaid hacker had recklessly caused this enormous loss he would have been liable under *Cox v Riley* but now escapes scot free because the 1990 Act does not extend to recklessly caused harm and he has not, presumably, impaired the "physical condition" of the computer. To some, and especially the proprietors of computer systems, it might seem odd in this case to say, "Well, there's nothing wrong with the computer. It *looks* exactly the same as it did yesterday. There's only one slight difference. It doesn't work."

4. Above, pp. 720, 721.
5. Law Com. No. 186, para. 3.78.
6. Above, p. 715, fn. 5.

20 Criminal Libels and Related Offences

The common law recognised four forms of criminal libel – blasphemous, defamatory, obscene and seditious. Lord Scarman regarded them as part of a group of criminal offences designed to safeguard the internal tranquillity of the kingdom; and thought that there was force in the "lawyer's conceptual argument" that the requirements of *mens rea* should be the same for all of them.[1] Regrettably the courts have not approached the offences consistently. If the purpose of the offences is the protection of internal tranquillity, that object has not always been kept clearly in view and the requirements of *mens rea* differ very significantly. Though all four offences still exist at common law, obscene libels are now in practice governed by the Obscene Publications Act 1959.

1 Blasphemy[2]

1) *Actus Reus*

It is a common law misdemeanour to publish blasphemous matter whether orally or in writing. Matter is blasphemous if it denies the truth of the Christian religion[3] or of the Bible[4] or the Book of Common Prayer,[5] or the existence of God. The earlier cases required no more than this for, as Stephen says, they

"all proceed upon the plain principle that the public importance of the Christian religion is so great that no one is allowed to deny its truth."[6]

The gist of the offence was said to be "a supposed tendency to shake the fabric of society generally."[7] Yet, while the law was stated in these broad terms, there is no recorded instance of a conviction for blasphemy where an

---

1. *Whitehouse v Gay News Ltd* (1979) 68 Cr App Rep 381 at 404 and 409, HL.
2. G. D. Nokes, *History of the Crime of Blasphemy*; Stephen, 2 HCL 469–476; Bailey, Harris and Jones, Ch. 9; Robertson, *Freedom, the Individual and the Law*, 210–214.
3. *Taylor* (1676) 1 Vent 293.
4. *Hetherington* (1841) 4 State Tr NS 563.
5. According to Russell, 1519; Archbold (39th ed.) §3401.
6. 2 HCL 475.
7. Per Lord Sumner in *Bowman v Secular Society Ltd* [1917] AC 406 at 459.

element of contumely and ribaldry was absent.[8] In the course of the nineteenth century it came to be held that matter denying the truth of Christianity, etc., will not be held criminal if it is expressed in decent and temperate language and not in such terms as are likely to lead to a breach of the peace. "If the decencies of controversy are observed, even the fundamentals of religion may be attacked without the writer being guilty of blasphemy."[9]

Stephen found himself unable to accept this milder view of the law because of the weight of the earlier authorities;[10] but the milder view found favour with the House of Lords in *Bowman v Secular Society Ltd*.[11] In that case it was held that a company formed to promote the secularisation of the state was not unlawful although one of its objects was to deny Christianity. Blasphemous words are punishable

> "for their manner, their violence, or ribaldry, or, more fully stated, for their tendency to endanger the peace then and there, to deprave public morality generally, to shake the fabric of society and to be a cause of civil strife."[12]

The application of this test would virtually abolish the crime because it is scarcely conceivable that any utterance regarding Christianity could seriously be expected to produce such drastic results today. In *Whitehouse v Gay News Ltd and Lemon*,[13] the first prosecution for over 60 years, the House of Lords applied a much less strict test. A publication is blasphemous if it is couched in indecent or offensive terms likely to shock and outrage the feelings of the general body of Christian believers in the community. There appears to be no need to prove any tendency to endanger the peace, still less "to shake the fabric of society". The publication in question, a poem and illustration vilifying Christ in his life and in his crucifixion, was, no doubt, extremely offensive to many people; but there was no indication that it had provoked or was likely to provoke violence and it would be ludicrous to suggest that it was likely to have any effect on the fabric of society.

In *Chief Metropolitan Stipendiary Magistrate, ex p Choudhury*[14] it was argued for the first time that the offence of blasphemy is applicable to religions other than Christianity. The court held that the law applies only to Christianity, and possibly only to the established church, though the latter point was not decided. The court had no power to extend the law to other religions and would not have exercised it if it had. Judicial decision is not an appropriate means of providing for a matter involving such complex issues of public policy. Accordingly, it was held that the chief magistrate

8. This was common ground in *Bowman v Secular Society Ltd*, see, for example, per Lord Sumner [1917] AC 406 at 460. Stephen says that the placards held to be blasphemous in *Cowan v Milbourn* (1867) LR 2 Exch 230 "could hardly have been expressed in less offensive language": 2 HCL at 474; but that was a civil action, and Lord Sumner and the Court of Appeal thought the decision wrong: [1917] AC at 463.
9. *Ramsay and Foote* (1883) 15 Cox CC 231 at 238, per Coleridge CJ.
10. 2 HCL 474, 475 and *Digest* (4th ed.), Art. 161.
11. [1917] AC 406.
12. Per Lord Sumner, [1917] AC at 466.
13. [1979] AC 617, [1979] 1 All ER 898, [1979] Crim LR 311 and commentary.
14. [1991] 1 QB 429, [1991] 1 All ER 306, DC.

had rightly refused to isue summonses alleging blasphemous libel against the religion of Islam by the author, Salman Rushdie, and the publishers of *The Satanic Verses*.

Whether or not the particular doctrines of Christian religions other than those of the established church are protected as such, an attack on Christianity generally may amount to the offence because that is the religion of the established church.[15] The established church is said to be unique because it is part of the constitution of the country, presumably part of "the fabric of society" which it is the object of the law to protect.

2) *Mens Rea*

In *Lemon and Gay News* the majority of the House of Lords held that the only *mens rea* that need be proved is an intention to publish the offending words. It is not necessary to prove that the defendant intended to attack Christianity or to shock and insult Christians or even that he knew that the words would or might have that effect. Lords Diplock and Edmund-Davies, dissenting, thought that the prosecution should be obliged to prove that D knew that this was the probable effect of the words. They considered that the decision of the majority turned the offence into one of strict liability, a charge which the majority denied. Presumably, however, it must be shown that D was aware of the presence and understood the meaning of the offending words. If they were in a foreign language and he believed they were a recipe for Christmas pudding, he would surely not be guilty.

3) *Reform of the Law*

Prosecutions for blasphemy have been extremely rare for over a hundred years[16] but several attempts to abolish the blasphemy laws have failed.[17] There is a strong case for their abolition. It is illogical that scurrilous publications relating to the Christian religion should be punishable because of their tendency to outrage the feelings of believers when similar publications relating to other religions are not. Christians are not alone in their susceptibility to outrage. On the other hand it would be wrong for the protection of the law to be extended to all religious beliefs, however weird. Events in Jonesville in Guyana in 1979 demonstrate that there may be religions which ought, in the public interest, to be vilified, however outraged their adherents might be. The rarity of prosecutions indicates that the Christian religion does not need the protection of the blasphemy laws. Other less strongly supported religions are well able to flourish in this country without it. The conclusion is that the law of blasphemy should be

15. *Gathercole* (1838) 2 Lew CC 237 (Alderson B).
16. *Pooley* (1857) 8 State Tr NS 1089; *Ramsay and Foote* (1883) 15 Cox CC 231; *Boulter* (1908) 72 JP 188; *Gott* (1922) 16 Cr App Rep 87 and *Lemon*, above.
17. R. S. W. Pollard, *Abolish the Blasphemy Laws*, 7.

abolished. The Law Commission, by a majority, has so recommended.[18] This would remove any legitimate grievances about the inequality of treatment of religions. The offences in the Public Order Act seem quite adequate to deal with any threat to public order. The two dissenting commissioners recommended that the common law offence be replaced by a new offence of publishing grossly abusive or insulting material relating to a religion with the purpose of outraging religious feelings.

2 Defamatory Libel

1) *Actus Reus*

A libel[19] is traditionally described as a writing[20] which tends to vilify a man and bring him into hatred, contempt and ridicule.[1] This definition has been thought to be inadequate in the law of tort where it is more likely that the test to be applied today would be that proposed by Lord Atkin:

"Would the words tend to lower the plaintiff in the estimation of right thinking members of society generally?"[2]

The traditional definition has, however, been accepted as representing the law of criminal libel in recent cases.[3]

The publication of a libel is a common law misdemeanour but by s. 5 of the Libel Act 1843, it is now punishable by no more than one year's imprisonment. It is also a tort[4] and the tortious aspect of libel is much more important. Criminal proceedings for libel are rare and are not encouraged by the courts. It was at one time thought that libel amounted to a criminal offence only if it was likely to result in a breach of the peace. It is now clear that this is not so except perhaps where the libel is published only to the person defamed,[5] or where the person defamed is dead. If criminal libel does require some additional constituent, it is that the libel must be "serious". If it is likely to provoke a breach of the peace or to disturb the peace of the community, then it is certainly serious; but it may be serious although it has no such tendency.[6] "Deliberate character assassination and the wild dissemination of defamatory matter by cranks" are – and, it is said,

---

18. Law Com. No. 145 (1985), "Offences against Religion and Public Worship".
19. See J. R. Spencer [1977] Crim LR 383 and 465.
20. Defamatory words published in the course of the performance of a play amount to a criminal libel unless the performance is given on a domestic occasion in a private dwelling: Theatres Act 1968, ss. 4 and 6. It is uncertain whether broadcasting (except from a script) can constitute criminal libel. The Defamation Act 1952, ss. 1 and 6, does not apply to criminal proceedings. The Faulks Committee had recommended that it should so apply.
   1. *Thorley v Lord Kerry* (1812) 4 Taunt 355.
   2. *Sim v Stretch* [1936] 2 All ER 1237 at 1240.
   3. *Goldsmith v Pressdram Ltd* [1977] QB 83 at 87, per Wien J; *Wells Street Stipendiary Magistrates' Court, ex p Deakin* [1980] AC 477 at 487, [1979] 2 All ER 497 at 502, per Viscount Dilhorne.
   4. See Salmond, Ch. 8, Street, Ch. 24 and Winfield, Ch. 12.
   5. Adams (1888) 22 QBD 66, CCR; Law Com. Working Paper No. 84, para. 38.
   6. *Wicks* [1936] 1 All ER 384 at 386. *Gleaves v Deakin* [1979] 2 All ER 497, HL.

ought to be – offences, whether or not the person defamed, or anyone else is likely to resort to unlawful violence.[7] It seems that seriousness is now part of the definition of the offence.[8] An examining magistrate should not commit for trial unless he is satisfied that the alleged libel is so serious as to justify a prosecution in the public interest.[9] Evidence of the truth of statements complained of, or of the general bad reputation of P, is not relevant at this stage: *Gleaves v Deakin*,[10] where the House did not find it necessary to decide whether the examining magistrate had acted rightly in admitting evidence of P's convictions. As evidence of truth and general reputation were inadmissible, it seems that in principle convictions ought also to have been excluded. The House thought that the consent of the Attorney-General to the bringing of a prosecution should be required but there are at present no general restrictions. Where the prosecution is of any person responsible for the publication of a newspaper for any alleged libel therein, the leave of a judge is required by s. 8 of the Law of Libel Amendment Act 1888. The judge should not exercise his discretion in favour of an applicant unless he is satisfied that (i) there is a clear prima facie case, (ii) the libel is so serious that it is proper for the criminal law to be invoked and (iii) that the public interest *requires* the institution of criminal proceedings. Wien J found these conditions to be satisfied in a case where the applicant occupied important public positions, where his integrity had been impugned and a criminal offence alleged against him and where a campaign of vilification had been carried on for months.[11]

Defamatory libel is best studied as a branch of the law of tort but it is necessary here to note the differences which exist between the crime and the tort. In the first place, libel is the only form of defamation which is indictable. Slander is not a crime.[12] The crime of libel is wider than the tort in at least two and possibly five respects.

(i) Publication to the person defamed is sufficient in crime but not in tort.[13] In tort, the gist of the matter is the loss of the plaintiff's reputation and this only occurs through publication to a third party; but a principal reason why libel is indictable is the danger to the public peace[14] and this may obviously be even greater where the publication is to the prosecutor himself than where it is to another.

(ii) The truth of the defamatory statement affords a complete defence (justification) in tort but in crime the defendant must prove not only that the statement is true but that it is for the public benefit that it be published. This is the effect of s. 6 of the Libel Act 1843, modifying

7. J. R. Spencer in *Reshaping the Criminal Law*, 285, quoted by Lord Edmund-Davies, [1979] 2 All ER at 505.
8. See, however, somewhat ambiguous remarks of Lord Dilhorne at [1979] 2 All ER at 501. Cf. Law Com. Working Paper No. 84, paras. 3.6–3.7.
9. [1979] 2 All ER 502 and 505.
10. Above, fn. 6.
11. *Goldsmith v Pressdram Ltd* [1977] QB 83, [1977] 2 All ER 557 (Wien J). Cf. *Desmond v Thorne* [1982] 3 All ER 268, [1983] 1 WLR 163 (Taylor J).
12. *Burford* (1669) 1 Vent 16; *Langley* (1704) 6 Mod Rep 124. But note that blasphemous or seditious spoken words, or words likely to cause a breach of the peace, are indictable.
13. *Adams* (1888) 22 QBD 66.
14. *Holbrook* (1878) 4 QBD 42 at 46; but cf. *Wicks*, above.

the common law under which it is probable that truth was not a defence to an indictment.

(iii) It is clear that the common law defence of privilege applies equally in crime as in tort[15] but it is not certain that the defence of fair comment on a matter of public interest is available. Wien J left the matter open in *Goldsmith v Pressdram Ltd*[16] and leading works say[17] that the defence may be relied on.[18]

(iv) A libel on a class of persons is not actionable unless the class is so small, like a body of trustees or directors, that it might be taken to refer to each member individually,[19] or it is otherwise so worded as to appear to refer to an individual. It is possible, however, that a libel intended to excite public hatred against a class, such as the clergy of Durham or the Justices of the Peace of Middlesex is indictable,[20] though no individual's reputation be harmed.

(v) It is not actionable to defame a dead person, but according to Coke[1] it is indictable, again because of a tendency to cause strife. Later decisions, however, suggest that this is so only if the libel is designed to bring the surviving relations of the deceased person into hatred or contempt[2] – in which case it seems to be a libel on them – or was actually intended to provoke or annoy the surviving relatives.[3]

2) *Vicarious Liability*

In other respects, the crime is narrower than the tort. In accordance with general principle, a master is liable in tort for libels published by his servant in the course of his employment.[4] It may be that vicarious liability also extended at common law to a criminal charge against the proprietor of a newspaper in respect of libels published by his servant.[5] However that may be, by the Libel Act 1843, s. 7, it is a defence to prove that the publication was made without D's authority, consent or knowledge and that the publication did not arise from want of due care or caution on his part. It seems to follow from this provision that D is liable for the acts of his

15. *Perry* (1883) 15 Cox CC 169 and *Rule* [1937] 2 KB 375.
16. [1977] QB 83 at 90. In [1977] 2 All ER 557 he is reported to have said, without citation of authority, that the defence does not apply; but his (one assumes) second thoughts, being stated in the Law Report, must prevail.
17. 28 Halsbury's Laws of England (4th edn.), para. 29–78; Archbold, para. 29–78; Russell, 803–805.
18. The Law Commission's provisional recommendation is that there should be no such defence in their proposed offence, which would require an intent to defame: Working Paper No. 84, 8–49.
19. *Knuppfer v London Express Newspapers Ltd* [1944] AC 116, [1944] 1 All ER 495.
20. *Williams* (1822) 5 B & Ald 595.
  1. *De Libellis Famosis*, (1605) 5 Co Rep 125a.
  2. *Topham* (1791) 4 Term Rep 126.
  3. *Ensor* (1887) 3 TLR 366; and see Stephen, *Digest* (4th ed.), 208 n.
  4. Above, p. 170.
  5. *Walter* (1799) 3 Esp 21; *Gutch, Fisher and Alexander* (1829) Mood & M 433. But cf. *Holbrook* (1877) 13 Cox CC 650.

servants within the scope of their authority unless the statutory conditions are satisfied.

3) *Mens Rea*

The defendant must have intended to publish the words which are alleged to be libellous. It is not enough that he intentionally published a book or paper in which they were contained.[6] It is not certain what further mental element is required. In *Wicks*[7] Du Parcq J said that the crime was one of strict liability but this was obiter and not supported by the authority cited.[8] It is submitted that D must at least know of the existence, or the possibility of the existence, of the facts which render the statement defamatory.[9] Other authorities suggest that there must be an actual intention to defame.[10] As publication to the victim is sufficient, it is difficult to see how this can be so in that type of case since there is no evidence of an intention to injure the victim's reputation. Arguably, that is a special case. Analogy with blasphemous libel, as defined in *Lemon*,[11] would suggest that an intention to defame is not required, analogy with seditious libel would suggest that it is.[12]

As noted above, a person may be held vicariously liable for libel if he fails to prove that the publication did not arise from his negligence; but this is not inconsistent with the opinion expressed above. It is not unknown for vicarious liability to attach to offences requiring *mens rea*[13] and it may be that *mens rea* has to be proved in the agent.

4) *Publication of Libel Known to be False*

The publication of a libel *known to be false* is a misdemeanour under s. 4 of the Libel Act 1843 punishable with two years' imprisonment. If it is not proved that D knew the libel to be false, or if it is true, D may be convicted of the common law offence and sentenced to not more than one year's imprisonment.[14]

6. *Munslow* [1895] 1 QB 758 at 765.
7. (1936) 25 Cr App Rep 168 at 173.
8. *Walter* (1799) 3 Esp 21.
9. So that there would be no criminal liability on the facts of *E. Hulton & Co v Jones* [1910] AC 20; *Cassidy v Daily Mirror Newspapers Ltd* [1929] 2 KB 331 or *Newstead v London Express Newspaper Ltd* [1940] 1 KB 377, [1939] 4 All ER 319.
10. *Abingdon* (1794) 1 Esp 226; *Creevey* (1813) 1 M & S 273; *Evans* (1821) 3 Stark 35; *Ensor* (1887) 3 TLR 366.
11. [1979] AC 617, [1979] 1 All ER 898.
12. Below, p. 749.
13. Above, p. 171.
14. *Boaler v R* (1888) 21 QBD 284.

3 Obscene Publications[15]

Obscenity was originally an ecclesiastical offence but it was held in *Curl*[16] that the publication of an obscene libel was a common law misdemeanour. The law is now to be found in the Obscene Publication Acts 1959 and 1964.

1) *What is Obscenity?*

The ordinary meaning of obscene is filthy, lewd, or disgusting. In law, the meaning is in some respects, narrower, in other respects possibly wider.

The 1959 Act, s. 1 (1), provides the test of obscenity:

"For the purposes of this Act an article[17] shall be deemed to be obscene if its effect or (where the article comprises two or more distinct items) the effect of any one of its items is, if taken as a whole, such as to tend to deprave and corrupt persons who are likely, having regard to all relevant circumstances, to read, see or hear the matter contained or embodied in it."

This retains, in substantially the same form, the test at common law laid down by Cockburn CJ, in *Hicklin*:[18]

"... I think the test of obscenity is this, whether the tendency of the matter charged as obscenity is to deprave and corrupt those whose minds are open to such immoral influences, and into whose hands a publication of this sort may fall."

It has been said that the test was largely ignored at common law and that, if matter was found to be "obscene" in the ordinary meaning of the word, the tendency to deprave and corrupt was presumed; but, if that be so, the effect of the statutory enactment of the definition has been to require proof of an actual tendency to deprave and corrupt.[19] In *Anderson*[20] (the case of the "Oz School Kids' Issue") the conviction was quashed because the judge left the jury with the impression that "obscene" meant "repulsive," "filthy," "loathsome," or "lewd." An article might be all of these and yet not have a tendency to deprave and corrupt. Indeed its very "obscenity" (in the popular sense) may, paradoxically, prevent it from being "obscene" (in the legal sense). If the article were so revolting that it would put anyone off the kind of depraved activity depicted (the "aversion argument") then it would have no tendency to deprave.[1]

---

15. Bailey, Harris and Jones, Ch. 5. N. St. John Stevas, *Obscenity and the Law* and [1954] Crim LR 817; C. H. Rolph, *The Trial of Lady Chatterley*; Robertson, *Freedom, the Individual and the Law*, Ch. 5; D. G. T. Williams, "The Control of Obscenity" [1965] Crim LR 471, 522.

16. (1727) 2 Stra 788; following *Sidley* (1663) 1 Sid 168; sub nom. *Sydlyes'* case. 1 Keb 620, a case of an indecent exhibition.

17. For the definition of "article", see below, p. 744.

18. (1868) LR 3 QB 360 at 371. This was an appeal from a decision of a recorder quashing an order of the justices for the destruction of certain pamphlets under the Obscene Publications Act 1857; below, p. 742.

19. *Director of Public Prosecutions v Whyte* [1972] 3 All ER 12 at 18, HL, per Lord Wilberforce.

20. [1972] 1 QB 304, [1971] 3 All ER 1152. See Tony Palmer, *The Trials of OZ* (1971).

1. *Calder and Boyars Ltd* [1969] 1 QB 151, [1968] 3 All ER 644; *Anderson*, above.

At the same time, it appears that the requirement that the article be "obscene" in the ordinary meaning of the word may have disappeared and that an article may be obscene within the statute if it has a tendency to deprave and corrupt, though it is not filthy, lewd or disgusting.

Until recently the law of obscenity was only invoked in relation to sexual depravity. The prosecutions invariably concerned publications of an erotic and pornographic kind. The words "deprave and corrupt" are clearly capable of bearing a wider meaning than this; and it has now been held that depravity and corruption is not confined to sexual depravity and corruption. In *Calder (John) Publications Ltd v Powell*[2] it was held that *Cain's Book* might properly be found obscene on the ground that it

". . . highlighted, as it were, the favourable effects of drug-taking, and, so far from condemning it, advocated it, and that there was a real danger that those into whose hands the book came might be tempted at any rate to experiment with drugs and get the favourable sensations highlighted by the book."

The difficulty about extending the notion of obscenity beyond sexual morality is that it is not now apparent where the law is to stop. It seems obvious that an article with a tendency to induce violence is now obscene;[3] and, if taking drugs is depravity, why not drinking, or, if evidence of its harmful effects accumulates, smoking? Whether the conduct to which the article tends amounts to depravity would seem to depend on how violently the judge (in deciding whether there was evidence of obscenity) and the jury (in deciding whether the article was obscene) disapproved of the conduct in question. It is now clear that depravity may be a mental state, not resulting in external action of any kind. On the contrary, the protection of the minds of the people is the primary object of the law. In *Director of Public Prosecutions v Whyte*[4] it was found that the articles would enable their readers to engage in private fantasies of their own, not involving overt sexual activity of any kind. It was held that they were obscene. That case also settled that an article may be obscene although it is directed only to persons who are already depraved. It is enough that it maintains a state of corruption which might otherwise be escaped.

"The Act is not merely concerned with the once for all corruption of the wholly innocent, it equally protects the less innocent from further corruption, the addict from feeding or increasing his addiction."[5]

Expert evidence of the medical effects of cocaine and the various ways of taking it is admissible because this is a matter which is outside the experience of the ordinary juryman.[6] But whether those effects constitute depravity and corruption – i.e., whether the article, whatever it is, is obscene – is exclusively a question for the jury. Expert evidence is not

2. [1965] 1 QB 509, [1965] 1 All ER 159.
3. Cf. *Director of Public Prosecutions v A and BC Chewing Gum Ltd* [1968] 1 QB 159, [1967] 2 All ER 504; *Calder and Boyars Ltd* [1969] 1 QB 151 at 172.
4. Above, fn. 19.
5. At p. 19, per Lord Wilberforce.
6. *Skirving* [1985] QB 819, [1985] 2 All ER 705, CA, criticised by R. T. H. Stone, [1986] Crim LR 139 at 142.

admissible on that issue,[7] except apparently in the case of material directed at very young children, when experts in child psychiatry may be asked what the effect of certain material on the minds of children would be.[8] That case is to be regarded as "highly exceptional and confined to its own circumstances."[9] The theory seems to be that a jury is as well able as an expert to judge the effect on an adult but not on a child. This does not mean that the jury should be left without guidance on the question. It would seem right that they should be reminded that "deprave and corrupt" are very strong words; that material which might lead morally astray is not necessarily corrupting;[10] and that they should keep in mind the current standards of ordinary decent people.[11] In the end, they have to make a judgment by what they believe to be the prevailing moral standard.

Nevertheless, much may depend on the tone of the judge's direction to the jury. In the case of *Martin Secker and Warburg*,[12] concerning the publication of *The Philanderer*, Stable J gave a direction to a jury which was acclaimed in the press for its enlightened attitude and was thought to be reassuring to those who fear that the criminal law as applied by the judges is out of touch with public opinion.[13] The learned judge told the jury:[14]

"... the charge is a charge that the tendency of the book is to corrupt and deprave. The charge is not that the tendency of the book is either to shock or to disgust. That is not a criminal offence. The charge is that the tendency of the book is to corrupt and deprave. Then you say: 'Well, corrupt and deprave whom?' to which the answer is: those whose minds are open to such immoral influences and into whose hands a publication of this sort may fall. What, exactly, does that mean? Are we to take our literary standards as being the level of something that is suitable for the decently brought up young female aged fourteen? Or do we go even further back than that and are we to be reduced to the sort of books that one reads as a child in the nursery? The answer to that is: Of course not. A mass of literature, great literature, from many angles, is wholly unsuitable for reading by the adolescent, but that does not mean that a publisher is guilty of a criminal offence for making those works available to the general public."

Dealing with the particular book, he said:[15]

"... the book does deal with candour or, if you prefer it, crudity with the realities of human love and of human intercourse. There is no getting away from that, and the Crown say: 'Well, that is sheer filth.' Is it? Is the act of sexual passion sheer filth? It may be an error of taste to write about it. It may be a matter in which, perhaps, old-fashioned people would

7. *Calder and Boyars Ltd* [1969] 1 QB 151, [1968] 3 All ER 644; *Anderson* [1972] 1 QB 304, [1971] 3 All ER 1152; *Director of Public Prosecutions v Jordan* [1976] 3 All ER 775.
8. *Director of Public Prosecutions v A and BC Chewing Gum Ltd* [1968] 1 QB 159, [1967] 2 All ER 504.
9. *Anderson* [1972] 1 QB 304 at 313.
10. *Knuller (Publishing, Printing and Promotions Ltd) v Director of Public Prosecutions* [1972] 2 All ER 898 at 932, 936.
11. Ibid., at 904.
12. [1954] 2 All ER 683, [1954] 1 WLR 1138.
13. See (1954) 17 MLR 571.
14. [1954] 2 All ER at 686.
15. Ibid., at 687, 688.

mourn the reticence that was observed in these matters yesterday, but is it sheer filth? That is a matter which you have to consider and ultimately to decide."

Other directions to juries in recent times, however, have been a good deal less liberal and it has been suggested that Stable J's is not the typical judicial attitude.[16] Nor is it so clear that the law does not require us to take our standards from "the decently brought up young female aged fourteen". The article is obscene if it has a tendency to deprave "persons who are likely . . . to read, see or hear the matter contained or embodied in it". Only if the number of readers likely to be corrupted is "so small as to be negligible" is the article not obscene.[17] It is certainly obscene if it has a tendency to deprave "a significant proportion" of those likely to read it.[18] It would not be obscene simply on the ground that it might tend to deprave "a minute lunatic fringe of readers".[19] If, however, a significant, though comparatively small, number of the likely readers were decently brought up fourteen-year-old-girls, then whether the book was obscene would turn on whether it was likely to deprave them.

The questions for the jury are of a highly speculative nature. How, for example, is the jury to say whether a significant proportion of the readers will be fourteen-year-old girls? The answer seems to depend on all kinds of matters of which the jury can, at best, have imperfect knowledge. The same article may or may not be obscene depending on the manner of publication. If it has a tendency to deprave fourteen-year-old girls, a bookseller who sells a copy to a club for fourteen-year-old girls is obviously publishing an obscene article; but if he sells the same book to the Conservative Club or a working men's club, this may not be so. The fact that the publisher (in the sense of the producer) of the book is acquitted of publishing an obscene libel, does not mean, then, that other subsequent "publishers" of the book do not commit an offence.

The actual intention of the author is irrelevant. If the article has a tendency to deprave a significant proportion of the readership, it does not matter how pure and noble the author's intent may have been,[20] the article is obscene. In *Martin Secker and Warburg* Stable J told the jury:[1]

"You will have to consider whether the author was pursuing an honest purpose and an honest thread of thought, or whether that was all just a bit of camouflage . . ."

This was too favourable to the defence, unless the jury were to take account of the author's intention, as it appeared in the book itself, as a factor which would have a bearing on whether people would be depraved.

It is now made perfectly clear by the Act that an "item" alleged to be obscene must be "taken as a whole" so that where an article consists of a single item, like a novel, the article must be judged as a whole. Where an

---

16. Street, *Freedom, the Individual and the Law* (5th ed., 1984), 122.
17. *Director of Public Prosecutions v Whyte* [1972] 3 All ER 12 at 21 and 25, per Lords Pearson and Cross.
18. *Calder and Boyars Ltd* [1969] 1 QB 151 at 168.
19. Ibid., at 984.
20. *Calder and Boyars Ltd* [1969] 1 QB 151 at 168–169. Cf. *Lemon*, above, p. 724.
 1. [1954] 2 All ER 683 at 688.

article, like a magazine, comprises a number of distinct items, each item must be tested individually; and if one item is found to be obscene, the whole article is obscene.[2]

2) Offences

It is an offence if D:
-   (i) publishes an obscene article whether for gain or not;[3] or
-   (ii) "has" an obscene article for publication for gain (whether gain to himself or gain to another).[4]

Making an obscene article is not an offence, as such; but those who participate in its manufacture may be liable as secondary parties to the publication, or the "having", which is a continuing offence.[5]

1 Publication

Section 1 (3) of the Obscene Publications Act 1959 provides:
"For the purposes of this Act a person publishes an article who—
-   (a) distributes, circulates, sells, lets on hire, gives, or lends it, or who offers it for sale or for letting on hire; or
-   (b) in the case of an article containing or embodying matter to be looked at or a record, shows, plays or projects it . . ."

> [The proviso exempting television and sound broadcasting was repealed by the Broadcasting Act 1990, s. 162]

If the charge alleges publication to a named person, it must be proved that the article had a tendency to deprave and corrupt that person.[6] If the article does not have a tendency to deprave the person to whom it is published, it will be obscene only if either—

(1) (a) there are "persons who are likely, having regard to all the relevant circumstances, to read, see or hear the matter contained or embodied in it" (whether they have done so or not) and (b) it will have a tendency to deprave and corrupt those persons;[7] or

(2) it has in fact been published to a person whom it is likely to deprave and corrupt, and this publication could reasonably have been expected to follow from publication by D.[8]

If D is appropriately charged, he may then be convicted of publishing an obscene article to those persons.

In Barker,[9] where D published certain photographs to P and the judge told the jury that the fact that P kept them under lock and key was unimportant, the conviction was quashed. If the jury had been told that

---

2. *Anderson* [1972] 1 QB 304 at 312, above, p. 730.
3. Obscene Publications Act 1959, s. 2 (1).
4. Ibid., s. 2 (1) as amended by the 1964 Act, s. 1 (1).
5. *Barton* [1976] Crim LR 514, CA.
6. *Director of Public Prosecutions v Whyte* [1972] 3 All ER 12 at 29, per Lord Salmon.
7. Ibid., s. 1 (1).
8. Obscene Publications Act 1959, s. 2 (6).
9. [1962] 1 All ER 748, [1962] 1 WLR 349.

they were to consider the tendency of the article to deprave and corrupt only P, the direction would seem to be unobjectionable. If, however, they were directed or left to suppose that they should consider its tendency to deprave and corrupt others, then the direction was clearly wrong. The fact that P kept the articles under lock and key was not *conclusive*, for he may have intended to produce them at some future time; but it was certainly *relevant* to the answer to proposition 1 (a) above.

If the article has no tendency to deprave and corrupt the person to whom it is published and neither of the conditions specified above is satisfied, then D must be acquitted. So in *Clayton and Halsey*[10] where P was an experienced police officer who testified that he was not susceptible to depravity or corruption and there was no evidence of publication, or likelihood of publication, to a third party, the Court of Criminal Appeal held that the case should have been withdrawn from the jury.[11] Lord Parker CJ said:[12]

"... while it is no doubt theoretically possible that a jury could take the view that even a most experienced officer, despite his protestations, was susceptible to the influence of the article yet, bearing in mind the onus and degree of proof in a criminal case, it would, we think, be unsafe and therefore wrong to leave that question to the jury."

2 Having an Obscene Article for Publication for Gain

This second type of offence was introduced by amendments made by the 1964 Act and was intended to deal with the difficulties arising from *Clayton and Halsey*. In fact the accused in that case were convicted of *conspiracy* to publish the articles, because the buyers they had in view were not incorruptible police officers. But the implications of the case were serious; for, where there was no evidence that D had conspired with another, it made it virtually impossible to get a conviction on the evidence of a policeman that the articles had been sold to him. Under the amendment it is now possible to charge D with *having* the article for publication for gain; and the incorruptibility of the particular police officer who purchases it will be irrelevant. The jury is unlikely to suppose that D kept these articles solely for sale to police officers; and they need only be satisfied that, having regard to all the relevant circumstances, (i) D contemplated publication to such a person as the article would have a tendency to deprave and corrupt, or (ii) that he contemplated publication from which a further publication to susceptible persons could reasonably be expected to follow (whether D in fact contemplated that further publication or not). By s. 1 (3) (b) of the 1964 Act:

"the question whether the article is obscene shall be determined by reference to such publication for gain of the article as in the circumstances it may reasonably be inferred he had in contemplation and to any

10. [1963] 1 QB 163, [1962] 3 All ER 500.
11. D, of course, did not know that he was dealing with an incorruptible police officer. He had *mens rea* and might now be guilty of an attempt under the Criminal Attempts Act 1981, above, p. 304.
12. [1963] 1 QB at 168, [1962] 3 All ER at 502.

further publication that could reasonably be expected to follow from it, but not to any other publication."

The meaning of "having" an article is elucidated by s. 1 (2) of the 1964 Act:

". . . a person shall be deemed to have an article for publication for gain if with a view to such publication he has the article in his ownership, possession or control."

Thus the owner of the shop in which the article is stocked may be convicted as the owner of the article, as well as his servant who has possession or control of it. The van driver who takes it from wholesaler to retailer may also be thought to be in control of it for the purposes of gain.

This overcomes another difficulty which arose under the 1959 Act. It was held[13] that a person who displays an obscene article in a shop window is not guilty of publishing it. Of the various ways of publishing referred to in s. 1 (3), the only one which could conceivably have been applicable was "offering for sale"; and it was held that "offer" must be construed in accordance with the law of contract,[14] under which the display of goods in a shop window is an "invitation to treat" and not an offer.[15] This decision, of course, remains good law; but now a charge might successfully be brought of having the obscene article for publication for gain, whether it had been displayed or not.

The proviso to section 1 (3) (b) formerly extended to film exhibitions taking place otherwise than in a private house. The effect of the amendment to the proviso by section 53 of the Criminal Law Act 1977 is that the exhibition of a film anywhere is a publication for the purposes of the Obscene Publications Act; but no prosecution under section 2 may be brought without the consent of the Director of Public Prosecutions, where the article is a moving picture film not less than 16 mm. wide and publication of it took place or could reasonably be expected to take place only in the course of a film exhibition.[16]

"Film exhibition" in s. 2[17] means any exhibition of moving pictures which is produced otherwise than by the simultaneous reception and exhibition of programmes included in a programme service within the meaning of the Broadcasting Act 1990.

If the film were such as to outrage public decency then its public showing was a common law offence. A local authority which, in performing its licensing duties, authorised the showing of an outrageously indecent film might have been guilty of aiding and abetting the offence.[18] A local authority has no duty to censor films, except in relation to children; but if it chooses to act, through its licensing powers, as a censor for adults, it must

13. *Mella v Monahan* [1961] Crim LR 175, following *Fisher v Bell* [1961] 1 QB 394, [1960] 3 All ER 731.
14. For a criticism of this ruling, see [1961] Crim LR at 181; cf. *Partridge v Crittenden* [1968] 2 All ER 421, [1968] 1 WLR 1204.
15. *Pharmaceutical Society of Great Britain v Boots Cash Chemists (Southern) Ltd* [1953] 1 QB 401, [1953] 1 All ER 482.
16. Obscene Publications Act 1959, s. 2 (3A).
17. As amended by the Cinemas Act 1985, Sch. 2.
18. *Greater London Council, ex p Blackburn* [1976] 3 All ER 184.

act in accordance with the law and not expressly permit the commission of an offence. Since the Criminal Law Act 1977, however, no proceedings may be brought for an offence at common law (including conspiracy) in respect of a film exhibition alleged to be obscene, indecent, offensive, disgusting or injurious to morality.[19] An indictment for statutory conspiracy, contrary to s. 1 of the Criminal Law Act 1977,[20] would lie in appropriate circumstances.

3) *Defences*

1 No Reasonable Cause to Believe Article Obscene

By s. 2 (5) of the 1959 Act and s. 1 (3) (a) of the 1964 Act, it is a defence for D to prove that he (i) had not examined the article and (ii) had no reasonable cause to suspect that it was such that his publication of it, or his having it, as the case may be, would make him liable to be convicted of an offence against s. 2. Both conditions must be satisfied; so if D has examined the article, his failure to appreciate its tendency to deprave and corrupt is no defence under these sections.

2 Public Good

Section 4 of the 1959 Act (as amended by the Criminal Law Act 1977) provides a defence of "public good":

"(1) Subject to subsection (1A) of this section a person shall not be convicted of an offence against section 2 of this Act ... if it is proved that publication of the article in question is justified as being for the public good on the ground that it is in the interests of science, literature, art or learning, or of other objects of general concern.

(2) It is hereby declared that the opinion of experts as to the literary, artistic, scientific or other merits of an article may be admitted in any proceedings under this Act either to establish or negative the said ground."

The defence becomes relevant only when the jury has decided that the book is obscene – that it has a tendency to deprave a significant proportion of those likely to read it. The Act assumes that this harm to a section of the community might be outweighed by the other considerations referred to in the section. The jury should be directed to consider first whether an article is obscene within s. 1. If not satisfied of that beyond reasonable doubt, they must acquit. If so satisfied, they should go on to consider whether, on a balance of probabilities, the publication of the article, though obscene, is for the public good.[1] The jury's task is then to

". . . consider, on the one hand, the number of readers they believe would tend to be depraved and corrupted by the book, the strength of the

---

19. Obscene Publications Act 1959, s. 2 (4A).
20. Above, p. 270.
   1. *Director of Public Prosecutions v Jordan* [1976] 3 All ER 775, HL.. Cf. *Sumner* [1977] Crim LR 362 (Judge Davies).

tendency to deprave and corrupt, and the nature of the depravity or corruption; on the other hand, they should assess the strength of the literary, sociological or ethical merit which they consider the book to possess. They should then weigh up all these factors and decide whether on balance the publication is proved to be justified as being for the public good."[2]

Expert evidence is not admissible in support of a defence under s. 4 to the effect that pornographic material is psychologically beneficial to persons who are sexually repressed, perverted or deviant, in that it relieves their sexual tensions and may divert them from anti-social activities. The House of Lords so held in *Director of Public Prosecutions v Jordan*.[3] The other "objects of general concern" must fall within the same area as those specifically mentioned. The effect on sexual behaviour and attitudes was a totally different area, covered in s. 1. The Court of Appeal[4] had reached the same conclusion on the ground that the same qualities relied on by the Crown to show that the article was obscene were being relied on by the defence to show that it was for the public good. To admit such evidence would be to allow every jury to decide for itself as a matter of public policy whether obscene material should be prohibited. Parliament has decided that it should – unless it possesses certain merits; and whatever doubt there may be as to the range of those merits, they clearly cannot include obscenity itself. "Merits" must mean qualities which show that the publication of the article is for the public good in that it tends to the advancement of an object of general concern. In *Penguin Books* Byrne J said that merits from a sociological, an ethical and an educational point of view were included.[5] This must now be read in the light of *Jordan*. The "other objects of general concern" must not only be such as conduce to the public good but must also be of "concern" to members of the public in general. The Court of Appeal in *Jordan*[6] appears to have assumed judicial knowledge that the public generally are not "concerned" with, or about, the relief of the sexually repressed. It is not clear whether "concerned" is interpreted to mean "interest in" or "activity in". According to the court, "The disposal of sewage is no doubt for the public good but it is not a matter with which the generality of the public is concerned." The general public is certainly interested in the disposal of sewage, at least in the sense that if it were not efficiently done, they would have a great deal to say about it. On the other hand, it is difficult to suppose that the general public could ever be active in the disposal of sewage. It is submitted, however, that "concern" ought to be interpreted to mean "interest". The general public are not active in literature, art or science, but the Act assumes, rightly, it is submitted, that these are objects of public concern.

2. *Calder and Boyars Ltd* [1969] 1 QB 151 at 172.
3. Above.
4. Sub nom. *Staniforth* [1976] 2 All ER 714, [1976] 2 WLR 849.
5. See *The Trial of Lady Chatterley* by C. H. Rolph, at 234; *Calder and Boyars Ltd* [1969] 1 QB 151 at 172; *John Calder (Publications) Ltd v Powell* [1965] 1 All ER 159 at 161.
6. [1976] 2 All ER 714 at 719, CA.

In *Reiter*,[7] the jury were asked to look at a large number of other books in order to decide whether the books which were the subject of the charge were obscene. The Court of Criminal Appeal held that this was wrong. It appears that it is still not permissible, under the Act, to prove that other books, which are just as obscene as the one in issue, are freely circulating;[8] but evidence relating to other books may now be admitted to establish the "climate of literature" in order to assess the literary merit of the book.[9]

In *Penguin Books*,[10] Crown counsel conceded in argument that the intention of the *author* in writing the book is relevant to the question of literary merit. If this is right, it must again[11] refer only to the intention as it appears in the book itself.

The onus of establishing the defence is on the accused and the standard of proof required is proof on a balance of probabilities.[12] The defence is not available on a charge of conspiracy to corrupt public morals; but Parliament has been assured that such a charge will not be brought so as to circumvent the defence.[13]

Subsection (1) does not apply where the article is a moving picture film or moving picture soundtrack or television or sound programme.[14] In the case of these articles a similar defence of public good is provided except that the interests which may justify publication are those of drama, opera, ballet or any other art, or of literature or learning.[15]

4) *Mens Rea*

1 At Common Law

In *Hicklin*[16] it was held that it was not necessary to establish that D's motive was to deprave and corrupt; and that, if he knowingly published that which had a tendency to deprave and corrupt, it was no defence that he had an honest and laudable intention in publishing the work in question. D, a member of the Protestant Electoral Union, sold[17] copies of *The Confessional Unmasked*. He argued that he did so with the intention, not of prejudicing good morals, but of exposing what he deemed to be the errors of the Church of Rome and, particularly, the immorality of the confessional. To this Cockburn CJ answered:

---

7. [1954] 2 QB 16, [1954] 1 All ER 741.
8. *Penguin Books* (1961) Rolph, op. cit., 127.
9. Ibid.
10. Rolph, op. cit., 87 and 123.
11. As with the question whether the book is obscene. Above, p. 733.
12. *Calder and Boyars Ltd*, above, at 171.
13. "That should be known by all who are concerned with the operation of the criminal law", per Lord Morris in *Knuller v Director of Public Prosecutions* [1972] 2 All ER 898 at 912. See Lord Diplock's doubts as to the efficacy of the assurance (924) and Lord Reid's opinion that it does not apply to conspiracy to outrage public decency (906).
14. "Moving picture soundtrack" means "any sound record designed for playing with a moving picture film, whether incorporated with the film or not", s. 4 (3).
15. Section 4 (1A). Cf. Theatres Act 1968, s. 3; below, p. 746; Broadcasting Act 1990, Sch 15.
16. (1868) LR 3 QB 360.
17. For the price he paid for them and not "for gain".

"Be it so. The question then presents itself in this simple form: May you commit an offence against the law in order that thereby you may effect some ulterior object which you have in view, which may be an honest and even a laudable one? My answer is, emphatically, no."[18]

The case did not decide, as is sometimes supposed, that no *mens rea* is required. The argument was not that D did not know the nature of the thing published nor even that he did not know that its natural consequence was to tend to deprave and corrupt; but that the publication was justified by his predominant intention of exposing the errors of the Church of Rome. Cockburn CJ indeed assumed that D *did* know what the effect of the publication would be:

". . . it is impossible to suppose that the man who published it must not have known and seen that the effect upon the minds of many of those into whose hands it would come would be of a mischievous and demoralising character."[19]

A man who knows that a certain result will follow may properly be said to intend[20] it or, at the very least, to be reckless. Blackburn J relied particularly upon *Vantandillo*,[1] which lays down that it is a misdemeanour to carry a person with a contagious disease through the street, though no intent to infect anyone be alleged; but in that case the court insisted that D should have "full knowledge"[2] of the fact of the contagious disease. *Hicklin*,[3] then, need not be taken to have decided more than that, if D publishes that which he knows will have a tendency to deprave and corrupt, it is no defence that he did so with the best of motives.

No case before the Act of 1959 decided anything to the contrary. In *Thomson*[4] the Common Serjeant admitted evidence of other books found on D's premises as tending to show that

"she sold this book with the intention alleged in the indictment [to corrupt morals], and not accidentally."

In *Barraclough*,[5] it was held unnecessary (but desirable) that the indictment should contain an allegation of intent, because the intent was implicit in the allegation of publishing obscenity.[6] In *De Montalk*,[7] D handed to a printer some poems he had written, intending to circulate about 100 copies, mostly to young people of both sexes ("literary people"). The printer sent the poems to the police and D was convicted. His appeal on the ground that there was no sufficient direction on intent was dismissed; but the headnote goes farther than the judgment in asserting that the jury should not be directed that they must find an intent to corrupt public morals. Crown counsel (later Byrne J) submitted merely that intention *was to be inferred*

---

18. (1868) LR 3 QB at 371, 372.
19. Ibid., at 372. If the law requires knowledge, this is now clearly a question for the jury: Criminal Justice Act 1967, s. 8; above, p. 86.
20. Above, p. 53.
1. (1815) 4 M & S 73.
2. Ibid., at 77.
3. Above, p. 730.
4. (1900) 64 JP 456 at 457.
5. [1906] 1 KB 201, CCR.
6. ". . . intent . . . is still part of the charge or the publication would not have been unlawful": per Darling J, ibid., at 212.
7. (1932) 23 Cr App Rep 182.

from the act of publication and that no affirmative evidence of intention need be given; and the court dismissed the appeal, saying that the law was accurately stated in *Barraclough*.[8] But in *Penguin Books*,[9] Byrne J held that, if D publishes an article which is obscene, the inference that he intends to deprave and corrupt is irrebuttable. Such an approach today would seem to be inconsistent with s. 8 of the Criminal Justice Act 1967;[10] but, though Byrne J used the language of proof, he was probably saying, in substance, that intent to deprave was not a constituent of the offence.[11] He conceded that the judgment in *De Montalk* was not very clear, but stated that the court came to the conclusion that there was nothing in the argument that the presumption was rebuttable, and that he was bound by that decision.

2 Under the Obscene Publications Act

In *Shaw v Director of Public Prosecutions*[12] D was charged with publishing an obscene article in the form of the *Ladies' Directory*. His appeal to the Court of Criminal Appeal[13] on the ground that the judge did not direct the jury to take into account D's "honesty of purpose" was dismissed. Ashworth J said:[14]

"If these proceedings had been brought before the passing of the Obscene Publications Act 1959, in the form of a prosecution at common law for publishing an obscene libel, it would no doubt have been necessary to establish an intention to corrupt. But the Act of 1959 contains no such requirement and the test of obscenity laid down in s. 1 (1) of the Act is whether the effect of the article is such as to tend to deprave and corrupt persons who are likely to read it. In other words obscenity depends on the article and not on the author."[15]

This, of course, is inconsistent with the view of Byrne J who, in *Penguin Books*,[16] conceived that he was applying the common law rule. According to the Court of Criminal Appeal's view, he was wrong about the common law, but reached the right result by accident, the common law having been revised by the Act! As a matter of fact, it seems that this was not the intention of Parliament.[17]

It was not necessary to the decision to decide that no *mens rea* was required. To rule that "honesty of purpose" is irrelevant is one thing and no more than was done in *Hicklin*; to decide that no *mens rea* with reference to depravity and corruption is necessary, is another. D's motives of benevolence towards the prostitutes whom he was assisting to ply their trade may have been wholly admirable but if he knew (as he must have

---

8. Above.
9. Above, p. 738.
10. Above, p. 86.
11. See the discussion of s. 8; above, pp. 86 and 347.
12. [1962] AC 220, [1961] 2 All ER 446; above, p. 291.
13. He was refused leave to appeal to the House of Lords on this count.
14. [1962] AC at 227, [1961] 1 All ER at 333, CCA.
15. The reference to the author is puzzling. Presumably "the publisher" is meant. They were one and the same in Shaw.
16. Above.
17. Street, *Freedom, the Individual and the Law* (3rd ed.) 141.

done!) that the inevitable result would be what the law regards[18] as depravity and corruption, he intended that result. Moreover, the test laid down in s. 1 (1) is not decisive, for this merely defines the *actus reus* and says nothing about *mens rea*. It is difficult, however, to dispute the conclusion of the Court of Criminal Appeal in the light of the defence provided by s. 2 (5).[19] If *mens rea* in the sense described above were required, this provision would be quite unnecessary. But the clear implication of s. 2 (5) is that D would be guilty (i) although he had examined the article and concluded that it had no tendency to deprave and corrupt if there were reasonable grounds on which he might have suspected that it would; (ii) although the jury thought it as likely as not that he did not suspect the article's tendency;[20] and (iii) although he had examined the article and failed to appreciate its tendency. Thus it appears likely that the Act, perhaps inadvertently, has restricted the requirement of *mens rea*. In *Anderson*,[1] the court thought it quite obvious that the jury had acquitted of conspiracy to corrupt public morals because they were not satisfied that there was the required intent to corrupt. But the court did not consider this fatal to the charge under the Obscene Publications Act and, indeed, considered whether they should uphold the conviction under s. 2 of the Criminal Appeal Act 1968 on the ground that no actual miscarriage of justice had occurred[2] – something they could hardly have done if the jury had negatived the intent necessary for the crime.

5) *Forfeiture of Obscene Articles*

The Obscene Publications Act 1857 provided a summary procedure for the forfeiture of obscene articles. That Act is replaced by s. 3 of the Obscene Publications Act 1959. The procedure is that an information on oath must be laid before a magistrate that there is reasonable ground for suspecting that obscene articles are *kept* in any premises, stall or vehicle in the justice's area *for publication for gain*.[3] The justice may then issue a warrant authorising a constable to search for and seize any articles which he has reason to believe to be obscene and to be kept for publication for gain. Such a warrant authorises only a single entry and a second entry in reliance on the warrant will be unlawful; but, in the absence of evidence of "oppression", the court has no discretion to exclude any evidence unlawfully obtained.[4]

18. Whether he knew the law so regarded it, is irrelevant. Cf. *Sancoff v Halford* [1973] Qd R 25.
19. Above, p. 737.
20. The onus of proof on a balance of probabilities is on D.
  1. Above, p. 730.
  2. [1971] 3 All ER 1152 at 1161.
  3. *Hicklin*'s case might thus now fall outside the Act. He sold the pamphlets for the price he paid for them and this was evidently considered not to be selling for gain: (1868) LR 3 QB at 368 and 374. But cf. p. 612, above.
  4. *Adams* [1980] QB 575, [1980] 1 All ER 473, CA.

Any articles seized must be brought before a justice for the same area. If the justice, after looking at the articles, decides they are not obscene, then the matter drops and the articles[5] are, no doubt, returned.[6] But if he thinks they may be obscene (and he need not come to a decided opinion at this stage) he may issue a summons to the occupier of the premises, etc., to appear before the court and show cause why the articles should not be forfeited. If the court is satisfied[7] that the articles, at the time they were seized, were obscene articles kept for publication for gain, it must order the articles to be forfeited. The power does not apply to any article which is returned to the person from whom it was seized.[8] The section applies to material destined for publication abroad.[9] The magistrates may thus be required to form an opinion as to the likely effect of the material on foreigners with different attitudes and customs but, in practice, they are likely to rely on their knowledge of human nature and unlikely to hold an article to be obscene where it is destined for country X and not obscene where it is destined for country Y.

The owner, author or maker of the articles, or any other person through whose hands they had passed before being seized, is entitled to appear and show cause why they should not be forfeited; and any person who appeared or was entitled to appear to show cause against the making of the order has a right of appeal to the Crown Court.

The defence of "public good" is available in proceedings for forfeiture;[10] but the decision is, of course, now in the hands of the justices and not in the hands of a jury. Thus, if proceedings for forfeiture are brought instead of an indictment, the author or publisher of a book can, in substance, be deprived of a right to jury trial.

There is not necessarily any uniformity of decision. One bench may pass a magazine or picture, while another condemns it.[11] In practice, it seems that the advice of the Director of Public Prosecutions is usually taken by the police before applying for a warrant. His advice is not *necessary* for it is thought undesirable that he should be in the position of a literary or moral censor.[12]

---

5. It is not necessary for each justice to read all the material, provided the whole is discussed and considered by them: *Olympia Press Ltd v Hollis* [1974] 1 All ER 108. On an appeal to the Crown Court, the judge may take a number of articles at random to sample, showing them to the defence as an indication of the basis on which he has reached his decision: *R v Snaresbrook Crown Court, ex p Metropolitan Police Commissioner* (1984) 79 Cr App Rep 184, DC. Cf. R. T. H. Stone, [1986] Crim LR 139.

6. *Thomson v Chain Libraries Ltd* [1954] 2 All ER 616, [1954] 1 WLR 999.

7. In *Thomson v Chain Libraries* [1954] 2 All ER 616 at 618, Hilbery J said that the onus of proof is on the person who appears to show cause. *Sed quaere?* The magistrate must be *satisfied* that the article is obscene.

8. Criminal Law Act 1977, Sch. 12.

9. *Gold Star Publications Ltd v Director of Public Prosecutions* [1981] 2 All ER 257, HL.

10. Obscene Publications Act 1959, s. 4 (1).

11. The same thing could of course occur in relation to proceedings on indictment. If another publisher were to be prosecuted for publishing *Lady Chatterley*, the decision in *Penguin Books* (above, p. 738) would not be relevant in evidence, let alone an estoppel; and another jury, hearing different expert evidence, might well arrive at a different conclusion.

12. Under the Prosecution of Offences Regulations 1978, reg. 6 (2) (e), a chief officer of police must report to the Director any alleged commission of an *offence* of obscenity.

Where, however, the article is a moving picture film in respect of which a prosecution under section 2 of the 1959 Act could not be instituted without the consent of the Director,[13] no order for forfeiture may be made unless the warrant under which the article was seized was issued on an information laid by or on behalf of the Director.[14]

6) *The Common Law of Obscene Libel*

The 1959 Act did not, in terms, abolish the common law misdemeanour of obscene libel, but provided in s. 2 (4):

"A person publishing an article shall not be proceeded against for an offence at common law consisting of the publication of any matter contained or embodied in the article where it is of the essence of the offence that the matter is obscene."

It might be thought that the intention was that, in future, all proceedings in respect of obscene publications should be brought under the Act. The subsection has not been so interpreted. In *Shaw v Director of Public Prosecutions*[15] it was relied on by the defence in relation to the first count alleging a common law conspiracy to corrupt public morals by the publication of the *Ladies' Directory*; that is, as was held, the publication of an obscene article. The answer to this argument, accepted by the Court of Criminal Appeal[16] and the House of Lords,[17] was that the conspiracy did not "consist of the publication" of the booklet; it consisted in the agreement to corrupt public morals by publishing it.

It thus appears that it would still be possible to bring a prosecution for conspiracy to publish an obscene libel (and possibly an incitement or attempt to do so). Such a prosecution should not be brought to evade the statutory defence of public good.[18]

7) *What is an Article?*

The 1959 Act provides by s. 1 (2):

"In this Act 'article' means any description of article containing or embodying matter to be read or looked at or both, any sound record, and any film or other record of a picture or pictures."

This includes a video cassette.[19] In *Straker v Director of Public Prosecutions*[20] it was held that while a negative *might* be within this definition,[1] it

13. See above, p. 736.
14. Obscene Publications Act 1959, s. 3 (3A).
15. [1962] AC 220.
16. [1962] AC at 235, 236.
17. [1962] AC at 268, 269, 290, 291.
18. Above, p. 739.
19. *A-G's Reference (No. 5 of 1980)* [1980] 3 All ER 816, [1981] 1 WLR 88.
20. [1963] 1 QB 926, [1963] 1 All ER 697, DC.
   1. Widgery LCJ had little doubt that this was so: *Derrick v Customs and Excise Commissioners* [1972] 2 WLR 359 at 361.

was not kept for "publication" as described in s. 3 (1) since it was not to be shown, played or projected,[2] but to be used for making prints. It could not, therefore, be forfeited under s. 3. This gap is closed by s. 2 of the 1964 Act which provides

"(1) The Obscene Publications Act 1959 (as amended by this Act) shall apply in relation to anything which is intended to be used, either alone or as one of a set, for the reproduction or manufacture therefrom of articles containing or embodying matter to be read, looked at or listened to, as if it were an article containing or embodying that matter so far as that matter is to be derived from it or from the set."

By s. 2 (2) of the 1964 Act an article is had or kept for publication

"if it is had or kept for the reproduction or manufacture therefrom of articles for publication".

The negatives in *Straker* clearly fall within this provision.

In *Conegate Ltd v Customs and Excise Comrs*[3] it was conceded that inflatable life-size dolls, though obscene, were not "articles". It has been suggested that the concession was wrong because the dolls, having faces painted on them, were to be "looked at". However the gist of the obscenity seems to lie in the use to which the dolls were intended to be put, rather than in their appearance.

8) *Posting Indecent or Obscene Matter*

It is an offence under the Post Office Act 1953, s. 11, punishable summarily by a fine not exceeding the statutory maximum and, on indictment, by imprisonment for twelve months, to

". . . send or attempt to send or procure to be sent a postal packet which:
(b) encloses any indecent or obscene print, painting, photograph, lithograph, engraving, cinematograph film, book, card or written communication, or any indecent or obscene article whether similar to the above or not . . ."

It was held in *Stanley*[4] that the words "indecent or obscene" in this section:

"convey one idea, namely offending against the recognised standards of propriety, indecent being at the lower end of the scale and obscene at the upper end of the scale . . .

. . . an indecent article is not necessarily obscene, whereas an obscene article must almost certainly be indecent."

Therefore the verdict of a jury holding that certain cinematograph films were not obscene (for the purposes of the Obscene Publications Act) but were indecent (for the purposes of the Post Office Act) was upheld.

If "indecent" comprehends everything which is obscene and more, the word "obscene" in the Act is redundant. "Obscene" here bears its ordinary

2. Section 1 (3) (b), above, p. 734.
3. [1987] QB 254, [1986] 2 All ER 688, [1986] Crim LR 562, DC.
4. [1965] 2 QB 327, [1965] 1 All ER 1035.

meaning[5] and so may not extend to material simply because it advocates drug-taking or violence[6] which would not ordinarily be described as "indecent".[7] On the other hand, such articles might well be said to offend against "recognised standards of propriety"; and, for the purposes of other legislation, abusive language and shouts in church alleging hypocrisy against the reader of the lesson[8] have been held to be "indecent". It is possible therefore that "indecent" is not confined to sexual indecency, but extends to other improper matter.

The test of indecency is objective and the character of the addressee is immaterial.[9] Indeed, the object of the section, looked at as a whole, seems to be the protection of Post Office employees against dangerous, deleterious or indecent articles.[10] It is evidently not limited to employees, however, since it is only in rare cases that they will have access to matter "enclosed" as para. (b) requires. Evidence is not admissible by any person to say what the effect of the article was on him. The jury do not need assistance. They are themselves "the custodians of the standards for the time being."[11]

The improper use of a public telecommunication system is a summary offence under the Telecommunications Act 1984, s. 43; and sending unsolicited matter describing human sexual techniques, or unsolicited advertisement of such matter, is an offence[12] under s. 4 of the Unsolicited Goods and Services Act 1971.

9) Obscenity in the Theatre

The Theatres Act 1968, which abolished censorship of the theatre, makes it an offence, punishable under s. 2, summarily with six months, and on indictment with three years' imprisonment, to present[13] or direct an obscene performance of a play. The definition of obscenity is the same as in s. 1 (1) of the Obscene Publications Act 1959,[14] except that attention is directed to the effect of the performance on the persons who are likely to *attend* it instead of "read, see or hear it". A defence of "public good" is provided by s. 3 which is the same as that under s. 4 of the 1959 Act,[15] except that the interests which may justify the performance are, as in the

---

5. *Anderson* [1971] 3 All ER 1152 at 1162. The judge's direction (above, p. 730) was thus correct so far as the "Post Office count" was concerned. *Stamford* [1972] 2 QB 391, [1972] 2 All ER 427.
6. Above, p. 731.
7. *Lees v Parr* [1967] 3 All ER 181n in (By-law).
8. *Abrahams v Cavey* [1968] 1 QB 479, [1967] 3 All ER 179 (Ecclesiastical Courts Jurisdiction Act 1860, s. 2); *Farrant* [1973] Crim LR 240.
9. *Straker* [1965] Crim LR 239, CCA; *Kosmos Publications Ltd v Director of Public Prosecutions* [1975] Crim LR 345.
10. *Stamford* [1972] 2 All ER 427 at 429.
11. Ibid., at p. 432.
12. *Director of Public Prosecutions v Beate Uhse (UK) Ltd* [1974] QB 158, [1974] 1 All ER 753.
13. Cf. *Grade v Director of Public Prosecutions* [1942] 2 All ER 118; above, p. 176.
14. Above, pp. 730–734.
15. Above, p. 737.

case of films, those of "drama, opera, ballet or any other art or of literature or learning".

A performance given "on a domestic occasion in a private dwelling" is excepted by s. 7 from the provisions of s. 2; and, by s. 8, proceedings may not be instituted except by or with the consent of the Attorney General.

If proceedings are to be brought in respect of the alleged obscenity of the performance of a play, they must be brought under the Act; for, by s. 2 (4), it precludes proceedings at common law (including conspiracy). A prosecution on indictment under s. 2 must be commenced within two years of the commission of the offence: s. 2 (3).

10) *Indecent Displays*

The Indecent Displays (Control) Act 1981 makes it an offence to make, cause or permit the public display of any indecent matter. Matter displayed in, or so as to be visible from, any public place is publicly displayed. A public place is one to which the public have or are permitted to have access, whether on payment or otherwise, except (a) where the payment is or includes payment for the display, or (b) the place is a shop or part of a shop to which the public can gain access only by passing an adequate warning notice, as specified in the Act. The Act is aimed at displays that people cannot avoid seeing as they go about their business – bookshop and sex shop window displays, cinema club posters, and so on. It does not apply to BBC or IBA television broadcasts, displays visible only from within an art gallery or museum, the performance of a play within the Theatres Act 1968 or a cinematograph exhibition as defined in the Cinematographic Act 1952. "Matter" is anything capable of being displayed except an actual human body or part of it. "Indecent" is not defined. Whether matter is indecent will no doubt be considered a matter of fact to be determined by applying the ordinary meaning of the word.[16]

11) *Other Statutes*

There are a number of other statutes under which summary proceedings may be, and are, instituted, where the safeguards of the Obscene Publications Acts do not apply. These include the Metropolitan Police Act 1839, s. 54, and the Children and Young Persons (Harmful Publications) Act 1955. No doubt there are also many local Acts and by-laws which may be invoked.[17]

---

16. Above, p. 745.
17. See, generally, Report of the Home Office Working Party on Vagrancy and Street Offences (1974).

12) *Outraging Public Decency*

It is now clear that the common law offence of outraging public decency
survives. An article outraging public decency is not necessarily obscene. It
may well outrage and disgust without having any tendency to deprave and
corrupt. In such a case, a prosecution for the common law offence is not
barred by s. 2(4) of the Obscene Publications Act.[18] It was so held in
Gibson[19] where in a commercial art gallery D exhibited "Human Earrings",
earrings made out of freeze-dried human foetuses. It was not suggested
that anyone was likely to be corrupted by the exhibition but, as the jury had
found, the public would be outraged by it. The defence of "public good"
under s. 4 (1) of the 1959 Act does not apply to the common law offence. An
article may have a tendency both to corrupt and to cause outrage. It seems
to follow that, in such a case, the protection of the Act can be avoided by
charging the common law offence. It can hardly be said that the "essence of
the offence" charged is that the article is obscene because the prosecution
do not have to prove obscenity in order to establish it; and, if obscenity is
not of the essence of the offence charged, the prosecution is not barred by
s. 2 (4).

a) *The actus reus.* An act outraging public decency must be proved. If no
such act is done, the offence is not committed, however outrageous D's
intentions or fantasies, as revealed, for example, in his private diaries.[20] It
might be different where the observers of ambiguous conduct are aware of
the actor's purpose. They might then be outraged by acts which, if not
known to be done with that purpose, would not be outrageously indecent.

At least two members of the public must have observed the outrageous
act. In *Lunderbech*[1] where D, masturbating in a children's playground, was
seen only by two police officers who did not testify that they were outraged,
the court said that where the act is plainly indecent and likely to disgust and
annoy, "the jury are entitled to infer such disgust and annoyance without
affirmative evidence that anyone was disgusted and annoyed". The so-
called "inference" is plainly fictitious. In *May*[2] (schoolmaster "behaving in
an indecent manner with a desk" in the presence of two boys) it was held to
be irrelevant that the two boys may have enjoyed the performance. The
effect seems to be that the offence is committed if the jury think the conduct
is outrageously indecent because it would disgust and annoy them, and
therefore the ordinary members of the public whom they represent, if they
witnessed it.

b) *Mens rea.* To the extent that *Lemon* declared blasphemy to be an offence
of strict liability, *Gibson* does the same for outraging public decency. D
must presumably be aware of the nature of the act he is doing. If Gibson
had not known that the earrings were made from human foetuses he would

---

18. Above, p. 744.
19. [1991] 1 All ER 439, [1991] Crim LR 738.
20. *Rowley* [1991] 4 All ER 649, [1991] Crim LR 785.
 1. [1991] Crim LR 784.
 2. (1989) 91 Cr App Rep 157, [1990] Crim LR 415.

presumably not have been guilty. But the case decides that it was not necessary to prove that he intended or foresaw that the effect of the exhibition would be to outrage public decency. As the court said, the practical effect of this ruling is not great. It is difficult to imagine a jury not being satisfied that D knew very well what the effect of his act would certainly be. But this does not justify dispensing with *mens rea*. Rather, it demonstrates that there is not that necessity which is sometimes urged as a justification for strict liability – i.e., that no one would be convicted if *mens rea* were required.

The court remarked that one reason why the early authorities are of little assistance is the existence before the enactment of s. 8 of the Criminal Justice Act 1967 of the presumption that a person intends the natural and probable consequences of his actions. The court failed to draw the inevitable conclusion from this premise. If, before 1967, intention need not be proved only because it was conclusively presumed, it is no longer presumed and must be proved.

4 Seditious Words and Libels

Sedition is closely related to the form of treason consisting in "levying war" against the Queen in her realm and may be a preliminary step towards that crime. There is probably no offence properly described as "sedition" in English law,[3] but the oral or written publication of words with a seditious intention is a common law misdemeanour and an agreement to further a seditious intention by doing any act is a conspiracy. The question then is what is seditious intention? Stephen[4] defined it as:

"... an intention to bring into hatred or contempt, or to excite disaffection against the person of, Her Majesty, her heirs or successors, or the government and constitution of the United Kingdom, as by law established, or either House of Parliament, or the administration of justice, or to excite Her Majesty's subjects to attempt, otherwise than by lawful means, the alteration of any matter in Church or State by law established, or to raise discontent or disaffection amongst Her Majesty's subjects, or to promote feelings of ill-will and hostility between different classes of such subjects.

An intention to shew that Her Majesty has been misled or mistaken in her measures, or to point out errors or defects in the government or constitution as by law established, with a view to their reformation, or to excite Her Majesty's subjects to attempt by lawful means the alteration of any matter in Church or State by law established,[5] or to point out, in order to their removal, matters which are producing, or have a tendency

---

3. Stephen, 2 HCL 298.
4. *Digest* (3rd ed.), Art. 93. See now 9th ed., Art. 114.
5. In the fourth and subsequent editions, Stephen inserted at this point "... or to incite any person to commit any crime in disturbance of the peace ...."

to produce, feelings of hatred and ill-will between classes of Her Majesty's subjects, is not a seditious intention."

This definition was approved by the criminal code Commissioners and followed by Cave J in his direction to the jury in *Burns*.[6]

a) *Mens rea*. In *Chief Metropolitan Stipendiary Magistrate, ex p Choudhury*[7] the Divisional Court, following the Supreme Court of Canada in *Boucher v R*,[8] held that:

"... the seditious intention on which a prosecution for seditious libel must be founded is an intention to incite to violence or to create public disturbance or disorder against His Majesty or the institutions of government. Proof of an intention to promote feelings of ill-will and hostility between different classes of subjects does not alone establish a seditious intention. Not only must there be proof of an incitement to violence in this connection but it must be violence or resistance or defiance for the purpose of disturbing constituted authority."

The court therefore upheld the decision of the magistrate that Salman Rushdie's *The Satanic Verses* was not a seditious libel because there was no evidence that it was an attack on the institutions of government. The earlier authorities were inconsistent,[9] one view being that an objective test was applicable, another that intention or recklessness would suffice. None of these authorities was binding on the Divisional Court and the above proposition represents the law. The strict requirement of *mens rea* is in marked contrast to the principles applicable to other varieties of common law libel.

b) *Actus reus*. It cannot be enough that the words are used with a seditious intention. There must also be an *actus reus*. That is, the words must have a tendency to incite public disorder. In deciding whether the words have this tendency, it is proper to look at all the relevant surrounding circumstances – the state of public feeling, the place, the mode of publication, and so on. Most important of all, the jury is entitled

"... to look at the audience addressed, because language which would be innocuous practically speaking, if used to an assembly of professors or divines, might produce a different result if used before an excited audience of young and uneducated men."[10]

On the other hand if the tendency of the words is to incite ordinary people to violence, it is no defence that the audience addressed was unaffected by the incitement:

"A man cannot escape from the consequences of uttering words with intent to excite people to violence solely because the persons to whom

6. (1886) 16 Cox CC 355 at 360.
7. [1991] 1 All ER 306 at 322–323, [1990] Crim LR 711, DC.
8. (1951) 2 DLR 369.
9. See the 6th edition of this book, 834–835.
10. *Aldred* (1909) 22 Cox CC 1 at 3, per Coleridge J.

they are addressed may be too wise or too temperate to be seduced into that violence."[11]

Thus words are seditious (i) if they are likely to incite ordinary men whether likely to incite the audience actually addressed or not; or (ii), if, though not likely to incite ordinary men, they are likely to incite the audience actually addressed.

D need not have himself written the libel. The crime may consist in the publication of the words of another with the appropriate intent. If the publisher has *mens rea* it is immaterial that the writer of the libel did not.[12]

Whether publication is necessary is not settled. In *Burdett*,[13] Holroyd J and Abbott CJ thought that the mere composition of the libel without publishing it was an offence. Earlier cases[14] supported this view but their authority was forcefully attacked by Sir James Scarlett, afterwards Lord Abinger.[15]

c) *Sedition and freedom of speech.* It is common for the judge to stress the importance of freedom of speech and of the press. In *Burns*,[16] Cave J said

"You will recollect how valuable a blessing the liberty of the press is to all of us, and sure I am that that liberty will meet no injury – suffer no diminution at your hands."

and in *Caunt*,[17] Birkett J's last words to the jury were:

"Two matters would seem to emerge over all others in this case.

First of all it is in the highest degree essential that nothing should be done in this court to weaken the liberty of the press; and secondly, remember at all times that it is the duty of the prosecution to prove his case beyond all reasonable doubt."[18]

11. *Burns* (1886) 16 Cox CC 355 at 365, per Cave J. In *Cohen* (1916) 34 WLR 210, it was held that, if the words were likely to be an incitement to an ordinary man, D was not entitled to the benefit of the steadfast loyalty of the person actually addressed.
12. (1789) 22 St Tr 300, per Eyre CB delivering the unanimous opinion of the judges.
13. (1820) 1 State Tr NS 1 at 122, 123 and 128, 139.
14. They are cited in argument, ibid., at 57.
15. Ibid.
16. (1886) 16 Cox CC 355 at 362.
17. (1947), reported in *An Editor on Trial* (Morecambe Press Ltd).
18. See also Coleridge J in *Aldred* (1909) 22 Cox CC 1 at 4.

21 Offences against Public Order

1 Offences under the Public Order Act 1986

The Public Order Act 1986 abolished the common law offences of riot, rout, unlawful assembly and affray and some statutory offences relating to public order[1] and replaced them with new offences. Three offences take the place of the four above-mentioned common law crimes. They are, in descending order of gravity, riot, violent disorder and affray. Riot requires the presence of 12 persons and violent disorder of 3, but affray may be committed where only the defendant is present. Riot is intended for exceptionally serious cases and no prosecution for it may be instituted except by or with the consent of the Director of Public Prosecutions. Notwithstanding the title of the Act, each offence may be committed in private as well as in public places and, though it is a constituent of each offence that the conduct (of the 12, or the 3, or the defendant, as the case may be) must be such as would cause a person of reasonable firmness present at the scene to fear for his personal safety, no person need actually be, or even be likely to be, at the scene.[2] Where no person is present, the court or jury has to answer a hypothetical question.

In riot and violent disorder the 12 or the 3 persons must be proved to have been present together, using or threatening unlawful violence. It must be proved that the accused intended to use violence or was aware that his conduct might be violent but it is unnecessary to prove any such mental element on the part of the remainder of the 12, or the 3, who are not charged.[3] It is sufficient to prove that their conduct was objectively unlawfully violent, or presented a threat of unlawful violence. In riot, however, a common purpose (which need not involve violence) must be proved in respect of 12 persons, though not all of them are charged.

It is probable that all three offences are continuing offences. It was held that a common law affray might continue for a considerable period of time and over a wide area. An indictment was not bad for duplicity where it

---

1. For the law before the 1986 Act, see the 5th edition of this work, Ch. 20; and for the background to the 1986 Act see the Home Office *Review of the Public Order Act and Related Legislation*, Cmnd. 7891 (1980) and Law Commission Working Paper No. 82 (1982) and Report, *Offences Relating to Public Disorder* (Law Com. No. 123, 1983). For detailed studies of the new law, see Richard Card, *Public Order: The New Law* (1987) and A. T. H. Smith, *Offences against Public Order* (1987).
2. Sections 1 (3) and (4), 2 (3) and (4) and 3 (3) and (4).
3. Section 6 (7); A. T. H. Smith, op. cit., 3–03.

alleged an affray on 31st August and 1st September "in divers streets".[4] It appeared in evidence that the accused were milling about, armed, uttering threats and fighting, from 8.30 p.m. to 12.30 a.m., over a radius of a quarter of a mile. This was held to be a single affray. Where the ingredients of the offence ceased to exist for a time, the affray was over; and, when those ingredients came into existence again, a second affray occurred. So, where the accused travelled in a coach to a number of sites where they created terror, there was an affray at each site. During the coach journeys there was no fighting and no one was put in fear.[5] It seems likely that the same principles will apply to the new statutory offence of affray and also to the offences of riot and violent disorder. Once the 12 or the 3, as the case may be, have used or threatened violence, the offence is constituted and will continue so long as they remain together (in the case of riot, for a common purpose) and at least one of them is continuing to use or threaten violence. One is enough, since it is provided that the persons present need not use or threaten violence simultaneously.

1) *Riot*

Riot is an indictable offence, punishable with ten years' imprisonment, or an unlimited fine, or both. It is defined by s. 1 of the Act as follows:

"(1) Where 12 or more persons who are present together use or threaten unlawful violence for a common purpose and the conduct of them (taken together) is such as would cause a person of reasonable firmness present at the scene to fear for his personal safety, each of the persons using unlawful violence for the common purpose is guilty of riot.

(2) It is immaterial whether or not the 12 or more use or threaten unlawful violence simultaneously.

(3) The common purpose may be inferred from conduct."

If 12 or more persons with a common purpose threaten unlawful violence but only one actually uses it, there is a riot but only one principal rioter. Since they have a common purpose, the rest may be guilty as secondary parties but this is not necessarily so. Suppose that they have all agreed – "Threats, yes, but actual violence, no." If D, for the common purpose, then uses violence, D commits riot but the rest are not necessarily guilty and, if D has clearly gone beyond the scope of the concerted action,[6] as by producing a knife or gun which the rest did not know he had with him, they will certainly not be guilty.

The gravity of riot depends on the presence of large numbers. The number, 12, is arbitrary and it will not usually be necessary to offer evidence of a head-count, for the offence is unlikely to be used except in the case of a large crowd when well in excess of 12 are using or threatening violence.

4. *Woodrow* (1959) 43 Cr App Rep 105.
5. *Jones* (1974) 59 Cr App Rep 120.
6. Above, p. 143.

By s. 8, in Part 1 of the Act:

"violence" means any violent conduct, so that—

(i) except in the context of affray, it includes violent conduct towards property as well as violent conduct towards persons, and

(ii) it is not restricted to conduct causing or intended to cause injury or damage but includes any other violent conduct (for example, throwing at or towards a person a missile of a kind capable of causing injury which does not hit or falls short).

Conduct which might well have caused injury or damage will clearly be capable of amounting to violence even though it was neither intended to, nor did, cause injury or damage. "Violent" movements of the body, where there is no possibility of any impact – as where D waves his fist at P who is across the street – are probably not "violence" but a threat of violence.

The common purpose need not be an unlawful one. It might be, for example, to persuade an employer to take back an employee whom he has wrongfully dismissed. But the violence, whether used or threatened, must be unlawful. Force reasonably used or threatened in self-defence or for the prevention of crime cannot found a charge of riot. There is no requirement that the 12 or more should have come together in pursuance of any agreement. They may have assembled by chance, and one by one, so long as, at some point when violence is used, they are present together with a common purpose and using or threatening violence.

The mental element of riot includes the common purpose. It must be proved that a person charged with riot shared that common purpose and that he (but not the other 11 or more) intended to use violence or was aware that his conduct might be violent.[7] The Act wisely avoids the ambiguous word, "reckless", but, in effect adopts the *Cunningham*[8] meaning of recklessness, thus keeping the law of riot, violent disorder and affray in line with offences against the person generally. Because the meaning of violence itself is uncertain it is not entirely clear what the requirement of awareness will exclude. Possibly a person who was not aware that his conduct would cause any risk of injury or damage would be held to be unaware that his conduct might be violent when it did in fact cause a risk of, or actual, damage or injury.

Exceptionally, s. 6 (5) and (6) make special provision for the intoxicated defendant.

"(5) For the purposes of this section a person whose awareness is impaired by intoxication shall be taken to be aware of that of which he would be aware if not intoxicated, unless he shows either that his intoxication was not self-induced or that it was caused solely by the taking or administration of a substance in the course of medical treatment.

(6) In subsection (5) "intoxication" means any intoxication, whether caused by drink, drugs or other means, or by a combination of means."

In effect, this spells out the common law rule for offences "of basic

7. Section 6 (1).
8. Above, p. 61.

intent"[9] but shifts the onus of proving that intoxication was involuntary to the defendant.[10] Yet if D denies that he had the alleged "purpose" because he was too drunk, s. 6 is inapplicable and the common law governs. If the indictment alleges only intent to use violence, that is presumably an allegation of a specific intent, so self-induced drunkenness would be an answer at common law; but D is still to be taken, apparently, to be aware of that of which he would be aware if not intoxicated; and, if the jury think he would have been aware that violence was a virtual certainty,[11] that is evidence on which they might find that he intended it. Thus intoxication might not be an answer even to an allegation of intentional violence.

1 The Riot (Damages) Act 1886

This Act provides that, where a house, shop or building in any police district, or property inside it, has been injured, stolen or destroyed "by any persons riotously and tumultuously assembled together", the owner shall be compensated out of the police rate. The word "riotously" is now to be construed in accordance with s. 1 of the Public Order Act 1986,[12] so the ambit of the 1886 Act is significantly reduced. No compensation is payable to a person whose property is damaged by a gang of eleven, tumultuously assembled. The assembly must be tumultuous as well as riotous. The word, "tumultuously", was added:

"... for the specific reason that it was intended to limit the liability of compensation to cases where the rioters were in such numbers and in such a state of agitated commotion, and were generally so acting, that the forces of law and order should have been well aware of the threat which existed, and, if they had done their duty, should have taken steps to prevent the rioters from causing damage."[13]

In fixing the amount of compensation regard must be had to the conduct of the claimant, in particular whether he took adequate precautions, or was a party to the riot, or offered any provocation. Where the claimant has received compensation from a third party, such as an insurance company, the sum payable under the 1886 Act is correspondingly reduced; but the third party is entitled to recover the sum so paid as if he had sustained the loss.

2) *Violent Disorder*

Violent disorder is an offence punishable on indictment with five years' imprisonment or an unlimited fine or both or, on summary conviction, with

---

9. Above, pp. 70 and 223.
10. Unless "shows", contrasted with "proves" elsewhere in the Act, implies a merely evidential burden.
11. Above, p. 54.
12. Above, p. 753. See s. 10 (1).
13. *J W Dwyer Ltd v Metropolitan Police District, Receiver* [1967] 2 QB 970, [1967] 2 All ER 1051 (Lyell J).

six months' imprisonment or the statutory maximum fine, or both. It is defined as follows by s. 2:

"(1) Where 3 or more persons who are present together use or threaten unlawful violence and the conduct of them (taken together) is such as would cause a person of reasonable firmness present at the scene to fear for his personal safety, each of the persons using or threatening unlawful violence is guilty of violent disorder.

(2) It is immaterial whether or not the 3 or more use or threaten unlawful violence simultaneously."

There need be no common purpose. Each of the three or more persons may have a different purpose or no purpose. At least three must be using or threatening *unlawful* violence,[14] so if one of only three persons present is acting in self-defence or the prevention of crime, no offence is committed.

It must be proved that D (but not the other two or more) intended to use or threaten violence or that he was aware that his conduct might be violent or threaten violence.[15] The intoxicated defendant is governed by s. 6 (5) and (6), considered above.[16]

In *Mahroof*[17] it seems to have been assumed that if three defendants are the only persons alleged to have been involved in the disorder and one of them is acquitted, the others must also be acquitted. This will usually be the case but it is not necessarily so. If the acquitted person was using or threatening unlawful violence but was not guilty on some other ground, the other two may still be convicted. The third person may be acquitted because he did not so intend to, and was not aware that he might, use or threaten violence (perhaps being involuntarily intoxicated) or had some other defence such as duress, insanity or that he was aged only 13 and lacked "mischievous discretion". Such cases are likely to be rare.

This offence is intended to be the normal charge for serious outbreaks of public disorder, riot being reserved for exceptionally serious cases, but it clearly covers many relatively minor disturbances. Consequently, it is triable either way.

3) *Affray*

Affray is punishable on indictment with three years' imprisonment or an unlimited fine or both, or, on summary conviction, with six months' imprisonment or the statutory maximum fine or both. It is defined as follows by s. 3:

"(1) A person is guilty of affray if he uses or threatens unlawful violence towards another and his conduct is such as would cause a person of reasonable firmness present at the scene to fear for his personal safety.

(2) Where 2 or more persons use or threaten the unlawful violence, it is the conduct of them taken together that must be considered for the purposes of subsection (1).

14. For the meaning of "violence", see above, pp. 754–755.
15. Section 6 (2).
16. P. 754.
17. [1989] Crim LR 72; cf. *Fleming and Robinson* [1989] Crim LR 658.

(3) For the purposes of this section a threat cannot be made by the use of words alone."

In this section, "violence" is limited to violence towards another person and does not include violence towards property.[18]

The offence envisages at least three persons: (i) the person using or threatening unlawful violence; (ii) a person towards whom the violence or threat is directed; and (iii) a person of reasonable firmness who need not actually be, or be likely to be, present at the scene. So where D swiped with a knife towards a constable, J, the question was not whether a person of reasonable firmness in J's shoes would have feared for his personal safety but whether this hypothetical third person, present in the room and seeing D's conduct towards J, would have so feared.[19] As at common law, affray is a public order offence for the protection of the bystander. There are other offences for the protection of persons at whom the violence is aimed.

Subsection (2) makes it clear that, where two or more use or threaten the unlawful violence, it is the conduct of all of them which must be considered in deciding whether it would cause a person of reasonable firmness to fear for his personal safety.

The mental element is D's intention to use or threaten violence or his awareness that his conduct may be violent or threaten violence. Where reliance is placed by the prosecution on subsection (2), it will probably be necessary to show that D's awareness extended to the conduct of the other persons or persons using or threatening violence.

The intoxicated defendant is governed by s. 6 (5) and (6), considered above.[20]

4) *Fear or Provocation of Violence*

It is an offence under s. 4, punishable on summary conviction with 6 months' imprisonment or a fine not exceeding level 5 on the standard scale, if a person:

(i) uses towards another person threatening, abusive or insulting words or behaviour, or

(ii) distributes or displays to another person any writing, sign or other visible representation which is threatening, abusive or insulting

with intent to cause that person to believe that immediate unlawful violence will be used against him or another by any person, or to provoke the immediate use of unlawful violence by that person or another, or whereby that person is likely to believe that such violence will be used or it is likely that such violence will be provoked.

The words in s. 4 (1) (a), "uses towards another person", mean "uses in the presence of and in the direction of another person directly . . ."; *Atkin v DPP*[21] where D told customs officers in his house that, if the bailiff in the

---

18. Section 8, above, pp. 754–755.
19. *Davison* [1992] Crim LR 31, CA.
20. P. 754.
21. (1989) 89 Cr App Rep 199, [1989] Crim LR 581, DC.

car outside came in, he was "a dead 'un". The bailiff, being informed, felt threatened, but the threat was not direct. Similarly under s. 4 (1) (b) the distribution or display must be made directly to a person present. Writing contained in an envelope is not a "display".[1]

a) *"Threatening, abusive or insulting"*. This is the first of eight offences under the Act of which "threatening, abusive or insulting" conduct is a principal constituent.[2] Whether conduct has this quality seems to be governed by an objective test. It has been noticed above[3] that a word describing the *actus reus* may imply a mental element. The Act, however, assumes that conduct or material may be threatening, abusive or insulting even though there is no evidence that the actor or author intended it to have, or was aware that it might have, that quality. When proof by the prosecution of such intention or awareness is required, the Act specifically so provides;[4] and, in other cases, it puts the burden on the defendant to prove that he did not suspect or have reason to suspect that it was threatening, abusive or insulting.[5]

The words, "threatening, abusive or insulting", which are taken from the repealed s. 5 of the Public Order Act 1936, are to be given their ordinary meaning. It has been said that it is not helpful to seek to explain them by the use of synonyms or dictionary definitions because "an ordinary sensible man knows an insult when he sees or hears it".[6] Whether particular conduct is "threatening", etc., is a question of fact. In *Brutus v Cozens*[7] D interrupted a tennis match to protest against apartheid and thereby angered the spectators. The House of Lords, reversing the Divisional Court, held that the finding of the magistrates that this was not "insulting" behaviour could not be disturbed because it was a not unreasonable finding of fact. If the magistrates had decided that the behaviour was insulting, it may be that their decision would have been equally beyond challenge.[8] Masturbation in the sight of a stranger in a public lavatory is capable of being insulting behaviour because the stranger might be a heterosexual who would be insulted at being taken for a homosexual.[9] It is immaterial that the stranger is a policeman who is on the look out for this sort of thing, or a homosexual, who is not at all insulted. Words cannot be insulting (or, presumably, threatening or abusive) unless there is "a human target which they strike" and it seems that D must be aware of that "human target", though he need not intend the conduct to be "insulting": *Masterson v Holding*,[10] where intimate "cuddling" by two homosexual men in Oxford Street at 1.55 a.m. on a June morning, in the presence of two young men and two young

1. *Chappell v DPP* (1989) 89 Cr App Rep 82.
2. Sections 4 (1), 5 (1), 18 (1), 19 (1), 20 (1), 21 (1), 22 (1), 23 (1).
3. P. 29.
4. Section 6 (3) and (4).
5. Sections 19, 20, 21, 22, 23.
6. *Brutus v Cozens* [1972] 2 All ER 1297 at 1300, per Lord Reid.
7. Above, fn. 6.
8. Per Lord Kilbrandon at 1303. Lord Reid, obiter, agreed with the magistrates' finding; but it does not follow that he would have held a contrary finding to be unreasonable.
9. *Parkin v Norman* [1982] 2 All ER 583 at 588–589, DC.
10. [1986] 3 All ER 39, [1986] 1 WLR 1017.

women, was held capable of being insulting. It may be, however, that, for the purposes of s. 4 (though not for any other offence under the Act), the words "towards another" require that the words or behaviour be directed against that other.[11]

It must be proved that D:

(i) intended his words or behaviour towards P to be, or was aware that they might be, threatening, abusive or insulting;[12] and

(ii) either—

  (a) that he intended P to believe that immediate unlawful violence would be used against him or another; or

  (b) that he intended to provoke the immediate use of unlawful violence by P or another; or

  (c) that P was likely to believe that such violence (i.e. *immediate unlawful violence*[13]) would be used; or

  (d) that it was likely that such violence would be provoked.

Although the section creates only one offence,[14] alternatives (a) and (b) require proof of intention whereas in alternatives (c) and (d) the test is objective. The belief specified must be the belief of the person threatened.[15]

Where D's awareness that his conduct might be threatening, abusive or insulting is impaired by intoxication, s. 6 (5) and (6)[16] apply.

The offence may be committed in a public or a private place, except where D acts inside a dwelling[17] and P is also inside that, or another, dwelling.[18] So in *Atkin v DPP*[19] the threat to the customs officers in D's house could not be the offence. Threatening gestures through the bedroom window to the neighbour in his bedroom window across the street do not amount to the offence. Where D is in a dwelling, it seems that, if the issue is raised, the prosecution must prove that D was aware that his conduct might be heard or seen by a person outside that or another dwelling.[20]

5) *Harassment, Alarm or Distress*

It is an offence under s. 5 (1), punishable on summary conviction with a fine not exceeding level 3 on the standard scale, if a person—

(i) uses threatening, abusive or insulting words or behaviour, or disorderly behaviour, or

---

11. Card, op. cit., 3. 11.
12. Section 6 (3).
13. *Horseferry Road Metropolitan Stipendiary Magistrate, ex p Siadatan* [1991] 1 QB 260, [1990] Crim LR 548, DC. (The publication of Salman Rushdie's *The Satanic Verses* was not an offence because it was not likely to provoke *immediate* violence.)
14. Section 7 (2).
15. *Loade v DPP* [1990] 1 QB 1052, [1990] 1 All ER 36, DC.
16. Above, pp. 754–755.
17. Defined in s. 8.
18. Section 4 (2). Delivery of a threatening letter to P's home is incapable of being an offence under s. 4 or s. 5: *Chappell v DPP* (1989) 89 Cr App Rep 82.
19. Above, p. 758.
20. Cf. s. 5 (3) (b), putting the onus of proof on D.

(ii) displays any writing, sign or other visible representation which is
threatening, abusive or insulting,

within the hearing or sight of a person likely to be caused harassment,
alarm or distress thereby.

This offence is wider than that under s. 4 in that it includes the further
alternative of "disorderly" behaviour; and it extends beyond apprehension
of violence to the causing of "harassment, alarm or distress". "Disorderly"
is, no doubt, another ordinary word of the English language to be given its
natural meaning and it will apply to acts of hooliganism likely to produce
the specified effect. There is no requirement that the conduct be directed
"towards another person"; but it must be proved that D intended his
conduct to be threatening, abusive, or insulting or disorderly or was aware
that it might be so.[21] Section 6 (5) and (6) apply to the intoxicated
defendant.[22] The prosecution must prove that D's conduct took place
within the hearing or sight of a person (who might be a policeman[23]) likely
to be caused harassment, alarm (for his own or a third party's[24] safety) or
distress; but it is then for D to prove, if he can, that he had no reason to
believe that there was any such person within hearing or sight. Once again,
the offence may be committed in a public or a private place, except where D
acts inside a dwelling and P is also inside that, or another, dwelling. It is a
defence for D to prove that he was inside a dwelling and that he had no
reason to believe that his conduct would be heard or seen outside that or
another dwelling.[1]

6) *Acts Intended or Likely to Stir up Racial Hatred*

Offences of inciting racial hatred were first introduced into the law by the
Race Relations Act 1965 which required proof of an intention to stir up
such hatred. Because of the difficulty of proving intent, the law was
amended by the Race Relations Act 1976 which replaced the requirement
of intent with an objective test. It was enough that the defendant's conduct
was likely to stir up racial hatred, whether he intended to do so or not. Part
III of the Public Order Act 1986 replaces the old law with six new offences.
They are all concerned with acts intended or likely to stir up racial hatred –
the objective test is retained throughout – and, by s. 17:

"In this Part, 'racial hatred' means hatred against a group of persons in
Great Britain defined by reference to colour, race, nationality (including
citizenship) or ethnic or national origins."

It will be noted that the offences do not extend to stirring up hatred
against religious groups as such but an attack on a particular religion, such
as the Jewish religion, might be interpreted as an attack on Jews. Under the
1976 Act it was held that the term, "ethnic", was to be construed relatively

21. Section 6 (3).
22. Above, pp. 754–755.
23. *DPP v Orum* [1988] 3 All ER 449, [1989] 1 WLR 88, DC.
24. *Lodge v DPP* (1988) Times, 26 October.
  1. Section 5 (3) (b).

widely and that the Sikhs, though originally a religious community, now constituted an ethnic group because they were a separate community with a long shared history and distinctive customs.[2]

Proceedings for an offence under Part III may not be instituted except by or with the consent of the Attorney General. Each offence is punishable on indictment with two years' imprisonment or an unlimited fine or both, or, on summary conviction with six months' imprisonment or a fine not exceeding the statutory maximum, or both.

The essence of each offence is that D does an act involving the use of threatening, abusive or insulting words, behaviour or material and either:

(i) he intends thereby to stir up racial hatred, or
(ii) having regard to all the circumstances racial hatred is likely to be stirred up thereby.

The offences are:

s. 18 – using threatening, abusive or insulting words or behaviour or displaying any written material which is threatening, abusive or insulting;

s. 19 – publishing or distributing written material which is threatening, abusive or insulting;

s. 20 – presenting or directing the public performance of a play which involves the use of threatening, abusive or insulting words or behaviour;

s. 21 – distributing or showing or playing a recording of visual images or sounds which are threatening, abusive or insulting;

s. 22 – providing a programme service for, or producing, or directing, a programme involving threatening, abusive or insulting visual images or sounds, or using the offending words or behaviour therein;

s. 23 – possessing written material, or a recording of visual images or sounds, which is threatening, abusive or insulting, with a view to its being, displayed, published, etc.

7) *Mens Rea and Proof of "Threatening, Abusive or Insulting"*

This part of the Act provides a variety of requirements of *mens rea* and proof in relation to the "threatening, abusive or insulting" quality of the material in question. We have seen that for offences under ss. 4 and 5 the prosecution must prove that D intended his conduct to have, or was aware that it might have, that quality.[3] In Part III this requirement applies only to an offence under s. 18 where D is not shown to have intended to stir up racial hatred. Where he is shown to have such an intention it appears that the test for "threatening, abusive or insulting" is wholly objective. There is a variation in s. 22. Where D is not shown to have intended to stir up racial hatred, the prosecution must prove that he knew or *had reason to suspect*

---

2. *Mandla v Dowell Lee* [1983] 2 AC 548, [1983] 1 All ER 1062.
3. Section 6 (3) and (4), above, p. 759.

that the material was threatening, abusive or insulting. Where he is shown to have such an intention the test is purely objective.

For offences under ss. 19, 20, 21 and 23, the prosecution need prove no intention or awareness with respect to "threatening, abusive or insulting", but it is a defence for a defendant, who is not shown to have intended to stir up racial hatred, to prove:

for s. 19, that he was not aware of the content of material and did not suspect or have reason to suspect that it was threatening, abusive or insulting;

for s. 20, that he did not know and had no reason to suspect that the offending words or behaviour were threatening, abusive or insulting;

for s. 21, that he was not aware of the content of the recording and did not suspect and had no reason to suspect that it was threatening, abusive or insulting; and

for s. 23 that he was not aware of the content of the written material or recording and did not suspect, and had no reason to suspect, that it was threatening, abusive or insulting.

2 Public Nuisance[4]

Public nuisance is a misdemeanour at common law triable either way.[5] It consists in,

". . . an act not warranted by law or an omission to discharge a legal duty, which act or omission obstructs or causes inconvenience or damage to the public in the exercise of rights common to all His Majesty's subjects."[6]

A person who has suffered particular damage as the result of a public nuisance can maintain an action for damages in tort;[7] and the major importance of public nuisance today is in the civil remedy which it affords.

1 Nature of Nuisance

The most common and important instance of a public nuisance is obstruction of the highway and this is more particularly considered below. But it also includes a wide variety of other interferences with the public; for example, the carrying on of an offensive trade which impregnates the air "with noisome offensive and stinking smoke" to the common nuisance of the public passing along the highway;[8] polluting a river with gas so as to destroy the fish and render the water unfit for drinking;[9] unnecessarily, and with full knowledge of the facts, exposing in a public highway a person

---

4. Brownlie, *Law of Public Order and National Security* (2nd ed., 1981), 75, 77.
5. Criminal Law Act 1977, s. 16 and Sch. 2.
6. Stephen, *Digest*, 184.
7. See Street, *Torts*, 313 et seq.
8. *White and Ward* (1757) 1 Burr 333. See also *Tysoe v Davis* [1983] Crim LR 684 (QBD).
9. *Medley* (1834) 6 C & P 292.

infected with a contagious disease;[10] taking a horse into a public place knowing that it has glanders and that that is an infectious disease;[11] sending food to market, knowing that it is to be sold for human consumption and that it is unfit for that purpose;[12] burning a dead body in such a place and such a manner as to be offensive to members of the public passing along a highway or other public place;[13] keeping a fierce and unruly bull in a field crossed by a public footway;[14] discharging oil into the sea in such circumstances that it is likely to be carried on to English shores and beaches;[15] by causing excessive noise and dust in the course of quarrying operations;[16] by giving false information as to the presence of explosives so as to cause actual danger or discomfort to the public;[17] and trespassing and sniffing glue in a school playground even in the absence of staff and pupils.[18]

A great many varieties of nuisance are now the subject of special legislation[19] and proceedings are unlikely to be brought at common law where there is a statutory remedy. But the common law may still be useful where no statute has intervened or where the penalty provided by statute is too slight.[20]

A public nuisance may be committed by omission, as by permitting a house near the highway to fall into a ruinous state[1] or by allowing one's land to accumulate filth, even though it is deposited there by others for whom D is not responsible.[2]

Whereas private nuisance always involves some degree of repetition or continuance,[3]

"an isolated act may amount to a public nuisance if it is done under such circumstances that the public right to condemn it should be vindicated."[4]

The interference with the public's rights must be substantial and unreasonable. Not every obstruction of the highway is a public nuisance:

"If an unreasonable time is occupied in the operation of delivering beer from a brewer's dray into the cellar of a publican, this is certainly a

10. *Vantandillo* (1815) 4 M & S 73.
11. *Henson* (1852) Dears CC 24.
12. *Stevenson* (1862) 3 F & F 106; otherwise if D did not intend it for human consumption: *Crawley* (1862) 3 F & F 109.
13. *Price* (1884) 12 QBD 247.
14. Archbold, §31–56.
15. *Southport Corporation v Esso Petroleum Co Ltd* [1954] 2 QB 182 at 197, [1954] 2 All ER 561 at 571, per Denning LJ (CA; reversed, [1956] AC 218, [1955] 3 All ER 894).
16. *A–G v PYA Quarries Ltd* [1957] 2 QB 169, [1957] 1 All ER 864.
17. *Madden* [1975] 3 All ER 155, CA. The court said "potential danger" to the public was not enough but that "actual risk" to the comfort of the public was. This is difficult to follow. Is not "potential" danger the same as risk? And should not risk be enough?
18. *Sykes v Holmes* [1985] Crim LR 791. DC (conduct capable of being a nuisance within s. 40 of the Local Government (Miscellaneous Provisions) Act 1982).
19. See, for example, Archbold, §§31–50 to 31–140.
20. Cf. obstruction of the highway, Highways Act 1980, s. 137, Town Police Clauses Act 1847, s. 28.
1. *Watts* (1703) 1 Salk 357.
2. *A–G v Tod Heatley* [1897] 1 Ch 560.
3. Per Denning LJ [1957] 2 QB at 192.
4. Ibid. In *Mutters* (1864) Le & Ca 491, a conviction was upheld where the indictment alleged that D, on a particular day, caused an explosion which scattered pieces of rock on to neighbouring dwelling-houses and the highway; but the indictment did allege that D allowed the stones to remain on the highway for several hours.

nuisance. A cart or wagon may be unloaded at a gateway; but this must be done with promptness. So as to the repairing of a house; – the public must submit to the inconvenience occasioned necessarily in repairing the house; but if this inconvenience is prolonged for an unreasonable time, the public have a right to complain and the party can be indicted for a nuisance."[5]

The interference with the public's rights must be caused by some unnecessary and unreasonable act or omission by D. In *Dwyer v Mansfield*[6] it was held that, when queues formed outside D's shop because he was selling only 1 lb of potatoes per ration book in view of the wartime scarcity, he was not liable because he was carrying on his business in a normal and proper way without doing anything unreasonable or unnecessary. The nuisance, if there was one, had been created not by D's conduct, but by the short supply of potatoes.[7] The result would be different if D sold ice-cream through the window of a shop, causing a crowd to gather on the pavement, because this is not a normal and proper way of carrying on business.[8]

2 The Public

Blackstone says that a public nuisance must be an annoyance to all the King's subjects.[9] This is obviously too wide for, if it were so, no public nuisance could ever be established. Denning LJ declared that the test is,

"... that a public nuisance is a nuisance which is so widespread in its range or so indiscriminate in its effect that it would not be reasonable to expect one person to take proceedings on his own responsibility to put a stop to it, but that it should be taken on the responsibility of the community at large."[10]

Whether an annoyance or injury is sufficiently widespread to amount to a public nuisance is a question of fact. In *Lloyd*,[11] where D's carrying on his trade caused annoyance to only three houses in Clifford's Inn, Lord Ellenborough said that this, if anything,[12] was a private nuisance, not being sufficiently general to support an indictment. But in the *PYA Quarries* case the nuisance was held to be sufficiently general where the inhabitants of about thirty houses and portions of two public highways were affected by dust and vibration. In *Madden* a telephone call stating that there was a bomb in a factory affected only eight security officers who could not be regarded as a class of the public.[13] If the call had stated that the bomb was

---

5. *Jones* (1812) 3 Camp 230, per Lord Ellenborough. And see *Cross* (1812) 3 Camp 224: "A stage-coach may set down or take up passengers in the street, this being necessary for the public convenience; but it must be done in a reasonable time": per Lord Ellenborough. For a similar statutory rule, see Public Service Vehicles Regulations 1936, reg. 7, and *Ellis v Smith* [1962] 3 All ER 954, [1962] 1 WLR 1486.
6. [1946] KB 437, [1946] 2 All ER 247.
7. *Sed quaere.* Would it be a defence to obstructing a pavement that D's strip-tease club was the only one in town?
8. *Fabbri v Morris* [1947] 1 All ER 315 (Highway Act 1835, s. 72).
9. *Commentaries*, iii, 216.
10. *A–G v PYA Quarries Ltd* [1957] 2 QB 169 at 191, [1957] 1 All ER 894 at 908.
11. (1802) 4 Esp 200.
12. The annoyance could be avoided by shutting the windows.
13. [1975] 3 All ER 155, CA. What if all the workers in the factory had been evacuated? See now, Criminal Law Act 1977, s. 51 (2); above, p. 427.

in a public place, such as a highway, from which the public were consequently excluded, it would seem that there would have been a public nuisance, even if few or no members of the public were in fact affected. Probably the same result should apply if the place were one to which the public have access on payment, such as a sports ground.

3 Mens Rea

It has been held that it is not necessary to establish that it was D's object to create a public nuisance. In *Moore*,[14] D was held liable where he organised pigeon-shooting on his land and, in consequence, great numbers of persons collected on the highway to shoot at pigeons as they escaped. Apparently this result (in 1832) was one which "the experience of mankind must lead anyone to expect."[15] Similarly the proprietor of a club[16] and of a theatre[17] have been held liable when the natural consequence of the nature of the entertainment provided within was to cause crowds or queues to gather outside and substantially to interfere with the public's use of the highway.

Although the authorities, on their face, suggest that D may be criminally liable in public nuisance for negligence, it would be dangerous to assume that this is necessarily and invariably so. References to "natural and probable consequences" are frequently ambiguous and may amount to no more than a finding of intention or recklessness. Modern civil cases on public nuisance certainly suggest that negligence is enough to establish civil liability. As the civil action involves establishing that the crime has been committed, this might be thought to settle the question. But it is not conclusive. While the plaintiff certainly has to establish the *actus reus* of public nuisance, it may well be that it is not necessary to prove the same degree of culpability as would be required in a criminal case. The rules in the civil action and the criminal prosecution are not necessarily the same. Thus Denning LJ tells us:

"In an action for a public nuisance, once the nuisance is proved, and the defendant is shown to have caused it, the legal burden is shifted to the defendant to justify or excuse himself."[18]

But in a criminal prosecution the principle of *Woolmington v Director of Public Prosecutions*[19] surely requires that, at most, there is only an evidential burden on D who sets up justification or excuse.[20] Similarly, it may be that, in some types of nuisance at least, a higher degree of culpability – intention or recklessness – must be proved. It is true that Blackburn J has said that

"the evidence which would maintain the action would also support the indictment";[1]

14. (1832) 3 B & Ad 184.
15. Per Littledale J.
16. *Bellamy v Wells* (1890) 60 LJ Ch 156.
17. *Lyons, Sons & Co. v Gulliver* [1914] 1 Ch 631.
18. *Southport Corpn v Esso Petroleum Co Ltd* [1954] 2 QB 182 at 197, [1954] 2 All ER 561 at 571.
19. [1935] AC 462; **SHC** 42; above, p. 28.
20. Another obvious difference is that the civil case may be made out on a balance of probabilities, but the criminal case must be proved beyond reasonable doubt.
1. *Stephens* (1866) LR 1 QB 702 at 710; below.

but that was a case where the proceedings were regarded as substantially civil in character.

Public nuisance covers a wide variety of different offences and it may be a mistake to assume that the same rules apply to all of them. In some of the cases, knowledge of the facts has been insisted upon.[2]

4 Vicarious Liability

In at least some types of public nuisance a master is liable for the acts of his servant, performed within the scope of employment, even though the mode of performance which creates the nuisance is contrary to the master's express orders. Thus in *Stephens*,[3] D was held liable for the obstruction by his servants of the navigation of a public river by depositing rubbish therein. The reason given was that the proceeding was, in substance, civil, the object being not to punish D but to prevent the continuation of the nuisance.[4] But Mellor and Shee JJ thought that there may be nuisances of such a character that this rule would not be applicable. Baty[5] criticises the ground of this decision and pertinently asks:

"who is to decide whether [the] prosecution is 'substantially civil' or tinged with criminology?"[6]

Certainly, prosecutions for obstructing the highway are by no means always civil in substance: frequently the object is the punishment of the offenders. In *Chisholm v Doulton*[7] Field J said that *Stephens* "must be taken to stand upon its own facts";[8] and the court held that, on a charge under the Smoke Nuisance (Metropolis) Act 1853 D was not criminally liable for the negligence of his servant in creating a nuisance. In cases of statutory nuisance D is vicariously liable only if the words of the statute require it.[9]

The rule imposing vicarious liability for public nuisance may thus be neither so firmly established nor so all-embracing as is sometimes supposed.

2. Above, pp. 762–763, fns. 10, 11 and 12.
3. (1866) LR 1 QB 702; see also *Medley* (1834) 6 C & P 292.
4. Does this involve an inquiry into the motives of the prosecutor? Or does it reflect the courts' own view of what is the proper remedy for the wrong in question?
5. *Vicarious Liability*, 204.
6. In *Russell* (1854) 3 E & B 942, Lord Campbell thought that the obstruction of navigation by building a wall was "a grave offence".
7. (1889) 22 QBD 736.
8. Ibid., at 740.
9. Cf. *Armitage Ltd v Nicholson* (1913) 23 Cox CC 416.

Index